The Broadview Anthology of
AMERICAN LITERATURE

Volume A
Beginnings to 1820

The Broadview Anthology of
AMERICAN LITERATURE

Volume A
Beginnings to 1820

GENERAL EDITORS:

Derrick R. Spires, Cornell University
Rachel Greenwald Smith, Saint Louis University
Joseph Rezek, Boston University
Christina Roberts, Seattle University
Justine S. Murison, University of Illinois, Urbana-Champaign
Laura L. Mielke, University of Kansas
Christopher Looby, University of California, Los Angeles
Rodrigo Lazo, University of California, Irvine
Alisha Knight, Washington College
Hsuan L. Hsu, University of California, Davis
Michael Everton, Simon Fraser University
Christine Bold, University of Guelph

broadview press

BROADVIEW PRESS – www.broadviewpress.com
Peterborough, Ontario, Canada

Founded in 1985, Broadview Press remains a wholly independent publishing house. Broadview's focus is on academic publishing: our titles are accessible to university and college students as well as scholars and general readers. With over 800 titles in print, Broadview has become a leading international publisher in the humanities, with world-wide distribution. Broadview is committed to environmentally responsible publishing and fair business practices.

Library and Archives Canada Cataloguing in Publication

Title: The Broadview anthology of American literature / general editors: Derrick Spires, Cornell University [and 11 others].
Other titles: Beginnings to Reconstruction
Names: Spires, Derrick Ramon, editor.
Description: Includes bibliographical references and index.
Identifiers: Canadiana (print) 20220161925 | Canadiana (ebook) 20220161984 | ISBN 9781039301573 (set) | ISBN 9781554814640 (Volume A ; softcover) | ISBN 9781770488274 (set ; PDF) | ISBN 9781770488250 (Volume A ; PDF)

Subjects: LCSH: American literature. | LCGFT: Literature.
Classification: LCC PS507 .B76 2022 | DDC 810.8—dc23

Broadview Press handles its own distribution in North America:
PO Box 1243, Peterborough, Ontario K9J 7H5, Canada
555 Riverwalk Parkway, Tonawanda, NY 14150, USA
Tel: (705) 743-8990; Fax: (705) 743-8353
email: customerservice@broadviewpress.com

For all territories outside of North America, distribution is handled by Eurospan Group.

Broadview Press acknowledges the financial support of the
Government of Canada for our publishing activities.

Canada

Cover design by Lisa Brawn
Typesetting by Alexandria Stuart

PRINTED IN CANADA

Contributing Editors and Writers

Managing Editors:	Laura Buzzard, Don LePan
Developmental Editors and Staff Writers:	Jennifer McCue, Brett McLenithan, Nora Ruddock, Helena Snopek, Maxwell Uphaus
General Academic and Textual Editors:	Joe Davies, Michel Pharand
Design Coordinator:	Alexandria Stuart

Associate General Editors:

Gina Caison Koritha Mitchell
Drew Lopenzina Benjamin Railton
John Marsh Kelly Wisecup

Contributing Editors:

David Anthony Clayton McCarl Ashley Reed
Kristin Boudreau Laura K. Muñoz Christopher B. Teuton
Scott Cave Tiffany Potter Willow White
Matthew Cohen Birgit Brander Rasmussen Caroline Wigginton
Alejandra Dubcovsky David Read Kelly Wisecup
Jenny Marie Forsythe

Contributing Writers:

Tim Cassedy Rodrigo Lazo Joseph Rezek
Michael Everton John Marsh Siân Silyn Roberts
Emily Farrell Zoe McKenna Jason Shaffer
Jenny Marie Forsythe Laura Mielke Alexandria Stuart
John R. Funchion Bethany Qualls Kelly Wisecup
Christopher Hager Ashley Reed Braedan Zimmer
Genevieve Kirk Andrew Reszitnyk

Layout and Typesetting:

Alexandria Stuart

Production Coordinators:

Tara Lowes Tara Trueman

Permissions Coordinator:

Jacqueline Kwan

Proofreaders:

Joe Davies Judith Earnshaw Michel Pharand
Bethany Qualls

Text Preparation:

Caileigh Broach Genevieve Kirk Jennifer McCue
Alexandria Stuart Braedan Zimmer

EDITORIAL ADVISORS:

Stephen Arch, Michigan State University

Faith Barrett, Duquesne University

Elise Bartosik-Vélez, Dickinson College

Ralph Bauer, University of Maryland

Jonathan Beecher Field, Clemson University

Martin Bickman, University of Colorado
Boulder

Alex Black, Hobart and William Smith Colleges

Hester Blum, Pennsylvania State University

Michael Branch, University of Nevada, Reno

Marcus Briggs-Cloud, Ekvn-Yefolecv

David Carlson, California State University,
San Bernardino

Stephen L. Carr, University of Pittsburgh

Ricia Anne Chansky, University of Puerto Rico
at Mayagüez

Matthew Cohen, University of Nebraska-
Lincoln

Michael Cohen, University of California,
Los Angeles

Karen Cook-Bell, Bowie State University

Jennifer Desiderio, Canisius College

Hasia R. Diner, New York University

Marcy Dinius, DePaul University

Michael G. Ditmore, Pepperdine, Seaver College

Virginia Dow, Liberty University

Jessica Edwards, University of Delaware

Benjamin Fagan, Auburn University

Stephanie Farrar, University of Wisconsin,
Eau Claire

Jean Ferguson Carr, University of Pittsburgh

Ed Folsom, University of Iowa

Gabrielle Foreman, Pennsylvania State
University

Granville Ganter, St. John's University

Jeffrey Glover, Loyola University Chicago

Charlotte Gordon, Endicott College

Kirsten Silva Gruesz, University of California,
Santa Cruz

Robert Gunn, University of Texas at El Paso

Christopher Hager, Trinity College

Faye Halpern, University of Calgary

Amy Hamilton, Northern Michigan University

Jason Haslam, Dalhousie University

John Hay, University of Nevada, Las Vegas

Andrew Higgins, State University of New York,
New Paltz

Zach Hutchins, Colorado State University

Coleman Hutchison, University of Texas
at Austin

Bruce Johansen, University of Nebraska Omaha

Susan Kalter, Illinois State University

Frank Kelderman, University of Louisville

Mary Lou Kete, University of Vermont

Pamela Kingsbury, University of North Alabama

Stephanie Kirk, Washington University in
St. Louis

Carmen Lamas, University of Virginia

Eric D. Lamore, University of Puerto Rico
at Mayagüez

Edward Larkin, University of Delaware

Kerry Larson, University of Michigan

Drew Lopenzina, Old Dominion University

John Mac Kilgore, Florida State University

John Marsh, Pennsylvania State University

Barbara McCaskill, University of Georgia

Jerome J. McGann, University of Virginia

Kevin McGuirk, University of Waterloo

Angelyn Mitchell, Georgetown University

Dennis Moore, Florida State University

Amy Morris, University of Cambridge

Muscogee Nation Historic and Cultural
Preservation Department

Scott Peeples, College of Charleston

Benjamin Railton, Fitchburg State University

Stephen Railton, University of Virginia

Colin Ramsey, Appalachian State University

David Read, University of Missouri

Todd Richardson, University of Texas,
Permian Basin

Siân Silyn Roberts, Queen's College, CUNY

Phillip Round, University of Iowa

John Saillant, Western Michigan University

James Salazar, Temple University

Geoffrey D. Sanborn, Amherst College

Timothy H. Scherman, Northeastern Illinois
University

Ana Schwartz, University of Texas at Austin

Seminole Nation Historic Preservation Office
E. Thomson Shields, Jr., East Carolina
 University
Reiner Smolinski, Georgia State University
Carole Lynn Stewart, Brock University
Matthew Teutsch, Piedmont University
Margaret Thickstun, Hamilton College
Zachary Turpin, University of Idaho
Abram Van Engen, Washington University
 in St. Louis
Lindsay Van Tine, Gilder Lehrman Institute of
 American History

Megan Walsh, St. Bonaventure University
James Warren, Washington and Lee University
Ed White, Tulane University
Edward Whitley, Lehigh University
Maria Windell, University of Colorado Boulder
Chad Wriglesworth, University of Waterloo
Jonathan Yeager, University of Tennessee at
 Chattanooga
Michael Ziser, University of California, Davis

CONTENTS

This anthology's online component is available at sites.broadviewpress.com/baalonline/

PREFACE . XXV

ACKNOWLEDGMENTS . XXXVII

AMERICA AND AMERICAN LITERATURE, BEGINNINGS TO 1820 XXXIX
 Indigenous North American Cultures and Literatures XXXIX
 Contact, and the Literatures of Contact. XLIII
 Religion in Early America . LIII
 Slavery and America: Beginnings to 1820 . LX
 "Begin the World Over Again": An Age of Rebellion and Revolution LXVI
 The Shape of a People . LXXIII
 "A State of Independency": The Republic's First Decades. LXXX
 Revolutionary Ideas, Enlightenment Thought online
 The Environment online
 Literary Genres, Beginnings to 1820 online
 Poetry
 Prose Fiction
 Prose Non-fiction
 Drama
 Language in America, Beginnings to 1820 online

TEXTS AND CONTEXTS: A CHRONOLOGICAL CHART . LXXXVII

INDIGENOUS ORAL AND VISUAL LITERATURES . 1
 Wampanoag . 3
 [Moshup Story] . 4
 [Moshup Story] . 4
 [Moshup Story] . 4
 Mi'kmaq . 5
 Petroglyph of Human Figure and Sun . 6
 Petroglyph Tracing . 6
 Page of a Mi'kmaq Prayer Book . 7
 Mohegan . 8
 Painted Wood-Splint Storage Basket . 8
 Haudenosaunee (Iroquois). 9
 from [Creation Story] . 10
 from "The Creation" online
 Origin of Folk Stories . 12
 Thanksgiving Address . 13
 Iroquois or Confederacy of the Five Nations. 15

Wampum Belts . 17
 Ha:yëwënta' (Hiawatha) Belt . 18
 Two Row Wampum . 18
 In Context: Interpreting the Two-Row Wampum [video selection] online
Ojibwe . 19
 from "The Birth of Nenabozho" . 20
 Nanabush Eats the Artichokes . 25
 Nanabozho . 26
 [Nanabush Story] [audio selection] online
 Ojibwe Pictographs . 29
Cherokee . 32
 Why the Possum's Tail Is Bare . 33
 Sequoyah, Cherokee Syllabary . 33
 [The Belt that Would Not Burn] . 34
Maya . 35
 from the Dresden Codex . 36
 from the Popol Vuh . 39
Navajo (Diné) . 40
 from the Creation Story . 41
 Tse' Hone / Newspaper Rock . 43
Coast Salish . 44
 Maiden of Deception Pass . 44
 [Samish version, translated into English] 45
 [English version] . 46
 Tracy Powell, The Maiden of Deception Pass 47
 Hul'q'umi'num House Post . 48
 Lummi House Post . 49
 Battle at Sea . 49
 Coyote and Rock [audio selection] online

CIVILIZATIONS IN CONTACT . 51
 Vinland online
 from Erik the Red's Saga
 from The Saga of the Greenlanders
 The Caribbean . 51
 from Christopher Columbus with Bartolomé de las Casas, Journal of the First
 Voyage to America . 53
 Christopher Columbus, Letter of Columbus to Various Persons Describing the Results
 of His First Voyage and Written on the Return Journey 57
 from Michele de Cuneo, letter [Concerning Columbus's Second Voyage] 60
 from Bartolomé de las Casas, A Short Account of the Destruction of the Indies 62
 Mexico . 66
 from Hernán Cortés, Second Letter to the Spanish Crown 68
 from the anonymous manuscript of Tlatelolco 72
 Florida and New Mexico . 77
 from Alonso Gregorio de Escobedo, La Florida 78
 from Inca Garcilaso de la Vega, La Florida del Inca 85

from Gaspar Pérez de Villagrá, *History of New Mexico* online
 The Pueblo Revolt .90
 Antonio de Otermín, letter on the Pueblo Revolt of 1680, 8 September 1680 . . .91
 How the Spaniards Came to Shung-Opovi, How They Built a Mission, and
 How the Hopi Destroyed the Mission .97
Northeastern Woodlands .100
 Lenni Lenape (Delaware) Accounts of the Arrival of the Whites102
 The Coming of the Whites .102
 Prediction of the Arrival of the White People .102
 Indian Account of the First Arrival of the Dutch at New York Island103
 from Thomas Hariot, *A Brief and True Report of the New Found Land of Virginia* . .105
 John White, Selected Watercolors .109
 Caleb Cheeshateaumauk, letter to the Society for the Propagation of the Gospel
 in New England, 1663 .114
 Mittark, Agreement of Mittark and His People Not to Sell Land to the English . . .114
 Handsome Lake, "How the White Race Came to America and Why the Gaiʹwiioʹ
 Became a Necessity" .115
 In Context: The Myth of Thanksgiving .118
 from Edward Winslow, "A Letter Sent from New England to a Friend in These
 Parts," *Mourt's Relation* .119
 from William Bradford, *Of Plymouth Plantation* .120
 Abraham Lincoln, A Proclamation, 3 October 1863120
New France online
 from Samuel de Champlain, *Voyages of Samuel Champlain*
 from *Relation of the Discoveries and Voyages of Cavalier de La Salle from 1679 to 1681*
 from Chrestien LeClercq, *New Relation of Gaspesia, with the Customs and Religion
 of the Gaspesian Indians*
California .123
 from Antonio de la Ascención, *A Brief Report of the Discovery in the South Sea*124
 from Pablo Tac, "Conversion of the San Luiseños of Alta California"128
 from Lorenzo Asisara with Thomas Savage, [Account of Mission Life]130

ÁLVAR NÚÑEZ CABEZA DE VACA .132
from *The Relación of Álvar Núñez Cabeza de Vaca* .134
 Chapter 4: How We Entered Inland .134
 from Chapter 5: How the Governor Left the Ships .136
 from Chapter 14: How Four Christians Departed .138
 Chapter 15: Of What Happened to Us in the Villa of Malhado139
 from Chapter 17: How the Indians Came Forth and Brought with Them Andrés
 Dorantes and Castillo and Estevanico .141
 Chapter 21: Of How We Cured Some Sick People Here141
 from Chapter 22: How They Brought Us Other Sick People the Next Day142
 from Chapter 26: Of the Nations and Languages .144
 from Chapter 27: Of How We Moved on and Were Well Received144
 Chapter 33: How We Came upon the Track of Christians145
 Chapter 34: Of How I Sent for the Christians .146
 from Chapter 36: Of How We Had Churches Built in That Land148

JOHN SMITH .150
 from *The General History of Virginia, New England, and the Summer Isles*153
 from The Third Book .153
 from Chapter 1 .153
 from Chapter 2: What Happened Till the First Supply156
 from Chapter 8: Captain Smith's Journey to Pamunkey163
 from The Fourth Book . online
 from The Sixth Book . online
 from A Description of New England . online
 In Context: Alternative Accounts of Wahunsonacock and Pocahontas online

WILLIAM BRADFORD .169
 from *Of Plymouth Plantation* .171
 from The First Book .171
 from Chapter 1: [The Separatist Interpretation of the Reformation in England] 171
 from Chapter 4: Showing the Reasons and Causes of Their Removal173
 Chapter 9: Of Their Voyage, and How They Passed the Sea; and of Their Safe
 Arrival at Cape Cod .174
 from Chapter 10: Showing How They Sought Out a Place of Habitation; and
 What Befell Them Thereabout .176
 from The Second Book .179
 from Chapter 11: The Remainder of Anno 1620 [The Mayflower Compact]
 [The Starving Time] [Indian Relations] .179
 from Chapter 12: Anno Domini 1621 [*Mayflower* Departs and Corn Planted]
 [Indian Diplomacy] [First Thanksgiving] .181
 from Chapter 14: Anno Domini 1623 [End of the "Common Course and
 Condition"] .183
 from Chapter 19: Anno Domini 1628 [A Visit from the Dutch] [Thomas
 Morton of Merrymount] .184
 from Chapter 25: Anno Domini 1634 [Captain Stone, the Dutch, and the
 Connecticut Indians] .187
 from Chapter 28: Anno Domini 1637 [The Pequot War]188
 from Chapter 32: Anno Domini 1642 [Wickedness Breaks Forth] [A Horrible
 Case of Bestiality] .190
 from Chapter 34: Anno Domini 1644 [Proposal to Remove to Nauset]191
 from *Of Plymouth Plantation* [selections from Chapters 1, 4, 9, 10, 11, 12, 13, 14,
 15, 19, 23, 28, 29, 32, 33, 34, and 35] . online
 In Context: *Mourt's Relation* .193
 from Edward Winslow and William Bradford, *A Relation or Journal of the Proceedings
 of the Plantation Settled at Plymouth in New England* [*Mourt's Relation*]193
 from Robert Cushman, *Reasons and Considerations Touching the Lawfulness of
 Removing out of England into the Parts of America* .199
 In Context: Mapping Colonial Conflict .204
 John Underhill, "The Figure of the Indians' Fort or Palizado in New England and
 the Manner of Destroying It by Captain Underhill and Captain Mason," *News
 from America* .204

John Tinker, Uncas, Wesawegun, Cassacinamon, Harry Wright, and Ninigret,
 "Plan of the Pequot Country and Testimony of Uncas, Cassacinamon,
 and Wesawegun" . 206
William Hubbard, *A Map of New-England* . 207

THOMAS MORTON . 208
 from *The New English Canaan* . 210
 The Author's Prologue online
 from Book 1 online
 from Chapter 1: Proving New England the Principal Part of All America
 Chapter 2: Of the Original of the Natives
 Chapter 4: Of Their Houses and Habitations
 Chapter 7: Of Their Childbearing
 Chapter 9: Of Their Pretty Conjuring Tricks
 Chapter 13: Of Their Magazines or Storehouses
 Chapter 16: Of Their Acknowledgement of the Creation, and Immortality of
 the Soul
 Chapter 18: Of Their Custom in Burning the Country
 Chapter 19: Of Their Inclination to Drunkenness
 Chapter 20: That the Savages Live a Contented Life
 from Book 3 . 210
 Chapter 14: Of the Revels of New Canaan . 210
 Chapter 15: Of a Great Monster Supposed to Be at Ma-re-Mount; and the
 Preparation Made to Destroy It. 213
 Chapter 16: How the Nine Worthies Put Mine Host of Ma-re-Mount into the
 Enchanted Castle at Plymouth, and Terrified Him with the Monster Briareus 215

JOHN WINTHROP . 217
 A Model of Christian Charity . 219
 from *The Journal of John Winthrop* online

ANNE HUTCHINSON . 229
 The Examination of Mrs. Anne Hutchinson at the Court at Newtown 231
 In Context: John Winthrop's Record of Anne Hutchinson's Testimony online

ROGER WILLIAMS . 236
 from *A Key into the Language of America* . 238
 from Chapter 1: Of Salutation . 241
 from Chapter 21: Of Religion, the Soul, Etc. 242
 from Chapter 29: Of Their War, Etc. 243
 from *The Bloody Tenet of Persecution* . 244
 Syllabus of the Work online
 from [Address] to the Right Honourable Both Houses of the High Court of
 Parliament . 244
 from Chapter 1 . 244
 from Chapter 2 . 245

from Chapter 9. .245
from Chapter 16. .246
from Chapter 39. .246
from Chapter 138. .247
Letter to the Town of Providence. .247
from *Hireling Ministry None of Christ's* online

ANNE BRADSTREET .249
Prologue .251
from The Four Monarchies online
An Elegy upon That Honourable and Renowned Knight, Sir Philip Sidney online
In Honour of That High and Mighty Princess, Queen Elizabeth of Most
 Happy Memory online
To the Memory of My Dear and Ever Honored Father Thomas Dudley Esq. online
Contemplations. .253
The Flesh and the Spirit. .257
The Author to Her Book .259
Before the Birth of One of Her Children. .259
To My Dear and Loving Husband. .260
A Letter to Her Husband, Absent upon Public Employment.260
Another [Letter to Her Husband, Absent upon Public Employment I] online
Another [Letter to Her Husband, Absent upon Public Employment II] online
To Her Father with Some Verses online
In Reference to Her Children, 23 June 1659 online
In Memory of My Dear Grand-Child Elizabeth Bradstreet261
In Memory of My Dear Grand-Child Anne Bradstreet261
On My Dear Grand-Child Simon Bradstreet. .261
For Deliverance from a Fever. .261
Some Verses upon the Burning of Our House, July 10th, 1666.262
As Weary Pilgrim online
To My Dear Children .263
from *Meditations Divine and Moral* .265

MICHAEL WIGGLESWORTH .269
from *The Diary of Michael Wigglesworth* .271
from *The Day of Doom Or, A Poetical Description of the Great and Last Judgment*279
from *Meat Out of the Eater* online

MARY ROWLANDSON. .283
The Sovereignty and Goodness of God. .285
In Context: Editions of Rowlandson's Narrative313
In Context: Picturing Mary Rowlandson. .314
In Context: Indigenous Experiences of Metacom's War.315
 from John Easton, letter to Josiah Winslow, 26 May 1675315
 James Quannapaquait with unnamed magistrates, *The Examination and Relation
 of James Quannapaquait, alias James Rumny-Marsh*.316

Massachusetts Council, order regarding Indigenous allies .318
Numphow and John Line, letter to Thomas Henchman, November 1675318
James Printer .319
 from Daniel Gookin, *An Historical Account of the Doings and Sufferings of the*
 Christian Indians in New England in the Years 1675, 1676, 1677320
 attributed to James Printer, note tacked to a tree, c. 1676320
 from Andrew Pittimee, Quanahpohkit, John Mague, and James Speen, petition to
 the Governor and Council of the Massachusetts Colony, June 1676321
 William Ahaton, petition to the Governor and Council of the Massachusetts
 Colony, July 1676 online
 from William Wannukhow, Joseph Wannukhow, and John Appamatahqeen,
 petition to the Boston Court of Assistants, 5 September 1676 online

EDWARD TAYLOR .322
 [Acrostic Love Poem to Elizabeth Fitch] online
 from *God's Determinations Touching His Elect* online
 from *Preparatory Meditations before My Approach to the Lord's Supper* online
 Upon a Spider Catching a Fly .324
 Upon a Wasp Chilled with Cold online
 Huswifery .324
 Upon Wedlock, and Death of Children .325
 The Ebb and Flow online

SOR JUANA INÉS DE LA CRUZ .326
 82: [Divina Lysi mía] / [My divine Lysis] .328
 92: [Silly, you men] .329
 92: [Hombres necios] / [Silly, you men] online
 165: [Semblance of my elusive love, hold still—] .330
 165: [Detente, Sombra de mi bien Esquivo] / [Semblance of my elusive love,
 hold still—] online
 In Context: The Frontispieces to Sor Juana's Published Works online
 from the Reply to Sor Philothea .330
 In Context: Sor Philothea's Letter to Sor Juana online

SAMUEL SEWALL online
 from *Diary of Samuel Sewall*
 The Selling of Joseph: A Memorial
 In Context: John Saffin's Response to *The Selling of Joseph*

COTTON MATHER .336
 from *The Wonders of the Invisible World* .338
 from Enchantments Encountered .338
 from The Trial of Martha Carrier .340
 In Context: The Salem Witch Trials online

CANASSATEGO .343
 from Speech at Lancaster, 26 June 1744 .345

from Speech at Lancaster, 4 July 1744 online
 In Context: Indigenous–Settler Negotiations in the Mid-Eighteenth Century 347
 from George Washington, *The Journal of Major George Washington* 347

JONATHAN EDWARDS .. 352
 Sinners in the Hands of an Angry God 354
 In Context: The Preaching of Jonathan Edwards 364
 [Personal Narrative] ... online
 from *A History of the Work of Redemption* online

JAMES ALBERT UKAWSAW GRONNIOSAW online
 *A Narrative of the Most Remarkable Particulars in the Life of James Albert Ukawsaw
 Gronniosaw, an African Prince, as Related by Himself*

ELIZABETH ASHBRIDGE ... 366
 Some Account of the Fore Part of the Life of Elizabeth Ashbridge 367
 In Context: Quaker Conversion Narratives 386

CONTEXTS: IMMIGRATION AND INDENTURED SERVITUDE online
 advertisement, *The Pennsylvania Gazette* from Thomas Lloyd, letter to Edmond Hector,
 (10 August 1738) 10 October 1756
 advertisement, *The Pennsylvania Gazette* from Gottlieb Mittelberger, *Gottlieb Mittelberger's
 (29 October 1766) Journey to Pennsylvania in the Year 1750 and
 notice, *New York Independent Journal* Return to Germany in the Year 1754*
 (24 January 1784)
 Elizabeth Sprigs, letter to John Sprigs,
 22 September 1756

LUCY TERRY .. 389
 Bars Fight ... 390
 In Context: Josiah Holland's Account of the Bars Fight online

JOHN MARRANT ... online
 A Narrative of the Lord's Wonderful Dealings with John Marrant, a Black

SAGOYEWATHA .. 391
 [Reply to the Missionary Jacob Cram] 393
 [Reply to President Washington, 31 March 1792] online

BENJAMIN FRANKLIN .. 396
 from *The New-England Courant* [The "Silence Dogood" Papers] online
 The Speech of Miss Polly Baker online
 The Way to Wealth: Preface to Poor Richard Improved online
 Rules by Which a Great Empire May Be Reduced to a Small One online
 Drinking Song .. online
 Remarks Concerning the Savages of North America 398
 On the Slave Trade ... 401
 from *The Autobiography* .. 403

Part 1 . 404
Part 2 . 441
The Autobiography [full text] online
The Autobiography [modernized text] online
In Context: Portraits of Benjamin Franklin . 452
In Context: Correspondence Between William Franklin and Benjamin Franklin online
In Context: Franklin's Cultural and Literary Influences online
In Context: France Mourns Benjamin Franklin online

SAMSON OCCOM . 455
[*Autobiographical Narrative*] . 458
from *A Sermon, Preached at the Execution of Moses Paul, an Indian* 462
The Sufferings of Christ . 466
The Most Remarkable and Strange State, Situation, and Appearance of Indian Tribes
 in This Great Continent . 467
Elm Bark Box . 468

SARAH KEMBLE KNIGHT . online
The Journal of Madame Knight
In Context: Boston and New York in the Early Eighteenth Century

J. HECTOR ST. JOHN DE CRÈVECOEUR . 469
from *Letters from an American Farmer* . 472
 from Letter 2: On the Situation, Feelings, and Pleasures of an American Farmer . . 472
 from Letter 3: What Is an American? . 475
 from Letter 4: Description of the Island of Nantucket online
 from Letter 9: Description of Charles-Town 483
 from Letter 10: On Snakes; and on the Hummingbird 490
 from Letter 12: Distresses of a Frontier Man online
 In Context: Nantucket and Charles-Town . 492
 In Context: Reactions to *Letters from an American Farmer* online
 In Context: Rationalizing Colonialism: Thomas Hobbes, John Locke, and
 George Washington . online

JOHN ADAMS AND ABIGAIL ADAMS . 494
from Abigail Adams to John Adams, 19 August 1774 496
from John Adams to Abigail Adams, 16 September 1774 online
John Adams to Abigail Adams, 29 October 1775 online
Abigail Adams to John Adams, 27 November 1775 496
Abigail Adams to John Adams, 31 March 1776 497
from John Adams to Abigail Adams, first letter of 3 July 1776 499
John Adams to Abigail Adams, second letter of 3 July 1776 499
John Adams to Abigail Adams, 7 February 1777 online
Abigail Adams to John Adams, 8 February 1777 online
John Adams to Thomas Jefferson, 2 September 1813 online
Thomas Jefferson to John Adams, 28 October 1813 online
John Adams to Thomas Jefferson, 15 November 1813 online

THOMAS PAINE . 501
 from *Common Sense* . 505
 Introduction . 505
 from Of the Origin and Design of Government in General, with Concise
 Remarks on the English Constitution . 505
 from Of Monarchy and Hereditary Succession . 507
 Thoughts on the Present State of American Affairs 509
 In Context: A Response to *Common Sense* . 514
 from Charles Inglis, *The Deceiver Unmasked* . 515
 from *The American Crisis* . 517
 from *Rights of Man*, Part Two . online
 from *The Age of Reason* . online

THOMAS JEFFERSON . 519
 from *The Autobiography of Thomas Jefferson* . 522
 A Declaration by the Representatives of the United States of America 522
 In Context: British and American Reactions to the Declaration of Independence 526
 from *Notes on the State of Virginia* . 531
 from Query 5: Its Cascades and Caverns? . online
 from Query 6: A Notice of the Mines and Other Subterraneous Riches 531
 from Query 8: The Number of its Inhabitants? online
 from Query 11: A Description of the Indians Established in That State? 534
 from Query 14: The Administration of Justice and Description of the Laws? 537
 from Query 17: The Different Religions Received into That State? online
 Query 18: The *Particular* Customs and Manners That May Happen to Be
 Received in That State? . 543
 from Query 19: The Present State of Manufactures, Commerce, Exterior and
 Interior Trade? . online
 In Context: Responses to Jefferson's *Notes on the State of Virginia* 544
 from review of "*Observations sur la Virginie*, par M.J., traduites de l'Anglais,"
 Mercure de France . 544
 from James McCune Smith, "On the Fourteenth Query of Thomas Jefferson's
 Notes on Virginia," *The Anglo-African Magazine* 545

THE FEDERALIST . 549
 from *The Federalist* . 550
 No. 1 [Alexander Hamilton] . 550
 No. 6 [Alexander Hamilton] . online
 No. 9 [Alexander Hamilton] . online
 No. 10 [James Madison] . 552
 No. 51 [James Madison] . online

VENTURE SMITH . 557
 A Narrative of the Life and Adventures of Venture, A Native of Africa 559

CONTEXTS: SLAVERY AND RESISTANCE .573

from King Alfonso I (Nzinga Mbemba) of
Kongo, letter to King João III of Portugal,
18 October 1526575

from Bartolomé de las Casas, *History of
the Indies* .575

from Bernardino de Manzanedo, dispatch
to King Charles I of Spain.576

from John Rolfe, letter to Sir Edwin Sandys,
January 1620 .578

from Edward Waterhouse, "A Declaration of the
State of the Colony and Affairs in Virginia" 578

from Richard Ligon, *A True and Exact
History of the Island of Barbados* online

from An Act for the Encouragement of the
Importation of White Servants online

John Saffin, "The Negroes Character"579

anonymous, letter to the *South Carolina
Gazette*, 14 October 1732579

from the South Carolina Negro Act (1740) online

from John Woolman, *Some Considerations
on the Keeping of Negroes*580

from James Grainger, *The Sugar-Cane*582

Belinda Sutton, "The Petition of Belinda,
an African" .584

Prince Hall, A Charge Delivered to the
African Lodge, 24 June 1797 online

from George Lawrence, An Oration on
the Abolition of the Slave Trade online

from William Hamilton, An Address to the New
York African Society for Mutual Relief online

from "Old Elizabeth," *Memoir of Old
Elizabeth, a Coloured Woman*585

from Jupiter Hammon, An Address to the
Negroes in the State of New York587

Benjamin Banneker, letter to Thomas
Jefferson, 19 August 1791588

from Peter Williams Jr., "An Oration on
the Abolition of the Slave Trade,"
1 January 1808590

from Boyrereau Brinch, *The Blind African
Slave, or Memoirs of Boyrereau Brinch,
Nick-named Jeffrey Brace*594

OLAUDAH EQUIANO OR GUSTAVUS VASSA .598

from *The Interesting Narrative of the Life of Olaudah Equiano*601

from Chapter 1 .601

Chapter 1 [full text] online

Chapter 2 .604

from Chapter 3 .611

from Chapter 3 [additional selections] online

from Chapter 4 .615

from Chapter 5 .618

Chapter 5 [full text] online

from Chapter 6 .623

from Chapter 7 .630

Chapter 7 [full text] online

from Chapter 8 .634

from Chapter 9 .635

from Chapter 9 [additional selections] online

from Chapter 10 online

from Chapter 11 online

from Chapter 12 online

In Context: Equiano's Narrative as a Philadelphia Abolitionist Pamphlet.640

In Context: Reactions to Olaudah Equiano's Work .641

[Note to Instructors: *The Interesting Narrative* is among over 400 available editions from Broadview, any one of which may be packaged together with this anthology volume.]

ABSALOM JONES .642

The Petition of the People of Colour .643

from A Thanksgiving Sermon online

RICHARD ALLEN AND ABSALOM JONES online
 from *A Narrative of the Proceedings of the Black People, During the Late Awful
 Calamity in Philadelphia*

RICHARD ALLEN online
 from "Confession of John Joyce, Alias Davis, Who Was Executed on Monday,
 the 14th of March, 1808"

HERMAN MANN AND DEBORAH SAMPSON online
 from *The Female Review*
 In Context: Picturing Deborah Sampson

CONTEXTS: REBELLIONS AND REVOLUTIONS . 646
 "Pontiac's War" . 647
 from anonymous [believed to be Robert
 Navarre], *Journal of the Pontiac
 Conspiracy* . 647
 from George III, The Royal Proclamation
 of 1763 . 650
 The Paxton Boys' Massacres online
 Benjamin Franklin, *A Narrative of the
 Late Massacres, in Lancaster County,
 of a Number of Indians, Friends of This
 Province, By Persons Unknown. With
 Some Observations on the Same*
 from *The Apology of the Paxton Volunteers,
 Adapted to the Candid and Impartial
 World*
 The Revolutionary War 652
 Patrick Henry, Virginia Stamp Act
 Resolutions online
 from John Dickinson, *Letters from a farmer
 in Pennsylvania to the Inhabitants of
 the British Colonies* online
 "Brutus," *To the Free and Loyal Inhabitants
 of the City and Colony of New York* online
 Announcement of the Formation of the
 Association of the Sons of Liberty in
 New York online
 Proceedings of Farmington, Connecticut,
 on the Boston Port Act online
 from George III, Speech to Parliament,
 30 November 1774 652
 from Response of the House of Commons,
 8 December 1774 653
 from William Wirt, *Sketches of the Life and
 Character of Patrick Henry* 654
 from Samuel Johnson, "Taxation No
 Tyranny: An Answer to the Resolutions
 and Address of the American Congress"
 online
 Benjamin Franklin 659
 "What Would Satisfy the Americans?" 659
 "Join, or Die" 659
 Poems and Songs 661

 anonymous ("A Son of Liberty"), "A
 New Song, Addressed to the Sons of
 Liberty, on the Continent of America;
 Particularly to the Illustrious,
 Glorious and Never to Be Forgotten
 Ninety-two of Boston" 661
 anonymous ("A Young Woman of
 Virginia"), "Virginia Banishing
 Tea" . 662
 Philip Freneau, from *American Liberty*
 online
 from Lemuel Haynes, "The Battle of
 Lexington" . 663
 Ruth Bryant, "An Address to the Sons of
 Liberty" online
 Ruth Bryant, "The American Maid's
 Choice" . 665
 Hannah Griffitts, "Upon Reading a
 Book Entitled *Common Sense*" . . 666
 Joseph Stansbury 666
 "Verses to the Tories" 666
 "The United States" 667
 Francis Hopkinson, "A Camp Ballad" 667
 Jonathan Odell, "The Old Year and
 the New: A Prophecy" 668
 Margaretta Faugères, "A Salute to the
 Fourteenth Anniversary of
 American Independence" 669
 from Dunmore's Proclamation, 1775 . . . 669
 from Edward Rutledge, letter to Ralph
 Izard, 8 December 1775 670
 Declaration by the Representatives of the
 People of the Colony and Dominion
 of Virginia, Assembled in General
 Convention, 14 December 1775 671
 from Samuel Seabury, *An Alarm to the
 Legislature of the Province of New York,
 Occasioned by the Present Political
 Disturbances in North America, Addressed
 to the Honourable Representatives in
 General Assembly Convened* online
 from Reverend John Lindsay, letter to Dr.
 William Robertson, 6 August 1776 . . 671

The Constitution of the United States online

from Noah Webster, *An Examination into the Leading Principles of the Federal Constitution* online

from Mercy Otis Warren, *History of the Rise, Progress, and Termination of the American Revolution* 672

from Joseph Plumb Martin, *A Narrative of Some of the Adventures, Dangers and Sufferings of a Revolutionary Soldier* online

The French Revolution, and the Revolutionary Call for Women's Rights 676

Declaration of the Rights of Man and of the Citizen . 676

from Mary Wollstonecraft, *A Vindication of the Rights of Woman* online

from Olympe de Gouges, The Declaration of the Rights of Woman online

"The Rights of Woman" in America 678

from Annis Boudinot Stockton, letter to her daughter [Julia Stockton Rush], 22 March 1793 678

from anonymous ("A Lady"), *The Philadelphia Minerva* 679

The Haitian Revolution 679

from Baron de Wimpffen, *A Voyage to Saint Domingo, in the Years 1788, 1789, and 1790* online

Toussaint Louverture, Proclamation, 29 August 1793 680

Thomas Jefferson on the Haitian Revolution, Selected letters 680

The Haitian Revolution in American Newspapers . 682

from Abraham Bishop, "The Rights of Black Men" 683

from Proclamation by Léger-Félicité Sonthonax, Civil Commissioner of the Republic, delegate to the French Islands of Leeward America, in order to restore order and public tranquility online

Declaration of the Independence of the Blacks of St. Domingo online

from Haitian Declaration of Independence online

from Jean-Jacques Dessalines, "Liberty or Death. Proclamation. Jean-Jacques Dessalines, Governor General, to the People of Hayti" 684

from Lenora Sansay, *Secret History, Or, the Horrors of St. Domingo* 686

from Charles Brockden Brown, "On the Consequences of Abolishing the Slave Trade to the West Indian Colonies" online

J. Barlow, selected engravings online

from Condy Raguet, "Account of the Massacre in St. Domingo in May 1806" online

from William Wells Brown, *St. Domingo: Its Revolutions and Its Patriots* 688

from Baron de Vastey, *The Colonial System Unveiled* online

Gabriel's Rebellion and Other Rebellions by Enslaved Americans 692

Newspaper Reports 692

from Robert Sutcliff, *Travels in Some Parts of North America in the Years 1804, 1805, and 1806.* 693

[Note to Instructors: *Secret History* is among over 400 available editions from Broadview, any one of which may be packaged together with this anthology volume.]

JUDITH SARGENT MURRAY . 694

"On the Equality of the Sexes" . 695

from *The Gleaner Contemplates the Future Prospects of Women in This "Enlightened Age"* 702

BRITON HAMMON . 704

A Narrative of the Uncommon Sufferings and Surprising Deliverance of Briton Hammon, A Negro Man. . 705

PHILIP FRENEAU . 710

from *A Poem on the Rising Glory of America* online

from *The Rising Glory of America* online

from *Some Account of the Capture of the Ship Aurora* online

from *The British Prison Ship* online

The Hurricane . 712

The Wild Honey Suckle . 712

The Indian Burying Ground . 712

On Mr. Paine's *Rights of Man* . 713

To Sir Toby .714
In Context: Slavery in the Caribbean. .716
On the Religion of Nature. .717
Reflections on the Gradual Progress of Nations from Democratical States to
 Despotic Empires online
On the Universality of Other Attributes of the God of Nature online

PHILLIS WHEATLEY .718
To Maecenas .719
To the University of Cambridge, in New-England. .720
To the King's Most Excellent Majesty .721
On Being Brought from Africa to America .721
On Imagination. .721
To the Right Honourable William, Earl of Dartmouth722
To S.M., a Young African Painter, on Seeing His Works723
A Farewell to America. To Mrs. S.W.. .723
To His Excellency General Washington .725
On the Death of General Wooster online
On the Death of the Rev. Mr. George Whitefield .726
Selected Letters .729
 to Obour Tanner, 19 May 1772 .729
 to Selina Hastings, 27 June 1773 .729
 to Colonel David Wooster, 18 October 1773 .730
 to Obour Tanner, 30 October 1773 .731
 to Samson Occom, 11 February 1774. .732
In Context: Preface to Phillis Wheatley's *Poems on Various Subjects, Religious and Moral* . .733
In Context: Reactions to Phillis Wheatley's *Poems on Various Subjects, Religious*
 and Moral online
On the Death of a Young Lady of Five Years of Age. .734
On the Death of a Young Gentleman .735
An Hymn to the Morning. .735
On Recollection .735

LEMUEL HAYNES. .737
 from *Liberty Further Extended: Or Free Thoughts on the Illegality of Slave-Keeping*738
 Universal Salvation: A Very Ancient Doctrine online

ROYALL TYLER online
 The Contrast, A Comedy; In Five Acts
 from *The Algerine Captive*

SUSANNA HASWELL ROWSON .744
 Slaves in Algiers; or, A Struggle for Freedom .746
 from *Charlotte Temple* online

Hannah Webster Foster. .772
 The Coquette; or, The History of Eliza Wharton .774
 In Context: Elizabeth Whitman online
 In Context: *The Coquette* and the Eighteenth-Century Seduction Novel online
 In Context: Eighteenth-Century Marriage Advice online
 from *The Boarding-School; Lessons of a Preceptress to Her Pupils* online

Popular Literature and Print Culture .848
 Bay Psalm Book. .848
 from the Preface .849
 Psalm 23 [King James Version] .851
 Psalm 23 [Bay Psalm Book] .851
 Samuel Sewall, ["Verses upon a New Century"]. .851
 Henry Timberlake, "A Translation of the War-Song" [of the Cherokee] online
 from Benjamin Harris, *The New England Primer* .853
 from Benjamin Franklin, *The Printer to the Reader*854
 anonymous ("A Lady"), "Woman's Hard Fate". .855
 anonymous, *New England Bravery* .855
 Samuel Davies, from "The Duty of Christians to Propagate their Religion Among
 Heathens, Earnestly Recommended to the Masters of Negro Slaves in Virginia" online
 Samuel Davies, from "The Rule of Equity" online
 Mary Nelson, "Forty Shillings Reward" .857
 In Context: Forty Shillings Reward .858
 Mercy Otis Warren, "A Thought on the Inestimable Blessing of Reason" online
 Mercy Otis Warren, "On a Survey of the Heavens" online
 from James Revel, "The Poor, Unhappy, Transported Felon"859
 from William Bartram, *Travels through North and South Carolina, Georgia, East and
 West Florida, the Cherokee Country, the Extensive Territories of the Muscogulges or
 Creek Confederacy, and the Country of the Chactaws* online
 from Philip Freneau, "The Country Printer" .861
 from George Washington, Farewell Address online
 anonymous, "Every Man His Own Politician". .861
 from *The Philadelphia Repository and Weekly Register*862
 L'Embonpoint .862
 The Mother .862
 from anonymous ("Volina"), "You Say We're Fond of Fops—Why Not?"863
 Samuel Woodworth, "The Patriotic Diggers". .863
 William Ellery Channing, sermons online
 from "The Moral Argument against Calvinism"
 from "A Discourse on Some of the Distinguishing Opinions of Unitarians"
 ["The Baltimore Sermon"]

Charles Brockden Brown online
 from *An Address to the Government of the US on the Cession of Louisiana to the French*
 Somnambulism: A Fragment
[Note to Instructors: *Ormond* and *Edgar Huntly* are among over 400 available editions from
Broadview, any one of which may be packaged together with this anthology volume.]

DAVID GEORGE ... online
 An Account of the Life of David George

MARY JEMISON .. online
 from A Narrative of the Life of Mrs. Mary Jemison
 In Context: Illustrating Jemison's Narrative

TECUMSEH .. 865
 Speech to William Henry Harrison 867
 Speech to the Osages ... 871

WASHINGTON IRVING .. 873
 from A History of New York ... 875
 from Chapter 5 .. 875
 Chapter 5 [full chapter] ... online
 The Wife .. 877
 Rip Van Winkle ... 881
 In Context: Images of Rip Van Winkle 891
 In Context: A German Source for "Rip Van Winkle" online
 English Writers on America ... online
 The Legend of Sleepy Hollow .. online
 Traits of Indian Character ... online

APPENDICES

 Reading Poetry .. online

[Note to Instructors and Students: See the anthology's companion website for further supplemental resources, including a selection of historical maps and an interactive timeline.]

 Glossary of Terms ... 895

 Glossary of Poetic Terms .. online

 Maps .. 910

 Permissions Acknowledgments ... 920

 Index of Authors and Titles ... 925

PREFACE

A FRESH APPROACH

To those with some awareness of the abundance of fresh material and lively debate in the field of American literary studies in recent decades, it may seem surprising that this abundance has not been more fully reflected in the number of multi-volume anthologies. Shorter anthologies have come and gone, but the decades since the first appearance of *The Norton Anthology of American Literature* in 1979 have seen the publication of only one other anthology of comparable size, *The Heath Anthology of American Literature*—which, like the Norton, has long been available in five volumes. There has, in short, been no expansion in the range of available multi-volume anthologies to match the expansion of content and of approach that has characterized the discipline itself; the number of writing guides and business communication textbooks has multiplied steadily (to the point where there are literally hundreds of available choices), while the number of comprehensive anthologies of American literature has remained at two.

For those of us who have been working for the past three years on *The Broadview Anthology of American Literature*, it is not difficult to understand why. The very expansion of the discipline has made the task of assembling and editing an anthology that fully and vibrantly reflects the ways in which American literary traditions are studied and taught an extraordinarily daunting one. The sheer amount of work involved is enormous, but so too is the amount of expertise that must be called on. With that background very much in mind, we decided when we embarked on this project to involve a large number of contributors in the process (as the pages following the title page to this volume attest), and to encourage a high degree of collaboration at every level. First and foremost have been the distinguished academics who serve as General Editors for the anthology, but in all there have been hundreds of people involved at various stages in advising, researching, drafting headnotes or annotations,

reviewing material, editing material, and carrying out the work of designing and typesetting the texts and other materials. That approach has allowed us to prepare a large anthology of high quality with unusual speed—but we have throughout remained acutely aware of the importance of maintaining a high degree of consistency. Material has been reviewed and revised in-house at Broadview, by outside editors, and by a variety of academics with an extraordinarily diverse range of backgrounds and academic specialities, as well as by members of the group of General Editors for the project as a whole. The aim has been not only to ensure accuracy but also to make sure that the same standards are applied throughout the anthology to matters such as extent and coverage in author introductions, level of annotation, tone of writing, and student accessibility.

The General Editors have throughout taken the lead in the process of making selections for the anthology. Along the way we have been guided by several core principles. We have endeavored to provide a selection that is broadly representative, while also being mindful of the importance of choosing texts that have the capacity to engage readers' interest today. We have included a select number of longer works (among them Mary Rowlandson's *Narrative*, Benjamin Franklin's *Autobiography*, Elizabeth Ashbridge's *Account*, Susanna Rowson's *Slaves in Algiers*, Hannah Webster Foster's *The Coquette*, Black Hawk's *Life*, Frederick Douglass's *Narrative*, Henry David Thoreau's *Walden*, Herman Melville's *Benito Cereno*, and Rebecca Harding Davis's *Life in the Iron Mills*) in their entirety. On the other hand, where inexpensive high-quality editions of particular works are available in our series of Broadview Editions, we have often decided to omit these works here, on the grounds that those wishing to teach one or more such works may easily order them in a special-price combination package with the anthology; on these grounds we have decided against including Hawthorne's *The Scarlet Letter*, for example. With a number of works (among them Olaudah Equiano's *Interesting Narrative*, Thomas Paine's *Common Sense*,

Harriet Beecher Stowe's *Uncle Tom's Cabin*, Harriet Jacobs's *Incidents in the Life of a Slave Girl*, and Herman Melville's *Moby-Dick*), we have provided a substantial selection of excerpts.

Overall, our aim has always been to present American literature in the round—literature from the South and West as well as the Northeast, literature by a wide range of black and Indigenous as well as white writers, literature by Hispanic writers, literature reflective of different sexual orientations, and popular literature as well as literature established by scholarly and pedagogical convention as "literary." We have aimed to represent all genres—including oral literature and oratory (for which we include a special section in Volume B) as well as prose nonfiction, fiction, poetry, and drama. Throughout, we have aimed to include a wide range of selections by lesser-known writers as well as a full selection of works long accepted as part of the canon. From Elizabeth Ashbridge and Venture Smith to Absalom Jones and Lemuel Haynes, and from José María Heredia to Elias Boudinot and Margaret Jane Mussey Sweat, you will find many writers here who are not represented in most general anthologies of American literature. Nor is the anthology's expanded range a matter only of including writers who have never been part of the established canon of American literature. We have also taken a fresh look at the history of the canon in other ways; we acknowledge, for example, the central place that Henry Wadsworth Longfellow held in the literary imagination of nine-teenth- and early twentieth-century America by according him more space than has any general anthology of American literature for at least a half century.

By this point, readers of this preface may well be wondering if the anthology could possibly manage to find space for the works they have long been accustomed to teaching, and have no wish to stop teaching: works by the likes of Bradstreet, Emerson, Poe, Hawthorne, Melville, Dickinson, and Whitman. The short answer is yes; indeed, the selection of works by these writers is, overall, at least as great as that in existing anthologies. The Melville section, for example, runs to over 140 pages, the Dickinson section to over 90 pages, the Whitman to over 120 pages.

But surely no anthology can offer *both* such an abundance of material by canonical writers *and* a much broader selection of underrepresented writers? How is such a sleight of hand possible? In part, the inclusion of a greater range of material is made possible simply by the format we have adopted; a two-column, large trim-size format allows us to include, in a similar number of pages, a greater amount of material than do the formats adopted by other anthologies. But even using a larger trim-size, no anthology that limited itself to two bound-book volumes covering the Beginnings to Reconstruction (a further three projected volumes will provide coverage to the present) could possibly do an adequate job of representing American literature so fully. The key point here is that the Broadview is emphatically *not* simply a bound-book anthology; for these first two periods the website component of the anthology includes well over a thousand pages of material. These website selections are not "add-ons" prepared to a lower editorial standard and meant to be accorded a subsidiary status; as their inclusion in the anthology's main table of contents suggests, they are an integral part of the anthology itself, presented in the same format, and edited and annotated according to the same principles as the material included in the bound book volumes. Our research has suggested that most of the authors and works which we have included as part of the anthology's website component are likely to be taught somewhat less frequently than are the authors and works included in the bound book volumes. But we fully expect that a majority of instructors will wish to teach at least *some* of the selections that are to be found in the anthology's online component rather than in the bound books. (In some cases, too, we have gone against what our research has suggested about current pedagogical practice, and have included in the bound-book volumes work by lesser-known writers who we believe deserve to be more widely taught—just as, in the other direction, we have included in the anthology's website component a number of works that have long been part of the established canon.) In the end, of course, instructors will make their own choices, with the needs of their own students in mind; our aim is simply to provide instructors with the widest possible range of materials to choose from, prepared to a high editorial standard, and accompanied by the widest possible range of contextual materials.

How does this hybrid approach work in practice? A few examples may help to make plain the various ways in which it can work. In volume A, excerpts from Cotton Mather's *The Wonders of the Invisible World* are included in the bound book, while a substantial package of contextual materials relating to the Salem Witch Trials is included in the anthology's online component; Parts 1 and 2 of Franklin's *Autobiography* are included in the bound book (together with "Remarks Concerning the Savages of North America" and "On the Slave Trade"), while the full *Autobiography* is made available in the anthology's website component. Four of Crèvecoeur's *Letters from an American Farmer* are included in the bound book, together with a small selection of contextual materials, while two more of the letters (and a good deal more contextual material) are included in the anthology's website component. In volume B, Catharine Maria Sedgwick's "Cacoethes Scribendi" is included in the bound book, while "Berkeley Jail," excerpts from *Hope Leslie*, and excerpts from "Slavery in New England" appear in the anthology's website component; substantial excerpts from Thoreau's *Walden* (together with "Resistance to Civil Government") are included in the bound book, while the complete text of *Walden* is made available in the anthology's website component, together with contextual materials and a number of other works (among them "A Plea for Captain John Brown," excerpts from *The Maine Woods*, excerpts from the journals, and excerpts from *A Yankee in Canada*). In a small number of cases, audio selections are included in the online component alongside written texts, in recognition of the value of oral traditions.

The online component of the anthology is also important when it comes to the overview introductions to each volume. At the request of the large number of instructors we consulted on this matter, these overviews cover significant developments in American history as well as developments in American literary history. Indeed (and somewhat to our surprise), a substantial majority of those we surveyed felt that it was more important to include overviews of key aspects of the historical background in the bound book volumes than it was to include overviews of the literary genres. The genre introductions for each period are thus included (together with certain of the historical

overview sections, and with an overview of the development of language during the period) in the anthology's website component.

The way in which we have treated the poets George Moses Horton and Sarah Piatt is a good example of the degree to which a hybrid approach makes possible unprecedented opportunities for an anthology to be truly inclusive. Neither of these two writers has at this point a clearly established place in the canon; there is no handful of poems by either poet that have become familiar to all Americanists and that are included again and again in anthologies. Horton, author of the first book by a black Southerner and one of the most interesting poetic voices of the mid-nineteenth century, is rarely included in anthologies of any sort; even *The Norton Anthology of African American Literature* accords him only four pages. Piatt is more widely recognized, and is now represented by at least one or two poems in most anthologies of American literature—but, with the partial exception of "The Palace-Burner," there is no consensus on which of her poems most deserve to be read and studied. For each of these poets we present well over a dozen selections—some in the bound book, others as part of the anthology's online component. Our hope is that this approach may facilitate wider reading by both instructors and students, perhaps leading to some lively class discussions as to which poems by each poet are most engaging, most interesting—and most deserving of finding a place in the American literary canon.

One further point about a "hybrid" anthology such as this one deserves to be made; when an anthology comprises both bound book and website components, there is no need to remove any author or any work from the anthology—ever. Almost every academic who has been teaching for a few years has experienced the frustration that occurs when a new edition of a favorite anthology appears—and some of the selections that have *made* it a favorite anthology have been removed. With this anthology (as with Broadview's acclaimed anthology of British literature), any selections that, upon publication of a new edition, no longer appear in the bound book anthology, will readily be found in the anthology's website component.

In a number of cases the distinctive format of the anthology facilitates the presentation of content in an

engaging and practical fashion. Notably, the adoption of a two-column format allows for different versions of texts to be presented in parallel column format. That provides an opportunity for ready comparison, for example, of the *Bay Psalm Book* version of Psalm 21 with the King James version; of Thomas Jefferson's original draft of the Declaration of Independence with the final text; and of various different versions of several of Emily Dickinson's poems. It provides an opportunity as well to show translated material alongside the original. We present several of Sor Juana's poems both in the Spanish originals and in a facing-column translation; we present Jane Johnston Schoolcraft's Ojibwe-language poems with her own English translations; we present Longfellow's English and Italian versions of "The Old Bridge at Florence" side by side; and we present the original Spanish text of Heredia's "To Washington" alongside an English translation specially prepared for this anthology. The translated material in the "Popular Literature and Print Culture" section of Volume B—Wilhelm Weitling's "The Little Communist" and an excerpt from Ignace Nau's poem of Haiti, "Dessalines"—is presented in the same way. Readers are thus provided with an accessible translation while at the same time being able to experience something of the flavor of the original, in a format that provides for maximum convenience in comparing the two.

The large trim-size, two-column format also allows for greater flexibility in the presentation of visual materials. Throughout we have aimed to make this an anthology that is fully alive to the visual aspects of print culture, and, more broadly, to the connections between literary and visual culture. Readers will thus find an abundance of illustrations from the original texts, of facsimiles of title pages, of newspaper clippings of relevant articles, and of other pertinent images. Wherever possible we include with each author headnote an image of the author—and, with authors such as Truth, Douglass, Whitman, and Longfellow, we include a portfolio of other author images. In all there are hundreds of black-and-white illustrations in each volume—and we include in each volume as well twelve pages of color images.

Visual materials are also a key component of the background contextual materials that form an important part of the anthology. These materials are presented in two ways. Several "Contexts" sections on particular topics or themes appear in each volume of the anthology, presented independent of any particular text or author. These include broadly based groupings of material on such topics as "Slavery and Resistance," "Gender and Sexuality," and "Expansion, Native American Expulsions, and 'Manifest Destiny.'" Groups of "In Context" materials, on the other hand, each relate to a particular text or author. They range from the "Indigenous Experiences of Metacom's War" (presented as "In Context" material accompanying Rowlandson's *Narrative*); to "Images of Rip Van Winkle"; to a fugitive slave advertisement for Harriet Jacobs; to a selection of materials on the California Gold Rush (presented as "In Context" material accompanying excerpts from the memoirs of Vicente Pérez Rosales); to a selection of "Nineteenth-Century Images of Whales and Whaling" and "The Story of the Essex" (both presented as "In Context" material accompanying the anthology's substantial selection of *Moby-Dick* excerpts).

For the most part these contextual materials are, as the word suggests, included purely with a view to setting texts in their broader literary, historical, and cultural context. In some cases, however, the materials included in "Contexts" sections are themselves literary works of considerable stature; such is the case, for example, with Boyrereau Brinch's memoirs of life as an enslaved person in New England (excerpted in the volume A section "Contexts: Slavery and Resistance"); with Gottlieb Mittelberger's account of his time in America (excerpted in the volume A section "Contexts: Immigration and Indentured Servitude"); with William Wells Brown's history of the Haitian Revolution and Joseph Plumb Martin's narrative of everyday life as a soldier during the Revolutionary War (both of which are excerpted in the volume A section "Contexts: Rebellions and Revolutions"); with *The Narrative of Bethany Veney: A Slave Woman* (excerpted in the volume B section "Contexts: Slavery and Abolition"); with Susan Fenimore Cooper's *Rural Hours* (excerpted in the volume B section "Contexts: Nature and the Environment"), and with the various excerpts of works by Frederick Law Olmsted that are included as contextual material. In the inclusion of

texts such as these, as well as in other ways, the anthology aims to encourage readers to explore the boundaries of the literary and the non-literary, and the issue of what constitutes a "literary text."

We also take a rather different approach to popular literature than do competing anthologies. For decades now, the leading college-level anthologies of American literature have been making some space for texts that were popular in the eighteenth or nineteenth centuries but dropped from view in the early twentieth; works such as *The Coquette*, *Clotel*, and *Ruth Hall* have found their way into anthologies—as, of course, has *Uncle Tom's Cabin*. This renewed interest in popular and influential works of other eras, though, has often not extended to works that remained highly popular well into the twentieth century. This is particularly true of poems; works such as Longfellow's *Hiawatha* and "Paul Revere's Ride" and Whitman's "O Captain, My Captain," which were etched into the memories of generations of Americans, have been considered somehow inappropriate for inclusion in twenty-first-century anthologies. That is not the approach we take here; *The Coquette*, *Clotel*, *Ruth Hall*, and *Uncle Tom's Cabin* are certainly to be found in this anthology, but so too are *Hiawatha*, "Paul Revere's Ride," and "O Captain, My Captain." And so too are dozens of other works of popular literature—some within author entries, others in the substantial "Popular Literature and Print Culture" sections that are included in both of these first two volumes. From early poems such as the anonymous broadsheet "New England Bravery, Being a Full and True Account of the Taking of the City of Louisbourg by the New England Forces," Mary Nelson's "Forty Shillings Reward," and James Revel's "The Poor, Unhappy, Transported Felon"; to John Greenleaf Whittier's "Snow-Bound" and Elizabeth Oakes Smith's "The Drowned Mariner"; from Susanna Rowson's *Charlotte Temple*, Lydia Maria Child's *Hobomok*, and the anonymously authored "Theresa, a Haytien Tale" to Solomon Northup's *Twelve Years a Slave*, Ann S. Stephens's *Malaeska: Indian Wife of the White Hunter*, George Lippard's *The Quaker City, or, The Monks of Monk Hall*, and John Rollin Ridge's *The Life and Adventures of Joaquín Murieta: The Celebrated California Bandit*, an extraordinarily wide range of popular texts is presented. Our aim is to provide a broad-ranging representation of American literature that includes as full a sense as possible of American literary history and print culture.

Nor does the anthology neglect oral literature and oral culture. We provide a remarkably wide-ranging selection of Indigenous and African American oral literatures, and we incorporate a diverse array of speeches in both volumes. In anthologizing oral literatures in written form, we have aimed to be as transparent as possible in identifying when—and by whom—the oral works were recorded, and where possible we have included versions produced by writers from the communities to whom the stories belong. In the case of Indigenous traditions, we have also included a variety of visual pieces (such as wampum, story poles, and painted boxes). Indigenous oral and visual literatures are concentrated at the beginning of the anthology's first volume in recognition of Indigenous cultural precedence, but we have also endeavored to recognize the continued presence of Indigenous peoples and the continuing vitality of these forms—both by including some stories in contemporary versions and by including further examples of Indigenous oral and visual literature throughout the anthology volumes.

"AMERICAN": "American" is of course a slippery term. As used in expressions such as "American history" and "American literature," "American" is typically understood to mean "relating to the United States of America," rather than to all of the Americas, from Cape Horn to the North Pole. But we adopt a broad definition of "American" in this anthology, offering coverage that begins with the literatures of the people who inhabited what is now the United States, and contiguous areas; we include the literatures of Indigenous peoples first of all, and then those of settler colonists from Spain, France, and elsewhere as well as from Britain.

The fact that the United States of America as an independent nation existed first on the eastern seaboard has traditionally led to a strong emphasis in the teaching of early American literature on the literature of the east coast—and especially of the Northeast. Americanists in recent decades have pushed to broaden that scholarly and pedagogical focus, and those efforts have been reflected in recent editions of

the main anthologies. This anthology partakes of that broadening, and carries it further. In our coverage of Indigenous literatures, for example, we provide a range of materials from groups in the South, the Southwest, and the Northwest as well as from the East and Northeast. Similarly, the "Civilizations in Contact" section includes extensive coverage of civilizations in contact throughout North America. Hispanic authors—among them Sor Juana Inés de la Cruz, José María Heredia, Vicente Pérez Rosales, and the anonymous author of *Xicoténcatl*—are here given considerably more space than they are conventionally accorded. More space too is provided for Indigenous voices. And, whereas many anthologies of the past have treated the writings of Indigenous authors primarily as contextual material, we have chosen to accord author entries to a significant number of Indigenous authors, including Canassatego, Sagoyewatha, Tecumseh, Jane Johnston Schoolcraft / Bamewawagezhikaquay, Mà-ka-tai-me-she-kià-kiàk / Black Hawk, Elias Boudinot / Gallegina, and John Rollin Ridge / Yellow Bird.

CHRONOLOGY, PERIODIZATION, AND REPRESENTATION: Like the other major anthologies of American literature, this anthology uses chronology as its primary organizing principle. But we nevertheless aim to challenge established conventions of periodization in important ways. Significantly, we end the first two volumes not at 1865 but rather with Reconstruction; we include in volume B a wide selection of material covering the 1865–77 period. The most common point at which to break the two halves of an American Literature survey course has long been the end of the Civil War in 1865, and all other American literature anthologies use 1865 as a break point. Why take a different approach? One reason is simply that the amount of literary material any full survey course must at least touch on keeps expanding. Some of that expansion occurs as a result of the ongoing process of recovering lesser-known antebellum authors and texts, but the majority occurs simply as a result of the march of time. Moving the break from 1865 to 1877 runs the risk of giving short shrift to some important pre-bellum writers and texts. On balance, however, more and more Americanists are coming round to the view that the higher priority is to give somewhat more weight to more recent material; it

is in part for that reason that an increasing number of institutions now break the survey at 1877 rather than 1865.

But achieving an appropriate balance between the more recent past and earlier eras is not the only reason for choosing 1877 rather than 1865 as a break point. The two dates send different messages as to the arc of American history—and of American literary history. Choosing 1865 as a break point suggests a new beginning, a fresh start, with America having finally put the wrenching issue of slavery behind it. Choosing the end of Reconstruction as a break point suggests, arguably, something closer to reality: that, much as slavery itself may have ended, the legacy of slavery carried on as an enormously powerful shaping force in American history and literature. In making this choice, we recognize that historians no longer see 1877 as representing a clean break point, a precise moment at which Reconstruction's hopes of achieving equality were dashed and Reconstruction's ideals finally betrayed. They and we see it rather as one important moment in a continuum. But choosing such a moment emphasizes the importance of that continuum to the history and the literature of America. That is not to suggest that other topics that have received more emphasis in other anthologies—industrialization and urbanization, for example, or realism and regionalism[1]—are unimportant; far from it. We are confident that the coverage we provide of these and other related topics compares favorably to that of any other available anthology. But throughout the anthology we accord a place of utmost

[1] Through to the end of the twentieth century, the degree to which anthologies of American literature placed very little emphasis on racial inequality after the end of the Civil War is striking. Through to at least its 1994 fourth edition, for example, *The Norton Anthology of American Literature* included in its introduction to the history and literature of 1865–1914 America just one short paragraph on "the problem of racial inequality, more specifically what came to be known as the 'Negro problem.'" The 11-line paragraph—included almost at the end of the introduction—includes a brief discussion of Booker T. Washington and W.E.B. Du Bois; in the rest of the introduction, the only mention of a black author is the appearance of Charles Chesnutt in a list of "southern local colorists." The introduction's emphasis is entirely on the economic "transformation of a nation" ushered in by the Civil War—on industrialization and urbanization, in short—and, in literature, on realism and naturalism and regionalism. The authors never use the word "slavery"—or, indeed, the word "Reconstruction."

significance to slavery, the legacy of slavery, and, more generally, the ongoing struggle for equality.

In taking this approach, we recognize that a majority of institutions still break the survey course at 1865; for that reason, we will also include material covering the period 1865–77 in the forthcoming volume C (the first volume covering the second half of the survey). Much as the editors of this anthology may feel that the end of Reconstruction is a more appropriate break point than 1865, we have no desire to inconvenience those working within the traditional framework of the American Literature survey.

At several points in the anthology, we challenge the traditional periodization of—and the traditional emphases on—the scholarship and the pedagogy of American literature through departures from strict chronology. The first three authors we included in volume B, for example, are William Apess, Catharine Sedgwick, and James Fenimore Cooper—in that order. Had we followed strict chronology according to each author's birthdate (the guideline through most of the anthology), that order would be reversed, with Cooper appearing first (just as he appears before Sedgwick and Apess in the Norton and in other leading anthologies). Cooper was born a few months earlier than Sedgwick in 1789, and Apess was born almost a decade later—in 1798. In part, it can be argued, Apess might justifiably precede the other two, despite having been born later, on the grounds that his best-known work, the memoir *A Son of the Forest*, recalls an earlier time—his childhood and youth in the very early years of the century. But we felt there was a more important reason for beginning with an Indigenous writer such as Apess. Presentation involves issues of representation, and this anthology aims to represent Indigenous perspectives—like those of African Americans and other previously under-represented groups—more fully and more prominently than has traditionally been done in presenting the chronology of American literature. Foregrounding Apess rather than Cooper at the opening of a volume is one important signal. Including Sedgwick before Cooper is another—a sign that we feel it to be at *least* as important to represent the traditions in nineteenth-century American literature that Sedgwick was so influential in forging as it is

to represent the influence of Cooper and his famous "Leatherstocking" series.

One other point is worth making about the presentation of William Apess in this anthology. We have chosen to foreground in the bound book portion of the anthology his "An Indian's Looking-Glass for the White Man" and excerpts from his *Eulogy on King Philip*; we do include excerpts from *Son of the Forest* in the anthology, but in the website component rather than in the bound book. That is not to suggest anything negative about *Son of the Forest* itself. But it is to run counter to what has long been a powerful tendency in anthologizing authors from underrepresented groups. Far too often, in our view, such authors (and such groups) are represented exclusively by memoirs and other autobiographical writings, while their analytical or argumentative works are ignored. Here as in other respects we aim to present American literature more fully and fairly than it often has been presented—and to represent Indigenous writers, black writers, and so on more fully and fairly than they have been represented. Readers will find an abundance of autobiographical writings in the pages of this anthology, by writers traditionally underrepresented as well as by canonical writers such as Jacobs and Douglass. But they will also find fiction, poetry, and analytic and argumentative writings by such authors as Lemuel Haynes, Elias Boudinot, Harriet Wilson, George Moses Horton, Maria Stewart, David Walker, Martin R. Delany, and John Rollin Ridge.

AMERICAN LITERATURE AND AMERICAN HISTORY IN THE TWENTY-FIRST CENTURY: This anthology is being published at a time when, in many parts of the U.S., broad-minded approaches to the teaching of American history, culture, and literature are under severe pressure. Most notably, it is argued in numerous states that the teaching of "divisive concepts" (as the phrasing of Oklahoma's legislation puts it) is to be discouraged in public institutions—at the post-secondary level as well as in schools. Students, it is argued, should not be exposed to "overly negative" portrayals of America— by which is often implied portrayals of the nation's checkered history with respect to gender equality, its dispossession and mistreatment of Indigenous peoples, and its long history of racial oppression. Even a cursory

glance through the contents of this anthology will be enough to make clear we do not share that view. In these as in other respects, we have made every effort to present American literature in the context of a full and honest presentation of American culture and American history—which, in our view, has to include a full acknowledgment of the central role that settler colonialism, slavery, and racial oppression have played in that history, from the arrival of enslaved people in St. Augustine in 1565 and in Jamestown in 1619 through to our own time. But we do not present only the negative: far from it. Throughout the anthology we present a wide range of the texts that have reflected—and have shaped—the development of American ideals. Yes, we present Crèvecoeur's farmer's reflections on slavery and his jaundiced comments on the American Revolution—but we present too the glowing reflections on the American character that he puts forward in his "What Is an American?" letter. Yes, we provide the background on how the matter of slavery came to be omitted from the Declaration of Independence—but, in presenting Jefferson's original draft as well as the final text, we encourage a full and open discussion of the document that has been foundational in shaping American ideals. Literature that is straightforwardly expressive of the highest of those ideals—from John Winthrop and Roger Williams, to Phillis Wheatley and Canassatego and Benjamin Franklin, and on to Abraham Lincoln, Julia Ward Howe, Walt Whitman, and many others—features prominently in the anthology. But we believe too that many of the high points in American history and literature have been moments of resistance. From Thomas Paine and Absalom Jones to Lemuel Haynes and Judith Sargent Murray, from Tecumseh and William Apess to Lydia Maria Child and Margaret Fuller, from Henry David Thoreau to William Lloyd Garrison, the Grimké sisters, and Sojourner Truth, and on to David Walker, Frederick Douglass, Rebecca Harding Davis, Frances Harper—the list is a long one—some of America's finest literature has come from writers who struggled for justice and, in doing so, placed themselves in eloquent opposition to the tendencies of their time.[1] Authors such as

these are featured prominently throughout the anthology; in this as in other respects, we have striven to take a broad view, and to present American literature—and America—in the round.

COURSE TEXT OPTIONS: Our primary aim has been to provide an anthology of extraordinary quality and extraordinary range for use in American Literature survey courses of the sort that are found in the vast majority of North American colleges and universities; we envisage the two-volume package of volumes A and B as being a popular choice for any course surveying American literature from its beginnings to 1865 (or, as some courses now do, to 1877). The breadth and depth of coverage provided in the hybrid anthology also make it an excellent choice for upper-year courses of various sorts—courses covering narrower periods, thematic courses, and so on. For courses surveying Transatlantic Literature rather than American Literature only, an attractive option may be to create a custom text (either electronically or through Broadview's bound custom coursepack option), bringing together an instructor's preferred readings from this anthology and from *The Broadview Anthology of British Literature*—the format of which is almost identical to that of *The Broadview Anthology of American Literature*. Together, these anthologies offer several thousand pages of material to choose from in assembling your own custom course text. (We offer an easy and intuitive Custom Text Builder, and our Custom Text Administrator welcomes inquiries.)

Even for many teaching a standard American Literature survey course, the Broadview custom text option may be an appealing one. If, for example, you typically build your survey course around a small number of complete works, together with a relatively modest number of poems, short stories, essays, etc., you might bring together the shorter materials in a custom text of 200 pages or so, and then choose a special price package of Broadview editions. (Broadview's list of American literature editions now includes more

1 We give considerably less prominence to the authors who reflect sides of the American character that virtually everyone today finds deeply repugnant—but even these we do not entirely hide from

view. In certain Contexts sections and as part of the anthology's website component readers can find, for example, excerpts from racist "anti-Indian" writings, excerpts from "anti-Tom" novels written in defense of slavery, and so on. Here too, our aim is to further in every way possible students' understanding of the literatures of America, both in the context of today and in their historical context.

than 80 titles, from *The Female American*, Equiano's *Interesting Narrative*, and Paine's *Common Sense* to Wharton's *The Age of Innocence* and Fitzgerald's *The Great Gatsby*.) Editions may be packaged together for a special discount—or, if you decide to choose just one or two editions for use with the anthology, the edition(s) may be packaged together with the anthology for a nominal additional charge.

EDITORIAL PROCEDURES, CONVENTIONS, AND APPARATUS

The in-house set of editorial guidelines for *The Broadview Anthology of American Literature* now runs to over 40 pages, covering everything from conventions for the spacing of marginal notes, to the use of small caps for the abbreviations CE and BCE, to the approach we have adopted to references in author headnotes to name changes. Perhaps the most important core principle in the introductions to the various volumes, in the headnotes for each author, in the introductions in "Contexts" sections, and in annotations throughout the anthology, is to endeavor to provide a sufficient amount of information to enable students to read and interpret these texts, but without making evaluative judgments or imposing particular interpretations. In practice that is all a good deal more challenging than it sounds; it is often extremely difficult to describe why a particular author is considered to be important without using language that verges on the interpretive or the evaluative. But it is a fine line that we have all agreed is worth trying to walk; we hope that readers will find that the anthology achieves an appropriate balance.

INTRODUCTIONS AND AUTHOR HEADNOTES: Introductory headnotes are provided for each author included in the anthology; each "Contexts" section includes its own substantial introduction; and each volume includes an introduction to the period as a whole. The overview introductions to each volume of the anthology endeavor to provide a sense not only of the broad picture of literary developments in the period, but also of the historical, social, and political background, and of the cultural climate. Readers should be cautioned that, while there is inevitably

some overlap between information presented here and information presented in the author headnotes, an effort has been made to avoid such repetition as much as possible; the introduction to each period should thus be read in conjunction with the author headnotes and the introductions to the Contexts sections.

We aim throughout to be factual in the information we provide in author headnotes, and not to direct students' response with a particular evaluative or interpretive emphasis. But at the same time, we aim to engage student interest by making clear the degree to which and the ways in which a particular author's works have provoked a deep response or excited controversy, whether in their own day or in more recent times. Of necessity we provide something by way of conventional biographies of the authors—an overview of each author's life and works. But we strive as well in each case to provide what might be called a biography of the texts themselves: a summary of the reception history for key works, and an indication of why—in their own day, in our era, and in the intervening decades—the works have been considered worthy of attention and engagement (or, in some cases, have been unjustly neglected).

ANNOTATION: It is also often difficult to make judgments as to where it is appropriate to provide an explanatory annotation for a word or phrase. Our policy has been to annotate where we believe that most second-year undergraduates are likely to have difficulty understanding the denotative meaning. (We have made it a practice not to provide notes discussing connotative meanings.) But in practice the vocabularies of undergraduates at any given level may vary enormously, both from institution to institution and within any given college or university class. Where a word might not be known to many students but is not extraordinarily unusual or obscure, we will leave it to students unfamiliar with the word to look up its meaning. In the other direction, we make it a practice to annotate seemingly familiar words where they are being used in a text in ways that many undergraduates may not be familiar with; if a child is described as having grown up in "mean circumstances," we will gloss *mean* as *humble, impoverished*. On the whole, we provide somewhat more annotation than most

competitors, and somewhat less interpretation. Again, we hope that readers will find that the anthology has struck an appropriate balance.

SPELLING AND PUNCTUATION: The level of capitalization in many seventeenth-, eighteenth-, and early nineteenth-century texts can be a distraction for students coming for the first time to the literature of these periods—as can the ways in which such texts are often punctuated. Our general policy has been to use modern conventions of capitalization, and to lightly modernize spelling and punctuation, while also providing samples of important texts in the original (and indicating in the margin where the original spelling and punctuation have been retained). Where capitalization and italicization are concerned, we have made an exception in the case of certain authors and texts—Benjamin Franklin's *Autobiography* is a notable example[1]—where spelling and punctuation choices are known (or believed on reliable authority) to represent conscious choice on the part of the author rather than simply reflecting the common practice of the time.

Much as spelling and punctuation in the great majority of texts included in the anthology are lightly modernized, we aim to provide for readers a real sense of the historical development of the language and of print culture. To that end we have included in each volume many examples of texts in their original form—in some cases through the use of pages shown in facsimile, in others by providing short passages in original spelling and punctuation as described above. We have also included a section on the history of the language as part of the introduction to each volume. And throughout the anthology we include materials—visual as well as textual—relating to the history of print culture. While the anthology is intended for English-language courses, we have also made an effort through facsimile pages and facing-column translations to gesture toward the diversity of languages that are encompassed in American literature, including Spanish, French, and Indigenous languages such as Ojibwe and Massachusett.

We of course use modern conventions of American spelling and punctuation in all material newly prepared for the anthology (period introductions, author headnotes, annotations, etc.). We have not, however, "Americanized" all spellings in the texts themselves; texts from earlier periods of course use spellings that we would now categorize as British rather than American, which have been retained. (Instructors who wish to discuss with their students the development of American spelling can thus find in the anthology a wealth of material that is relevant.)

THE ETHICS AND POLITICS OF ANNOTATION, CAPITALIZATION, ETC.: Anthologies of American literature have traditionally allowed many offensive words or phrases (racist, sexist, anti-Semitic, anti-Muslim, anti-gay, etc.) either to pass entirely without comment, or to be glossed with apologist comments that leave the impression that such terms were excusable in the past, and may even be unobjectionable in the present. Most obviously, many anthologies print "the n-word" where it appears in various texts without remarking on its presence; our view is that, where such terms appear, they should be annotated, with a footnote making clear the degree to which such terms are highly offensive—and saying something as well about the history of their use. Derogatory comments about Jews and money and about the supposed cultural inferiority of Indigenous peoples are other examples. *The Broadview Anthology* endeavors in such cases, first of all, not to allow such words and phrases to pass without comment; and second, to gloss without glossing over. A few unacceptable slurs—such as the word "savage"—are unfortunately so omnipresent that we have elected not to gloss them at every usage.

Issues of ethics and politics often arise as well over debated points of present-day usage. Some of these—such as the decision whether or not to use "slave"—involve word choice. Our policy has been to avoid the use of this noun wherever possible; "enslaved people" may be somewhat more wordy than "slaves," but it has the advantage of emphasizing the essential humanity of those being referred to.

Other issues involve capitalization. As is the case with many other issues in the often-fraught history of racial and ethnic terminology, there may here be

[1] For those who may prefer to teach the *Autobiography* with modernized spelling and punctuation, we provide a lightly modernized text in the anthology's website component.

reasonable arguments that point in somewhat different directions. After much discussion, we have decided to capitalize the word "Indigenous" wherever it has been judged an appropriate term to use, but to refer wherever possible to specific groups (Ojibwe, Diné, etc.). We have chosen not to capitalize "black," however (except, of course, where it is capitalized in the literary texts themselves); though many respected media outlets have in recent years made it a policy to capitalize "black," our view is that the capitalization of "black" may be taken to implicitly encourage the highly questionable assumption that a single, monolithic "black" ethnicity or culture exists.

TEXTS: Each author entry concludes with a note on the text(s), addressing issues regarding different versions and source texts. In some cases, we have also used footnotes to clarify one or more textual issues or to indicate what translation has been used. Copyright information for texts and translations that are not in the public domain is provided on the website and within the bound books, in a section listing Permissions Acknowledgments.

We make it a practice to include the date when the work was first made public, whether through publication in print or, in the case of dramatic works, made public through the first performance of the play (or in the case of oratory, when the speech was first delivered). Where that date is known to differ substantially from the date of composition, a note to this effect is included in parentheses.

TIMELINES: The "Texts and Contexts" timelines provide in each volume a convenient parallel reference guide to the dates of literary texts and historical developments.

GLOSSARY: Here we have adopted an integrated approach, including political and religious terms along with literary ones in a convenient general glossary. While we recognize that googling for information of this sort is often the student's first resort (and we recognize too the value of searching the web for the wealth of background reference information available there), we also recognize that information culled from the Internet is often far from reliable; it is our intent, through this glossary, through our introductions and headnotes, and through the wealth of accessible annotation in the anthology, to provide as part of the anthology a reliable core of information in the most convenient and accessible form possible.

MAPS: Also appearing within each of the bound books are a selection of maps specially prepared for this anthology.

ONLINE COMPANION MATERIALS: In addition to the website component of the anthology itself, the main anthology website includes a range of companion materials. "Reading Poetry" provides a concise but comprehensive introduction to the study of poetry; it includes discussions of diction, imagery, poetic figures, and of various poetic forms, as well as offering an introduction to prosody. We provide as well a comprehensive glossary of poetic terms. Also appearing online is a selection of historical maps; these may supplement the maps in the bound book volumes in a variety of interesting ways. Additional companion materials on the anthology website include an interactive timeline and lists of the anthology's contents grouped by theme and author background.

ACKNOWLEDGMENTS

In addition to those whose assistance is acknowledged formally on the contributors' pages following the title page of this anthology, and those who were kind enough to grant permission to reprint copyrighted material (listed in the Permission Acknowledgments at the back of each volume) the General Editors and all of us in-house at Broadview owe an enormous debt of gratitude to the hundreds of academics who have offered advice and assistance at various stages of this project. In particular, we would like to express our appreciation and our thanks to the following:

Mary Grace Albanese, Binghamton University, State University of New York

Christopher Apap, Oakland University

Stephen Arch, Michigan State University

Marybeth Baggett, Liberty University

Brad Bannon, University of Tennessee, Knoxville

Margarita Barcelo, Metropolitan State University of Denver

Wesley Beal, Lyon College

Phillip Beard, Auburn University

William Bedford Clark, Texas A&M University

Ann Beebe, University of Texas at Tyler

Martin Bickman, University of Colorado, Boulder

John Blair, Texas State University

Anne Boyd Rioux, University of New Orleans

Nicholas Bradley, University of Victoria

Ashlee Brand, Cuyahoga Community College

Vince Brewton, University of North Alabama

Miriam Brown Spiers, Kennesaw State University

Michelle Burnham, Santa Clara University

Sandra Burr, Northern Michigan University

Cari Carpenter, West Virginia University

Vincent Casaregola, St. Louis University

John Casey, University of Illinois, Chicago

Abigail Chandler, University of Massachusetts Lowell

Mary Chapman, University of British Columbia

Schuyler Chapman, Glenville State College

Ben Child, Colgate University

Amanda Claybaugh, Harvard

Jim Coby, Indiana University

Michael Cohen, University of California, Los Angeles

Jeffrey Lamar Coleman, St. Mary's College of Maryland

Melissa Daniels-Rauterkus, University of Southern California

Clark Davis, University of Denver

David Davis, Mercer University

Richard De Prospo, Washington College

Christopher Diller, Berry College

Joseph A. Dimuro, University of California, Los Angeles

Don Dingledine, University of Wisconsin, Oshkosh

Kathleen Donegan, University of California, Berkeley

Virginia Dow, Liberty University

Paul Downes, University of Toronto

J. Michael Duvall, College of Charleston

Amy Earhart, Texas A&M University

S. Max Edelson, University of Virginia

Gregory Eiselein, Kansas State University

Berton Emerson, Whitworth University

Anna Esquivel, Jackson State Community College

Mike Everton, Simon Fraser University

Vera Foley, Gustavus Adolphus College

Laura Furlan, University of Massachusetts, Amherst

Brian Gazaille, University of Oregon

Lisa Gordis, Barnard College

Robin Grey, University of Illinois, Chicago

John Griffith, University of Washington

Christopher Hager, Trinity College

Kenneth Haley, Paris Junior College

Faye Halpern, University of Calgary

William Hammersmith, Liberty University

Lawrence Hanley, San Francisco State University

Lucas Hardy, Youngstown State University

Tamara Harvey, George Mason University

Jason Haslam, Dalhousie University

Heather Hathaway, Marquette University

John Hay, University of Las Vegas, Nevada

Desiree Henderson, University of Texas at Arlington

Melvin Hill, University of Tennessee at Martin

Andrew Hoberek, University of Missouri

Michael Hoberman, Fitchburg State University

Larry Howe, Roosevelt University

Zach Hutchins, Colorado State University

Coleman Hutchison, University of Texas at Austin

Gordon Hutner, University of Illinois

Mark Kamrath, University of Central Florida

Amelia Katanski, Kalamazoo College

Pam Kingsbury, University of North Alabama

Dana Kinnison, University of Missouri

Nadine M. Knight, College of the Holy Cross

Andrew Kopec, Purdue University, Fort Wayne

Cynthia Kuhn, Metropolitan State University, Denver

Kimberli Lawson, Brigham Young University

William Lawton, James Madison University

Hellen Lee, California State University, Sacramento

Lisa Logan, University of Central Florida

Laura Lorhan, University of California, Los Angeles

Christopher Love, University of Alabama

David Magill, Longwood University

Joshua Masters, University of West Georgia

Kristin Matthews, Brigham Young University

Barbara McCaskill, University of Georgia

Gabrielle McIntire, Queen's University

Diego Millan, Washington and Lee University

Keith Mitchell, University of Massachusetts, Lowell

Koritha Mitchell, Ohio State University

Lisa Moody, Southeastern Louisiana University

Heather Moulton, Central Arizona College

Erich Nunn, Auburn University

Nadia Nurhussein, Johns Hopkins University

Jeffrey Ostler, University of Oregon

Keri Overall, Weatherford College

Robert Dale Parker, University of Illinois, Urbana-Champaign

Jason Payton, University of Georgia

KJ Peters, Loyola Marymount University

Ben Railton, Fitchburg State University

Arthur Redding, York University

Peter Reed, University of Mississippi

James Riemer, Marshall University

Sian Roberts, Queens College

Elizabeth Robinson, Tennessee Technological University

Karen Roggenkamp, Texas A&M University-Commerce

Eric Russell, Central Michigan University

Elissa Minor Rust, Portland Community College

Debra Ryals, Pensacola State College

James Salazar, Temple University

Jennifer Schell, University of Alaska, Fairbanks

Sarah Schuetze, University of Wisconsin, Green Bay

Susan Schulten, University of Denver

Ormond Seavey, George Washington University

Jason Shaffer, United States Naval Academy

Cherene Sherrard-Johnson, University of Wisconsin-Madison

Mark Silverberg, Cape Breton University

Scott Simkins, Auburn University

Avery Slater, University of Toronto

Scott Slawinski, Western Michigan University

Angela Sorby, Marquette University

Derrick Spires, University of Illinois at Urbana-Champaign

Sunny Stalter-Pace, Auburn University

Nicole Stamant, Agnes Scott College

Jordan Stein, Fordham University

Carole Lynn Stewart, Brock University

Nancy Sweet, California State University, Sacramento

Brynnar Swenson, Butler University

Matthew Teutsch, Auburn University

Brianna Thompson, Kenyon College

David Thoreen, Assumption University

Michael Thurston, Smith College

Kathryn Walkiewicz, University of California, San Diego

Sarah Wasserman, University of Delaware

Ed White, Tulane University

Natasha Whitton, Southeastern Louisiana University

Caroline Wigginton, University of Mississippi

Maria Windell, University of Colorado, Boulder

Nathan Wolff, Tufts University

Chad Wriglesworth, University of Waterloo

Joan Wylie Hall, University of Mississippi

Hilary Wyss, Trinity College

Elissa Zellinger, Texas Tech University

Michael Ziser, University of California, Davis

America and American Literature, Beginnings to 1820

[Overview introductory sections on the following topics appear in the website component of the anthology:

Revolutionary Ideas, Enlightenment Thought
The Environment
Language in America, Beginnings to 1820

Literary Genres, Beginnings to 1820
 Poetry
 Prose Fiction
 Prose Non-fiction
 Drama]

Indigenous North American Cultures and Literatures

"My elders say this was how our world was created," writes Cherokee scholar Christopher B. Teuton:

> Before there was this solid earth on which we live, the place we call Elohi, there was only Galunlati, the Sky World, which exists high above the arch of the Sky-Vault. A long time ago, before humans, the ancient animals grew crowded in there; they needed more space to live and grow. … In the ancient time they were still changing; this was before their forms were finally shaped by their thoughts and actions.

The animals held a council and agreed to search the "vast world of water" below them to find a place where they could live. One by one, the animals failed in their search until Dayunisi, the small and unassuming water beetle, dove into the water and brought up a handful of mud from the depths:

> She places that dark mud on the surface of the dark blue water, and with the help of others it begins to spread out in all directions, growing and drying. And it becomes the world on which we now stand[.] …

All of the hundreds of Indigenous cultures in North America have their own narratives of creation. Each is unique, but there are sometimes commonalities; many, for example, feature an "earth diver" who, like the water beetle, obtains materials for the first land from deep under water. Some include the emergence of humankind from an underground realm, or a series of emergences into a series of higher worlds. According to Lakota tradition, while the earth was being prepared for human habitation, people lived underground in a spirit lodge; those who emerged too early were punished by transformation into buffalo, who would sustain the humans who came up to the land at the appropriate time. In Tlingit oral literature, the world was created by Raven, but it was in darkness until Raven cleverly stole the stars, moon, and sun to light it.

For many Indigenous peoples of North America, chronological precision is unimportant to traditional knowledge, and it is simply not a part of the narratives of origin—and, often, migration—that tell how each people came to be in its homeland. (Ethnological and archaeological consensus, too, are not specific as to when human society first emerged on the continent, though the earliest estimates are that it did so more than thirty thousand years ago.) But Indigenous traditional literatures evoke a deep, complex past and a history of environmental and cultural change. Some stories suggest that the people they belong to have been rooted in the same place from their very beginning; others suggest evolution through a series of metaphorical or geographical movements, and sometimes through merging or cultural interchange with other groups encountered along the way. Chickasaw knowledge-keepers, for example, say that their people traveled from the west under guidance from the Creator until they had crossed a great river, when there was disagreement as to where they should stop; those who stopped first became the Choctaw Nation, and those who continued eastward became Chickasaw.

Some migration stories are far less literal. The Diné (Navajo) creation story, for instance, involves the emergence of people from a dark first world into a succession of supernatural realms until they reach the Fifth World, where humans now live; in the Fourth World, they first encounter the Pueblo people. Some scholars see parallels between this Indigenous account and settler ethnographic accounts, which hold that the people of the Navajo Nation are descended from Athapaskans who journeyed from subarctic North America before settling in the Dinétah (an area including parts of what are now also called New Mexico, Colorado, Utah, and Arizona). There, they developed diplomatic relations with the Pueblo people whose civilization had long been established in the region; the Diné came to flourish not far from places abandoned early in the second millennium CE by Ancestral Puebloans, whose civilization had served as a continental center of trade and who had left behind massive buildings—many with hundreds of rooms—and hundreds of miles of roads.

Cultural exchange and historical change like this occurred in every part of North America. In the first half of the second millennium CE, there were many hundreds of different languages spoken on the continent by thousands of distinct cultures. Every type of landscape, from woodland to tundra to desert, supported a diversity of cultures—a diversity reflected in the fact that agricultural societies had cultivated as many as seven hundred species of corn alone (a staple crop across much of the continent). Agriculture, sometimes facilitated by vast irrigation systems, fed the Aztec Empire and other city-states in what would later be called Mexico and the southern U.S., while many peoples of the plains, the coast, and the northern woodlands regions developed specialized hunting and gathering skills, often practicing these skills alongside agriculture. Some peoples constructed imposing cities, while others moved freely through large territories, and some traveled seasonally between temporary settlements and permanent villages. Political systems were

This photograph, taken as part of the Historic American Buildings Survey in the mid-twentieth century, shows the ruins of Pueblo Bonito, the largest of the "great houses" built by Ancestral Puebloans. The complex, built between 850 and 1150, was four storeys tall and had more than 350 rooms on the ground floor alone.

equally varied, including small bands loosely linked by intermarriage; the aristocratic, expansionist Aztec Empire; and the democratic Haudenosaunee (Iroquois Confederacy), whose Great Law of Peace provides for each of its five (later, six) component nations to send delegates to a Grand Council where decisions affecting the whole Confederacy are made by consensus.

Such structures were not impervious to change; far from it. The fact that we do not in many cases have detailed written records of the histories of Indigenous societies should not be taken to suggest that those societies were static—that their histories began to unfold only with the arrival of Europeans. Take, for example, the case of the Great Law of Peace of the Haudenosaunee. When Europeans first encountered these peoples, their Great League was a long-established understanding—effectively, a pact of mutual non-aggression. But that had not always been the case; indeed, the formation of the pact had been preceded by a long period of wars and recriminations among the five—a period described in the Dekanawida legend (as set down in English in the early twentieth century by Mohawk Seth Newhouse and revised by Onondaga-Tuscarora Albert Cusick):

> The Ongweoweh [the original people] had fought long and bravely. So long had they fought that they became lustful for war, and many times Endeka-Gakwa, the Sun, came out of the East to find them fighting. It was thus because the Ongweoweh were so successful that they said the Sun loved war and gave them power. All the Ongweoweh fought other nations, sometimes together and sometimes singly, and oftimes they fought among themselves. … Everywhere there was peril and everywhere mourning. Men were ragged with sacrifice and the women scarred with the flints, and everywhere there was misery. Feuds with outer nations, feuds with brother nations, feuds of sister towns and feuds of families and of clans made every warrior a stealthy man who liked to kill. Then in those days there was no great law.

It was after a long period of such conflict that the prophet Dekanawida and his disciple Hayonhwatha (variously spelled Deganawida and Hiawatha, respectively) arranged a series of meetings of the feuding nations, and managed to negotiate a lasting peace accord—the Great Law of Peace.

Historians have not reached a consensus as to precisely when these momentous developments occurred; some say that the peak period of feuding among the Five Nations occurred in the fifteenth century, and the peace efforts of Deganawida and Hiawatha in the early sixteenth century, while others argue that the same succession of events transpired as much as several centuries earlier. But all agree that the events chronicled in the legend of Deganawida were crucial to the formation of what became the most powerful and influential Indigenous group in the northeast of the continent.

Diplomatic and economic links between Indigenous groups throughout the continent spanned vast distances; trade networks allowed for the movement of resources including seashells, ceramics, buffalo hides from the Great Plains, and fish oil from the Pacific Northwest. Turquoise, a valuable gemstone mined by Puebloans, was used as a trade currency as far north as the Great Lakes and as far south as the Aztec Empire. Trade was facilitated by roads spanning much of the continent, such that from Muscogee lands in present-day Georgia it was possible to trace travel routes all the way to the Pacific coast, where a road connected what is now northern Mexico to present-day Alaska.

North American Indigenous traditional literatures are as diverse and complex as the cultures they belong to, but generally speaking, oral literature historically played—and continues to play—a prominent role in Indigenous cultural expression. In the centuries before colonization, as now, Indigenous oral literatures spanned many genres, including songs; political speeches; chants, rituals, and other ceremonial works; and stories. It can serve a vast range of aesthetic, cultural, and spiritual aims, as Anishinaabe (Ojibwe) academic Niigaanwewidam James Sinclair describes:

> Now, as before, stories reflect the experiences, thoughts, and knowledge important to Anishinaabeg, and collectively map the creative and critical relationships, and philosophies and histories of kin. Among other reasons, stories create, define, and maintain our relations with each other and the world around us, and when shared, cause us to reflect, to learn, to grow, as families, communities, and a People. Stories also

indicate where we are in the universe, how we got here/there, and often indicate where we need to go.

Many peoples' most important works of oral literature have a long history of performance by skilled practitioners in a ceremonial context. Some such ceremonies, and the narratives they incorporate, can extend over multiple days; a recitation of the Haudenosaunee Great Law of Peace might take a week to ten days, while some Diné ceremonies last nine. Scholar Drew Lopenzina argues that ceremonial narratives play an important and distinctive role in the perpetuation of culture and of human and natural relationships:

> ... [W]hen the storyteller relates the creation of the world in a ceremonial setting, it is perceived not as mere invocation of ancient occurrences, but rather as an indispensable component of the world's continuance. It is the ceremony that keeps the world in motion, informing all its beings of right action and a proper ordering of events. The story itself is generative and it may change with each telling, just as the world itself is changing and reshaping the narrative order of our existence, but it is framed within a certain form and tradition that must be properly understood and enacted for the ceremony itself to be successful.

The ability of a story to change with each iteration, within the framework of tradition, is part of the particular power of oral literature. Each expert performance of a traditional Indigenous oral story—whether it occurs today or six hundred years ago—partakes of a long cultural lineage that shapes the content of the story and the method of its performance. But each performance is also shaped by the choices of the storyteller, whose gestures, vocal inflections, phrasing, and selection of what story elements to emphasize can all reflect the historical and cultural moment, the needs of the audience, and other aspects of the specific context in which the story is told.

Scholars have often attempted to impose universal categories on Indigenous stories. Culture hero stories, for example, are so called because they feature figures whose actions shape the world, such as Gluskap, who, according to the traditions of the Wabanaki Confederacy, played a role in the world's creation, taught humans the

skills they needed to live, and has saved humans from various monsters—often by transforming them into animals after defeating them. In Indigenous literature, culture heroes often overlap with trickster figures—multifaceted beings who are clever and powerful, but tend to be led astray by their appetites in ways that can be variously funny, ribald, sinister, philosophically profound, and morally or practically instructive. Tricksters may also be creators, like Raven of Tlingit stories, and they may have a shaping effect on the world after its creation, like Coyote, who brings death and sickness into the world in the stories of Maidu people, Caddo people, and many others. But while there are commonalities in the figures and motifs that appear in the traditional literatures of different Indigenous cultures, each must be understood as its own independent body of literature founded in the landscape, history, and moral and aesthetic standards of its people.

Nowhere are Indigenous literatures more diverse than in the vast array of visual modes of communication that peoples have developed across the continent. Ideas, stories, histories, diplomatic agreements, and messages of all kinds have long been recorded and communicated in literary forms specific to particular regions or nations. These forms include symbolic carvings and engravings, painted baskets, tattoos, scrolls, wampum belts and strings, maps, books, arrangements of stones or sticks—all carrying meanings legible to those with the knowledge necessary to read them. For example, many peoples of Dawnland (an Algonquian name for what are now New England, the Canadian Maritime provinces, and parts of Quebec) possess pictographic traditions with many uses, including map-making and long-distance communication. Pictographs inscribed into a tree might indicate where the author had experienced a successful hunt, or inform friends and family of the length and destination of the author's journey. Further north, Innu tshissinuatshitakana (message sticks), pieces of spruce placed according to symbolic conventions, were similarly developed to communicate with fellow travelers.

Many traditional literacies occupy a space between what European tradition would consider writing and visual art, sometimes combining visual with oral forms as well. Mayan writing, developed in Mesoamerica as early as the first millennium BCE, is so complex that

interpreting books aloud was an art form of its own: glyphs represented both syllabic sounds and entire words or concepts, and books incorporated pictures as well as glyphs that together conveyed the text's complete meaning. Among Haudenosaunee and other Northern woodlands peoples, an important form of communication and record-keeping is wampum—purple and white shell beads that can be patterned so as to convey ideas. For many hundreds of years, belts of wampum woven in symbolic patterns have been made to document diplomatic agreements and other significant events. The full meaning of the pattern is preserved in oral tradition, as wampum keepers in each generation learn to read the belts, using them as a guide to memory that enables them to speak at length on the knowledge held in the wampum. In the case of diplomatic agreements, wampum readings can function as diplomatic events in themselves, in which the involved parties gather to hear, discuss, and reinvigorate the agreement made concrete in the belt.

Many traditions recognize visual literacy as possessing a sacred power. In Anishinaabe tradition, for example, images inscribed on birchbark scrolls record important spiritual and historical knowledge; the scrolls, kept by the Midéwiwin or Great Medicine Society, serve as a complement to an oral tradition in which one must be educated in order to interpret them. Diné ceremonies generally employ both sacred chants and sandpaintings, detailed and symbolically rich images made by dropping sand, pollen, and other colored powders in precise ways. These sacred visual texts are intended to be destroyed in the course of the ceremony, and are sufficiently powerful that it is considered dangerous to oneself and one's community to capture them in permanent form.

The colonization of the Americas brought about a great deal of loss in Indigenous literatures, as the actions of settler-colonists—sometimes intentionally—destroyed whole cultures and interfered in numerous ways with the knowledge-keeping practices of the cultures that survived. Colonization also brought change to Indigenous literatures, as Indigenous people adapted European languages, genres, and forms of writing to their purposes, and as each people's oral and visual traditions have continued to evolve through centuries of political and cultural upheaval.

CONTACT, AND THE LITERATURES OF CONTACT

As Lenape elder Nora Thompson Dean recounted in the late twentieth century,

> Long ago there was a Lenape man who had remarkable powers. He would often go and meditate. He was able to foresee the future. One day he told his people, "Soon we will have visitors. They will be real white, fair-skinned people, and they will come from the east in a huge vessel. They are a people who will change our way of life."
>
> Not many people believed him, but finally one day the Lenape people saw a ship coming in. And when these men got out of their boat, the Lenape people were much amazed as they had light skin, blue eyes, and light hair. They were very stunned and dumbfounded, but most of the Lenape were so glad that these visitors had come that they put down furs for them to walk on.

The arrival of Europeans elicited various reactions on different parts of the continent—surprise, aggression, and gracious welcome among them. But one common thread is undeniable: contact brought tremendous change to Indigenous ways of life, as well as to the ways of life of the Europeans who came to the Americas. Christopher Columbus and his crew were not the first white people to reach the Atlantic coast of the Americas; Norse people, having established themselves on Greenland slightly before 1000 CE, had briefly settled in small numbers on the northeastern North American coast, while seafarers from various regions of the western European seaboard, including England and the Basque country, may have fished the Grand Banks off the coast of Newfoundland in the late Middle Ages. The extraordinary and destructive cultural, environmental, and political transformation initiated by Columbus's arrival in the Caribbean in 1492, however, was different from anything that had come before.

Columbus's actions during his early voyages presaged much of what was to follow as Europeans explored and colonized what they would call the New World: on his first voyage, he took Taíno prisoners and established a military base on Hispaniola, where Haiti and the Dominican Republic are now located; he subsequently enslaved hundreds of Taíno people for sale in

Mayans invented paper around 500 CE, and Mayan cities possessed libraries housing thousands of books. During the colonial era, almost all of these were deliberately destroyed by Spanish clergy. This image shows two pages from one of the few books known to have survived, known as the Paris Codex (for the city where it is now kept). Among other things, the codex contains precise astronomical information and a calendar denoting the appropriate rituals for a 360-year period.

This wampum belt, known as the Dust Fan Belt, is kept by the Onondaga Nation. According to its keepers, it was made at the foundation of the Haudenosaunee Confederacy, and its imagery evokes the confederacy's principles. The Onondaga interpret the belt as evoking two powerful symbols, first of the Tree of Peace, a giant white pine that was uprooted at the foundation of the Haudenosaunee Confederacy of Five Nations. Into the cavity of the uprooted pine, the nations threw their weapons of war, which were then buried when the tree was replanted; an eagle was placed at the top to guard the Confederacy against potential dangers. The white pine is also symbolic of the Confederacy itself, as the tree's needles grow in bundles of five, the number of nations originally in the Confederacy. The pattern of the belt also suggests the shape of a dust fan, a reminder of the need for clear vision. There is no beginning or ending to the belt—the pattern continues beyond its borders—suggesting the long continuity of the Confederacy and its values.

Spain. Believing there to be vast gold deposits in one area of Hispaniola, he demanded each of its inhabitants produce as tribute an impossible quota of gold—and cut off the hands of those who inevitably failed. Before 1500, more than half of the island's Indigenous population was dead, mostly due to execution, forced overwork, or suicide, and the Spanish began to bring in enslaved Africans to replace them as a source of labor. "Who in future generations will believe this?" wrote the friar and historian Bartolomé de las Casas, reflecting on the scale of the destruction. "I myself writing as a knowledgeable eyewitness can hardly believe it."

Columbus's ventures marked the beginning of an age of exploration and colonization by European powers. These efforts were dominated by Spain in the sixteenth century, and increasingly by England from the seventeenth century onward, though many other nations competed to secure for themselves the labor, resources, and land of the Americas. Often, Indigenous people were affected by colonization even before their own territories were occupied, as invasive species, disruptions to trade patterns, and, above all, foreign diseases caused immense suffering, dramatically reduced Indigenous populations, and created political and economic instability. The shrewdest colonizers—who were, in the early phases of colonization, vastly outnumbered by Indigenous people—did not hesitate to take advantage of these weaknesses, or to exploit pre-existing diplomatic tensions between Indigenous groups.

The Spanish conquistador Hernán Cortés, for example, would have had very little chance at defeating the powerful Aztecs with only the small force at his command—and did, in fact, fail disastrously in his early attempts. But the capital city of Tenochtitlan was soon ravaged by smallpox and famine, and Cortés formed an alliance with the nearby Tlaxcalans, who saw an opportunity to free themselves from Aztec dominance. With ten thousand Tlaxcalan warriors and mere hundreds of Spanish soldiers, Cortés massacred

Illustration from *The General History of the Things of New Spain*, sixteenth century. Known as the Florentine Codex for the city in which it is now held, *The General History of the Things of New Spain* is a massive compendium of Aztec history, culture, and knowledge written in Spanish and Nahuatl (the language spoken by Aztecs). The book is the result of a decades-long collaboration between the Spanish friar Bernardino de Sahagún and dozens of Nahua scholars and artist-scribes. The illustration reproduced here depicts an epidemic of smallpox that occurred shortly after Europeans introduced the disease to the Americas. Most of the book is lavishly colored, but the last portion, from which this image was taken, is not; another epidemic struck, forcing the book's creators to sequester themselves, and they ran out of pigment before completing the project.

the people of Tenochtitlan in 1521. Less than a decade later, an anonymous poet wrote of the siege in Nahuatl (the language spoken by Aztecs):

> Broken spears lie in the roads;
> we have torn our hair in our grief.
> The houses are roofless now, and their walls
> are red with blood.
>
> Worms are swarming in the streets and plazas,
> and the walls are splattered with gore.
> The water has turned red, as if it were dyed,
> and when we drink it,
> it has the taste of brine. ...

The European settler-colonizing presence spread quickly: after failed attempts earlier in the century, Spanish colonizers founded presidios (fortified settlements) at St. Augustine, Florida, in 1565 and Santa Fe, New Mexico, in 1610. Exploration of the Pacific, led by Spanish and Portuguese explorers, was not as thorough as Atlantic exploration, but by the late sixteenth century Spain's trade routes crossed both Pacific and Atlantic Oceans, with some ships stopping to replenish their fresh water on the California coast as they completed the treacherous route between the Philippines and South America. The English, too, explored the Pacific coast, primarily as privateers seeking Spanish trade goods—though Sir Francis Drake alarmed the Spanish government in 1579 by making diplomatic contact with Indigenous inhabitants of northern California and declaring it "Nova Albion" (New England). (As it turned out, California would indeed be settled by the Spanish, beginning in the mid-eighteenth century with the presidio of San Diego.)

As they staked their claims, colonists frequently overwrote North American place names with their own; California, for example, was named for a fictional island described in the early sixteenth-century Spanish romance *Las Sergas de Esplandián*:

> Know, then, that, on the right hand of the Indies, there is an island called California, very close to the side of the Terrestrial Paradise, and it was peopled by black women, without any man among them, for they lived in the fashion of Amazons. ... Their arms were all of gold, and so was the harness

of the wild beasts which they tamed and rode. For, in the whole island, there was no metal but gold.

Many colonizers, especially in the early period, were motivated by genuine belief in myths such as that of the fantastically wealthy city of El Dorado, which was sought by Antonio de Berrio, Walter Ralegh, and numerous other explorers.

English settler-colonization did not begin in earnest until the seventeenth century, when English colonizers established settlements concentrated in the Caribbean; in what are now Virginia and the Carolinas; and in New England, the location of Plymouth Colony (1620), the Massachusetts Bay Colony (1630), and several others. When John Smith named this last region "New England" in 1616, English settlement in North America was far from fully established. On the contrary, the small population of early colonists in New England and Virginia frequently struggled merely to survive. With little knowledge of the landscape or the local economies, they relied on the knowledge of Indigenous people—some they had kidnapped and some they communicated with peacefully—and on Indigenous food stores, both stolen and traded for. As John Smith wrote in 1617, "had the savages not fed us" the Virginia colonists "directly [would have] starved." On the New England coast, Indigenous homes still significantly outnumbered settler-colonist dwellings a decade after the arrival of the *Mayflower*. Cultural interchange was multidirectional: Indigenous people adopted aspects of European homes and fortifications; Europeans adopted canoes; wampum came to be used as a currency across the region; and pidgins (simple languages used for trade) developed out of different, mutually intelligible Indigenous languages, influencing both Indigenous and European speech.

Even as English settlement became more developed, power relations in New England were far from straightforward. The Narragansett, Abenaki, Pequot, Mohegan, Wampanoag, and several other Indigenous peoples who lived there each had their own internal and external conflicts, diplomatic connections, and agendas, and some found opportunities for advancement in forming alliances with colonist communities. Colonists turned diplomatic instabilities to their advantage, most infamously during the genocidal Pequot War (1636–38). An alliance of English colonies

This map, which appeared in John Smith's *A Description of New England* (1616), is the first to apply the name "New England" to the region formerly known to colonists as "North Virginia." The map features place names selected by the teenaged Prince Charles (1600–49), later King Charles I, and Smith included a table showing "the correspondence of the old names to the new." Most of the place names assigned on the map were not retained in the long term, but a few were: Accomack, for example, was renamed Plymouth, and the Massachusets River was to be known as the Charles.

including Massachusetts and Plymouth singled out the powerful Pequot for elimination and formed an alliance with the Narragansett and Mohegan, pre-existing enemies of the Pequot. The Indigenous allies of the English were appalled when the war culminated in the Mystic Massacre, during which English soldiers set fire to the Pequot fortress and killed everyone inside, including children and civilians as well as warriors. The Narragansett disclaimed the massacre, declaring that the English were "too furious, and slay[ed] too many men," but the damage was done: the English enslaved the survivors, forbade them from calling themselves Pequot, and demanded that all Indigenous people of the area bring them the heads of any Pequot they discovered. The war brought about a fundamental shift in the region's power relations by revealing what the English were capable of, and even the Narragansett and Mohegan, who had entered the war thinking themselves equal allies, ended in a position of subservience. To the Indigenous groups who had been neutral in the conflict, the English had replaced the Pequot as the dominant group in the area; the Montaukett sachem Wyandanch, for example, agreed to give the colonists "tribute, as we did the Pequots."

On the European side, too, conflicts were multi-faceted. The Dutch settlers of New Netherland were threateningly near to the New England colonies, and in the mid-seventeenth century, New Netherlanders found themselves confronting, according to council minutes, "on the one side the war with the savages and on the other side the approach of the English." According to colony records, the English similarly feared that "at the same time they shall fall upon the English: the Dutch from their ships, the Indians by land." Enmity even arose between colonies of the same parent nations, as demonstrated in the bitter rivalry between the Puritan-dominated Plymouth Colony and the nearby, relatively secular colony of Ma-re Mount. Thomas Morton, Ma-re Mount's founder, hosted revelries for both settler and Indigenous people, to whom he also sold guns; Plymouth colonists disapproved so strongly of these actions that they eventually arrested him and sent him back to England as an accused criminal.

In other contact regions of North America, as in New England, settler-colonists—often from more than one European nation—shared with diverse Indigenous groups a complex web of trade, cultural interchange, conflict, and brutality. In Florida, for example, the vast La Chua Ranch, operated by Spanish, Mexican, Native American, and enslaved African people, was at the center of a trade not only in beef but also in Cuban rum and Indigenous-grown corn. In the Great Lakes region, French missionaries converted large numbers of Wendat (Huron) people and allied with them against their Haudenosaunee rivals. There, too, the French were vastly outnumbered by Indigenous people and relied on them for the success of their colonial enterprise; as Mary McKey, a Wendat elder, phrased it in an oral history, "When the white man was first seen here, in the old time, he began to barter with our ancestors. Nowhere could he step without coming across some red man."

In European literature of contact, writers attempted to understand but also to lay claim to an unfamiliar land, and occasionally to condemn but more often to advocate colonization. The accuracy of narratives of discovery varies tremendously, but all are shaped at least to some degree by the agendas of their authors and by the European cultural and literary frameworks they used to interpret what they witnessed. Columbus's first letter of discovery (1493), for example, is an explicit request to the Spanish monarchy to finance further expeditions. Its description of his exploits bears the influence of earlier travel narratives set largely in Asia, such as *The Travels of Marco Polo* (c. 1300) and *The Travels of Sir John Mandeville* (mid-fourteenth century), reflecting Columbus's belief that he had reached the Asian coast. Cortés, in his "Letters of Relation" (1519–26)—another blatant attempt to secure royal support through the medium of print—describes the Aztec ruler Moctezuma's palace as having "a large patio, laid with pretty tiles in the manner of a chessboard." This feature is unlike anything in Indigenous Mesoamerica but quite common in the architecture of the Moors, an enemy whom the Spanish monarchy had recently defeated in Granada. *The General History of Virginia, New England, and the Summer Isles* (1624), John Smith's account of his prominent role in the establishment of Jamestown and his later experiences in other English settlements, includes some self-aggrandizing passages that similarly call into question the accuracy of his

Samuel de Champlain, "Defeat of the Iroquois at Lake Champlain," 1613. Samuel de Champlain, an explorer who played a key role in the early colonization of New France, was also an artist and writer who illustrated his own accounts of his experiences. The above image depicts Champlain at the center of a battle in which Haudenosaunee warriors were defeated by a group consisting of a few French people and a number of Wendat, Innu, and Algonquin people. Champlain described the incident as follows:

When I saw [the Haudenosaunee] make a move to draw their bows upon us, I took aim with my arquebus and shot straight at one of the three chiefs, and with this shot two fell to the ground and one of their companions was wounded who died thereof a little later. I had put four bullets into my arquebus. As soon as our people saw this shot so favourable for them, they began to shout so loudly that one could not have heard it thunder, and meanwhile the arrows flew thick on both sides. The Iroquois were much astonished that two men should have been killed so quickly, although they were provided with shields made of cotton thread woven together and wood, which were proof against their arrows. This frightened them greatly. As I was reloading my arquebus, one of my companions fired a shot from within the woods, which astonished them again so much that, seeing their chiefs dead, they lost courage and took to flight, abandoning the field and their fort, and fleeing into the depth of the forest, whither I pursued them and laid low still more of them. Our Indians also killed several and took ten or twelve prisoners.

work. Most famous among these is an encounter with Wahunsonacock, chief of the Powhatan Confederacy, who, according to Smith, was about to execute him when the chief's daughter, Pocahontas, supposedly risked her own life to prevent the execution.

Alongside personal and national ambition, religious conviction was a key motive for colonization—and one that was often invoked in discovery and settlement accounts. To some Spanish colonizers, bringing Catholicism to Indigenous people was the predominant goal; according to the memoirs of Bernal Díaz del Castillo, a participant in the conquest of Tenochtitlan, the conquistadors came "to serve God and his Majesty, to give light to those who were in the darkness"—if also, Castillo adds, "to grow rich as all men desire to do." Though Spanish missions and civil governments were often in conflict, the twin purposes of wealth and proselytization were in many respects complementary, as Spanish missionaries tended to make the closest contact with Indigenous villages, cultivating diplomatic relationships with Indigenous groups as potential sources of labor. In the Great Lakes region at the center of New France, religious proselytization motivated missionaries to learn Indigenous languages and ways of living; this facilitated the development of the diplomatic and economic relationships underlying the fur trade. Many of the settlers of New England were Puritans, Protestants who believed the Anglican Church to be corrupted by Catholic influence. They saw settlement in the New World as a way to establish a spiritually upright society in which they could live according to their principles. For these settlers, their experiences paralleled those of the Israelites, God's chosen people, recounted in the Bible: hardships were tests of faith, and successes were signs that their colonization of the land was willed by divine providence.

"Many good religious devout men have made it a great question," John Smith acknowledged in his *Advertisements for the Unexperienced Planters of New England, or Any Where* (1631), "as a matter of conscience, by what warrant they might go to possess those countries, which are none of theirs, but the poor salvages [savages']." Indeed, writings about colonization often struggled to justify the exploitation, dispossession, and killing of Indigenous people, especially as these facts conflicted with settler-colonists' belief in

Seal of the Massachusetts Bay Colony, 1629. The original seal of the Massachusetts Bay Colony, developed when the colony received its charter in 1629, depicts an Indigenous man saying "come over and help us." He holds an arrow pointing down, a symbol of peace.

their religious purpose or their political right to the territory. The justifications colonists used were sometimes mutually contradictory. Robert Cushman, a Plymouth supporter, argued that there was a spiritual imperative to "conver[t] ... the heathens" but also described the land as "empty." At the same time, many colonists went so far as to interpret the devastating epidemics that swept Indigenous communities as a divine blessing that reflected God's support for the settlers. Even the relatively Indigenous-friendly colonist Thomas Morton praised "the wondrous wisdom and love of God, ... shown by sending to the place his Minister [i.e., disease], to sweep away by heaps the Salvages." Belief that God had granted them the right to settle North America was used to excuse even extreme violence; John Underhill, a soldier who commanded the

massacre of the Pequot, wrote that "We had sufficient light from the word of God for our proceedings."

Often, narratives of discovery were inconsistent in the degree to which they acknowledged that North America was even occupied. John Smith wrote, for example, that settlers should come because "the country of the Massachusetts" was a "Paradise … for here are many isles all planted with corn; groves, mulberries, salvage gardens, and good harbors." On the other hand, William Bradford, a leader of the Plymouth colonists, wrote of "those vast and unpeopled countries of America, which are fruitful and fit for habitation, being devoid of all civil inhabitants, where there are only salvage and brutish men, which range up and down, little otherwise than the wild beasts of the same." Even as, in actuality, the English relied on Indigenous knowledge and resources to establish their settlements, they argued that the Indigenous inhabitants had limited rights to the land because they had failed to cultivate it. Cushman claimed that "[t]hey are not industrious, neither have art, science, skill or faculty to use either the land or the commodities of it, but all spoils, rots, and is marred for want of manuring, gathering, ordering, etc."

Even the size of European territorial claims could represent a distortion of the facts. Seventeenth-century New France, for example, consisted of only a few settlements, but the French claimed to have "discovered" and to possess a vast area of the North American interior. For much of the colonial period, the reach of colonists beyond the east coast and the southern portion of the continent was limited, and much of North America remained mostly or wholly Indigenous in population. As late as 1782, J. Hector St. John de Crèvecoeur marveled that

> Many ages will not see … the unknown bounds of North America entirely peopled. Who can tell how far it extends? … for no European foot has as yet travelled half the extent of this mighty continent!

The continent was, of course, already "peopled." For the societies of the north and west, disruptions were relatively small in the first centuries, but for those in contact regions change was harsh and abrupt. Some Indigenous people migrated out of contact regions, others tried military resistance, and others attempted to make economic and diplomatic opportunities for themselves out of the changes. For many, this latter approach involved selectively adopting European cultural practices, including writing in European languages. In Mexico, scribes who were already trained in their own complex writing system quickly acquired the alphabet used by the Spanish. Through their early adoption, they preserved pre-contact works as well as accounts of colonization that might otherwise not have survived in written form, as Spanish clergy systematically destroyed Aztec and Mayan books.

In New England, many seventeenth-century sachems enlisted settlers to write diplomatic letters on their behalf, and some Indigenous students soon began to seek a European education that would help them advocate for their communities. A number of these students attended Harvard. The college had a mandate to educate them for the purposes of proselytization, but they learned Latin, Hebrew, and Greek and studied classical literature and philosophy as well as Christian theology. North America's first printing

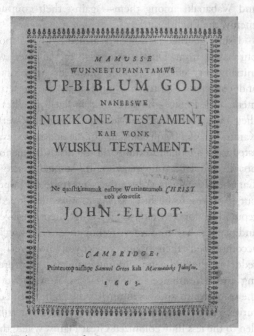

Title page of *Mamusse Wunneetupanatamwe Up-Biblum God*, also known as the Eliot Indian Bible or Algonquian Bible, 1663.

press, the Cambridge Press, was operated by Wowaus, a Nipmuc man also known as James Printer. Among its publications was the first Bible to be printed in North America, an Algonquian translation known as the Eliot Indian Bible (1663) for its overseer, the Puritan settler John Eliot, but written largely by Indigenous scholars.

Some Indigenous groups responded to settler-colonial encroachment with immediate violence. The Calusa of what the Spanish called La Florida, for example, responded aggressively to almost every Spanish attempt at diplomatic or missionary engagement, a strategy that kept them independent until the early eighteenth century. More often, Indigenous groups were friendly at first, but came to consider diplomatic efforts futile as settler-colonists claimed dominance over ever-expanding territory and demonstrated their willingness to exploit and brutalize Indigenous people. One famous early attempt at a military solution to the threat posed by colonization was King Philip's War (1675–76), named for the Wampanoag sachem Metacom (also known as King Philip). Metacom's leadership helped to unite a large number of New England Indigenous peoples—Nipmuc, Narragansett, and Wabanaki among them—against their common enemy, the English settlers.

Using guerilla tactics and armed with weapons purchased from Dutch colonists, the alliance was initially very effective, killing hundreds of colonists and completely destroying more than fifteen settlements. The English, however, had Indigenous allies of their own, including the Mohegan and the powerful Kanien'kehá:ka (Mohawk), and in the end they devastated their opponents, killing thousands of Indigenous people and enslaving many more, some for sale to Caribbean colonists. A lucrative slave trade developed, but it proved to be brief as the captives developed a reputation for tenaciously resisting their enslavers, and planters began to refuse to buy them. The English accomplished their main objectives, however, in reducing the Indigenous population and discouraging armed resistance to colonization. At the end of the seventeenth and beginning of the eighteenth centuries, people from more than thirty east coast tribes fled to the less fully colonized Great Plains, where they formed hybrid cultures with the tribes already living there. Through this migration, they achieved almost another hundred years relatively free from the direct interference of settler-colonists.

While in reality Indigenous people faced captivity in much larger numbers than colonists, the colonial genre of the "Indian captivity narrative," typically written by and for white readers, focuses on the sufferings of colonists held captive by Indigenous groups. The genre began to develop not long after North American colonization itself, with the earliest first-person captivity accounts published in the mid-sixteenth century. *The Relation of Álvar Núñez Cabeza de Vaca* (1542) was a particularly early and influential firsthand narrative. In it, Cabeza de Vaca recounts the growth of his Catholic faith and of his respect for Indigenous peoples during the eight years he spent lost between what the Spanish called La Florida and Mexico, including a period of enslavement in what is now Texas. The secondhand narrative of Juan Ortiz, retold by numerous authors but most famously in Inca Garcilaso de la Vega's *La Florida del Inca* (1605), was also influential. Ortiz's account of his capture by the people of Uzita, where the daughter of the cacique (chief) saves him from execution, may have inspired John Smith's account of his salvation by Pocahontas.

In English, the most influential early captivity narrative by far was Mary Rowlandson's *The Sovereignty and Goodness of God* (1682), an account of her abduction and captivity during King Philip's War. Rowlandson's story established a pattern that many (though not all) English-language captivity narratives would follow: a white protagonist, especially a white woman, whose suffering is the primary subject of the account; a focus on the testing and development of the protagonist's Christian faith; and detailed but also frequently inaccurate and racist depictions of Indigenous people and cultures. In this respect, captivity narratives are like much of the early American literary canon, in which Indigenous experiences of contact are usually obscured or distorted. These experiences are, however, more directly communicated in colonial-era Indigenous people's own writings and nonalphabetic works; in their dictated letters, transcribed speeches, and legal documents; and in oral histories that Native American peoples continue to preserve.

RELIGION IN EARLY AMERICA

When the subject of religion among the settlers of what would become the United States arises, the Puritans of New England come to many minds first. Primary school students dress up as Pilgrims and learn how these early English settlers journeyed from Europe to the New World in search of religious liberty. But long before the Plymouth settlers arrived aboard the Mayflower in 1620, or even before their fellow English colonists in Virginia founded Jamestown in 1607, Spanish-speaking Catholics had traversed North America, seeking to convert—and to conquer—the Indigenous peoples of Florida and much of what are now the states of Texas, New Mexico, Arizona, and California. Indeed, throughout the sixteenth and seventeenth centuries, many of the areas that would eventually become the United States were explored and settled by French- and Spanish-speaking Catholics. Maryland, founded in 1632 as a Catholic colony, is estimated to have had a Catholic population of 3,000 in 1700; the combined Catholic population of what are now the southwestern states, Louisiana, and Florida, though difficult to estimate, was certainly far, far larger. Indeed, the oldest known Christian church in what is now the continental United States stands, not in Plymouth or Jamestown, but in Santa Fe: San Miguel Mission, built between 1610 and 1626.

Though the Puritans may not deserve quite so central a place in early American history as they have often been accorded, there is no question of their importance. The Puritans were not originally a denomination unto themselves, but rather a large group within the established Church of England; they took their name from their desire to purify the church by ridding it of its more "popish" or Roman Catholic elements. They embraced the doctrines laid out by John Calvin, a French theologian who argued from biblical proofs that only a small number of individuals (the "elect") had been predestined for salvation from the time they were born. Because the Puritans felt that the Church of England's clerical hierarchy discouraged individual congregations from making their own decisions, they organized their churches as congregational polities, in which each male member of the church participated in decision-making. (This organization was less egalitarian

Timothy H. O'Sullivan, *The Church of San Miguel, Santa Fe,* 1873.

than it sounds, since only those who had proven they were among the elect could be members of the church.) And because they objected to the sumptuous display in Anglican church decoration and clerical dress, the Puritans held their services in unadorned meeting-houses and would not even allow musical instruments during worship. Though they had been persecuted for their religious beliefs in England, this did not make the Puritans more inclined toward religious tolerance when they reached America. The Massachusetts Bay colonists, for instance, drove Quakers and members of other denominations out of the colony, and banished dissenters such as Roger Williams and Anne Hutchinson. In creating such laws and following such practices, British colonies in North America were following the same sorts of discriminatory patterns that had long been followed in Britain itself.

Whether Catholic or Protestant, European migrants to North America offered the conversion of natives as a primary goal of exploration and settlement. They regarded Indigenous peoples as heathens or pagans who needed both the light of Christian revelation and the refinement of European civilization. Because they regarded Indigenous religions as devilish, European

Tituba and the Children.

Tituba, a central figure in the Salem Witch Trials, as she was imagined in a nineteenth-century engraving.

Few episodes in American history have sparked greater or longer lasting interest than the Salem witch trials of 1692–93, in which thirty people were found guilty of witchcraft following the accusations of several young women. Nineteen of the convicted were executed and one more was pressed to death for refusing to confess. Horrific as this episode was, it pales by comparison with various seventeenth-century outbreaks of hysteria over alleged witchcraft in Europe (in the Bamberg witch trials alone, some 1,000 people are believed to have been executed).

The causes of such outbreaks are still widely discussed and disputed; anxiety over emergent capitalism and the rise of scientific rationalism have been suggested, as have (in the case of the Salem episode) issues of race and trauma. Certain of the accusers had evidently been captured for some time by an Abenaki group and during that period had been traumatized by witnessing various atrocities. Tituba, one of the first three women accused of witchcraft and a key figure in the saga, is now believed to have been of Arawak (northeastern South American Indigenous) background, and to have come to Salem after some time enslaved in Barbados.

Important literary works with a connection to this historical episode include Nathaniel Hawthorne's 1835 story "Young Goodman Brown" and Arthur Miller's 1953 play *The Crucible*. For more on this subject, see the section "In Context: The Salem Witch Trials" in the online component of this anthology.

colonists could not see the commonalities shared by their cultures. Indigenous North Americans possessed complex cosmologies that nearly always included faith in a Supreme Being responsible for Creation, belief in other, lesser supernatural entities, and visions of an afterlife. In outline, then, Indigenous belief systems had a good deal in common with those of Christians, whether Catholic or Protestant, who also believed in a Supreme Being, in angels and other lesser supernatural beings, and in an afterlife of either punishment or reward. Rather than appreciating these shared spiritual traits, however, European settlers sought either to graft a Christian cosmology onto native beliefs and practices or to eradicate them altogether. English settlers in New England frequently combined their conversion efforts with "civilizing" requirements: natives who converted were expected to adopt English standards of dress and kinship and to come out of their tribal homes to

The Serra Chapel at the Mission San Juan Capistrano, built of adobe blocks, which dates from 1777–83. The Spanish decided in 1768 to colonize "Alta California" ("Upper California"); they had already established missions in Baja California. The Spanish approach to colonization was highly structured, and (in theory at least) powerfully oriented toward conversion of the Indigenous peoples to Christianity. Forts ("Presidios") were established at San

Diego, Santa Barbara, Monterrey, and San Francisco, with each of the four presidios responsible for the defense of several substantial Catholic missions, each to be run by the Franciscan order. The Padre of each mission assumed overall authority for the surrounding area; the declared plan was, after a ten-year transition period, to hand over control of lands claimed by each mission to the Indigenous population—though in practice, no plan to cede control was ever enacted.

Church authorities at these missions made much of the large numbers baptized, but scholars now believe that a relatively small percentage of the local population were true converts to Catholicism; most are thought to have adhered to their traditional religion, which—like Catholicism—posited an all-powerful Creator, and vested substantial secular authority in the local religious leaders.

The Spanish influx into Alta California was led by Franciscan missionary Junípero Serra (1713–84), who established the first nine Spanish missions in the area. Serra (after whom the chapel shown above is named) has become a highly controversial figure. He has been widely condemned by anti-colonialists as an oppressor of Indigenous peoples in Alta California—and for his earlier work for the Inquisition in Mexico. But he has long been lauded by Catholic authorities for the number of people who converted to Catholicism on his watch and for his enthusiasm for the work of conversion; when he first came into contact with unbaptized Indigenous peoples (in San Diego, in 1769), he wrote that he "kissed the ground and thanked God for giving me what I have longed for for so many years." He was declared a saint by Pope Francis in 2015.

form villages of "praying Indians" at the outskirts of English settlements. While Catholic missionaries were less insistent on erasing native cultural forms, their conversion efforts also often proceeded through violent means: historians now estimate that, by the late eighteenth century, genizaros—Indigenous people in what are now the southwestern states who had been "de-tribalized," usually by being enslaved—accounted for one-third of the population of New Mexico.

As English colonists on the Eastern seaboard drove Indigenous people off their land and became more politically and territorially entrenched, they created

strong ties between church and state by establishing one religion as official. It was the Puritan church—officially named the Congregational Church—that became the established church in Massachusetts, Connecticut, and New Hampshire. In most of the other colonies (which had been founded largely from economic motives), including South Carolina, North Carolina,[1] Georgia, Virginia, and, somewhat later, Maryland, the Anglican Church (the Church of England) became the

1 From 1669 to 1712 these were a single colony—Carolina—that was divided into two provinces.

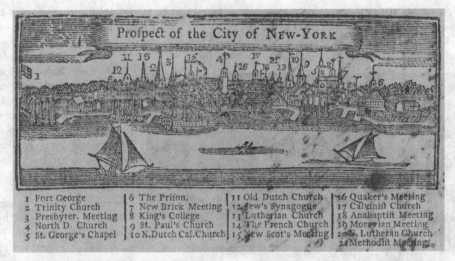

Prospect of the City of New-York

1 Fort George	6 The Prison.	11 Old Dutch Church	16 Quaker's Meeting
2 Trinity Church	7 New Brick Meeting	12 Jew's Synagogue	17 Calvinist Church
3 Presbyter. Meeting	8 King's College	13 Lutheran Church	18 Anabaptist Meeting
4 North D. Church	9 St. Paul's Church	14 The French Church	19 Moravian Meeting
5 St. George's Chapel	10 N. Dutch Cal. Church	15 New Scot's Meeting	20 N. Lutheran Church
			21 Methodist Meeting.

New York City (woodblock), 1771. Broadly speaking, England's mainland colonies may be divided into three groups: New England colonies, in which Puritans dominated and in which the Congregational Church was accorded established status; southern colonies, in which mainstream Anglicans dominated and the Church of England became the established church; and the middle colonies, in which no denomination was accorded the status of an established religion. New York does not quite fit the pattern; although the Church of England became the established religion in several counties of New York, it was never adopted by the colony as a whole. In the Hudson Valley and some other areas, the Dutch Reformed Church remained strong, while in various northern and western areas Lutherans predominated. As this 1771 image illustrates, New York City offered (by eighteenth-century standards) a spiritual smorgasbord.

established religion.[1] That did not simply mean that one church had slightly favored status over others. It typically meant that all citizens were required to support the established church through the payment of tithes or other taxes; it also often meant that those who did not belong to the established church were precluded from holding public office. In some colonies, restrictions went a good deal further. In Virginia, all white Virginians were required not only to pay taxes to support the established church, but also to be members of it and to attend services. Prejudice against those suspected of belonging to other denominations sometimes ran high; in the 1760s and 1770s, for example, those alleged to be Baptist were frequently subject to physical violence.

In most colonies, then, freedom of religion was an entirely alien concept; the formation of churches in non-approved denominations was in many cases prohibited, as in some cases was private worship. Even in colonies that had embraced the concept of "liberty of conscience" and not established any Christian denomination as the state religion, "liberty of conscience" was a long way removed from twenty-first-century notions of religious freedom. Colonies such as New Jersey and Georgia proclaimed that "liberty of conscience" applied to all except "papists" (as Catholics were derogatively termed), and the practice of non-Christian religions such as Judaism and Islam was often outlawed entirely.

There were two notable exceptions to this rule. In 1636 The Colony of Rhode Island and Providence Plantations (as it was officially known), founded by Roger Williams, became the first English colony to

[1] The Anglican Church was also the established faith in Maine (which became part of Massachusetts in 1691 and did not separate from it until 1820). Vermont—an unorganized area on the edge of the New England and New York colonies until 1777, when it briefly declared itself an independent republic—was largely Puritan / Congregationalist, but it required only that office holders "profess the Protestant religion." In Delaware there was no officially established religion, but Anglicans came eventually to predominate. In New Jersey too there was no established religion, and in this case a variety of Christian denominations flourished, with Presbyterians the largest group and Quakers the second largest. In Pennsylvania, William Penn (1644–1718) founded a Quaker colony, but its laws mandated religious tolerance.

declare freedom of religion for all Christian denominations—including Catholicism. But religious freedom in Rhode Island went further still; there was no prohibition placed on non-Christian religions. In his writings, Williams expressed the view that "none of the papists, Protestants, Jews, or Turks" should be forced to come to "prayers or worship, nor be compelled from their own particular prayers or worship." In other words, the world of religion would be kept entirely separate from the world of politics and law. This principle of the separation of church and state—a "wall of separation between the garden of the church and the wilderness of the world," in Williams's words—would later be enshrined in the First Amendment to the U.S. Constitution.

The second major exception was Pennsylvania, the charter for which was granted in 1681 to William Penn, who sought a safe haven far from England for himself and other members of the Society of Friends (also known as the Quakers). The charter provided a substantial measure of religious freedom, and its provisions created a lasting difference between Pennsylvania and all other colonies except Rhode Island—a difference that did not please everyone. The dissatisfied immigrant Gottlieb Mittelberger, for instance, writing in the early 1750s, complained that the "preachers throughout Pennsylvania ha[d] no power to punish anyone, or to compel anyone to go to church," with the result that "many sects lead people astray, and ma[de] them heterodox."[1] And yet, as Mittelberger begrudgingly admitted, religious tolerance seemed to result in greater general kindliness: "To speak truth, one seldom hears a quarrel among [the Pennsylvanians]. ... Americans live more quietly and peacefully together than the Europeans—and all this is the result of the

The first Jewish cemetery in America was established in Rhode Island in 1677, and the first synagogue—the Touro Synagogue, the interior of which is pictured here—in the same colony in 1763.

liberty which they enjoy and which makes them all equal."

If church and state were so closely entwined in the majority of the colonies, and freedom of religion such an alien concept in all but a few, how did it come to pass that the United States, after it was founded, could so swiftly embrace the principle of religious freedom?[2] One reason was simply that, even among those who would have preferred that America establish a single religion, there was no agreement as to *which* religious denomination it should be. Theological differences even between Protestant denominations could be rancorous and protracted, making the choice of a single established sect all but impossible. Another reason was

[1] To illustrate his point, Mittelberger described "a German neighbor, who had been a Lutheran but had re-baptized himself in running water; some time afterwards he circumcised himself and believed only in the Old Testament; finally, however, shortly before his death, he baptized himself again by sprinkling water upon his head." The different modes of baptism suggest that Mittelberger's neighbor had cycled through a number of different Protestant denominations that conducted their baptismal ceremonies differently. The references to circumcision and to belief "only in the Old Testament" suggest that the neighbor flirted with Judaism, which requires that male believers be circumcised; the Jewish Bible is roughly co-extensive with the Christian Old Testament.

[2] Article 1 of the 1791 Bill of Rights (the First Amendment to the Constitution) declares that "Congress shall make no law respecting an establishment of religion, or prohibiting the free exercise thereof."

that rates of religiosity in early America were highly inconsistent from one decade to the next. The religious observances of seventeenth-century Christians—whether of Puritans in New England, Quakers in Pennsylvania, or Anglicans in the southern colonies—were generally restrained in character. But in the 1730s and 1740s a series of revivals swept both the North American colonies and Western Europe. This period, known as the Great Awakening, saw a marked increase in religious practice in the colonies.

Beginning in the Massachusetts church led by Jonathan Edwards, a Congregationalist minister and theologian, the revival soon attracted preachers from both North America and England who sought to fan the flames of religious fervor. Like Edwards, the English evangelists John Wesley and George Whitefield (both Anglicans) sought to engage the emotions as well as the souls and minds of their listeners. But unlike Edwards, who quickly became concerned about what he considered the excesses of the revival he himself had sparked, Wesley and Whitefield sought to take preaching and religious instruction beyond the walls of the church (traveling widely and often preaching outdoors) and to inspire a spirit of intense personal commitment in believers. Whitefield, like Edwards, embraced a Calvinist theology: though he preached passionately to anyone who would listen, only the elect, both men believed, would be enabled to heed Christ's call. Wesley, by contrast, preached an Arminian theology that emphasized that salvation was open to all—not just to a predestined elect. A new denomination—the Methodists—developed out of Wesley's teaching, and within other denominations the evangelical revival movement became so powerful that it divided both the Congregationalists and the Presbyterians in two, with evangelical factions within both denominations breaking away from the traditional mainstream.

In the second half of the century, however, the revival quickly lost strength; far fewer Americans were attending outdoor revival meetings in the 1770s than had done so in the 1740s. And for the most part, they did not return to the churches of traditional Christian denominations. The result was that by the late eighteenth century, it is estimated, no more than 10 per cent of Americans were churchgoers. The Revolutionary decades were arguably the most secular

John Wollaston, *George Whitefield*, c. 1742. Whitefield was one of the most powerful figures of the Great Awakening—on both sides of the Atlantic. A close associate of John Wesley, he chose to go his own way, preaching to large crowds outdoors rather than affiliating with any church. He was universally agreed to possess extraordinary power as a speaker, as the actor David Garrick's fervently expressed wish attests: "I would give a hundred guineas, if I could say 'Oh!' like Mr. Whitefield." Whitefield has sometimes been called America's first celebrity. Accounts of his preaching filled newspapers from Maine to Georgia; Benjamin Franklin wrote in his autobiography of hearing Whitefield preach; and Phillis Wheatley first gained fame in Boston for her poem "Elegy on the Death of the Rev. Mr. George Whitefield."

era in American history. During these decades, many influential Americans adopted deism—the view that humans should base their faith on reason, and that reason justifies belief in a Supreme Being who is responsible for Creation, but that much of what is recounted in the Bible cannot be confirmed by human means. Some deists, such as Thomas Paine, rejected Christianity and all other organized religion and came to believe that God, having created the world, played no part in human affairs thereafter; others, such as Thomas Jefferson, continued to believe in the historical reality of Jesus Christ and the moral efficacy of his teachings but nevertheless held beliefs far removed from those of any traditional Christian denomination. James Madison and Benjamin Franklin were also deists; indeed, historian Jill Lepore has concluded that "most of the Founding Fathers were deists," though she concedes that "not all of them were as skeptical as Jefferson" about the value of traditional Christianity.

Regardless of their varying, occasionally skeptical attitudes towards traditional religious belief, the founders nevertheless recognized religion as a central aspect of social life, and the new Constitution, while prohibiting a federal establishment of religion, did nothing to interfere with state church establishments, some of which persisted into the early decades of the nineteenth century. But men like Jefferson, Madison, and many of their contemporaries also possessed a then-unprecedented openness toward non-Christian religions. Royall Tyler's popular 1797 novel *The Algerine Captive*, for instance, stages a debate between a Christian adherent and a Muslim mullah; while the Christian feels he should be able to best the mullah easily, he finds himself confounded by the logic of the other man's arguments. John Adams, negotiating real-life protection for Americans traveling off the coast of North Africa, included the following wording in the 1797 Treaty of Tripoli:

> As the government of the United States of America is not in any sense founded on the Christian Religion, as it has in itself no character of enmity against the laws, religion or tranquility of Musselmen [Muslims], and as the said States never have entered into any war or act of hostility against any Mehomitan [Muslim] nation, it is declared by the parties that no pretext arising from religious

opinions shall ever produce an interruption of the harmony existing between the two countries.

And in 1784, Massachusetts author Hannah Adams published *A View of Religions*, an early work of comparative religious studies that, instead of dismissing or denigrating non-Christian religions, sought to understand them on their own terms.

This respect rarely extended to the religious traditions of the enslaved people who were brought from Africa to labor in the American colonies. As many as twenty per cent of them may have been followers of Islam, but the majority almost certainly did not hold monotheistic beliefs. The religious traditions in many areas of West Africa (the center of the trade in enslaved people on the east side of the Atlantic) were animistic: adherents of religions that allow for the possibility of objects and places as well as living creatures possessing spiritual qualities—of things and places being in a real sense alive.[1] It is unclear for how long or to what extent animism and other elements of African religions persisted in the religious practices of African Americans; with families subject to dispersal at the whim of enslavers, with high death rates, and with precious little time available to carry on traditions, much was inevitably lost. In certain cases, however—particularly in areas in which Catholic missionaries allowed or even encouraged the blending of Christian with non-Christian religious elements—hybrid sets of religious beliefs set down deep roots. Such was the case with Voodoo (originally "Vaudou") in Haiti, and also with Santeria in Cuba.

It is also possible to see elements of animism persisting in the spirituals through which enslaved African Americans began in the eighteenth century to express

[1] It may also be worth noting that some variants of Christianity have certain affinities with animism. Such is arguably the case with the sort of Nature-worship that we often associate with English Romantic poetry, or with certain moods of the spirituality of transcendentalists such as Emerson. Here, for example, is how Emerson expresses (in "Woodnotes II") the view that a "Universal Spirit" is not a Supreme Being sitting above the natural world, but is rather embedded in every aspect of nature:

> He is the axis of the star;
> He is the sparkle of the spar;
> He is the heart of every creature;
> He is the meaning of each feature;
> And his mind is the sky.

John Rose, *The Old Plantation*, (Beaufort County, South Carolina), c. 1785.

a distinctive brand of Christianity. Spirituals such as "Roll, Jordan, Roll" have often been read with reference to the institution of slavery, as in the Bible, crossing the Jordan River marked the entrance of the formerly enslaved Israelites into the "Promised Land" where they would be free. But in the river and in the tree of life with which the spiritual begins, it does not seem too much of a stretch to hear traces of West African animism. In one spiritual, African American voices proclaimed: "If you want to find Jesus, go in the wilderness," subverting a Methodist hymn about coming *out of* the wilderness. Through small acts of meaning-making like this, many enslaved people combined West African spiritual traditions with Christian doctrine and practice, building religions that were uniquely their own.

SLAVERY AND AMERICA: BEGINNINGS TO 1820

[See also this volume's "Contexts: Slavery and Resistance" section.]

Until relatively recently, American slavery has been associated mainly with the period leading up to the Civil War—the period of Frederick Douglass's *Narrative*, of Harriet Beecher Stowe's *Uncle Tom's Cabin*, and of Solomon Northup's *Twelve Years a Slave*. Many Americans have tended to think of slavery as a "peculiar institution"[1] that, horrible as it undoubtedly

[1] This term is thought to have been first used by the Southern politician John C. Calhoun, an outspoken defender of slavery; while he was Vice President during the years 1825–32, Calhoun began to refer both to the "peculiar labor" of enslaved people and to the "peculiar domestic institution" of slavery in the Southern states. The intent was to suggest that, however pernicious slavery might be in other contexts or in other parts of the world, the form it had taken in the American South was entirely benign—and, in any case, was "peculiar" to that region and could not be judged by outsiders.

A 1671 engraving of St. Augustine.

was, existed for only a limited time in America, and left few lingering after-effects. But the more thoroughly American history is explored, the more clear it becomes that this long-held view of slavery flies in the face of the facts. Slavery played a central role in American life from long before the United States existed, and the legacy of slavery has carried on through to our own day.

In the Thirteen Colonies, the system known as chattel slavery began not in the late eighteenth century but "about the latter end of August" in 1619, when a ship called the *White Lion*, carrying "twenty and odd" enslaved Africans, arrived in the colony of Virginia. (In Portuguese- and Spanish-controlled territories, African chattel slavery was by that time long established. The Portuguese had first enslaved West African people in 1441; enslaved African people had first arrived in St. Augustine in Spanish Florida in 1565.) Early on, systems of chattel slavery were not codified to the extent they later would be, and such slavery was not fully racialized in the way that it later became; English colonists in

America, for example, purchased slaves not only from Africa but also from various Native American peoples.[1]

In the late 1600s the Thirteen Colonies began to codify the status of enslaved people—and of all black people, whether enslaved or not. Between 1662 and 1723 Virginia passed a series of laws that declared enslaved people to be property; determined that any child born to an enslaved mother would be enslaved from birth; and restricted the rights of black people who were not enslaved. By 1723, a "free" black person would be required to pay at least as much tax as a white person, but would not be free to own property, vote, occupy any position of civil or ecclesiastical authority, or marry a white person. Other colonies enacted similar laws, firmly embedding racism into American

[1] Certain forms of slavery had been common among Native American peoples before the arrival of Europeans; those captured in war, for example, were often then enslaved. But Native American practices did not classify enslaved people as property (or "chattel")—and did not regard "slave" as a status that would be passed on from generation to generation.

society long before the Revolution. That was the case not only in the South, but also in much of the North. In New York City, for example (where the Dutch had introduced slavery, with the English later codifying it), enslaved people made up 20 per cent of the city's population by the middle of the eighteenth century.

When the Northern colonies finally did move to abolish slavery, in most cases they adopted a policy of gradualism. In some states emancipation legislation affected only those born after it was enacted, so that those who were already enslaved when the legislation was passed would remain enslaved for life; thus it was, for example, that in Pennsylvania (which in 1780 became the first of the Thirteen Colonies to pass legislation abolishing slavery) there were still enslaved people in the late 1840s. In other states, legislation to "free" enslaved people altered their status not to "free person"—let alone to "citizen"[1]—but rather to indentured servant, and mandated that the children of enslaved people were also required to spend extended periods as indentured servants. In New Jersey, the last of the Northern states to pass such legislation, formerly enslaved people became "apprenticed for life"; considerable numbers were still effectively enslaved when the Civil War broke out.

While the role of slavery in Northern states has been underemphasized, it remains true that the role played by enslaved people was far more prominent in the Southern states. In New Jersey, the Northern state with the highest concentration of enslaved people, these constituted 6 per cent of the population in 1800; in South Carolina, the Southern state with the highest concentration, 42 per cent of the population was enslaved. Overwhelmingly, Southern enslaved people worked on farms or—especially from the late eighteenth and early nineteenth centuries—on large plantations. It would be difficult to exaggerate the value of the labor provided by enslaved people. Florida slaveholder and plantation owner Zephaniah Kingsley—author in the 1820s of one of the most popular proslavery tracts—was among those who were quite straightforward on that score:

> In short, the greatest value of agricultural product for export, and nearly all the springs of national and individual prosperity, flow from slave labor[.] … The labor of the negro, under the wholesome restraint of intelligent direction, is like a constant stream[.] …

Engraved portrait of Alice, an enslaved Pennsylvanian woman, 1804. Born around 1686 to enslaved parents who had been brought to Philadelphia from Barbados, Alice—who lacked a surname but was known as Alice of Dunk's Ferry, after the ferry crossing where she collected tolls for her enslaver—died, still enslaved, in 1802 (more than twenty years after Pennsylvania adopted a law to gradually abolish slavery in 1780). In her later years, she became a well-known recounter of stories about colonial Pennsylvania's early days—"being," as the writer Isaiah Thomas (in one of whose works this portrait was published) put it, "a sensible intelligent woman, and having a good memory."

[1] This word was left undefined in the American constitution, but beginning in the late 1780s the practice developed in most states of classifying "Negroes" (along with women, children, and Indigenous people) as "inhabitants" who were not to be allowed the privilege of voting or otherwise participating in government. Not until the Fourteenth Amendment was passed in 1868 did that situation begin to change.

1. Negre qui ejambe le tabac.
2. Negre qui torque le tabac.
3. Negre qui le met en rolle.
4. Tabac a la pente.

Anonymous eighteenth-century engraving showing enslaved black people processing harvested tobacco. While American slavery is today often associated with cotton cultivation, the cotton industry only took off—and began making large demands on the labor of enslaved African Americans—at the very end of the eighteenth century. For most of the seventeenth and eighteenth centuries, tobacco was the primary cash crop produced by enslaved labor throughout much of the American South—including in areas, such as Virginia, where cotton production never became widespread.

If slavers such as Kingsley were frank about how much economic benefit enslaved people provided them with, they were utterly disingenuous when they asserted that slavery amounted to "wholesome restraint." Every American schoolchild nowadays has some sense of the physical brutality to which enslaved people were subjected. But the full extent of the systemic cruelty is still often not appreciated; many today, for example, remain unaware of the degree to which family life was often made utterly impossible for enslaved people, as parents and children were sold off separately.

As slavery became more widespread in the eighteenth century, restrictions on the lives of enslaved people became tighter and tighter. In South Carolina, for example, a substantial 1739 uprising of enslaved people—the Stono Rebellion—prompted the government to pass an updated version of the law known as the "Negro Act"—more formally, An Act for the Better Ordering and Governing of Negroes and Other Slaves in this Province. The 1740 version expanded considerably on the previous iterations of the act in several respects; notably, it prohibited enslaved people from assembling in groups, and made it illegal to teach any slave how to write:

> ... [T]he having of slaves taught to write, or suffering them to be employed in writing, may be attended with great inconveniences; Be it therefore enacted by the authority aforesaid, That all and every person and persons whatsoever, who shall hereinafter teach or cause any slave or slaves to be taught to write, or shall use or employ any slave as a scribe in any manner of writing whatsoever, hereafter taught to write, every such person and persons, shall, for every such offense, forfeit the sum of one hundred pounds current money.

The South Carolina legislation was subsequently used as a model for similar legislation in Georgia and other states.

By 1776, then, the institution of slavery had become very firmly entrenched in America. The ironies, paradoxes, and contradictions inherent in the manner in which America's founders dealt with the issue of slavery—or, perhaps more accurately, refused to deal with it—have been the subject of much discussion. At its center is the figure of Thomas Jefferson, a believer in the superiority of whites over blacks, and an enslaver who fathered numerous children with Sally Hemings, whom he had enslaved, but also the drafter of the Declaration of Independence, with its ringing assertion that "all men are created equal." In the original draft of that document Jefferson also included a clause denouncing the British king for allowing slavery, an "execrable commerce" and an "assemblage of horrors." That clause was, as Jefferson recounted later, "struck out in compliance to South Carolina and Georgia," though he admitted that representatives of the Northern states had not fought to retain it. Between 1777 and 1804 those Northern states all enacted legislation that would bring about emancipation within their borders (albeit extremely gradually). And many whites during this era—in the South as well as the North—expected as well as hoped that slavery would somehow fade away in every state. But no state was willing to press for an end to slavery throughout the nation sooner rather than later—and, once the three-fifths clause was embedded in the Constitution (see below), it is doubtful if any could have succeeded in doing so had they tried.

In 1808, following Britain, the United States abolished the transatlantic slave trade; people could no longer be brought legally from Africa to America to be sold into slavery.[1] But that move did not bring with it any improvement in conditions for enslaved people in America; for many, indeed, conditions became even worse. The cotton and sugar industries were both growing rapidly in the early nineteenth century, and both were characterized by extraordinarily harsh conditions; in short order, enslaved people were literally worked

A remnant of the signage for one of the New Orleans slave markets still exists at the corner of St Louis and Chartres in the French Quarter: the faint outline ("…change") of what was once the sign for the Slave Exchange at the St. Louis Hotel.

to death. That the slaveholders continued after 1808 to be able to obtain replacements was due to the growth of America's internal slave trade—which, unlike the transatlantic trade, remained entirely legal. In certain of the Atlantic states—most notably, Virginia, where the soil had become depleted after generations of tobacco growing, and where there grew to be three times as many enslaved women as enslaved men—supplying the internal slave trade became a highly profitable business. From early adolescence onward, women were expected to be pregnant continually; sexual partners were chosen for them—or, in many cases, they were raped by their enslavers. Their children were then shipped to the Gulf Coast to be sold at the New Orleans slave market—the most important source of labor for the sugar and cotton industries.

Before 1820 the literature of slavery is far less voluminous than it is in the 1820–60 period, but it includes a number of foundational texts. Chief among them is Olaudah Equiano's *Interesting Narrative*, published in 1789 in London and three years later in New York, but the writings of others who were enslaved also deserve attention, among them the narratives of Ukawsaw Gronniosaw (*A Narrative of the Most Remarkable Particulars in the Life of James Albert Ukawsaw Gronniosaw, an African Prince, as Related by Himself,*

[1] Considerable numbers of enslaved people from abroad continued to be brought into the United States illegally—some smuggled through Atlantic ports, some brought from (Spanish-controlled) Florida and Texas.

For Sale,

THE under mentioned Property, situate in the parish of Plaquemine, to wit:
A fine Sugar Plantation and Saw Mill, having 50 arpents front on the river with the usual depth for 30, and a double concession for 20 arpents, situate at 8 leagues from New Orleans and on the same side ; together with
 51 head of Slaves
 12 yoke of Draught Oxen
 32 Horses or mules
 6 Carts and all the Plantation Tools necessary.

Notice of sale, *Louisiana State Gazette* (New Orleans), 1 November 1819. The sale of enslaved people through auction at slave markets grew steadily through the late eighteenth and early nineteenth centuries, but many enslaved people were also sold—as in this case—along with the plantation where they were enslaved.

1772); of Venture Smith (*A Narrative of the Life and Adventures of Venture, a Native of Africa: But Resident above Sixty Years in the United States of America, Related by Himself*, 1798); and of Jeffrey Brace (*The Blind African Slave, Or Memoirs of Boyrereau Brinch, Nicknamed Jeffrey Brace, as Told to Benjamin F. Prentiss, Esq.*). These early slave narratives are a varied group; in the late eighteenth and early nineteenth centuries the slave narrative genre had not yet become firmly established—and the narratives of enslaved people were not inextricably associated with the abolitionist cause in the ways that they later came to be. The theme of Christian spiritual development figures prominently in a number of these early narratives. Gronniosaw's narrative, for example, was published not in order to promote antislavery causes, but to demonstrate (as Calvinist preacher Walter Shirley puts it in his preface to the volume) that God may choose to save "those whom he hath foreknown" even in "those benighted parts of the world where the gospel of Jesus Christ hath never reached"; as Shirley would have it, God undertook to bring Gronniosaw "by a way he knew not, out of darkness into His marvelous light." Equiano's narrative did spur antislavery feeling to some degree when it was published—but it appears to have done so only in Britain. The American edition, published

in 1792, excited little interest, and to the extent that it did, it seems to have been valued as a travel narrative as much as for what Equiano has to say about slavery (see the author headnote on Equiano for a discussion of the reception history of the book). The narratives of Venture Smith and of Jeffrey Brace are more tightly focused on the subject of slavery than are those of Gronniosaw or Equiano, but they appear to have attracted little attention on publication. Interestingly, Smith's story is framed in the preface as of importance less for drawing attention to the horrors of slavery in the way that later slave narratives do (with their extended descriptions of whippings and other horrific abuses), than it is for demonstrating the lost potential that slavery represented for a "great mind" such as Smith's:

> The subject of the following pages, had he received only a common education, might have been a man of high respectability and usefulness; and had his education been suited to his genius, he might have been an ornament and an honor to human nature. … It may perhaps, not be unpleasing to see the efforts of a great mind wholly uncultivated, enfeebled and depressed by slavery, and struggling under every disadvantage—the reader may here see a Franklin and a Washington, in a state of nature, or rather in a state of slavery.

All four of these narratives are represented in the pages of this anthology—as are Phillis Wheatley's poems on the subject of slavery. Included as well are a number of commentaries on slavery by black writers such as clergymen Absalom Jones (*The Petition of People of Color*) and Lemuel Haynes (*Liberty Further Extended: Or Free Thoughts on the Illegality of Slave-keeping*). It was black writers such as Jones and Haynes who pointed out most directly the contradictions inherent in the approach to freedom taken by America's founders: "Liberty" in Haynes's words, "is equally as precious to a black man as it is to a white one, and bondage equally as intolerable to the one as it is to the other." Haynes's text, though, remained unpublished.

The writings of eighteenth and early nineteenth-century white authors on the subject of slavery— J. Hector St. John de Crevècoeur and Thomas Jefferson notable among them—are also represented

The Female Combatants, 1776. This illustration, probably printed in London, was published in the early days of the American Revolution; it depicts the incipient conflict as a face-off between an elegantly dressed older woman, representing Britain, and a younger, bare-breasted and tattooed woman in Indigenous garb, representing the American colonies. The British figure declares, "I'll force you to Obedience you Rebellious Slut," while the American figure responds, "Liberty, Liberty forever Mother while I exist." Notably, while the illustration appropriates Native American imagery to represent the American colonies, it leaves out of the picture the actual Indigenous peoples who were caught between—and variously manipulated, exploited, or attacked by—the rebellious colonies and their "mother country."

substantially in these pages. It is striking, however, that the highest profile late-eighteenth works of fiction and drama on the subject of slavery, Susanna Rowson's 1794 *Slaves in Algiers* and Royall Tyler's 1797 *The Algerine Captive*, concern the enslavement of white people in North Africa rather than the enslavement of black people in America.

"BEGIN THE WORLD OVER AGAIN": AN AGE OF REBELLION AND REVOLUTION

[See also this volume's "Contexts: Rebellions and Revolutions" section.]

To the white European colonizers of North America in the seventeenth and early eighteenth centuries, rebellions and revolts were occurrences to be feared. The pattern was largely the same: members of an oppressed group rebelled against oppressors of European background. Examples include the 1680 Pueblo Revolt against Spanish rule; the 1729 Natchez revolt against French rule; the 1663 rebellion of enslaved Africans (together with indentured servants) in Virginia; the 1712 rebellion of enslaved Africans (together with Native Americans) in New York; the 1739 rebellion of enslaved Africans in South Carolina; and Metacom's Rebellion of 1675–78 (also known as King Philip's War—see above under "Contact, and the Literatures of Contact"). Colonizers reacted to such events by waging War against Indigenous nations, passing strict slave codes, and terrorizing the black population. Although these rebellions were largely defeated, their legacy helped set the stage for the complicated era historians often call the "age of revolutions," beginning with the American Revolution (1775–83) and ending with the European revolutions of the mid-nineteenth century.

It is one irony of American history, though not a surprising one, that when colonists in mainland North America[1] rebelled against British rule, they largely sidelined, ignored, and continued to terrorize members of the oppressed groups who had fought, and

[1] It is sometimes forgotten that Britain had in the 1770s not thirteen but twenty-six American colonies, ranging from icy Newfoundland in the north to Grenada, just off the coast of South America. Britain considered her Caribbean possessions—especially sugar-producing Barbados—to be the most valuable.

continued to fight, for a better life. Indeed, the American Revolution was first understood as a rebellion. The idea that colonists might revolt against the "mother country," as white people across the economic spectrum did in the 1770s, and as the Spanish colonists of Mexico did in 1810, was inconceivable almost right up until those events actually happened. Even when the conflict now known as the American Revolution began, it was not until the British were finally defeated that it came to be understood as a Revolutionary War or a War of Independence.

The most radical event of the age of revolutions occurred not in British North America but in Haiti, the former French colony of Saint-Domingue, where between 1791 and 1804 enslaved Africans overthrew French rule, eradicated the institution of slavery, defeated Napoleon's attempts at re-enslavement, and established the first independent black nation in the Americas (and the second independent nation in the Americas overall, after the U.S.). While the Haitian Revolution aimed to overthrow white supremacy, the American Revolution was initially not a matter of high principles. When Britain began to directly tax the colonies[1]—particularly the Thirteen Colonies that it had paid for an army to defend against the French in the war of 1756–63—the resistance was at first merely economic. Soon came an appeal to a broader principle about self-sovereignty—not just "No taxation!" but instead "No taxation without representation." With the Declaration of Independence of 1776 would come the most powerful principle: "all men are created equal" and possess the "inalienable rights" to "life, liberty, and the pursuit of happiness." The success of a war that white men fought nominally for that grand principle influenced revolutionary movements in Europe, the Americas, and around the world, while Haitian independence was largely dismissed and denigrated—except by black people in the African diaspora who continued to look to it for inspiration.

During the long years of the American Revolution itself, the conflict also played out as a "civil war," as J. Hector St. John de Crèvecoeur's American farmer

called it in 1782. Particularly in states such as New York and Pennsylvania, a great many people, much as they might dislike the measures imposed by Britain, did not favor a complete break with the Crown. The Quaker poet Hannah Griffitts, for example, who had stood in resolute opposition to measures such as the Sugar Act and the Townsend Duties, was in 1776 just as resolute in her opposition to Thomas Paine's arguments for independence; in her poem "Upon Reading a Book Entitled Common Sense" she argues that there is "subtlety" (in the now-archaic sense of treachery or cunning) in "ev'ry page of this fallacious tale." Overall, historians have estimated that some 20 per cent of American free citizens remained loyal to Britain, with up to 45 per cent becoming active supporters of independence.[2]

About 20 per cent of the non-Indigenous population of 1770s North America[3] was enslaved rather than free, and enslaved people seem to have supported independence in much smaller numbers. Once the British announced, in November 1775, that anyone who escaped slavery and joined the British army would thereby attain their freedom, the black American population was overwhelmingly (if very quietly) pro-British. Many enslaved people did escape and try to join the British forces; although many were re-captured, several thousand remained free and did indeed join the British. (Two of the most important black American writers of the time, Phillis Wheatley and Lemuel Haynes, are in this respect both interesting exceptions—supporters of the Patriot rather than Loyalist cause.) At the end of the war, the 75,000 Loyalists to the crown who left the United States at war's end included between 15,000 and 20,000 formerly enslaved people.

While the Declaration of Independence expressed with great eloquence the classic Enlightenment principles of equality, the clarity of its rhetoric also effectively

[1] The now-infamous series of taxes included those imposed under the Sugar Act (1764); the Stamp Act (1765); the Townshend Acts of 1767 and 1768; and the series of 1774 measures known as the "Coercive Acts" in Britain and as the "Intolerable Acts" in the American colonies.

[2] Estimates of the percentage of the population that remained loyal to the Crown are generally based on enlistment figures or other indicators of the behavior of the male citizenry. Did women support or oppose independence in the same proportion as men? The anecdotal evidence is unclear, and we have no statistical indicators.

[3] The Indigenous population living within American borders may still have been as large as 500,000 in the late eighteenth century, though estimates of the Indigenous population at any time before Native Americans were fully included in the census (in 1900) vary widely.

John Singleton Copley, *The Death of Major Peirson, 6 January 1781*, 1783. Copley (1738–1815), an American-born artist, made his name as a portrait painter in New England but moved to Britain in 1774, never to return. This painting depicts the defense of the British island of Jersey against invading French forces (allied to the rebellious Thirteen Colonies) during the Revolutionary War. The inclusion of a black man in the British ranks, while of debatable historical accuracy in terms of this specific battle, reflects the real participation of black Americans on the British side of the war.

Portrait of an unidentified American Revolutionary War sailor, c. 1780. Many black people—including the writers Olaudah Equiano and Briton Hammon—served in the British navy or on merchant ships during the eighteenth century. Because of their frequently extensive maritime experience, black Americans, both free and enslaved, were recruited to the navy of the Thirteen Colonies from the very start of the Revolutionary War; while some performed menial jobs, others became ships' pilots—a skilled and prestigious position. The American Revolutionary naval officer James Barron, in his memoirs, identified several black men whom he served with as "courageous patriots who ... in justice to their merits should not be forgotten," including "Captain" Mark Starlins, an enslaved man who became a pilot. Other African Americans, however, served in the British Royal Navy, in the belief that—in the reported words of one black fisherman and pilot who was executed in Charleston in 1775 for allegedly plotting a pro-British insurrection—"the War was come to help the poor Negroes."

obscured not only the hypocrisy inherent in that document (as an argument for equality that pertained only to white men) but also a complicated history of rebellion and revolution that preceded and followed the year 1776. Some of the most talented writers of the age engaged with that history as it immediately unfolded and also for decades to come.

What is the difference between a revolt or rebellion and a revolution? The best short answer is perhaps that a revolution succeeds; a rebellion doesn't. But the word "revolution" has come to suggest something more: it has typically been applied to changes in society that are about much more than mere power. As we have grown used to thinking of it, a revolution is founded in some way on a set of ideas.

There were many reasons why the balance of opinion in the thirteen North American colonies finally swung decisively in 1776 toward open rebellion, but the most important was arguably the influence of a short pamphlet whose author claimed to offer "nothing more than simple facts, plain arguments, and common sense." Thomas Paine's *Common Sense*, published in January of 1776, went through twenty-five editions in under a year; it was by far the best-selling pamphlet in an era when the norm was to share books, pamphlets, and newspapers rather than for individuals to purchase their own copy. (Historians debate how many copies were sold—Paine himself guessed that the number was 120,000, but the current thinking is now in the range of 40,000–70,000.) Paine argued more persuasively than anyone else that Britain could never be expected to act in the interest of American colonies; that the principle of hereditary succession on which the British monarchy was founded was foolish and wicked; that in the colonies "the *law* ought to be king"; and that "a government of our own" was the "natural right" of the people. More perhaps than any other writer, he ensured that a rebellion became an ideas-based revolution. *Common Sense* provided the world with a rhetoric of Revolution that survives to this day. To his fellow colonists, he wrote:

> We have it in our power to begin the world over again. A situation, similar to the present, hath not happened since the days of Noah until now. The birth day of a new world is at hand.

John Singleton Copley, *Paul Revere*, c. 1770. Revere (1735–1818) was a prosperous and well-respected silversmith both before and after the famous role he played in the American Revolution. See the In Context materials accompanying Henry Wadsworth Longfellow's poem "The Midnight Ride of Paul Revere" (in the online component of this anthology, Volume B) for Revere's own account.

In the American Revolution, the primary principle of "freedom" that the rebels were fighting for was self-governance—independence from their colonial rulers.[1] In another pamphlet, *American Liberty; A Poem* (1775),

[1] Particularly given that it was the British forces who offered freedom to enslaved Americans willing to fight for their side in the war, the vocabulary of the era's literature is often deeply paradoxical; Freneau is among the many patriots who write of America fighting to escape the "slavery" of control by Britain but have nothing to say on the subject of offering freedom to Americans who are literally enslaved. The ironies are particularly tangled in Freneau's case; horrified by the cruelties of slavery in the West Indies that he witnessed when he traveled there in 1776 (and that he wrote about in his "Sir Toby" poems), Freneau nevertheless did not at the time call for the abolition of slavery—and indeed he later became an enslaver himself when he lived in New Jersey. He did free his enslaved people, however, before New Jersey in 1804 passed a law mandating gradual emancipation.

John Singleton Copley, *John Adams*, 1783. In this painting, Adams— the American commissioner to the negotiations that produced the Treaty of Paris that ended the Revolutionary War—is shown gesturing toward a map of his newly independent country. The statue in the background contains imagery of peace, including an olive branch and a lowered torch. Adams was later appointed the first American ambassador to Britain; when a counterpart assumed that he had family in England, he replied:

> Neither my father nor mother, grandfather or grand- mother, great grandfather or great grandmother, nor any other relation that I know of, nor care a farthing for, has been in England these one hundred and fifty years; so that you see I have not one drop of blood in my veins, but what is American.

Philip Freneau set out a vision of the future that many held—a vision of a nation that gives "all for freedom," that frees itself from the chains of control by Britain, and that thereby emboldens itself to expand in all directions, including out west by colonizing lands ruled by sovereign Native American nations. Freneau's rhetoric embodies the central paradox of the revolution, which was that the vision of freedom it attempted to universalize in fact was white supremacist and inherently, if silently, limited to white men:

> Thrice happy we who long attacks have stood
> And swam to Liberty thro' seas of blood;
> The time shall come when strangers rule no more,
> Nor cruel mandates vex from Britain's shore;
> When Commerce shall extend her short'ned wing,
> And her free freights from every climate bring;
> When mighty towns shall flourish free and great,
> Vast their dominion, opulent their state;
> When one vast cultivated region teems,
> From ocean's edge to Mississippi's streams[.] …

In the same year that Freneau issued his *American Liberty* pamphlet, John Adams urged "the people of every colony" to "set up governments of their own, under their own authority; for the people [are] the source of all authority." But who exactly were "the people"? Enslaved people were not considered part of "the people"—and neither were women. Nor, indeed, were all adult white males accorded full rights. Though some states—notably Pennsylvania—went further than others in declaring rights for all, even in Pennsylvania the right to vote was restricted to those who were resident in the state and paid taxes. States

such as Massachusetts required that men own property in order to vote, or to hold office. The United States was making unprecedented strides in the direction of what we now call democracy—but many elite Americans maintained a powerful fear of it. Following Aristotle[1] and a long tradition of European thought, they saw in unrestrained democracy the danger of "mob rule." It was a fear that was reinforced in the 1790s by the course that the French Revolution ended up taking.

The freedoms that were fought for in France beginning in 1789 were considerably more wide-ranging than those which had motivated the American Revolution, even though the National Assembly in France drew heavily on the Declaration of Independence in its own Declaration of the Rights of Man and the Citizen (a document that Thomas Jefferson helped his friend the Marquis de Lafayette draft when Jefferson was the American Minister to France). Not just monarchical rule but economic and social hierarchies of any sort were under attack. "Men are born and remain free and equal in rights," Article 1 of the Declaration states; "social distinctions," it added, "may be founded only upon the general good." For a time, many radicals in the United States voiced a degree of pride at the obvious debt the French owed to American revolutionary rhetoric. That enthusiasm was dampened considerably beginning in 1793, however, as the horrific violence known as "the terror" began.

Even as France descended into violence, a new group of revolutionaries were fighting in Saint-Domingue to transform the brutal slave regime that had long terrorized the majority of the colony's inhabitants. Saint-Domingue was the center of Caribbean sugar production—and the center too of the region's most horrific levels of oppression. Its population was composed of approximately 30,000 white people, approximately 30,000 free people of color, and some 500,000 enslaved black people. While some of the white colonists of Saint-Domingue petitioned the central government in France for the same kinds of rights white colonists in America had achieved, Toussaint Louverture, a former slave, held the great

radical ambition to abolish slavery and extend equal rights to all. While the long tradition of slave revolt and rebellion in the Americas lay behind the ambitions and actions of Louverture, he also credited events in France as an inspiration. Louverture's initial aim was to rule an autonomous Haiti as a colonial governor still within the French Empire. Several articles in the Haitian Constitution of 1801 (known as "Toussaint's Constitution") make his radicalism quite clear:

> There cannot exist slaves on this territory, servitude is therein forever abolished. All men[2] are born, live and die free and French.

> There shall exist no distinction other than those based on virtue and talent, and other superiority afforded by law in the exercise of a public function.

> The law is the same for all whether in punishment or in protection.

These demands, backed up by military might, terrified white people all over the Atlantic world, and especially in those portions of the United States with large enslaved black populations. The Haitian Revolution unfolded over many years, and at different stages involved interventions by the British and the Spanish as well as by numerous factions within Haiti itself; the Haitian army defeated Napoleon's final attempt at invasion in 1803. Jean Jacques Dessalines, a former slave, declared total independence from France on 1 January 1804. (Louverture had earlier been captured and imprisoned in France, where he died in 1803.)

The events in Saint-Domingue inspired considerable fear in the American south, and the United States government remained hostile to Haitian autonomy throughout the nineteenth century (during the Revolution, the U.S. provided both arms and financial aid to the losing cause). Haiti also inspired a number

[1] Aristotle posited three broad types of government: a monarchy—the corrupt version of which is a tyranny; an aristocracy—the corrupt version of which is an oligarchy; and a polity—the corrupt version of which is a democracy.

[2] Like the revolutionary declarations of America and France, those of Haiti made no mention of women. The European and English trail blazers in that regard were the 1791 *Declaration of the Rights of Woman and the Female Citizen* (French: *Déclaration des droits de la femme et de la citoyenne*) by Olympe de Gouges and Mary Wollstonecraft's *A Vindication of the Rights of Woman* (1792). Of note is the fact that Judith Sargent Murray's *On the Equality of the Sexes* (1790) predates both of these works—though there is no evidence that either de Gouges or Wollstonecraft was aware of Murray's work.

of revolts in the United States on the part of enslaved black people—and horrific reprisals on the part of enslavers. But it did not entirely sour white American opinion generally on "the spirit of revolution." In the second decade of the nineteenth century freedom continued (as Thomas Paine had predicted it would) to be "hunted round the globe." The period 1810–25 saw successful revolutions and the establishment of numerous republics in former Spanish and Portuguese colonies throughout much of Central and South America. Americans for the most part celebrated the creation of these new free republics, saw the situation of the South Americans as parallel to their own struggles against a colonial oppressor, and swelled with pride at the part they saw themselves as having played in inspiring the revolutionary activity. "If national policy forbids our lending active and open service to their cause," the *Alexandria Gazette* opined in 1817, "it may surely be permitted us to wish them success, and … afford them our prayers and wishes."

Below the surface of this pan-American revolutionary camaraderie, however, lay a number of unresolved tensions. Some of these were rooted in ethnicity and religion. Most of the newly independent republics were Spanish speaking, and in all of them the Catholic Church was prominent—whereas English-speaking Americans were overwhelmingly Protestant, and often virulently anti-Catholic when it came to matters closer

Toussaint Louverture, c. 1800. This engraving was made as part of a series of portraits of generals of the French Revolution.

Engraved portrait of Simón Bolívar, 1819. Known as *El Libertador* (The Liberator), Bolívar (1783–1830) successfully led the struggles of what are now Venezuela, Bolivia, Colombia, Ecuador, Peru, and Panama for independence from Spain. While he drew inspiration from the American Revolution and admired George Washington (to whom he has often been compared), Bolívar was disturbed by American slavery, which he encountered when he visited the U.S. in 1807; while fighting for Venezuelan independence in 1816, he proclaimed "absolute freedom for the slaves who have groaned under the Spanish yoke during the three previous centuries"—on the condition that all emancipated enslaved men of military age join the independence struggle.

to home. The Monroe Doctrine, established in 1823, rejected European rule in the Americas but paternalistically cast the United States as protector of the hemisphere. A further source of tension was slavery; though circumstances in the new Central American and South American republics were in every case very different from those in Haiti, the new republics in almost every case resolved to abolish slavery—typically, through the same sort of gradualist approach that the Northern U.S. states were following. That put them very much at odds with attitudes increasingly being adopted by whites in the Southern states, where slavery (which had often in the eighteenth century been defended on circumstantial grounds, as an institution that for the moment represented the least of all possible evils) was increasingly defended as a positive good. These tensions in American public opinion would be brought to the surface in the 1820s, when the newly formed Democratic Party began to vigorously stir up feeling against the Central and South American republics on the bases of religion and of race.

By then the American Revolution itself had become a subject of historical romance and playful literary satire. In Washington Irving's "Rip Van Winkle," the eponymous hero famously sleeps through the Revolution and wakes up only to find all the great social changes it established both bothersome and bewildering. But especially among enslaved people in the Americas, who continued to rebel, and also throughout Europe—whose autocratic regimes contended with numerous revolutions from below—a great hope lived on, that ordinary people can somehow begin the world over again.

THE SHAPE OF A PEOPLE

American literature from the colonial and early national periods serves as an illuminating record of how residents understood themselves as people and as *a* people. Oral narratives, folk songs, political records, life writing, fictional narratives, sermons, poetry, scientific prose, and so many other writings from this era take up fundamental questions: What is the basis for community and how does it perpetuate itself? Which individuals are recognized by and included in

a community, why, and how? What are the obligations of individuals to their communities and vice versa?

The shape of the people in colonial North America was never static. The original inhabitants of the lands claimed by Europeans—from the Taínos of the Caribbean to the Salish of the Pacific Northwest to the Mi'kmaq in present-day Maine and the Canadian Atlantic Provinces—had their own understandings of personhood and community. One finds in oral literatures such as the Diné (Navajo) creation story and the Wampanoag "Origin of the Island of Nantucket" accounts of how a people is formed and sustained through the natural environment. A wide range of Indigenous metaphysics informed diplomatic and martial responses of various tribes to the arrival of Europeans—and to the disease, war, and displacement they brought to Indigenous peoples. As waves of European settlers and enslaved Africans arrived in North America over three centuries, the Native American population decreased by as much as 90 per cent. Native Americans pursued their own migrations and alliances, forming new communities and political structures in the interest of survival.

According to one scholarly estimate, from the seventeenth century through to the Revolutionary War the net[1] migration of Europeans to British North America (including the Caribbean) was in the range of 700,000 Europeans immigrated. Immigrants to what would become the Thirteen Colonies came primarily from England in the first half of the seventeenth century; in the eighteenth century they came increasingly from Scotland, Ireland, and the Rhineland (now part of Germany) as well. After 1650, the majority of these European immigrants were indentured servants, contractually obligated to labor for a term in exchange for the cost of their relocation. The vast majority of immigrating servants were men, with a ratio of roughly 4:1 in the seventeenth century. Indeed, men outnumbered women among Euro-American immigrants in every North American colony, including New England, to which more family units migrated. This demographic

[1] It is important to use net figures in considering totals; considerable numbers of immigrants returned to Europe after spending a few years in America. (Gottlieb Mittelberger, for example, whose observations are quoted in the next paragraph, emigrated from the Duchy of Württemberg in what is now Germany in 1750, but returned to Württemberg in 1754.)

Benjamin West, *Penn's Treaty with the Indians*, 1771–72. The legendary "Great Treaty" negotiated between the Lenni Lenape (Delaware) leader Tamanend and William Penn, the founder of Pennsylvania, is frequently celebrated in art and literature, perhaps most famously in this painting by Benjamin West. In the mid-seventeenth century, the Lenape occupied territory from New York to Maryland, including what became eastern Pennsylvania. Unlike the overwhelming majority of colonists, who wholly disregarded the prior land claims of Indigenous populations, Penn paid the Lenape for their territory in Pennsylvania; nonetheless, conflict between the colonists and the Lenape continued during Penn's lifetime and afterward—and usually the Lenape were forced to give way to the colonists' desires. No text of a "Great Treaty" survives, but a wampum belt given to Penn by the Lenape as part of peace negotiations in 1682 is depicted below.

Shackamoxon Treaty Belt [Penn Wampum Belt], 1682.

imbalance gradually leveled out over the eighteenth century.

The transport of indentured servants and the sale of their contracts was a significant business, and the merchants engaged in this business did not shy away from treating their indentured passengers as commodities. Often, prospective immigrants were imprisoned as soon as they signed their contracts and confined until their ship's departure in case they thought better of their decision. On the ship itself, profit was maximized at the cost of extremely cramped conditions and subpar food and water in insufficient quantities. The German immigrant Gottlieb Mittelberger offers a vivid picture of the deplorable circumstances:

> [D]uring the voyage there is on board these ships terrible misery, stench, fumes, horror, vomiting, many kinds of sea-sickness, fever, dysentery, headache, heat, constipation, boils, scurvy, cancer [i.e., cankers], mouth-rot, and the like, all of which come from old and sharply salted food and meat, also from very bad and foul water, so that many die miserably.

Conditions could be better than those Mittelberger describes, but they could also be worse. In one particularly egregious example, the *Sea-Flower* departed from Ireland in 1741 with more than one hundred indentured passengers; the trip to Boston took four months, several weeks longer than expected, and by the time the *Sea-Flower* arrived more than half the passengers had starved to death. A few had eaten their shipmates.

Why did migrants lease their own freedom to undertake such voyages? Some were taken in by the rhetoric of those who profited from the indenture system; Mittelberger speaks disparagingly of "those who suffer themselves to be persuaded and enticed away by the man-thieves" who convince them that "roasted pigeons will fly into their mouths in America or Pennsylvania without their working for them." But for many migrants, the prospects were genuinely worse at home. For the least wealthy Europeans, standards of living were very poor in the sixteenth and seventeenth centuries as land that had once been held in common was privatized and rural peasants were forced into the cities. In England, where circumstances were especially bad, more than half of the nation's peasant class was

without land by the beginning of the seventeenth century, and the number rose as the century progressed. Overpopulation in urban centers fostered rampant disease, while frequent food shortages and price increases left many people unable to afford to feed themselves. Even so, some regretted the decision to try their luck in America; Richard Frethorne, a twelve-year-old indentured servant writing home to his parents, told them that "people cry out day and night—Oh! That they were in England without their limbs—and would not care to lose any limb to be in England again, yea, though they beg from door to door." Frethorne—like many other indentured servants in the colonies—did not survive his term of servitude.

Indentured servants found their rights and freedoms severely curtailed in America. Servants' masters commonly whipped, beat, raped, and otherwise abused them, and they could not marry without permission. Nonetheless, for some indentured servants, America did provide a greater degree of opportunity than they would have had in Europe. In early seventeenth-century Maryland, for example, many servants acquired land and political standing in the community after completing their contracts. But such opportunities diminished through the century as class divisions solidified; by the mid-seventeenth century, Maryland immigrants who had completed indentures were much less likely to end up acquiring their own land than to become tenant farmers, continuing to work for the landowning classes that had exploited them as indentured labor. Similar patterns can be found throughout the colonies. In Boston, for example, in the 1680s, the top one per cent of the population possessed about 25 per cent of the wealth in the city; by 1770, that number had risen to 44 per cent of the city's wealth.

Transportation to America was also common as a punishment for a wide range of crimes committed in Britain, and by some estimates a full quarter of the British immigrants to America in the eighteenth century were convicts. Like indenture, transportation was a profitable system of unfree labor; merchants were paid by the government to transport prisoners and, upon arrival in America, could then sell the convicts for the duration of their sentences (usually seven years). Many convicts attempted to escape, even though the

penalty for returning to Britain before one's sentence expired was death.

Between 1600 and 1776, more than three million enslaved Africans were forcibly brought to British colonies, with about 660,000 arriving in mainland North America. From the beginning, the lot of enslaved Africans was worse than that of indentured Europeans, but, especially in the first half of the seventeenth century, enslaved black people and indentured white people often found a great deal of common ground in their experiences. Initially, enslaved and indentured people frequently socialized together, formed romantic relationships, ran away together, and occasionally rebelled together. This community between indentured and enslaved people made colonial elites uneasy, and they encouraged division between white and black people with a variety of laws. Interracial sex was punishable by whipping as early as 1630 in Virginia, while laws prohibiting marriage between black and white people began to be passed throughout the colonies in the 1660s. Indentured servants also, increasingly, received privileges that were denied to enslaved

people; white servants, for example, were sometimes permitted to join militias while enslaved people were not, and white defendants generally received lesser sentences than black defendants for the same crimes. In the early eighteenth century, colonies passed laws requiring indentured servants' masters to furnish them with goods upon completion of the indenture—while for black people enslavement had become lifelong and hereditary.

While the majority of those who came to early America were taken by force or driven by economic motives, scholars of American literature long privileged the writings and history of the Puritans and related Protestant groups who came to New England for a different reason: to live according to their religious beliefs without interference. These British immigrants who led the colonization of the Algonquian homelands understood themselves to have entered into a covenant with God as a chosen people, to be obligated to obey God's Law and to live in close community with one another. In 1630, John Winthrop offered the Puritans founding Massachusetts Bay Colony a scriptural type

Robert W. Weir, *Embarkation of the Pilgrims*, 1843, U.S. Capitol Rotunda.

for their social formation: a body of distinct parts "knit together by [Christ's] bond of love." That love took the form of placing the welfare of the community above all else. Residents who were not church members were literally known as Strangers, and early on the Puritan leadership expelled Quakers, Catholics, Antinomians, and others who disagreed with ministers. The concept of covenanted community contributed to the remarkable success of Anglo-Protestant colonization in New England, despite high mortality, harsh weather, theological disagreements, military conflict, and conflict with British investors and the crown. Accounts of faith-based resilience abound in the literature of New England, from the poetry of Anne Bradstreet to the captivity narrative of Mary Rowlandson.

The focus on New England writing in the study of early American literature has contributed to a long-lasting narrative of American exceptionalism (the belief that America is in important ways exceptional—not merely different but extraordinarily different, and in ways that mark it as superior). This belief in America's fundamental difference is commonly traced back to Winthrop's now-famous assertion that the Massachusetts Bay Colony "shall be as a city upon a hill. The eyes of all people are upon us." According to this narrative, the covenanted communities of Winthrop and others—freedom-seeking dissenters chosen by God and committed to one another—gave rise over time to freedom-loving revolutionaries who envisioned a nation conceived in liberty. Certainly, many participants in the American Revolution claimed for America a unique and important place in history, arguing that its deliberate foundation on a set of developed political principles set it apart from other nations that had evolved organically. Alexander Hamilton put it this way:

> It seems to have been reserved to the people of this country, by their conduct and example, to decide the important question, whether societies of men are really capable or not of establishing good government from reflection and choice, or whether they are forever destined to depend for their political constitutions on accident and force.

The idea of the U.S. as a political experiment and an example to the world has been ubiquitous in American

Engraving from Pere Joseph François Lafitau, *Customs of the American Indians Compared with the Customs of Primitive Times* (*Moeurs des Sauvages Amériquains, Comparées aux Moeurs des Premiers Temps*), 1724. This engraving from the work of an eighteenth-century French ethnologist shows a European imagining of the peace negotiations that led to the foundation of the Haudenosaunee Confederacy. It shows leaders from five Iroquois nations (Cayuga, Mohawk, Oneida, Onondaga, and Seneca) assembled around Dekanawida, a leader of the negotiations.

politics since the Revolution, but the phrase "city upon a hill" did not become a commonplace shorthand for this idea until the mid-twentieth century, when it was revived by John F. Kennedy. Since then, American politicians from Ronald Reagan to Barack Obama have used it in key speeches.

Alongside the narrative of exceptional American community, the narrative of the exceptional individual has been a part of American literature since the colonial era. This idea is particularly prominent in works from the Chesapeake and Mid-Atlantic regions such as John Smith's self-promotional *General History of Virginia, New England, and the Summer Isles* (1624), in which Smith presents himself as a rugged hero who pursues his vision of righteous, thrilling conquest in the face of immense opposition. Benjamin Franklin (who was born in Boston but made his name in Philadelphia) produced an *Autobiography* (1791) that some have read as evidence that the nation was made great through citizens' dogged pursuit of self-interest and self-improvement.

In recent decades, scholars of American literary history have looked more broadly at the different literatures of American communities before 1820. They have taken a more expansive approach to reading the Puritan works that have long been part of the canon—reading, for example, with an eye to the Indigenous voices that are overwritten in William Bradford's account of the Pequot War or Rowlandson's account of King Philip's War. And they have broadened the canon considerably.

Even among the white settlers of New England, not everyone was a Puritan; Thomas Morton's *New English Canaan* (1637), for instance, offers an alternative vision of a society in which there is no place for Puritan religious authority, for the practice of indentureship, or for the violent expulsion of Indigenous neighbors. Examples abound beyond seventeenth-century New England. In the eighteenth-century life writing of Quakers Elizabeth Ashbridge and John Woolman, for instance, we learn about the alternative social structures created through Quaker faith and receive firsthand testimony as to the cruelties of indentureship, as to violence against women (both domestic and public), and as to the practice of slavery. Indigenous oral literatures preserve the knowledge of various forms of political community practiced across the continent—including that of the Iroquois Confederacy (Haudenosaunee), a democratic governmental system established centuries before the Continental Congress. Indigenous political ideologies are also reflected in the transcribed speeches of powerful rhetoricians such as Sagoyewatha / Red Jacket (Seneca), Canassatego (Onondaga), and Tecumseh (Shawnee).

Early African American expression has in the past been approached primarily through the neoclassical poetry of Phillis Wheatley and through Olaudah Equiano's *Interesting Narrative* (1789), with an emphasis placed on individual resistance to oppression. In recent decades, the range of African American voices and genres included under the umbrella of "American Literature" has expanded, as has the understanding of African American writing in civic contexts. In addition to Wheatley's and Equiano's groundbreaking publications, readers take up such contributions of African Americans as Belinda Sutton's 1783 petition to the Massachusetts General Court—of interest both as an autobiography and as, some argue, the first successful petition for slavery reparations—and the life writings of preachers such as John Marrant and David George.

Some black writers argued openly against African American oppression, but by its very publication even the most conservative African American writing testified against the commonly held view that, as Benjamin Banneker phrased it in a widely circulated letter to Thomas Jefferson, black people were "scarcely capable of mental endowments." (Banneker, a free-born African American, presented his achievements in surveying and astronomy as evidence against this view.) Oral forms of literature also retained an important place in African American literature of the period, from rhetorically powerful sermons and abolitionist speeches (which often appeared in print as well) to works such as Lucy Terry's "Bars Fight" (composed c. 1746), a ballad that was preserved in oral tradition for more than a century before its print publication.

Title page of Samson Occom's *A Sermon Preached at the Execution of Moses Paul, an Indian*, 1772. Samson Occom, a Mohegan minister and community leader, is now best known for his autobiographical narrative, unpublished until the twentieth century. He was, however, famous in his lifetime as a preacher, and the text of his *Sermon Preached at the Execution of Moses Paul* (1772) is generally acknowledged to be the first bestseller by a Native American. The text appeared in a remarkable nineteen editions; the title page pictured here is from the fourth.

Title page of Benjamin Banneker's 1795 *Almanac*. Banneker, a self-taught mathematician, published a series of almanacs (annual publications including, among other things, astronomical and weather information for the coming year). His 1795 volume features a woodcut portrait of the author.

Engraving by Hébert after Auguste Raffet, *Attack and Capture of the Crête-à Pierrot*, 1839.

If American exceptionalism has understood the Revolutionary era and the first decades of the republic as establishing unprecedented freedom for early Americans, then an expanded body of American literature makes plain the founding exclusions as well as inclusions. Thomas Paine imagined a people formed out of shared emotion and rational discernment—that is, out of a *common sense* that would sustain them in revolution and in the work of nation building. But Abigail Adams suspected that when men alone were entrusted with that work, they would omit their female compatriots. In 1776, she wrote to her husband, who was away at the Continental Congress, that in addition to declaring independence from Britain they should also "Remember the Ladies, and be more generous and favorable to them than your ancestors." Sure enough, patriarchal tyranny did not end in the revolutionary era. A little over a decade later, as the founding fathers framed the U.S. Constitution in the late 1780s, they assumed the political agency of "We the people" for men alone and established that an enslaved American would constitute 3/5 of a person for the purposes of representation. Subsequently, the U.S. refused to recognize in 1804 the newly established and first black-led republic in the Americas, Haiti, despite a supposedly shared commitment to liberty and equality.

One evocative account of the shape of the people at the end of the eighteenth century is J. Hector St. John de Crèvecoeur's *Letters from an American Farmer* (1782), in which the fictional Farmer James poses the question "What then is the American, this new man?" and concludes that he is a European immigrant transformed by the freedom and prosperity the land affords. His love of country, James insists, is inspired by the fact that "his labour is founded on the basis of nature, SELF-INTEREST." Yet in travels to South Carolina, James witnesses slavery's brutal negation of black personhood. When, at the end of *Letters*, Revolutionary War approaches his farmstead, James and his family flee to a nearby Native American community, determining they had best ride out the brutal war among a people less impacted—at least in Crèvecoeur's romantic telling—by the disagreement between the British crown and colonists who wished to form their own nation.

By the first decades of the nineteenth century, two interrelated questions from the Revolution remained: Who was considered equal to whom? And who would enjoy true liberty? There was not a single shape to American society, though there were many narratives or theories of who belonged and how they understood their communal identity. If anything was certain, it was the perpetual possibility of reshaping "a people"— of reimagining community by way of individual rights and public values.

"A State of Independency": The Republic's First Decades

What was created in 1776 when the Continental Congress issued the Declaration of Independence? While Thomas Jefferson's ringing words have served as an inspiration for democratic ideals ever since, they did not at the time herald an intent to form a democratic nation in anything like the modern sense. In practice, the claim that "all men" possessed "certain inalienable rights" was understood to apply only to adult white males. Nor did the founders intend in 1776 to create a nation state in anything like the modern sense; the Declaration was consistently plural in its language, referring to the former colonies as "free and independent states," with no suggestion of any overarching body that would speak for them all collectively. Similarly, the Articles of Confederation that the Continental Congress adopted in 1777 (and that were ratified by the individual states over the next four years) asserted the "sovereignty, freedom, and independence" of each of the individual states, not of the collective entity. The colonies had entered collectively into what was often termed a "state of independency," but the national government existed almost exclusively as an entity to conduct the war and other matters of foreign affairs; it had no power over any of the individual states in any sphere, and no power to levy taxes or to undertake any other financial or economic measures.

Before long it became clear that more power would need to be granted to the federal government if the Confederation were to last—that a national government would need to have the power to regulate commerce and to raise money without relying solely on contributions from the individual states, and that a

judiciary and other permanent national institutions would need to be created. But what should be the extent, and the limits, of federal power?

When a Constitutional Convention was finally held in May 1787 and a Constitution for the United States proposed, the debate about this question was fierce. Under the constitution's provisions, the individual states would be barred from charging import or export taxes, interfering with property rights, or in any way obstructing interstate commerce. Moreover, in the statement of purpose drafted by Gouverneur Morris (a native New Yorker who represented Pennsylvania at the convention), the national government was tasked with overarching duties such as establishing justice, promoting the general welfare of the people, and securing the blessings of liberty; the preamble, which in its original draft had referred to "We, the people of the states of New-Hampshire, Massachusetts, Rhode Island and Providence Plantations, Connecticut, New York," etc., was given a more collectivist emphasis: "We, the people of the United States ..."

Supporters of the proposed constitution, known as the Federalists, put their case persuasively—most notably in the 85 essays by Alexander Hamilton, James Madison, and John Jay that were collectively known as *The Federalist Papers*. But to many, the proposed constitution's provisions granted too much power to the national government, and did too little to protect the rights of individual citizens—rights that had been given robust expression in the constitutions of many of the individual states. It was in that context that Madison, in order to win support for ratification, proposed that the first Congress put into place a Bill of Rights, "to make the Constitution better in the opinion of those who are opposed to it." The ten amendments that together constitute the Bill of Rights were put forward in 1789; among other things, they protect "freedom of speech, or of the press," protect "the right of the people peaceably to assemble," prohibit "unreasonable searches and seizures," protect the right to not "be deprived of life, liberty, or property, without due process of law," and assure anyone accused of a crime of the right to "a speedy and public trial." In the 1780s the Bill of Rights was a constitutional add-on, but it has come in the twentieth and twenty-first centuries to be regarded as of central importance to the Constitution.

By 21 June 1788 the Constitution in its original form had been ratified by the required number of states; by 15 December 1791 the Bill of Rights had also been ratified by the required number of states.

The numbers in the different States, according to the most accurate accounts which could be obtained by the late Federal Convention, were as follow :	
In New-Hampshire,	102,000
In Massachusetts,	360,000
In Rhode-Island,	58,000
In Connecticut,	202,000
In New-York,	238,000
In New-Jersey,	130,000
In Pennsylvania,	360,000
In Delaware,	37,000
In Maryland, (including three-fifths of 80,000 negroes)	218,000
In Virginia, (including three-fifths of 280,000 negroes)	420,000
In North-Carolina, (including three-fifths of 60,000 negroes)	200,000
In South-Carolina, (including three-fifths of 80,000 negroes)	150,000
In Georgia, (including three-fifths of 20,000 negroes)	90,000

From the *Hartford Courant*, 25 February 1788; similar notices appeared in newspapers throughout the states.

The Constitution's "We, the people" preamble was understood to exclude the Indigenous peoples of North America (excepting those few who had accepted assimilation and were paying taxes), and also to exclude enslaved people. The words "person," "persons," and "people" in the Bill of Rights were understood similarly. Enslaved people do appear in the Constitution obliquely when they are referred to in the notorious "three-fifths" clause, according to the terms of which additional political power was granted to slave-holding states. Enslaved people themselves were of course granted no political power and no rights. But whenever population was taken into account (in apportioning each state's number of representatives in the House of Representatives, and each state's number of votes for the presidential electoral college), slave states would be granted representation based on the total number of their white population plus "three fifths of all other persons." The three-fifths clause played a key role in maintaining slavery—and in giving Southern states an outsized say in national politics up to the Civil War.

In the debates over the Constitution, the "Federalists" and the "Anti-Federalists" were loose groupings of individuals, not organized political parties. In these early days of the republic most Americans had strong feelings against "faction"—what we would call division along party lines. There were thus no parties in the nation's earliest days; those who had been elected gave speeches and voted as independent individuals, not as the members of any formal group. But in the years following the ratification of the Constitution and the Bill of Rights, large, informal groupings took shape—most notably, on one side, supporters of the ideas that George Washington, Alexander Hamilton, and John Adams (who succeeded Washington as President) gave voice to, and on the opposing side, supporters of the ideas that Thomas Jefferson and James Madison gave voice to. Washington, Hamilton, and Adams advocated a relatively strong central government, a standing army, a national bank, and other measures to bring order to the monetary and financial system, and support for manufacturing and other industries. Pointing to the excesses of the French Revolution, they opposed measures that would broaden the franchise so as to allow men who did not own property to vote, and they tended to think of inequality not as an issue to be addressed but as an inevitable, even desirable feature of any properly functioning society. Federalist preacher (and textbook author) Jedediah Morse made this principle quite explicit in *A Discourse, Delivered at the African Meeting House in Boston, July 14 1808*:

> Distinctions of rank and condition in life are requisite to the perfection of the social state. There must be rulers and ruled, masters and servants, rich and poor. ... There is nevertheless a kind of equality among the members: all are free; all are useful and necessary; all are to be regarded and honored according to their station and use.[1]

Jefferson and Madison, on the other hand, were more sympathetic to democratic and egalitarian ideals, more supportive of farmers (both slaveholding Southern plantation owners and small "yeomen" owning family farms), and suspicious of institutions such as a permanent national army or a national bank, which they regarded as signs of a dangerous centralization of power in the hands of the federal government.

In the 1790s these loose groupings coalesced into two political parties: the Federalists, supporting Washington and Hamilton, and the Republicans,[2] supporting Jefferson and Madison. Disagreements between the two became more and more heated as the decade wore on, and partisans on both sides accused their opponents of holding treasonous views. The fiercely contested 1800 election turned largely on the Federalists' imposition of several pieces of legislation that aimed to reduce dissent. The Alien and Sedition Acts of 1798 made it more difficult to obtain American citizenship and gave the federal government broad powers to imprison or deport non-citizens and to prosecute those expressing views critical of the government. The resolution of the election was extraordinarily complicated and prolonged, but in the end Thomas Jefferson was elected president, on the slogan "Jefferson and Liberty."

The election of Jefferson is commonly thought of as a watershed moment in American history—not least of all because it demonstrated that a peaceful transition of power could be accomplished in the young republic. (Jefferson's endeavor to bring unity to the fractious country was demonstrated by his famous declaration, "We are all republicans, we are all federalists.") But it has also often been seen as a triumph of democratic ideals and of the values of "the common man" over what had become the overly controlling habits of Adams and the Federalists. Jefferson did pardon those who had been convicted under the Sedition Act (which Congress allowed to expire in 1801), and he restored the period required before one could obtain citizenship to five years from fourteen. But his administration proved to be no more willing than those of Washington or Adams had been to respect the rights of Indigenous peoples or of free African Americans.

[1] Morse made these statements in the course of arguing that freeing enslaved people should not be imagined to entail a general leveling of society. (While asserting repeatedly that, for all people, "the greatest slavery is sin," Morse celebrated the abolition of the international slave trade and expressed hope that the "gradual and ultimate extinction of African slavery" would come to pass.)

[2] The Republican party of this era (also known as the Democratic-Republican Party) broke up in the 1820s; the Republican Party that was founded in 1854 and that still exists today is an entirely different entity.

Early nineteenth-century criteria as to who counted as a citizen and who could vote were extremely narrow by modern standards—and they narrowed even further during the years Jefferson was in power (1801–09). In most states only citizens who owned a considerable amount of property (fifty acres or more was a common requirement) were allowed to vote. In the early years of the republic many states did not specify that "citizen"

The Providential Detection, c. 1797–1800. This anti-Jeffersonian political cartoon depicts Thomas Jefferson being prevented by an American eagle (and by God, symbolized by an eye peering out of a cloud in the top right corner) from burning the U.S. Constitution on an "Altar to Gallic Despotism"—referring to the radical and, to Federalists, extremist policies of the French Revolution, which influenced Jeffersonian Republicanism. The document Jefferson is dropping from his right hand, labeled "To Mazzei," refers to a private letter Jefferson wrote to his friend Philip Mazzei in 1796, in which he condemned the "Anglo-Monarchico-Aristocratic party"—i.e., the Federalists—currently controlling the U.S. government; the letter's publication in 1797 made Jefferson the target of intense Federalist criticism.

was intended to mean "white male"; in several states (theoretically at least) both women and free black people could vote.[1] By 1807, however, almost every state had passed legislation specifically restricting the franchise to white men, excluding women and black people of either sex from voting. Overall, then, it is difficult to argue that democratic vistas widened in America in the early nineteenth century.

Nowhere are the paradoxes inherent in Jeffersonian "democratic ideals" more evident than in the history of American expansion during this period. Federalists in this era were wary of expansion, fearing the unpredictable consequences of taking on new responsibilities and of trying to assimilate the inhabitants of new territories. Jefferson, on the other hand, was keen to acquire more land for the white farmers and would-be western settlers who were a key constituency for the Republicans, envisaging "an empire of liberty" that would eventually stretch to the Pacific. For white would-be settlers on western lands, he made this prospect more appealing by requiring settlers to purchase no more than 160 acres of public land (compared to the former requirement of 640 acres) with a down payment of only $16 and at a price of $2 an acre—or sometimes less. (By contrast, when land was purchased under the terms of treaties imposed on Indigenous peoples, the price was typically no more than 2 cents per acre; Jefferson wrote in 1803 that he felt it "important to press on the Indians, as steadily and strenuously as they can bear, the extension of our purchases.")

The primary U.S. territorial acquisition for which Jefferson was responsible, the Louisiana Purchase of 1803, has often been seen primarily through the lens of the negotiations between Jefferson's government and that of Napoleon; it should also be seen in an international context that includes the Caribbean as well as Europe and continental North America—and it should be seen as part of a process rather than in isolation. In the 1780s and 1790s the Spanish authorities in

[1] The original constitutions of Massachusetts, New Hampshire, Vermont, and Maine had all granted the vote to free black people, but by the early nineteenth century they all passed legislation denying black people the right to vote. In New Jersey, both free black males and property-owning women were able to vote until 1807; thereafter, the franchise was restricted to white men—as it was in New York, Pennsylvania, Connecticut, Maryland, Tennessee, and North Carolina.

James Peale, *The Artist and His Family*, 1795. This paint-ing of Peale, his wife Mary, and five of their eventual six children helped promote the ideology of "Republican Motherhood": the idea that women had a key role to play in fostering the fledgling U.S.'s republican values by instilling these values in their children. "Republican Motherhood" vested women's traditional domestic roles with great political importance while reinforcing the belief that the private home, rather than the public sphere, was women's proper place—a belief conveyed in this painting by the way in which only Peale himself looks outward at the painting's viewer, while his wife confines her focus to her children.

Florida and Louisiana,[1] anxious that the white popula-tions there not be heavily outnumbered by Indigenous people and enslaved people, were eager to attract white American settlers. At the urging of Jefferson (then Secretary of State), President George Washington

made a show of complaining of "this seduction of our inhabitants" while secretly encouraging white Americans to settle in those Spanish territories. "I wish a hundred thousand of our inhabitants would accept the invitation," Jefferson wrote; "it will be the means of delivering to us peaceably, what may otherwise cost us a war." When in 1801 France acquired the Louisiana territory from Spain the fundamentals did not change.[2] Indeed, the transfer of colonial control ended up has-tening the process by which the U.S. acquired the vast territory. The unexpectedly stiff resistance that Napoleon's French forces had met when they tried to retake Haiti from the enslaved people who had rebelled there[3] persuaded Napoleon that he could not afford to defend the huge territory of Louisiana at the same time as he was fighting a war in Europe. Thanks very largely to the strength of a black-led revolution that the American government deplored, the United States was able to buy all of Louisiana for a mere $15 million. For the most part, of course, the French were selling land that was not theirs to sell; the colonial powers had laid claim to the vast Louisiana territory without having negotiated treaties with its Indigenous inhabit-ants that could give them any legitimate claim to own-ership. But such niceties did not trouble Jefferson or the American Congress any more than they had the European colonial powers.

The acquisition of the Louisiana Territory repre-sented the most substantial expansion of the United States during the first decades of the new republic, but Americans looked to expand in a number of other directions as well during these years—to the south and to the north as well as westward. The War of 1812 has traditionally not been framed as a war of American expansionism; at the time, indeed, works of popular literature such as Samuel Woodworth's "The Patriotic Diggers" framed it as a defensive war in the face of British aggression. But were it not for American expan-sionism the war would surely not have occurred; its roots lie in the spread of white settlement westward in the late eighteenth and early nineteenth centuries.

1 "Louisiana" initially referred to a vast area of the North American interior, stretching from the Great Lakes to the Gulf of Mexico and from the Appalachian to Rocky Mountains, explored and colonized by France in the late seventeenth and eighteenth centuries (the name "Louisiana" came from King Louis XIV of France). The Louisiana Territory purchased by the U.S. in 1803 comprised only part of this, but still consisted of a huge stretch of land between the Mississippi and the Rockies, of which the present-day U.S. state of Louisiana is only the southernmost portion.

2 France had previously ceded the Louisiana Territory to Spain in 1762.

3 For more on the Haitian Revolution and its impact on American history and literature, see the "Contexts: Revolutions and Rebellions" section of this volume.

UNDER MY WINGS EVERY THING PROSPERS

J.L. Bouqueto de Woiseri, *Under My Wings Everything Prospers*, 1803. The Louisiana Purchase was widely and often extravagantly praised. At a 10 August 1803 gathering of the citizens of Lexington, Kentucky, to celebrate the purchase, for example, the following toast was made: "To Thomas Jefferson, President of the United States. Can he, by whose wise measures we have acquired a new world, continue still to have enemies?"

The above painting of New Orleans by a local artist dates from just after the Louisiana Purchase. The bird holding the banner is a somewhat puzzling feature. The bald eagle had been selected as the national symbol of the United States in 1782; the bird pictured here is clearly not a mature bald eagle, though it is possible that it is a juvenile. (Not until they are three to five years old do bald eagles acquire their distinctive white head feathers.)

Without any formal authorization, close to 400,000 American settler colonists had by 1800 taken land west of the Appalachians. It was in response to these encroachments that a number of allied Indigenous peoples challenged the Americans in a succession of wars, culminating in what became known as Tecumseh's War (see the Tecumseh author entry). And it was in large part in response to British support (some real, some imagined) for this Indigenous resistance[1] that the U.S. in 1812 declared war on Britain. Kentuckian Henry Clay, the leader of the congressional group known as the War Hawks, argued bluntly to his fellow congressmen that the "conquest of Canada" could readily be accomplished even "by the militia of Kentucky acting alone," and that Congress should act to "extinguish the torch that lights up savage warfare,"

and to "acquire the entire fur trade connected with that country [i.e., the entire fur trade in Canada]." The Federalists and not a few Republicans thought Clay and the War Hawks to be misguided extremists, but in the end the War Hawks prevailed; the bill authorizing the declaration of war passed in the Senate by 19 to 13.

The war itself was inconclusive; when it ended in 1815 the boundary between the United States and the British colonies to the north was unchanged. But the end of the war did not bring an end to American expansionism. As had happened in what became Ohio, and as would happen later in what would become the state of Texas, American settlers had also begun without formal authorization in the late eighteenth century to spill over the country's southern border; many thousands had settled in the Spanish colonies of East Florida and West Florida (whose combined area extended from St. Augustine on the Atlantic coast to what is now southeastern Louisiana). Though the territories

[1] This account is necessarily oversimplified; other irritants included a variety of disputes over trade and shipping issues.

Julia Plantou (artist) and Alexis Chataigner (engraver), *Peace of Ghent 1814 and Triumph of America*, c. 1815. This elaborate allegorical image projects a celebratory, patriotic view of the Peace of Ghent, the treaty between Britain and the United States that ended the War of 1812. At the right, Columbia, the allegorical representation of the U.S., is being crowned with the laurels of victory; at the left, Britannia, the allegorical representation of Britain, is being compelled to accept peace terms by Minerva and Hercules—Roman gods personifying, respectively, wisdom and strength.

were nominally under Spanish control, fewer than 15,000 Spanish settlers lived there (most of them in the centers of St. Augustine, Pensacola, and Mobile); those of Spanish descent were substantially outnumbered by Seminole, Muscogee (Creek), and other Indigenous peoples, together with "maroons" who had escaped from slavery. (In the eighteenth century, Spain had held out the prospect of freedom to enslaved Africans in British colonies, on the condition that they convert to Catholicism.) Americans who settled in the Floridas coveted what they saw as underutilized land, and feared that the maroons would foment unrest among those still enslaved. But by 1810 many thousands of white Americans who had settled in Spanish territory

in the Floridas were chafing at Spanish laws—not least of all the web of laws designed to protect enslaved workers from mistreatment. When in that year a group of Americans in West Florida rebelled against Spanish rule and declared themselves to be "a free and independent state," the administration of President James Madison invaded, and Congress annexed what had been a large part of West Florida to the United States. A similar process unfolded over the course of the next decade in the remainder of West Florida and in East Florida; through pressure, subterfuge, and outright war (against the Muscogee and the Seminole as well as the Spanish), the United States had by 1821 acquired the entirety of the two Floridas.

Texts and Contexts:
A Chronological Chart

In the chart below, dates generally refer to the year when a work was first made public, whether published in print or, in the case of speeches and plays, made public through the first performance. Where that date is known to differ substantially from the date of composition, the difference is generally noted; for manuscript works whose exact date of composition is unknown, we have provided an estimated date range.

For the convenience of those who may wish to look slightly beyond the chronological boundaries of this volume, the following chart carries through to the Indian Removal Act of 1830.

TEXTS		CONTEXTS	
before 10,500 BCE	The oral traditions of North American Indigenous people can in some cases be traced back to the last Ice Age	before 10,500 BCE	Migration of small groups from Asia to the Americas over several thousand years
		c. 3000 BCE –500 BCE	Red Paint Culture flourishes in the Northeast
		c. 200–900	Peak of Maya civilization; city of Teotihuacàn flourishes
		c. 700–1600	Mississippian Culture flourishes in Midwest and Southeast
		c. 750 CE	Ancestral Puebloans of the Southwest begin living in pueblo complexes
		982–1015	Norse people establish settlements in North America and encounter Inuit, Beothuk, Mi'kmaq
c. 1021–1154	Maya Codex of Mexico		
		c. 1142–1500	Formation of Haudenosaunee (Iroquois) Confederacy (exact date is controversial)
c. 1200–1250	Dresden Codex	c. 1200–1400	Ndee (Apache) and Diné (Navajo) migrate into Southwest
			Beginning of the migration of the Ojibwe people from the Atlantic to the Great Lakes

	c. 1300–	Peak of Aztec civilization. City of
	1521	Tenochtitlan is capital of the Aztec Empire until capture by the Spanish in 1521
	1492	Christopher Columbus reaches San Salvador (called Guanahaní by the Indigenous population), an island in the Bahamas, suspecting he has reached Asia
		European diseases begin to devastate the Indigenous population of the Americas, which is estimated to have numbered between 50 and 100 million before European contact
1493	Columbus, *Letter on the First Voyage*	
c. 1500–1600	*Florentine Codex*	
	1500	Spain and Portugal begin establishing colonies in Central America, the Caribbean, and South America. Increasingly, captives are shipped from Africa and enslaved, joining and/or replacing enslaved Indigenous people
1507	Map by Martin Waldseemüller uses the word "America" for the first time (after explorer Amerigo Vespucci)	
	1508	Ponce de León explores Puerto Rico
	1513	Ponce de León explores Florida
	1519–21	Hernán Cortés conquers the Aztec empire
	1521	Permanent Spanish settlement founded at San Juan, Puerto Rico
	1525	First voyage of a slave ship directly from Africa to the Americas
	1526	A Spanish expedition to present-day South Carolina includes enslaved Africans; the Africans' rebellion prevents the Spanish from establishing a colony, and they abandon it a year later
1528	Anonymous, *Annals of Tlatelolco*	
	1534–36	Jacques Cartier explores the St. Lawrence River and the coasts of modern-day eastern Canada and Maine
	1539	First printing press in the Americas set up in Mexico City; it is used to print documents related to the church and the viceregal government
		Hernando de Soto invades Florida
	1540	Hernando de Alarcón's voyage to Baja California and the Colorado River begins

1542 Álvar Núñez Cabeza de Vaca, *The Relation of Álvar Núñez Cabeza de Vaca*

1542 Juan Rodríguez Cabrillo's voyage to California begins

1552 Bartolome de las Casas, *A Short Account of the Destruction of the Indies*

1558–1603 Reign of Elizabeth I

1565 Permanent Spanish settlement founded at St. Augustine, Florida; approximately 800 Spanish colonists bring with them approximately 50 enslaved Africans

1585 English colonizers land on Roanoke Island near modern-day North Carolina but abandon the settlement a year later

1587 Second expedition to Roanoke, led by John White (later called the Lost Colony due to the disappearance of the colonists)

1588 Thomas Hariot, *A Brief and True Report of the New Found Land of Virginia*

1603–10 Samuel de Champlain explores the St. Lawrence River and Acadia, establishing a settlement in the Bay of Fundy (1604) and founding Quebec (1608)

1605 Inca Garcilaso de la Vega, *La Florida del Inca*

1607 The Virginia Company establishes a settlement at Jamestown

Under the leadership of Wahunsonacock, Powhatan people provide food and supplies to starving Jamestown colonists

1609 Henry Hudson explores Staten Island, Manhattan Island, and river valley of what is known today as the Hudson River

1610 Gaspar de Villagrá, *Historia de la Nueva Mexico*

1610–14 First Anglo-Powhatan War

1611 King James Bible (a new translation prompted in part by English Puritans)

1612 First commercial tobacco crop grown in Jamestown

1613 Samuel de Champlain, *The Voyages of the Sieur de Champlain*

1613 Two Row Wampum establishes the Convenant Chain between settlers and member nations of the Haudenosaunee

1619 "20. and odd" enslaved persons from the African Kingdom of Ndongo, or "Angola," arrive in Virginia aboard a privateer ship flying the Dutch flag

1624 John Smith, *The General History of Virginia, New England, and the Summer Isles*

1630 John Winthrop, "A Model of Christian Charity" (pub. 1838)

1630–50 William Bradford's journal, *Of Plymouth Plantation* (pub. 1856)

1637 Thomas Morton, *New English Canaan*

1640 *Bay Psalm Book*

1643 Roger Williams, *A Key into the Language of America*

1650 Anne Bradsteet, *The Tenth Muse*

1620 Approximately 100 Separatists arrive aboard the *Mayflower*, found Plymouth Colony

1621 Settlers and local Wampanoag together celebrate successful harvest

1622–26 Second Anglo-Powhatan War

1624 First permanent Dutch settlement in New Netherland (later called New York)

1630–43 English Puritans establish Massachusetts Bay Colony.

1634 First English settlers arrive in Maryland

1636 Harvard College founded

1636–38 Pequot War between the Pequot tribe and English colonists from the Massachusetts Bay, Plymouth, and Connecticut colonies (with Narragansett and Mohegan allies)

Mystic Massacre of 1637; colonists set fire to a Pequot fort, killing most of the occupants (between 500 and 700 Pequot)

1637 *Desire*, first slave ship built in the American colonies, sets sail for the British West Indies

1638 First printing press arrives in the colonies

Anne Hutchinson tried, convicted, and banished for challenging Puritan religious beliefs

1641 Massachusetts legalizes slavery; it is the first British colony to do so

Sugar exports from the Caribbean begin

1642–51 English Civil War

1644–46 Third Anglo-Powhatan War

1649 Execution of Charles I of England

1651 Thomas Hobbes's *Leviathan* is published in London

1660 Restoration of British monarchy; end of Puritan rule in England

1662	Michael Wigglesworth, *The Day of Doom*	1662	Hereditary slavery established in Virginia
1663	Algonquian-language Bible (first Bible printed in North America)	1663	Rebellion by enslaved blacks and white indentured servants in Virginia
1673–1729	Samuel Sewall's *Diary* (pub. 1878–82)	1675–76	Metacom's War (King Philip's War)
		1676	Bacon's Rebellion
		1680	Pueblo Revolt
		1681	William Penn founds Pennsylvania
1682	Mary Rowlandson, *A Narrative of the Captivity and Restoration of Mrs. Rowlandson*		
1682–1725	Edward Taylor, *Preparatory Meditations* (pub. 1939, 1960)		
		1688	Quakers pass first formal antislavery resolution
		1689	John Locke's *Second Treatise of Government* is published in London
		1689–97	King William's War
1692	Sor Juana Inés de la Cruz, *First Dream*	1692–93	Salem witchcraft trials
1693	Cotton Mather, *The Wonders of the Invisible World*		
		1694	Rice cultivation introduced in the Carolinas
		1695	Gold discovered in Brazil
1702	Cotton Mather, *Magnalia Christi Americana*	1702–13	Queen Anne's War
		1708	South Carolina becomes first English colony with a black majority
		1718	French found New Orleans
		1720–80	Peak years of the slave trade to British North America
		1722	Tuscarora join the Haudenosaunee
		1726–56	The Great Awakening
1741	Jonathan Edwards, "Sinners in the Hands of an Angry God"	1744–48	King George's War
c. 1746	Lucy Terry, "Bars Fight" (pub. 1854)		
		1752	Benjamin Franklin invents the lightning rod

1754–63 French and Indian War

 Seven Years' War

1760 Briton Hammon, *A Narrative of the Uncommon
 Sufferings, and Surprizing Deliverance of Briton
 Hammon, A Negro Man*

1760–1820 Reign of King George III

1761 Jupiter Hammon, "An Evening Thought: Salvation
 by Christ, with Penitential Cries"

1762–1801 John and Abigail Adams's correspondence (pub.
 1840, 1875)

1763 Pontiac's rebellion

 Royal Proclamation of 1763

1765 Stamp Act

1767 Survey of Mason-Dixon line completed

1769 Father Junípero Serra founds Mission San Diego
 (first Spanish mission in "Alta California")

1770 Boston Massacre

1772 James Gronniosaw, *A Narrative of the Most
 Remarkable Particulars in the Life of James Albert
 Ukawsaw Gronniosaw, an African Prince, as Related
 by Himself*

 Samson Occom, *Sermon Preached at the Execution
 of Moses Paul*

1773 Phillis Wheatley, *Poems on Various Subjects*

1773 Boston Tea Party

1774 First Continental Congress

1775 American Revolutionary War begins

 Anthony Benezet founds America's first abolition-
 ist society (Benjamin Franklin becomes its presi-
 dent in 1787)

1776 Thomas Paine, *Common Sense*

 Declaration of Independence

1777 The Stars and Stripes is adopted as the national
 flag by the Continental Congress

 Vermont Republic abolishes slavery

1780s Annis Boudinot Stockton publishes poems in vari-
 ous newspapers

1782 J. Hector St. John de Crèvecoeur, *Letters from an American Farmer*

1783 Treaty of Paris ends the Revolutionary War; Britain cedes the Northwest Territory to the United States, doubling the land area of the new country

1785 John Marrant, *A Narrative of the Lord's Wonderful Dealings with John Marrant, a Black*

1786 Philip Freneau, *Poems*

 Jupiter Hammon, "Address to the Negroes of New York State"

1787 Thomas Jefferson, *Notes on the State of Virginia*

 Royall Tyler, *The Contrast*

1787 U.S. Constitution signed at constitutional convention in Philadelphia; ratified a year later by 9 of 13 states

 Free African Society founded by Absalom Jones and Richard Allen

1787–88 Alexander Hamilton, James Madison, and John Jay, *The Federalist* papers

1789 Olaudah Equiano, *The Interesting Narrative of the Life of Olaudah Equiano* (American edition pub. 1792)

1789 French Revolution begins

 George Washington elected first president

 Bill of Rights (ratified 1791)

1790 Judith Sargent Murray, "On the Equality of the Sexes"

1790 U.S. Supreme Court meets for first time

 First U.S. census; population of 3.9 million (including 694,280 enslaved people; Indigenous people are not counted)

1791 Benjamin Franklin, *Autobiography* (Part 1 is first published in France in translation; Parts 1, 2, and 3 are published in English in 1817)

 Susanna Haswell Rowson, *Charlotte Temple*

1791 Washington, D.C., established as U.S. capital

 Haitian Revolution begins

1792 United States Dollar approved as currency

 New York Stock Exchange founded

1793 U.S. Congress passes first Fugitive Slave Act

1794 Patent issued for Eli Whitney's cotton gin

1795 First Naturalization Act, restricting citizenship to free white persons

1797 Hannah Webster Foster, *The Coquette*

1798 Venture Smith, *A Narrative of the Life and Adventures of Venture, A Native of Africa*

 Charles Brockden Brown, *Wieland*

1798 Alien and Sedition Acts

1799	Code of Handsome Lake (Gaihwi:io), orally transmitted with the aid of wampum
1805	Sagoyewatha, "Reply to the Missionary Jacob Cram"
1808	Leonora Sansay, *Secret History; or, the Horrors of St. Domingo*
1814	Francis Scott Key, "The Star-Spangled Banner"
1817	William Cullen Bryant, "Thanatopsis"
	First Cherokee Women's Petition (a second and third followed in 1818 and 1831)

1799	Napoleon Bonaparte seizes power in France
1800	Thomas Jefferson elected President
1803	Louisiana Purchase
1804	Haitian Declaration of Independence
1804–06	Lewis and Clark expedition, aided by Shoshone guide Sacagawea
1807	United States Congress passes Act Prohibiting Importation of Slaves (went into effect 1808)
	Britain passes Act for the Abolition of the Slave Trade (went into effect 1808)
1808	Under the leadership of Tecumseh and proclaiming the teachings of Tenskwatawa, Tecumseh's confederacy evolves to promote tribal unity and the rejection of English-American culture
1810	Mexican War of Independence begins
1812–14	War of 1812
1813–14	Creek War
1814	Burning of Capitol Building in Washington
	Francis Cabot Lowell introduces new systems to the textile industry at the Boston Manufacturing Company
1815	Nathan Hale founds the *North American Review*, the nation's first literary magazine
	Battle of Waterloo
1816–18	First Seminole War
1819	First steamship to cross the Atlantic
	Spain cedes East Florida to the United States and renounces claim to West Florida
	Attorney General of Upper Canada confirms that formerly enslaved people who have fled the United States and entered Upper Canada are "protected by the laws of England" and cannot be forced to return

1820	Washington Irving, *The Sketch Book*		1820	Missouri Compromise admits Missouri to the union as a slave state, Maine as a free state, and prohibits slavery in all new states in the Louisiana Purchase lands north of latitude 36° 30′
1821	William Cullen Bryant, *Poems*		1821	Mexico becomes independent
				Sequoyah creates syllabary for the Cherokee language
			1823	President James Monroe proclaims that the United States will consider any attempt by European powers to expand the area under their control in the Western hemisphere as a threat to the "health and safety" of the United States
1824	Mary Jemison, *A Narrative of the Life of Mary Jemison* Lydia Maria Child, *Hobomok*			
1825	José María Heredia, "Niagara"		1825	Erie Canal opens
1826	Elias Boudinot, "An Address to the Whites" James Fenimore Cooper, *The Last of the Mohicans* Jane Johnston Schoolcraft begins to publish poems in *The Literary Voyager*		1826	American Temperance Society founded Landscapes by Thomas Cole exhibited at the American Academy of the Fine Arts
1827	James John Audubon begins to publish *The Birds of America* David Cusick, *Sketches of Ancient History of the Six Nations* Lydia Sigourney, *Poems* Catharine Sedgwick, *Hope Leslie*		1827	Last enslaved people in New York state freed *Freedom's Journal* founded
			1827–28	The newspaper *The Cherokee Phoenix* founded (Elias Boudinot, editor)
			1828	First performances of "Jump Jim Crow" by Thomas Dartmouth Rice
1829	William Apess, *A Son of the Forest* David Walker, *An Appeal to the Coloured Citizens of the World* Cherokee Council, "Memorial of the Cherokees" George Moses Horton, *The Hope of Liberty*		1829	First steam locomotive to operate on a U.S. railroad, "The Stourbridge Lion" Slavery abolished in Mexico
			1830	Indian Removal Act

Opening of Baltimore and Ohio Railroad (first U.S. railway chartered for commercial transportation)

Louis A. Godey begins publishing *The Lady's Book* (subsequently known as *Godey's Lady's Book* and as *Godey's Magazine and Lady's Book*)

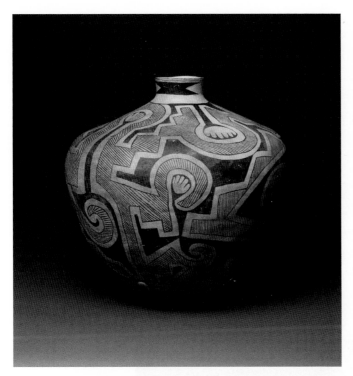

Ancestral Pueblo storage jar, c. 1050–1100. This Ancestral Pueblo storage jar, likely used to preserve food in preparation for drought, is painted in a style known as "Socorro black-on-white" for the region of the Upper Rio Grande Valley where it originated. The abstract pattern on the jar probably references the movement of water, with the black portions evoking clouds while the lines represent rain; the hand-shaped symbol may be the painter's personal mark.

Shingwaukonse, Mishipeshu with canoe and serpents, c. early nineteenth century. This rock painting, part of an important Ojibwe pictograph site at Agawa Rock on the east coast of Lake Superior, depicts the powerful spirit Mishipeshu, sometimes called the Great Lynx, who governs the dangerous waters of Lake Superior and possesses the region's copper. The prominent shaman and chief Shingwaukonse (1773–1854) told the anthropologist Henry Rowe Schoolcraft that, while many of Agawa Rock's paintings are substantially older, he himself had drawn Mishipeshu as part of a ritual to gather power before leading a resistance effort against copper miners. Indigenous knowledge-keepers and settler anthropologists have also found a variety of other meanings in the image.

Alejo Fernández, *The Virgin of the Navigators*, 1531–36. This painting forms the central panel of an altarpiece painted by the prominent Seville-based artist Alejo Fernández under a commission from the House of Trade, the government entity that oversaw the commercial aspects of the Spanish Empire. Scholars continue to discuss the identities of the figures sheltered under the Virgin Mary's cloak, but some of the most likely candidates include Hernán Cortés, leader of the conquest of Mexico, on a bent knee in a red cape; Charles I of Spain (also Holy Roman Emperor as Charles V) behind Cortés with a red beard; explorer Amerigo Vespucci, holding a cane; and, in a gold robe, Christopher Columbus. Behind these figures are Indigenous people of the Americas. One possible explanation for their simple cloth attire, unlike anything Indigenous Americans would have worn in daily life, is that they are dressed for baptism.

John White, *The Manner of Their Fishing*, c. 1585. English artist John White accompanied the first attempt to colonize Roanoke Island, off the coast of what is now North Carolina, where he made watercolors such as this one depicting the plants, animals, and Indigenous people of the region. Etchings based on his paintings were made for a 1590 edition of Thomas Hariot's *A Brief and True Report of the New Found Land of Virginia* (first published in 1588), an account of the same expedition; these etchings circulated widely and strongly influenced European understandings of the Americas and the people who lived there. In Hariot's caption for the etching based on this painting, he notes a number of the fishing methods depicted, including the building of fishing weirs, rows of stakes placed in the water so as to trap fish. He writes of them that "[t]here was never seen among us so cunning a way to take fish," commenting that "it is a pleasant sight to see the people, sometimes wading, and going sometimes sailing in those rivers, which are shallow and not deep, free from all care of heaping up riches for their posterity, content with their state, and living friendly together of those things which god of his bounty has given to them, yet without giving him any thanks according to his desert."

For further examples of John White's work and selections from Hariot's *Brief and True Report*, see "Civilizations in Contact" elsewhere in this anthology.

Anonymous, *Elizabeth Clarke Freake and Baby Mary*, 1671–74. Anonymous, *John Freake*, 1671–74.

The anonymous painter of these works, sometimes known as the "Freake Painter" in reference to them, painted around ten portraits in the Boston area in the early 1670s; the painter appears to have received English training in the Elizabethan style of portraiture, which was no longer popular in England by this time. The subjects of the portraits, John Freake and Elizabeth Clarke Freake, were Boston Puritans whose wealth is reflected in the expensive and fashionable clothing they wear. Elizabeth was born near Boston to a wealthy merchant family, and John, who had immigrated to Boston from England, was also a very successful merchant. Elizabeth originally held a fan in her portrait, but it was altered a few years later to include her youngest daughter.

Detail, anonymous casta painting, eighteenth century. Popular among eighteenth-century Spanish elites in the Americas, casta paintings represent complex racial classifications or "castes" through a series of images showing the offspring of various mixed-race couples. Each set begins with white, black, and Indigenous parents, applying separate terms to their children and grandchildren in various racial combinations. Like many sets of casta paintings do, the image reproduced here includes sixteen classifications:

1. Spaniard with Indigenous person: Mestizo.
2. Mestizo with Spaniard: Castizo.
3. Castizo with Spaniard: Spaniard.
4. Spaniard with African: Mulatto.
5. Mulatto with Spaniard: Morisca ("Moorish").
6. Morisca with Spaniard: Chino (literally "Chinese").
7. Chino with Indigenous person: Salta atrás ("throwback").
8. Salta atrás with Mulatto: Lobo ("wolf").
9. Lobo with Chino: Gíbaro.
10. Gíbaro with Mulatto: Albarazado ("white-spotted").
11. Albarazado with African: Cambujo.
12. Cambujo with Indigenous person: Zambiaga.
13. Zambiaga with Loba: Calpamulato.
14. Calpamulto with Cambujo: Tente en el aire ("hold yourself in the air").
15. Tente en el aire with Mulatto: No te entiendo (literally "I don't understand you").
16. No te entiendo with Indigenous person: Torna atrás ("return backwards").

Beyond terms such as "mestizo" and "mulatto," this precise (and, generally speaking, offensive) terminology was little used in practice, but its complexity can be taken as an indication of eighteenth-century Euro-American fascination both with race and with taxonomy. The categories also reflect differences in Spanish racism toward Indigenous and black people: most casta paintings assert that a person with one Indigenous grandparent could be considered Spanish, while a person with one African grandparent could not.

Agostino Brunias, *Free Women of Colour with Their Children and Servants in a Landscape*, c. 1770–96. The Italian-born painter Agostino Brunias spent much of his career on Dominica and other Caribbean islands colonized by Britain. His paintings, which often focus on the islands' mixed-race elites, had admirers on both sides of the abolition debate. His proslavery audience in Europe and the colonies enjoyed his idyllic and exotic depictions of plantation life—and the absence of any representation of the brutality of slavery. At the same time, his work was welcomed by black and mixed-race Caribbeans who appreciated his celebration of the Creole culture emerging in the region; the Haitian revolutionary Touissant Louverture, for example, wore a jacket with buttons featuring miniature scenes painted by Brunias.

Robert Dighton, *Keep Within Compass and You Shall Be Sure, to Avoid Many Troubles which Others Endure*, 1784 and 1785. Designed by the painter and printmaker Robert Dighton and printed by the London publisher Carington Bowles, these images circulated widely in the colonies as well as in Britain, appearing not only as prints but also on everyday objects such as fans and teapots. The man in the print on the left points to sacks of coins; on the edge of the illustration are smaller scenes of a man ruined by gambling, a man being robbed by a prostitute, a ship crashed on rocks, and prisoners in jail. The woman in the print on the right holds a book that reads "The Pleasures of Imagination Realized"; the chest at her feet is labeled "The Reward of Virtue." The scenes surrounding her feature women ruined by gambling, dropping a baby in a bout of drunkenness, being arrested by watchmen, and performing manual labor in prison.

Joshua Johnson, *Adelina Morton*, c. 1810. Generally considered the first known professional African American painter, Joshua Johnson was born into slavery in Maryland, and after his enslaver (who was also his father) granted him his freedom he earned his living making portraits of Baltimore elites. In one newspaper advertisement offering his services, he writes that, "As a self-taught genius, deriving from nature and industry his knowledge of the Art; and having experienced many insuperable obstacles in the pursuit of his studies, it is highly gratifying to him to make assurances of his ability to execute all commands with an effect, and in a style, which must give satisfaction."

Charlotte Cardner, Quaker School Sampler, 1813. At the beginning of the nineteenth century, the New York Female Association, a Quaker organization, founded New York's first public school for girls—a project motivated by the Quaker belief that education should be accessible to all. Students learned reading, writing, arithmetic, and embroidery; the latter skill is evident in this sampler made for one of the school's patrons.

Prudence Punderson, *The First, Second, and Last Scene of Mortality*, c. 1776–83. Needlework artist Prudence Punderson's family supported the British side during the American Revolution, and as a result they were forced to flee their home in Connecticut. While living in exile and relative poverty in Long Island, Punderson created her best-known works, including this self-portrait. On the right, Punderson appears as a baby, cared for by a servant (probably an enslaved woman named Jenny, whom the family owned); in the center, she appears as an adult drawing at a table; on the left is depicted a covered mirror above a coffin bearing the initials "P.P." The interior depicted is likely based on the home the Pundersons left behind in Connecticut, as their Long Island lodgings would not have been so comfortable. As soon as the war ended, Punderson returned to Connecticut and married; she died less than a year later, at the age of 26.

Anonymous, *Benjamin Hawkins and the Creek Indians*, c. 1805. In 1796, Benjamin Hawkins, a former senator, was appointed "Principal Temporary Agent for Indian Affairs South of the Ohio River" and charged with implementing the so-called "plan of civilization," according to which the Indigenous peoples of the region would replace hunting and Indigenous farming practices with a Euro-American style of farming cash crops and keeping livestock. On the surface, this plan was intended to help Indigenous groups flourish economically—ignoring the fact that they were quite capable of supporting themselves already—but the covert goal was to undermine Indigenous claims to hunting lands to make more room for settler-colonists. Hawkins saw himself as an ally to the Indigenous groups and believed the "plan of civilization" was the best way forward, since the other likely possibility was the violent expulsion of the Indigenous peoples from the region. He moved to a Muscogee-Creek community, where he found that many people were already selectively adopting Euro-American farming practices and appreciated his support. Disagreement among the Muscogee about how to respond to the "plan of civilization" culminated in a civil war (1813–14); the U.S. government intervened brutally and forced the Muscogee to sign a treaty that ceded two-thirds of their land. Hawkins resigned in protest.

Anonymous Chinese artist after John James Barralet, *Apotheosis of Washington*, early nineteenth century (original c. 1802). After George Washington's death in 1799, the commemoration of his life and passing became a tremendously fashionable subject for artists. The print this work is based on, by the Irish-born illustrator John James Barralet, was so popular that it was issued several times. One copy was taken to China to be copied onto porcelain—or, in examples such as the one reproduced here, glass—for sale in the United States. The work depicts Washington lifted from his tomb by allegorical figures of Immortality and Father Time; in the background are figures of Faith, Hope, and Charity. In front of the tomb are an Indigenous figure and Lady Liberty, who holds a liberty cap on a pole, a symbol of the revolution. Liberty and the Indigenous man are placed in poses reminiscent of the sleeping soldiers often depicted in scenes of Christ's resurrection, while the image of Washington ascending on a cloud, aided by winged figures, reflects typical images of the Virgin Mary being taken up into heaven.

John Quidor, *The Return of Rip Van Winkle*, 1849. New York painter John Quidor devoted much of his career to depicting scenes from literature, especially from the work of Washington Irving—most famously "The Legend of Sleepy Hollow" (1820) and "Rip Van Winkle" (1819), the latter of which was a popular subject for nineteenth-century artists generally. In this interpretation of Rip's dramatic homecoming following his twenty-year nap, Quidor frames the character's extreme body language with the chaos and change occasioned by the American Revolution. See Washington Irving's author section, elsewhere in this anthology, for another Quidor painting based on "Rip Van Winkle."

John Lewis Krimmel, *Independence Day Celebration in Centre Square*, 1819. Born in Germany, John Lewis Krimmel emigrated to Philadelphia in 1809, where he became best-known for his scenes of everyday life. This painting of the city's 1819 Fourth of July celebrations shows a crowd engaging in the festivities while, on the right, a woman attempts to distribute temperance literature. On the left, a black child runs away from the scene—an allusion to the risk of racist violence that generally kept African American Philadelphians from participating in city revelries such as this. In the central foreground, officers of the army and navy point to a Pennsylvania flag, a portrait of George Washington, and banners referencing American victories in the War of 1812 (1812–15).

INDIGENOUS ORAL AND VISUAL LITERATURES

Indigenous traditional literatures are the oldest literatures produced on the North American continent, and they are still heard, read, interpreted, translated, and published in Indigenous nations today, as part of continuous literary and intellectual histories, political deliberations, and ceremonies. These literatures appear in a vast array of media, each with their own complex aesthetics, from oral literatures—told in hundreds of languages across the continent—to visual texts, some of which use alphabetic writing and some of which use nonalphabetic forms. Nonalphabetic Indigenous traditional literatures include, for example, carved house posts, painted baskets, pictographic texts, and wampum belts; they can express narratives and ideas, record laws, and document events, among other purposes. The stories told in traditional literatures—both oral and written—are enormously varied, ranging from stories of the creation of the world and of humans and other animals to stories of how communities and cultures were formed, stories of alliances and conflicts among Indigenous communities and other historical events, and stories engaging with questions of how people should live.

Indigenous traditional literatures challenge conceptions of "America" and of "American literature" oriented around European colonization and settlement and around alphabetic writing. In many recent American literature anthologies, including this one, a cluster of "traditional literatures" from several tribal traditions is located in the opening pages as a signal of their firstness. Yet before the late twentieth century, it was far more common for anthologies to ignore Native American literatures and position works by the Virginia settler John Smith or the Massachusetts Bay colony settler John Winthrop as the first American literatures. When these older anthologies did acknowledge Indigenous literary traditions, they rarely depicted Indigenous people as authors and presented traditional literatures without context. To take just a few examples, the 1968 anthology *O Brave New World: American Literature 1600–1840* begins with a section titled "The Mythological Inheritance," which consists of captivity narratives by colonists, including John Smith's 1624 *Generall History of Virginia*. In 1976, the anthology *Colonial American Literature from Wilderness to Independence* opened with a section titled "Before the Settlers" that placed two "Indian Myths" alongside European travel narratives and an excerpt from William Shakespeare's *The Tempest*. These selections gave the impression that Indigenous traditional literatures were scarce and that settlers' narratives were better suited to exemplify early literatures from the Americas. In 1989, the *Heath Anthology* was the first to begin with a section—titled "Native American Traditions"—featuring Indigenous literatures from across the continent and acknowledging Indigenous peoples' place as the first peoples of the land.

Foregrounding traditional literatures can complicate the linear timelines through which American literary histories are often told, in which European settlement is soon followed by nation formation and in which "American" (i.e., settler) literatures replace Indigenous ones. Contrary to those linear timelines, Indigenous traditional literatures existed long before settler literatures, and their complex histories of retelling, translation, and publication reach into the present. As active, living texts, they invoke a tense that Timothy Powell, in his collaborations with Eastern Band Cherokee storyteller Freeman Owle, calls "ancient present tense." By this, Powell and Owle mean that Indigenous stories have roots that go back for thousands of years, and when those stories are told, they bring "this deep past into the immediacy of the present," as if the events are occurring now.[1] Traditional literatures require an understanding of literary history that transcends linear time to account for stories' active tellings and retellings in Indigenous communities and for the ways that Indigenous stories bring multiple timescales together. At the same

[1] See Timothy Powell, William Weems, and Freeman Owle, "Native/American Digital Storytelling: Situating the Cherokee Oral Tradition within American Literary History," *Literary Compass* 4.1 (2007).

time, interpreting traditional literatures in the context of the specific tribal communities and histories to which they belong can call into question the category of "American literature" itself: traditional literatures not only originate from a period before the existence of an "America" but also are cultivated and kept within Indigenous tribal nations that have histories, governance systems, languages, and cultural practices distinct from those of settler nation states such as the United States and Canada.

European settlers have often evaluated Indigenous literatures in terms of a binary between oral literature—which settlers saw as untrustworthy and ephemeral—and written literature, which they saw as superior and more durable. In fact, traditional literatures cannot be understood according to this binary: traditional stories and knowledge are carefully preserved over centuries in oral form, and traditional literatures have always existed in a wide array of non-alphabetic visual forms as well, as shown in many of the following selections including pictographs, petroglyphs, wampum, and wood carvings. In this sense, traditional literatures exemplify what Cherokee scholar Christopher B. Teuton calls the "textual continuum," a spectrum of oral, graphic (pictographic, hieroglyphic, and other non-alphabetic texts), and alphabetic texts.[1] This multi-media continuum also corresponds to practices of preserving knowledge, making new knowledge, and questioning knowledge. Teuton explains that "The oral and graphic build on the premise that oral discourses are living forms of cultural knowledge, kept alive in the memory of members of a group; graphic discourses record tradition for posterity, to live beyond the lives of those who record them." Meanwhile, what Teuton calls the "critical impulse" questions and disrupts, making the process of keeping knowledge one of continual construction, rather than of static reproduction.

Many of the works gathered here were recorded in English alphabetic script between the eighteenth and twenty-first centuries. Each of these versions reflects a centuries-long process of translation and circulation by Indigenous people and, sometimes, European settlers. The traditional literatures selected here were first told in an Indigenous language, and they continue to be told in Indigenous languages such as Anishinaabemowin, Wôpanâak, Mohegan, K'iche', Onöndowa'ga:' Gawë:nö' (Seneca), and Kanien'kéha (Mohawk). They were also, at various points in their histories, translated and transcribed in English, Spanish, or French, often by Indigenous intellectuals or knowledge keepers who made strategic decisions about when and how to translate stories and circulate them in manuscript or in print networks. Some of these decisions occurred in the context of pressure from settler historians and anthropologists to record and "preserve" Indigenous literatures. At other times, settlers themselves transcribed Indigenous stories or made copies of pictographic texts, usually to serve their own research interests. Such stories recorded by settlers should be read with an especially critical eye; as scholar Craig Womack suggests, because they reflect the recorder's own separation from the stories' culture of origin, they are often stripped of important cultural context and rendered as "artifacts" rather than living works.[2]

In the eighteenth and nineteenth centuries, settlers often acted under the assumption that Indigenous people could not maintain their own literary histories. Yet despite the destruction of Indigenous codices by Spanish priests, boarding schools throughout the U.S. and Canada that were deliberately designed to separate Indigenous children from their own communities and traditions, and many other settler efforts to eliminate Indigenous people and cultures, Indigenous peoples and stories survived. And Indigenous writers, artists, and historians continue to engage with traditional literatures today, renewing the stories again.

⌘ ⌘ ⌘

[1] See Christopher B. Teuton, *Deep Waters: The Textual Continuum in American Indian Literature* (University of Nebraska Press, 2010).

[2] For an example of this issue discussed in detail, see Womack's *Red on Red: Native American Literary Separatism* (University of Minnesota Press, 1999).

Wampanoag

The following stories of geologic and oceanic formation come from Wampanoag homelands in what is now southern New England, and they describe the formation of the islands, coasts, cliffs, mainlands, and waterways composing Wampanoag lands. As these stories indicate, the ocean has long been important to Wampanoag people, in part as a source of food complementing the corn, beans, and squash that Wampanoag women planted and harvested on land. The stories contain ecological knowledge for using the resources of the land and sea.

Wampanoag people had at least a century of experience observing and interacting with Europeans before the 1620s, when the Plymouth colony was established on Wampanoag lands whose inhabitants had moved inland to avoid deadly epidemics probably introduced by earlier colonists. Some of the first Wampanoag people to learn English speech and customs did so under duress: more than once in the early decades of the seventeenth century, dozens of Wampanoag people were kidnapped by Europeans and forcibly taken to Europe. Among these were Epenow, who became a resistance leader after his escape, and Tisquantum (often known as Squanto), who became a translator for diplomatic negotiations between the Plymouth colonists and the Wampanoag sachem Ousemequin (often referred to by his title, Massasoit). Wampanoag leaders including Ousemequin, Wamsutta, Metacom (or Philip), and the women leaders Weetamoo and Awashonks continued to rely on diplomacy as colonists sought to expand their settlements further onto Wampanoag lands and those of other Native polities. In 1675, the colonial insistence on expansion instigated King Philip's War, in which the colonies forcibly asserted claims to Indigenous lands and killed, imprisoned, or sold into slavery hundreds of Wampanoag and other Indigenous people.

The following stories were relayed in the nineteenth century by Wampanoag people on Noepe (now also called Martha's Vineyard), attesting to the survival of Wampanoag people and stories despite colonization and war. They describe Moshup, the powerful giant who created the island of Noepe and who lived at the southern end of the island, at Aquinnah. Moshup created the island and the rock formations in the bay by drawing lines in the water with his toe or, in another version, by slowly dragging his foot in the water. The colorful red cliffs at Aquinnah are stained with the blood of whales Moshup killed by throwing them against the cliffs, and Moshup provided for the Wampanoag people living on the island, teaching them how to fish. Noepe was a site of refuge from the violence of King Philip's War, and the island remained a Wampanoag place even after the Englishman Thomas Mayhew established a settlement on the island in 1642. Mayhew's descendants worked with local Wampanoag leaders to create Christian communities that continued to be shaped by Wampanoag practices and beliefs, and Mayhew children learned Wôpanâak as Wampanoag children learned English. Members of the Aquinnah Tribe of Gay Head, a federally recognized tribe, continue to live near the cliffs that Moshup stained red.

Two of the Moshup stories below appeared in print without attribution to their source, but one provides some significant details about the chain of transmission: the story attributed to Thomas Cooper has been communicated from a grandmother to her grandson, even as this story (like the two others reprinted here) is also filtered through colonial transcribers and their perspectives. Despite colonists' limitations in understanding Wampanoag stories, these accounts of Moshup attest to the ways that Wampanoag people kept the stories alive by circulating them among family members and strategically seeing them into print.

[MOSHUP STORY]
as recorded by William Baylies, *Description of Gay Head*
(1793)

In former times, the Indian God, Moiship, resided in this part of the island. ... To keep up his fires, he pulled up the largest trees by the roots; on which, to satisfy his hunger, he broiled the whale, and the great fish of the sea, throwing out the refuse sufficient to cover several acres. He did not consume all himself; but with a benevolent hand, often supplied them with food ready cooked. To facilitate the catching these fish, he threw many large stones, at proper distances, into the sea, on which he might walk with greater ease to himself. This is now called the devil's bridge. On a time, an offering was made to him of all the tobacco on Martha's Vineyard, which having smoked, he knocked the snuff out of this pipe, which formed Nantucket.[1] When the Christian religion took place in the island, he told them, as light had come among them, and he belonged to the kingdom of darkness, he must take his leave; which to their great sorrow, he accordingly did; and has never been heard of since. ...

[MOSHUP STORY]
as recorded by anonymous, "Origin of the Island of Nantucket"[2] (1787)

On the west end of Martha's Vineyard, are high cliffs of variegated coloured earths, known by the name of Gayhead. On the top of the hill is a large cavity, which has the appearance of the crater of an extinguished volcano, and there are evident marks of former subterraneous fires. The Indians who live about this spot have a tradition that a certain deity resided there before the Europeans came into America, that his name was *Manshop*; that he used to step out on a ledge of rocks which ran into the sea, and take up a whale, which he broiled for his own eating on the coals of the aforesaid volcano, and often invited the Indians to dine with him, or gave them the relicks of his meal. That once to shew their gratitude to *Manshop* for his very great kindness to them, they made an offering to him of all the tobacco which grew upon the island in one season. This was scarcely sufficient to fill his great pipe, but he received the present very graciously, smoked his

pipe, and turned out the ashes of it in to the sea, which formed the island of Nantucket. Upon the coming of the Europeans into America, *Manshop* retired in disgust, and has never since been seen.

[MOSHUP STORY]
as recorded by Benjamin Bassett, *Fabulous Traditions and Customs of the Indians of Martha's Vineyard* (1806)

The following fabulous Traditions and Customs of the Indians of Martha's Vineyard, were communicated to BENJAMIN BASSET, Esq. of Chilmark, by Thomas Cooper, a half blooded Indian, of Gay Head, aged about sixty years; and which, he says, he obtained of his grandmother, who, to use his own expression, was a stout girl, when the English came to the island.

The first Indian who came to the Vineyard, was brought thither with his dog on a cake of ice. When he came to Gay Head, he found a very large man, whose name was Moshup. He had a wife and five children, four sons and one daughter; and lived in the Den. He used to catch whales, and then pluck up trees, and make a fire, and roast them. The coals of the tree, and the bones of the whales, are now to be seen. After he was tired of staying here, he told his children to go and play ball on a beach that joined Noman's Land to Gay Head. He then made a mark with his toe across the beach at each end, and so deep, that the water followed, and cut away the beach; so that his children were in fear of drowning. They took their sister up, and held her out of the water. He told them to act as if they were going to kill whales; and they were all turned into killers (a fish so called). The sister was dressed in large stripes. He gave them a strict charge always to be kind to her. His wife mourned the loss of her children so exceedingly, that he threw her away. She fell upon Seconet, near the rocks, where she lived some time, exacting contribution of all who passed by water. After a while she was changed into a stone. The entire shape remained for many years. But after the English came, some of them broke off the arms, head, etc. but the most of the body remains to this day. Moshup went away nobody knows whither. He had no conversation with the Indians, but was kind to them, by sending whales, etc. ashore to them to eat. But after they grew thick around him he left them.

[1] *Nantucket* Island near Martha's Vineyard.

[2] *Nantucket* Island near Martha's Vineyard.

Mi'kmaq

The examples below of Mi'kmaq petroglyphs, or pictographs carved on rocks, attest to the material and spatial qualities of Indigenous writing systems. Pictographic writing systems are not alphabetic, meaning that they are not oriented by letters representing sounds that combine to form words; instead, they include images that represent ideas. Indigenous people in the northeast, including Mi'kmaq people, traced pictographs on rocks as well as on birchbark. Petroglyphs such as the ones below could serve several purposes: as maps that oriented travelers in place and in stories; as signals that someone had already traveled along the route; and as territorial markers. For the Mi'kmaq—whose homelands extend throughout the oceans and northeastern coast of what are now eastern Canada and the United States, and whose knowledge of river and ocean travel took them along the east coast as far as what is now Florida—petroglyphs are part of what Abenaki scholar Lisa Brooks calls a "spatialized writing system" that "represented the relationships between people, between places, between humans and nonhumans, between the waterways that joined them."[1]

Europeans observed Mi'kmaq writing systems carefully with the goal of using them to represent European concepts. Seventeenth-century French priest Chrestien LeClercq developed an ideographic script, inspired by his observation of older Mi'kmaq writing practices, that spread quickly in Mi'kmaq communities. LeClercq's goal in developing the script was to translate prayer books that could be used to convert Mi'kmaq people to Catholicism; his books attest to the influence of Indigenous writing systems on European practices of translation. Mi'kmaq people used the writing system for their own ends, which included but were not limited to religious practices.

Mi'kmaq people made contact with Europeans as early as the sixteenth century, and they conducted diplomacy with both French and British officials as European nations vied for access to Indigenous lands and trading networks. Alliances with the French provided some protection against British settlers and soldiers who sought to claim Mi'kmaq lands. Mi'kmaq leaders continued diplomacy even when the British founded Halifax, Nova Scotia, in 1749 and Governor Edward Cornwallis attempted a genocidal campaign to eliminate Mi'kmaq people by offering a bounty to British settlers for killing them. Treaties made with British, French, and U.S. governments in the eighteenth and nineteenth centuries protected hunting and fishing rights throughout Mi'kmaq territories and provided a foundation for more recent court decisions affirming Mi'kmaq sovereignty. These protections came after an extended period in which Canada and the U.S. refused to honor those treaties and instituted policies to remove Mi'kmaq people from their lands and require Mi'kmaq children to attend boarding schools intended to force their assimilation to settler culture. Mi'kmaq territories currently extend to Newfoundland, St Pierre et Miquelon, Nova Scotia, New Brunswick, the Magdalen archipelago, and the Gaspé Peninsula of Quebec, with traditional homelands reaching to the state of Maine in the United States. Alongside this insistence on political sovereignty, Mi'kmaq artists such as Louis Esme Cruz continue to use pictographs in their visual art, attesting to the ways Mi'kmaq people are keeping their writing systems alive.

[1] See Lisa Brooks, *The Common Pot: The Recovery of Native Space in the Northeast* (University of Minnesota Press, 2008).

PETROGLYPH OF HUMAN FIGURE AND SUN
Bedford, Nova Scotia (undated)

PETROGLYPH TRACING
traced by George Creed (1888)

The undated petroglyph represented in this tracing evokes a fish and four sticks that were inscribed on a rock pointing to the west; with two sticks lying across them. This may communicate the message "I am going fishing to the west for two days."

PAGE OF A MI'KMAQ PRAYER BOOK
(c. 1790)

Mohegan

The basket pictured here is woven from wood splints and painted with pink, green, and white images of medallions, trails, and plants. Its design, decoration, and construction process reflect Mohegan textual traditions that extend far beyond alphabetic literature: as the Cree scholar Stephanie Fitzgerald points out, the Mohegan word for painting, wuskuswang, is also the word for writing. Alphabetic literature—such as the work of the Mohegan minister Samson Occom, included elsewhere in this anthology—can be understood as a newcomer to a longstanding textual tradition that includes painted images on baskets, pictographs inscribed on rocks and birchbark, and wampum belts.

The process of making a basket requires one to select a log, soak it, strip the bark, and weave the strips together before painting the basket. This work is collaborative, often performed by women (though in the nineteenth century more men also made baskets to support their communities). Basket making is a time for sharing stories and knowledge, some of which are inscribed in images on the baskets themselves. As Mohegan women Gladys Tantaquidgeon and Jayne Fawcett note, basket makers adorn their baskets by drawing on a "Mohegan symbolic 'vocabulary,'" which includes designs that tell certain stories.[1] For example, the domed medallions on this basket represent the four directions; the leaves and pink dots represent strawberries and other plants that sustain Mohegan people; and the trails represent the trail of life as well as specific Mohegan journeys.

PAINTED WOOD-SPLINT STORAGE BASKET
(c. 1817)

[1] See Gladys Tantaquidgeon and Jayne G. Fawcett, "Symbolic Motifs on Painted Baskets of the Mohegan-Pequot," *A Key into the Language of Woodsplint Baskets,* eds. Ann McMullen and Russell G. Handsman (American Indian Archaeological Institute, 1987).

Haudenosaunee (Iroquois)

The works below come from the Haudenosaunee or Iroquois Confederacy ("Iroquois" is derived from the word French colonists called Haudenosaunee people; "Haudenosaunee" is the peoples' own name for themselves). The Confederacy originally consisted of five nations, the Seneca, Mohawk, Onondaga, Oneida, and Cayuga, who formed a league by uniting around the Great Law of Peace. The Five Nations later accepted the Tuscarora nation into the Confederacy. The Tuscarora had historical and linguistic ties to Haudenosaunee people, and when, in the early eighteenth century, British settlers began to invade Tuscarora lands in the Carolinas, the Confederacy agreed to provide protection, and Tuscarora moved north in 1722 to become one of the Six Nations. The Confederacy still exists today, having survived the 1779–80 Sullivan Campaign, a series of scorched earth campaigns by American forces on Haudenosaunee lands and fields during the U.S. Revolutionary War, which destroyed nearly all the villages of the Onondaga, Cayuga, and Seneca. Haudenosaunee people also lived through a series of illegal land cessions and removals in the nineteenth century, the forced education of Haudenosaunee children in boarding schools, and sweeping anti-Indian laws in Canada and the United States that denied legal rights to Indigenous people. Despite these events, as the selection of Haudenosaunee literatures here attests, Haudenosaunee people are keeping stories of their creation and of the Confederacy's formation alive.

The Haudenosaunee story of the world's creation is, as Susan M. Hill (Mohawk) comments, not only an account of how the world began; it also "holds many of our beliefs regarding the relationship intended to exist between humans and the rest of the natural world."[1] The stories regarding the formation of the Haudenosaunee Confederacy continue this account of the relationship among humans and with the natural world. These stories tell how the Peacemaker and his helper Hiawatha united Haudenosaunee people during a time when they were ruled by greed and violence. The Peacemaker brought the Great Law of Peace, which provided the Haudenosaunee with means for resolving conflict through peace rather than war and established practices of good governance and leadership. The more recently recorded versions of "The Creation"[2] and "Thanksgiving Address" attest to the ways that Haudenosaunee people continue to tell and live by these stories and to recite and share the precedents established in the Great Law. The Thanksgiving Address is spoken in greeting and gratitude to all of creation, to recognize the reliance of humans on the natural world and to bring those assembled into agreement. The Address is also invoked before ceremonies and government meetings.

Haudenosaunee people have maintained these stories and laws for generations, in the form of oral texts, speeches, and wampum belts as well as, in more recent centuries, written texts. The works gathered here represent an attempt to reflect, as far as possible, the range of forms Haudenosaunee stories take. The first two works were written by Seneca and Tuscarora men who translated stories into English and, at least in part, into terms white settler readers could comprehend. They are less authors—in the sense of a writer who owns their work—than linguistic and cultural translators who continued longstanding practices of sharing, remembering, and transcribing stories and laws. Some Haudenosaunee people, such as the Seneca scholar Arthur C. Parker and his great-uncle Ely S. Parker, collaborated with white anthropologists whose work was deeply distorted by colonialist ideology and often positioned Haudenosaunee people as racially and culturally inferior. The Parkers used these collaborations to circulate versions of Haudenosaunee stories of the world's creation and of the formation of the Haudenosaunee Confederacy, even as anthropologists' assumptions and queries sometimes framed those stories' final forms. By contrast, some printed versions of Haudenosaunee stories were strictly Haudenosaunee productions: the first edition of Cusick's *Sketches of the Ancient History of the Six Nations*, for example, was translated, printed, and distributed

[1] See Susan M. Hill, *The Clay We Are Made Of: Haudenosaunee Land Tenure on the Grand River* (University of Manitoba Press, 2017).

[2] This selection appears in the anthology's website component.

by Tuscarora people in New York. Cusick described his process of writing and translating *Sketches* as one undertaken to provide a history of the Six Nations from a Haudenosaunee perspective. He wrote in his preface that he "had long been waiting" for some of "my people" to write a history, and when he found that no such history existed, Cusick himself "determined to commence the work." Cusick's preface emphasizes the importance of tribal histories told by tribal members, an act that laid the groundwork for more recent editions of Haudenosaunee histories and stories.

from [CREATION STORY]
as recorded and translated by David Cusick, *Sketches of the Ancient History of the Six Nations* (1827)

PART I
A TALE OF THE FOUNDATION OF THE GREAT ISLAND, NOW NORTH AMERICA—THE TWO INFANTS BORN, AND THE CREATION OF THE UNIVERSE

Among the ancients there were two worlds in existence. The lower world was in great darkness—the possession of the great monster—but the upper world was inhabited by humankind; and there was a woman conceived[1] and would have the twin born. When her travail[2] drew near, and her situation seemed to produce a great distress on her mind, and she was induced by some of her relations to lay herself on a mattress which was prepared, so as to gain refreshments to her wearied body; but while she was asleep the very place sunk down towards the dark world.

The monsters of the great water were alarmed at her appearance of descending to the lower world; in consequence all the species of the creatures were immediately collected into where it was expected she would fall. When the monsters were assembled, and they made consultation, one of them was appointed in haste to search the great deep, in order to procure some earth, if it could be obtained; accordingly the monster descends, which succeeds, and returns to the place. Another requisition was presented, who would be capable to secure the woman from the terrors of the great water, but none was able to comply except a large turtle came forward and made proposal to them to endure her lasting weight, which was accepted.

The woman was yet descending from a great distance. The turtle executes[3] upon the spot, and a small quantity of earth was varnished on the back part of the turtle. The woman alights on the seat prepared, and she receives a satisfaction.[4] While holding her, the turtle increased every moment and became a considerable island of earth, and apparently covered with small bushes. The woman remained in a state of unlimited darkness, and she was overtaken by her travail to which she was subject.

While she was in the limits of distress one of the infants in her womb was moved by an evil opinion and he was determined to pass out under the side of the parent's arm, and the other infant in vain endeavored to prevent his design. The woman was in a painful condition during the time of their disputes, and the infants entered the dark world by compulsion, and their parent expired in a few moments. They had the power of sustenance without a nurse,[5] and remained in the dark regions.

After a time the turtle increased to a great Island and the infants were grown up, and one of them possessed with a gentle disposition, and named Enigorio, i.e. the good mind. The other youth possessed an insolence of character, and was named Enigonhahetgea, i.e. the bad mind. The good mind was not contented to remain in a dark situation, and he was anxious to create a great light in the dark world; but the bad mind was desirous that the world should remain in a natural state.

The good mind determines to prosecute his designs, and therefore commences the world of creation. At first he took the parent's head, (the deceased) of which he created an orb, and established it in the centre of the

1 *conceived* I.e., pregnant (with twins).

2 *travail* Labor of childbirth.

3 *executes* Carries out the plan.

4 *satisfaction* I.e., solution to her problem.

5 *a nurse* Someone to provide them with milk.

firmament,[1] and it became of a very superior nature to bestow light to the new world (now the sun), and again he took the remnant of the body and formed another orb, which was inferior to the light (now moon). In the orb a cloud of legs appeared to prove it was the body of the good mind (parent). The former was to give light to the day and the latter to the night; and he also created numerous spots of light (now stars): these were to regulate the days, nights, seasons, years, etc.

Whenever the light extended to the dark world the monsters were displeased and immediately concealed themselves in the deep places, lest they should be discovered by some human beings. The good mind continued the works of creation, and he formed numerous creeks and rivers on the Great Island, and then created numerous species of animals of the smallest and the greatest, to inhabit the forests, and fishes of all kinds to inhabit the waters. When he had made the universe he was in doubt respecting some beings to possess the Great Island; and he formed two images of the dust of the ground in his own likeness, male and female, and by his breathing into their nostrils he gave them the living souls, and named them Ea-gwe-howe, i.e. a real people; and he gave the Great Island all the animals of game for their maintenance; and he appointed thunder to water the earth by frequent rains, agreeable of the nature of the system; after this the Island became fruitful and vegetation afforded the animals subsistence.

The bad mind, while his brother was making the universe, went throughout the Island and made numerous high mountains and falls of water, and great steeps, and also creates various reptiles which would be injurious to mankind; but the good mind restored the Island to its former condition. The bad mind proceeded further in his motives and he made two images of clay in the form of humankind; but while he was giving them existence they became apes; and when he had not the power to create mankind he was envious against his brother; and again he made two of clay. The good mind discovered his brother's contrivances, and aided in giving them living souls[2] (it is said these had the most knowledge of good and evil).

The good mind now accomplishes the works of creation, notwithstanding the imaginations of the bad mind were continually evil; and he attempted to enclose all the animals of game in the earth, so as to deprive them from mankind; but the good mind released them from confinement (the animals were dispersed, and traces of them were made on the rocks near the cave where it was closed).

The good mind experiences that his brother was at variance with the works of creation, and feels not disposed to favor any of his proceedings, but gives admonitions of his future state. Afterwards the good mind requested his brother to accompany him, as he was proposed to inspect the game, etc., but when a short distance from their nominal residence, the bad mind became so unmanly that he could not conduct his brother anymore.

The bad mind offered a challenge to his brother and resolved that who gains the victory should govern the universe; and appointed a day to meet the contest. The good mind was willing to submit to the offer, and he enters the reconciliation with his brother; which he falsely mentions that by whipping with flags would destroy his temporal life;[3] and he earnestly solicits his brother also to notice the instrument of death, which he manifestly relates by the use of deer horns, beating his body he would expire. On the day appointed the engagement commenced, which lasted for two days: after pulling up the trees and mountains as the track of a terrible whirlwind, at last the good mind gained the victory by using the horns, as mentioned the instrument of death, which he succeeded in deceiving his brother and he crushed him in the earth; and the last words uttered from the bad mind were, that he would have equal power over the souls of humankind after death; and he sinks down to eternal doom, and became the Evil Spirit. After this tumult the good mind repaired to the battle ground, and then visited the people and retires from the earth.

1 *firmament* Sky or heavens.

2 [Cusick's note] It appears by the fictitious accounts, that the said beings became civilized people and made their residence in the southern parts of the Island; but afterwards they were destroyed by the barbarous nations, and their fortifications were ruined unto this day.

3 *he falsely ... life* He says that a whipping with rushes (grasslike plants) would kill him, which is a lie.

ORIGIN OF FOLK STORIES
as recorded by Arthur C. Parker, *Seneca Myths and Folk Tales*
(1923)

There was once a boy who had no home. His parents were dead and his uncles would not care for him. In order to live this boy, whose name was Gaqka, or Crow, made a bower of branches for an abiding place and hunted birds and squirrels for food.

He had almost no clothing but was very ragged and dirty. When the people from the village saw him they called him Filth-Covered-One, and laughed as they passed by, holding their noses. No one thought he would ever amount to anything, which made him feel heavy-hearted. He resolved to go away from his tormentors and become a great hunter.

One night Gaqka found a canoe. He had never seen this canoe before, so he took it. Stepping in he grasped the paddle, when the canoe immediately shot into the air, and he paddled above the clouds and under the moon. For a long time he went always southward. Finally the canoe dropped into a river and then Gaqka paddled for shore.

On the other side of the river was a great cliff that had a face that looked like a man. It was at the forks of the river where this cliff stood. The boy resolved to make his home on the top of the cliff and so climbed it and built a bark cabin.

The first night he sat on the edge of the cliff he heard a voice saying, "Give me some tobacco." Looking around the boy, seeing no one, replied, "Why should I give tobacco?"

There was no answer and the boy began to fix his arrows for the next day's hunt. After a while the voice spoke again, "Give me some tobacco."

Gaqka now took out some tobacco and threw it over the cliff. The voice spoke again: "Now I will tell you a story."

Feeling greatly awed the boy listened to a story that seemed to come directly out of the rock upon which he was sitting. Finally the voice paused, for the story had ended. Then it spoke again saying, "It shall be the custom hereafter to present me with a small gift for my stories." So the boy gave the rock a few bone beads. Then the rock said, "Hereafter when I speak, announcing that I shall tell a story you must say, 'Nio,' and as I speak you must say 'Hĕⁿ'',' that I may know that you

are listening. You must never fall asleep but continue to listen until I say 'Dā´neho nigagā´is.' (So thus finished is the length of my story.) Then you shall give me presents and I shall be satisfied."

The next day the boy hunted and killed a great many birds. These he made into soup and roasts. He skinned the birds and saved the skins, keeping them in a bag.

That evening the boy sat on the rock again and looked westward at the sinking sun. He wondered if his friend would speak again. While waiting he chipped some new arrow-points, and made them very small so that he could use them in a blow gun. Suddenly, as he worked, he heard the voice again. "Give me some tobacco to smoke," it said. Gaqka threw a pinch of tobacco over the cliff and the voice said, "Hau'nio," and commenced a story. Long into the night one wonderful tale after another flowed from the rock, until it called out, "So thus finished is the length of my story." Gaqka was sorry to have the stories ended but he gave the rock an awl made from a bird's leg and a pinch of tobacco.

The next day the boy hunted far to the east and there found a village. Nobody knew who he was but he soon found many friends. There were some hunters who offered to teach him how to kill big game, and these went with him to his own camp on the high rock. At night he allowed them to listen to the stories that came forth from the rock, but it would speak only when Gaqka was present. He therefore had many friends with whom to hunt.

Now after a time Gaqka made a new suit of clothing from deer skin and desired to obtain a decorated pouch. He, therefore, went to the village and found one house where there were two daughters living with an old mother. He asked that a pouch be made and the youngest daughter spoke up and said, "It is now finished. I have been waiting for you to come for it." So she gave him a handsome pouch.

Then the old mother spoke, saying, "I now perceive that my future son-in-law has passed through the door and is here." Soon thereafter, the younger woman brought Gaqka a basket of bread and said, "My mother greatly desires that you should marry me." Gaqka looked at the girl and was satisfied, and ate the bread.

The older daughter was greatly displeased and frowned in an evil manner.

That night the bride said to her husband, "We must now go away. My older sister will kill you for she is jealous." So Gaqka arose and took his bride to his own lodge. Soon the rock spoke and began to relate wonder stories of things that happened in the old days. The bride was not surprised, but said, "This standing rock, indeed, is my grandfather. I will now present you with a pouch into which you must put a trophy for every tale related."

All winter long the young couple stayed in the lodge on the great rock and heard all the wonder tales of the old days. Gaqka's bag was full of stories and he knew all the lore of former times.

As springtime came the bride said, "We must now go north to your own people and you shall become a great man." But Gaqka was sad and said, "Alas, in my own country I am an outcast and called by an unpleasant name." The bride only laughed, saying, "Nevertheless we shall go north."

Taking their pelts and birdskins, the young couple descended the cliff and seated themselves in the canoe. "This is my canoe," said the bride. "I sent it through the air to you."

The bride seated herself in the bow of the canoe and Gaqka in the stern. Grasping a paddle he swept it through the water, but soon the canoe arose and went through the air. Meanwhile the bride was singing all kinds of songs, which Gaqka learned as he paddled.

When they reached the north, the bride said, "Now I shall remove your clothing and take all the scars from your face and body. She then caused him to pass through a hollow log, and when Gaqka emerged from the other end he was dressed in the finest clothing and was a handsome man.

Together the two walked to the village where the people came out to see them. After a while Gaqka said, "I am the boy whom you once were accustomed to call 'Cia''dōdă'.' I have now returned." That night the people of the village gathered around and listened to the tales he told, and he instructed them to give him small presents and tobacco. He would plunge his hand in his pouch and take out a trophy, saying, "Ho ho'! So here is another one!" and then looking at his trophy would relate an ancient tale.

Everybody now thought Gaqka a great man and listened to his stories. He was the first man to find out all about the adventures of the old-time people. That is why there are so many legends now.

THANKSGIVING ADDRESS

as crafted by Rokwaho (Dan Thompson) and translated by John Stokes and Kanawahienton (David Benedict) (1993)

(Ohén:ton Karihwatéhkwen—Words Before All Else)

THE PEOPLE

Today we have gathered and we see that the cycles of life continue. We have been given the duty to live in balance and harmony with each other and all living things. So now, we bring our minds together as one as we give greetings and thanks to each other as People. *Now our minds are one.*

THE EARTH MOTHER

We are all thankful to our Mother, the Earth, for she gives us all that we need for life. She supports our feet as we walk about upon her. It gives us joy that she continues to care for us as she has from the beginning of time. To our Mother, we send greetings and thanks. *Now our minds are one.*

THE WATERS

We give thanks to all the Waters of the world for quenching our thirst and providing us with strength. Water is life. We know its power in many forms— waterfalls and rain, mists and streams, rivers and oceans. With one mind, we send greetings and thanks to the spirit of Water. *Now our minds are one.*

THE FISH

We turn our minds to all the Fish life in the water. They were instructed to cleanse and purify the water. They also give themselves to us as food. We are grateful that we can still find pure water. So, we turn now to the

Fish and send our greetings and thanks.
Now our minds are one.

THE PLANTS

Now we turn toward the vast fields of Plant life. As far as the eye can see, the Plants grow, working many wonders. They sustain many life forms. With our minds gathered together, we give thanks and look forward to seeing Plant life for many generations to come.
Now our minds are one.

THE FOOD PLANTS

With one mind, we turn to honor and thank all the Food Plants we harvest from the garden. Since the beginning of time, the grains, vegetables, beans and berries have helped the people survive. Many other living things draw strength from them too. We gather all the Plant Foods together as one and send them a greeting and thanks.
Now our minds are one.

THE MEDICINE HERBS

Now we turn to all the Medicine Herbs of the world. From the beginning, they were instructed to take away sickness. They are always waiting and ready to heal us. We are happy there are still among us those special few who remember how to use these plants for healing. With one mind, we send greetings and thanks to the Medicines and to the keepers of the Medicines.
Now our minds are one.

THE ANIMALS

We gather our minds together to send greetings and thanks to all the Animal life in the world. They have many things to teach us as people. We see them near our homes and in the deep forests. We are glad they are still here and we hope that it will always be so.
Now our minds are one.

THE TREES

We now turn our thoughts to the Trees. The Earth has many families of Trees who have their own instructions and uses. Some provide us with shelter and shade, others with fruit, beauty and other useful things. Many people of the world use a Tree as a symbol of peace and strength. With one mind, we greet and thank the Tree life.
Now our minds are one.

THE BIRDS

We put our minds together as one and thank all the Birds who move and fly about over our heads. The Creator gave them beautiful songs. Each day they remind us to enjoy and appreciate life. The Eagle was chosen to be their leader. To all the Birds—from the smallest to the largest—we send our joyful greetings and thanks.
Now our minds are one.

THE FOUR WINDS

We are all thankful to the powers that we know as the Four Winds. We hear their voices in the moving air as they refresh us and purify the air we breathe. They help to bring the change of seasons. From the four directions they come, bringing us messages and giving us strength. With one mind, we send our greetings and thanks to the Four Winds.
Now our minds are one.

THE THUNDERERS

Now we turn to the west where our Grandfathers, the Thunder Beings, live. With lightning and thundering voices, they bring with them the water that renews life. We bring our minds together as one to send greetings and thanks to our Grandfathers, the Thunderers.
Now our minds are one.

THE SUN

We now send greetings and thanks to our eldest Brother, the Sun. Each day without fail he travels the

sky from east to west, bringing the light of a new day. He is the source of all the fires of life. With one mind, we send greetings and thanks to our Brother, the Sun.
Now our minds are one.

GRANDMOTHER MOON

We put our minds together and give thanks to our oldest Grandmother, the Moon, who lights the night-time sky. She is the leader of women all over the world, and she governs the movement of the ocean tides. By her changing face we measure time, and it is the Moon who watches over the arrival of children here on Earth. With one mind, we send greetings and thanks to our Grandmother, the Moon.
Now our minds are one.

THE STARS

We give thanks to the Stars who are spread across the sky like jewelry. We see them in the night, helping the Moon to light the darkness and bringing dew to the gardens and growing things. When we travel at night, they guide us home. With our minds gathered together as one, we send greetings and thanks to all the Stars.
Now our minds are one.

THE ENLIGHTENED TEACHERS

We gather our minds to greet and thank the Enlightened Teachers who have come to help throughout the ages. When we forget how to live in harmony, they remind us of the way we were instructed to live as people. With one mind, we send greetings and thanks to these caring Teachers.
Now our minds are one.

THE CREATOR

Now we turn our thoughts to the Creator, or Great Spirit, and send greetings and thanks for all the gifts of Creation. Everything we need to live a good life is here on this Mother Earth. For all the love that is still around us, we gather our minds together as one and send our choicest words of greetings and thanks to the Creator.
Now our minds are one.

CLOSING WORDS

We have now arrived at the place where we end our words. Of all the things we have named, it was not our intention to leave anything out. If something was forgotten, we leave it to each individual to send such greetings and thanks in their own way.
Now our minds are one.

IROQUOIS OR CONFEDERACY OF THE FIVE NATIONS
as recorded by Ely S. Parker (manuscript c. 1848)

By the tradition of the Five Nations it appears that in their early history, they were frequently engaged in petty wars one with another, as well also with tribes living north of the lakes. The Five Nations, on account of their small numbers, suffered more by these wars than their neighbors, until there sprang up among the Onondagas a man more formidable in war than a whole tribe or nation. He consequently became the terror of all the surrounding nations, especially of the Cayugas and Senecas. This man, so formidable and whose cabin was as impregnable as a tower, is said to have had a head of hair, the ends of each terminating in a living snake; the ends of his fingers, and toes, his ears, nose and lips, eyebrows and eyelashes all terminated in living snakes. He required in war, no bow and arrow, no battle axe or war club, for he had but to look upon his enemies, and they fell dead—so great was the power of the snakes that enshrouded him. He was a warrior by birth, and by his great power he had become the military despot of all the surrounding nations. And when he marched against his enemies they fled before his fatal sight.

Among the Onondagas there lived a man renowned for his wisdom, and his great love of peace. For a long time he had watched with great anxiety the increasing power of this military despot who on account of his snakey habiliments,[1] was known by the applicable name Tadodahoh, or Atotahoh, signifying tangled because the snakes seemed to have tangled themselves into his hair; he saw bands of noble warriors fall before his fatal look. He revolved in his mind by what means he could take from the Tadodahoh his power, and also

[1] *habiliments* Attire.

to divest him of his snakey appendages. He well knew that he could not wrest his power from him, unless he could put into his hands some means by which he could still exercise power and influence. He therefore concluded to call a general council, of the Five Nations, and to invite to this council the Tadodahoh, at which council he proposed to lay before the wise men a plan of Union that would secure not only amity and peace among themselves, and a perpetual existence as a confederacy, but they would render themselves formidable and superior in power to any nation on the Continent. He accordingly called a council to be held upon the east bank of the Onondaga Lake, and to this council the Tadodahoh was invited, who it is said lived near the shores of Lake Ontario a short distance from Irondequoit Bay. He accepted the invitation and proceeded to the place. He occupied the council grounds alone, for no one would approach near to him, although great numbers had come to attend. The projector of the alliance alone proceeded to the grounds and into the presence of the Tadodahoh. He proceeded to divulge his plan when he was informed that his daughter had died whom he had left at home sick. He drew his robe about him, covering himself completely, and mourned for her. (His style of mourning was afterwards adopted by the Confederacy as the custom to mourn for sachems just before another was to be installed in his place.) He mourned night and day, and in his mourning which he did in a kind of song, he repeated the whole plan of Union. And when he had finished, no one of the wise men seemed to understand or comprehend his meaning and objects. Daganowedah, the projector of the play of alliance, being provoked at their dullness of comprehension, which resulted more from their ignorance of civil matters than dullness of comprehension, arose in the night and travelled towards the east. He had not travelled far when he struck a small lake, and anyone could go around it sooner than to cross it in a canoe. Yet he chose to make a canoe of bark and go across it. It seems that he did not wish to deviate from a straight line. While he was crossing the lake, his canoe ran upon what he supposed to be a sand bar; he put his paddle down into the water to ascertain the cause of the stopping of the boat; in taking out his paddle he found a quantity of small shells, he took pains to put

a sufficient quantity into his canoe, and after going ashore, he made a pouch of a young deer skin, and put these shells into it, after having first made a number of belts, and put the rest into strings of equal lengths. To this he gave the name of wampum, and the belts and strings he had made of the shells, he converted into the records of his wise sayings and the entire plan of his project of alliance.

He then proceeded on his journey, and he had not travelled far when he came to an Indian castle.[1] Without calling a council he began to rehearse his plan of alliance, by means of his belts and strings of wampum. But the people of this castle were unable to comprehend the benefits of his project, and talked of him as crazy. When he heard what they were saying concerning him, he proceeded on his journey, sorrowing that he could not find a people who would listen to the words of wisdom. He at length came to another settlement, which was one of the Mohawk castles. Here again he rehearsed his plan of Union. Still his sayings were incomprehensible to that people. They however listened carefully for the purpose of ascertaining what it was that he could talk so long upon. All that they could understand of it, was the manner in which councils were to be called. A council was accordingly called and he invited to attend. They invited him for the purpose of giving him an opportunity to say in council and before a large number what he had been so long saying in the open fields. But after he had taken his seat in council and nothing was said or done, no exchange of wampum belts (for he had lent them a belt with which to call a council), he arose and again went into the fields and there repeated his speeches. He concluded by saying that they too were ignorant, and knew nothing about transacting civil matters. This was reported to the Grand Chief of the Mohawks and again he called another council and invited Daganowedah. When the council was opened and the wise man had taken his seat, the Mohawk Chief presented to him a belt of wampum, with a request that whatever he should have to say, should be said in open council. If he was a messenger from another tribe, they would hear in open council what were their wishes. He merely replied that he was the messenger of no one; that he had conceived a noble plan of alliance, but had not

[1] *castle* Most important village of a given Indigenous group.

found a nation wise enough to comprehend its benefits and thus he had travelled and should continue so to travel until he found support. He then rehearsed in open council his plan of Union which though they could not comprehend it, was pronounced by all to be a noble project. Daganowedah the Onondaga wise man was immediately adopted into the Mohawk Nation, nor could the Onondagas afterwards claim him, since they first rejected his project of Alliance. He was also made a chief of the Mohawk Nation, and was to exercise equal power with the original Mohawk chief. They were to live in the same lodge, and to be in every respect, equals.

But he had lived with the original chief but a short time, when he was ordered about as though he had been a mere servant. To this a free spirit will ever revolt, he therefore left him, and again went into the fields. He was asked why he left the house of his friend. He replied that he had not been treated as a friend or visitor, but as a slave. The original chief begged his pardon, and solicited him to return. He did, and was thenceforth treated with great regard. Daganowedah at length suggested the propriety of sending runners to the west, from whence he had come, to ascertain what may be doing from whence he had come. He wanted runners to go and seek the smoke of the council fire. The chief of the Mohawks at once called upon some runners to go towards the west in search of the smoke of a council fire. The guardian bird of the runners was the heron; they accordingly took upon themselves the form of herons. They went towards the west, but flying too high they did not see the smoke of the council fire of Onondaga. They proceeded as far west as Sandusky in Ohio, where they were unable to transform or change themselves again into men. Another set of runners were then sent out who took upon them the form or shape of crows. They found the smoke of the council fire at Onondaga and so reported.

Daganowedah then proposed to send a few runners to the council to inform them that they had found a wise man of the Onondaga nation, who had conceived a plan of Union, and to request that he might be heard before the Great Tadodahoh. This was done; and as soon as the council at Onondaga heard where their wise man had gone, they sent a deputation to recall him. Daganowedah had in the mean time made arrangement with the Mohawk Chief to act as his spokesman when they should be in council. He was also to take the lead in the file, and to perform all the duties necessary to the completion of the Alliance, but he was to act as Daganowedah should direct. His reason for choosing a spokesman, was that he had not been heard when the council first opened, and that probably they might listen to a wise man of the Mohawks. To this arrangement the Mohawk agreed. He agreed also to divest Tadodahoh of his snakes, and to make him as other men, except that he should clothe him in civil power as the Head of the Confederacy that should be formed. They then proceeded with a delegation of the Mohawks to the council grounds at Onondaga. When they had arrived they addressed Tadodahoh the great military despot. The Mohawk divested him of his snakes, and for this reason he was styled Hayowenthah, or one who takes away or divests.

The plan of alliance was at first simple. It provided for the establishment of a confederacy, enjoying a democratic form of government. The civil and legislative power was to be vested in a certain number of wise men who should be styled civil sachems, and the military and executive power in another set of men who should be styled military sachems. The Union was to be established as a family organization, the Mohawks, Onondagas and Senecas to compose the Fathers and the Cayugas and Oneidas the children. This plan was adopted.

WAMPUM BELTS

These images of wampum belts (white, purple, and black beads made from quahog shells and whelk and woven together) represent important texts of diplomacy, law, and memory. Wampum belts encode Haudenosaunee history, political agreements, and cultural knowledge. According to Haudenosaunee histories, Hiawatha received wampum when he was grieving the loss of his three daughters and wife. The Peacemaker taught him how to string wampum beads together and how to conduct ceremonies to clear the mind and heart and assuage grief. Hiawatha brought wampum to Haudenosaunee people, using the Condolence Ceremony to clear peoples' minds, eyes, ears, and throats of grief and negativity.

Wampum belts also record alliances and other political agreements. For example, the Two Row Belt pictured here records the first treaty, made in 1613, between the Haudenosaunee Confederacy and a settler nation, in this case Dutch settlers. As Seneca-descended scholar Penelope Kelsey has explained, the two dark lines represent the Haudenosaunee and Dutch, respectively. These lines do not share common origins, and they do not intersect, but they are fashioned from the same materials. The belt records an agreement between two different peoples who will continue to pursue different paths while existing together; it is a map for how the two peoples will interact. The Two Row wampum recognizes settler practices but insists on maintaining specifically Haudenosaunee practices and knowledge for Haudenosaunee people.

While some settler translators learned and participated in wampum protocols in order to respect their powerful diplomatic purposes, settlers, including anthropologists and ethnographers working closely within these communities, also stole belts, removing some to museums and keeping others in private collections. Haudenosaunee people continue to work to secure the return of stolen belts to the Confederacy; some have been recovered, while others remain in settler institutions. The belts depicted here are held by the Onondaga Nation.

Ha:yëwënta' (Hiawatha) Belt

Two Row Wampum

Ojibwe

Ojibwe tribal nations are part of the Anishinaabeg peoples, the linguistically and historically related peoples who include the Ojibwe, Odawa, and Potawatomi tribal nations. There are now multiple Ojibwe tribal nations on homelands stretching from the Great Lakes to the Plains and extending across more recent boundary lines between the United States and Canada. Ojibwe stories place the peoples' origin in the northeast. After the receding of the glaciers at the end of the last ice age, Ojibwe people traveled west, keeping pictographic records that show a migration route following rivers from the Atlantic to the upper Great Lakes. By the time some of the stories included here were recorded in print in the nineteenth century, Ojibwe tribes had hundreds of years of experience pursuing diplomacy and conflict with other Indigenous nations, including but not limited to the Haudenosaunee and Dakota, and with the French, British, and United States traders and settlers who desired access to Indigenous trading routes and homelands.

Anishinaabemowin, the language Ojibwe people speak, differentiates among several kinds of stories: aadizookaanag are traditional stories that carry values and philosophies, while dibaajimowinan are historical in nature, including family and tribal stories.[1] The stories below are aadizookaanag, traditional stories of creation and of the Ojibwe hero or trickster Nanaboozhoo (also spelled Nanabush and Nenabozho). These stories articulate the values people need to live well together and demonstrate the behaviors that build or destroy communities. And these stories continue in the work of Ojibwe writers and artists today: as the poet Heid E. Erdrich writes, "We write into and out of a great telling that brings us stories and songs, that teaches us to look and listen. This is not some mystic tradition; it is simply how it is to be aware of where you are, who you are, and who your people are when they create with words."[2]

The stories selected here center around Nanaboozhoo, a shape-shifting figure who can take human and animal forms. These selections also highlight the range of Nanaboozhoo stories, from his role in creation stories to some of the humorous adventures he undertakes. Many of Nanaboozhoo's stories are funny, ribald accounts in which he plays the role of a prankster. Nanaboozhoo can be self-interested, pursuing his own appetites and desires, but he can also be selfless. His actions often escape usual human expectations for behavior, and their surprising qualities can encourage listeners to understand a problem or phenomenon from a new perspective or to realize that their current expectations may be limited.[3]

William Jones and George Copway, the Indigenous scholars who recorded for print some of the stories and pictographs included here, did so as part of work that also included translating and defending Ojibwe linguistic and historical knowledge. Jones is a Meskwakie (or Fox) man who studied with the anthropologist Franz Boas at Columbia University before becoming the first Indigenous anthropologist to work at Chicago's Field Museum. Jones made Anishinaabemowin dictionaries that Ojibwe people use today for language study; he also kept linguistic and botanical records on the Field Museum's collections of seeds from Meskwakie people, which are being used today in the Field Museum's rematriation (or return) of seeds to the Meskwakie.

George Copway, a Mississauga Ojibwe missionary and writer, also recorded Ojibwe pictographs and histories that Ojibwe people continue to study and use today. His transcription of pictographs appears in his history of Ojibwe people, *The Traditional History and Characteristic Sketches of the Ojibway Nation*. Far from the decontextualized ethnographic reporting that characterized many settler histories of Ojibwe people, Copway's *Traditional History* defended pictographic writing systems against settlers' disparaging of them. Copway represented Ojibwe people as drawing on multiple

[1] See Jill Doerfler, Niigaanwewidam James Sinclair, and Heidi Kiiwetinepinesiik Stark, "Bagijige: Making an Offering," in their 2013 collection *Centering Anishinaabeg Studies: Understanding the World Through Stories*.

[2] See Heid E. Erdrich, "Name': Literary Ancestry as Presence," *Centering Anishinaabeg Studies*.

[3] For further discussion of Nanaboozhoo, see John Borrows, "The Trickster: Integral to a Distinctive Culture," *Forum Constitutionnel* 8.2 (1997).

forms of inscription and communication, from pictographs to wampum to alphabetic writing. Ojibwe leaders used pictographs representing their clans, or patrilineal kinship identities, to sign treaties with European and North American settler nations, while pictographs carved on stone marked territory, sent messages, and recorded songs. Copway's own work exemplifies the diverse languages and media in which Ojibwe literatures appear: he participated in a Great Lakes network of Ojibwe Methodists who translated English-language hymns into Anishinaabemowin and who wrote some of the first English-language Ojibwe histories and personal autobiographies. Copway's history, as well as his autobiography and political writings in defense of Ojibwe peoples, are part of an extensive and ongoing Ojibwe literary tradition, in both English and Anishinaabemowin.

from "THE BIRTH OF NENABOZHO"
as told by Waasaagoneshkang, recorded by William Jones, and translated by Rand Valentine, from *Voices from Four Directions: Contemporary Translations of the Native Literatures of North America* (2004)

The following story was told near Pelican Lake, Minnesota, in the early twentieth century by Waasaagoneshkang (Ojibwe: He Who Leaves the Imprint of His Foot Shining in the Snow), an Ojibwe man who spent his formative years near the border between Minnesota and Ontario. Waasaagoneshkang dictated this and many other traditional stories to the anthropologist William Jones; the version excerpted here is a 2004 translation by the linguist Rand Valentine based on Jones's transcription.

I

Once some people were living in a wigwam, an old woman and her daughter.
And at some point she said to her daughter,
 "Listen, my daughter, be on your guard.
 Take careful heed of what I'm about to tell you.
 I'm terribly afraid, I fear for your well-being.
 Never ever sit facing the west when you go outside
 to relieve yourself.[1]
 Something bad will happen to you if you sit facing
 in that direction.
 That's the basis of my fear for you.
 Take heed of what I'm telling you,
 because you could bring great harm on yourself.
 That's what I want to tell you now."

Well, it seems that that young woman was exceedingly careful.

No man ever came within sight of her.
But then once she forgot,
 and at that instant she heard the wind rushing
 toward her.
And she felt the rush of a cool breeze there at her going out.
And she leapt to her feet.
 "Mother, look at me, this state I'm in.
 Perhaps it's happened to me as you said it might."

Well, the old woman said to her daughter:
 "Oh, most assuredly you've brought great harm on
 yourself!"

And the old woman began to weep.
 "That's how it is, you've brought harm on your
 body.
 Listen to what's going to happen to you.
 Beings have entered your body, and that's what has
 left you so pitiable.
 They're not humans, those who entered your body.
 And it won't be long until they're born.
 Alas, it's the very ones I feared."

Well, after a while the old woman heard the sound of them arguing with each other.
And then she knew for sure that her daughter wouldn't survive.
She heard them arguing;
 there within her daughter's belly they rumbled.
And this they were heard to say:
 "It's I who shall be firstborn!"
"No" was heard another,
 "You will not be firstborn—*I* shall be!"

And always the old woman wept when she heard them contending in this way.
She knew what a large number they were.

[1] [Valentine's note] Nenabozho's brothers and father were traditionally associated with the cardinal points of the compass.

Well, as they spoke they pushed each other back,
 seeking in vain to exit.
Some of them said: "Don't! We're going to harm our
 mother.
 Let us exit in an orderly fashion," some said, in
 vain.

But those who wanted to be firstborn weren't happy
 with this.
And so they declared that they would exit through
 various routes.
One of them saw a light.
 "Well, as for me, I'm going straight in that
 direction."
And so as they contended as to who would be
 firstborn,
 they tore their mother apart.

And some time later as the old woman was looking
 about,
 she found a bit of blood.
And so she peeled some birch bark.
And into the birch bark she placed the blood, repeat-
 edly folding the bark,
 and then she laid it away.

Well, from time to time she took a look at it.
And once, when she unwrapped it,
 she beheld a child.
And she was spoken to by the child,
 this is what she was told:
 "Grandmother!"
she was told when she was spoken to.

And then it spoke to her again:
"Do you know who I am?
Why, I am Nenabozho."

2

So the old woman began to raise him.
And at some point he said to his grandmother:
 "Might you not know of people living anywhere
 here on the earth?"

"Yes," he was told by his grandmother,
 "across Gichigami there are people."[1]

"And by any chance might they not be in possession
 of fire?"

"Yes," he was told by his grandmother,
 "most certainly they possess fire."

And this he said to his grandmother:
 "Well, guess what, I'm going to go get that fire!"
 he said to his grandmother.

And this his grandmother said to him:
 "You won't be able to do it.
 They keep very close guard over their home.
 There's an old man living there.
 Every day he works at making a net.
 He never goes out but always remains inside.
 But he has two daughters; they're the only ones
 who ever venture out."

And this he said to his grandmother:
 "Nevertheless, I'm going,"
 he said to his grandmother.

"Very well," he was told by his grandmother.

Well, at some point then he said:
 "Let Gichigami freeze over,
 let Gichigami freeze as thick as a sheet of birch
 bark covering the lodge."

And truly, it happened just as he said.

"And this is what I'll look like," he said.
 "I'll look like a bunny."

And then truly, that's how he looked.

And so he set off across the ice,
 and most assuredly he didn't break through.

[1] [Valentine's note] I use the Ojibwe designation for Lake Superior, Gichigami, throughout, assuming that it is known from Longfellow's *The Song of Hiawatha*, though the correct pronunciation is GitCh—ih—guh—mih or gih—Chi—guh—mih, with all the *i*s short as in English *pin*.

And eventually he came in sight of where the people
 were living.
And when he arrived at the place from which they
 drew their water,
 he arranged this at the place where they would
 come to draw their water:
 he was thrown up on the shore by Gichigami;
 he was rolled up there, precisely where the woman
 drew her water.

And this he said: "Let her find me irresistibly cute."

And so he lay in wait for her to come to fetch water.

And what do you know, but indeed he saw her walk-
 ing toward him.
And when she arrived where he was,
 she drew up some water.
And he was noticed by her,
 and he was picked up by her,
And so, he was wrung out by her,
 and he was carried away home,
 tucked inside the bosom of her dress, he was.

And when he had been taken inside the lodge,
 indeed he beheld an old man sitting there.
And, truly, the old man was making a net.
And the woman said this to her elder sister:
 "Look at this!"
 She said secretly to her elder sister.

 "Look at what I found, a little bunny rabbit!"

And this she was told by her elder sister:
 "Our father's going to take us to task,"
 she was told by her elder sister;
 that is, secretly she was told this by her elder sister.

And then she searched inside the bosom of her dress,
and she extracted him and set him down beside the
 fire to dry off his fur.

And the women were laughing it up,
 they found the bunny so irresistibly cute.
And as a result, they were discovered by their father.
 "Pipe down!" he told them.

"Take a look at this bunny!"

"What!" they were told by their father.
 "Haven't you heard that manitous[1] were recently
 born?
 And might not this indeed be one of them?
 Go and put it outside,"
 they were told by their father.

But this the woman said:
 "How could it be that a bunny rabbit be a
 manitou?"
 she said to her father.

And this he said:
 "Truly you're not in the habit of listening.
 Have you never noticed how advanced in years I
 am?"

But this is what the woman did:
 she exposed the bunny to the heat of the fire,
 and to make its fur dry,
 she kept turning it over and over by the fire.

And this then thought Nenabozho:
"I must be dry by now."

Well, the women kept amusing themselves with him.

And this he thought: "Let a spark fall on me!"

And truly a spark alit on him.
And after he was on fire,
 he leaped out of the lodge.

And the women said this:
 "Look, it's racing out with the fire!"
 they said to their father.

"Oh, no!" said the old man.
 "Truly you don't know how to listen,
 even though people try to tell you.
 Undoubtedly it's a manitou,
 come to rob us of our fire!"

[1] *manitous* Spirits.

And the old man leaped up
 and ran to his canoe,
 intending to toss it into the water.
But it was of no use,
 because the water had been frozen into ice.

And so they were left to watch helplessly
 as far out in the midst of the great expanse of
 Gichigami,
 it began to flicker with a blue flame,
 until it faded from their sight.
They were utterly helpless to do anything.

And he came in sight of where they were staying.
And this he had said to his grandmother before set-
 ting off:
 "Be prepared because I may indeed return with
 fire,"
 he had said to his grandmother.

And so he spoke to her as he came in sight of their
 home;
 this he said to his grandmother upon entering:
 "Extinguish me, grandma, I'm on fire!"
And that is how they came to have fire.

And this said Nenabozho:
 "And thus shall the rabbit appear mottled in the
 summer."

3

And thus they came to be in possession of fire.

And Nenabozho remained there with his
 grandmother,
 and all this time the waters of Gichigami were
 heaving.
Seated-Rabbit is the name of that portion of
 Gichigami.
And always he went there to sit.

And this he said to his grandmother:
 "So be it, Grandma, that this be the duration of
 my being a rabbit."

And at that place there was evidently a promontory,
 and there on the height of the rock he would sit.
Indeed, that is the appearance that the rock has there.
And then he said,
 "Seated-Rabbit is what the people shall call it."

And afterward he took on human form.
But no longer did he have the appearance of a child.
And this he said to his grandmother:
 "Do you know who I am?"

"No," he was told.

"I am Nenabozho."

And this he said to his grandmother:
 "Can it really be that I am an only child?"
 he said to his grandmother.

"Yes," he was told.
 "Truly you're an only child," he was told.

And this he answered:
 "Can you tell me this, then?"
he said to his grandmother,
 "Might not I have had a father?"

"Yes," he was told,
 "but whoever it might have been was not visible,"
 he was told.

And this too he was told,
 "She who was your mother is dead.
 That's all I can tell you.
 I would not hide anything from you."

And this Nenabozho said to her:
 "How could it be that I be an only child?
 You must be hiding something from me,"
 he said to his grandmother.

And then he said:
 "Why do you do this,
 hiding from me what transpired with us?
 But be that as it may, I haven't forgotten what
 happened.

I know that I have brothers.
So tell me the truth of what happened to us."

Well, these words frightened the old woman.
And this she said to her grandchild:
 "Very well, I will tell you,
 it's true that you weren't alone when you were
 born.

"As truly as I speak,
 this is what happened to you:
You and your brothers killed your mother when you
 were born.
But steadfastly I held to what I had purposed,
and that is why I have raised you."

And this he said to his grandmother:
 "Oh, so that's what happened to me at my birth!
 It was not I who killed my mother."

And then he thought:
 "I'm going to go looking for those brothers of
 mine,"
 he thought.

Well, then he said to his grandmother,
 "I'm going to go look for the one who made me
 an orphan."

"Don't!" his grandmother said in vain to him.
 "What is to be gained in your doing this,
 going into battle against your brother?"

"Nevertheless," he said, "I'm going to do it."

And then he set to work making his arrows.
And when he had prepared,
 he set off;
 directly to the south he went,
 because he knew that that was where his brother
 was.

And when he was near the home of his brother,
 he made four caches of arrows.

And then he came to the place where his brother was.

And Nenabozho said, "So, are you ready to do battle
 with me?"

"Indeed," his brother said to him.

"Well, then, let the battle begin."

And so they began fighting,
 and they were firing at each other.
And as he was being forced back,
 Nenabozho came to the place where his arrows
 were,
 where he had cached them.

And from there in turn he drove the other back,
 almost to the place where he lived,
 Nenabozho drove him back.

And from there once more Nenabozho was driven
 back,
 once again he was driven back to a place where
 he had cached his arrows.
And once more, futilely, he drove the other back,
 near to where he lived.

And then once more Nenabozho was driven back,
 until yet again he reached a cache of arrows.

And at that point he thought:
 "It seems likely now that I'll be vanquished."
He had only a very few arrows left,
 and they were very small.

And so he began to weep.

And this he thought:
 "It's likely now that I'll be killed,"
 he thought.

And then he was addressed by the weasel.
 "What's the matter with you,
 you look as if you've been weeping, Nenabozho,"
 he was told by the weasel.
 "Nothing's going to happen to you.
 Listen, I'll tell you what you must do,"
 said the weasel to him.

"Listen, shoot him there …"
"Shoot him at the base of his hair knot."

So then Nenabozho gave a war cry.
And no sooner had he begun driving his brother back,
 than he shot him at the base of the hair knot.
And his brother fell forward.
Nenabozho raced up to him,
 and this he said: "Die!"

And this he was told by his brother:
 "You're doing vast harm to those who are yet to
 live."
And his brother wept;
 he wept for the people.
In vain he sought to avoid being killed.

But Nenabozho was thoroughly determined to kill
 him.

And at last he succeeded in killing his younger sibling.
And for a short time his brother was out of his wits.

And Nenabozho said,
 "In return, you will be leader over there
 where those who cease to live will come.
 It's there you shall be,
 and there you shall be leader."

And then after his brother had consented,
 he said to him,
 "You've done vast harm to the people who are
 soon to live."

"Well, the earth would fill up with people.
 And where might those people live who are soon
 to be born?
 That is why it shall come to pass that people die,
 because otherwise the earth would soon be
 filled,
 and although we could arrange it such that
 only the aged might die among those who are
 to come,
 nowhere would they have room were this to
 come to pass.

You see, that's why they will also die while yet
 children.
Yes, that is what I foresee,
that it will happen thus to those who are soon to die,
that it will happen as it now does with you.
Because it is only a change of place from one earth
 to another.
Where you are those who have ceased to live shall
 meet you." …

NANABUSH EATS THE ARTICHOKES
as told by Waasaagoneshkang, recorded and translated by
William Jones, and revised by Ridie Wilson Ghezzi, *Coming
to Light: Contemporary Translations of the Native Literatures
of North America* (1994)

And then he went slowly along upon his way.
Now presently he saw some creatures.
 "What are you called?"
 he said to them.
 "Wonder if you may be eaten."

"Yes,"
 they said to him.

And then he was told,
 "Yes, we really are eaten."

 "Well, what is your effect after a lot of you is eaten?"

 "We have no effect.
 Then we make one farty in the stomach."
And then he ate them.
 Well, he was told they were good to eat.
Eventually he ate his fill and left them.
 "You really have a pleasing taste,"
 he said to them.

And then he kept straight along upon his way.
Now presently while traveling along,
 suddenly at the rear,
 "PO!"
 came a sound.
He started running.
 "Who made that noise?"
 he thought.

He was getting far on the run.
Again he was traveling along.
 "PO!"
 was the sound something made.
He whirled around.
 "Who made that noise?"
 he thought.

Again he was traveling along.
 Suddenly he farted.
 He started running.
 "Well, I will leave the one making that noise
 behind,"
 he thought.

Just as he was about to slow up,
 suddenly again,
 "PO!"
 came a sound.
Then he became afraid.
 "Well, I will look for the one making that sound,"
 he thought.

He lay in wait for it beside the path.
Then he went back a little ways.

And then he watched for it beside the path.
Suddenly again he heard some creature at his back.
 Then quickly came the sound:
 "PO!"
He leaped to his feet.
 "Holy smoke! Wonder what's following me.
 Must be a great manitou!"[1]
 he thought.

He started running at top speed.
While he was running,
 suddenly again,
 "PO!"
He landed a great distance off.
He whirled around.
Well he did not see the one that he tried in vain to hit.
Suddenly again there at his back he heard something.
 "PO!"

[1] *great manitou* Powerful spirit.

 "Holy smoke!"
 he thought.

He started running.
Then there where he started running,
 "PO!"
 "Holy smoke!"
 he thought.

He started running really fast.
He ran a short way. He ran fast.
Then quickly toward him the same sound.
 "PO!"
At last at every step he took,
 "PO!"
 "PO!"
 "PO!"
 "PO!"
 "PO!"

"Then it is just what my little brothers told me
 when I saw the artichokes:
 'We make people farty in the stomach,'
 I was told.
Hey, I am farting!
Then that is when the people,
 my uncles,
 shall say to the end of the world."

While he was traveling along,
suddenly again,
 "PO!"
"Hey, I am farting!"

NANABOZHO
as told by Charles Kawbawgam, translated by Jacques
LePique, and recorded by Homer H. Kidder, from *Ojibwa
Narratives of Charles and Charlotte Kawbawgam and Jacques
LePique, 1893–1895* (published 1994)

Ojibwe hereditary chief Charles Kawbawgam
(d. 1902) was born in the early nineteenth cen-
tury on the northern shore of Lake Superior and
spent most of his life on the southern side of the
lake. The following is one of many stories he
told to the white Michigan-born scholar Homer
H. Kidder (1874–1950) in Ojibwe. Kidder

spoke no Ojibwe and Kawbawgam spoke no English; Kawbawgam's words were translated by his brother-in-law, Jacques LePique, who was of mixed heritage and spoke several languages. Kidder then revised the translations to remove what he considered the "peculiarities" of LePique's French-Canadian inflected English. The narratives remained in manuscript form until the publication of *Ojibwa Narratives of Charles and Charlotte Kawbawgam and Jacques LePique, 1893–1895*, edited by Arthur P. Bourgeois, in 1994.

Nanabozho had a young wolf whom he called his nephew.[1] They lived on the shore of a lake and, when it froze over, he told the wolf that he must never cross it on the ice.

"Early or late," said he, "always go around this lake, for at the bottom are spirits who are my enemies and, if they should catch you on the ice, they would kill you."

But once, coming home late from hunting, the wolf struck across the lake. In the middle, the ice went to pieces beneath him, broken by the spirits, and the wolf was drowned.

Then Nanabozho gave a long cry and mourned aloud. All through the winter and the spring, he would go about the lake moaning for his nephew, seeking in his mind a plan to be revenged. He could not rest till revenged.

He knew that in the summer, on the hottest days, the spirits rose from the bottom of the lake to the surface, and he found a beach where they used to sleep in the sun. There, on a hot day, he changed himself into a pine stub, with the stoutest roots, and there he waited.

By and by, as the sun got higher, the spirits began to look out from the water, one after another, frogs, toads, lizards, and snakes, also bears, skunks, beavers and others, for although they were spirits, they came to the top in the shapes of animals. The last to come was in the form of a snow white panther, Mishi Bizi, the chief of the water spirits. He looked all about and, seeing the pine stub, said to the others: "Look at that stub. What do you think of it?"

The spirits answered: "We have never seen it before. It may be Nanabozho."[2]

The chief sent a *Mishi Ginabig*, the great serpent, on shore to try the stub. He was one of the strongest among them. He had immense antlers and he was as big as the largest pines. He coiled himself around the stub and hugged it with all his might, but Nanabozho did not make a sound.

The Mishi Ginabig said: "This is not Nanabozho." But the chief sent a still more powerful spirit, a yellow bear, who went at the stub and tore it with his claws till Nanabozho had to hold his breath to keep from howling. He would not cry out because his heart was set on revenge. He had a terrible will for revenge.

The yellow bear said: "No, no! This is not Nanabozho." Still the chief was not satisfied. He sent the most powerful spirit of them all, a monstrous red bear. Nothing could stand before him, rocks or trees. He rushed at the stub again and again, being sure that if it was Nanabozho he could knock it down, but the roots were so strong that he could not budge it. So the red bear gave up too. He said: "This cannot be Nanabozho."

All this time the spirits had been floating in the water, but now they believed they were safe and came out on the beach. There they lay in a ring around the white panther and one by one, they fell asleep. Then Nanabozho took his own shape and strung his bow. Jumping over the spirits, he shot an arrow into the body of Mishi Bizi, near the heart. The panther roared and Nanabozho leaped over the others into the woods, while the spirits dove into the lake.

Nanabozho believed that he had killed his enemy and avenged the wolf. His heart was glad.

One day, meeting Mishi Bizi's grandmother, the Frog Woman, he saw that she had been crying. He said: "What's the matter?" He supposed it was the death of Mishi Bizi that made her cry. She answered: "My grandson was shot by Nanabozho and the arrow is still in him. I am doctoring him. If it hadn't been for me, he would have died." So Nanabozho knew that Mishi Bizi was still alive.

[1] [Kidder's note] How Nanabozho came to have a wolf is told in a version of this story related to my father in the [eighteen] sixties by Jacques LePique[.] …

[2] [Kidder's note] At this point Kawbawgam says: "Nanabozho must have had more power than the spirits for they could not tell whether it was Nanabozho or not."

The old woman was packing a load of basswood bark and Nanabozho asked her what she was going to do with it.

She answered: "I am going to make a string and run it through the woods, tied on the trees, so that we can see if Nanabozho touches it somewhere."

"But don't you suppose," said he, "That Nanabozho would see your string and would keep from touching it?"

"Maybe you are Nanabozho yourself," said the Frog Woman.

"Oh, no! I'm not Nanabozho," said he. "I am only telling you what I would do if I were Nanabozho. But what happens if Nanabozho does touch the string?"

"Why then, perhaps I could tell where he is," said the Frog Woman. "We are going to send a shower of rocks, so that Nanabozho will be killed."

"You must think Nanabozho is a fool," said he. "Couldn't he hide somewhere till the stones stopped falling?"

The old woman then felt pretty sure she was talking with Nanabozho, but he laughed and said: "No, no. I never saw this Nanabozho. I'm just saying what I would do if I were Nanabozho."

Next day he met her again and asked her when the rocks were going to fall. She answered: "Tomorrow."

So Nanabozho piled trees across a narrow ravine, and when the shower of rocks began, he went underneath and sat there till it was over. Before that, there were no great rocks on the earth. It was then that they fell where we see them today, such as the Pictured Rocks, Sugar Loaf, the Gull Rock,[1] and the rest.

When the spirits found that Nanabozho was not killed by the rain of rocks, they sent a terrible winter, hoping to freeze him to death. This was the first winter. Snow covered all the earth. But Nanabozho made snow shoes, the first ever made. He could run on the snow, while deer and other animals were stuck in drifts. So he had plenty of game, and when the spirits sent chickadees to see if he was still alive, he pelted them with balls of fat.

When the winter was over, Nanabozho met the Frog Woman once more and asked her what was going

to happen. She said: "The spirits are going to flood the world, and Nanabozho will be drowned."

The old woman was on her way to a cave where the spirits lived under the lake. She told him that she went there to doctor her grandson every evening when the door of the cave opened. Nanabozho asked her where she kept her medicine rattle in the cave, and when she had told him, he said he would like to hear the song that she sang when she doctored her grandson. So she sang her medicine song, and when Nanabozho had learned it, he killed her and flayed her. Then he put on the Frog Woman's skin, dove into the lake, and swam down to the cave of the spirits.

In the cave, the spirits were in human form, but when they went out they put on animal form, because in that form they had more power. The door of the cave opened only between daylight and dark, when the Frog Woman used to come to doctor Mishi Bizi. Nanabozho was at the door when it opened, and he walked in, dressed in the skin of the Frog Woman.

Two frogs were on guard inside the door. They said: "Our grandmother looks like Nanabozho."

He struck them with the old woman's staff to make them keep still. He said: "It is crying all day that makes my skin so wrinkled."

He called for the medicine rattle, and singing the song of the Frog Woman, he came close to Mishi Bizi as if to doctor him. Then seizing the arrow, he drove it into the heart of the panther and killed him. Then he ran out of the cave and escaped.

When the flood came, Nanabozho climbed the highest mountain. But the water rose to the top of the mountain. Then Nanabozho climbed a tall pine, but the water rose to the top of the tree. Nanabozho said to the pine: "Brother, stretch." And the tree stretched his own length. Three times, when the water rose to the top, the pine stretched his own length. But the fourth time, the tree said that he could stretch no more. Soon the water reached Nanabozho's waist, then his neck. When it was almost up to his mouth, Nanabozho saw a blue heron and said: "Brother, drink up all the water you can hold." Then the heron took his fill and sank from sight.

At the same time, seeing a beaver, Nanabozho said to him, "Dive and fetch me up some earth, so that I can make a new world." The beaver dove but the

[1] *Pictured Rocks, Sugar Loaf, the Gull Rock* Cliffs, a mountain, and an island, respectively, in northern Michigan.

water was so deep that he could not reach the bottom. He came up dead, and Nanabozho blew on him and brought him back to life. Then an otter swam by and Nanabozho sent him down also to get some earth. But the otter, too, came up dead and Nanabozho blew on him and brought him to life. At last Nanabozho saw a muskrat and said to him: "Brother, dive quickly and bring me up some earth, so that I may make a new world. Otherwise we must all die." The muskrat came up dead, but his paws were closed tight, holding a little earth. Nanabozho blew on him and brought him to life. Then he took the earth brought up by the muskrat and, holding it out on his hand, prayed to the Great Spirit for the hottest day that ever came. So the earth dried on his hand and Nanabozho blew it out on the water, and made a new world.

This was the world where we live today. By the flood, the people of the old earth were drowned and the Great Spirit put upon the new earth the father and mother of the people of this earth.

When Nanabozho stepped on the new land, he saw the blue heron lying on the shore with his belly swelled to immense size by the water he had swallowed. Nanabozho kicked him in the belly and the water poured out in such a stream that Nanabozho had to run away to keep from being drowned.

Nanabozho lived many years on the new earth and at last disappeared. Nobody knows where he went, but the Indians do not believe that he is dead, for when they are without food, they can get what they need by praying to Nanabozho. So he must be living somewhere in the spirit world.

Ojibwe Pictographs

recorded and translated by George Copway, from *The Traditional History and Characteristic Sketches of the Ojibway Nation* (1851)

3.

This is one of their war songs, which might read in English thus:

1.

I will haste to the land of the foe,
With warriors clad with the bow.

2.

I will drink the blood of their very heart;
I will change their joy into sorrow's smart
Their braves, their sires will I defy,
And a Nation's vengeance satisfy.

They are in their homes, now happy and free;
No frowning cloud o'er their camp they see;
Yet the youngest of mine shall see the tall
Braves, scattered, wandering, and fall.

The warrior is represented by the figure of a man with a bow about him, and arrows in his hand; with the plume of the eagle waving over his head, indicative of his acquaintance with war life. The next figure represents a watching warrior, equally brave, but the heart is represented as dead. The curve of his mouth shows that

he is shouting. The next figure represents a person with long hair, an indication that the best of the enemy's warriors were to fall, and their wail must be heard like the wail of a woman. The wigwam with its smoke curling upwards, indicates a council fire and the defiance of an attack. The other wigwams are seen without fire; and the black one signifies silence and death.

When I was young I was taught this, and while singing I could, in imagination, see the enemy, though none were within a hundred miles. …

… These are some of the figures used by us in writing. With these, and from others of a similar class, the Ojibways can write their war and hunting songs.

An Indian well versed in these can send a communication to another Indian, and by them make himself as well understood as a pale face can by letter.

There are over two hundred figures in general use for all the purposes of correspondence. Material things are represented by pictures of them.

Sea, water.

Sky, heaven.

River, stream.

Land.

Great Spirit, every where.

Sun.

Moon.

Stars.

Noon.

Sunrise.

Sunset.

Life. Death.

Sickness.

Man.

Woman.

Smooth water, Clear day.

Bad Spirit, water god.

Fish.

Bear.

Invitations to Indians to come and worship in the spring are made in the following form:

The whole story would thus read:

"Hark to the words of the Sa-ge-mah."
"The Great Medicine Lodge will be ready in eight days."
"Ye who live in the woods and near the Lakes and by streams of water, come with your canoes or by land to the worship of the Great Spirit."

In the above, the wigwam and the medicine pale or worship, represent the depositories of medicine, record and work. The Lodge is represented with men in it; the dots above indicate the number of days.

These picture representations were used by the Ojibways until the introduction of European manners among them. …

Cherokee

By the time Cherokee people first made contact with colonists in 1540, Cherokees had been living in what is now called southern Appalachia for thousands of years and had established numerous permanent communities supported by a combination of hunting, fishing, and agriculture, structured around a two-season rhythm of summer and winter. Cherokee oral stories convey values and wisdom that have been shaped by relationship to the landscape over this long duration, and that continue to evolve as Cherokee history unfolds. According to Cherokee scholar Sandra Muse Isaacs, two key principles that recur in her people's oral traditions are Gadugi, a community-oriented commitment to generosity and support of other beings, and Duyvkta, the "right path" of harmony, balance, self-respect, and care for oneself as well as others.

Cherokee people also have a long tradition of writing. An indispensable contributor to this tradition is the blacksmith, silversmith, warrior, inventor, and political figure Sequoyah (c. 1770–1843), best known as the creator of the Cherokee Syllabary, a method of writing in the Cherokee language that he developed and popularized in the early nineteenth century. According to ethnographic accounts, Sequoyah created the syllabary independently, inspired by European writing systems, but Cherokee oral history holds that he was also inspired by an earlier form of writing that had been used by some Cherokee knowledge-keepers. Each symbol in Sequoyah's system represents an entire syllable, which makes it far more efficient to learn than the English alphabet; it spread quickly and was adopted by a majority of Cherokee speakers by the mid-1820s. It contributed to the development of a written constitution for the nation, completed in 1827, and to the creation of the bilingual Cherokee-English newspaper the *Cherokee Phoenix*, founded in 1828. The syllabary remains in common use today.

By the time the stories presented here were recorded in English in the late nineteenth and twentieth centuries, a series of atrocities perpetrated by the American government had wreaked havoc on Cherokee culture for generations. The most infamous of these, known as Expulsion or Removal, occurred in the late 1830s, as the majority of Cherokee people were forced to leave their homes and travel west of the Mississippi River; thousands of people died of disease and starvation during the journey or shortly afterward. As a result of these events, there are now Western Cherokee-speaking communities in Oklahoma, where the people were forcibly relocated, and Eastern Cherokee-speaking communities in the original homeland of Appalachia, as some resisters had managed to escape expulsion.

Myths of the Cherokee, the collection from which the first of the stories below was taken, was compiled by the white ethnographer James Mooney, who spent several years with the Eastern Band of Cherokees in the mountains of North Carolina toward the end of the nineteenth century. During this time, Mooney worked with a number of knowledgeable storytellers, most notably the shaman A'yûñ'inĭ (Swimmer). It appears that Mooney pressured the storytellers he worked with to share restricted knowledge, but also that they were motivated by a desire to preserve a record of their literature, which was then under threat from the pressures of colonization; present-day Cherokee scholars disagree regarding the extent to which Mooney exploited his collaborators. Mooney believed himself to be preserving the literature of a dying culture, but in fact Cherokee oral traditions continue to flourish—and continue to evolve to reflect the events of recent centuries, including the era of expulsion, as the story told by Lloyd Sequoyah below illustrates.

WHY THE POSSUM'S TAIL IS BARE
as recorded by James Mooney, *Myths of the Cherokee* (1902)

James Mooney writes of the following text that "This story was heard from several informants, east and west. In one variant the hair clipping was done by the Moth, and in another by the spells of the Snail, who is represented as a magician. The version here given is the most common."

The Possum used to have a long, bushy tail, and was so proud of it that he combed it out every morning and sang about it at the dance, until the Rabbit, who had had no tail since the Bear pulled it out, became very jealous and made up his mind to play the Possum a trick.

There was to be a great council and a dance at which all the animals were to be present. It was the Rabbit's business to send out the news, so as he was passing the Possum's place he stopped to ask him if he intended to be there. The Possum said he would come if he could have a special seat, "because I have such a handsome tail that I ought to sit where everybody can see me." The Rabbit promised to attend to it and to send someone besides to comb and dress the Possum's tail for the dance, so the Possum was very much pleased and agreed to come.

Then the Rabbit went over to the Cricket, who is such an expert hair cutter that the Indians call him the barber, and told him to go next morning and dress the Possum's tail for the dance that night. He told the Cricket just what to do and then went on about some other mischief.

In the morning the Cricket went to the Possum's house and said he had come to get him ready for the dance. So the Possum stretched himself out and shut his eyes while the Cricket combed out his tail and wrapped a red string around it to keep it smooth until night. But all this time, as he wound the string around, he was clipping off the hair close to the roots, and the Possum never knew it.

When it was night the Possum went to the town-house where the dance was to be and found the best seat ready for him, just as the Rabbit had promised. When his turn came in the dance he loosened the string from his tail and stepped into the middle of the floor.

The drummers began to drum and the Possum began to sing, "See my beautiful tail." Everybody shouted and he danced around the circle and sang again, "See what a fine color it has." They shouted again and he danced around another time, singing, "See how it sweeps the ground." The animals shouted more loudly than ever, and the Possum was delighted. He danced around again and sang, "See how fine the fur is." Then everybody laughed so long that the Possum wondered what they meant. He looked around the circle of animals and they were all laughing at him. Then he looked down at his beautiful tail and saw that there was not a hair left upon it, but that it was as bare as the tail of a lizard. He was so much astonished and ashamed that he could not say a word, but rolled over helpless on the ground and grinned, as the Possum does to this day when taken by surprise.

SEQUOYAH, CHEROKEE SYLLABARY (NINETEENTH CENTURY)

This syllabary was hand-written by Sequoyah himself.

[THE BELT THAT WOULD NOT BURN]
as told by Lloyd Sequoyah and transcribed by Barbara R.
Duncan, *Living Stories of the Cherokee* (1998)

> The following narrative was recounted by
> Cherokee Medicine Man Lloyd Sequoyah
> during a discussion with lawyers in support of
> a suit attempting to stop the Tennessee Valley
> Authority from building the Tellico Dam and
> flooding many culturally significant Cherokee
> sites. (The suit failed; the dam was constructed
> and the land flooded.)

Years ago,
 during the time when the whites were coming
 into this country,
 things were hard for the Cherokee.
One day, an old man came to the city of Old Echota,[1]
 and he called all the people into the townhouse to
 hear him speak.
Before he spoke he took a wampum belt
 and threw it up over two of the crossbeams
 between the posts that held up the seven-sided
 council house.
He told the people that times were hard for them,
 and that they would get harder.
But they would survive as a people, he said,
 if they would follow the traditional way of the
 Cherokee people:
 Duyukta, the path of harmony, of being in
 balance.

They asked him what the wampum belt meant, and
 he explained.
The man and woman on one end of the belt represent
 the Cherokee people.
The white path of beads down the center of the belt
 represents Duyukta, the path of harmony, of being
 in balance.
The black beads on both sides of the white path
 represents all the things that you can do
 to stray from the path of being in harmony.
The checkerboard of squares at the other end of the
 belt
 represents all the good things that will come to
 you
 at the end of life's journey
 if you stay on the path of harmony.
He said that
 as long as the Cherokee people stayed on the path
 of harmony and balance,
 and the wampum belt survived,
 that the Cherokee would survive as a people.
As he finished speaking the wampum belt burst into
 flame.
The people were horrified,
 thinking this signified the end of them as a people.
But when the flames died down,
 they saw that the belt was still intact:
 all of the beads, threads, and deerskin backing.
And they knew they would survive as a people
 if they would follow the path of harmony and
 balance.

[1] *Old Echota* Cherokee town and political center from the 1740s
to the late 1780s, when settler-colonists drove out most of the popu-
lation. Echota was one of the places flooded by the construction of
the Tellico Dam.

Maya

Mayan people, who live in Central America today, are the descendants of Mayans who built an extensive series of cities that were flourishing by 1200 BCE, thousands of years before Europeans knew about or attempted to conquer the Americas. Probably by the first millennium BCE, Mayans also developed a system of hieroglyphic writing, which survives in stone carvings and in a small number of books. Mayan books generally incorporate both illustration and hieroglyphic writing on each page, and the line between these forms is blurred: illustrations often feature some hieroglyphic elements, while the interpretation of hieroglyphs can be affected by painterly visual elements (such as, in the case of humanoid figures, position or facial expression). In addition, a single glyph (a hieroglyphic symbol) may have multiple phonetic meanings apart from its meaning as an ideogram (a character that represents an idea). The interpretation of a hieroglyphic text is thus a complex art requiring skills that were taught only to members of the aristocracy. Mayan bookmaking flourished until the practice was violently curtailed by colonization: Spanish priests burned vast numbers of Mayan codices as part of the conquest of Mayan cities, peoples, and ways of life, and the priests sought to replace the hieroglyphic writing systems and stories told in codices with the Spanish language and alphabetic writing systems. Of the hundreds of Mayan books that existed in the sixteenth century, only a few are believed to have survived to the present day.

The surviving text of the *Popol Vuh* (K'iche': Council Book) is based on an alphabetic work made by K'iche' Mayan intellectuals in the 1550s. The work, which is in alphabetic text in the K'iche' language, is a translation of a hieroglyphic text containing astronomical knowledge as well as stories of creation, human emergence, and Mayan history. Rather than transcribing the meaning of individual glyphs, the translators recorded what might have been said by a reader interpreting the hieroglyphic text aloud. The K'iche' intellectuals who translated their stories and histories into alphabetic script had learned alphabetic writing from Spanish missionaries, who hoped not to facilitate the recording of Mayan stories but to convert Mayan people to Catholicism. For the K'iche' transcribers of the *Popol Vuh*, this was an act of turning alphabetic writing to Indigenous ends, to ensure the perpetuation of Mayan literature and knowledge.

Between 1701 and 1715, the Dominican priest Francisco Ximénez saw the K'iche' manuscript and made a copy, to which he added a Spanish translation. The manuscript transcribed and translated by Ximénez remained in the possession of the Dominican order until the closing of monasteries in 1830, when it was sent to Guatemala City, then to France, and in 1911 to the Newberry Library in Chicago, where it resides today. The manuscript held at the Newberry remains the only surviving copy of the *Popol Vuh* of which scholars are currently aware.

The *Popol Vuh* is an epic that tells of the beginning of the cosmos and earth; the making of humans; and stories of the beings who inhabited the earth before humans existed and who model behavior that humans might emulate or avoid. The gods attempt several times to make humans, first creating beings who squawk and chatter, then a being made of mud, and beings made of wood. Finally, they mold figures out of a corn paste, and these figures become humans. In addition to these stories of creation and the earth's formation, the *Popol Vuh* relates the histories of the Mayan people in what is now Guatemala, up to the first few decades of conquest and contact with the Spanish. The Newberry Library recently digitized the *Popol Vuh*, and Mayan and other scholars continue to study the text, both in this digital form and by consulting published editions. Knowledge of the text is continually being corrected and updated, as scholars work with Mayan language experts and knowledge keepers to correct translations and understand the *Popol Vuh*'s relation to hieroglyphic texts.

from THE DRESDEN CODEX (C. THIRTEENTH CENTURY)

One of very few books to survive Christian missionaries' systematic destruction of Mayan literature, the Dresden Codex is best known for its accurate and extensive astronomical tables; the second page below is from a series of tables predicting solar eclipses. The only full-page illustration in the codex, also reproduced below, depicts a flood.

from THE POPOL VUH
as translated by Dennis Tedlock, *Popol Vuh* (1985 translation
of original text c. 1550)

The passage reprinted here, from near the
beginning of the *Popol Vuh*, introduces the
gods' first attempt at creation (it would take
them four tries to succeed in creating human
beings). The translation the excerpt is drawn
from, published in 1985, is the product of a
collaboration between white American ethnog-
rapher and poet Dennis Tedlock and K'iche'
daykeeper Andres Xiloj, who gave Tedlock
extensive training in Mayan culture as well as
collaborating on the interpretation of the text
itself. Tedlock's extensive glossary and transla-
tor's notes are not reprinted here in full, but are
occasionally quoted below.

THIS IS THE ACCOUNT, here it is:
 Now it still ripples, now it still murmurs, ripples,
it still sighs, still hums, and it is empty under the sky.

Here follow the first words, the first eloquence:

There is not yet one person, one animal, bird, fish,
crab, tree, rock, hollow, canyon, meadow, forest. Only the
sky alone is there; the face of the earth is not clear. Only
the sea alone is pooled under all the sky; there is nothing
whatever gathered together. It is at rest; not a single thing
stirs. It is held back, kept at rest under the sky.

Whatever there is that might be is simply not there:
only the pooled water, only the calm sea, only it alone
is pooled.

Whatever might be is simply not there: only
murmurs, ripples in the dark, in the night. Only the
Maker, Modeler alone, Sovereign Plumed Serpent, the
Bearers, Begetters[1] are in the water, a glittering light.
They are there, they are enclosed in quetzal[2] feathers,
in blue-green.

Thus the name, "Plumed Serpent." They are great
knowers, great thinkers in their very being.

And of course there is the sky, and there is also the
Heart of Sky.[3] This is the name of the god, as it is spoken.

[1] *Maker, Modeler ... Begetters* "Maker," "Modeler," "Bearers,"
and "Begetters" are here all epithets applied to a group of gods that
includes Sovereign Plumed Serpent (Tepeu Cucumatz).

[2] *quetzal* Brilliantly colored bird with long tail plumes.

[3] *Heart of Sky* Epithet for the god Hurricane (Hurakan), who
is also described as a trio of gods or divine aspects: Thunderbolt

And then came his word, he came here to the
Sovereign Plumed Serpent, here in the blackness, in
the early dawn. He spoke with the Sovereign Plumed
Serpent, and they talked, then they thought, then they
worried. They agreed with each other, they joined their
words, their thoughts. Then it was clear, then they
reached accord in the light, and then humanity was
clear, when they conceived the growth, the generation
of trees, of bushes, and the growth of life, of human-
kind, in the blackness, in the early dawn, all because
of the Heart of Sky, named Hurricane. Thunderbolt
Hurricane comes first, the second is Newborn
Thunderbolt, and the third is Raw Thunderbolt.

So there were three of them, as Heart of Sky, who
came to the Sovereign Plumed Serpent, when the dawn
of life was conceived:

"How should it be sown, how should it dawn? Who
is to be the provider, nurturer?"

"Let it be this way, think about it: this water should
be removed, emptied out for the formation of the
earth's own plate and platform, then comes the sowing,
the dawning of earth. But there will be no high days
and no bright praise for our work, our design, until the
rise of the human work, the human design," they said.

And then the earth arose because of them, it was
simply their word that brought it forth. For the form-
ing of the earth they said "Earth." It arose suddenly,
just like a cloud, like a mist, now forming, unfolding.
Then the mountains were separated from the water,
all at once the great mountains came forth. By their
genius alone, by their cutting edge[4] alone they carried
out the conception of the mountain-plain, whose face
grew instant groves of cypress and pine.

Hurricane, Newborn Thunderbolt, and Raw Thunderbolt.

[4] *genius ... cutting edge* Tedlock notes that the word *naual*, here
translated as "genius," refers to "the spiritual essence or character of
a person, animal, plant, stone, or geographical place." *Naual* is here
and elsewhere in the *Popol Vuh* paired with *puz* (here translated as
"cutting edge"), which "refers to the cutting open of flesh with a
knife and is the primary term for the act of heart sacrifice." He goes
on to explain that, "[w]hen used together, *puz* and *naual* are met-
onyms for shamanic power, referring to the ability to make genius
or spiritual essence visible or audible by means of ritual." Here, the
use of *puz* "implies that 'the mountains were separated from the
water' through an act resembling the extraction of the heart (or other
organs) from a sacrifice."

Navajo (Diné)

Much of the Navajo (Diné) creation story takes place between the four sacred mountains that define the limits of Dinétah, the Navajo traditional homeland, which spans parts of what are now also called Arizona, Colorado, New Mexico, and Utah. Traditional Navajo ways of life involve seasonal movement through this land. Initially, hunting and gathering were the only sources of food, but Navajo people also adopted agriculture from their Pueblo neighbors, and later, adopted the keeping of livestock herds from the Spanish, whom they first encountered in the late sixteenth century. Having resisted colonization by violent Spanish forces for more than a century, Navajo people began to face hostility from U.S. forces in the mid-1800s, and in 1863 were compelled to surrender to the U.S. The military forced them to march to central New Mexico, where they were held in an internment camp for four years; many people died both on the march, known as the Long Walk, and as a result of conditions in the camp, where sanitation, provisions, and shelter were inadequate. After four years, the Navajo were permitted to return to a reservation in a portion of Dinétah; since then, they have expanded their territory to include more of their traditional homeland.

An extended telling of the creation story plays a central role in the Blessingway rite, an important ceremony known in the Diné language as hózhóojí, meaning "way of hózhó." The complex philosophical concept of hózhó, meaning something like "beauty," "harmony," or "goodness," is taught and made manifest through the telling of the creation story and the other actions of the rite. Navajo anthropologist Rain Parrish describes the "interrelationships of stories, chants and rituals" as part of this process:

> At the beginning of the ceremony the practitioners introduce the surroundings
> of the dwellings, and the practitioner and patient's relationship to the natural
> and supernatural worlds. The origin of the Navajo is traced and we then return
> to the present world. The story of the myths is related with all its appropriate
> rituals. The key to the restoration of harmony and well being is in carefully
> acquiring the knowledge or ritual actions and their powers. By participating in
> this process, by actualizing the myths, we are composing a profound sense of
> unity with spirit and substance.

The Blessingway is one of many traditional ceremonies incorporating song, poetry, movement, and drypainting (visual art made by dropping sand and other colored powders). All the elements of a given ceremony are informed by the specific narratives included in it, which are often episodes drawn from the creation story. Ceremonies differ dramatically in duration—some last one night, while the Blessingway takes nine days. They also differ in many other respects; the drypaintings of the Blessingway are a few inches across, for example, while some drypaintings used in other ceremonies are so large that they must be painted in buildings made for the purpose. Specific ceremonies have particular functions, including to establish harmony, to cure sickness, or to oppose evil.

The portion of the creation story transcribed below is from *Navajo Creation Myth: The Story of the Emergence*, an early-twentieth-century collaboration between the white anthropologist Mary Cabot Wheelwright and the Navajo knowledge-keeper Hasteen Klah. Klah escaped attending the boarding schools intended to force assimilation to settler culture that were inflicted on many of his peers, and instead received training in traditional practices; as a nádleehí, a person whose gender does not fully conform to the roles of either men or women, he developed an unusual breadth of expertise that encompassed weaving (traditionally a women's art) as well as ceremony (traditionally conducted by men). Fearing that his knowledge, threatened by boarding schools and other oppressive government tactics, would be otherwise lost, Klah disregarded prohibitions against the sharing of ceremonial knowledge in order to record, with Wheelwright, not only the creation story itself but also an extensive body of drypaintings and other ceremonial practices.

from THE CREATION STORY
as recorded by Hasteen Klah with Mary C. Wheelwright,
Navajo Creation Myth: The Story of the Emergence (1942)

The creation story begins with the creation of the First World, followed by the emergence of beings from that place into a series of higher worlds, until they reach the Fourth World (or, in some versions, the Fifth), where people currently live. The episode transcribed below begins after the birth of twins to Estsan-ah-tlehay, Changing Woman, an important figure in the narrative. At this point in the story the world is plagued by numerous monsters, which the twins will eventually slay.

from BIRTH OF NAYENEZGANI AND TOHBACHISCHIN

When they were sixteen years old, they were ... quite grown up, and they looked so much alike no one could tell them apart. They wanted very much to find out who their father was. They asked this four times before the Sun had risen, but their mother was ashamed to tell them. But when the Sun had come up about half way, she pointed to it and said: "That is your father."

Etsay-Hasteen[1] made the twins bows and arrows, and they went about hunting and enjoying themselves. Once in their wanderings they came close to the edge of the mountain and they saw a Yehtso, a Gray Monster, coming up, and they shot at him with their bows and arrows and he was so frightened that he ran away.

One day when they were out hunting, Begochiddy[2] met them and sitting down between them said: "The Sun is your father and you must go and visit him." To help them, and to tell them what would happen in the future, and to show them the way, he gave them wind spirits, Niltche-beyazh. And he gave Nayenezgani the elder, the rainbow, Natseelit, to carry him wherever he wanted to go. And he gave Tohbachischin a ray of light, Shah-bekloth. He told the boys that when they came to their father's house they would be shown all sorts of clothing and other things, but that they must choose only the flint armor, Bezh; the lightning arrows,

Iknee-kah; and the stone knife, also the big cyclones and the big hail, and the kehtahn or magic cigarette named Kehtahn-de-konth; and he repeated: "You must be sure to ask for that." (Their mother, Estsan-ah-tlehay, did not know that they were starting on this journey.) ...

[The twins journey to the house of the Spirit of the Sun.]

from TEST OF THE TWINS BY THE SUN

Inside on the east side of the house there was a black cloud rolled up, on the south side a blue cloud, on the west a yellow cloud, and on the north a white cloud. The twins met the Moon spirit there, though the moon itself was not present as it was wandering about. And the Spirit asked them: "What are you doing here, my boys? Your father is a fierce man and I will try to protect you." So the Spirit wrapped the two boys in the white cloud to hide them.

After they were hidden in the white cloud, the Sun Spirit came in and asked the Moon Spirit: "Who was speaking?" and the Moon Spirit answered: "No one except myself." The Sun Spirit did not believe this and went to the black cloud and unrolled it but found nothing there, and he unrolled the south cloud and the west cloud, and finally in the north cloud he found the boys. He seized them by the hair of their heads and threw them against some great spikes of obsidian which were turned edge-wise like knives set in the floor at the east side of the hogahn.[3] He said: "I hope these boys are my sons" (for if they were really his sons they would not be hurt by anything). They were not harmed by the knives; and then the Sun Spirit threw them onto the knives on the south, west and north, and they were still unharmed.

The Sun Spirit called the Moon spirit and said: "Uncle, heat the sweat-house." So the Moon Spirit heated the sweat-house, and on one side he dug a hole large enough to contain the two boys and covered it with a little Moon. He brought the boys over to the sweat-house and showed them the hole where they could hide, and they hid themselves in it. Then the Sun

[1] *Etsay-Hasteen* The first man.

[2] *Begochiddy* Introduced earlier in the narrative as the "great god."

[3] *hogahn* Dwelling constructed from wood and mud.

Spirit came to the house bringing a jug of water and poured it on a bar of obsidian which had been heated red hot; and it filled the house with much steam, and he asked the boys: "Are you too warm in there?" and the boys answered: "No." He asked this of the boys four times and they answered each time: "No, we are all right," so the Sun Spirit went back to his hogahn and the boys came out of the sweat-house.

Each night while they were at the Sun's house they slept on the roof, and they had a robe of white clouds to cover them and the Sun Spirit gave them another robe also, but they were very cold there and would have frozen except that the Otter Woman came and gave them her fur robe to spread over them. It hailed and stormed all night, and the Sun thought that they would be frozen, but thanks to the fur robe which the Otter Woman gave them, they were warm.

When the Sun went into his home again, he filled a turquoise pipe, a white shell pipe, an abalone pipe, and a jet pipe with poison smoke. On their way back to the Sun's house from the sweat-house, the twins met a caterpillar who gave them some medicine weeds to eat so that they could not be killed if they smoke the poison pipes of the Sun. Back in the Sun's house again the boys were given a blue pipe to smoke, and the Sun lighted it with a little Sun. They smoked all of the pipes easily.

Finding that he could not kill them with the poison smoke, the Sun Spirit caught the boys by the hair and threw them into a big black jar on the east side of the room. He then hung a huge stone by a stream of water to the roof over the jar and let the stone fall to crush the twins; but when he looked into the jar, he saw the boys in it unharmed. He tried this four times, and even made the great stone drop more heavily but he could not hurt the twins. Then he took the boys into his arms, holding one on either side of him, for he knew now that they were really his sons, because they had not been harmed by his tests.

The Sun Spirit had four children by a spirit woman named Yoodi-yenai, who had been in the Fourth World. Her eldest daughter was called Turquoise Girl, Doklizhe-etahdeh, and the younger was called White Shell Girl, Yolthkai-etahdeh. The older boy was called Abalone Boy, Dichithli-eshki, and the younger boy was called Jet Boy, Baszhini-eshki. The Sun Spirit said to his daughters: "Bring some water to your brothers," and the Turquoise Girl brought a blue basket and a jug of water, and the White Shell Girl brought a white basket and a jug of water, and also they brought soap-root, and the twins washed their hair and their sisters bathed them and dried them first with fine white corn meal and then with corn pollen. Then the Sun and his spirit wife went to the eastern room and brought the sweet-smelling flowers with which they rubbed the twins. And they were made beautiful and looked just like the other children of the Sun. And they sat down on a turquoise bench. The Sun Spirit told his daughters to feed the twins and they gave them Yolthkai-tahn (corn meal mush, ceremonially called White-Shell-Food).

The Sun Spirit then asked the twins: "Why did you come to me?" And they answered: "There are monsters killing all of our people and we want to be able to kill them." The Sun Spirit did not answer but took the boys to the east room which was reached by steps. He opened the door, and there they saw many rainbows, and the Sun Spirit asked the twins if that was what they wanted, but the boys said: "No, we do not want that sort of thing." Then the Sun took them to a door at the south and opened it, and there were many plants, corn, beans, and so forth. And the Sun Spirit said: "Is that what you wanted?" The boys said: "No." So the west door was opened, and there they saw clothing and jewelry, and the Sun asked them: "Did you come for this sort of thing?" And they said: "No"; but the boys had forgotten what they wanted and the Sun then showed them many more things.

Then Niltche-beyaz, the Spirit Wind, spoke in their ears and said: "Begochiddy told you to ask for flint armor and the other weapons." So they said to the Sun: "We want the flint armor and the stone knife, lightning arrows, cyclones, hail, and the magic kehtahn." The Sun said to them: "What do you want them for? They are dangerous." And they answered: "We want to dress in that armor and use the weapons to kill the giants and the monsters." When the twins answered thus, the Sun Spirit sat down with his head in his hands and said sadly: "You must not kill your brother," for he claimed the giants as his children. But finally he decided to grant their request and said: "Very well, I will give you what you have asked for." And he taught them how to wear the armor, and how to

shoot the lightning arrows, and how to use the stone knife, the big hail, the cyclones, and also how to use the magic kehtahn. And they then told him how they were going to kill the monsters, the bears, and other creatures who were harming the people.

Then the Sun Spirit gave them the gifts that they had asked for and they started to go back to Tsoll-tsilth on the clouds, the Sun accompanying them. And when they reached there, they rested above the mountain sitting on the clouds, and the Sun Spirit asked them many questions to test their cleverness. He pointed to Siss-nah-jini and asked them its name and the boys answered correctly. The Sun asked the names of all the mountains and they named them correctly. He also pointed to Huerfano Peak[1] below and the boys recognized their home, so the Sun was satisfied that they were intelligent and asked them no more questions.

TSE' HONE / NEWSPAPER ROCK

Known in Diné (Navajo) as Tse' Hone (rock that tells a story), this rock contains a large collection of petroglyphs that were carved over a period of more than a thousand years, and by a variety of peoples, including Ancestral Puebloans, Fremont people, Diné (Navajo) people, Pueblo people, and Europeans, among other groups. Tse' Hone is in present-day Utah, to the north of the Diné homeland.

[1] *Huerfano Peak* Sacred mountain at the center of the Navajo homeland.

Coast Salish

The homelands of the numerous tribes of the Coast Salish extend along the Northwest Coast from the Salish Sea in what is now called southern British Columbia to the northern coast of what is now Oregon. The Coast Salish peoples are culturally diverse, and there are more than ten Coast Salish languages: the stories that appear below in English translation were originally told in Samish and Lushootseed, two of these languages. One commonality among Coast Salish peoples is a close relationship to the land and waterways, which have historically been temperate and abundant, offering an array of salmon, berries and roots, shellfish, and other foods that people tended to harvest by moving seasonally, spending the rainy winters in permanent villages of cedar plank buildings.

In addition to the practical woodworking used to build homes and canoes, Coast Salish peoples have a diverse range of carving traditions. For some peoples, these traditions include the carving of freestanding poles and house posts (posts embedded in the wall of a building) that convey information through symbolic conventions. Poles and house posts can communicate the identity and kinship ties of the carving's owner; they can also convey cultural knowledge, including stories and history. In some carving traditions, story poles—the poles that tell stories—are read in a linear fashion: the front is read from the bottom up, and then the back is read from the top down. Traditional Coast Salish oral stories, too, are governed by conventions that vary by region and language group. Salish narrative structure, for instance, tends to organize events in groups of four or, in some tribes, groups of five. Traditional storytelling approaches tend to be highly theatrical, with conventionally stylized voices sometimes adopted for specific characters; in Lushootseed stories, for example, Raven speaks with a nasal tone.

Coast Salish peoples and white settlers first encountered each other in the eighteenth century, and colonization of the region began in earnest in the nineteenth century. Because Coast Salish peoples live on either side of the Canada-U.S. border, and some have large population centers such as Vancouver and Seattle in their traditional territories, individual tribes had varied experiences of colonization. There are, however, some common threads—including a systematic effort to eliminate Coast Salish culture by banning essential practices such as the potlatch and by forcing children to attend boarding schools, where they were required to assimilate to settler culture and prevented from speaking their own languages. As a result, some Coast Salish languages are no longer spoken and others have very few fluent speakers, but many tribes are making heroic efforts to salvage their languages; Samish, for example, a Straits Salish dialect that had only three fluent speakers in 2018, is being revitalized through an education program conducted by the tribe. The stories reprinted below are drawn from the 2008 collection *Salish Myths and Legends: One People's Stories*, edited by Terry Thompson and Steven M. Egesdal, part of a community of Indigenous and non-Indigenous scholars hoping to help sustain Coast Salish oral traditions and their languages.

MAIDEN OF DECEPTION PASS

as told by Victor Underwood Sr. and edited by Brent Galloway, *Salish Myths and Legends* (2008)

The traditional territory of the Samish people, on Washington's northern coast, includes a portion of the Salish sea, the Cascades Mountains, and part of the San Juan Islands. The following telling of "Maiden of Deception Pass" was edited by Brent Galloway. Both versions reproduced here were told in 1984 by Victor Underwood Sr., a Samish-speaking man born on Orcas Island, one of the San Juan Islands. Underwood told the story three times: briefly in English, then in Samish, and then more fully in English. The Samish telling appears below in English translation, followed by the longer English version.

The biggest tribe then were the Samish,
Well-respected people.
They're big.
So they're there.

Those that go aren't just sitting around home.
They go to a place where they go to fish.
They're looking to eat fish.
They get to the place where they're going.
That's where they were working.
All of them want to get some food for the
 children.
Those people are gathered there.
They get the fish, anything, everything on the sea-
 bottom right here, the sea-bottom food.
The Samish never get hungry.
They always get their food for their children.

Then she[1] saw a powerful monster right here on
 the sea bottom.
He wished for the woman.
She went into the water to bathe.
So she was grabbed.
Then he went taking her down to put her at the
 sea bottom.
He wanted to get as a spouse a woman from here,
 out of the water.

He went to go to her parents.

Then he asked, "I want to take your daughter as
 my wife.
She is a good child."

So the mother said, "I don't want my daughter to
 go.
I want her here with us."
So the monster from here on the sea bottom said,
 "I want to take your daughter.
If you don't give me your daughter, then it will be
 impossible for you to
get any food from here down on the bottom,
 anything.

I am the king of what's on the bottom here where
 I am.
I am the one supplying you folks's food.
If you won't give me your daughter, then therefore
 lots will be hungry.
Then your people will be all the same."

And so they answered for their own daughter.

So their daughter was taken away.
And then all their many relatives got the food
 easily.
It was just easy for them to get the food from
 down there at the bottom.

So when their daughter comes up out of the water
 she sees them.
Whenever their daughter is ready to come up out
 of the water it gets cold inside.
It gets cold.
Then her own parents already know it.

"My dear daughter must be coming here.
She got here,
it's really true."

And he saw green seaweed growing from her face.
Everything was growing,
coming,
coming out,
growing from her face.
Mussels too.

So he said, "Child, it's enough.
You can't always come see us.
You're always staying home and resting there.
Look at us because we're showing
And don't worry about anything there.
I know that you are all right where you're at when
 you are there.
I guess that's the way you're being taken when
 you're going to where
your relatives are at.
You've helped them (your relatives).
He's feeding them every kind of food.
You can leave us alone.

[1] *she* I.e., a Samish maiden.

Really, you're going to be happy when you're there
 down below."
That's all I'm going to say.
The story is over

[ENGLISH VERSION]

As I say, Samish was the biggest tribe, you know. It's
the biggest tribe they ever had that I was told. I was
told by my grandfather. It was the biggest tribe. They
had houses, houses all around, that's in Guemes.[1] And I
seen … I lived in Guemes when I was a kid. But I seen
the poles but I never seen the houses. And the Samish
used to be together all the time.

And they went to Deception Pass, that's where their
fishing grounds was. There was a big village there; they
stayed right there. They do a lot of fishing. Everything
is what they eat from the sea, everything they want.
They had everything there, mussels and all that, every-
thing of seafood they can eat. They have always had it
there.

One day this girl, daughter of this, one of the old
people, went down the beach. She would stay down on
the beach for … goes down every day. Every day she
goes down there. Pretty soon she went down the beach
and went into the water, washing. Somebody grabbed
her and she looked and it was a hand. So they dragged
her down, dragged her down the beach, down under
the water. When she got down there she felt the water
when she was going, but after she got down it was just
like the way we are now, you see. She looked back and
seen all her people, seen the village; everything was,
you know, it was just the same as we are today. So this
man told her—he was a nice looking man—"I been
watching you. I been watching you every day when
you come down. And I had kind of worked on you
so you can come down." Well them days people used
to work on somebody that they want to get ahold of.
They work on them. I wouldn't know how to say it,
but the Indians had their own way. They had their own
power. If they want anybody, well, they work on it so
they can come down. So they talked and he says, "Well
I want to marry you. So I'm going to go up and ask
your parents if you can, you can come down with me."

So they went up. They got up and people were kind
of worried about their daughter and can feel that cold
cold in the house before he walked in. He walked in
and they seen him, a good-looking man, and he talked
to the parents. He says, "I had your daughter down
below." He says, "I'm the king of the sea." He says, "I'm
the king of everything that you eat, everything, the
fish, everything that you got down below to eat." And
he says, "I look after it. I'm the king. And if you don't
let me have your daughter," he says, "your people are
going to starve. You wouldn't get nothing out of me.
There'll be no fish or anything that you eat." So they
talked it over and says, "Well yeah, I guess you can go."

So they took her daughter down, and she comes
up to see their parents. They done that for I wouldn't
know how long. It just took quite a while, in a way to
go down, up, up and see their parents. Pretty soon the
barnacles started to grow, the weeds started to grow on
her thigh. So the old man says, "You better not come
back." He says, "We're okay. You say you can see us, so
we're all fine here." He says that to her because she[2] felt
bad her daughter was turning to sea, like. That's why
they told her not to come back.

So Samish had lots to eat, everything they need;
everything they need they go get out, even after, after-
time people, Samish, used to go over and call her name,
"Qʷəl'ásəl'wət, we want something to eat." They č'í:təŋ
(thanked her) when I want something that's going to
come we need. Now the Samish people never starve.
They get all the food they want. They go out and get
it. Even if they're traveling through there's supposed to
have been real swift water, and they talk to her, kind
of talk to her that they're from the tribe. The water
settles down; they can go right up with their canoe.
No trouble at all because they believed her, she's down
there. They called her name. That's how people used to
go. That's all far as I can remember. Yeah.

[1] *Guemes* Small island near Orcas Island.

[2] *she* I.e., the maiden's mother.

Tracy Powell, The Maiden of Deception Pass (1983)

This story pole, carved by Samish carver Tracy Powell in 1983, is on Rosario Beach, in traditional Samish territory on the Washington coast.

HUL'Q'UMI'NUM HOUSE POST (PHOTOGRAPHED C. 1914)

Hul'q'umi'num traditional territory includes southeastern Vancouver Island and part of the opposite mainland coast, as well as the nearby Gulf Islands. This house post, photographed in Kw'amutsun on Vancouver Island, Canada, depicts a human head with minks, animals associated with a cleansing rite. The post is one of five that were initially attached to the home of the prominent shaman Puykwilum and later moved to the house of his son, Edward Paul. The posts were eventually acquired by the British Columbia Museum.

LUMMI HOUSE POST (MID-NINETEENTH CENTURY)

This house post belonged to Chief Chowitsoot of the Lummi people, whose traditional territory is on the northernmost part of the Washington coast. The image carved on the post, an illustration of the chief's wealth, depicts the sun carrying valuables.

BATTLE AT SEA

as told by Wilson George and edited by Vi Hilbert (taqʷšǝblu) and Thomas M. Hess, *Salish Myths and Legends* (2008)

The traditional home of the Suquamish people, Dxʷsǝq̓ʷǝb (Lushootseed: place of the clear salt water), is on the Kitsap Peninsula in northern Washington. A Suquamish man born on the peninsula, Wilson George was living on the Tulalip Reservation north of Seattle when, in 1950, he allowed the recording of the following account of a battle that occurred in the region in the first half of the nineteenth century. In the 1980s, Upper Skagit elder and scholar Vi Hilbert transcribed the recording in its original Lushootseed, and the white linguist Thomas M. Hess translated it into English.

These were my forebears, these people whom I'm going to tell you about. They were my ancestors. One time they were visited by a large party from ʔǝhiw̓

and elsewhere about the southern reaches of Puget Sound. They addressed my famous forefather.

"We ought to raid those people from up the coast! We should all combine our forces. Let us be the ones to avenge their attacks. If you, esteemed sir, are of like mind, your warriors and ours could go; we could retaliate."

Then the great Kitsap[1] replied, "Yes! I understand. I hear what you worthy leaders are saying. I hear your counsel about raiding those notorious people to the north. They believe they can lord it over all of us with impunity. Not so! We have our own view of things— our own! Whoever thinks to fight us should know that we too can fight.

"If your minds concur in this, then I too will go. I and my warriors will accompany your leaders. If they go, we go. We will go and we will fight."

So they went. They set out. First they went to the Klallam[2] who were invited to join this force. They crossed the Straits of Juan de Fuca. They came to Sooke.[3] The warriors there were also invited to join forces. They were told, "You ought to accompany us. We are going after those arrogant ones who have been raiding us."

Their destination was there—what is called Vancouver today. The Native People's name was different, but I can't call it by its real name because my memory has grown short. It is short. I don't remember things well. And I don't remember the name of that place belonging to those people. But they were the ones to be raided. They were the ones my forefathers were seeking for revenge.

Now it was discovered! It was their own land that was to be raided—not someone else's. But, they too were on their way to perpetrate yet another attack on the Klallam.

The two war parties met each other. The two large groups intent on harming each other met out on the Straits. Those from Vancouver spoke. "Oh, let us not

[1] *Kitsap* Prominent nineteenth-century Suquamish chief known for his skill in diplomacy and war.

[2] *Klallam* Coast Salish group with numerous settlements on the northern Washington coast and on Vancouver Island (now in Canada), northwest of Washington.

[3] *Sooke* Home of the T'Sou-ke people on the southern part of Vancouver Island.

fight. We are too far from our land and you people also are too far from your land. It is better not to do battle here. If you give us a young man, it would be good. Or if it be a woman, we could be the ones to provide a young man for a marriage."

Some of our party replied, "We do not want it that way. We have come for revenge. We will fight you people. If you are good enough to give battle, that is what we should do. We will fight right here on the water—out from shore, here. In our canoes we will fight."

Then the wise Kitsap addressed his people. "Beware! These, our adversaries, are from this region and they are strong at sea. We cannot prevail in a battle with them on the water. And yet, we are the mighty ones with reputations to uphold. We have come to fight. We cannot simply go home without so much as a shot. That would not be good for our name. Therefore, I think that we must engage them in battle for that is what we have come to do."

Those from Vancouver answered. They spoke, "So be it. The heart of the worthy Kitsap is good. We too are willing to join battle. If they fight us, we fight!" Then they fought. The battle began on the water. There they fought. And always the people of Ɂǝhiẃ were overwhelmed. Always they were outmaneuvered. Also their spears were too short. (Sqʷiǝx̌b is what we call them; "spear" is the whiteman's word for them.) And ours were too short. But those belonging to the warriors from Vancouver were longer. Our spears were inadequate but they used theirs to overturn our canoes. And our warriors drowned.

As for Kitsap, he fought with bow and arrow. Once his arrows were spent, he would go to where the currents eddied in the riptide, and he gathered up the arrows that were floating there. He would grab a lot of arrows drifting there to reuse. He could refill his quiver. Doing this, Kitsap got the better of his foe. The ones from the north could not prevail over him.

He would feign a retreat, and they would come after him. He would pretend to flee and they would give chase. That way he would draw one enemy canoe after another away from the protection of their fellows,

and he would pick off the man in the stern of each canoe. And these steersmen, shot by Kitsap's arrows, would roll out of their canoes. Without a man to steer, the canoes would swing broadside. Then Kitsap would pick them off one by one as they sat in their canoes. They would die. Kitsap was slaughtering them. His own people did not die. Those with him survived—all but one.

Only one was shot. He was shot right in the eye, the one in the stern of one of Kitsap's canoes. He grabbed that arrow and pulled it out. With it came his eye. It came out. His name was Tǝlibut. Tǝlibut was the name of the man whose eye came out. He was Kitsap's brother. He paddled a couple more strokes, then toppled into the water. But a man sitting near him caught him and pulled him back into the canoe. He didn't have an eye. He was dead. The seating shifted. A new man took the stern. Someone else took the place of Tǝlibut.

Meanwhile, Kitsap fought on. He was pursued. He would retreat; and they thought he was trying to leave, to retreat. As they would draw near, he would shoot the man in the stern, who would slump down dead and be pushed over the side.

As his arrows were used up, Kitsap would go to the spot where many floated in the tide. He gathered them up and used those enemy arrows to kill them.

Finally, someone among the enemy realized what was happening. He called out. "Kitsap is not really retreating! On the contrary, he wants to be chased. And as for me, I've had it. I'm finished. You should stop too. No one can kill Kitsap. His spirit power is too great. It is ferocious. It is not like that of ordinary men.

"You guys see how he is shot at? He just flips our arrows away. They do not enter his body. Or else it is his hair. It's only his hair. All our arrows just lodge in his hair. He pulls them out and reuses them on us. We're just giving him arrows to kill us with!

"Quit now, you guys. Kitsap has beaten us. Stop now, my people. This battle should end now!"

Then Kitsap stopped too and went home.

I'm finished. This ends my telling.

Civilizations in Contact

The Caribbean

Christopher Columbus never recanted his claim that the Caribbean islands he reached in his world-changing 1492 expedition were on the east coast of Asia. Like the early explorers and colonists who came after him, he interpreted the unfamiliar places and people he encountered in terms familiar to him. He had set out from Portugal believing Japan was less than 3,000 miles away (a quarter of the actual distance) and with expectations of what he would find there that had been shaped by his reading. From the writings of Marco Polo, who had visited Asia in the late thirteenth century, he expected to find the prosperous kingdom of a Great Khan, abundant with spices and gold. In *The Travels of Sir John Mandeville* (mid-fourteenth century), a widely read travel narrative that merged fact with fantastical fiction, he read of Southeast Asian islands populated by "folk of diverse shape and marvelously disfigured"—one-eyed giants, headless people with eyes in their shoulders, and people with enormous lips or ears. But the *Travels* also described places of great wealth and magnificence, including a Christian empire in India and an "isle, great and good and plenteous" where the people are unfamiliar with Christianity but are "full of all virtue, and they eschew all ... sins."

Echoes of the monsters and riches Columbus had read about appear in his accounts of his own travels, including in his personal journal and in his public letter describing his first voyage, both of which are represented in translation below. The letter was published in numerous editions in the 1490s, and its purpose was largely to maintain public support for Columbus's operations, which were financed with the help of the Spanish queen, Isabella I of Castile. Thus, it reflects the religious and economic goals that Columbus and the monarchy shared. Columbus was invested in the possibility of bringing Catholicism to new peoples, a missionary project he appears to have personally believed in and that provided what was seen as an honorable purpose for his voyages and settlement attempts. Profit was another key motive for his exploration and colonization—a motive that would sometimes complement and sometimes contradict the goal of religious conversion. Belief in the importance of conversion provided justification for Spanish control of the Indigenous people whose labor colonization relied upon, but it also made the exploitation of the Taíno controversial, since many Spanish people, including Isabella I, thought it immoral to enslave those they had converted to Catholicism.

With some exceptions, the Taíno and other Indigenous groups the European crew encountered on the first voyage received them peacefully, though Columbus frequently took Indigenous prisoners. When he departed the island now known as Haiti and the Dominican Republic, he left a fortified encampment occupied by a small number of crew members who were all killed before his return. When Columbus undertook his second voyage in 1494, he returned to the island with a much larger number of settlers, many of whom were prisoners released on the condition of their participation in the colonizing project. He established the colony of Hispaniola with the intention of extracting vast quantities of gold, but the island did not turn out to be the wellspring of gold and other expensive goods that he had expected. He attempted to increase the colony's profits by exploiting the Taíno people who lived there; clinging to his belief that the island concealed extraordinary gold deposits, he required every Taíno person over 14 to produce a nearly unachievable quota of gold and imposed gruesome punishment on those who refused or failed to comply. Colonists also enslaved Taíno and other Indigenous people to sell in Spain, and many settlers raped or undertook at best dubiously consensual relationships with Indigenous women. In a letter excerpted below, the Italian aristocrat Michele de Cuneo, a friend of Columbus who participated in the second voyage,

offers a chillingly matter-of-fact account of sexual violence and enslavement perpetrated by the colonists.

Conditions for the Taíno worsened in 1499, when Columbus returned to Hispaniola on a third voyage to find the settlers in rebellion against him, forcing him to implement a system whereby control over the land and people was parcelled out to individual settlers. This was soon codified into the encomienda system, according to which the Indigenous laborers were nominally free and said to receive the benefits of civilization and Christianity as recompense for their work. But in reality, the system was tantamount to slavery. Columbus himself—never as skilled a leader as he was a sailor—was soon ousted from power altogether and sent back to Spain to face criminal charges. He regained enough status to make one more voyage across the Atlantic, but he was forbidden to return to Hispaniola and instead focused his exploration on the Central American mainland. This expedition was plagued by shipwreck and mutiny, and Columbus spent more than a year stranded on Jamaica before he was finally rescued. His health compromised by the experience, he returned to Spain, where he died two years later. He had explored a remarkable amount of territory, encompassing much of the Caribbean and portions of the South and Central American coast, and he had amassed a great deal of personal wealth, but he continued to resent his loss of authority in Hispaniola.

Another participant in the early settlement of Hispaniola was Bartolomé de las Casas, a Spanish merchant's son who first came to the colony in 1502 and crossed the Atlantic many times in the following decades. Initially a participant in the conquest of the Caribbean and a plantation opera-tor under the encomienda system, and also educated as a priest, Las Casas came to believe that the violent and exploitative way the Spanish treated Indigenous people in the colonies was profoundly sinful. He gave up his own encomienda and took up a campaign against the oppression he had witnessed and participated in. Las Casas remained focused on this cause for the rest of his life, and in numerous writings and speeches he attempted to convince both colonists and Spanish authorities of the injustice of their behavior toward Indigenous populations. His views intensified as his career progressed: once a proponent of the enslavement of Africans (who were more resistant to European diseases) as a replacement for Indigenous enslavement, he came to oppose slavery altogether, and to advocate not just freedom from slavery but also limited self-governance for colonized Indigenous societies.

Las Casas had some impact on the policies of the Church and of the Spanish state. He joined the Dominican order and took up a leadership role in missionary efforts in the colonies, serving for a time as bishop in the Mexican colony of Chiapas. The pressure he placed on the government contributed to some attempts at political change, the most significant of which was the passage of the New Laws of the Indies (1542). These laws were intended to free most Indigenous people from enslavement and would have substantially reformed settler-Indigenous relations in other important ways, but the reaction to them in the colonies was so forceful that the laws were soon partially repealed. Seeking a wider audience for his appeals, Las Casas published the arguments and testi-mony he had given in support of the New Laws as *A Short Account of the Destruction of the Indies* in 1552. Presented as an account of Las Casas's personal experience, the book is also a persuasive document intended not only to evoke the extent of the atrocities committed by colonists but also to convince readers of the humanity of the Indigenous victims. For Spanish authorities, it was at this time an open question whether Indigenous people should be considered worthy of the rights accorded to other peoples. In 1550 Las Casas had, at the request of the monarchy, formally debated the theologian Juan Ginés de Sepúlveda, who argued that Indigenous people were naturally suited to enslavement, describing them as "*homunculi* in whom hardly a vestige of humanity remains."

As Las Casas hoped, *Destruction of the Indies* was widely read both in Spain and, in translation, in other European countries. It was both influential and controversial. Some considered Las Casas a heretic or a traitor—and, indeed, his forceful condemnation of Spanish actions in the colonies would long be used by Spain's Protestant enemies as fodder for the "Black legend," a distorted narrative that exaggerated the evils committed by the Spanish Empire while downplaying those of Protestant colonizing nations. But Las Casas also found an audience sympathetic to his aims, and

his work is considered an important contribution to the development of the philosophy of universal human rights.

The following section begins with excerpts from Columbus's diary of his first voyage to North America, a document that bears the mark both of Columbus and of Las Casas. While the full, original text of the diary has not survived, a substantial portion of the record is preserved in an abridged copy made by Las Casas, probably several decades after Columbus's death. Las Casas intersperses passages quoted directly from the diary with his own summaries of omitted portions, and scholars continue to debate the extent to which his objectivity as an editor might have been compromised by his own strong views. In the passages included below, direct quotations from Columbus appear in quotation marks.

⌘⌘⌘

from Christopher Columbus with Bartolomé de las Casas, *Journal of the First Voyage to America*[1]

Friday, 12th of October

The vessels were hove to,[2] waiting for daylight; and on Friday they arrived at a small island of the Lucayos,[3] called, in the language of the Indians, Guanahani.[4] Presently they saw naked people. The Admiral[5] went on shore in the armed boat, and Matin Alonso Pinzon, and Vicente Yañez, his brother, who was captain of the *Niña*. The Admiral took the royal standard,[6] and the captain went with two banners of the green cross, which the Admiral took in all the ships as a sign, with an F and a Y[7] and a crown over each letter, one on one side of the cross and the other on the other. Having landed, they saw trees very green, and much water, and fruits of diverse kinds. The Admiral called to the two captains, and to the others who leaped on shore, and to Rodrigo Escovedo, secretary of the whole fleet, and to Rodrigo Sanchez of Segovia, and said that they should bear faithful testimony that he, in presence of all, had taken, as he now took, possession of the said island for the King and for the Queen his Lords, making the declarations that are required, as is now largely set forth in the testimonies which were then made in writing.

Presently many inhabitants of the island assembled. What follows is in the actual words of the Admiral in his book of the first navigation and discovery of the Indies. "I," he says, "that we might form great friendship, for I knew that they were a people who could be more easily freed and converted to our holy faith by love than by force, gave to some of them red caps, and glass beads to put round their necks, and many other things of little value, which gave them great pleasure, and made them so much our friends that it was a marvel to see. They afterwards came to the ship's boats where we were, swimming and bringing us parrots, cotton threads in skeins, darts, and many other things; and we exchanged them for other things that we gave them, such as glass beads and small bells. In fine,[8] they took all, and gave what they had with good will. It appeared to me to be a race of people very poor in everything. They go as naked as when their mothers bore them, and so do the women, although I did not see more than one young girl. All I saw were youths, none more

[1] Translated by Clements R. Markham, 1893.

[2] *hove to* I.e., stopped.

[3] *Lucayos* Spanish name for the Taíno people who inhabited the islands.

[4] *Guanahani* The island renamed San Salvador by Columbus.

[5] *Admiral* Columbus, given the title of Admiral of the Ocean Sea in recognition of his 1492 exploration.

[6] *standard* Flag.

[7] *an F and a Y* Signifying King Ferdinand II of Aragon and Queen Isabella I of Castile, the Catholic monarchs of Spain. The flag described here, featuring a green cross and the monarchs' initials, represented Columbus's fleet.

[8] *In fine* In short.

than thirty years of age. They are very well made, with very handsome bodies, and very good countenances.[1] Their hair is short and coarse, almost like the hairs of a horse's tail. They wear the hairs brought down to the eyebrows, except a few locks behind, which they wear long and never cut. They paint themselves black, and they are the color of the Canarians,[2] neither black nor white. Some paint themselves white, others red, and others of what color they find. Some paint their faces, others the whole body, some only round the eyes, others only on the nose. They neither carry nor know anything of arms, for I showed them swords, and they took them by the blade and cut themselves through ignorance. They have no iron, their darts being wands without iron, some of them having a fish's tooth at the end, and others being pointed in various ways. They are all of fair stature and size, with good faces, and well made. I saw some with marks of wounds on their bodies, and I made signs to ask what it was, and they gave me to understand that people from other adjacent islands came with the intention of seizing them, and that they defended themselves. I believed, and still believe, that they come here from the mainland to take them prisoners. They should be good servants and intelligent, for I observed that they quickly took in what was said to them, and I believe that they would easily be made Christians, as it appeared to me that they had no religion. I, our Lord being pleased, will take hence, at the time of my departure, six natives for your Highness, that they may learn to speak. I saw no beast of any kind except parrots, on this island." The above is in the words of the Admiral.

Saturday, 13th of October
"... They brought skeins of cotton thread, parrots, darts, and other small things which it would be tedious to recount, and they give all in exchange for anything that may be given to them. I was attentive, and took trouble to ascertain if there was gold. I saw that some of them had a small piece fastened in a hole they have in the nose, and by signs I was able to make out that to the south, or going from the island to the south, there

was a king who had great cups full, and who possessed a great quantity. I tried to get them to go there, but afterwards I saw that they had no inclination. I resolved to wait until tomorrow in the afternoon and then to depart, shaping a course to the S.W., for, according to what many of them told me, there was land to the S., to the S.W., and N.W., and that the natives from the N.W. often came to attack them, and went on to the S.W. in search of gold and precious stones. ..."

Sunday, 14th of October
"At dawn I ordered the ship's boat and the boats of the caravels[3] to be got ready, and I went along the coast of the island and to the N.N.E., to see the other side, which was on the other side to the east, and also to see the villages. Presently I saw two or three, and the people all came to the shore, calling out and giving thanks to God. Some of them brought us water, others came with food, and when they saw that I did not want to land, they got into the sea, and came swimming to us. We understood that they asked us if we had come from heaven. One old man came into the boat, and others cried out, in loud voices, to all the men and women, to come and see the men who had come from heaven, and to bring them to eat and drink. Many came, including women, each bringing something, giving thanks to God, throwing themselves on the ground and shouting to us to come on shore. But I was afraid to land, seeing an extensive reef of rocks which surrounded the island, with deep water between it and the shore forming a port large enough for as many ships as there are in Christendom,[4] but with a very narrow entrance. It is true that within this reef there are some sunken rocks, but the sea has no more motion than the water in a well. In order to see all this I went this morning, that I might be able to give a full account to your Highnesses, and also where a fortress might be established. I saw a piece of land which appeared like an island, although it is not one, and on it there were six houses. It might be converted into an island in two days, though I do not see that it would be necessary, for these people are very simple as regards the use of arms, as your Highnesses will see from the

1 *countenances* Facial appearances.

2 *Canarians* Canary Islanders. In 1492, Castile was in the last few years of a decades-long campaign to conquer the Canary Islands, which the monarchy achieved complete control over in 1496.

3 *caravels* Portuguese sailing ships designed for exploration. The *Pinta* and *Niña* were this type of ship.

4 *Christendom* The entire Christian world.

seven that I caused to be taken, to bring home and learn our language and return; unless your Highnesses should order them all to be brought to Castile,[1] or to be kept as captives on the same island; for with fifty men they can all be subjugated and made to do what is required of them. Close to the above peninsula there are gardens of the most beautiful trees I ever saw, and with leaves as green as those of Castile in the month of April and May, and much water. I examined all that port, and afterwards I returned to the ship and made sail. I saw so many islands that I hardly knew how to determine to which I should go first. Those natives I had with me said, by signs, that there were so many that they could not be numbered, and they gave the names of more than a hundred. At last I looked out for the largest, and resolve to shape a course for it, and so I did. It will be distant five leagues[2] from this of *San Salvador*, and the others some more, some less. All are very flat, and all are inhabited. The natives make war on each other, although these are very simple-minded and handsomely-formed people."

Tuesday, 27th of November
… The Admiral also says: "How great the benefit that is to be derived from this country would be, I cannot say. It is certain that where there are such lands there must be an infinite number of things that would be profitable. But I did not remain long in one port, because I wished to see as much of the country as possible, in order to make a report upon it to your Highnesses; and besides, I do not know the language, and these people neither understand me nor any other in my company; while the Indians I have on board often misunderstand. Moreover, I have not been able to see much of the natives, because they often take to flight. But now, if our Lord pleases, I will see as much as possible, and will proceed by little and little, learning and comprehending; and I will make some of my followers learn the language. For I have perceived that there is only one language up to this point. After they understand the advantages, I shall labor to make all these people Christians. They will become so readily, because they have no religion nor idolatry, and your

Highnesses will send orders to build a city and fortress, and to convert the people. I assure your Highnesses that it does not appear to me that there can be a more fertile country nor a better climate under the sun, with abundant supplies of water. This is not like the rivers of Guinea, which are all pestilential. I thank our Lord that, up to this time, there has not been a person of my company who has had so much as a headache, or been in bed from illness, except an old man who has suffered from the stone[3] all his life, and he was well again in two days. I speak of all three vessels. If it will please God that your Highnesses should send learned men out here, they will see the truth of all I have said. I have related already how good a place Rio de Mares[4] would be for a town and fortress, and this is perfectly true; but it bears no comparison with this place, nor with the Mar de Nuestra Señora.[5] For here there must be a large population, and very valuable productions, which I hope to discover before I return to Castile. I say that if Christendom will find profit among these people, how much more will Spain, to whom the whole country should be subject. Your Highnesses ought not to consent that any stranger should trade here, or put his foot in the country, except Catholic Christians, for this was the beginning and end of the undertaking; namely, the increase and glory of the Christian religion, and that no one should come to these parts who was not a good Christian." …

Sunday, 16th of December
At midnight the Admiral made sail with the land-breeze to get clear of that gulf.[6] Passing along the coast of Española on a bowline,[7] for the wind had veered to the east, he met a canoe in the middle of the gulf, with a single Indian in it. The Admiral was surprised how he could have kept afloat with such a gale blowing. Both

[1] *Castile* Kingdom in Spain at the time of writing.

[2] *leagues* One league is approximately three miles, and three nautical miles at sea.

[3] *the stone* Kidney stones.

[4] *Rio de Mares* Name Columbus gave to the area surrounding a bay he encountered while exploring Cuba.

[5] *Mar de Nuestra Señora* Name Columbus gave to a region of numerous mountainous islands.

[6] *made sail … that gulf* Due to unfavorable winds, Columbus had struggled to depart from his anchorage near what is now Port-de-Paix, Haiti.

[7] *on a bowline* With the sails tied so as to move the boat close to the opposite direction of the wind.

the Indian and his canoe were taken on board, and he was given glass beads, bells, and brass trinkets, and taken in the ship, until she was off a village 17 miles from the former anchorage, where the Admiral came to again. The village appeared to have been lately built, for all the houses were new. The Indian then went on shore in his canoe, bringing the news that the Admiral and his companions were good people; although the intelligence had already been conveyed to the village[.] … Presently more than five hundred natives with their king came to the shore opposite the ships, which were anchored very close to the land. Presently one by one, then many by many, came to the ship without bringing anything with them, except that some had a few grains of very fine gold in their ears and noses, which they readily gave away. The Admiral ordered them all to be well treated; and he says: "for they are the best people in the world, and the gentlest; and above all I entertain the hope in our Lord that your Highnesses will make them all Christians, and that they will be all your subjects, for as yours I hold them." He also saw that they all treated the king with respect, who was on the seashore. The Admiral sent him a present, which he received in great state. He was a youth of about 21 years of age, and he had with him an aged tutor, and other councillors who advised and answered him, but he uttered very few words. One of the Indians who had come in the Admiral's ship spoke to him, telling him how the Christians had come from Heaven, and how they came in search of gold, and wished to find the island of Baneque.[1] He said that it was well, and that there was much gold in the said island. He explained to the alguazil[2] of the Admiral that the way they were going was the right way, and that in two days they would be there; adding, that if they wanted anything from the shore he would give it them with great pleasure. This king, and all the others, go naked as their mothers bore them, as do the women without any covering, and these were the most beautiful men and women that had yet been met with. They are fairly white, and if they were clothed and protected from the sun and air, they would be almost as fair as people in Spain. This land is cool, and the best that words

can describe. It is very high, yet the top of the highest mountain could be ploughed with bullocks;[3] and all is diversified with plains and valleys. In all Castile there is no land that can be compared with this for beauty and fertility. All this island, as well as the island of Tortuga, is cultivated like the plain of Cordova. They raise on these lands crops of yams, which are small branches, at the foot of which grow roots like carrots, which serve as bread. They powder and knead them, and make them into bread; then they plant the same branch in another part, which again sends out four or five of the same roots, which are very nutritious, with the taste of chestnuts. Here they have the largest the Admiral had seen in any part of the world, for he says that they have the same plant in Guinea. At this place they were as thick as a man's leg. All the people were stout and lusty, not thin, like the natives that had been seen before, and of a very pleasant manner, without religious belief. The trees were so luxuriant that the leaves left off being green, and were dark coloured with verdure. It was a wonderful thing to see those valleys, and rivers of sweet water, and the cultivated fields, and land fit for cattle, though they have none, for orchards, and for anything in the world that a man could seek for.

In the afternoon the king came on board the ship, where the Admiral received him in due form, and caused him to be told that the ships belonged to the Sovereigns of Castile, who were the greatest princes in the world. But neither the Indians who were on board, who acted as interpreters, nor the king, believed a word of it. They maintained that the Spaniards came from Heaven, and that the Sovereigns of Castile must be in Heaven, and not in this world. They placed Spanish food before the king to eat, and he ate a mouthful, and gave the rest to his councillors and tutor, and to the rest who came with him.

"Your Highnesses may believe that these lands are so good and fertile, especially these of the island of Española,[4] that there is no one who would know how to describe them, and no one who could believe if he had not seen them. And your Highnesses may believe that this island, and all the others, are as much yours as Castile. Here there is only wanting a settlement and

[1] *Baneque* Indigenous people had told the explorers that a great deal of gold could be found on this island.

[2] *alguazil* Member of a ship's crew responsible for policing.

[3] *bullocks* Castrated bulls.

[4] *Española* Hispaniola, now the location of Haiti and the Dominican Republic.

the order to the people to do what is required. For I, with the force I have under me, which is not large, could march over all these islands without opposition. I have seen only three sailors land, without wishing to do harm, and a multitude of Indians fled before them. They have no arms, and are without warlike instincts; they all go naked, and are so timid that a thousand would not stand before three of our men. So that they are good to be ordered about, to work and sow, and do all that may be necessary, and to build towns, and they should be taught to go about clothed and to adopt our customs."

—WRITTEN 1492–93

Christopher Columbus, *Letter of Columbus to Various Persons Describing the Results of His First Voyage and Written on the Return Journey*[1]

Since I know that you will be pleased at the great success with which the Lord has crowned my voyage, I write to inform you how in thirty-three days I crossed from the Canary Islands to the Indies, with the fleet which our most illustrious sovereigns gave me. I found very many islands with large populations and took possession of them all for their Highnesses; this I did by proclamation and unfurled the royal standard.[2] No opposition was offered.

I named the first island that I found "San Salvador," in honour of our Lord and Saviour who has granted me this miracle. The Indians call it "Guanahani." The second island I named "Santa Maria de Conception," the third "Fernandina," the fourth "Isabela" and the fifth "Juana"; thus I renamed them all.[3]

When I reached Cuba, I followed its north coast westwards, and found it so extensive that I thought this must be the mainland, the province of Cathay.[4] Since there were no towns or villages on the coast, but only

small groups of houses whose inhabitants fled as soon as we approached, I continued on my course, thinking that I should undoubtedly come to some great towns or cities. We continued for many leagues[5] but found no change, except that the coast was bearing me northwards. This I wished to avoid, since winter was approaching and my plan was to journey south. As the wind was carrying me on I decided not to wait for a change of weather but to turn back to a remarkable harbor which I had observed. From here I sent two men inland to discover whether there was a king or any great cities. They travelled for three days, finding only a large number of small villages and great numbers of people, but nothing more substantial. Therefore they returned.

I understood from some Indians whom I had captured elsewhere that this was an island, and so I followed its coast for 107 leagues to its eastward point. From there I saw another eighteen leagues eastwards which I then named "Hispaniola." I crossed to this island and followed its northern coast eastwards for 188 leagues continuously, as I had followed the coast of Cuba. All these islands are extremely fertile and this one is particularly so. It has many large harbors finer than any I know in Christian lands, and many large rivers. All this is marvelous. The land is high and has many ranges of hills, and mountains incomparably finer than Tenerife.[6] All are most beautiful and various in shape, and all are accessible. They are covered with tall trees of different kinds which seem to reach the sky. I have heard that they never lose their leaves, which I can well believe, for I saw them as green and lovely as they are in Spain in May; some were flowering, some bore fruit and others were at different stages according to their nature. It was November but everywhere I went the nightingale and many other birds were singing. There are palms of six or eight different kinds—a marvelous sight because of their great variety—and the other trees, fruit and plants are equally marvelous. There are splendid pine woods and broad fertile plains, and there is honey. There are many kinds of birds and

[1] Translated by J.M. Cohen, 1969.

[2] *standard* Flag.

[3] *The second … them all* These names reference Catholic saints, with the exception of islands named for King Ferdinand II of Aragon and Queen Isabella I of Castile, the Catholic monarchs of Spain, who supported Columbus's venture.

[4] *Cathay* China.

[5] *leagues* One league is approximately three miles, and three nautical miles at sea.

[6] *Tenerife* One of the Canary Islands, and the last to be conquered by Castile; its people surrendered to the Castilian monarchy in 1496.

varieties of fruit. In the interior are mines and a very large population.

Hispaniola is a wonder. The mountains and hills, the plains and meadow lands are both fertile and beautiful. They are most suitable for planting crops and for raising cattle of all kinds, and there are good sites for building towns and villages. The harbors are incredibly fine and there are many great rivers with broad channels and the majority contain gold. The trees, fruits and plants are very different from those of Cuba. In Hispaniola there are many spices and large mines of gold and other metals. …

The inhabitants of this island, and all the rest that I discovered or heard of, go naked, as their mothers bore them, men and women alike. A few of the women, however, cover a single place with a leaf of a plant or piece of cotton which they weave for the purpose. They have no iron or steel or arms and are not capable of using them, not because they are not strong and well built but because they are amazingly timid. All the weapons they have are canes cut at seeding time, at the end of which they fix a sharpened stick, but they have not the courage to make use of these, for very often when I have sent two or three men to a village to have conversation with them a great number of them have come out. But as soon as they saw my men all fled immediately, a father not even waiting for his son. And this is not because we have harmed any of them; on the contrary, wherever I have gone and been able to have conversation with them, I have given them some of the various things I had, a cloth and other articles, and received nothing in exchange. But they have still remained incurably timid. True, when they have been reassured and lost their fear, they are so ingenuous and so liberal with all their possessions that no one who has not seen them would believe it. If one asks for anything they have they never say no. On the contrary, they offer a share to anyone with demonstrations of heartfelt affection, and they are immediately content with any small thing, valuable or valueless, that is given them. I forbade the men to give them bits of broken crockery, fragments of glass or tags of laces, though if they could get them they fancied them the finest jewels in the world. One sailor was known to have received gold to the weight of two and a half castellanos[1] for the

tag of a breeches lace, and other received much more for things of even less value. For newly minted blancas[2] they would give everything they possessed, even two or three castellanos of gold or an arroba[3] or two of spun cotton. They even took bits of broken hoops from the wine barrels and, as simple as animals, gave what they had. This seemed to me to be wrong and I forbade it.

I gave them a thousand pretty things that I had brought, in order to gain their love and incline them to become Christians. I hoped to win them to the love and service of their Highnesses and of the whole Spanish nation and to persuade them to collect and give us of the things which they possessed in abundance and which we needed. They have no religion and are not idolaters; but all believe that power and goodness dwell in the sky and they are firmly convinced that I have come from the sky with these ships and people. In this belief they gave me a good reception everywhere, once they had overcome their fear; and this is not because they are stupid—far from it, they are men of great intelligence, for they navigate all those seas, and give a marvelously good account of everything—but because they have never before seen men clothed or ships like these.

As soon as I came to the Indies, at the first island I discovered I seized some natives, intending them to inquire and inform me about things in these parts. These men soon understood us, and we them, either by speech or signs, and they were very useful to us. I still have them with me, and despite all the conversation they have had with me they are still of the opinion that I come from the sky and have been the first to proclaim this wherever I have gone. The others have gone running from house to house and to the neighboring villages shouting: "Come, come and see the people from the sky," so, once they were reassured about us, all have come, men and women alike, and not one, old or young, has remained behind. All have brought us something to eat and drink which they have given with a great show of love. In all the islands they have very many canoes like oared fustas.[4]

[1] *castellanos* Castilian gold coins.

[2] *blancas* Castilian copper coins.

[3] *arroba* Unit measuring weight; the precise weight of an arroba varied by region, but was in the range of two to three dozen pounds.

[4] *fustas* Long, narrow ships with mast and sails, used by the Portuguese for expedition and cargo.

They are of various sizes, some as large as a fusta of eighteen benches. But they are not as broad, since they are hollowed out of a single tree. A fusta would not be able to keep up with them, however, for they are rowed at an incredible speed. In these they travel and transport their goods between the islands, which are innumerable. I have seen some of these canoes with eighty men in them, all rowing.

In all these islands I saw no great difference in the looks of the people, their customs or their language. On the other hand, all understand one another, which will be of singular assistance in the work of their conversion to our holy faith, on which I hope your Highnesses will decide, since they are very well disposed towards it.

I have already told of my voyage of 107 leagues in a straight line from west to east along the coast of Cuba, according to which I reckon that the island is larger than England and Scotland put together.

One of these provinces is called Avan and there the people are born with tails, and these provinces cannot have a length of less than fifty or sixty leagues, according to the information I received from those Indians whom I have with me and who know all the islands.

The other island, Hispaniola, is greater in circumference than the whole of Spain from Collioure to Fuenterabia[1] in the Basque province, since I travelled along one side for 188 great leagues in a straight line from west to east.

These islands are richer than I yet know or can say and I have taken possession of them in their Majesties' name and hold them all on their behalf and as completely at their disposition as the Kingdom of Castile. In the island of Hispaniola I have taken possession of a large town which is most conveniently situated for the goldfields and for communications with the mainland both here, and there in the territories of the Grand Khan,[2] with which there will be very profitable trade. I have named this town Villa de Navidad and have built a fort there. Its fortifications will by now be finished and I have left sufficient men to complete them. They have arms, artillery and provisions for more than a year, and a fusta; also a skilled shipwright who can build more.

I have established warm friendship with the king of that land, so much so, indeed, that he was proud to call me and treat me as a brother. But even should he change his attitude and attack the men of La Navidad, he and his people know nothing about arms and go naked, as I have already said; they are the most timorous people in the world. In fact, the men that I have left there would be enough to destroy the whole land, and the island holds no dangers for them so long as they maintain discipline.

In all these islands the men are seemingly content with one woman, but their chief or king is allowed more than twenty. The women appear to work more than the men and I have not been able to find out if they have private property. As far as I could see whatever a man had was shared among all the rest and this particularly applies to food.

I have not found the human monsters which many people expected. On the contrary, the whole population is very well made. They are not Negroes as in Guinea, and their hair is straight, for where they live the sun's rays do not strike too harshly, but they are strong nevertheless, despite the fact that Hispaniola is 20 to 21 degrees from the Equator.[3]

There are high mountains in these islands and it was very cold this winter but the natives are used to this and withstand the weather, thanks to their food, which they eat heavily seasoned with very hot spices. Not only have I found no monster but I have had no reports of any except the island called "Quaris," which is the second as you approach the Indies from the east, and which is inhabited by a people who are regarded in these islands as extremely fierce and who eat human flesh. They have many canoes in which they travel throughout the islands of the Indies, robbing and taking all they can. They are no more ill-shaped than any other natives of the Indies, though they are in the habit of wearing their hair long like women. They have

[1] *Collioure ... Fuenterabia* Collioure and Fuenterabia (now Hondarríbia) are today at opposite ends of the border between France and Spain; Collioure is on the east coast, and Fuenterabia is on the west coast.

[2] *Grand Khan* I.e., the Mongolian emperor. At the time of writing, Columbus persisted in his belief that he had reached Asia.

[3] *despite ... Equator* Reference to longstanding European beliefs that the equatorial region was too hot to allow for human flourishing. Some who held these beliefs thought the region was entirely uninhabitable; others thought it was populated by monstrous or weak and unhealthy races.

bows and arrows with the same canes as the others, tipped with splinters of wood, for the lack of iron which they do not possess. They behave most savagely to the other peoples but I take no more account of them than the rest. It is these men who have relations with the women of Matinino, where there are no men and which is the first island you come to on the way from Spain to the Indies. These women do not follow feminine occupations but use cane bows and arrows like those of the men and arm and protect themselves with plates of copper, of which they have much.

In another island, which I am told is larger than Hispaniola, the people have no hair. Here there is a vast quantity of gold, and from here and the other islands I bring Indians as evidence.

In conclusion, to speak only of the results of this very hasty voyage, their Highnesses can see that I will give them as much gold as they require, if they will render me some very slight assistance; also I will give them all the spices and cotton they want, and as for mastic,[1] which has so far been found only in Greece and the island of Chios and which the Genoese authorities have sold at their own price, I will bring back as large a cargo as their Highnesses may command. I will also bring them as much aloes as they ask and as many slaves, who will be taken from the idolaters. I believe also that I have found rhubarb and cinnamon and there will be countless other things in addition, which the people I have left there will discover. For I did not stay anywhere unless delayed by lack of wind except at the town of La Navidad, which I had to leave secure and well established. In fact I should have done much more if the ships had been reasonably serviceable, but this is enough.

Thus the eternal God, Our lord, grants to all those who walk in his way victory over apparent impossibilities, and this voyage was pre-eminently a victory of this kind. For although there was much talk and writing of these lands, all was conjectural, without ocular evidence. In fact, those who accepted the stories judged rather by hearsay than on any tangible information. So all Christendom will be delighted that our Redeemer has given victory to our most illustrious King and Queen and their renowned kingdoms, in this great

matter. They should hold great celebrations and render solemn thanks to the Holy Trinity with many solemn prayers, for the great triumph which they will have, by the conversion of so many peoples to our holy faith and for the temporal benefits which will follow, for not only Spain, but all Christendom will receive encouragement and profit.

This is a brief account of the facts.

Written in the caravel[2] off the Canary Islands.
15 February 1493

At your orders
The Admiral

After this was written, when I was already in Spanish waters, I was struck by such a strong south-south-west wind that I was compelled to lighten ship,[3] but today by a great miracle I made the port of Lisbon, from which I decided to write letters to their Highnesses. Throughout the Indies, I have always found weather like that of May; I went there in thirty-three days and returned in twenty-eight. I met with no storms except these which held me up for fourteen days, beating about in these seas. The sailors here say that there has never been so bad a winter nor so many ships lost.

Written on 4 March
—1493

from Michele de Cuneo, letter [Concerning Columbus's Second Voyage][4] (1495)

From [the] island of Guadalupe, which belongs to the Caribs,[5] we set sail on 10 November and on the 13th of the same month we came to another island of Caribs very beautiful and fertile, and we arrived at a very beautiful harbor. As soon as the Caribs saw us they ran away to the mountains like those of the other island and they emptied their houses, into which we went and took whatever pleased us. In these few days we found many islands where we did not go

[1] *mastic* Tree resin used to make varnish, as well as for other purposes.

[2] *caravel* Ship.

[3] *lighten ship* I.e., throw cargo and other heavy items into the water; a lighter ship can withstand stormy weather more easily.

[4] Translated by Samuel Eliot Morison, 1963.

[5] *Caribs* Kalinago people, neighbors and historical enemies of the Taíno people.

ashore. A few times we anchored, that is, for the night; and when we did not anchor we kept the ship hove-to,[1] and this in order not to make any headway and for fear of running afoul of the said islands, to which, because they were close one to the other the Lord Admiral gave the name of Eleven Thousand Virgins; and to the one previously mentioned, Santa Cruz.

One of those days while we were lying at anchor we saw coming from a cape a canoe, that is to say a boat, which is how they call it in their language, going along with oars so that it looked like a well-manned bergantino,[2] on which there were three or four Carib men with two Carib women and two Indian slaves, of whom (that is the way the Caribs treat their other neighbors in those other islands), they had recently cut the genital organ to the belly, so that they were still sore; and we having the flagship's boat ashore, when we saw that canoe coming, quickly jumped into the boat and gave chase to that canoe. While we were approaching her the Caribs began shooting at us with their bows in such manner that, had it not been for the shields, half of us would have been wounded. But I must tell you that to one of the seamen who had a shield in his hand came an arrow, which went through the shield and penetrated his chest three inches, so that he died in a few days. We captured that canoe with all the men, and one Carib was wounded by a spear in such a way that we thought he was dead, and cast him for dead into the sea, but instantly saw him swim. In so doing we caught him and with the grapple hauled him over the bulwarks of the ship where we cut his head with an axe. The other Caribs, together with those slaves, we later sent to Spain. While I was in the boat I captured a very beautiful Carib woman, whom the said Lord Admiral gave to me, and with whom, having taken her into my cabin, she being naked according to their custom, I conceived desire to take pleasure. I wanted to put my desire into execution but she did not want it and treated me with her finger nails in such a manner that I wished I had never begun. But seeing that, to tell you the end of it all, I took a rope and thrashed her well, for which she raised such unheard of screams that you would not have believed your ears. Finally we came to an agreement in such manner that

I can tell you that she seemed to have been brought up in a school of harlots. To that cape of that island the Admiral gave the name Cape of the Arrow because of the one who had died of the arrow. …

… Sailing to Hispaniola I was the first to sight land. Therefore the Lord Admiral in that very place ordered us ashore at a cape where there was an excellent harbor and he called it el cavo de San Michele Saonese,[3] out of respect for me, and this he wrote down in his book. Sailing always along the coast we found mountainous shores and good harbors and several times we landed, and everywhere we found innumerable people of the usual sort. And thus ranging the coast toward our settlement we found not too far from a cape a very beautiful island which also I was the first to sight, the which was some 25 leagues in circumference, and again out of love for me, the Lord Admiral called it *La Bella Saonese*. He gave it to me as a present; and I took possession of it according to the appropriate modes and forms, as the Lord Admiral was doing of the other islands in the name of His Majesty the King, that is by virtue of a document signed by a notary public. On the above mentioned island I uprooted grass and cut trees and planted the cross and also the gallows, and in the name of God I baptized it with the name *La Bella Saonese*. And well it is called beautiful for in it there are 37 villages with at least 30,000 souls; and all this too the Lord Admiral noted down in his book. …

When our caravels[4] in which I wished to go home had to leave for Spain, we gathered together in our settlement 1600 people male and female of those Indians, of whom, among the best males and females, we embarked on our caravels on 17 February 1495, 550 souls. Of the rest who were left the announcement went around that whoever wanted them could take as many as he pleased; and this was done. And when everybody had been supplied there were some 400 of them left to whom permission was granted to go wherever they wanted. Among them there were many women who had infants at the breast. They, in order to better escape us, since they were afraid we would turn

[1] *hove-to* With sails positioned to inhibit movement.

[2] *bergantino* Sailing ship.

[3] *el cavo … Saonese* The cape of St. Michael of Savona. Cuneo was from Savona, in northern Italy.

[4] *caravels* Ships.

to catch them again, left their infants anywhere on the ground and started to flee like desperate people; and some fled so far that they were removed from our settlement of Isabela 7 or 8 days beyond mountains and across huge rivers; wherefore from now on scarcely any will be had. Among these people who were taken was one of their kings with two chiefs, who it was decided should be killed with arrows on the following day, so they were tied up; but in the night they knew so well how to gnaw one another's ropes with their teeth, that they were freed from their bonds and escaped. ...

Meanwhile I departed for Spain with those caravels. Sailing with terrible and contrary winds we had to turn back thrice so that we spent a month among those islands. Wherefore, seeing the few provisions that we had, we turned north and proceeded in that direction for about 600 Roman miles;[1] and when it pleased God the winds turned favorable to our sails and we passed from the island of Boriquen to the island of Madeira in 23 days. But when we reached the waters around Spain about 200 of those Indians died, I believe because of the unaccustomed air, colder than theirs. We cast them into the sea. The first land we saw was Cape Spartel and very soon after we reached Cadiz, in which place we disembarked all the slaves, half of whom were sick. For your information they are not working people and they very much fear cold, nor have they long life. ...
—1495

from Bartolomé de las Casas, *A Short Account of the Destruction of the Indies*[2]

[PREFACE]

The Americas were discovered in 1492, and the first Christian settlements established by the Spanish the following year. It is accordingly forty-nine years now since Spaniards began arriving in numbers in this part of the world. They first settled the large and fertile island of Hispaniola, which boasts six hundred leagues[3]

of coastline and is surrounded by a great many other large islands, all of them, as I saw for myself, with as high a native population as anywhere on earth. Of the coast of the mainland, which, at its nearest point, is a little over two hundred and fifty leagues from Hispaniola, more than ten thousand leagues had been explored by 1541, and more are being discovered every day. This coastline, too, was swarming with people and it would seem, if we are to judge by those areas so far explored, that the Almighty selected this part of the world as home to the greater part of the human race.

God made all the peoples of this area, many and varied as they are, as open and as innocent as can be imagined. The simplest people in the world—unassuming, long-suffering, unassertive, and submissive—they are without malice or guile, and are utterly faithful and obedient both to their own native lords and to the Spaniards in whose service they now find themselves. Never quarrelsome or belligerent or boisterous, they harbour no grudges and do not seek to settle old scores; indeed, the notions of revenge, rancor, and hatred are quite foreign to them. At the same time, they are among the least robust of human beings: their delicate constitutions make them unable to withstand hard work or suffering and render them liable to succumb to almost any illness, no matter how mild. Even the common people are no tougher than princes or than other Europeans born with a silver spoon in their mouths and who spend their lives shielded from the rigors of the outside world. They are also among the poorest people on the face of the earth; they own next to nothing and have no urge to acquire material possessions. As a result they are neither ambitious nor greedy, and are totally uninterested in worldly power. Their diet is every bit as poor and as monotonous, in quantity and in kind, as that enjoyed by the Desert Fathers.[4] Most of them go naked, save for a loincloth to cover their modesty; at best they may wrap themselves in a piece of cotton material a yard or two square. Most sleep on matting, although a few possess a kind of hanging net, known in the language of Hispaniola as a hammock. They are innocent and pure in mind and have a lively intelligence, all of which makes them particularly receptive to learning and understanding the truths of our Catholic faith and to being instructed

[1] *Roman miles* Unit of distance slightly shorter than a modern mile.

[2] Translated by Nigel Griffin, 1992.

[3] *leagues* One league is approximately three miles.

[4] *Desert Fathers* Early Christian hermits who lived very austerely.

in virtue; indeed, God has invested them with fewer impediments in this regard than any other people on earth. Once they begin to learn of the Christian faith they become so keen to know more, to receive the Sacraments, and to worship God, that the missionaries who instruct them do truly have to be men of exceptional patience and forbearance; and over the years I have time and again met Spanish laymen who have been so struck by the natural goodness that shines through these people that they frequently can be heard to exclaim: "These would be the most blessed people on earth if only they were given the chance to convert to Christianity."

It was upon these gentle lambs, imbued by the Creator with all the qualities we have mentioned, that from the very day they clapped eyes on them the Spanish fell like ravening wolves upon the fold, or like tigers and savage lions who have not eaten meat for days. The pattern established at the outset has remained unchanged to this day, and the Spaniards still do nothing save tear the natives to shreds, murder them and inflict upon them untold misery, suffering and distress, tormenting, harrying and persecuting them mercilessly. We shall in due course describe some of the many ingenious methods of torture they have invented and refined for this purpose, but one can get some idea of the effectiveness of their methods from the figures alone. When the Spanish first journeyed there, the indigenous population of the island of Hispaniola stood at some three million; today only two hundred survive. The island of Cuba, which extends for a distance almost as great as that separating Valladolid from Rome,[1] is now to all intents and purposes uninhabited; and two other large, beautiful and fertile islands, Puerto Rico and Jamaica, have been similarly devastated. Not a living soul remains today on any of the islands of the Bahamas, which lie to the north of Hispaniola and Cuba, even though every single one of the sixty or so islands in the group, as well as those known as the Isles of Giants and others in the area, both large and small, is more fertile and more beautiful than the Royal Gardens in Seville and the climate is as healthy as anywhere on earth. The native population, which once numbered some five hundred thousand, was wiped out by forcible expatriation to the island of Hispaniola, a policy adopted by the Spaniards in an endeavor to make up losses among the indigenous population of that island. One God-fearing individual was moved to mount an expedition to seek out those who had escaped the Spanish trawl and were still living in the Bahamas and to save their souls by converting them to Christianity, but, by the end of a search lasting three whole years, they had found only the eleven survivors I saw with my own eyes. A further thirty or so islands in the region of Puerto Rico are also now uninhabited and left to go to rack and ruin as a direct result of the same practices. All these islands, which together must run to over two thousand leagues, are now abandoned and desolate.

On the mainland, we know for sure that our fellow-countrymen have, through their cruelty and wickedness, depopulated and laid waste an area which once boasted more than ten kingdoms, each of them larger in area than the whole of the Iberian Peninsula. The whole region, once teeming with human beings, is now deserted over a distance of more than two thousand leagues: a distance, that is, greater than the journey from Seville to Jerusalem and back again.

At a conservative estimate, the despotic and diabolical behaviour of the Christians has, over the last forty years, led to the unjust and totally unwarranted deaths of more than twelve million souls, women and children among them, and there are grounds for believing my own estimate of more than fifteen million to be nearer the mark.

There are two main ways in which those who have traveled to this part of the world pretending to be Christians have uprooted these pitiful peoples and wiped them from the face of the earth. First, they have waged war on them: unjust, cruel, bloody and tyrannical war. Second, they have murdered anyone and everyone who has shown the slightest sign of resistance, or even of wishing to escape the torment to which they have subjected him. This latter policy has been instrumental in suppressing the native leaders, and, indeed, given that the Spaniards normally spare only women and children, it has led to the annihilation of all adult males, whom they habitually subject to the harshest and most iniquitous and brutal slavery that man has ever devised for his fellow-men, treating them, in fact, worse than animals. All the many and infinitely varied

[1] *Valladolid from Rome* Valladolid, in western Spain, is about a thousand miles from Rome; Cuba is close to 800 miles long.

ways that have been devised for oppressing these peoples can be seen to flow from one or other of these two diabolical and tyrannical policies.

The reason the Christians have murdered on such a vast scale and killed anyone and everyone in their way is purely and simply greed. They have set out to line their pockets with gold and to amass private fortunes as quickly as possible so that they can then assume a status quite at odds with that into which they were born. Their insatiable greed and overweening[1] ambition know no bounds; the land is fertile and rich, the inhabitants simple, forbearing and submissive. The Spaniards have shown not the slightest consideration for these people, treating them (and I speak from first-hand experience, having been there from the outset) not as brute animals—indeed, I would to God they had done and had shown them the consideration they afford their animals—so much as piles of dung in the middle of the road. They have had as little concern for their souls as for their bodies, all the millions that have perished having gone to their deaths with no knowledge of God and without the benefit of the Sacraments. One fact in all this is widely known and beyond dispute, for even the tyrannical murderers themselves acknowledge the truth of it: the indigenous peoples never did the Europeans any harm whatever; on the contrary, they believed them to have descended from the heavens, at least until they or their fellow-citizens had tasted, at the hands of these oppressors, a diet of robbery, murder, violence, and all other manner of trials and tribulations.

HISPANIOLA

As we have said, the island of Hispaniola was the first to witness the arrival of the Europeans and the first to suffer the wholesale slaughter of its people and the devastation and depopulation of the land. It all began with the Europeans taking native women and children both as servants and to satisfy their own base appetites; then, not content with what the local people offered them of their own free will (and all offered as much as they could spare), they started taking for themselves the food the natives contrived to produce by the sweat of their brows, which was in all honesty little enough. Since

what a European will consume in a single day normally supports three native households of ten persons each for a whole month, and since the newcomers began to subject the locals to other vexations, assaults, and iniquities, the people began to realize that these men could not, in truth, have descended from the heavens. Some of them started to conceal what food they had, others decided to send their women and children into hiding, and yet others took to the hills to get away from the brutal and ruthless cruelty that was being inflicted on them. The Christians punched them, boxed their ears and flogged them in order to track down the local leaders, and the whole shameful process came to a head when one of the European commanders raped the wife of the paramount chief of the entire island. It was then that the locals began to think up ways of driving the Europeans out of their lands and to take up arms against them. Their weapons, however, were flimsy and ineffective both in attack and in defence (and, indeed, war in the Americas is no more deadly than our jousting, or than many European children's games) and, with their horses and swords and lances, the Spaniards easily fended them off, killing them and committing all kinds of atrocities against them.

They forced their way into native settlements, slaughtering everyone they found there, including small children, old men, pregnant women, and even women who had just given birth. They hacked them to pieces, slicing open their bellies with their swords as though they were so many sheep herded into a pen. They even laid wagers on whether they could manage to slice a man in two at a stroke, or cut an individual's head from his body, or disembowel him with a single blow of their axes. They grabbed suckling infants by the feet and, ripping them from their mothers' breasts, dashed them headlong against the rocks. Others, laughing and joking all the while, threw them over their shoulders into a river, shouting: "Wriggle, you little perisher." They slaughtered anyone and everyone in their path, on occasion running through a mother and her baby with a single thrust of their swords. They spared no one, erecting especially wide gibbets[2] on which they could string their victims up with their feet just off the ground and then burn them alive thirteen at a time, in honour of our Saviour and the twelve

[1] *overweening* Overly proud.

[2] *gibbets* I.e., wooden frames upon which bodies could be hung.

Apostles, or tie dry straw to their bodies and set fire to it. Some they chose to keep alive and simply cut their wrists, leaving their hands dangling, saying to them: "Take this letter"—meaning that their sorry condition would act as a warning to those hiding in the hills. The way they normally dealt with the native leaders and nobles was to tie them to a kind of griddle consisting of sticks resting on pitchforks driven into the ground and then grill them over a slow fire, with the result that they howled in agony and despair as they died a lingering death.

It once happened that I myself witnessed their grilling of four or five local leaders in this fashion (and I believe they had set up two or three other pairs of grills alongside so that they might process other victims at the same time) when the poor creatures' howls came between the Spanish commander and his sleep. He gave orders that the prisoners were to be throttled, but the man in charge of the execution detail, who was more bloodthirsty than the average common hangman (I know his identity and even met some relatives of his in Seville), was loath to cut short his private entertainment by throttling them and so he personally went round ramming wooden bungs[1] into their mouths to stop them making such a racket and deliberately stoked the fire so that they would take just as long to die as he himself chose. I saw all these things for myself and many others besides. And, since all those who could do so took to the hills and mountains in order to escape the clutches of these merciless and inhuman butchers, these mortal enemies of humankind trained hunting dogs to track them down—wild dogs who would savage a native to death as soon as look at him, tearing him to shreds and devouring his flesh as though he were a pig. These dogs wrought havoc among the natives and were responsible for much carnage. And when, as happened on the odd occasion, the locals did kill a European, as, given the enormity of the crimes committed against them, they were in all justice fully entitled to, the Spanish came to an unofficial agreement among themselves that for every European killed one hundred natives would be executed.

The Kingdoms of Hispaniola

… Indeed, they invented so many new methods of murder that it would be quite impossible to set them all down on paper and, however hard one tried to chronicle them, one could probably never list a thousandth part of what actually took place. All I can say is that I know it to be an incontrovertible fact and do here so swear before Almighty God, that the local peoples never gave the Spanish any cause whatever for the injury and injustice that was done to them in these campaigns. On the contrary, they behaved as honorably as might the inmates of a well-run monastery, and for this they were robbed and massacred, and even those who escaped death on this occasion found themselves condemned to a lifetime of captivity and slavery. I would go further. It is my firm belief that not a single native of the island committed a capital offence, as defined in law, against the Spanish while all this time the natives themselves were being savaged and murdered. Despite the enormous provocation, very few of the natives, I hazard, were guilty of even those sins which do not lie within the ambit[2] of human law but are properly the province of God, such as hatred and anger, or the thirst for revenge against those who committed such enormities upon them. It is my own experience of these peoples, gained over many years, that they are no more given to impetuous actions or to harboring thoughts of retribution than are boys of ten or twelve years of age. I know beyond any shadow of a doubt that they had, from the very beginning, every right to wage war on the Europeans, while the Europeans never had just cause for waging war on the local peoples. The actions of the Europeans, throughout the New World, were without exception wicked and unjust: worse, in fact, than the blackest kind of tyranny.

After the fighting was over and all the men had been killed, the surviving natives—usually, that is, the young boys, the women, and the children—were shared out between the victors. One got thirty, another forty, a third as many as a hundred or even twice that number; everything depended on how far one was in the good books of the despot who went by the title of governor. The pretext under which the victims were parceled out in this way was that their new masters would then be

[1] *bungs* Plugs.

[2] *ambit* Scope.

in a position to teach them the truths of the Christian faith; and thus it came about that host of cruel, grasping and wicked men, almost all of them pig-ignorant, were put in charge of these poor souls. And they discharged this duty by sending the men down the mines, where working conditions were appalling, to dig for gold, and putting the women to labor in the fields and on their master's estates, to till the soil and raise the crops, properly a task only for the toughest and strongest of men. Both women and men were given only wild grasses to eat and other unnutritious foodstuffs. The mothers of young children promptly saw their milk dry up and their babies die; and, with the women and the men separated and never seeing each other, no new children were born. The men died down the mines from overwork and starvation, and the same was true of the women who perished out on the estates. The islanders, previously so numerous, began to die out as would any nation subjected to such appalling treatment. For example, they were made to carry burdens of three and four arrobas[1] for distances of up to a hundred or even two hundred leagues, and were forced to carry their Christian masters in hammocks, which are like nets slung from the shoulders of the bearers. In short, they were treated as beasts of burden and developed huge sores on their shoulders and backs as happens with animals made to carry excessive loads. And this is not to mention the floggings, beatings, thrashings, punches, curses and countless other vexations and cruelties to which they were routinely subjected and to which no chronicle could ever do justice nor any reader respond save with horror and disbelief.

It is of note that all these island territories began to go to the dogs once news arrived of the death of our most gracious Queen Isabella, who departed this life in 1504. Up to then, only a small number of provinces had been destroyed through unjust military action, not the whole area, and news of even this partial destruction had by and large been kept from the Queen, because, she—may her soul rest in peace—took a close personal interest in the physical and spiritual welfare of the native peoples, as those of us who lived through those years and saw examples of it with our own eyes can attest. There is one other general rule in all this, and it is that, wherever the Spaniards set foot, right throughout the Americas, they subjected the native inhabitants to the cruelties of which we have spoken, killing these poor and innocent people, tyrannizing them, and oppressing them in the most abominable fashion. The longer they spent in the region the more ingenious were the torments, each crueller than the last, that they inflicted on their victims, as God finally abandoned them and left them to plummet headlong into a life of full-time crime and wickedness.

—1552

Mexico

In 1519, the Aztec[2] city of Tenochtitlan was the center of an ambitious and complex political network extending coast to coast in central Mexico and as far south as present-day Guatemala, encompassing millions of people and a variety of languages and cultures. The splendor and sophistication of Tenochtitlan were marvelous to the small contingent of Spanish troops, led by the conquistador Hernán Cortés, who visited the city that year—and who, less than two years later, would be responsible for its destruction. The massacre of the city's population was a key turning point in the establishment of New Spain, placing Spain on a trajectory to colonize large swaths of the western hemisphere. Western histories of this important moment in the Spanish conquest have often treated the fall of Tenochtitlan as a foregone conclusion resulting from European technological superiority, but the reality was quite different, as both Spanish and Nahua writings suggest.

[1] *three and four arrobas* Around 44 to 60 kilograms.

[2] The Nahuatl-speaking people who dominated what Western historians later named the Aztec Empire called themselves Mexica. Because the Aztec political system also incorporated numerous other cultures, this anthology uses the familiar "Aztec" in reference to the political system and Mexica in reference to the Mexica people.

Cortés's journey to Mexico had inauspicious beginnings. A minor nobleman's son without prospects in Spain, Cortés traveled as a young man to the Caribbean, where he participated in the conquest of Cuba. Cortés and the governor of Cuba, Diego Velázquez de Cuéllar, had a fraught relationship, and Velázquez chose Cortés to lead an expedition to Mexico but then thought better of his decision. Cortés, learning that Velázquez had changed his mind, left anyway—departing illegally and with insufficient provisions—before the governor could stop him. Upon his arrival in Mexico, he fought and negotiated his way inland toward Tenochtitlan, conquering some communities and forming alliances with others. Essential to his diplomatic efforts was Malintzin, also known as La Malinche, an enslaved woman who was given to Cortés early in his venture by the Mayan cacique (lord) of Pontonchán (near where Cortés landed on the Mexican coast). Malintzin, able to speak Nahuatl in the style of an Aztec noble, became an interpreter and advisor for Cortés, who benefited tremendously from her rhetorical skill and her insight into Mexico's political complexities. Through a combination of force and diplomacy, the Spanish obtained numerous allies among the peoples who paid the Aztecs tribute, some more willingly than others; most importantly, they formed an alliance with the people of Tlaxcala, the Aztecs' most powerful longstanding enemies.

Initially, interactions between the Spanish and the Mexica in Tenochtitlan were ostensibly peaceful: the Spanish were invited to enter the Aztec capital and, for half a year, they unofficially ruled through their manipulation of its Great Speaker, Moctezuma II. (Moctezuma's motivations—and the extent to which he may have been physically coerced—remain unclear; Western accounts often suggest that he thought the Spanish were gods, but this is highly unlikely.) Relations became openly hostile when, while Cortés was out of the city, his troops massacred thousands of upper-class Aztecs during a major religious festival. Cortés returned in time to experience the Aztec response—known in Spanish histories as the Noche Triste (Night of Sorrows)—as the Spanish were driven out of Tenochtitlan, hundreds of them killed as they fled down the causeways that connected the island city to the mainland. But here, as in other battles, the Spanish benefited tremendously from a difference between Spanish and Mexica ideologies of war. While the Spanish attempted to kill as many of their enemies as possible in order to subjugate them, the Mexica soldiers sought to capture their enemies alive for ritual sacrifice. The focus on capture—much more difficult than killing an opponent outright—allowed for the survival of many Spanish troops, even when they were seriously outnumbered, and Cortés himself was wounded in capture attempts but never killed. Meanwhile, strategies utterly reprehensible to the Aztecs, such as surprise attacks on civilians and the use of sieges to weaken an opponent, raised the body count dramatically in favor of Spanish forces.

After the Noche Triste, the Spanish regrouped in Tlaxcala. Meanwhile, smallpox ravaged the Indigenous populations of Mexico, a catastrophe that disproportionately impacted Tenochtitlan. Cortés returned to the city and set up a siege that lasted almost three months, deploying disease and famine against its occupants, and hoping to obtain a surrender. But the Spanish had proven themselves so unpredictably violent and, by Mexica standards, dishonorable, that the people of the city resisted at every opportunity. Unwilling to back down, Cortés continued to batter the city and its people, writing regretfully that "We could not but be saddened by their determination to die." Finally, he ordered an attack in which his army—a few hundred Spanish soldiers and many thousands of predominantly Tlaxcalan allies—descended on the starving, largely unarmed survivors of the siege and killed, by Cortés's estimation, forty thousand in a single day.

The first excerpt below, a description of Tenochtitlan, is drawn from Cortés's Second Letter to the Spanish Crown, part of a series of four or five letters he wrote describing the conquest of Mexico (it is not clear whether he actually authored a lost "First Letter," as he claims at the beginning of the second). A conquistador's relación (or relation) was, conventionally, an official report to the government that plainly outlined the author's activities, and Cortés was unusual in making his relación in an extended, narrative form intended to appeal to a broad audience—though he wrote it in a direct style quite unlike the ornate, erudite mode common to Spanish literature during the period. The contents of the relación should not be taken as straightforwardly factual, as the primary purpose of the letters was to justify his actions to the monarchy and to the public. At the time Cortés wrote

the Second Letter, in the fall of 1520, his troops had been expelled from Tenochtitlan, and he was far from succeeding in his attempted conquest; he was also still acting without legal authority and had recently thwarted an attempt by the Cuban governor to have him arrested. Cortés's expressions of wonder at Tenochtitlan may well be genuine, as other Spanish accounts suggest a similar degree of astonishment at Aztec civilization, but his report is also very likely embellished out of a desire to demonstrate his value to the monarchy as the Aztecs' prospective conqueror. Partly because Cortés's relaciónes were so successful in enhancing his own reputation and publicly justifying his disregard of government directives, the monarchy banned publication of the letters in the late 1520s as part of a larger campaign to control the narrative of colonization through censorship.

In the selections below, Cortés's description of Tenochtitlan is followed by a description of key events of the conquest from the perspective of some of the conquered. The account, sometimes referred to as the *Annals of Tlatelolco*, is an anonymous text written in alphabetic Nahuatl. Its authors were probably noble inhabitants of Tlatelolco, a city that occupied the same island as Tenochtitlan and was closely connected to it, though Tlatelolcas had a cultural identity separate from the people of Tenochtitlan. The account may have been recorded as early as 1528—a testament to the speed with which the region's Nahua scholars, already literate in their own writing system, acquired alphabetic literacy—though some portions may have been composed orally even closer to the time of the city's fall. While the manuscript laments tremendous destruction, death, and loss, its very existence is also a testament to the continuation of Nahua culture despite the Spanish conquest. In particular, the famous lament known as "Broken Spears," included in the text, exemplifies a pre-conquest poetic tradition in which, as an alternative to achievement as warriors, individuals could secure fame by capturing historic events and important deeds in eloquent verse. Though the Spanish secured the Aztec capital in 1521, Nahua culture remained dominant in Mexico for some time, and many Indigenous communities continued to resist colonization. Despite centuries of efforts on the part of Spanish colonizers to eliminate classical Nahuatl, more than a million people in Mexico speak the language's modern descendants.

from Hernán Cortés, Second Letter to the Spanish Crown[1]

[T]he] great city of Temixtitan[2] is built on ... [the salt lake,[3] and no matter by what road you travel there are two leagues[4] from the main body of the city to the mainland. There are four artificial causeways leading to it, and each is as wide as two cavalry lances. The city itself is as big as Seville or Córdoba. The main streets are very wide and very straight; some of these are on the land, but the rest and all the smaller ones are half on land, half canals where they paddle their canoes. All the streets have openings in places so that the water may pass from one canal to another.

Over all these openings, and some of them are very wide, there are bridges made of long and wide beams joined together very firmly and so well made that on some of them ten horsemen may ride abreast.

Seeing that if the inhabitants of this city wished to betray us they were very well equipped for it by the design of the city, for once the bridges had been removed they could starve us to death without our being able to reach the mainland, as soon as I entered the city I made great haste to build four brigantines,[5] and completed them in a very short time. They were such as could carry three hundred men to the land and transport the horses whenever we might need them.

This city has many squares where trading is done and markets are held continuously. There is also one square twice as big as that of Salamanca, with arcades all around, where more than sixty thousand people

[1] Translated by Anthony Pagden, 1971.

[2] *Temixtitan* Aztec capital city Tenochtitlan.

[3] *salt lake* Lake Texcoco.

[4] *leagues* One league is approximately three miles.

[5] *brigantines* Sailing ships.

come each day to buy and sell, and where every kind of merchandise produced in these lands is found; provisions as well as ornaments of gold and silver, lead, brass, copper, tin, stones, shells, bones, and feathers. They also sell lime,[1] hewn and unhewn stone, adobe bricks, tiles, and cut and uncut woods of various kinds. There is a street where they sell game and birds of every species found in this land: chickens, partridges and quails, wild ducks, fly-catchers, widgeons,[2] turtledoves, pigeons, cane birds, parrots, eagles and eagle owls, falcons, sparrow hawks and kestrels, and they sell the skins of some of these birds of prey with their feathers, heads and claws. They sell rabbits and hares, and stags and small gelded dogs which they breed for eating.

There are streets of herbalists where all the medicinal herbs and roots found in the land are sold. There are shops like apothecaries', where they sell ready-made medicines as well as liquid ointments and plasters. There are shops like barbers' where they have their hair washed and shaved, and shops where they sell food and drink. There are also men like porters to carry loads. There is much firewood and charcoal, earthenware braziers and mats of various kinds like mattresses for beds, and other, finer ones, for seats and for covering rooms and hallways. There is every sort of vegetable, especially onions, leeks, garlic, common cress and watercress, borage, sorrel, teasels[3] and artichokes; and there are many sorts of fruit, among which are cherries and plums like those in Spain.

They sell honey, wax, and a syrup made from maize canes, which is as sweet and syrupy as that made from the sugar cane. They also make syrup from a plant which in the islands is called maguey,[4] which is much better than most syrups, and from this plant they also make sugar and wine, which they likewise sell. There are many sorts of spun cotton, in hanks of every color, and it seems like the silk market at Granada, except here there is a much greater quantity. They sell as many colors for painters as may be found in Spain and all of excellent hues. They sell deerskins, with and without

the hair, and some are dyed white or in various colors. They sell much earthenware, which for the most part is very good; there are both large and small pitchers, jugs, pots, tiles and many other sorts of vessel, all of good clay and most of them glazed and painted. They sell maize both as grain and as bread and it is better both in appearance and in taste than any found in the islands or on the mainland. They sell chicken and fish pies, and much fresh and salted fish, as well as raw and cooked fish. They sell hen and goose eggs, and eggs of all the other birds I have mentioned, in great numbers, and they sell tortillas made from eggs.

Finally, besides those things which I have already mentioned, they sell in the market everything else to be found in this land, but they are so many and so varied that because of their great number and because I cannot remember many of them nor do I know what they are called I shall not mention them. Each kind of merchandise is sold in its own street without any mixture whatever; they are very particular in this. Everything is sold by number and size, and until now I have seen nothing sold by weight. There is in this great square a very large building like a courthouse, where ten or twelve persons sit as judges. They preside over all that happens in the markets, and sentence criminals. There are in this square other persons who walk among the people to see what they are selling and the measures[5] they are using; and they have been seen to break some that were false.

There are, in all districts of this great city, many temples or houses for their idols. They are all very beautiful buildings, and in the important ones there are priests of their sect who live there permanently; and, in addition to the house for the idols, they also have very good lodgings. All these priests dress in black and never comb their hair from the time they enter the priesthood until they leave; and all the sons of the persons of high rank, both the lords and honored citizens also, enter the priesthood and wear the habit from the age of seven or eight years until they are taken away to be married; this occurs more among the first-born sons, who are to inherit, than among the others. They abstain from eating things, and more at some times of

[1] *lime* Substance used for a variety of purposes, including the processing of corn.

[2] *widgeons* Ducks.

[3] *teasels* Cortés probably is likening a local plant to the golden thistle, a spiny, edible plant that is native to Spain but not Mexico.

[4] *maguey* Agave.

[5] *measures* I.e., devices used to determine the appropriate quantities in an exchange of goods.

the year than at others; and no woman is granted entry nor permitted inside these places of worship.

Amongst these temples there is one, the principal one, whose great size and magnificence no human tongue could describe, for it is so large that within the precincts, which are surrounded by a very high wall, a town of some five hundred inhabitants could easily be built. All round inside this wall there are very elegant quarters with very large rooms and corridors where their priests live. There are as many as forty towers, all of which are so high that in the case of the largest there are fifty steps leading up to the main part of it; and the most important of these towers is higher than that of the cathedral of Seville. They are so well constructed in both their stone and woodwork that there can be none better in any place, for all the stonework inside the chapels where they keep their idols is in high relief, with figures and little houses, and the woodwork is likewise of relief and painted with monsters and other figures and designs. All these towers are burial places of chiefs, and the chapels therein are each dedicated to the idol which he venerated.

There are three rooms within this great temple for the principal idols, which are of remarkable size and stature and decorated with many designs and sculptures, both in stone and in wood. Within these rooms are other chapels, and the doors to them are very small. Inside there is no light whatsoever; there only some of the priests may enter, for inside are the sculptured figures of the idols, although, as I have said, there are also many outside.

The most important of these idols, and the ones in whom they have most faith, I had taken from their places and thrown down the steps; and I had those chapels where they were cleaned, for they were full of the blood of sacrifices; and I had images of Our Lady and of other saints put there, which caused Mutezuma[1] and the other natives some sorrow. First they asked me not to do it, for when the communities learned of it they would rise against me, for they believed that those idols gave them all their worldly goods, and that if they were allowed to be ill treated, they would become angry and give them nothing and take the fruit from the earth leaving the people to die of hunger. I made them understand through the interpreters how deceived they

were in placing their trust in those idols which they had made with their hands from unclean things. They must know that there was only one God, Lord of all things, who had created heaven and earth and all else and who made all of us; and He was without beginning or end, and they must adore and worship only Him, not any other creature or thing. And I told them all I knew about this to dissuade them from their idolatry and bring them to the knowledge of God our Saviour. All of them, especially Mutezuma, replied that they had already told me how they were not natives of this land, and that as it was many years since their forefathers had come here, they well knew that they might have erred somewhat in what they believed, for they had left their native land so long ago; and as I had only recently arrived from there, I would better know the things they should believe, and should explain to them and make them understand, for they would do as I said was best. Mutezuma and many of the chieftains of the city were with me until the idols were removed, the chapel cleaned and the images set up, and I urged them not to sacrifice living creatures to the idols, as they were accustomed, for, as well as being most abhorrent to God, Your Sacred Majesty's laws forbade it and ordered that he who kills shall be killed. And from then on they ceased to do it, and in all the time I stayed in that city I did not see a living creature killed or sacrificed.

The figures of the idols in which these people believe are very much larger than the body of a big man. They are made of dough from all the seeds and vegetables which they eat, ground and mixed together, and bound with the blood of human hearts which those priests tear out while still beating. And also after they are made they offer them more hearts and anoint their faces with the blood. Everything has an idol dedicated to it, in the same manner as the pagans who in antiquity honored their gods. So they have an idol whose favor they ask in war and another for agriculture; and likewise for each thing they wish to be done well they have an idol which they honor and serve.

There are in the city many large and beautiful houses, and the reason for this is that all the chiefs of the land, who are Mutezuma's vassals, have houses in the city and live there for part of the year; and in addition there are many rich citizens who likewise have very good houses. All these houses have very large and

[1] *Mutezuma* Moctezuma II, Aztec emperor (r. c. 1502–20).

very good rooms and also very pleasant gardens of various sorts of flowers both on the upper and lower floors.

Along one of the causeways to this great city run two aqueducts made of mortar. Each one is two paces wide and some six feet deep, and along one of them a stream of very good fresh water, as wide as a man's body, flows into the heart of the city and from this they all drink. The other, which is empty, is used when they wish to clean the first channel. Where the aqueducts cross the bridges, the water passes along some channels which are as wide as an ox; and so they serve the whole city.

Canoes paddle through all the streets selling the water; they take it from the aqueduct by placing the canoes beneath the bridges where those channels are, and on top there are men who fill the canoes and are paid for their work. At all the gateways to the city and at the places where these canoes are unloaded, which is where the greater part of the provisions enter the city, there are guards in huts who receive a *certum quid*[1] of all that enters. I have not yet discovered whether this goes to the chief or to the city, but I think to the chief, because in other markets in other parts I have seen this tax paid to the ruler of the place. Everyday, in all the markets and public places there are many workmen and craftsmen of every sort, waiting to be employed by the day. The people of this city are dressed with more elegance and are more courtly in their bearing than those of the other cities and provinces, and because Mutezuma and all those chieftains, his vassals, are always coming to the city, the people have more manners and politeness in all matters. Yet so as not to tire Your Highness with the description of the things of this city (although I would not complete it so briefly), I will say only that these people live almost like those in Spain, and in as much harmony and order as there, and considering that they are barbarous and so far from the knowledge of God and cut off from all civilized nations, it is truly remarkable to see what they have achieved in all things.

Touching Mutezuma's service and all that was remarkable in his magnificence and power, there is so much to describe that I do not know how to begin even to recount some part of it; for, as I have already said, can there be anything more magnificent than that this barbarian lord should have all the things to be found under the heavens in his domain, fashioned in gold and silver and jewels and feathers; and so realistic in gold and silver that no smith in the world could have done better, and in jewels so fine that it is impossible to imagine with what instruments they were cut so perfectly; and those in feathers more wonderful than anything in wax or embroidery.

I have not yet been able to discover the extent of the domain of Mutezuma, but in the two hundred leagues which his messenger traveled to the north and to the south of this city his orders were obeyed, although there were some provinces in the middle of these lands which were at war with him. But from what I have discovered, and what he had told me, I imagine that his kingdom is almost as big as Spain, for he sent messengers from the region of Putunchan, which is the Grijalba River, seventy leagues to a city which is called Cumantan commanding the inhabitants thereof to offer themselves as vassal to Your Majesty, and that city is 230 leagues from the capital; the remaining 150 leagues have been explored by Spaniards on my orders. The greater part of the chiefs of these lands and provinces, especially those from close by, resided, as I have said, for most of the year in this capital city, and all or most of their eldest sons were in the service of Mutezuma. In all these domains he had fortresses garrisoned with his own people, and governors and officials to collect the tributes which each province must pay; and they kept an account of whatever each one was obliged to give in characters and drawings on the paper which they make, which is their writing. Each of these provinces paid appropriate tributes in accordance with the nature of the land; thus Mutezuma received every sort of produce from those provinces, and he was so feared by all, both present and absent, that there could be no ruler in the world more so.

He had, both inside the city and outside, many private residences, each one for a particular pastime, and as well made as I can describe—as is befitting so great a ruler. The palace inside the city in which he lived was so marvelous that it seems to me impossible to describe its excellence and grandeur. Therefore, I shall not attempt to describe it at all, save to say that in Spain there is nothing to compare with it. …

[1] *certum quid* Latin: certain sum.

... He had another very beautiful house, with a large patio, laid with pretty tiles in the manner of a chessboard. There were rooms nine feet high and as large as six paces square. The roofs of each of these houses are half covered with tiles which the other half is covered by well-made latticework. In each of these rooms there was kept a bird of prey of every sort that is found in Spain, from the kestrel to the eagle, and many others which have never been seen there. There were large numbers of each of these birds, and in the covered part of each of the rooms was a stick like a perch, and another outside beneath the latticework, and they were on one during the night or when it rained and on the other during the day when the sun was out. All these birds were given chickens to eat each day and no other food. In this house there were several large low rooms filled with big cages, made from heavy timbers and very well joined. In all, or in most of them, were large numbers of lions, tigers, wolves, foxes and cats of various kinds which given as many chickens to eat as they needed. Another three hundred men looked after these birds and animals. There was yet another house where lived many deformed men and women, among which were dwarfs and hunchbacks and others with other deformities; and each manner of monstrosity had a room to itself; and likewise there were people to look after them. I shall not mention the other entertainments which he has in this city, for they are very many and of many different kinds. ...

—1522

from the anonymous manuscript of Tlatelolco[1]

THE ARRIVAL OF CORTES

Year 13-Rabbit.[2] The Spaniards were sighted off the coast.

Year 1-Canestalk.[3] The Spaniards came to the palace at Tlayacac. When the Captain arrived at the palace, Motecuhzoma[4] sent the Cuetlaxteca[5] to greet him and to bring him two suns as gifts. One of these suns was made of the yellow metal, the other of the white. The Cuetlaxteca also brought him a mirror to be hung on his person, a gold collar, a great gold pitcher, fans and ornaments of quetzal[6] feathers and a shield inlaid with mother-of-pearl.

The envoys made sacrifices in front of the Captain. At this, he grew very angry. When they offered him blood in an "eagle dish," he shouted at the man who offered it and struck him with his sword. The envoys departed at once.

All the gifts which the Cuetlaxteca brought to the Captain were sent by Motecuhzoma. That is why the Cuetlaxteca went to meet the Captain at Tlayacac: he was only performing his duties as a royal envoy.

Then the Captain marched to Tenochtitlan.[7] He arrived here during the month called Bird, under the sign of the day 8-Wind. When he entered the city, we gave him chickens, eggs, corn, tortillas and drink. We also gave him firewood and fodder for his "deer." Some of these gifts were sent by the lord of Tenochtitlan, the rest by the lord of Tlatelolco.

Later the Captain marched back to the coast, leaving Don Pedro de Alvarado[8]—The Sun—in command.

THE MASSACRE IN THE MAIN TEMPLE

During this time, the people asked Motecuhzoma how they should celebrate their god's fiesta.[9] He said: "Dress him in all his finery, in all his sacred ornaments."

During this same time, The Sun commanded that Motecuhzoma and Itzcohuatzin, the military chief of

[1] Translated into English by Lysander Kemp (1962, 1992) with reference to a 1956 Spanish translation by Angel Maria Garibay K.

[2] *13-Rabbit* 1518, according to the European calendar. Aztec solar years proceed in groups of 52, further divided into groups of 13 under the zodiac signs of rabbit, canestalk, knife, and house.

[3] *1-Canestalk* 1519, according to the European calendar.

[4] *Motecuhzoma* Moctezuma II, Aztec emperor (r. c. 1502–20).

[5] *Cuetlaxteca* The specific identity of this individual representative is unclear, but the Cuetlaxteca were allies of the Mexica.

[6] *quetzal* Large, vibrantly colored bird with feathers highly valued by the Mexica.

[7] *Tenochtitlan* Aztec capital city.

[8] *Don Pedro de Alvarado* Notoriously brutal conquistador (c. 1485–1541). The Aztecs nicknamed him after the sun god Tonatiuh, possibly in reference to Alvarado's light-colored hair.

[9] *fiesta* I.e., public religious holiday.

Map of Tenochtitlan, 1524. This map was originally published with a Latin translation of Cortés's letters. While the style is clearly European, scholars have speculated as to whether it is based on an Indigenous map or on a sketch by a member of Cortés's crew.

Tlatelolco, be made prisoners. The Spaniards hanged a chief from Acolhuacan named Nezahualquentzin. They also murdered the king of Nauhtla,[1] Cohualpopocatzin, by wounding him with arrows and then burning him alive.

For this reason, our warriors were on guard at the Eagle Gate. The sentries from Tenochtitlan stood at one side of the gate, and the sentries from Tlatelolco at the other. But messengers came to tell them to dress the figure of Huitzilopochtli.[2] They left their posts and went to dress him in his sacred finery: his ornaments and his paper clothing.

When this had been done, the celebrants began to sing their songs. That is how they celebrated the first day of the fiesta. On the second day they began to sing again, but without warning they were all put to death. The dancers and singers were completely unarmed. They brought only their embroidered cloaks, their turquoises, their lip plugs, their necklaces, their clusters of heron feathers, their trinkets made of deer hooves. Those who played the drums, the old men, had brought their gourds of snuff and their timbrels.[3]

The Spaniards attacked the musicians first, slashing at their hands and faces until they had killed all of them. The singers—and even the spectators—were also killed. This slaughter in the Sacred Patio went on for three hours. Then the Spaniards burst into the rooms of the temple to kill the others: those who were carrying water, or bringing fodder for the horses, or grinding meal, or sweeping, or standing watch over this work.

The king Motecuhzoma, who was accompanied by Itzcohuatzin and by those who had brought food for the Spaniards, protested: "Our lords, that is enough! What are you doing? These people are not carrying shields or macanas.[4] Our lords, they are completely unarmed!"

The Sun treacherously murdered our people on the twentieth day after the Captain left for the coast. We allowed the Captain to return to the city in peace.

But on the following day we attacked him with all our might, and that was the beginning of the war.

THE NIGHT OF SORROWS

The Spaniards attempted to slip out of the city at night, but we attacked furiously at the Canal of the Toltecs, and many of them died. This took place during the fiesta of Tecuilhuitl.[5] The survivors gathered first at Mazatzintamalco[6] and waited for the stragglers to come up.

Year 2-Flint. This was the year in which Motecuhzoma died. Itzcohuatzin of Tlatelolco died at the same time.

The Spaniards took refuge in Acueco, but they were driven out by our warriors. They fled to Teuhcalhueyacan and from there to Zoltepec. Then they marched through Citlaltepec and camped in Temazcalapan, where the people gave them hens, eggs and corn. They rested for a short while and marched on to Tlaxcala.[7]

Soon after, an epidemic broke out in Tenochtitlan. Almost the whole population suffered from racking coughs and painful, burning sores. …

THE FIGHTING IS RENEWED

The Spaniards made ready to attack us, and the war broke out again. They assembled their forces in Cuepopan[8] and Cozcacuahco. A vast number of our warriors were killed by their metal darts. Their ships sailed to Texopan, and the battle there lasted three days. When they had forced us to retreat, they entered the Sacred Patio of Tlilancalco [Black House], where we strung up the heads of our lords the Spaniards. The second was in Acacolco, where we strung up Spanish

[1] *Nauhtla* Region that recently had been conquered by the Aztecs.

[2] *Huitzilopochtli* Major Aztec deity and patron god of Tenochtitlan.

[3] *timbrels* Percussion instruments.

[4] *macanas* Clubs made of wood.

[5] *fiesta of Tecuilhuitl* Period of ritual feasting.

[6] *Mazatzintamalco* One of the dikes outside Tenochtitlan that prevented the city from flooding.

[7] *The Spaniards … Tlaxcala* Roughly speaking, in this passage the Spanish travel eastward from Tenochtitlan, stopping in places that are subject to Tenochtitlan and therefore might be persuaded to support its enemies. They arrive in Tlaxcala, a state that retained its independence from the Aztec Empire but remained in tension with it.

[8] *Cuepopan* Neighborhood in Tenochtitlan that was often the site of battles.

heads and the heads of two of their horses. The third was in Zacatla, in front of the temple of the earth-goddess Cihuacoatl, where we strung up the heads of Tlaxcaltecas.

The women of Tlatelolco joined in the fighting. They struck at the enemy and shot arrows at them; they tucked up their skirts and dressed in the regalia of war.

The Spaniards forced us to retreat. Then they occupied the market place. The Tlatelolcas—the Jaguar Knights, the Eagle Knights, the great warriors—were defeated, and this was the end of the battle. It had lasted five days, and two thousand Tlatelolcas were killed in action. During the battle, the Spaniards set up a canopy for the Captain in the market place. They also mounted a catapult on the temple platform.

EPIC DESCRIPTION OF THE BESIEGED CITY

And all these misfortunes befell us. We saw them and wondered at them; we suffered this unhappy fate.

Broken spears lie in the roads;
we have torn our hair in our grief.
The houses are roofless now, and their walls
are red with blood.

Worms are swarming in the streets and plazas,
and the walls are splattered with gore.
The water has turned red, as if it were dyed,
and when we drink it,
it has the taste of brine.

We have pounded our hands in despair
against the adobe walls,
for our inheritance, our city, is lost and dead.
The shield of our warriors were its defense,
but they could not save it.

We have chewed dry twigs and salt grasses;
we have filled our mouths with dust and bits of
 adobe;
we have eaten lizards, rats and worms. ...

When we had meat, we ate it almost raw. It was scarcely on the fire before we snatched it and gobbled it down.

They set a price on all of us: on the young men, the priests, the boys and girls. The price of a poor man was only two handfuls of corn, or ten cakes made from mosses or twenty cakes of salty couch-grass. Gold, jade, rich cloths, quetzal feathers—everything that once was precious was now considered worthless.

The captains delivered several prisoners of war to Cuauhtemoc[1] to be sacrificed. He performed the sacrifices in person, cutting them open with a stone knife.

THE MESSAGE FROM CORTES

... Three of the great chiefs said to Cuauhtemoc: "Our prince, the Spaniards have sent us one of the magistrates, Xochitl the Acolnahuacatl. It is said that he has a message for you."

Cuauhtemoc asked them: "What is your advice?"

The chiefs all began to shout at once: "Let the message be brought here! We have made auguries with paper and with incense! The captain who seized Xochitl should bring us the message!"

The captain was sent to question Xochitl in the Temple of the Woman. Xochitl said: "The 'god'[2] and La Malinche[3] send word to Cuauhtemoc and the other princes that there is no hope for them. Have they no pity on the little children, the old men, the old women? What more can they do? Everything is settled.

"You are to deliver women with light skins, corn, chickens, eggs and tortillas. This is your last chance. The people of Tenochtitlan must choose whether to surrender or be destroyed."

The captain reported this message to Cuauhtemoc and the lords of Tlatelolco. The lords deliberated among themselves: "What do you think about this? What are we to do?"

THE CITY FALLS

Cuauhtemoc said to the fortune tellers: "Please come forward. What do you see in your books?"

1 *Cuauhtemoc* Aztec emperor (r. 1520–21).

2 *The 'god'* I.e., Cortés.

3 *La Malinche* Nahua woman who played a key role in the Spanish Conquest, acting as an interpreter, advisor, and diplomat on behalf of Cortés.

One of the priests replied: "My prince, hear the truth that we tell you. In only four days we shall have completed the period of eighty days. It may be the will of Huitzilopochtli that nothing further shall happen to us. Let us wait until these four days have passed."

But then the fighting broke out again. The captain of Huitznahuac—the same Huasteco[1] who had brought in Xochitl—renewed the struggle. The enemy forced us to retreat to Amaxac.[2] When they also attacked us there, the general flight began. The lake was full of people, and the roads leading to the mainland were all crowded.

Thus the people of Tenochtitlan and Tlatelolco gave up the struggle and abandoned the city. We all gathered in Amaxac. We had no shields and no *macanas*, we had nothing to eat and no shelter. And it rained all night.

THE PEOPLE FLEE THE CITY

Cuauhtemoc was taken to Cortés along with three other princes. The Captain was accompanied by Pedro de Alvarado and La Malinche.

When the princes were made captives, the people began to leave, searching for a place to stay. Everyone was in tatters, and the women's thighs were almost naked. The Christians searched all the refugees. They even opened the women's skirts and blouses and felt everywhere: their ears, their breasts, their hair. Our people scattered in all directions. They went to neighboring villages and huddled in corners in the houses of strangers.

The city was conquered in the year 3-House. The date on which we departed was the day 1-Serpent in the ninth month.

The lords of Tlatelolco went to Cuauhtitlan.[3] Even the greatest captains and warriors left in tatters. The women had only rags to cover their heads, and they had patched together their blouses out of many-colored scraps. The chiefs were grief-stricken and mourned to one another: "We have been defeated a second time!"
—1528

Illustration showing parents fleeing the siege of Tenochtitlan with their children, from *The General History of the Things of New Spain* [Florentine Codex], sixteenth century.

[1] *Huasteco* The Huastec people of what is now northeastern Mexico were conquered by the Aztecs in the mid-fifteenth century.

[2] *Amaxac* In the northern part of Tlatelolco. The Amaxac Road leads out of Tlatelolco to the mainland.

[3] *Cuauhtitlan* City-state north of Tenochtitlan; also part of the Aztec Empire.

Florida and New Mexico

Spain established a strong footing in Mexico and the Caribbean early in the sixteenth century, and the empire concentrated most of its further colonization efforts to the south of those colonies. But in the sixteenth and seventeenth centuries Spanish explorers and colonizers were also the most significant European presence in the southern part of what is now the continental United States. Exploration began early: the first Spanish expedition to what is now Florida, in 1513, was led by Juan de Ponce de León, a conquistador who had already amassed an incredible fortune as governor of Puerto Rico, where he exploited the Indigenous people to mine gold. Ponce de León named the region La Florida and claimed it for Spain on his first voyage; he returned in 1521 with the intention to settle, but his attempt was thwarted by the armed resistance of local Calusa people, who killed him. Another attempted conquest failed in 1528—and among the survivors was Álvar Núñez Cabeza de Vaca, who spent years traveling from what is now the Florida panhandle to Mexico, interacting closely with many Indigenous peoples during his journey. After his eventual return to Spain, Cabeza de Vaca published a report of his experiences that helped to inspire further exploration north of what is now Mexico.

In 1540, a major exploration of the southwest was led by Francisco Vázquez de Coronado, whose party included several hundred Spanish people and three times as many Indigenous allies. Coronado explored much further east and west, but he based his operations in what are now Arizona and New Mexico, in the territory of people the Spanish called Pueblos. Pueblos share an architectural style, living in communal complexes made of adobe—which the Spanish called "pueblos," meaning "villages"—but are not, as the Spanish assumed, a single culture. In the mid-sixteenth century they had no shared government, significantly different religious and cultural practices, and at least four distinct language groups, though many used similar irrigation methods that allowed them to flourish in the dry landscape. Coronado took Zuni, Hopi, and other Puebloan villages by force, displacing the communities within and taking their food. When the people resisted, Coronado's troops retaliated by destroying whole villages—about a dozen by the time the expedition returned to Mexico, in 1542, without establishing a permanent settlement.

While Coronado approached the center of the continent from the west, another Spanish expedition approached it from the east, led by the conquistador Hernando de Soto, who had already made a fortune pillaging the Incan capital city in Peru. De Soto's expedition traversed much of the territory of the prosperous Mississippian peoples, ancestors of a number of present-day Indigenous peoples including the Cherokee, Chickasaw, Choctaw, Muscogee (Creek), and Seminole. As they went, de Soto and his troops burned and looted villages, seeking all manner of wealth but especially gold and people to enslave. They provoked a great deal of armed resistance from Choctaw, Chickasaw, and other communities, but made it as far as present-day Texas before returning to Mexico (though de Soto himself died of an illness on the way). Like Coronado's expedition, de Soto's troops did not establish a permanent settlement, nor did they make a serious attempt to understand the cultures or geography of the places they visited; their primary goal was the acquisition of riches.

The Spanish returned to both regions, however, with greater ambitions. In 1565, Spanish settlers founded the colony of St. Augustine, which would eventually become the city of the same name, in La Florida. Other attempted settlements were short-lived; the Calusa, Ai, Tequesta, and Timucua of the region were unimpressed with the missionaries who attempted to convert them to Christianity—not to mention angered by the thefts and assaults committed by Spanish soldiers—and resisted violently and effectively. By 1587 only St. Augustine remained, though missionaries would exert substantial influence over many communities in the following century. Efforts to establish the colony of "New Mexico" began in the late 1590s, with a group of settlers who appropriated the pueblos of Indigenous communities. Dependent on these communities for food and shelter, the settlers enforced their dominance brutally; their behavior provoked resistance, which they subdued with even greater brutality. These earliest settlements failed, and the settler population became concentrated in Santa Fe, declared the capital of the province in 1610.

In theory, Spain had laws in place to protect Indigenous people from enslavement and brutal mistreatment, and to maintain government control over when and how Indigenous lands were seized. In practice, in both Florida and New Mexico, these laws were neither very effective nor well enforced. Indigenous people were often caught between the conflicting religious and secular powers in the colonies. Governments in both colonies required Indigenous subjects to perform labor for the good of the colony—a practice that settlers in positions of power often exploited for personal gain—and outright enslavement of Indigenous people, while illegal, was nonetheless a common practice among settlers. New Mexico also employed an encomienda system, in which individual settlers were given a right to collect tribute from an Indigenous community—a right that they often exercised, illegally, by essentially enslaving community members.

Some Indigenous individuals and communities were motivated to convert to Catholicism out of a hope that the missionaries would serve as a buffer between them and the brutality and disruption presented by commercial colonists (though many were also persuaded by the missionaries' power and zeal and saw no conflict between their own spirituality and Christian beliefs). Though conversion was generally not directly coerced, once converts were baptized into the community they were subject to the will of the missionaries and their soldiers, who administered corporal punishment and recaptured converts who tried to leave. Converts endured severely curtailed personal freedoms and the destruction of their community's sacred objects by missionaries who wanted to disrupt what they viewed as heathen cultural practices. The missionaries also relied on their converts' forced labor to build, sustain, and enrich the mission.

Oppressed in multiple directions, groups of Pueblos and Indigenous Floridians rebelled numerous times throughout the seventeenth century. Generally speaking, linguistic and cultural differences made it difficult for Indigenous groups to organize large-scale resistance, with the notable exception of the Pueblo Revolt of 1680, in which many diverse communities united to drive the settlers out, achieving more than a decade of independence for the region, which the Spanish then recolonized under terms somewhat more favorable to the Pueblos. The last decades of the seventeenth century also brought a shift in power dynamics in La Florida, as many Indigenous people joined with English settlers in a long campaign against the Spanish. This alliance substantially diminished the power of the Spanish in the region, but the English soon proved to be no less exploitative; they enslaved many of their own allies to sell to other English colonies.

from Alonso Gregorio de Escobedo, *La Florida*

La Florida is an epic poem written by Franciscan missionary Alonso Gregorio de Escobedo (dates unknown) between the 1590s and the 1610s. The 37 cantos and some 21,000 verses in this poem give an account of Escobedo's time living at the Spanish fort of St. Augustine from roughly 1587 to 1593. They follow the octava real rhyme scheme, a poetic form Spanish renaissance writers appropriated from Italian epic to tell heroic Spanish stories. However, *La Florida* is a poem without a clear hero. It is a record of violent attempts to invade a region that is now called the Florida peninsula, enslave Indigenous people, and force them to convert to Christianity. The poem is also

a record of the enduring and continued presence of Indigenous people in this region. Unpublished in Escobedo's lifetime, the poem existed only in manuscript form for centuries and was not published in full until the scholar Alexandria Sununu prepared a critical edition in 1993. However, it is of increasing interest to scholars of Spanish colonial history and literature.

The place Escobedo calls "La Florida" did not exist. "La Florida" is the name Spanish invaders gave to a broad expanse of land that they never fully saw, much less understood. This place was, and still is, the home of numerous Indigenous people who controlled vast networks of trade, diplomacy, and information that stretched far across North America.

The English translation of Canto 26 that is presented here reveals a tension within

Escobedo's writings. He is torn, from stanza to stanza, between admiration for Indigenous people and his desire to justify and perpetuate a violent missionization project. Canto 26 appears in a section of the poem that blends Escobedo's literary, historical, and proto-ethnographic perspectives on Indigenous people, mainly Timucua, Guale, and Mocama, living around St. Augustine in the sixteenth century. Escobedo sometimes refers to Indigenous people as cimarrones in this poem. Here, the word cimarrón connotes a functioning Indigenous world beyond European control, like the Muskogean speaking people who lived far from Spanish influence and resisted invasion. This word shows Spanish efforts to transfer their own status as outsiders onto the people whose homelands they attempted to invade, as well as the difficulties they faced in trying to control Indigenous land and people. Thus the word cimarrón indicates the power of Indigenous people to refuse and oppose invasion and conquest.

Escobedo presents his descriptions of the customs and practices of Indigenous peoples as facts; he claims to base the information in this canto on his first-hand experiences. However, Escobedo had only a very narrow view of a vast and dynamic Indigenous world. He likely stayed close to the Spanish fort, unable to travel a significant distance beyond those walls without armed guards. At best, he had a limited understanding of neighboring Indigenous languages. While he might have seen some of the things he describes up close, it is likely that much of the information Escobedo presented in his poem was hearsay.

Like most colonial sources, *La Florida* touts knowledge and control of an Indigenous world, but ends up revealing more about European limitations and perspectives. Escobedo's poem is thus an excellent primary source for exploring the Spanish mindset, and a far more complicated one for locating Indigenous voices and stories.

Note on the Text
The English translation included below was created by Scott Cave, Alejandra Dubcovsky, Jenny Marie Forsythe, Clayton McCarl, and Laura Muñoz for this anthology. It is the result of a collaborative effort among these translators, and it presents one possible English translation among many others that may be yet to come.

Our group of translators chose to include our English version of this canto in its entirety, without censoring or removing any of its content. This means that we have endeavored not to conceal the violence and racism of histories of Spanish, European, and Anglo-American invasion in this region. We have also prioritized foregrounding what the text is saying over how the text is saying it. In Spanish, Escobedo's poem is discordant and heterogeneous; it combines many different types of discourse and poetic devices. Our English version is more stylistically consistent. For better or for worse, we have resolved many of the ambiguities in the poem for the sake of clarity.

The translators gratefully acknowledge colleagues in the Muscogee Nation Historic and Cultural Preservation Department and in the Seminole Nation Historic Preservation Office along with Mr. Marcus Briggs-Cloud of Ekvn-Yefolecv for talking with us about this canto and for sharing ideas that have shaped this translation. As a result of this collaborative process, we have departed from the anthology's usual approach to annotation; the notes below include a small amount of interpretive commentary intended to help students understand the text from a perspective that centers Indigenous histories and futures. The translators acknowledge that any mistakes or inaccuracies in this translation are completely our own.

Canto 26

This canto describes the location and climate of La Florida, with the rituals and ceremonies of the Native Indians, including the way
they go into battle against our people.

5 Ask and you will receive, without a doubt.
But those who do not ask judiciously will see
God close the door to them forever,
because their petition comes from malice.

But the door to His heart will always be open
10 to the humble servant, whom He receives tenderly.
Humility is such an excellent virtue
that it conquers even almighty God.

I beg God to guide me, for I aim to sing
of Indian rituals and bravery.
15 He knows my ignorance, and I also confess it.
May His great hand favor me
so that as my story unfolds here,
so that as my poor mind finds words,
I may persuade every faithful Christian
20 to value having faith and to scorn being pagan.

What story will we tell on judgement day,
those of us baptized on this earth,
if you and I are more full of vice
than those who have never seen the light of faith?
25 "How can this be!" God will say, "It is the charge
of every soldier in my army
to follow me at any cost into battle.
How can you abandon me for earthly pleasures?"

If the Indian, the Turk, the Moor[1] are condemned,
30 It is not surprising, because they do not know God.
But for half the world to fall! It makes me cry,
it pierces my soul, and it terribly tarnishes as
 injudicious
those who know and then reject the treasure
that our kingdom of Castile enjoys.
35 It is a painful, bitter, and sorrowful fate
that the faithful should die just like the unfaithful.

Of non-Christians I will tell what I feel
are particularly extraordinary cases,
the cases of great importance
40 which duly deserve to be written down.
I will not only take as my instrument
their pitiful stories and their rituals,
but also the ornamentation of their bodies
and their ruinous, shameful ways of living.

45 The Christian is stunned by how far they are lost.
The Christian's invincible soul hangs in suspense,

and with good reason he moans and sighs
and lights up the sky with his tears.
He begs God to cease His wrath
50 if God is indeed trying to destroy idolaters,
because every person on the coast
is purposefully walking into hell.

The coast of La Florida is dangerous.
It is surrounded by mountains and swamps.
55 The people who live there are warlike.
They are such fierce enemies of Christians,
that if perhaps someone dares venture out
through the mountains without fearing the pagans,
if by chance he comes back alive, he will have
60 A chest full of arrows, much to his displeasure.

The unfaithful are not as fierce as they once were;
now they pretend to be more pious.
Gunpowder broke through their defenses.
Gunpowder will straighten out a traitor.
65 When gunpowder rains down on the head
of the bravest and most spirited man,
it forces him to be virtuous if he is insolent
and obedient if he is disobedient.

They are partial to women: a stupid vice!
70 Each one enjoys as many as he wants.
Fornication is their exercise and their glory.
The Indian suffers and dies for this disgrace.
They practice fornication like it's their job.
If you look for disgrace, you will find it with them.
75 They transgress the laws of nature.
They betray the people of Spain.

I knew a cacique[2] who had
a pregnant daughter and a pregnant mother.[3]
The whole inconstant rabble does this
80 because it is their wicked custom.

[1] *Moor* Muslims from Spain and North Africa. In this poem, it is used as a slur to refer to non-Christians.

[2] *cacique* Taíno: chief or leader. It is one of many Taíno words in this poem and in Spanish colonial records from across the Americas that reflect the Spanish practice of appropriating Indigenous words and using them in a broader lexicon of conquest.

[3] *pregnant ... mother* Escobedo implies that an Indigenous man impregnated both his mother and his daughter. It is possible that Escobedo is misunderstanding matrilineal kinship practices and trying to make them fit into a model consistent with Spanish and patriarchal ideas.

If I ever spoke against this great evil,
they scorned me like I was nothing,
They said, "what gives us pleasure,
will never be wrong, only right."

85 They are great friends of the truth-teller.
Like liars, they don't tell the truth.
They are enemies of justice and truth:
gossipers, story-tellers, rebels.
Sometimes they bear false witness,
90 and sometimes they betray their leaders.
I know them as if I were their mother:
they are a cruel and bloody people.

If through their good or our bad fortune
they capture one of our soldiers,
95 they do not stop at killing him.
They rob him of his head,
and, with one fingernail, hard and strong,
from either on the left or right hand,
they will tear off his delicate scalp.[1]
100 This is the prize the Indian anticipates.

For them it's a heroic and rare feat
(the one that I just wrote down).
The killer receives a strange honor.
He is commended for the rest of his life.
105 He marks his dark face with a stripe
dyed with his own blood,
and it reaches from his chin to his forehead.
This is a sign of his courage.

He is light and swift as a deer
110 and strong as a rocky mountain.
He is solidly woven from thick muscles,
equal in strength to any Spaniard.
To doubt this would be as foolish
as believing the dishonest man,
115 or the false and pernicious fortune teller.

When a little baby is born,
his mother dives into the sea with ease
and she washes herself to get relief,
she washes her body and also her head.
120 She is totally free of fear or suspicion
that the cold pounding water
could be strong enough to hurt her.[2]
Instead, the water holds her like a bath.

And rising out of the sea she shines
125 as if she had never been submerged,
and her features light up more beautifully
than if she had rested for a year in bed.
Then she washes every bit of her new son;
she washes his hands and feet and face.
130 And carrying him in her arms,
she gives him a thousand hugs.

The most distinguished man wears clothing
cut for him by his own wretched mother
and handed down from his most ancient ancestor.
135 And throughout his life he wears no other clothes,
not even a hat to cover his brow,
and in this way he weathers the cold and the sun,
barefoot and with only a cloth
that covered a deer before becoming leather.

140 This is the garment he uses to cover
his private parts, and even so
the bow and stern are still visible
to anyone who is looking out for them.
These men toss out their hair like a cape.
145 Each one appears wild and fierce.
If they lived this way as a form of Christian penance,
God would see their sacrifice and heal them.

The women wear clothes made of Spanish moss,
a plant that grows in abundance on the oak tree
150 and is used as summer clothes.
In winter their clothes show excessive pride.
They wear this moss on foot, leg, and hand,
and this covering serves their vanity above all else.

[1] *with one fingernail ... scalp* While European invaders attempted to demonize Indigenous people with distorted accounts of them taking the scalps of their enemies, in fact Europeans spread the practice and engaged in it themselves. Many scholars have argued that, contrary to the views conventionally held by settler-colonists, the practice was unknown in the Americas before Europeans introduced it.

[2] *the cold ... hurt her* Escobedo likely reveals his own fear of water here. Most Spanish invaders were not able to swim and bathed infrequently.

Their miserable dress is unbearable to Spaniards
155 because it has a detestable odor.

A certain task is assigned to women:
they must look for adequate food
so that the Indian can eat comfortably
alongside his children and his people.
160 The *bárbaro*[1] rests in sleep as deep
as a tomb, untroubled by searching for food.
He sleeps so freely and pleasantly
that no worry ever can disturb him.[2]

Oh, how happy would the faithful Spaniard be
165 if he could live with such serenity,
if he did not vainly follow greed,
but instead imitated the blind pagan.
If the seeing man succumbs to
greed, which brings dissatisfaction,
170 he might yet see that in desire we find death,
and in renouncing everything, good luck.

How miserable is this life
for the Indian without Jesus Christ, divine Lord,
and without the pleasure of clothes or food
175 for everlasting nourishment of the body.
What pleasure can these people of La Florida have
if they are lacking the joy of bread and wine,
if all they eat is fish without salt?
Salt is a condiment these people do not have.[3]

180 La Florida is full of swamps.
A hundred thousand arms of the sea flow through it
such that even those who get closest
cannot find one inch of dry land.

But then the flatlands and rivers appear,
185 where a beautiful patch of oysters rests,
uncovered for six hours
until the water hides it like a curtain.

Because there is a great quantity of oysters,
they make a fine mortar from the shells
190 that they construct great walls with it,
and repair the broken parts of any home.
The piles of shells are uncountable
and the mortar is so fine that anyone would think it
as good as that which is used here in the East
195 even though it comes from the West.[4]

Every Indian has a bohío,[5] a house
(In Castilian we call this a vile small house).
The door faces into the south wind near the river
because they're extraordinarily afraid of the north
 wind.
200 Of all the winds that blow it's the coldest.
We have winds like this too in Castile.
Many witnesses will swear it,
and we can believe them; they are friends.

Yet another wind harasses and pursues
205 all who live in that land.
It is the enemy of every Spaniard.
It is war-like in its frigidity.
It has an extraordinary effect on the body
We call it the Nor'easter, and if it grabs you,
210 whether you're a poor Indian or a Christian, it leaves
 you
without mouth and feet, without eyes and hands.

In this great cold, hands disappear.
They lose their warmth and strength.
There are no eyes, eyes lose their ability
215 to see the grandeur of the sky.
There are no feet, feet are clumsy and delirious.
They walk with a sluggish gait.

[1] *bárbaro* Spanish: barbarian; a slur used to refer to Indigenous people, much like the words "sauvage" and "savage" which later French, English, and Anglo-American invaders used to denigrate Indigenous people.

[2] *He sleeps ... disturb him* Escobedo's representation of a gendered division of labor shows his limited and incomplete understanding of Indigenous ways of living, and it reveals his assumption that life was only about work and the search for wealth.

[3] *Salt ... do not have* This detail about fresh food without preservatives points to the importance of Indigenous diets and foodways. It also gives credence to ongoing fights for Indigenous food sovereignty and the rights of Indigenous people to fish, hunt, and live in relationship to land as they have always done.

[4] *The piles ... the West* The traditional practice of using natural material from shells in construction of homes underscores the present-day rights of Indigenous people to live in non-toxic environments, in structures that will not cause harm as they break down, and in an ecologically good relationship to land.

[5] *bohío* Taíno: house.

There is no mouth, only a mouth full of sores,
one that can't eat without great pain.

220 If a Spaniard dressed in our style
dares not leave his home for even an hour
although he may have business in the plaza
how, will these sinful people fare,
when they are hunted by the cold wind?
225 For they dwell in nakedness;
they have no coat nor comfort.
Their only cloak is the empty sky.

And yet they resist the cold wind.
These Indians sleep on the ground,
230 and a small fire is a presence
that spills across the entire bohío.
All together they drink in the merciful
warm ember, or rather the tall flame,
until Apollo[1] sends his rays to clothe
235 this sad and wretched nation.

When the dark night draws near,
the most important and knowledgeable people
gather together to drink cacina[2]
in a house used for that purpose.
240 Everyone who likes it once returns two thousand
times to drink it again, for it is so precious
and helps to treat kidney stones
and is very sweet and tasty.

It is from a tree I regard as small
245 filled with great vitality and potential,
created by my infinite God
for the purpose of comforting the poor Indian.
Anyone afflicted by hunger
would be satisfied when they drink this
250 and filled with great strength for a while
and no longer troubled by hunger.

After the cacina is toasted
in a pot in the middle of the fire

and sprinkled with clear water
255 according to the customs of the Indians,
it is given to the poorest among them
who drink it sweetly and with great gusto,
and because this cacina is the first to be prepared
it is stronger than the ones that follow.

260 They put the leaves of the same tree in the fire
and this gives them enough warmth
and they drink this cacina calmly.
Those who came to the fire sad and miserable,
now happily begin a new batch,
265 and once again joyfully thank the cacique,
for the sweet and smooth drink he has gifted them.
No matter how much they drink, it is never
 disagreeable.

They make a third batch in the same way.
It is a drink of much more benefit
270 than the second or the first batch
because it is cooler and milder in the chest.
It is so good that even the cacique waits
to drink it and is satisfied
and glad to hear the joyful cries
275 given by his happy people.

He receives the drink in a strange fashion,
because when he is handed the cup,
the vassal who attends him makes three
gestures of reference as if to a benign god.
280 The cacique is not worthy of this praise,
though he may be worthy of the drink.
He is so attached to the cup that after a while
he becomes its foolish servant.

On these occasions the Indian is aloof.
285 That is how he acts to command respect.
To me this seems at odds with courtesy,
and it strikes me as very flawed.
The master and the servant are sinners,
each one in this pair is imperfect,
290 but in spirit and courage there is none
more brave to be found anywhere.

The proof of this truth is made evident
if the cimarrón Indian of La Florida

1 *Apollo* Greek god associated with the sun, poetry, and
eloquence.

2 *cacina* Local Indigenous word related to cultural practices that
should only be discussed within the community, and that Escobedo
would therefore not have understood.

goes naked to battle our people
295 who normally wear armor.
Because he is so brave, he uses his arrows
to attempt to take their lives.
If he, too, were wearing strong armor,
his resistance to Spain would be even greater.

300 It's astonishing to see an unarmed man
dressed only in the armor of his ferocity
go into battle without hesitation, calmly,
demonstrating the nobility of his spirit.
With only his macana[1] in his right hand,
305 trusting entirely in his own agility,
he goes out (like a fierce bull when provoked)
to end the life of the Christian who provokes him.

The macana is a thick and strong rod
of only four hands long
310 encrusted with a round flat stone so sharp that
nothing is hard enough to resist it.
It will kill the man who wears the strongest armor.
Whoever doesn't run from it is lacking wisdom,
for its blow is such that I can guarantee
315 it will shatter a thick wall.

And it's certain that the warrior is mad
who goes into battle unarmed
without carrying anything to resist
the cruel and quick enemy.
320 For you see, only being in his presence
would terrify the boldest Spaniard,
because the red paint the warrior wears
is his helmet, shield, and breastplate.

The Christian seeks to kill
325 the Western man of fearless spirit
who goes into battle
as if he were out of his senses.
If our men are brave, the Indian is strong,
blasphemous, vile, rude,
330 he incites us to kill him
because he attacks us senselessly.

Our Spanish people go into battle with weapons,
cotton chest guards and coarse cloth,

a great helmet covering their faces,
335 a visor cut according to their chosen design,
and in their left hand the broad sword
they often employ to win laurels and trophies.
And the Spaniard waits for his opponent
and his opponent waits to deliver him to death.

340 The Western Indian is so skillful
in landing his arrows square in the face
of the vassals of King Philip of Austria,[2]
that their lives will end if they aren't careful.
The arrow never bends on its path
345 because this nation is so unparalleled
in aiming, and they always shoot with anger.
To wound in the eyebrow, they hit the eye.

If through the very tiny window
the Spaniard has in his helmet
350 the skillful cimarrón hangs his arrow
with incredible, unheard of accuracy,
who would not then fear such a danger!
But a man who carries his face uncovered
would lose his life for this madness
355 and gain a humble grave.

Oh, how many soldiers skilled in war,
did these most brave infidels
bury in their land.
They always treated them with cruelty!
360 For only in the flat hill or mountain
our faithful often brought death to them
and to avenge himself, the cruel, malevolent Indian
took their lives on the road.

And because now the night is showing herself
365 I want to put an end to my words
until God with His strong right hand
gives light to this hemisphere and her regions.
With my pen as my guide, I will write
of these cimarrones, of their rituals and their vile
 customs.
370 Although we will pass through quickly
we will not stray a single step from the truth.
—MANUSCRIPT C. 1590–1610

[1] *macana* Taíno: wooden weapon or agricultural tool.

[2] *King Philip of Austria* Philip ruled several countries (including Spain as Philip II) in the latter half of the sixteenth century.

from Inca Garcilaso de la Vega, *La Florida del Inca*

The Peruvian historian Inca Garcilaso de la Vega (1539–1616) was born in Cuzco, Peru, in 1539 and baptized as Gómez Suárez de Figueroa. Garcilaso's mother, Isabel Chimpu Ocllo (c. 1523–71), was the granddaughter of Inca ruler Túpac Yupanqui and the cousin of Inca ruler Atahualpa (c. 1502–33). The Spanish conquistador Hernando de Soto had a profound impact on Garcilaso's family; de Soto participated in the 1532 capture and eventual execution of Garcilaso's relative Atahualpa, and he used wealth stolen from Atahualpa and the Inca to fund his infamous invasion of what is now called the Florida peninsula. Many years later, de Soto's exploits provided the subject matter for Garcilaso's first book, *La Florida del Inca*, about de Soto and the Indigenous people whose homelands he invaded.

Garcilaso became a historian by listening to people talk, but he didn't start writing histories until he was in his forties. When he was around twenty years old, he emigrated to Spain, his father's country. While he was in Madrid to petition the Crown for recognition of his military services, Garcilaso came across an old acquaintance named Gonzalo Silvestre (d. 1592). Silvestre had been a participant in the de Soto invasion of Florida and later traveled to Peru. He likely met a young Garcilaso in Cuzco and told him stories about Florida. After the two men met again in Spain, Garcilaso took a series of trips across Andalusia to listen to Silvestre's stories and to write down an account of the de Soto invasion and of many Indigenous people who resisted Spanish invaders, fought against them, and also helped them survive. Garcilaso called his version of this history *La Florida del Inca*, the Inca's Florida. He explained in his book's subtitle that it was a "History of the Adelantado Hernando de Soto, Governor and Captain General of the Kingdom of Florida, and of other heroic Spanish and Indian gentlemen." When the prominent printer Pedro Craesbeeck published *La Florida del Inca* in Lisbon in 1605, it was the first history of the Americas by an American-born historian to be produced on a printing press. It was also the

first time Garcilaso used his new chosen name, Inca Garcilaso de la Vega, in print.

The two chapters included here tell Garcilaso's version of the story of Vasco Porcallo de Figueroa (c. 1495–c. 1550) and Hirrihigua (dates unknown). Vasco Porcallo was a Spanish enslaver and planter who left his plantation in Trinidad, Cuba, to join de Soto's invasion, and Hirrihigua was the Indigenous leader of a town that shared his name near what is now called Tampa Bay. In the sixteenth century, the Tampa Bay area was the home of people non-Indigenous anthropologists have called Tocobaga. It was a linguistically diverse place where speakers of many varieties of Timucuan and Muskogean languages crossed paths. According to Garcilaso, Hirrihigua defeated Vasco Porcallo without ever coming near him, thanks in part to a powerful information network that he and other Indigenous people controlled and used to protect themselves from Spanish invaders.

Indigenous people have lived in Florida continuously from time immemorial to the present. When Garcilaso wrote *La Florida del Inca* in the late sixteenth century, he acknowledged that the European invasion of Africa and the Americas had already profoundly transformed the lives and cultures of European invaders and of Indigenous peoples. In the centuries after his book was published, Indigenous people from the peninsula and beyond have survived enslavement, war, and forced migrations. They have traveled throughout the southeast and the Caribbean, married across communities, adapted and changed. There are important cultural, linguistic, and historical connections between the Indigenous people Garcilaso references in *La Florida del Inca* and present-day Muskogean-speaking Tribes and Nations indigenous to the American Southeast.

NOTE ON THE TEXT

Garcilaso wrote long, complex sentences using punctuation conventions that are different from the ones we use today. For example, Garcilaso often used commas and not periods to indicate pauses between ideas. This translation adapts the structure of Garcilaso's text for contemporary readers. Each sentence in the source text becomes a paragraph in this translation, and

each paragraph break in the source text becomes a section break here.

The following text was translated by Jenny Marie Forsythe for Broadview Press in 2021. The source text for this translation comes from the 1605 Lisbon edition of *La Florida del Inca*, which is available online through the John Carter Brown library catalogue. A facsimile copy of an early manuscript version of *La Florida del Inca* published by Miguel Maticorena Estrada in 2015 was an important reference guide for this translation.

The translator gratefully acknowledges Ida Altman, Aaron Broadwell, Alejandra Dubcovsky, and Christina Sampson for their help with questions about Florida languages and histories as well as Isabel Gómez, Laura Muñoz, Víctor Spezzini, and members of the UCLA Diversifying the Classics Project for their help workshopping this translation.

CHAPTER II
WHAT HAPPENED TO THE LIEUTENANT GENERAL WHO WAS GOING TO CAPTURE A CURACA

One day, when Governor Hernando de Soto was in the town of Cacique Hirrihigua, he heard a warning and certain news that the Cacique[1] had gone off to the hills not far from the army.

The lieutenant general Vasco Porcallo de Figueroa was a very aggressive and honor-hungry man, and he wanted to go after Hirrihigua. He wanted to revel in the glory of carrying him out of the forest either by kindness or by force. The Governor tried to intervene and told him he would send another captain, but Vasco Porcallo insisted that he wanted to go himself. And so

[1] *Cacique* Garcilaso includes a note elsewhere in his text to define the words "cacique" and "curaca" and to explain why he uses them interchangeably: "This name curaca, in the general language of the Indians of Peru, means the same as cacique in the language of the island of Hispaniola and its environs, which is 'lord of vassals.' And as I am an Indian of Peru and not of Santo Domingo or its surroundings, it will be permitted that I introduce some terms from my language in my work, so that it is evident that I am Native to that land and not to the other." "Curaca" and "cacique" were not terms used in the languages of what is now called the Florida peninsula; parallel terms in the languages of people indigenous to this place include "parucusi," in the Timucua language, and "mekko," in Mvskoke.

he named the soldiers and infantrymen he wanted to take with him, and he left the camp with great vigor and even greater hope that he would either take prisoner or make friends with the Curaca Hirrihigua. Hirrihigua had spies who told him that Vasco Porcallo and many other Castilians were coming after him, and so he sent them a message to implore them not to go any further. Hirrihigua explained that he was in a secure place where, no matter how much they tried, they couldn't get to him because there were many bad paths through streams, swamps, and forests between them. And so he requested and implored them to turn back before some disgraceful thing happened to them if, for example, they entered into a place they weren't able to leave again. The messenger said that Hirrihigua said that he gave them this warning not because he feared them or was afraid they would capture him, but rather because he wanted to reward them for the favor and grace they had done him earlier when they did not harm or damage his land and vassals as much as they might have.

The Cacique Hirrihigua sent so many messages to Vasco Porcallo that his messengers nearly caught up with each other on their way to deliver them. But the more the messengers multiplied, the more the lieutenant general wanted to press onward. He heard the exact opposite of what the messages said. He persuaded himself that the messages spoke of the Curaca's fear of not being able to escape him rather than of his courtesy or friendly intent.

With these imaginings, Vasco Porcallo hurried as he walked, acting like a pair of spurs to everyone who went with him, until they arrived at a large and bad swamp. Passing through the swamp was difficult for everyone, but Vasco Porcallo insisted that they enter, and tried to move them to follow his example. He was once an experienced soldier and he knew that to be a captain who was obeyed during difficulties he didn't have any better choice than to go ahead of his soldiers, even though it was reckless. So he dug his heels into his horse and entered hurriedly into the swamp, and many others entered after him. But when the lieutenant general was just a few steps in, his horse fell down with him on it, and both of them nearly drowned. Those who followed on foot were on mud, mire, silt,

and slime so they couldn't swim quickly to help him. They sank if they tried to swim through the mud, mire, silt, and slime, and the ones on horseback couldn't get near enough to favor him for the same reason, and they all ran the same risk, except that Vasco Porcallo risked much more, because he was carrying weapons and covered in mud, mire, silt, and slime, and because his horse had fallen on top of one of his legs and was drowning him sideways and keeping him from using his own body.

Vasco Porcallo escaped this danger more through divine mercy than through human intervention. When he saw himself covered in mud with all hope of capturing the Cacique gone, and when he saw that the Indian had not gone out to fight him with weapons, but only with words shot through friendly channels, and when he saw that he was still defeated—expelled, and ashamed of himself, filled with thoughts and melancholy—he ordered the people to return. Then he saw the memory of the great property and rest and delights he had left behind in his house collide with the anger of his disgrace. Then he saw that he was no longer a youth, and that the greater part of his life was already past, and that all or most of the work to come in that conquest would be like the work of that day or worse. Then he saw that he didn't have any need to take on that work willingly, because he had done enough work already. Then it seemed right to him to return to his house and leave that journey for the youths all around him.

He went down the road with these imaginings. He spoke them out loud to himself and sometimes to his public, repeating over and over the names of the two Curacas: Hirrihigua and Urribarracuxi,[1] dismembering them syllable by syllable, and swapping out their letters so that the sounds came out more closely resembling what he wanted to infer. He went down the road saying: *Hurri Harri, Hurri Higa, Burra coxa, Hurri Harri, devil take this land forever where the only names I ever heard are horrid, vile, and donkey, swear I can't finish this story. No more paths and no more patterns, portents cancel pleasant presents. To work? To eat? If that's*

your only option. Or to take refuge in the honor of running over, I'm running over with riches, and honor for my whole life, even never after ever.

With these words and others like them, repeated many times, the army arrived. Later, Vasco Porcallo asked the Governor for permission to go back to the island of Cuba.

The General gave it to him with the same openness and grace with which he received his offer for the conquest. With his permission, he gave him the little galleon *San Anton* that he used to leave.

Vasco Porcallo doled out his own weapons, horses, other equipment, and table service to the gentleman and soldiers of his choosing. Since he was a very rich and noble man, he had taken a particularly good and outstanding table service.

He ordered that all the supplies and provisions he had taken from his house for his person and family be left to the soldiers.

He ordered a natural son of his named Gómez Suárez de Figueroa, whose mother was an Indian of Cuba, to stay and continue on the journey with the Governor. He left him two horses, weapons, and other necessary things for the conquest.

And ever after, his son performed like a very good gentleman and soldier in all things, like father like son. He served with much promptness in all the occasions that arose. After the Indians killed the horses, he always walked on foot without wanting to accept a borrowed horse from the General or from any other person. He wouldn't take any other gift or favor either, even when he became injured and in great need, for it seemed to him that all the gifts they made and offered didn't come close to compensating the services and benefits his father made in common and in particular to the whole army, of which the Governor remained anguished and full of desire to make gifts and offerings to this gentleman. But the spirit of Gómez Suárez de Figueroa was so strange and elusive that he never even wanted to receive anything from anyone.

[1] *Urribarracuxi* Name of another Indigenous leader and of a town that shares his name.

Theodor de Bry, *Floridae Americae Provinciae Recens a Exactissima* (*American Province of Florida, Recent and Exact*), 1591.

CHAPTER 12
THE RELATION THAT BALTASAR DE GALLEGOS SENT ABOUT WHAT HE HAD DISCOVERED

In a very short time, the things we've told drew to a close, and Vasco Porcallo set sail. He took back all the Spaniards, and Indians, and Blacks that he brought with him to serve him, and he left behind the soldiers' perceptions of him. Their perceptions were not of his cowardice, because that didn't fit with his spirit, but rather of his instability. Like on the island of Cuba, when he offered himself for the conquest and ran off with ambition overflowing, ready to abandon his house, wealth, and riches for new things even though he didn't need them.

Always in such serious cases, resolutions that ignore the prudence and advice of friends do tend to cause fits of rage, and desperate regrets do accompany harm and damage and bring much infamy to the one who carries them out. Because if this gentleman had seen before he left his house what he saw after he left his house to make him return to his house, no one else would have seen what happened, and he wouldn't have unsettled his body in the decline and loss of his reputation and the dissipation of his wealth. Because he could have employed his reputation and wealth in the same journey with more prudence and better advice and brought greater praise and honor to himself. But who will tame a wild beast?

And who can give advice to the free and powerful, confident in themselves, and persuaded that just as

they have great material wealth, they must also have spiritual wealth in equal measure, and further still that a deficiency in wealth for men who do not have it, must also equal a deficiency in their wisdom and discretion?

That is why rich men don't ask for advice, don't want to receive it, and don't have eyes to see the ones who might give it to them.

The day after Vasco Porcallo departed, four gentlemen arrived with orders from Baltasar de Gallegos to give the relation of what they had seen and heard in the lands they had traveled.

The four gentlemen gave a very complete relation that cheered the Spanish; because they reported all things in favor of their aspirations and conquest; save one thing that they noted, that ahead of the town of Urribarracuxi there was a very large swamp that was extremely difficult to cross.

Everyone rejoiced over the good news, and they responded to the subject of the swamp, saying that God had given man ingenuity and tricks to flatten and pass through any difficulties that presented themselves.

After this relation of news, the Governor ordered a decree that notice be given to start walking after three days passed.

He ordered Gonzalo Silvestre and twenty other horsemen to go tell Baltasar de Gallegos that on the fourth day the army would depart and follow him.

Since the Governor had to leave the town of Hirrihigua, it was necessary to construct a post and station people there to defend it and to guard the weapons, supplies, and munitions of the army—because they had stolen a great quantity of all these—and also to guard the caravel and the two brigantines[1] that were in the bay so they were not left unprotected.

He appointed the captain Pedro Calderón to this post. He made him commander of earth and sea. He put everything in these two parts in his charge, and he left him forty spearmen and eighty infantrymen (not counting the sailors of the three ships) to defend and guard the post. He gave them orders to stay there without going anywhere else until they sent word of new orders. And he ordered that they endeavor to always

have peace with the Indians of the region, and not to have war for any reason, even if they had to dissimulate many things and suffer much contempt, and in particular he ordered them to indulge the Curaca Mucozo[2] and make entirely good friends with him.

Once the Governor gave this order, which the captain Pedro Calderón obeyed like a good captain and soldier, the Governor left the bay of Espíritu Santo/Tampa Bay and the town of Hirrihigua, he walked toward the town of Mucozo, and he arrived there for a visit on the morning of the third day of his journey.

Mucozo knew de Soto was coming, and he came out to receive him with many tears and feelings on his departure. He pleaded that he would stay in his town that day, but the Governor did not want to go to the trouble of dealing with so many people. He told Mucozo that he needed to keep going because he had already counted the days, that he hoped he would stay with God, and that he left in his service the captain and soldiers who stayed in the town of Hirrihigua. He thanked him again for what he had done for him, and his army, and the interpreter Juan Ortiz.[3] The Governor embraced him very tenderly and made signs of the great love he owed to this famous Indian's kindness. Mucozo shed many tears, even though he tried to hold them back, and he kissed the Governor's hands, and used many words to signify the pain of his absence. He spoke some of these words, saying: that he did not know how to say which had been greater, the pleasure of having known him and received him as lord, or the pain of seeing his lordship leave without being able to follow him. And as a last favor, he asked to be remembered.

Once he said goodbye to the General, Mucozo spoke to the other captains and principal gentleman. For a good while he told them of the sadness and solitude in which they left him, and he asked that the Sun would show them the way and triumph in all its works.

With that, the good Mucozo stayed put.

[1] *caravel … brigantines* Sailing ships.

[2] *Mucozo* Name of another Indigenous leader in this region and of a town that Garcilaso's text places near the town of Hirrihigua.

[3] *Juan Ortiz* Spanish soldier who was stranded near what is now called Tampa Bay during a disastrous invasion attempt led by Pánfilo de Narváez; he lived there for more than a decade until he was found by de Soto's forces and became one of his interpreters.

And the Governor moved on toward the town of Urribarracuxi, without seeing anything along the way that was fit to be remembered.

From the bay of Espíritu Santo/Tampa Bay to the town of Urribarracuxi, they always walked to the Northeast, which is to the north and twisting a little bit towards where the Sun rises.

It must be noted that this path and all the other paths that are told in this history cannot give precise measurements, and they cannot be used to blame me if something else appears afterwards, when this land is won and God has been served. Although I did my entire due diligence to be able to record these paths with certainty, it was not possible to reach a definitive version because, since the primary intention that came to these Castilians was to conquer that land and look for gold and silver, they did not give their attention to any other thing besides silver and gold. In the name of silver and gold they neglected other things that were more important for them, such as marking the land.

And that is enough to defend myself for not writing with the certainty that I have desired and that was necessary.

—1605

The Pueblo Revolt

In the 1660s and 70s, Pueblo people struggled as an extensive drought brought food shortages, along with Navajo and Apache raiders seeking to feed their own communities—hardships that exacerbated the burdens of colonization as the Spanish continued to demand labor and resources from the Pueblos. Many Pueblos returned with renewed vigor to their longstanding spiritual practices, including, importantly, ritual dances in which the dancers embody specific katsinas (spirits) in order to bring rain. Missionaries' brutal attempts to stamp out these rituals and persecute their leaders served only to galvanize Pueblo rejection of Catholicism. This combination of circumstances provoked an unprecedented mass resistance known as the Pueblo Revolt of 1680.

The organization of the revolt was an extraordinary feat involving dozens of independent villages and a number of distinct cultures, including several mutually unintelligible languages. Before 1680, these barriers had prevented Indigenous people—who vastly outnumbered settlers in New Mexico—from coordinating their efforts against the Spanish. At the center of this organizational effort was Po'pay, a Tewa man from Ohkay Owingeh (San Juan Pueblo) who, in 1675, was one of almost fifty religious leaders whipped for witchcraft and sentenced to enslavement. Before the leaders could be sold, a group of Pueblo warriors successfully demanded their release from prison, and Po'pay went into hiding in Taos, a pueblo far north of Santa Fe, the locus of Spanish power in the region. Here, according to accounts some Pueblo people gave to the Spanish, he communed with spirits including Po'se yemu, a teacher of traditions and bringer of rain who is revered in most Pueblo cultures. Po'pay coordinated the attack with the help of a circle of war captains recruited from many different Pueblos.

The Spanish learned that an attack was coming but did not anticipate its scale, and they were both unprepared and wholly outnumbered. Within weeks, the rebellion had ended in a decisive victory for the Pueblos, who killed hundreds of colonists and two-thirds of the missionaries but allowed the majority of the 2,500 settlers and their remaining Pueblo allies to flee hundreds of miles south to El Paso, on the southern border of New Mexico. The success of the rebellion was in many respects unprecedented, and the sudden loss of an entire established province dismayed Spanish settlers and authorities. In a letter reprinted in translation below, the province's governor, Antonio de Otermín, describes this loss from a Spanish perspective and attempts to justify his failure to prevent what was, in Spanish eyes, an unthinkable catastrophe.

The extent of the provocations the Pueblos endured and the violence with which they responded are reflected in the account of one community's participation in the rebellion given below by Hopi scholar Edmund Nequatewa, from his oral literature collection *Truth of a Hopi* (1936). As Nequatewa's story suggests, a key motive for the rebels was religion—a desire both to expel oppressive missionaries and to revitalize traditional spirituality. In many

communities, the victors burned churches, destroyed Christian relics, rebuilt their kivas (underground ritual buildings), and relearned the important ceremonial dances that missionaries had only partially succeeded in erasing from community knowledge. Many people ceremonially washed themselves in the river to cleanse themselves of their Catholic baptism. In 1681, Fray Francisco de Ayeta, who traveled to New Mexico as part of a failed reconquest attempt, reported that "not a sign has been visible of [the Pueblos] ever having been Christians." Spanish influence was not, however, entirely erased. The Pueblos—almost all of whom had been born under Spanish rule and many of whom had Spanish as well as Indigenous heritage—did choose to maintain some technologies, crops, and livestock of Spanish origin.

The Pueblos succeeded in maintaining their independence for thirteen years. A reconquest campaign beginning in 1692 secured most of New Mexico for Spain—with the exception of Hopi, which remained independent for another century. Even though the rebels did not achieve permanent independence for New Mexico, they did substantially improve conditions under colonialism; afraid to provoke another rebellion, the colonial government did not reinstate the exploitative encomienda system, and missionaries were less violent in their efforts to suppress Pueblo spiritual practices.

NOTE ON THE TEXTS

The text of the letter of Antonio de Otermín appears as translated in C.W. Hackett's *Historical Documents Relating to New Mexico, Nueva Vizcaya, and Approaches Thereto, to 1773*; the story by Nequatewa is based on the version appearing in his collection *Truth of a Hopi*. Spelling and punctuation have been modernized in accordance with the practices of this anthology.

Antonio de Otermín, letter on the Pueblo Revolt of 1680, 8 September 1680

My very reverend father, Sir, and friend, most beloved Fray Francisco de Ayeta:[1]

The time has come when, with tears in my eyes and deep sorrow in my heart, I commence to give an account of the lamentable tragedy, such as has never before happened in the world, which has occurred in this miserable kingdom and holy *custodia*,[2] His Divine Majesty[3] having thus permitted it because of my grievous sins. Before beginning my narration I desire, as one obligated and grateful, to give your reverence the thanks due for the demonstrations of affection and kindness which you have given in your solicitude in ascertaining and inquiring for definite notices about both my life and those of the rest in this miserable kingdom, in the midst of persistent reports which had been circulated of the deaths of myself and the others, and for sparing neither any kind of effort nor large expenditures. For this, only Heaven can reward your reverence, though I do not doubt that his Majesty (may God keep him) will do so.

After I sent my last letter to your reverence by the *maese de campo*,[4] Pedro de Leyba, while the necessary things were being made ready alike for the escort and in the way of provisions, for the most expeditious dispatch of the returning carts and their guards, as your reverence had enjoined me, I received information that a plot for a general uprising of the Christian Indians was being formed and was spreading rapidly. This was wholly contrary to the existing peace and tranquility in this miserable kingdom, not only among the Spaniards and natives, but even on the part of the heathen enemy, for it had been a long time since they had done us any considerable damage. It was my misfortune that I learned of it on the eve of the day set for the beginning

[1] *Fray Francisco de Ayeta* Custos (guardian) of the New Mexico missions from 1676 to 1683.

[2] *custodia* Administrative area that had its own government but was also subject to the authority of a province. New Mexico was under the authority of the province of Santo Evangelio, in Mexico.

[3] *His Divine Majesty* I.e., God.

[4] *maese de campo* Spanish: field master, a high-ranking military official.

of the said uprising, and though I immediately, at that instant, notified the lieutenant general on the lower river and all the other *alcaldes mayores*[1]—so that they could take every care and precaution against whatever might occur, and so that they could make every effort to guard and protect the religious ministers and the temples—the cunning and cleverness of the rebels were such, and so great, that my efforts were of little avail. To this was added a certain degree of negligence by reason of the [report of the] uprising not having been given entire credence, as is apparent from the ease with which they captured and killed both those who were escorting some of the religious,[2] as well as some citizens in their houses, and, particularly, in the efforts that they made to prevent my orders to the lieutenant general passing through. This was the place where most of the forces of the kingdom were, and from which I could expect some help, but of three orders which I sent to the said lieutenant general, not one reached his hands. The first messenger was killed and the others did not pass beyond Santo Domingo,[3] because of their having encountered on the road the certain notice of the deaths of the religious who were in that convent, and of the *alcalde mayor*, some other guards, and six more Spaniards whom they captured on that road. Added to this is the situation of this kingdom which, as your reverence is aware, makes it so easy for the said [Indian] alcaldes[4] to carry out their evil designs, for it is entirely composed of *estancias*,[5] quite distant from one another.

On the eve [of the day] of the glorious San Lorenzo,[6] having received notice of the said rebellion from the governors of Pecos and Tanos, who said that two Indians had left the Theguas, and particularly the pueblos of Thesuque,[7] to which they belonged, to notify them to come and join the revolt, and that they [the governors] came to tell me of it and of how they were unwilling to participate in such wickedness and treason, saying that they now regarded the Spaniards as their brothers, I thanked them for their kindness in giving the notice and told them to go to their pueblos and remain quiet. I busied myself immediately in giving the said orders which I mentioned to your reverence, and on the following morning as I was about to go to mass there arrived Pedro Hidalgo,[8] who had gone to the pueblo of Thesuque, accompanying Father Fray Pio, who went there to say mass. He told me that the Indians of the said pueblo had killed the said Father Fray Pio and that he himself had escaped miraculously. [He told me also] that the said Indians had retreated to the sierra with all the cattle and horses belonging to the convent, and with their own.

The receipt of this news left us all in the state that may be imagined. I immediately and instantly sent the *maese de campo*, Francisco Gómez, with a squadron of soldiers sufficient to investigate this case and also to attempt to extinguish the flame of the ruin already begun. He returned here on the same day, telling me that [the report] of the death of the said Fray Juan Pio was true. He said also that there had been killed that same morning Father Fray Tomás de Torres, *guardián*[9] of Nambé, and his brother, with the latter's wife and a child, and another resident of Taos, and also Father Fray Luis de Morales, *guardián* of San Ildefonso, and the family of Francisco de Anaya;[10] and in Poxuaque Don Joseph de Goitia, Francisco de Ximénez,[11] his wife and family, and Doña Petronila de Salas[12] with ten sons and daughters; and that they had robbed and profaned the convents and [had robbed] all the haciendas[13] of

[1] *alcaldes mayores* I.e., government officials with authority over one of the regions into which New Mexico was divided (with the exception of Santa Fe, which had its own municipal government).

[2] *religious* I.e., religious officials.

[3] *Santo Domingo* Spanish name for Kewa Pueblo, about 35 miles southwest of Santa Fe.

[4] *the said … alcaldes* I.e., Indigenous officials involved in the revolt.

[5] *estancias* Ranches.

[6] *On the eve … Lorenzo* St. Lawrence's feast day is 10 August.

[7] *Pecos and Tanos … Thesuque* Unless otherwise indicated, all the places mentioned in this passage are Indigenous communities.

[8] *Pedro Hidalgo* Spanish soldier.

[9] *guardián* Official in charge of a mission.

[10] *Franciso de Anaya* Spanish military captain.

[11] *Francisco de Ximénez* Spanish military captain.

[12] *Doña Petronila de Salas* Spanish woman born in New Mexico.

[13] *haciendas* Estates.

those murdered and also all the horses and cattle of that jurisdiction and La Cañada.[1]

Upon receiving this news I immediately notified the *alcalde mayor* of that district to assemble all the people in his house in a body, and told him to advise at once the *alcalde mayor* of Los Taos to do the same. On this same day I received notice that two members of a convoy had been killed in the pueblo of Santa Clara, six others having escaped by flight. Also at the same time the *sargento mayor*,[2] Bernabe Marquez, sent to ask me for assistance, saying that he was surrounded and hard pressed by the Indians of the Queres and Tanos nations.[3] Having sent the aid for which he asked me, and an order for those families of Los Cerrillos[4] to come to the villa, I instantly arranged for all the people in it and its environs to retire to the *casas reales*.[5] Believing that the uprising of the Tanos and Pecos might endanger the person of the reverend father custodian, I wrote him to set out at once for the villa, not feeling reassured even with the escort which the lieutenant took, at my orders, but when they arrived with the letter they found that the Indians had already killed the said father custodian; Father Fray Domingo de Vera; Father Fray Manuel Tinoco, the minister *guardián* of San Marcos, who was there; and Father Fray Fernando de Velasco, *guardián* of Los Pecos, near the pueblo of Galisteo, he having escaped that far from the fury of the Pecos. The latter killed in that pueblo Fray Juan de la Pedrosa, two Spanish women, and three children. There died also at the hands of the said enemies in Galisteo Joseph Nieto, two sons of *Maestre de Campo* Leiva, Francisco de Anaya, the younger, who was with the escort, and the wives of *Maestre de Campo* Leiva and Joseph Nieto, with all their daughters and families. I also learned definitely on this day that there had died in the pueblo of Santo Domingo Fathers Fray Juan de Talabán, Fray Francisco Antonio Lorenzana, and Fray Joseph de Montesdoca, and the *alcalde mayor*,

Andrés de Peralta, together with the rest of the men who went as escort.

Seeing myself with notices of so many and such untimely deaths, and that not having received any word from the lieutenant-general was probably due to the fact that he was in the same exigency and confusion, or that the Indians had killed most of those on the lower river, and considering also that in the pueblo of Los Taos the fathers *guardianes* of that place and of the pueblo of Pecuries might be in danger, as well as the *alcalde mayor* and the residents of that valley, and that at all events it was the only place from which I could obtain any horses and cattle—for all these reasons I endeavored to send a relief of soldiers. Marching out for that purpose, they learned that in La Cañada, as in Los Taos and Pecuries, the Indians had risen in rebellion, joining the Apaches of the Achos nation. In Pecuries they had killed Francisco Blanco de la Vega; a *mulata* belonging to[6] the *maese de campo*, Francisco Xavier; and a son of the said *mulata*. Shortly thereafter I learned that they also killed in the pueblo of Taos the father *guardián*, Fray Francisco de Mora, and Father Fray Mathías Rendón, the *guardián* of Pecuries; and Fray Antonio de Pro; and the *alcalde mayor*, as well as another fourteen or fifteen soldiers, along with all the families of the inhabitants of that valley, all of whom were together in the convent. Thereupon I sent an order to the *alcalde mayor*, Luis de Quintana, to come at once to the villa with all the people whom he had assembled in his house, so that, joined with those of us who were in the *casas reales*, we might endeavor to defend ourselves against the enemy's invasions. It was necessarily supposed that they would join all their forces to take our lives, as was seen later by experience.

On Tuesday, the thirteenth of the said month, at about nine o'clock in the morning, there came in sight of us in the suburb of Analco,[7] in the cultivated field of the hermitage[8] of San Miguel, and on the other side of the river from the villa, all the Indians of the Tanos and Pecos nations and the Querez of San Marcos, armed and giving war-whoops. As I learned that one of

[1] *La Cañada* Spanish name given to the settlements in the Santa Cruz River valley, north of Santa Fe.

[2] *sargento mayor* Sergeant major.

[3] *Queres and Tanos nations* Keres territory includes a number of pueblos to the southwest of Santa Fe; Southern Tewa (also known as Tano) territory is to the south of Santa Fe.

[4] *Los Cerrillos* Spanish name given to a district south of Santa Fe.

[5] *casas reales* Spanish: royal houses; i.e., the governor's palace.

[6] *mulata* Person of mixed black and white heritage; *belonging to* I.e., employed or enslaved by.

[7] *Analco* Settlement near Santa Fe inhabited by Tlaxcalans (Indigenous Mexicans) who had accompanied the Spanish colonists.

[8] *hermitage* I.e., church.

the Indians who was leading them was from the villa and had gone to join them shortly before, I sent some soldiers to summon him and tell him on my behalf that he could come to see me in entire safety, so that I might ascertain from him the purpose for which they were coming. Upon receiving this message he came to where I was, and, since he was known, as I say, I asked him how it was that he had gone crazy too—being an Indian who spoke our language, was so intelligent, and had lived all his life in the villa among the Spaniards, where I had placed such confidence in him—and was now coming as a leader of the Indian rebels. He replied to me that they had elected him as their captain, and that they were carrying two banners, one white and the other red, and that the white one signified peace and the red one war. Thus if we wished to choose the white it must be [upon our agreeing] to leave the country, and if we chose the red, we must perish, because the rebels were numerous and we were very few; there was no alternative, inasmuch as they had killed so many religious and Spaniards.

On hearing this reply, I spoke to him very persuasively, to the effect that he and the rest of his followers were Catholic Christians, [asking] how they expected to live without the religious; and said that even though they had committed so many atrocities, still there was a remedy, for if they would return to obedience to his Majesty they would be pardoned; and that thus he should go back to this people and tell them in my name all that had been said to him, and persuade them to [agree to] it and to withdraw from where they were; and that he was to advise me of what they might reply. He came back from there after a short time, saying that his people asked that all classes of Indians who were in our power be given up to them, both those in the service of the Spaniards and those of the Mexican nation of that suburb of Analco. He demanded also that his wife and children be given up to him, and likewise that all the Apache men and women whom the Spaniards had captured in war [be turned over to them], inasmuch as some Apaches who were among them were asking for them. If these things were not done they would declare war immediately, and they were unwilling to leave the place where they were because they were awaiting the Taos, Percuries, and Theguas nations, with whose aid they would destroy us.

Seeing his determination, and what they demanded of us, and especially the fact that it was untrue that there were any Apaches among them, because they were at war with all of them, and that these parleys were intended solely to obtain his wife and children and to gain time for the arrival of the other rebellious nations to join them and besiege us, and that during this time they were robbing and sacking what was in the said hermitage and the houses of the Mexicans, I told him (having given him all the preceding admonitions as a Christian and a Catholic) to return to his people and say to them that unless they immediately desisted from sacking the houses and dispersed, I would send to drive them away from there. Whereupon he went back, and his people received him with peals of bells and trumpets, giving loud shouts in sign of war.

With this, seeing after a short time that they not only did not cease the pillage but were advancing toward the villa with shamelessness and mockery, I ordered all the soldiers to go out and attack them until they succeeded in dislodging them from that place. Advancing for this purpose, they joined battle, killing some at the first encounter. Finding themselves repulsed, they took shelter and fortified themselves in the said hermitage and the houses of the Mexicans, from which they defended themselves a part of the day with the firearms that they had and with arrows. Having set fire to some of the houses in which they were, thus having them surrounded and at the point of perishing, there appeared on the road from Thesuque a band of the people whom they were awaiting, who were all the Teguas. Thus it was necessary to go to prevent these latter from passing on to the villa, because the *casas reales* were poorly defended; whereupon the said Tanos and Pecos fled to the mountains and the two parties joined together, sleeping that night in the sierra of the villa. Many of the rebels remained dead and wounded, and our men retired to the *casas reales* with one soldier killed and the *maese de campo*, Francisco Gómez, and some fourteen or fifteen soldiers wounded, to attend them and entrench and fortify ourselves as best we could.

On the morning of the following day, Wednesday, I saw the enemy come down all together from the sierra where they had slept, toward the villa. Mounting my horse, I went out with the few forces that I had to

meet them, above the convent. The enemy saw me and halted, making ready to resist the attack. They took up a better position, gaining the eminence[1] of some ravines and thick timber,[2] and began to give war-whoops, as if daring me to attack them.

I paused thus for a short time, in battle formation, and the enemy turned aside from the eminence and went nearer the sierras, to gain the one which comes down behind the house of the *maese de campo*, Francisco Gómez. There they took up their position, and this day passed without our having any further engagements or skirmishes than had already occurred, we taking care that they should not throw themselves upon us and burn the church and the houses of the villa.

The next day, Thursday, the enemy obliged us to take the same step as on the day before of mounting on horseback in fighting formation. There were only some light skirmishes to prevent their burning and sacking some of the houses which were at a distance from the main part of the villa. I knew well enough that these dilatory tactics were to give time for the people of the other nations who were missing to join them in order to besiege and attempt to destroy us, but the height of the places in which they were, so favorable to them and on the contrary so unfavorable to us, made it impossible for us to go and drive them out before they should all be joined together.

On the next day, Friday, the nations of the Taos, Pecuries, Hemes,[3] and Querez having assembled during the past night, when dawn came more than 2,500 Indians fell upon us in the villa, fortifying and entrenching themselves in all its houses and at the entrances of all the streets, and cutting off our water, which comes through the *arroyo*[4] and the irrigation canal in front of the *casas reales*. They burned the holy temple and many houses in the villa. We had several skirmishes over possession of the water, but, seeing that it was impossible to hold even this against them, and almost all the soldiers of the post being already wounded, I endeavored to fortify myself in the *casas*

reales and to make a defense without leaving their walls. [The Indians were] so dexterous[5] and so bold that they came to set fire to the doors of the fortified tower of Nuestra Señora de las Casas Reales,[6] and, seeing such audacity, and the manifest risk that we ran of having the *casas reales* set on fire, I resolved to make a sally[7] into the plaza of the said *casas reales* with all my available force of soldiers, without any protection, to attempt to prevent the fire which the enemy was trying to set. With this endeavor we fought the whole afternoon, and, since the enemy, as I said above, had fortified themselves and made embrasures[8] in all the houses, and had plenty of arquebuses,[9] powder, and balls, they did us much damage. Night overtook us and God was pleased that they should desist somewhat from shooting us with arquebuses and arrows. We passed this night, like the rest, with much care and watchfulness, and suffered greatly from thirst because of the scarcity of water.

On the next day, Saturday, they began at dawn to press us harder and more closely with gunshots, arrows, and stones, saying to us that now we should not escape them, and that besides their own numbers, they were expecting help from the Apaches whom they had already summoned. They fatigued us greatly on this day, because all was fighting, and above all we suffered from thirst, as we were already oppressed by it. At nightfall, because of the evident peril in which we found ourselves by their gaining the two stations where cannon were mounted, which we had at the doors of the *casas reales*, aimed at the entrances of the streets, in order to bring them inside it was necessary to assemble all the forces that I had with me, because we realized that this was their [the Indians'] intention. Instantly all the said Indian rebels began a chant of victory and raised war-whoops, burning all the houses of the villa, and they kept us in this position the entire night, which I assure your reverence was the most horrible that could be thought of or imagined, because the

[1] *eminence* Height.

[2] *timber* I.e., trees.

[3] *Hemes* Towa-speaking people whose territory is located to the east of Santa Fe.

[4] *arroyo* Desert creek or river.

[5] *dexterous* I.e., cunning.

[6] *Nuestra … Reales* Spanish: Our Lady of the Royal Palace; i.e., the church.

[7] *sally* Sudden attack made by a force that is under siege.

[8] *embrasures* Openings made in a fortification so that fighters can shoot out.

[9] *arquebuses* Long guns similar to muskets.

whole villa was a torch and everywhere were war chants and shouts. What grieved us most were the dreadful flames from the church and the scoffing and ridicule which the wretched and miserable Indian rebels made of the sacred things, intoning the *alabado*[1] and the other prayers of the church with jeers.

Finding myself in this state, with the church and the villa burned, and with the few horses, sheep, goats, and cattle which we had without feed or water for so long that many had already died, and the rest were about to do so, and with such a multitude of people, most of them children and women, so that our numbers in all came to about a thousand persons, perishing with thirst—for we had nothing to drink during these two days except what had been kept in some jars and pitchers that were in the *casas reales*—surrounded by such a wailing of women and children, with confusion everywhere, I determined to take the resolution of going out in the morning to fight with the enemy until dying or conquering. Considering that the best strength and armor were prayers to appease the Divine wrath, though on the preceding days the poor women had made them with such fervor, that night I charged them to do so increasingly, and told the father *guardián* and the other two religious to say mass for us at dawn, and exhort all alike to repentance for their sins and to conformance with the Divine will, and to absolve us from guilt and punishment. These things being done, all of us who could mounted our horses, and the rest [went] on foot with their arquebuses, and some Indians who were in our service with their bows and arrows, and in the best order possible we directed our course toward the house of the *maese de campo*, Francisco Xavier, which was the place where (apparently) there were the most people and where they had been most active and boldest. On coming out of the entrance to the street it was seen that there was a great number of Indians. They were attacked in force, and though they resisted the first charge bravely, finally they were put to flight, many of them being overtaken and killed. Then turning at once upon those who were in the streets leading to the convent, they also were put to flight with little resistance. The houses in the direction of the house of the said *maese de campo*, Francisco Xavier, being still full of Indians who had taken refuge in them, and

seeing that the enemy with the punishment and deaths that we had inflicted upon them in the first and second assaults were withdrawing toward the hills, giving us a little room, we laid siege to those who remained fortified in the said houses. Though they endeavored to defend themselves, and did so, seeing that they were being set afire and that they would be burned to death, those who remained alive surrendered and much was made of them. The deaths of both parties in this and the other encounters exceeded three hundred Indians.

Finding myself a little relieved by this miraculous event, although I had lost much blood from two arrow wounds which I had received in the face and from a remarkable gunshot wound in the chest on the day before, I immediately had water given to the cattle, the horses, and the people. Because we now found ourselves with very few provisions for so many people, and without hope of human aid, considering that our not having heard in so many days from the people on the lower river would be because of their all having been killed, like the others in the kingdom, or at least of their being or having been in dire straits, with the view of aiding them and joining with them into one body, so as to make the decisions most conducive to his Majesty's service, on the morning of the next day, Monday, I set out for La Isleta,[2] where I judged the said comrades on the lower river would be. I trusted in Divine Providence, for I left without a crust of bread or a grain of wheat or maize,[3] and with no other provision for the convoy of so many people except four hundred animals and two carts belonging to private persons, and, for food, a few sheep, goats, and cows.

In this manner, and with this fine provision, besides a few small ears of maize that we found in the fields, we went as far as the pueblo of La Alameda,[4] where we learned from an old Indian whom we found in a maize-field that the lieutenant-general with all the residents of his jurisdictions had left some fourteen or fifteen days before to return to El Paso[5] to meet the

[1] *alabado* Praise hymn.

[2] *La Isleta* Spanish name given to a Tiwa Pueblo more than 70 miles southwest of Santa Fe.

[3] *maize* Corn.

[4] *La Alameda* Spanish name given to a Tiwa Pueblo about 60 miles southwest of Santa Fe.

[5] *El Paso* Settlement at the southern border of New Mexico, about 300 miles south of Santa Fe.

carts. This news made me very uneasy, alike because I could not be persuaded that he would have left without having news of me as well as of all the others in the kingdom, and because I feared that from his absence there would necessarily follow the abandonment of this kingdom. On hearing this news I acted at once, sending four soldiers to overtake the said lieutenant-general and the others who were following him, with orders that they were to halt wherever they should come up with them. Going in pursuit of them, they overtook them at the place of Fray Cristóbal.[1] The lieutenant-general, Alonso Garcia, overtook me at the place of Las Nutrias,[2] and a few days' march thereafter I encountered the *maese de campo*, Pedro de Leiva, with all the people under his command, who were escorting these carts and who came to ascertain whether or not we were dead, as your reverence had charged him to do, and to find me, ahead of the supply train. I was so short of provisions and of everything else that at best I should have had a little maize for six days or so.

Thus, after God, the only succor and relief that we have rests with your reverence and in your diligence. Wherefore, and in order that your reverence may come immediately, because of the great importance to God and the king of your reverence's presence here, I am sending the said *maese de campo*, Pedro de Leyba, with the rest of the men whom he brought so that he may come as escort for your reverence and the carts or mule-train in which we hope you will bring us some assistance of provisions. Because of the haste which the case demands I do not write at more length, and for the same reason I cannot make a report at present concerning the above to the señor viceroy,[3] because the *autos*[4] are not verified and there has been no opportunity to conclude them. I shall leave it until your reverence's arrival here. For the rest I refer to the account which will be given to your reverence by the father secretary, Fray Buene Ventura de Berganza. I am slowly overtaking the other party, which is sixteen leagues from here, with the view of joining them and discussing whether

or not this miserable kingdom can be recovered. For this purpose I shall not spare any means in the service of God and of his Majesty, losing a thousand lives if I had them, as I have lost my estate and part of my health, and shedding my blood for God. May He protect me and permit me to see your reverence in this place at the head of the relief. September 8, 1680. Your servant, countryman, and friend kisses your reverence's hand.

Don Antonio de Otermín
—1680

HOW THE SPANIARDS CAME TO SHUNG-OPOVI,[5] HOW THEY BUILT A MISSION, AND HOW THE HOPI DESTROYED THE MISSION
as recorded by Edmund Nequatewa in *Truth of a Hopi* (1936)

It may have taken quite a long time for these villages to be established. Anyway, every place was pretty well settled down when the Spanish came. The Spanish were first heard of at Zuni[6] and then at Awatovi.[7] They came on to Shung-opovi, passing Walpi.[8] At First Mesa, Si-kyatki was the largest village then, and they were called Si-kyatki, not Walpi. The Walpi people were living below the present village on the west side. When the Spaniards came, the Hopi thought that they were the ones they were looking for—their white brother, the Bahana,[9] their savior.

The Spaniards visited Shung-opovi several times before the missions were established. The people of Mishongovi[10] welcomed them so the priest who was with the white men built the first Hopi mission at

[1] *Fray Cristóbal* Stopping place about halfway between Santa Fe and El Paso.

[2] *Las Nutrias* Stopping place about 50 miles south of La Alameda.

[3] *viceroy* I.e., senior government official in charge of New Spain.

[4] *autos* Legal documents.

[5] *SHUNG-OPOVI* One of the villages of Second Mesa, one of the three mesas (flat-topped elevated areas) where Hopi villages are located.

[6] *Zuni* Pueblo of the Zuni people, southeast of the Hopi mesas.

[7] *Awatovi* A large, important village before Spanish conquest, Awatovi was destroyed near the end of the eighteenth century and was never rebuilt.

[8] *Walpi* Hopi village on the First Mesa.

[9] *Bahana* According to Nequatewa, the Bahana (the "white man") came into the world at the same time as the Hopi people and left to find great knowledge; the true Bahana would one day return bearing this knowledge and would "make peace and do away with all evil."

[10] *Mishongovi* Another village of the Second Mesa.

Mishongovi. The people of Shung-opovi were at first afraid of the priests but later they decided he was really the Bahana, the savior, and let him build a mission at Shung-opovi.

Well, about this time the Strap Clan were ruling at Shung-opovi and they were the ones that gave permission to establish the mission. The Spaniards, whom they called Castilla, told the people that they had much more power than all their chiefs and a whole lot more power than the witches. The people were very much afraid of them, particularly if they had much more power than the witches. They were so scared that they could do nothing but allow themselves to be made slaves. Whatever they wanted done must be done. Any man in power that was in this position the Hopi called *Tota-achi*, which means a grouchy person that will not do anything himself, like a child. They couldn't refuse, or they would be slashed to death or punished in some way. There were two *Tota-achi*.

The missionary did not like the ceremonies. He did not like the Kachinas[1] and he destroyed the altars and the customs. He called it idol worship and burned up all the ceremonial things in the plaza.

When the Priests started to build the mission, the men were sent away over near the San Francisco peaks to get the pine or spruce beams. These beams were cut and put into shape roughly and were then left till the next year when they had dried out. Beams of that size were hard to carry and the first few times they tried to carry these beams on their backs, twenty to thirty men walking side by side under the beam. But this was rather hard in rough places and one end had to swing around. So finally they figured out a way of carrying the beam in between them. They lined up two by two with the beam between the lines. In doing this, some of the Hopis were given authority by the missionary to look after these men and to see if they all did their duty. If any man gave out on the way he was simply left to die. There was great suffering. Some died for lack of food and water, while others developed scabs and sores on their bodies.

It took a good many years for them to get enough beams to Shung-opovi to build the mission. When this

mission was finally built, all the people in the village had to come there to worship, and those that did not come were punished severely. In that way their own religion was altogether wiped out, because they were not allowed to worship in their own way. All this trouble was a heavy burden on them and they thought it was on account of this that they were having a heavy drought at this time. They thought their gods had given them up because they weren't worshiping the way they should.

Now during this time the men would go out pretending they were going on a hunting trip and they would go to some hiding place, to make their prayer offerings. So today, a good many of these places are still to be found where they left their little stone bowls in which they ground their copper ore to paint the prayer sticks. These places are called *Puwa-kiki*, cave places. If these men were caught they were severely punished.

Now this man, Tota-achi (the Priest), was going from bad to worse. He was not doing the people any good and he was always figuring what he could do to harm them. So he thought out how the water from different springs or rivers would taste and he was always sending some man to these springs to get water for him to drink, but it was noticed that he always chose the men who had pretty wives. He tried to send them far away so that they would be gone two or three days, so it was not very long until they began to see what he was doing. The men were even sent to the Little Colorado River[2] to get water for him, or to Moencopi.[3] Finally, when a man was sent out he'd go out into the rocks and hide, and when the night came he would come home. Then, the priest, thinking the man was away, would come to visit his wife, but instead the man would be there when he came. Many men were punished for this.

All this time the priest, who had great power, wanted all the young girls to be brought to him when they were about thirteen or fourteen years old. They had to live with the priest. He told the people they would become better women if they lived with him for

[1] *Kachinas* Katsinas, spirits who play a central role in Hopi belief. Katsina dances (in which masked dancers embody katsinas) were particular targets of suppression by missionaries.

[2] *Little Colorado River* River almost 50 miles away from Shung-opovi at its closest points.

[3] *Moencopi* Moenkopi Wash is a tributary of the Little Colorado River; it is now the site of a Hopi village about 50 miles west of Shung-opovi.

about three years. Now one of these girls told what the Tota-achi were doing and a brother of the girl heard of this and he asked his sister about it, and he was very angry. This brother went to the mission and wanted to kill the priest that very day, but the priest scared him and he did nothing. So the Shung-opovi people sent this boy, who was a good runner, to Awatovi to see if they were doing the same thing over there, which they were. So that was how they got all the evidence against the priest.

Then the chief at Awatovi sent word by this boy that all the priests would be killed on the fourth day after the full moon. They had no calendar and that was the best way they had of setting the date. In order to make sure that everyone would rise up and do this thing on the fourth day the boy was given a cotton string with knots in it and each day he was to untie one of these knots until they were all out and that would be the day for the attack.

Things were getting worse and worse so the chief of Shung-opovi went over to Mishongnovi and the two chiefs discussed their troubles. "He is not the savior and it is your duty to kill him," said the chief of Shung-opovi. The chief of Mishongnovi replied, "If I end his life, my own life is ended."

Now the priest would not let the people manufacture prayer offerings, so they had to make them among the rocks in the cliffs out of sight, so again one day the chief of Shung-opovi went to Mishongnovi with tobacco and materials to make prayer offerings. He was joined by the chief of Mishongnovi and the two went a mile north to a cave. For four days they lived there heartbroken in the cave, making pahos.[1] Then the chief of Mishongnovi took the prayer offerings and climbed to the top of the Corn Rock and deposited them in the shrine, for according to the ancient agreement with the Mishongnovi people it was their duty to do away with the enemy.

He then, with some of his best men, went to Shung-opovi, but he carried no weapons. He placed his men at every door of the priest's house. Then he knocked on the door and walked in. He asked the priest to come out but the priest was suspicious and would not come out. The chief asked the priest four times and each time the priest refused. Finally, the priest said, "I think you are up to something."

The chief said, "I have come to kill you." "You can't kill me," cried the priest, "you have no power to kill me. If you do, I will come to life and wipe out your whole tribe."

The chief returned, "If you have this power, then blow me out into the air; my gods have more power than you have. My gods have put a heart into me to enter your home. I have no weapons. You have your weapons handy, hanging on the wall. My gods have prevented you from getting your weapons."

The old priest made a rush and grabbed his sword from the wall. The chief of Mishongnovi yelled and the doors were broken open. The priest cut down the chief and fought right and left but was soon overpowered, and his sword taken from him.

They tied his hands behind his back. Out of the big beams outside they made a tripod. They hung him on the beams, kindled a fire and burned him.

1 *pahos* Prayer feathers, which are ritually prepared and then used for ceremonial purposes.

Northeastern Woodlands

In the northeastern part of North America, the first Indigenous people to come into contact with early modern Europeans were probably Beothuk, whose home settlers would come to call Newfoundland. Beothuk people may have made contact with English sailors or Basque whalers even before Columbus landed in the Caribbean, but they certainly had solidified trade relationships with Europeans early in the sixteenth century—as did Mi'kmaq people, whose territory extended from Newfoundland to what is now Maine. Many Indigenous peoples further inland and further south along the coast made first contact with European explorers and settlers as the sixteenth century unfolded, and some experienced first contact in the seventeenth century. The transcriptions below of Lenni Lenape (Delaware) oral accounts of "the arrival of the whites" likely reflect encounters with English explorer Henry Hudson's Dutch-financed expedition in 1609. The Lenape accounts appear below in three versions, told and transcribed in the nineteenth, twentieth, and twenty-first centuries. In some versions of the account, the settlers steal land from the Lenape using a trick from classical legend: they asked for as much land as could be encompassed by an animal hide, then, having obtained agreement, cut up the hide into small strips to enclose a larger territory. Scholars disagree as to whether Europeans really attempted to employ this ruse or whether this part of the story is a later addition, borrowed from Western tradition as a metaphor for settlers' actual behavior.

North of La Florida, European attempts to establish settler-colonies were largely not successful until the seventeenth century. But while they did not result in permanent settlements, sixteenth-century explorations and colonization attempts in northeastern North America did inform literary depictions of the continent and its people that would shape the way Europeans thought and wrote about the "New World" in following centuries. Mathematician, scientist, and navigator Thomas Hariot's *A Brief and True Report of the New Found Land of Virginia* (1588), for example, written after his participation in the first failed Roanoke colony in what is now North Carolina, was the first published account of a visit to the Americas to be written in English. As such, it helped to establish a pattern for English-language documents that, as its title page indicates, were addressed to "the adventurers, favourers, and wellwillers of the action, for the inhabiting and planting" of North American settlements. Like many of the later pro-colonization pamphlets it influenced, Hariot's report focuses on the economic advantages colonization could offer to settlers and traders, and most of the document addresses the land's natural resources and suitability for farming. In the portion of the pamphlet excerpted here, Hariot discusses the region's Algonquian-speaking peoples with an eye to their potential as allies or enemies of English colonies. He was better prepared than most of the English to forge connections with the colony's Indigenous neighbors, having learned Algonquian from the Croatoan chief Manteo and the Roanoke Wanchese, when the two Indigenous men had made a diplomatic visit to London in 1584. Hariot's account, together with the watercolors made by the painter John White based on his experiences of the same Roanoke expedition, constitute the most detailed surviving observations of Indigenous lives by very early English colonists. White's paintings in particular, which were published as engravings in later printings of Hariot's book, had a shaping influence on the way the English imagined Indigenous people during the era.

In seventeenth-century Dawnland—known to English settlers as New England—English settlers were somewhat less focused on religious conversion than their French counterparts to the north,[1] and Puritan attempts at proselytization were largely not as effective as those of Catholic missionaries in other regions. One early attempt at indoctrination of the local Indigenous people was undertaken at Harvard, which in the 1660s began to offer an education in Christian religion and ancient Western languages to Indigenous students, most of whom were members of prominent families seeking insight into the culture of the encroaching settler-colonists. Of the first class of such students, many died, some at least in part because of the unfamiliar way of living; the only one to

[1] See the online component of this anthology for materials related to French colonization centered on the St. Lawrence and Great Lakes regions.

graduate, a Wampanoag sachem's son named Caleb Cheeshateaumauk, died of tuberculosis the following year. During his time at Harvard, Cheeshateaumauk is believed to have authored the oldest surviving document written by an Indigenous person in the English colonies: a letter to the Society for the Propagation of the Gospel in New England, an English organization that funded conversion efforts such as those undertaken at Harvard. Cheeshateaumauk's letter, written in Latin, reflects its author's education in Western classics as well as his family background in diplomacy.

The Society for the Propagation of the Gospel in New England also funded a translation of the Bible into Massachusett, an undertaking accomplished by the missionary John Eliot and a team of Indigenous translators, many of whom were Harvard students. Eliot's missionary efforts led some Massachusett-speaking Indigenous groups not only to adopt Christianity but also to adopt alphabetic writing in the Massachusett language. One such piece of writing is the legal document reprinted below, according to which the sachem Mittark and his community made a formal agreement never to sell their territory in Aquinnah (Gay Head). In 1703, when two community members attempted to sell their portions of the land, other residents of Gay Head brought forward this document to argue against the legality of the sale. The commission deciding the case heard testimony that the document was in fact a forgery written after Mittark's death; the document was then declared invalid and the sales were allowed to proceed. While it remains unclear whether the document is the 1681 agreement it purports to be or a forgery made two decades later, it is in either case an illustrative example of an Indigenous community harnessing the power of the written document to advocate for itself in an English colonial system that did not recognize the legitimacy of Indigenous forms of record-keeping. While many Indigenous people in other tribes near the English colonies also wrote or dictated letters and other documents for diplomatic purposes, Massachusett-speakers were unusual in the extent of their early adoption of alphabetic literacy. The body of legal and religious documents written in Massachusett from the mid-seventeenth to mid-eighteenth centuries is expansive enough that, in the twenty-first century, it is now being used to facilitate the language's revival after a period of extinction.

Even as Indigenous communities and individuals were quick to make strategic use of the written word, oral tradition never ceased to play a key role in Indigenous literary cultures. The continued importance of orality—and the fact that oral literature continued to develop in response to historical change even as traditional elements were preserved—is illustrated by the career of the Seneca prophet Handsome Lake in the late eighteenth and early nineteenth centuries. Handsome Lake's teachings, known as the Gai'wiio' (Good Message), merge traditional Haudenosaunee practice with Christian (and especially Quaker) influences. Also known as the Code of Handsome Lake, the teachings were carried orally by Handsome Lake and then by his followers; they were eventually written down in the mid-nineteenth century but are still recited formally by adherents. The final selection below is a story that was first transcribed for publication with the Code in 1913, having been passed from Handsome Lake to his relative Chief Edward Cornplanter, who told it to the Seneca scholar Arthur C. Parker. First told hundreds of years after European and Indigenous people encountered each other on the continent's northeastern coast, the story reflects on early colonization and its consequences.

Lenni Lenape (Delaware) Accounts of the Arrival of the Whites

Each of the following accounts of first contact between Lenni Lenape and European people is mediated in a number of ways. The first was told by Willie Longbone (1868–1946), a fluent Lenape-speaker of Oklahoma, who made extensive recordings of his people's language and literature with the assistance of the settler anthropologist Carl Vogelin; the translation was made by Jim Rementer, a settler scholar who has worked for decades on the preservation and revitalization of the Lenape language. The second version, also transcribed by Rementer, is based on the storytelling of Nora Thompson Dean (1907–84), a prominent Lenape knowledge-keeper. These two accounts from the twentieth- and twenty-first centuries are followed by a much earlier version, by the English-born John Heckewelder (1743–1823), a missionary for the Moravian Church who included it in his book on the Lenape and neighboring peoples; he did not give the name of the storyteller who told him the account. This last version communicates at least as much about Heckewelder's own views of the Lenape as it does about Lenape perspectives on Europeans.

THE COMING OF THE WHITES
as told in 1939 by Willie Longbone, recorded by Carl Vogelin, and translated by Jim Rementer, from *Algonquian Spirit: Contemporary Translations of the Algonquian Literatures of North America* (2005)

A long time ago when the whites came across the water the Lenape did not know that they were coming. One man said in his vision song, "Someone wants to come to see us. He will come across the water." A warrior said, "I'll kill him when I see him."

The next year they saw a ship coming in this direction, and the chief [who had the vision] said, "Now that's the one. The one coming is our elder brother," but the warrior said, "Not mine!" When the whites had arrived, the warrior began to say, "I want to overpower him," but the man [chief] said, "This one is our older brother, that's what I said! [Na nën ndëluwèn.]" The white man said, "Oh, [repeating the Lenape word

ndëluwèn], you must be a Delaware!" That is the reason they began to call the Lenape "Delaware." [At this point the sound on the record becomes very distorted, but then it resumes as] "What do you want?" He [the white man] said, "I want a little piece of land, only as much as a cowhide will cover. Will you give it to me?"

[The Lenape answered], "Oh yes, we can give you that much." Ah, but they did not use just the cowhide. They began to cut it into little thin strips so that when stretched out it encircled a large piece of land. [End of recording.]

PREDICTION OF THE ARRIVAL OF THE WHITE PEOPLE
as transcribed by Jim Rementer from multiple tellings by Nora Thompson Dean, from *Algonquian Spirit: Contemporary Translations of the Algonquian Literatures of North America* (2005)

Long ago there was a Lenape man who had remarkable powers. He would often go and meditate. He was able to foresee the future. One day he told his people, "Soon we will have visitors. They will be real white, fair-skinned people, and they will come from the east in a huge vessel. They are a people who will change our way of life."

Not many people believed him, but finally one day the Lenape people saw a ship coming in. And when these men got out of their boat, the Lenape people were much amazed as they had light skin, blue eyes, and light hair. They were very stunned and dumbfounded, but most of the Lenape were so glad that these visitors had come that they put down furs for them to walk on.

But some Lenape wanted to kill the white people and said, "We don't want these people here. We'll just kill them." But the powerful man said, "No, they came to me in a vision. We will not kill them. They might be our brothers. They might bring us good things. They are going to bring us good things, eventually. We want to treat them good."

And so they did. They put furs down for the white people to sit and walk on. They gave the white people seeds, food, and other things they needed. That's the way the prediction was told a long time ago about the arrival of the white people.

INDIAN ACCOUNT OF THE FIRST ARRIVAL OF THE DUTCH AT NEW YORK ISLAND

as recorded by John Heckewelder, *History, Manners, and Customs of the Indian Nations Who Once Inhabited Pennsylvania and the Neighboring States* (1818)

The Lenni Lenape claim the honour of having received and welcomed the Europeans on their first arrival in the country, situated between New England and Virginia. It is probable, however, that the Mahicanni or Mohicans, who then inhabited the banks of the Hudson, concurred in the hospitable act. The relation I am going to make was taken down many years since from the mouth of an intelligent Delaware Indian, and may be considered as a correct account of the tradition existing among them of this momentous event. I give it as much as possible in their own language.[1]

A great many years ago, when men with a white skin had never yet been seen in this land, some Indians who were out a fishing, at a place where the sea widens, espied at a great distance something remarkably large floating on the water, and such as they had never seen before. These Indians immediately returning to the shore, apprised their countrymen of what they had observed, and pressed them to go out with them and discover what it might be. They hurried out together, and saw with astonishment the phenomenon which now appeared to their sight, but could not agree upon what it was; some believed it to be an uncommonly large fish or animal, while others were of opinion it must be a very big house floating on the sea. At length the spectators concluded that this wonderful object was moving towards the land, and that it must be an animal or something else that had life in it; it would therefore be proper to inform all the Indians on the inhabited islands of what they had seen, and put them on their guard. Accordingly they sent off a number of runners and watermen to carry the news to their scattered chiefs, that they might send off in every direction for the warriors, with a message that they should come immediately. These arriving in numbers, and having themselves viewed the strange appearance, and observing that it was actually moving towards the entrance of the river or bay; concluded it to be a remarkably large

house in which the Mannitto (the Great or Supreme Being) himself was present, and that he probably was coming to visit them.[2] By this time the chiefs were assembled at York island, and deliberating in what manner in which they should receive their Mannitto on his arrival. Every measure was taken to be well provided with plenty of meat for a sacrifice. The women were desired to prepare the best victuals.[3] All the idols or images were examined and put in order, and a grand dance was supposed not only to be an agreeable entertainment for the Great Being, but it was believed that it might, with the addition of a sacrifice, contribute to appease him if he was angry with them. The conjurers were also set to work, to determine what this phenomenon portended, and what the possible result of it might be. To these and to the chiefs and wise men of the nations, men, women, and children were looking up for advice and protection. Distracted between hope and fear, they were at a loss what to do; a dance, however, commenced in great confusion. While in this situation, fresh runners arrive declaring it to be a large house of various colours, and crowded with living creatures. It appears now to be certain, that it is the great Mannitto, bringing them some kind of game,[4] such as he had not given them before, but other runners soon after arriving declare that it is positively a house full of human beings, of quite a different colour from that of the Indians, and dressed differently from them; that in particular one of them was dressed entirely in red, who must be the Mannitto himself. They are hailed from the vessel in a language they do not understand, yet they shout or yell in return by way of answer, according to the custom of their country; many are for running off to the woods, but are pressed by others to stay, in order not to give offence to their visitor, who might find them out and destroy them. The house, some say, large canoe, at last stops, and a canoe of a

[2] [Heckewelder's note] Henry Hudson, a British navigator and discoverer in the employ of the Dutch East India Company, sailed from Amsterdam in command of the *Half Moon*, in April of 1609, in search of a north-eastern passage. Foiled by the ice in the higher latitudes, he turned southwards, and in September anchored in New York bay.

[3] *victuals* Foods.

[4] *game* I.e., animals for hunting.

[1] *in their own language* I.e., following their manner of telling.

smaller size comes on shore with the red man, and some others in it; some stay with his canoe to guard it. The chiefs and wise men, assembled in council, form themselves into a large circle, towards which the man in red clothes approaches with two others. He salutes them with a friendly countenance,[1] and they return the salute after their manner. They are lost in admiration; the dress, the manners, the whole appearance of the unknown strangers is to them a subject of wonder; but they are particularly struck with him who wore the red coat all glittering with gold lace, which they could in no manner account for. He, surely, must be the great Mannitto, but why should he have a white skin? Meanwhile, a large *Hackhack*[2] is brought by one of his servants, from which an unknown substance is poured out into a small cup or glass, and handed to the supposed Mannitto. He drinks—has the glass filled again, and hands it to the chief standing next to him. The chief receives it, but only smells the contents and passes it on to the next chief, who does the same. The glass or cup thus passes through the circle, without the liquor being tasted by anyone, and is upon the point of being returned to the red clothed Mannitto, when one of the Indians, a brave man and a great warrior, suddenly jumps up and harangues the assembly on the impropriety of returning the cup with its contents. It was handed to them, says he, by the Mannitto, that they should drink out of it, as he himself had done. To follow his example would be pleasing to him; but to return what he had given them might provoke his wrath, and bring destruction on them. And since the orator believed it for the good of the nation that the contents offered them should be drunk, and as no one else would do it, he would drink it himself, let the consequence be what it might; it was better for one man to die, than that a whole nation should be destroyed. He then took the glass, and bidding the assembly a solemn farewell, at once drank up its whole contents. Every eye was fixed on the resolute chief, to see what effect the unknown liquor would produce. He soon began to stagger, and at last fell prostrate on the ground. His companions now bemoan his fate, he falls into a sound

sleep, and they think he has expired. He wakes again, jumps up and declares, that he has enjoyed the most delicious sensations, and that he never before felt himself so happy as after he had drunk the cup. He asks for more, his wish is granted; the whole assembly then imitate him, and all become intoxicated.

After this general intoxication had ceased, for they say that while it lasted the whites had confined themselves to their vessel, the man with the red clothes returned again, and distributed presents among them, consisting of beads, axes, hoes, and stockings such as the white people wear. They soon became familiar with each other, and began to converse by signs. The Dutch made them understand that they would not stay here, that they would return home again, but would pay them another visit the next year, when they would bring them more presents, and stay with them awhile; but as they could not live without eating, they should want a little land of them to sow seeds, in order to raise herbs and vegetables to put into their broth. They went away as they had said, and returned in the following season, when both parties were much rejoiced to see each other; but the whites laughed at the Indians, seeing that they knew not the use of the axes and hoes they had given them the year before; for they had these hanging to their breasts as ornaments, and the stockings were made use of as tobacco pouches. The whites now put handles to the former for them, and cut trees down before their eyes, hoed up the ground, and put the stockings on their legs. Here, they say, a general laughter ensued among the Indians, that they had remained ignorant of the use of such valuable implements, and had borne the weight of such heavy metal hanging to their necks, for such a length of time. They took every white man they saw for an inferior Mannitto attendant upon the supreme Deity who shone superior in the red and laced clothes.

As the whites became daily more familiar with the Indians, they at last proposed to stay with them, and asked only for so much ground for a garden spot as, they said, the hide of a bullock would cover or encompass, which hide was spread before them. The Indians readily granted this apparently reasonable request; but the whites then took a knife, and beginning at one end of the hide, cut it up to a long rope, not thicker than a child's finger, so that by the time the whole was cut

[1] *countenance* Facial expression.

[2] [Heckewelder's note] Hackhack is properly a gourd; but since they have not seen glass bottles and decanters, they call them by the same name.

up, it made a great heap; they then took the rope at one end, and drew it gently along, carefully avoiding its breaking. It was drawn out into a circular form, and being closed at its ends, encompassed a large piece of ground. The Indians were surprised at the superior wit of the whites,[1] but did not wish to contend with them about a little land, as they had still enough themselves. The white and red men lived contentedly together for a long time, though the former from time to time asked for more land, which was readily obtained, and thus they gradually proceeded higher up the Mahicannittuck,[2] until the Indians began to believe that they would soon want all their country, which in the end proved true.

from Thomas Hariot, *A Brief and True Report of the New Found Land of Virginia*[3]

OF THE NATURE AND MANNERS OF THE PEOPLE

It resteth I speak[4] a word or two of the natural inhabitants, their natures and manners, leaving large discourse thereof until time more convenient hereafter: now only so far forth, as that you may know, how that they in respect of troubling our inhabiting and planting, are not to be feared; but that they shall have cause both to fear and love us, that shall inhabit with them.

They are a people clothed with loose mantles[5] made of deer skins, and aprons of the same round about their middles; all else naked; of such a difference of statures only as we in England; having no edge tools or weapons of iron or steel to offend us withal, neither know they how to make any: those weapons that they have, are only bows made of Witch-hazel, and arrows of reeds; flat edged truncheons also of wood about a yard long, neither have they anything to defend themselves

but targets[6] made of barks; and some armors made of sticks wickered[7] together with thread.

Their towns are but small, and near the sea coast but few, some containing but 10 or 12 houses, some 20; the greatest that we have seen have been but of 30 houses; if they be walled it is only done with barks of trees made fast to stakes, or else with poles only fixed upright and close one by another.

Their houses are made of small poles made fast[8] at the tops in round form after the manner as is used in many arbories[9] in our gardens in England, in most towns covered with barks, and in some with artificial[10] mats made of long rushes; from the tops of the houses down to the ground. The length of them is commonly double to the breadth, in some places they are but 12 and 16 yards long, and in other some we have seen of four and twenty.

In some places of the country one only town belongeth to the government of a *Wiróans* or chief Lord; in other some two or three, in some six, eight, and more; the greatest *Wiróans* that yet we had dealing with had but eighteen towns in his government, and able to make not above seven or eight hundred fighting men at the most: The language of every government is different from any other, and the farther they are distant the greater is the difference.

Their manner of wars amongst themselves is either by sudden surprising one another most commonly about the dawning of the day, or moonlight; or else by ambushes, or some subtle devices:[11] Set battles are very rare, except it fall out where there are many trees, where either part may have some hope of defence, after the delivery of every arrow, in leaping behind some or other.

If there fall out any wars between us and them, what their fight is likely to be, we having advantages against so many manner of ways, as by our discipline, our strange weapons and devices else; especially by ordnance great and small, it may be easily imagined; by

[1] [Heckewelder's note] These Dutchmen were probably acquainted with what is related of Queen Dido in ancient history, and thus turned their classical knowledge to a good account. [According to classical legend, Dido founded Carthage by obtaining land using a similar trick.]

[2] *Mahicannittuck* Known to settlers as the Hudson River.

[3] The present text is based on the first edition (1588).

[4] *It resteth I speak* It remains for me to speak.

[5] *mantles* Cloaks or other loose garments.

[6] *targets* Light shields.

[7] *wickered* I.e., woven.

[8] *fast* Secure.

[9] *arbories* Orchards.

[10] *artificial* Human-made.

[11] *devices* Stratagems.

the experience we have had in some places, the turning up of their heels against us in running away was their best defence.

In respect of us they are a people poor, and for want[1] of skill and judgement in the knowledge and use of our things, do esteem our trifles before things of greater value: Notwithstanding in their proper manner considering the want of such means as we have, they seem very ingenious; for although they have no such tools, nor any such crafts, sciences and arts as we; yet in those things they do, they show excellency of wit. And by how much they upon due consideration shall find our manner of knowledges and crafts to exceed theirs in perfection, and speed for doing or execution, by so much the more is it probable that they should desire our friendships and love, and have the greater respect for pleasing and obeying us. Whereby may be hoped if means of good government be used, that they may in short time be brought to civility, and the embracing of true religion.

Some religion they have already, which although it be far from the truth, yet being as it is, there is hope it may be the easier and sooner reformed.

They believe that there are many Gods which they call *Montóac*, but of different sorts and degrees; one only chief and great God, which hath been from all eternity. Who as they affirm when he purposed to make the world, made first other gods of a principal order to be as means and instruments to be used in the creation and government to follow; and after the Sun, Moon, and Stars, as petty gods and the instruments of the other order more principal. First they say were made waters, out of which by the gods was made all diversity of creatures that are visible or invisible.

For mankind they say a woman was made first, which by the working of one of the gods, conceived and brought forth children: And in such sort they say they had their beginning.

But how many years or ages have passed since, they say they can make no relation, having no letters nor other such means as we to keep records of the particularities of times past, but only tradition from father to son.

They think that all the gods are of human shape, and therefore they represent them by images in the forms of men, which they call *Kewasówok* (one alone is called *Kewás*); them they place in houses appropriate or temples which they call *Machicómuck*; where they worship, pray, sing, and make many times offerings unto them. In some *Machicómuck* we have seen but one *Kewás*, in some two, and in other some three; the common sort think them to be also gods.

They believe also the immortality of the soul, that after this life as soon as the soul is departed from the body according to the works it hath done, it is either carried to heaven the habitacle[2] of gods, there to enjoy perpetual bliss and happiness, or else to a great pit or hole, which they think to be in the furthest parts of their part of the world toward the sunset, there to burn continually: the place they call *Popogusso*.

For the confirmation of this opinion, they told me two stories of two men that had been lately dead and revived again, the one happened but few years before our coming into the country of a wicked man which having been dead and buried, the next day the earth of the grave being seen to move, was taken up again; who made the declaration where his soul had been, that is to say very near entering into *Popogusso*, had not one of the gods saved him and gave him leave to return again, and teach his friends what they should do to avoid that terrible place of torment.

The other happened in the same year we were there, but in a town that was threescore miles from us, and it was told me for strange news that one being dead, buried and taken up again as the first, showed that although his body had lain dead in the grave, yet his soul was alive, and had traveled far in a long broad way, on both sides whereof grew most delicate and pleasant trees, bearing more rare and excellent fruits than ever he had seen before or was able to express, and at length came to most brave and fair houses near which he met his father, that had been dead before, who gave him great charge to go back again and show his friends what good they were to do to enjoy the pleasures of that place, which when he had done he should after come again.

What subtlety soever be in the *Wiroances* and Priests, this opinion worketh so much in many of the common and simple sort of people that it maketh them have great respect to their Governors, and also

[1] *want* Lack.

[2] *habitacle* Home.

great care what they do, to avoid torment after death, and to enjoy bliss; although notwithstanding there is punishment ordained for malefactors, as stealers, whoremongers, and other sorts of wicked doers; some punished with death, some with forfeitures, some with beating, according to the greatness of the facts.

And this is the sum of their religion, which I learned by having special familiarity with some of their priests. Wherein they were not so sure grounded, nor gave such credit to their traditions and stories but through conversing with us they were brought into great doubts of their own, and no small admiration of ours, with earnest desire in many, to learn more than we had means for want of perfect utterance in their language to express.

Most things they saw with us, as mathematical instruments, sea compasses, the virtue of the lodestone in drawing iron,[1] a perspective glass[2] whereby was showed many strange sights, burning glasses,[3] wildfire works,[4] guns, books, writing and reading, spring clocks that seem to go of themselves, and many other things that we had, were so strange unto them, and so far exceeded their capacities to comprehend the reason and means how they should be made and done, that they thought they were rather the works of gods than of men, or at the leastwise they had been given and taught us of the gods. Which made many of them to have such opinion of us, as that if they knew not the truth of god and religion already, it was rather to be had from us, whom God so specially loved than from a people that were so simple, as they found themselves to be in comparison of us. Whereupon greater credit was given unto that we spake of concerning such matters.

Many times and in every town where I came, according as I was able, I made declaration of the contents of the Bible; that therein was set forth the true and only GOD, and his mighty works, that therein was contained the true doctrine of salvation through Christ, with many particularities of Miracles and chief points of religion, as I was able to then utter, and

thought fit for the time. And although I told them the book materially and of itself was not of any such virtue, as I thought they did conceive, but only the doctrine therein contained; yet would many be glad to touch it, to embrace it, to kiss it, to hold it to their breasts and heads, and stroke over all their body with it; to show their hungry desire of that knowledge which was spoken of.

The *Wiroans* with whom we dwelt called Wingina, and many of his people would be glad many times to be with us at our prayers, and many times call upon us both in his own town, as also in others whither he sometimes accompanied us, to pray and sing Psalms; hoping thereby to be partaker of the same effects which we by that means also expected.

Twice this *Wiroans* was so grievously sick that he was like to die, and as he lay languishing, doubting of any help by his own priests, and thinking he was in such danger for offending us and thereby our god, sent for some of us to pray and be a means to our God that it would please him either that he might live or after death dwell with him in bliss, so likewise were the requests of many others in the like case.

On a time also when their corn began to wither by reason of a drought which happened extraordinarily, fearing that it had come to pass by reason that in some thing they had displeased us, many would come to us and desire us to pray to our God of England, that he would preserve their corn, promising that when it was ripe we also should be partakers of the fruit.

There could at no time happen any strange sicknesses, losses, hurts, or any other cross[5] unto them, but that they would impute to us the cause or means thereof for offending or not pleasing us.

One other rare and strange accident, leaving others, will I mention before I end, which moved the whole country that either knew or heard of us, to have us in wonderful admiration.

There was no town where we had any subtle device practised against us, we leaving it unpunished or not revenged (because we sought by all means possible to win them by gentleness) but that within a few days after our departure from every such town, the people began to die very fast, and many in short space; in some towns about twenty, in some forty, in some sixty,

[1] *virtue … iron* Power of magnets to attract iron.

[2] *perspective glass* Viewing device used to see distant objects more clearly, or a viewing device used to produce an interesting distortion or other visual effect.

[3] *burning glasses* Lenses or mirrors that can be used to start fires.

[4] *wildfire works* Flammable substances used as a weapon of war.

[5] *cross* Adversity.

and in one six score, which in truth was very many in respect of their numbers. This happened in no place that we could learn but where we had been, where they used some practice against us, and after such time; the disease also so strange, that they neither knew what it was, nor how to cure it; the like by report of the oldest men in the country never happened before, time out of mind. A thing specially observed by us as also by the natural inhabitants themselves.

Insomuch that when some of the inhabitants which were our friends and especially the *Wiroans* Wingina had observed such effects in four or five towns to follow their wicked practises, they were persuaded that it was the work of our God through our means, and that we by him might kill and slay whom we would without weapons and not come near them.

And thereupon when it had happened that they had understanding that any of their enemies had abused us in our journeys, hearing that we had wrought no revenge with our weapons, and fearing upon some cause the matter should so rest: did come and entreat us that we would be a means to our God that they as others that had dealt ill with us might in like sort die; alleging how much it would be for our credit and profit, as also theirs; and hoping furthermore that we would do so much at their requests in respect of the friendship we profess them.

Whose entreaties although we showed that they were ungodly, affirming that our God would not subject himself to any such prayers and requests of men: that indeed all things have been and were to be done according to his good pleasure as he had ordained: and that we to show ourselves his true servants ought rather to make petition for the contrary, that they with them might live together with us, be made partakers of his truth and serve him in righteousness; but notwithstanding in such sort, that we refer that as all other things, to be done according to his divine will and pleasure, and as by his wisdom he had ordained to be best.

Yet because the effect fell out so suddenly and shortly after according to their desires, they thought nevertheless it came to pass by our means, and that we in using such speeches unto them did but dissemble the matter, and therefore came unto us to give us thanks in their manner that although we satisfied them

not in promise, yet in deeds and effect we had fulfilled their desires.

This marvelous accident in all the country wrought so strange opinions of us, that some people could not tell whether to think us gods or men, and the rather because that all the space of their sickness, there was no man of ours known to die, or that was especially sick: they noted also that we had no women amongst us, neither that we did care for any of theirs.[1]

Some therefore were of opinion that we were not born of women, and therefore not mortal, but that we were men of an old generation many years past then risen again to immortality.

Some would likewise seem to prophesy that there were more of our generation yet to come, to kill theirs and take their places, as some thought the purpose was by that which was already done.

Those that were immediately come after us they imagined to be in the air, yet invisible and without bodies, and that they by our entreaty and for the love of us did make the people die in that sort as they did by shooting invisible bullets into them.

To confirm this opinion their physicians to excuse their ignorance in curing the disease, would not be ashamed to say, but earnestly make the simple people believe, that the strings of blood that they sucked out of the sick bodies, were the strings wherewithal the invisible bullets were tied and cast.

Some also thought that we shot them ourselves out of our pieces[2] from the place where we dwelt, and killed the people in any such town that had offended us as we listed,[3] how far distant from us soever it were.

And other some said that it was the special work of God for our sakes, as we ourselves have cause in some sort to think no less, whatsoever some do or may imagine to the contrary, especially some astrologers knowing of the eclipse of the sun which we saw the same year before in our voyage thitherward, which unto them appeared very terrible. And also of a comet which began to appear but a few days before the beginning of the said sickness. But to conclude them from being the

[1] *neither that ... of theirs* I.e., they also noted that we did not show sexual interest in the women of their communities.

[2] *pieces* Firearms.

[3] *listed* Wished.

special causes of so special an accident[1] there are farther reasons than I think fit at this present to be alleged.

These their opinions I have set down the more at large that it may appear unto you that there is good hope they may be brought through discreet dealing and government to the embracing of the truth, and consequently to honour, obey, fear and love us.

And although some of our company towards the end of the year, showed themselves too fierce, in slaying some of the people, in some towns, upon causes that on our part, might easily enough have been borne withal: yet notwithstanding because it was on their part justly deserved, the alteration of their opinions generally and for the most part concerning us is the less to be doubted.[2] And whatsoever else they may be, by carefulness of ourselves need nothing at all to be feared.[3]

The best nevertheless in this as in all actions besides is to be endeavoured and hoped, and of the worst that may happen notice to be taken with consideration, and as much as may be eschewed.

—1588

John White, Selected Watercolors

The English artist and colonist John White participated in the first two attempts to found an English colony in the Americas, on Roanoke Island, off the coast of present-day North Carolina. White himself would lead the second attempt, which famously ended in disaster with the disappearance of the entire colony's population while he was in England obtaining more supplies. The following illustrations were based on observations made during his first voyage, in 1585, when he was commissioned to document the people, plants, and animals the settlers encountered. White appears to have aimed for accuracy in his depictions, but his drawings tend to focus on elements of particular relevance to the colonizing project—potential sources of food, prospective trade goods and

markets, and Indigenous technologies. The Roanoke Colony was established on territory belonging to Roanoke people, but there were many Indigenous groups in the area, and White also visited nearby towns such as Secotan and Pomeiooc. White's watercolors provided the basis for a series of etchings included in a 1590 edition of Hariot's *Brief and True Report*; these etchings circulated widely and had a significant impact on the way Europeans thought about and portrayed Indigenous people in the following centuries.

This illustration of a prominent woman and her daughter in Pomeiooc shows the woman holding a gourd; Hariot identifies it as "a gourd full of some kind of pleasant liquor" but such vessels typically held water. The woman's daughter holds an English doll of high quality—likely a gift recognizing her high status. Hariot's caption notes that the young girls of the community "are greatly delighted with puppets and babes [dolls] which were brought out of England."

1 *accident* Event, especially one that occurs by chance.

2 *doubted* Feared.

3 *by carefulness ... feared* I.e., they are so attentive in caring for us that we need not fear them.

This illustration shows the Algonquian-speaking community of Secoton. White's descriptions identify, from top to bottom, "Their ripe corn," "Their green corn," and "Corn newly sprung"; "Their sitting at meat"; "Their place of solemn prayer"; "The house wherein the tomb of their herounds [chiefs] standeth"; and "A ceremony in their prayers with strange gestures and songs, dancing about posts carved on the tops like men's faces."

This image, titled "Their Sitting at Meat," does not specify a particular community, but shows people enjoying foods commonly eaten along the coast near Roanoke Island. Hariot writes that "Their meat [food] is maize sodden … of very good taste, deer's flesh, or of some other beast, and fish. They are very sober in their eating, and drinking, and consequently very long lived because they do not oppress nature."

White drew this map of the region surrounding Roanoke based on measurements taken by Hariot and probably other surveyors.

[Catawba Deerskin Map], based on a 1721 original. This map is a paper copy of a lost deerskin original presented by Catawba people to Francis Nicholson, governor of the colony of South Carolina, in 1721. The map shows Indigenous nations between Charles Town in South Carolina (represented to the south at the left side of the map) and Virginia (represented to the northwest in the bottom right corner of the map).

Caleb Cheeshateaumauk, letter to the Society for the Propagation of the Gospel in New England,[1] 1663

Most honored benefactors,

Historians tell of Orpheus, the musician and outstanding poet, that he received a lyre from Apollo, and that he was so excellent with it that he moved the forests and rocks by his song. He made huge trees follow behind him, and indeed rendered tamer the most ferocious beasts. After he took up the lyre he descended into the nether world, lulled Pluto and Proserpina with his song, and led Eurydice, his wife, out of the underworld into the upper.[2] The ancient philosophers say that this serves as a symbol to show how powerful are the force and virtue of education and refined literature in the transformation of the nature of barbarians. They are like trees, rocks, and brute beasts, and a substantive change (metamorphosis) must be effected in them. They have to be secured like tigers and must be induced to follow.[3]

God delegated you to be our patrons, and He endowed you with all wisdom and intimate compassion, so that you might perform the work of bringing blessings to us pagans, who derive our life and origin from our forebears. We used to be naked in soul and body, alien from all humanity, led around in the desert by all sorts of errors.

Oh threefold and fourfold most illustrious and most loving men, what kind of thanks, if not the greatest and most immense, should we give you, for you have supported us with an abundance of all things for our education and for the sustenance of our bodies. You have poured forth immense—the greatest—resources.

And we will especially give great thanks to God the most excellent and highest, who has revealed the sacred scriptures to us, and who has shown to us the Lord Jesus Christ, who is the way of truth and of life.[4] Besides all this, another hope is left us through the depths of divine mercy: that we may become instruments to spread and propagate the gospel among our kin and neighbors, so that they also may know God, and Christ.

Even though we cannot commensurately reciprocate your kindness and that of our other benefactors, we do hope, however. We are not left alone praying before God with importunate supplications for those pious and merciful men who are still in old England, who disbursed so much gold and silver for us to obtain the salvation of our souls, and for you as well, who were instruments like aqueducts in bestowing all these benefits on us.

Most devoted to your dignity:

Caleb Cheeshateaumauk

—1663

Mittark, Agreement of Mittark and His People Not to Sell Land to the English[5]

I am Muttaak, sachem of Gay Head and Nashaquitsa[6] as far as Wanemessit. Know this all people. I Muttaak and my chief men[7] and my children and my people, these are our lands. Forever we own them, and our posterity forever shall own them. I Muttaak and we the chief men, and with our children and all our

[1] Translation by Wolfgang Hochbruck and Beatrix Dudensing-Reichel, 1992, 1996.

[2] *Historians tell ... the upper* The story of Orpheus and Eurydice appears in numerous classical sources, including Ovid's *Metamorphoses*. Orpheus is permitted to retrieve his dead wife from the underworld on the condition that he not look back at her as she follows him to the surface; he looks back slightly before she reaches the world of the living, and she vanishes. Some early and medieval Christian interpretations of the story, which position Orpheus as a Christ-like or priest-like figure saving souls from hell, do not include this ending; *Apollo* Ancient Greek god associated with the sun and poetry; *Pluto and Proserpina* Latin names for the king and queen of the underworld in classical mythology.

[3] *They are like ... to follow* See Horace's *The Art of Poetry* (19 BCE), in which Orpheus is described as "the priest and Interpreter of the gods" who "deterred the savage race of men from slaughters and inhuman diet" and was "once said to tame tigers and furious lions."

[4] *who is the ... life* See John 14.6: "Jesus saith unto him, I am the way, the truth, and the life: no man cometh unto the Father, but by me."

[5] Translated by Ives Goddard and Kathleen Joan Bragdon, 1988.

[6] *Gay Head and Nashaquitsa* Territory on the southwestern portion of Noepe, now also called Martha's Vineyard, off the coast of Massachusetts.

[7] *chief men* Members of a sachem's council.

[common] people[1] [present], have agreed that no one [shall] sell land. But if anyone larcenously sells land, you shall take [back] your land, because it is forever your possession. But if anyone does not keep this agreement, he shall fall [and] have nothing more of this land at Gay Head and Nashaquitsa at all forever. I Muttaak and we the chief men, and our posterity, [say]: And it shall be so forever. I Ummuttaak say this, and my chief men: if any of these sons of mine protects my sachemship, he shall forever be a sachem. But if [any of] my sons does not protect my sachemship and sells it, he shall fall forever. And we chief men say this, and our sachem: if any of these sons of ours protects our chieftainship, he shall forever be a chief man. But if any of our sons does not protect our chieftainship and sells it, he shall fall forever. I Umuttaag, sachem, say this and my chief men; [this is] our agreement. We say it before God. It shall be so forever. I Ummuttaak, this is my hand [X], on the date September 11, 1681.

We chief men say this [and] our sachem; this is our agreement. [We say it] before God. It shall be so forever. These are our hands [X — X — X].

I John Keeps am a witness and this is my hand concerning the agreement of Ummuttaak and his chief men of Gay Head and Nashaquitsa, all [and] both. I Puttukquannan am a witness. I witnessed this agreement of Ummuttaak and his chief men of Gay Head and Nashaquitsa, both. No one forever [shall] sell it; they [shall] keep it. I Puttakquannan, this is my hand [X].

I Sasauwapinnoo am a witness. I witnessed the agreement of Ummuttaak and his chief men of Gay Head and Nashaquitsa, all [and] both. I Sasauwapinnoo, my hand.

—1681

Mittark, Agreement of Mittark and His People Not to Sell Land to the English, 1681. An English translation of this Massachusett-language legal document appears above.

HANDSOME LAKE, "HOW THE WHITE RACE CAME TO AMERICA AND WHY THE GAI´WIIO´[2] BECAME A NECESSITY"

originally told by Handsome Lake in the early nineteenth century; appearing here as told by Chief Edward Cornplanter (So-son-do-wa) to Arthur C. Parker for *The Code of Handsome Lake, the Seneca Prophet* (1913)

Now this happened a long time ago across the great salt sea, odji ke'dāgi ga, that stretches east. There is, so it seems, a world there and soil like ours. There in the great queen's country where swarmed many people—so many that they crowded upon one another and had no place for hunting—there lived a great queen. Among her servants was a young preacher of the queen's religion, so it is said.

[1] *[common] people* People subject to the sachem. The consent of the common people was essential to decisions regarding the dispensation of land; *[common]* Words believed to be erroneously omitted by the clerk who copied the document have been inserted in square brackets.

[2] *GAI´WIIO´* Literally "Good Message," the religious movement founded by Handsome Lake.

Now this happened. The great queen requested the preacher to clean some old volumes which she had concealed in a hidden chest. So he obeyed and when he had cleaned the last book, which was at the bottom of the chest, he opened it and looked about and listened, for truly he had no right to read the book and wanted no one to detect him. He read. It was a great book and told him many things which he never knew before. Therefore he was greatly worried. He read of a great man who had been a prophet and the son of the Great Ruler. He had been born on the earth and the white men to whom he preached killed him. Now moreover the prophet had promised to return and become the King. In three days he was to come and then in forty to start his kingdom. This did not happen as his followers had expected and so they despaired. Then said one chief follower, "Surely he will come again sometime, we must watch for him."

Then the young preacher became worried for he had discovered that his god was not on earth to see. He was angry moreover because his teachers had deceived him. So then he went to the chief of preachers and asked him how it was that he had deceived him. Then the chief preacher said, "Seek him out and you will find him for indeed we think he does live on earth." Even so, his heart was angry but he resolved to seek.

On the morning of the next day he looked out from the opening of his room and saw out in the river a beautiful island and he marveled that he had never seen it before. He continued to gaze and as he did he saw among the trees a castle of gold and he marveled that he had not seen the castle of gold before. Then he said, "So beautiful a castle on so beautiful an isle must indeed be the abode of him whom I seek." Immediately he put on his clothes and went to the men who had taught him and they wondered and said, "Indeed it must be as you say." So then together they went to the river and when they came to the shore they saw that it was spanned by a bridge of shining gold. Then one of the great preachers fell down and read from his book a long prayer and arising he turned his back upon the island and fled for he was afraid to meet the lord. Then with the young man the other crossed the bridge and he knelt on the grass and he cried loud and groaned his prayer but when he arose to his feet he too fled and would not look again at the house—the castle of gold.

Then was the young man disgusted and boldly he strode toward the house to attend to the business which he had in mind. He did not cry or pray and neither did he fall to his knees for he was not afraid. He knocked at the door and a handsome smiling man welcomed him in and said, "Do not be afraid of me." Then the smiling man in the castle of gold said, "I have wanted a young man such as you for some time. You are wise and afraid of nobody. Those older men were fools and would not have listened to me (direct) though they might listen to some one whom I had instructed. Listen to me and most truly you shall be rich. Across the ocean that lies toward the sunset is another world and a great country and a people whom you have never seen. Those people are virtuous, they have no unnatural evil habits and they are honest. A great reward is yours if you will help me. Here are five things that men and women enjoy: take them to these people and make them as white men are. Then shall you be rich and powerful and you may become the chief of all great preachers here."

So then the young man took the bundle containing the *five things* and made the bargain. He left the island and looking back saw that the bridge had disappeared and before he had turned his head the castle had gone and then as he looked the island itself vanished.

Now then the young man wondered if indeed he had seen his lord for his mind had been so full of business that he had forgotten to ask. So he opened his bundle of five things and found a flask of rum, a pack of playing cards, a handful of coins, a violin and a decayed leg bone. Then he thought the things very strange and he wondered if indeed his lord would send such gifts to the people across the water of the salt lake; but he remembered his promise.

The young man looked about for a suitable man in whom to confide his secret and after some searching he found a man named Columbus and to him he confided the story. Then did Columbus secure some big canoes and raise up wings and he sailed away. He sailed many days and his warriors became angry and cried that the chief who led them was a deceiver. They planned to behead him but he heard of the plan and promised that on the next day he would discover the new country. The next morning came and then did Columbus discover America. Then the boats turned back and reported their find to the whole world. Then

did great ships come, a good many. Then did they bring many bundles of the five things and spread the gifts to all the men of the great earth island.

Then did the invisible man of the river island laugh and then did he say, "These cards will make them gamble away their wealth and idle their time: this money will make them dishonest and covetous and they will forget their old laws: this fiddle will make them dance with their arms about their wives and bring about a time of tattling and idle gossip: this rum will turn their minds to foolishness and they will barter their country for baubles; then will this secret poison eat the life from their blood and crumble their bones." So said the invisible man he was Hanĭsse'ono, the evil one.

Now all this was done and when afterward he saw the havoc and the misery his work had done he said, "I think I have made an enormous mistake for I did not dream that these people would suffer so." Then did even the devil himself lament that his evil had been so great.

So after the swarms of white men came and misery was thrust upon the Ongwe-oweh[1] the Creator was sorry for his own people whom he had molded from the soil of the earth of this Great Island, and he spoke to his four messengers and many times they tried to tell right men the revelations of the Creator but none would listen. Then they found our head man sick. Then they heard him speak to the sun and to the moon and they saw his sickness. Then they knew that he suffered because of the cunning evils that Hanĭsse'ono had given the Ongwe-oweh. So then they knew that he was the one. He was the one who should hear and tell Gai'wiio'. But when Ganio'dai'io'[2] spoke the evil being ceased his lament and sought to obstruct Gai'wiio', for he claimed to be master.

The Gai'wiioi' came from Hodiänok'doo^n Hĕd'iohe', the Great Ruler, to the Hadiöyă'geono^n, the four messengers.[3] From them it was transmitted to Ganio'dai'io', Handsome Lake who taught it to Skandyo^n''gwadĭ (Owen Blacksnake) and to his own grandson, Sos'heowă (James Johnson). Blacksnake taught it to Henry Stevens (Ganishando), who taught it to Soson'dowa, Edward Cornplanter. "So I know that I have the true words and I preach them," adds Cornplanter.

Seneca pouch, early nineteenth century. This pouch, embroidered with an image of the twin brothers central to the Haudenosaunee creation story, references internal divisions among the Haudenosaunee during the American Revolution (1765–91), when members disagreed as to whether to support the American or British sides.

[1] *Ongwe-oweh* Literally, "original people," i.e., the Haudenosaunee.

[2] *Ganio'dai'io'* Handsome Lake.

[3] *four messengers* Beings who delivered the Creator or Great Ruler's message to Handsome Lake.

In Context

The Myth of Thanksgiving[1]

The American celebration of Thanksgiving has changed over the course of the four centuries since the "first Thanksgiving" of 1621. The holiday has come to represent for many people a celebration of food, family, and friends—all centered on the story and iconography of a myth concerning the Pilgrims of Plymouth and their "friendly relations" with the Wampanoag people of what came to be known as New England. Parades, pageants, costumes, and other revelries have often attended the holiday, perpetuating a myth of harmonious relationships between the Wampanoag and the Puritans and a subsequent gradual, benevolent expansion of the European colony across the territory that became the United States, in the course of which Indigenous peoples gave up their lands and gradually disappeared. Yet very little of this story is based in truth. The first Thanksgiving feast took place during a brief time when a treaty of mutual defense existed between the Pilgrims and the Wampanoag, in what was otherwise a long history of slaughter, domination, and duplicity on the part of the colonists.

The earliest roots of what developed into the American holiday of Thanksgiving can be traced to two accounts of the Plymouth colony's plentiful harvest of 1621, excerpts of which are both printed below: a letter by Edward Winslow printed in *Mourt's Relation* (1622), and a journal entry by Governor William Bradford in *Of Plymouth Plantation* (1651). The successful harvest of 1621, the year following the colonists' first arrival in Plymouth, was crucial to the survival of the fledgling community. For Puritans, a day of Thanksgiving was a solemn occasion declared by the community at any time of year when it saw evidence of God's favor in worldly events. The day would be dedicated to fasting and prayer; similarly, the community would declare days of humiliation or penitence, in which the people would pray for forgiveness when outward events revealed signs that God was displeased. Neither Winslow nor Bradford identified the event they described as a day of Thanksgiving; as there was feasting involved, it was evidently not a formal Thanksgiving but more a day of social celebration. Winslow relates how the sachem of the Wampanoag, Massasoit, came to see the colonists with ninety men. The Wampanoag had made a mutual defense pact with the Pilgrims the year before, and, when the Wampanoag heard gunfire at the colony, brought an army to aid in the colonists' defense. Finding the gunfire was not hostile, the Wampanoag brought additional food to the feast and stayed for three days.

This peaceful meeting was not repeated on a yearly basis, and there was little future occasion to celebrate harmony with the Indigenous peoples of the area. The Puritans continued to hold Thanksgivings and Humiliations, but in response to events in the moment—for example, when grateful for their victories in battle against the friends they had feasted with in 1621. The Thanksgiving held in 1676 was one such occasion, when the Pilgrims stuck the head of Metacom, the son of Massasoit, on a spike, where it was to stay for twenty-five years. The settlers also worked ceaselessly to acquire Indigenous lands using dubious methods, including threats, violence, debt, and false promises.

The modern holiday of Thanksgiving was shaped by more than simply the "origin story" of the 1621 Wampanoag-Pilgrim feast. In 1841, a Unitarian minister named Alexander Young wrote notes in his copy of *Mourt's Relation*, to the effect that the celebration described by Winslow was the "first thanksgiving ... of New England." Then, two decades later, a magazine editor named Sarah Josepha Hale repurposed this language and wrote a letter urging

[1] The editors are indebted to Philip Deloria's excellent article "The Invention of Thanksgiving: Massacres, Myths, and the Making of the Great November Holiday" (*The New Yorker*, 18 November 2019).

Abraham Lincoln to declare a national Thanksgiving holiday to celebrate the union. In 1863, Lincoln agreed. He declared that there would be a national holiday on the last Thursday of November—"Thanksgiving"—a day of national unity in the midst of civil war. Families and friends gathered to share foodways, customs, and leisure activities, and also to pray and mourn the losses from the ongoing civil conflict. From that point on, Thanksgiving began to resemble the holiday we are familiar with today, a celebration of American identity, family, food, and sport. By the early twentieth century, the story of the 1621 feast was woven within this unionist fabric, and the holiday gradually became increasingly celebratory and consumerist, having mainly lost the undertones of war remembrance that Lincoln had urged.

For the Wampanoag and other Indigenous nations of New England, Thanksgiving is observed as a National Day of Mourning. Since 1970, the United American Indians of New England have held protests and vigils on Thanksgiving; Linda Coombs, a member of the Wampanoag nation, has powerfully described what the holiday has come to represent for her people: "When the colonists came over in the 17th century, they had to get rid of us in one form or fashion or another, whether it was converting us, moving us, annihilating us, or shipping us out of the country into slavery, and I just wish people knew that, because this history is not yet well known, but that's what it took for America to be what it is today and for people to sit down to have their Thanksgiving dinner."[1]

from Edward Winslow, "A Letter Sent from New England to a Friend in These Parts," 12 December 1621, published in *Mourt's Relation* (1622)

Loving, and old friend,

Although I received no letter from you by this ship, yet forasmuch as I know you expect the performance of my promise, which was, to write unto you truly and faithfully of all things, I have therefore at this time sent unto you accordingly. …

You shall understand, that in this little time, that a few of us have been here, we have built seven dwelling-houses, and four for the use of the plantation, and have made preparation for diverse[2] others. We set the last spring some twenty acres of Indian corn, and sowed some six acres of barley and peas, and according to the manner of the Indians, we manured our ground with herrings or rather shads, which we have in great abundance, and take with great ease at our doors. Our corn did prove[3] well, and God be praised, we had a good increase of Indian corn, and our barley indifferent good, but our peas not worth the gathering, for we feared they were too late sown, they came up very well, and blossomed, but the sun parched them in the blossom.

Our harvest being gotten in, our governor[4] sent four men on fowling, that so we might after a special manner rejoice together after we had gathered the fruit of our labors; they four in one day killed as much fowl, as with a little help beside, served the company almost a week, at which time amongst other recreations, we exercised our arms, many of the Indians coming amongst us, and among the rest their greatest King Massasoit,[5] with some ninety men, whom for three days we entertained and feasted, and they went out and killed five deer, which they brought to the plantation and bestowed on our governor,

[1] Quoted in Olivia B. Waxman, "400 Years after the 'First Thanksgiving,' the Tribe that Fed the Pilgrims Continues to Fight for Its Land amid Another Epidemic," 23 November 2020, *Time Magazine*.

[2] *diverse* Several.

[3] *prove* Thrive.

[4] *governor* William Bradford (1590–1657).

[5] *King Massasoit* Sachem of the Wampanoag confederacy, also known as Ousamequin (c. 1581–1661).

and upon the captain, and others. And although it be not always so plentiful as it was at this time with us, yet by the goodness of God, we are so far from want that we often wish you partakers of our plenty. …

Your loving friend,

E.W.

William Bradford, from Chapter 12 Anno Domini 1621, *Of Plymouth Plantation* (1856; written 1630–51)

They began now to gather in the small harvest they had, and to fit up their houses and dwellings against winter, being all well recovered in health and strength and had all things in good plenty. For as some were thus employed in affairs abroad, others were exercised in fishing, about cod and bass and other fish, of which they took good store, of which every family had their portion. All the summer there was no want; and now began to come in store of fowl, as winter approached, of which this place did abound when they came first (but afterward decreased by degrees). And besides waterfowl there was great store of wild turkeys, of which they took many, besides venison, etc. Besides they had about a peck[1] a meal a week to a person, or now since harvest, Indian corn to that proportion. Which made many afterwards write so largely of their plenty here to their friends in England, which were not feigned but true reports.

Abraham Lincoln, A Proclamation, 3 October 1863

The year that is drawing towards its close, has been filled with the blessings of fruitful fields and healthful skies. To these bounties, which are so constantly enjoyed that we are prone to forget the source from which they come, others have been added, which are of so extraordinary a nature, that they cannot fail to penetrate and soften even the heart which is habitually insensible to the ever watchful providence of Almighty God. In the midst of a civil war of unequalled magnitude and severity, which has sometimes seemed to foreign States to invite and to provoke their aggression,[2] peace has been preserved with all nations, order has been maintained, the laws have been respected and obeyed, and harmony has prevailed everywhere except in the theatre of military conflict; while that theatre has been greatly contracted by the advancing armies and navies of the Union. Needful diversions of wealth and of strength from the fields of peaceful industry to the national defence, have not arrested the plough, the shuttle[3] or the ship; the axe has enlarged the borders of our settlements, and the mines, as well of iron and coal as of the precious metals, have yielded even more abundantly than heretofore. Population has steadily increased, notwithstanding the waste that has been made in the camp, the siege and the battlefield; and the country, rejoicing in the consciousness of augmented strength and vigor, is permitted to expect continuance of years with large increase of freedom. No human counsel hath devised nor hath any mortal hand worked out these great things. They are the gracious gifts of the Most High God, who, while dealing with us in anger for our sins, hath nevertheless remembered mercy. It has seemed to me fit and proper that they should be solemnly, reverently and gratefully acknowledged as with one heart and one voice by the whole American People. I do therefore invite my fellow citizens in every part of the United States, and also those who are at sea and those who are sojourning in foreign lands, to set apart and observe the last Thursday of November next, as a day of Thanksgiving and Praise to our beneficent Father who dwelleth

[1] *peck* Unit of measurement equivalent to about eight quarts.

[2] *foreign States … aggression* Confederate forces had hoped for military support from Britain and France, a threat that never materialized.

[3] *shuttle* I.e., the shuttle used on a loom for weaving.

in the Heavens. And I recommend to them that while offering up the ascriptions[1] justly due to Him for such singular deliverances and blessings, they do also, with humble penitence for our national perverseness and disobedience, commend to His tender care all those who have become widows, orphans, mourners or sufferers in the lamentable civil strife in which we are unavoidably engaged, and fervently implore the interposition of the Almighty Hand to heal the wounds of the nation and to restore it as soon as may be consistent with the Divine purposes to the full enjoyment of peace, harmony, tranquility and Union.

In testimony whereof, I have hereunto set my hand and caused the Seal of the United States to be affixed.

Thomas Nast, *Thanksgiving-Day*, 26 November 1863. This print was inserted as a centerfold in *Harper's Weekly* in 1863, after Lincoln's Thanksgiving Proclamation of the same year. Lady Liberty at prayer is the central figure, with other groups of citizens also praying in the surrounding vignettes, including, at the bottom, a group of enslaved people praying for freedom and giving thanks for emancipation (the Emancipation Proclamation had been issued by Lincoln on 1 January 1863).

[1] *ascriptions* I.e., prayers (an ascription is the term for the closure of a sermon, when the speaker offers thanks and praise to God).

J.L.G. Ferris, *The First Thanksgiving, 1621*, c. 1912–15. This painting presents an idealized, roman-
tic depiction of the Wampanoag and Plymouth settlers sharing a meal ("the first Thanksgiving") at
Plymouth—though the presence of various weapons in the image hints at the precariousness of peace.
Ferris produced this painting as part of a series, *Pageant of a Nation*, that presented key moments in
U.S. history. Many aspects of this painting have been proven historically inaccurate—for example,
there is no evidence that women took part in the feast, and the Wampanoag did not wear feathered
headdresses. Their clothes in the painting, too, are more typical of tribes from the Plains.

National Day of Mourning plaque, 1998. This plaque was erected by the town of Plymouth as part
of a settlement with the United American Indians of New England, after peaceful protesters had
been arrested on Thanksgiving Day in Plymouth on 27 November 1997. The settlement not only
led to all charges being dropped against the protesters and to the erection of this plaque, but also,
according to the statement by the United American Indians of New England, to other reparations:
"Plymouth has acknowledged our right to walk on our own land without a permit on National Day
of Mourning. Plymouth has agreed to make the truth part of its celebration of the pilgrim myth of
thanksgiving. Under the terms of this agreement, we will have a number of important opportunities
to address the lies and inaccuracies about 'thanksgiving' and the history of Indigenous peoples that
have been disseminated not only in Plymouth but throughout the country. We are confident that this
agreement represents a tremendous victory for the struggle of Native people to have our voices heard
and respected."

California

Many Indigenous peoples of what settlers called California—an exceptionally linguistically and culturally diverse region—were aware of Europeans long before the Spanish made any serious attempt to colonize the area. Spain first claimed and began to explore Baja California (Lower California, a long peninsula that is now part of Mexico) in the 1530s, and Alta California (Upper California, a large area including the present state of California) in the 1540s, but it did not actually establish settlements in Baja California until the late 1690s, or in Alta California until the mid-1700s. News of their colonization efforts elsewhere, however, preceded the Spanish. In 1542, when the crew of Spanish explorer Juan Rodríguez Cabrillo became the first Europeans to land on the Alta California coast, the Kumeyaay people who lived there were already wary of white explorers. Cabrillo wrote that his informants had heard reports from the interior of "men like us ... traveling about, bearded, clothed and armed ... killing many native Indians."

Compared to Central America, known to be rich in resources, California did not appear to the Spanish government to be a profitable place to settle. Initially, it was primarily of interest to Spain for its position on the trade route from the Philippines to Mexico; it took months to cross the Pacific, and by the time Spanish crews reached North America they were often in desperate need of rest and fresh water. In 1602, the merchant Sebastián Vizcaíno led an expedition north from Baja California, charting the coastline and seeking a site for a Spanish outpost where ships could pause on their way from Asia toward Mexico. Vizcaíno imposed many of the place names that are commonly used today—including that of Monterey Bay, the site he proposed for settlement. Vizcaíno's expedition is described in the excerpt below from *A Brief Report of the Discovery in the South Sea* (1620) by Fray Antonio de la Ascención, a cosmographer and Carmelite priest who contributed to the journey in both religious and mapmaking capacities. In his *Brief Report* and other writings, Ascención enthusiastically endorsed settlement—and proposed that the Carmelite order take a lead role in the conversion of Indigenous people. These recommendations were not followed, as the Spanish government decided instead to invest in a search for rumored islands in the central Pacific, closer to the midpoint of the trade route from Asia to Mexico. While Ascención did not shape official policy as he intended, his work influenced many seventeenth- and eighteenth-century Spanish writers' perceptions of California.

Indigenous life on the Alta California coast continued with relatively little direct interference from settlers until a Spanish colonization effort began in the late 1760s, prompted largely by fears that British, Dutch, or Russian colonists might infringe on Spanish claims to the region. In other parts of the Americas, the importance of religious conversion had receded somewhat in Spain's approach to colonization, with military and other secular institutions gaining in prominence. But Franciscan missionaries, led by the friar Junípero Serra and supported by soldiers, dominated the colonization of "New California." The settlers were vastly outnumbered; as late as the 1780s there were a few hundred Spanish people and about 20,000 Indigenous people on the California coast. California's Franciscan missionaries, hoping to stamp out thoughts of rebellion, often employed brutal whippings, brandings, and other corporal punishment to maintain their authority. Mission life, for the Indigenous neophytes (converts living in the mission) was structured by forced labor that some Euro-American accounts likened to enslavement; as the explorer Jean-François de Lapérouse wrote, "The men and women are collected by the sound of a bell; a missionary leads them to work, to the church, and to all their exercises." Missionaries interfered extensively in community and family life, requiring neophytes to live in gender segregated barracks out of a concern for Indigenous morality—while at the same time Junípero Serra lamented his inability to stop his colonists from raping the converts. Neophytes died in large numbers due to overcrowding, malnutrition, and disease, while others fled, and some mounted resistance movements. Despite this, the mission populations grew, as food shortages, political instability, and other external factors pushed

more people to convert. By the time the California missions were dissolved in 1834, their operators had effectively enslaved about 90,000 people.

A brief history of one mission's establishment, excerpted below, is offered in the writings of Pablo Tac, a Luiseño (Payómkawichum) scholar who was born in 1820 at Mission San Luis Rey de Francia, in his home territory of Quechla (near what is now San Diego). Tac studied first in Mexico City, then in Rome at the Collegium Urbanum de Propaganda Fide (Urban College for the Propagation of the Faith), a cosmopolitan environment where students from across Europe, Asia, and America prepared for the priesthood together. At the Collegium, Tac developed his own approach to writing Luiseño, which had previously been solely an oral language, and he wrote a Luiseño grammar in Spanish and Latin. This language guide is interspersed with Spanish-language writings on Luiseño history and culture. Tac's work appears to give equal weight to pre-contact and Christianized Indigenous practices, with, for example, descriptions of longstanding dance traditions appearing alongside Christian verses.

The excessive brutality that sometimes occurred in missions—and the resistance it was met with—is suggested in the excerpt below from an interview with Lorenzo Asisara, a man born in 1819 into the Indigenous population of Mission Santa Cruz. Asisara served unpaid as a musician and a priests' assistant until the mission's dissolution and was working as a ranch hand when he was interviewed in 1877 by the Cuban-born American historian Thomas Savage. Savage recorded Asisara's description of the mission under a succession of administrators, many of them kinder and more well-liked than Father Olbes, who features in the account below.

from Antonio de la Ascención, *A Brief Report of the Discovery in the South Sea*[1]

10

We went forward,[2] making the exploration carefully and slowly, because head winds impeded it. Other ports and islands were discovered along the coast, and all along it there were many Indians, who signalled us with smoke columns and other signs; but, in order to reach Cape Mendocino,[3] everything was left to be examined on our return. Finally, after much labor we reached the port of San Diego, which is very good and capacious and offers many very good advantages for Spanish settlement. Here the ships were cleaned and oiled again, the place being quiet, and there being many friendly and affable Indians there. They use bows and arrows and appear warlike and valiant, since,

notwithstanding they came to see us every day, they always treated us with so great a distrust that they never had complete confidence in us. They pronounced so very well in our language what they heard us speak that anyone hearing them and not seeing them would say they were Spaniards. Every day they would come in order that we might give them some of the fish we caught in the net, and they would go away quietly after they had helped to haul it in.

The harbor is large and secure, and has a large beach within, like an island of sand, which the sea covers at high tide. In the sand on this beach there is a great quantity of yellow pyrites,[4] all full of holes, a sure sign that in the neighboring mountain and adjacent to this port there are gold mines; for the water, when it rains, brings it from the mountains, and the whole watershed converges here. On the sandy beach which I said was in this harbor we found some large pieces, like adobe, brown or dark red in color, and very light in weight, like dried cowdung. They had neither a good nor a bad

[1] Translated by Herbert Bolton, 1916.

[2] *We went forward* At this point in the narrative, the expedition is traveling up the west coast of Baja California (a peninsula that is now part of Mexico, south of the state of California) toward San Diego.

[3] *Cape Mendocino* In what is now the northern part of the state of California.

[4] *pyrites* Iron sulfide minerals also called "fool's gold" for their gold color, and frequently found near real gold deposits.

odor, and they are said to be amber.[1] If this is so, there are great riches and an abundance of amber here.

There are many different kinds of fish, of very good taste and flavor, such as ray, sea-horse, lobster, crab, *guitarras*,[2] sardine, turtle, and many other kinds. There is much wild game for hunting and fowling; and there are many large, grassy pastures. The Indians paint themselves white, and black, and dark London blue.[3] This color comes from certain very heavy blue stones, which they grind very fine, and, dissolving the powder in water, make a stain, with which they daub the face and make on it lines which glisten like silver ribbons. These stones seem to be of a rich silver ore, and the Indians told us by signs that from similar stones a people living inland, of form and figure like our Spaniards, bearded, and wearing collars and breeches, and other fine garments like ours, secured silver in abundance, and that they had a name for it in their own language. To ascertain whether these Indians knew silver, the general showed them some silver bowls and a plate. They took it in their hands and spun it around, and, pleased by the sound, said it was good, and was the same as that possessed and valued highly by the people of whom they had told us. Then he put in their hands a pewter bowl, but when they struck it the sound did not please them and, spitting, they wanted to throw it into the sea.

The people of whom the Indians told us might have been foreigners, Hollanders or English, who had made their voyage by the Strait of Anian and might be settled on the other coast of this land, facing the Mediterranean Sea of California.[4] Since the realm is narrow, as has been said, it may be that the other sea is near that place; for the Indians offered to guide and take us to the place where they say the people are settled. If this is so, it is probable they have large interests and profits there, since their voyage is so long

and difficult. Still, it is true that by passing through the Strait of Anian and reaching their land by the latitude, their voyage is only half as long as that from the port of San Juan de Ulúa[5] to Spain. This will be clearly seen from evidence furnished by the globe. In this case, it will be to his Majesty's[6] interest to endeavor to assure himself of the fact: first, in order to know the route, and secondly, in order to expel from there such dangerous enemies, lest they contaminate the Indians with their sects and liberty of conscience,[7] by which great harm to their souls will follow, whereby instructing them and leading them in the paths of the true law of God will be made very difficult. Besides this, his Majesty will be able to secure many other advantages, as I shall show later.

II

After we left the Port of San Diego we discovered many islands placed in a line, one behind another. Most of them were inhabited by many friendly Indians, who have trade and commerce with those of the mainland. It may be that they are vassals of a petty king who came with his son from the mainland in a canoe with eight oarsmen, to see us and to invite us to go to his land, saying that he would entertain us and provide us with anything which we needed and he possessed. He said that he came to see us on account of what the inhabitants of these islands had reported to him. There are many people in this land, so many that the petty king, seeing that there were no women on the ships, offered by signs to give to everyone ten women apiece if they would all go to his land, which shows how thickly populated it all is. And besides, all along, day and night, they made many bonfires, the sign in use among them to call people to their land. Since there was no convenient port where the ships could be secure in the country whence this petty king came, the acceptance of his invitation was deferred until the return voyage.

1 *amber* I.e., ambergris, a secretion produced by sperm whales that is valuable as an ingredient in perfume.

2 *guitarras* Guitarfish, a type of ray with a wide, pointed head and small wings.

3 *London blue* Shade of blue-black.

4 *Mediterranean* I.e., almost entirely surrounded by land; *Strait of Anian ... Sea of California* Ascención believed California to be an island bounded by the Strait of Anian to the north and the Mediterranean Sea of California to the east.

5 *San Juan de Ulúa* Site of a Spanish colonial fortress established in the 1530s on the eastern coast of Mexico. It is about 5,500 miles from San Juan de Ulúa to Spain.

6 *his Majesty* King Philip III of Spain (r. 1598–1621).

7 *their sects* I.e., branches of Protestantism; *liberty of conscience* Freedom to act according to one's own ethical and religious beliefs—a tenet more strongly associated with Protestantism than with Catholicism.

Thereupon we went forward with our voyage, and at the end of some days arrived at a fine port, which was named Monterrey. It is in latitude 37°, in the same climate and latitude as Seville. This is where the ships coming from the Philippines to New Spain[1] come to reconnoitre. It is a good harbor, well sheltered, and supplied with water, wood, and good timber, both for masts and ship building, such as pines, live oaks, and great white oaks, large and frondose,[2] and many black poplars on the banks of a river that nearby enters the sea and was named the Carmelo. In climate, in birds and game, in variety of animals and trees, in everything it is essentially like our Old Spain. When the ships from China arrive at this place they have already sailed four months and they come in need of repairs, which in this harbor they can make very well, and with perfect convenience; therefore it would be a very good thing for the Spaniards to settle this port for the assistance of navigators, and to undertake the conversion to our Holy Faith of those Indians, who are numerous, docile, and friendly. And from here they might trade and traffic with the people of China and Japan, opportunity for that being favorable because of propinquity.[3]

The land of this country is very fertile and has good pastures and forests, and fine hunting and fowling. Among the animals there are large, fierce bears, and other animals called elks, from which they make elk-leather jackets, and others of the size of young bulls, shaped and formed like deer, with thick, large horns. There were many Castilian roses[4] here. There are pretty ponds of fresh water. The mountains near this port were covered with snow, and that was on Christmas day. On the beach was a dead whale, and at night some bears came to feed on it.

There are many fish here, and a great variety of mollusks among the rocks; among them were certain barnacles, or large shells, fastened to the lowest part of the rocks. The Indians hunt for them to extract from their contents to eat. These shells are very bright, of fine mother-of-pearl.[5] All along this coast, there is a great abundance of sea-wolves or dogs,[6] of the size of a yearling calf. They sleep on the water, and sometimes go ashore to take the sun; and there they place their sentinel in order to be secure from enemies. The Indians clothe themselves in the skins of these animals, which are healthful, fine, beautiful, and convenient. Finally, I will say that this is a good and commodious port, and might be settled, but this should be done in the way which I shall set forth hereafter. ...

13
The Method to Be Observed in Subduing and Settling the Realm of the Californias

All this realm of the Californias can be pacified and settled, and by this means and by the preaching of the Holy Gospel its natives can be led to the fold of our Holy Mother, the Roman Catholic Church, and converted to our Holy Catholic Faith. Now, in order that this may become an accomplished fact, and that his Majesty may effect it at a moderate expense, that which must be commanded, ordered, and provided is as follows:

There should be prepared and equipped in the port of Acapulco two small vessels of two hundred tons burden, and a frigate, with boats and skiffs for their service; and they should be abundantly supplied with stores and munitions of war, as well as with food, rigging, canvas, and everything that may seem necessary for settling in infidel and heathen lands.

While these things are being provided and prepared, there should be raised in Mexico as many as two hundred soldiers, care being taken that they should be good seamen, and also that they be old soldiers, expert and experienced as well in arms as in seamanship, in order that all, uniformly and without distinction, may aid in everything as occasion may offer. And let care be taken that they be good and honorable men in order that on the journey both on sea and land there may be peace, union, and brotherhood among all. Plenty

[1] *Philippines to New Spain* The Mexican colonies of New Spain facilitated trade between the Philippines and Spain; the route crossed the Pacific northeast from Manila and turned south toward Acapulco when it reached the California coast.

[2] *frondose* Leafy.

[3] *propinquity* Nearness.

[4] *Castilian roses* The California wild rose, whose flowers are pink with five petals, resembles some rose species native to western Europe.

[5] *certain barnacles ... of fine mother-of-pearl* Several species of abalone are native to the California coast.

[6] *sea-wolves or dogs* Probably sea lions or seals.

of men of these parts and talents will very easily be found in Mexico if his Majesty will increase their pay in proportion as the double service they have to render demands, and if their pay and allowance be given them punctually when due.

The duty of raising this troop should be assigned to one or two captains, good Christians and God-fearing men, and persons of merit, who have served his Majesty faithfully on other occasions, in war on land as well as in the fleets at sea. To them should be entrusted the appointment of officers to accompany them, who should be persons they are satisfied will perform their service in a Christian and careful manner, and men of experience, who know how to fulfill the offices committed to them, for on these officers depend the good order and discipline of the soldiers. This expedition must be entrusted to a person of courage and talents, of long experience, and accustomed to such charges, in order that he may know how to treat all with love and dignity, and each one individually as his character deserves. Let care be taken that such a person be God-fearing, scrupulous in his conscience, and zealous in the service of his Majesty and in the things relating to the conversion of these souls. To a person of these qualities can be given the office of general of the armada, to whom all, both captains and soldiers, will be subject, and whom they will obey in everything, and whose orders they will follow.

To the general, captains, soldiers, and all who go on this expedition, must be given express order and command that they shall hold themselves in strict obedience and subjection to the religious who are in their company, and that without their order, counsel, and advice, war may not be made, or the heathen Indians be otherwise molested, even if they should give occasion, in order that by this means matters may be conducted with peace and Christianity, and with love and quiet, which is the method to be used in the pacification of that realm, and in the preaching of the Holy Gospel, to which end and aim these expenses and preparations are directed. Not to do this, but the contrary, will be to waste everything, to lose time, and to render the expenditure ineffectual, as has been found by experience many times in this New Spain, in other conquests and pacifications of new lands, whereby God our Lord has been more injured than served.

14

The religious who should go on this expedition are the Discalced of Our Lady of Carmel,[1] the ones to whom are entrusted by his Majesty the conversion, instruction, and teaching of the Indians of this realm 'of the Californias. On this first entrance there should be six religious, four priests and two lay brothers;[2] and it will be requested of the superiors of this order, in the name of his Majesty, that those whom they assign and appoint for this voyage be persons such as the occasion and enterprise demand, holy, affable, full of love and wisdom, that they may know how to counsel, guide and direct these souls, and to deal with such cases as may present themselves conformably with sound Catholic doctrine.

By observing the indulgences[3] and benefits which the Supreme Pontiffs[4] have granted in favor of new conversions, for their greater increase, these holy friars, with their piety, modesty, simplicity, and religious graciousness, will succeed in winning the wills and hearts of both general and captains, as well as of all the soldiers, in order thereby to lead them in the holy path of virtue; and may they with loving arguments persuade and admonish all, before embarking, to confess their sins and receive the most holy sacrament of the Eucharist,[5] with all the devotion and inclination possible, offering their souls and lives to the service of his divine Majesty, asking of him success for their voyage and expedition. By doing this, with the proper spirit and devotion, the religious will make themselves lords over the hearts and wills of all, and will have authority over all to keep them in peace, love, and unity; and if perchance there should be any dissension among them,

[1] *Discalced of Our Lady of Carmel* Religious order to which Ascensión belonged.

[2] *lay brothers* Members of a religious order who perform secular functions.

[3] *indulgences* Pardon from some or all of the punishment in purgatory that is, according to Catholic doctrine, due to sinners even when their sins have been forgiven. Indulgences can be obtained in a variety of ways and the Church has, at times, offered them for participation in colonizing projects.

[4] *Supreme Pontiffs* Popes.

[5] *Eucharist* Christian sacrament commemorating the Last Supper; Roman Catholics believe they receive the body and blood of Jesus in the form of bread and wine.

they will calm it at once with discretion, and thus animosities, vexations, and enmities, and the mutinies, insurrections, and disobedience to superiors which ordinarily occur on such enterprises, will be avoided.

These religious will be provided with everything necessary for their voyage, such as vessels for saying mass and administering the sacraments, books and vestments and, in particular, something in the way of delicacies that they may have wherewith to give the sick if there should be any. Likewise, there should be taken on board at the coast of his Majesty a quantity of trifles, Flemish trinkets, such as beads of colored glass, artificial garnets, hawks' bells,[1] mirrors, knives, cheap scissors, Parisian tops, and some articles of clothing.

These things should be divided among the religious and soldiers, so that in places where they may go on shore or where they may choose sites for settlements in the lands of the heathen, they may distribute them, with signs of love and good will, in the name of his Majesty, in order that with these pleasing gifts the heathen Indians may come to feel love and affection for the Christians, and may realize that they are coming to their lands to give them of that which they bring, and not to take away their possessions, and may understand that they are seeking the good of their souls. This is a measure of great importance, to the end that the Indians may become quiet, humane, and peaceable, and obey the Spaniards without opposition or repugnance, and receive with pleasure those who go to preach to them the Holy Gospel and the mysteries of our Holy Catholic faith; to the end, moreover, that the Indians may be grateful and thankful, and, in recompense and pay for what is given them, may assist with whatever of value they may have in their land, things to eat as well as other articles, as they did with us.

With this preparation, the soldiers and religious should embark in the ships provided, no woman going or embarking with them, to avoid offenses to God and dissensions between one another. With the ocean currents that run toward the entrance of California, even if winds favorable to navigation should fail, one can within a month at the most succeed in landing in the Bay of San Bernabé,[2] which is at Cape San Lucas and the extremity of California, the point best fitted for the first settlement.

—1620

from Pablo Tac, "Conversion of the San Luiseños of Alta California"[3]

It is known from history that the first missionaries to go to California were the Jesuits, and the first among them was Father Juan Salvatierra,[4] renowned in the history of California for his acts of piety. The Dominican Fathers arrived in Baja California and the Franciscan Fathers in Alta California. The Franciscan Fathers of whom I speak here in Mexico are called the Fernandino Fathers, because the college or monastery where they are found is called the Convent of San Fernando King of Spain. These Fathers arrived in Alta California, and one of them arrived in our region, which we call *Quechla*—which is why we call ourselves *quechnajuichom*, which is to say "inhabitants of Quechla"—when we were at peace; because there was always war, always conflict day and night with those who spoke other languages. It appears that our enemies were those who today are called Diegueños by the Spanish and *quichamcauichom* by us, which means "those of the south."

Before going to battle, they painted themselves to be fearsome to their enemies, and they captured their enemies either when they were sleeping or when the men were away from home, the women remaining alone, and they killed women, elders, and children. This done, they then burned the huts, fleeing back to their homes. Their weapons were bows and arrows, and certain wooden swords, wooden lances that in our language are called *uacatom*. The bows were made of strong wood that could not be easily broken, and were so long that they reached all the way to the shoulders of the men[.] ...

[1] *hawks' bells* Small, round bells typically made of copper. They were initially used in falconry but were commonly distributed as trade goods by Spanish explorers and colonizers.

[2] *Bay of San Bernabé* Now the Bay of San José del Cabo, near Cabo San Lucas.

[3] Translated by Lisbeth Haas, 2011.

[4] *Father Juan Salvatierra* Jesuit missionary (1648–1717) who founded the first missions in Baja California.

Pablo Tac, drawing of the eagle dance, 1840. In this illustration from his history and grammar, Tac depicts the eagle dance, which he describes in his text as "the most difficult":

In this dance one person dances. … Every four to seven paces, there is an elder who ensures that the dancer does not fall, which can easily happen, since he must look up at the sky, with one foot raised and the other on the ground, and with one arm in the air and the other toward the earth. So must he walk around that circle, which is made of people who want to see the dance.

Louis Choris, *Danse des Californiens*, 1816–18. The German-Russian painter Louis Choris traveled as a documentary artist on an 1816 Russian exploration of North America's Pacific coast. This watercolor depicts Ohlone people dancing at Mission San Francisco de Asís in what is now San Francisco.

With these arms they went to war, which we still have today. Life then was miserable, because there were always conflicts. The God that was worshipped then was the Sun, and Fire. Thus we lived in the forests, until God All Merciful released us from these miseries, through Father Antonio Peyri,[1] [the] Catalan who arrived in our country in the afternoon with seven Spanish soldiers.

As the missionary was arriving with a few people to our country, our captain, seeing them from afar, and also the others, became scared, but they did not flee, nor did they take up arms to kill them, but seated they watched them. But when those men approached, then did our captain rise (because he had been seated with the others) and meet them. They stop, and then the captain begins to speak with the missionary, perhaps saying in his language *hichsom ivà haluon, pulùchajam chom quiñai*, "What is it that you seek here? Leave our country!" But they did not understand him, and they also responded in Spanish. And the captain began using hand signals, and the Fernandino, understanding him, gave him gifts, and in this manner, he became his friend. The captain, turning to his people, must have spoken well of the whites (I believe), and for this reason they let them sleep here. There were no stone houses then but only huts (it is said). That was the happy day we saw white people, called by us *Sosabitom*. O merciful God, why did you leave us for so many centuries, years, months, and days in darkness, after you'd come to the world, blessed may you be from this day for centuries to come.

The Fernandino Father stayed in our country with the small entourage he brought, and he made himself a hut, and here he lived for many days. In the morning he would say his Mass, and afterward, he would ruminate on how he would baptize them, and where he would put his House the Church, and how he would manage with five thousand souls (which were all the Indians), how he would provide for them, and seeing how all this could be done. Having the captain as his friend, he feared nothing. This was a great blessing, that the Indians did not kill the Spaniards when they arrived, and very admirable, because they had never wanted other people to live with them, which is why

up to those days they were waging war. That is how he wished it, he who can only love. I don't know if he baptized them before building the church or after having done it, but I believe he baptized them before building it.

He was now great friends with the captain, and also loved by the neophytes.[2] They could understand him some, when he as their father ordered them to bring stones from the sea (which was not far) for the foundations, make bricks, roof tiles, cut rafters, reeds, and other necessary things. They did it, with the master artisans who helped them, and within a few years they finished working. ...

—1840

from Lorenzo Asisara with Thomas Savage, [Account of Mission Life][3]

The interview excerpted below was conducted by the historian Thomas Savage as part of a much more substantial interview with Asisara's friend José María Amador, a gold miner of Spanish descent. Asisara's and Amador's accounts were combined into a manuscript titled *Memorias sobre la Historia de California* (*Memoirs of the History of California*), but the work remained unpublished until the twenty-first century.

After the death of Father Quintana in 1812, Father Olbes served as minister at the mission, as I earlier stated. He was a very suspicious man and very mean. One night, he decided to take the key of the dormitory in order to lock in the single men; accompanying him was the corporal of the guard to protect him. The corporal, Ignacio Peralta, took roll call of everyone who was in the dormitory to see if anyone was missing and find out who this person was. One individual, by the name of Dámaso, was missing; he was in the habit of playing cards and he was late because he wanted to get some food before going to the dormitory. Father Olbes and the corporal waited for him for a few minutes, less than thirty minutes. When Dámaso came back, the Father harshly asked him to tell him where he had been. The Indian responded that he had been waiting

[1] *Father Antonio Peyri* One of the first missionaries at the Mission San Luis Rey de Francia, where Pablo Tac was born.

[2] *neophytes* Newly converted people.

[3] Translated by Gregorio Mora-Torres, 2005.

for a meal that his relatives were going to give him. The [Indian] alcaldes[1] reported that he had been missing from work from noon until the evening because he had gone to play cards. The priest asked him if this was true and Dámaso responded affirmatively, that he had been missing but that he had gone in search of wood to bring to the house where he was being fed. "I am now going to punish you," Father Olbes said, "not on your ass, but on your belly." Dámaso responded: "No, Father, there is no reason for you to punish me in the belly. I went to find some wood for the people that feed me; I have not committed any other offense." The Father ordered the alcaldes to grab him in order to punish him; the Indian resisted, claiming that he had done nothing wrong. The priest insisted that he be punished. The others who were in the dormitory shouted to Dámaso in the Indian language, "Do not let yourself be caught, nor punished." The Father turned around to see what the Indians were saying.

He ordered that Dámaso be caught through the use of force but [the latter] resisted, telling the alcaldes, "Let the Father catch me, and let him punish me himself." The Father, however, insisted that the alcaldes do the punishment, but they, since they understood what those in the jayunte[2] were saying, did not dare to obey the priest. Then, an Indian called Crisanto, the uncle of Dámaso, shouted at him, "do not let them." Father Olbes, then, ordered the alcaldes, "get that one, also." He grabbed the alcaldes and pushed them to go and get Crisanto. The alcaldes were afraid of an insurrection of the Indians against the Father and themselves. At this point, the corporal unsheathed his sword in order to get Crisanto but he [the latter] got away, saying "F——! Let's kill them." Everyone from the jayunte

got up and got ready to attack the corporal, the priest, and the alcaldes. They started to pick up roof tiles and the Father took off running in one direction; the corporal dropped his sword and fled despite the clamor of the Reverend, "Corporal! Corporal!" But this one, who was more cowardly than the devil, was fleeing as fast as he could; the alcaldes also [ran] seeking their safety. The Indians were throwing tiles at the corporal and the alcaldes but no rock was thrown at the priest or the others to hurt them, only to scare them. A lot of rocks were thrown at the bells. Father Olbes kept shouting, "Corporal!" at every instant while running hard and did not stop until he reached his house.

The Indians wanted to instill fear in him so that he would not resort to so many floggings because Father Olbes was a firm believer in giving cruel lashings. He was never satisfied with prescribing fewer than fifty lashes, sometimes on the buttocks, and quite frequently on the belly. This, he enjoyed very much.

Even children between the ages of eight to ten, he would order that they receive twenty-five lashes at the hands of a strong man, on the buttocks or the belly, according to his fancy of the moment.

After the flight of Father Olbes and his defenders, the Indian bachelors went to their jayunte to sleep, saying, "Let's go to sleep, for tomorrow it is certain that we will be punished." On the following morning, the Father and the corporal came back and asked about who came up with the idea of stoning them. No one answered him. The Father gave them a lecture and then they went to hear mass at the church; everyone was now forgiven from punishment. …

—1877

[1] *alcaldes* Indigenous people with authority over the other Indigenous inhabitants of the mission. Typically, alcaldes were elected by the mission's Indigenous community, but the missionaries decided who could be nominated.

[2] *jayunte* Men's quarters.

Álvar Núñez Cabeza de Vaca

c. 1490 – c. 1560

In 1542, a work was published in Spain to widespread acclaim, *La relación y comentarios* ["The Account and Commentaries"], a text which told of the travels of a small group of failed conquistadors through the peopled wilderness of North America. To the surprise of many in Europe, the would-be colonizers were, on numerous occasions, assisted by the Indigenous peoples of the region, who seemed to possess substantial riches. One of the few survivors of a disastrous Spanish expedition to colonize Florida (a name that during this period referred to a vast swath of unexplored territory north of New Spain, stretching from the Florida Peninsula to the Pacific coast), Álvar Núñez Cabeza de Vaca was the Spanish explorer and political leader who composed this account. Widely read by Spanish politicians, explorers, and missionaries for its detailed information on the geography, material resources, and Indigenous cultures of North America, the *relación* won its author great fame and political rewards, and inspired many to become conquistadors.

Born in Jerez de la Frontera, Castile (now Spain), Cabeza de Vaca was a member of a minor aristocratic family. In 1527—six years after the Spanish conquest of the Aztec Empire—he was appointed treasurer and chief constable for the expedition of Pánfilo de Narváez, who had been directed by the Spanish king to "discover and conquer and settle" the coast of the Gulf of Mexico. In April 1528, the expedition landed near modern-day Tampa Bay, Florida, then marched inland in search of plunder. Their provisions ran low, and the colonizers suffered serious losses from disease, starvation, environmental hazards, and conflicts with Indigenous groups. By November 1528, only eighty of the approximately six hundred original expeditioners were left alive.

Weakened by illness and hunger, Cabeza de Vaca and a few other survivors had by then made it to an island off the coast of present-day Texas, where they threw themselves upon the mercy of the local Indigenous people. At times, he and his companions were permitted to engage in trade or made to perform faith healing, which they accomplished by reciting Christian prayers over the bodies of the sick. On other occasions, he and his cohort were enslaved, beaten, and forced to perform difficult labor; he was also separated from his companions on several occasions. In September 1534, Cabeza de Vaca and the three others who remained alive—two Spaniards named Andrés Dorantes de Carranza and Alonso del Castillo Maldonado, and an enslaved Moroccan named Estevanico—escaped their captors and set out to connect with the Spanish settlements in what is now western Mexico.

Over the course of their journey, the travelers appear to have earned a reputation among the Indigenous population as faith healers and amassed hundreds of followers, for whom there may have been a religious or ritual element to the relationship. The journey came to an end in the spring of 1536, when Cabeza de Vaca and his party stumbled upon a group of Spanish enslavers near the Gulf of California. Having arrived in Spanish colonial territory, Cabeza de Vaca was disgusted by the mistreatment of local Indigenous peoples, a fact that he claims caused conflict between him and certain New Spanish authorities. Nevertheless, he joined with resident Franciscan missionaries to begin the work of Christianizing the population, commanding them to "build churches and put crosses in them." While here, Cabeza de Vaca and the two other Spanish survivors of the Narváez expedition produced a joint report of the mission, presenting it to the New Spanish viceroy.

In the summer of 1537, Cabeza de Vaca returned home to Spain, where he presented the king a new report on his experiences—one he hoped would win him political favor. A detailed version of this report was released to the public in 1542 as *La relación y comentarios*. A further modified edition of that text was published in 1555 under the title *Naufragios* ["Shipwrecks"]. In an effort to ensure that his report would be "of no trivial value for those who go in [the king's] name to subdue those countries," Cabeza de Vaca made mention of everything that might prove profitable to Spain. He described the various Indigenous

nations' languages, physical attributes, forms of social organization, and approaches to war, while taking careful stock of their wealth, agriculture, and material resources.

In 1540, Cabeza de Vaca was appointed governor of Rio de la Plata—today, Paraguay—a region in which Spanish authorities feared warfare with Indigenous peoples was likely to break out. His subjects chafed under his administration, and he was arrested in April 1544 and sent to Spain in chains. In 1551, he was found guilty of political misconduct by the Royal Council of the Indies and stripped of his titles. In 1555, he released an account of his governorship, *Comentarios* ["Commentaries"], which presented him as an honest and peaceful administrator, who was resented by his subordinates for the kindness and mercy he showed in his dealings with Indigenous peoples.

Cabeza de Vaca's self-portrayal as a champion of Indigenous people has proven controversial. Throughout the *relación*, he frequently alludes to their virtuousness, and emphasizes that it is possible to "bring them to a knowledge of the true faith and true Lord." Some scholars maintain that Cabeza de Vaca genuinely appreciated the Indigenous peoples' humanity, suggesting that he advocated for cooperation with—rather than domination of—the Indigenous communities. According to this point of view, the *relación* should be seen as an apology for a peaceful form of colonization, which ought to be considered in conjunction with works such as Bartholomé de las Casas's 1542 text *Brevísima relación de la destrucción de las Indias* ["A Short Account of the Destruction of the Indies"]. Other scholars view Cabeza de Vaca's sympathetic remarks toward Indigenous peoples more cynically, arguing that his remarks were part of a rhetorical strategy to curry favor with the imperial administration. In the eyes of these scholars, rather than view the *relación* as a humane reflection upon the customs of Indigenous nations, we should see it as the reflections of a failed conqueror, whose sole aim was to get away from a population he viewed as irredeemably alien.

Whatever Cabeza de Vaca's true views on Indigenous peoples, the information that he provided about the people and land of North America proved invaluable in Spanish colonization efforts. His report to the king provided intelligence that was used during Hernando de Soto's 1539 expedition to Florida, Fray Marcos de Niza's 1539 search for the legendary Seven Cities of Gold (which was aided by Cabeza de Vaca's former companion Estevanico), and Francisco Vásquez de Coronado's expedition into modern-day Arizona and New Mexico. The ultimate effect of *La relación* was to accelerate the conquest, forced conversion, and displacement of the very people Cabeza de Vaca claimed to admire.

NOTE ON THE TEXT: The excerpts presented below are reprinted with permission from Volume 1 of *Alvar Núñez Cabeza de Vaca: His Account, His Life, and the Expedition of Pánfilo de Narváez* (1999), translated into English by Rolena Adorno and Patrick Charles Pautz. Their translation is based on the 1542 Zamora edition of Cabeza de Vaca's *Relación*.

⌘⌘⌘

from *The Relación of Álvar Núñez Cabeza de Vaca*

The account that Álvar Núñez Cabeza de Vaca gave of what occurred in the Indies on the expedition of which Pánfilo de Narváez served as governor, from the year [15]27 to [15]36, when he returned to Seville with three members of his company.

Holy, Imperial, Catholic Majesty:[1]

Among as many princes as we know there have been in the world, I think none could be found whom men have tried to serve with truer will or greater diligence and desire than we see men honoring Your Majesty today. It is quite evident that this is not without great cause and reason; nor are men so ignorant that all of them blindly and arbitrarily pursue this course, since we see not only countrymen, whom faith and duty oblige to do this, but even foreigners strive to exceed their efforts. But even when the desire and will of all makes them equal in this matter, beyond the particular advantage that anyone can secure for himself, there is a very great disparity not caused by the shortcoming of any one of them, but only by fortune, or more certainly through no fault of one's own, but only by the will and judgment of God, where it happens that one may come away with more notable services than he expected, while to another everything occurs so to the contrary that he cannot demonstrate any greater witness to his intention than his diligence, and even this is sometimes so obscured that it cannot make itself evident. For myself I can say that on the expedition that by command of Your Majesty I made to the mainland, well I thought that my deeds and services would be as illustrious and self-evident as those of my ancestors, and that I would not have any need to speak in order to be counted among those who with complete fidelity and great solicitude administer and carry out the mandates of Your Majesty, and whom you favor. But since neither my counsel nor diligence prevailed in order that the endeavor upon which we were embarked be completed as service to Your Majesty, and since no expedition of as many as have

gone to those lands ever saw itself in such grave dangers or had such a wretched and disastrous end as that which God permitted us to suffer on account of our sins, I had no opportunity to perform greater service than this, which is to bring to Your Majesty an account of all that I was able to observe and learn in the nine years that I walked lost and naked through many and very strange lands, as much regarding the locations of the lands and provinces and the distances among them, as with respect to the foodstuffs and animals that are produced in them, and the diverse customs of many and very barbarous peoples with whom I conversed and lived, plus all the other particulars that I could come to know and understand, so that in some manner Your Majesty may be served. Because although the hope that I had of coming out from among them was always very little, my care and effort to remember everything in details was always very great. This I did so that if at some time our Lord God should wish to bring me to the place where I am now,[2] I would be able to bear witness to my will and serve Your Majesty, inasmuch as the account of it all is, in my opinion, information not trivial for those who in your name might go to conquer those lands and at the same time bring them to knowledge of the true faith and the true Lord and service to Your Majesty. I wrote all this with such sure knowledge that although some very novel things may be read in it, very difficult for some to believe, they can absolutely give them credence and be assured that I am in everything brief rather than lengthy, and it will suffice for this purpose to have offered it to Your Majesty as such, for which I ask that it be received in the name of service, because this alone is what a man who came away naked could carry out with him.

CHAPTER 4
HOW WE ENTERED INLAND

And the next day[3] the governor[4] decided to go inland to explore the land and see what it contained. The commissary, the inspector of mines, and I went with

[1] *Holy, Imperial, Catholic Majesty* Charles V, who served as Holy Roman emperor from 1519 to 1556 and as king of Spain from 1515 to 1556.

[2] *the place where I am now* I.e., his home in Castile.

[3] *the next day* The expeditioners landed near modern-day Tampa Bay, Florida, on 12 April 1528. Their intended destination after leaving Cuba had been the Río de las Palmas (believed to be the present-day Río Soto la Marina in northeastern Mexico), where they intended to establish a settlement, but poor weather had landed the ships on the opposite end of the Gulf of Mexico.

[4] *the governor* Pánfilo de Narváez, leader of the expedition.

him, with forty men, and among them six horsemen, whose horses were of little use to us. We followed to the north until, at the hour of vespers,[1] we arrived at a very large bay[2] that seemed to us to go far inland. We remained there that night, and the next day we returned to where the ships and crew were stationed. The governor ordered that the brigantine[3] go along the coast toward Florida and look for the port that Miruelo, the pilot, had said he knew. But he had already miscalculated, and he did not know where we were nor where the port was. And the brigantine was ordered, in case it did not find the port, to travel to Havana and pick up Álvaro de la Cerda's ship,[4] and after taking on some provisions, to come to search for us. When the brigantine had departed, the same group of us as before, along with some others, again went inland, and we followed along the coast of the bay we had found and, having gone four leagues,[5] we took four Indians. And we showed them maize to see if they recognized it, because up to that point we had not seen any sign of it. They told us that they would take us to where it can be found. And thus they took us to their village, which is at the back of the bay near there and in which they showed us a little maize that was not yet ready to harvest. There we found many crates belonging to Castilian[6] merchants, and in each one of them was the body of a dead man, and the bodies were covered with painted deer hides. This seemed to the commissary to be a type of idolatry, and he burned the crates with the bodies in them. We also found pieces of linen cloth and plumes that seemed to be from New Spain. In addition, we found samples of gold. By means of signs we asked the Indians where those things had come from. They indicated to us by gestures that very far away from there there was a province called Apalachen,[7] in which there was much gold, and they made signs to

indicate that there were very great quantities of everything we held in esteem. They said that in Palachen[8] there was great bounty. And taking those Indians as guides we departed from there. And going some ten or twelves leagues we found another village of fifteen houses where there was a good-sized plot of sown maize that was ready to be harvested, and we also found some that was dry. And after being there two days, we returned to where the comptroller and the crew and the ships were located, and we told the comptroller and the pilots about what we had seen and the news that the Indians had given us. And the next day, which was the first of May, the governor called aside the commissary, the comptroller, and the inspector, and myself, as well as a sailor named Bartolomé Fernández, and a notary named Jerónimo de Alaniz. And thus all together, he told us that it was his will to enter inland, and that the ships should go along the coast until they arrived at the port,[9] and that the pilots said and believed that going in the direction of the Río de Palmas they were very close to there. And on this matter he requested that we give him our opinion. I responded that it seemed to me that by no means should he leave the ships without first assuring that they remained in a secure and inhabited port, and that he should take notice that the pilots were not convinced, nor were they all affirming the same thing, nor did they know where they were, and that beyond all this, the horses were in such condition that we could not make use of them in any need that might present itself, and that above all we were traveling mute, that is, without interpreters, through an area where we could hardly make ourselves understood by the Indians or learn about the land what we desired to know, and that we were entering into a land about which we had no information, nor did we know what it was like, nor what was stored in it, nor by what people it was populated, nor in which part of it we were located, and that beyond all this, we did not have adequate provisions to enter a place of which we were ignorant, because having seen the stores of the ships, no more than a pound of hardtack and another of salt pork could be given to each man as a ration to take in exploring the land, and that in my opinion we should set sail and go

[1] *vespers* In Catholic worship, the evening prayer.

[2] *a very large bay* I.e., Tampa Bay.

[3] *brigantine* Type of small sailing ship that can also be rowed.

[4] *Álvaro de la Cerda's ship* Ship that had been left behind in Havana, Cuba.

[5] *leagues* One league is equivalent to approximately three miles.

[6] *Castilian* From Castile, a region of Spain (the Kingdom of Spain had been formed from the union of the Kingdoms of Aragon and Castile in 1516).

[7] *Apalachen* Region in what is now called the Florida Panhandle.

[8] *Palachen* I.e., Apalachen.

[9] *the port* I.e., on the Río de las Palmas.

to seek a port and a land better for settling, since what we had seen was in itself as unpopulated and as poor as any place that had been discovered in those parts. To the commissary it seemed quite the opposite, he saying that it was not necessary to embark, but rather that, always going along the coast, they should go in search of the port (because the pilots said that going in the direction of Pánuco[1] it would not be but ten or fifteen leagues from there, and that it was not possible, always going along the coast, for us to miss it, because they said that it entered twelve leagues inland), and that the first ones to find it should wait there for the others, and that to embark was to tempt God, because since we departed from Castile we had suffered so many hardships and had experienced so many storms, so many losses of ships and men until arriving there, and that for these reasons he should go along the coast until reaching the port and that the ships with the other men should go along the same route until arriving at the same port. To all the others who were there assembled it seemed appropriate to do this in this manner, except for the notary, who said that, rather than abandoning the ships, they should be left in a known and secure port and in an area that was inhabited; that once this was done, he [the governor] could enter inland and do whatever seemed best to him. The governor followed his opinion as well as what the others counseled him. I, having seen his resolution, requested on behalf of Your Majesty that he not leave the ships without their being in port and secure, and thus I asked that my request be certified by the notary we had there with us. He [the governor] responded that since he agreed with the assessment of the majority of the other officials and the commissary, I had no right to make these demands of him. And he asked the notary to certify that on account of there not being adequate foodstuffs in that land to establish a settlement or a port for the ships, he was moving the settlement that he had established there and was going with it in search of the port and of land that would be better. And then he commanded that the people who were going to go with him be advised to supply themselves with whatever was necessary for the journey. And when this was done, in the presence of those who were there he said to me that since I objected so much and feared the inland expedition, I should stay and take charge of the ships and the people who remained on them and settle the land if I arrived before him. I refused to do this. And after having gone from there that same afternoon, saying that it did not seem to him that he could entrust it to anyone else, he sent me a messenger to say that he was beseeching me to take charge of it. And he, seeing that in spite of entreating me so much I still declined to accept it, asked me why I avoided doing so, to which I responded that I refused to take that responsibility because I was certain and knew that he would not see the ships again nor the ships him, and that I understood this on seeing how unprepared they were to go inland, and that I was more willing than he and the others to expose myself to danger and endure whatever he and the others were to endure than to take charge of the ships and give occasion that it be said, as I had opposed the overland expedition, that I remained out of fear, for which my honor would be under attack, and that I preferred risking my life to placing my honor in jeopardy. He, seeing that he could not prevail upon me, beseeched many others to speak with me about it and beg me to do it, to whom I responded the same as I had to him. And thus, through his lieutenant, he dispatched an order by which an *alcalde*[2] he brought with him, named Caravallo, was to remain with the ships.

from Chapter 5
How the Governor Left the Ships

Saturday, the first of May, the same day that this happened, he [the governor] commanded that each one of those who was to go with him be given two pounds of hardtack and half a pound of salt pork. And thus we set out to enter inland. We took with us a total of three hundred men. Among them went the commissary, Fray Juan Suárez, and another friar, who was called Fray Juan de Palos, and three clerics, and the [royal] officials. We the horsemen who went with them numbered forty. And thus we traveled with those provisions, which we carried for fifteen days without finding anything to eat other than hearts of palm of

[1] *Pánuco* The crew also hoped eventually to reach the Spanish settlement of Santisteban de Puerto on the Río Pánuco—also on the opposite side of the Gulf of Mexico, south of the Río de las Palmas.

[2] *alcalde* Town government official with administrative and judicial powers.

the type found in Andalusia.[1] During this entire time we did not find a single Indian, nor did we see a single house or village. And at the end [of the fifteen days] we came to a river[2] that we crossed by swimming on rafts with very great difficulty. It took us an entire day to cross it because it had a very strong current. Having crossed to the other side, nearly two hundred Indians, more or less, confronted us. The governor went out to them, and after having spoken to them by means of signs, they gestured to us in such a way that we had to turn on them. And we captured five or six of them, and these Indians took us to their houses, which were a half league from there, where we found great quantities of maize ready to be harvested. And we gave infinite thanks to our Lord for having aided us in so great a need, because since we were most certainly new to these hardships, beyond the fatigue we suffered, we came very worn out from hunger. … [W]e departed from there, always going in pursuit of that province of Apalachen that the Indians had told us about, taking as guides the ones from among them whom we had captured. And thus we walked until the seventeenth of June, during which time we found no Indians who dared to face us. And there, a native lord, carried on the shoulders of an Indian and covered with a painted deer hide, came forth to meet us. He brought with him many people, and before him they came playing reed flutes. And thus he arrived to where the governor was and he spent an hour with him. And by gestures we gave him to understand that we were going to Palachen, and by those which he made, it seemed to us that he was an enemy of the people of Apalachen, and that he would go to help us against them. We gave him beads and bells and other items in exchange, and he gave the governor the deerskin garment he was wearing, and thus he returned. And we went following him in the direction that he took. That night we reached a river that was very deep and very wide and had a very strong current. And because we did not dare to cross it with rafts, we made a canoe for the purpose, and it took us a day to cross it. And if the Indians had wanted to attack us, they could easily have obstructed our passage, and even with their help we had great difficulty. One of the horsemen, who was named Juan Velázquez, a native of Cuéllar,[3] because he did not want to wait, went into the river on his horse, and the current, since it was strong, swept him off his horse, and he held tight to the reins, and thus he drowned and drowned the horse as well. And those Indians of that lord, who was called Dulchanchellin, found the horse and told us where we could find him [Velázquez] downstream, and thus they went to retrieve him. And his death gave us much grief, because up to that point none of us had perished. The horse fed many that night. Once departed from there, we arrived the next day at the village of that lord, and there he sent us maize. That night, where they went to get water, they shot at one of our Christians, and God willed that they not wound him. The next day we left from there without even one of the Indians of that area appearing, because all of them had fled. But following our course, there appeared Indians who came prepared for war. And although we called to them, they refused to return or even hold their ground, but, rather, they retreated, following us along the same road we were traveling. The governor left some of the horsemen behind as an ambush on the road, so that as the Indians passed, they assaulted them and took three or four Indians. And we took these Indians as guides from that point onward; they took us through land very difficult to maneuver and glorious to see, because in it there are very great forests, and the trees wonderfully tall, and there are so many that are fallen upon the ground that they hindered our progress, so that we could not pass without making many detours and having very great difficulty. Of those trees that were not downed, many were split from top to bottom by lightning bolts that strike in that land where there are always great storms and tempests. With these difficulties we walked until the day after the Day of Saint John,[4] when we arrived within sight of Apalachen without being perceived by the Indians of the area. We gave many thanks to God upon seeing ourselves so near it (believing that what they had told us about that land was true, that there the great hardships that we had suffered would end), as much because of the long and difficult road we had walked as because of the great hunger we had suffered. Because although sometimes we found maize, most

[1] *Andalusia* Province of southern Spain.

[2] *a river* The Withlacoochee River in what is now central Florida.

[3] *Cuéllar* Prominent town in north-central Spain.

[4] *the Day of Saint John* Catholic feast day in honor of Saint John the Baptist, observed on 24 June.

of the time we walked seven or eight leagues without finding any. And there were many among us who, apart from the great fatigue and hunger they suffered and, since there was no other recourse, had wounds on their backs from carrying their weapons on their shoulders. But on finding ourselves where we desired to be, and where they told us there were so many foodstuffs and so much gold, it seemed to us that a great portion of our hardship and weariness had been lifted from us. …

[The expeditioners remain briefly in Apalachen, raiding a village for supplies and warring with the Indigenous inhabitants. They then continue their journey in search of the Río de las Palmas, with many members of the expedition dying of hunger and thirst along the way. At the end of an arduous sea voyage, during which many more men die, the expeditioners finally land on an island off the coast of what is now Texas. The Indigenous inhabitants of the region prove willing to lend their aid to the weakened crew; it now being winter, they determine to remain on the island until conditions improve.]

from Chapter 14
How Four Christians Departed

… [T]he weather turned so cold and there were such great storms that the Indians could not pull up the roots.[1] And from the waterways where they fished there was no yield whatsoever. And as the houses were so unprotected, the people began to die. And five men who were in Xamho on the coast came to such dire need that they ate one another until only one remained, who because he was alone, had no one to eat him. The names of these men were: Sierra, Diego López, Corral, Palacios, Gonzalo Ruiz. The Indians became very upset because of this and it produced such a great scandal among them that without a doubt, if at the start they had seen it, they would have killed them, and all of us would have been in grave danger. Finally, in a very short time, of us eighty men who arrived there from both ends [of the island], only fifteen remained alive. And after these men had died, a stomach ailment befell the Indians of the land, from which half of them died. And they thought that we

were the ones who had killed them. And taking this to be very true, they planned among themselves to kill those of us who remained. When they came to put it into effect, an Indian in whose possession I had been placed told them that they should not believe that we were the ones who killed them, because if we had such power, we would not have allowed so many of our own to die, as they saw, without our being able to prevent it, and that since no more than a few of us now remained, and since none of us did any harm or ill, the best thing to do would be to leave us alone. And our Lord God granted that the others followed this advice and opinion, and thus they were diverted from their intention. To this island we gave the name Malhado.[2] The people we found there are large and well proportioned. They have no weapons other than bows and arrows, which they employ with great skill. The men have one pierced nipple and some have both pierced. And through the hole they make, they wear a reed up to two and a half spans long and as thick as two fingers. They also have their lower lip pierced and a piece of reed as thin as half a finger placed in it. The women are given to hard work. They inhabit this island from October to the end of February. They sustain themselves on the roots that I have mentioned, which they dig out from under water in November and December. They have waterways and they do not have fish apart from this period; from then on they eat the roots. At the end of February they go to other places to look for food because at that time the roots begin to sprout and become inedible. These people love their children more and treat them better than any people in the world. And when it happens that one of their children dies, the parents and the relatives and all the rest of the people weep. And the weeping lasts a whole year, that is, each day in the morning before sunrise, first the parents begin to weep, and after this the entire community also weeps. And they do this at noon, and at daybreak. And after a year of mourning has passed, they perform the honors of the dead and wash and cleanse themselves of the ashes they wear. They mourn all the dead in this manner, except for the elderly, to whom they pay no attention, because they

1 *pull up the roots* I.e., harvest root vegetables.

2 *Malhado* Spanish: Misfortune. Many historians have posited that Malhado, or the Isle of Misfortune, is present-day Galveston Island, off the Texas coast near present-day Houston; others have suggested different possibilities.

say they have lived past their time, and from them no gain is to be had, rather, they occupy land and deprive the children of their share of the food. Their custom is to bury their dead, except those among them who are physicians,[1] whose remains they burn. And while the fire burns, they all dance and make a great celebration. And afterward they pulverize the bones. And a year later, upon paying homage to them, they all lacerate themselves, and to the relatives they give the powdered bones so that they may drink them in water. Each of them has one wife. Among them, the physicians are the most unconstrained; they can have two or three wives, among whom there is great friendship and harmony. When one gives his daughter in marriage, from the day that the one who takes her as his wife marries her, everything that he kills hunting or fishing is taken by his wife to the house of her father without daring to take or eat anything of it. And from the house of the father-in-law, food is brought to the husband, and in all this time [neither] the father-in-law nor the mother-in-law enters his house, nor is he to enter the house of any of his in-laws. And if it should happen that they meet anywhere, they veer a crossbow's shot from their course, and as they go distancing themselves from one another, they carry their heads lowered and their eyes to the ground, because they consider it a bad thing to see or speak with one another. The women are at liberty to communicate and converse with their parents-in-law and relatives. And this custom is common from the island [of Malhado] to more than fifty leagues inland. They have another custom, which is that when a child or sibling dies, in the household in which the death occurs they cease to seek food for three months, but rather they allow themselves to starve. And their relatives and neighbors supply them with the food they are to eat. And because in the time we were there so many of them died, in most of the houses there was very great hunger in the effort to also keep their custom and ceremony. And those who sought food, in

spite of their great labors, could find but very little, because the weather was so severe. And for this reason, the Indians who held me left the island, and in some canoes crossed to the mainland to certain bays that had many oysters. And for three months of the year they eat nothing else and drink very bad water. There is a great scarcity of firewood, and there are mosquitoes in great abundance. Their houses are built of woven reeds on top of beds of oyster shells. And they sleep on them on animal skins, if they happen to have them. And thus we were there until the end of April when we went to the seacoast where we ate blackberries the entire month, during which time they do not cease to perform their *areitos*[2] and celebrations.

CHAPTER 15
OF WHAT HAPPENED TO US IN THE VILLA OF MALHADO[3]

On that island about which I have spoken, they tried to make us physicians without examining us or asking us for our titles, because they cure illnesses by blowing on the sick person, and with that breath of air and their hands they expel the disease from him. And they demanded that we do the same and make ourselves useful. We laughed about this, saying that it was a mockery and that we did not know how to cure. And because of this, they took away our food until we did as they told us. And seeing our resistance, an Indian told me that I didn't know what I was saying when I said that what he knew how to do would do no good, because the stones and other things that the fields produce have powers, and that he, by placing a hot stone on the abdomen, restored health and removed pain, and that it was certain that we,[4] because we were

[1] *physicians* The original Spanish word here, "físico," would have had a somewhat broader meaning for Cabeza de Vaca than "physician" does today. Adorno and Pautz note that "físico" indicated a person who (according to the thirteenth-century Castilian statutory code *Siete Partidas*) understood "the nature of things and their interactions; knowing such things, one can do much good and remove evil, particularly preserving the life and health of men and preventing them from falling ill."

[2] *areitos* Religious songs and dances. The word is derived from the Taíno language, spoken by various Indigenous peoples in the Caribbean, but was adopted by Spanish colonists in reference to many different Indigenous cultures.

[3] *THE VILLA OF MALHADO* The use of the term "villa" (town) here is misleading and may be the result of an editor's error; the Spanish did not establish any sort of municipality on the island they named Malhado.

[4] *we* I.e., human beings (including both the Spanish travelers and the Indigenous people).

men, had greater virtue and capacity.[1] In short, we found ourselves in such need that we had to do it, without fearing that anyone would bring us to grief for it. The manner in which they perform cures is as follows: on becoming sick, they call a physician and after being cured they not only give him everything they possess, but they also seek things to give him from among their relatives. What the physician does is to make some incisions where the sick person has pain, and then sucks all around them. They perform cauterizations with fire, which is a thing among them considered to be very effective, and I have tried it and it turned out well for me. And after this, they blow upon the area that hurts, and with this they believe that they have removed the malady. The manner in which we performed cures was by making the sign of the cross over them and blowing on them, and praying a Pater Noster and an Ave Maria,[2] and as best we could, beseeching our Lord God that he grant them health and move them to treat us well. Our Lord God in his mercy willed that all those on whose behalf we made supplication, after we had made the sign of the cross over them, said to the others that they were restored and healthy, and on account of this they treated us well, and refrained from eating in order to give their food to us, and they gave us skins and other things. The hunger that we suffered there was so extreme that many times I went three days without eating anything, and they also suffered the same, and it seemed impossible to me to remain alive, although many times afterward, I found myself in even greater hunger and necessity, as I will recount later.

The Indians who held Alonso del Castillo and Andrés Dorantes and the others who had remained alive, since they spoke another language and were of a different lineage,[3] crossed to a different part of the mainland to eat oysters, and they remained there until the first day of the month of April, and afterward they returned to the island, which is probably about two leagues from there at the point where the water is the widest, and the island is a half league wide and five long. All the people of this land go about naked. Only the women cover part of their bodies with a type of fiber that grows on trees.[4] The young women cover themselves with deerskins. They are people who freely share what they have with one another. There is no lord among them. All who are of a single lineage band together. On the island live people of two different languages: some are called of Capoques, and the others, of Han. They have as a custom that, when they know one another and meet from time to time, before they speak they weep for half an hour and when this is done, the one who receives the visit rises first and gives to the other everything he possesses, and the other receives it. And a little while later he goes away with it, and it even happens sometimes that after receiving the goods, they part without speaking a single word. They have other strange customs, but I have told the most important and most notable ones so that I may go and tell what else happened to us.

[Too ill to continue the journey with the other survivors of the Narváez expedition, Cabeza de Vaca is left alone with the Capoque and the Han on Malhado for several years, during which he is subjected to hard labor. Eventually he flees to the mainland to live with a people he identifies as the Charruco, where he is treated well and allowed to work and travel freely as a merchant. In the spring of 1533 he is reunited with Castillo, Dorantes, and an enslaved Christian Moroccan named Estevanico, who join him as the final four survivors of the Narváez expedition. Cabeza de Vaca's account becomes interspersed with the other men's accounts of their own journeys until this point. In the following segment, Dorantes and Castillo recall their own encounter with a Spanish traveler named Figueroa, who tells of the demise of Narváez and the other expeditioners.]

[1] *greater virtue and capacity* I.e., than the stones and other natural healing objects.

[2] *a Pater Noster and an Ave Maria* Latin names for the Lord's Prayer (literally, the Our Father) and the Hail Mary.

[3] *The Indians ... a different lineage* Upon their first arrival on the island they later name Malhado, Cabeza de Vaca and his crew encounter these two other expeditioners who had become separated from the initial expedition. Cabeza de Vaca identifies the Indigenous peoples by whom del Castillo and Dorantes are held as the Yguase and the Mariame.

[4] *fiber that grows on trees* Probably Spanish moss.

from Chapter 17
How the Indians Came Forth and Brought with Them Andrés Dorantes and Castillo and Estevanico

… [Figueroa told Dorantes, Castillo, and the other five] that being with these Indians, he learned from them that with the Mariames there was a Christian who had crossed over from the other side, and [that] he [Figueroa] had found him [the Christian] with the ones who were called Quevenes, and that this Christian was Hernando de Esquivel, a native of Badajoz,[1] who had come in the company of the commissary. And [Figueroa told them] that he had learned from Esquivel about the end to which the governor and the comptroller and the others had come. And he [Esquivel] told him [Figueroa] that the comptroller and the friars had capsized in their raft between the rivers, and coming down along the coast, the raft of the governor landed on the shore with his men, and he [the governor] went with his raft until they arrived at that large inlet,[2] and that there he again boarded the men and crossed them from the other side, and went back for the comptroller and the friars and all the others. And he [Esquivel] told how being disembarked, the governor had revoked the authority of the comptroller and his lieutenant, and he gave the command to a captain whom he had with him, named Pantoja, and that the governor remained on his raft and refused that night to come on land. And a helmsman and a page who was ill remained with him, and on the raft they had neither water nor anything to eat, and at midnight the north wind blew so strongly that it took the raft out to sea without anyone seeing it, because it had no grapnel except for a rock, and that nothing more was ever heard of it. And [Esquivel told Figueroa] that having seen this, the people who remained on land went down the coast, and that because they found such a great barrier of water, with great difficulty they made small rafts in which they crossed to the other side, and that going ahead, they arrived to a point of a woods at the edge of the water, and that they found Indians who, as they saw them coming, put their houses in their canoes and crossed from the other side to the coast. And the Christians,

seeing the weather as it was, because it was the month of November, stopped at this wood, because they found water and firewood and some crayfish and shellfish, where, from cold and from hunger, they began little by little to die. Beyond this, Pantoja, who had remained as lieutenant, treated them very badly. And not being able to endure it, Sotomayor (the brother of Casco Porcallo, the one from the island of Cuba), who had come on the expedition as camp master, set against him and gave Pantoja such a blow that it killed him, and thus they went on dying. And the flesh of those who died was jerked by the others. And the last one to die was Sotomayor, and Esquivel made jerky of him, and eating of him [of Sotomayor], he [Esquivel] maintained himself until the first of March, when an Indian of those who had fled from there came to see if they were dead, and he took Esquivel with him. And while he [Esquivel] was in the custody of this Indian, Figueroa spoke to him. And he [Figueroa] learned from him [Esquivel] all that we have told. And he [Figueroa] urged him [Esquivel] to come with him to go together along the route to Pánuco, which Esquivel refused to do, saying that he had learned from the friars that Pánuco lay behind, and thus he remained there. …

Chapter 21
Of How We Cured Some Sick People Here

That same night that we arrived,[3] some Indians came to Castillo and said to him that they suffered a malady of the head, begging him to cure them. And after he had made the sign of the cross over them and commended them to God, at that point the Indians said that all the sickness had left them. And they went to their houses and brought many prickly pears and a piece of venison, a thing that we could not identify. And when this news was spread among them, many other sick people came that night to be cured. And each one brought a piece of venison. And there were so many of them that we did not know where to put the meat. We gave thanks to God because each day his mercy and blessings were increasing. And after the

[1] *Badajoz* City in western Spain, near the Portuguese border.

[2] *that large inlet* Espiritu Santo Bay, south of Galveston Bay.

[3] *arrived* In the country of an Indigenous people Cabeza de Vaca identifies as the Avavare, in what is now southern Texas. The four survivors live in this region during the winter of 1534/35.

cures were completed, they began to dance and make their *areitos* and celebrations, which lasted until sunrise of the following day. And the celebration held on account of our arrival lasted for three days. And at the end of them, we asked them about the land that lay ahead, and about the people that we would find in it, and the sources of food that were in it. They responded to us that throughout that entire land there were many prickly pears, but that the season was already over, and that there were no people because they had all gone to their homes, having already collected the prickly pears, and that the land was very cold and in it there were very few hides. Seeing that winter and cold weather were already upon us, we decided to spend it with these Indians. Five days after we had arrived there, they left to hunt for other prickly pears where there were other people of different nations and tongues. And traveling five days with very great hunger because there were no prickly pears nor any other fruit along the route, we arrived at a river where we put up our houses. And after setting them up, we went to look for the fruit of some trees, which is like [the fruit of] a vetch.[1] And since through all this land there are no trails, I stopped to investigate it more fully; the people returned and I remained alone, and going to look for them, that night I got lost. And it pleased God that I found a tree aflame, and warmed by its fire I endured the cold that night, and in the morning I gathered a load of firewood, and I took two firebrands and again looked for the people. And I continued in this manner for five days, always with my lighted torch and load of wood, so that if my fire died in a place where there was no firewood (since in many areas there was none), I would have the means to make other firebrands and I would not remain without a light, because against the cold I had no other recourse since I went naked as I was born. And for the night I had this defense, that is, I went to the groves of the wood near the rivers, and stopped in them before sunset. And in the earth I dug a pit with the butt of a timber and in it I threw a great deal of firewood from the trees that grow in great quantity there. And I gathered much dry wood fallen from the trees, and around that pit I placed four fires like the points of a cross. And I made an effort and took care to rekindle the fire from time to time, and from the long grass that grows there I made some bundles to cover myself in that hole. And in this way I protected myself from the cold of night. And during one of them, the fire fell on the grass with which I was covered. And while I was sleeping in the pit the fire began to burn fiercely, and despite the great haste that I made to get out, my hair nevertheless received the sign of the danger in which I had been. In this entire time I did not eat a mouthful of food, nor did I find anything that I could eat, and since my feet were bare, they bled a great deal. And God took pity upon me, that in all this time the north wind did not blow, because otherwise it would have been impossible for me to survive. And at the end of five days, I arrived at a bank of a river where I found my Indians, for they and the Christians had already taken me for dead, and they were convinced that some viper had bitten me. All took great pleasure in seeing me, especially the Christians, and they told me that until then, they had traveled with great hunger, that this was the reason they had not searched for me, and that night they gave me to eat some of the prickly pears they had. And the next day we departed from there and went to where we found many prickly pears with which all satisfied their great hunger. And we gave many thanks to our Lord because his succor never failed us.

from CHAPTER 22
How They Brought Us Other Sick People the Next Day

… And since throughout the land nothing was talked about except the mysteries that God our Lord worked through us, people came from many places to seek us out so that we could cure them. … [S]ome Indians of the Susolas came to us, and they begged Castillo to go and cure a wounded man and other sick people, and they said that among them there was one who was very near his end. Castillo was a very cautious physician, particularly when the cures were threatening and dangerous. And he believed that his sins would prevent the cures from turning out well every time. The Indians told me that I should go to cure them because they held me in esteem, and they remembered that I had cured them at the nut-gathering grounds, and because of that, they had given us nuts and hides, and

1 *vetch* Class of plants often cultivated for their beans, such as the broad bean.

this had happened when I came to join the Christians. And thus I had to go with them, and Dorantes and Estevanico went with me. And when I arrived near their huts, I saw the sick man whom we were going to cure, who was dead, because there were many people around him weeping and his house was undone, which is the sign that the owner is dead. And thus when I arrived, I found the Indian, his eyes rolled back in his head, and without any pulse, and with all the signs of death; so it seemed to me, and Dorantes said the same. I removed a mat that he had on top of him, with which he was covered. And as best I could, I beseeched our Lord to be served by giving health to that man and to all the others among them who were in need. And after having made the sign of the cross and blown on him many times, they brought me his bow and they gave it to me along with a basket of crushed prickly pears. And they took me to cure many others who had sleeping sickness, and they gave me two other baskets of prickly pears, which I gave to our Indians who had come with us. And having done this, we returned to our lodgings. And our Indians, to whom I had given the prickly pears, remained there, and at nighttime they returned to their houses and said that that one who had been dead and whom I had cured in their presence had arisen revived and walked about and eaten and spoken with them, and that as many as I had cured had become well and were without fever and very happy. This caused very great wonder and fear, and in all the land they spoke of nothing else. All those to whom this report arrived came looking for us so that we could cure them and make the sign of the cross over their children. And when the Indians who were in the company of ours, who were the Culthalcuches, had to return to their land, before leaving, they offered us all the prickly pears that they had gathered for their journey without keeping even one for themselves. And they gave us flints as long as a span and a half, which they use for cutting, and it is an object of very great esteem among them. They beseeched us to remember them and to ask God to always keep them well, and we promised them that we would do so, and with this they departed the most contented people in the world, having given us all the best things they had. We were with those Avavares Indians eight months. And this reckoning we made by the moon. In all this time

people came from many areas looking for us. And they said that truly we were children of the sun. Until then Dorantes and the black man[1] had not performed any cures, but on account of the great demands made on us, [the Indians] coming from many places to look for us, we all became physicians, although in boldness and daring to perform any cure I was the most notable among them. And we never cured anyone who did not say that he was better, and they had so much confidence that they would be cured if we performed the cures, that they believed that as long as we were there, none of them would die. These and the rest whom we had left behind told us something very strange, and by the explanation they put together for us, it seemed that it had occurred some fifteen or sixteen years earlier; that they said that through that land went a man they call an evil being, and that he was small in body and that he had a beard, although they were never able to see his face clearly, and that when he came to the house where they were, their hair stood on end and they trembled, and afterward he appeared at the door of the house with a flaming firebrand. And later that man came in and took whichever one of them he wanted, and he gave them three large incisions in the sides with a very sharp flint, a hand wide and two spans long. And he placed his hand into those wounds and pulled out their entrails, and that he cut off a piece, more or less a span long, and threw the part that he cut off into the fire, and afterward he made three cuts in the arm, and the second one he made in the crook of the arm, and dislocated it. And a little while afterward, he set it back into place, and he placed his hands over the wounds, and they told us that later they were healed, and that many times when they danced, he appeared among them, sometimes in the costume of a woman, and other times dressed as a man, and when he wanted, he picked up the *buhío*, or house, and raised it into the air, and a little while afterward he dropped it and it fell with a great blow. They also told us that many times they gave him food to eat and that he never ate anything, and that they asked him where he came from and where he had his house, and he showed them a cleft in the earth and said that his house was there

[1] *the black man* Estevanico, the enslaved Moroccan who was among the four survivors. Cabeza de Vaca most often refers to him simply as *el negro*, or "the black man."

below. We laughed a great deal about these things they told us, making fun of them. And since they saw that we did not believe them, they brought many of those who had said that he had taken them, and we saw the scars of the cuts that he had made in the places and in the manner they had said. We told them that he was an evil person. And in the best manner that we could, we gave them to understand that, if they believed in God our Lord and were Christians like us, they would not be afraid of him, nor would he dare to come and do those things to them, and they could be assured that as long as we were in the land, he would not dare to appear in it. With this they were very pleased, and they lost a great deal of the fear they had. … I have already said how, throughout this entire land, we went about naked, and since we were not accustomed to it, like serpents we changed our skins twice a year. And with the sun and wind, there appeared on our chests and backs some very great ulcerations, which caused us very great distress on account of the large loads we carried, which were very heavy and caused the ropes to cut into the flesh of our arms. And the land is so rugged and impassable that many times when we gathered fire-wood in the dense thickets, when we finished taking it out we were bleeding in many places from the thorns and brambles that we encountered, for wherever they ensnared us they broke our skin. Sometimes it happened to me that, after shedding much blood in gathering wood, I could not haul it out, either on my back or by dragging it. I did not have, when I saw myself in these difficulties, any other remedy or consolation but to think about the Passion of our Redeemer Jesus Christ and the blood he shed for me, and to consider how much greater had been the torment that he suffered from the thorns, than that which I had to endure at that time. I traded with these Indians by making combs for them, and with bows[.] …

from CHAPTER 26
OF THE NATIONS AND LANGUAGES

… In the time that thus I was among these people, I saw a wicked behavior, and it is that I saw one man married to another, and these are effeminate, impotent men. And they go about covered like women, and they perform the tasks of women, and they do not use a bow, and they carry very great loads. And among these we saw many of them, thus unmanly as I say, and they are more muscular than other men and taller; they suffer very large loads. …

from CHAPTER 27
OF HOW WE MOVED ON AND WERE WELL RECEIVED

… And at sunset we arrived[1] at a hundred houses of Indians, and before we arrived, all the people who were in them came out to receive us with so much shouting that it was a fright and vigorously slapping their thighs. They carried pierced gourds with stones inside, which is the item of highest celebration, and they do not take them out except to dance or to cure, nor does anyone but they dare to use them. And they say that those gourds have virtue and that they come from the sky, because throughout that land there are none nor do they know where they might be, but only that the rivers bring them when they flood. So great was the fear and agitation that these people experienced that with some trying to arrive more quickly than others to touch us, they crowded us so much that they nearly could have killed us. And without letting our feet touch the ground, they carried us to their houses. And they fell so much upon us and pressed us in such a manner that we went into the houses they had prepared for us. And we did not consent in any way to their making more celebrations with us that night. They spent that entire night dancing and performing *areitos* among themselves. And the next morning they brought us all the people of that village for us to touch and make the sign of the cross over them, as we had done to the others with whom we had been. And after this was done, they gave many arrows to the women of the other village who had come with theirs. The next day we left there, and all the people of the village went with us. And when we arrived at other Indians we were very well received as we had been by the previous ones. And thus they gave us some of the things they had and the deer they had killed that day. And among these people we saw a new custom, and it is that the ones who were with us took from those who came to be cured their bows and arrows and shoes and

[1] *we arrived* By this point, the four survivors have made their way to a region on the northeast coast of what is now Mexico.

beads if they brought them. And after having taken them, they placed those people before us, so that we might cure them. And once cured, they went away very content, saying that they were healed. Thus we departed from those Indians and we went to others by whom we were very well received, and they brought us their sick, who, on our making the sign of the cross over them, said they were healed. And anyone who did not improve believed that we could cure him. And with what the others whom we cured told them, they made such merriment and dancing that they did not let us sleep. Departing from these people, we went to many other houses, and at this point another new custom commenced, and it is that receiving us very well, those who came with us began to treat the others very badly, taking their possessions and sacking their houses without leaving them any single thing. About this we were much distressed to see the bad treatment that was given to those who thus received us, and also because we feared that that practice would be or would cause some altercation and scandal among them. But since we were powerless to remedy it or to dare to punish those who did it, for the time being we had to endure it until we had more authority among them. And also the same Indians who lost their households, on seeing our sadness, consoled us by saying that we should not be grieved by that, because they were so content to have seen us that they considered that their possessions had been well employed, and that farther ahead they would be compensated by others who were very rich. Along this entire road we had very great difficulty because of the many people who followed us. And we could not flee from them, although we tried, because the quickness with which they came to touch us was very great. …

[Cabeza de Vaca and the others continue to traverse what is now northern Mexico, nearing the Gulf of California.]

CHAPTER 33
HOW WE CAME UPON THE TRACK OF CHRISTIANS

After we saw clear signs of Christians and we understood that we were very near them, we gave many thanks to God our Lord for wanting to take us out of so sad and wretched a captivity. And may the pleasure we felt on this account be judged by every man when he considers the time we spent in that land and the dangers and hardships we endured. That night I entreated one of my companions to go after the Christians who were going through the area where we were leaving the land secured. And it was a three-day journey. This they judged a troublesome undertaking, excusing themselves because of fatigue and hardship and in spite of the fact that each one of them would be able to do it better than I, on account of being hardier and younger. But seeing their will, the next day in the morning I took with me the black man and eleven Indians, and following the train of the Christians that I found, I passed through three places where they had slept. And this day I went ten leagues. And the next morning I reached four Christians on horseback who experienced great shock upon seeing me so strangely dressed and in the company of Indians. They remained looking at me a long time, so astonished that they neither spoke to me nor managed to ask me anything. I told them to take me to their captain. And thus we went half a league from there, where their captain, Diego de Alcaraz, was. And after I had spoken to him, he said that he was very lost there because it had been many days since he had been able to take any Indians[1] and that there was no way to go because among them there began to be great need and hunger. I told him how Dorantes and Castillo remained behind at a place ten leagues from there with many people who had brought us. And he then sent out three horsemen and fifty Indians of those they were bringing. And the black man returned with them to guide them. And I remained there and I asked that they certify for me the year and the month and day that I had arrived there, and the manner in which I had come, and thus they did it. From this river to the village of the Christians, which is called San Miguel,[2] which is under the governance of the province they call Nueva Galicia, there are thirty leagues.

[1] *take any Indians* The men Cabeza de Vaca encounters are New Spanish slavers who depended on their captives to act as guides.

[2] *San Miguel* Town in what is now central Mexico, then part of Nueva Galicia, an autonomous kingdom of New Spain.

Chapter 34
Of How I Sent for the Christians

Five days later, Andrés Dorantes and Alonso del Castillo arrived with those who had gone for them. And they brought with them more than six hundred people who were from that settlement that the Christians had caused to ascend into the highlands, and they went about hidden throughout the land. And those who had come with us to that point had taken them out of the mountains and turned them over to the Christians, and they had sent away all the other peoples whom they had brought there. And when they had arrived to where I was, Alcaraz beseeched me to call the people of the villages that are found on the bank along the river, who went hidden through the mountains of the land, and command them to bring food to eat, although this was not necessary because they always took care to bring us all they could. And we sent out our messengers to call them, and six hundred people came who brought us all the maize they could obtain. And they brought it in some clay-sealed pots in which they had buried and hidden it. And they brought us everything else they had, but we refused to take any of it except the food. And we gave everything else to the Christians so that they could distribute it among themselves. And after this we suffered many annoyances and great disputes with them, because they wanted to enslave the Indians we brought with us. And with this anger, on parting we left many Turkish bows that we carried, and many leather pouches and arrows among them the five made from emeralds that we inadvertently left, and thus we lost them. We gave the Christians many bison robes and other things that we carried. We had great difficulty convincing the Indians to return to their homes and secure themselves and sow their maize. They did not want but to go with us until leaving us with other Indians, as they were accustomed to doing, because if they returned without doing this, they feared they would die, and going with us, they feared neither the Christians nor their lances. The Christians were disturbed by this, and they made their interpreter tell them that we were of the same people as they, and that we had been lost for a long time, and that we were people of ill fortune and no worth, and that they were the lords of the land whom the Indians were to serve

and obey. But of all this the Indians were only superficially or not at all convinced of what they told them. Rather, some talked with others among themselves, saying that the Christians were lying, because we came from where the sun rose, and they from where it set; and that we cured the sick, and that they killed those who were well; and that we came naked and barefoot, and they went about dressed and on horses and with lances; and that we did not covet anything but rather, everything they gave us we later returned and remained with nothing, and that the others had no other objective but to steal everything they found and did not give anything to anyone. And in this manner, they conveyed everything about us and held it in high esteem to the detriment of the others. And thus they responded to the Christians' interpreter and they made known the same thing to those through a language that they had among them by which we understand one another. And those who speak it we call Primahaitu, which we found used in more than four hundred leagues of those we had traveled, and we found no other in all that distance. Finally, it was not possible to convince the Indians that we were the same as the other Christians, and with much effort and insistence we made them return to their homes, and we ordered them to secure themselves and settle their villages, and to sow and work the land since, because of being abandoned, it was now very overgrown with vegetation, for that land is without doubt the best of any to be found in these Indies and the most fertile and abundant in foodstuffs. And they sow three times a year. They have many fruits and many beautiful rivers and many other very good waterways. There are great indications and signs of mines of gold and silver. The people are of very good inclinations. Those who are friends of the Christians serve them very willingly. They are very well disposed, much more so than those of Mexico. And, finally, it is a land that lacks nothing in order to be very good. When we dispatched the Indians, they told us that they would do what we commanded and would settle their villages if the Christians would let them. And thus I declare and affirm as true that if they should not do it, the Christians will be to blame. And after we had sent them away the Christians sent us off under the guard of an *alcalde* who was named Ceberos and three other Christians with him, from which it is evident how much men's thoughts

THE RELACIÓN OF ÁLVAR NÚÑEZ CABEZA DE VACA 147

deceive them, for we went to them seeking liberty and when we thought we had it, it turned out to be so much to the contrary. And in order to remove us from conversation with the Indians, they led us through areas depopulated and overgrown so that we would not see what they were doing nor their conduct, because they had conspired to go and attack the Indians whom we had sent away reassured and in peace. And they carried it out just as they had planned it. They led us through those dense thickets for two days without water, lost without a path. And we all thought that we would perish from thirst, and seven men died from it, and many friends that the Christians brought with them were unable, until noon of the following day, to reach the place where we found water that night. And we walked with them twenty-five leagues, a little more or less. And at the end of them, we arrived at a village of peaceful Indians. And the *alcalde* who was leading us left us there, and he went on ahead another three leagues to a settlement called Culiacán[1] where Melchior Díaz, *alcalde mayor* and captain of that province, was. Upon learning of our escape and arrival, he departed later that night and came to where we were, and he wept a great deal with us, praising God our Lord for having shown so much mercy to us. And he spoke to us and treated us very well. And on behalf of the governor, Nuño de Guzmán, as well as his own, he offered us everything that he had and could. And he [Melchior Díaz] showed much sorrow at the bad reception and treatment we had received from Alcaraz and the others we had found. And we took it for certain that if he had been there, what was done to us and the Indians would have been prevented. And after that night, the next day we departed for Auhacán[2] and the *alcalde mayor* beseeched us earnestly to stop there; that in doing so we would perform a very great service to God our Lord and Your Majesty, because the land was abandoned and not cultivated and all of it greatly destroyed, and the Indians went about hidden and in flight through the highlands without wanting to come and settle

themselves in their villages; and [he asked] that we have them called together and order them on behalf of God and Your Majesty to come and settle the plain and work the land. To us this seemed very difficult to put into effect, because we did not bring any Indian of ours or any of those who usually accompanied us and were skilled in these matters. Finally we entrusted this to two Indians of those whom they held captive there, who were of that land, and these Indians had been with the Christians when we first arrived to them, and they saw the people who accompanied us and learned from them about the great authority and influence that through all those lands we had possessed and exercised, and the wonders that we had worked and the sick people we had cured and many other things. And with these [two] Indians we commanded other Indians of the settlement to together go and call the Indians who had taken refuge in the sierras and those of the Río Petachán, where we found the Christians,[3] and tell them to come to us because we desired to speak to them. And so that they could go in safety and the others come forth, we gave them a very large gourd of those that we carried in our hands, which was our principal insignia and emblem of our great estate. And taking this gourd they set out and went through the area for seven days, and at the end of them, they returned and brought with them three lords, of those who were taking refuge in the sierras, who brought along fifteen men. And they brought us beads and turquoises and plumes. And the messengers told us that they had not found the natives of the river where we had come out because the Christians had again made them flee to the highlands. And Melchior Díaz told the interpreter to speak on our behalf to those Indians and tell them how we came on behalf of God who is in heaven, and how we had walked through the world for nine years, telling all the people we had found to believe in God and serve him because he was Lord of all things in the world, and that he blessed and rewarded the good, and punished the bad with perpetual fire, and that when the good died, he carried them to heaven where no one would die or be hungry or cold or thirsty or have any other need whatsoever, but rather, would have the greatest glory that one could

[1] *Culiacán* San Miguel de Culiacán, city in what is now the northwestern Mexican province of Sinaloa, near the coast of the Gulf of California.

[2] *Auhacán* Approximation of the Nahuatl name Culhuacán, a village south of the New Spanish city of San Miguel de Culiacán and sometimes also called Culiacán by the Spanish.

[3] *where we found the Christians* I.e., where they had met Diego de Alcaraz and the other enslavers.

imagine, and that those who did not want to believe in him or obey his commandments would be cast by him under the ground in the company of demons and into a great fire that would never cease, but rather torment them forever, and that beyond this, if they desired to be Christians and serve God our Lord in the manner in which we commanded them, that the Christians would take them as brothers and treat them very well, and we would order them [the Christians] not to provoke them or take them out of their lands, but rather to be their great friends, but that if they did not want to do this, the Christians would treat them very badly and carry them off as slaves to other lands.[1] To this they responded to the interpreter that they would be very good Christians and serve God. And when asked to what they gave reverence and made sacrifices and whom they asked for water in their maize fields and health for themselves, they responded that it was to a man who was in the sky. We asked them what his name was. And they said it was Aguar, and that they believed that he had created the whole world and all the things in it. We again asked them how they knew this. And they responded that their fathers and grandfathers had told it to them, that for a long time they had known about this, and they knew that that man sent water and all good things. We told them that the one to whom they referred we called God, and that thus they should call him and serve and adore him as we commanded and they would be well served by it. They responded that they understood everything very well and that thus they would do it. And we ordered them to come down from the sierras and to come forward confidently and in peace, and populate the land and put up their houses and in the midst of them make one for God and put a cross at the entrance, like the one we had there, and that when Christians came there, to come out and receive them with the crosses in their hands, without their bows and without weapons, and take them to their houses and give them whatever they had to eat, and in this way they [the Christians] would not do

them harm but rather would be their friends. And they said that thus they would do it as we commanded it. And the captain gave them robes and treated them very well, and thus they returned, taking the two who were captives and who had gone as messengers. This occurred in the presence of the notary they had there and many other witnesses.

from CHAPTER 36
OF HOW WE HAD CHURCHES BUILT IN THAT LAND

When the Indians returned, all those of that province who were friends of the Christians, since they had news of us, came to see us. And they brought us beads and plumes. And we commanded them to build churches and put crosses in them, because until then they had not made them. And we had them bring the children of the most important lords and baptize them. And afterward, the captain made a solemn oath to God to neither make nor consent to making any incursion nor to take slaves in that land or among people whom we had secured, and that this he would uphold and fulfill until His Majesty and the governor Nuño de Guzmán or the viceroy[2] in his name acted to comply with what would best serve God our Lord and His Majesty. And after the children had been baptized, we departed for the *villa* of San Miguel, where, when we arrived, Indians came who told us how many people were coming down from the sierras and populating the plain and making churches and crosses and doing everything we had commanded them. And each day we received news of how this was being most fully carried out and accomplished. And after we had been there fifteen days, Alcaraz arrived with the Christians who had gone on that raid. And they told the captain how the Indians were down from the sierras and had populated the plain, and they had found populous villages that earlier were abandoned and deserted, and that the Indians came out to receive them with crosses in their hands and took them to their houses and shared with them what they had. And they slept with them there that night. Astonished by such a new development and by what the Indians told them about how they were

[1] *And Melchior Díaz ... other lands* The speech given by the interpreter and summarized by Cabeza de Vaca here was known as the requerimiento ("requirement"), a standard text first created in 1513 that was required by Spanish law to be read out before the Indigenous population on all colonial expeditions, intended to legitimize the violent conquest of those who would not convert to Christianity.

[2] *the viceroy* Antonio de Mendoza y Pancheco (1495–1552), the first viceroy of New Spain.

now secured, he ordered that they do them no harm and thus they took leave.

May God our Lord in his infinite mercy grant, in all the days of Your Majesty and under your authority and dominion, that these people come and be truly and with complete devotion subject to the true Lord who created and redeemed them. And we hold it for certain that it will be so, and that Your Majesty will be the one who is to put this into effect, that it will not be so difficult to do, because in the two thousand leagues that we traveled by land and through the sea on the rafts and another ten months that we went through the land

without stopping once we were no longer captives, we found neither sacrifices nor idolatry. …

[H]aving arrived in Compostela, the governor received us very well and from the provisions he had gave us some clothes, which I was unable to wear for many days, nor were we able to sleep but on the ground. And after ten or twelve days had passed, we left for Mexico.[1] And along the entire road we were well treated by the Christians. And many came out to see us along the roads and gave thanks to God our Lord for having delivered us from so many dangers. …

—1542

[1] *Mexico* I.e., Mexico-Tenochtitlan, the former Aztec capital that had been captured by Hernán Cortés during the Conquest of the Aztec Empire in 1521.

JOHN SMITH
1580 – 1631

In 1624, fifteen years after his departure in disgrace from the Jamestown colony, John Smith published *The General History of Virginia, New England, and the Summer Isles* in England, commenting on his experiences of the emerging colonization endeavor, on his ambivalent relationship with the region's Native American leaders, and on what he saw as the shameful failures of the people in charge of the colony. "Had we been in Paradise itself, with those governors," he scoffed, "it would not have been much better." The *General History* was Smith's third publication based on his colonial experiences, and he would go on to write several more over the next seven years, earning a reputation both as a writer who had played a significant role in the colonial endeavor and as one who could not be trusted to report the truth. Smith's complex legacy has become only more fraught in the centuries since his death, and he has been simultaneously derided as a self-aggrandizing braggart and hailed as a founding figure of American history and literature.

Smith was baptized in Willoughby, Lincolnshire on 9 January 1580, the first son of well-to-do tenant farmers George and Alice Rickard Smith. Though educated at a respectable grammar school and encouraged by his parents to pursue a merchant career, Smith would later describe himself as having a mind "set upon brave adventures." Shortly after his father's death in 1596, Smith left England and joined a company of soldiers fighting the Spanish in the war for Dutch independence; in 1600 he joined the Habsburg armies in the war against the Ottoman Empire. In his later autobiographical works Smith would colorfully describe his many exploits across northern and eastern Europe, which included the "good success" of decapitating three Turkish soldiers in single combat as well as a subsequent period of enslavement which took him as far as what is now southern Russia before he managed to kill his captor and escape. For his feats of daring in the Long Turkish War, Smith was awarded a coat of arms for which he devised his own motto: "Vincere est vivere"—"To conquer is to live."

Smith's American ventures began in 1606, after King James I of England had signed the "First Charter of Virginia," granting settlement rights in North America to the newly formed Virginia Company. Impressed by Smith's experience, the company's partners named him to the governing committee of the new settlement, making him something of an exception in a group made up primarily of wealthy gentlemen. In December of that year Smith joined the company's first colonial expedition. Tensions between Smith and the upper-class governors began early in the voyage—he was accused of planning a mutiny during the voyage and briefly sentenced to death—and they persisted throughout the next several years, even after Smith was elected to the Company's presidency in September 1608.

The colonists struggled immensely to establish themselves; some historians (and Smith himself) have attributed this to their poor work ethic and lack of competent leadership, though others have pointed out that the Company arrived in Virginia during a period of severe drought. Regardless, Smith's presidency was certainly more austere than that of his predecessors, who had relied primarily on supply missions from England for their survival. By contrast, Smith emphasised agricultural labor and famously declared that "he that will not work shall not eat." Smith also developed a wide knowledge of the region's geography, and cultivated important if frequently ambivalent trade relationships with the local Algonquian nations, including with various leaders of the Powhatan Confederacy; as he writes in a letter to Queen Anne published in the *General History*, "had the savages not fed us, we directly [would have] starved."

By 1609, however, Smith had—like many of the colony's previous leaders—been discredited in the eyes of the council; he was wounded in a gunpowder explosion that autumn, and returned to England in October. He would never visit Virginia again, though he traveled to New England in 1614 on another colonizing venture (and planned other voyages there).

The events of 1606–08 were first recorded in Smith's *A True Relation of Such Occurrences and Accidents of Note as Happened in Virginia* (1608). He revisited this subject several times, most famously in his *General History*, which was published many years after his removal from the colony. It expands significantly on the earlier work, and includes the famous, previously unmentioned account of his near-execution by Powhatan chief Wahunsonacock (sometimes spelled Wahunsenacawh); according to his 1624 account, Smith was on the point of being clubbed to death when the chief's favored young daughter (a historical figure known by several names—Pocahontas, most famously, but also Amonute, Matoaka, and Lady Rebecca Rolfe), put "his head in her arms, and laid her own upon his to save him from death."

Smith's aims as a writer were manifold; in part, he sought to elevate himself as an exemplary colonist, while also—especially in his later writings—publicizing the various failures of his rivals in Jamestown. Texts such as the *General History* were produced within an established tradition of writings about the emerging colonial effort. To that point the genre had mostly comprised works by writers who had themselves never made the Atlantic crossing: as Smith proudly declared, "I am no compiler by hearsay, but have been a real actor."

Smith's later years as a would-be adventurer, however, were marked more by frustration than by triumph. He failed to persuade the Pilgrims to choose him as their guide in 1620, and he failed in a 1621 petition to the London Company to recompense him for his services in Virginia; repeated attempts to regain employment with that Company also proved fruitless. After his last trip to North America, which formed the basis of his *A Description of New England* (1616), he remained in England as a writer. He published the successful *An Accidence, or the Pathway to Experience Necessary for All Young Seamen* (1626), a manual of sailors' terms, and followed up with *A Sea Grammar* (1627), the first sailor's handbook in English. He remained a tireless self-promoter; his autobiography, *The True Travels, Adventures, and Observations of Captain John Smith, in Europe, Asia, Africa, and America, from* Anno Domini *1593 to 1629*, appeared in 1630. Smith's last work, *Advertisements for the Inexperienced Planters of New England, or Anywhere* (1631), again saw him setting himself up as a model for the planters of the "New World."

Smith never married or had children, and died in London on 21 June 1631. His reputation by that point was mixed; his publications had certainly helped spur English interest in the colonization of New England, but his unreliability as a writer was already widely suspected. David Lloyd's ballad *The Legend of Captain Jones*—widely believed to be a satire of Smith—was published the same year that he died.

It was in the nineteenth century that American writers and historians began to perceive and extol Smith as a national hero; Southern author William Gilmore Simms, for instance, declared Smith the "Founder of Virginia" in his 1846 *The Life of Captain John Smith*. Smith's adventures in Jamestown and among the Indigenous peoples of Virginia were the subject for numerous stage plays and works of poetry in the 1800s. In particular, many white writers began to romanticize the story of his relationship with Pocahontas (who had in fact married another English colonist, John Rolfe, in 1614).

In the 1860s and 70s, however, some historians began again to cast doubt upon Smith's reliability as a writer, beginning a scholarly feud that continued well into the early twentieth century. The feud was to a large extent fueled by cultural conflicts between the anti-Smith North and the pro-Smith South. In 1930, prolific Massachusetts-based historian Samuel Eliot Morison concluded that Smith was "a liar, if you will, but a thoroughly cheerful and generally harmless liar." Today, scholars are more likely to concede that Smith provides what he believes to be a factually accurate account of his travels, though his work is inevitably tainted by colonialist as well as other biases—as well as by ambition. Despite the heated debates that still circulate about Smith, about his writings, and about the colonial mission itself, he continues to occupy a prominent position in the mythology of America.

———

NOTE ON THE TEXT: The excerpts from *The General History of Virginia, New England, and the Summer Isles* are based on the 1624 edition; various transcriptions, including that of the University of North Carolina's Documenting the South project and that prepared by Philip Barbour for his three-volume *Complete Works of John Smith* (1986) have been consulted, as have some older editions (notably Edward Arber and A.G. Bradley's 1910 *Travels and Works of Captain John Smith*). Spelling and punctuation have largely been modernized in accordance with the practices of this anthology, although we have left Smith's rambling sentence structures intact in many cases where modern punctuation practice would call for more periods (and fewer colons, semi-colons, and commas). In the text of Chapter 2 we include a passage in which Smith's original spelling and punctuation have been preserved.

The editors gave serious consideration to the question of whether the speeches by Wahunsonacock (also known as Powhatan) that are embedded within the Smith text should be presented independent of that text; given that the speeches are not reported in other sources and have come down to us in no other form than that mediated by Smith, however, we decided that it would be preferable to present them only in that context. A fuller discussion of the role Wahunsonacock played in the history of the area now known as Virginia is provided in the anthology's online component along with excerpts from Smith's *A True Relation of Such Occurrences and Accidents of Note as Hath Happened in Virginia*.

⌘ ⌘ ⌘

from *The General History of Virginia, New England, and the Summer Isles*

from The Third Book

from Chapter 1

It might well be thought, a country so fair (as Virginia is) and a people so tractable[1] would long ere this have been quietly possessed, to the satisfaction of the adventurers,[2] and the eternizing of the memory of those that effected it. But because all the world does see a defailment,[3] this following treatise shall give satisfaction to all indifferent[4] readers, how the business hath been carried [out]: where no doubt they will easily understand and answer to their question, how it came to pass there was no better speed and success in those proceedings.

Captain Bartholomew Gosnold, one of the first movers[5] of this plantation, having many years solicited many of his friends, but found small assistance, at last prevailed with some gentlemen, as Captain John Smith,[6] Mr. Edward-Maria Wingfield, Mr. Robert Hunt,[7] and diverse others, who depended[8] a year upon his projects; but nothing could be effected, till by their great charge and industry, it came to be apprehended by certain of the nobility, gentry, and merchants, so that his Majesty, by his letters patents, gave commission for establishing councils, to direct here [in London]; and to govern, and to execute there [in Virginia].[9] To effect this, was spent another year, and by that [time] three ships were provided, one of 100 tons, another of 40, and a pinnace[10] of 20. The transportation of the company was committed to Captain Christopher Newport, a mariner well practiced for the western parts of America. But their orders for government[11] were put in a box, not to be opened, nor the governors known, until they arrived in Virginia.

On the 19 of December, 1606 we set sail from Blackwall,[12] but by unprosperous winds were kept six weeks in the sight of England; all which time Mr. Hunt, our preacher, was so weak and sick that few expected his recovery. Yet although he were but twenty miles from his habitation ([at] the time we were in the Downs[13]) and notwithstanding the stormy weather, nor the scandalous imputations (of some few, little better than atheists, of the greatest rank[14] amongst us) suggested against him,[15] all this could never force from him so much as a seeming desire to leave the business, but [he] preferred the service of God, in so good a voyage, before any affection[16] to contest with his godless foes, whose disastrous designs[17] (could they have prevailed) had even then overthrown the business, so many discontents did then arise, had he not with the water of patience, and his godly exhortations (but chiefly by his true devoted examples) quenched those flames of

1 *tractable* Tame, easily governable.

2 *quietly possessed* Peacefully colonized; *adventurers* Investors in the colony.

3 *all the world … defailment* I.e., all the world has perceived this venture to have been a failure.

4 *indifferent* Impartial, open-minded.

5 *first movers* Initiators.

6 *Captain John Smith* Smith frequently refers to himself in the third person throughout this text, possibly in part because the *General History* incorporated writing from several other authors.

7 *Mr. Edward-Maria Wingfield* Soldier and Member of Parliament in England (1550–1631); *Mr. Robert Hunt* Minister who joined the Virginia expedition (1568–1608).

8 *diverse* Various; *depended* Anticipated.

9 *his Majesty* King James I of England (1566–1625); *by his letters … Virginia* In 1606 James I signed the First Charter of Virginia, granting the colonists of the Virginia Company land rights in America. The charter also established corresponding ruling councils in London and Virginia, whose members, while needing to meet the King's approval, could govern relatively freely.

10 *pinnace* Small sailing vessel, generally with two masts, usually meant to accompany a larger ship. The pinnace was named the *Discovery*; the two other, larger ships were the *Susan Constant*, on board which Smith sailed, and the *Godspeed*.

11 *orders for government* I.e., decisions regarding who would be appointed to the colony's governing council.

12 *Blackwall* I.e., Blackwall Yarn, a shipyard on the River Thames.

13 *the Downs* Anchorage off the coast of Kent in the English Channel, in which ships might seek shelter from storms before venturing into the open ocean.

14 *greatest rank* Highest status.

15 *nor … against him* It was rumored that Hunt had committed adultery with his servant in England, among other accusations.

16 *affection* Inclination.

17 *designs* Schemes.

envy and dissention. We watered at the Canaries;[1] we traded with the savages at Dominica;[2] three weeks we spent in refreshing ourselves amongst these West-India Isles. In Guadeloupe we found a bath so hot, as in it we boiled pork as well as over the fire. And at a little isle called Monito, we took from the bushes with our hands near two hogsheads[3] full of birds in three or four hours. In Nevis, Mona, and the Virgin Isles we spent some time, where, with a loathsome beast like a crocodile (called an iguana), tortoises, pelicans, parrots, and fishes, we daily feasted. Gone from thence in search of Virginia, the company was not a little discomforted, seeing the mariners had 3 days passed their reckoning[4] and found no land, so that Captain Ratcliffe (captain of the pinnace) rather desired to bear up the helm to return for England, than [to] make further search. But God the guider of all good actions, forcing them by an extreme storm to hull[5] all night, did drive them by his providence to their desired port, beyond all their expectations, for never any of them had seen that coast.

The first land they made they called Cape Henry,[6] where thirty of them, recreating[7] themselves on shore, were assaulted by five savages, who hurt two of the English very dangerously. That night was the box opened,[8] and the orders read, in which Bartholomew Gosnold, John Smith, Edward Wingfield, Christopher Newport, John Ratcliffe, John Martin, and George Kendall were named to be the Council, and [instructed] to choose a President amongst them for a year, who with the Council should govern. Matters of moment[9] were to be examined by a jury, but determined by the major part of the Council, in which the President had two voices.[10] Until the 13 of May they sought a place to plant[11] in. Then the Council was sworn; Mr. Wingfield was chosen President, and an oration made, [explaining] why Captain Smith was not admitted of the Council as the rest.[12]

Now falleth every man to work: the Council contrive[13] the fort, the rest cut down trees to make place to pitch their tents; some provide clapboard to relade[14] the ships, some make gardens, some nets, etc. The savages often visited us kindly. The President's overweening jealousy[15] would admit no exercise at arms, or fortification, but the boughs of trees cast together in the form of a half moon by the extraordinary pains and diligence of Captain Kendall. Newport, Smith, and twenty others were sent to discover the head of the river: by diverse small habitations they passed, [and] in six days they arrived at a town called Powhatan, consisting of some twelve houses, pleasantly seated on a hill; before it three fertile isles, about it many of their cornfields; the place is very pleasant, and strong by nature; of this place the Prince is called Powhatan,[16] and his people

[1] *watered* Supplied the ship with fresh water; *Canaries* The Canary Islands, an archipelago off the southern coast of present-day Morocco.

[2] *savages at Dominica* The Carib people were at the time the inhabitants of this Caribbean island; Smith uses the pejorative word "savage" indiscriminately to name the Indigenous inhabitants of any location.

[3] *near two hogsheads* Almost two barrels.

[4] *3 days … reckoning* I.e., it had been three days since their calculated date of arrival.

[5] *hull* Ride by force of the wind alone with furled sails.

[6] *Cape Henry* Named for King James's son, Henry Frederick (1594–1612), this cape on the coast of Virginia, along with Cape Charles, forms the entrance to Chesapeake Bay.

[7] *recreating* Refreshing or restoring their physical health.

[8] *the box opened* An unusual aspect of the venture was that Smith and the others had sailed with a box that contained a list of those the Virginia Company had appointed to govern the colony, and had been given strict instructions not to open the box and read the list until they had arrived.

[9] *moment* Immediate importance.

[10] *voices* Votes.

[11] *plant* Settle.

[12] *why Captain Smith … as the rest* During the voyage Smith had been charged with sedition, treason, and a plot to "make himself king," and had consequently been sentenced to death. When orders arrived from London assigning Smith a leadership position in the colony, he was reprieved from his sentence, though not immediately permitted to take his seat on council.

[13] *contrive* Designed. (In this passage Smith alternates between present and past verb tenses.)

[14] *clapboard* Thin, overlapping wooden planks used in building as protection from the elements; *relade* Reload.

[15] *overweening jealousy* Excessive prudence; the council had been warned by the English investors to avoid inciting any conflict with the local Indigenous peoples.

[16] *Prince … Powhatan* The chief's personal name was Wahunsonacock; that the English referred to him simply as "Powhatan" was likely the result of a misunderstanding based on him having been introduced to them as the Chief of Powhatan.

Powhatans; to this place the river is navigable, but higher[1] within a mile, by reason of the rocks and isles, there is not passage for a small boat; this they call the Falls. The people in all parts kindly intreated[2] them, till being returned within twenty miles of Jamestown, they [the Powhatans] gave just cause of jealousy,[3] but had God not blessed the discoverers otherwise than those at the fort, there had then been an end of that plantation; for at the fort, where they arrived the next day, they found 17 men hurt, and a boy slain by the savages, and had it not chanced [that] a cross-bar shot[4] from the ships struck down a bough from a tree amongst them [the Powhatans], that caused them to retire, our men had all been slain, being securely all at work, and their arms in dry vats.[5]

Hereupon the President was contented the fort should be palisaded,[6] the ordnance mounted,[7] his men armed and exercised, for many were the assaults and ambuscades[8] of the savages, and our men by their disorderly straggling were often hurt, when the savages by the nimbleness of their heels well escaped. What toil we had, with so small a power to guard our workmen a-day, watch all night, resist our enemies, and effect our business, to relade the ships, cut down trees, and prepare the ground to plant our corn,[9] etc., I refer to the reader's consideration. Six weeks being spent in this manner, Captain Newport (who was hired only for our transportation) was to return [to England] with the ships. Now Captain Smith, who all this time from their departure from the Canaries was restrained as a prisoner upon the scandalous suggestions of some of the chief [colonists] (envying his repute), who feigned[10] [that] he intended to usurp the government, murder the Council, and make himself king; that his confederates[11] were dispersed in all the three ships; and that diverse of his confederates that revealed it, would affirm it. For this he was committed as a prisoner; thirteen weeks he remained thus suspected, and by that time the ships should return they [the Council members] pretended out of their commiserations[12] to refer him to the Council in England to receive a check,[13] rather than by particulating[14] his designs make him so odious to the world, as to touch his life, or utterly overthrow his reputation. But he so much scorned their charity, and publicly defied the uttermost of their cruelty, [that] he wisely prevented their policies, though he could not suppress their envies, yet so well he demeaned[15] himself in this business, as all the company did see his innocence, and his adversaries' malice, and those suborned to accuse him accused his accusers of subornation; many untruths were alleged against him; but being so apparently disproved, begat a general hatred in the hearts of the company against such unjust commanders that the President was adjudged to give him £200 so that all he [President Wingfield] had was seized upon, in part of satisfaction, which Smith presently returned to the store for the general use of the colony. Many were the mischiefs that daily sprung from their ignorant (yet ambitious) spirits; but the good doctrine and exhortation of our preacher Mr. Hunt reconciled them, and caused Captain Smith to be admitted of the Council; the next day all received the Communion,[16] the day following the savages voluntarily desired peace, and Captain Newport returned for England with news; leaving in Virginia 100 [colonists] the 15 of June 1607.

By this observe:
Good men did ne'r their country's ruin bring.

[1] *higher* Upstream.

[2] *intreated* Treated.

[3] *jealousy* Anger and mistrust.

[4] *cross-bar shot* Cannonball with a spike protruding from either side.

[5] *arms* Weapons; *dry vats* Storage containers.

[6] *palisaded* Enclosed by a wooden fence.

[7] *ordnance mounted* Cannon or other large artillery positioned for use.

[8] *ambuscades* Ambushes.

[9] *corn* Grain (such as the seeds of wheat and barley); it is only through trade with the Native Americans that the colonists begin to consume maize.

[10] *feigned* Falsely alleged.

[11] *confederates* Alleged co-conspirators.

[12] *commiserations* Compassion.

[13] *check* Reprimand.

[14] *particulating* Making known in detail.

[15] *demeaned* Conducted.

[16] *received the Communion* Took part in the Eucharist, the Christian sacrament in which blessed bread and wine are ingested.

But when evil men shall injuries begin;
Not caring to corrupt and violate
The judgements'-seat for their own lucre's[1] sake:
Then look that country cannot long have peace,
Though for the present it have rest and ease.[2] …

from CHAPTER 2
WHAT HAPPENED TILL THE FIRST SUPPLY

Being thus left to our fortunes, it fortuned that within ten days[3] scarce ten amongst us could either go,[4] or well stand, such extreme weakness and sickness oppressed us. And thereat none need marvel, if they consider the cause and reason, which was this: whilst the ships stayed, our allowance was somewhat bettered by a daily proportion of biscuit, which the sailors would pilfer to sell, give, or exchange with us, for money, sassafras, furs, or love.[5] But when they departed, there remained neither tavern, beer-house, nor place of relief, but the common kettle.[6] Had we been as free from all sins as [we were from] gluttony and drunkenness, we might have been canonized for Saints; but our President would never have been admitted,[7] for engrossing to his private[8] oatmeal, sack, oil, *aqua vitæ*,[9] beef, eggs, or what not, but the kettle;[10] that indeed he allowed

equally to be distributed, and that was half a pint of wheat, and as much barley boiled with water for a man a day, and this, having fried some 26 weeks in the ship's hold, contained as many worms as grains; so that we might truly call it rather so much bran than corn.[11] Our drink was water,[12] our lodgings castles in the air. With this lodging and diet, our extreme toil in bearing and planting palisades, so strained and bruised us, and our continual labour in the extremity of the heat had so weakened us, as were cause sufficient to have made us as miserable in our native country, or any other place in the world. From May to September, those that escaped lived upon sturgeon, and sea-crabs; fifty [men] in this time we buried. The rest, seeing the President's projects[13] to escape these miseries in our pinnace by flight[14] (who all this time had neither felt want nor sickness) so moved our dead spirits, as we deposed him, and established Ratcliffe in his place (Gosnold being dead Kendall deposed).[15] Smith newly recovered, Martin and Ratcliffe were by his care preserved and relieved, and the most of the soldiers recovered, with the skillful diligence of Mr. Thomas Wotton our surgeon[16] general. But now was all our provision spent, the sturgeon gone, all helps abandoned, each hour expecting the fury of the savages; when God, the patron of all good endeavours, in that desperate extremity so changed the hearts of the savages that they brought such plenty of their fruits, and provision, as no man wanted.[17]

And now where some affirmed it was ill done of the Council to send forth men so badly provided, this incontradictable reason will show them plainly they are too ill advised to nourish such ill conceits. First, the

[1] *lucre's* Profit's.

[2] *Then look … ease* Smith quotes a translation of Greek poet Theognis of Megara (c. 6th century BCE) found in Martin Fotherby's *Atheomastix: Clearing Four Truths against Atheists and Infidels* (1622), a work that seems to be the source of most of the poetic quotations Smith includes in the *General History*.

[3] *within ten days* I.e., by 25 June 1607 (within ten days of Captain Newport's 15 June departure for England to give news of the colony and to bring back fresh supplies).

[4] *go* Walk.

[5] *pilfer* Plunder or steal; *sassafras* Tree native to eastern North America and Asia, whose leaves, roots, and bark were used for medicinal purposes; *love* Presumably, sexual favors provided by the settlers for the sailors.

[6] *common kettle* I.e., collective supplies.

[7] *would never … admitted* I.e., would not have been admitted to sainthood.

[8] *engrossing to his private* Keeping for his personal use.

[9] *sack* White wine from Spain; *aqua vitæ* Latin: water of life; term for a variety of alcoholic distillates, such as brandy or whisky.

[10] *but the kettle* Except the communal supplies.

[11] *so that … than corn* I.e., the grains had been so damaged by worms and rot that there was not much left other than the bran, or husks.

[12] *Our drink … water* I.e., as opposed to beer or wine, the preferred beverages of the colonists and indeed what the noun "drink" would ordinarily refer to.

[13] *the President's projects* I.e., Wingfield's plans.

[14] *flight* I.e., retreat; running away.

[15] *Gosnold being … Kendall deposed* Gosnold had died in August of 1607, while Kendall had been removed from the council and arrested under a charge of mutiny; as later described by Smith, he was soon executed.

[16] *surgeon* Medical doctor (without the specific connotation of specializing in surgery).

[17] *as no man wanted* Such that no man was in need.

fault of our going was our own, what could be thought fitting or necessary we had, but what we should find, or want, or where we should be, we were all ignorant [of], and supposing to[1] make our passage in two months, with victual to live,[2] and the advantage of the spring to work; we were at sea five months, where we both spent our victual and lost the opportunity of the time and season to plant, by the unskillful presumption of our ignorant transporters, that understood not at all what they undertook.

Such actions have ever since the world's beginning been subject to such accidents, and everything of worth is found full of difficulties, but nothing so difficult as to establish a Commonwealth so far remote from men and means, and where men's minds are so untoward[3] as neither do well [to] themselves, nor suffer others.

But to proceed. The new President[4] and Martin, being little beloved, of weak judgment in dangers, and less industry[5] in peace, committed the managing of all things abroad[6] to Captain Smith; who by his own example, good words, and fair promises, set some to mow, others to bind thatch, some to build houses, others to thatch them, himself always bearing the greatest task for his own share, so that in short time he provided most of them lodgings, neglecting any for himself.

This done, seeing [that] the savages' superfluity[7] begin to decrease, [Smith] (with some of his workmen) shipped himself in the shallop[8] to search the country for trade. The want of the language,[9] knowledge to manage his boat without sails, the want of a sufficient power (knowing the multitude of the savages), apparel for his men, and other necessaries, were infinite impediments, yet no discouragement. Being but six or seven

in company he went down the river to Kecoughtan,[10] where at first they scorned him as a famished man, and would in derision offer him a handful of corn, a piece of bread, for their [the colonists'] swords and muskets, and such like proportions also for their apparel. But seeing by trade and courtesy there was nothing to be had, he made bold to try such conclusions as necessity enforced, though contrary to his commission:[11] [Smith] let fly[12] his muskets, [and] ran his boat on shore, whereat they all fled into the woods. So marching towards their houses, they might see great heaps of corn;[13] much ado[14] he had to restrain his hungry soldiers from present taking of it, expecting as it happened that the savages would assault them, as not long after they did with a most hideous noise. Sixty or seventy of them, some [painted] black, some red, some white, some parti-coloured,[15] came in a square order, singing and dancing out of the woods, with their *Okee* (which was an idol made of skins, stuffed with moss, all painted and hung with chains and copper) borne before them: and in this manner being well-armed, with clubs, targets,[16] bows and arrows, they charged the English, that so kindly received them,[17] with their muskets loaded with pistol shot, that down fell their God, and diverse[18] lay sprawling on the ground; the rest fled again to the woods, and ere long sent one of their *Quiyoughkasoucks*[19] to offer peace, and redeem their *Okee*. Smith told them, [that] if only six of them would come unarmed and load his boat, he would not

[1] *supposing to* Having assumed we would.

[2] *victual to live* Provisions necessary to survive.

[3] *untoward* Unruly or inept.

[4] *new President* I.e., Ratcliffe.

[5] *industry* Industriousness; willingness to work.

[6] *abroad* I.e., beyond the palisade.

[7] *superfluity* Generosity.

[8] *shallop* Smaller, shallow-water boat used for communications to and from a larger ship.

[9] *want of the language* Not knowing the local language.

[10] *Kecoughtan* Village on the mouth of the James River, home to the Kecoughtan people, who were part of the Powhatan Confederacy and whose leader or weroance was Pochins, son of Wahunsonacock.

[11] *commission* Instructions.

[12] *let fly* Fired.

[13] *towards their … heaps of corn* Towards the Powhatan houses, they [Smith's soldiers] could see great heaps of grain.

[14] *ado* Difficulty.

[15] *parti-coloured* Multicolored (i.e., wearing body paint).

[16] *targets* Shields.

[17] *that so kindly received them* Who responded to their attack in the same manner (i.e., as strongly).

[18] *diverse* Several of them.

[19] *Quiyoughkasoucks* Smith uses this term in various contexts throughout his writings, sometimes to refer to Algonquian deities, and sometimes, as here, to refer to their priests. "Quiyoughcohannock" is also the name of a member tribe of the Powhatan Confederacy.

only be their friend, but restore [to] them their *Okee*, and give them beads, copper, and hatchets besides; which on both sides was to their contents performed, and then they brought him venison, turkeys, wild fowl, bread, and what they had, singing and dancing in sign of friendship till they departed. In his return he discovered the town and country of Warraskoyack.[1]

Thus God unboundless by his power,
Made them thus kind, would us devour.

Smith, perceiving [that]—notwithstanding their late[2] misery—not any [of the colonists] regarded but from hand to mouth[3] (the company being well recovered), caused the pinnace to be provided with things fitting to get provision for the year following; but in the interim he made 3 or 4 journeys and discovered the people of Chickahominy.[4] Yet what he carefully provided the rest carelessly spent. Wingfield and Kendall living in disgrace, seeing all things at random[5] in the absence of Smith ... strengthened themselves with[6] the sailors and other confederates to regain their former credit and authority, or at least such means aboard the pinnace (being fitted to sail as Smith had appointed for trade) to alter her course and to go for England. Smith, unexpectedly returning, had the plot discovered[7] to him, [and] much trouble he had to prevent it, till with store of saker[8] and musket shot he forced them [to] stay or sink in the river, which action cost the life of Captain Kendall. These brawls are so disgustful, as some will say they were better forgotten, yet all men of good judgement will conclude [that] it were better their baseness should be manifest to the world, than the business bear the scorn and shame of their excused disorders.[9] The President and Captain Archer[10] not long after intended also to have abandoned the country, which project also was curbed and suppressed by Smith. The Spaniard never more greedily desired gold than he [Smith] victual, nor his soldiers more to abandon the country, than he to keep it.[11] But, finding plenty of corn in the river of Chickahominy where hundreds of savages in diverse places stood with baskets expecting his coming, and now the winter approaching, the rivers became so covered with swans, geese, ducks, and cranes, that we daily feasted with good bread, Virginia peas, pumpkins, and putchamins,[12] fish, fowl, and diverse sorts of wild beasts as fat as we could eat them: so that none of our Tuftaffety humorists[13] desired to go for England.

But our comedies never endured long without a tragedy; some idle exceptions[14] being muttered against Captain Smith, for not discovering the head of Chickahominy River, and taxed[15] by the Council to be too slow in so worthy an attempt.[16] The next voyage he proceeded so far that with much labour by cutting of trees asunder he made his passage, but when his barge could pass no farther, he left her in a broad bay out of danger of shot, commanding none should go ashore till his return: himself with two English and two savages went up higher in a canoe, but he was not long absent

[1] *Warraskoyack* Village on the mouth of the Pagan River, a tributary of the James River.

[2] *late* Recent.

[3] *regarded but ... to mouth* I.e., considered anything beyond their immediate needs.

[4] *Chickahominy* Region along the Chickahominy River, which flows south into the James River and was named after the nation who inhabited it.

[5] *at random* In disorder.

[6] *strengthened themselves with* Made themselves popular among.

[7] *discovered* Revealed.

[8] *saker* Shot for cannon.

[9] *it were better ... disorders* I.e., it would be better to let the guilt of the responsible persons be known, rather than have the entire company be seen as at fault.

[10] *Captain Archer* Gabriel Archer (1575–1609/10) had traveled to New England with Bartholomew Gosnold in 1602, and was among the first colonists at Chesapeake Bay in 1607; well-known as a rival to Smith, he left for England with Captain Christopher Newport on a so-called Supply Mission. Archer returned the next year and the rivalry continued until he died in the brutal following winter.

[11] *The Spaniard ... keep it* Smith desired to provide food for the colony as eagerly as Spaniards desire gold, and Smith just as strongly to preserve the colony as his soldiers to abandon it. (Contemporary stereotypes among the English often depicted Spanish people as cruel and greedy, especially during the early period of American colonization when the British and Spanish empires were in conflict.)

[12] *putchamins* Persimmons.

[13] *Tuftaffety humorists* Frivolous, luxury-loving people; *Tuftaffety* Variety of taffeta, a high-end silk fabric.

[14] *exceptions* Complaints.

[15] *taxed* Accused.

[16] *so ... attempt* Such an important duty.

but[1] his men went ashore, whose want of government[2] gave both occasion and opportunity to the savages to surprise one George Cassen,[3] whom they slew, and much failed not to have cut off the boat and all the rest. Smith little dreaming of that accident, being got to the marshes at the river's head, twenty miles in the desert,[4] had his[5] two men slain (as is supposed) sleeping by the canoe, whilst himself by fowling sought them victual, who finding he was beset with 200 savages, two of them he slew, still defending himself with the aid of a savage his guide, whom he bound to his arm with his garters, and used him as a buckler,[6] yet he was shot in his thigh a little, and had many arrows that stuck in his clothes but no great hurt, till at last they took him prisoner. When this news came to Jamestown, much was their sorrow for his loss, few expecting what ensued. Six or seven weeks those barbarians kept him prisoner; many strange triumphs and conjurations they made of him, yet he so demeaned himself amongst them, as he not only diverted them from surprising the fort, but procured his own liberty, and got himself and his company such estimation amongst them, that those savages admired him more than their own *Quiyoughkasoucks*. The manner how they used and delivered him, is as followeth.

The savages having drawn from George Cassen whither Captain Smith was gone, prosecuting that opportunity they followed him with 300 bowmen, conducted by the King of Pamunkey,[7] who in divisions searching the turnings of the river, found Robinson and Emry by the fireside; those they shot full of arrows and slew. Then finding the Captain, as is said, that used the savage that was his guide as his shield (three of them being slain and diverse others so galled[8]), all the rest would not come near him. Thinking thus to have returned to his boat, regarding them, as he marched, more than his way, [he] slipped up to the middle in an oozy creek, and his savage with him, yet durst[9] they not come to him till, being near dead with cold, he threw away his arms. Then according to their composition they drew him forth and led him to the fire, where his men were slain. Diligently they chafed his benumbed limbs. He demanding for their Captain, they showed him Opechancanough, King of Pamunkey, to whom he gave a round ivory double compass dial. Much they marveled at the playing of the fly[10] and needle, which they could see so plainly, and yet [could] not touch it, because of the glass that covered them. But when he demonstrated by that globe-like jewel the roundness of the earth, and skies, the sphere of the sun, moon, and stars, and how the sun did chase the night round about the world continually; the greatness of the land and sea, the diversity of nations, variety of complexions, and how we were to them antipodes,[11] and many other such like matters, they all stood as amazed with admiration. Notwithstanding, within an hour after they tied him to a tree, and as many as could stand about him prepared to shoot him; but the King holding up the compass in his hand, they all laid down their bows and arrows, and in a triumphant manner led him to Orapaks,[12] where he was after their manner kindly feasted, and well used.[13]

Their order in conducting him was thus; Drawing themselves all in fyle, the King in the middest had all their Peeces[14] and Swords borne before him. Captaine *Smith* was led after him by three great Salvages, holding him fast by each arme: and on each side six went in fyle with their Arrowes nocked.[15] But arriving at the Towne (which was but onely thirtie or fortie hunting houses made of Mats, which they remove as they please, as we our tents) all the women and children

original spelling

1 *but* Until.

2 *want of government* Lack of discipline.

3 *George Cassen* Listed as a "labourer" in the records of the Jamestown colonists.

4 *desert* Wilderness.

5 [Smith's note] Jehu Robinson and Thomas Emry, slain. [*had his* Found his.]

6 *buckler* Shield.

7 *King of Pamunkey* Opechancanough, younger brother of Chief Wahunsonacock and chief of the Pamunkey, an Algonquian-speaking tribe, part of the Powhatan Confederacy.

8 *galled* Injured.

9 *durst* Dared.

10 *fly* Card showing the points on a compass.

11 *antipodes* Living on the opposite side of the earth.

12 *Orapaks* Village further west, near the head of the Chickahominy River.

13 *used* Treated.

14 *Peeces* Firearms.

15 *Arrowes nocked* Arrows notched (onto their bowstrings).

staring to behold him, the souldiers first all in fyle performed the forme of a *Bissom*[1] so well as could be; and on each flanke, officers as Serieants[2] to see them keepe their order. A good time they continued this exercise, and then cast themselves in a ring, dauncing in such severall[3] Postures, and singing and yelling out such hellish notes and screeches; being strangely painted, every one [had] his quiver of Arrowes, and at his backe a club; on his arme a Fox or an Otters skinne, or some such matter for his vambrace;[4] their heads and shoulders painted red, with Oyle and *Pocones*[5] mingled together, which Scarlet-like colour made an exceeding handsome shew; his Bow in his hand, and the skinne of a Bird with her wings abroad[6] dryed, tyed on his head, a peece of copper, a white shell, a long feather, with a small rattle growing at the tayles of their snakes tyed to it, or some such like toy. All this while *Smith* and the King stood in the middest guarded, as before is said, and after three dances they all departed. *Smith* they conducted to a long house, where thirtie or fortie tall fellowes did guard him, and ere long more bread and venison was brought him then would have served twentie men, I thinke his stomacke at that time was not very good; what he left they put in baskets and tyed over his head. About midnight they set the meate againe before him, all this time not one of them would eate a bit with him, till the next morning they brought him as much more, and then did they eate all the old, & reserved the new as they had done the other, which made him thinke they would fat him to eat him. Yet in this desperate estate to defend him from the cold, one [whose name was] Maocassater brought him his gowne, in requitall of[7] some beads and toyes *Smith* had given him at his first arrivall in *Virginia*.

Two days after a man would have slain him (but that the guard prevented it) for the death of his son, to whom they conducted him [Smith] to recover the poor man then breathing his last. Smith told them that at Jamestown he had a water would do it,[8] if they would let him fetch it, but they would not permit that; but made all the preparations they could to assault Jamestown, craving his advice, and for recompense he should have life, liberty, land, and women. In part of a table book[9] he wrote his mind to them at the fort,[10] what was intended, how they should follow that direction to affright the messengers, and without fail send him such things as he wrote for. And an inventory with them. The difficulty and danger, he told the savages, of the mines, great guns, and other engines exceedingly affrighted them, yet according to his request they went to Jamestown, in as bitter weather as could be of frost and snow, and within three days returned with an answer.

But when they came to Jamestown, seeing men sally[11] out as he had told them they would, they fled; yet in the night they came again to the same place where he had told them they should receive an answer, and such things as he had promised them, which they found accordingly, and with which they returned with no small expedition,[12] to the wonder of them all that heard it, that he could either divine,[13] or the paper could speak. Then they led him to the Youghtanunds, the Mattapanients, the Piankatanks, the Nantaughtacunds, and Onawmanients upon the rivers of Rappahannock, and Potomac, over all those rivers, and back again by diverse other several nations, to the King's habitation at Pamunkey, where they entertained him with most strange and fearful conjurations:

As if near led to hell,
Amongst the devils to dwell.[14]

[1] *Bissom* Military formation in which soldiers march in a twisting line.

[2] *Serieants* Sergeants.

[3] *severall* Various.

[4] *vambrace* Forearm armor.

[5] *Pocones* Dyes made from the roots of any of several eastern North American plants.

[6] *abroad* Spread out.

[7] *in requitall of* In return for.

[8] *water ... it* I.e., medicine.

[9] *table book* Notebook.

[10] *In part ... the fort* He took a page from his notebook and wrote a warning to the colonists at the fort.

[11] *sally* Rush.

[12] *expedition* Promptness.

[13] *divine* Communicate through magic.

[14] *As if ... dwell* Smith paraphrases a translation of the Roman poet Seneca (c. 4 BCE–65 CE) found in Martin Fotherby's *Atheomastix*.

Not long after, early in a morning a great fire was made in a long house, and a mat spread on the one side, as on the other; on the one they caused him to sit, and all the guard went out of the house, and presently came skipping in a great grim fellow, all painted over with coal, mingled with oil; and many snakes' and weasels' skins stuffed with moss, and all their tails tied together, so as they met on the crown of his head in a tassel; and round about the tassel was as a coronet of feathers, the skins hanging round about his head, back, and shoulders, and in a manner covered his face, with a hellish voice and a rattle in his hand. With most strange gestures and passions he began his invocation, and environed the fire with a circle of meal;[1] which done, three more such like devils came rushing in with the like antic tricks, painted half black, half red; but all their eyes were painted white, and some red strokes like mutchatos[2] along their cheeks. Round about him those fiends danced a pretty while, and then came in three more as ugly as the rest, with red eyes, and white strokes over their black faces, at last they all sat down right against him; three of them on the one hand of the chief priest, and three on the other. Then all with their rattles began a song, which ended, the chief priest laid down five wheat corns.[3] Then, straining his arms and hands with such violence that he sweat, and his veins swelled, he began a short oration.[4] At the conclusion they all gave a short groan; and then laid down three grains more. After that, began their song again, and then another oration, ever laying down so many corns as before, till they had twice encircled the fire; that done, they took a bunch of little sticks prepared for that purpose, continuing still their devotion, and at the end of every song and oration, they laid down a stick betwixt the divisions of corn. Till night, neither he nor they did either eat or drink, and then they feasted merrily, with the best provisions they could make. Three days they used this ceremony; the meaning whereof, they told him, was to know if he intended them well or no. The circle of meal signified their country, the circles of corn the bounds of the sea, and the sticks his country.

They imagined the world to be flat and round, like a trencher,[5] and they in the midst. After this they brought him a bag of gunpowder, which they carefully preserved till the next spring, to plant as they did their corn, because they would be acquainted with the nature of that seed. Opitchapam the King's brother invited him to his house, where, with as many platters of bread, fowl, and wild beasts as did environ him,[6] he bid him welcome; but not any of them would eat a bit with him, but put up all the remainder in baskets. At his return to Opechancanough's, all the King's women, and their children flocked about him for their parts,[7] as a due by custom to be merry with such fragments.

But his waking mind in hideous dreams did
 oft see wondrous shapes,
 Of bodies strange, and huge in growth, and
of stupendous makes.[8]

At last they brought him to Werowocomoco,[9] where was Powhatan, their emperor. Here more than two hundred of those grim courtiers stood wondering at him, as [if] he had been a monster; till Powhatan and his train had put themselves in their greatest braveries.[10] Before a fire upon a seat like a bedstead, he sat covered with a great robe, made of rarowcun[11] skins, and all the tails hanging by. On either hand did sit a young wench of 16 to 18 years, and along on each side [of] the house two rows of men, and behind them as many women, with all their heads and shoulders painted red; many of their heads bedecked with the white down of birds; but everyone with something, and a great chain of white beads about their necks. At his entrance before the King, all the people gave a great

1 *meal* Ground maize.

2 *mutchatos* Mustaches.

3 *corns* Kernels.

4 *oration* Prayer.

5 *trencher* Plate.

6 *as did environ him* As it took to encircle him.

7 *parts* Gifts or offerings.

8 *But his ... makes* Smith quotes Fotherby's translation of Roman poet Lucretius (c. 99–c. 55 BCE).

9 *Werowocomoco* Village on the York River, Powhatan's political center.

10 *braveries* Fine formal costumes.

11 *rarowcun* Raccoon. This English word is derived from an Algonquian word which Smith attempts to represent with various spellings throughout his writings.

shout. The Queen of Appamatuck[1] was appointed to bring him water to wash his hands, and another brought him a bunch of feathers, instead of a towel to dry them. Having feasted him after their best barbarous manner they could, a long consultation was held, but the conclusion was [that] two great stones were brought before Powhatan. Then as many as could laid hands on him [Smith] dragged him to them, and thereon laid his head, and being ready with their clubs to beat out his brains, Pocahontas, the King's dearest daughter, when no entreaty could prevail, got his head in her arms, and laid her own upon his to save him from death; whereat the emperor was contented he should live to make him hatchets, and her bells, beads, and copper; for they thought him as well of[2] all [these] occupations as themselves. For the King himself will make his own robes, shoes, bows, arrows, pots; plant, hunt, or do anything so well as the rest.

> They say he bore a pleasant show,
> But sure his heart was sad.
> For who can pleasant be, and rest,
> That lives in fear and dread:
> And having life suspected, doth
> It still suspected lead.[3]

Two days after, Powhatan having disguised himself in the most fearfulest manner he could, [he] caused Captain Smith to be brought forth to a great house in the woods, and there upon a mat by the fire to be left alone. Not long after, from behind a mat that divided the house was made the most dolefulest[4] noise he ever heard; then Powhatan, more like a devil than a man, with some two hundred more as black as himself, came unto him and told him now they were friends, and presently he should go to Jamestown to send him two great guns, and a grindstone, for which he would give

him the country of Capahowosick,[5] and forever esteem him as[6] his son Nantaquoud. So to Jamestown with 12 guides Powhatan sent him. That night they quartered[7] in the woods, he still expecting (as he had done all this long time of his imprisonment) every hour to be put to one death or other, for all their feasting. But almighty God (by his divine providence) had mollified the hearts of those stern barbarians with compassion. The next morning betimes they came to the fort, where Smith, having used the savages with what kindness he could, he showed Rawhunt, Powhatan's trusty servant, two demi-culverins[8] and a millstone to carry [to] Powhatan. They found them somewhat too heavy; but when they did see him discharge them, being loaded with stones, among the boughs of a great tree loaded with icicles, the ice and branches came so tumbling down that the poor savages ran away half dead with fear. But at last we regained some conference with them, and gave them such toys; and sent to Powhatan [and] his women and children such presents as gave them in general full content.

Now in Jamestown they were all in combustion,[9] the strongest preparing once more to run away with the pinnace; which with the hazard of his life, with saker falcon and musket shot, Smith [was] forced now the third time to stay or sink. Some, no better than they should be, had plotted with the President the next day to have put him to death by the Levitical law,[10] for the lives of Robinson and Emry, pretending the fault was his that had led them to their ends: but he quickly took such order with such lawyers[11] that he laid them by the heels,[12] till he sent some of them prisoners for England. Now every once in four or five days, Pocahontas with her attendants brought him so much provision that

1 *Queen of Appamatuck* Opossunoquonuske, leader of this Algonquian-speaking tribe which resided along the Appomattox River.

2 *as well of* I.e., as skilled at.

3 *They say … lead* Smith paraphrases Fotherby's translation of Greek playwright Euripides (c. 480–406 BCE).

4 *dolefulest* Doleful; sorrowful.

5 *Capahowosick* Village located just southwest of Werowocomoco on Smith's map of Virginia.

6 *as* I.e., as well as.

7 *quartered* I.e., took up quarters; lodged.

8 *demi-culverins* Large, long cannons.

9 *combustion* Disorder.

10 *Levitical law* See Leviticus 24.17: "And he that killeth any man shall surely be put to death."

11 *lawyers* Those who execute Mosaic law (the laws set down in the first five books of the Torah or Old Testament, including the Book of Leviticus).

12 *laid them … heels* Arrested them.

saved many of their lives, that else for all this had[1] starved with hunger.

> Thus from numb death our good God sent relief,
> The sweet assuager of all other grief.[2]

His relation[3] of the plenty he had seen, especially at Werawocomoco, and of the state and bounty of Powhatan (which till that time was unknown), so revived their dead spirits (especially [the story of] the love of Pocahontas)[4] [that] all men's fear was abandoned. Thus you may see what difficulties still crossed any good endeavour: and the good success of the business being thus oft brought to the very period of destruction; yet you see by what strange means God hath still delivered it. As for the insufficiency of them admitted in Commission, that error could not be prevented by the Electors,[5] there being no other choice, and all strangers to each other's education, qualities, or disposition. And if any deem it a shame to our nation to have any mention made of those enormities, let them peruse the histories of the Spaniards' discoveries and plantations, where they may see how many mutinies, disorders, and dissentions have accompanied them, and crossed their attempts. …

from CHAPTER 8
CAPTAIN SMITH'S JOURNEY TO PAMUNKEY

… The 12 of January we arrived at Werowocomoco, where the river was frozen near half a mile from the shore; but to neglect[6] no time, the President[7] with his barge so far had approached by breaking the ice, as the ebb left him amongst those oozy shoals. Yet rather than to lie there frozen to death, by his own example he taught them to march near middle deep, a flight shot through this muddy frozen ooze. When the barge floated, he appointed two or three to return her aboard the pinnace. Where, for want of water in melting the ice, they made fresh water, for the river there was salt. But in this march Mr. Russell (whom none could persuade to stay behind), being somewhat ill, and exceeding heavy, so overtoiled himself as the rest had much ado (ere he got ashore) to regain[8] life into his dead benumbed spirits. Quartering in the next houses we found, we sent to Powhatan for provision, who sent us plenty of bread, turkeys, and venison; the next day having feasted us after his ordinary manner, he began to ask us when we would be gone, saying he [had] sent not for us, neither had he any corn; and his people much less.[9] Yet for forty swords he would procure us forty baskets. The President, showing him the men there present that brought him the message and conditions, asked Powhatan how it chanced he became so forgetful; thereat the King concluded the matter with a merry laughter, asking for our commodities, but none he liked without guns and swords, valuing a basket of corn more precious than a basket of copper; saying he could eat his corn, but not the copper.

Captain Smith, seeing the intent of this subtle[10] savage, began to deal with him after this manner:

> Powhatan, though I had many courses to have made my provision, yet believing your promises to supply my wants, I neglected all to satisfy your desire: and to testify my love, I sent you my men for your building, neglecting mine own. What your people had you have increased, forbidding them our trade: and now you think by consuming the time, we shall consume for want, not having to fulfill your strange demands. As for swords and guns, I told you long ago I had none to spare; and you must know those I have can keep me from want: yet steal or wrong you

1 *else for all this had* Otherwise would have.

2 *Thus from … grief* The first line appears to be Smith's own, while the second is quoted from Fotherby's translation of Euripides.

3 *relation* Telling the story.

4 *especially … Pocahontas* I.e., especially Smith's relation of Pocahontas's apparent love for him.

5 *them admitted in Commission* Those appointed to govern the colony in the Virginia Company's original instructions; *Electors* Those elected by the Virginia Company's stockholders to direct the company's business.

6 *neglect* Waste.

7 *the President* Smith, who had been elected President the previous September.

8 *regain* Restore.

9 *saying … less* Pretending that he had not sent for us, that he did not have any grain, and that his people had much less food [than they needed].

10 *subtle* Cunning.

I will not, nor dissolve that friendship we have mutually promised, except you constrain us by our bad usage.

The King, having attentively listened to this discourse, promised that both he and his country would spare him what he could, the which within two days they should receive. "Yet Captain Smith," sayeth the King,

> some doubt I have of your coming hither that makes me not so kindly seek to relieve you as I would. For many do inform me [that] your coming hither is not for trade but to invade my people, and possess my country, who dare not come to bring you corn, seeing you thus armed with your men. To free us of this fear, leave aboard your weapons, for here they are needless, we being all friends, and forever Powhatans.[1]

With many such discourses they spent the day, quartering that night in the King's houses. The next day he renewed his building, which he little intended should proceed. For, the Dutchmen[2] finding his plenty, and knowing our want, and perceiving his preparations to surprise us, little thinking we could escape both him and famine; to obtain his favour, revealed to him so much as they knew of our estates and projects, and how to prevent them. One of them being of so great a spirit, judgement, and resolution, and a hireling that was certain of his wages for his labour, and ever well used both he and his countrymen; that the President knew not whom better to trust; and not knowing any fitter for that employment, had sent him as a spy to discover Powhatan's intent, then little doubting his honesty, nor could ever be certain of his villainy till near half a year after.

Whilst we expected the coming in of the country, we wrangled out of the King ten quarters[3] of corn for a copper kettle, the which the President perceiving him much to affect,[4] valued it at a much greater rate. But in regard of his scarcity he would accept it [the corn], provided we should have as much more the next year, or else the country of Monacan.[5] Wherewith each seemed well contented, and Powhatan began to expostulate the difference of peace and war after this manner:

> Captain Smith, you may understand that I, having seen the death of all my people thrice, and not any one living of these three generations but myself; I know the difference of peace and war better than any in my country. But now I am old and ere long must die; my brethren, namely Opitchapam, Opechancanough, and Kecoughtan, my two sisters, and their two daughters, are distinctly each other's successors. I wish their experience [to be] no less than mine, and your love to them no less than mine to you. But this bruit from Nansemond,[6] that you are come to destroy my country, so much affrighteth all my people as they dare not visit you. What will it avail[7] you to take that by force [which] you may quickly have by love, or to destroy them that provide you food? What can you get by war, when we can hide our provisions and fly to the woods, whereby you must famish, by wronging us your friends? And why are you thus jealous[8] of our loves, seeing us unarmed, and [that we] both do, and are willing still to feed you, with that [which] you cannot get but by our labours? Think you I am so simple not to know it is better to eat good meat, lie well, and sleep quietly with

[1] *being all … Powhatans* Chief Wahunsonacock had previously adopted Smith as a son and granted him chiefdom over Capahowosick, a nearby village on the York River. Some historians believe that what Smith had understood to be his near execution by Chief Wahunsonacock earlier was in fact an adoption ritual.

[2] *the Dutchmen* With the second supply ship Jamestown had imported several "Dutchmen" (elsewhere Smith indicates that they were from Germany), as well as several Polish people, to work as builders and artisans. Smith later came to believe that the Dutchmen had betrayed him to Powhatan.

[3] *quarters* Units of measure used for grains and other dry commodities.

[4] *affect* Admire.

[5] *Monacan* Siouan-speaking tribe who were at this time in conflict with the Powhatan Confederacy.

[6] *bruit* Rumor; *Nansemond* Tribe under the Powhatan Confederacy who lived along the Nansemond River, a tributary of the James; in 1608 the English had raided their town in search of corn, burning and destroying their houses and canoes.

[7] *avail* Benefit.

[8] *jealous* Mistrustful.

my women and children, laugh and be merry with you, have copper, hatchets, or what I want being your friend, than be forced to fly from all, to lie cold in the woods, feed upon acorns, roots, and such trash, and be so hunted by you, that I can neither rest, eat, nor sleep; but my tired men must watch, and if a twig but break, everyone cryeth, "there commeth Captain Smith"? Then must I fly I know not whither: and thus with miserable fear end my miserable life, leaving my pleasures to such youths as you, which through your rash unadvisedness may quickly as miserably end, for want of that [which] you never know where to find. Let this therefore assure you of our loves, and every year our friendly trade shall furnish you with corn; and now also, if you would come in friendly manner to see us, and not thus with your guns and swords as to invade your foes.

To this subtle discourse, the President thus replied:

Seeing [that] you will not rightly conceive of our words, we strive to make you know our thoughts by our deeds; the vow I made you of my love, both myself and my men have kept. As for your promise, I find it every day violated by some of your subjects. Yet we, finding your love and kindness, our custom is so far from being ungrateful, that, for your sake only, we have curbed our thirsting desire of revenge; else had they[1] known as well the cruelty we use to our enemies, as our true love and courtesy to our friends. And I think your judgment sufficient to conceive, as well by the adventures we have undertaken, as by the advantage we have (by our arms) of yours: that had we intended you any hurt, long ere this we could have effected it. Your people coming to Jamestown are entertained[2] with their bows and arrows without any exceptions; we esteeming it with you as it is with us, to wear our arms as our apparel. As for the danger of our enemies, in such wars consist our chiefest pleasure. For your riches we have no use; as for

the hiding your provision, or by your flying to the woods, we shall not so unadvisedly starve as you conclude; your friendly care in that behalf is needless, for we have a rule to find beyond your knowledge.[3]

Many other discourses they had, till at last they began to trade. But the King, seeing his will would not be admitted as a law, [neither] our guard dispersed, nor our men disarmed, he (sighing) breathed his mind once more in this manner:

Captain Smith, I never use any Weroance[4] so kindly as yourself, yet from you I receive the least kindness of any. Captain Newport gave me swords, copper, clothes, a bed, towels, or what I desired; ever taking what I offered him, and would send away his guns when I entreated him. None doth deny to lie at my feet, or refuse to do what I desire, but only you, of whom I can have nothing but what you regard not,[5] and yet you will have whatsoever you demand. Captain Newport you call father, and so you call me; but I see for all us both you will do what you list,[6] and we must both seek to content you. But if you intend [to be] so friendly as you say, send hence your arms, that I may believe you; for you see the love I bear you doth cause me thus nakedly[7] to forget myself.

Smith, seeing this savage but trifle the time to cut his throat,[8] procured the savages to break the ice, that his boat might come to fetch his corn and him, and gave order for more men to come on shore, to surprise the King, with whom also he but trifled the time till his men were landed, and to keep him from suspicion, entertained the time with this reply:

1 *they* I.e., Wahunsonacock's people.

2 *entertained* Armed.

3 *we have … knowledge* I.e., we have ways beyond your knowledge to acquire provisions.

4 *Weroance* Algonquin word for "chief" or "leader."

5 *what you regard not* What you don't want; worthless things.

6 *list* Want.

7 *nakedly* Defenselessly.

8 *but trifle … throat* Only putting in time before cutting his throat.

Powhatan you must know, as I have but one God, I honour but one King; and I live not here as your subject, but as your friend to pleasure you with what I can. By the gifts you bestow on me, you gain more than by trade: yet would you visit me as I do you, you should know it is not our custom, to sell our courtesies as a vendible commodity. Bring all your country with you for your guard; I will not dislike it as being over jealous. But to content you, tomorrow I will leave my arms, and trust to your promise. I call you father indeed, and as a father you shall see I will love you: but the small care you have of such a child caused my men persuade me to look to myself.

By this time Powhatan, having knowledge his men were ready, whilst the ice was a breaking, with his luggage, women and children, fled. Yet to avoid suspicion, [he] left two or three of the women talking with the Captain, whilst he secretly ran away, and his men that secretly beset the house. Which being presently discovered to Captain Smith, with his pistol, sword, and target he made such a passage among these naked devils, that at his first shot, they next him tumbled one over another, and the rest quickly fled, some one way, some another: so that without any hurt, only accompanied with John Russell, he obtained the *corps de guard*.[1] When they [the Powhatans] perceived him so well escaped, and with his eighteen men (for he had no more with him ashore) to the uttermost of their skill they sought excuses to dissemble the matter: and Powhatan to excuse his flight and the sudden coming of this multitude, sent our Captain a great bracelet and a chain of pearl, by an ancient orator that bespoke us to this purpose, perceiving even then from our pinnace, a barge and men departing and coming unto us.

Captain Smith, our Weroance is fled, fearing your guns, and knowing when the ice was broken there would come more men, sent these numbers but to guard his corn from stealing, that might happen without your knowledge:

now, though some be hurt by your misprision,[2] yet Powhatan is your friend and so will forever continue. Now, since the ice is open, he would have you send away your corn, and if you would have his company, send away also your guns, which so affrighteth his people, that they dare not come to you as he promised they should.

Then having provided baskets for our men to carry our corn to the boats, they kindly offered their service to guard our arms, that none should steal them. A great many they were of goodly well proportioned fellows, as grim as devils; yet the very sight of cocking our matches,[3] and being to let fly, a few words caused them to leave their bows and arrows to our guard, and bear down our corn on their backs; we needed not importune them to make dispatch.[4] But our barges being left on the ooze by the ebb,[5] caused us [to] stay till the next high-water, so that we returned again to our old quarter. Powhatan and his Dutchmen, [who were] bursting with desire to have the head of Captain Smith, for if they could but kill him, they thought all was theirs, neglected not any opportunity to effect his purpose. The Indians with all the merry sports they could devise, spent the time till night; then they all returned to Powhatan, who all this time was making ready his forces to surprise the house and him at supper. Notwithstanding, the eternal all-seeing God did prevent him, and by a strange means. For Pocahontas, his dearest jewel and daughter, in that dark night came through the irksome woods, and told our Captain great cheer should be sent us by and by, but Powhatan and all the power he could make would after come kill us all, if they that brought it could not kill us with our own weapons when we were at supper. Therefore, if we would live, she wished us presently to be gone. Such things as she delighted in, he [Smith] would have given her, but with the tears running down her cheeks she said she durst not be seen to have any; for if Powhatan should know it, she were but dead, and so she ran away by herself as she came.

1 *corps de guard* French: guardhouse; military construction which defends the entrance to a fort.

2 *misprision* Misconduct.

3 *cocking our matches* Readying our firearms for use.

4 *needed ... dispatch* I.e., it was not necessary to insist that they do as the colonists wish and bear the corn.

5 *ebb* Tide.

Within less than an hour came eight or ten lusty[1] fellows, with great platters of venison and other victual, very importunate to have us put out our matches (whose smoke made them sick) and sit down to our victual. But the Captain made them taste every dish, which [having been] done he [then] sent some of them back to Powhatan, to bid him make haste, for he was prepared for his coming. As for them, he knew they came to betray him at his supper: but he would prevent them and all their other intended villainies, so that they might be gone. Not long after came more messengers, to see what news; not long after them [came] others. Thus we spent the night as vigilantly as they, till it was high-water, yet [we] seemed to the savages as friendly as they to us[.] …

—1624

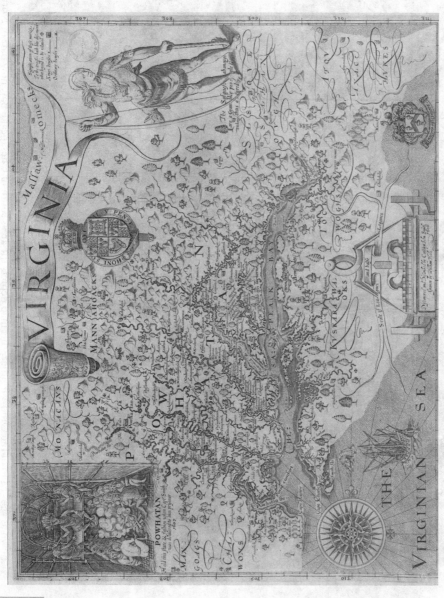

John Smith's map of Virginia was first published in 1612, and also included a "description of the country, the commodities, people, government and religion." In the upper left-hand corner of the map is a depiction of Wahunsonacock as he is said to have appeared when Smith was his prisoner. The image was later reproduced in Smith's *General History.*

1 *lusty* Strong, vigorous.

Known as the "Map of the Ould Virginia," this map depicts the areas south of Chesapeake Bay, now part of North Carolina, that had been settled under Sir Walter Ralegh's patent in the 1580s. The whole image, which was designed by Robert Vaughan for Smith's *General History*, also includes numerous depictions of Smith's encounters with the Powhatan and other Indigenous peoples around Virginia.

—1624

WILLIAM BRADFORD

1590 – 1657

One of the famous group of settlers who came to Cape Cod on the *Mayflower*, William Bradford was a Puritan Separatist, writer, and politician who served for decades as the governor of Plymouth, one of the earliest European settlements in New England. His historical account of the journey and the first thirty years of settlement—*Of Plymouth Plantation* (1630–51)—helped shape the mythology of early American history. Bradford himself soon became mythologized as the "father of American history"; Cotton Mather described him in 1702 as an Adam figure, "the father of them all," and also as a Moses, "the leader of a people in a wilderness." While the Puritans' colonialist belief in their divine right to settle America has been soundly criticized, Bradford's journal is still widely considered foundational to the American story, and an early example of the Puritan consciousness that shaped New England history for generations.

Bradford was born in 1590 in Austerfield, Yorkshire, to a family with considerable farmland. Orphaned as a child, he was brought up by two of his uncles. He loved to read and began to study the Geneva Bible at an early age; at seventeen, he joined a Separatist Puritan congregation. Unlike most Puritans, who sought to reform the Anglican Church from within, the Separatists took their beliefs far enough to break with the established church—a move that was considered treasonous, putting them at odds not only with the powerful clergy but also with the government.

Persecution of Separatists under King James I led Bradford's community (known as the Scrooby congregation) to move to Holland, a country that allowed them religious freedom. They went first to Amsterdam in 1607, and then to Leiden, where Bradford became a weaver. He struggled financially until he inherited his family's estate in 1611, and two years later he married Dorothy May, an Englishwoman living in Amsterdam. Most members of the Scrooby congregation, however, continued to find it difficult to earn a living in Leiden, and they worried that their children might be assimilated into Dutch culture and lose their English Separatist identity. Bradford was among a group of community members who decided to leave Leiden and establish a new colony in what is now New York State, in part of a region the English then referred to as Virginia. These "Pilgrims" departed in 1620, having obtained a grant of land from the English government and secured financing through a profit-sharing agreement with the Merchant Adventurers, a London trading company.

Instead of Virginia, however, the *Mayflower* touched down at Cape Cod. Prevented by the weather from sailing further south, the leaders of the community decided to settle in a place they called Plymouth, known to the local Indigenous people as Patuxet. Many historians think that the settlement might have encountered more resistance from Indigenous people had not an epidemic killed ninety per cent of the Patuxet (the local Wampanoag band) between 1617 and 1619, leaving the area sparsely populated when the Pilgrims arrived. Instead, relationships with Indigenous people would prove crucial for the colony's survival, as Indigenous supporters taught the colonists how to fish, how to cultivate the land, and other essential skills. This help was sorely needed: in the first year after arrival, more than half of the hundred settlers died of scurvy and other illnesses. Bradford survived a serious illness, but his wife drowned in November 1620 when she fell off the deck of the *Mayflower*, which was moored in Plymouth harbor.

Following the death of John Carver, the first governor of Plymouth, Bradford was elected to take up the role; he would serve as governor for thirty of the first thirty-five years of the colony's existence. The governor, along with his elected assistants, made crucial decisions on the colony's behalf, including political and economic decisions, but also practical everyday ones about land allocation and farming practices; the governor also presided as a judge over criminal and civil disagreements. Bradford proved to be an effective leader, making careful decisions to ensure the colony's survival; he was also, however, capable of ruthlessness—of sentencing a community member to death for bestiality, for example. His dealings with the neighboring Indigenous peoples, while he intended them to be fair and measured,

were nonetheless affected by his racial and religious prejudices. The Plymouth community grew over the course of Bradford's lifetime from the 101 *Mayflower* passengers in 1620 to 1,360 members in 1657. By the end of his life, however, he was distressed by the number of new settlements unconnected to the Separatist church; Baptists and Quakers, for example, had begun to form their own congregations. This splintering of the original intimate church community was, for him, a source of sorrow and regret.

In 1630, Bradford began writing *Of Plymouth Plantation*, which tells the story of the settlers' journey from Holland and of the first thirty years of colonization. The narrative resolutely keeps its focus on the colony's economic prosperity and moral status, revealing little about Bradford's own personal life. He speaks of himself in the third person, barely mentioning his wife's death, and there is no mention at all of his remarriage to Alice Southworth or of the births of his three children (he and his first wife had left their first son in Holland, but he eventually followed Bradford to America). *Of Plymouth Plantation* records, in Bradford's "plain style" of writing, detailed and vivid accounts of the voyage, contact with Indigenous peoples, the work of settlement, and various iconic incidents, some of which made their way into American mythology.

Of Plymouth Plantation is composed of two books, the first detailing the Pilgrims' journey and early days of settlement, and the second providing a year-by-year account of the principal concerns of the colony. Book One is written confidently in the genre of providential histories not uncommon among Puritans at the time, in which the hand of God is at times clearly, and at other times mysteriously, guiding events. The histories recorded in the Bible are the most important precursors of this kind of writing; the story in Exodus, for example, of the people of Israel escaping captivity in Egypt, was for Bradford and other American Puritans a prefiguration of their own journey across the sea to find religious freedom. In taking up the genre, Bradford was influenced by earlier providential histories such as John Foxe's *Acts and Monuments* (1563), a popular work that told the stories of Protestant martyrs in sixteenth-century England. Book Two of *Plymouth Plantation*, however, shifts away from a providential tone and style, coming to resemble an economic history, as Bradford finds himself detailing the complex financial and political negotiations of Plymouth with its various trade partners: Indigenous communities, nearby settlements, and the Merchant Adventurers in England. Book Two also becomes more elegiac in tone, as Bradford struggles to square the gradual dissolution of the community with his faith in Plymouth's God-given destiny.

The manuscript of *Of Plymouth Plantation* was passed down in Bradford's family for several generations. The family made it available to seventeenth- and eighteenth-century historians such as Nathaniel Morton, Cotton Mather, and Thomas Prince, and it remained a central source for information about the early years of New England history (along with Edward Winslow's 1622 publication *A Relation or Journal of the Beginning and Proceedings of the English Plantation Settled at Plymouth in New England*, to which Bradford also contributed). The manuscript made its way to a Boston library, from which it is thought to have been stolen by a British soldier during the Boston occupation of 1775–76. New England scholars had a copy of the first portion of the text but considered the rest lost until 1855, when they noticed that British scholars were citing it. Thus began a 42-year-long legal battle to return the text to America. This conflict was finally decided in favor of the United States in 1897, when the manuscript was returned and placed in the Massachusetts State House, where it remains.

Because the manuscript was outside America for so many decades, *Of Plymouth Plantation* was not printed in its entirety until 1856. Once published, it was received with enthusiasm both as a literary work and as a valuable history of early New England. Its readership increased further with the publication of an accessible scholarly edition of Bradford's history by Worthington C. Ford in 1912, and by the 1960s the book was on most course syllabi dealing with American studies. In the twentieth century, Bradford came to be more appreciated as a literary writer, with greater attention being paid to his style and influences. Scholars have also argued that Bradford's narrative has influenced writers of immigration such as Willa Cather, as well as writers of "frontier" fiction such as Catherine Maria Sedgwick and James Fenimore Cooper. As a document of colonialism, the bias inherent in Bradford's work has come into focus, and *Of Plymouth Plantation* has been compared to other colonial narratives outside of New England, such as Álvar Núñez Cabeza de Vaca's *La relación y comentarios* (1542). Indigenous responses to the text have also enriched the critical dialogue; Cherokee writer Betty Booth Donahue argues in *Bradford's Indian Book* (2011), for example, that the structure of the text is profoundly influenced by Indigenous forms of storytelling.

In 1647, Bradford stopped adding entries to *Of Plymouth Plantation*, but he continued to write, composing dialogues and poems on theological topics. While not generally considered exceptional in literary terms, these works are often read for further insight into the colonial period and into Bradford's roles—as historiographer, politician, and writer—in shaping our perceptions of early American history. Bradford died in Plymouth in 1657, where a stone monument on Burial Hill commemorates his contributions to the community. In his last poem, "Epitaphium Meum" ("My Epitaph"), he describes himself as "a man of sorrows," waiting for his "happy change." Despite the disappointment he felt at the dispersal of the Plymouth community, he passed down his history in the hope that the Pilgrims' story would be an example to future generations: "As one small candle may light a thousand, so the light here kindled hath shone unto many, yea in some sort to our whole nation." Bradford's text remains a rich resource for readers seeking to understand the complex cultural, economic, political, and religious histories of early America.

NOTE ON THE TEXT: Several editions of Bradford's *Of Plymouth Plantation* have been consulted in the preparation of the text reprinted here, including Worthington Chauncey Ford's 1912 edition and Samuel Eliot Morison's 1952 edition. Spelling and punctuation have been lightly modernized in accordance with the practices of this anthology.

⌘ ⌘ ⌘

from *Of Plymouth Plantation*

And first of the occasion and inducements there unto; the which that I may truly unfold, I must begin at the very root and rise of the same. The which I shall endeavour to manifest in a plain style, with singular regard unto the simple truth in all things; at least as near as my slender judgment can attain the same.

from THE FIRST BOOK

from CHAPTER 1
[THE SEPARATIST INTERPRETATION OF THE REFORMATION IN ENGLAND, 1550–1607]

It is well known unto the godly and judicious, how since the first breaking out of the light of the gospel[1] in our honourable nation of England (which was the first of nations whom the Lord adorned therewith, after the gross darkness of popery which had covered and overspread the Christian world), what wars, and oppositions ever since, Satan hath raised, maintained, and continued against the Saints,[2] from time to time, in one sort or other. Sometimes by bloody death and cruel torments; other whiles imprisonments, banishments, and other hard usages; as being loath his kingdom should go down, the truth prevail and the churches of God revert to their ancient purity and recover their primitive order, liberty, and beauty. …

Mr. Foxe[3] recordeth how that besides those worthy martyrs and confessors which were burned in Queen Mary's days[4] and otherwise tormented, "Many (both students and others) fled out of the land to the number of 800, and became several congregations, at Wesel, Frankfurt, Basel, Emden, Markpurge, Strasburg and Geneva, etc." Amongst whom (but especially those

1 *first breaking out … gospel* Dawn of Protestantism. The Church of England, a Protestant church, was founded in the 1530s, though Protestant ideology had taken hold in some quarters in England in the preceding decades.

2 *Saints* Term used by some Puritan sects to describe their members; Bradford is using it here more generally to refer to Protestants. The implication is that members are themselves saints and do not need priests to act as intermediaries between them and God.

3 [Bradford's note] Acts and Mon[uments]: pag. 1587 edition 2. [This book is commonly known as *The Book of Martyrs* (first published in 1563), an account of Christian martyrs in Western history; it was written by John Foxe, an English historian and member of the clergy.]

4 *burned in Queen Mary's days* Mary I (1516–58) was a Roman Catholic, and in her attempt to reverse the Reformation set in motion by her father, Henry VIII, she burned almost 300 Protestant dissenters at the stake. Upon Queen Mary's death, her half-sister Elizabeth became Queen, and England became Protestant again.

at Frankfurt) began that bitter war of contention and persecution about the ceremonies and service book,[1] and other popish and antichristian stuff, the plague of England to this day, which are like the high places in Israel which the prophets cried out against, and were their ruin.[2] ...

And this contention died not with Queen Mary, nor was left beyond the seas. But at her death these people[3] returning into England under gracious Queen Elizabeth, many of them being preferred to bishoprics and other promotions according to their aims and desires, that inveterate hatred against the holy discipline of Christ in His church[4] hath continued to this day. Insomuch that for fear it should prevail, all plots and devices have been used to keep it out, incensing the Queen and State against it as dangerous for the commonwealth; and that it was most needful that the fundamental points of religion should be preached in those ignorant and superstitious times. And to win the weak and ignorant they might retain diverse harmless ceremonies; and though it were to be wished that diverse things were reformed, yet this was not a season for it. And many the like, to stop the mouths of the more godly, to bring them on to yield to one ceremony after another, and one corruption after another; by these wiles beguiling some and corrupting others till at length they began to persecute all the zealous professors[5] in the land (though they knew little what this discipline meant) both by word and deed, if they would not submit to their ceremonies and become slaves to them and their popish trash, which have no ground in the Word of God, but are relics of that man of sin.[6] And the more the light of the gospel grew, the more they urged their subscriptions to[7] these corruptions. So as (notwithstanding all their former pretenses and fair colors) they whose eyes God had not justly blinded might easily see whereto these things tended. And to cast contempt the more upon the sincere servants of God, they opprobriously[8] and most injuriously gave unto and imposed upon them that name of Puritans, which is said the Novatians[9] out of pride did assume and take unto themselves. And lamentable it is to see the effects which have followed. Religion hath been disgraced, the godly grieved, afflicted, persecuted and many exiled; sundry[10] have lost their lives in prisons and other ways. On the other hand, sin hath been countenanced; ignorance, profaneness, and atheism[11] increased, and the papists encouraged to hope again for a day. ...

So many, therefore, of these professors as saw the evil of these things in these parts, and whose hearts the Lord had touched with heavenly zeal for His truth, they shook off this yoke of antichristian bondage, and as the Lord's free people joined themselves (by a covenant of the Lord) into a church estate, in the fellowship of the gospel, to walk in all His ways made known, or to be made known unto them, according to their best endeavours, whatsoever it should cost them, the Lord assisting them. And that it cost them something this ensuing history will declare. ...

Yet seeing themselves thus molested, and that there was no hope of their continuance there, by a joint consent they resolved to go into the Low Countries, where they heard was freedom of religion for all men; as also

[1] *contention ... service book* Puritans such as Bradford objected to many practices of the Church of England, including its rituals, Book of Common Prayer, and hierarchical clergy; they considered such things to be distractions reminiscent of Catholicism.

[2] *high places in Israel ... ruin* See 1 Kings 13.1–3. These passages describe the coming of a "man of God" who speaks against the altars in "high places" in Bethel, where idolatrous worship and sacrifice took place; the man of God predicts the coming of a prophet, Josiah, who will destroy these idols and their worshippers.

[3] *these people* Anglican Protestants who had fled England to avoid persecution under Queen Mary.

[4] *holy discipline ... His church* I.e., the discipline and practices of Puritan congregations.

[5] *professors* Those who openly claim to believe in Christianity.

[6] *Word of God* I.e., the Gospels; *that man of sin* Following Martin Luther's lead, Puritans viewed the Pope, and the church he leads, as the "man of sin," the antichrist—a figure opposed to Christ that seeks to supplant him at the Second Coming. See 2 Thessalonians 2.3–4.

[7] *subscriptions to* Approvals of.

[8] *opprobriously* Scornfully.

[9] *Novatians* Followers of Novatian (200–58), a Greek theologian whose sect did not allow lapsed Christians to be accepted back into the rites of communion.

[10] *sundry* Many.

[11] *atheism* In the seventeenth century, the term was used to refer not only to a disbelief in God, but more broadly to godlessness, wickedness, or corruption.

how sundry from London and other parts of the land had been exiled and persecuted for the same cause, and were gone thither, and lived at Amsterdam and in other places of the land. So after they had continued together about a year, and kept their meetings every Sabbath in one place or other, exercising the worship of God amongst themselves, notwithstanding all the diligence and malice of their adversaries, they seeing they could no longer continue in that condition, they resolved to get over into Holland as they could. Which was in the year 1607 and 1608; of which more at large in the next chapter.

from CHAPTER 4
SHOWING THE REASONS AND
CAUSES OF THEIR REMOVAL

After they had lived in this city[1] about some eleven or twelve years (which is the more observable being the whole time of that famous truce between that state and the Spaniards)[2] and sundry of them were taken away by death and many others began to be well stricken in years (the grave mistress of Experience having taught them many things), those prudent governors with sundry of the sagest members began both deeply to apprehend their present dangers and wisely to foresee the future and think of timely remedy. In the agitation of their thoughts, and much discourse of things hereabout, at length they began to incline to this conclusion: of removal to some other place. Not out of any newfangledness or other such like giddy humor by which men are oftentimes transported to their great hurt and danger, but for sundry weighty and solid reasons, some of the chief of which I will here briefly touch.

And first, they saw and found by experience the hardness of the place and country to be such as few in comparison would come to them, and fewer that would bide it out and continue with them. For many that came to them, and many more that desired to be with them, could not endure that great labour and hard fare, with other inconveniences which they underwent and were contented with. … For many, though they desired to enjoy the ordinances of God in their purity and the liberty of the gospel with them, yet (alas) they admitted of bondage with danger of conscience, rather than to endure these hardships. Yea, some preferred and chose the prisons in England rather than this liberty in Holland with these afflictions. But it was thought that if a better and easier place of living could be had, it would draw many and take away these discouragements. Yea, their pastor would often say that many of those who both wrote and preached now against them, if they were in a place where they might have liberty and live comfortably, they would then practice as they did.

Secondly. They saw that though the people generally bore all these difficulties very cheerfully and with a resolute courage, being in the best and strength of their years; yet old age began to steal on many of them; and their great and continual labours, with other crosses and sorrows, hastened it before the time. So as it was not only probably thought, but apparently seen, that within a few years more they would be in danger to scatter, by necessities pressing them, or sink under their burdens, or both. And therefore according to the divine proverb, that a wise man seeth the plague when it cometh, and hideth himself, Proverbs 22.3, so they like skillful and beaten soldiers were fearful either to be entrapped or surrounded by their enemies so as they should neither be able to fight nor fly. And therefore thought it better to dislodge betimes[3] to some place of better advantage and less danger, if any such could be found.

Thirdly. As necessity was a taskmaster over them so they were forced to be such, not only to their servants but in a sort to their dearest children, the which as it did not a little wound the tender hearts of many a loving father and mother, so it produced likewise sundry sad and sorrowful effects. For many of their children that were of best dispositions and gracious inclinations, having learned to bear the yoke in their youth[4] and willing to bear part of their parents' burden, were oftentimes so oppressed with their heavy labours that though their minds were free and willing, yet their bodies bowed under the weight of the same,

[1] *this city* Leiden, Holland.

[2] *truce between … Spaniards* The Twelve Years' Truce (1609–21), a break in the hostilities of the Eighty Years' War between Spain and the Southern Netherlands.

[3] *betimes* Quickly, before it was too late.

[4] *bear the yoke in their youth* See Lamentations 3.27.

and became decrepit in their early youth, the vigour of nature being consumed in the very bud as it were. But that which was more lamentable, and of all sorrows most heavy to be borne, was that many of their children, by these occasions and the great licentiousness of youth in that country,[1] and the manifold temptations of the place, were drawn away by evil examples into extravagant and dangerous courses, getting the reins off their necks and departing from their parents. Some became soldiers, others took upon them far voyages by sea, and others some worse courses tending to dissoluteness and the danger of their souls, to the great grief of their parents and dishonour of God. So that they saw their posterity would be in danger to degenerate and be corrupted.

Lastly (and which was not least), a great hope and inward zeal they had of laying some good foundation, or at least to make some way thereunto, for the propagating and advancing the gospel of the kingdom of Christ in those remote parts of the world; yea, though they should be but even as stepping-stones unto others for the performing of so great a work.

These and some other like reasons moved them to undertake this resolution of their removal; the which they afterward prosecuted with so great difficulties, as by the sequel will appear. …

CHAPTER 9
OF THEIR VOYAGE, AND HOW THEY PASSED THE SEA; AND OF THEIR SAFE ARRIVAL AT CAPE COD

September 6. These troubles[2] being blown over, and now all being compact together in one ship,

they put to sea again with a prosperous wind, which continued diverse days together, which was some encouragement unto them; yet, according to the usual manner, many were afflicted with seasickness. And I may not omit here a special work of God's providence. There was a proud and very profane young man, one of the seamen, of a lusty,[3] able body, which made him the more haughty; he would always be contemning the poor people in their sickness and cursing them daily with grievous execrations; and did not let to tell them that he hoped to help to cast half of them overboard before they came to their journey's end, and to make merry with what they had; and if he were by any gently reproved, he would curse and swear most bitterly. But it pleased God before they came half seas over, to smite this young man with a grievous disease, of which he died in a desperate manner, and so was himself the first that was thrown overboard. Thus his curses light on his own head, and it was an astonishment to all his fellows for they noted it to be the just hand of God upon him. …

But to omit other things (that I may be brief) after long beating at sea they fell with that land which is called Cape Cod; the which being made and certainly known to be it, they were not a little joyful. After some deliberation had amongst themselves and with the master of the ship, they tacked about and resolved to stand for the southward (the wind and weather being fair) to find some place about Hudson's River[4] for their habitation. But after they had sailed that course about half the day, they fell amongst dangerous shoals and roaring breakers, and they were so far entangled therewith as they conceived themselves in great danger; and the wind shrinking upon them withal, they resolved to bear up again for the Cape and thought themselves happy to get out of those dangers before night overtook them, as by God's providence they did. And the next day they got into the Cape Harbor[5] where they rid in safety.

[1] *great licentiousness … country* The English Puritans objected to many aspects of Dutch life, particularly their habit of socializing after church on Sundays, which the Puritans felt ought to be kept holy and spent in contemplation. There was also concern among the Puritan leaders that if they remained in the Netherlands their children would eventually become Dutch and not English, which they wanted to prevent.

[2] *These troubles* In Book 1, Chapters 7–8 (omitted here) the Pilgrims set sail in two ships. The smaller one, the *Speedwell*, leaks, and they return to Dartmouth, England, to have it repaired. A second sailing produces the same result, and the ships return to Plymouth, England, where the *Speedwell* is deemed unseaworthy. Some of its passengers decide not to take the journey after all, but some board the larger ship (the *Mayflower*), which then becomes rather crowded with passengers, crew, and supplies.

[3] *lusty* Strong and healthy.

[4] *Hudson's River* Prominent waterway in New York state and the *Mayflower*'s original destination.

[5] *Cape Harbor* Today called Provincetown Harbor.

A word or two by the way of this cape. It was thus first named by Captain Gosnold and his company,[1] Anno[2] 1602, and after by Captain Smith[3] was called Cape James; but it retains the former name amongst seamen. Also, that point which first showed those dangerous shoals unto them they called Point Care, and Tucker's Terror; but the French and Dutch to this day call it Malabar[4] by reason of those perilous shoals and the losses they have suffered there.

Being thus arrived in a good harbor, and brought safe to land, they fell upon their knees and blessed the God of Heaven[5] who had brought them over the vast and furious ocean, and delivered them from all the perils and miseries thereof, again to set their feet on the firm and stable earth, their proper element. And no marvel if they were thus joyful, seeing wise Seneca[6] was so affected with sailing a few miles on the coast of his own Italy, as he affirmed, that he had rather remain twenty years on his way by land than pass by sea to any place in a short time, so tedious and dreadful was the same unto him.[7]

But here I cannot but stay and make a pause, and stand half amazed at this poor people's present condition; and so I think will the reader, too, when he well considers the same. Being thus passed the vast ocean, and a sea of troubles before in their preparation (as may be remembered by that which went before), they had now no friends to welcome them nor inns to entertain or refresh their weatherbeaten bodies no houses or much less towns to repair to, to seek for succor. It is recorded in Scripture[8] as a mercy to the Apostle[9] and his shipwrecked company, that the barbarians showed them no small kindness in refreshing them, but these savage barbarians, when they met with them (as after will appear) were readier to fill their sides full of arrows than otherwise. And for the season it was winter, and they that know the winters of that country know them to be sharp and violent, and subject to cruel and fierce storms, dangerous to travel to known places, much more to search an unknown coast. Besides, what could they see but a hideous and desolate wilderness, full of wild beasts and wild men—and what multitudes there might be of them they knew not. Neither could they, as it were, go up to the top of Pisgah[10] to view from this wilderness a more goodly country to feed their hopes; for which way soever they turned their eyes (save upward to the heavens) they could have little solace or content in respect of any outward objects. For summer being done, all things stand upon them with a weatherbeaten face, and the whole country, full of woods and thickets, represented a wild and savage hue. If they looked behind them, there was the mighty ocean which they had passed and was now as a main bar and gulf to separate them from all the civil parts of the world. If it be said they had a ship to succor them, it is true; but what heard they daily from the master and company? But that with speed they should look out a place (with their shallop[11]) where they would be, at some near distance; for the season was such as he would not stir from thence till a safe harbor was discovered by them, where they would be, and he might go without danger; and that victuals[12] consumed apace but he must and would keep sufficient for themselves and their return. Yea, it was muttered by some that if they got not a place in time, they would turn them and their goods ashore and leave them. Let it also be considered what weak hopes of supply and succor they left behind them, that might

[1] [Bradford's note] Because they took much of that fish there. [I.e., they caught a great deal of codfish there.]

[2] *Anno* Latin: Year.

[3] *Captain Gosnold* Bartholomew Gosnold (1571–1607), English explorer and lawyer, led the first recorded European expedition to Cape Cod; *Captain Smith* John Smith (c. 1580–1631), English explorer, author, and cartographer.

[4] *Point Care … Malabar* These names probably refer to Nauset Harbor, Cape Cod.

[5] *blessed the God of Heaven* See Daniel 2.19.

[6] *Seneca* Seneca the Younger (c. 4 BCE–65 CE), a Roman stoic philosopher.

[7] [Bradford's note] Epistle 53. [Bradford is paraphrasing from Seneca's "Epistle 53" from *The Moral Epistles to Lucius* (c. 65 CE).]

[8] [Bradford's note] Acts 28[.2].

[9] *the Apostle* Paul the Apostle (c. 5–c. 64 or 67), also known as Saint Paul, an early Christian missionary who is traditionally considered the author of thirteen books of the New Testament.

[10] *Pisgah* Mount Pisgah. On its peak, God shows Moses the Promised Land. See Deuteronomy 34.1–4.

[11] *shallop* Open row-boat used in shallow waters to move between a larger boat and land.

[12] *victuals* Food or provisions.

bear up their minds in this sad condition and trial they were under; and they could not but be very small. It is true, indeed, the affections and love of their brethren at Leiden was cordial and entire towards them, but they had little power to help them or themselves; and how the case stood between them and the merchants at their coming away hath already been declared.[1]

What could now sustain them but the Spirit of God and His grace? May not and ought not the children of these fathers rightly say: "Our fathers were Englishmen which came over this great ocean, and were ready to perish in this wilderness; but they cried unto the Lord, and He heard their voice and looked on their adversity,"[2] etc. "Let them therefore praise the Lord, because He is good: and His mercies endure forever."[3] "Yea, let them which have been redeemed of the Lord, show how He hath delivered them from the hand of the oppressor. When they wandered in the desert wilderness out of the way, and found no city to dwell in, both hungry and thirsty, their soul was overwhelmed in them. Let them confess before the Lord His loving kindness and His wonderful works before the sons of men."[4]

from CHAPTER 10
SHOWING HOW THEY SOUGHT OUT A PLACE OF HABITATION; AND WHAT BEFELL THEM THEREABOUT

Being thus arrived at Cape Cod the 11th of November, and necessity calling them to look out a place for habitation (as well as the master's and mariners' importunity); they having brought a large shallop with them out of England, stowed in quarters in the ship, they now got her out and set their carpenters to work to trim her up; but being much bruised and shattered in the ship with foul weather, they saw she would be long in mending. Whereupon a few of them tendered themselves to go by land and discover those nearest places, whilst the shallop was in mending; and the rather because as they went into that harbor there seemed to be an opening some two or three leagues off, which the master judged to be a river.[5] It was conceived there might be some danger in the attempt, yet seeing them resolute, they were permitted to go, being sixteen of them well armed under the conduct of Captain Standish,[6] having such instructions given them as was thought meet.[7]

They[8] set forth the 15th of November; and when they had marched about the space of a mile by the sea side, they espied five or six persons with a dog coming towards them, who were savages; but they fled from them and ran up into the woods, and the English followed them, partly to see if they could speak with them, and partly to discover if there might not be more of them lying in ambush. But the Indians seeing themselves thus followed, they again forsook the woods and ran away on the sands as hard as they could, so as they could not come near them but followed them by the tracks of their feet sundry miles and saw that they had come the same way. So, night coming on, they made their rendezvous and set out their sentinels, and rested in quiet that night; and the next morning followed their tracks till they had headed a great creek[9] and so left the sands, and turned another way into the woods. But they still followed them by guess, hoping to find their dwellings; but they soon lost both them and themselves, falling into such thickets as were ready to tear their clothes and armor in pieces; but were most distressed for want of drink. But at length they found

[1] *how the case stood ... been declared* The relationship between the Pilgrims and the Merchant Adventurers—the group of capitalists led by Thomas Weston (c. 1584–c. 1647) who helped fund Plymouth Plantation—had fallen out over several conditions of their agreement. Most contentiously, the Adventurers changed the original agreement that would grant the Pilgrims ownership of their houses and lands (and the profits made from them) after seven years; an amendment to that original agreement stated that such property would be *divided* between the Pilgrims and the Adventurers after seven years. The disagreement between the parties delayed the *Mayflower*'s departure and did not end amicably, with Weston refusing any further financial aid.

[2] [Bradford's note] Deuteronomy 26.5,7.

[3] *Let them therefore praise ... endure forever* See Psalm 106.1.

[4] [Bradford's note] Psalm 107.1–5, 8.

[5] *river* From where the Pilgrims were, the land near Plymouth looks like an island in certain conditions, hence the assumption a river divides the land from the sea.

[6] *Captain Standish* Myles Standish (c. 1584–1656), English ex-soldier hired by the Merchant Adventurers as a military advisor to the Pilgrims. He became a good friend and supporter to the Pilgrims.

[7] *meet* Suitable.

[8] *They* Bradford was included in this group.

[9] *headed a great creek* Went around the source of the creek, in this case East-Harbor Creek.

water and refreshed themselves, being the first New England water they drunk of, and was now in great thirst as pleasant unto them as wine or beer had been in foretimes.

Afterwards they directed their course to come to the other shore, for they knew it was a neck of land they were to cross over, and so at length got to the seaside and marched to this supposed river, and by the way found a pond of clear, fresh water, and shortly after a good quantity of clear ground where the Indians had formerly set corn, and some of their graves. And proceeding further they saw new stubble where corn had been set the same year, also they found where lately a house had been, where some planks and a great kettle was remaining, and heaps of sand newly paddled[1] with their hands. Which, they digging up, found in them diverse fair Indian baskets filled with corn, and some in ears, fair and good, of diverse colors, which seemed to them a very goodly sight (having never seen any such before). This was near the place of that supposed river they came to seek, unto which they went and found it to open itself into two arms with a high cliff of sand in the entrance but more like to be creeks of salt water than any fresh, for aught they saw; and that there was good harborage for their shallop, leaving it further to be discovered by their shallop, when she was ready. So, their time limited them being expired, they returned to the ship lest they should be in fear of their safety; and took with them part of the corn and buried up the rest. And so, like the men from Eshcol, carried with them of the fruits of the land and showed their brethren;[2] of which, and their return, they were marvelously glad and their hearts encouraged.

After this, the shallop being got ready, they set out again for the better discovery of this place,[3] and the master of the ship desired to go himself. So there went some thirty men but found it to be no harbor for ships but only for boats. There was also found two of their houses covered with mats, and sundry of their implements in them, but the people were run away and could not be seen.[4] Also there was found more of their corn and of their beans of various colors; the corn and beans they brought away, purposing to give them full satisfaction[5] when they should meet with any of them as, about some six months afterward they did, to their good content.

And here is to be noted a special providence of God, and a great mercy to this poor people, that here they got seed to plant them corn the next year, or else they might have starved, for they had none nor any likelihood to get any till the season had been past, as the sequel did manifest. Neither is it likely they had had this, if the first voyage had not been made, for the ground was now all covered with snow and hard frozen; but the Lord is never wanting unto His in their greatest needs; let His holy name have all the praise.

The month of November being spent in these affairs, and much foul weather falling in, the 6th of December they sent out their shallop again with ten of their principal men[6] and some seamen, upon further discovery, intending to circulate that deep bay of Cape Cod. The weather was very cold and it froze so hard as the spray of the sea lighting on their coats, they were as if they had been glazed. Yet that night betimes they got down into the bottom of the bay, and as they drew near the shore they saw some ten or twelve Indians very busy about something. They landed about a league or two from them, and had much ado to put ashore anywhere—it lay so full of flats. Being landed, it grew late and they

1 *paddled* Flattened down. In Champlain's *Voyages* (1632), the author notes that Indigenous peoples of this area would dig large sand trenches, put their corn in grass sacks, and cover it with several feet of sand, thereby preserving it very effectively.

2 *Eshcol … brethren* In Numbers 13, God tells Moses to send men to explore the land of Canaan, which God gives to the Israelites. The leaders of the various tribes set out and explore the wilderness, bringing back grapes, pomegranates, and figs to prove to their people the fertility of the land they found. See Numbers 13.23–26.

3 *this place* This second expedition explored the areas around the Pamet and Little Pamet Rivers, returning to Cape Cod Harbor on 30 November.

4 *their houses … could not be seen* This area was inhabited by Nauset people, who spoke the Massachusett language; their round wigwams were constructed with bent boughs stuck into the ground on each side, interwoven with smaller boughs and covered with mats of woven bark. The implements mentioned were likely for farming and fishing.

5 *satisfaction* Payment.

6 *ten of their principal men* According to *Mourt's Relation* (1622), a first-hand account of the colony's beginnings, these were Standish, Carver, Bradford, Edward Winslow, John Tilley, Edward Tilley, John Howland, Richard Warren, Steven Hopkins, Edward Doten, John Alderton, Thomas English, Clarke, Copin, and four more unnamed sailors.

made themselves a barricado with logs and boughs as well as they could in the time, and set out their sentinel and betook them to rest, and saw the smoke of the fire the savages made that night. When morning was come they divided their company, some to coast along the shore in the boat, and the rest marched through the woods to see the land, if any fit place might be for their dwelling. They came also to the place where they saw the Indians the night before, and found they had been cutting up a great fish like a grampus,[1] being some two inches thick of fat like a hog, some pieces where of they had left by the way. And the shallop found two more of these fishes dead on the sands, a thing usual after storms in that place, by reason of the great flats of sand that lie off.

So they ranged up and down all that day, but found no people, nor any place they liked. When the sun grew low, they hasted out of the woods to meet with their shallop, to whom they made signs to come to them into a creek hard by,[2] the which they did at high water; of which they were very glad, for they had not seen each other all that day since the morning. So they made them a barricado as usually they did every night, with logs, stakes and thick pine boughs, the height of a man, leaving it open to leeward, partly to shelter them from the cold and wind (making their fire in the middle and lying round about it) and partly to defend them from any sudden assaults of the savages, if they should surround them; so being very weary, they betook them to rest. But about midnight, they heard a hideous and great cry, and their sentinel called "Arm! arm!" So they bestirred them and stood to their arms and shot off a couple of muskets, and then the noise ceased. They concluded it was a company of wolves or such like wild beasts, for one of the seamen told them he had often heard such a noise in Newfoundland.

So they rested till about five of the clock in the morning; for the tide, and their purpose to go from thence, made them be stirring betimes. So after prayer they prepared for breakfast, and it being day dawning it was thought best to be carrying things down to the boat. But some said it was not best to carry the arms down, others said they would be the readier, for they

had lapped them up in their coats from the dew; but some three or four would not carry theirs till they went themselves. Yet as it fell out, the water being not high enough, they laid them down on the bank side and came up to breakfast.

But presently, all on the sudden, they heard a great and strange cry, which they knew to be the same voices they heard in the night, though they varied their notes; and one of their company being abroad came running in and cried, "Men, Indians! Indians!" And withal, their arrows came flying amongst them. Their men ran with all speed to recover their arms, as by the good providence of God they did. In the meantime, of those that were there ready, two muskets were discharged at them, and two more stood ready in the entrance of their rendezvous but were commanded not to shoot till they could take full aim at them. And the other two charged again with all speed, for there were only four had arms there, and defended the barricado, which was first assaulted. The cry of the Indians was dreadful, especially when they saw their men run out of the rendezvous towards the shallop to recover their arms, the Indians wheeling about upon them. But some running out with coats of mail on, and cutlasses in their hands, they soon got their arms and let fly amongst them and quickly stopped their violence. Yet there was a lusty man, and no less valiant, stood behind a tree within half a musket shot, and let his arrows fly at them; he was seen [to] shoot three arrows, which were all avoided. He stood three shots of a musket, till one taking full aim at him and made the bark or splinters of the tree fly about his ears, after which he gave an extraordinary shriek and away they went, all of them. They[3] left some to keep the shallop and followed them about a quarter of a mile and shouted once or twice, and shot of two or three pieces, and so returned. This they did that they might conceive that they were not afraid of them or any way discouraged.

Thus it pleased God to vanquish their enemies and give them deliverance; and by His special providence so to dispose that not any one of them were either hurt or hit, though their arrows came close by them and on every side [of] them; and sundry of their coats, which hung up in the barricado, were shot through and through. Afterwards they gave God solemn thanks and

[1] *grampus* Name applied to several species of whale and dolphin.

[2] *creek* Herring River, also called Great Meadow Creek; *hard by* Nearby.

[3] *They* The English.

praise for their deliverance, and gathered up a bundle of their arrows and sent them into England afterward by the master of the ship, and called that place the First Encounter. …

from THE SECOND BOOK

The rest of this History (if God give me life and opportunity) I shall, for brevity's sake, handle by way of annals,[1] noting only the heads of principal things, and passages as they fell in order of time, and may seem to be profitable to know or to make use of. And this may be as the Second Book.

from CHAPTER 11
THE REMAINDER OF ANNO 1620
[THE MAYFLOWER COMPACT][2]

I shall a little return back, and begin with a combination made by them before they came ashore; being the first foundation of their government in this place. Occasioned partly by the discontented and mutinous speeches that some of the strangers[3] amongst them had let fall from them in the ship: That when they came ashore they would use their own liberty, for none had power to command them, the patent they had being for Virginia and not for New England, which belonged to another Government, with which the Virginia Company had nothing to do.[4] And partly that such an act by them done, this their condition considered,[5] might be as firm as any patent, and in some respects more sure.

[1] *annals* A narrative of events organized according to year.

[2] *MAYFLOWER COMPACT* Written agreement created by the male passengers of *The Mayflower*, declaring that, once disembarked, they intended to live together within a common political body governed by laws and a constitution.

[3] *strangers* Those who traveled on *The Mayflower* but were not members of the Separatist congregation.

[4] *patent … nothing to do* The Pilgrims had brought a patent—a land grant from the King—for "the Northern parts of Virginia," but weather forced a landing further north, outside the jurisdiction specified in the patent. In this state of legal uncertainty, some of the ship's passengers threatened to abandon the group once they reached land. The Mayflower Compact averted this threat of mutiny.

[5] *this … considered* Considering their circumstances.

The form was as followeth:

IN THE NAME OF GOD, AMEN.

We whose names are underwritten, the loyall subjects of our dread[6] soveraigne Lord, King James, by the grace of God of Great Britain, France and Ireland king, defender of the faith, etc.

Haveing undertaken, for the glorie of God and advancement of the Christian faith and honour of our king and countrie, a voyage to plant the first colonie in the Northerne parts of Virginia, doe by these presents[7] solemnly and mutualy in the presence of God, and one of another, covenant and combine our selves together into a civill body politick, for our better ordering and preservation and furtherance of the ends aforesaid; and by vertue hereof to enacte, constitute, and frame such just and equall lawes, ordinances, acts, constitutions and offices, from time to time, as shall be thought most meete and convenient for the generall good of the Colonie, unto which we promise all due submission and obedience. In witness whereof we have hereunder subscribed our names at Cape-Codd, the 11 of November, in the year of the raigne of our soveraigne lord, King James, of England, France and Ireland, the eighteenth, and of Scotland the fifty-fourth. Anno Dom. 1620.

After this they chose, or rather confirmed, Mr. John Carver (a man godly and well approved amongst them) their Governor for that year. And after they had provided a place for their goods, or common store (which were long in unlading for want of boats, foulness of winter weather and sickness of diverse) and begun some small cottages for their habitation; as time would admit, they met and consulted of laws and orders, both for their civil and military government as the necessity of their condition did require, still adding thereunto as urgent occasion in several times, and as cases did require.

In these hard and difficult beginnings they found some discontents and murmurings arise amongst some, and mutinous speeches and carriages[8] in other; but they were soon quelled and overcome by the

[6] *dread* Revered.

[7] *by these presents* In these statements.

[8] *carriages* Ways of behaving.

original spelling

wisdom, patience and just and equal[1] carriage of things by the Governor and better part, which clave[2] faithfully together in the main.

[THE STARVING TIME]

But that which was most sad and lamentable was, that in two or three months' time half of their company died, especially in January and February, being the depth of winter, and wanting houses and other comforts; being infected with the scurvy and other diseases which this long voyage and their inaccomodate condition had brought upon them. So as there died sometimes two or three of a day in the foresaid time, that of 100 and odd persons, scarce fifty remained. And of these, in the time of most distress, there was but six or seven sound persons who to their great commendations be it spoken, spared no pains night nor day, but with abundance of toil and hazard of their own health, fetched them wood, made them fires, dressed them meat, made their beds, washed their loathsome clothes, clothed and unclothed them. In a word, did all the homely and necessary offices for them which dainty and queasy stomachs cannot endure to hear named; and all this willingly and cheerfully, without any grudging in the least, showing herein their true love unto their friends and brethren; a rare example and worthy to be remembered. Two of these seven were Mr. William Brewster, their reverend Elder, and Myles Standish, their Captain and military commander, unto whom myself and many others were much beholden in our low and sick condition. And yet the Lord so upheld these persons as in this general calamity they were not at all infected either with sickness or lameness. And what I have said of these I may say of many others who died in this general visitation, and others yet living; that whilst they had health, yea, or any strength continuing, they were not wanting to any that had need of them. And I doubt not but their recompense is with the Lord. ...

[INDIAN RELATIONS]

All this while the Indians came skulking about them, and would sometimes show themselves aloof off, but when any approached near them, they would run away; and once they stole away their tools where they had been at work and were gone to dinner. But about the 16th of March, a certain Indian came boldly amongst them and spoke to them in broken English, which they could well understand but marveled at it. At length they understood by discourse with him, that he was not of these parts, but belonged to the eastern parts where some English ships came to fish, with whom he was acquainted and could name sundry of them by their names, amongst whom he had got his language. He became profitable to them in acquainting them with many things concerning the state of the country in the east parts where he lived, which was afterwards profitable unto them; as also of the people here, of their names, number and strength, of their situation and distance from this place, and who was chief amongst them. His name was Samoset.[3] He told them also of another Indian whose name was Squanto,[4] a native of this place, who had been in England and could speak better English than himself.

Being, after some time of entertainment and gifts dismissed, a while after he came again, and five more with him, and they brought again all the tools that were stolen away before, and made way for the coming of their great Sachem, called Massasoit.[5] Who, about four or five days after, came with the chief of his friends and other attendance, with the aforesaid Squanto. With whom, after friendly entertainment and some gifts given him, they made a peace with him (which hath now continued this 24 years) in these terms:

3 *Samoset* Sagamore—a type of chief—of the Pemaquid Abenaki people (c. 1590–1653). Samoset's people lived in what is now Maine.

4 *Squanto* Tisquantum (1585–1622), a member of the Patuxet tribe that lived in the area around Plymouth. Squanto was kidnapped by English sailors in 1617 and returned to New England in 1619 to find his village empty as the result of an epidemic.

5 *Sachem* High chief; *Massasoit* Sachem of the Wampanoag (c. 1581–1661).

1 *equal* Impartial.

2 *clave* Cleaved, stuck.

1. That neither he nor any of his should injure or do hurt to any of their people.

2. That if any of his did any hurt to any of theirs, he should send the offender, that they might punish him.

3. That if anything were taken away from any of theirs, he should cause it to be restored; and they should do the like to his.

4. If any did unjustly war against him, they would aid him; if any did war against them, he should aid them.

5. He should send to his neighbors confederates to certify them of this, that they might not wrong them, but might be likewise comprised in the conditions of peace.

6. That when their men came to them, they should leave their bows and arrows behind them.

After these things he returned to his place called Sowams,[1] some 40 miles from this place, but Squanto continued with them and was their interpreter and was a special instrument sent of God for their good beyond their expectation. He directed them how to set their corn, where to take fish, and to procure other commodities, and was also their pilot to bring them to unknown places for their profit, and never left them till he died. …

from CHAPTER 12
ANNO DOMINI 1621
[*MAYFLOWER* DEPARTS AND CORN PLANTED]

They now began to dispatch the ship away which brought them over, which lay till about this time, or the beginning of April.[2] The reason on their parts why she stayed so long, was the necessity and danger that lay upon them; for it was well towards the end of December before she could land anything here, or they able to receive anything ashore. Afterwards, the 14th of January, the house which they had made for a general rendezvous by casualty fell afire, and some were fain to retire aboard for shelter; then the sickness began to fall sore amongst them, and the weather so bad as they could not make much sooner any dispatch. Again, the Governor and chief of them, seeing so many die and fall down sick daily, thought it no wisdom to send away the ship, their condition considered and the danger they stood in from the Indians, till they could procure some shelter; and therefore thought it better to draw some more charge[3] upon themselves and friends than hazard all. The master and seamen likewise, though before they hasted[4] the passengers ashore to be gone, now many of their men being dead, and of the ablest of them (as is before noted), and of the rest many lay sick and weak; the master durst not put to sea till he saw his men begin to recover, and the heart of winter over.

Afterwards they (as many as were able) began to plant their corn, in which service Squanto stood them in great stead, showing them both the manner how to set it, and after how to dress and tend it. Also he told them, except they got fish and set with it in these old grounds it would come to nothing.[5] And he showed them that in the middle of April they should have store enough come up the brook by which they began to build, and taught them how to take it,[6] and where to get other provisions necessary for them. All which they found true by trial and experience. Some English seed they sowed, as wheat and peas, but it came not to good, either by the badness of the seed or lateness of the season or both, or some other defect. …

[INDIAN DIPLOMACY]

Having in some sort ordered their business at home, it was thought meet to send some abroad to see their new friend Massasoit, and to bestow upon him some gratuity[7] to bind him the faster unto them; as also that hereby they might view the country and see in what

[1] *Sowams* This village is now named Warren, Rhode Island.

[2] *the ship … April* The *Mayflower* sailed from New Plymouth on 5 April and reached England on 6 May.

[3] *charge* Expense.

[4] *hasted* Hurried.

[5] *fish … come to nothing* Squanto taught them to use fish as fertilizer for the crops. In Captain John Smith's *Advertisements for the Unexperienced*, he wrote that in New England they "stick at every plant of corn, a herring or two; which cometh in that season in such abundance, they may take more than they know what to do with." It was a very effective method to gain high yields of corn.

[6] *he showed them … how to take it* Squanto taught the settlers how to set up a fishing weir across the brook to catch large quantities of migrating herring in the spring.

[7] *gratuity* Gift.

manner he lived, what strength he had about him, and how the ways were to his place, if at any time they should have occasion. So the second of July they sent Mr. Edward Winslow and Mr. Hopkins,[1] with the foresaid Squanto for their guide; who gave him a suit of clothes and a horseman's coat, with some other small things, which were kindly accepted; but they found but short commons[2] and came both weary and hungry home. For the Indians used then to have nothing so much corn as they have since the English have stored[3] them with their hoes, and seen their industry in breaking up new grounds therewith.[4]

They found his place to be forty miles from hence, the soil good and the people not many, being dead and abundantly wasted in the late great mortality, which fell in all these parts about three years before the coming of the English, wherein thousands of them died. They not being able to bury one another, their skulls and bones were found in many places lying still above ground where their houses and dwellings had been, a very sad spectacle to behold. But they brought word that the Narragansetts[5] lived but on the other side of that great bay, and were a strong people, and many in number, living compact together, and had not been at all touched with this wasting plague.

About the later end of this month, one John Billington lost himself in the woods, and wandered up and down some five days, living on berries and what he could find. At length he light on an Indian plantation twenty miles south of this place, called Manomet; they conveyed him further off, to Nauset among those people that had before set upon the English when they were coasting whilst the ship lay at the Cape, as is before noted. But the Governor caused him to be inquired for among the Indians, and at length Massasoit sent word

where he was, and the Governor sent a shallop for him and had him delivered. Those people[6] also came and made their peace; and they gave full satisfaction to those whose corn they had found and taken when they were at Cape Cod.

Thus their peace and acquaintance was pretty well established with the natives about them. …

[First Thanksgiving[7]]

They began now to gather in the small harvest they had, and to fit up their houses and dwellings against winter, being all well recovered in health and strength and had all things in good plenty. For as some were thus employed in affairs abroad, others were exercised in fishing, about cod and bass and other fish, of which they took good store, of which every family had their portion. All the summer there was no want; and now began to come in store of fowl, as winter approached, of which this place did abound when they came first (but afterward decreased by degrees). And besides waterfowl there was great store of wild turkeys, of which they took many, besides venison, etc. Besides they had about a peck[8] a meal a week to a person, or now since harvest, Indian corn to that proportion. Which made many afterwards write so largely of their plenty here to their friends in England, which were not feigned but true reports.

1 *Mr. Hopkins* Stephen Hopkins (1581–1644), an English tanner and merchant recruited to join the Pilgrims by the Company of Merchant Adventurers.

2 *short commons* Scarce rations, little food.

3 *stored* Supplied.

4 *industry … therewith* The Indigenous peoples in this area used clamshells to till the earth for their corn; the English supplied them with hoes, which dig up more earth more quickly. There are records, however, suggesting that cultivation by clamshell was superior than that which resulted from European tools.

5 *Narragansetts* Algonquian tribe living in what is now Rhode Island.

6 *Those people* I.e., the Nauset.

7 *First Thanksgiving* The feast described here is not explicitly identified as a "thanksgiving" in Bradford's account, but it was a practice of Puritan congregations to declare days of thanksgiving—special days set aside for prayer, to thank God for favorable events such as a good harvest. The modern holiday is based on this tradition. See also "The Myth of Thanksgiving," included in the "Civilizations in Contact" section of this volume.

8 *peck* Unit of measurement for dry goods, equivalent to about eight dry quarts.

from CHAPTER 14
ANNO DOMINI 1623
[END OF THE "COMMON COURSE AND CONDITION"[1]]

All this while no supply was heard of, neither knew they when they might expect any. So they began to think how they might raise as much corn as they could, and obtain a better crop than they had done, that they might not still thus languish in misery. At length, after much debate of things, the Governor (with the advice of the chiefest amongst them) gave way that they should set corn every man for his own particular,[2] and in that regard trust to themselves; in all other things to go on in the general way as before. And so assigned to every family a parcel of land, according to the proportion of their number, for that end, only for present use (but made no division for inheritance) and ranged all boys and youth under some family. This had very good success, for it made all hands very industrious, so as much more corn was planted than otherwise would have been by any means the Governor or any other could use, and saved him a great deal of trouble, and gave far better content. The women now went willingly into the field, and took their little ones with them to set corn; which before would allege weakness and inability; whom to have compelled would have been thought great tyranny and oppression.

The experience that was had in this common course and condition, tried sundry years and that amongst godly and sober men, may well evince the vanity of that conceit of Plato's and other ancients, applauded by some of later times; that the taking away of property and bringing in community into a commonwealth would make them happy and flourishing; as if they were wiser than God.[3] For this community (so far as it was) was found to breed much confusion and discontent and retard much employment that would have been to their benefit and comfort. For the young men, that were most able and fit for labor and service, did repine that they should spend their time and strength to work for other men's wives and children without any recompense. The strong, or man of parts, had no more in division of victuals and clothes than he that was weak and not able to do a quarter the other could; this was thought injustice. The aged and graver men to be ranked and equalized in labors and victuals, clothes, etc., with the meaner and younger sort, thought it some indignity and disrespect unto them. And for men's wives to be commanded to do service for other men, as dressing their meat, washing their clothes, etc., they deemed it a kind of slavery, neither could many husbands well brook[4] it. Upon the point all being to have alike, and all to do alike, they thought themselves in the like condition, and one as good as another; and so, if it did not cut off those relations that God hath set amongst men, yet it did at least much diminish and take of the mutual respects that should be preserved amongst them. And would have been worse if they had been men of another condition. Let none object this is men's corruption, and nothing to the course itself. I answer, seeing all men have this corruption in them, God in His wisdom saw another course fitter for them. ...

[1] *COMMON COURSE AND CONDITION* The economic system at Plymouth was from the beginning one in which all members labored for the common stock—each person worked and contributed, and everyone was fed and clothed and housed. This began to cause some tension in the colony among those who felt that not all members were contributing equally (and that harder work was not rewarded with more gain).

[2] *every man for his own particular* Each man for himself, i.e., all members would harvest—and keep—their own crops.

[3] *conceit of Plato's ... wiser than God* In Jean Bodin's *Les Six livres de la République* (1576), a translated copy of which Bradford owned, Bodin writes: "But he [Plato] understood not that by making all

things thus common, a Commonweal must needs perish: for nothing can be public, where nothing is private." In *Republic*, Plato argues that the ruling classes should give up private property to ensure their transcendence of personal interest, and that their needs would be taken care of by the state.

[4] *brook* Tolerate.

from CHAPTER 19
ANNO DOMINI 1628
[A VISIT FROM THE DUTCH[1]]

This year the Dutch sent again unto them from their Plantation both kind letters, and also diverse commodities, as sugar, linen cloth, holland, finer and coarser stuffs,[2] etc. They came up with their bark to Manomet, to their house there,[3] in which came their Secretary, Rasier, who was accompanied with a noise of trumpeters and some other attendants, and desired that they would send a boat for him, for he could not travel so far overland. So they sent a boat to Scusset[4] and brought him to the Plantation with the chief of his company. And after some few days' entertainment he returned to his bark, and some of them went with him and bought sundry of his goods. After which beginning thus made, they sent oftentimes to the same place and had intercourse together for diverse years. And amongst other commodities they vended much tobacco for linen cloth, stuffs, etc., which was a good benefit to the people, till the Virginians found out their Plantation.[5]

But that which turned most to their profit, in time, was an entrance into the trade of wampumpeag.[6]

For they now bought about £50 worth of it of them, and they told them how vendible it was at their fort Orania, and did persuade them they would find it so at Kennebec.[7] And so it came to pass in time, though at first it stuck,[8] and it was two years before they could put off this small quantity, till the inland people[9] knew of it; and afterwards they could scarce ever get enough for them, for many years together. And so this with their other provisions cut off their trade quite from the fishermen, and in great part from other of the straggling planters. And strange it was to see the great alteration it made in a few years among the Indians themselves; for all the Indians of these parts and the Massachusetts had none or very little of it, but the sachems and some special persons that wore a little of it for ornament. Only it was made and kept among the Narragansetts and Pequots, which grew rich and potent by it, and these people were poor and beggarly and had no use of it. Neither did the English of this Plantation or any other in the land, till now that they had knowledge of it from the Dutch, so much as know what it was, much less that it was a commodity of that worth and value. But after it grew thus to be a commodity in these parts, these Indians fell into it also, and to learn how to make it; for the Narragansetts do gather the shells of which they make it from their shores. And it hath now continued a current commodity about this 20 years, and it may prove a drug[10] in time.

In the meantime, it makes the Indians of these parts rich and powerful and also proud thereby, and fills them with pieces,[11] powder and shot, which no laws can restrain, by reason of the baseness of sundry unworthy persons, both English, Dutch and French, which may turn to the ruin of many. Hitherto the Indians of these parts had no pieces nor other arms but their bows

[1] THE DUTCH The Netherlands had begun explorations in North America around the same time as the English, in the early years of the seventeenth century. The Dutch established their first settlement in 1615 on Castle Island, near what is now Albany, New York. By 1623 they had claimed a province, New Netherland, which spanned the East Coast from eastern Virginia to southwest Cape Cod. In 1626, the Dutch bought Manhattan from the Lenape people and created a new port that they named New Amsterdam, expanding to the Bronx, Brooklyn, and Long Island.

[2] holland Type of linen manufactured in the Netherlands; stuffs Fabrics.

[3] their house there Dutch trading post at Cushenoc, now called Augusta, Maine.

[4] Scusset Creek that ends in Cape Cod Bay, and that was used by canoes to move between Cape Cod Bay and Buzzards Bay.

[5] Virginians ... Plantation I.e., until the Virginians—who supplied Plymouth with tobacco—began to trade directly with the Dutch at their Plantation in Manhattan.

[6] [Bradford's note] Peag. [Wampumpeag, now commonly called wampum, are shell-beads strung together, used in seventeenth-century America by Indigenous peoples and settlers as currency. Wampum also has a long history among many Indigenous peoples as a means of record-keeping, story-telling, naming, and other decorative and ceremonial purposes.]

[7] Orania Dutch Fort Orange, present day Albany; Kennebec The Plymouth Plantation had just secured a patent to set up a trading post on the Kennebec River, near Augusta, Maine.

[8] it stuck I.e., the wampum did not "move," was not used in trade.

[9] inland people Wampum was made primarily by the coastal peoples, particularly the Narragansett, Pequot, Montaukett, and Shinnecock. At the time of Bradford's writing, it had only recently been introduced to the inland tribes.

[10] drug Product that has lost its trade value.

[11] pieces Guns.

and arrows, nor of many years after; neither durst they scarce handle a gun, so much were they afraid of them. And the very sight of one (though out of kilter[1]) was a terror unto them. But those Indians to the east parts, which had commerce with the French, got pieces of them, and they in the end made a common trade of it. And in time our English fishermen, led with the like covetousness, followed their example for their own gain. But upon complaint against them, it pleased the King's Majesty to prohibit the same by a strict proclamation, commanding that no sort of arms or munition should by any of his subjects be traded with them.

[Thomas Morton of Merrymount]

About some three or four years before this time, there came over one Captain Wollaston (a man of pretty parts[2]) and with him three or four more of some eminency, who brought with them a great many servants, with provisions and other implements for to begin a plantation. And pitched themselves in a place within the Massachusetts which they called after their Captain's name, Mount Wollaston. Amongst whom was one Mr. Morton,[3] who it should seem had some small adventure of his own or other men's amongst them, but had little respect amongst them, and was slighted by the meanest servants. Having continued there some time, and not finding things to answer their expectations nor profit to arise as they looked for, Captain Wollaston takes a great part of the servants and transports them to Virginia, where he puts them off at good rates, selling their time to other men; and writes back to one Mr. Rasdall (one of his chief partners and accounted their merchant) to bring another part of them to Virginia likewise, intending to put them off there as he had done the rest. And he, with the consent of the said Rasdall, appointed one Fitcher to be his Lieutenant and govern the remains

of the Plantation till he or Rasdall returned to take further order thereabout. But this Morton abovesaid, having more craft than honesty (who had been a kind of pettifogger of Furnival's Inn[4]) in the others' absence watches an opportunity (commons being but hard[5] amongst them) and got some strong drink and other junkets[6] and made them a feast; and after they were merry, he began to tell them he would give them good counsel. "You see," saith he, "that many of your fellows are carried to Virginia, and if you stay till this Rasdall return, you will also be carried away and sold for slaves[7] with the rest. Therefore I would advise you to thrust out this Lieutenant Fitcher, and I, having a part in the Plantation, will receive you as my partners and consociates; so may you be free from service, and we will converse, plant, trade, and live together as equals and support and protect one another," or to like effect. This counsel was easily received, so they took opportunity and thrust Lieutenant Fitcher out o'doors, and would suffer him to come no more amongst them, but forced him to seek bread to eat and other relief from his neighbours till he could get passage for England.

After this they fell to great licentiousness and led a dissolute life, pouring out themselves into all profaneness. And Morton became Lord of Misrule,[8] and maintained (as it were) a School of Atheism. And after they had got some goods into their hands, and got much by trading with the Indians, they spent it as vainly in quaffing and drinking, both wine and strong waters[9]

[1] *out of kilter* Not in working order.

[2] *pretty parts* Many talents.

[3] *Mr. Morton* Thomas Morton (1579–1647) was a lawyer and author of *The New English Canaan* (1637). His religion—traditional Anglican—his libertinism, and his interest in integrating his community with the Indigenous population, placed him at odds with the Puritans from Plymouth. For Morton's account of these events, see the excerpts from *The New English Canaan* included in this anthology.

[4] *pettifogger of Furnival's Inn* A "pettifogger" is a derogatory name for a lawyer, suggesting one that deals in trivial cases using dubious practices; Furnival's Inn was a place where lawyers studied and boarded in London. Morton actually studied at Clifford's Inn, where he befriended the playwright Ben Jonson (1572–1637) and became part of the hedonistic culture that surrounded the Inns of Court at that time.

[5] *commons … hard* Provisions being meager.

[6] *junkets* Sweet dishes.

[7] *slaves* I.e., indentured servants. The tobacco crop in Jamestown, Virginia, required a substantial labor force to plant and harvest, and in Bradford's era that labor was provided by indentured servants from Britain as well as by enslaved Africans and Native Americans.

[8] *Lord of Misrule* Person appointed to rule over the Feast of Fools, a feast day widely celebrated across Europe, which involved feasting, partying, and a great deal of drinking. The festival was banned by Henry VIII, restored by Mary I, and banned again by Queen Elizabeth I.

[9] *strong waters* Hard liquors.

in great excess (and, as some reported) £10 worth in a morning. They also set up a maypole,[1] drinking and dancing about it many days together, inviting the Indian women for their consorts, dancing and frisking together like so many fairies, or furies, rather; and worse practices. As if they had anew revived and celebrated the feasts of the Roman goddess Flora, or the beastly practices of the mad Bacchanalians.[2] Morton likewise, to show his poetry composed sundry rhymes and verses, some tending to lasciviousness, and others to the detraction and scandal of some persons, which he affixed to this idle or idol maypole. They changed also the name of their place, and instead of calling it Mount Wollaston they call it Merry-mount, as if this jollity would have lasted ever. But this continued not long, for after Morton was sent for England (as follows to be declared) shortly after came over that worthy gentleman Mr. John Endecott, who brought over a patent under the broad seal for the government of the Massachusetts. Who, visiting those parts, caused that maypole to be cut down and rebuked them for their profaneness and admonished them to look there should be better walking. So they or others now changed the name of their place again and called it Mount Dagon.[3]

Now to maintain this riotous prodigality and profuse excess, Morton, thinking himself lawless, and hearing what gain the French and fishermen made by trading of pieces, powder and shot to the Indians, he as the head of this consortship began the practice of the same in these parts. And first he taught them how to use them, to charge and discharge, and what proportion of powder to give the piece, according to the size or bigness of the same; and what shot to use for fowl and what for deer. And having thus instructed them, he employed some of them to hunt and fowl for him, so as they became far more active in that employment than any of the English, by reason of their swiftness of foot and nimbleness of body, being also quick-sighted and by continual exercise well knowing the haunts of all sorts of game. So as when they saw the execution that a piece would do, and the benefit that might come by the same, they became mad (as it were) after them and would not stick to give any price they could attain to for them; accounting their bows and arrows but baubles in comparison of them.

And here I may take occasion to bewail the mischief that this wicked man began in these parts, and which since, base covetousness prevailing in men that should know better, has now at length got the upper hand and made this thing common, notwithstanding any laws to the contrary. So as the Indians are full of pieces all over, both fowling pieces, muskets, pistols, etc. They have also their moulds to make shot of all sorts, as musket bullets, pistol bullets, swan and goose shot, and of smaller sorts. Yea some have seen them have their screw-plates[4] to make screw-pins themselves when they want them, with sundry other implements, wherewith they are ordinarily better fitted and furnished than the English themselves. Yea, it is well known that they will have powder and shot when the English want it nor cannot get it; and that in a time of war or danger, as experience hath manifested, that when lead hath been scarce and men for their own defense would gladly have given a groat[5] a pound, which is dear enough, yet hath it been bought up and sent to other places and sold to such as trade it with the Indians at 12d[6] the pound. And it is like they give 3s or 4s[7] the pound, for they will have it at any rate. And these things have been done in the same times when some of their neighbours and friends are daily killed by the Indians, or are in danger thereof and live but at the Indians' mercy. ...

[1] *maypole* Wooden pole erected throughout Europe as a sign of spring renewal. The symbol derived from pagan traditions and was thus regarded as idolatrous by Puritans. In seventeenth-century England, the maypole was at the center of a dispute between royalist cultural conservatives, who viewed the maypole as an English tradition that reinforced the authority of the English crown, and religious cultural reformers, who believed that the maypole was a pagan practice in need of eradication.

[2] *Flora* Roman goddess of spring and fertility; *Bacchanalians* Revelers attending Bacchanalia, festivals of the Roman god Bacchus, who was associated with ecstasy and wine. These ancient initiatory rites involved ecstatic experiences, drunkenness, and sexual freedom.

[3] *Mount Dagon* Dagon is an ancient fertility god, described in the Bible as the god of the Philistines, antagonists of the biblical Israelites. See Judges 16.23.

[4] *screw-plates* Steel plates with differently sized threaded holes used to make screws (here, for fastening the parts of a gun together).

[5] *groat* Equal to four pence; in a London pub at the time, this could buy you a meal and a pint of beer.

[6] *12d* Twelve pence.

[7] *3s or 4s* Three or four shillings (each shilling contains twelve pence).

So sundry of the chief of the straggling plantations, meeting together, agreed by mutual consent to solicit those of Plymouth (who were then of more strength than them all) to join with them to prevent the further growth of this mischief, and suppress Morton and his consorts before they grew to further head and strength. Those that joined in this action, and after contributed to the charge of sending him for England, were from Piscataqua, Naumkeag, Winnisimmet, Wessagusset, Nantasket[1] and other places where any English were seated. Those of Plymouth being thus sought to by their messengers and letters, and weighing both their reasons and the common danger, were willing to afford them their help though themselves had least cause of fear or hurt. So, to be short, they first resolved jointly to write to him, and in a friendly and neighbourly way to admonish him to forbear those courses, and sent a messenger with their letters to bring his answer.

But he was so high as he scorned all advice, and asked who had to do with him, he had and would trade pieces with the Indians, in despite of all, with many other scurrilous terms full of disdain. They sent to him a second time and bade him be better advised and more temperate in his terms, for the country could not bear the injury he did. It was against their common safety and against the King's proclamation. He answered in high terms as before; and that the King's proclamation was no law, demanding what penalty was upon it. It was answered, more than he could bear—His Majesty's displeasure. But insolently he persisted and said the King was dead[2] and his displeasure with him, and many the like things. And threatened withal that if any came to molest him, let them look to themselves for he would prepare for them.

Upon which they saw there was no way but to take him by force; and having so far proceeded, now to give over would make him far more haughty and insolent. So they mutually resolved to proceed, and obtained of the Governor of Plymouth to send Captain Standish and some other aid with him, to take Morton by force. The which accordingly was done. But they found him to stand stiffly in his defense, having made fast his doors, armed his consorts, set diverse dishes of powder and bullets ready on the table; and if they had not been over-armed with drink, more hurt might have been done. They summoned him to yield, but he kept his house and they could get nothing but scoffs and scorns from him. But at length, fearing they would do some violence to the house, he and some of his crew came out, but not to yield but to shoot; but they were so steeled with drink as their pieces were too heavy for them. Himself with a carbine,[3] overcharged and almost half filled with powder and shot, as was after found, had thought to have shot Captain Standish; but he stepped to him and put by his piece and took him. Neither was there any hurt done to any of either side, save that one was so drunk that he ran his own nose upon the point of a sword that one held before him, as he entered the house; but he lost but a little of his hot blood.

Morton they brought away to Plymouth, where he was kept till a ship went from the Isle of Shoals for England, with which he was sent to the Council of New England, and letters written to give them information of his course and carriage. And also one was sent at their common charge to inform their Honours more particularly and to prosecute against him. But he fooled of the messenger, after he was gone from hence, and though he went for England yet nothing was done to him, not so much as rebuked, for aught was heard, but returned the next year. Some of the worst of the company were dispersed and some of the more modest kept the house till he should be heard from. But I have been too long about so unworthy a person, and bad a cause.

from CHAPTER 25
ANNO DOMINI 1634
[CAPTAIN STONE, THE DUTCH, AND THE CONNECTICUT INDIANS]

… I am now to relate some strange and remarkable passages. There was a company of people lived in the country up above in the River of Connecticut a great way from their trading house there, and were enemies to those Indians which lived about them, and of whom they stood in some fear, being a stout people. About a thousand of them had enclosed themselves in a fort

[1] *Piscataqua … Nantasket* Places on the coast of New England.

[2] *King was dead* James I had died in 1625.

[3] *carbine* Medium-sized gun (mid-way between a pistol and a larger musket).

which they had strongly palisadooed[1] about. Three or four Dutchmen went up in the beginning of winter to live with them, to get their trade and prevent them for bringing it to the English or to fall into amity with them; but at spring to bring all down to their place. But their enterprise failed. For it pleased God to visit these Indians with a great sickness and such a mortality that of a thousand, above nine and a half hundred of them died, and many of them did rot above ground for want of burial. And the Dutchmen almost starved before they could get away, for ice and snow; but about February they got with much difficulty to their trading house; whom they kindly relieved, being almost spent with hunger and cold. Being thus refreshed by them diverse days, they got to their own place and the Dutch were very thankful for this kindness.

This spring also, those Indians that lived about their trading house there,[2] fell sick of the small pox and died most miserably; for a sorer disease cannot befall them, they fear it more than the plague. For usually they that have this disease have them in abundance, and for want of bedding and linen and other helps they fall into a lamentable condition as they lie on their hard mats, the pox breaking and mattering[3] and running one into another, their skin cleaving by reason thereof to the mats they lie on. When they turn them, a whole side will flay off at once as it were, and they will be all of a gore blood, most fearful to behold. And then being very sore, what with cold and other distempers, they die like rotten sheep. The condition of this people was so lamentable and they fell down so generally of this disease as they were in the end not able to help one another, no not to make a fire nor to fetch a little water to drink, nor any to bury the dead. But would strive as long as they could, and when they could procure no other means to make fire, they would burn the wooden trays and dishes they ate their meat in, and their very bows and arrows. And some would crawl out on all fours to get a little water, and sometimes die by the way and not be able to get in again. But of those of the English house, though at first they were afraid of the infection, yet seeing their woeful and sad condition and hearing their pitiful cries and lamentations, they

had compassion of them, and daily fetched them wood and water and made them fires, got them victuals whilst they lived; and buried them when they died. For very few of them escaped, notwithstanding they did what they could for them to the hazard of themselves. The chief sachem himself now died and almost all his friends and kindred. But by the marvelous goodness and providence of God, not one of the English was so much as sick or in the least measure tainted with this disease, though they daily did these offices for them for many weeks together. And this mercy which they showed them was kindly taken and thankfully acknowledged of all the Indians that knew or heard of the same. And their masters here did much commend and reward them for the same.

<div style="text-align:center">

from CHAPTER 28
ANNO DOMINI 1637
[THE PEQUOT WAR]

</div>

In the fore part of this year, the Pequots[4] fell openly upon the English at Connecticut, in the lower parts of the river, and slew sundry of them as they were at work in the fields, both men and women, to the great terror of the rest; and went away in great pride and triumph, with many high threats. They also assaulted a fort at the river's mouth, though strong and well defended; and though they did not there prevail, yet it struck them with much fear and astonishment to see their bold attempts in the face of danger. Which made them in all places to stand upon their guard and to prepare for resistance, and earnestly to solicit their friends and confederates in the Bay of Massachusetts to send them speedy aid, for they looked for more forcible assaults. Mr. Vane, being then Governor, writ from their General Court to them here to join with them in this war. To which they were cordially willing, but took opportunity to write to them about some former things, as well as present, considerable hereabout. …

In the meantime, the Pequots, especially in the winter before, sought to make peace with the Narragansetts, and used very pernicious arguments to move them thereunto: as that the English were strangers and began to overspeed their country, and would

[1] palisadooed Fortified.

[2] their trading house there Plymouth trading house, at Windsor.

[3] mattering Oozing pus.

[4] Pequots Indigenous people living in what is now southeastern Connecticut.

deprive them thereof in time, if they were suffered to grow and increase. And if the Narragansetts did assist the English to subdue them, they did but make way for their own overthrow, for if they were rooted out, the English would soon take occasion to subjugate them. And if they would hearken to them they should not need to fear the strength of the English, for they would not come to open battle with them but fire their houses, kill their cattle and lie in ambush for them as they went abroad upon their occasions; and all this they might easily do without any or little danger to themselves. The which course being held, they well saw the English could not long subsist but they would either be starved with hunger or be forced to forsake the country. With many the like things; insomuch that the Narragansetts were once wavering and were half minded to have made peace with them, and joined against the English. But again, when they considered how much wrong they had received from the Pequots, and what an opportunity they now had by the help of the English to right themselves; revenge was so sweet unto them as it prevailed above all the rest, so as they resolved to join with the English against them, and did.

The Court here agreed forthwith to send fifty men at their own charge; and with as much speed as possibly they could, got them armed and had made them ready under sufficient leaders, and provided a bark to carry them provisions and tend upon them for all occasions. But when they were ready to march, with a supply from the Bay, they had word to stay; for the enemy was as good as vanquished and there would be no need.

I shall not take upon me exactly to describe their proceedings in these things, because I expect it will be fully done by themselves who best know the carriage and circumstances of things. I shall therefore but touch them in general. From Connecticut, who were most sensible of the hurt sustained and the present danger, they set out a party of men, and another party met them from the Bay, at the Narragansetts', who were to join with them. The Narragansetts were earnest to be gone before the English were well rested and refreshed, especially some of them which came last. It should seem their desire was to come upon the enemy suddenly and undiscovered. There was a bark of this place, newly put in there, which was come from Connecticut, who did encourage them to lay hold of the Indians' forwardness,

and to show as great forwardness as they, for it would encourage them, and expedition might prove to their great advantage. So they went on, and so ordered their march as the Indians brought them to a fort[1] of the enemy's (in which most of their chief men were) before day. They approached the same with great silence and surrounded it both with English and Indians, that they might not break out; and so assaulted them with great courage, shooting amongst them, and entered the fort with all speed. And those that first entered found sharp resistance from the enemy, who both shot at and grappled with them; others ran into their houses and brought out fire and set them on fire, which soon took in their mat; and standing close together, with the wind all was quickly on a flame, and thereby more were burnt to death than was otherwise slain. It burnt their bowstrings and made them unserviceable; those that escaped the fire were slain with the sword; some hewed to pieces, others run through with their rapiers, so as they were quickly dispatched and very few escaped. It was conceived they thus destroyed about 400 at this time. It was a fearful sight to see them thus frying in the fire and the streams of blood quenching the same, and horrible was the stink and scent thereof; but the victory seemed a sweet sacrifice,[2] and they gave the praise thereof to God, who had wrought so wonderfully for them, thus to enclose their enemies in their hands and give them so speedy a victory over so proud and insulting an enemy. …

That I may make an end of this matter, this Sassacus (the Pequots' chief sachem) being fled to the Mohawks, they cut off his head, with some other of the chief of them, whether to satisfy the English or rather the Narragansetts (who, as I have since heard, hired them to do it) or for their own advantage, I well know not; but thus this war took end. The rest of the Pequots were wholly driven from their place, and some of them submitted themselves to the Narragansetts and lived under them. Others of them betook themselves to the Mohegans under Uncas, their sachem, with the approbation of the English of Connecticut, under whose protection Uncas lived; and he and his men had been faithful to them in this war and done them very good service. But this did so vex the Narragansetts,

1 *fort* This was Fort Mystic, on the bank of the Mystic River.

2 *sweet sacrifice* See Leviticus 2.2.

that they had not the whole sway over them, as they have never ceased plotting and contriving how to bring them under; and because they cannot attain their ends, because of the English who have protected them, they have sought to raise a general conspiracy against the English, as will appear in another place. ...

from CHAPTER 32
ANNO DOMINI 1642
[WICKEDNESS BREAKS FORTH]

Marvelous it may be to see and consider how some kind of wickedness did grow and break forth here, in a land where the same was so much witnessed against and so narrowly looked unto, and severely punished when it was known, as in no place more, or so much, that I have known or heard of; insomuch as they have been somewhat censured even by moderate and good men for their severity in punishments. And yet all this could not suppress the breaking out of sundry notorious sins (as this year, besides other, gives us too many sad precedents and instances), especially drunkenness and uncleanness.[1] Not only incontinency[2] between persons unmarried, for which many both men and women have been punished sharply enough, but some married persons also. But that which is worse, even sodomy and buggery[3] (things fearful to name) have broke forth in this land oftener than once.

I say it may justly be marveled at and cause us to fear and tremble at the consideration of our corrupt natures, which are so hardly bridled, subdued and mortified; nay, cannot by any other means but the powerful work and grace of God's Spirit. But (besides this) one reason may be that the Devil may carry a greater spite against the churches of Christ and the gospel here, by how much the more they endeavour to preserve holiness and purity amongst them and strictly punisheth the contrary when it ariseth either in church or commonwealth; that he might cast a blemish and stain upon them in the eyes of [the] world, who use to be rash in judgment. I would rather think thus, than that Satan hath more power in these heathen lands, as

some have thought, than in more Christian nations, especially over God's servants in them.

2. Another reason may be, that it may be in this case as it is with waters when their streams are stopped or dammed up. When they get passage they flow with more violence and make more noise and disturbance than when they are suffered to run quietly in their own channels; so wickedness being here more stopped by strict laws, and the same more nearly looked unto so as it cannot run in a common road of liberty as it would and is inclined, it searches everywhere and at last breaks out where it gets vent.

3. A third reason may be, here (as I am verily persuaded) is not more evils in this kind, nor nothing near so many by proportion as in other places; but they are here more discovered and seen and made public by due search, inquisition and due punishment; for the churches look narrowly to their members, and the magistrates over all, more strictly than in other places. Besides, here the people are but few in comparison of other places which are full and populous and lie hid, as it were, in a wood or thicket and many horrible evils by that means are never seen nor known; whereas here, they are, as it were, brought into the light and set in the plain field, or rather on a hill, made conspicuous to the view of all. ...

[A HORRIBLE CASE OF BESTIALITY]

And after the time of the writing of these things befell a very sad accident of the like foul nature in this government, this very year, which I shall now relate. There was a youth whose name was Thomas Granger. He was servant to an honest man of Duxbury, being about 16 or 17 years of age. (His father and mother lived at the same time at Scituate.) He was this year detected of buggery, and indicted for the same, with a mare, a cow, two goats, five sheep, two calves and a turkey. Horrible it is to mention, but the truth of the history requires it. He was first discovered by one that accidentally saw his lewd practice towards the mare. (I forbear particulars.) Being upon it examined and committed, in the end he not only confessed the fact with that beast at that time, but sundry times before and at several times with all the rest of the forenamed in his indictment. And this his free confession was not only in private to the

[1] *uncleanness* Sexual impurity.

[2] *incontinency* Lack of self-restraint.

[3] *buggery* Anal intercourse, as well as any intercourse with an animal.

magistrates (though at first he strived to deny it) but to sundry, both ministers and others; and afterwards, upon his indictment, to the whole court and jury; and confirmed it at his execution. And whereas some of the sheep could not so well be known by his description of them, others with them were brought before him and he declared which were they and which were not. And accordingly he was cast by the jury and condemned, and after executed about the 8th of September, 1642. A very sad spectacle it was. For first the mare, and then the cow, and the rest of the lesser cattle were killed before his face, according to the law, Leviticus 20.15; and then he himself was executed. The cattle were all cast into a great and large pit that was digged of purpose for them, and no use made of any part of them.

Upon the examination of this person and also of a former that had made some sodomitical attempts upon another, it being demanded of them how they came first to the knowledge and practice of such wickedness, the one confessed he had long used it in old England; and this youth last spoken of said he was taught it by another that had heard of such things from some in England when he was there, and they kept cattle together. By which it appears how one wicked person may infect many, and what care all ought to have what servants they bring into their families.

But it may be demanded how came it to pass that so many wicked persons and profane people should so quickly come over into this land and mix themselves amongst them? Seeing it was religious men that began the work and they came for religion's sake? I confess this may be marveled at, at least in time to come, when the reasons thereof should not be known; and the more because here was so many hardships and wants met withal. I shall therefore endeavour to give some answer hereunto.

1. And first, according to that in the gospel, it is ever to be remembered that where the Lord begins to sow good seed, there the envious man will endeavour to sow tares.[1]

2. Men being to come over into a wilderness, in which much labor and service was to be done about building and planting, etc., such as wanted help in that respect, when they could not have such as they would, were glad to take such as they could; and so, many untoward servants, sundry of them proved, that were thus brought over, both men and womenkind who, when their times were expired, became families of themselves, which gave increase hereunto.

3. Another and a main reason hereof was that men, finding so many godly disposed persons willing to come into these parts, some began to make a trade of it, to transport passengers and their goods, and hired ships for that end. And then, to make up their freight and advance their profit, cared not who the persons were, so they had money to pay them. And by this means the country became pestered with many unworthy persons who, being come over, crept into one place or other.

4. Again, the Lord's blessing usually following His people as well in outward as spiritual things (though afflictions be mixed withal) do make many to adhere to the People of God, as many followed Christ for the loaves' sake (John 6.26)[2] and a "mixed multitude" came into the wilderness with the People of God out of Egypt of old (Exodus 12.38).[3] So also there were sent by their friends, some under hope that they would be made better; others that they might be eased of such burdens, and they kept from shame at home, that would necessarily follow their dissolute courses. And thus, by one means or other, in 20 years' time, it is a question whether the greater part be not grown the worser? …

<div align="center">

from CHAPTER 34
ANNO DOMINI 1644
[PROPOSAL TO REMOVE TO NAUSET]

</div>

Mr. Edward Winslow was chosen Governor this year.

Many having left this place (as is before noted) by reason of the straitness and barrenness of the same and their finding of better accommodations elsewhere more suitable to their ends and minds; and sundry others

[1] *tares* Weeds that resemble wheat when first growing. See Matthew 13.24–30.

[2] *John 6.26* "Jesus answered them, and said, Verily verily I say unto you, Ye seek me not, because ye saw the miracles, but because ye ate of the loaves, and were filled."

[3] *Exodus 12.38* "And a great multitude of sundry sorts of people went out with them, and sheep, and beeves [oxen], and cattle in great abundance."

still upon every occasion desiring their dismissions, the church began seriously to think whether it were not better jointly to remove to some other place than to be thus weakened and as it were insensibly dissolved.[1] Many meetings and much consultation was held hereabout, and diverse were men's minds and opinions. Some were still for staying together in this place, alleging men might here live if they would be content with their condition, and that it was not for want or necessity so much that they removed as for the enriching of themselves. Others were resolute upon removal and so signified that here they could not stay; but if the church did not remove, they must. Insomuch as many were swayed rather than there should be a dissolution, to condescend to a removal if a fit place could be found that might more conveniently and comfortably receive the whole, with such accession of others as might come to them for their better strength and subsistence; and some such-like cautions and limitations.

So as, with the aforesaid provisos, the greater part consented to a removal to a place called Nauset, which had been superficially viewed and the good will of the purchasers to whom it belonged obtained, with some addition thereto from the Court. But now they began to see their error, that they had given away already the best and most commodious places to others, and now wanted themselves. For this place was about 50 miles from hence, and at an outside of the country remote from all society; also that it would prove so strait as it would not be competent to receive the whole body, much less be capable of any addition or increase; so as, at least in a short time, they should be worse there than they are now here. The which with sundry other like considerations and inconveniences made them change their resolutions. But such as were before resolved upon removal took advantage of this agreement and went on, notwithstanding; neither could the rest hinder them, they having made some beginning.[2]

And thus was this poor church left, like an ancient mother grown old and forsaken of her children, though not in their affections yet in regard of their bodily presence and personal helpfulness; her ancient members being most of them worn away by death, and these of later time being like children translated into other families, and she like a widow left only to trust in God. Thus, she that had made many rich became herself poor.

—1856 (WRITTEN 1630–51)

[1] *Many having left ... insensibly dissolved* The leaders of Plymouth encouraged newcomers to establish new towns, but they had wanted the original church and community to remain cohesive. The land near Plymouth, however, was not conducive to expansion, and the wharfs and harbor at Boston were better for commerce— leading to the gradual diminishment of both population and trade at Plymouth.

[2] *made some beginning* Those who left for Nauset (now called Eastham) purchased the rights for the land from Mattaquason, sachem of Monamoyick. The church at Nauset was the third church to branch away from the original Plymouth church; the first two were Duxbury and Marshfield.

IN CONTEXT

Mourt's Relation

This journal, written between November 1620 and November 1621, describes the landing of the *Mayflower* and the early days of Plymouth Plantation. While scholars generally believe that William Bradford (1590–1657) contributed to the journal, particularly to the earlier sections, the primary author is Edward Winslow (1595–1655), a *Mayflower* passenger who was also heavily involved in the government of the new colony. The *Relation* was published anonymously in England in 1622, and at that time it was attributed to George Morton (1585–1624)—also known as Mourt—who had signed the prefatory "Letter to the Reader" at the beginning of the volume. This led to the journal becoming popularly known as *Mourt's Relation*. Highly valued as a literary and historical document in its own right, the book is also of interest when read in conjunction with Bradford's later description of the same events in *Of Plymouth Plantation* (1651).

from Edward Winslow and William Bradford, *A Relation or Journal of the Proceedings of the Plantation Settled at Plymouth in New England* [*Mourt's Relation*][1] (1622)

Wednesday, the sixth of September, the winds coming east-north-east, a fine small gale, we loosed from Plymouth,[2] having been kindly entertained and courteously used by diverse[3] friends there dwelling, and after many difficulties in boisterous storms, at length, by God's providence, upon the ninth of November following, by break of the day we espied land which we deemed to be Cape Cod, and so afterward it proved. And the appearance of it much comforted us, especially seeing so goodly a land, and wooded to the brink of the sea. It caused us to rejoice together, and praise God that had given us once again to see land. And thus we made our course south-south-west, purposing to go to a river ten leagues to the south of the Cape,[4] but at night the wind being contrary, we put round again for the bay of Cape Cod: and upon the 11th of November we came to an anchor in the bay, which is a good harbor and pleasant bay, circled round, except in the entrance which is about four miles over from land to land, compassed about to the very sea with oaks, pines, juniper, sassafras, and other sweet wood; it is a harbor wherein a thousand sail of ships may safely ride. There we relieved ourselves with wood and water, and refreshed our people, which our shallop[5] was fitted to coast the bay, to search for a habitation; there was the greatest store of fowl that ever we saw.

And every day we saw whales playing hard by[6] us, of which in that place, if we had instruments and means to take them, we might have made a very rich return, which to our great grief we wanted.[7] Our master and his mate, and others experienced in fishing, professed we might have made three or four

[1] Several editions of *Mourt's Relation* have been consulted in the preparation of the text reprinted here, including Dwight Heath's 1963 edition and Henry Martyn Dexter's 1865 edition.

[2] *Plymouth* Referring here to the harbor city of Plymouth, England.

[3] *diverse* Various.

[4] *river … south of the Cape* In *Of Plymouth Plantation*, Bradford suggests they were looking for the Hudson River. The distance from Cape Cod to that river, however, is much greater than ten miles.

[5] *shallop* Open row-boat used in shallow waters to move between a larger boat and land.

[6] *hard by* Near.

[7] *wanted* Lacked.

thousand pounds' worth of oil; they preferred it before Greenland whale-fishing, and purpose the next winter to fish for whale here. For cod we assayed,[1] but found none; there is good store, no doubt, in their season. Neither got we any fish all the time we lay there, but some few little ones on the shore. We found great mussels, and very fat and full of sea-pearl, but we could not eat them, for they made us all sick that did eat, as well sailors as passengers; they caused to cast and scour,[2] but they were soon well again. …

Wednesday, the 15th of November, they[3] were set ashore, and when they had ordered themselves in the order of a single file and marched about the space of a mile, by the sea they espied five or six people with a dog, coming towards them, who were savages, who when they saw them, ran into the wood and whistled the dog after them, etc. First they supposed them to be Master Jones,[4] the master, and some of his men, for they were ashore and knew of their coming, but after they knew them to be Indians they marched after them into the woods, lest other of the Indians should lie in ambush; but when the Indians saw our men following them, they ran away with might and main and our men turned out of the wood after them, for it was the way they intended to go, but they could not come near them. They followed them that night about ten miles by the trace of their footings, and saw how they had come the same way they went, and at a turning perceived how they ran up a hill, to see whether they followed them. At length night came upon them, and they were constrained to take up their lodging, so they set forth three sentinels, and the rest, some kindled a fire, and others fetched wood, and there held our rendezvous that night.

In the morning so soon as we could see the trace,[5] we proceeded on our journey, and had the track until we had compassed the head of a long creek, and there they took into another wood, and we after them, supposing to find some of their dwellings, but we marched through boughs and bushes, and under hills and valleys, which tore our very armor in pieces, and yet could meet with none of them, nor their houses, nor find any fresh water, which we greatly desired, and stood in need of, for we brought neither beer nor water with us, and our victuals was only biscuit and Holland cheese, and a little bottle of aquavitae,[6] so as we were sore athirst. About ten o'clock we came into a deep valley, full of brush, wood-gaile,[7] and long grass, through which we found little paths or tracks, and there we saw a deer, and found springs of fresh water, of which we were heartily glad, and sat us down and drunk our first New England water with as much delight as ever we drunk drink in all our lives.

When we had refreshed ourselves, we directed our course full south, that we might come to the shore, which within a short while after we did, and there made a fire, that they in the ship might see where we were (as we had direction[8]) and so marched on towards this supposed river. And as we went in another valley we found a fine clear pond of fresh water, being about a musket shot broad and twice as long. There grew also many fine vines, and fowl and deer haunted there; there grew much sassafras. From thence we went on, and found much plain ground, about fifty acres, fit for plow, and some signs where the Indians had formerly planted their corn. After this, some thought it best, for nearness of the river, to go down and travel on the sea sands, by which means some of our men were tired, and lagged behind. So we stayed and gathered them up, and struck into the land again, where we found a little path to certain heaps of sand, one whereof was covered with old mats, and had a wooden thing like a mortar whelmed[9] on the top of it,

[1] *assayed* Tried.

[2] *cast and scour* Vomit and suffer from diarrhea.

[3] *they* Sixteen men, under Captain Myles Standish (c. 1584–1656), a military advisor to the Pilgrims, were sent out to explore the land to see if it was fit for habitation. William Bradford was among them.

[4] *Master Jones* Christopher Jones (1570–1622), captain of the *Mayflower*.

[5] *trace* Tracks.

[6] *aquavitae* Strong alcohol, such as whiskey or brandy.

[7] *wood-gaile* Likely bayberry, a shrub in the same family as sweet gale.

[8] *as we had direction* As we had been instructed to do.

[9] *whelmed* Upside-down.

and an earthen pot laid in a little hole at the end thereof. We, musing what it might be, digged and found a bow, and, as we thought, arrows, but they were rotten. We supposed there were many other things, but because we deemed them graves, we put in the bow again and made it up as it was, and left the rest untouched, because we thought it would be odious unto them to ransack their sepulchres.

We went on further and found new stubble, of which they had gotten corn this year, and many walnut trees full of nuts, and great store of strawberries, and some vines. Passing thus a field or two, which were not great, we came to another which had also been new gotten, and there we found where a house had been, and four or five old planks laid together; also we found a great kettle[1] which had been some ship's kettle and brought out of Europe. There was also a heap of sand, made like the former—but it was newly done, we might see how they had paddled it with their hands—which we digged up, and in it we found a little old basket full of fair Indian corn, and digged further and found a fine great new basket full of very fair corn of this year, with some thirty-six goodly ears of corn, some yellow, some red, and others mixed with blue, which was a very goodly sight. The basket was round, and narrow at the top; it held about three or four bushels, which was as much as two of us could lift up from the ground, and was very handsomely and cunningly made. But whilst we were busy about these things, we set our men sentinel in a round ring, all but two or three which digged up the corn. We were in suspense what to do with it and the kettle, and at length, after much consultation, we concluded to take the kettle and as much of the corn as we could carry away with us; and when our shallop came, if we could find any of the people, and come to parley[2] with them, we would give them the kettle again, and satisfy them for their corn. So we took all the ears, and put a good deal of the loose corn in the kettle for two men to bring away on a staff; besides, they that could put any into their pockets filled the same. The rest we buried again, for we were so laden with armor that we could carry no more. …

In the morning we took our kettle and sunk it in the pond, and trimmed our muskets, for few of them would go off because of the wet, and so coasted[3] the wood again to come home, in which we were shrewdly puzzled, and lost our way. As we wandered we came to a tree, where a young sprit[4] was bowed down over a bow, and some acorns strewed underneath. Stephen Hopkins[5] said it had been to catch some deer. So as we were looking at it, William Bradford being in the rear, when he came looked also upon it, and as he went about, it gave a sudden jerk up, and he was immediately caught by the leg. It was a very pretty device, made with a rope of their own making and having a noose as artificially[6] made as any roper in England can make, and as like ours as can be, which we brought away with us. In the end we got out of the wood, and were fallen about a mile too high above the creek, where we saw three bucks, but we had rather have had one of them. We also did spring[7] three couple of partridges, and as we came along by the creek we saw great flocks of wild geese and ducks, but they were very fearful of us. So we marched some while in the woods, some while on the sands, and other while in the water up to the knees, till at length we came near the ship, and then we shot off our pieces, and the long boat came to fetch us. Master Jones and Master Carver[8] being on the shore, with many of our people, came to meet us. And thus we came both weary and welcome home, and delivered in our corn into the store, to be kept for seed, for we knew not how to come by any, and therefore were very glad, purposing, so soon as we could meet with any inhabitants of that place, to make them large satisfaction. …

[1] *kettle* Cauldron or pot.

[2] *parley* Talk; negotiate.

[3] *coasted* Walked along the edge of.

[4] *sprit* Young, flexible tree.

[5] *Stephen Hopkins* Passenger on the *Mayflower* who had previous experience as a settler, having lived for four years in Virginia from 1610–14.

[6] *artificially* Skillfully.

[7] *spring* Flush from cover.

[8] *Master Carver* John Carver (1584–1621) was the first governor of Plymouth.

... [W]e marched to the place where we had the corn formerly, which place we called Cornhill, and digged and found the rest, of which we were very glad. We also digged in a place a little further off, and found a bottle of oil. We went to another place which we had seen before, and digged, and found more corn, viz.[1] two or three baskets full of Indian wheat,[2] and a bag of beans, with a good many of fair wheat ears. Whilst some of us were digging up this, some others found another heap of corn, which they digged up also, so as we had in all about ten bushels, which will serve us sufficiently for seed. And sure it was God's good providence that we found this corn, for else we know not how we should have done, for we knew not how we should find or meet with any Indians, except it be to do us a mischief. Also, we had never in all likelihood seen a grain of it if we had not made our first journey, for the ground was now covered with snow, and so hard frozen that we were fain with our cutlasses[3] and short swords to hew and carve the ground a foot deep, and then wrest it up with levers, for we had forgot to bring other tools. Whilst we were in this employment, foul weather being towards, Master Jones was earnest to go aboard, but sundry[4] of us desired to make further discovery and to find out the Indians' habitations. So we sent home with him our weakest people, and some that were sick, and all the corn, and eighteen of us stayed still, and lodged there that night, and desired that the shallop might return to us next day and bring us some mattocks[5] and spades with them.

The next morning we followed certain beaten paths and tracks of the Indians into the woods, supposing they would have led us into some town, or houses. After we had gone a while, we light[6] upon a very broad beaten path, well nigh two feet broad. Then we lighted all our matches and prepared ourselves, concluding that we were near their dwellings, but in the end we found it to be only a path made to drive deer in, when the Indians hunt, as we supposed.

When we had marched five or six miles into the woods and could find no signs of any people, we returned again another way, and as we came into the plain ground we found a place like a grave, but it was much bigger and longer than any we had yet seen. It was also covered with boards, so as we mused what it should be, and resolved to dig it up, where we found, first a mat, and under that a fair bow, and there another mat, and under that a board about three quarters[7] long, finely carved and painted, with three tines, or broaches,[8] on the top, like a crown. Also between the mats we found bowls, trays, dishes, and such like trinkets. At length we came to a fair new mat, and under that two bundles, the one bigger, the other less. We opened the greater and found in it a great quantity of fine and perfect red powder, and in it the bones and skull of a man. The skull had fine yellow hair still on it, and some of the flesh unconsumed; there was bound up with it a knife, a packneedle,[9] and two or three old iron things. It was bound up in a sailor's canvas cassock,[10] and a pair of cloth breeches. The red powder was a kind of embalment, and yielded a strong, but not offensive smell; it was as fine as any flour. We opened the less bundle likewise, and found of the same powder in it, and the bones and head of a little child. About the legs and other parts of it was bound strings and bracelets of fine white beads; there was also by it a little bow, about three quarters long, and some other odd knacks. We brought sundry of the prettiest things away with us, and covered the corpse up again. After this, we digged in sundry like places, but found no more corn, nor any thing else but graves.

1 *viz.* Abbreviation of the Latin *videlicet*, meaning "namely" or "that is to say."

2 *Indian wheat* Corn.

3 *cutlasses* Short, slightly curved swords.

4 *sundry* Various.

5 *mattocks* Sturdy pick-like tools used to loosen up tough ground.

6 *light* Happened.

7 *three quarters* I.e., three quarters of a yard.

8 *tines, or broaches* Sharp points.

9 *packneedle* Large, strong needle that could be used to sew tough cloth.

10 *cassock* Cloak.

There was variety of opinions amongst us about the embalmed person. Some thought it was an Indian lord and king. Others said the Indians have all black hair, and never any was seen with brown or yellow hair. Some thought it was a Christian of some special note, which had died amongst them, and they thus buried him to honor him. Others thought they had killed him, and did it in triumph over him.

Whilst we were thus ranging and searching, two of the sailors, which were newly come on the shore, by chance espied two houses which had been lately dwelt in, but the people were gone. They, having their pieces and hearing nobody, entered the house and took out some things, and durst not stay but came again and told us. So some seven or eight of us went with them, and found how we had gone within a flight shot[1] of them before. The houses were made with long young sapling trees, bended and both ends stuck into the ground. They were made round, like unto an arbor, and covered down to the ground with thick and well-wrought mats, and the door was not over a yard high, made of a mat to open. The chimney was a wide open hole in the top, for which they had a mat to cover it close when they pleased. One might stand and go upright in them. In the midst of them were four little trunches[2] knocked into the ground, and small sticks laid over, on which they hung their pots, and what they had to seethe.[3] Round about the fire they lay on mats, which are their beds. The houses were double matted, for as they were matted without, so were they within, with newer and fairer mats. In the houses we found wooden bowls, trays and dishes, earthen pots, handbaskets made of crabshells wrought together, also an English pail or bucket; it wanted a bail,[4] but it had two iron ears. There was also baskets of sundry sorts, bigger and some lesser, finer and some coarser; some were curiously wrought with black and white in pretty works, and sundry other of their household stuff. We found also two or three deer's heads, one whereof had been newly killed, for it was still fresh. There was also a company of deer's feet stuck up in the houses, harts' horns,[5] and eagles' claws, and sundry such like things there was, also two or three baskets full of parched acorns, pieces of fish, and a piece of a broiled herring. We found also a little silk grass, and a little tobacco seed, with some other seeds which we knew not. Without was sundry bundles of flags,[6] and sedge, bulrushes, and other stuff to make mats. There was thrust into a hollow tree two or three pieces of venison, but we thought it fitter for the dogs than for us. Some of the best things we took away with us, and left the houses standing still as they were.

So it growing towards night, and the tide almost spent, we hasted with our things down to the shallop, and got aboard that night, intending to have brought some beads and other things to have left in the houses, in sign of peace and that we meant to truck[7] with them, but it was not done, by means of our hasty coming away from Cape Cod. But so soon as we can meet conveniently with them, we will give them full satisfaction. Thus much of our second discovery. …

About five o'clock in the morning we began to be stirring, and two or three which doubted whether their pieces would go off or no made trial of them, and shot them off, but thought nothing at all. After prayer we prepared ourselves for breakfast and for a journey, and it being now the twilight in the morning, it was thought meet[8] to carry the things down to the shallop. Some said it was not best to carry the armor down; others said they would be readier; two or three said they would not carry theirs till they went themselves, but mistrusting nothing at all. As it fell out, the water not being high enough, they laid the things down upon the shore and came up to breakfast. Anon, all upon a sudden, we heard a great and

[1] *flight shot* Distance a shot would fly.

[2] *trunches* Stakes.

[3] *seethe* Boil.

[4] *bail* Handle.

[5] *harts' horns* Antlers from male deer.

[6] *flags* Reeds.

[7] *truck* Trade.

[8] *meet* Appropriate.

strange cry, which we knew to be the same voices,[1] though they varied their notes. One of our company, being abroad, came running in and cried, "They are men! Indians! Indians!" and withal, their arrows came flying amongst us. Our men ran out with all speed to recover their arms, as by the good providence of God they did. In the meantime, Captain Miles Standish, having a snaphance[2] ready, made a shot, and after him another. After they two had shot, other two of us were ready, but he wished us not to shoot till we could take aim, for we knew not what need we should have, and there were four only of us which had their arms there ready, and stood before the open side of our barricade, which was first assaulted. They thought it best to defend it, lest the enemy should take it and our stuff, and so have the more vantage against us. Our care was no less for the shallop, but we hoped all the rest would defend it; we called unto them to know how it was with them, and they answered, "Well! Well!" every one and, "Be of good courage!" We heard three of their pieces go off, and the rest called for a firebrand to light their matches. One took a log out of the fire on his shoulder and went and carried it unto them, which was thought did not a little discourage our enemies. The cry of our enemies was dreadful, especially when our men ran out to recover their arms; their note was after this manner, "Woach woach ha ha hach woach." Our men were no sooner come to their arms, but the enemy was ready to assault them.

There was a lusty man and no whit less valiant, who was thought to be their captain, stood behind a tree within half a musket shot of us, and there let his arrows fly at us. He was seen to shoot three arrows, which were all avoided, for he at whom the first arrow was aimed, saw it, and stooped down and it flew over him; the rest were avoided also. He stood three shots of a musket. At length one took, as he said, full aim at him, and after which he gave extraordinary cry and away they went all. We followed them about a quarter of a mile, but we left six to keep our shallop, for we were careful about our business. Then we shouted all together two several times, and shot off a couple of muskets and so returned; this we did that they might see we were not afraid of them nor discouraged.

Thus it pleased God to vanquish our enemies and give us deliverance. By their noise we could not guess that they were less than thirty or forty, though some thought that they were many more. Yet in the dark of the morning we could not so well discern them among the trees, as they could see us by our fireside. We took up eighteen of their arrows which we have sent to England by Master Jones, some whereof were headed with brass, others with harts' horn, and others with eagles' claws. Many more no doubt were shot, for these we found were almost covered with leaves; yet, by the especial providence of God, none of them either hit or hurt us though many came close by us and on every side of us, and some coats which hung up in our barricade were shot through and through.

So after we had given God thanks for our deliverance, we took our shallop and went on our journey, and called this place, The First Encounter. ...

The 11th of June we set forth,[3] the weather being very fair: but ere we had been long at sea, there arose a storm of wind and rain, with much lightning and thunder, insomuch that a spout[4] arose not far from us: but, God be praised, it dured[5] not long, and we put in that night for harbor at a place called Cummaquid,[6] where we had some hope to find the boy. Two savages were in the boat with us, the one was Tisquantum, our interpreter, the other Tokamahamon,[7] a special friend. It being night before we came in, we anchored in the midst of the bay, where we were dry at low water. In the morning we espied

1 *same voices* The night before the group had been woken by "a great and hideous cry."

2 *snaphance* Gun with a flint-lock.

3 *we set forth* Ten of the company goes to "the kingdom of Nauset, to seek a boy that had lost himself in the woods." The boy was John Billington, who was being held in a Nauset community in what is now Cape Cod.

4 *spout* Waterspout.

5 *dured* Endured, lasted.

6 *Cummaquid* Later renamed Barnstable, Massachusetts, by settlers.

7 *Tisquantum* Also known as Squanto (1585–1622), a member of the Patuxet tribe that lived in the area around Plymouth. Squanto was kidnapped by English sailors in 1617 and returned to New England in 1619; *Tokamahamon* Wampanoag guide chosen by the sachem Massasoit to give aid to the Plymouth settlers.

savages seeking lobsters, and sent our two interpreters to speak with them, the channel being between them; where they told them what we were, and for what we were come, willing them not at all to fear us, for we would not hurt them. Their answer was, that the boy was well, but he was at Nauset; yet since we were there they desired us to come ashore and eat with them; which, as soon as our boat floated, we did, and went six ashore, having four pledges for them in the boat. They brought us to their sachem or governor, whom they call Iyanough,[1] a man not exceeding twenty-six years of age, but very personable, gentle, courteous, and fair conditioned, indeed not like the savage, save for his attire; his entertainment was answerable to his parts, and his cheer[2] plentiful and various.

One thing was very grievous unto us at this place; there was an old woman, whom we judged to be no less than a hundred years old, which came to see us because she never saw English, yet could not behold us without breaking forth into great passion, weeping and crying excessively. We demanding the reason of it, they told us she had three sons who, when Master Hunt[3] was in these parts, went aboard his ship to trade with him, and he carried them captives into Spain (for Tisquantum at this time was carried away also) by which means she was deprived of the comfort of her children in her old age. We told them we were sorry that any Englishman should give them that offense, that Hunt was a bad man, and that all the English that heard of it condemned him for the same: but for us, we would not offer them any such injury though it would gain us all the skins[4] in the country. So we gave her some small trifles, which somewhat appeased her. ...

from Robert Cushman, *Reasons and Considerations Touching the Lawfulness of Removing out of England into the Parts of America*[5] (1622)

This tract was appended to printed versions of *Mourt's Relation* and attributed to the author "R.C." Most scholars identify this author as Robert Cushman (1579–1625), the business agent for the colony, who brought the manuscript of the *Relation* with him when he returned to England in 1622. Cushman's tract has long been placed in the genre of "promotional" literature outlining the benefits of immigration from England to the colonies. Critic Andrew Delbanco, however, argues that the tract belongs to the genre of "cases of conscience," literature that debates the morality of a given question or action, in this case whether it is moral or not to leave one's homeland in search of a better life. The tract is organized as a sermon, using scripture to support the claims made in favor of emigration. It contains an early expression of the "empty domicile" theory—the idea that Indigenous lands were empty wildernesses that could rightfully be taken by Europeans without payment or permission.

For as much as many exceptions are daily made against the going into and inhabiting of foreign desert[6] places, to the hindrances of plantations abroad, and the increase of distractions at home, it is not

[1] *Iyanough* Iyannough (c. 1598–1623) was sachem to the Mattachiest tribe, a Wampanoag people who lived near Cummaquid.

[2] *cheer* Food and drink.

[3] *Master Hunt* Thomas Hunt, a shipmaster, who took twenty-seven Indigenous people and sold them as slaves in Spain.

[4] *skins* Beaver skins.

[5] Several editions of *Mourt's Relation* have been consulted in the preparation of the text reprinted here, including Dwight Heath's 1963 edition and Henry Martyn Dexter's 1865 edition. While Cushman's biblical annotation has been retained in footnotes, some of his marginal notes have been omitted from this text.

[6] *desert* Wild, uninhabited.

amiss that some which have been ear-witnesses of the exceptions made, and are either agents or abettors of such removals and plantations, do seek to give content to the world, in all things that possibly they can.

And although the most of the opposites[1] are such as either dream of raising their fortunes here, to that than which there is nothing more unlike, or such as affecting their home-born country so vehemently, as that they had rather with all their friends beg, yea, starve in it, than undergo a little difficulty in seeking abroad; yet are there some who, out of doubt in tenderness of conscience, and fear to offend God by running before they be called, are straitened[2] and do straiten others from going to foreign plantations. …

And being studious for brevity, we must first consider that whereas God of old did call and summon our fathers by predictions, dreams, visions, and certain illuminations to go from their countries, places, and habitations, to reside and dwell here or there, and to wander up and down from city to city, and land to land, according to his will and pleasure, now there is no such calling to be expected for any matter whatsoever, neither must any so much as imagine that there will now be any such thing.[3] God did once so train up his people, but now he doth not, but speaks in another manner, and so we must apply ourselves to God's present dealing, and not to his wonted[4] dealing; and as the miracle of giving manna ceased when the fruits of the land became plenty, so God, having such a plentiful storehouse of directions in his holy word, there must not now any extraordinary revelations be expected.[5] But now the ordinary examples and precepts of the Scriptures, reasonably and rightly understood and applied, must be the voice and word that must call us, press us, and direct us in every action.

Neither is there any land or possession now, like unto the possession which the Jews had in Canaan,[6] being legally holy and appropriated unto a holy people, the seed of Abraham, in which they dwelt securely and had their days prolonged, it being by an immediate voice said, that he (the Lord) gave it them as a land of rest after their weary travels, and a type of eternal rest in heaven but now there is no land of that sanctimony, no land so appropriated, none typical, much less any that can be said to be given of God to any nation as was Canaan, which they and their seed must dwell in, till God sendeth upon them sword or captivity. But now we are all in all places strangers and pilgrims, travellers and sojourners, most properly, having no dwelling but in this earthen tabernacle; our dwelling is but a wandering, and our abiding but as a fleeting, and in a word our home is nowhere, but in the heavens, in that house not made with hands, whose maker and builder is God, and to which all ascend that love the coming of our Lord Jesus.[7]

1 *the opposites* Those opposed to emigration.

2 *straitened* Restricted.

3 [Cushman's note] Genesis 12.1–2 and 35.1; Matthew 2.19; Psalm 105.13. [Genesis 12.1–2: "For the Lord had said unto Abram, Get thee out of thy country, and from thy kindred, and from thy father's house unto the land that I will show thee. / And I will make of thee a great nation, and will bless thee, and make thy name great, and thou shalt be a blessing." In Genesis 35.1, God tells the patriarch Jacob to "go up to Bethel and dwell there, and make there an altar unto God." In Matthew 2.19–21, an angel appears to Joseph and tells him to flee Egypt and travel to Israel with his family. Psalm 105.13 describes the people of Israel walking "about from nation to nation, from one kingdom to another people." Unless otherwise indicated, all biblical passages quoted in the footnotes to this selection are from the Geneva Bible.]

4 *wonted* Customary; i.e., past.

5 [Cushman's note] Hebrew 1.1–2; Joshua 5.12. [Hebrews 1.1: "At sundry times and in diverse manners God spake in the old time to our fathers by the Prophets: in these last days he hath spoken unto us by his Son." "Manna" refers to a food God provides to sustain the Israelites as they wander the wilderness; in Joshua 5.12, God ceases to bestow manna once the Israelites are able to feed themselves.]

6 [Cushman's note] Genesis 17.8. [In this passage God says to the patriarch Abraham, "And I will give thee and thy seed after thee the land, wherein thou art a stranger, even all the land of Canaan, for an everlasting possession, and I will be their God."]

7 [Cushman's note] 2 Corinthians 5.1–3. ["For we know that if our earthly house of this tabernacle be destroyed, we have a building given of God, that is, an house not made with hands, but eternal in the heavens. For therefore we sigh, desiring to be clothed with our house, which is from heaven. Because that if we be clothed, we shall not be found naked."]

Though then there may be reasons to persuade a man to live in this or that land, yet there cannot be the same reasons which the Jews had, but now as natural, civil and religious bands tie men, so they must be bound, and as good reasons for things terrene[1] and heavenly appear, so they must be led. And so here falleth in our question, how a man that is here born and bred, and hath lived some years, may remove himself into another country.

I answer, a man must not respect only to live, and do good to himself, but he should see where he can live to do most good to others; for, as one saith, "He whose living is but for himself, it is time he were dead." Some men there are who of necessity must here live, as being tied to duties, either to church, commonwealth, household, kindred, etc. But others, and that many, who do no good in none of those, nor can do none, as being not able, or not in favor, or as wanting opportunity, and live as outcasts, nobodies, eye-sores, eating but for themselves, teaching but themselves, and doing good to none, either in soul or body, and so pass over days, years, and months, yea, so live and so die. Now such should lift up their eyes and see whether there be not some other place and country to which they may go to do good and have use towards others of that knowledge, wisdom, humanity, reason, strength, skill, faculty, etc., which God hath given them for the service of others and his own glory. …

But some will say, what right have I to go live in the heathens' country?

Letting pass the ancient discoveries, contracts and agreements which our Englishmen have long since made in those parts, together with the acknowledgment of the histories and chronicles of other nations, who profess the land of America from the Cape de Florida unto the Bay of Canada (which is south and north three hundred leagues and upwards, and east and west further than yet hath been discovered) is proper to the King of England—yet letting that pass, lest I be thought to meddle further than it concerns me, or further than I have discerning, I will mention such things as are within my reach, knowledge, sight and practise, since I have travailed in these affairs.

And first, seeing we daily pray for the conversion of the heathens, we must consider whether there be not some ordinary means and course for us to take to convert them, or whether prayer for them be only referred to God's extraordinary work from heaven. Now it seemeth unto me that we ought also to endeavor and use the means to convert them, and the means cannot be used unless we go to them or they come to us; to us they cannot come, our land is full; to them we may go, their land is empty.

This then is a sufficient reason to prove our going thither to live lawful: their land is spacious and void, and there are few and do but run over the grass, as do also the foxes and wild beasts. They are not industrious, neither have art, science, skill or faculty to use either the land or the commodities of it, but all spoils, rots, and is marred for want of manuring, gathering, ordering, etc. As the ancient patriarchs therefore removed from straiter places into more roomy, where the land lay idle and waste, and none used it, though there dwelt inhabitants by them (as Genesis 13.6,11,12, and 34.21, and 41.20), so is it lawful now to take a land which none useth, and make use of it.

And as it is a common land or unused, and undressed[2] country, so we have it by common consent, composition and agreement, which agreement is double. First, the imperial governor Massasoit,[3] whose circuits[4] in likelihood are larger than England and Scotland, hath acknowledged the King's Majesty of England to be his master and commander, and that once in my hearing, yea, and in writing, under his hand to Captain Standish,[5] both he and many other kings which are under him, as Paomet, Nauset, Cummaquid, Narraganset, Nemasket,[6] etc., with diverse others that dwell about the bays of

[1] *terrene* Earthly.

[2] *undressed* I.e., uncultivated.

[3] *Massasoit* Sachem of the Wampanoag (c. 1581–1661). He allied with the Pilgrims at Plymouth, forging a peace that lasted until his death in 1661. His advice and support were crucial to the colony's survival.

[4] *circuits* Circumference of lands.

[5] *Captain Standish* Myles Standish (c. 1584–1656), English ex-soldier hired as a military advisor to the Pilgrims.

[6] *Paomet, Nauset, … Nemasket* Names of local Indigenous peoples, some of whom were part of the Wampanoag Confederacy.

Patuxet[1] and Massachusetts. Neither hath this been accomplished by threats and blows, or shaking of sword and sound of trumpet, for as our faculty that way is small, and our strength less, so our warring with them is after another manner, namely by friendly usage, love, peace, honest and just carriages,[2] good counsel, etc., that so we and they may not only live in peace in that land, and they yield subjection to an earthly prince, but that as voluntaries[3] they may be persuaded at length to embrace the Prince of Peace, Christ Jesus, and rest in peace with him forever.[4]

Secondly, this composition[5] is also more particular and applicatory, as touching ourselves there inhabiting: the emperor,[6] by a joint consent, hath promised and appointed us to live at peace where we will in all his dominions, taking what place we will, and as much land as we will, and bringing as many people as we will, and that for these two causes. First, because we are the servants of James, King of England, whose the land (as he confesseth) is; second, because he hath found us just, honest, kind and peaceable, and so loves our company; yea, and that in these things there is no dissimulation on his part, nor fear of breach (except our security engender in them some unthought of treachery, or our uncivility provoke them to anger) is most plain in other relations, which show that the things they did were more out of love than out of fear.

It being then, first, a vast and empty chaos; secondly, acknowledged the right of our sovereign king; thirdly, by a peaceable composition in part possessed of diverse of his loving subjects, I see not who can doubt or call in question the lawfulness of inhabiting or dwelling there, but that it may be as lawful for such as are not tied upon some special occasion here, to live there as well as here. Yea, and as the enterprise is weighty and difficult, so the honor is more worthy, to plant a rude[7] wilderness, to enlarge the honor and fame of our dread[8] sovereign, but chiefly to display the efficacy and power of the Gospel, both in zealous preaching, professing, and wise walking under it, before the faces of these poor blind infidels.

As for such as object the tediousness of the voyage thither, the danger of pirates' robbery, of the savages' treachery, etc., these are but lions in the way,[9] and it were well for such men if they were in heaven, for who can show them a place in this world where iniquity shall not compass them at the heels,[10] and where they shall have a day without grief,[11] or a lease of life for a moment; and who can tell, but God, what dangers may lie at our doors, even in our native country, or what plots may be abroad, or when God will cause our sun to go down at noon-days,[12] and in the midst of our peace and security, lay upon us some lasting scourge for our so long neglect and contempt of his most glorious Gospel?

But we have here great peace, plenty of the Gospel, and many sweet delights, and variety of comforts. ...

[1] *Patuxet* The Plymouth colony was established on the territory of the Patuxet, a Wampanoag people.

[2] *carriages* Behaviors.

[3] *voluntaries* Willing participants.

[4] [Cushman's note] Psalms 110.3 and 48.3. [Psalm 110.3: "Thy people shall come willingly at the time of assembling thine army in holy beauty: the youth of thy womb shall be as the morning dew"; Psalm 48.3: "In the palaces thereof God is known for a refuge."]

[5] *composition* Agreement, peaceful arrangement.

[6] *the emperor* I.e., Massasoit.

[7] *rude* Uncivilized.

[8] *dread* Revered.

[9] [Cushman's note] Proverbs 22.13. ["The slothful man saith, A lion is without, I shall be slain in the street."]

[10] [Cushman's note] Psalm 49.5. ["Wherefore should I fear in the evil days, when iniquity shall compass me about, as at mine heels?"]

[11] [Cushman's note] Matthew 6.34. ["Care not then for the morrow, for the morrow shall care for itself: the day hath enough with his own grief."]

[12] [Cushman's note] Amos 8.9. ["And in that day, saith the Lord God, I will even cause the Sun to go down at noon: I will darken the earth in the clear day."]

True indeed, and far be it from us to deny and diminish the least of these mercies, but have we rendered unto God thankful obedience for this long peace, whilst other peoples have been at wars?[1] Have we not rather murmured, repined, and fallen at jars amongst ourselves, whilst our peace hath lasted with foreign power? Was there ever more suits in law, more envy, contempt and reproach than nowadays? Abraham and Lot departed asunder when there fell a breach betwixt them,[2] which was occasioned by the straitness of the land; and surely, I am persuaded that howsoever the frailties of men are principal in all contentions, yet the straitness of the place is such as each man is fain[3] to pluck his means, as it were, out of his neighbor's throat; there is such pressing and oppressing in town and country, about farms, trades, traffic, etc., so as a man can hardly any where set up a trade but he shall pull down two of his neighbors.

To conclude, without all partiality, the present consumption[4] which groweth upon us here, whilst the land groaneth under so many close-fisted and unmerciful men, being compared with the easiness, plainness and plentifulness in living in those remote places, may quickly persuade any man to a liking of this course, and to practise a removal, which being done by honest, godly and industrious men, they shall there be right heartily welcome, but for other of dissolute and profane life, their rooms are better than their companies.[5] For if here,[6] where the Gospel hath been so long and plentifully taught, they are yet frequent in such vices as the heathen would shame to speak of, what will they be when there is less restraint in word and deed? My only suit[7] to all men is, that whether they live there or here, they would learn to use this world as they used it not,[8] keeping faith and a good conscience, both with God and men, that when the day of account shall come, they may come forth as good and fruitful servants, and freely be received, and enter into the joy of their Master.

[1] [Cushman's note] 2 Chronicles 32.25. [In 2 Chronicles 32, God saves Hezekiah, King of Judah, from a sickness, but when Hezekiah is insufficiently grateful his kingdom is threatened with divine punishment.]

[2] [Cushman's note] Genesis 13.9–10. [In Genesis 13.9, Abraham resolves a dispute over shared pasture by giving Lot a portion of the Promised Land so that each patriarch can establish a separate settlement.]

[3] *fain* Glad.

[4] *consumption* Decay.

[5] *rooms are better than their companies* Proverbial phrase meaning their absences are preferable to their presences.

[6] *here* I.e., in England.

[7] *suit* Plea.

[8] *use this world as they used it not* See 1 Corinthians 7.31, which urges "they that use this world" to act "as though they used it not," i.e., as though they did not need or care about earthly things.

IN CONTEXT

Mapping Colonial Conflict

The following are historical mappings of conflicts between settlers and Indigenous peoples in seventeenth-century New England. The first map depicts the genocide of the Pequot known as the Mystic Massacre (1637); the second documents Indigenous oral records of the boundaries of Pequot territory before the Pequot War (1636–38); and the third is a settler map marking sites of conflict across New England.

John Underhill, "The Figure of the Indians' Fort or Palizado in New England and the Manner of Destroying It by Captain Underhill and Captain Mason," *News from America* (1638)

John Underhill and John Mason, colonists from Connecticut, led a genocide of the Pequots at their fortress on the Mystic River on 26 May 1637, killing everyone inside—including children and the elderly. The death toll of 400 people constituted a large percentage of the Pequot population, and the attack marked a devastating turning point in the Pequot War; after the massacre, almost all surviving Pequots were hunted down and killed or enslaved by settlers and their Indigenous allies, and were for a time not permitted to call themselves Pequot. It was not until 1983 that the Mashantucket Pequot Tribal Nation was recognized by the federal government; another tribal nation, the Eastern Pequot, is still pursuing federal recognition.

This map depicting the massacre appeared in Underhill's *News from America*, an account of his experiences as a militia captain during the Pequot War. Underhill describes the Mystic Massacre as follows:

Captain Mason entering into a wigwam, brought out a firebrand, after he had wounded many in the house, then he set fire on the west side where he entered, myself set fire on the south end with a train of powder. The fires of both meeting in the center of the fort blazed most terribly, and burnt all in the space of half an hour; many courageous fellows were unwilling to come out, and fought most desperately through the pallisadoes, so as they were scorched and burnt with the very flame, and were deprived of their arms, in regard the fire burnt their very bowstrings, and so perished valiantly: mercy they did deserve for their valour, could we have had opportunity to have bestowed it; many were burnt in the Fort, both men, women, and children, others forced out, and came in troops to the Indians [the colonists' Narragansett and Mohegan allies], twenty, and thirty at a time, which our soldiers received and entertained with the point of the sword; down fell men, women, and children. Those that scaped us, fell into the hands of the Indians, that were in the rear of us; it is reported by themselves, that there were about four hundred souls in this Fort, and not above five of them escaped out of our hands. Great and doleful was the bloody sight to the view of young soldiers that never had been in war, to see so many souls lie gasping on the ground so thick in some places, that you could hardly pass along. It may be demanded, Why should you be so furious (as some have said) should not Christians have more mercy and compassion? But I would refer you to David's war, when a people is grown to such a height of blood, and sin against God and man … there he hath no respect to persons, but harrows them, and saws them, and puts them to the sword, and the most terriblest death that may be: sometimes the Scripture declares women and children must perish with their parents; sometime[s] the case alters: but we will not dispute it now. We had sufficient light from the word of God for our proceedings.

John Tinker, Uncas, Wesawegun, Cassacinamon, Harry Wright, and Ninigret, "Plan of the Pequot Country and Testimony of Uncas, Cassacinamon, and Wesawegun" (1662)

This image shows the extent of Pequot territory before the Pequot War, with testimony of Uncas, Cassacinamon, and Wesawegun regarding the borders of the land. The map is made by the war's victors: the colonists and the Mohegan and the Narragansett, the Indigenous tribes that fought alongside the colonists. The 1638 Treaty of Hartford had declared Pequot territory to be the property of the English colonists. In 1662, however, there was conflict among the colonists after Charles II issued the Connecticut charter, which transferred the Pequot lands from Massachusetts to Connecticut. There were disagreements among the colonists as to the extent of the land, and disagreements between the Mohegan and the Narragansett as well, who each claimed some portion of the land as spoils of war. To help sort out the various claims, Indigenous leaders were gathered together at the General Court in New London to document their knowledge of the territory's boundaries. John Tinker and Harry Wright, two colonial representatives, were joined by Uncas; other signatories to the map were Pequot survivors Wesawegun and Cassacinamon. The following is a lightly modernized transcription of the writing on the map:

In New London this 4th of August 1662 Woncass [Uncas] Sagamore of Mohegan by request of Captain George Denison appeared before me, and this above draft being drawn he declared to my understanding and affirmed that at what time the English did conquer the Pequids [Pequots], their country did reach to a brook called Weex-co-da-wa, which brook falls into the end of that water or pond called Nekeequoweese, and that the land falling between that and the pond called Teapanocke, called by them Muxquota, is and was then Pequot land, the same is affirmed by Cassacinamon, and that he being then a boy used there to drive their (to say for the Pequots) deer into that neck of land, also Wesawegun affirmeth the same, and that eastward of that brook Weexcodawa, is and was Narragansett land belonging to Ninagrads [Ninigret] and his heirs by marriage of Hermon Garret's sister:

John Tinker, Assist.

—Woncase [Uncas] his mark
—Cassasinomon his mark
—Wesawegun his mark

William Hubbard, A Map of New-England (1677)

This is the first map printed in America, issued by Boston printer John Foster. It was an illustration in English-born writer and clergy member William Hubbard's book *The Present State of New England: Being a Narrative of the Troubles with the Indians* (1677). The description in the upper right corner identifies the map as "the first that ever was here [in America] cut, and done by the best pattern that could be had, which being in some places defective, it made the other less exact: yet doth it sufficiently show the situation of the country, and conveniently well the distance of places." The crowns on the map mark European settlements; the numbers mark places where there had been conflicts with Indigenous peoples.

Thomas Morton

c. 1576 – c. 1647

To the Pilgrim settlers of America, Thomas Morton was more than just a rival colonist and trader: he was a debauched villain, a "Lord of Misrule," who presided over a settlement that Plymouth governor William Bradford derided as a "School of Atheism." A lawyer, trader, and staunch Royalist, Morton established the colony of Ma-re Mount in what is now Quincy, Massachusetts. In his own words, Ma-re Mount was a place of "revels and merriment" where European and Indigenous people were encouraged to commingle. In *New English Canaan*, the only book he is known to have published, Morton reflects upon his time in Ma-re Mount, outlines his impressions of the natural environment and Indigenous peoples of America, and skewers the customs of his Puritan and Separatist rivals. He promises his readers that America holds tremendous economic opportunities—opportunities that England could capitalize upon if only it would cease to leave the region in the hands of religious radicals.

Little is known about Morton's early life. He was probably born between 1576 and 1579 in southwestern England to a minor aristocratic family. Near the last decade of the sixteenth century, he attended Clifford's Inn in London, where he studied law and the classics. He reputedly spent several years practicing law, and, in 1621, he married the wealthy widow Alice Miller. After a messy dispute with Alice's son over her estate, Morton became estranged from his wife and set out for New England.

In 1624, Morton helped to establish a trading post called Mount Wollaston at a location known as Passonagessit, on land that had been occupied by Massachusett people before disease introduced by French and English colonizers ravaged the community. (Morton described the plague as evidence of the "wondrous wisdom and love of God," clearing the region for English habitation.) Within two years of Mount Wollaston's establishment, Morton seized control of the settlement. In 1627, he rechristened it "Ma-re Mount"; Bradford and the Pilgrims of Plymouth sneeringly referred to the settlement as "Merrymount" and regarded it as a hive of licentious merrymaking. Unlike the Pilgrims and Puritans, who saw the American environment as, to borrow Bradford's expression, "a hideous and desolate wilderness," Morton regarded it as a place where earthly pleasures could—indeed, *should*—be savored. In his view, the English and the Indigenous peoples of the region could come together through their shared enjoyment of "good hospitality" and "all manner of Revels."

On 1 May 1627, to the dismay of the Pilgrims of the nearby Plymouth Colony, Morton erected an 80-foot-high maypole in commemoration of May Day—a pagan celebration that coincided with the Anglican festival of Saints Philip and Jacob. Morton, according to his own account, "brewed a barrel of excellent beer, and provided a case of bottles to be spent, with other good cheer, for all comers of that day." For days, white and Indigenous traders danced beneath the maypole, and many couplings took place, nearly all of them between European men and Algonquian women. In Plymouth, Bradford noted with disgust that at Ma-re Mount Europeans and Native Americans, "danc[ed] and frisk[ed] together like so many fairies, or furies." Morton, for his part, approved of the interracial unions, which he described as "harmless mirth." At Ma-re Mount, sex functioned as a trading commodity: many European traders saw it as an incentive to come to Morton's settlement rather than another, while the little surviving evidence of Indigenous perspectives on the matter suggests that Indigenous traders—including the women who participated—tended to view it as a means to secure enduring commercial relationships.

For more than a year, the maypole towered over Ma-re Mount, standing "as a fair sea-mark" that visually distinguished the settlement from Plymouth Colony. European and Indigenous traders alike found Ma-re Mount to be an attractive location to exchange wares, in part because Morton was willing to engage in practices that his neighbors found morally and legally dubious. Morton offered European traders an opportunity to engage in revelry—something they were never going to experience in Plymouth. To Indigenous traders, Morton provided guns—items King James I had prohibited the English from

supplying to Native Americans. In disregarding this prohibition, Morton not only armed a community with whom the Pilgrims were on unsteady diplomatic terms, but also caused the price of lead to rise dramatically. In the eyes of the Puritans and Separatists of New England, Ma-re Mount was an economic, as well as moral, threat.

In 1628, after another raucous May Day celebration was held in Ma-re Mount, a detachment of soldiers from Plymouth arrested Morton and marooned him off the coast of New Hampshire. The maypole was cut down, and the settlement renamed "Mount Dagon," in reference to the god of the Philistines, antagonists of the biblical Israelites. In 1629, after eluding punishment in England, Morton returned to Massachusetts, where he resumed his participation in the fur trade. In 1630, the Puritan Governor John Winthrop called for Morton to be taken into custody, and he was again sent to England to face trial. In England, Morton escaped prosecution and—along with several powerful political allies—participated in a successful suit to have the Massachusetts Bay Company's charter revoked, though this did little to halt the growth of Puritan power in the colony.

In 1637, Morton published *New English Canaan*, an assemblage of essays, poems, and mock-heroic narratives about his experiences in America, which was printed only once during Morton's lifetime, by a Dutch printer. Although *New English Canaan* is based upon legal briefs that Morton assembled during his suit against the Massachusetts Bay Company, the text's language is vivid and playful in the style of English court literature of the period, making frequent reference to both classical and modern works, including Homer's *Odyssey* and Cervantes's *Don Quixote*. Morton denounces the Puritans and Pilgrims of New England and exhorts Britain to dominate the American fur trade. He represents America as a pastoral environment, idealizing the rugged landscape and favorably contrasting the culture of the Indigenous peoples with that of his Puritan and Pilgrim rivals. "I have found the Massachusetts Indians more full of humanity than the Christians," Morton writes, "and have had much better quarter with them." Although Morton's descriptions of the Massachusett nation are often to some degree complimentary, they are also frequently inaccurate and rife with presumptions of European cultural superiority, interspersing truthful observations with wild speculations, misinterpretations, and stereotypes.

In 1643, as Puritans took hold of the reins of power in England, Morton left once more for America. He was again arrested and imprisoned, but released after he promised to leave Massachusetts forever. Morton spent the final years of his life in Maine.

New English Canaan was not published in the United States until 1830, but the triumph of the Puritans over Morton's Anglican allies ensured that Morton would be remembered from the seventeenth century onward as a libertine and a lawless rapscallion. For much of the nineteenth century, he was recollected, as Lydia Maria Child phrased it in 1824, as a "thoughtless and dissipated" figure "who had rather dance around the Maypole" than heed the "truths of the gospel." Ma-re Mount figured in the American imaginary as an almost mythical space, about which Nathaniel Hawthorne wrote in his 1837 story "The Maypole of Merrymount." For twentieth- and twenty-first-century scholars, Morton remains a subject of fascination for his resistance to the dominant cultural norms of the Puritans and Pilgrims. He is remarkable among early American writers for his observant, almost loving, descriptions of the natural landscape and Indigenous peoples of New England. "The more I looked the more I liked," Morton reflected. "If this land be not rich, then is the whole world poor."

NOTE ON THE TEXT: The text of the work presented here is based on the 1883 edition published by the Prince Society and edited by Charles Francis Adam Jr.; Jack Dempsey's 1999 edition has also been consulted. Most translations of Massachusett words and phrases are based upon those provided in James Hammond Trumbull's 1903 *Natick Dictionary*. Spelling and punctuation have been modernized in accordance with the practices of this anthology. For ease of reading, names of people and places have also been modernized, and Morton's marginal notes have been removed.

⌘⌘⌘

from *The New English Canaan*

from BOOK 3

CHAPTER 14
OF THE REVELS OF NEW CANAAN

The inhabitants of Passonagessit[1] (having translated the name of their habitation from that ancient savage name to Ma-re Mount,[2] and being resolved to have the new name confirmed for a memorial to after ages) did devise amongst themselves to have it performed in a solemn manner, with revels and merriment after the old English custom; [they] prepared to set up a maypole upon the festival day of Philip and Jacob,[3] and therefore brewed a barrel of excellent beer and provided a case of bottles, to be spent, with other good cheer, for all comers of that day. And because they would have it in a complete form, they had prepared a song fitting to the time and present occasion. And upon May Day they brought the maypole to the place appointed, with drums, guns, pistols and other fitting instruments, for that purpose; and there erected it with the help of savages, that came thither of purpose to see the manner of our revels. A goodly pine tree of 80 foot long was reared up, with a pair of buck horns nailed on somewhat near unto the top of it: where it stood, as a fair sea mark for directions how to find out the way to mine host[4] of Ma-re Mount.

And because it should more fully appear to what end it was placed there, they had a poem in readiness made, which was fixed to the maypole, to show the new name confirmed upon that plantation; which, although it were made according to the occurrents[5] of the time, it, being enigmatically composed, puzzled the Separatists[6] most pitifully to expound it, which (for the better information of the reader) I have here inserted.

THE POEM

Rise Oedipus,[7] and, if thou canst, unfold
What means Charybdis underneath the mold,[8]
When Scylla[9] solitary on the ground
(Sitting in form of Niobe)[10] was found,
Till Amphitrite's darling[11] did acquaint

[1] *The inhabitants of Passonagessit* I.e., Passonagessit's mixed community of European settlers and Indigenous traders.

[2] *having translated ... Ma-re Mount* It is unclear whether, as Morton claims, "Ma-re Mount" is a translation of *Passonagessit*, the Massachusett name for the place. The Massachusett phrase *pasco-naig-és-it* can be translated as "place near the little point"; if *Passonagessit* derives from this phrase, then Ma-re Mount, as an anglicized version of a Latin phrase for "hill by the sea," is a somewhat faithful translation. However, given that Morton consistently misuses or misrepresents Indigenous words and practices, he cannot be trusted on this account. Some scholars have suggested that "Ma-re Mount" evokes multiple layers of puns, often sexual in nature; for example, an allusion to the act of "mounting" may hint at a vulgar union with Mary, the mother of Christ.

[3] *maypole* Wooden pole erected throughout Europe as a sign of rejoicing. The symbol derived from pagan traditions and was thus regarded as idolatrous by Puritans and Pilgrims. In seventeenth-century England, the maypole was at the center of a dispute between royalist cultural conservatives, who viewed the maypole as an English tradition that reinforced the authority of the English crown, and religious cultural reformers, who believed that the maypole was a vulgar practice in need of eradication; *Philip and Jacob* Two of Jesus' apostles. Their feast day is observed in England on the first of May, which is also the date of May Day, a traditional spring celebration with roots in pagan practices.

[4] *mine host* Morton's nickname, which he shares with Shakespeare's character Sir John Falstaff, a notorious womanizer and glutton.

[5] *occurrents* Poetic fashions.

[6] *Separatists* Calvinist Protestants who believed it was necessary to separate from the Church of England; the American branch of Separatists are known as Pilgrims.

[7] *Oedipus* Character in ancient Greek literature who ends a plague by solving the difficult riddle of the Sphinx.

[8] *Charybdis* In ancient Greek mythology, a sea monster (or, in some versions, an enormous whirlpool) who sits opposite another monster, Scylla, on either site of a narrow strait. Morton later suggests that Charybdis was the husband of Scylla, though in most versions of the story they are both women; *mold* Ground.

[9] *Scylla* In some versions of her myth, Scylla was a beautiful woman who refused many suitors until a jealous witch transformed her into a monster; in other versions she was transformed into a dangerous rock.

[10] *Niobe* Figure in ancient Greek myth whose children were killed by the gods; in some versions of the story, she then turned to stone. Algonquian legend also features a woman transformed to stone while grieving the death of her children: Squant, who turned into a seaside cliff near Ma-re Mount.

[11] *Amphitrite* Ancient Greek goddess of the sea; *Amphitrite's darling* Probably Aphrodite, ancient Greek goddess of love, who was born from sea foam.

Grim Neptune[1] with the tenor of her plaint,
And caused him send forth Triton[2] with the sound
Of trumpet loud, at which the seas were found
So full of Protean[3] forms that the bold shore
10 Presented Scylla a new paramour[4]
So strong as Samson[5] and so patient
As Job[6] himself—directed thus, by fate,
To comfort Scylla so unfortunate.
I do profess, by Cupid's beauteous mother,[7]
15 Here's Scogan's choice[8] for Scylla, and none other;
Though Scylla's sick with grief, because no sign
Can there be found of virtue masculine.
Esculapius[9] come; I know right well
His labour's lost when you may ring her knell.
20 The fatal sisters'[10] doom none can withstand,
Nor Citharea's[11] power, who points to land
With proclamation that the first of May
At Ma-re Mount shall be kept holiday.

The setting up of this Maypole was a lamentable
spectacle to the precise Separatists that lived at new
Plymouth. They termed it an idol; yea, they called
it the Calf of Horeb,[12] and stood at defiance with the
place, naming it Mount Dagon;[13] threatening to make
it a woeful mount and not a merry mount.

The riddle, for want of Oedipus, they could not
expound; only they made some explication of part of
it, and said by it was meant Sampson Job, the carpenter
of the ship that brought over a woman to her husband,
that had been there long before and thrived so well that
he sent for her and her children to come to him; where
shortly after he died: having no reason, but because of
the sound of those two words;[14] when as (the truth is)
the man they applied it to was altogether unknown to
the author.

There was likewise a merry song made, which (to
make their revels more fashionable) was sung with a
chorus, every man bearing his part; which they per-
formed in a dance, hand in hand about the maypole,
whiles one of the company sung and filled out the
good liquor, like Ganymede and Jupiter.[15]

THE SONG

Drink and be merry, merry, merry boys;
Let all your delight be in Hymen's[16] joys;
Io[17] to Hymen, now the day is come,
About the merry maypole take room.
5 Make green garlands, bring bottles out
And fill sweet nectar[18] freely about.
Uncover thy head and fear no harm

[1] *Neptune* Possible allusion to James I (r. England 1603–25), who was represented as Neptune in Ben Jonson's masque *Neptune's Triumph for the Return of Albion* (unperformed, written 1624).

[2] *Triton* Son of Amphitrite and Poseidon, the ancient Greek equivalent of Neptune; he also acts as Poseidon's herald.

[3] *Protean* I.e., various, changeable; a reference to Proteus, a shape-changing ocean-dweller of classical myth.

[4] *paramour* Lover.

[5] *Samson* Biblical figure renowned for his strength. Samson, an Israelite, loves Delilah, who betrays him to the Philistines, enemies of his people; in response, he destroys the Philistine temple. See Judges 14–16.

[6] *Job* Biblical figure who endures a series of extreme misfortunes. See Job 1–42.

[7] *Cupid's beauteous mother* Venus, the Roman equivalent of Aphrodite.

[8] *Scogan's choice* John Scogan was the court fool of Edward IV. He was said to have been sentenced to hang but permitted to choose the tree upon which his hanging would take place: he was spared execution after he was unable to find a satisfactory tree. "Scogan's choice" thus refers to a choice among a limited range of bad options.

[9] *Esculapius* Asclepius, ancient Greek god of medicine. According to some accounts, he was capable of resurrecting the dead.

[10] *fatal sisters* In ancient Greek mythology, three sisters known as the Fates determined the life spans of all living beings.

[11] *Citharea* Aphrodite.

[12] *Calf of Horeb* Golden idol in the shape of a calf to which biblical Israelites prayed, breaking the commandments given to them by God. See Exodus 32.1–8 and Psalm 106.19–20.

[13] *Mount Dagon* Dagon was a Mesopotamian god of fertility, who was worshipped by the Philistines, a nation depicted in the Bible as one of the foremost antagonists of the Ancient Israelites.

[14] *because … two words* I.e., the Pilgrims mistakenly believed that part of the poem was about Sampson Job, a carpenter on one of the ships that carried settlers from England to America, because of the references to Samson and Job in the poem.

[15] *Ganymede* Cup-bearer to the gods in Ancient Greek mythology, and the most beautiful of all mortals; *Jupiter* King of the gods in ancient Roman mythology. Jupiter abducted Ganymede and granted him immortality because of his beauty.

[16] *Hymen* Ancient Greek god of marriage.

[17] *Io* Joyful exclamation appearing in classical poetry.

[18] *nectar* Drink of the gods in classical mythology.

For here's good liquor to keep it warm.

Then drink and be merry, etc.

10 Io to Hymen, etc.

Nectar is a thing assigned

By the deity's own mind

To cure the heart oppressed with grief,

And of good liquors is the chief.

15 Then drink, etc.

Io to Hymen, etc.

Give to the melancholy man

A cup or two of 't now and then;

This physic[1] will soon revive his blood,

20 And make him be of a merrier mood.

Then drink, etc.

Io to Hymen, etc.

Give to the nymph that's free from scorn

No Irish stuff nor Scotch over worn.[2]

25 Lasses in beaver coats come away,

Ye shall be welcome to us night and day.

To drink and be merry, etc.

Io to Hymen, etc.

This harmless mirth[3] made by young men (that lived in hope to have wives brought over to them, that would save them a labour to make a voyage to fetch any over) was much distasted of the precise Separatists, that keep much ado about the tithe of mint and cumin,[4] troubling their brains more than reason would require about things that are indifferent:[5] and from that time sought occasion against my honest host of Ma-re Mount, to overthrow his undertakings and to destroy his plantation quite and clean.[6] But because they presumed with their imaginary gifts (which they have out of Phao's

box)[7] they could expound hidden mysteries, to convince them of blindness, as well in this as in other matters of more consequence, I will illustrate the poem, according to the true intent of the authors of these revels, so much distasted by those moles.[8]

Oedipus is generally received for the absolute reader of riddles, who is invoked: Scylla and Charybdis are two dangerous places for seamen to encounter, near unto Venice; and have been by poets formerly resembled to man and wife. The like license the author challenged for a pair of his nomination, the one lamenting for the loss of the other as Niobe for her children. Amphitrite is an arm of the sea, by which the news was carried up and down of a rich widow, now to be taken up or laid down. By Triton is the fame spread that caused the suitors to muster, (as it had been to Penelope of Greece)[9] and, the coast lying circular, all our passage to and fro is made more convenient by sea than land. Many aimed at this mark; but he that played Proteus best and could comply with her humor must be the man that would carry her; and he had need have Sampson's strength to deal with a Delilah, and as much patience as Job that should come there, for a thing that I did observe in the life-time of the former.[10]

But marriage and hanging (they say) comes by destiny and Scogan's choice tis better [than] none at all. He that played Proteus (with the help of Priapus)[11] put their noses out of joint, as the proverb is.

And this the whole company of the revelers at Ma-re Mount knew to be the true sense and exposition of the riddle that was fixed to the maypole, which the Separatists were at defiance with. Some of them affirmed that the first institution thereof was in memory of a whore;[12] not knowing that it was a trophy

[1] *physic* Medicine.

[2] *Irish stuff* Fabric made in Ireland; *Scotch* Fabric made in Scotland; *over worn* Worn out.

[3] *harmless mirth* I.e., couplings of European traders and Indigenous women.

[4] *the tithe of mint and cumin* I.e., every insignificant detail. See Matthew 23.23: "Woe unto you, scribes and Pharisees, hypocrites! For ye pay tithe of mint and anise and cumin, and have omitted the weightier matters of the law, judgment, mercy and faith."

[5] *indifferent* Of no consequence, unimportant.

[6] *quite and clean* Completely.

[7] *Phao's box* In classical myth, Phao obtains an ointment that makes him appear to be much more attractive than he actually is.

[8] *moles* Proverbially blind animals.

[9] *Penelope of Greece* Wife of Odysseus, the protagonist of Homer's *Odyssey*; she is beset by many suitors when Odysseus is presumed dead.

[10] *the former* Probably, the rich widow's former husband.

[11] *Priapus* Ancient Greek god of livestock and male genitalia.

[12] *a whore* I.e., Flora, an ancient Roman fertility goddess whose celebrations involved a dance performed by prostitutes. Early Christians claimed that Flora herself was a prostitute who became so wealthy she was worshipped as a god (see Lactantius's *Divine Institutes* 20).

erected at first in honor of Maja,[1] the Lady of Learning which they despise, vilifying the two universities[2] with uncivil terms, accounting what is there obtained by study is but unnecessary learning; not considering that learning does enable men's minds to converse with elements of a higher nature than is to be found within the habitation of the mole.

CHAPTER 15
OF A GREAT MONSTER SUPPOSED TO BE AT MA-RE-MOUNT; AND THE PREPARATION MADE TO DESTROY IT

The Separatists, envying the prosperity and hope of the plantation at Ma-re Mount (which they perceived began to come forward, and to be in a good way for gain in the beaver trade), conspired together against mine host especially (who was the owner of that plantation) and made up a party against him; and mustered up what aid they could, accounting of him as of a great monster.

Many threatening speeches were given out both against his person and his habitation, which they divulged should be consumed with fire: And taking advantage of the time when his company (which seemed little to regard their threats) were gone up into the inlands to trade with the savages for beaver, they set upon my honest host at a place called Wessaguscus,[3] where, by accident,[4] they found him. The inhabitants there were in good hope of the subversion of the plantation at Ma-re Mount (which they principally aimed at) and the rather because my host was a man that endeavored to advance the dignity of the Church of England;[5] which they (on the contrary part) would labour to vilify with uncivil terms: envying[6] against

the sacred Book of Common Prayer, and my host that used it in a laudable[7] manner amongst his family, as a practice of piety.

There he would be a means to bring sacks to their mill (such is the thirst after beaver) and helped the conspirators to surprise mine host (who was there all alone), and they charged him, (because they would seem to have some reasonable cause against him to set a gloss upon[8] their malice) with criminal things; which indeed had been done by such a person, but was of their conspiracy; mine host demanded of the conspirators who it was that was author of that information, that seemed to be their ground for what they now intended. And because they answered they would not tell him, he as peremptorily replied, that he would not say whether he had, or he had not done as they had been informed.

The answer made no matter (as it seemed) whether it had been negatively or affirmatively made; for they had resolved what he would suffer, because (as they boasted) they were now become the greater number: they had shaken off their shackles of servitude, and were become masters and masterless people. It appears they were like bears' whelps in former time, when mine host's plantation was of as much strength as theirs, but now (theirs being stronger) they (like overgrown bears) seemed monstrous. In brief, mine host must endure to be their prisoner until they could contrive it so that they might send him for England (as they said), there to suffer according to the merit of the fact which they intended to father upon him; supposing (belike) it would prove a heinous crime.

Much rejoicing was made that they had gotten their capital enemy (as they concluded him), whom they purposed to hamper in such sort that he should not be able to uphold his plantation at Ma-re Mount. The conspirators sported themselves at my honest host, that meant them no hurt, and were so jocund[9] that

[1] *Maja* Maia was the mother of Hermes, an ancient Greek god associated with learning, among many other attributes; she was celebrated during the month of May, which some have suggested was named for her.

[2] *two universities* Oxford and Cambridge, universities at which classical literature was studied.

[3] *Wessaguscus* Location near Ma-re Mount that came to be known as Weymouth, Massachusetts, by English settlers.

[4] *accident* Chance.

[5] *my host ... of England* I.e., Morton was an Anglican.

[6] *envying* Holding resentment.

[7] *laudable* Pun on the name of William Laud (1573–1645), the Archbishop of Canterbury, one of the principal religious enemies of the Puritans and Separatists, and the head of the commission to which Morton and his allies lobbied to have the charter of the Massachusetts Bay Company revoked.

[8] *set a gloss upon* Explain.

[9] *jocund* Cheerful.

they feasted their bodies, and fell to tippling[1] as if they had obtained a great prize; like the Trojans when they had the custody of Epeius's pine-tree horse.[2] Mine host feigned grief, and could not be persuaded either to eat or drink; because he knew emptiness would be a means to make him as watchful as the geese kept in the Roman Capital:[3] whereon, the contrary part, the conspirators would be so drowsy that he might have an opportunity to give them a slip, instead of a tester.[4] Six persons of the conspiracy were set to watch mine host at Wessaguscus: But he kept waking; and in the dead of night (one lying on the bed for further surety), up gets mine host and got to the second door that he was to pass, which, notwithstanding the lock, he got open, and shut it after him with such violence that it affrighted some of the conspirators. The word, which was given with an alarm, was, he's gone, he's gone, what shall we do, he's gone! The rest (half asleep) start up in a maze,[5] and, like rams, ran their heads one at another full butt in the dark.

Their grand leader, Captain Shrimp,[6] took on most fury. The Captain ripped and tore his clothes for anger, to see the empty nest, and their bird gone. The rest were eager to have torn their hair from their heads; but it was so short that it would give them no hold.[7] Now Captain Shrimp thought in the loss of this prize (which he accounted his masterpiece) all his honor would be lost forever. In the meantime mine host was got home to Ma-re Mount through the woods, eight miles round about the head of the river Monatoquit that parted the two plantations, finding his way by the help of the lightning (for it thundered as he went terribly), and there he prepared powder, three pounds dried, for his present employment, and four good guns for him and the two assistants left at his house with bullets of several sizes, three hundred or thereabouts, to be used if the conspirators should pursue him thither. And these two persons promised their aid in the quarrel, and confirmed that promise with health in good *rosa solis*.[8]

Now Captain Shrimp, the first Captain in the Land (as he supposed), must do some new act to repair this loss and to vindicate his reputation, which had sustained blemish by this oversight, begins now to study, how to repair or survive his honor: in this manner, calling of council, they conclude.

He takes eight persons more to him, and (like the nine worthies[9] of New Canaan) they embark with preparation against Ma-re-Mount, where this monster of a man, as their phrase was, had his den. The whole number, had the rest not been from home, being but seven, would have given Captain Shrimp (a quondam drummer)[10] such a welcome as would have made him wish for a drum as big as Diogenes's tub,[11] that he might have crept into it out of sight. Now the nine worthies are approached, and mine host prepared: having intelligence by a savage, that hastened in love from Wessaguscus to give him notice of their intent. One of mine host's men proved a craven: the other had proved his wits to purchase a little valor, before mine host had observed his posture.

The nine worthies coming before the den of this supposed monster (this seven headed hydra,[12] as they termed him) and began, like Don Quixote[13] against the windmill, to beat a parley, and to offer quarter, if

1 *tippling* Drinking alcohol excessively.

2 *Epeius's pine-tree horse* The Trojan War of ancient Greek myth concluded when the Greek Epeius built a wooden horse in which he and other soldiers hid. After the Trojans brought the horse into their stronghold, thinking it to be a gift, the Greek soldiers emerged and slaughtered them.

3 *geese kept ... Roman Capital* Ancient Roman legend held that in 390 BCE, an attack upon Rome by the Gauls was foiled when the geese on Capitoline Hill alerted the Roman defenders.

4 *give them ... of a tester* Pun on "slip," which refers to escape but also means "counterfeit coin." A tester is a coin of small value.

5 *maze* Disoriented state.

6 *Captain Shrimp* Myles Standish (c. 1584–1656), the military leader of the Pilgrims at Plymouth; Morton's nickname likely refers to his short height and pink skin tone.

7 *it was ... no hold* Separatists considered it shamefully immodest for men to have long hair.

8 *rosa solis* Liqueur flavored with the sundew plant.

9 *nine worthies* Nine heroes considered by medieval Europeans to be exemplary in virtue.

10 *quondam drummer* Occasional drummer.

11 *Diogenes's tub* Diogenes famously slept outdoors in a large storage jar (in later retellings, a tub).

12 *hydra* Many-headed monster in Greek myth who would grow two new heads after one had been sliced off.

13 *Don Quixote* Protagonist of Cervantes's *Don Quixote*. Having lost his mind, Don Quixote imagines himself to be a knight and attempts to joust with windmills, believing them to be giants.

mine host would yield; for they resolved to send him for England and had him lay by his arms.

But he (who was the son of a soldier), having taken up arms in his just defense, replied that he would not lay by those arms, because they were so needful at sea, if he should be sent over. Yet, to save the effusion of so much worthy blood, as would have issued out of the veins of these 9 worthies of New Canaan, if mine host should have played upon them out at his port holes (for they came within danger like a flock of wild geese, as if they had been tailed[1] one to another, as colts to be sold at a fair), mine host was content to yield upon quarter; and did capitulate with them in what manner it should be for more certainty, because he knew what Captain Shrimp was.

He expressed that no violence should be offered to his person, none to his goods, nor any of his household but that he should have his arms and what else was requisite for the voyage, which, their herald returns,[2] it was agreed upon and should be performed.

But mine host no sooner had felt open the door, and issued out, but instantly Captain Shrimp and the rest of the worthies stepped to him, laid hold of his arms, and had him down: and so eagerly was every man bent against him (not regarding any agreement made with such a carnal man) that they fell upon him as if they would have eaten him: some of them were so violent that they would have a slice with scabbard and all for haste; until an old soldier (of the Queen's,[3] as the proverb is) that was there by accident, clapped his gun under the weapons and sharply rebuked these worthies for their unworthy practices. So the matter was taken into more deliberate consideration. Captain Shrimp, and the rest of the nine worthies, made themselves (by this outrageous riot) masters of mine host of Ma-re Mount, and disposed of what he had at his plantation. This they knew (in the eye of the savages) would add to their glory, and diminish the reputation of mine honest host, whom they practiced[4] to be rid of

upon any terms, as willingly as if he had been the very hydra of the time.

CHAPTER 16
HOW THE NINE WORTHIES PUT MINE HOST OF MA-RE-MOUNT INTO THE ENCHANTED CASTLE AT PLYMOUTH, AND TERRIFIED HIM WITH THE MONSTER BRIAREUS[5]

The nine worthies of New Canaan having now the law in their own hands (there being no general governor in the land; nor none of the Separation that regarded the duty they owe their sovereign, whose natural born subjects they were, though translated out of Holland,[6] from whence they had learned to work all to their own ends, and make a great show of religion, but no humanity) for they were now to sit in council on the cause.

And much it stood mine honest host upon to be very circumspect, and to take Eacus[7] to task for that his voice was more allowed of than both the other: and had not mine host confounded all the arguments that Eacus could make in their defence, and confuted him that swayed the rest, they would have made him unable to drink in such manner of merriment any more. So that following this private counsel, given him by one that knew who ruled the rest, the hurricane ceased that else would split his pinnace.[8]

A conclusion was made and sentence given that mine host should be sent to England a prisoner. But when he was brought to the ships for that purpose, no man durst be so foolhardy as to undertake carry him. So these worthies set mine host upon an island,[9] without gun, powder, or shot or dog or so much as a knife to get anything to feed upon, or any other

1 *tailed* Tied by the tail.

2 *returns* Reports; *their herald returns* I.e., according to the messenger sent by Standish.

3 *of the Queen's* I.e., from the generation that served under Queen Elizabeth I.

4 *practiced* Schemed.

5 *BRIAREUS* Giant, hundred-handed monster of Greek mythology.

6 *none of … their sovereign* None among the Separatists who considered James I their king; *translated out of Holland* Before journeying to America, the Pilgrims had attempted to settle in the Netherlands.

7 *Eacus* In Greek mythology, Eacus was one of the three judges in Hades, the land of the dead. Morton may be using the name to refer to Samuel Fuller (c. 1580–1633), a Pilgrim physician and deacon.

8 *pinnace* Small boat.

9 *upon an island* Morton was abandoned on the Isles of Shoals off the coast of New Hampshire.

clothes to shelter him with at winter than a thin suit which he had on at that time. Home he could not get to Ma-re Mount. Upon this Island he stayed a month at least, and was relieved by savages that took notice that mine host was a sachem of Pasonagessit, and would bring bottles of strong liquor to him, and unite themselves into a league of brotherhood with mine host; so full of humanity are these infidels before those Christians. From this place for England sailed mine host in a Plymouth ship (that came into the land to fish upon the coast) that landed him safe in England at Plymouth: and he stayed in England until the ordinary time for shipping to set forth for these parts, and then returned: no man being able to tax him of anything. But the worthies (in the meantime) hoped they had been rid of him.

—1637

JOHN WINTHROP
1588 – 1649

As governor of the newly formed Massachusetts Bay Colony, John Winthrop famously envisaged the community as a "city upon a hill" to be observed by all, and with the potential to become such "a praise and glory that men shall say of succeeding plantations, 'may the Lord make it like that of New England.'" A lawyer, Puritan lay theologian, and civil magistrate, Winthrop was recognized during his lifetime not as a writer but as a political figure who had an outsized effect upon the early development of colonial New England. He had a role in many of the religious and political controversies that marked the fledgling years of New England's colonization—controversies that continue to resonate within American society, on subjects from religion and the state to the ideal balance between personal freedom and social responsibility. In the centuries following Winthrop's death, his writing came to be appreciated for its articulation of a Puritan worldview, and for its contributions to the historical record of early New England.

Winthrop was born in a rural English village in 1588 to devout Calvinist parents, his father the younger son of a minor landowning family. Winthrop had a comfortable upbringing and a rigorous education, and at age fourteen he gained admittance to Trinity College in Cambridge, intending to become a minister. This education was interrupted at seventeen, when he married Mary Forth; he later turned his attention to studying law. He would outlive three wives, marrying Thomasine Clopton in 1615, Margaret Tyndal in 1618, and Martha Rainsborough in 1648; among them, his wives would bear sixteen children, only half of whom lived to adulthood.

In 1613, Winthrop came into ownership of his family's estate in Groton, Suffolk—lands which had been expropriated from the Catholic Church and sold to Winthrop's grandfather—where he served as Lord of the Manor. Winthrop felt a calling to participate in public life, reflecting that "surer peace and joy in Christianity must not aim at a condition retired from the world." In 1615 he was appointed to the Suffolk Commission of the Peace, and in 1627 he was named attorney for the Court of Wards.

During this time, Winthrop grew increasingly concerned with the kingdom's spiritual welfare. Like other Puritans, he was alarmed by the policies of James I and his successor Charles I, both of whom had shifted the Church of England away from Calvinist orthodoxy. Winthrop became convinced that it would be necessary to emigrate from England in order to live a godly life. By 1629, he was meeting with the Massachusetts Bay Company, a group of Puritans who had already begun to establish their own commonwealth in America. Winthrop quickly rose to prominence within the company and in October 1629 was elected governor. The following year, on a ship with about 700 fellow emigrants, he set sail for America to assume command of the colony itself.

Tradition holds that while en route to the colony, Winthrop delivered the inspirational lay sermon *A Model of Christian Charity*, which includes his description of the American colony as "a city upon a hill." The ideas in *A Model of Christian Charity* were not particularly groundbreaking to Winthrop's audience, and the sermon was not remarked upon by his contemporaries—or even by Winthrop himself in his journals. This makes it difficult if not impossible to confirm the date of the sermon's composition and delivery—if indeed he ever delivered it—and some scholars have questioned whether Winthrop was even the sermon's author, positing such figures as the minister George Phillips, his fellow passenger, as more likely candidates. Though the text circulated among some readers during Winthrop's lifetime, no seventeenth-century response hints at the impact the sermon would have in later centuries.

Winthrop ultimately served as Governor of Massachusetts for twelve non-consecutive annual terms during the colony's first two decades. His leadership was instrumental in bringing the first large waves of English settlers into the Massachusetts Bay Colony. In his role as a colonial leader, Winthrop participated in numerous political and theological clashes, many of them involving dissenters such as Thomas Morton, Roger Williams, and Anne Hutchinson. Winthrop was neither the most nor the least tolerant colonial leader in New England at the time: while he despised what he called their "dangerous errors" in matters of religion, he nevertheless professed respect for the "bold spirit" and "godl[iness]" of radical figures such as Williams and Hutchinson. Winthrop's chief concern was to preserve the cohesion of the Puritan commonwealth, and believed that it was necessary "to entertain all means that may conduce to [its] welfare … and to keep off whatever appears to tend to [its] damage."

In addition to the colony's internal social and religious crises, Winthrop was involved in conflicts between the colonists and the Indigenous nations of the region: the colony occupied territory that belonged to Massachusett, Nipmuc, and other Algonquian-speaking peoples. Relations between the settlers and Indigenous people were relatively friendly in the first few years, during which Winthrop entertained a few Algonquian leaders at his home but had little sustained communication with them. The Pequot War of 1636–38, however, demanded a greater degree of diplomacy; Winthrop appealed to Roger Williams, who convinced the Narragansett people to join the fight against their traditional rivals, the Pequot, in an alliance that also included the Mohegan and all the other New England colonies. At the conclusion of the Pequot War, Winthrop oversaw the enslavement of Pequot captives, some of whom were kept by the victors (including Winthrop himself), while others were exchanged in Barbados for enslaved people from Africa.

Throughout the decades he spent in the government of the Massachusetts Bay Colony, Winthrop kept a journal. He began the project as he crossed the Atlantic, intending to record his experience of the journey so he could tell later waves of settlers what to expect. He then decided to continue the journal as a record of the colony's foundation; gradually the journal developed from an up-to-the-minute diary into a work more closely resembling a historical account. By the second volume, Winthrop's notes indicate that he had come to consider his project to be a sacred history documenting the suffering and eventual triumph of God's "subjects and soldiers." The work was thus part of a tradition of earlier Christian historians such as the English Protestant John Foxe, whose *Acts and Monuments* (1563), commonly known as the *Book of Martyrs* for its focus on the persecution of righteous Christians, was beloved by Puritan readers.

Winthrop's journal includes a wealth of information not found in the colony's official records, including the details of political controversies too sensitive for official documentation. Given the spiritual purpose of his task, Winthrop strove to be candid, and this often makes the journal both engaging and informative—though it is by no means unbiased, as he often takes great pains to justify his political decisions and show his opponents to have been in the wrong. Winthrop, who died in March 1649 after a lengthy illness, worked on the journal right up until the last weeks of his life, when he became too ill to write.

None of the writing for which Winthrop would come to be remembered was in circulation at the time of his death. Though later portions of his journal seem to have been intended for wider readership, the work did not appear in print until 1790, when the first two of his three journal notebooks were published. In 1825/26, after the third was rediscovered, all three volumes were released under the title *Winthrop's Journal, The History of New England from 1630–1649*. Winthrop's account began to shape conceptions of American history even before its first printing—the manuscript was frequently lent out to scholars of New England history—and since its publication it has been more widely considered invaluable as a historical record. *A Model of Christian Charity* remained unpublished even longer, finally appearing in print in 1838, while Winthrop's other writings were published as the *Winthrop Papers* in 1929–47.

In the early eighteenth century, Winthrop was lionized as a historical and spiritual figure; in 1702, fellow Puritan Cotton Mather praised him for "a certain *greatness of soul*, which rendered him grave, generous, courageous, resolved, well-applied, and every way a *gentleman* in his demeanour." More recently, his popular image has been more complex; he is envisioned by some as a repressive authoritarian, and by others as a pragmatic moderate within the context of the seventeenth-century Puritan political spectrum.

A major contributor to his enduring reputation is the rise in popularity of *A Model of Christian Charity*, which since the mid-twentieth century has been required reading for many students of American history and literature. Now often invoked as an early example of American exceptionalism, Winthrop's characterization of his colony as a "city upon a hill" continues to strike a deep patriotic chord, and twentieth-century American leaders such as John F. Kennedy and Ronald Reagan quoted the phrase in their own speeches.

NOTE ON THE TEXT: This text of *A Model of Christian Charity* is based upon the 1838 version published by the Massachusetts Historical Society. Biblical references are taken from the 1599 Geneva Bible, the translation of the Christian scriptures that Winthrop would have used.

⌘ ⌘ ⌘

A Model of Christian Charity

God Almighty, in his most holy and wise providence,[1] hath so disposed of the condition of mankind, as in all times some must be rich, some poor, some high and eminent in power and dignity; others mean and in submission.

THE REASON HEREOF

1 *Reas.*[2] First, to hold conformity with the rest of his world, being delighted to show forth the glory of his wisdom in the variety and difference of the creatures,[3] and the glory of his power in ordering all these differences for the preservation and good of the whole, and the glory of his greatness, that as it is the glory of princes to have many officers, so this great king will have many stewards, counting himself more honored in dispensing his gifts to man by man, than if he did it by his own immediate hands.

2 *Reas.* Secondly, that he might have the more occasion to manifest the work of his Spirit: first upon the wicked in moderating and restraining them, so that the rich and mighty should not eat up the poor, nor the poor and despised rise up against and shake off their yoke. Secondly, in the regenerate,[4] in exercising his graces in them, as in the great ones, their love, mercy, gentleness, temperance etc., in the poor and inferior sort, their faith, patience, obedience, etc.

3 *Reas.* Thirdly, that every man might have need of others, and from hence they might be all knit more nearly together in the bonds of brotherly affection. From hence it appears plainly that no man is made more honorable than another or more wealthy etc., out of any particular and singular respect to himself, but for the glory of his creator and the common good of the creature, man. Therefore God still reserves the property of these gifts to himself as [in] Ezekiel 16.17.[5] He there calls wealth, "his gold and his silver," and Proverbs 3.9,[6] he claims their service as his due, "Honor the Lord with thy riches," etc.—all men being thus (by divine providence) ranked into two sorts, rich and poor; under the first are comprehended all such as are able to live comfortably by their own means duly improved; and all others are poor according to the former distribution.

There are two rules whereby we are to walk one towards another: justice and mercy. These are always distinguished in their act and in their object, yet may they both concur in the same subject in each respect; as sometimes there may be an occasion of showing mercy to a rich man in some sudden danger or distress, and

1 *providence* Divine control and foreknowledge.

2 *Reas.* Reason.

3 *creatures* Created beings.

4 *the regenerate* Those saved, or reborn, through the sacrifice of Jesus Christ.

5 *Ezekiel 16.17* "Thou hast also taken thy fair jewels of my gold and of my silver, which I had given thee, and madest to thyself images of men, and didst commit whoredom with them."

6 *Proverbs 3.9* "Honour the Lord with thy riches, and with the first fruits of all thine increase."

also doing of mere justice to a poor man in regard of some particular contract, etc.

There is likewise a double law by which we are regulated in our conversation[1] towards another: in both the former respects, the law of nature and the law of grace, or the moral law or the law of the gospel, to omit the rule of justice as not properly belonging to this purpose otherwise than it may fall into consideration in some particular cases. By the first of these laws, man as he was enabled so withal is commanded to love his neighbor as himself.[2] Upon this ground stands all the precepts of the moral law, which concerns our dealings with men. To apply this to the works of mercy, this law requires two things. First, that every man afford his help to another in every want or distress; secondly, that he perform this out of the same affection which makes him careful of his own goods, according to the words of our Savior (Matthew 7.12): "whatsoever ye would that men should do to you."[3] This was practiced by Abraham and Lot in entertaining the angels and the old man of Gibeah.[4]

The law of grace or of the gospel hath some difference from the former (the law of nature), as in these respects: First, the law of nature was given to man in the estate of innocence—this of the gospel in the estate of regeneracy.[5] Secondly, the former propounds one man to another, as the same flesh and image of God. This as a brother in Christ also, and in the communion of the same Spirit, and so teacheth to put a difference between Christians and others. "Do good to all, especially to the household of faith."[6] Upon this ground the Israelites were to put a difference between the brethren of such as were strangers, though not of the Canaanites.[7]

Thirdly, the law of nature would give no rules for dealing with enemies, for all are to be considered as friends in the state of innocence, but the gospel commands love to an enemy. Proof: "If thine enemy hunger, feed him; Love your enemies, do good to them that hate you." Matthew 5.44.[8]

This law of the gospel propounds likewise a difference of seasons and occasions. There is a time when a Christian must sell all and give to the poor, as they did in the Apostles' times.[9] There is a time also when Christians (though they give not all yet) must give beyond their ability, as they of Macedonia, 2 Corinthians 8.[10] Likewise, community of perils calls for extraordinary liberality, and so doth community in some special service for the church. Lastly, when there is no other means whereby our Christian brother may be relieved in his distress, we must help him beyond our ability rather than tempt God in putting him upon[11] help by miraculous or extraordinary means.

This duty of mercy is exercised in the kinds:[12] giving, lending and forgiving.[13]

Question: What rule shall a man observe in giving in respect of the measure?

[1] *conversation* Way of behaving in society.

[2] *love his neighbor as himself* See Matthew 19.19: "Honour thy father, and mother: and, Thou shalt love thy neighbour as thyself"; and Matthew 5.43: "Ye have heard that it hath been said, Thou shalt love thy neighbour, and hate thine enemy."

[3] *whatsoever ye … to you* See Matthew 7.12: "Therefore whatsoever ye would that men should do to you: even so do ye to them: for this is the Law and the Prophets."

[4] *Abraham … of Gibeah* In Genesis 18, Abraham is a gracious host to three angels who visit him in human form. In Genesis 19, Abraham's nephew Lot hosts two angels, whom he defends from an angry mob, offering his own daughters to the mob in place of his guests. Judges 19 includes the story of an old man in Gibeah who similarly shelters travelers and defends them from a horde of "wicked" people, offering his own daughter to placate them.

[5] *estate of innocence* I.e., state before original sin; *estate of regeneracy* I.e., state of salvation through Christ.

[6] *Do good … of faith* See Galatians 6.10.

[7] *Canaanites* People of Canaan, the Promised Land of the Israelites, who were expelled upon the Israelites' arrival. God instructed the Israelites to have "no compassion" for the Canaanites, and to "utterly destroy them." See Deuteronomy 7.1–4.

[8] *Matthew 5.44* The full text reads, "But I say unto you, Love your enemies, bless them that curse you, do good to them that hate you, and pray for them which hurt you, and persecute you."

[9] *There is a time … Apostles' times* See Luke 18.22, where Jesus tells a rich man seeking eternal life to "Sell all that ever thou hast, and distribute unto the poor, and thou shalt have treasure in heaven, and come follow me."

[10] *2 Corinthians 8* Winthrop refers to verses 1–3: "We do you also to wit, brethren, of the grace of God bestowed upon the Churches of Macedonia. Because in great trial of affliction their joy abounded, and their most extreme poverty abounded unto their rich liberality. For to their power (I bear record) yea, and beyond their power they were willing."

[11] *putting him upon* I.e., forcing our brother to rely upon.

[12] *kinds* Categories.

[13] *forgiving* I.e., of a debt.

Answer: If the time and occasion be ordinary he is to give out of his abundance. "Let him lay aside as God hath blessed him."[1] If the time and occasion be extraordinary, he must be ruled by them; taking this withal, that then a man cannot likely do too much, especially if he may leave himself and his family under probable means of comfortable subsistence.

Objection: A man must lay up for posterity, the fathers lay up for posterity and children, and he is worse than an infidel that provideth not for his own.[2]

Answer: For the first, it is plain that it being spoken by way of comparison, it must be meant of the ordinary and usual course of fathers, and cannot extend to times and occasions extraordinary. For the other place the Apostle[3] speaks against such as walked[4] inordinately, and it is without question, that he is worse than an infidel who through his own sloth and voluptuousness shall neglect to provide for his family.

Objection: "The wise man's eyes are in his head," saith Solomon,[5] "and foreseeth the plague"; therefore he must forecast and lay up against evil times when he or his may stand in need of all he can gather.

Answer: This very argument Solomon useth to persuade to liberality (Ecclesiastes 11[6]), "Cast thy bread upon the waters ... for thou knowest not what evil may come upon the land." Luke [16.9], "Make you friends of the riches of iniquity ..."[7] You will ask how this

shall be? Very well. For first he that gives to the poor, lends to the Lord[8] and he will repay him even in this life an hundredfold to him or his. "The righteous is ever merciful and lendeth, and his seed enjoyeth the blessing,"[9] and besides we know what advantage it will be to us in the day of account when many such witnesses shall stand forth for us to witness the improvement of our talent.[10] And I would know of those who plead so much for laying up for time to come, whether they hold that to be gospel Matthew [6.19],[11] "Lay not up for yourselves treasures upon earth," etc. If they acknowledge it, what extent will they allow it? If only to those primitive[12] times, let them consider the reason whereupon our Savior grounds it. The first is that they are subject to the moth, the rust, the thief. Secondly, they will steal away the heart: "where the treasure is there will your heart be also."

The reasons are of like force at all times. Therefore the exhortation must be general and perpetual, withallways in respect of the love and affection to riches and in regard of the things themselves when any special service for the church or particular distress of our brother do call for the use of them; otherwise it is not only lawful but necessary to lay up as Joseph did[13] to have ready upon such occasions, as the Lord (whose stewards we are of them) shall call for them from us. Christ gives us an instance of the first, when he sent his disciples for the donkey, and bids them answer the

[1] *Let him ... blessed him* See 1 Corinthians 16.2.

[2] *he is worse ... his own* See 1 Timothy 5.8; *infidel* Unbeliever.

[3] *Apostle* St. Paul, traditionally considered the author of many books of the New Testament, including 1 Timothy.

[4] *walked* Lived one's life. See Ephesians 5.15: "Take heed therefore that ye walk circumspectly, not as fools, but as wise."

[5] *Solomon* King of Israel who is traditionally considered the author of Ecclesiastes and a contributor to Proverbs. See Ecclesiastes 2.14 and Proverbs 22.3 for the passages quoted.

[6] *Ecclesiastes 11* See Ecclesiastes 11.1–2: "Cast thy bread upon the waters: for after many days thou shalt find it. Give a portion to seven, and also to eight: for thou knowest not what evil shall be upon the earth."

[7] *Make you ... iniquity* See Luke 16.9: "Make you friends with the riches of iniquity, that when ye shall want, they may receive you into everlasting habitations." This statement follows the parable of a steward who is about to lose his position keeping his master's accounts; the steward alters the records to reduce the debts owed to his master, thus ensuring that he will be taken in by his master's debtors.

[8] *he that gives ... Lord* See Proverbs 19.17: "He that hath mercy upon the poor, lendeth unto the Lord: and the Lord will recompense him that which he hath given."

[9] *The righteous ... the blessing* See Psalms 37.26.

[10] *improvement of our talent* Increase of our riches and wealth. See Matthew 25.14–30, a parable in which a master gives each of his servants coins; he rewards the servants who increase their wealth by lending it and punishes the one who hoards it instead.

[11] *Matthew [6.19]* See Matthew 6.19–21: "Lay not up treasures for yourselves upon the earth, where the moth and canker corrupt, and where thieves break through and steal: But lay up for yourselves treasures in heaven, where neither moth nor rust doth corrupt, and where thieves do not break through nor steal. For where your treasure is, there will your heart be also."

[12] *primitive* I.e., early. The early Christian period was often called the era of the "primitive church," with no connotation of inferiority.

[13] *lay up as Joseph did* Joseph, son of Jacob and Rachel, rose from slavery to high office in the pharaoh's court. He averted a crisis by storing grain in anticipation of a famine. See Genesis 41.

owner thus, "the Lord hath need of him."[1] So when the Tabernacle[2] was to be built, he sends to his people to call for their silver and gold, etc., and yields no other reason but that it was for his work. When Elisha comes to the widow of Sareptah[3] and finds her preparing to make ready her pittance for herself and family, he bids her first provide for him, he challenges first God's part which she must first give before she must serve her own family. All these teach us that the Lord looks that when he is pleased to call for his right in any thing we have, our own interest we have must stand aside till his turn be served. For the other, we need look no further than to that of 1 John 3.17, "He who hath this world's goods and seeth his brother to need and shuts up his compassion from him, how dwelleth the love of God in him?" Which comes punctually to this conclusion: If thy brother be in want and thou canst help him, thou needst not make doubt of what thou shouldst do; if thou lovest God thou must help him.

Question: What rule must we observe in lending?

Answer: Thou must observe whether thy brother hath present or probable or possible means of repaying thee, if there be none of those, thou must give him according to his necessity, rather than lend [to] him as he requires.[4] If he hath present means of repaying thee, thou art to look at him not as an act of mercy, but by way of commerce, wherein thou art to walk by the rule of justice; but if his means of repaying thee be only probable or possible, then he is an object of thy mercy, thou must lend him, though there be danger of losing it. Deuteronomy 15.7–8: "If any of thy brethren be poor ... thou shalt lend him sufficient." That men might not shift off this duty by the apparent hazard, he tells them that though the year of Jubilee[5] were at hand (when he must remit it, if he were not able to repay it before), yet he must lend him, and that cheerfully.[6] It may not grieve thee to give him, saith he. And because

some might object, why so I should soon impoverish myself and my family, he adds, with all thy work, etc., for our Savior said (Matthew 5.42),[7] "From him that would borrow of thee turn not away."

Question: What rule must we observe in forgiving?[8]

Answer: Whether thou didst lend by way of commerce or in mercy, if he hath nothing to pay thee, thou must forgive (except in cause where thou hast a surety or a lawful pledge). Deuteronomy 15.1–2—Every seventh year the creditor was to quit that which he lent to his brother if he were poor, as appears in verse 4: "Save when there shall be no poor with thee." In all these and like cases, Christ gives a general rule (Matthew 7.12), "Whatsoever ye would that men should do to you, do ye the same to them."

Question: What rule must we observe and walk by in cause of community of peril?[9]

Answer: The same as before, but with more enlargement towards others and less respect towards ourselves and our own right. Hence it was that in the primitive church they sold all, had all things in common, neither did any man say that which he possessed was his own. Likewise in their return out of the captivity, because the work was great for the restoring of the church and the danger of enemies was common to all, Nehemiah[10] directs the Jews to liberality and readiness in remitting their debts to their brethren, and disposing liberally to such as wanted, and stand not upon their own dues which they might have demanded of them. Thus did some of our forefathers in times of persecution in England, and so did many of the faithful of other churches, whereof we keep an honorable remembrance of them; and it is to be observed that both in Scriptures and latter stories of the churches that such as have been most bountiful to the poor saints, especially in those extraordinary times and occasions, God hath left them highly commended to posterity, as Zaccheus, Cornelius, Dorcas, Bishop Hooper, the

1 *the Lord hath need of him* See Luke 19.31.

2 *Tabernacle* Tent containing the Ark of the Covenant, the vessel that held the Ten Commandments. See Exodus 25.

3 *the widow of Sareptah* See 1 Kings 17.

4 *requires* I.e., requests.

5 *Jubilee* Biblically mandated observance supposed to occur every 50 years where debts and enslaved people are released and fields left uncultivated. See Leviticus 25.

6 *though the year ... cheerfully* See Deuteronomy 15.7–10.

7 *Matthew 5.42* The full passage reads: "Give to him that asketh, and from him that would borrow of thee, turn not away."

8 *forgiving* I.e., forgiving debt.

9 *in cause ... of peril* I.e., in situations when the community is in danger.

10 *Nehemiah* An Old Testament prophet, Nehemiah oversaw repairs on the walls of Jerusalem and persuaded moneylenders to think of the common good and charge no interest.

Cutler of Brussels and diverse others.[1] Observe again that the Scripture gives no caution to restrain any from being over liberal this way; but all men to the liberal and cheerful practice hereof by the sweeter promises; as to instance one for many (Isaiah 58.6–9) "Is not this the fast I have chosen to loose the bonds of wickedness, to take off the heavy burdens, to let the oppressed go free and to break every yoke ... to deal thy bread to the hungry and to bring the poor that wander into thy house, when thou seest the naked to cover them ... and then shall thy light brake forth as the morning and thy health shall grow speedily, thy righteousness shall go before God, and the glory of the Lord shalt embrace thee; then thou shall call and the Lord shall answer thee," etc. [Isaiah 58.]10: "If thou pour out thy soul to the hungry, then shall thy light spring out in darkness, and the Lord shall guide thee continually, and satisfy thy soul in draught, and make fat thy bones, thou shalt be like a watered garden, and they shalt be of thee that shall build the old waste places," etc. On the contrary most heavy curses are laid upon such as are straitened[2] towards the Lord and his people (Judges 5.23), "Curse ye Meroshe ... because they came not to help the Lord." "He who shutteth his ears from hearing the cry of the poor, he shall cry and shall not be heard."[3] Matthew 25: "Go ye cursed into everlasting fire," etc. "I was hungry and ye fed me not."[4] 2 Corinthians 9.6: "He that soweth sparingly shall reap sparingly."

Having already set forth the practice of mercy according to the rule of God's law, it will be useful to lay open the grounds of it also, being the other part of the Commandment and that is the affection from which this exercise of mercy must arise, the Apostle tells us that this love is the fulfilling of the law,[5] not that it is enough to love our brother and so no further; but in regard of the excellency of his parts giving any motion to the other as the soul to the body and the power it hath to set all the faculties at work in the outward exercise of this duty; as when we bid one make

the clock strike, he doth not lay hand on the hammer, which is the immediate instrument of the sound, but sets on work the first mover or main wheel; knowing that will certainly produce the sound which he intends. So the way to draw men to the works of mercy, is not by force of argument from the goodness or necessity of the work; for though this cause may enforce a rational mind to some present act of mercy, as is frequent in experience, yet it cannot work such a habit in a soul, as shall make it prompt upon all occasions to produce the same effect, but by framing these affections of love in the heart which will as naturally bring forth the other, as any cause doth produce the effect.

The definition which the Scripture gives us of love is this: Love is the bond of perfection.[6] First it is a bond or ligament.[7] Secondly, it makes the work perfect. There is no body but consists of parts and that which knits these parts together, gives the body its perfection, because it makes each part so contiguous to others as thereby they do mutually participate with each other, both in strength and infirmity, in pleasure and pain. To instance in the most perfect of all bodies: Christ and his church make one body. The several parts of this body considered a part before they were united, were as disproportionate and as much disordering as so many contrary qualities or elements, but when Christ comes, and by his spirit and love knits all these parts to himself and each to other, it is become the most perfect and best proportioned body in the world (Ephesians 4.15–16).[8] Christ, by whom all the body being knit together by every joint for the furniture thereof, according to the effectual power which is in the measure of every perfection of parts, a glorious body without spot or wrinkle; the ligaments hereof being Christ, or his love, for Christ is love (1 John 4.8).[9] So this definition is right. Love is the bond of perfection.

[1] *Zaccheus ... and diverse others* Christian martyrs.

[2] *straitened* I.e., unsympathetic.

[3] *He who ... be heard* See Proverbs 21.13.

[4] *Go ye cursed ... me not* See Matthew 25.41–45, where Jesus equates refusal to help the poor and in need with refusal to help Jesus himself.

[5] *love is ... the law* See Romans 13.10.

[6] *Love is ... perfection* See Colossians 3.14.

[7] *ligament* Connection.

[8] *Ephesians 4.15–16* "But let us follow the truth in love, and in all things, grow up into him, which is the head, that is, Christ. By whom all the body being coupled and knit together by every joint, for the furniture thereof ... receiveth increase of the body, unto the edifying of itself in love."

[9] *1 John 4.8* "He that loveth not, knoweth not God, for God is love."

From hence we may frame these conclusions. 1. First of all, true Christians are of one body in Christ (1 Corinthians 12[.12]). Ye are the body of Christ and members of their part. All the parts of this body being thus united are made so contiguous in a special relation as they must needs partake of each other's strength and infirmity; joy and sorrow, weal and woe. If one member suffers, all suffer with it, if one be in honor, all rejoice with it. Secondly, the ligaments of this body which knit together are love. Thirdly, no body can be perfect which wants its proper ligament. Fourthly, all the parts of this body being thus united are made so contiguous in a special relation as they must needs partake of each other's strength and infirmity, joy and sorrow, weal and woe. 1 Corinthians 12.26: If one member suffers, all suffer with it; if one be in honor, all rejoice with it. Fifthly, this sensitivity and sympathy of each other's conditions will necessarily infuse into each part a native desire and endeavor, to strengthen, defend, preserve and comfort the other.

To insist a little on this conclusion being the product of all the former, the truth hereof will appear both by precept and pattern. 1 John 3.16, "We ought to lay down our lives for the brethren." Galatians 6.2, "Bear ye one another's burdens and so fulfill the law of Christ." For patterns we have that first of our Savior who, out of his good will in obedience to his father, becoming a part of this body and being knit with it in the bond of love, found such a native sensitivity of our infirmities and sorrows as he willingly yielded himself to death to ease the infirmities of the rest of his body, and so healed their sorrows. From the like sympathy of parts did the Apostles and many thousands of the Saints lay down their lives for Christ. Again the like we may see in the members of this body among themselves. Romans 9—Paul could have been contented to have been separated from Christ, that the Jews might not be cut off from the body. It is very observable what he professeth of his affectionate partaking with every member; "Who is weak" (saith he) "and I am not weak? Who is offended and I burn not?"[1] And again (2 Corinthians 7.13), "Therefore we are comforted because ye were comforted." Of Epaphroditus[2] he

speaketh (Philippians 2.25–30) that he regarded not his own life to do him service. So Phebe[3] and others are called the servants of the church. Now it is apparent that they served not for wages, or by constraint, but out of love. The like we shall find in the histories of the church, in all ages; the sweet sympathy of affections which was in the members of this body one towards another; their cheerfulness in serving and suffering together; how liberal they were without repining, harbourers without grudging, and helpful without reproaching; and all from hence, because they had fervent love amongst them; which only makes the practice of mercy constant and easy.

The next consideration is how this love comes to be wrought. Adam in his first estate[4] was a perfect model of mankind in all their generations, and in him this love was perfected in regard of the habit. But Adam, himself rent[5] from his Creator, rent all his posterity also one from another; whence it comes that every man is born with this principle in him to love and seek himself only, and thus a man continueth till Christ comes and takes possession of the soul and infuseth another principle, love to God and our brother, and this latter having continual supply from Christ, as the head and root by which he is united, gets predominant in the soul, so by little and little expels the former. 1 John 4.7 "Love cometh of God and every one that loveth is born of God," so that this love is the fruit of the new birth, and none can have it but the new creature. Now when this quality is thus formed in the souls of men, it works like the Spirit upon the dry bones. Ezekiel 37.7—"Bone came to bone."[6] It gathers together the scattered bones, or perfect old man Adam,[7] and knits them into one body again in Christ, whereby a man is become again a living soul.

[1] *Who ... I burn not?* See 2 Corinthians 11.29.

[2] *Epaphroditus* In his letter to the Philippians, Paul writes of Epaphroditus that "for the work of Christ he was near unto death,

and regarded not his life, to fulfill that service which was lacking on your part toward me" (Philippians 2.30).

[3] *Phebe* Paul praises the service of Phebe, a deacon in the early Church. See Romans 16.1–2.

[4] *first estate* State of innocence, before the first sin.

[5] *rent* Torn away.

[6] *Bone came to bone* See Ezekiel 37.1–10, in which Ezekiel revives a field of dry bones to form a living army.

[7] *old man Adam* Adam, the first human, guilty of original sin (as opposed to Jesus Christ, sometimes called "new Adam" in reference to his role as redeemer of original sin).

The third consideration is concerning the exercise of this love, which is twofold, inward or outward. The outward hath been handled in the former preface of this discourse. From unfolding the other we must take in our way that maxim of philosophy, "*simile simili gaudet*,"[1] or like will to like; for as of things which are turned with disaffection to each other, the ground of it is from a dissimilitude or arising from the contrary or different nature of the things themselves; for the ground of love is an apprehension of some resemblance in the things loved to that which affects it. This is the cause why the Lord loves the creature, so far as it hath any of his Image in it; he loves his elect[2] because they are like himself, he beholds them in his beloved son. So a mother loves her child, because she thoroughly conceives a resemblance of herself in it. Thus it is between the members of Christ; each discerns, by the work of the Spirit, his own Image and resemblance in another, and therefore cannot but love him as he loves himself. Now when the soul, which is of a sociable nature, finds anything like to itself, it is like Adam when Eve was brought to him. She must be one with himself. "This is flesh of my flesh"[3] (saith he) "and bone of my bone." So the soul conceives a great delight in it; therefore she desires nearness and familiarity with it. She hath a great propensity to do it good and receives such content[4] in it, as fearing the miscarriage of her beloved, she bestows it in the inmost closet of her heart. She will not endure that it shall want any good which she can give it. If by occasion she be withdrawn from the company of it, she is still looking towards the place where she left her beloved. If she heard it groan, she is with it presently. If she find it sad and disconsolate, she sighs and moans with it. She hath no such joy as to see her beloved merry and thriving. If she see it wronged, she cannot hear it without passion. She sets no bounds to her affections, nor hath any thought of reward. She finds recompense enough in the exercise of her love towards it. We may see this acted to life in Jonathan

and David.[5] Jonathan a valiant man endued[6] with the spirit of love, so soon as he discovered the same spirit in David had presently his heart knit to him by this ligament of love; so that it is said he loved him as his own soul, he takes so great pleasure in him, that he strips himself to adorn his beloved. His father's kingdom was not so precious to him as his beloved David, David shall have it with all his heart. Himself desires no more but that he may be near to him to rejoice in his good. He chooseth to converse with him in the wilderness even to the hazard of his own life, rather than with the great Courtiers in his father's palace. When he sees danger towards him, he spares neither rare pains nor peril to direct it. When injury was offered his beloved David, he would not bear it, though from his own father. And when they must part for a season only, they thought their hearts would have broke for sorrow, had not their affections found vent by abundance of tears. Other instances might be brought to show the nature of this affection; as of Ruth and Naomi,[7] and many others; but this truth is cleared enough.

If any shall object that it is not possible that love shall be bred or upheld without hope of requital, it is granted; but that is not our cause; for this love is always under reward. It never gives, but it always receives with advantage. First, in regard that among the members of the same body, love and affection are reciprocal in a most equal and sweet kind of commerce. Secondly, in regard of the pleasure and content that the exercise of love carries with it, as we may see in the natural body. The mouth is at all the pains[8] to receive and mince the food which serves for the nourishment of all the other parts of the body; yet it hath no cause to complain; for first the other parts send back, by several passages, a due proportion of the same nourishment, in a better form for the strengthening and comforting the mouth. Secondly, the labor of the mouth is accompanied with such pleasure and content as far exceeds the pains it takes. So is it in all the labor of love among Christians.

1 *simile simili gaudet* Medieval Latin proverb roughly meaning "like rejoices in like."

2 *elect* People chosen to receive salvation.

3 *This is flesh of my flesh* In Christian doctrine, God created Eve from Adam's rib. See Genesis 2.22–23.

4 *content* Satisfaction, contentment.

5 *Jonathan and David* Jonathan defies his father to maintain his friendship with David in 1 Samuel 19.

6 *endued* Endowed.

7 *Ruth and Naomi* After the death of her son, Naomi urges his widow, Ruth, to return to her parents. She chooses instead to remain with Naomi. See Ruth 1.16.

8 *at all the pains* Solely responsible for the labor.

The party loving, reaps love again, as was showed before, which the soul covets more than all the wealth in the world. Thirdly, nothing yields more pleasure and content to the soul than when it finds that which it may love fervently; for to love and live beloved is the soul's paradise both here and in heaven. In the state of wedlock there be many comforts to learn out of the troubles of that condition; but let such as have tried the most, say if there be any sweetness in that condition comparable to the exercise of mutual love.

From the former considerations arise these conclusions: First, this love among Christians is a real thing, not imaginary. Secondly, this love is as absolutely necessary to the being of the body of Christ, as the sinews and other ligaments of a natural body are to the being of that body. Thirdly, this love is a divine, spiritual, nature; free, active, strong, courageous, permanent; undervaluing[1] all things beneath its proper object; and of all the graces, this makes us nearer to resemble the virtues of our heavenly father. Fourthly, it rests in the love and welfare of its beloved. For the full certain knowledge of those truths concerning the nature, use, and excellency of this grace, that which the holy ghost hath left recorded, 1 Corinthians 13,[2] may give full satisfaction, which is needful for every true member of this lovely body of the Lord Jesus, to work upon their hearts by prayer, meditation, continual exercise at least of the special [influence] of this grace, till Christ be formed in them and they in him, all in each other, knit together by this bond of love.

It rests now to make some application of this discourse, by the present design, which gave the occasion of writing of it. Herein are four things to be propounded; first the persons, secondly the work, thirdly the end,[3] fourthly the means.

First, for the persons. We are a company professing ourselves fellow members of Christ, in which respect only, though we were absent from each other many miles, and had our employments as far distant, yet we ought to account ourselves knit together by this bond of love and live in the exercise of it, if we would have comfort of our being in Christ. This was notorious in the practice of the Christians in former times; as is testified of the Waldenses,[4] from the mouth of one of the adversaries Aeneas Sylvius "*mutuo ament pene antequam norunt*,"[5] they used to love any of their own religion even before they were acquainted with them.

Secondly, for the work we have in hand. It is by a mutual consent, through a special overvaluing providence[6] and a more than an ordinary approbation of the churches of Christ, to seek out a place of cohabitation and consortship[7] under a due form of government both civil and ecclesiastical. In such cases as this, the care of the public must oversway all private respects, by which, not only conscience, but mere civil policy, doth bind us. For it is a true rule that particular estates cannot subsist in the ruin of the public.

Thirdly, the end is to improve our lives to do more service to the Lord; the comfort and increase of the body of Christ, whereof we are members, that ourselves and posterity may be the better preserved from the common corruptions of this evil world, to serve the Lord and work out our salvation under the power and purity of his holy ordinances.

Fourthly, for the means whereby this must be effected. They are twofold, a conformity with the work and end we aim at. These we see are extraordinary, therefore we must not content ourselves with usual ordinary means. Whatsoever we did, or ought to have done, when we lived in England, the same must we do, and more also, where we go. That which the most in their churches maintain as truth in profession only, we must bring into familiar and constant practice; as in this duty of love, we must love brotherly without dissimulation, we must love one another with a pure heart fervently. We must bear one another's burdens. We must not look only on our own things, but also

[1] *undervaluing* I.e., considering to be inferior.

[2] *1 Corinthians 13* This chapter extols the virtue of love, concluding, "And now abideth faith, hope, and love, even these three: but the greatest of these is love" (1 Corinthians 13.13).

[3] *end* Purpose.

[4] *Waldenses* Christian sect founded in the late twelfth century. Its members were persecuted by the Catholic Church, and the movement later adopted the theology of the Protestant Reformation.

[5] *Aeneas Sylvius* Historian and scholar Pope Pius II (Aeneas Sylvius Piccolomini, 1405–64); *mutuo ament pene antequam norunt* Latin phrase more accurately rendered as "*mutuo solent amare pene antequam norunt*." Winthrop follows the phrase with its translation.

[6] *overvaluing providence* I.e., providence that exceeds everything else in value.

[7] *consortship* Fellowship.

on the things of our brethren. Neither must we think that the Lord will bear with such failings at our hands as he doth from those among whom we have lived; and that for these three reasons: First, in regard of the more near bond of marriage between him and us, wherein he hath taken us to be his, after a most strict and peculiar manner, which will make him the more jealous of our love and obedience. So he tells the people of Israel, you only have I known of all the families of the earth, therefore will I punish you for your transgressions.[1] Secondly, because the Lord will be sanctified in them that come near Him. We know that there were many that corrupted the service of the Lord; some setting up altars before his own; others offering both strange fire and strange sacrifices also; yet there came no fire from heaven, or other sudden judgment upon them, as did upon Nadab and Abihu,[2] whom yet we may think did not sin presumptuously. Thirdly, when God gives a special commission he looks to have it strictly observed in every article; When he gave Saul a commission to destroy Amaleck,[3] He indented[4] with him upon certain articles, and because he failed in one of the least, and that upon a fair pretense, it lost him the kingdom, which should have been his reward, if he had observed his commission.

Thus stands the cause between God and us. We are entered into covenant with him for this work. We have taken out a commission. The Lord hath given us leave to draw our own articles. We have professed to enterprise these and those accounts, upon these and those ends. We have hereupon besought him of favor and blessing. Now if the Lord shall please to hear us,

and bring us in peace to the place we desire, then hath he ratified this covenant and sealed our commission, and will expect a strict performance of the articles contained in it; but if we shall neglect the observation of these articles which are the ends we have propounded, and, dissembling with our God, shall fall to embrace this present world and prosecute our carnal intentions, seeking great things for ourselves and our posterity, the Lord will surely break out in wrath against us, and be revenged of such a people, and make us know the price of the breach of such a covenant.

Now the only way to avoid this shipwreck, and to provide for our posterity, is to follow the counsel of Micah,[5] to do justly, to love mercy, to walk humbly with our God. For this end, we must be knit together, in this work, as one man. We must entertain each other in brotherly affection. We must be willing to abridge ourselves of our superfluities, for the supply of others' necessities. We must uphold a familiar commerce together in all meekness, gentleness, patience and liberality. We must delight in each other; make others' conditions our own; rejoice together, mourn together, labor and suffer together, always having before our eyes our commission and community in the work, as members of the same body. So shall we keep the unity of the spirit in the bond of peace. The Lord will be our God, and delight to dwell among us, as his own people, and will command a blessing upon us in all our ways, so that we shall see much more of his wisdom, power, goodness and truth, than formerly we have been acquainted with. We shall find that the God of Israel is among us, when ten of us shall be able to resist a thousand of our enemies; when he shall make us a praise and glory that men shall say of succeeding plantations, "may the Lord make it like that of New England." For we must consider that we shall be as a city upon a hill.[6] The eyes of all people are upon us. So that if we shall deal falsely with our God in this work we have undertaken, and so cause him to withdraw his present help from us, we shall be made a story and a by-word through the world. We shall open the mouths of enemies to speak evil of

1 *you only ... your transgressions* See Amos 3.2.

2 *Nadab and Abihu* In Leviticus 9–10, the high priest Aaron is instructed to make offerings, which God sends a fire to consume; Aaron's sons, Nadab and Abihu disregard God's instructions by lighting their own fire at the altar. See Leviticus 10.1–2: "But Nadab and Abihu, the sons of Aaron ... offered strange fire before the Lord, which he had not commanded them. Therefore a fire went out from the Lord, and devoured them."

3 *commission to destroy Amaleck* In 1 Samuel 15, God (speaking through the prophet Samuel) instructs Saul, King of Israel, to destroy all the people of Amalek and their livestock. Saul has most of the Amalekites killed but spares the king of Amalek and the best of the livestock; as a punishment, God declares that Saul will cease to be king of Israel.

4 *indented* Made a binding agreement.

5 *counsel of Micah* See Micah 6.8: "He hath showed thee, O man, what is good, and what the Lord requireth of thee: surely to do justly, and to love mercy, and to humble thyself, to walk with thy God."

6 *city upon a hill* See Matthew 5.14: "Ye are the light of the world. A city that is set on an hill, cannot be hid."

the ways of God, and all professors for God's sake. We shall shame the faces of many of God's worthy servants, and cause their prayers to be turned into curses upon us till we be consumed out of the good land whither we are going.

I shall shut up this discourse with that exhortation of Moses,[1] that faithful servant of the Lord, in his last farewell to Israel, Deuteronomy 30. "Beloved, there is now set before us life and death, good and evil," in that we are commanded this day to love the Lord our God, and to love one another, to walk in his ways and to keep his Commandments and his ordinance and his laws, and the articles of our covenant with Him, that we may live and be multiplied, and that the Lord our God may bless us in the land whither we go to possess it. But if our hearts shall turn away, so that we will not obey, but shall be seduced, and worship other Gods, our pleasure and profits, and serve them; it is propounded unto us this day, we shall surely perish out of the good land whither we pass over this vast sea to possess it.

Therefore let us choose life,
 that we, and our seed
 may live, by obeying his
 voice and cleaving to him,
for he is our life and our prosperity.[2]

—1838 (WRITTEN 1630)

[1] *Moses* One of the most important Hebrew prophets, best known for delivering the Israelites from captivity in Egypt to the promised land, and for transmitting God's laws to the people.

[2] *Beloved, there is now … our prosperity* This passage paraphrases Deuteronomy 30.15–20.

Anne Hutchinson

1591 – 1643

To the leaders of the Massachusetts Bay Colony, Anne Hutchinson was an unspeakably vile woman, an "American Jezebel" and an "instrument of Satan." The figurehead of a theological controversy that divided Massachusetts Bay Puritans, Hutchinson was long remembered as a symbol of the supposedly monstrous consequences of outspoken religious criticism and of what writer Nathaniel Hawthorne later called her "feminine ambition." Today, she is considered one of the first significant American public women—one who voiced her spiritual convictions in opposition to a powerful and patriarchal church and government.

Hutchinson was born in Lincolnshire, England, the daughter of Anglican deacon Francis Marbury and his second wife Bridget; both her parents were from prominent families. A religious conformist in his old age, Marbury had been far more rebellious in his youth, when he defied the Bishop of London and was imprisoned for heresy. It appears that he gave Anne an uncommonly rigorous education for a woman of the time, including reading, writing, and biblical interpretation. In her early twenties, she married cloth merchant William Hutchinson.

In 1612, Hutchinson began attending Saint Botolph's Church in Boston, Lincolnshire, where the young, dynamic minister John Cotton proclaimed a radical Puritan spiritual message. Upon hearing Cotton's sermons, which pronounced the freely given grace of God to be the sole pathway to salvation, Hutchinson began to see the Anglican clergy as an alliance of "antichrists"—a view common among the most fervid Puritans. She also found a mentor in her similarly radical brother-in-law, the preacher John Wheelwright.

In 1633, Cotton fled to North America to escape religious persecution. The following year, Hutchinson joined him, along with her husband and ten children—as did Wheelwright and his family. They settled in Boston, the capital of the Massachusetts Bay Colony and a refuge for Puritans. Hutchinson quickly became a leading member of the Church of Boston, serving the community as a widely sought spiritual counselor, healer, and midwife. She hosted discussion groups in which she and other parishioners debated ecclesiastical matters, beginning with discussion of Cotton's sermons but quickly extending beyond them; it wasn't long before Hutchinson and her group began to criticize many of the colony's church leaders for their spiritual failings. Hutchinson hosted both mixed-gender and women-only groups, and she ran the latter meetings herself—a practice that was not outside the bounds of Puritan propriety but that in Hutchinson's case proved threatening to church officials. Even her political enemy John Winthrop conceded that Hutchinson was "a woman of a ready wit and a bold spirit" but maintained that she was disseminating "dangerous errors," which spread like "Plague" from women to men.

Hutchinson's disagreement with the colony's religious authorities stemmed from deep-seated theological concerns: she differed from the colony's ministers—with the exception of outliers such as Cotton and Wheelwright—on the question of how one could know that one had been saved by God. The established view was that one might never be certain during one's lifetime, but could find evidence of salvation by examining one's thoughts and actions for evidence of "sanctification"—godly behavior that demonstrated the presence of God's grace. This, Hutchinson claimed, was incorrect: in her view, people who had been saved would know it immediately, never doubt their salvation, and therefore have no need to scrutinize their actions for evidence. In this way, Hutchinson took an extreme position on the question of whether "works" (an individual's good acts) or "grace" (given unconditionally by God) were necessary for a person to be saved. Generally, Puritans considered souls to be saved by grace alone, not works, but Hutchinson went further: to her, the established ministers, by suggesting that individual behavior could be interpreted as evidence of the presence of grace, were essentially endorsing works as a part of salvation.

Hutchinson's position was endorsed by Henry Vane the Younger, a youthful aristocrat who served for a single year as colonial governor. With his support, she attracted a large following, and underlying tensions blossomed into a heated, public controversy—one long known as the Antinomian Controversy,[1] now more often called the Free Grace Controversy. The conflict escalated in early 1637, when Wheelwright delivered a lay sermon that denounced all the colony's ministers, with the exception of Cotton.

Massachusetts's rulers took action. In May of 1637, Vane was succeeded as governor by John Winthrop, who sought to quash dissent in the colony. In August, the ministers in power held a council enumerating and denouncing the "erroneous opinions" of the Free Grace proponents. Cotton was forced to tone down his sermons, and, that autumn, Wheelwright was banished. Many of his and Hutchinson's allies were brought to trial as well, though most received lesser punishments. Hutchinson, too, was tried by civil authorities.

At her two-day trial, held in November, Hutchinson expertly cited scripture to defend herself. On the first day, several ministers testified to the erroneous views they had heard her express. At the beginning of the second day, she shrewdly demanded that the ministers testify again—this time under oath—and tension heightened in the court as many of the witnesses were reluctant to do so. With the question of the repeated testimonies still unresolved, a few people were allowed to speak on Hutchinson's behalf; one of these was John Cotton, whose longwinded and awkward testimony was by no means unambiguous in support of her. Hutchinson interrupted him with an extraordinary testimony of her own, during which she avowed that she had received direct revelations from God and prophesied that ruin would come to the colony should the ministers continue to persecute her. After this apparently heretical and treasonous statement, the trial concluded fairly quickly; two of the previous day's witnesses agreed to repeat their testimonies under oath, and soon afterward Hutchinson was declared "deluded by the devil" and sentenced to banishment.

Hutchinson spent four months under house arrest and was then excommunicated at a second trial conducted by church officials. She and some of her supporters left for Aquidneck Island, where fellow Free Grace proponents were already at work on a new colony. They had been invited to settle there by Roger Williams, who had been banished from Massachusetts for his religious views two years earlier and had since founded his own colony on another part of Aquidneck. Together, these settlements would develop into Rhode Island.

According to Winthrop, in Aquidneck Hutchinson delivered lay sermons on Sundays to a mixed-gender audience—now openly defying Puritan gender norms—and continued to condemn the Massachusetts Bay churches. During these years, she also experienced a series of misfortunes, including a stillbirth, which Massachusetts authorities triumphantly interpreted as signs of God's disapproval. In 1641, her husband died. In 1642, as Massachusetts threatened to take over Rhode Island, Hutchinson left the new settlement and traveled with many of her children to New Netherland. She settled near what is now Westchester, New York, on territory whose ownership was contested by the local Siwanoy people. The following year, in retaliation for a Dutch massacre of a Lenape village, a Siwanoy raiding party attacked Hutchinson's homestead. All except her nine-year-old daughter Susanna were killed.

No writing by Hutchinson is known to have survived, but several of her contemporaries recorded their experiences of the Free Grace Controversy. The best-known of these accounts are given by John Winthrop in his *Journal* and in *A Short Story of the Rise, Reign, and Ruin of the Antinomians, Familists and Libertines* (1644), his extended argument against the positions held by Hutchinson and her allies. For political expediency, the accounts of Winthrop and others tended to heap blame upon Hutchinson while downplaying the importance of players such as Cotton (who remained an influential Boston minister) and Vane (who had returned to England and become politically powerful there). As a result, she was long demonized by conformists, while her memory inspired radicals such as Quaker activist Mary Dyer.

Hutchinson's reputation in the nineteenth century is suggested in a sketch by Hawthorne, who ambivalently describes her as "a woman of extraordinary talent and strong imagination" and as "a burden too grievous for our fathers." Twentieth-century accounts were similarly clouded by sexism: some scholars

[1] Antinomianism is the belief that those who have been saved by grace are not obligated to follow moral codes.

represented her as a mere accessory to Cotton, while in 1962 Emery Battis, in what was for decades the standard account of the Free Grace Controversy, argued that Hutchinson's increased extremism was a symptom of menopause. Some recent scholars champion Hutchinson as a proto-feminist combating a patriarchal church, while others present her as a liberal fighting a repressive theocracy. Others have seen her not as a progressive but as a committed Puritan whose radicalism and conviction exceeded even that of other Puritans.

NOTE ON THE TEXT: The transcript of Hutchinson's civil trial survives in two forms, neither entirely reliable. One is a condensed account by John Winthrop included as part of *A Short Story of the Rise, Reign, and Ruin of the Antinomians, Familists and Libertines.* The other, more extensive account appears as an appendix to *History of the Colony and Province of Massachusetts Bay* (1767), by the prominent historian Thomas Hutchinson, Hutchinson's own great-grandson. Thomas Hutchinson, who collected documents of historical import, claimed that his transcript was based upon "an ancient manuscript of the trial at large, having been preserved," but unfortunately this manuscript no longer survives and its authorship remains a mystery. Selections from the appendix to Thomas Hutchinson's book appear below; the editors have consulted the text as it appears in Hutchinson's *History* and in David D. Hall's *The Antinomian Controversy, 1636–1638: A Documentary History* (1990). Portions of Winthrop's account are included in the online portion of this anthology as contextual material.

⌘ ⌘ ⌘

The Examination of Mrs. Anne Hutchinson at the Court at Newtown

MR. WINTHROP, GOVERNOR. Mrs. Hutchinson, you are called here as one of those that have troubled the peace of the commonwealth and the churches here; you are known to be a woman that hath had a great share in the promoting and divulging of those opinions that are causes of this trouble, and to be nearly joined not only in affinity and affection with some of those the court had taken notice of and passed censure upon, but you have spoken diverse things, as we have been informed, very prejudicial to the honour of the churches and ministers thereof, and you have maintained a meeting and an assembly in your house that hath been condemned by the general assembly as a thing not tolerable nor comely in the sight of God nor fitting for your sex, and notwithstanding that was cried down you have continued the same. Therefore we have thought good to send for you to understand how things are, that if you be in an erroneous way we may reduce[1] you that so you may become a profitable member here among

us. Otherwise if you be obstinate in your course that then the court may take such course that you may trouble us no further. Therefore I would intreat you to express whether you do not hold and assent in practice to those opinions and factions that have been handled in court already, that is to say, whether you do not justify Mr. Wheelwright's sermon and the petition.[2]

MRS. HUTCHINSON. I am called here to answer before you but I hear no things laid to my charge.

GOV. I have told you some already and more I can tell you.

[MRS. H.] Name one, Sir.

GOV. Have I not named some already?

MRS. H. What have I said or done?

GOV. Why for your doings, this you did harbour and countenance those that are parties in this faction that you have heard of.

[1] *reduce* Restore to correct spiritual conduct.

[2] *Mr. Wheelwright's ... petition* Earlier in 1637, Hutchinson's brother-in-law John Wheelwright was tried in court after delivering a rebellious sermon critical of most Massachusetts church authorities. His supporters submitted a petition arguing, among other things, that Wheelwright's actions were a matter of "conscience"—that is, of personal spiritual belief—and that it was therefore inappropriate to try him in civil court before he was tried by the church. The court dismissed the petition, and Wheelwright was convicted and banished for "contempt and sedition."

[MRS. H.] That's matter of conscience, Sir.

GOV. Your conscience you must keep or it must be kept for you. ...

GOV. Why do you keep such a meeting at your house as you do every week upon a set day?

MRS. H. It is lawful for me to do so, as it is all your practices, and can you find a warrant for yourself[1] and condemn me for the same thing? ...

GOV. For this, that you appeal to our practice you need no confutation. ... [B]ut I will say that there was no meeting of women alone, but your meeting is of another sort for there is sometimes men among you.

MRS. H. There was never any man with us.

GOV. Well, admit there was no man at your meeting and that you was sorry for it, there is no warrant for your doings, and by what warrant do you continue such a course?

MRS. H. I conceive there lies a clear rule in Titus, that the elder women should instruct the younger,[2] and then I must have a time wherein I must do it.

GOV. All this I grant you, I grant you a time for it, but what is this to the purpose that you Mrs. Hutchinson must call a company together from their callings to come to be taught of you?

MRS. H. Will it please you to answer me this and to give me a rule, for then I will willingly submit to any truth. If any come to my house to be instructed in the ways of God what rule have I to put them away?

GOV. But suppose that a hundred men come unto you to be instructed; will you forbear to instruct them?

MRS. H. As far as I conceive I cross a rule in it.

GOV. Very well, and do you not so here?

MRS. H. No Sir, for my ground is they are men.

GOV. Men and women all is one for that, but suppose that a man should come and say, "Mrs. Hutchinson, I hear that you are a woman that God hath given his grace unto and you have knowledge in the word of God, I pray instruct me a little," ought you not to instruct this man?

MRS. H. I think I may. Do you think it not lawful for me to teach women and[3] why do you call me to teach the court?

GOV. We do not call you to teach the court but to lay open yourself.

MRS. H. I desire you that you would then set me down a rule by which I may put them away that come unto me and so have peace in so doing.

GOV. You must show your rule to receive them.

MRS. H. I have done it.

GOV. I deny it because I have brought more arguments than you have. ...

MRS. H. ... [I]f you look upon the rule in Titus it is a rule to me. If you convince me that it is no rule I shall yield.

GOV. You know that there is no rule that crosses another, but this rule crosses that in the Corinthians.[4] But you must take it in this sense: that elder women must instruct the younger about their business, and to love their husbands and not to make them to clash.

MRS. H. I do not conceive but that it is meant for some public times.

GOV. Well, have you no more to say but this?

MRS. H. I have said sufficient for my practice.

GOV. Your course is not to be suffered for, besides that we find such a course as this to be greatly prejudicial[5] to the state, besides the occasion that it is to seduce many honest persons that are called to those meetings and your opinions, being known to be different from the word of God, may seduce many simple souls that resort unto you. Besides that the occasion which hath come of late hath come from none but such as have frequented your meetings, so that now they are flown off from magistrates and ministers, and this since they have come to you. And besides

1 *a warrant for yourself* Justification for your own actions.

2 *clear rule ... younger* See Titus 2.1–5, where it is presented as "wholesome doctrine" that "the elder women" be "teachers of honest things. That they may instruct the young women to be sober minded, that they love their husbands, that they love their children, that they be discrete, chaste, keeping at home, good and subject unto their husbands, and the word of God be not evil spoken of." Unless otherwise indicated, biblical quotations included in footnotes to this selection are from the 1560 Geneva Bible, which appears to be the translation Hutchinson references most frequently in this transcript.

3 *and* But then.

4 *that in the Corinthians* See 1 Corinthians 14.34–35: "Let your women keep silence in the Churches: for it is not permitted unto them to speak: but they ought to be subject, as also the Law saith. And if they will learn anything, let them ask their husbands at home: for it is a shame for women to speak in the Church."

5 *prejudicial* Harmful.

that it will not well stand with the commonwealth that families should be neglected for so many neighbours and dames and so much time spent. We see no rule of God for this. We see not that any should have authority to set up any other exercises besides what authority hath already set up, and so what hurt comes of this you will be guilty of and we for suffering you.

MRS. H. Sir, I do not believe that to be so.

GOV. Well, we see how it is. We must therefore put it away from you,[1] or restrain you from maintaining this course.

MRS. H. If you have a rule for it from God's word you may.

GOV. We are your judges, and not you ours and we must compel you to it. …

[The trial continues into a second day, and several witnesses are questioned, including John Cotton, whose examination Hutchinson interrupts with the following speech.]

MRS. H. If you please to give me leave I shall give you the ground of what I know to be true. Being much troubled to see the falseness of the constitution of the church of England, I had like to have turned separatist.[2] Whereupon I kept a day of solemn humiliation and pondering of the thing; this scripture was brought unto me—he that denies Jesus Christ to be come in the flesh is antichrist.[3] This I considered of and in considering found that the papists[4] did not deny him to be come in the flesh, nor we did not deny him—who then was antichrist? Was the Turk[5] antichrist only? The Lord knows that I could not open[6] scripture; he must by his prophetical office open it unto me. So after that being unsatisfied in the thing, the Lord was pleased to bring this scripture out of the Hebrews: He that denies the testament denies the testator,[7] and in this did open unto me and give me to see that those which did not teach the new covenant[8] had the spirit of antichrist, and upon this he did discover[9] the ministry unto me; and ever since, I bless the Lord, he hath let me see which was the clear ministry and which the wrong. Since that time I confess I have been more choice[10] and he hath let me to distinguish between the voice of my beloved and the voice of Moses, the voice of John Baptist[11] and the voice of antichrist, for all those voices are spoken of in scripture. Now if you do condemn me for speaking what in my conscience I know to be truth I must commit myself unto the Lord.

MR. NOWELL.[12] How do you know that was the spirit?

[1] *put it away from you* I.e., remove it from you, put it out of your mind.

[2] *turned separatist* Become part of a movement to separate from the state-sponsored Church of England.

[3] *he that … antichrist* See 1 John 4.3. In his first epistle, John argues against those who claim that Jesus was not both fully human and fully God, but instead a spirit who only had the appearance of humanity. In the Geneva Bible, footnotes to 1 John 4 interpret this passage as applying to ministers (described as "[t]hey which boast that they have the spirit to preach or prophesy"), who possess "the spirit of God" only if they preach that Christ is both human and divine; *antichrist* One who falsely pretends to be Christ, but who in fact denies and subverts Jesus' message.

[4] *papists* Disparaging term for Catholics.

[5] *the Turk* Hutchinson uses the word as a stand-in for "Muslim."

[6] *open* I.e., explicate in the manner of a minister. Puritan sermons generally involved the close examination of a passage from the Bible.

[7] *He that … testator* I.e., those who deny the existence of a testament declared by God for humanity deny the existence and death of the one who established the testament, Jesus. See Hebrews 9.16–18.

[8] *new covenant* The covenant of grace established between God and humankind, according to which God freely dispenses his grace and saves the elect. According to Puritan theology, the covenant of grace was established by Christ, who atoned for humanity's sins by sacrificing himself, thereby making it possible for the righteous to attain salvation. The covenant of grace replaced the covenant of works, the first covenant between God and humanity, according to which God granted eternal life in exchange for obedience. This earlier covenant was broken after Adam, the first human, defied God.

[9] *discover* Reveal.

[10] *choice* Discerning.

[11] *my beloved* I.e., Jesus. See Song of Songs 2.8. and 5.2 in the King James Bible for references to "the voice of my beloved"; *Moses* Hebrew prophet who first delivered God's law and the ten commandments to the ancient Israelites; *John Baptist* Prophet who first announced the coming of Christ.

[12] *MR. NOWELL* Increase Nowell, one of the magistrates judging Hutchinson's trial; he also served as court secretary.

MRS. H. How did Abraham know that it was God that bid him offer his son, being a breach of the sixth commandment?[1]

DEP. GOV. THOMAS DUDLEY.[2] By an immediate voice.

MRS. H. So to me by an immediate revelation.

DEP. GOV. THOMAS DUDLEY. How! an immediate revelation.

MRS. H. By the voice of his own spirit to my soul. I will give you another scripture, Jeremiah 46.27–28[3]—out of which the Lord showed me what he would do for me and the rest of his servants. But after he was pleased to reveal himself to me I did presently, like Abraham, run to Hagar.[4] And after that he did let me see the atheism[5] of my own heart, for which I begged of the Lord that it might not remain in my heart, and being thus, he did show me this (a twelvemonth after) which I told you of before. Ever since that time I have been confident of what he hath revealed unto me.

… another place out of Daniel 7 and he … and for us all,[6] wherein he showed me the sitting of the judgment and the standing of all high and low before the Lord and how thrones and kingdoms were cast down before him. When our teacher[7] came to New-England it was a great trouble unto me, my brother Wheelwright being put by also. I was then much troubled concerning the ministry under which I lived, and then that place in the 30th of Isaiah was brought to my mind. Though the Lord give thee bread of adversity and water of affliction yet shall not thy teachers be removed into corners any more, but thine eyes shall see thy teachers.[8] The Lord giving me this promise and they being gone there was none then left that I was able to hear, and I could not be at rest but I must come hither.[9] Yet that place of Isaiah did much follow me, though the Lord give thee the bread of adversity and water of affliction. This place lying I say upon me, then this place in Daniel was brought unto me and did show me that though I should meet with affliction yet I am the same God that delivered Daniel out of the lion's den,[10] I will also deliver thee.

Therefore I desire you to look to it, for you see this scripture fulfilled this day, and therefore I desire you that as you tender the Lord and the church and commonwealth to consider and look what you do. You have power over my body but the Lord Jesus hath power over my body and soul; and assure yourselves thus much, you do as much as in you lies to put the Lord Jesus Christ from you, and if you go on in this course you begin, you will bring a curse upon you and your posterity, and the mouth of the Lord hath spoken it.

DEP. GOV. THOMAS DUDLEY. What is the scripture she brings?

MR. STOUGHTON.[11] Behold I turn away from you.

[1] *Abraham … commandment* In Genesis 22.1–2, God speaks directly to Abraham, ordering him to offer his own son as a sacrifice. This would break the commandment "Thou shalt not kill."

[2] *THOMAS DUDLEY* One of the magistrates judging Hutchinson's trial.

[3] *Jeremiah 46.27–28* "But fear not thou, O my servant Jacob, and be not thou afraid, O Israel: for behold, I will deliver thee from a far country, and thy seed from the land of their captivity, and Jacob shall return and be in rest, and prosperity, and none shall make him afraid. Fear thou not, O Jacob my servant, saith the Lord, for I am with thee, and I will utterly destroy all the nations, whither I have driven thee: but I will not utterly destroy thee, but correct thee by judgment, and not utterly cut thee off."

[4] *run to Hagar* I.e., choose the covenant of works instead of the covenant of grace. The biblical patriarch Abraham had one son with his servant, Hagar, and one son with his wife, Sarai. The annotations accompanying Galatians 4.21–24 in the Geneva Bible link the covenant of works to Hagar and the covenant of grace to Sarai.

[5] *atheism* In the seventeenth century, the term was used to refer not only to a disbelief in God, but more broadly to godlessness, wickedness, or corruption.

[6] *… another … us all* The manuscript was unclear here, and may have been deliberately defaced; *Daniel 7* This portion of Daniel describes a vision of four kingdoms, depicted as beasts, that will hold great power on earth but be conquered by divine judgment. The "little horn" (Daniel 7.8) of the fourth, most terrible beast is often interpreted as an image of the antichrist.

[7] *our teacher* John Cotton, who left England in 1633.

[8] *Though the … teachers* See Isaiah 30.20 (King James Bible).

[9] *must come hither* Hutchinson and her family left England for Massachusetts in 1634.

[10] *Daniel … lion's den* See Daniel 6. Daniel's political rivals contrive to have him imprisoned overnight in a den of lions as a means of execution; God protects him because of his faith, and he emerges unharmed.

[11] *MR. STOUGHTON* Israel Stoughton, one of the magistrates at the trial.

Mrs. H. But now having seen him which is invisible I fear not what man can do unto me.[1]

Gov. Daniel was delivered by miracle; do you think to be delivered so too?

Mrs. H. I do here speak it before the court. …

Gov. The case is altered and will not stand with us now, but I see a marvellous providence of God to bring things to this pass that they are. We have been hearkening about the trial of this thing and now the mercy of God by a providence hath answered our desires and made her to lay open herself and the ground of all these disturbances to be by revelations[.] … [T]he ground work of her revelations is the immediate revelation of the spirit and not by the ministry of the word,[2] and that is the means by which she hath very much abused the country[.] …

Gov. The court hath already declared themselves satisfied concerning the things you hear, and concerning the troublesomeness of her spirit and the danger of her course amongst us, which is not to be suffered.

Therefore if it be the mind of the court that Mrs. Hutchinson for these things that appear before us is unfit for our society, and if it be the mind of the court that she shall be banished out of our liberties[3] and imprisoned till she be sent away, let them hold up their hands.

[Thirty-seven of the forty magistrates and deputies in attendance vote to banish Hutchinson, with two votes against and one abstention.]

Gov. Mrs. Hutchinson, the sentence of the court you hear is that you are banished from out of our jurisdiction as being a woman not fit for our society, and are to be imprisoned till the court shall send you away.

Mrs. H. I desire to know wherefore I am banished?

Gov. Say no more. The court knows wherefore and is satisfied.

—1767 (TRANSCRIPT OF 1637 TRIAL)

[1] *But now … unto me* See Hebrews 11.27, which says of Moses, "By faith he forsook Egypt, and feared not the fierceness of the king: for he endured, as he that saw him which is invisible."

[2] *[T]he ground … of the word* I.e., the teachings she is spreading are not grounded in the instruction of a minister.

[3] *our liberties* The area subject to our jurisdiction; i.e., the Massachusetts Bay Colony.

ROGER WILLIAMS
c. 1603 – 1683

Long before the separation of church and state was proclaimed by American founders, Roger Williams attested the need for "a wall of separation between the Garden of the church and the wilderness of the world." Like other Massachusetts Puritans such as John Winthrop and John Cotton, Williams was deeply committed to the truth of his Puritan beliefs. But whereas Winthrop had envisaged a government that would foster correct worship, Williams held up a different ideal: the removal of everything, including state interference, that might stand in the way of each individual's relationship to God. Though his ideas were too radical even for most other Puritans, he managed to found a colony that put them into practice—and, a century after his death, his work would influence the shape of American government.

Born around 1603 to a respected middle-class family, Williams was raised in one of London's centers of Separatist activity, the Smithfield district. He entered Cambridge University's Pembroke College with the assistance of prominent jurist Sir Edward Coke, and went on to earn scholarships for his skill in Latin, Hebrew, and Greek. He graduated with a BA in 1627, but he soon abandoned his MA and began to focus on Puritan theology and practice; he took holy orders and began serving as a chaplain two years later. His beliefs grew increasingly radical: Williams came to oppose any formal connection between the Church of England and the state, and he advocated freedom of worship—dangerous opinions to hold in the political landscape of the time.

Williams married Mary Barnard, a reverend's daughter, in 1629, and shortly thereafter the two set sail for Massachusetts Bay Colony, seeking the freedom to worship safely. Williams was a charming and charismatic speaker, and many in Massachusetts welcomed the intelligent, scholarly, and pious preacher. He was offered the prestigious post of minister at Boston's First Church, but turned the post down, saying that he "durst not officiate to an unseparated people." His belief that Puritans must separate from the Church of England was deeply controversial, as such a move would destabilize the colony's relationship with its parent country. He also expressed other controversial views: he thought, for instance, that the English king had no power to grant colonists ownership of Native Americans' lands, a position that called the colony's legitimacy into question. He asserted, too, that the authority of civil magistrates should be limited to civil matters, not extending to religious belief or practice. Not surprisingly, these ideas were threatening to those who followed Governor John Winthrop's vision for a highly structured society administered by Puritan believers with the guidance of the clergy. Williams's attempt to find a congregation with whom he could speak openly took him to Salem, then to Plymouth, and back to Salem again.

Williams's conflict with Winthrop and with the General Court of the Massachusetts Bay Colony escalated, and in 1635 he was indicted for "heresy and divisiveness." (He and Winthrop nonetheless remained lifelong friends—and even political allies—who frequently exchanged letters.) Williams avoided deportation by fleeing south, and he was welcomed by the people of Narragansett Bay. He purchased land from the Narragansett chiefs Canonicus and Mianotonomo in what is now Rhode Island, and named his new home Providence; here he and Mary raised six children. The settlers of Providence were largely on good terms with the Narragansett, and during the Pequot War (1636–38) Williams's diplomacy secured them as allies with the English colonists against the Pequot. (After the war, he would also be instrumental in persuading the Narragansett to help recapture escaped Pequot slaves.)

Williams remained committed to the separation of religion and government, advocating freedom from persecution even for those whose views he despised (among them Quakers, whom he called "the cursed sect"). Providence became a sanctuary for Quakers, Baptists, Jews, and other religious minorities who found the Massachusetts colony too oppressive. Increasing suppression in Massachusetts brought

an influx of Puritan dissenters such as Anne Hutchinson, some of whom founded the new settlements of Pocasset (later Portsmouth) and Newport nearby. Williams himself abandoned the idea of membership in any specific church, though he remained deeply devout in his own beliefs.

In 1643, encroachment by the Massachusetts Bay Colony forced Williams to return to England to seek a charter for the colony of Rhode Island (which included Providence and the other tolerant settlements). During this voyage he gathered what he knew of Narragansett language and customs into *A Key into the Language of America* (1643), which has become one of his best-known works. Ostensibly a phrasebook, the *Key* also examines Narragansett culture, language, beliefs, and other elements of life. It is a remarkable example of what we would now call anthropology and provides considerable insight into early relations between Indigenous Americans and Europeans. In the twentieth century, it would be a useful source of information for a revival of Narragansett language and culture.

While in London, Williams wrote another major work: the 400-page *Bloody Tenet of Persecution, for Cause of Conscience, in a Conference between Truth and Peace* (1644). This thorough articulation of his views on freedom of religion was part of an ongoing debate on the subject with Massachusetts Puritan minister John Cotton that would extend into the next decade. While Williams succeeded in obtaining a charter for Rhode Island, there remained significant resistance in England to the idea of religious toleration: *The Bloody Tenet* was greeted with public outrage, and Parliament ordered all copies burned. Williams's argument nonetheless had an impact on the debate in England, and it is likely that his ideas influenced those of prominent English intellectuals such as John Milton (1608–74) and, later, John Locke (1632–1704).

Williams returned to Providence in 1644. For several decades, his friendly relations with the Narragansett helped to cultivate a generally peaceful relationship between the Indigenous peoples and the English settlers of the region. During King Philip's War (1675–76), his diplomatic efforts finally failed; the New England settlers massacred a Narragansett village, and in response the Narragansett joined other tribes in attacking and burning Providence. Williams lived to see his home rebuilt, though he never recovered financially. The Narragansett numbers, however, were severely depleted. Many died during the conflict, and Williams oversaw the sale of many of the captives into indentured servitude in Rhode Island—or outright slavery on English plantations in the Caribbean. The few remaining Narragansett were forced to flee their land.

Williams spent his last years living in poverty in Providence, where he died around 1683. He was a prolific writer throughout his life, but much of his work became scattered after his death. Shortly after the Civil War, a group in Rhode Island collected his works and compiled them in a six-volume set released as *The Complete Writings of Roger Williams* (1867). Later editions were expanded into seven volumes. Since the publication of his collected works, many scholars have praised Williams as a liberal ahead of his time for his views on colonization and religious freedom, while others have stressed the need to interpret his ideas in the context of his extremely devout seventeenth-century theology.

A few colonies founded after Rhode Island adopted similar statements of religious toleration, and at the time of the American Revolution the nation's founders embraced Williams's ideal as it had been adapted by Locke and other liberal theorists. More than a century after Williams's death, the First Amendment to the United States Constitution would declare that "Congress shall make no law respecting an establishment of religion, or prohibiting the free exercise thereof."

NOTE ON THE TEXTS: The text of *A Key into the Language of America* is based upon the 1643 edition. For "Letter to the Town of Providence," both *The Complete Writings of Roger Williams*, vols. 1 and 7 (1963) and Calvin Davis's *On Religious Liberty: Selections from the Works of Roger Williams* (2008) have been consulted. The text of *The Bloody Tenet* is based upon the 1848 edition published by J. Haddo. Spelling and punctuation have been modernized in accordance with the practices of this anthology.

⌘ ⌘ ⌘

from *A Key into the Language of America*[1]

To my Dear and Well-beloved Friends and Country-men, in Old and New England.

I present you with a key; I have not heard of the like,[2] yet framed, since it pleased God to bring that mighty continent of America to light. Others of my country-men have often, and excellently, and lately written of the country (and none that I know beyond the good-ness and worth of it).

This key respects the native language of it, and happily[3] may unlock some rarities concerning the natives themselves, not yet discovered.

I drew the materials in a rude lump at sea, as a pri-vate help to my own memory, that I might not by my present absence lightly lose what I had so dearly bought in some few years' hardship, and charges among the barbarians; yet being reminded by some, what pity it were to bury those materials in my grave at land or sea; and withal, remembering how often I have been importuned by worthy friends, of all sorts, to afford them some help this way. I resolved (by the assistance of the most high) to cast those materials into this key, pleasant and profitable for all, but especially for my friends residing in those parts.

A little key may open a box, where lies a bunch of keys. With this I have entered into the secrets of those countries, wherever English dwell about two hundred miles, between the French and Dutch plantations; for want of this, I know what gross mistakes myself and others have run into.

There is a mixture of this language north and south, from the place of my abode, about six hundred miles; yet within the two hundred miles (aforementioned) their dialects do exceedingly differ; yet no so, but (within that compass) a man may, by this help, con-verse with thousands of natives all over the country; and

by such converse it may please the Father of Mercies[4] to spread civility and (in his own most holy season) Christianity; for one candle will light ten thousand, and it may please God to bless a little leaven[5] to season the mighty lump of those peoples and territories.

It is expected, that having had so much converse with these natives, I should write some little of them.

Concerning them (a little to gratify expectation), I shall touch upon four heads:

First, by what names they are distinguished.

Secondly, their original[6] and descent.

Thirdly, their religion, manners, customs, etc.

Fourthly, that great point of their conversion.

To the first, their names are of two sorts:

First, those of the English giving: as natives, savages, Indians, wildmen (so the Dutch call them *wilden*), Abergeny[7] men, pagans, barbarians, heathen.

Secondly, their names which they give themselves.

I cannot observe that they ever had (before the coming of the English, French or Dutch amongst them) any names to difference themselves from strang-ers, for they knew none; but two sorts of names they had, and have amongst themselves:

First, general, belonging to all natives, as *Nínnuock, Ninnimissinnûwock, Eniskeetompaŭwog*, which signifies Men, Folk, or People.

Secondly, particular names, peculiar to several nations, of them amongst themselves, as Nanhiggan̆uck, Massachusêuck, Cawasumsêuck, Cowwesğuck, Quin-tikóok, Qunnipiğuck, Pequttóog, etc.

They have often asked me, why we call them Indians, natives, etc. And understanding the reason, they will call themselves Indians, in opposition to English, etc.

For the second head proposed, their original and descent:

From Adam and Noah[8] that they spring, it is granted on all hands.

1 Subtitled *An Help to the Language of the Natives in That Part of America, Called New England.*

2 *I have ... the like* Williams's *Key* was the first substantial English-language text to study Indigenous languages in detail, although William Wood's 1634 *New England's Prospect* did dedicate five pages to the subject.

3 *respects* Is concerned with; *happily* Perhaps.

4 *Father of Mercies* I.e., God.

5 *leaven* Literally, a raising agent, such as yeast. Cf. Matthew 13.33: "The kingdom of heaven is like unto leaven, which a woman took, and hid in three measures of meal, till the whole was leavened."

6 *original* Origin.

7 *Abergeny* Aboriginal.

8 *Adam* According to Christian tradition, the first human cre-ated by God; *Noah* Biblical figure who, under God's direction, spared himself and a small number of humans and other animals from a flood that destroyed all other living beings. Cf. Genesis 7.23.

But for their later descent, and whence they came into those parts, it seems as hard to find, as to find the wellhead of some fresh stream, which running many miles out of the country to the salt ocean, hath met with many mixing streams by the way. They say, themselves, that they have sprung and grown up in that very place, like the very trees of the wilderness.

They say that their great god Kautántowwì created those parts, as I observed in the chapter of their religion. They have no clothes, books, nor letters, and conceive their fathers never had; and therefore they are easily persuaded that the God that made Englishmen is a greater God, because He hath so richly endowed the English above themselves. But when they hear that about sixteen hundred years ago, England and the inhabitants thereof were like unto themselves, and since have received from God, clothes, books, etc. they are greatly affected with a secret hope concerning themselves.

Wise and judicious men, with whom I have discoursed, maintain their original to be northward from Tartaria:[1] and at my now taking ship, at the Dutch plantation, it pleased the Dutch Governor (in some discourse with me about the natives) to draw their line from Iceland, because the name Sackmakan (the name for an Indian prince, about the Dutch) is the name for a prince in Iceland.

Other opinions I could number up: under favour I shall present (not mine opinion, but) my observations to the judgment of the wise.

First, others (and myself) have conceived some of their words to hold affinity with the Hebrew.[2]

Secondly, they constantly anoint their heads as the Jews did.

Thirdly, they give dowries for their wives, as the Jews did.

Fourthly (and which I have not so observed amongst other nations as amongst the Jews, and these): they constantly separate their women (during the time of their monthly sickness) in a little house alone by themselves four or five days, and hold it an irreligious thing for either father or husband or any male to come near them.

They have often asked me if it be so with women of other nations, and whether they are so separated, and for their practice they plead nature and tradition. Yet again I have found a greater affinity of their language with the Greek tongue.

2. As the Greeks and other nations, and ourselves call the seven stars (or Charles' Wain, the Bear)[3] so do they *Mosk* or *Paukunnawaw*, the Bear.

3. They have many strange relations of one Wétucks,[4] a man that wrought great miracles amongst them, and walking upon the waters, etc., with some kind of broken resemblance to the Son of God.

Lastly, it is famous that the Sowwest (*Sowaniu*) is the great subject of their discourse, from thence their traditions. There they say (at the southwest) is the court of their great god Kautántowwìt. At the southwest are their forefathers' souls; to the southwest they go themselves when they die; from the southwest came their corn, and beans out of their great god Kautántowwìt's field; and indeed the further northward and westward from us their corn will not grow, but to the southward better and better. I dare not conjecture in these uncertainties. I believe they are lost, and yet hope (in the Lord's holy season) some of the wildest of them shall be found to share in the blood of the Son of God. To the third head, concerning their religion, customs, manners etc. I shall here say nothing, because in those 32 chapters of the whole book,[5] I have briefly touched those of all sorts, from their birth to their burials, and have endeavored (as the nature of the work would give way) to bring some short observations and applications home to Europe from America.

Therefore fourthly, to that great point of their conversion, so much to be longed for, and by all New English so much pretended,[6] and I hope in truth.

1 *Tartaria* Region of Central Asia.

2 *affinity with the Hebrew* Many Europeans hypothesized a connection between Native Americans and the ancient Israelites.

3 *Charles' ... Bear* Charlemagne's wagon, the constellation Ursa Major, also known as The Great Bear.

4 *Wétucks* Legendary giant of Narragansett oral literature, called Moshup by neighboring tribes; he has transformative powers and his actions are said to have shaped the geographical features of the region.

5 *whole book* The *Key*.

6 *by all ... much pretended* Reference to exaggerated claims about the conversion of Indigenous people made by the Puritans, most notably in the 1643 text *New England's First Fruits*.

For myself I have uprightly labored to suit my endeavors to my pretenses, and of later times (out of desire to attain their language) I have run through varieties of intercourses with them day and night, summer and winter, by land and sea. Particular passages tending to this, I have related diverse,[1] in the chapter of their religion.

Many solemn discourses I have had with all sorts of nations of them, from one end of the country to another (so far as opportunity, and the little language I have could reach).

I know there is no small preparation in the hearts of multitudes of them. I know their many solemn confessions to myself, and one to another of their lost wandering conditions. I know strong convictions upon the consciences of many of them, and their desires uttered that way.

I know not with how little knowledge and grace of Christ the Lord may save, and therefore, neither will despair, nor report much.

But since it hath pleased some of my worthy countrymen to mention (of late in print) Wequash,[2] the Péquot captain, I shall be bold so far to second their relations, as to relate mine own hopes of him (though I dare not be so confident as others).

Two days before his death, as I passed up to Qunníhticut River, it pleased my worthy friend Mr. Fenwick[3] (whom I visited at his house in Saybrook Fort at the mouth of that river) to tell me that my old friend Wequash lay very sick. I desired to see him, and himself was pleased to be my guide two miles where Wequash lay.

Amongst other discourse concerning his sickness and death (in which he freely bequeathed his son to Mr. Fenwick) I closed with him concerning his soul: he told me that some two or three years before he had lodged at my house, where I acquainted him with the condition of all mankind, and his own in particular; how God created man and all things; how man fell from God, and of his present enmity against God, and

the wrath of God against him until repentance. Said he, "Your words were never out of my heart to this present," and said he, "Me much pray to Jesus Christ." I told him so did many English, French, and Dutch, who had never turned to God, nor loved Him. He replied in broken English: "Me so big naughty heart, me heart all one stone!"; savory expressions using to breathe from compunct[4] and broken hearts, and a sense of inward hardness and unbrokenness. I had many discourses with him in his life, but this was the sum of our last parting until our General Meeting.[5]

Now, because this is the great inquiry of all men: What Indians have been converted? What have the English done in those parts? What hopes of the Indians receiving the knowledge of Christ?

And because to this question, some put an edge from the boast of the Jesuits in Canada and Maryland, and especially from the wonderful conversions made by the Spaniards and Portugals in the West Indies; besides what I have here written, as also, beside what I have observed in the chapter of their religion, I shall further present you with a brief additional discourse concerning this great point, being comfortably persuaded that the Father of Spirits, who was graciously pleased to persuade Japhet (the Gentiles) to dwell in the tents of Shem[6] (the Jews), will, in His holy season (I hope approaching), persuade these gentiles of America to partake of the mercies of Europe, and then shall be fulfilled what is written by the prophet Malachi,[7] from the rising of the sun (in Europe) to the going down of the same (in America), My name shall be great among the Gentiles. So I desire to hope and pray.

Your unworthy countryman,
Roger Williams

[1] *I have … diverse* I have recounted a variety.

[2] *Wequash* Member of the Pequot tribe who famously converted to Christianity. Wequash's conversion was given special attention by the authors of *New England's First Fruits*.

[3] *Qunníhticut* Connecticut; *Mr. Fenwick* George Fenwick (c. 1603–57), an English politician and early colonizer of Connecticut.

[4] *compunct* Pricked by knowledge of wrongdoing.

[5] *General Meeting* Reunion at Judgment Day.

[6] *Japhet* Noah's third son, traditionally seen as the progenitor of European, and some Asian, peoples; *Shem* Noah's eldest son, considered the progenitor of Semitic peoples. Cf. Genesis 9.27.

[7] *written by … Malachi* Cf. Malachi 1.11: "For from the rising of the sun even unto the going down of the same my name shall be great among the Gentiles; and in every place incense shall be offered unto my name, and a pure offering: for my name shall be great among the heathen, saith the Lord of hosts."

Directions for the Use of the Language

1. A dictionary or grammar way I had consideration of, but purposely avoided, as not so accommodate to the benefit of all, as I hope this form is.

2. A dialogue also I had thoughts of, but avoided for brevity's sake, and yet (with no small pains) I have so framed every chapter and the matter of it, as I may call it an implicit dialogue.

3. It is framed chiefly after the Narrogánset dialect, because most spoken in the country, and yet (with attending to the variation of peoples and dialects) it will be of great use in all parts of the country.

4. Whatever your occasion be either of travel, discourse, trading, etc., turn to the table which will direct you to the proper chapter.

5. Because the life of all languages is in the pronunciation, I have been at the pains and charges[1] to cause the accents, tones, or sounds to be affixed (which some understand, according to the Greek language, acutes, graves, circumflexes), for example in the second leaf,[2] in the word *Ewò* (He): the sound or tone must not be put on *E* but *wò* where the grave accent is.

In the same leaf, in the word *Ascowequássin*, the sound must not be on any of the syllables, but on *quáss*, where the acute or sharp sound is.

In the same leaf in the word *Anspaumpmaúntam*, the sound must not be on any other syllable but *maún*, where the circumflex or long sounding accent is.

6. The English for every Indian word or phrase stands in a straight line directly against the Indian: yet sometimes there are two words for the same thing (for their language is exceeding copious, and they have five or six words sometimes for one thing) and then the English stands against them both: for example in the second leaf,

Cowáunckamish and *Cuckquénamish.*	I pray your favour.

from Chapter 1
Of Salutation

Observation

The Natives are of two sorts (as the English are). Some more rude and clownish,[3] who are not so apt to salute, but upon salutation resalute[4] lovingly. Others, and the general, are sober and grave, and yet cheerful in a mean,[5] and as ready to begin a salutation as to resalute, which yet the English generally begin, out of desire to civilize them.

What cheer *Nétop?* is the general salutation of all English toward them. *Nétop* is friend.

Netompaüog	Friends.

They are exceedingly delighted with salutations in their own language.

Neèn, Keèn, Ewò	I, you, he.
Keén ka neen	You and I.
Asco wequássin	
Asco wequassunnúm-mis	Good morrow.
Askuttaaquompsin?	How do you?
Asnpaumpmaúntam	I am very well.
Taubot paump maúntaman	I am glad you are well.
Cowaúnckamish	My service to you. …

From these courteous salutations observe in general: There is a savour[6] of civility and courtesy even amongst these wild Americans, both amongst themselves and towards strangers.

More Particular

1. The courteous pagan shall condemn
Uncourteous Englishmen,
Who live like foxes, bears and wolves,
Or lion in his den.

2. Let none sing blessings to their souls,
For that they courteous are:
The wild barbarians with no more
Than nature, go so far:

[1] *I have … charges* I have worked painstakingly under a heavy load.

[2] *leaf* Page.

[3] *rude and clownish* Rustic and unrefined.

[4] *salute* Offer a greeting; *resalute* Return a greeting.

[5] *in a mean* On average, typically.

[6] *savour* Understanding.

3. If nature's sons both wild and tame,
 Humane and courteous be:
 How ill becomes it sons of God
 To want[1] humanity?

from CHAPTER 21
OF RELIGION, THE SOUL, ETC.

Manìt-manittó-wock | God, Gods

Obs.[2] He that questions whether God made the World, the Indians will teach him. I must acknowledge I have received in my converse with them many confirmations of those two great points, Hebrews 11.6.[3] viz.:[4]

1. That God is.

2. That he is a rewarder of all them that diligently seek him.

They will generally confess that God made all: but then in special, although they deny not that Englishman's God made English Men, and the Heavens and Earth there! yet their Gods made them and the Heaven, and Earth where they dwell.

Nummusquauna- | God is angry
múckqun manit | with me?

Obs. I have heard a poor Indian lamenting the loss of a child at break of day, call up his wife and children and all about him to lamentation, and with abundance of tears cry out! O God thou hast taken away my child! thou art angry with me: O turn thine anger from me, and spare the rest of my children.

If they receive any good in hunting, fishing, harvest etc. they acknowledge God in it.

Yea, if it be but an ordinary accident, a fall, etc. they will say God was angry and did it. *Musquantum manit.* God is angry. But herein is their Misery.

First they branch their Godhead[5] into many Gods.
Secondly, attribute it to creatures.

First, many Gods: they have given me the names of thirty seven … which in their solemn worships they invocate as:

Kautántowwit The great South-West God, to whose house all souls go, and from whom came their corn, beans, as they say.

Wompanand	The Eastern God.
Chekesuwànd	The Western God.
Wunnauaméanit	The Northern God.
Sowwanànd	The Southern God.
Wetuómanit	The House God.

Even as the Papists have their he and she saint protectors as St. George, St. Patrick, St. Denis, Virgin Mary,[6] etc.

Squáuanit	The Woman's God.
Muckquachuck-	The Children's God.
quànd	

Obs. I was once with a Native dying of wound, given him by some murderous English (who robbed him and run him through with a rapier, from whom in the heat of his wound, he at present escaped from them, but dying of his wound, they suffered death at new Plymouth, in New England) this native dying called much upon Muckquachuckquànd, which of other natives I understood (as they believed) had appeared to the dying young man, many years before, and bid him whenever he was in distress call upon him.

Secondly, as they have many of these feigned deities: so worship they the creatures in whom they conceive doth rest some deity:

Keesuckquànd	The Sun God.
Nanepaushat	The Moon God.
Paumpágussit	The Sea.
Yotáanit	The Fire God.

Supposing that Deities be in these, etc.

When I have argued with them about their Fire-God: can it, say they, be, but this fire must be a God, or divine power, that out of a stone will arise in a spark, and when a poor naked Indian is ready to starve with cold in the house and especially in the woods, often saves his life, doth dress all our food for us, and if it be angry will burn the house about us, yea if a spark fall into the dry wood, burns up the country, (though this burning of the wood to them they count a benefit both

1 *want* Lack.

2 *Obs.* Observation.

3 *Hebrews 11.6* "But without faith it is impossible to please him: for he that cometh to God must believe that he is, and that he is a rewarder of them that diligently seek him."

4 *viz.* Abbreviation of the Latin videlicet, meaning "namely," or "that is to say."

5 *Godhead* God's essence; in Christianity the term is often used in reference to the trinity, God understood as a unified whole made up of three "persons": father, son, and holy spirit.

6 *St. George … Virgin Mary* Saints of the Catholic Church.

for destroying of vermin, and keeping down the weeds and thickets)? …

Besides there is a general custom amongst them, at the apprehension of any excellency in men, women, birds, beasts, fish, etc. to cry out *Manittóo*, that is, it is a God, as thus if they see one man excel others in wisdom, valour, strength, activity etc. they cry out *Manittóo*, a God: and therefore when they talk amongst themselves of the English ships, and great buildings, of the plowing of their fields, and especially of books and letters, they will end thus: *Manittôwock*, they are Gods; *Cummanitôo*, you are a God, etc. A strong conviction natural in the soul of man, that God is filling all things, and places, and that all excellencies dwell in God, and proceed from him, and that they only are blessed who have that Jehovah their portion.

from CHAPTER 29
OF THEIR WAR, ETC.

Obs. Their wars are far less bloody and devouring than the cruel wars of Europe; and seldom twenty slain in a pitched field:[1] partly because when they fight in a wood every tree is a buckler.[2]

When they fight in a plain, they fight with leaping and dancing, that seldom an arrow hits, and when a man is wounded, unless he that shot follows upon the wounded, they soon retire and save the wounded: and yet having no Swords, nor guns, all that are slain are commonly slain with great valour and courage: for the conqueror ventures into the thickest, and brings away the head of his enemy.

Niss-nissoke	Kill kill.
Kunnish	I will kill you.
Kunnishickqun ewò	He will kill you.
Kunnishickquock	They will kill you.
Siuckissûog	They are stout men.
Nickummissũog	They are weak.
Nnickummaunámaûog	I shall easily vanquish them.
Neene núppamen	I am dying?
Cowaúnckamish	Quarter, quarter.
Kunnanaumpasúmmish	Mercy, mercy.
Kekuttokaûntá	Let us parley.

Aquétuck	Let us cease arms.
Wunnishaũnta	Let us agree.
Cowammáunsh	I love you.
Wunnêtu ntá	My heart is true.
Tuppaûntash	Consider what I say.
Tuppaûntamoke	Do you all consider.
Cummequaunum cummittamussussuck ka cummuckiaûg	Remember your wives and children.
Eatch kèen anawâyean	Let all be as you say.
Cowawwunnaúwem	You speak truly.
Cowauôntam	You are a wise man.
Wetompátitea	Let us make friends.

General Observations of Their Wars

How dreadful and yet how righteous is it with the most righteous judge of the whole world, that all the generations of men being turned enemies against, and fighting against him who gives them breath and being, and all things (whom yet they cannot reach, should stab, kill, burn, murder and devour each other)?

More Particular

The Indians count of men as dogs,
It is no wonder then:
They tear out one another's throats!
But now that English men,
(That boast themselves God's children, and
Members of Christ to be)
That they should thus break out in flames.
Sure 'tis a mystery!
The second sealed mystery or red horse,[3]
Whose rider hath power and will,
To take away peace from earthly men,
They must each other kill.

—1643

1 *pitched field* I.e., planned battle.

2 *buckler* Shield.

3 *second sealed … red horse* In Revelation, John envisions God opening seven seals, each of which precipitates a cataclysmic event. The second seal releases a rider on a red horse who signifies War. Cf. Revelation 6.3–4.

from *The Bloody Tenet of Persecution*

from [ADDRESS] TO THE RIGHT HONOURABLE BOTH HOUSES OF THE HIGH COURT OF PARLIAMENT

Right Honourable and Renowned Patriots,
Next to saving of your souls in the lamentable shipwreck of mankind, your task as Christians is to save the souls, but as magistrates the bodies and goods, of others.[1]

Many excellent discourses have been presented to your fathers' hands and yours, in former and present parliaments. I shall be humbly bold to say, that, in what concerns your duties as magistrates towards others, a more necessary and seasonable debate was never yet presented. …

Most noble senators; your fathers, whose seats you fill, are mouldered, and mouldering their brains, their tongues, etc., to ashes in the pit of rottenness: they and you must shortly, together with two worlds of men, appear at the great bar.[2] It shall then be no grief of heart that you have now attended to the cries of souls, thousands oppressed, millions ravished, by the acts and statutes concerning souls not yet repealed—of bodies impoverished, imprisoned, etc., for their souls' belief: yea, slaughtered on heaps for religious controversies, in the wars of present and former ages. …

It cannot be denied to be a pious and prudential act for your Honours, according to your conscience, to call for the advice of faithful counsellors in the high debates concerning your own, and the souls of others.

Yet, let it not be imputed as a crime for any suppliant to the God of heaven for you, if, the humble sense of what their souls believe, they pour forth, amongst others, these three requests at the throne of grace:

First. That neither your Honours, nor those excellent and worthy persons whose advice you seek, limit the Holy One of Israel to their apprehensions, debates, conclusions, rejecting or neglecting the humble and faithful suggestions of any, though as base as spittle and

clay, with which sometimes Christ Jesus opens the eyes of them that are born blind.[3]

Secondly. That the present and future generations of the sons of men may never have cause to say that such a parliament, as England never enjoyed the like, should model the worship of the living eternal, and invisible God, after the bias of any earthly interest, though of the highest concernment[4] under the sun. And yet saith the learned Sir Francis Bacon (however otherwise persuaded, yet thus he confesseth), "Such as hold pressure of conscience, are guided therein by some private interests of their own."[5]

Thirdly. [That] whatever way of worshipping God your own consciences are persuaded to walk in, yet, from any bloody act of violence to the consciences of others, it may never be told at Rome nor Oxford, that the parliament of England hath committed a greater rape than if they had forced or ravished the bodies of all the women in the world. …

from CHAPTER 1

Truth. In what dark corner of the world, sweet Peace, are we two met? How hath this present evil world banished me from all the coasts and quarters of it? And how hath the righteous God in judgment taken thee from the earth? Revelation 6.4.[6]

Peace. It is lamentably true, blessed Truth, the foundations of the world have long been out of course: the gates of earth and hell have conspired together to intercept our joyful meeting and our holy kisses. With what a wearied, tired wing have I flown over nations, kingdoms, cities, towns, to find out precious Truth!

1 *your task … of others* I.e., in your capacity as a Christian you have the obligation to save other people's souls, but in your role as a magistrate you are obliged only to preserve other people's bodies and goods.

2 *great bar* Court of heaven.

3 *spittle and … blind* Cf. John 9.6–7: "When he had thus spoken, he spat on the ground, and made clay of the spittle, and he anointed the eyes of the blind man with the clay, And said unto him, Go, wash in the pool of Siloam (which is by interpretation, sent). He went his way therefore, and washed, and came seeing."

4 *concernment* Significance.

5 *Francis Bacon* English philosopher, scientist, and jurist (1561–1626) best known for his contributions to the development of the scientific method; *Such as … their own* Cf. Francis Bacon's 1625 essay "Of Unity in Religion."

6 *Revelation 6.4* "And there went out another horse that was red: and power was given to him that sat thereon to take peace from the earth, and that they should kill one another: and there was given unto him a great sword."

Truth. The like inquiries in my flights and travels have I made for Peace, and still am told she hath left the earth and fled to heaven.

Peace. Dear Truth, what is the earth but a dungeon of darkness, where Truth is not?

Truth. And what is the Peace thereof but a fleeting dream, thine ape[1] and counterfeit? …

from CHAPTER 2

… *Truth.* Sweet Peace, what hast thou there?

Peace. Arguments against persecution for cause of conscience.

Truth. And what there?

Peace. An answer to such arguments, contrarily maintaining such persecution for cause of conscience.[2]

Truth. These arguments against such persecution, and the answer pleading for it, [are] written, as Love hopes, from godly intentions, hearts, and hands, yet in a marvelously different style and manner—the arguments against persecution in milk, the answer for it, as I may say, in blood.

The author of these arguments against persecution, as I have been informed, being committed by some then in power close prisoner to Newgate,[3] for the witness of some truths and of Jesus, and having not the use of pen and ink, wrote these arguments in milk, in sheets of paper brought to him by the woman, his keeper, from a friend in London as the stopples[4] of his milk bottle.

In such paper, written with milk, nothing will appear; but the way of reading it by fire being known to this friend who received the papers, he transcribed and kept together the papers, although the author himself could not correct, nor view what himself had written.

It was in milk, tending to soul nourishment, even for babes and sucklings in Christ.

It was in milk, spiritually white, pure and innocent, like those white horses of the word of truth and meekness, and the white linen or armor of righteousness, in the army of Jesus, Revelation 6 and Revelation 19.[5]

It was in milk, soft, meek, peaceable, and gentle, tending both to the peace of souls, and the peace of states and kingdoms.

Peace. The answer, though I hope out of milk-pure intentions, is returned in blood—bloody and slaughterous conclusions—bloody to the souls of all men, forced to the religion and worship which every civil state or commonweal agrees on, and compels all subjects to, in a dissembled uniformity.[6]

Bloody to the bodies, first of the holy witnesses of Christ Jesus, who testify against such invented worships.

Secondly, of the nations and people slaughtering each other for their several respective religions and consciences.

from CHAPTER 9

Peace. It will here be said, whence then ariseth civil dissensions and uproars about matters of religion?

Truth. I answer: When a kingdom or state, town or family, lies and lives in the guilt of a false god, false Christ, false worship, no wonder if sore eyes be troubled at the appearance of the light, be it never so sweet. No wonder if a body full of corrupt humours be troubled at strong, though wholesome, physic[7]—if persons sleepy and loving to sleep be troubled at the

1 *ape* Imitator.

2 *Arguments against … of conscience* Peace refers to "An Humble Supplication to the King's Majesty," a text written by an anonymous prisoner that argues against the state enforcement of religious uniformity, and John Cotton's "The Answer of Mr. John Cotton," which argues the opposite position.

3 *close prisoner … Newgate* Confined prisoner at Newgate Prison, in London, England.

4 *stopples* Plugs.

5 *Revelation 6* Cf. Revelation 6.2: "And I saw, and behold a white horse: and he that sat on him had a bow; and a crown was given unto him: and he went forth conquering, and to conquer"; *Revelation 19* Cf. Revelation 19.11–14: "And I saw heaven opened, and behold a white horse; and he that sat upon him *was* called Faithful and True, and in righteousness he doth judge and make war. … And he *was* clothed with a vesture dipped in blood: and his name is called The Word of God. And the armies *which were* in heaven followed him upon white horses, clothed in fine linen, white and clean."

6 *commonweal* Commonwealth; *dissembled uniformity* I.e., false and counterfeit—because compelled—uniformity of worship.

7 *humours* Vital fluids that were believed to determine a person or animal's health; *physic* Medicine.

noise of shrill, though silver, alarums.[1] ... Whereas, good eyes are not so troubled at light; vigilant and watchful persons, loyal and faithful, are not so troubled at the true, no, nor at a false religion of Jew or Gentile.

Secondly. Breach of civil peace may arise when false and idolatrous practices are held forth, and yet no breach of civil peace from the doctrine or practice, or the manner of holding forth, but from that wrong and preposterous way of suppressing, preventing, and extinguishing such doctrines or practices by weapons of wrath and blood, whips, stocks, imprisonment, banishment, death, etc.; by which men commonly are persuaded to convert heretics, and to cast out unclean spirits, which only the finger of God can do, that is, the mighty power of the Spirit in the word.

Hence the town is in an uproar, and the country takes the alarum to expel that fog or mist of error, heresy, blasphemy, as is supposed, with swords and guns. Whereas it is light alone, even light from the bright shining Sun of Righteousness,[2] which is able, in the souls and consciences of men, to dispel and scatter such fogs and darkness. ...

from CHAPTER 16

Peace. ... First, saith he [the Apostle Paul], such a person [who professes religious errors] is to be tolerated till God may be pleased to reveal his truth to him.

Truth. This is well observed by you: for indeed this is the very ground why the apostle calls for meekness and gentleness towards all men, and toward such as oppose themselves, 2 Timothy 2.25;[3] because there is a peradventure,[4] or may be; "It may be, God may *give them repentance.*" That God hath shown mercy to one,

may show mercy to another. It may be, that eyesalve[5] that anointed one man's eyes who was blind and opposite, may another as blind and opposite. He that hath given repentance to the husband, may give it to his wife, etc.

Hence the soul that is lively and sensible of mercy received to itself in former blindness, opposition, and enmity against god, cannot but be patient and gentle toward the Jews, who yet deny the Lord Jesus to be come, and justify their forefathers in murdering of him; toward the Turks,[6] who acknowledge Christ a great prophet, yet less than Mahomet; yea, to all the several sorts of anti-Christians, who set up many a false Christ instead of him; and, lastly, to the pagans, and wildest sorts of the sons of men, who have not yet heard of the Father, nor the Son; and to all these sorts, Jews, Turks, anti-Christians, pagans, when they oppose the light presented to them, in the sense of its own former opposition, and that God peradventure[7] may at last give repentance. I add, such a soul will not only be patient, but earnestly and constantly pray for all sorts of men, that out of them God's elect may be called to the fellowship of Christ Jesus; and, lastly, not only pray, but endeavour, to its utmost ability, their participation of the same grace and mercy. ...

from CHAPTER 39

... *Truth.* I argue from this place of Timothy[8] in particular, thus:

First. If the civil magistrates be Christians, or members of the church, able to prophesy in the church of Christ, then, I say as before, they are bound by this command of Christ to suffer opposition to their doctrine with meekness and gentleness, and to be so far from striving to subdue their opposites with the civil sword, that they are bound with patience and meekness to wait, if God peradventure will please to grant repentance unto their opposites. ...

Secondly. Be they oppositions within, and church members, as the answerer speaks, become slanderous in

1 *silver* Pleasant-sounding; *alarums* Alarms.

2 *Sun of Righteousness* Cf. Malachi 4.2: "But unto you that fear my name shall the Sun of righteousness arise with healing in his wings; and ye shall go forth, and grow up as calves of the stall."

3 *Timothy 2.25* Cf. 2 Timothy 2.24–26: "And the servant of the Lord must not strive; but be gentle unto all men, apt to teach, patient, in meekness instructing those that oppose themselves; if God peradventure will give them repentance to the acknowledging of the truth; and that they may recover themselves out of the snare of the devil, who are taken captive by him at his will."

4 *peradventure* Possibility.

5 *eyesalve* Eye medicine. (Cf. Revelation 3.18: "[A]noint thine eyes with eyesalve, that thou mayest see.")

6 *Turks* Muslims.

7 *peradventure* Possibly.

8 *Timothy* Cf. 2 Timothy 2.24–26, quoted above.

doctrine (I speak not of scandals against the civil state, which the civil magistrate ought to punish), it is the Lord only, as this scripture to Timothy implies, who is able to give them repentance, and recover them out of Satan's snare. To which end also, he hath appointed those holy and dreadful censures in his church or kingdom. True it is, the sword may make, as once the Lord complained, Isaiah 10, a whole nation of hypocrites; but to recover a soul from Satan by repentance, and to bring them from anti-Christian doctrine or worship to the doctrine or worship Christian in the least true internal or external submission, that only works the all-powerful God, by the sword of his spirit in the hand of his spiritual officers.

from CHAPTER 138

Peace. If English ground must yet be drunk with English blood, oh! Where shall Peace repose her wearied head and heavy heart?

Truth. Dear Peace, if thou find welcome, and the God of peace miraculously please to quench these all-devouring flames, yet where shall Truth find rest from cruel persecutions?

Peace. Oh! Will not the authority of holy scriptures, the commands and declarations of the Son of God, therein produced by thee, together with all the lamentable experiences of former and present slaughters, prevail with the sons of men, especially with the sons of peace, to depart from the dens of lions, and mountains of leopards, and to put the bowels,[1] if not of Christianity, yet of humanity each to other?

Truth. Dear Peace, Habakkuk's fishes[2] keep their constant bloody game of persecutions in the world's mighty ocean; the greater taking, plundering, swallowing up the lesser. Oh! happy he whose portion is the God of Jacob![3] who hath nothing to lose under the sun;[4] but hath a state, a house, an inheritance, a name, a crown, a life, past all the plunderers', ravishers', murderer's reach and fury!

Peace. But lo! Who's there?

Truth. Our sister *Patience*, whose desired company is as needful as delightful. It is like the wolf will send up the scattered sheep in one; the common pirate gather up the loose and scattered navy; the slaughter of the witnesses by that bloody beast[5] unite the Independents and Presbyterians.

The God of peace, the God of truth, will shortly seal this truth, and confirm this witness, and make it evident to the whole world—

THAT THE DOCTRINE OF PERSECUTION FOR CAUSE OF CONSCIENCE IS MOST EVIDENTLY AND LAMENTABLY CONTRARY TO THE DOCTRINE OF CHRIST JESUS, THE PRINCE OF PEACE. AMEN.

—1644

Letter to the Town of Providence

In 1654, Providence formed a citizen militia and fined anyone who refused to join. Opponents of this compulsory military service—one of whom was Williams's brother—cited the colony's policy on freedom of conscience as justification for their refusal to participate. The controversy is probably what induced Williams to write the following letter, in which he clarifies the position on religious freedom he took in earlier works such as *The Bloody Tenet*.

LETTER TO THE TOWN OF PROVIDENCE,
c. JANUARY 1655

Loving Friends and Neighbors,

[1] *bowels* Considered the site of one's compassion.

[2] *Habakkuk's fishes* Human beings. Cf. Habakkuk 1.13–14: "Thou art of purer eyes than to behold evil, and canst not look on iniquity: wherefore lookest thou upon them that deal treacherously, and holdest thy tongue when the wicked devoureth the man that is more righteous than he? And makest men as the fishes of the sea, as the creeping things, that have no ruler over them?"

[3] *God of Jacob* Phrase frequently used in the Bible to refer to God; *Jacob* Hebrew patriarch from whom, according to Christian tradition, the Israelites were descended.

[4] *under the sun* This phrase is used frequently in Ecclesiastes to refer to the worldly realm; see, for example, Ecclesiastes 5.18. "[I]t is good and comely for one to eat and to drink, and to enjoy the good of all his labour that he taketh under the sun all the days of life, which God giveth him: for it is his portion."

[5] *slaughter of ... bloody beast* According to Revelation, at the end of history two witnesses will prophecy in the name of God, and then be slaughtered by a ten-horned beast. Cf. Revelation 11.3–7. Earlier in *The Bloody Tenet*, Williams interprets the beast as a symbol of the civil magistrates who persecute faithful Christians.

It pleases God yet to continue this great liberty of our town meetings, for which we ought to be humbly thankful and to improve these liberties to the praise of the Giver, and to the peace and welfare of the town and colony, without our own private ends. I thought it my duty to present you with this my impartial testimony and answer to a paper sent [to] you the other day from my brother[1]—that it is blood-guiltiness and against the rule of the Gospel to execute judgment upon transgressors against the private or public weal.

That ever I should speak or write a tittle,[2] that tends to such an infinite liberty of conscience, is a mistake, and which I have ever disclaimed and abhorred. To prevent such mistakes, I shall at present only propose this case:

There goes many a ship to sea, with many hundred souls in one ship, whose weal[3] and woe is common, and is a true picture of a commonwealth, or a human combination or society. It hath fallen out sometimes, that both Papists and Protestants, Jews and Turks, may be embarked in one ship; upon which supposal[4] I affirm, that all the liberty of conscience, that ever I pleaded for, turns upon these two hinges—that none of the Papists, Protestants, Jews, or Turks, be forced to come to the ship's prayers of worship, nor compelled from their own particular prayers or worship, if they practice any.

I further add, that I never denied, that notwithstanding this liberty, the commander of this ship ought to command the ship's course, yea, and also command that justice, peace and sobriety, be kept and practiced, both among the seamen and all the passengers. If any of the seamen refuse to perform their services, or passengers to pay their freight; if any refuse to help, in person or purse, towards the common charges or defence; if any refuse to obey the common laws and orders of the ship, concerning their common peace or preservation; if any shall mutiny and rise up against their commanders and officers; if any should preach or write that there ought to be no commanders or officers, because all are equal in Christ, therefore no masters nor officers, no laws nor orders, nor corrections nor punishments[5]—I say, I never denied, but in such cases, whatever is pretended, the commander or commanders may judge, resist, compel and punish such transgressors, according to their deserts and merits. This if seriously and honestly minded, may, if it so please the Father of lights, let in some light to such as willingly shut not their eyes.

I remain studious of your common peace and liberty. —1655

[1] *my brother* Robert Williams (1604–80), Roger Williams's brother and a conscientious objector to compulsory military service.

[2] *tittle* Minute amount.

[3] *weal* Well-being.

[4] *Papists* Catholics; *Turks* Muslims; *supposal* Hypothesis.

[5] *if any should preach … nor punishments* Allusion to the Antinomian perspective that God's chosen people are not subject to the law.

ANNE BRADSTREET

c. 1612 – 1672

A Puritan colonist born in England, Anne Bradstreet is distinguished as one of the first poets to write in English in North America. As such, she has always been closely associated with the historical archive of early colonial America. But why do we read Anne Bradstreet in the modern world? For many decades now, a lively debate has centered on that question. Is it merely for historical and sociological reasons— "because she was the first American poet, and a woman at that" (as Louisa Hall puts it)? Or is her poetry of real value to us today *as poetry*?

Though Bradstreet was praised by some in her own time as an accomplished versifier, her work attracted little attention in the seventeenth and eighteenth centuries, and for much of the nineteenth and early twentieth centuries discussions of her poetry tended to be politely patronizing. The 1858 *American Cyclopedia* praised her "singular quaintness"; William P. Trent's 1904 *Brief History of American Literature* concluded that she "was a good, true woman, well read in the poets of her day, and possessed of genuine though very slight literary powers." Then, in the 1950s and 60s the poet John Berryman reimagined Bradstreet's life through the 57 stanzas of his 1956 "Homage to Mistress Bradstreet"—and brought a new bluntness to discussions of what he described at one point as Bradstreet's "spiritless poems." He went on in a 1965 essay to characterize Bradstreet as a "boring, high minded Puritan woman who may have been our first American poet but was not a good one." (It was "as a woman," rather than "as a poetess" that Bradstreet interested Berryman.) A number of poets and literary scholars piled on, describing Bradstreet's verse as "dull," "awkward," "insipid"—at best, "endearingly competent." But in the 1960s and 70s those critics met with a strong riposte; in 1966, for example, Ann Stanford argued that Bradstreet's work was characterized by powerful tensions—a "clash of feeling and dogma that keeps her poetry alive." In 1967 the distinguished poet Adrienne Rich made a strong case that Bradstreet's more personal work in particular displayed both honesty and emotional intensity. Late twentieth-century feminist critics fleshed out the picture of a poet of considerable range, and in this century Eavan Boland persuasively argued in a 2006 essay for the merits of "the neighbourly, definite voice" with which Bradstreet tells her story. (Boland's 2012 poem "Becoming Anne Bradstreet" makes the case in a different fashion for the earlier poet's "home truths.")

Bradstreet was born Anne Dudley in Northampton, England, to Dorothy Yorke and Thomas Dudley. In 1619 her father became steward to the Earl of Lincoln, and Anne lived in comfort on the Earl's estate in her youth. Though not educated formally, she was an ardent reader and made use of her access to an extensive library, encouraged by her parents to pursue learning in many subjects. She married her father's assistant, Cambridge graduate Simon Bradstreet, in 1628; two years later, the couple joined her parents and hundreds of other Puritan colonists on a journey to join the new Massachusetts Bay Colony in America.

Their ship, the *Arbella*, arrived in Salem after three difficult months. The eighteen-year-old Bradstreet, as she later wrote, "found a new world and new manners at which my heart rose [in revolt]. But after I was convinced it was the way of God, I submitted to it and joined the church at Boston." Bradstreet's body of work gives expression, from a variety of angles, both to her Puritan beliefs and to her experience of everyday life in seventeenth-century America.

We do not know if Bradstreet wrote any poems before she came to America; the first of her extant poems, "Upon a Fit of Sickness," was composed in 1632, when she was twenty. After their first years in Salem, the family lived in several increasingly remote communities, including Charlestown, Newtown, and Ipswich; they eventually settled in Andover (now called North Andover). Bradstreet and her husband also began to establish their own family, with their first child Samuel born in 1633 and seven more following over the next nineteen years (all of whom, remarkably, survived into adulthood). Bradstreet's

husband and father both worked as administrators in the colony, spending a great deal of time away from home and often leaving her as the sole manager of the household; she nonetheless found time to compose poems, which she shared with her social circle but made no effort to publish. (Print technology was not yet well established in America, and even in Europe authors often still preferred to circulate manuscripts by hand rather than have them printed).

In 1650, a collection of Bradstreet's poems was published in London under the title *The Tenth Muse Lately Sprung Up in America*. The publication seems to have been orchestrated by several friends, chief among them her brother-in-law John Woodbridge, who had brought copies of a number of her poems with him when he returned to England. In his epistle to the reader, Woodbridge expresses his rationale:

> … I fear the displeasure of no person in the publishing of these poems but the author, without whose knowledge, and contrary to her expectation, I have presumed to bring to public view, what she resolved should (in such a manner) never see the sun; but I found [that various people] had gotten some scattered papers … [and] were likely to have sent forth broken pieces, to the author's prejudice, which I thought to prevent, as well as to pleasure those that earnestly desired the view of the whole.

Though some have suggested that Bradstreet herself may have approved of Woodbridge's actions, most scholars have taken the evidence at face value and concluded that Bradstreet very likely did indeed (as she later put it in her poem "The Author to Her Book") find herself "blushing" at the unexpected and unplanned publication.

Whatever the circumstances of its publication, the writing in the collection demonstrates not only the author's facility with poetic forms but also her very considerable knowledge of philosophy, history, science, and literature. Her "quaternions" (four-part poems) discuss the four elements, seasons, humors of human beings, and stages of life; her elegies praise such figures as Elizabeth I and Sir Philip Sidney; and her "Dialogue Between Old England and New" depicts the political relationship between her old and new homes as personified by a mother and daughter. Though *The Tenth Muse* was a commercial success for the printer, it would be the only collection of Bradstreet's work published during her lifetime.

The poems in *The Tenth Muse* are largely public poems, but Bradstreet's writing could also be highly personal, drawing on her life experiences as a wife, mother, and Puritan, and including elegies for her parents, poems responding to the deaths of several grandchildren, and love letters to her husband. (The publication history has led many to assume that the formal, public poems were essentially apprentice work, and that it was only later in her life that Bradstreet's writing took a personal turn, but recent scholarship has shown that there can be no precise correlation of her public poems and her personal poems with different stages of her life.) With her children as her imagined audience, she wrote *Meditations Divine and Moral*, a work containing observations and wisdom which she hoped could serve as a guide for her descendants after her death. Also among her unpublished writings were poems documenting personal trials (such as the fire that destroyed her home), as well as happy occasions such as her son's safe return from a trip to England. In addition to providing a glimpse into Bradstreet's lived experiences, her personal poems are notable for the tensions between their speaker's attachment to earthly life and a Puritan insistence that heavenly concerns take priority over all temporal ones.

Rich, Boland, and numerous others have been of the view that Bradstreet's public poetry is less successful aesthetically than her more personal poems—but on that subject too there has been lively disagreement, with Louisa Hall and others suggesting that what earlier commentators had read as instances of poetic incompetence (in, for example, Bradstreet's early elegies) are in fact "purposeful strategies"—intentional breaches of formal literary convention. A spirit of lively engagement with the poetry itself, then, has increasingly come to prevail in discussions of Bradstreet, with the pious and patronizing voices that were for so long dominant now increasingly relegated to the sidelines.

At sixty, Bradstreet succumbed to consumption. Six years later, her writing was published in North America for the first time as *Several Poems Compiled with Great Wit and Learning* (1678), a volume that

brought together the poems from *The Tenth Muse* both with poems not previously published—some of which (such as the love poems to her husband) the editors acknowledged that she "never meant should come to public view"—and with various later poems about Bradstreet's life. Other personal poems, however, remained in the possession of her son Simon; these would not appear in print until 1867, when John Harvard Ellis published a complete collection of her writing.

Not many material artifacts from Bradstreet's life remain—her place of burial is unmarked and no portraits of her as an adult have survived.

NOTE ON THE TEXTS: Unless otherwise noted, the texts here are based on those found in the 1678 edition of *Several Poems Compiled with Great Variety of Wit and Learning, Full of Delight Wherein Especially is Contained a Compleat Discourse, and Description of the Four Elements, Constitutions, Ages of Man, Seasons of the Year, Together with an Exact Epitome of the Three by a Gentlewoman in New-England*—or, in the case of poems not included in the seventeenth-century publications, the 1867 John Harvard Ellis edition of *The Works of Mrs. Bradstreet in Prose and Verse* (the first collection to include her later, personal poems). The ordering of the texts follows that found in these volumes—though, as scholars such as Margaret Olofson Thickstun have pointed out, we do not have any evidence that Bradstreet had any input herself into this ordering—or, indeed, whether she was responsible for the titles assigned to many of the poems.

Transcriptions of the 1678 volume may be found both on the University of Michigan Early English Books site and the University of Pennsylvania Celebration of Women Writers site. Other editions consulted include the 1897 Frank E. Hopkins edition (with introduction by Charles Eliot Norton) of *Poems of Mrs. Bradstreet, Together with Her Prose Remains*, and the 1967 Jeannine Hensley edition (with introduction by Adrienne Rich) of *The Works of Anne Bradstreet*. Thickstun was among those who raised concerns over some of the editorial practices followed in the Hensley volume; she has now published a new edition of Bradstreet's work—*Anne Bradstreet, Poems and Meditations* (2019)—which addresses those concerns, presenting the works in ways that helpfully clarify their publication history for the reader. (The editors of this anthology gratefully acknowledge Thickstun's assistance.)

Spelling and punctuation have been modernized in accordance with the practices of this anthology.

⌘ ⌘ ⌘

Prologue[1]

1

To sing of wars, of captains, and of kings,
 Of cities founded, commonwealths begun,
For my mean° pen are too superior things, *humble*
And how they all, or each, their dates have run:
5 Let poets and historians set these forth,
My obscure verse shall not so dim their worth.

2

But when my wond'ring eyes and envious heart
Great Bartas'[2] sugared lines do but read o'er,

Fool, I do grudge, the muses did not part
10 'Twixt him and me that over-fluent store;[3]
A Bartas can do what a Bartas will,
But simple I, according to my skill.

3

From school-boy's tongue, no rhetoric we expect,
Nor yet a sweet consort° from broken strings, *harmony*
15 Nor perfect beauty where's a main defect,
My foolish, broken, blemished Muse so sings;
And this to mend, alas, no art is able,
'Cause nature made it so irreparable.

[1] This poem serves as the prologue for *The Tenth Muse* (1650).

[2] *Bartas* Guillaume de Salluste, seigneur du Bartas (1544–90), French writer of epic poetry.

[3] *muses* Nine classical sister goddesses responsible for the arts; *did not ... store* Did not divide between the two of us the overabundance of talent they gave him.

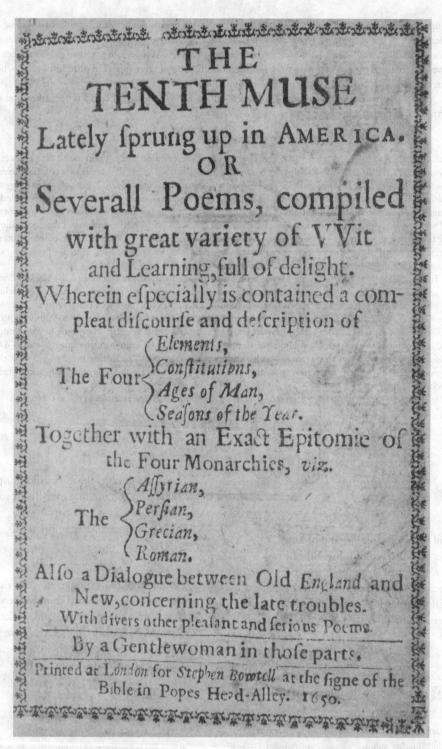

THE TENTH MUSE

Lately sprung up in AMERICA.

OR

Severall Poems, compiled

with great variety of VVit
and Learning, full of delight.
Wherein especially is contained a compleat discourse and description of

The Four
{ *Elements,*
Constitutions,
Ages of Man,
Seasons of the Year. }

Together with an Exact Epitomie of the Four Monarchies, *viz.*

The
{ *Assyrian,*
Persian,
Grecian,
Roman. }

Also a Dialogue between Old *England* and New, concerning the late troubles.
With divers other pleasant and serious Poems.

By a Gentlewoman in those parts.

Printed at *London* for *Stephen Bowtell* at the signe of the Bible in Popes Head-Alley. 1650.

Title page of the 1650 edition of *The Tenth Muse.*

4

Nor can I, like that fluent sweet-tongued Greek[1]
20 Who lisped at first, speak afterwards more plain;
By art, he gladly found what he did seek,
A full requital of his striving pain:
Art can do much, but this maxim's most sure,
A weak or wounded brain admits no cure.

5

25 I am obnoxious° to each carping tongue *vulnerable*
Who says my hand a needle better fits.
A poet's pen, all scorn, I should thus wrong;
For such despite° they cast on female wits: *spite*
If what I do prove well, it won't advance,
30 They'll say it's stol'n, or else, it was by chance.

6

But sure the antique Greeks were far more mild,
Else of our sex, why feignèd° they those nine,[2] *invented*
And poesy made, Calliope's[3] own child,
So 'mongst the rest, they placed the arts divine:
35 But this weak knot they will full soon untie,
The Greeks did nought, but play the fool and lie.[4]

7

Let Greeks be Greeks, and women what they are,
Men have precedency, and still excel,
It is but vain unjustly to wage war;
40 Men can do best, and women know it well.
Preeminence in each, and all is yours,
Yet grant some small acknowledgement of ours.

8

And oh, ye high flown quills that soar the skies,
And ever with your prey, still catch your praise,
45 If e'er you deign these lowly lines your eyes,

Give wholesome parsley wreath, I ask no bays:[5]
This mean and unrefined stuff of mine,
Will make your glistering gold but more to shine.
—1650, 1678

Contemplations

1

Sometime now past in the autumnal tide,
When Phoebus wanted but one hour to bed,[6]
The trees all richly clad, yet void of pride,
Were gilded o'er by his rich golden head.
5 Their leaves and fruits seemed painted, but was true,
Of green, of red, of yellow, mixèd hue;
Rapt° were my senses at this delectable view. *overwhelmed*

2

I wist° not what to wish, yet sure thought I, *knew*
If so much excellence abide below,
10 How excellent is he that dwells on high,
Whose power and beauty by his works we know?
Sure he is goodness, wisdom, glory, light,
That hath this under world so richly dight:° *decorated*
More Heaven than Earth was here, no winter and no
 night.

3

15 Then on a stately oak I cast mine eye,
Whose ruffling top the clouds seemed to aspire;[7]
How long since thou wast in thine infancy?
Thy strength, and stature, more thy years admire;[8]
Hath hundred winters passed since thou wast born?
20 Or thousand since thou breakest thy shell of horn?
If so, all these as nought, eternity doth scorn.

[1] *fluent ... Greek* Demosthenes of Athens (384–322 BCE), famous orator, who suffered from a speech defect and trained himself to speak clearly.

[2] *those nine* I.e., the Muses.

[3] *Calliope* Muse of epic poetry.

[4] *But this ... lie* I.e., my critics will pull apart my argument by dismissing the ancient Greeks as liars and fools.

[5] *bays* In classical times, wreaths of bay laurel were awarded for poetic and other achievements.

[6] *Phoebus wanted but one hour to bed* I.e., the sun was only an hour away from setting; Phoebus is a name given to the classical god Apollo, referring to his role as sun god.

[7] *the clouds seemed to aspire* Seemed to try to reach to the clouds.

[8] *Thy strength ... admire* Your strength and stature, and even more so your years, give rise to admiration. (The use of the verb *admire* in this way, meaning cause someone to feel admiration or wonder, is now obsolete.)

4

Then higher on the glistering sun I gazed,
Whose beams was shaded by the leafy tree.
The more I looked, the more I grew amazed,
25 And softly said, what glory's like to thee?
Soul of this world, this universe's eye,
No wonder some made thee a deity:
Had I not better known, (alas), the same had I.[1]

5

Thou as a bridegroom from thy chamber rushes,
30 And as a strong man joys to run a race,[2]
The morn doth usher thee, with smiles and blushes;
The Earth reflects her glances in thy face.
Birds, insects, animals with vegative,[3]
Thy heat from death and dullness doth revive:
35 And in the darksome womb of fruitful nature dive.

6

Thy swift annual and diurnal course,
Thy daily straight, and yearly oblique path,
Thy pleasing fervor, and thy scorching force,
All mortals here the feeling knowledge hath.[4]
40 Thy presence makes it day, thy absence night,
Quaternal seasons causèd by thy might:
Hail creature, full of sweetness, beauty and delight.

7

Art thou so full of glory that no eye
Hath strength thy shining rays once to behold?
45 And is thy splendid throne erect so high
As to approach it, can no earthly mold?° *form, thing*
How full of glory then must thy creator be,
Who gave this bright light luster unto thee?
Admired, adored for ever, be that majesty.

8

50 Silent alone, where none or° saw, or heard, *either*
In pathless paths I led my wand'ring feet,
My humble eyes to lofty skies I reared
To sing some song, my mazèd° muse *bewildered*
 thought meet.° *appropriate*
My great Creator I would magnify,
55 That nature had thus decked liberally:
But ah, and ah, again, my imbecility!

9

I heard the merry grasshopper then sing,
The black-clad cricket, bear a second part;
They kept one tune, and played on the same string,
60 Seeming to glory in their little art.
Shall creatures abject thus their voices raise
And in their kind resound their maker's praise:
Whilst I, as mute, can warble forth no
 higher lays?° *songs, poems*

10

When present times look back to ages past,
65 And men in being fancy those are dead,[5]
It makes things gone perpetually to last,
And calls back months and years that long since fled.
It makes a man more agèd in conceit,° *imagination*
Than was Methuselah, or's grand-sire great,[6]
70 While of their persons and their acts his mind doth
 treat.

11

Sometimes in Eden fair, he seems to be,
Sees glorious Adam there made Lord of all,
Fancies the Apple, dangle on the Tree,
That turn'd his Sovereign to a naked thral.° *slave*
75 Who like a miscreant's driven from that place,

[1] *Had I not better ... had I* If I had not known better (i.e., been told of the existence of a Christian God), I'm sorry to say that I too would have treated the great tree as a god.

[2] *Thou as ... a race* See Psalm 19.1–5: "The heavens declare the glory of God; and the firmament sheweth his handiwork. ... In them he set a tabernacle for the sun, / Which is as a bridegroom coming out of his chamber, and rejoiceth as a strong man to run a race."

[3] *animals with vegative* The animal as well as the plant world.

[4] *All mortals ... hath* I.e., all mortal beings on earth feel this knowledge.

[5] *men in ... dead* Living people think of (or imagine) those who are dead.

[6] *Methuselah* Old Testament figure said to have lived to be 969 years old (Genesis 5.27); *or's grand-sire great* Or his great grand-father. Methuselah's great grandfather, Mahalaleel, lived 895 years (Genesis 5.17), though the speaker may be alluding to Adam, from whom Methuselah is of course also descended.

original spelling/punctuation

— original spelling/punctuation

To get his bread with pain, and sweat of face:[1]
A penalty impos'd on his backsliding Race.

12

Here sits our Grandame in retired place,[2]
And in her lap, her bloody Cain[3] new born,
The weeping Imp oft looks her in the face,
Bewails his unknown hap,° and fate forlorn; *fortune*
His Mother sighs, to think of Paradise,
And how she lost her bliss, to be more wise,
Believing him that was, and is, Father of lyes.[4]

13

85 Here Cain and Abel come to sacrifice,
Fruits of the earth and fatlings[5] each do bring,
On Abel's gift the fire descends from skies,
But no such sign on false Cain's offering;
With sullen hateful looks he goes his ways,
90 Hath thousand thoughts to end his brother's days,
Upon whose blood his future good he hopes to raise.

14

There Abel keeps his sheep, no ill he thinks,
His brother comes, then acts his fratricide,
The virgin Earth, of blood her first draught drinks
95 But since that time she often hath been cloyed;[6]
The wretch with ghastly face and dreadful mind
Thinks each he sees will serve him in his kind,
Though none on Earth but kindred near then could
 he find.

15

Who fancies not his looks now at the bar,[7]
100 His face like death, his heart with horror fraught,
Nor malefactor° ever felt like war, *evildoer*
When deep despair with wish of life hath fought,
Branded with guilt, and crushed with
 treble° woes, *triple*
A vagabond to land of Nod he goes,
105 A city builds,[8] that walls might him secure from foes.

16

Who thinks not oft upon the fathers' ages,
Their long descent, how nephews' sons they saw,
The starry observations of those sages,
And how their precepts to their sons were law,
110 How Adam sighed to see his progeny,
Clothed all in his black sinful livery,[9]
Who neither guilt nor yet the punishment
 could fly.° *escape*

17

Our life compare we with their length of days
Who to the tenth of theirs doth now arrive?[10]
115 And though thus short, we shorten many ways,
Living so little while we are alive;
In eating, drinking, sleeping, vain delight—
So, unawares, comes on perpetual night,
And puts all pleasures vain unto eternal flight.

18

120 When I behold the heavens as in their prime,
And then the earth (though old) still clad in green,
The stones and trees, insensible of time,
Nor age nor wrinkle on their front are seen;
If winter come, and greenness then do fade,
125 A spring returns, and they more youthful made;

[1] *To get … face* Part of the condemnation spoken by God after driving Adam and Eve out of the Garden of Eden for eating the forbidden fruit: "In the sweat of thy face shalt thou eat bread" (Genesis 3.19).

[2] *our Grandame … place* Our grandmother (i.e., Eve), in the location she inhabited after she was exiled.

[3] *Cain* One of Adam and Eve's sons. In Genesis 4.1–16, when his brother Abel's sacrifice of a lamb pleased God more than Cain's offering of crops, Cain became enraged and killed Abel. After becoming the first murderer, Cain was forced to wander the earth as an exile.

[4] *Father of lyes* Title bestowed on the devil in John 8.44. In Genesis 3.15, a serpent convinced Eve to eat the forbidden fruit that would give her knowledge of good and evil; in conventional interpretations of the Bible, this serpent is equated with the devil.

[5] *fatlings* Young animals raised for meat.

[6] *cloyed* Sickened, especially by over-feeding.

[7] *at the bar* Before the judge.

[8] *land of … builds* Cain finally settled in a location east of Eden known as Nod, where he built a city and named it after his son Enoch (Genesis 4.16–17).

[9] *Clothed … livery* I.e., Adam's children wear his sinfulness as if wearing his house uniform; they have inherited his sinfulness.

[10] *Our life … arrive* The early patriarchs of the Old Testament were said to have enjoyed lifespans of hundreds of years.

But man grows old, lies down, remains where once
 he's laid.

19

By birth more noble than those creatures all,
Yet seems by nature and by custom cursed,
No sooner born, but grief and care makes fall
130 That state obliterate he had at first;
Nor youth, nor strength, nor wisdom spring again,
Nor habitations long their names retain,
But in oblivion to the final day[1] remain.

20

Shall I then praise the heavens, the trees, the earth
135 Because their beauty and their strength last longer?
Shall I wish there, or never to had birth,
Because they're bigger, and their bodies stronger?
Nay, they shall darken, perish, fade and die,
And when unmade, so ever shall they lie,
140 But man was made for endless immortality.

21

Under the cooling shadow of a stately elm
Close sat I by a goodly river's side,
Where gliding streams the rocks did overwhelm;
A lonely place, with pleasures dignified.
145 I once that loved the shady woods so well,
Now thought the rivers did the trees excel,
And if the sun would ever° shine, there *always*
 would I dwell.

22

While on the stealing stream I fixed mine eye,
Which to the longed-for ocean held its course,
150 I marked nor crooks nor rubs[2] that there did lie
Could hinder aught,° but still augment its force. *anything*
"O happy flood," quoth I, "that holds thy race
Till thou arrive at thy belovèd place,
Nor is it rocks or shoals that can obstruct thy pace,

23

155 "Nor is't enough, that thou alone mayst slide,
But hundred brooks in thy clear waves do meet,
So hand in hand along with thee they glide
To Thetis'[3] house, where all embrace and greet.
Thou emblem true of what I count the best,
160 O could I lead my rivulets[4] to rest,
So may we press to that vast mansion, ever blest."

24

Ye fish which in this liquid region 'bide,
That for each season have your habitation,
Now salt, now fresh where you think best to glide
165 To unknown coasts, to give a visitation,
In lakes and ponds, you leave your numerous
 fry;° *hatchlings*
So nature taught, and yet you know not why,
You wat'ry folk that know not your felicity.

25

Look how the wantons frisk to taste the air,[5]
170 Then to the colder bottom straight they dive;
Eftsoon° to Neptune's[6] glassy hall repair *soon after*
To see what trade the great ones there do drive,
Who forage o'er the spacious sea-green field,
And take the trembling prey before it yield,
175 Whose armour is their scales, their spreading fins their
 shield.

26

While musing thus with contemplation fed,
And thousand fancies buzzing in my brain,
The sweet-tongued Philomel[7] perched o'er my head,
And chanted forth a most melodious strain
180 Which rapt me so with wonder and delight,
I judged my hearing better than my sight,
And wished me wings with her a while to take my
 flight.

1 *final day* I.e., Judgment Day, for which bodies will be resurrected and reunited with souls.

2 *marked nor crooks … rubs* Observed that neither bends nor obstructions.

3 *Thetis* Classical sea nymph.

4 *rivulets* Small branches of a river or stream.

5 *wantons … air* The lively ones leap up above the surface.

6 *Neptune* Classical sea god.

7 *Philomel* Nightingale, so named for the Greek mythological figure Philomela, who was transformed into a nightingale.

27

"O merry bird," (said I) "that fears no snares,
That neither toils nor hoards up in thy barn,[1]
185 Feels no sad thoughts nor
 cruciating° cares *tormenting, painful*
To gain more good or shun what might thee harm.
Thy clothes ne'er wear, thy
 meat° is everywhere, *food (of any sort)*
Thy bed a bough, thy drink the water clear,
Reminds not what is past, nor what's to come dost
 fear.

28

190 "The dawning morn with songs thou dost
 prevent,° *anticipate*
Sets hundred notes unto thy feathered crew,
So each one tunes his pretty instrument,
And warbling out the old, begins anew,
And thus they pass their youth in summer season,
195 Then follow thee into a better region,
Where winter's never felt by that sweet airy legion."

29

Man at the best a creature frail and vain,
In knowledge ignorant, in strength but weak,
Subject to sorrows, losses, sickness, pain,
200 Each storm his state, his mind, his body break,
From some of these he never finds cessation,
But day or night, within, without, vexation,
Troubles from foes, from friends, from dearest, near'st
 relation.

30

And yet this sinful creature, frail and vain,
205 This lump of wretchedness, of sin and sorrow,
This weather-beaten vessel wracked with pain,
Joys not in hope of an eternal morrow;
Nor all his losses, crosses, and vexation,
In weight, in frequency and long duration
210 Can make him deeply groan for that divine
 translation.° *transformation*

31

The mariner that on smooth waves doth glide,
Sings merrily, and steers his barque° with ease, *ship*
As if he had command of wind and tide,
And now becomes great master of the seas;
215 But suddenly a storm spoils all the sport,
And makes him long for a more quiet port,
Which 'gainst all adverse winds may serve for fort.

32

So he that saileth in this world of pleasure,
Feeding on sweets, that never bit of th' sour,
220 That's full of friends, of honour and of treasure,
Fond° fool, he takes this earth ev'n *silly*
 for heav'n's bower,[2]
But sad affliction comes and makes him see
Here's neither honour, wealth, nor safety;
Only above is found all with security.

33

225 O Time the fatal wrack° of mortal things, *ruination*
That draws oblivion's curtains over kings;
Their sumptuous monuments, men know them not,
Their names without a record are forgot,
Their parts, their ports, their pomp's all laid in th'
 dust
230 Nor wit, nor gold, nor buildings 'scape time's rust;
But he whose name is graved in the white stone[3]
Shall last and shine when all of these are gone.
—1678

The Flesh and the Spirit

In secret place where once I stood
Close by the banks of lacrim flood° *flood of tears*
I heard two sisters reason on
Things that are past, and things to come;
5 One Flesh was called, who had her eye
On worldly wealth and vanity;
The other Spirit, who did rear
Her thoughts unto a higher sphere:

[1] *That neither toils … thy barn* See Matthew 6.28.

[2] *bower* Shaded, comfortable sanctuary.

[3] *white stone* See Revelation 2.17: "To him that overcometh will I give … a white stone, and in the stone a new name written."

Sister, quoth Flesh, what liv'st thou on,
10 Nothing but meditation?
Doth contemplation feed thee so
Regardlessly to let earth go?[1]
Can speculation satisfy
Notion without reality?
15 Dost dream[2] of things beyond the moon
And dost thou hope to dwell there soon?
Hast treasures there laid up in store
That all in the world thou count'st but poor?
Art fancy-sick[3] or turned a sot° fool
20 To catch at shadows which are not?
Come, come, I'll show unto thy sense,
Industry hath its recompense.° compensation
What canst desire, but thou may'st see
True substance in variety?
25 Dost honour like? Acquire the same,
As some to their immortal fame:
And trophies to thy name erect
Which wearing time shall ne'er deject.
For riches dost thou long full sore?
30 Behold enough of precious store.
Earth hath more silver, pearls, and gold
Than eyes can see, or hands can hold.
Affect's thou pleasure?[4] Take thy fill,
Earth hath enough of what you will.
35 Then let not go what thou may'st find,
For things unknown, only in mind.

Spirit: Be still thou unregenerate[5] part,
Disturb no more my settled heart,
For I have vowed, (and so will do)
40 Thee as a foe, still to pursue.
And combat with thee will and must,
Until I see thee laid in the dust.
Sisters we are, yea twins we be
Yet deadly feud twixt thee and me;
45 For from one father are we not,

Thou by old Adam wast begot,[6]
But my arise is from above
Whence my dear father I do love.
Thou speak'st me fair but hat'st me sore;
50 Thy flatt'ring shows I'll trust no more.
How oft thy slave, hast thou me made,
When I believed what thou hast said,
And never had more cause of woe
Than when I did what thou bad'st do.[7]
55 I'll stop mine ears at these thy charms
And count them for my deadly harms.
Thy sinful pleasures I do hate,
Thy riches are to me no bait,
Thine honours do nor will I love;[8]
60 For my ambition lies above.
My greatest honour it shall be
When I am victor over thee,
And triumph shall, with laurel head,[9]
When thou my captive shalt be led,
65 How I do live, thou need'st not scoff,
For I have meat° thou know'st not of; food
The hidden manna[10] I do eat;
The word of life it is my meat.
My thoughts do yield° me more give
 content° contentment
70 Than can thy hours in pleasure spent.
Nor are they shadows which I catch,
Nor fancies vain at which I snatch.
But reach at things that are so high,
Beyond thy dull capacity;
75 Eternal substance I do see,
With which enrichèd I would be:

[1] *Doth contemplation … earth go* I.e., are you fed so full by contemplation that you can thoughtlessly ignore earthly things?

[2] *Dost dream* Do you dream.

[3] *Art fancy-sick* Are you imagining things?

[4] *Affect's thou pleasure?* Do you seek pleasure?

[5] *unregenerate* Not recognized as a member of God's elect.

[6] *Adam wast begot* Spirit suggests here that Flesh is a descendant of Adam, the first human, and is thus contaminated by Adam's original sin of disobedience to God.

[7] *bad'st do* Bids or commands me to do.

[8] *Thine honours do … love* I.e., I will not honor you, nor will I love you. Both the 1650 and 1678 editions read "Thine honours do …" but this may be a misprint for "Thine honors due," which would offer other interpretations.

[9] *laurel head* In Ancient Greece and Rome, laurels were traditionally granted those victorious in athletic competitions or in battle.

[10] *manna* In the Book of Exodus, manna was the food God provided for the Israelites during their forty years wandering the desert. Cf. Exodus 16.1 and Psalm 78.24–25.

Mine eye doth pierce the heavens, and see
What is invisible to thee.
My garments are not silk nor gold,
80 Nor such like trash which earth doth hold,
But royal robes I shall have on,
More glorious than the glistering° sun; *gleaming*
My crown not diamonds, pearls, and gold,
But such as angels' heads enfold.
85 The city where I hope to dwell,
There's none on earth can parallel;
The stately walls both high and strong,
Are made of precious jasper stone,
The gates of pearl, both rich and clear,
90 And angels are for° porters there; *act as*
The streets thereof transparent gold,
Such as no eye did e're behold,
A crystal river there doth run,
Which doth proceed from the Lamb's[1] throne:
95 Of life, there are the waters sure,
Which shall remain forever pure;
Nor° sun, nor moon, they have no need, *of*
For glory doth from God proceed:
No candle there, nor yet torch light,
100 For there shall be no darksome night.

From sickness and infirmity,
For evermore they shall be free,
Nor withering age shall e're come there,
But beauty shall be bright and clear.
105 This city pure is not for thee,
For things unclean there shall not be:
If I of heaven may have my fill,
Take thou the world, and all that will.
—1678

The Author to Her Book[2]

Thou ill-formed offspring of my feeble brain,
Who after birth did'st by my side remain,

Till snatched from thence by friends, less wise than true
Who, thee abroad, exposed to public view,[3]
5 Made thee in rags, halting to th' press to trudge,
Where errors were not lessened (all may judge).
At thy return my blushing was not small,
My rambling brat (in print) should mother call,
I cast thee by as one unfit for light,
10 Thy visage was so irksome in my sight;
Yet being mine own, at length affection would
Thy blemishes amend, if so I could:
I washed thy face, but more defects I saw,
And rubbing off a spot, still made a flaw.
15 I stretched thy joints to make thee even feet,[4]
Yet still thou run'st more hobbling than is meet;° *suitable*
In better dress to trim thee was my mind,
But nought save home-spun cloth, i' th' house I find.
In this array, 'mongst vulgars[5] mayst thou roam.
20 In critics' hands, beware thou dost not come;
And take thy way where yet thou art not known,
If for thy father asked, say, thou hadst none:
And for thy mother, she alas is poor,
Which caused her thus to send thee out of door.
—1678

Before the Birth of One of Her Children

All things within this fading world hath end,
Adversity doth still our joys attend;
No ties so strong, no friends so clear and sweet,
But with death's parting blow is sure to meet.
5 The sentence passed is most irrevocable,
A common thing, yet oh, inevitable;
How soon, my dear, death may my steps attend,[6]
How soon't may be thy lot to lose thy friend,

1 *Lamb's* Jesus is often referred to as the "Lamb of God," as he offered himself as a sacrifice for the atonement of humankind's sin. Cf. John 1.29 and Revelation 22.3.

2 This poem first appeared in the posthumous *Several Poems* (1678), a collection that included both new writing and revised versions of previously published poems.

3 *Till … view* Bradstreet's first book, *The Tenth Muse* (1650), was published in London, apparently without her knowledge or permission. Her brother-in-law John Woodbridge had brought her writings to England and arranged for the publication.

4 *make thee … feet* Make your poetic rhythm regular. (Poetic feet are units made up of stressed and unstressed syllables in regular patterns; they are the building blocks of accentual syllabic meter.)

5 *vulgars* Common people.

6 *How soon … attend* Reference to the dangers associated with childbirth; it is estimated that the odds of a seventeenth-century woman dying while giving birth were greater than [continued …]

We both are ignorant, yet love bids me
10 These farewell lines to recommend to thee,
That when that knot's untied that made us one,
I may seem thine, who in effect am none.
And if I see not half my days that's due,
What nature would, God grant to yours and you;
15 The many faults that well you know I have,
Let be interred in my oblivious grave;
If any worth or virtue were in me,
Let that live freshly in thy memory,
And when thou feel'st no grief, as I no harms,
20 Yet love thy dead, who long lay in thine arms,
And when thy loss shall be repaid with gains,
Look to my little babes, my dear remains.
And if thou love thyself, or loved'st me,
These oh protect from step dame's[1] injury.
25 And if chance to thine eyes shall bring this verse,
With some sad sighs honour my absent hearse;[2]
And kiss this paper for thy love's dear sake,
Who with salt tears this last farewell did take.
—1678

To My Dear and Loving Husband

If ever two were one, then surely we.
If ever man were loved by wife, then thee;
If ever wife was happy in a man,
Compare with me, ye women, if you can.
5 I prize thy love more than whole mines of gold,
Or all the riches that the East doth hold.
My love is such that rivers cannot quench,
Nor ought° but love from thee give recompense. *anything*
Thy love is such I can no way repay,
10 The heavens reward thee manifold, I pray.
Then while we live, in love let's so persever,
That when we live no more, we may live ever.
—1678

1% per birth. (Given that most women gave birth several times, the lifetime risk for a woman was much higher.)

[1] *step dame* Stepmother.

[2] *hearse* Frame upon which a body was placed during a funeral; in Puritan funerary practices, prose and poems in praise of the deceased were sometimes pinned to the hearse. "Hearse" can also refer to the dead body itself.

A Letter to Her Husband, Absent upon Public Employment[3]

My head, my heart, mine eyes, my life, nay more,
My joy, my magazine of earthly store,[4]
If two be one, as surely thou and I,
How stayest thou there, whilst I at Ipswich[5] lie?
5 So many steps, head from the heart to sever,
If but a neck, soon should we be together:
I, like the earth this season, mourn in black,
My sun is gone so far in's° zodiac,[6] *in its*
Whom whilst I joyed, nor storms, nor frosts I felt,
10 His warmth such frigid colds did cause to melt.
My chilled limbs now numbèd lie forlorn;
Return, return sweet Sol from Capricorn;[7]
In this dead time, alas, what can I more
Than view those fruits which through thy heat I bore?[8]
15 Which sweet contentment yield me for a space,
True living pictures of their father's face.
O strange effect! now thou art southward gone,
I weary grow, the tedious day so long;
But when thou northward to me shalt return,
20 I wish my sun may never set, but burn
Within the Cancer[9] of my glowing breast,
The welcome house of him my dearest guest.
Where ever, ever stay, and go not thence,
Till nature's sad decree shall call thee hence;
25 Flesh of thy flesh, bone of thy bone,[10]
I here, thou there, yet both but° one. *only*
—1678

[3] *Public Employment* Civil service. Bradstreet's husband Simon worked as an administrator for the Massachusetts Bay Colony, and often traveled to the outlying communities.

[4] *magazine … store* Storehouse of earthly values.

[5] *Ipswich* Isolated community in Massachusetts.

[6] *zodiac* Ring of constellations extending across the sky; the sun appears to travel through each in the course of a year.

[7] *Sol* Sun; also the name of the Roman sun god; *Capricorn* Goat-shaped constellation marking the portion of the sky in which the sun appears from late December through most of January.

[8] *those fruits … bore* I.e., the speaker's children.

[9] *Cancer* Crab-shaped constellation marking the portion of the sky in which the sun appears from late June through much of July.

[10] *Flesh … thy bone* See Genesis 2.23: "And Adam said, This is now bone of my bones, and flesh of my flesh: she shall be called Woman."

In Memory of My Dear Grand-Child Elizabeth Bradstreet, Who Deceased August, 1665 Being a Year and Half Old

1

Farewell dear babe, my heart's too much content,[1]
Farewell sweet babe, the pleasure of mine eye,
Farewell fair flower that for a space was lent,
Then ta'en away unto Eternity.
5 Blest babe, why should I once bewail thy fate,
Or sigh thy days so soon were terminate,
Sith° thou art settled in an everlasting state? *since*

2

By nature trees do rot when they are grown.
And plums and apples throughly° ripe do fall, *thoroughly*
10 And corn and grass are in their season mown,
And time brings down what is both strong and tall.
But plants new set to be eradicate,
And buds new blown° to have so short a date, *blossomed*
Is by his hand alone that guides nature and fate.
—1678

In Memory of My Dear Grand-Child Anne Bradstreet, Who Deceased June 20, 1669, Being Three Years and Seven Months Old

With troubled heart and trembling hand I write,
The heavens have changed to sorrow my delight.
How oft with disappointment have I met,
When I on fading things my hopes have set?
5 Experience might 'fore this have made me wise,
To value things according to their price:
Was ever stable joy yet found below,° *i.e., on Earth*
Or perfect bliss without mixture of woe?
I knew she was but as a withering flower,
10 That's here today, perhaps gone in an hour;
Like as a bubble, or the brittle glass,
Or like a shadow turning as it was.
More fool then I to look on that was lent
As if mine own, when thus impermanent.

[1] *my heart's too much content* I.e., who gave my heart too much happiness.

15 Farewell dear child, thou ne'er shall come to me;
But yet a while, and I shall go to thee.
Meantime my throbbing heart's cheered up with this:
Thou with thy Saviour art in endless bliss.
—1678

On My Dear Grand-Child Simon Bradstreet, Who Died on 16 November, 1669, Being but a Month and One Day Old

No sooner come, but gone, and fall'n asleep,
Acquaintance short, yet parting caused us weep,
Three flowers, two scarcely blown,[2] the last i'th' bud,
Cropped by th' Almighty's hand; yet is he good.
5 With dreadful awe before him let's be mute,
Such was his will, but why, let's not dispute,
With humble hearts and mouths put in the dust,
Let's say he's merciful, as well as just.
He will return, and make up all our losses,
10 And smile again, after our bitter crosses.
Go pretty babe, go rest with sisters twain;° *two*
Among the blest in endless joys remain.
—1678

For Deliverance from a Fever

When sorrows had begirt° me round, *beseiged*
And pains within and out,
When in my flesh no part was found,[3]
Then didst Thou rid me out.[4]
5 My burning flesh in sweat did boil,
My aching head did break,
From side to side for ease I toil,
So faint I could not speak.
Beclouded was my soul with fear

[2] *two scarcely blown* Two of Bradstreet's other grandchildren died in early childhood; her poems in response to their deaths are included above; *blown* Blossomed.

[3] *no part was found* No attribute was found. The meaning of *part* in this context is not entirely clear, and there are several archaic meanings of the word; to read it as meaning *quality* or *attribute* (as the word is used in the phrase *a person of many parts*) seems plausible.

[4] *didst Thou rid me out* Then did you [God] clean me out.

10 Of Thy displeasure sore,
 Nor could I read my evidence
 Which oft I read before.
 "Hide not Thy face from me!" I cried,
 "From burnings keep my soul.
15 Thou know'st my heart, and hast me tried;° *tested*
 I on Thy mercies roll."
 "O heal my soul," Thou know'st I said,
 "Though flesh consume to nought,
 What though in dust it shall be laid,
20 To glory 't shall be brought."
 Thou heard'st, Thy rod Thou didst remove
 And spared my body frail
 Thou show'st to me Thy tender love,
 My heart no more might quail.
25 O, praises to my mighty God,
 Praise to my Lord, I say,
 Who hath redeemed my soul from pit,° *damnation*
 Praises to Him for aye.° *forever*
 —1867

Some Verses upon the Burning of Our House, July 10th, 1666[1]

In silent night when rest I took
For sorrow near I did not look,
I wakened was with thund'ring noise
And piteous shrieks of dreadful voice.
5 That fearful sound of "fire" and "fire,"
 Let no man know is my desire.
 I, starting up, the light did spy,
 And to my God my heart did cry
 To strengthen me in my distress
10 And not to leave me succourless.° *without aid*
 Then, coming out, beheld a space[2]

The flame consume my dwelling place,
And when I could no longer look,
I blest his name that gave and took,
15 That laid my goods now in the dust.
 Yea, so it was, and so 'twas just.
 It was His own, it was not mine,
 Far be it that I should repine;
 He might of all justly bereft,
20 But yet sufficient for us left.
 When by the ruins oft I past
 My sorrowing eyes aside did cast
 And here and there the places spy
 Where oft I sat and long did lie:
25 Here stood that trunk, and there that chest,
 There lay that store I counted best.
 My pleasant things in ashes lie,
 And them behold no more shall I.
 Under thy roof no guest shall sit,
30 Nor at thy table eat a bit.
 No pleasant tale shall e'er be told,
 Nor things recounted done of old.
 No candle e'er shall shine in thee,
 Nor bridegroom's voice e'er heard shall be.
35 In silence ever shalt thou lie,
 Adieu, adieu, all's vanity.
 Then straight I 'gin my heart to chide,
 And did thy wealth on earth abide,
 Didst fix thy hope on mould'ring dust,
40 The arm of flesh didst make thy trust?
 Raise up thy thoughts above the sky
 That dunghill mists away may fly.
 Thou hast a house on high erect,
 Framed by that mighty architect,
45 With glory richly furnished
 Stands permanent, though this be fled.
 It's purchasèd and paid for too
 By Him who hath enough to do.
 A price so vast as is unknown
50 Yet by his gift is made thine own.
 There's wealth enough, I need no more;
 Farewell my pelf,° farewell my store. *worldly riches*
 The world no longer let me love;[3]
 My hope and treasure lies above.
 —1867

[1] The following poem appears in a handwritten collection of Bradstreet's personal writings known as the Andover Manuscript, which contains some texts in Bradstreet's own hand, and others—including this poem—transcribed by her son Simon from papers that are now lost. The full text of the heading given the poem by Simon Bradstreet reads as follows: "Here follow some verses upon the burning of our house, July 10th, 1666. Copied out of a loose paper." This and the other poems from the Andover Manuscript were first published in 1867.

[2] *beheld a space* Saw that within a brief time.

[3] *The world ... me love* Let me love the world no longer.

To My Dear Children[1]

This book by any yet unread,
I leave for you when I am dead,
That, being gone, here you may find
What was your living mother's mind.
Make use of what I leave in love
And God shall bless you from above.

A.B.

My dear children:
Knowing by experience that the exhortations of parents take most effect when the speakers leave to speak,[2] and those especially sink deepest which are spoke latest—and being ignorant whether on my death-bed I shall have opportunity to speak to any of you, much less to all—thought it the best, whilst I was able, to compose some short matters (for what else to call them I know not) and bequeath [them] to you, that[3] when I am no more with you, yet I may be daily in your remembrance (although that is the least in my aim in what I now do), but that[4] you may gain some spiritual advantage by my experience. I have not studied in this you read to show my skill, but to declare the truth—not to set forth myself, but the glory of God. If I had minded the former, it had been perhaps better pleasing to you,—but seeing the last is the best, let it be best pleasing to you. The method I will observe shall be this—I will begin with God's dealing with me from my childhood to this day. In my young years, about 6 or 7 as I take it, I began to make conscience of my ways, and what I knew was sinful, as[5] lying, disobedience to parents, etc., I avoided it. If at any time I was overtaken with the like evils, it was a great trouble. I could not be at rest till by prayer I had confessed it unto God.

I was also troubled at the neglect of private duties,[6] though too often tardy that way.[7] I also found much comfort in reading the scriptures, especially those places I thought most concerned my condition, and as I grew to have more understanding, so the more solace I took in them.

In a long fit of sickness which I had on my bed I often communed with my heart, and made my supplication to the most high,[8] who set me free from that affliction.

But as I grew up to be about 14 or 15 I found my heart more carnal, and sitting loose from God, vanity, and the follies of youth take hold of me. About 16, the Lord laid his hand sore[9] upon me, and smote me with the smallpox. When I was in my affliction, I besought the Lord, and confessed my pride and vanity and he was entreated of me, and again restored me. But I rendered not to him according to the benefit received.

After a short time I changed my condition and was married, and came into this country, where I found a new world and new manners, at which my heart rose. But after I was convinced it was the way of God, I submitted to it and joined to the church at Boston.

After some time I fell into a lingering sickness like a consumption, together with a lameness, which correction I saw the Lord sent to humble and try me and do me good; and it was not altogether ineffectual.

It pleased God to keep me a long time without a child, which was a great grief to me, and cost me many prayers and tears before I obtained one, and after him gave me many more, of whom I now take the care, that as I have brought you into the world, and with great pains, weakness, cares, and fears, brought you to this, I now travail[10] in birth again of you till Christ be formed in you.

Among all my experiences of God's gracious dealings with me I have constantly observed this, that he

[1] This short poem and prose message appears to have been transcribed by Bradstreet's son Simon from an earlier manuscript in Bradstreet's own hand; "To My Dear Children" was first published along with the other Andover Manuscript material in the 1867 collection *The Works of Anne Bradstreet in Prose and Verse*.

[2] *leave to speak* Cease to speak.

[3] *that* So that.

[4] *but that* Only so that.

[5] *as* Such as.

[6] *private duties* Prayers, devotions.

[7] *though too often tardy that way* I.e., though I was often slower than I should have been (to feel guilty for neglecting my duties).

[8] *most high* I.e., God.

[9] *sore* Heavily.

[10] *travail* Labor. The apostle Paul uses this metaphor in Galatians 4.19 ("My little children, of whom I travail in birth again until Christ be formed in you").

hath never suffered[1] me long to sit loose from him, but by one affliction or other hath made me look home, and search what was amiss, so usually thus it hath been with me that I have no sooner felt my heart out of order, but I have expected correction for it, which most commonly hath been upon my own person, in sickness, weakness, pains, sometimes on my soul, in doubts and fears of God's displeasure, and my sincerity towards him. Sometimes he hath smote a child with sickness, sometimes chastened by losses in estate,[2]—and these times (through his great mercy) have been the times of my greatest getting and advantage, yea I have found them the times when the Lord hath manifested the most love to me. Then have I gone to searching, and have said with David, Lord search me and try me,[3] see what ways of wickedness are in me, and lead me in the way everlasting; and seldom or never but I have found either some sin I lay under which God would have reformed, or some duty neglected which he would have performed. And by his help I have laid vows and bonds upon my soul to perform his righteous commands.

If at any time you are chastened of God, take it as thankfully and joyfully as in greatest mercies, for if ye be His, ye shall reap the greatest benefit by it. It hath been no small support to me in times of darkness when the Almighty hath hid His face from me, that yet I have had abundance of sweetness and refreshment after affliction, and more circumspection in my walking after I have been afflicted. I have been with God like an untoward[4] child, that no longer than the rod has been on my back (or at least in sight) but I have been apt to forget him and myself too. Before I was afflicted I went astray, but now I keep thy statutes.[5]

I have had great experience of God's hearing my prayers, and returning comfortable answers to me, either in granting the thing I prayed for, or else in satisfying my mind without it; and I have been confident it hath been from him, because I have found my heart through his goodness enlarged in thankfulness to him.

I have often been perplexed that I have not found that constant joy in my pilgrimage and refreshing which I supposed most of the servants of God have; although he hath not left me altogether without the witness of his holy spirit, who hath oft given me his word and set to his seal that it shall be well with me. I have sometimes tasted of that hidden manna[6] that the world knows not, and have set up my Ebenezer,[7] and have resolved with myself that against such a promise, such tastes of sweetness, the gates of Hell shall never prevail. Yet have I many times sinkings and droopings, and not enjoyed that felicity that sometimes I have done. But when I have been in darkness and seen no light, yet have I desired to stay myself upon the Lord. And, when I have been in sickness and pain, I have thought if the Lord would but lift up the light of his countenance upon me, although he ground me to powder, it would be but light to me; yea, oft have I thought [that] if I were in hell itself, and could there find the love of God toward me, it would be a heaven. And, could I have been[8] in heaven without the love of God it would have been a hell to me; for in truth, it is the absence and presence of God that makes heaven or hell.

Many times hath Satan troubled me concerning the verity of the scriptures, many times by atheism: how could I know whether there was a God? I never saw any miracles to confirm me, and those which I read of— how did I know but they were feigned? That there is a God my reason would soon tell me by the wondrous works that I see, the vast frame of the heaven and the earth, the order of all things, night and day, summer and winter, spring and autumn, the daily providing for this great household upon the earth, the preserving and directing of all to its proper end. The consideration of

[1] *suffered* Allowed.

[2] *sometimes chastened by losses in estate* Sometimes rebuked (me) by making me suffer financial losses.

[3] *David … try me* King David was a biblical king of Israel. Several biblical psalms are attributed to him, including the one to which Bradstreet refers here, Psalm 26.

[4] *untoward* Unruly, disobedient.

[5] *I keep thy statutes* Bradstreet alludes to Psalm 119.8, a prayer offered to God by one who obeys God and "keep[s] [his] statutes."

[6] *manna* In the Book of Exodus, manna was the food God provided for the sustenance of the Israelites during their forty years wandering the desert. See Exodus 16.31 and Psalm 78.24–25.

[7] *Ebenezer* Hebrew for "stone of help," a commemoration of the assistance of God. See 1 Samuel 7.12.

[8] *could I have been* If I could have been.

these things would with amazement certainly resolve me that there is an Eternal Being.

But how should I know He is such a God as I worship in Trinity, and such a savior as I rely upon? Though this hath thousands of times been suggested to me, yet God hath helped me ever. I have argued this with myself. That there is a God, I see. If ever this God hath revealed himself, it must be in his word, and this must be it, or none. Have I not found that operation by it that no human invention can work upon the soul? Hath not judgments befallen diverse[1] who have scorned and condemned it? Hath it not been preserved through all ages maugre[2] all the heathen tyrants and all of the enemies who have opposed it? Is there any story but that which shows the beginnings of times, and how the world came to be as we see? Do we not know the prophecies in it fulfilled, which could not have been so long foretold by any but God himself?

When I have got over this block, then have I another pot in my way: that, admit[3] this be the true God whom we worship, and that be His word, yet why may not the Popish religion[4] be the right? They have the same God, the same Christ, the same word; they only interpret it one way, we another. This hath sometimes stuck with me, and more it would, but the vain fooleries that are in their religion, together with their lying miracles and cruel persecutions of the saints, which admit were they as they term them, yet not so to be dealt withal. The consideration of these things and many the like would soon turn me to my own religion again. But some new troubles I have had since the world has been filled with blasphemy, and sectaries,[5] and some who have been accounted sincere Christians have been carried away with them, that[6] sometimes I have said, "Is there faith upon the earth?" and I have not known what to think. But then I have remembered the words of Christ that so it must be, and that, if it were possible, the very elect[7] should be deceived. "Behold, saith our Savior, I have told you before." That hath stayed my heart, and I can now say, "Return, O my soul, to thy rest; upon this rock Christ Jesus will I build my faith,[8] and if I perish, I perish." But I know all the powers of Hell shall never prevail against it. I know whom I have trusted, and whom I have believed, and that He is able to keep that I have committed to his charge. Now to the king, immortal, eternal, and invisible, the only wise God, be honor and glory forever and ever![9] Amen.

This was written in much sickness and weakness, and is very weakly and imperfectly done, but, if you can pick any benefit out of it, it is the mark which I aimed at.[10]

—1867

from *Meditations Divine and Moral*[11]

1

There is no object that we see, no action that we do, no good that we enjoy, no evil that we feel, or fear, but we may make some spiritual advantage of all, and he that makes such improvement is wise as well as pious.

5

It is reported of the peacock that priding himself in his gay feathers he ruffles them up, but spying his black feet, he soon lets fall his plumes, so he that glories in his gifts and adornings should look upon his corruptions, and that will damp his high thoughts.

[1] *diverse* Different kinds of people.

[2] *maugre* In spite of.

[3] *admit* Even if it is admitted that.

[4] *the Popish religion* Roman Catholicism.

[5] *sectaries* Dissenters; those of different religious sects.

[6] *have been carried away with them, that* Have been so persuaded by them (i.e., by these dissenting versions of Christianity) that.

[7] *elect* Those who have been predestined by God for salvation.

[8] *upon this … my faith* Bradstreet alludes to Matthew 16.18, in which Jesus says to his disciple Peter, "And I say also unto thee, That thou art Peter, and upon this rock I will build my church; and the gates of hell shall not prevail against it."

[9] *Now to … forever and ever* Bradstreet echoes Paul's address to God in the epistle Philippians 4.20.

[10] *it is the mark which I aimed at* (Then I have achieved) the goal I aimed at.

[11] This series of meditations, which Bradstreet left to her son Simon in the hopes they might prove instructional to her children after her death, were first published in the 1867 collection *The Works of Anne Bradstreet in Prose and Verse*.

6

The finest bread hath the least bran, the purest honey the least wax, and the sincerest Christian the least self-love.

8

Downy beds make drowsy persons, but hard lodging keeps the eyes open; a prosperous state makes a secure Christian, but adversity makes him consider.

9

Sweet words are like honey, a little may refresh, but too much gluts the stomach.

10

Diverse children have their different natures; some are like flesh which nothing but salt will keep from putrefaction, some again like tender fruits that are best preserved with sugar. Those parents are wise that can fit their nurture according to their nature.

12

Authority without wisdom is like a heavy axe without an edge, fitter to bruise than polish.

13

The reason why Christians are so loath to exchange this world for a better is because they have more sense than faith; they see what they enjoy, they do but hope for that which is to come.

16

That house which is not often swept makes the cleanly inhabitant soon loathe it, and that heart which is not continually purifying itself is no fit temple for the spirit of God[1] to dwell in.

19

Corn,[2] till it have passed through the mill and been ground to powder, is not fit for bread. God so deals with his servants: he grinds them with grief and pain till they turn to dust, and then are they fine manchet[3] for his mansion.

27

It is a pleasant thing to behold the light, but sore eyes are not able to look upon it; the pure in heart shall see God, but the defiled in conscience shall rather choose to be buried under rocks and mountains than to behold the presence of the Lamb.[4]

31

Iron, till it be throughly heated, is incapable to be wrought; so God sees good to cast some men into the furnace of affliction, and then beats them on his anvil into what frame he pleases.

38

Some children are hardly weaned;[5] although the teat be rubbed with wormwood[6] or mustard, they will either wipe it off, or else suck down sweet and bitter together. So it is with some Christians; let God embitter all the sweets of this life, that so they might feed upon more substantial food, yet they are so childishly sottish[7] that they are still hugging and sucking these empty breasts, that God is forced to hedge up their way with thorns or lay affliction on their loins that so they might shake hands with the world before it bid them farewell.

40

The spring is a lively emblem of the resurrection: after a long winter we see the leafless trees and dry stocks (at the approach of the sun) to resume their former vigour and beauty in a more ample manner than what they

[1] *God* Capitalized here in accordance with modern practice and the conventions of this anthology. It may be worth noting, however, that Bradstreet is consistent in using a lower case "g" when she mentions "God" in the manuscript of the *Meditations*.

[2] *Corn* Grain.

[3] *manchet* Bread made of finely ground flour.

[4] *the Lamb* I.e., Jesus Christ.

[5] *hardly weaned* Difficult to wean.

[6] *wormwood* Bitter herb.

[7] *sottish* I.e., addicted (as to alcohol).

lost in the autumn. So shall it be at that great day after a long vacation, when the Sun of righteousness shall appear, those dry bones shall arise in far more glory than that which they lost at their creation, and in this transcends the spring, that their leaf shall never fail nor their sap decline.

48

There is nothing admits of more admiration, than God's various dispensation of his gifts among the sons of men, betwixt whom he hath put so vast a disproportion that they scarcely seem made of the same lump, or sprung out of the loins of one Adam: some set in the highest dignity that mortality is capable of, and some again so base that they are viler than the earth; some so wise and learned that they seem like angels among men, and some again so ignorant and sottish that they are more like beasts than men; some pious saints; some incarnate devils, some exceeding beautiful, and some extremely deformed; some so strong and healthful that their bones are full of marrow and their breasts of milk, and some again so weak and feeble that while they live, they are accounted among the dead, and no other reason can be given of all this but so it pleased Him, whose will is the perfect rule of righteousness.

51

The eyes and the ears are the inlets or doors of the soul, through which innumerable objects enter, yet is not that spacious room filled, neither doth it ever say it is enough, but like the daughters of the horseleech, cries "give, give"[1] and which is most strong; the more it receives the more empty it finds itself, and sees an impossibility, ever to be filled, but by Him, in whom all fullness dwells.

53

He that is to sail into a far country, although the ship, cabin, and provision be all convenient and comfortable for him, yet he hath no desire to make that his place of residence, but longs to put in at that port where his business lies; a Christian is sailing through this world unto his heavenly country, and here he hath many conveniences and comforts but he must beware of desiring to make this the place of his abode, lest he meet with such tossings that may cause him to long for shore. Before he sees land we must therefore be here as strangers and pilgrims, that we may plainly declare that we seek a city above, and wait all the days of our appointed time till our change shall come.

60

He that would be content with a mean[2] condition must not cast his eye upon one that is in a far better estate[3] than himself, but let him look upon him that is lower than he is, and if he see that such a one bears poverty comfortably it will help to quiet him. But if that will not do, let him look on his own unworthiness and that will make him say with Jacob, "I am less than the least of thy mercies."[4]

62

As man is called the little world so his heart may be called the little commonwealth; his more fixed and resolved thoughts are like to inhabitants, his slight and flitting thoughts are like passengers that travel to and fro continually; here is also the great court of justice erected, which is always kept by Conscience, who is both accuser, excuser, witness, and judge, whom no bribes can pervert, nor flattery cause to favour but as he finds the evidence, so he absolves or condemns; yea so absolute is this Court of Judicature, that there is no appeal from it—no, not to the court of heaven itself, for if our conscience condemn us, He also who is greater than our conscience will do it much more, but he that would have boldness to go to the throne of grace to be accepted there must be sure to carry a certificate from the court of conscience that he stands right there.

67

All the works and doings of God are wonderful, but none more awful than his great work of election and

[1] *horseleech … give* See Proverbs 30.15: "The horseleach hath two daughters, crying, Give, give. There are three things that are never satisfied, yea, four things say not, It is enough."

[2] *mean* Low.

[3] *estate* Situation.

[4] *Jacob … mercies* See Genesis 32.10.

reprobation.[1] When we consider how many good parents have had bad children, and again how many bad parents have had pious children, it should make us adore the sovereignty of God, who will not be tied to time nor place, nor yet to persons, but takes and chooses, when and where and whom He pleases. It should also teach the children of godly parents to walk with fear and trembling, lest they through unbelief fall short of a promise. It may also be a support to such as have or had wicked parents, that if they abide not in unbelief, God is able to graft[2] them in. The upshot of all should make us with the Apostle to admire the justice and mercy of God and say how unsearchable are His ways and His footsteps past finding out.[3]

71

All weak and diseased bodies have hourly mementos of their mortality, but the soundest of men have likewise their nightly monitor, by the emblem of death, which is their sleep (for so is death often called) and not only their death but their grave is lively represented before their eyes. By beholding their bed, the morning may mind them of the resurrection, and, the sun approaching, of the appearing of the Sun of righteousness,[4] at whose coming they shall all rise out of their beds, the long night shall fly away, and the day of eternity shall never end. Seeing these things must be, what manner of persons ought we to be, in all good conversation?

72

As the brands[5] of a fire, if once severed, will of themselves go out although you use no other means to extinguish them, so distance of place, together with length of time (if there be no intercourse[6]) will cool the affections of intimate friends, though there should be no displeasance between them.

77

God hath by his providence so ordered, that no one country hath all commodities within itself, but what it wants, another shall supply, that so there may be a mutual commerce through the world. As it is with countries so it is with men, there was never yet any one man that had all excellences, let his parts natural and acquired, spiritual and moral, be never so large, yet he stands in need of something which another man hath (perhaps meaner[7] than himself)—which shows us [that] perfection is not below, and also that God will have us beholden one to another.
—1867

[1] *wonderful* Wonder-inspiring; *awful* Awe-inspiring; *election and reprobation* Choosing who will be granted salvation and who will be refused.

[2] *graft* Grafting involves inserting a piece of one plant into the stock of another, so that the roots of the latter can sustain the former.

[3] *the Apostle* Paul, whose Epistle to the Romans is referenced; *admire ... finding out* See Romans 11.33: "O the depth of the riches both of the wisdom and knowledge of God! how unsearchable are his judgments, and his ways past finding out!"

[4] *Sun of righteousness* See Malachi 4.2.

[5] *brands* Segments of burning wood.

[6] *no intercourse* No contact; no social intercourse.

[7] *meaner* Lower.

MICHAEL WIGGLESWORTH

1631 – 1705

Nicknamed "Mr. Doomsday," Michael Wigglesworth was a poet, diarist, doctor, and minister, best known during his life and for centuries afterward for *The Day of Doom* (1662), a 224-stanza poem about Judgment Day. The poem was a bestseller, and it was read, heard, memorized, and recited by generations of Americans. Described by Cotton Mather as a "feeble little shadow of a man," Wigglesworth experienced intense anxiety, spiritual agony, and physical illness through most his life, but he nonetheless served the community of Malden, Massachusetts, as minister and doctor for fifty years, while also maintaining his wider reputation as a scholar and poet in the Massachusetts Bay colony.

Wigglesworth was born in Yorkshire, England, a place he later described as "ungodly … where children had learnt wickedness betimes [early]." The family were Nonconformists and faced religious persecution, leading them to emigrate to New England, where they settled in New Haven, Connecticut. Wigglesworth was sent to school with Ezekiel Cheever, a renowned Puritan schoolmaster, for a few years, until Wigglesworth's father was injured in 1641; at this time, Wigglesworth went home to help with the farm. He was not well-suited to farm work, however, and his father sent him back to school, where he prepared for college, eventually entering Harvard in 1647. Wigglesworth graduated first in his class and pursued graduate studies, first in medicine and then, after a conversion experience in 1650, in preparation for the ministry.

Wigglesworth remained at Harvard until 1653 and took on work as a tutor; his students included young men who later became prominent leaders in the Bay colony, including Eleazer and Increase Mather. It was during this period that Wigglesworth began to keep a diary, which he maintained until 1657. Regular diary-writing was a common practice among Puritans and was encouraged as a means of spiritual self-examination and meditation. For Wigglesworth, this included an intense and agonizing acknowledgment of what he felt was excessive fondness for his students (all of whom were male), and of the sexual dreams and nocturnal ejaculations that plagued him while asleep. Ejaculation, when it occurred outside of marriage or for any purpose other than procreation, was considered sinful by Puritans, and "sodomy and buggery" were practices punishable by death. In 1646, less than ten years before Wigglesworth began the diary, a man named William Plaine from New Haven was executed for "corrupt[ing] a great part of the youth by masturbations." In this context, it is not surprising that Wigglesworth repressed and feared his feelings, and remarks in the diary that touched on sexuality were written in a shorthand code. The encoded portions, which used a form of shorthand developed by the seventeenth-century stenographer Thomas Shelton, were not interpreted until 1951, when the scholar Edward S. Morgan published his translated edition. The diary also bears witness to the extreme sensitivity of conscience that kept Wigglesworth in a constant state of anxiety and doubt—he worries at length, for example, about a neighbor's barn door flapping in the wind: Was it Wigglesworth's duty to close it, or would that offend his neighbor, by suggesting that he wasn't taking good enough care of his property?

In 1655, Wigglesworth married his cousin Mary Reyner, and also accepted an invitation to serve as minister of the Malden congregation; his first daughter, Mercy, was born in 1656. Wigglesworth's mental anguish continued, however, and also manifested physically. By 1658, he felt too weak to preach and appear in public, and some members of the Malden congregation began to question whether he was fit to serve as their teacher and minister; their doubts were based on his weak health, but also on his extreme theological conservatism. Wigglesworth quieted these concerns by writing an open letter to the community, but he continued to be unable to preach, a situation that caused him great unease of mind. New England was at the beginning of the period known as the "Great Declension," when there was concern that the religious purpose that had guided the original founders of the colonies was fracturing

and falling away. Increased crime, witchcraft, erratic weather, and a higher mortality rate contributed to a conviction that God was delivering judgment against this slackening of religious fervor. In response, ministers developed the "jeremiad," a new form of fiery sermon warning listeners that God would judge and punish such behavior. Wigglesworth, unable to deliver such jeremiads from the pulpit, took to poetry as a means of expressing his concerns for his community, and of offering the teaching he could not deliver in person.

Following his wife's death in 1659, Wigglesworth began writing more intensely, publishing *The Day of Doom* in 1662. Composed at least partially in response to New England's supposed religious backsliding, the poem is a verse jeremiad, intended as a stern rebuke and warning to the community. Within a year, 1800 copies were sold; only the Bible and the Bay Psalm Book sold as briskly and circulated as widely in the Massachusetts Bay Colony. The poem, with its dwelling on punishment and its focus on Christ as judge, may feel harsh and alien to modern readers; to its original audience, however, the sermonic dimension of the poem was part of its appeal. Written in an accessible, plain style, and using the catchy ballad meter used in most hymns, the poem attained a broad audience. One in twenty people in the colony owned a copy, but it was shared, heard, and memorized by a far greater number still.

Wigglesworth's next major volume of poems, *Meat Out of the Eater* (1670), sold almost as well, going through four editions before 1689. A series of meditations on the meaning to be found in the hardships sent by God, the title poem "Meat Out of the Eater" took its place within the flourishing Puritan genre of affliction literature. Meditating on the difficulties of life was a central spiritual practice at the time, and diaries, poems, and other narratives of affliction were read in tandem with the Bible as a means of bolstering faith and enduring troubles. John Foxe's *Acts and Monuments* (1563), which recorded the martyrdoms of persecuted European Protestants, is perhaps the most famous example, but most major Puritan writers touch on this theme at various times in their work, including William Bradford, Anne Bradstreet, and Edward Taylor.

Wigglesworth described the 1670s as a "dreary, unproductive, and lonely" time, but this unhappy period ended in 1679 when he married—to the astonishment of the community—his young housekeeper Martha Mudge. The ensuing scandal caused Wigglesworth to offer his resignation, but the Malden church eventually decided to keep Wigglesworth as minister. Four daughters were born in the six years that followed, and a son in 1689. In 1684–85, Wigglesworth became stronger in health and began preaching and appearing in public. Of this recovery, Cotton Mather later wrote that "It pleased God ... wondrously to restore his Faithful Servant. He that had been for ... years almost *Buried Alive*, comes abroad again." Wigglesworth was offered the presidency of Harvard, which he refused. After his second wife's death, he was married a third time, to Sybil Avery in 1691; the couple had a son in 1693. Throughout this time, Wigglesworth gained in reputation and influence throughout the colony. In 1704 and 1705 he wrote his final poems, "Death Expected and Welcomed" and "A Farewell to the World." He died in 1705, and Cotton Mather preached the eulogy, entitled "A Faithful Man, Described and Rewarded."

Wigglesworth's poetry retained its hold on the Puritan imagination for several generations, and new editions of *The Day of Doom* continued to be printed into the nineteenth century. By the mid-nineteenth century, however, critical opinions had turned decidedly against the Puritan sensibility, and against Wigglesworth in particular. Critic Moses Coit Tyler, for example, pronounced in 1879 that Wigglesworth's "blazing and sulphurous" poetry was "quite lacking in art ... a sort of cheap melody, a shrill, reverberating clatter"; and by 1929 Kenneth B. Murdock wrote that *The Day of Doom* is notable only for "its sulphurousness, the cruelty of its doctrine, and its harping on the horrors of hell." Wigglesworth's readership and critical esteem continued to plummet during the twentieth century, until the publication of his encoded diary in the mid-twentieth century sparked renewed interest in his work. For centuries Wigglesworth had been caricatured as a fire-and-brimstone, ranting, rather miserable Puritan, and the diary offered a more complex picture of a man who, while fully committed to Puritan ideology, was at the same time suffering terribly within its strictures.

NOTE ON THE TEXTS: Excerpts from *The Diary of Michael Wigglesworth, 1653–1657* are based on the 1951 edition by Edward S. Morgan, published by the Colonial Society of Massachusetts. Morgan's edition was the first to decipher Wigglesworth's encoded diary entries; sections that were originally in code appear here in italics. *The Day of Doom* is based on the last authoritative edition overseen by Wigglesworth, the fifth edition of the poem printed in 1701 by B. Green and J. Allen. The standard scholarly edition published in 1989 by Ronald A. Bosco was also consulted. Spelling and punctuation have been modernized in accordance with the practices of this anthology.

⌘⌘⌘

from *The Diary of Michael Wigglesworth*

[FEBRUARY 1653]

If the unloving carriages[1] of my pupils can go so to my heart as they do; how then do my vain thoughts, my detestable pride, my *unnatural filthy lust that are so oft and even this day in some measure stirring in me*[2] how do these grieve my lord Jesus that loves me infinitely more than I do them?[3] Do I take it heavily that my love is so lightly made of? Ah! Lord Jesus how fearful is my despising of thy dying love, of thy love in giving me thy self after thou seemest to have cast me off forever? Ah! I cannot love thee, not fear to sin against thee, although thou exercise me with such crosses, as again this day, wherein I may read my own ill carriages toward thee. And dost thou yet make any beam of thy love break out toward me, after any fears? Nay have so oft and so long comforted myself with thy love amidst my daily sins. The enmity and contrariety of my heart to seeking thee in earnest, with my want of dear affection to thee, these make me afraid. But thou did give me thy self in the Lord's supper, thou didst give me a heart (though vile) to lay hold of the desiring all from thee, and this gives me hope, blessed be thy name. …

[15 FEBRUARY 1653]

Pride I feel still again and again abounding, self-admiration, though destroying myself daily. God gracious and bountiful in bestowing, in directing me and mine, but I unthankfully wickedly making God's gifts subservient to my vain glory. Ah Lord I am vile, I desire to abhor myself (o that I could!) before thee for these things. *I find such unresistable torments of carnal lusts or provocation unto the ejection of seed that I find myself unable to read anything to inform me about my distemper because of the prevailing or rising of my lusts. This I have procured to myself.*[4] *God hath brought this to my eye this day. Thou hast destroyed thy self but in me is thy help; Lord let me find help in thee though I have destroyed myself by my iniquity.* …

[17 FEBRUARY 1653]

I took a good deal of time this day to look thoroughly into the vileness of that sin of pride. And see that which might make me go mourning all my days, yet I can find little heart breaking for it, nor power against it. I found my spirit in a troubled perplexed sunken frame this day, propense[5] to fretting: yet so sensual and mind so full of vain thoughts, as I could not get my heart into a praying frame,[6] a little at length the Lord did breathe this evening, and gives me to see the riches of his love continued, though I continue my provocations. And oh that I could see still more of my own

[1] *carriages* Behaviors.

[2] *unnatural … in me* Sections of the following excerpts are italicized; these are parts of the diary written in the shorthand code Wigglesworth used.

[3] *them* Here, possibly referring to Wigglesworth's students or to his own lust and "vain thoughts."

[4] *procured to myself* Brought upon myself.

[5] *propense* Inclined.

[6] *frame* I.e., frame of mind.

vileness, and the sweet love of my gracious God, whom woe is me I abuse.

The last night a filthy dream and so pollution[1] escaped me in my sleep for which I desire to hang down my head with shame and beseech the Lord not to make me possess the sin of my youth and give me into the hands of my abomination. I find both pride in special so monstrous prevalent again and again this day, and vain thoughts together with weariness of the length of duties in the morning, also sensual outgoings of heart or proneness thereto, and so to crossness and peevishness, slighting of others, lashing out in too much eagerness of spirit in discourse, dishonouring God and shaming myself thereby; in a word, my heart and words and actions go wholly out of frame, and void of anything of God, that I see my sin is above measure sinful; I loathe myself, and could even take vengeance of myself for these abominations. …

[25–27 FEBRUARY 1653]

… After noon God pleased to give some affection and to warm my heart a little with the love and grace of Christ coming and dwelling amongst us. Yet in the fore part of the sermon I found my spirit so distracted with vain thoughts and so disquieted within me, because one of my pupils was ill and absent from the ordinances,[2] that I could not attend to the word, I could not cry for help scarcely to heaven nor see the evil of those impatient disquietments, yet I desired a heart to cry for help, and the Lord set me free at length from them, yet sundry[3] times this day pride prevailed over me. And some fears because I feel not love to God as I should, but more love to man, lest I should love man more than God. I am laden with a body of death, and could almost be willing to be dissolved and be with Christ freed from this sinful flesh, save that I fear my state[4] and have some misgivings; yet I desire to be made sincere, what is amiss, Lord amend! Assure me of thy love that I may be prepared for life or death.

[2 MARCH 1653]

This day was brought news of that dreadful disaster at Boston by fire;[5] which came to pass the very night before Mr. Mitchel's[6] lecture concerning God['s] judgements, and how abused they aggravate sin. Thus God seals his word with his dreadful works; my heart was much affected and dejected within me upon deep thoughts of these things and what I had heard God speak to me in his word (for he met with sundry of my sins and gave dreadful examples of God's judgments that should have warned me from them), yet afterward, o amazing prodigious, overpowering prevalency of wickedness! Pride again, and again most fearfully after all those shakings, awakenings, and almost sinkings of spirit, discovered its power over me. Ah Lord! my king, my God, thee thee I provoke, and wert thou not a God indeed, infinite in thy grace, fire and brimstone, or a flood of wrath had seized on me long ere now. Why hast thou not plucked away from me by some sad stroke my dearest ones? Am I better, nay how far am I viler than they to whom thou hast done this, my want of watchfulness against, or my boldness to vain thought, I am afraid of. …

[5 APRIL 1653]

… On Thursday morning the Lord was pleased to give me somewhat a heart-breaking meditation of him. So that I thought, And will the Lord now again return and embrace me in the arms of his dearest love? Will he fall upon my neck and kiss me? For he was pleased to give in some secret and silent evidence of his love.

But ah wretched backsliding heart! What evil hast thou found in God that thy love and affection to him are so quickly cold? That thou secretly departest from him not savouring the things of God, going a-whoring in thy desires after vanities, seeking thy self, like an empty vine bringing forth fruit to thy self? I abhor myself before the Lord for my shameless pride, especially now when God is abasing me. …

[1] *pollution* I.e., nocturnal ejaculation.

[2] *ordinances* Religious services; sacraments.

[3] *sundry* Several.

[4] *state* Status, in terms of salvation.

[5] *disaster … by fire* On 14 January 1653, a fire in Boston killed three children and destroyed many buildings.

[6] *Mr. Mitchel* Jonathan Mitchel (1624–68) was an influential pastor of the Cambridge Congregational Church, preaching to the Harvard community as well as to those living nearby.

[12 JUNE 1653] SABBATH

And why do vain thoughts still lodge within me upon thy day, amidst thy worship? Ah my God, why is there yet such a profane spirit let loose to trample my soul under foot, as that I cannot see the evils, be sensible of the plagues of my own heart when I am waiting to hear thee speak in thy ordinances? When I should receive good from thee, I grow unsensible of my need of grace for myself: hence I mind with greater affection what concerneth others' good than my own. My heart is no sooner beginning to be awakened, affected, broken for my sins (as it began yesterday) but my goodness (if any there be) is like the morning dew that is dried up. …

[4–5 JULY 1653]

In the 2 next days I found so much of a spirit of pride and secret joying in some conceived excellence in myself which is too hard for me and I can't prevail over and also so much secret vice and vain thoughts in holy duties and thereby weariness of them and such filthy lust also flowing from my fond affection to my pupils while in their presence on the third day after noon that I confess myself an object of God's loathing as my sin is of my own and pray God make it so more to me

[14–15 OCTOBER 1653]

Friday morning. I had some fears in my spirit about the immutability of God's love in case I should fall away from him; but the Lord did in some measure clear the absolute stability thereof from the scripture.[1] In the forenoon[2] I met with great difficulties in my studies and my strength failed me, I besought the Lord for his help, and though in the forenoon I could make nothing of it, yet afternoon I was exceedingly helped and my work made marvelous easy. But ah! ungrateful heart, I take God's name in vain in my nearest approaches to him and profane his ordinances: for this I am not able to stand before him. God brought to my mind in special (being at a private meeting[3]) my want of love and dutifulness to my parents, which I begged pardon of.

And the very next morning news is brought me of my father's death. Whereupon I set my self to confess before the Lord my sins against him in want of natural affections to, and sympathy with, my afflicted parents, in my not prizing them and their life which God hath graciously continued so long. My great request is for pardon of all former sins, and present deliverance from a stupid frame of spirit unsensible of God's visitation and my own loss in losing such [a] friend. My humble supplication is to the Lord to sanctify his hand to me and all of us whom it concerns and to become a father of the fatherless and husband to the widow. My Father died the first of October.

[24 OCTOBER 1653]

… On the 2d day at night in my sleep I dreamed of the approach of the great and dreadful day of judgment; and was thereby exceedingly awakened in spirit (as I thought) to follow God with tears and cries until he gave me some hopes of his gracious good will toward me.

[12 MARCH 1654]

The sabbath I found God awakening and quickening my heart to cry to him for more sanctifying grace seeing it cometh only by Christ; and the reason why I have so little I was told is from security, sloth and fulness of self or the creature.[4] The sabbath evening and the next day I was much distressed in conscience, seeing a stable door of Mr. Mitchel's beat to and fro with the wind, whether I should out of duty shut it or not; no temptations perplex me so sorely as such like, when I am not clear concerning my duty.

My fear is lest my will should blind reason. This made me seriously and solemnly cry to Heaven for light to my mind, and grace to obey with cheerfulness all God's will. And still I cry, Lord leave me not to err from thy ways.

[1] *the Lord … from the scripture* I.e., biblical study reassured Wigglesworth that God's love is immutable. God and Christ's unchangeable natures are discussed in many places in the Bible.

[2] *forenoon* Morning.

[3] *private meeting* Religious gathering held in a private home rather than a public meeting house.

[4] *creature* Created being (as opposed to God, the creator).

Subdue the enmity of my heart in tender mercy for thy name sake: pity my poor fainting decaying body. My strength and my heart even fail within me by these temptations and the difficulty of my studies (which by distraction I cannot attend freely) and the continued perverseness[1] of my pupils. Lord hear me, for I have none but thee. ...

[2–3 April 1654]

Sabbath. The wise God who knoweth how to tame and take down proud and wanton hearts, suffered me to be sorely buffeted with the like temptation as formerly about seeing some doors blow to and fro with the wind in some danger to break, as I think; I cannot tell whether it were my duty to give them some hint that own them. When I think 'tis a common thing, and that 'tis impossible but that the owners should have oft seen them in that case, and heard them blow to and fro, and that it is but a trivial matter, and that I have given a hint to one that dwells in the house, and he maketh light of it; and that it would rather be a seeming to check others' mindlessness of their own affairs, and lastly that there may be special reasons for it that I know not; why the case seemeth clear that 'tis not my duty, yet I am sorely afraid I should regard iniquity in my heart, and God upon this eclipseth the sweet beams of his love, he hideth his face and I am troubled. I would not for all the world be a worker of any one iniquity. He hideth his face justly from a wretch that could not prize it, but am bold to wax wanton and proud when I have it. But Lord pity my languishing soul and feeble spirits and frail body ready to fail under the blow of thy hand if thou rebuke.

I still find pride and whorish departure from God prevail, though not in the particular of marriage[2] as before but Lord make me watchful Lord make me spiritual by all thy dispensations.

[25 April 1654]

[Wigglesworth travels home from a trip to New Haven.]

... Coming through the wilderness we were overtaken with a great and dreadful tempest of rain and wind. Where I beheld the mighty power of God as well by land as by sea. For all the trees of the forest bowed and bended like a bow over our heads as we rode along and diverse[3] we heard fall; and about 40 I suppose we saw in our way that were newly blown down. I thought how good it was to have this great God for a man's friend, For lo! how easily he could arm all his creatures against his enemies? And at this time the Lord let in sweet peace and confidence into my heart in the hopes of his favour. For which taste of his sweetness I will bless his name as long as I live. ...

[5 August 1654]

But ah how apt am I to kick with the heel Jesurun[4] like and lightly to esteem the rock of my salvation? How soon have I forgotten his wonderful works? A mind distracted with a thousand vanities sabbath days and weekdays when I should be musing of the things of God. But where is my sorrow and bitter mourning for these profanations of God's ordinances? A thing so grievous to my God. It hath been some grief to me that I am so unprofitable a servant, that I cannot serve God in my calling aiming at his glory and doing it as his work. I have begged this mercy but alas! I cannot attain it, but I lose myself and my love to God amidst my multitude of occasions. My heart is hurried now this way, now that way by diverse lusts; one while anxiously solicitous, another while pleasing myself with this or that creature, this or that project, but ah! Where is my walking with God, and rejoicing in the light of his countenance? And now good Lord have mercy on me! How unfit am I to sanctify a sabbath, with such a carnal heart, such dead and dull affections, such

1 *perverseness* Obstinacy.

2 *particular of marriage* Term used euphemistically to refer to ejaculation, which Puritans believed should only occur for the purpose of procreation within marriage.

3 *diverse* Several, many.

4 *Jesurun* Another name for the people of Israel used in the Old Testament. See Deuteronomy 32.15: "But Jeshurun waxed fat, and kicked: thou art waxen fat, thou art grown thick, thou art covered with fatness; then he forsook God which made him, and lightly esteemed the Rock of his salvation."

distracting thoughts as possess and fill my mind, such a faint and feeble body? And how much more unfit to partake of a sacrament? I am afraid I shall abuse it: at least get no good by it. But the same carnal, secure, vain sensual, slothful, proud, unbelieving, unthankful, unfruitful frame remain in me still. ...

[15 FEBRUARY 1655]

... To continue in a single estate[1] is both uncomfortable many ways and dangerous (as I conceive) to my life, and exposeth to sin, and contrary to engagement of affections, and friends' expectations, and liable to the harsh censure of the world that expecteth the quite contrary: To change my condition[2] endangers to bring me into a pining and loathsome disease,[3] to a wretched life and miserable death, the beginnings whereof I do already feel at sometimes, and dread more than death; and consequently I fear it would be injurious to another besides myself, whom I least desire to injure.

[23 FEBRUARY 1655]

I was much carried away with too much frothiness and love to vanity on Thursday and Friday, having cheerful company in the house with me. *I found myself much overborn with carnal concupiscence[4] nature being suppressed for I had not had my afflux[5] in 12 nights. Friday night it came again without any dream that I know of. Yet after it I am still inclined to lust. The Lord help me against it and against discouragement by it and against temptations of another nature and disquietments.*

1 *estate* State.

2 *change my condition* I.e., marry.

3 *loathsome disease* Wigglesworth thought he had gonorrhea, which in classical medical texts referred not to a sexually transmitted infection but to a condition in which the sufferer cannot control the frequency of ejaculation. It was thought that the disease led to sluggishness, impotence, and eventual paralysis. Wigglesworth appears to have agonized over the question of whether marriage would improve or aggravate his condition (see the diary entry for 17 April 1655, below).

4 *concupiscence* Strong desire, especially sinful desire for worldly pleasure.

5 *afflux* Flow; in this context, ejaculation, particularly nocturnal emission.

[17 APRIL 1655]

On the Sabbath day morning, (having prepared to preach the 2 days before and fully intending it) I awaked with a very sore throat, so that I perceived my mouth was stopped for that day. Mr. Stow[6] being in the town by a providence supplied the place. It was a sacrament day[7] and I ventured out (hooded) before noon, but afternoon *again* durst not. I kept house all that week, being much pained in swallowing my spittle, and so overflowed with rheum[8] that if I forbore spitting my throat grew painful with dryness. This illness marred my stomach utterly (especially by the nauseous taste of the phlegm at the beginning and latter end thereof), mightily enfeebled my spirits, wasted my moisture and made me feverish. I used principally burnt wine,[9] which almost set me in a swoon diverse times, yet I think did me good. At the latter end of the week growing something better I ventured out to Wethersfield[10] hooded, whence I had a horse brought me according to agreement on Monday, and on Tuesday I set forth for the Bay.[11] The motives that hastened me were these. 1. I found my illness[12] continue and no means there to help me. 2ly I conceived journeying might do me good as much as physic,[13] if I could keep from cold. 3. To redeem[14] the spring time for marrying or taking physic, or both. God brought me through comfortably in 2 days from Springfield to Roxbury,[15] much bettered (though wearied) with my journey. Staying a day in the Bay and consulting with Mr. Alcock[16] (who advised to proceed with the business of marriage in the 1st place) I

6 *Mr. Stow* Samuel Stow, a Connecticut minister.

7 *sacrament day* Day on which Communion was taken.

8 *rheum* Mucous.

9 *burnt wine* Brandy.

10 *Wethersfield* Town in central Connecticut, now known as Old Wethersfield.

11 *the Bay* Massachusetts Bay Colony.

12 *illness* His supposed gonorrhea.

13 *physic* Medicine.

14 *redeem* To make good use of.

15 *Springfield to Roxbury* Springfield and Roxbury were towns in Massachusetts; Roxbury is now part of Boston.

16 *Mr. Alcock* Physician (1627–67) who treated Wigglesworth.

reached Rowley[1] on the Saturday. / On Monday ensuing I dined and discoursed with Mr. Rogers[2] about the great business. He could by no means concur with the other physicians in advising first to marriage and afterward to taking physic, for many reasons by him alleged; but thought it meet 1. to rectify the habit[3] of my body and afterward to proceed. I was distressed at the hearing of his opinion, because it still made the case more difficult. I prayed to the God of heaven and such was his mercy to me, that after a little reasoning about the case, and fuller declaration of my illness etc. Mr. Rogers his mind was quite altered, and he declared himself free and ready to further the consummation thereof[4] with all possible speed. And so he contrived the business and wrought it with them whom it concerned, that it was then published,[5] and I was to return again and be contracted the next Friday sennight.[6] And so I left my friends with determination so to return. Yet after I was gone from thence, my own weakness (which formerly perplexed me at such times) setting in with Mr. Rogers his scruples did much trouble me, and cause me to question, whether it were my way to marry, before the use of more means, and to run such a hazard as that of my life and health without an apparent necessity, before I had tried the utmost that physic could do. I repaired to Mr. Alcock with all speed again to speak with him and object unto him for my farther satisfaction.

1: He told me that he hoped my disease might be cured by physic; but it would be a long and tedious and far more difficult cure, than he hoped it would be by marriage, and astringent cordials afterward. And he had no heart to go the farther way about when as he might have a nearer way by providence offered him.

2: He told me diverse experiences of the success of this course in like distempers. An example of one just affected like myself before his marriage, who was grievously perplexed with it, yet went on with it and did very well after, and hath diverse children living at this day. And so of diverse others who have taken this course with good success.

3: He told me that mine was not vera Gon: as he could prove nor the excretio (*which happened by the presence of such a friend*) seminis but quasi sudor partium genitatium: as a little alum will cause the mouth to fill with water, so a little acrimony gathering there, causeth humours to flow thither amain, which might come away in great quantity, and yet there be plenty of veri seminis behind.[7] And so I found it to be.

4ly. He told me that which made me so fearful, made him fearless, and gave him the more hopes, that marriage would take away the cause of that distemper, which was naturalis impulsus seu instinctus irresistibilis.[8]

These things together with the consideration. 1. Of my unsettled condition[9] wherein I cannot attend rules of physic with any conveniency. 2ly Of the great charge and expenses I must be at for a continued course of physic and diet better than ordinary. 3ly Of my inability with comfort and honesty to live long as I am single. 4ly Of the little hopes to prevail against rebellious nature, which is disquieted rather than overcome by physic in statu presenti.[10] These things make it pretty clear to me that God calleth to a speedy change of my condition, which I therefore desire to attend as a duty that God calleth unto, leaving my life and health in his hands. And oh! that I had a meek spirit to submit to his

1 *Rowley* Town in eastern Massachusetts.

2 *Mr. Rogers* Another physician.

3 *habit* Condition.

4 *consummation thereof* Accomplishment of Wigglesworth's marriage.

5 *published* Announced publicly by means of marriage banns.

6 *contracted* Married; *next Friday sennight* Friday of the next week.

7 *mine was not … behind* I.e., I did not have true gonorrhea, as far as he could tell, and the bodily excretion (which happened as a result of a desirable person's presence) was not semen but a kind of sweat of the genital parts: as a bit of alum (a mineral salt) causes one's mouth to water, so an irritating substance gathering in the genitals causes bodily fluids to flow out forcefully, potentially in great quantity, leaving plenty of true semen behind.

8 *naturalis impulsus seu instinctus irresistibilis* Latin: a natural or normal drive, or rather irresistible instinct.

9 *unsettled condition* Wigglesworth did not yet have a settled home at this time.

10 *in statu presenti* Latin: in my present circumstances.

good pleasure. A believing heart! and a judicious mind to see clearly that this is my way at all times.

[18 May 1655]

At the time appointed with fear and trembling I came to Rowley to be marryed.[1] The great arguments unto me were, 1: Physicians counsel: 2ly the institution of marryage by god himself for the preservation of purity and chastity, which with most humble and hearty prayers I have begged and stil wilbeg of the Lord. so that I went about the business which god call'd me to attend And consummated it now is by the will of god May 18. 1655. / oh Lord! let my cry come up unto thee for all the blessings of a marryed estate, A heart sutable thereto, chastity especially thereby, and life and health if it be thy will. oh crown thy own ordinance with thy blessing, that it may appear it is not in vain to wait upon thee in the wayes of thy own appointment *I feel the stirrings and strongly of my former distemper even after the use of marriage*[2] *the next day which makes me exceeding afraid. I know not how to keep company with my dearest friend but it is with me as formerly in some days already.*[3] oh pitty the poorest and vilest of thy creatures for the Lords sake, And let not thy servants be a curs each to other but a blessing in this new relation …

[July 1655]

… About the 17th of July I went to the Bay carrying my wife with me. Where much of God appeared, both in our comfortable going and return (though I much feared the prevailing of rheum to my great affliction, yet the Lord prevented it) and also much of God in expediting my occasions;[4] which were with the physician, about a parcel of corn disposing of (which providence had taken good order for in my absence),

and about Malden Invitation;[5] blessed be God for all his benefits. But oh my ill requitals of the Lord's love! Much frothiness, pride, *carnal lusts also exceeding* prevailing *Lord forgive my intemperance in the use of marriage for thy son's sake.*

[15 September 1655]

God will guide and provide.
He hath done so in troubles as great as these and therefore he can do it and will do it.
In memorial of his former mercies received in answer to prayer and of all his goodness hitherto I will erect
A pillar to the praise of his grace
O Dulcis memoria difficultatis praeteritae!
Olim haec (quae nunc incumbent mala, haec inquam)
Meminisse juvabit.
Quae mala nunc affligunt, postea in Laudem dei, nostramque voluptatem cedent
Quis triumphum caneret, quis spoliis onustus rederet victor, si numquam dimicaret?[6]

EBEN
September 15

EZER[7]
1655

Hitherto the Lord

hath happen me

[1] *marryed* Wigglesworth married his cousin, Mary Reyner.

[2] *use of marriage* I.e., sex within marriage.

[3] *I feel … already* While the rest of this passage appears with the original spelling and punctuation, the italicized text is translated from the shorthand code Wigglesworth used; *my dearest friend* Here, Wigglesworth's wife.

[4] *occasions* Reasons for going.

[5] *Malden Invitation* Invitation to become the minister at the Congregational church in Malden.

[6] *O Dulcis …dimicaret?* Latin: O sweet memory of troubles gone by! / Those troubles (I say this because new sins will press upon me) it will benefit me to have remembered. / Those sins that now dash me to the earth, afterwards may turn into praise of God, and give place to our own pleasure. / Who might sing the triumph, who comes back a victor burdened with the spoils, if he never struggled?

[7] *EBEN EZER* Hebrew: stone of help, the name of a stone erected by Samuel to mark the victory of the Israelites over the Philistines. See 1 Samuel 7.12: "Then Samuel took a stone, and set it between Mizpeh and Shen, and called the name of it Ebenezer, saying, Hitherto hath the Lord helped us."

SABBATH. SEPTEMBER 16. [1655]

*Some night pollution escaped me notwithstanding my
earnest prayer to the contrary which brought to mind my
old sins now too much forgotten (as near as I remember
the thoughts that then I had) together with my later sins
unto seeming one that had received so many mercies from
the Lord O unthankfulness unthankfulness when shall I
get rid of thee. ...*
—1653–57

Manuscript page from Wigglesworth's diary, 15–16 September 1655.

from *The Day of Doom*[1]
*Or, A Poetical Description of the Great
and Last Judgment. With a Short
Discourse about Eternity.*

[The Infants' Plea and God's Response]

166[2]

Then to the Bar,[3] all they drew near
 who died in Infancy,
And never had or° good or bad *either*
 effected pers'nally,
5 But from the womb unto the tomb
 were straightway carried,
(Or at the last ere they transgressed)
 who thus began to plead:

167[4]

If for our own transgression,
 or disobedience,
10 We here did stand at thy left-hand[5]
 just were the recompense:
But Adam's guilt[6] our souls hath spilt,
 his fault is charged° on us; *blamed*

15 And that alone hath overthrown,
 and utterly undone us.

168

Not we, but he, ate of the Tree,
 whose fruit was interdicted:
Yet on us all of his sad Fall,
20 the punishment's inflicted.
How could we sin that had not been
 or how is his sin our,° *ours*
Without consent, which to prevent,
 we never had a pow'r?

169[7]

25 O great Creator, why was our Nature
 depraved and forlorn?
Why so defiled, and made so vild° *vile*
 whilst we were yet unborn?
If it be just, and needs we must
30 transgressors reckoned be,
Thy Mercy, Lord, to us afford,
 which sinners hath set free.

170

Behold we see Adam set free,
 and saved from his trespass,
35 Whose sinful Fall hath split us all,
 and brought us to this pass.
Canst thou deny us once to try,
 or Grace to us to tender,° *offer*
When he finds grace before thy face,
40 that was the chief offender?

171[8]

Then answered the Judge most dread,
 God doth such doom forbid,
That men should die eternally

1 *Doom* Judgment.

2 [Wigglesworth's marginal note] Reprobate infants plead for themselves. Revelation 2.12, 15 compared with Romans 5.12, 14; 9.11, 13. [A "reprobate" in Calvinist theology is one who is predestined for damnation.]

3 *Bar* I.e., bar of judgment, tribunal. In the Last Judgment, Christ sits as judge and pronounces each soul as destined for heaven or hell.

4 [Wigglesworth's marginal note] Ezekiel 18.2. ["The fathers have eaten sour grapes, and the children's teeth are set on edge." Biblical quotations included in footnotes to this selection are from the Geneva Bible, used by Puritans of Wigglesworth's era more often than the King James.]

5 *stand ... left-hand* On Judgment Day the blessed are placed at Christ's right hand and the damned on his left. See Matthew 25.31–46.

6 *Adam's guilt* Adam and Eve, the first humans, disobey God by eating fruit from the Tree of Knowledge, committing the "original sin" for which, in some Christian theology, all the children of Adam (i.e., all humankind) bear the guilt and suffer the consequences: according to Calvinist Puritanism, people are in a state of sin and alienation from God from the moment of conception. Only the

elect—those predestined to be saved—are granted salvation from this condition.

7 [Wigglesworth's marginal note] Psalm 51.5. ["Behold, I was born in iniquity; / And in sin hath my mother conceived me."]

8 [Wigglesworth's marginal note] Their argument taken off. Ezekiel 18.20. ["The same soul that sinneth, shall die: the son shall not bear the iniquity of the father, neither shall the father bear the iniquity of the son."] Romans 5.12, 19.

for what they never did.
45 But what you call old Adam's Fall,
 and only his Trespass,
You call amiss to call it his,
 both his and yours it was.

172[1]

He was designed of all mankind
50 to be a public head,
A common root, whence all should shoot,
 and stood in all their stead.
He stood and fell, did ill or well,
 not for himself alone,
55 But for you all, who now his Fall,
 and trespass would disown.

173

If he had stood, then all his brood
 had been establishèd
In God's true love, never to move,
60 nor once awry to tread:
Then all his race my Father's Grace,
 should have enjoyed for ever,
And wicked sprites by subtle sleights° *tricks*
 could them have harmèd never.

174

65 Would you have grieved to have received
 through Adam so much good,
As had been your for evermore,
 if he at first had stood?
Would you have said, we ne'er obeyed,
70 nor did thy Laws regard;
It ill befits with benefits,
 us, Lord, so to reward?

175

Since then to share in his welfare,
 you could have been content,
75 You may with reason share in his treason,

and in the punishment.
Hence you were born in state forlorn,[2]
 with Natures so depraved:[3]
Death was your due, because that you[4]
80 had thus yourselves behaved.

176[5]

You think if we had been as he,
 whom God did so betrust,
We to our cost would ne'er have lost
 all for a paltry Lust.
85 Had you been made in Adam's stead,
 you would like things have wrought,
And so into the self-same woe,
 yourselves and yours have brought.

177

I may deny you once to try,[6]
90 or Grace to you to tender,[7]
Though he finds Grace before my face,[8]
 who was the chief offender:
Else should my Grace cease to be Grace;
 for it should not be free,
95 If to release whom I should please,
 I have no liberty.

[2] [Wigglesworth's marginal note] Romans 5.12. ["Wherefore, as by one man sin entered into the world, and death by sin, and so death went over all men: in whom all men have sinned."]

[3] [Wigglesworth's marginal note] Psalm 51.5.

[4] [Wigglesworth's marginal note] Genesis 5.3. [An annotation on this verse in the Geneva Bible suggests that Adam's son possesses Adam's "own likeness" in both "his creation" and "his corruption."]

[5] [Wigglesworth's marginal note] Matthew 23.30–31. ["And say, If we had been in the days of our fathers, we would not have been partners with them in the blood of the Prophets. So then ye be witnesses unto yourselves, that ye are the children of them that murdered the Prophets."]

[6] [Wigglesworth's marginal note] Romans 9.15, 18. ["For he saith to Moses, I will have mercy on him, to whom I will show mercy: and will have compassion on him, on who I will have compassion. … Therefore he hath mercy on whom he will, and whom he will he hardeneth."]

[7] [Wigglesworth's marginal note] The free gift.

[8] [Wigglesworth's marginal note] Romans 5.15. ["But yet the gift is not so as is the offense: for if through the offense of that one, many be dead, much more the grace of God, and the gift by grace, which is by one man Jesus Christ, hath abounded unto many."]

[1] [Wigglesworth's marginal note] 1 Corinthians 15.48–49. ["As is the earthly, such are they that are earthly: and as is the heavenly, such are they also that are heavenly. And as we have born the image of the earthly, so shall we bear the image of the heavenly."]

178

If upon one what's due to none
 I frankly shall bestow,
And on the rest shall not think best,
 Compassion's skirts to throw.
100 Whom injure I? Will you envy,
 and grudge at others weal?° *good fortune*
Or me accuse, who do refuse
 yourselves to help and heal?

179[1]

105 Am I alone of what's my own,
 no Master or no Lord?
Or if I am, how can you claim
 what I to some afford?
Will you demand Grace at my hand,
110 and challenge what is mine?
Will you teach me whom to set free,
 & thus my Grace confine?

180

You sinners are, and such a share[2]
 as sinners may expect,[3]
115 Such you shall have; for I do save[4]
 none but mine own Elect.[5]
Yet to compare your sin with their,[6]
 who lived a longer time,[7]

I do confess yours is much less,
120 though every sin's a crime.

181[8]

A crime it is, therefore in bliss
 you may not hope to dwell;
But unto you I shall allow
 the easiest room in Hell.
125 The glorious King thus answering,
 they cease, and plead no longer:[9]
Their Consciences must needs confess
 his Reasons are the stronger.

182[10]

Thus all men's pleas the Judge with ease
130 doth answer and confute,
Until that all, both great and small,
 are silencèd and mute
Vain hopes are cropped, all mouths are stopped
 sinners have ought° to say, *nothing*
135 But that 'tis just, and equal most
 they should be damned for ay.° *always*

183

Now what remains, but that to pains
 and everlasting smart,° *affliction*
Christ should condemn the sons of men,
140 which is their just desert;
Oh rueful plights of sinful wights!° *people*
 Oh wretches all forlorn:
'T had happy been they ne'er had seen
 the Sun, or not been born.

[1] [Wigglesworth's marginal note] Matthew 20.15. ["Is it not lawful for me to do as I will with mine own? Is thine eye evil, because I am good?" An annotation on this passage clarifies that "for the Hebrews by an evil eye, meant envy."]

[2] [Wigglesworth's marginal note] Psalm 58.3. ["The wicked are strangers from the womb: even from the belly have they erred, and speak lies."]

[3] [Wigglesworth's marginal note] Romans 6.23. ["For the wages of sin is death: but the gift of God is eternal life, through Jesus Christ our Lord."]

[4] [Wigglesworth's marginal note] Galatians 3.10. [According to Calvinist theology, these and the following passages from Romans and Revelation relate to the idea that only the elect, whom God has predestined for salvation, will be saved from original sin and its consequences by God's freely given grace.]

[5] [Wigglesworth's marginal note] Romans 8.29–30; 11.7.

[6] [Wigglesworth's marginal note] Revelation 21.27.

[7] [Wigglesworth's marginal note] Luke 12.48. ["But he that knew it not, and yet did commit things worthy of stripes, shall be beaten with few stripes: for unto whomsoever much is given, of him shall be much required, and to whom men much commit, the more of him will they ask."]

[8] [Wigglesworth's marginal note] Matthew 11.22. [In this passage, Jesus contrasts unbelieving cities with Jewish cities whose people have failed to repent, claiming that God will judge the latter more harshly.]

[9] [Wigglesworth's marginal note] The wicked all convinced and put to silence. Romans 3.19. Matthew 22.12.

[10] [Wigglesworth's marginal note] Behold the formidable estate of all the ungodly, as they stand hopeless and helpless before an impartial Judge, expecting their final sentence. Revelation 6.16–17.

184

145 Yea, now it would be good they could
 themselves annihilate,
 And cease to be, themselves to free
 from such a fearful state.
 Oh happy dogs, and swine, and frogs:
150 Yea serpents' generation,° *offspring*
 Who do not fear this doom to hear,
 And sentence of Damnation!
 —1662

MARY ROWLANDSON
1637 – 1711

The Sovereignty and Goodness of God, Puritan settler Mary Rowlandson's narrative of her time held hostage by an Indigenous community, was the first prose work by a woman to be published in English in British North America. An immediate success on both sides of the Atlantic, it would become one of the most popular works of early American literature. Rowlandson's dramatic story has been read as spiritual allegory, anti-Indigenous propaganda, ethnographic document, and historical record. It is today widely acknowledged to be, as a narrative, among the most vivid accounts of early New England settler experience—and, as a cultural artifact, among the seventeenth century's most deeply fraught examples of the rhetoric of colonization.

Born in England in 1637, Rowlandson sailed for the Massachusetts Bay Colony as a young child with her parents John and Joan White in 1639. The Whites were part of a massive wave of Puritan migration to a region the Indigenous peoples already living there called Dawnland. The early Europeans who came to Dawnland encountered thriving Indigenous communities and trade networks; they brought with them diseases that soon devastated the coastal communities, a catastrophe the Puritans interpreted as evidence of divine support for their invasion of the region. The Whites, who settled in Salem, acquired a significant amount of land over the next thirteen years, but they wanted more. In 1653, they left their son in charge and moved to the new town of Lancaster, situated fifty miles inland on Nipmuc territory.

In 1660, the English monarchy was restored to power, ending the Puritan regime in England. As a result, Puritan migration to Dawnland increased—as did tensions with the region's Indigenous occupants, the Nipmuc, Narragansett, and Wampanoag. A longstanding alliance between the Wampanoag and the English deteriorated after the death of sachem Ousamequin (known to settlers by his title Massasoit) in 1662. Ousamequin was succeeded by his eldest son Wamsutta, who soon died mysteriously, with many suspecting he had been poisoned. His younger brother Metacom (called "King Philip" by the English) and other Indigenous leaders—such as Pocasset saunkskaw (female sachem) Weetamoo, who also appears in Rowlandson's narrative—built an alliance to defend their territories, resources, and ways of life.

A wave of Indigenous resistance formed and began to crest in the summer of 1675. The ensuing conflict, now known as King Philip's War, lasted a year and devastated the region, leaving about five percent of the colonists and as many as forty percent of the Indigenous inhabitants dead. Many of the Indigenous survivors were either distributed among colonists as indentured servants, or shipped to Bermuda or the West Indies to be sold into slavery.

Settler histories tended to treat King Philip's War as an isolated event ending in a decisive victory for colonists, but the arc of resistance—and of tragedy—is a long one. Indigenous peoples had been resisting colonization in multiple ways long before 1675 and would continue to do so afterward. But the odds against them only grew; over the course of the seventeenth century the Indigenous population of what the colonizers now called "New England" fell from almost 150,000 to fewer than 10,000 (their numbers reduced by disease and starvation even more than by armed conflict), while the number of colonists rose from nothing to well over 50,000.

Rowlandson's narrative opens dramatically at the beginning of the attack that led to her capture. Eliding the context of Puritan expansion, it presents the attack as senseless violence perpetrated by "merciless Heathens" whom she describes in dehumanizing terms as "hell-hounds" and "ravenous beasts." The Preface, not written by Rowlandson, holds to the same racist ideas, even as it acknowledges the context of colonial violence that preceded and precipitated the attack: "the Narrhagansets were now driven quite from their own Country, and all their provisions there hoarded up, to which they durst not at present return, and being so numerous as they were, soon devoured those to whom they went [i.e., the Nipmuc], whereby both the one and their other were now reduced to extreme straits."

At the time of the attack on Lancaster, Rowlandson was in charge of her large household because her husband, Joseph Rowlandson, had traveled to Boston with several other men from the settlement to ask for military reinforcements. The property was already partially garrisoned, but it could not withstand the attack that came on 10 February 1676. An alliance of Nipmuc, Narragansett, and Wampanoag fighters killed several inhabitants and took hostage twenty-four others, among them Mary Rowlandson and three of her children. Following her capture, Rowlandson was separated from her two older children, while six-year-old Sarah, who had been badly injured in the attack, died in her arms nine days later. Rowlandson was held jointly in captivity by Weetamoo and her husband, the Narragansett sachem Quinnapin. Over the next eleven weeks she traveled widely with her captors; all frequently went hungry, and they undertook a level of physical exertion far beyond what the average Puritan woman would have been used to.

In early May, Rowlandson was ransomed for a sum of twenty pounds, a price she set herself at the request of her captors. The Rowlandson family never returned to Lancaster; they lived in Boston for ten months before moving to Connecticut. Joseph Rowlandson died not long thereafter. As was common among settlers, Rowlandson soon remarried. In 1679, she became Mrs. Samuel Talcott, marrying a former officer who had served in the colonial militia during the war. She outlived her second husband and died in 1711.

Rowlandson likely began writing the memoir of her capture not long after her release. At first, Rowlandson's account circulated in manuscript form, but public demand for her narrative grew, and it was published in 1682 under the title *The Sovereignty and Goodness of God, together with the Faithfulness of His Promises Displayed; Being a Narrative of the Captivity and Restoration of Mrs. Mary Rowlandson*. Puritans generally thought it inappropriate for writings by women to appear in print unless under the auspices of male authority; in its published form Rowlandson's narrative was preceded by a male-authored preface and followed by the text of her husband's final sermon. The anonymous preface—thought by most modern scholars to be the work of influential preacher, historian, and colonial administrator Increase Mather—emphasized Rowlandson's appropriately modest reluctance to publish, and described the book as a work of pious public service that offered important lessons on faith and providence. Mather also saw into print several other settler captivity narratives that, like Rowlandson's, vilify Indigenous people and argue for a return to Puritan orthodoxy.

Structured as a series of twenty "Removes"—each one recounting the travels of Rowlandson and her captors from one camp to another—Rowlandson's narrative dramatically depicts her emotional trauma and details her spiritual as well as her physical journey. Puritans tended to see mourning as a sinful and even idolatrous attachment to worldly relationships, and to be of the view that believers ought instead to celebrate God's will. It is in this context that Rowlandson portrays her efforts to come to terms with her own suffering; she makes liberal use of biblical references and quotations to reaffirm her faith.

The Sovereignty and Goodness of God was an immediate success. The first Boston edition sold out quickly, leading to the publication of two more editions in Cambridge, Massachusetts, that same year, and one more in England. In the first of many renamings and re-envisionings of Rowlandson's account, the English edition was retitled as *A True History of the Captivity and Restoration of Mrs. Mary Rowlandson, A Minister's Wife in New-England. Wherein Is Set forth, The Cruel and Inhumane Usage She Underwent amongst the Heathens, for Eleven Weeks Time: And Her Deliverance from Them*. The new title repositioned the narrative to appeal to a more religiously diverse audience, and foregrounded its exotic appeal as an eyewitness account. In the eighteenth century, as nationalist sentiment intensified, Rowlandson's narrative was seen as a dramatic depiction of the struggle of Anglo-American civilization against Indigenous "savagery." Once again, a shift in interpretive emphasis was reflected in the titles given the work; *A Narrative of the Captivity, Sufferings, and Removes of Mrs. Mary Rowlandson, Who Was Taken Prisoner by the Indians with Several Others, and Treated in the Most Barbarous and Cruel Manner by These Vile Savages* is one late eighteenth-century example.

In the early twentieth century, critics began increasingly to value Rowlandson's text for its historical and ethnographic significance. A 1903 edition, for example, suggested in its introduction that the work was "an authentic and graphic delineation of the manners and customs of the primitive children of the soil from whom our ancestors relentlessly wrested their beautiful and beloved heritage in order to enrich

us and our posterity." From the late twentieth century onwards, Rowlandson's account has been increasingly studied by literary scholars and historians not only for its portrayal of the trauma of war, but also for the ways in which it is shaped by cultural prejudices and by the ideology of colonization.

Today, Rowlandson's narrative is acknowledged to have played a central role in setting the pattern for an entire literary genre—the "Indian captivity narrative." Conventions of the genre include a focus on the perspective and suffering of white captives; a tendency towards dehumanizing and racist representations of Native Americans—portrayals often presented in order to justify colonial violence; and detailed, but also biased descriptions of Indigenous customs and ways of life. Arguably, use of the term "Indian captivity narrative" has had the effect of obscuring the much higher incidence of captivity experienced by Indigenous people and other people of color in colonial America. Indigenous people's accounts of their abduction, enslavement, forced indenture, imprisonment, and occasional deliverance are to be found embedded in legal documents, verse, sermons, letters, and Native American oral histories, but during Rowlandson's era these narratives were not generally published for white readers. The fact that settler readers frequently devoured the stories of captives such as Rowlandson but rarely encountered the stories of Indigenous captives is one of the many ironies surrounding Rowlandson's narrative. Increasingly, it is because of such ironies (rather than in spite of them) that the text is recognized as foundational to early American culture.

———————

NOTE ON THE TEXT: The text of the work presented below is based on the second "corrected and amended" edition of Rowlandson's *The Sovereignty and Goodness of God, together, with the Faithfulness of His Promises Displayed; Being a Narrative of the Captivity and Restoration of Mrs. Mary Rowlandson*, published in Cambridge, Massachusetts in 1682; this is the earliest surviving edition. Spelling and punctuation have been modernized in accordance with the practices of this anthology. Biblical citation formats have been made consistent for the sake of clarity. Rowlandson's inconsistent capitalization of the second-person pronoun when referring to God has been retained. Italics have been removed except when signifying foreign-language words or when clearly intended for emphasis.

⌘ ⌘ ⌘

The Sovereignty and Goodness of God, together, with the Faithfulness of His Promises Displayed; Being a Narrative of the Captivity and Restoration of Mrs. Mary Rowlandson

THE PREFACE TO THE READER[1]

It was on Tuesday Feb. 1, 1675,[2] in the afternoon, when the Narragansetts' quarters (in or toward the Nipmuc country, whither they are now retired for fear of the English army lying in their own country) were the second time beaten up by the forces of the United Colonies,[3] who thereupon soon betook themselves to flight, and were all the next day pursued by the English, some overtaken and destroyed. But on Thursday Feb. 3rd, the English having now been six days on their march from their headquarters at Wickford, in the Narragansett country, toward and

———————

[1] This preface is generally thought to have been written by Increase Mather (1639–1723), the influential Puritan minister who was partially responsible for the publication of Rowlandson's narrative.

[2] *Tuesday Feb. 1, 1675* By the modern Gregorian calendar, 11 February 1676. England continued to observe the Julian calendar until 1752, long after the Gregorian calendar had been adopted by most other European countries and colonies. (The discrepancy in the year is accounted for by the fact that, according to the Julian calendar, the new year began on 25 March.)

[3] *United Colonies* Also known as the New England Confederation, the United Colonies of New England was founded in 1643 and allied the Puritan colonies of Massachusetts Bay, Plymouth, Connecticut, and New Haven for military, political, and religious reasons. (The Puritan-dominant but religiously tolerant colony of Rhode Island was excluded from the alliance.)

after the enemy, and provision grown exceeding short, insomuch that they were fain to kill some horses for the supply, especially of their Indian friends, they were necessitated to consider what was best to be done. And about noon (having hitherto followed the chase as hard as they might) a council was called, and though some few were of another mind, yet it was concluded by far the greater part of the council of war, that the army should desist the pursuit and retire, the forces of Plymouth and the Bay[1] to the next town of the Bay, and Connecticut forces to their own next towns; which determination was immediately put in execution. The consequent whereof, as it was not difficult to be foreseen by those that knew the causeless enmity of these barbarians against the English, and the malicious and revengeful spirit of these heathen: so it soon proved dismal.

The Narragansetts were now driven quite from their own country, and all their provisions there hoarded up, to which they durst not at present return, and being so numerous as they were, soon devoured those to whom they went,[2] whereby both the one and other were now reduced to extreme straits, and so necessitated to take the first and best opportunity for supply, and very glad, no doubt, of such an opportunity as this, to provide for themselves, and make spoil of the English at once; and seeing themselves thus discharged of their pursuers, and a little refreshed after their flight, the very next week on Thursday Feb. 10, they fell with mighty force and fury upon Lancaster: which small town, remote from aid of others, and not being garrisoned as it might, the army being now come in, and as the time indeed required (the design[3] of the Indians against that place being known to the English some time before) was not able to make effectual resistance: but notwithstanding utmost endeavour of the inhabitants, most of the buildings were turned into ashes; many people (men, women and children) slain, and others captivated.[4] The most solemn and remarkable part of this tragedy, may that justly be reputed, which

fell upon the family of that reverend servant of God, Mr. Joseph Rowlandson, the faithful Pastor of Christ in that place, who being gone down to the council of the Massachusetts to seek aid for the defence of the place, at his return found the town in flames, or smoke, his own house being set on fire by the enemy, through the disadvantage of a defective fortification, and all in it consumed: his previous yoke-fellow,[5] and dear children, wounded and captivated (as the issue evidenced, and following narrative declares) by these cruel and barbarous savages. A sad catastrophe! Thus all things come alike to all: none knows either love or hatred by all that is before him. It is no new thing for God's precious ones to drink as deep as others, of the cup of common calamity. Take just Lot[6] (yet captivated) for instance beside others. But it is not my business to dilate[7] on these things, but only in few words introductively to preface to the following script, which is a narrative of the wonderfully awful, wise, holy, powerful, and gracious providence of God, towards that worthy and precious gentlewoman, the dear consort of the said Reverend Mr. Rowlandson, and her children with her, as in casting of her into such a waterless pit, so in preserving, supporting, and carrying through so many such extreme hazards, unspeakable difficulties and disconsolateness, and at last delivering her out of them all, and her surviving children also. It was a strange and amazing dispensation, that the Lord should so afflict his precious servant and handmaid; it was as strange, if not more, that he should so bear up the spirits of his servant under such bereavements and of his handmaid under such captivity, travels and hardships (much too hard for flesh and blood) as he did, and at length deliver and restore. But he was their Saviour, who hath said, *When thou passest through the Waters, I will be with thee, and through the Rivers, they shall not overflow thee: When thou walkest through the fire thou shalt not be burnt, nor shall the flame kindle upon thee*, Isaiah 43.2.; and again, *He woundeth and his hands make whole. He shall deliver thee in six troubles, yea in seven there shall no evil touch thee: In Famine*

[1] *the Bay* I.e., the Massachusetts Bay Colony.

[2] *devoured those … they went* I.e., depleted the food supply of the allied tribes, including the Nipmuc.

[3] *design* Plan; objective.

[4] *captivated* I.e., taken captive.

[5] *yoke-fellow* Wife (i.e., Mary Rowlandson).

[6] *just Lot* Virtuous biblical figure who is held captive during the conflict sometimes known as the War of Nine Kings; see Genesis 14.12–16.

[7] *dilate* Expound upon; discuss at length.

he shall redeem thee from Death, and in War from the power of the sword. Job 5.18–20. Methinks this dispensation doth bear some resemblance to those of Joseph, David, and Daniel, yea, and of the three children[1] too, the stories whereof do represent us with the excellent textures of divine providence, curious pieces of divine work: and truly so doth this, and therefore not to be forgotten, but worthy to be exhibited to, and viewed, and pondered by all, that disdain not to consider the operation of his hands.

The works of the Lord (not only of creation, but of providence also, especially those that do more peculiarly concern his dear ones, that are as the apple of his eye, as the signet[2] upon His hand, the delight of his eyes, and the object of his tenderest care) are great, sought out of all those that have pleasure therein. And of these verily this is none of the least.

This narrative was penned by the gentlewoman herself, to be to her a memorandum of God's dealing with her, that she might never forget, but remember the same, and the several[3] circumstances thereof, all the days of her life. A pious scope which deserves both commendation and imitation: some friends having obtained a sight of it, could not but be so much affected with the many passages of working providence discovered therein, as to judge it worthy of public view, and altogether unmeet[4] that such works of God should be hid from present and future generations. And therefore, though this gentlewoman's modesty would not thrust it into the press, yet her gratitude unto God made her not hardly persuadable to let it pass, that God might have his due glory, and others benefit by it as well as herself. I hope by this time none will cast any reflection[5] upon this gentlewoman, on the score of this publication of her affliction and deliverance.

If any should, doubtless they may be reckoned with the nine lepers, of whom it is said, *Were there not ten cleansed, where are the nine? but one returning to give God thanks.*[6] Let such further know that this was a dispensation of public note, and of universal concernment, and so much the more, by how much the nearer this gentlewoman stood related to that faithful Servant of God, whose capacity and employment was public in the house of God, and his name on that account of a very sweet savour in the Churches of Christ, who is there of a true Christian spirit, that did not look upon himself much concerned in this bereavement, this captivity in the time thereof, and in his deliverance when it came, yea more than in many others; and how many are there, to whom so concerned, it will doubtless be a very acceptable thing to see the way of God with this gentlewoman in the aforesaid dispensation, thus laid out and portrayed before their eyes.

To conclude whatever any coy phantasies may deem, yet it highly concerns those that have so deeply tasted, how good the Lord is, to enquire with David, *What shall I render to the Lord for all his benefits to me?* Psalm 116.12. He thinks nothing too great; yea, being sensible of his own disproportion to the due praises of God he calls in help. *Oh, magnify the Lord with me, let us exalt his Name together*, Psalm 34.3. And it is but reason, that our praises should hold proportion with our prayers: and that as many hath helped together by prayer for the obtaining of his mercy, so praises should be returned by many on this behalf; and forasmuch as not the general but particular knowledge of things makes deepest impression upon the affections, this narrative particularizing the several passages of this providence will not a little conduce thereunto. And therefore holy David in order to the attainment of that end, accounts himself concerned to declare what God had done for his soul, Psalm 66.16. *Come and hear, all ye that fear God, and I will declare what God hath done for my soul*, i.e. *for his life*, see verses 9–10. *He holdeth our soul in life, and suffers not our feet to be moved, for thou our God hast proved us, thou hast tried us, as silver is tried.*[7] Life-mercies are

1. *Joseph, David, and Daniel* Heroic biblical figures who are saved by divine intervention in Genesis 39, 1 Samuel 17, and Daniel 6, respectively; *the three children* Shadrach, Meshach, and Abednego are three youths who are cast into a burning furnace as punishment for their worship of God, but their lives are saved by divine intervention; see Daniel 3.

2. *signet* Ring into which a mold is fixed for the stamping of wax seals.

3. *several* Different; individual.

4. *unmeet* Inappropriate.

5. *reflection* Criticism; censure.

6. *Were there … give God thanks* See Luke 17.11–19: Jesus heals ten lepers, but only one of them—a Samaritan—comes back to praise and thank God for his healing.

7. *as silver is tried* To "try" in this context means to extract a metal by means of heat.

heart-affecting mercies, of great impression and force, to enlarge pious hearts in the praises of God, so that such know not how but to talk of God's acts, and to speak of and publish[1] his wonderful works. Deep troubles, when the waters come into thy soul, are wont to produce vows: vows must be paid. *It is better not vow, than vow and not to pay.*[2] I may say, that as none knows what it is to fight and pursue such an enemy as this, but they that have fought and pursued them: so none can imagine what it is to be captivated, and enslaved to such atheistical, proud, wild, cruel, barbarous, brutish—in one word—diabolical creatures are these, the worst of the heathen; nor what difficulties, hardships, hazards, sorrows, anxieties and perplexities do unavoidably wait upon such a condition, but those that have tried it. No serious spirit then (especially knowing anything of this gentlewoman's piety) can imagine but that the vows of God are upon her. Excuse her then if she come thus into public, to pay those vows. Come and hear what she hath to say.

I am confident that no friend of divine Providence will ever repent his time and pains spent in reading over these sheets, but will judge them worth pursuing again and again.

Here, Reader, you may see an instance of the Sovereignty of God, who doth what he will with his own as well as others; and who may say to him, *What dost thou?*[3] Here you may see an instance of the faith and patience of the Saints, under the most heart-sinking trials; here you may see, the promises are breasts full of consolation, when all the world besides is empty, and gives nothing but sorrow. That God is indeed the supreme Lord of the world, ruling the most unruly, weakening the most cruel and savage, granting his people mercy in the sight of the unmerciful, curbing the lusts of the most filthy, holding the hands of the violent, delivering the prey from the mighty, and gathering together the outcasts of Israel. Once and again you have heard, but here you may see, *that power belongeth unto God*; that our God is the God of Salvation, and to him belong the issues from Death. That our God is in the Heavens, and doth whatever pleases him.

Here you have Sampson riddle exemplified, and that great promise, Romans 8.28. verified, *Out of the Eater comes forth meat, and sweetness out of the strong.*[4] The worst of evils working together for the best good. How evident is it that the Lord hath made this gentlewoman a gainer by all this affliction, that she can say, 'tis good for her, yea better that she hath been, than that she should not have been, thus afflicted.

Oh how doth God shine forth in such things as these!

Reader, if thou gettest no good by such a declaration as this, the fault must needs be thine own. Read therefore; peruse, ponder, and from hence lay up something from the experience of another, against thine own turn comes, that so thou also through patience and consolation of the Scripture mayest have hope.

TER AMICAM[5]

A NARRATIVE OF THE CAPTIVITY AND RESTORATION OF MRS. MARY ROWLANDSON

On the tenth of February 1675 came the Indians with great numbers upon Lancaster. Their first coming was about sunrising; hearing the noise of some guns, we looked out; several houses were burning, and the smoke ascending to Heaven. There were five persons taken in one house; the father, and the mother and a sucking child, they knocked on the head; the other two they took and carried away alive. There were two others, who being out of their garrison upon some occasion were set upon; one was knocked on the head, the other escaped. Another there was who running along was shot and wounded, and fell down; he begged of them his life, promising them money (as they told me), but they would not hearken to him but knocked him in head, and stripped him naked, and split open his bowels. Another seeing many of the Indians about his barn, ventured and went out, but was quickly shot down. There were three others belonging to the same

[1] *publish* I.e., proclaim, announce.

[2] *It is … to pay* See Ecclesiastes 5.5.

[3] *What dost thou?* See Job 9.12.

[4] *Sampson riddle … the strong* Reference to the riddle Samson poses to the Philistines in Judges 14.14, which itself refers back to an incident in which Samson killed a lion and later found a swarm of bees that had nested in its carcass and made honey. His reference to Romans 8.28 is to the moment in which the apostle Paul promises that "And we know that all things work together for good to them that love God, to them who are the called according to his purpose."

[5] *TER AMICAM* Apparently a misprint for "Per Amicam," meaning "For my friend."

garrison who were killed; the Indians getting up upon the roof of the barn, had advantage to shoot down upon them over their fortification. Thus these murderous wretches went on, burning and destroying before them.

At length they came and beset our own house, and quickly it was the dolefullest day that ever mine eyes saw. The house stood upon the edge of a hill; some of the Indians got behind the hill, others into the barn, and others behind anything that could shelter them; from all which places they shot against the house, so that the bullets seemed to fly like hail; and quickly they wounded one man among us, then another, and then a third. About two hours (according to my observation, in that amazing time) they had been about the house before they prevailed to fire it (which they did with flax and hemp, which they brought out of the barn, and there being no defence about the house, only two flankers[1] at two opposite corners, and one of them not finished). They fired it once, and one ventured out and quenched it, but they quickly fired it again, and that took. Now is that dreadful hour come, that I have often heard of (in time of war, as it was the case of others), but now mine eyes see it. Some in our house were fighting for their lives, others wallowing in their blood, the house on fire over our heads, and the bloody heathen ready to knock us on the head, if we stirred out. Now might we hear mothers and children crying out for themselves, and one another, *Lord, what shall we do?* Then I took my children (and one of my sisters, hers) to go forth and leave the house: but as soon as we came to the door and appeared, the Indians shot so thick that the bullets rattled against the house, as if one had taken an handful of stones and threw them, so that we were fain to give back.[2] We had six stout dogs belonging to our garrison, but none of them would stir, though another time, if any Indian had come to the door, they were ready to fly upon him and tear him down. The Lord hereby would make us the more acknowledge his hand, and to see that our help is always in him. But out we must go, the fire increasing, and coming along behind us, roaring, and the Indians gaping before us with their guns, spears and hatchets to devour us. No sooner were we out of the house, but my brother in law (being before wounded, in defending the house, in or near the throat) fell down dead, whereat the Indians scornfully shouted, and hallowed,[3] and were presently upon him, stripping off his clothes, the bullets flying thick, one went through my side, and the same (as would seem) through the bowels and hand of my dear child[4] in my arms. One of my elder sister's children, named William, had then his leg broken, which the Indians perceiving, they knocked him on head. Thus were we butchered by those merciless heathen, standing amazed, with the blood running down to our heels. My eldest sister being yet in the house, and seeing those woeful sights, the infidels hauling mothers one way, and children another, and some wallowing in their blood: and her elder son telling her that her son William was dead, and my self was wounded, she said, *And Lord let me die with them*; which was no sooner said, but she was struck with a bullet, and fell down dead over the threshold. I hope she is reaping the fruit of her good labours, being faithful to the service of God in her place. In her younger years she lay under much trouble upon spiritual accounts, till it pleased God to make that precious Scripture take hold of her heart, 2 Corinthians 12.9, *And he said unto me my Grace is sufficient for thee.* More then twenty years after I have heard her tell how sweet and comfortable that place was to her. But to return: the Indians laid hold of us, pulling me one way, and the children another, and said, *Come go along with us*; I told them they would kill me; they answered, if I were willing to go along with them, they would not hurt me.

Oh the doleful sight that now was to behold at this house! *Come, behold the works of the Lord, what desolations he has made in the Earth.*[5] Of thirty-seven persons who were in this one house, none escaped either present death, or a bitter captivity, save only one, who might say as he, Job 1.15. *And I only am escaped alone to tell the News.* There were twelve killed, some shot, some stabbed with their spears, some knocked down with their hatchets. When we are in prosperity, oh the little that we think of such dreadful sights, and to see our dear friends and relations lie bleeding out their

[1] *flankers* Projecting defense structures.

[2] *fain to give back* Obliged to retreat.

[3] *hallowed* Hallooed; shouted.

[4] *my dear child* Sarah Rowlandson, about six-and-a-half years old.

[5] *Come ... in the Earth* See Psalm 46.8.

heart-blood upon the ground. There was one who was chopped into the head with a hatchet, and stripped naked, and yet was crawling up and down. It is a solemn sight to see so many Christians lying in their blood, some here, and some there, like a company of sheep torn by wolves. All of them stripped naked by a company of hell-hounds, roaring, singing, ranting and insulting, as if they would have torn our very hearts out; yet the Lord by his Almighty power preserved a number of us from death, for there were twenty-four of us taken alive and carried captive.

I had often before this said, that if the Indians should come, I should choose rather to be killed by them than taken alive, but when it came to the trial my mind changed; their glittering weapons so daunted my spirit, that I chose rather to go along with those (as I may say) ravenous beasts, than that moment to end my days; and that I may the better declare what happened to me during that grievous captivity, I shall particularly speak of the several removes[1] we had up and down the wilderness.

The First Remove

Now away we must go with those barbarous creatures, with our bodies wounded and bleeding, and our hearts no less than our bodies. About a mile we went that night, up upon a hill within sight of the town, where they intended to lodge. There was hard by a vacant house (deserted by the English before, for fear of the Indians). I asked them whether I might not lodge in the house that night? to which they answered, *What, will you love English men still?* This was the dolefullest night that ever my eyes saw. Oh, the roaring, and singing and dancing, and yelling of those black creatures in the night, which made the place a lively resemblance of hell. And as miserable was the waste that was there made, of horses, cattle, sheep, swine, calves, lambs, roasting pigs, and fowls (which they had plundered in the town), some roasting, some lying and burning, and some boiling to feed our merciless enemies, who were joyful enough though we were disconsolate. To add to the dolefulness of the former day, and the dismalness of the present night, my thoughts ran upon my losses and sad bereaved condition. All was gone: my husband

gone (at least separated from me, he being in the Bay; and to add to my grief, the Indians told me they would kill him as he came homeward), my children gone, my relations and friends gone, our house and home and all our comforts within door, and without, all was gone except my life, and I knew not but the next moment that might go too. There remained nothing to me but one poor wounded babe, and it seemed at present worse than death that it was in such a pitiful condition, bespeaking compassion, and I had no refreshing for it, nor suitable things to revive it. Little do many think what is the savageness and brutishness of this barbarous enemy! even those that seem to profess more than others among them, when the English have fallen into their hands.

Those seven that were killed at Lancaster the summer before upon a Sabbath day, and the one that was afterward killed upon a weekday, were slain and mangled in a barbarous manner, by one-eyed John, and Marlborough's Praying Indians, which Capt. Mosely brought to Boston, as the Indians told me.[2]

The Second Remove

But now, the next morning, I must turn my back upon the town, and travel with them into the vast and desolate wilderness, I knew not whither. It is not my tongue or pen can express the sorrows of my heart, and bitterness of my spirit, that I had at this departure: but God was with me in a wonderful manner, carrying me along and bearing up my spirit, that it did not quite fail. One of the Indians carried my poor wounded babe upon a horse; it went moaning all along, *I shall die, I shall die.* I went on foot after it, with sorrow that cannot be expressed. At length I took it off the horse, and carried it in my arms till my strength failed, and I fell down with it. Then they set me upon a horse with my wounded child in my lap, and there being no furniture[3]

1 *removes* Changes of place.

2 *Those seven ... Indians told me* On 22 August 1675, a group of Nipmuc and Wampanoag warriors carried out the first significant attack on the town of Lancaster, killing seven colonists. The Indigenous fighters were led by Nipmuc sachem Monoco, known to the English as "One-Eyed John"; many of the English also suspected, probably falsely, the involvement of Nipmuc "Praying Indians"—Indigenous converts to Christianity—from the town of Marlborough.

3 *furniture* I.e., saddle, stirrups, etc.

upon the horse's back, as we were going down a steep hill, we both fell over the horse's head, at which they like inhumane creatures laughed, and rejoiced to see it, though I thought we should there have ended our days, as overcome with so many difficulties. But the Lord renewed my strength still, and carried me along, that I might see more of his power; yea, so much that I could never have thought of, had I not experienced it.

After this it quickly began to snow, and when night came on, they stopped: and now down I must sit in the snow, by a little fire, and a few boughs behind me, with my sick child in my lap; and calling much for water, being now (through the wound) fallen into a violent fever. My own wound also growing so stiff, that I could scarce sit down or rise up; yet so it must be, that I must sit all this cold winter night upon the cold snowy ground, with my sick child in my arms, looking that every hour would be the last of its life; and having no Christian friend near me, either to comfort or help me. Oh, I may see the wonderful power of God, that my Spirit did not utterly sink under my affliction: still the Lord upheld me with his gracious and merciful Spirit, and we were both alive to see the light of the next morning.

THE THIRD REMOVE

The morning being come, they prepared to go on their way: One of the Indians got up upon a horse, and they set me up behind him, with my poor sick babe in my lap. A very wearisome and tedious day I had of it, what with my own wound, and my child's being so exceeding sick, and in a lamentable condition with her wound. It may be easily judged what a poor feeble condition we were in, there being not the least crumb of refreshing that came within either of our mouths, from Wednesday night to Saturday night, except only a little cold water. This day in the afternoon, about an hour by sun, we came to the place where they intended, *viz.*[1] an Indian town called Wenimesset, northward of Quahaug. When we were come, oh the number of pagans (now merciless enemies) that there came about me, that I may say as David, Psalm 27.13, *I had fainted, unless I had believed*, etc. The next day was the

Sabbath: I then remembered how careless I had been of God's holy time: how many Sabbaths I had lost and misspent, and how evilly I had walked in God's sight; which lay so close unto my spirit, that it was easy for me to see how righteous it was with God to cut off the thread of my life, and cast me out of his presence forever. Yet the Lord still showed mercy to me, and upheld me; and as he wounded me with one hand, so he healed me with the other. This day there came to me one Robert Pepper (a man belonging to Roxbury) who was taken in Captain Beers his fight,[2] and had been now a considerable time with the Indians; and up with them almost as far as Albany, to see King Philip, as he told me, and was now very lately come into these parts. Hearing, I say, that I was in this Indian town, he obtained leave to come and see me. He told me, he himself was wounded in the leg at Captain Beers his fight; and was not able some time to go, but as they carried him, and as he took oaken leaves and laid to his wound, and through the blessing of God he was able to travel again. Then I took oaken leaves and laid to my side, and with the blessing of God it cured me also; yet before the cure was wrought, I may say, as it is in Psalm 38.5–6, *My wounds stink and are corrupt, I am troubled, I am bowed down greatly, I go mourning all the day long.* I sat much alone with a poor wounded child in my lap, which moaned night and day, having nothing to revive the body, or cheer the spirits of her, but instead of that, sometimes one Indian would come and tell me one hour, that *Your master will knock your child in the head*, and then a second, and then a third, *Your master will quickly knock your child in the head.*

This was the comfort I had from them, miserable comforters are ye all, as he said.[3] Thus nine days I sat upon my knees, with my babe in my lap, till my flesh was raw again; my child being even ready to depart this sorrowful world, they bade me carry it out to another wigwam (I suppose because they would not be troubled with such spectacles), whither I went with a very heavy heart, and down I sat with the picture of death in my lap. About two hours in the night, my sweet babe, like a lamb, departed this life, on Feb. 18,

[1] *viz.* Abbreviation for the Latin videlicet, meaning "namely" or "that is to say."

[2] *Robert Pepper … his fight* I.e., Robert Pepper, a man from the town of Roxbury, Massachusetts, who was taken captive during a battle with Captain Richard Beers's troops.

[3] *This was … as he said* See Job 16.1–2.

1675, it being about six years and five months old. It was nine days from the first wounding, in this miserable condition, without any refreshing of one nature or other, except a little cold water. I cannot but take notice, how at another time I could not bear to be in the room where any dead person was, but now the case is changed; I must and could lie down by my dead babe, side by side all the night after. I have thought since of the wonderful goodness of God to me, in preserving me in the use of my reason and senses, in that distressed time, that I did not use wicked and violent means to end my own miserable life. In the morning, when they understood that my child was dead, they sent for me home to my master's wigwam (by my master in this writing must be understood Quanopin, who was a Sagamore,[1] and married King Philip's wife's sister;[2] not that he first took me, but I was sold to him by another Narraganset Indian, who took me when first I came out of the garrison). I went to take up my dead child in my arms to carry it with me, but they bid me let it alone: there was no resisting, but go I must and leave it. When I had been at my master's wigwam, I took the first opportunity I could get, to go look after my dead child: when I came I asked them what they had done with it? then they told me it was upon the hill: then they went and showed me where it was, where I saw the ground was newly digged, and there they told me they had buried it. There I left that child in the wilderness, and must commit it, and myself also in this wilderness-condition, to him who is above all. God having taken away this dear child, I went to see my daughter Mary, who was at this same Indian town, at a wigwam not very far off, though we had little liberty or opportunity to see one another; she was about ten years old, and taken from the door at first by a Praying Indian and afterward sold for a gun. When I came in sight, she would fall a-weeping; at which they were provoked, and would not let me come near her, but bade me be gone; which was a heart-cutting word to me. I had one child dead, another in the wilderness, I knew not where, the

third they would not let me come near to: *Me* (as he said) *have ye bereaved of my children, Joseph is not, and Simeon is not, and ye will take Benjamin also, all these things are against me.*[3] I could not sit still in this condition, but kept walking from one place to another. And as I was going along, my heart was even overwhelmed with the thoughts of my condition, and that I should have children, and a nation which I knew not ruled over them. Whereupon I earnestly entreated the Lord, that he would consider my low estate, and show me a token for good, and if it were his blessed will, some sign and hope of some relief. And indeed quickly the Lord answered, in some measure, my poor prayers; for as I was going up and down mourning and lamenting my condition, my son came to me, and asked me how I did; I had not seen him before, since the destruction of the town, and I knew not where he was, till I was informed by himself, that he was amongst a smaller parcel of Indians, whose place was about six miles off. With tears in his eyes, he asked me whether his sister Sarah was dead; and told me he had seen his sister Mary; and prayed me, that I would not be troubled in reference to himself. The occasion of his coming to see me at this time, was this: There was, as I said, about six miles from us, a small plantation[4] of Indians, where it seems he had been during his captivity; and at this time, there were some forces of the Indians gathered out of our company, and some also from them (among whom was my son's master) to go to assault and burn Medfield. In this time of the absence of his master, his dame brought him to see me. I took this to be some gracious answer to my earnest and unfeigned desire. The next day, *viz.* to this, the Indians returned from Medfield, all the company, for those that belonged to the other small company, came through the town that now we were at. But before they came to us, oh! the outrageous roaring and hooping[5] that there was. They began their din about a mile before they came to us. By their noise and hooping they signified how many they had destroyed (which was at that time twenty-three). Those that were with us at home, were gathered together as soon as they heard the hooping, and every time that the other went over their number, these at

[1] *Sagamore* Algonquian political leader; the term is sometimes used interchangeably with Sachem.

[2] *King Philip's wife's sister* The Wampanoag *saunkskaw*, or female sachem, Weetamoo (c. 1635–76); the Narraganset Quinnapin was her fourth and final husband.

[3] *Me … against me* See Genesis 42.36.

[4] *plantation* I.e., settlement.

[5] *hooping* Whooping.

home gave a shout, that the very earth rung again; and thus they continued till those that had been upon the expedition were come up to the Sagamore's wigwam; and then, oh, the hideous insulting and triumphing that there was over some English men's scalps that they had taken (as their manner is) and brought with them. I cannot but take notice of the wonderful mercy of God to me in those afflictions, in sending me a Bible. One of the Indians that came from Medfield fight, had brought some plunder, came to me, and asked me, if I would have a Bible, he had got one in his basket. I was glad of it, and asked him, whether he thought the Indians would let me read? He answered, yes; so I took the Bible, and in that melancholy time, it came into my mind to read first the 28th chapter of Deuteronomy,[1] which I did; and when I had read it, my dark heart wrought on this manner: That there was no mercy for me, that the blessings were gone, and the curses come in their room,[2] and that I had lost my opportunity. But the Lord helped me still to go on reading till I came to Chapter 30, the seven first verses, where I found, *There was mercy promised again, if we would return to him by repentance; and though we were scattered from one end of the Earth to the other, yet the Lord would gather us together, and turn all those curses upon our Enemies.* I do not desire to live to forget this Scripture, and what comfort it was to me.

Now the Indians began to talk of removing from this place, some one way, and some another. There were now, besides myself, nine English captives in this place (all of them children, except one woman). I got an opportunity to go and take my leave of them; they being to go one way, and I another, I asked them whether they were earnest with God for deliverance, they told me, they did as they were able, and it was some comfort to me, that the Lord stirred up children to look to him. The woman, *viz.* Goodwife[3] Joslin, told me she should never see me again, and that she

could find in her heart to run away; I wished her not to run away by any means, for we were near thirty miles from any English town, and she very big with child, and had but one week to reckon,[4] and another child in her arms, two years old, and bad rivers there were to go over, and we were feeble with our poor and coarse entertainment.[5] I had my Bible with me, I pulled it out, and asked her whether she would read; we opened the Bible and lighted on Psalm 27, in which Psalm we especially took notice of that, *ver. ult.*, *Wait on the Lord, Be of good courage, and he shall strengthen thine Heart, wait I say on the Lord.*[6]

THE FOURTH REMOVE

And now I must part with that little company I had. Here I parted from my daughter Mary (whom I never saw again till I saw her in Dorchester, returned from captivity), and from four little cousins and neighbours, some of which I never saw afterward: the Lord only knows the end of them. Amongst them also was that poor woman before mentioned, who came to a sad end, as some of the company told me in my travel: she having much grief upon her spirit, about her miserable condition, being so near her time,[7] she would be often asking the Indians to let her go home; they not being willing to that, and yet vexed with her importunity, gathered a great company together about her, and stripped her naked, and set her in the midst of them; and when they had sung and danced about her (in their hellish manner) as long as they pleased, they knocked her on head, and the child in her arms with her; when they had done that, they made a fire and put them both into it, and told the other children that were with them, that if they attempted to go home, they would serve them in like manner. The children said she did not shed one tear, but prayed all the while. But to return to my own journey, we travelled about half a day or little more, and came to a desolate place in the wilderness, where there were no wigwams or inhabitants

[1] *28th chapter of Deuteronomy* The first 30 chapters of this book consist of sermons delivered by Moses to the Israelites; the first verse of chapter 28 is, "And it shall come to pass, if thou shalt hearken diligently unto the voice of the Lord thy God, to observe and to do all his commandments which I command thee this day, that the Lord thy God will set thee on high above all nations of the earth."

[2] *in their room* I.e., in their place.

[3] *Goodwife* Polite form of address for a married woman of ordinary social status.

[4] *but one week to reckon* I.e., one week remaining in her pregnancy.

[5] *entertainment* Food and other provisions.

[6] *ver. ult.* Latin: final verse; *Wait on … the Lord* See Psalm 27.14.

[7] *being so near her time* I.e., having so recently given birth.

before; we came about the middle of the afternoon to this place; cold and wet, and snowy, and hungry, and weary, and no refreshing, for man, but the cold ground to sit on, and our poor Indian cheer.

Heart-aching thoughts here I had about my poor children, who were scattered up and down among the wild beasts of the forest. My head was light and dizzy (either through hunger or hard lodging, or trouble or all together), my knees feeble, my body raw by sitting double night and day, that I cannot express to man the affliction that lay upon my spirit, but the Lord helped me at that time to express it to himself. I opened my Bible to read, and the Lord brought that precious Scripture to me, Jeremiah 31.16: *Thus saith the Lord, refrain thy voice from weeping, and thine eyes from tears, for thy work shall be rewarded, and they shall come again from the Land of the Enemy.* This was a sweet cordial to me, when I was ready to faint, many and many a time have I sat down, and wept sweetly over this Scripture. At this place we continued about four days.

THE FIFTH REMOVE

The occasion (as I thought) of their moving at this time, was, the English army it being near and following them; for they went, as if they had gone for their lives, for some considerable way, and then they made a stop, and chose some of their stoutest men, and sent them back to hold the English army in play whilst the rest escaped. And then, like Jehu, they marched on furiously,[1] with their old, and with their young: some carried their old decrepit mothers, some carried one, and some another. Four of them carried a great Indian upon a bier; but going through a thick wood with him, they were hindered, and could make no haste; whereupon they took him upon their backs, and carried him, one at a time, till they came to Banquaug River. Upon a Friday, a little after noon, we came to this river. When all the company was come up, and were gathered together, I thought to count the number of them, but they were so many, and being somewhat in motion, it was beyond my skill. In this travel,

because of my wound, I was somewhat favoured in my load; I carried only my knitting work and two quarts of parched meal: Being very faint I asked my mistress to give me one spoonful of the meal, but she would not give me a taste. They quickly fell to cutting dry trees, to make rafts to carry them over the river, and soon my turn came to go over. By the advantage of some brush which they had laid upon the raft to sit upon, I did not wet my foot (which many of themselves at the other end were mid-leg deep), which cannot but be acknowledged as a favour of God to my weakened body, it being a very cold time. I was not before acquainted with such kind of doings or dangers. *When thou passeth through the waters I will be with thee, and through the Rivers they shall not overflow thee,* Isaiah 43.2. A certain number of us got over the river that night, but it was the night after the Sabbath before all the company was got over. On the Saturday they boiled an old horse's leg which they had got, and so we drank of the broth, as soon as they thought it was ready, and when it was almost all gone, they filled it up again.

The first week of my being among them, I hardly ate anything; the second week, I found my stomach grow very faint for want of something; and yet it was very hard to get down their filthy trash; but the third week, though I could think how formerly my stomach would turn against this or that, and I could starve and die before I could eat such things, yet they were sweet and savoury to my taste. I was at this time knitting a pair of white cotton stockings for my mistress, and had not yet wrought[2] upon a Sabbath day. When the Sabbath came they bade me go to work; I told them it was the Sabbath day, and desired them to let me rest, and told them I would do as much more tomorrow; to which they answered me, they would break my face. And here I cannot but take notice of the strange providence of God in preserving the heathen; they were many hundreds, old and young, some sick, and some lame; many had papooses[3] at their backs. The greatest number at

[1] *they marched on furiously* See 2 Kings 9.20: "He came even unto them, and cometh not again: and the driving is like the driving of Jehu the son of Nimshi; for he driveth furiously." Jehu was King of Israel from c. 842–c. 815 BCE.

[2] *wrought* I.e., done work.

[3] *papooses* The word *papoòs* was recorded in Roger Williams's *A Key into the Language of America* in 1643, where it was listed as the Narragansett word for "child." The term became popular with colonists as a general referent for any Native American child, but eventually took on a distinctly negative connotation—though it would have been considered a more-or-less neutral term by Rowlandson and her contemporaries.

this time with us were squaws,[1] and they travelled with all they had, bag and baggage, and yet they got over this river aforesaid; and on Monday they set their wigwams on fire, and away they went. On that very day came the English army after them to this river, and saw the smoke of their wigwams, and yet this river put a stop to them. God did not give them courage or activity to go over after us. We were not ready for so great a mercy as victory and deliverance; if we had been, God would have found out a way for the English to have passed this river, as well as for the Indians with their squaws and children, and all their luggage. *Oh that my People had hearkened to me, and Israel had walked in my ways, I should soon have subdued their Enemies, and turned my hand against their Adversaries.* Psalm 81.13–14.

THE SIXTH REMOVE

On Monday (as I said) they set their wigwams on fire, and went away. It was a cold morning, and before us there was a great brook with ice on it; some waded through it, up to the knees and higher, but others went till they came to a beaver dam, and I amongst them, where through the good providence of God, I did not wet my foot. I went along that day mourning and lamenting, leaving farther my own country, and travelling into the vast and howling wilderness, and I understood something of Lot's wife's temptation, when she looked back.[2] We came that day to a great swamp, by the side of which we took up our lodging that night. When I came to the brow of the hill that looked toward the swamp, I thought we had been come to a great Indian town (though there were none but our own company). The Indians were as thick as the trees; it seemed as if there had been a thousand hatchets going at once. If one looked before one, there was nothing but Indians, and behind one, nothing but Indians, and so on either hand, I myself in the midst, and no Christian soul near me, and yet how hath the Lord preserved me in safety? *Oh the experience that I have had of the goodness of God, to me and mine!*

THE SEVENTH REMOVE

After a restless and hungry night there, we had a wearisome time of it the next day. The swamp by which we lay was, as it were, a deep dungeon, and an exceeding high and steep hill before it. Before I got to the top of the hill, I thought my heart and legs and all would have broken, and failed me. What through faintness and soreness of body, it was a grievous day of travel to me. As we went along, I saw a place where English cattle had been: that was comfort to me, such as it was. Quickly after that we came to an English path, which so took with me, that I thought I could have freely lain down and died. That day, a little after noon, we came to Squaukheag, where the Indians quickly spread themselves over the deserted English fields, gleaning what they could find; some picked up ears of wheat that were crickled[3] down, some found ears of Indian corn; some found groundnuts,[4] and others sheaves of wheat that were frozen together in the shock, and went to threshing of them out. My self got two ears of Indian corn, and whilst I did but turn my back, one of them was stolen from me, which much troubled me. There came an Indian to them at that time, with a basket of horse liver. I asked him to give me a piece. *What*, says he, *can you eat horse liver?* I told him I would try, if he would give a piece, which he did, and I laid it on the coals to roast; but before it was half ready, they got half of it away from me, so that I was fain to take the rest and eat it as it was, with the blood about my mouth, and yet a savoury bit it was to me. *For to the hungry Soul every bitter thing is sweet.*[5] A solemn sight methought it was, to see fields of wheat and Indian

1 *squaws* The earliest recorded use of the word "squaw" in English was in *Mourt's Relation* (1622), where it is used as an adjective roughly analogous to "Native American female." The term's etymology has been widely contested, though it is generally agreed that it was borrowed by colonists from the Massachusett *squa*, and from similar words in other Algonquian languages. While the term's use by English speakers in Rowlandson's era was, like *papoose*, intended to be generally neutral, over time the word developed a severely derogatory connotation and an association with various negative stereotypes of Indigenous women.

2 *Lot's wife's … looked back* See Genesis 19.24; Lot's wife looks back as the family flees the city of Sodom—which is being destroyed by God for its inhabitants' wickedness—and is turned into a pillar of salt.

3 *crickled* Crackled; broken.

4 *groundnuts* Tuberous vegetables that bear some resemblance to potatoes, native to North America and part of the staple diets of many Indigenous people at the time.

5 *For to … is sweet* See Proverbs 27.7.

corn forsaken and spoiled, and the remainders of them to be food for our merciless enemies. That night we had a mess of wheat for our supper.

THE EIGHTH REMOVE

On the morrow morning we must go over the river, i.e. Connecticut, to meet with King Philip. Two canoes full they had carried over; the next turn I myself was to go, but as my foot was upon the canoe to step in, there was a sudden outcry among them, and I must step back; and instead of going over the river, I must go four or five miles up the river farther Northward. Some of the Indians ran one way, and some another. The cause of this route was, as I thought, their espying some English scouts who were thereabout. In this travel up the river, about noon, the company made a stop, and sat down; some to eat, and others to rest them. As I sat amongst them, musing of things past, my son Joseph unexpectedly came to me. We asked of each other's welfare, bemoaning our doleful condition, and the change that had come upon us. We had husbands and father, and children, and sisters, and friends, and relations, and house, and home, and many comforts of this life; but now we may say, as Job, *Naked came I out of my Mother's womb, and naked shall I return: The Lord gave, the Lord hath taken away, Blessed be the Name of the Lord*.[1] I asked him whether he would read; he told me, he earnestly desired it, I gave him my Bible, and he lighted upon that comfortable Scripture, Psalm 118.17–18. *I shall not die but live, and declare the works of the Lord: the Lord hath chastened me sore, yet he hath not given me over to death*. Look here, Mother (says he), did you read this? And here I may take occasion to mention one principal ground of my setting forth these lines: even as the Psalmist says, *To declare the Works of the Lord*, and his wonderful power in carrying us along, preserving us in the wilderness, while under the enemy's hand, and returning of us in safety again. And His goodness in bringing to my hand so many comfortable and suitable Scriptures in my distress. But to return. We travelled on till night; and in the morning, we must go over the river to Philip's crew.

When I was in the canoe, I could not but be amazed at the numerous crew of pagans that were on the bank on the other side. When I came ashore, they gathered all about me, I sitting alone in the midst. I observed they asked one another questions, and laughed, and rejoiced over their gains and victories. Then my heart began to fail: and I fell a-weeping, which was the first time, to my remembrance, that I wept before them. Although I had met with so much affliction, and my heart was many times ready to break, yet could I not shed one tear in their sight, but rather had been all this while in a maze,[2] and like one astonished. But now I may say as, Psalm 137.1: *By the Rivers of Babylon, there we sate down: yea, we wept when we remembered Zion*. There one of them asked me why I wept; I could hardly tell what to say. Yet I answered, they would kill me. No, said he, none will hurt you. Then came one of them and gave me two spoonfuls of meal to comfort me, and another gave me half a pint of peas, which was more worth than many bushels at another time. Then I went to see King Philip. He bade me come in and sit down, and asked me whether I would smoke it (a usual compliment nowadays amongst saints and sinners), but this no way suited me. For though I had formerly used tobacco, yet I had left it ever since I was first taken. It seems to be a bait the Devil lays to make men lose their precious time. I remember with shame how formerly, when I had taken two or three pipes, I was presently ready for another, such a bewitching thing it is; but I thank God, he has now given me power over it. Surely there are many who may be better employed than to lie sucking a stinking tobacco-pipe.

Now the Indians gather their forces to go against Northampton. Overnight one went about yelling and hooting to give notice of the design.[3] Whereupon they fell to boiling of groundnuts and parching of corn (as many as had it) for their provision; and in the morning away they went. During my abode in this place, Philip spoke to me to make a shirt for his boy, which I did, for which he gave me a shilling. I offered the money to my master, but he bade me keep it, and with it I bought a piece of horse flesh. Afterwards he asked me to make a cap for his boy, for which he invited me

[1] *Naked came … the Lord* God allowed Satan to inflict numerous hardships upon the devout Job, as a test of his faithfulness; the line referenced comes from Job 1.21.

[2] *in a maze* I.e., in amazement; in shock.

[3] *design* Plan.

to dinner. I went, and he gave me a pancake, about as big as two fingers; it was made of parched wheat, beaten and fried in bear's grease, but I thought I never tasted pleasanter meat[1] in my life. There was a squaw who spoke to me to make a shirt for her *sannup*,[2] for which she gave me a piece of bear. Another asked me to knit a pair of stockings, for which she gave me a quart of peas. I boiled my peas and bear together, and invited my master and mistress to dinner; but the proud gossip, because I served them both in one dish, would eat nothing, except one bit that he gave her upon the point of his knife. Hearing that my son was come to this place, I went to see him, and found him lying flat upon the ground. I asked him, how he could sleep so? He answered me, that he was not asleep, but at prayer, and lay so that they might not observe what he was doing. I pray God he may remember these things now he is returned in safety. At this place (the sun now getting higher), what with the beams and heat of the sun, and the smoke of the wigwams, I thought I should have been blind, I could scarce discern one wigwam from another. There was here one Mary Thurston of Medfield, who seeing how it was with me, lent me a hat to wear; but as soon as I was gone, the squaw who owned that Mary Thurston came running after me, and got it away again. Here was the squaw that gave me one spoonful of meal. I put it in my pocket to keep it safe. Yet notwithstanding somebody stole it, but put five Indian corns in the room of it, which corns were the greatest provisions I had in my travel for one day.

The Indians returning from Northampton, brought with them some horses, and sheep, and other things which they had taken. I desired them, that they would carry me to Albany, upon one of those horses, and sell me for powder; for so they had sometimes discoursed. I was utterly hopeless of getting home on foot, the way that I came. I could hardly bear to think of the many weary steps I had taken, to come to this place.

[1] *meat* In the seventeenth century, a word that could be used to refer to any meal, regardless of whether or not it included animal meat.

[2] *sannup* Massachusett: husband (or, more generally, any married man).

THE NINTH REMOVE

But instead of going either to Albany or homeward, we must go five miles up the river, and then go over it. Here we abode a while. Here lived a sorry Indian, who spoke to me to make him a shirt; when I had done it, he would pay me nothing. But he living by the riverside, where I often went to fetch water, I would often be putting of him in mind, and calling for my pay; at last he told me, if I would make another shirt, for a papoose not yet born, he would give me a knife, which he did when I had done it. I carried the knife in, and my master asked me to give it him, and I was not a little glad that I had any thing that they would accept of, and be pleased with. When we were at this place, my master's maid came home; she had been gone three weeks into the Narraganset country, to fetch corn, where they had stored up some in the ground. She brought home about a peck and half of corn. This was about the time that their great captain, Naananto, was killed in the Narraganset country. My son being now about a mile from me, I asked liberty to go and see him. They bade me go, and away I went; but quickly lost myself, travelling over hills and through swamps, and could not find the way to him. And I cannot but admire at the wonderful power and goodness of God to me, in that, though I was gone from home, and met with all sorts of Indians, and those I had no knowledge of, and there being no Christian soul near me; yet not one of them offered the least imaginable miscarriage to me. I turned homeward again, and met with my master; he showed me the way to my son. When I came to him I found him not well; and withal he had a boil on his side, which much troubled him. We bemoaned one another a while, as the Lord helped us, and then I returned again. When I was returned, I found myself as unsatisfied as I was before. I went up and down mourning and lamenting: and my spirit was ready to sink, with the thoughts of my poor children; my son was ill, and I could not but think of his mournful looks, and no Christian friend was near him, to do any office of love for him, either for soul or body. And my poor girl, I knew not where she was, nor whether she was sick, or well, or alive, or dead. I repaired under these thoughts to my Bible (my great comfort in that time) and that Scripture came to my

hand, *Cast thy burden upon the Lord, and He shall sustain thee*, Psalm 55.22.

But I was fain to go and look after something to satisfy my hunger, and going among the wigwams, I went into one, and there found a squaw who showed herself very kind to me, and gave me a piece of bear. I put it into my pocket, and came home, but could not find an opportunity to broil it, for fear they would get it from me, and there it lay all that day and night in my stinking pocket. In the morning I went to the same squaw, who had a kettle of groundnuts boiling; I asked her to let me boil my piece of bear in her kettle, which she did, and gave me some groundnuts to eat with it; and I cannot but think how pleasant it was to me. I have sometime seen bear baked very handsomely among the English, and some liked it, but the thoughts that it was bear, made me tremble; but now that was savoury to me that one would think was enough to turn the stomach of a brute creature.

One bitter cold day, I could find no room to sit down before the fire. I went out, and could not tell what to do, but I went in to another wigwam, where they were also sitting round the fire, but the squaw laid a skin for me, and bid me sit down, and gave me some groundnuts, and bade me come again; and told me they would buy me, if they were able, and yet these were strangers to me that I never saw before.

THE TENTH REMOVE

That day a small part of the company removed about three quarters of a mile, intending further the next day. When they came to the place where they intended to lodge, and had pitched their wigwams, being hungry I went again back to the place we were before at, to get something to eat, being encouraged by the squaw's kindness, who bade me come again; when I was there, there came an Indian to look after me, who when he had found me, kicked me all along. I went home and found venison roasting that night, but they would not give me one bit of it. Sometimes I met with favour, and sometimes with nothing but frowns.

THE ELEVENTH REMOVE

The next day in the morning they took their travel, intending a day's journey up the river. I took my load at my back, and quickly we came to wade over the river, and passed over tiresome and wearisome hills. One hill was so steep that I was fain to creep up upon my knees, and to hold by the twigs and bushes to keep myself from falling backward. My head also was so light, that I usually reeled as I went; but I hope all these wearisome steps that I have taken, are but a forewarning to me of the heavenly rest. *I know, O Lord, that thy judgments are right, and that thou in faithfulness hast afflicted me*, Psalm 119.71.[1]

THE TWELFTH REMOVE

It was upon a Sabbath-day morning that they prepared for their travel. This morning I asked my master whether he would sell me to my husband; he answered me *Nux*,[2] which did much rejoice my spirit. My mistress, before we went, was gone to the burial of a papoose, and returning, she found me sitting and reading in my Bible; she snatched it hastily out of my hand, and threw it out of doors. I ran out and catched it up, and put it into my pocket, and never let her see it afterward. Then they packed up their things to be gone, and gave me my load; I complained it was too heavy, whereupon she gave me a slap in the face, and bade me go. I lifted up my heart to God, hoping the Redemption was not far off, and the rather because their insolency grew worse and worse.

But the thoughts of my going homeward (for so we bent our course) much cheered my spirit, and made my burden seem light, and almost nothing at all. But (to my amazement and great perplexity) the scale was soon turned; for when we had gone a little way, on a sudden my mistress gives out, she would go no further, but turn back again, and said I must go back again with her; and she called her *sannup*, and would have had him gone back also, but he would not, but said he would go on, and come to us again in three days. My spirit was, upon this, I confess, very impatient, and

[1] *119.71* The actual citation is Psalm 119.75.

[2] *Nux* Yes.

almost outrageous.[1] I thought I could as well have died as went back; I cannot declare the trouble that I was in about it, but yet back again I must go. As soon as I had an opportunity, I took my Bible to read, and that quieting Scripture came to my hand, Psalm 46.10—*Be still, and know that I am God*—which stilled my spirit for the present. But a sore time of trial, I concluded, I had to go through. My master being gone, who seemed to me the best friend that I had of an Indian, both in cold and hunger, and quickly so it proved. Down I sat, with my heart as full as it could hold, and yet so hungry that I could not sit neither. But going out to see what I could find, and walking among the trees, I found six acorns, and two chestnuts, which were some refreshment to me. Towards night I gathered me some sticks for my own comfort, that I might not lie a-cold; but when we came to lie down they bade me to go out, and lie somewhere else, for they had company (they said) come in more than their own. I told them, I could not tell where to go. They bade me go look; I told them, if I went to another wigwam they would be angry, and send me home again. Then one of the company drew his sword, and told me he would run me through if I did not go presently. Then was I fain to stoop to this rude fellow, and to go out in the night, I knew not whither. Mine eyes have seen that fellow afterwards walking up and down Boston, under the appearance of a Friend-Indian, and several others of the like cut. I went to one wigwam, and they told me they had no room. Then I went to another, and they said the same. At last an old Indian bade me to come to him, and his squaw gave me some groundnuts; she gave me also something to lay under my head, and a good fire we had: and through the good providence of God, I had a comfortable lodging that night. In the morning, another Indian bade me come at night, and he would give me six groundnuts, which I did. We were at this place and time about two miles from Connecticut River. We went in the morning to gather groundnuts, to the river, and went back again that night. I went with a good load at my back (for they when they went, though but a little way, would carry all their trumpery[2] with them). I told them the skin was off my back, but I

had no other comforting answer from them than this, that it would be no matter if my head were off too.

THE THIRTEENTH REMOVE

Instead of going toward the Bay, which was that I desired, I must go with them five or six miles down the river into a mighty thicket of brush, where we abode almost a fortnight. Here one asked me to make a shirt for her papoose, for which she gave me a mess of broth, which was thickened with meal made of the bark of a tree, and to make it the better, she had put into it about a handful of peas, and a few roasted groundnuts. I had not seen my son a pretty while, and here was an Indian of whom I made inquiry after him, and asked him when he saw him. He answered me, that such a time his master roasted him, and that himself did eat a piece of him, as big as his two fingers, and that he was very good meat. But the Lord upheld my spirit under this discouragement, and I considered their horrible addictedness to lying, and that there is not one of them that makes the least conscience of speaking of truth. In this place, on a cold night, as I lay by the fire, I removed a stick that kept the heat from me; a squaw moved it down again, at which I looked up, and she threw a handful of ashes in mine eyes. I thought I should have been quite blinded, and have never seen more, but lying down, the water run out of my eyes, and carried the dirt with it, that by the morning, I recovered my sight again. Yet upon this, and the like occasions, I hope it is not too much to say with Job, *Have pity upon me, have pity upon me, O ye my Friends, for the Hand of the Lord has touched me.*[3] And here I cannot but remember how many times sitting in their wigwams, and musing on things past, I should suddenly leap up and run out, as if I had been at home, forgetting where I was, and what my condition was. But when I was without, and saw nothing but wilderness, and woods, and a company of barbarous heathens, my mind quickly returned to me, which made me think of that spoken concerning Sampson, who said, *I will go out and shake myself as at other times, but he wist not that the Lord was departed from him.*[4] About this time I began to think that all my hopes of restoration

[1] *outrageous* Outraged.

[2] *trumpery* Trifling objects; trash.

[3] *Have pity … touched me* See Job 19.21.

[4] *I will … from him* See Judges 16.20; *wist* Knew.

would come to nothing. I thought of the English army, and hoped for their coming, and being taken by them, but that failed. I hoped to be carried to Albany, as the Indians had discoursed before, but that failed also. I thought of being sold to my husband, as my master spake, but instead of that, my master himself was gone, and I left behind, so that my spirit was now quite ready to sink. I asked them to let me go out and pick up some sticks, that I might get alone, and pour out my heart unto the Lord. Then also I took my Bible to read, but I found no comfort here neither, which many times I was wont to find. So easy a thing it is with God to dry up the streams of Scripture-comfort from us. Yet I can say, that in all my sorrows and afflictions, God did not leave me to have my impatience work towards himself, as if his ways were unrighteous. But I knew that he laid upon me less than I deserved. Afterward, before this doleful time ended with me, I was turning the leaves of my Bible, and the Lord brought to me some Scriptures, which did a little revive me, as that Isaiah 55.8, *For my thoughts are not your thoughts, neither are your ways my ways, saith the Lord.* And also that, Psalm 37.5, *Commit thy way unto the Lord, trust also in him, and he shall bring it to pass.* About this time they came yelping from Hadley, where they had killed three Englishmen, and brought one captive with them, *viz.* Thomas Read. They all gathered about the poor man, asking him many questions. I desired also to go and see him; and when I came, he was crying bitterly, supposing they would quickly kill him. Whereupon I asked one of them, whether they intended to kill him; he answered me, they would not. He being a little cheered with that, I asked him about the welfare of my husband; he told me he saw him such a time in the Bay, and he was well, but very melancholy. By which I certainly understood (though I suspected it before) that whatsoever the Indians told me respecting him was vanity and lies. Some of them told me he was dead, and they had killed him; some said he was married again, and that the governor wished him to marry, and told him he should have his choice, and that all persuaded I was dead. So like were these barbarous creatures to him who was a liar from the beginning.[1]

As I was sitting once in the wigwam here, Philip's maid came in with the child in her arms, and asked me to give her a piece of my apron, to make a flap for it. I told her I would not. Then my mistress bade me give it, but still I said no; the maid told me if I would not give her a piece, she would tear a piece off it. I told her I would tear her coat then. With that my mistress rises up, and takes up a stick big enough to have killed me, and struck at me with it, but I stept out, and she struck the stick into the mat of the wigwam. But while she was pulling of it out, I ran to the maid and gave her all my apron, and so that storm went over.

Hearing that my son was come to this place, I went to see him, and told him his father was well, but very melancholy. He told me he was as much grieved for his father as for himself; I wondered at his speech, for I thought I had enough upon my spirit in reference to myself, to make me mindless of my husband and everyone else, they being safe among their friends. He told me also, that a while before, his master (together with other Indians) were going to the French for powder;[2] but by the way the Mohawks met with them, and killed four of their company, which made the rest turn back again, for which I desire that myself and he may bless the Lord; for it might have been worse with him, had he been sold to the French, than it proved to be in his remaining with the Indians.[3]

I went to see an English youth in this place, one John Gilberd of Springfield. I found him lying without doors,[4] upon the ground. I asked him how he did? He told me he was very sick of a flux,[5] with eating so much blood. They had turned him out of the wigwam, and with him an Indian papoose, almost dead (whose parents had been killed), in a bitter cold day, without fire or clothes: the young man himself had nothing on but his shirt and waistcoat. This sight was enough to melt a heart of flint. There they lay quivering in the cold, the youth round like a dog, the papoose stretched out, with his eyes and nose and mouth full of dirt, and yet alive,

[1] *him who was ... the beginning* I.e., Satan.

[2] *powder* I.e., gunpowder.

[3] *going to the French ... the Indians* Rowlandson expresses common Puritan anti-Catholic prejudice by suggesting that living under the rule of the Mohawk, who had allied themselves with the New England Confederation, would be preferable to capture by the Catholic French.

[4] *without doors* Outdoors.

[5] *flux* Early name for dysentery, a disease characterized by severe diarrhea and bleeding.

and groaning. I advised John to go and get to some fire; he told me he could not stand, but I persuaded him still, lest he should lie there and die, and with much ado I got him to a fire, and went myself home. As soon as I was got home, his master's daughter came after me, to know what I had done with the English man. I told her I had got him to a fire in such a place. Now had I need to pray Paul's Prayer, 2 Thessalonians 3.2, *That we may be delivered from unreasonable and wicked men.* For her satisfaction I went along with her, and brought her to him; but before I got home again, it was noised about, that I was running away and getting the English youth along with me; that as soon as I came in, they began to rant and domineer, asking me where I had been, and what I had been doing? and saying they would knock him on the head. I told them I had been seeing the English youth, and that I would not run away. They told me I lied, and taking up a hatchet, they came to me, and said they would knock me down if I stirred out again, and so confined me to the wigwam. Now may I say with David, 2 Samuel 24.14, *I am in a great strait.* If I keep in, I must die with hunger, and if I go out, I must be knocked in head. This distressed condition held that day, and half the next; and then the Lord remembered me, whose mercies are great. Then came an Indian to me with a pair of stockings that were too big for him, and he would have me ravel them out, and knit them fit for him. I showed myself willing, and bid him ask my mistress if I might go along with him a little way; she said yes, I might, but I was not a little refreshed with that news, that I had my liberty again. Then I went along with him, and he gave me some roasted groundnuts, which did again revive my feeble stomach.

Being got out of her sight, I had time and liberty again to look into my Bible, which was my guide by day, and my pillow by night. Now that comfortable Scripture presented itself to me, Isaiah 54.7: *For a small moment have I forsaken thee, but with great mercies will I gather thee.* Thus the Lord carried me along from one time to another, and made good to me this precious promise, and many others. Then my son came to see me, and I asked his master to let him stay a while with me, that I might comb his head, and look over him, for he was almost overcome with lice. He told me, when I had done, that he was very hungry, but I had nothing

to relieve him; but bid him go into the wigwams as he went along, and see if he could get anything among them. Which he did, and it seems tarried a little too long, for his master was angry with him, and beat him, and then sold him. Then he came running to tell me he had a new master, and that he had given him some groundnuts already. Then I went along with him to his new master, who told me he loved him, and he should not want. So his master carried him away, and I never saw him afterward, till I saw him at Pascataqua in Portsmouth.

That night they bade me go out of the wigwams again; my mistress's papoose was sick, and it died that night, and there was one benefit in it, that there was more room. I went to a wigwam, and they bade me come in, and gave me a skin to lie upon, and a mess of venison and groundnuts, which was a choice dish among them. On the morrow they buried the papoose, and afterward, both morning and evening, there came a company to mourn and howl with her: though I confess, I could not much condole with them. Many sorrowful days I had in this place, often getting alone. *Like a Crane or a Swallow, so did I chatter: I did mourn as a Dove, mine eyes fail with looking upward. Oh, Lord I am oppressed, undertake for me,* Isaiah 38.14. I could tell the Lord as Hezekiah, verse 3. *Remember now O Lord, I beseech thee, how I have walked before thee in truth.* Now had I time to examine all my ways: my conscience did not accuse me of unrighteousness toward one or other, yet I saw how in my walk with God, I had been a careless creature. As David said, *Against thee, thee only have I sinned;*[1] and I might say with the poor publican, *God be merciful unto me a sinner.*[2] On the Sabbath days, I could look upon the sun and think how people were going to the house of God, to have their souls refreshed; and then home, and their bodies also: but I was destitute of both; and might say as the poor prodigal, *He would fain have filled his belly with the husks that the Swine did eat, and no man gave unto him,* Luke 15.16. For I must say with him, *Father I have sinned against Heaven, and in thy sight,* verse 21. I remembered how on the night before and after the Sabbath, when my family was about me, and relations and neighbours with us, we could pray and sing, and then refresh our

[1] *As David … sinned* See Psalm 51.4.

[2] *poor publican … a sinner* See Luke 18.13.

bodies with the good creatures of God; and then have a comfortable bed to lie down on; but instead of all this, I had only a little swill for the body, and then like a swine, must lie down on the ground. I cannot express to man the sorrow that lay upon my spirit, the Lord knows it. Yet that comfortable Scripture would often come to my mind, *For a small moment have I forsaken thee, but with great mercies will I gather thee.*[1]

THE FOURTEENTH REMOVE

Now must we pack up and be gone from this Thicket, bending our course toward the Bay-towns I haveing nothing to eat by the way this day, but a few crumbs of Cake, that an Indian gave my girls the same day we were taken. She gave it me, and I put it in my pocket: there it lay, till it was so mouldy (for want of good baking) that one could not tell what it was made of; it fell all to crumbs, & grew so dry and hard, that it was like little flints; & this refreshed me many times, when I was ready to faint. It was in my thoughts when I put it into my mouth, that if ever I returned, I would tell the World what a blessing the Lord gave to such mean food. As we went along, they killed a Deer, with a young one in her. they gave me a piece of the Fawn, and it was so young and tender, that one might eat the bones as well as the flesh, and yet I thought it very good. When night came on we sate down; it rained, but they quickly got up a Bark Wigwam, where I lay dry that night. I looked out in the morning, and many of them had line[2] in the rain all night, I saw by their Reaking. Thus the Lord dealt mercifully with me many times, and I fared better than many of them. In the morning they took the blood of the Deer and put it into the Paunch, and so boyled it; I could eat nothing of that, though they ate it sweetly. And yet they were so nice[3] in other things, that when I had fetcht water, and had put the Dish I dipt the water with, into the Kettle of water which I brought, they would say, they would knock me down; for they said, it was a sluttish trick.[4]

THE FIFTEENTH REMOVE

We went on our travel. I having got one handful of groundnuts for my support that day they gave me my load, and I went on cheerfully (with the thoughts of going homeward), having my burden more on my back than my spirit. We came to Baquang River again that day, near which we abode a few days. Sometimes one of them would give me a pipe, another a little tobacco, another a little salt, which I would change for a little victuals.[5] I cannot but think what a wolfish appetite persons have in a starving condition: for many times when they gave me that which was hot, I was so greedy, that I should burn my mouth, that it would trouble me hours after, and yet I should quickly do the same again. And after I was thoroughly hungry, I was never again satisfied. For though sometimes it fell out,[6] that I got enough, and did eat till I could eat no more, yet I was as unsatisfied as I was when I began. And now could I see that Scripture verified (there being many Scriptures which we do not take notice of, or understand till we are afflicted) Micah 6.14. *Thou shalt eat and not be satisfied.* Now might I see more than ever before, the miseries that sin hath brought upon us. Many times I should be ready to run out against the heathen, but the Scripture would quiet me again, Amos 3.6. *Shall there be evils in the City, and the Lord hath not done it?* The Lord help me to make a right improvement of His Word, and that I might learn that great lesson, Micah 6.8–9, *He hath shewed thee (Oh Man) what is good, and what doth the Lord require of thee, but to do justly, and love mercy, and walk humbly with thy God? Hear ye the rod, and who hath appointed it.*

THE SIXTEENTH REMOVE

We began this remove with wading over Baquag River; the water was up to the knees, and the stream very swift, and so cold that I thought it would have cut me in sunder. I was so weak and feeble that I reeled as I went along, and thought there I must end my days at last, after my bearing and getting through so many difficulties. The Indians stood laughing to see me staggering along, but in my distress the Lord gave me experience

[1] *For a ... gather thee* See Isaiah 54.7.

[2] *line* Lain.

[3] *nice* Scrupulous; having refined tastes or habits.

[4] *sluttish* Unclean or disgusting; *trick* Thoughtless or stupid action.

[5] *victuals* Food.

[6] *it fell out* It so happened.

original spelling

of the truth, and goodness of that promise, Isaiah 43.2, *When thou passest thorough the Waters, I will be with thee, and through the Rivers, they shall not overflow thee.* Then I sat down to put on my stockings and shoes, with the tears running down mine eyes, and many sorrowful thoughts in my heart, but I got up to go along with them. Quickly there came up to us an Indian, who informed them that I must go to Wachusett to my master, for there was a letter come from the council to the Sagamores about redeeming the captives, and that there would be another in fourteen days, and that I must be there ready. My heart was so heavy before that I could scarce speak or go in the path; and yet now so light that I could run. My strength seemed to come again, and recruit my feeble knees, and aching heart; yet it pleased them to go but one mile that night, and there we stayed two days. In that time came a company of Indians to us, near thirty, all on horseback. My heart skipped within me, thinking they had been Englishmen at the first sight of them, for they were dressed in English apparel, with hats, white neckcloths, and sashes about their waists, and ribbons upon their shoulders; but when they came near, there was a vast difference between the lovely faces of Christians, and the foul looks of those heathens, which much damped my spirit again.

THE SEVENTEENTH REMOVE

A comfortable remove it was to me, because of my hopes. They gave me a pack, and along we went cheerfully, but quickly my will proved more than my strength; having little or no refreshing, my strength failed me, and my spirit were almost quite gone. Now may I say with David, Psalm 119.22–24, *I am poor and needy, and my heart is wounded within me. I am gone like the shadow when it declineth: I am tossed up and down like the locusts; my knees are weak through fasting, and my flesh faileth of fatness.*[1] At night we came to an Indian town, and the Indians sat down by a wigwam discoursing, but I was almost spent, and could scarce speak. I laid down my load, and went into the wigwam, and there sat an Indian boiling of horses' feet (they being wont to eat the flesh first, and when the feet were old and dried, and they had nothing else, they would

cut off the feet and use them). I asked him to give me a little of his broth, or water they were boiling in; he took a dish, and gave me one spoonful of samp,[2] and bid me take as much of the broth as I would. Then I put some of the hot water to the samp, and drank it up, and my spirit came again. He gave me also a piece of the ruff or ridding[3] of the small guts, and I broiled it on the coals; and now may I say with Jonathan, *See, I pray you, how mine eyes have been enlightened, because I tasted a little of this honey,* 1 Samuel 14.29. Now is my Spirit revived again, though means be never so inconsiderable, yet if the Lord bestow his blessing upon them, they shall refresh both soul and body.

THE EIGHTEENTH REMOVE

We took up our packs and along we went, but a wearisome day I had of it. As we went along I saw an Englishman stripped naked, and lying dead upon the ground, but knew not who it was. Then we came to another Indian town, where we stayed all night. In this town there were four English children, captives; and one of them my own sister's. I went to see how she did, and she was well, considering her captive condition. I would have tarried that night with her, but they that owned her would not suffer it. Then I went into another wigwam, where they were boiling corn and beans, which was a lovely sight to see, but I could not get a taste thereof. Then I went to another wigwam, where there were two of the English children; the squaw was boiling horses' feet, then she cut me off a little piece, and gave one of the English children a piece also. Being very hungry I had quickly eat[4] up mine, but the child could not bite it, it was so tough and sinewy, but lay sucking, gnawing, chewing and slabbering of it in the mouth and hand; then I took it of the child, and eat it myself, and savoury it was to my taste. Then I may say as Job, chapter 6.7, *The things that my soul refused to touch, are as my sorrowful meat.* Thus the Lord made that pleasant refreshing, which another time would have been an abomination. Then I went home to my mistress's wigwam, and they told me I disgraced my master with begging, and if I did so any more, they

[1] *I am ... of fatness* This is actually from Psalm 109.

[2] *samp* Cornmeal porridge.

[3] *ruff or ridding* Parts that were being cast aside.

[4] *eat* Ate.

would knock me in head. I told them, they had as good knock me in head as starve me to death.

THE NINETEENTH REMOVE

They said, when we went out, that we must travel to Wachusett this day. But a bitter weary day I had of it, travelling now three days together, without resting any day between. At last, after many weary steps, I saw Wachusett hills, but many miles off. Then we came to a great swamp, through which we travelled up to the knees, in mud and water, which was heavy going to one tired before. Being almost spent, I thought I should have sunk down at last, and never got out; but I may say, as in Psalm 94.18, *When my foot slipped, thy mercy, O Lord held me up*. Going along, having indeed my life, but little spirit, Philip, who was in the company, came up and took me by the hand, and said, *Two weeks more and you shall be Mistress again*. I asked him, if he spoke true? he answered, *Yes, and quickly you shall come to your master again*; who had been gone from us three weeks. After many weary steps we came to Wachusett, where he was, and glad I was to see him. He asked me, when I washed me? I told him not this month, then he fetched me some water himself, and bid me wash, and gave me the glass[1] to see how I looked, and bid his squaw give me something to eat: so she gave me a mess of beans and meat, and a little groundnut cake. I was wonderfully revived with this favour showed me, Psalm 106.46, *He made them also to be pitied, of all those that carried them Captives*.

My master had three squaws, living sometimes with one, and sometimes with another one, this old squaw, at whose wigwam I was, and with whom my master had been those three weeks. Another was Wettimore,[2] with whom I had lived and served all this while. A severe and proud dame she was, bestowing every day in dressing herself neat as much time as any of the gentry of the land: powdering her hair, and painting her face, going with necklaces, with jewels in her ears, and bracelets upon her hands. When she had dressed herself, her work was to make girdles of wampum and beads. The third squaw was a younger one, by whom he had two papooses. By that time I was refreshed by the old squaw, with whom my master was, Wettimore's maid came to call me home, at which I fell a-weeping. Then the old squaw told me, to encourage me, that if I wanted victuals, I should come to her, and that I should lie there in her wigwam. Then I went with the maid, and quickly came again and lodged there. The squaw laid a mat under me, and a good rug over me; the first time I had any such kindness showed me. I understood that Wettimore thought that if she should let me go and serve with the old squaw, she would be in danger to lose not only my service, but the redemption-pay[3] also. And I was not a little glad to hear this, being by it raised in my hopes, that in God's due time there would be an end of this sorrowful hour. Then came an Indian, and asked me to knit him three pair of stockings, for which I had a hat, and a silk handkerchief. Then another asked me to make her a shift, for which she gave me an apron.

Then came Tom and Peter, with the second letter from the council, about the captives. Though they were Indians, I got them by the hand, and burst out into tears. My heart was so full that I could not speak to them; but recovering myself, I asked them how my husband did, and all my friends and acquaintance? They said, *They are all very well, but melancholy*. They brought me two biscuits, and a pound of tobacco. The tobacco I quickly gave away; when it was all gone, one asked me to give him a pipe of tobacco, I told him it was all gone; then began he to rant and threaten. I told him when my husband came I would give him some. *Hang him rogue* (says he), *I will knock out his brains, if he comes here*. And then again, in the same breath they would say, that if there should come an hundred without guns, they would do them no hurt. So unstable and like madmen they were. So that fearing the worst, I durst not send to my husband, though there were some thoughts of his coming to redeem and fetch me, not knowing what might follow; for there was little more trust to them then to the master they served. When the letter was come, the Saggamores met to consult about the captives, and called me to them to enquire how much my husband would give to redeem me, when I came I sat down among them, as I was wont to do, as their manner is. Then they bade me stand up, and said, they were the General Court.

[1] *glass* Mirror.

[2] *Wettimore* I.e., Weetamoo.

[3] *redemption-pay* I.e., the ransom price.

They bid me speak what I thought he would give. Now knowing that all we had was destroyed by the Indians, I was in a great strait: I thought if I should speak of but a little, it would be slighted, and hinder the matter; if of a great sum, I knew not where it would be procured. Yet at a venture, I said twenty pounds, yet desired them to take less; but they would not hear of that, but send that message to Boston, that for twenty pounds I should be redeemed. It was a Praying Indian that wrote their letter for them. There was another Praying Indian, who told me, that he had a brother, that would not eat horse, his conscience was so tender and scrupulous (though as large as hell, for the destruction of poor Christians). Then he said, he read that Scripture to him, 2 Kings, 6.25: *There was a famine in Samaria, and behold they besieged it, until an Ass's head was sold for fourscore pieces of silver, and the fourth part of a Kab[1] of Doves' dung, for five pieces of silver.* He expounded this place to his brother, and showed him that it was lawful to eat that in a famine which is not at another time. And now, says he, he will eat horse with any Indian of them all. There was another Praying Indian who, when he had done all the mischief that he could, betrayed his own father into the English hands, thereby to purchase his own life. Another Praying Indian was at Sudbury fight,[2] though, as he deserved, he was afterward hanged for it. There was another Praying Indian so wicked and cruel as to wear a string about his neck, strung with Christians' fingers. Another Praying Indian, when they went to Sudbury fight, went with them, and his squaw also with him, with her papoose at her back. Before they went to that fight, they got a company together to Powwow; the manner was as followeth. There was one that kneeled upon a deer skin, with the company round him in a ring who kneeled, and striking upon the ground with their hands, and with sticks, and muttering or humming with their mouths. Besides him who kneeled in the ring, there also stood one with a gun in his hand. Then he on the deerskin made a speech, and all manifested assent to it: and so they did many times together. Then they bade him with the gun go out of the ring, which he did, but when he was out, they called him in again; but he seemed to make a stand, then they

called the more earnestly, till he returned again. Then they all sang. Then they gave him two guns, in either hand one. And so he on the deerskin began again; and at the end of every sentence in his speaking, they all assented, humming or muttering with their mouths, and striking upon the ground with their hands. Then they bade him with the two guns go out of the ring again; which he did, a little way. Then they called him in again, but he made a stand; so they called him with greater earnestness, but he stood reeling and wavering as if he knew not whether he should stand or fall, or which way to go. Then they called him with exceeding great vehemency, all of them, one and another: after a little while he turned in, staggering as he went, with his arms stretched out, in either hand a gun. As soon as he came in, they all sang and rejoiced exceedingly a while. And then he upon the deer skin made another speech, unto which they all assented in a rejoicing manner: and so they ended their business, and forthwith went to Sudbury fight. To my thinking they went without any scruple, but that they should prosper, and gain the victory. And they went out not so rejoicing, but they came home with as great a victory. For they said they had killed two captains and almost an hundred men. One Englishman they brought along with them: and he said, it was too true, for they had made sad work at Sudbury, as indeed it proved. Yet they came home without that rejoicing and triumphing over their victory, which they were wont to show at other times, but rather like dogs (as they say) which have lost their ears. Yet I could not perceive that it was for their own loss of men. They said they had not lost above five or six, and I missed none, except in one wigwam. When they went, they acted as if the Devil had told them that they should gain the victory: and now they acted as if the Devil had told them they should have a fall. Whether it were so or no, I cannot tell, but so it proved, for quickly they began to fall, and so held on that summer, till they came to utter ruin. They came home on a Sabbath day, and the Powwow[3] that kneeled upon the deer skin came home (I may say, without abuse) as black as the Devil. When my master came home, he came to me and bid me make a shirt for his papoose, of a Holland-laced pillowbeer.[4] About that time there

[1] *Kab* Measurement of volume.

[2] *Sudbury fight* Battle that took place in the town of Sudbury, Massachusetts on 21 April 1676.

[3] *Powwow* Shaman.

[4] *Holland-laced pillowbeer* Pillowcase made from Dutch linen.

came an Indian to me and bid me come to his wigwam at night, and he would give me some pork and ground-nuts. Which I did, and as I was eating, another Indian said to me, he seems to be your good friend, but he killed two Englishmen at Sudbury, and there lie their clothes behind you. I looked behind me, and there I saw bloody clothes, with bullet-holes in them; yet the Lord suffered not this wretch to do me any hurt. Yea, instead of that, he many times refreshed me: five or six times did he and his squaw refresh my feeble carcass. If I went to their wigwam at any time, they would always give me something, and yet they were strangers that I never saw before. Another squaw gave me a piece of fresh pork, and a little salt with it, and lent me her pan to fry it in; and I cannot but remember what a sweet, pleasant and delightful relish that bit had to me, to this day. So little do we prize common mercies when we have them to the full.

THE TWENTIETH REMOVE

It was their usual manner to remove, when they had done any mischief, lest they should be found out: and so they did at this time. We went about three or four miles, and there they built a great wigwam, big enough to hold an hundred Indians, which they did in prepa-ration to a great day of dancing. They would say now amongst themselves, that the Governor would be so angry for his loss as Sudbury, that he would send no more about the captives, which made me grieve and tremble. My sister being not far from the place where we now were, and hearing that I was here, desired her master to let her come and see me; and he was will-ing to it, and would go with her. But she being ready before him, told him she would go before, and was come within a mile or two of the place; then he over-took her, and began to rant as if he had been mad, and made her go back again in the rain, so that I never saw her till I saw her in Charlestown. But the Lord requited many of their ill doings, for this Indian, her master, was hanged afterward at Boston. The Indians now began to come from all quarters, against their merry dancing day. Among some of them came one Goodwife Kettle. I told her my heart was so heavy that it was ready to break. So is mine too, said she, but yet said, I hope we shall hear some good news shortly. I could hear how earnestly my sister desired to see me, and I as earnestly desired to see her: and yet neither of us could get an opportunity. My daughter was also now about a mile off, and I had not seen her in nine or ten weeks, as I had not seen my sister since our first taking. I earnestly desired them to let me go and see them: yea, I intreated, begged, and persuaded them, but to let me see my daughter; and yet so hard hearted were they, that they would not suffer it. They made use of their tyrannical power whilst they had it: but through the Lord's wonderful mercy, their time was now but short.

On a Sabbath day, the sun being about an hour high in the afternoon, came Mr. John Hoar[1] (the Council permitting him, and his own forward spirit inclining him) together with the two fore-mentioned Indians, Tom and Peter, with their third letter from the Council. When they came near, I was abroad. Though I saw them not, they presently called me in, and bade me sit down and not stir. Then they catched up their guns, and away they ran, as if an enemy had been at hand, and the guns went off apace. I manifested some great trouble,[2] and they asked me what was the matter? I told them, I thought they had killed the Englishman (for they had in the meantime informed me that an Englishman was come). They said, *No*; they shot over his horse, and under, and before[3] his horse; and they pushed him this way and that way, at their pleasure, showing what they could do. Then they let them come to their wigwams. I begged of them to let me see the Englishman, but they would not. But there was I fain to sit their pleasure. When they had talked their fill with him, they suffered me to go to him. We asked each other of our welfare, and how my husband did, and all my friends? He told me they were all well, and would be glad to see me. Amongst other things which my husband sent me, there came a pound of tobacco, which I sold for nine shillings in money: for many of the Indians, for want of tobacco, smoked hemlock and ground ivy. It was a great mistake in any who thought I sent for tobacco: for through the favour of God, that

[1] *Mr. John Hoar* Prominent Massachusetts militia leader and lawyer.

[2] *manifested some great trouble* I.e., had the appearance of being in great distress.

[3] *before* In front of.

desire was overcome. I now asked them, whether I should go home with Mr. Hoar? They answered *No*, one and another of them: and it being night, we lay down with that answer; in the morning, Mr. Hoar invited the Sagamores to dinner; but when we went to get it ready, we found that they had stolen the greatest part of the provision Mr. Hoar had brought, out of his bags, in the night: And we may see the wonderful power of God, in that one passage,[1] in that when there was such a great number of the Indians together, and so greedy of a little good food, and no English there, but Mr. Hoar and myself, that there they did not knock us in the head, and take what we had, there being not only some provision, but also trading-cloth,[2] a part of the twenty pounds agreed upon. But instead of doing us any mischief, they seemed to be ashamed of the fact, and said, it were some *matchit*[3] Indian that did it. Oh, that we could believe that there is no thing too hard for God! God showed his power over the heathen in this, as he did over the hungry lions when Daniel was cast into the den.[4] Mr. Hoar called them betime to dinner, but they ate very little, they being so busy in dressing themselves, and getting ready for their dance, which was carried on by eight of them, four men and four squaws. My master and mistress being two. He was dressed in his Holland shirt, with great laces sewed at the tail of it, and he had his silver buttons, his white stockings, his garters were hung round with shillings, and he had girdles of wampum upon his head and shoulders. She had a kersey[5] coat, and [was] covered with girdles of wampum from the loins upward; her arms from her elbows to her hands were covered with bracelets, there were handfuls of necklaces about her neck, and several sorts of jewels in her ears. She had fine red stockings, and white shoes, her hair powdered and face painted red, that was always before black. And all the dancers were after the same manner. There were two other singing and knocking

on a kettle for their music. They kept hopping up and down one after another, with a kettle of water in the midst, standing warm upon some embers, to drink of when they were dry. They held on till it was almost night, throwing out wampum to the standers by. At night I asked them again, if I should go home? They all as one said No, except[6] my husband would come for me. When we were lain down, my master went out of the wigwam, and by and by sent in an Indian called James the Printer,[7] who told Mr. Hoar that my master would let me go home tomorrow, if he would let him have one pint of liquors. Then Mr. Hoar called his own Indians, Tom and Peter, and bid them go and see whether he would promise it before them three: and if he would, he should have it; which he did, and he had it. Then Philip smelling the business called me to him, and asked me what I would give him, to tell me some good news, and speak a good word for me. I told him, I could not tell what to give him, I would anything I had, and asked him what he would have? He said, two coats and twenty shillings in money, and half a bushel of feed corn, and some tobacco. I thanked him for his love: but I knew the good news as well as the crafty fox. My master, after he had had his drink, quickly came ranting into the wigwam again, and called for Mr. Hoar, drinking to him, and saying, *He was a good man*; and then again he would say, *Hang him rogue*. Being almost drunk, he would drink to him, and yet presently say he should be hanged. Then he called for me; I trembled to hear him, yet I was fain to go to him, and he drank to me, showing no incivility. He was the first Indian I saw drunk all the while that I was amongst them. At last his squaw ran out, and he after her, round the wigwam, with his money jingling at his knees, but she escaped him. But having an old squaw, he ran to her; and so through the Lord's mercy, we were no more troubled that night. Yet I had not a comfortable night's rest, for I think I can say, I did not sleep

1 *passage* Event.

2 *trading-cloth* Pieces of cloth used as a form of currency.

3 *matchit* From *machétu* (recorded in Williams's *Key*, probably Narragansett): poor.

4 *as he … the den* See Daniel 6, where God sends an angel to restrain the lions in whose den the prophet Daniel has been imprisoned.

5 *kersey* Rough woven fabric made from wool.

6 *except* Unless.

7 *James the Printer* James Printer (1640–1709), born Wowaus, was a literate Nipmuc Christian who had become well known among Massachusetts colonials for his printing of the first translation of the Bible into the Massachusett language in 1663. He appears to have come to sympathize with Metacom's cause over the course of the war, and he subsequently worked as an interpreter and scribe for Metacom, for which many of the English colonists branded him as a traitor.

for three nights together. The night before the letter came from the council, I could not rest. I was so full of fears and troubles, God many times leaving us most in the dark, when deliverance is nearest: yea, at this time I could not rest night nor day. The next night I was overjoyed, Mr. Hoar being come, and that with such good tidings. The third night I was even swallowed up with the thoughts of things, *viz.* that ever I should go home again; and that I must go, leaving my children behind me in the wilderness; so that sleep was now almost departed from mine eyes.

On Tuesday morning they called their General Court (as they call it) to consult and determine whether I should go home or no. And they all as one man did seemingly consent to it, that I should go home, except Philip, who would not come among them.

But before I go any further, I would take leave to mention a few remarkable passages of providence, which I took special notice of in my afflicted time.

1. Of the fair opportunity, lost in the long march, a little after the fort fight, when our English army was so numerous, and in pursuit of the enemy, and so near as to take several and destroy them, and the enemy in such distress for food, that our men might track them by their rooting in the earth for groundnuts whilst they were flying for their lives. I say, that then our army should want provision, and be forced to leave their pursuit and return homeward; and the very next week, the enemy came upon our town, like bears bereft of their whelps, or so many ravenous wolves, rending us and our lambs to death. But what shall I say? God seemed to leave his people to themselves, and order all things for his own holy ends. *Shall there be evil in the City and the Lord hath not done it?*[1] *They are not grieved for the affliction of Joseph, therefore shall they go Captive, with the first that go Captive.*[2] It is the Lord's doing, and it should be marvelous in our eyes.

2. I cannot but remember how the Indians derided the slowness and dullness of the English army, in its setting out. For after the desolations at Lancaster and Medfield, as I went along with them, they asked me when I thought the English army would come after them? I told them I could not tell. It may be they will come in May, said they. Thus did they scoff at us, as if the English would be a quarter of a year getting ready.

3. Which also I have hinted before, when the English army with new supplies were sent forth to pursue after the enemy, and they understanding it, fled before them till they came to Baquaug River, where they forthwith went over safely; that that river should be impassable to the English. I can but admire to see the wonderful providence of God in preserving the heathen for farther affliction to our poor country. They could go in great numbers over, but the English must stop: God had an over-ruling hand in all those things.

4. It was thought if their corn were cut down, they would starve and die with hunger; and all their corn that could be found was destroyed, and they driven from that little they had in store, into the woods in the midst of winter; and yet how to admiration did the Lord preserve them for his holy ends, and the destruction of many still amongst the English! Strangely did the Lord provide for them, that I did not see (all the time I was among them) one man, woman, or child die with hunger.

Though many times they would eat that, that a hog or a dog would hardly touch, yet by that God strengthened them to be a scourge to his people.

The chief and commonest food was groundnuts. They eat also nuts and acorns, harty choaks,[3] lily roots, ground-beans, and several other weeds and roots, that I know not.

They would pick up old bones and cut them to pieces at the joints, and if they were full of worms and maggots, they would scald them over the fire to make the vermin come out, and then boil them, and drink up the liquor, and then beat the great ends of them in a mortar, and so eat them. They would eat horses' guts and ears, and all sorts of wild birds which they could catch; also bear, venison, beaver, tortoise, frogs, squirrels, dogs, skunks, rattlesnakes—yea, the very bark of trees—besides all sorts of creatures, and provision which they plundered from the English. I can but stand in admiration to see the wonderful power of God, in providing for such a vast number of our enemies in the wilderness, where there was nothing to

[1] *Shall ... done it* See Amos 3.6.

[2] *They are ... Captive* See Amos 6.6–7.

[3] *harty choaks* Artichokes; presumably referring to what is also known today as the Jerusalem artichoke or sunchoke, a wild-growing tuber.

be seen, but from hand to mouth. Many times in a morning, the generality of them would eat up all they had, and yet have some further supply against they wanted. It is said, Psalm 81.13–14. *Oh, that my People had hearkened to me, and Israel had walked in my ways, I should soon have subdued their Enemies, and turned my hand against their Adversaries.* But now our perverse and evil carriages in the sight of the Lord, have so offended him, that instead of turning his hand against them, the Lord feeds and nourishes them up to be a scourge to the whole land.

5. Another thing that I would observe is the strange providence of God in turning things about when the Indians was at the highest, and the English at the lowest. I was with the enemy eleven weeks and five days, and not one week passed without the fury of the enemy, and some desolation by fire and sword upon one place or other. They mourned (with their black faces) for their own losses, yet triumphed and rejoyced in their inhumane, and many times devilish cruelty to the English. They would boast much of their victories, saying that in two hours time they had destroyed such a captain and his company at such a place; and such a captain and his company in such a place; and such a captain and his company in such a place; and boast how many towns they had destroyed, and then scoff and say, *They had done them a good turn, to send them to Heaven so soon.* Again, they would say, *This summer that they would knock all the rogues in the head, or drive them into the sea, or make them fly the country*; thinking surely, Agag-like, *The bitterness of Death is past.*[1] Now the heathen begins to think all is their own, and the poor Christians' hopes to fail (as to man) and now their eyes are more to God, and their hearts sigh heaven-ward, and to say in good earnest, *Help, Lord, or we perish.* When the Lord had brought his people to this, that they saw no help in anything but himself, then he takes the quarrel into his own hand; and though they had made a pit, in their own imaginations, as deep as hell for the Christians that summer, yet the Lord hurled themselves into it. And the Lord had not so many ways before to preserve them, but now he hath as many to destroy them.

But to return again to my going home, where we may see a remarkable change of providence. At first they were all against it, except my husband would come for me; but afterwards they assented to it, and seemed much to rejoice in it. Some asked me to send them some bread, others some tobacco, others shaking me by the hand, offering me a hood and scarf to ride in; not one moving hand or tongue against it. Thus hath the Lord answered my poor desire, and the many earnest requests of others put up unto God for me. In my travels an Indian came to me, and told me, if I were willing, he and his squaw would run away, and go home along with me. I told him no, I was not willing to run away, but desired to wait God's time, that I might go home quietly, and without fear. And now God hath granted me my desire. O the wonderful power of God that I have seen, and the experience that I have had. I have been in the midst of those roaring lions and savage bears that feared neither God, nor man, nor the Devil; by night and day, alone and in company; sleeping all sorts together; and yet not one of them ever offered me the least abuse of unchastity to me, in word or action. Though some are ready to say I speak it for my own credit; but I speak it in the presence of God, and to his glory. God's power is as great now, and as sufficient to save, as when he preserved Daniel in the lions' den; or the three children in the fiery furnace. I may well say as his Psalm 107.12, *Oh give thanks unto the Lord for he is good, for his mercy endureth for ever.* Let the redeemed of the Lord say so, whom he hath redeemed from the hand of the enemy, especially that I should come away in the midst of so many hundreds of enemies quietly and peaceably, and not a dog moving his tongue. So I took my leave of them, and in coming along my heart melted into tears, more than all the while I was with them, and I was almost swallowed up with the thoughts that ever I should go home again. About the sun going down, Mr. Hoar and myself, and the two Indians, came to Lancaster, and a solemn sight it was to me. There had I lived many comfortable years amongst my relations and neighbours, and now not one Christian to be seen, nor one house left standing. We went on to a arm house that was yet standing, where we lay all night: and a comfortable lodging we had, though nothing but straw to lie on. The Lord preserved us in safety that night, and raised

[1] *The bitterness of Death is past* See 1 Samuel 15.32. Agag, king of Amalek, thought his life had been spared after his defeat by Saul, but he was then killed by Samuel.

us up again in the morning, and carried us along, that before noon, we came to Concord. Now was I full of joy, and yet not without sorrow; joy to see such a lovely sight, so many Christians together, and some of them my neighbours. There I met with my brother, and my brother in law, who asked me if I knew where his wife was? Poor heart! he had helped to bury her, and knew it not; she being shot down by the house was partly burnt, so that those who were at Boston at the desolation of the town, and came back afterward and buried the dead, did not know her. Yet I was not without sorrow, to think how many were looking and longing, and my own children amongst the rest, to enjoy that deliverance that I had now received; and I did not know whether ever I should see them again. Being recruited[1] with food and raiment, we went to Boston that day, where I met with my dear husband; but the thoughts of our dear children, one being dead, and the other we could not tell where, abated our comfort each to other. I was not before so much hemmed in with the merciless and cruel heathen, but now as much with pitiful, tender-hearted, and compassionate Christians. In that poor, and distressed, and beggarly condition I was received in, I was kindly entertained in several houses; so much love I received from several (some of whom I knew, and others I knew not) that I am not capable to declare it. But the Lord knows them all by name: The Lord reward them sevenfold into their bosoms of his spirituals, for their temporals.[2] The twenty pounds, the price of my redemption, was raised by some Boston gentlemen, and Ms. Usher, whose bounty and religious charity I would not forget to make mention of. Then Mr. Thomas Shepard of Charlestown received us into his house, where we continued eleven weeks; and a father and mother they were to us. And many more tender-hearted friends we met with in that place. We were now in the midst of love, yet not without much and frequent heaviness of heart for our poor children, and other relations, who were still in affliction. The week following, after my coming in, the governor and Council sent forth to the Indians again, and that not without success; for they brought in my sister, and Goodwife Kettle. Their not knowing where our children were was a sore trial to us still, and

yet we were not without secret hopes that we should see them again. That which was dead[3] lay heavier upon my spirit, than those which were alive and amongst the heathen; thinking how it suffered with its wounds, and I was no way able to relieve it, and how it was buried by the heathen in the wilderness from[4] among all Christians. We were hurried up and down in our thoughts. Sometime we should hear a report that they were gone this way, and sometimes that, and that they were come in, in this place or that. We kept enquiring and listning to hear concerning them, but no certain news as yet. About this time the Council had ordered a day of public thanksgiving: though I thought I had still cause of mourning, and being unsettled in our minds, we thought we would ride toward the Eastward, to see if we could hear anything concerning our children. And as we were riding along (God is the wise disposer[5] of all things) between Ipswich and Rowly we met with Mr. William Hubbard,[6] who told us that our son Joseph was come in to Major Waldren's,[7] and another with him, which was my sister's son. I asked him how he knew it? He said, the Major himself told him so. So along we went till we came to Newbury; and their minister being absent, they desired my husband to preach the thanksgiving for them; but he was not willing to stay there that night, but would go over to Salisbury, to hear further, and come again in the morning, which he did, and preached there that day. At night, when he had done, one came and told him that his daughter was come in at Providence.[8] Here was mercy on both hands. Now hath God fulfilled that precious Scripture which was such a comfort to me in my distressed condition, when my heart was ready to sink into the earth (my children being gone I could not tell whither), and my knees trembling under me. *And I was walking through the valley of the shadow of Death.*[9] Then the Lord brought, and now has fulfilled that

1 *recruited* Refreshed.

2 *for their temporals* I.e., in return for their worldly generosity.

3 *That which was dead* I.e., Rowlandson's daughter Sarah.

4 *from* Away from.

5 *disposer* Ruler; one who puts things in order.

6 *Mr. William Hubbard* Minister—and later a historian of King Philip's War—based in Ipswich, Massachusetts (1621–1704).

7 *Major Waldren* Colonial soldier Richard Waldron (1615–89).

8 *Providence* I.e., the settlement in Rhode Island.

9 *And I … of Death* See Psalm 23.4.

reviving word unto me: Thus saith the Lord, *Refrain thy voice from weeping, and thine eyes from tears, for thy Work shall be rewarded*, saith the Lord, *and they shall come again from the Land of the Enemy*.[1] Now we were between them, the one on the East, and the other on the West; our son being nearest, we went to him first, to Portsmouth, where we met with him, and with the Major also, who told us he had done what he could, but could not redeem him under seven pounds, which the good people thereabouts were pleased to pay. The Lord reward the Major, and all the rest, though unknown to me, for their labour of love. My sister's son was redeemed for four pounds, which the Council gave order for the payment of. Having now received one of our children, we hastened toward the other. Going back through Newbury, my husband preached there on the Sabbath day, for which they rewarded him many fold.

On Monday we came to Charlestown, where we heard that the governor of Rhode Island had sent over for our daughter, to take care of her, being now within his jurisdiction, which should not pass without our acknowledgments. But she being nearer Rehoboth than Rhode Island, Mr. Newman went over, and took care of her, and brought her to his own house. And the goodness of God was admirable to us in our low estate, in that he raised up passionate friends on every side to us, when we had nothing to recompense any for their love. The Indians were now gone that way, that it was apprehended dangerous to go to her. But the carts which carried provision to the English army, being guarded, brought her with them to Dorchester, where we received her safe: blessed be the Lord for it, for great is his power, and He can do whatsoever seemeth him good. Her coming in was after this manner: She was travelling one day with the Indians, with her basket at her back; the company of Indians were got before her, and gone out of sight, all except one squaw; she followed the squaw till night, and then both of them lay down, having nothing over them but the heavens, and under them but the earth. Thus she travelled three days together, not knowing whither she was going, having nothing to eat or drink but water, and green hirtle-berries.[2] At last they came into Providence, where she was kindly entertained by several of that town. The Indians often said that I should never have her under twenty pounds; but now the Lord hath brought her in upon free cost, and given her to me the second time. The Lord make us a blessing indeed, each to others.[3] Now have I seen that Scripture also fulfilled, Deuteronomy 30.4–7. *If any of thine be driven out to the outmost parts of heaven, from thence will the Lord thy God gather thee, and from thence will he fetch thee. And the Lord thy God will put all these curses upon thine enemies, and on them which hate thee, which persecuted thee.* Thus hath the Lord brought me and mine out of that horrible pit, and hath set us in the midst of tender-hearted and compassionate Christians. It is the desire of my soul, that we may walk worthy of the mercies received, and which we are receiving.

Our family being now gathered together (those of us that were living), the South Church in Boston hired an house for us. Then we removed from Mr. Shepard's, those cordial friends, and went to Boston, where we continued about three quarters of a year. Still the Lord went along with us, and provided graciously for us. I thought it somewhat strange to set up housekeeping with bare walls; but as Solomon says, *Money answers all things*;[4] and that we had through the benevolence of Christian friends, some in this town, and some in that, and others; and some from England; that in a little time we might look, and see the house furnished with love. The Lord hath been exceeding good to us in our low estate, in that when we had neither house nor home, nor other necessaries, the Lord so moved the hearts of these and those towards us, that we wanted neither food, nor raiment for our selves or ours, Proverbs 18.24. *There is a Friend which sticketh closer than a Brother.* And how many such friends have we found, and now living amongst? And truly such a friend have we found him to be unto us, in whose house we lived, *viz.* Mr. James Whitcomb, a friend unto us near hand, and afar off.

[1] *Thus saith … the Enemy* See Jeremiah 31.16.

[2] *hirtle-berries* Whortleberries; any of a number of species in the genus *Vaccinium*, which includes huckleberries and blueberries.

[3] *each to others* I.e., to each other.

[4] *Money answers all things* See Ecclesiastes 10.19.

I can remember the time, when I used to sleep quietly without workings in my thoughts, whole nights together, but now it is other ways with me. When all are fast[1] about me, and no eye open, but his who ever waketh, my thoughts are upon things past, upon the awful dispensation of the Lord towards us; upon his wonderful power and might, in carrying of us through so many difficulties, in returning us in safety, and suffering none to hurt us. I remember in the night season, how the other day I was in the midst of thousands of enemies, and nothing but death before me; it is then hard work to persuade myself, that ever I should be satisfied with bread again. But now we are fed with the finest of the wheat, and, as I may say, *With honey out of the rock.*[2] Instead of the husk, we have the fatted calf. The thoughts of these things in the particulars of them, and of the love and goodness of God towards us, make it true of me, what David said of himself, Psalm 6.6. *I watered my Couch with my tears.* Oh! the wonderful power of God that mine eyes have seen, affording matter enough for my thoughts to run in, that when others are sleeping mine eyes are weeping.

I have seen the extreme vanity of this world.[3] One hour I have been in health, and wealth, wanting nothing; but the next hour in sickness and wounds, and death, having nothing but sorrow and affliction.

Before I knew what affliction meant, I was ready sometimes to wish for it. When I lived in prosperity, having the comforts of the world about me, my relations by me, my heart cheerful, and taking little care for anything; and yet seeing many, whom I preferred before myself, under many trials and afflictions, in sickness, weakness, poverty, losses, crosses, and cares of the world, I should be sometimes jealous least I should have my portion in this life, and that Scripture would come to my mind, Hebrews 12.6. *For whom the Lord loveth he chasteneth, and scourgeth every Son whom he receiveth.* But now I see the Lord had his time to scourge and chasten me. The portion of some is to have their afflictions by drops, now one drop and then another, but the dregs of the cup, the wine of astonishment: like a sweeping rain that leaveth no food, did the Lord prepare to be my portion. Affliction I wanted, and affliction I had full measure (I thought), pressed down and running over: yet I see, when God calls a person to anything, and through never so many difficulties, yet he is fully able to carry them through and make them see, and say they have been gainers thereby. And I hope I can say in some measure, as David did, *It is good for me that I have been afflicted.*[4] The Lord hath showed me the vanity of these outward things. That they are the vanity of vanities, and vexation of spirit; that they are but a shadow, a blast, a bubble, and things of no continuance. That we must rely on God himself, and our whole dependence must be upon him. If trouble from smaller matters begin to arise in me, I have something at hand to check myself with, and say, why am I troubled? It was but the other day that if I had had the world, I would have given it for my freedom, or to have been a servant to a Christian. I have learned to look beyond present and smaller troubles, and to be quieted under them, as Moses said, Exodus 14.13. *Stand still and see the salvation of the Lord.*

FINIS

—1682

[1] *fast* I.e., fast asleep.

[2] *fed with ... the rock* See Psalm 81.16.

[3] *vanity of this world* Seventeenth-century meanings of *vanity* are only distantly related to the sense in which the word is most commonly used nowadays (i.e., to denote excessive regard for one's physical appearance). In the way that it is frequently used in sixteenth- and seventeenth-century translations of Ecclesiastes and other books of the Bible, *vanity* derives from a Hebrew word meaning *mist* or *vapor*—by extension, anything that does not last long, and that is insubstantial. According to Christian doctrine, all earthly things fall into that category.

[4] *It is ... afflicted* See Psalm 119.71.

IN CONTEXT

Editions of Rowlandson's Narrative

Only eight pages of the first edition of *The Sovereignty and Goodness of God*, published in Boston in 1682, have survived to today. Three more editions were, however, published that same year, two in Cambridge, Massachusetts, and one in London.

Title page to the first of two editions—called, respectively, the "second Addition" and the "second edition"—printed by Cambridge printer Samuel Green in 1682. Together, these two printings sold over one thousand copies.

Title page to the London edition of Rowlandson's narrative, also printed in 1682.

IN CONTEXT

Picturing Mary Rowlandson

Editions of Rowlandson's narrative continued to be reissued well into the eighteenth century. Two such editions were notably accompanied by illustrations that seem intended to portray Rowlandson, though both these portrayals took significant liberties with the text's account of events.

This edition of Rowlandson's narrative, retitled to suit the tastes of the revolutionary era, was first released in 1773 (though the title page reproduced below is from a 1791 reprinting). Here, Rowlandson—who did not engage in combat at any point during the Lancaster raid—is depicted single-handedly fighting off a group of attackers armed with tomahawks and rifles.

A

NARRATIVE

OF THE

Captivity, Sufferings, and Removes,

OF

Mrs. *Mary Rowlandfon,*

Who was taken Prifoner by the *Indians ;* with feveral others ; and treated in the moft barbarous and cruel Manner by thofe vile *Savages:* With many other remarkable Events during her Travels.

Written by her own Hand, for her private Ufe, and fince made public at the earneft Defire of fome Friends, and for the Benefit of the Afflicted.

BOSTON:

Re-printed and fold by THOMAS and JOHN FLEET, at the Bible and Heart, Cornhill, 1791.

This image was initially created for the frontispiece of a 1762 book called *The Life and Adventures of a Female Soldier*, which told the story of Hannah Snell, an English woman who had famously donned men's clothing and joined the British Navy earlier in the century. In 1770 the engraving was reused by the same printer in a new edition of Rowlandson's narrative; note the musket and gunpowder horn, the British flag over the fort in the distance, and the figure's distinctly eighteenth-century clothing, including a cocked hat.

IN CONTEXT

Indigenous Experiences of Metacom's War

Far more Indigenous people than settlers were held captive during and after King Philip's War. Some were taken as captives by other Indigenous people, sometimes including their own relations, but most were held captive by English settlers in a variety of ways: they were held in appalling conditions in internment camps; they were imprisoned for acts of war on the basis of little to no evidence; and, especially after the war, they were enslaved in large numbers.

Many of the documents included below relate to the forms of captivity experienced by "praying Indians," Indigenous allies of the English who had converted to Christianity and partially adopted European ways of living. These Indigenous Christians occupied a uniquely uncomfortable position in the conflict. As they struggled to maintain the diplomatic relationships they had entered into with the English, they often found themselves siding against their own relatives from outside the "praying towns"; some were even taken and held as captives by Metacom's forces. But the English—far more likely than Indigenous people to view the world in racial terms—tended to lump their Indigenous enemies and allies together and did not trust the Indigenous Christians regardless of their efforts to prove their loyalty. During the war, the English interned hundreds of their Indigenous allies, most infamously transporting many hundreds to Deer Island on the Massachusetts coast where, inadequately provisioned and deprived of their usual livelihoods, about half died over the winter.

By the summer of 1676, English forces were roaming the countryside capturing or killing Indigenous combatants, non-combatants, and allies almost indiscriminately. The petitions at the end of this selection represent the efforts of Indigenous leaders with longstanding relationships to the English—many of whom had gone to extraordinary lengths to aid the English side during the war—to negotiate the safe surrender of their families and communities. These efforts did succeed in obtaining some individuals' lives and freedoms, but overall the English were ruthless in punishing as criminals almost any Indigenous people who could not concretely prove their constant loyalty to the English, including those who had surrendered in response to offers of amnesty. Many were publicly executed, indentured for long periods (a fate especially common for children), or enslaved for life and either kept locally or forcibly transported for sale in Barbados, Bermuda, and other colonies.

NOTE ON THE TEXTS: Unless otherwise indicated, the editors have consulted several sources, including the manuscript versions, in preparing the following texts for the anthology; we are especially indebted to the work of Lisa Brooks, who discusses many of them in her landmark work *Our Beloved Kin: A New History of King Philip's War* (2018) and includes many of them on a website associated with the book. Several of the selections below are based on their transcriptions in *An Historical Account of the Doings and Sufferings of the Christian Indians in New England in the Years 1675, 1676, 1677* (1677) by Daniel Gookin, who was "Superintendent of the Praying Indians" and whose account of King Philip's War is more sympathetic and reliable than most other settler accounts from the period.

from John Easton, letter to Josiah Winslow, 26 May 1675

John Easton, Deputy Governor of Rhode Island, wrote the following letter to Plymouth Governor Josiah Winslow on behalf of Weetamoo, the saunkskaw (woman sachem) of the Pocasset, a Wampanoag tribe. Written a month before King Philip's War began, the letter articulates the concerns that would lead Weetamoo to join the war against the English: namely

that English settlements were, increasingly, interfering with Pocasset territory and disrupting Pocasset livelihoods. Weetamoo had substantial troops at her disposal and played a major role in King Philip's War until her death during the conflict; she also appears (as Wettimore) in Rowlandson's *Narrative*.

Friend Josiah Winslow, Governor of Plymouth Colony,

Weetamoo the queen of Pocasset and her husband showed me a letter—Constant Southworth[1] and other names to it, dated April 30, 75—by which they have great fear of oppression from the English, [so] that they could not tell how to trust me, but [feared] that I would to please the English join to do them wrong. ... [W]hat they would now have [as] their bounds north and south is to maintain a river at each end by which they have great dependence for fish, but are free to accommodate thee or whom they shall admit with thee of four mile square of land at least[.] ... But by having their other bounds confirmed in their records they shall agree to what more they will give them. They prefer so fair and as it appeareth to me desire only of you what is their reasonable due that I have large hope you will not deny it, and to have the difference decided as to them it may appear not to be by such as determine in their own case.[2] I am persuaded both may be so satisfied. I am largely engaged in myself to manifest to them that I am not false, but to endeavor they may have right according to English law, and hope it will not be in any opposition to your desires or to your rule in your colony. I know about 60 have confirmed to the queen's right to be to a far greater tract of land beside what now she and they would be contented with. ...

John Easton

James Quannapaquait with unnamed magistrates, *The Examination and Relation of James Quannapaquait, alias James Rumny-Marsh*[3] (January 1676)

James Quannapaquait and Job Kattenanit, two Indigenous Christians being held at Deer Island, were enlisted as spies and sent to learn about the plans of Metacom's followers; after their service, they were sent back to Deer Island. Quannapaquait's extensive account of their experiences, excerpted here, was recorded by the magistrates who heard his testimony, and offers insight into the experiences and motivations of Indigenous people on both sides of King Philip's War.

The examination and relation of James Quannapaquait, alias James Rumny-Marsh, being one of the Christian Indians belonging to Natick;[4] taken the 24th day of January 1675/6,[5] on which day he returned from his journey (for this man and another called Job of Magunkaquog,[6] a Christian man also)

[1] *Constant Southworth* Treasurer of the Plymouth Colony. Southworth was one of many people in the colony hoping to expand their own land holdings into Pocasset territory.

[2] *to have ... own case* I.e., I hope you will agree to have the dispute resolved by judges who will not appear to decide the matter according to their own interests.

[3] The present text is based upon the version reprinted in Josiah Howard Temple's *History of North Brookfield, Massachusetts* (1887).

[4] *Natick* Indigenous praying community.

[5] *1675/6* The writers here employ the practice of dual dating, which accounts for the fact that the date of the beginning of the new year varied among countries still using the Julian calendar, such as Britain and its colonies, where the new year was marked on 25 March.

[6] *Magunkaquog* Indigenous praying community.

were sent forth by order of the council of Massachusetts upon the last of December (as spies) to discover the enemies' quarters and motions and his state and condition, and to gain what intelligence they could; for which end they had particular instruction. Though when first they were moved to go [on] this journey, they saw it would be a hazardous undertaking, and that they should run the hazard of their lives in it, yet they were willing to venture upon these and like considerations. First, that they might declare their readiness to serve the English. Secondly, one of them, namely Job, had three children (even all he had) that were carried away with the Hassanamesit Indians and, as he conceived were with the enemy, and he was willing to know their state as well as the condition of the praying Indians of Hassanamesit and Magunkaquog that were he thought in the power of the enemy. Third, they hoped to suggest something in order to the enemy's submission to the English and making peace if they found the enemy in a temper fit for it. And if that could be effected then they hoped the poor Christian Indians at the Deer Island and in other places possibly might be restored to their places again, and be freed from much suffering they are now in by this war, and thereby the jealousies[1] that the English have now of them might be removed. These and other reasons induced them to run this adventure for which also if they returned in safety they had a promise of a reward.

They doubted[2] the Indian enemy would mistrust them for spies, and that they would move the fight for them against the English, unto which doubts they were advised to tell the Indian enemy a lamentable story (and yet agreeable to truth) of their deep sufferings by the English; that Job was imprisoned several days (as he was) where he suffered much, though he had served the English faithfully as an interpreter and in actual arms being with the Mohegans at the fight near Secunke with Philip, the beginning of August last, but imprisonment and suspicions the English had of him was part of his reward for that service to the English. …

… [Y]et after all these services both they and their wives and children and all their country men that lived at Natick were mistrusted by the English and thereupon (at a few hours warning) brought away from their place and fort and houses at Natick and carried down in boats to Deer Island, leaving and losing much of their substance, cattle, swine, horse and corn, and at the island were exposed to great sufferings having little wood for fuel, a bleak place and poor wigwams such as they could make a shift to make themselves with a few mats. And here at the island had very little provision, many of them, and diverse other sorrows and troubles they were exposed to, and were about 350 souls men, women, and children; and that now having an opportunity to get off the island they came to see how things were with the Indians in the woods; and if they preferred them to fight with and for them they were advised to manifest all readiness and forwardness and not show any averseness. Things being thus prepared these two spies were sent away without arms excepting hatchets and with a little parched meal[3] for provision. …

… At this place among these Indians they found all the Christian Indians belonging to Hassanamesit and Magunkaquog, which are about 40 men and about 80 women and children; these praying Indians were carried away by the enemy. Some went willingly, others of them unwillingly, as they told him, for before they went away they were in a great strait, for if they came to the English they knew they should be sent to Deer Island, as others were, and their corn being at such a distance about 40 miles from Boston, it could not be caried to sustain their lives and so they should be in danger to famish and others feared they should be sent away to Barbados, or other places. And to stay at Hassanamesit these Indians or enemies would not permit them, but said they must have the corn, but promised them if they would go with them they should not die but be preserved. These being in this condition most of them thought it best to go with them though they feared death every way. …

Further he saith that he understood by the chief men and old men yet they were inclinable to have peace again with the English, but the young men (who are their principal soldiers) say "We will have no peace. We are all or most of us alive yet and the English have killed very few of us last summer. Why shall

[1] *jealousies* Suspicions.

[2] *doubted* Feared.

[3] *parched meal* Dried ground grain.

we have peace to be made slaves, and either be killed or sent away to sea to Barbadoes, etc.? Let us live as long as we can and die like men, and not live to be enslaved." ...

Massachusetts Council, order regarding Indigenous allies [1] (30 August 1675)

> Even before the Massachusetts Council began to confine its Indigenous allies to sites such as Deer Island, it imposed substantial restrictions on their freedom of movement. The following Massachusetts Council order was imposed near the beginning of the war.

At a Council held in Boston, August 30th, 1675

The Council judging it of absolute necessity for security of the English and Indians in amity with us, that they be restrained their usual commerce with the English and hunting in the woods, during the time of hostility with those that are our enemies; do order, that all those Indians that are desirous to approve themselves faithful to the English be confined to the several places underwritten, until the Council shall take further order, and that they so order the setting of their wigwams that they may stand compact in one place of their plantations respectively, where it may be best for their own provision and defence, and that none of them do presume to travel above one mile from the centre of such of their dwellings unless in company of some English, or in their service, excepting for gathering in their corn with one Englishman in company, on peril of being taken as our enemies, or their abettors. And in case any of them be taken without the limits aforesaid except as above said, and do lose their lives, or be otherwise damnified[2] by English or Indians; the Council do hereby declare that they shall account themselves wholly innocent, and their blood, or other damage by them sustained, will be upon their own heads. Also, it shall not be lawful for any Indians that are now in amity with us to entertain any strange Indians, or to receive any of our enemies' plunder, but shall from time to time make discovery thereof to some English[3] that shall be appointed for that end to sojourn with them, on penalty of being accounted our enemies, and to be proceeded against as such.

Also, whereas it is the manner of the heathen that are now in hostility with us, contrary to the practice of civil nations, to execute their bloody insolences by stealth, and skulking in small parties, declining all open decision of the controversy, either by treaty or by the sword; the Council do therefore order, that after the publication of the provision aforesaid, it shall be lawful for any person, whether English or Indian, that shall find any Indian travelling in any of our towns or woods, contrary to the limits above-named, to command them under their guard and examination, or to kill and destroy them as they best may or can. The Council hereby declaring, that it will be most acceptable to them that none be killed or wounded that are willing to surrender themselves into custody.

The places of the Indians' residence are Natick, Punkapoag, Nashobah, Wamesit, and Hassanamesit. And if there be any that belong to other places, they are to repair to some one of these.

By the Council.

Edward Rawson, *Secretary*.

Numphow and John Line, letter to Thomas Henchman, November 1675

> In November 1675, a group of vigilantes from Chelmsford attacked the people of Wamesit, a nearby praying town. The vigilantes falsely believed people from Wamesit to be responsible for

[1] The present text is based on the version included in Gookin's *Historical Account*.

[2] *damnified* Injured.

[3] *but shall ... English* Unless they declare it to an English person.

the burning of a barn full of hay and grain, and in retaliation they shot six noncombatants, including a child who died of his wounds. This was not the first retaliatory attack Chelmsford had made on Wamesit, its ostensible ally, but for many in Wamesit it was the last straw. The following letter was written by Wamesit leaders Numphow and John Line as they led a group north in an attempt to escape conflict with the English. The letter is addressed to Thomas Henchman, a Chelmsford resident with authority over Wamesit, who at the request of the Massachusetts Council had sent a messenger, Wepocositt, to try to persuade them to come back.

First, Numphow, and John a Line, we send a messenger to you again (Wepocositt) with this answer, we cannot come home again, we go towards the French, we go where Wannalancet[1] is; the reason is we went away from our home, we had help from the Council, but that did not do us good, but we had wrong by the English. Secondly, the reason is we went away from the English, for when there was any harm done in Chelmsford, they laid it to us, and said we did it, but we know ourselves we never did any harm to the English, but we go away peaceably and quietly. Thirdly, as for the Island,[2] we say there is no safety for us, because many English be not good, and may be they come to us and kill us, as in the other case. We are not sorry for what we leave behind, but we are sorry the English have driven us from our praying to God and from our teacher. We did begin to understand a little of praying to God. We thank humbly the Council. We remember our love to Mr. Henchman and James Richardson.[3]

James Printer

James Printer, also known to his Nipmuc community as Wowaus, began an apprenticeship at Cambridge Press at a young age. During his career there he worked on, among many other texts, the first Bible published in North America. Though he attempted to maintain neutrality during King Philip's War, Printer was held captive by both sides. First, he was one of eleven Indigenous Christians who were falsely accused of a 1675 raid on Lancaster, the settlement where Rowlandson would herself be abducted in another attack later in the war. As Daniel Gookin's account below details, these falsely accused men, Printer included, were incarcerated for weeks and almost killed by an angry mob during the trial that ultimately found all but one of them innocent. After Printer returned to his hometown of Hassanamesit, which had become a praying community allied with the English, he and other residents were captured by Metacom's fighters. During his captivity Printer appears to have come to sympathize with the resisters' aims and to have worked as a scribe on Metacom's behalf; the note reprinted below is widely attributed to him.

Printer never gave up his ties to the English. After the war, he helped to negotiate amnesty for some of the Indigenous survivors and returned to his trade of typesetting. One of the works he would eventually typeset was Rowlandson's *The Sovereignty and Goodness of God*.

[1] *Wannalancet* Penacook sachem (c. 1619–97) who had led his community north to what is now New Hampshire, hoping to escape the English. Generally speaking, the areas immediately to the north of the English colonies on the Atlantic coast were occupied by the French or disputed between the French and English.

[2] *the Island* Deer Island, where the English forced many of their Indigenous allies to live during the war.

[3] *James Richardson* Chelmsford resident who, along with Henchman, had been given some authority over the Wamesit community. The burned barn belonged to him, but he had maintained his belief in the innocence of the people of Wamesit and attempted to act as their ally.

from DANIEL GOOKIN, *AN HISTORICAL ACCOUNT OF THE DOINGS AND SUFFERINGS OF THE CHRISTIAN INDIANS IN NEW ENGLAND IN THE YEARS 1675, 1676, 1677* (1677)

… [T]he pretence for seizing these fifteen Marlborough Indians and sending them down as prisoners was this, that eleven of them had committed a notorious murder upon seven English persons at Lancaster upon a Lord's day, August 22nd. The next and immediate accuser of these Indians was one David, an Indian, one of the fifteen, who being suspected for shooting at a lad belonging to the English of Marlborough that was sent out by his master to look up some sheep, this David being apprehended by the aforesaid captain upon the former suspicion, and fastened to a tree to be shot to death, and fearing to drink of the same cup as his brother Andrew had done a fortnight before, being shot to death by some soldiers at the same place. … But David, as aforesaid, being fastened to a tree, and guns bent at him, feared death, and being offered a reprieve if he would confess truth, he promised something, and so was unbound, and then accused eleven of the Indians then at the fort, and now prisoners, to be murderers of the English at Lancaster before mentioned; "but," said he, "I did not see it done, neither was I there, but I heard some speak so."

David was hereupon released from present death, but yet was sent down prisoner with the rest, and being examined before the Council, he at first owned[1] that he had said so to the Captain, at Marlborough; but afterward, upon the trial before the court and jury, he said he had accused those Indians falsely. Indeed some of the accused Indians, particularly one named James Akompanet, a very understanding fellow, pleaded in behalf of himself and the rest, that what David said against them, was, first, to save his own life when he was bound to the tree, secondly, to revenge himself of them because they had seized upon his brother Andrew, and his son, and delivered them to the English, one whereof was put to death, and the other sent out of the country, a slave.

… [All the people on] trial were acquitted, except one man, who was found guilty of being accessory to the murder; but this man, named Joseph Spoonant, was tried by another jury, not the same that tried the others. Upon what ground the jury went, I know not; but the man was sold for a slave and sent out of the country. Also, the first adviser of them all, called David, was condemned to be sold, his crime alleged for suspicion of shooting an Irish boy at Marlborough, and for accusing the others falsely; but all the rest were discharged. …

But before this business was fully examined and issued, the clamors of the people were very great upon this occasion, and all things against those praying Indians accused (as one of the most intelligent of the magistrates said) were represented as very great, as things appear in mist or fog. Some men were so violent that they would have had these Indians put to death by martial law, and not tried by a jury, though they were subjects under the English protection, and not in hostility with us; others had received such impressions in their minds, that they could hardly extend charity to the jurors and magistrates that acquitted them. … Although I mention the story of this matter in this place, yet it was towards the latter end of September, before these Indians were tried and acquitted, all which time they remained in prison, under great sufferings. …

ATTRIBUTED TO JAMES PRINTER, NOTE TACKED TO A TREE, C. 1676

Though English man hath provoked us to anger and wrath and we care not though we have war with you this 21 years—for there are many of us, 300 of which have fought with you at this town. We have nothing but our lives to lose, but thou hast many fair houses, cattle, and much good things.

[1] *owned* Admitted.

from Andrew Pittimee, Quanahpohkit, John Mague, and James Speen, petition to the Governor and Council of the Massachusetts Colony,[1] June 1676

In the following petition, a group of Indigenous officers who had served on the English side attempt to secure the freedom of a number of individuals being imprisoned by the English. The subjects of the petition include "Captain Tom" Wuttasacomponom, a Hassanamesit leader who had been held captive twice during the war. First, he was captured by Metacom's forces when they invaded Hassanamesit; he and his family eventually escaped or were freed but, they would later say, were too afraid to return to the English. In the spring of 1676, Indigenous scouts working for the English found him and his family and brought them in.

The success of the petition was limited but significant. The English publicly hanged Wuttasacomponom but did free the women and children the officers had requested. English authorities also responded to the suggestion "that others that are out, and love the English, may be encouraged to come in" by implementing a two-week period during which Indigenous individuals could request amnesty from the settlers. This negotiation undoubtedly saved some lives—though, as they would discover, those seeking amnesty could not be assured of a friendly reception.

To the Honourable the Governor and Council of the Massachusetts Colony, Assembled at Boston this —— of June 1676

The humble petition of Andrew Pittimee, Quanahpohkit, *alias* James Rumney Marsh, John Magus, and James Speen, officers unto the Indian soldiers, now in your service, with the consent of the rest of the Indian soldiers being about eighty men;

Humbly imploreth your favour and mercies to be extended to some of the prisoners taken by us, (most of them) near Lancaster, Marlborough, etc., in whose behalf we are bold to supplicate your Honours. And we have three reasons for this humble supplication. First, because the persons we beg pardon for, as we are informed, are innocent, and have not done any wrong or injury unto the English, all this war time, only were against their wills taken and kept among the enemy. Secondly, because it pleased your Honours to say to some of us, to encourage us to fidelity and activity in your service, that you would be ready to do anything for us that was fit for us to ask and you to grant. Thirdly, that others that are out, and love the English, may be encouraged to come in. More that we humbly intercede for, is the lives and liberties of those few of our poor friends and kindred, that, in this time of temptation and affliction, have been in the enemy's quarters; we hope it will be no grief of heart to you to show mercy, and especially to such who have (as we conceive) done no wrong to the English. If we did think, or had any ground to conceive that they were naught, and were enemies to the English, we would not intercede for them, but rather bear our testimony against them, as we have done. We have (especially some of us) been sundry times in your service to the hazard of our lives, both as spies, messengers, scouts, and soldiers, and have through God's favour acquitted ourselves faithfully, and shall do as long as we live endeavour with all fidelity to fight in the English cause, which we judge is our cause, and also God's cause, to oppose the wicked Indians, enemies to God and all goodness. In granting this our humble request, you will much oblige us who desire to remain,

Your Honour's Humble and Faithful Servants

Andrew Pittimee,
James Quanapohkhit,
Job,
John Magus,
James Speen

[1] The present text is based on the version included in Gookin's *Historical Account*.

EDWARD TAYLOR

c. 1643 – 1729

In a 1674 love letter to Elizabeth Fitch, the woman who would become his wife, Edward Taylor declared that though his heart belonged ultimately to God, he wished to share all his worldly devotion with Fitch. "[T]hough my love within my breast is so large that my heart is not sufficient to contain it," he wrote, "yet I can make it no more room to ride in than to squeeze it up betwixt my black ink and white paper." Balancing abstract spiritual aspirations with reflections upon everyday concerns and bodily delights, the writing of Edward Taylor puts the lie to the stereotype that the Puritans of colonial America were joyless and cold. A Puritan minister and a poet whose work went unpublished until the twentieth century, Taylor is now recognized as one of the foremost religious poets in colonial America. Taylor is known not only for the artistry of his lyrics, but also for his ability to infuse deeply felt emotions of love and longing into dense theological meditations.

Taylor was born in or around Sketchley, Leicester, England. Little is known about his early life, except that he was educated by a Puritan teacher, and that he briefly served as a schoolmaster in Bagworth, Leicester—a position he was obliged to abandon after he refused to take an oath of loyalty to the Crown and Church of England. Like many other Reformed Protestants who became dissenters after the restoration of the British monarchy in 1660, Taylor was unwilling to defer to the Church of England's theological and hierarchical governance. In April 1668, he left for Boston, the capital of the Massachusetts Bay Colony and a refuge for religious nonconformists. He spent his first days in the colony as the guest of Increase Mather, a Puritan spiritual leader, with whom he would forge a lifelong friendship. Taylor was soon admitted to Harvard as a mature student, and during his time there he wrote elegies for several Harvard officials.

Soon after Taylor's graduation in 1671, the newly incorporated town of Westfield requested a minister. Mather advised Taylor to go, and he accepted the position, albeit "not without much apprehension": Westfield was isolated, both geographically and intellectually, from the rest of the colony, and the journey to the town was treacherous. After he arrived, Taylor gradually began to serve his congregation as pastor and physician, and eventually to start the process of establishing a formal church. He became smitten with Elizabeth Fitch, a Connecticut pastor's daughter who shared his interest in poetry, and the two married in 1674. Many of Taylor's early poems express his overflowing love for both Elizabeth and God. These early poems are formally inventive, often including complex visual elements. Many are acrostics, inspired by the sampler patterns that women would embroider to practice their needlework; the acrostics accompanied each letter of the alphabet with a corresponding verse, just as needlework samplers stitched out each letter.

Taylor offered moral and spiritual support to Westfield's inhabitants as the town was threatened during King Philip's War (1675–78), in which an anti-colonial coalition of Wampanoag, Narragansett, and several other tribes led by the Wampanoag sachem Metacom (also known as King Philip) fought an alliance of New England colonists, Mohegan, and Pequot. (The Pocomtuc, whose home territory included the site of Westfield, were part of the Indigenous alliance, and they were forced to flee the area at the war's conclusion.) After the war, Taylor was able to establish a church in Westfield, but his personal life remained difficult: all of the eight children he had with Elizabeth would die before their father, and Elizabeth herself died in 1689. Some of Taylor's most personal poems are elegies written to memorialize people dear to him, including his children, his wife, and his friends and colleagues. Taylor remarried in 1692; he would have six children with his second wife, Ruth Wyllys, a member of a prominent political family.

Throughout these events, Taylor persisted in his work as a minister. As a Puritan, he adhered to a form of Christianity known as Covenant Theology: he believed that humans were born sinful as a result

of the failure of the first people, Adam and Eve, to live up to their covenant with God. Because of Adam and Eve's disobedience, humans were unable to have any effect upon their own salvation. Eternal life was extended to a small, predestined group of humans as a result of God's mercy, through what Puritans called "the Covenant of Grace." Taylor's beliefs were fairly typical for a Puritan minister of his time, with one notable exception. Although Taylor welcomed all community members to attend religious services, he—like some of his more conservative Puritan peers—considered only those who publicly affirmed that they had had a personal experience of God's grace to be participating members of the church. Taylor addresses this matter in *God's Determinations Touching His Elect* (c. 1682), which dramatizes the trials and triumphs of God's chosen people, the elect, as they experience salvation.

In the 1680s, Taylor began to write private devotional poetry as a means of focusing his mind before he went out to preach. Scholars believe that most of these *Preparatory Meditations* had a corresponding sermon, although the majority of these sermons have been lost. Taylor's meditations adhere to a very strict form: all are composed of six-line stanzas written in iambic pentameter. These devotional poems share many characteristics with British metaphysical poetry—wit, intricacy, and a productive synergy of thought and feeling. In particular, Taylor's poems suggest the influence of George Herbert, an Anglican whose work was popular among Puritan readers and would likely have been available to Taylor. (Taylor himself owned only one book of English poetry: a volume by the colonial poet Anne Bradstreet.)

With the exception of his elegies, some of which were read publicly on the occasion of the departed person's funeral, Taylor's work was for the most part not widely distributed in his own time. He did, however, gather all his poems carefully into leather-bound manuscripts; upon his death in 1729, these were bequeathed to his son-in-law Isaac Stiles and then inherited by his grandson Ezra Stiles. Stiles, who became president of Yale, arranged for the poems to be stored in the Yale library and the library of Westfield, where they remained until the twentieth century. In 1937, Taylor's manuscripts were discovered by the scholar Thomas H. Johnson, who published a selection of the work in 1939. After the work was released, Taylor was quickly recognized as a skilled poetic technician who challenged the idea, then current among Americanists, that Puritan literature lacked passion and sophistication. His work, which yokes together the language and imagery of the everyday and the divine, often produces complex and startling images. His poems are now often read within the contexts of early American and Puritan culture, as well as within the larger context of seventeenth-century metaphysical verse.

NOTE ON THE TEXTS: Several editions have been consulted in the preparation of this work; among them are the second edition of Donald E. Stanford's *The Poems of Edward Taylor* (1963), Lewis Turco's *Poetry: An Introduction Through Writing* (1973), and Taylor's original manuscripts. Spelling and punctuation have been modernized in accordance with the practices of this anthology.

⌘ ⌘ ⌘

Upon a Spider Catching a Fly

Thou sorrow, venom elf.° *small creature*
 Is this thy ploy,
To spin a web out of thyself
 To catch a fly?
5 For why?

I saw a pettish° wasp *fretful*
 Fall foul therein.
Whom yet thy whorlpins[1] did not [clasp]
 Lest he should fling
10 His sting.

But as afraid, remote
 Didst stand hereat
And with thy little fingers stroke
 And gently tap
15 His back.

Thus gently him didst treat
 Lest he should pet,° *take offense*
And in a froppish, waspish[2] heat
 Should greatly fret[3]
20 Thy net.

Whereas the silly fly,
 Caught by its leg
Thou by the throat took'st hastily
 And 'hind the head
25 Bite dead.

This goes to pot, that not:
 Nature doth call.[4]
Strive not above what strength hath got
 Lest in the brawl
30 Thou fall.

This fray seems thus to us.
 Hell's spider gets
His entrails spun to whip cords thus

35 And wove to nets
 And sets.

To tangle Adam's race[5]
 In's stratagems
To their destructions, spoiled, made base
 By venom things
40 Damned sins.
But mighty, gracious Lord
 Communicate
Thy grace to break the cord, afford
 Us glory's gate
45 And state.

We'll nightingale[6] sing like
 When perched on high
In glory's cage, thy glory, bright,
 [And] thankfully,
50 For joy.
—1939 (WRITTEN C. 1680–85)

Huswifery[7]

Make me, O Lord, thy spinning wheel[8] complete.
 Thy holy word my distaff[9] make for me
Make mine affections thy swift flyers[10] neat
 And make my soul thy holy spool[11] to be.
5 My conversation make to be thy reel[12]
And reel the yarn thereon spun of thy wheel.

Make me thy loom then, knit° therein this twine: *weave*
 And make thy Holy Spirit, Lord, wind quills:[13]

1 *whorlpins* I.e., legs; a whorlpin is a component of a spinning wheel.

2 *froppish* Ill-tempered; *waspish* Irritable, spiteful.

3 *fret* Damage by tearing or chafing.

4 *This goes … call* I.e., this one thing gets eaten, that other thing does not: nature decides.

5 *Adam's race* Humanity, which is, according to the Bible, descended from the first man, Adam.

6 *nightingale* Bird, renowned for its beautiful singing, that eats spiders.

7 *Huswifery* Housewifery, the duties of a housewife.

8 *spinning wheel* Device for making thread from fibers.

9 *distaff* Component of a spinning wheel that holds unspun fibers.

10 *flyers* Component of a spinning wheel that twists the fibers into thread.

11 *spool* Component of a spinning wheel on which the thread is wound.

12 *reel* Device used to hold finished thread.

13 *quills* Spindles on which yarn is wound.

Then weave the web thyself. The yarn is fine.
10 Thine ordinances make my fulling mills.[1]
 Then dye the same in heavenly colours
 choice,° *of high quality*
 All pinked with varnished[2] flowers of paradise.

 Then clothe therewith mine understanding, will,
 Affections, judgment, conscience, memory
15 My words, and actions, that their shine may fill
 My ways with glory and thee glorify.
 Then mine apparel shall display before ye
 That I am clothed in holy robes for glory.
 —1939 (WRITTEN C. 1680–85)

Upon Wedlock, and Death of Children

A curious knot[3] God made in paradise,
 And drew it out enameled° neatly fresh. *shining, glossy*
It was the true-love knot,[4] more sweet than spice
 And set with all the flowers of grace's dress.
5 It's wedden's° knot, that ne'er can be *wedding's*
 untied.
 No Alexander's sword can it divide.[5]

The slips[6] here planted, gay and glorious grow:
 Unless an hellish breath do singe their plumes
Here primrose, cowslips, roses, lilies blow° *bloom*
10 With violets and pinks that void° perfumes *emit*
 Whose beauteous leaves o'erlaid with honey dew.
 And chanting birds chirp out sweet music true.

When in this knot I planted was, my stock° *plant, stem*

[1] *ordinances* I.e., religious practices commanded by God;
fulling mills Places where impurities are removed from cloth.

[2] *pinked* Adorned; *varnished* Embellished.

[3] *curious* Beautiful, skilfully made; *knot* Ornate garden.

[4] *true-love knot* Knotted cord symbolic of love, sometimes used
to commemorate weddings.

[5] *No Alexander's … divide* Reference to the legendary Gordian
knot, which was so complicated no one could untie it. According to
tradition, it was undone only by the Macedonian leader Alexander
the Great, who simply cut the knot apart.

[6] *slips* Cuttings of old plants for growing new plants.

 Soon knotted,° and a manly flower out *budded*
 break.[7]
15 And after it my branch again did knot
 Brought out another flower its sweet breathed mate.
 One knot gave one t'other the t'other's place.
 Whence checkling° smiles fought in *laughing*
 each others face.

 But oh! a glorious hand from glory came
20 Guarded with angels, soon did crop° *harvest*
 this flower[8]
 Which almost tore the root up of the same
 At that unlooked for, dolesome,° *woeful*
 darksome hour.
 In prayer to Christ perfumed it did ascend,
 And angels bright did it to heaven tend.
25 But pausing on't, this sweet perfumed my thought,
 Christ would in glory have a flower,
 choice,° prime, *high quality*
 And having choice, chose this my branch forth brought:
 Lord, take't. I thank thee, thou tak'st aught of mine,
 It is my pledge in glory, part of me
30 Is now in it, Lord, glorified with thee.

 But praying o'er my branch, my branch did sprout
 And bore another manly flower,[9] and gay
 And after that another, sweet brake out,
 The which the former hand soon got away.
35 But oh! the tortures, vomit, screechings, groans,
 And six weeks fever would pierce hearts like stones.[10]

 Griefe o're doth flow: & nature fault would finde
 Were not thy Will, my Spell Charm, Joy & Gem:
 That as I said, I say, take, Lord, they're thine.
40 I piecemeale pass to Glory bright in them.
 I joy, may I Sweet Flowers for Glory breed,
 Whether thou getst them green, or lets them Seed.
 —1939 (WRITTEN C. 1682)

[7] *manly flower out break* Taylor's son Samuel was born in 1675
and survived into adulthood.

[8] *crop this flower* Taylor's daughter Elizabeth died in 1677, just
before her first birthday.

[9] *another manly flower* Taylor's son James was born in 1678. He
lived into adulthood.

[10] *But oh … stones* Taylor's fourth child Abigail died in 1682 at age
one.

—original spelling—

Sor Juana Inés de la Cruz

1648 – 1695

During the latter decades of the seventeenth century, Sor Juana Inés de la Cruz, a Hieronymite nun based in Mexico City, was among the best-known writers in the Spanish-speaking world. Her poetry and plays, on themes ranging from the religious to the secular, were read and performed at the courts in both New Spain and Madrid. Though her status as a woman writer certainly invoked criticism from conservative religious leaders, for much of her career her work was overwhelmingly well-received, and Sor Juana herself was praised as the "Tenth Muse of America."

Juana Inés Ramírez was born in the village of San Miguel Nepantla in 1648, the daughter of unmarried parents; baptised as a "daughter of the Church," she went by her mother's surname and was brought up by her mother and various wealthier maternal relatives. Extremely precocious as a child, Juana claimed in her autobiographical writings to have learned to read and write at the age of three. Different historical sources conflict as to the order of events, but it is clear that as a child she read voraciously from her grandfather's substantial library, that she mastered Latin at a young age, and that around the age of eight or ten she was sent to the viceregal court in Mexico City, where she astonished the high society with her wit, intellectual avidity, and vivacious personality, and where she wrote her first poems. It was during this period that she was introduced to the New Spanish vicereine, Leonor Carreto, and later to her successor, María Luisa Manrique de Lara Y Gonzaga—both of whom would become important patrons of Juana's writing. Sor Juana, who wrote love poetry with both male and female subjects, dedicated several passionate lyrics to María Luisa.

Given her apparently rich life at court—and lack of any particularly strong religious inclination—Juana's choice to enter the monastic life may seem puzzling. It is worth noting, however, that the Catholic convents of New Spain were a common refuge for young women who were either unwilling or unable to marry. In 1667 Juana entered the Discalced Carmelite order as a novice, but found the lifestyle there far too austere, and left after only three months. Two years later, however, she joined the Convent of Santa Paula (later San Jéronimo), which was known for its comparative leniency in the enforcement of rules. Here she lived for the remaining twenty-six years of her life, taking on the name Sor (Sister) Juana Inés de la Cruz (of the Cross).

Though officially cloistered from the outside, secular world, in reality the convent allowed its members a large degree of connectedness to the Mexican metropolis, as well as a greater amount of independence than would have been available to them as either married or unmarried laywomen. The nuns were accorded private cells, often consisting of several rooms, were allowed to acquire personal possessions such as jewelry and books, and were often given paid work; Sor Juana, for instance, was employed as the convent's accounts keeper. Though they were expected to adhere to a regular schedule of prayer and to participate in some communal meals and needlework sessions, they were also permitted to spend much of their time alone, and to receive visitors in the convent's outer parlor. Many of the sisters had personal servants, and Sor Juana herself owned at least one enslaved maidservant during her time at the convent. During her apparently ample personal time, Sor Juana studied the sciences, mathematics, philosophy, architecture, music theory, theology, and literature, over the years amassing one of the largest private libraries in the colonial Americas. Perhaps most significantly, she kept up a vibrant correspondence with the outside world, including with several New Spanish viceroyals, who corresponded with her both from New Spain and from the court at Madrid.

Throughout the 1680s, Sor Juana took advantage of her close personal connection to New Spain's colonial nobility, and her literary writings became highly sought after at the Mexican court. Her writings included plays, various forms of secular and religious song to be performed at courtly ceremonies and religious services, odes in honor of important personages or public occasions, and lyric poems—many of them dealing with romantic themes. Her work reflects mastery of a Baroque Mexican literary aesthetic, which includes highly ornate, often exaggerative language, intricate metaphors, and copious references to classical literature and philosophy; some of her villancicos (poetic compositions sung during religious services) also incorporate the Indigenous Nahuatl language. Though her works show the influence of eminent Spanish Baroque poets such as Luis de Góngora, poems such as her epic *First Dream* (first published 1692) have also been likened by recent scholars to the works of much-later symbolist poets such as Stéphane Mallarmé and modernist poets such as T.S. Eliot; *First Dream*, a mythologically inspired, gender-fluid depiction of a soul's pursuit of intellectual knowledge, has also been extensively analyzed for its resonances with later feminist thought.

Little evidence has survived to indicate a first date of composition for many of Sor Juana's works. A first volume of her poetry was published in Spain in 1689 as *The Overflowing of the Castalian Spring, by the Tenth Muse of America* (the "Castalian Spring" refers to a fountain in Greek mythology said to inspire poetic genius). Two more volumes would follow, with the *Second Volume of Her Works* published in Seville in 1692 and *Fame and Posthumous Works of the Mexican Phoenix* in Madrid in 1700. Sor Juana's name became mired in controversy near the end of 1690, when her tract criticizing a sermon by venerated Portuguese Jesuit António Vieira was published without her consent. The document raised the ire of a number of religious authority figures, who began to pressure her to desist from her literary and intellectual interests. It is unclear whether Sor Juana continued to write after 1691; she fell into relative obscurity until her death during an epidemic in 1695.

Over the following two centuries, Sor Juana was largely ignored by scholars and readers; no volumes of her poetry were re-issued between 1725 and 1940. Interest in her oeuvre was reignited in the mid-twentieth century, especially after the publication of Mexican poet Octavio Paz's influential biography *Sor Juana, or The Traps of Faith* in 1982. Since then, her poetry has been extensively studied by both Mexican and international scholars, and Sor Juana has become regarded once again as one of the most important figures of seventeenth-century colonial literature.

NOTE ON THE TEXTS: The English-language texts presented below are based upon those appearing in Alan S. Trueblood's edition, *A Sor Juana Anthology* (1988), whose translations are in turn based on the Spanish versions appearing in *Obras selectas* (Georgina Sabat de Rivers and Elias L. Rivers, 1976) and *Obras completas* (Alfonso Méndez Plancarte, 1952 and 1955). Trueblood's in-line biblical citations (in the *Reply to Sor Philothea*) have not been retained, although biblical references are noted in footnotes where relevant, in accordance with the practices of this anthology; Trueblood's in-line translations of Latin material quoted by Sor Juana have been moved to the footnotes. The Spanish-language poem presented here is based on the version first published in *Inundacion Castalida de la Unica Poetisa, Musa Dezima, Soror Juana Inés de la Cruz* (1689). The spelling and punctuation of the Spanish have not been modernized.

⌘ ⌘ ⌘

82

Expressa su respecto amoroso, y dize el sentido en que llama suya, à la Señora Virreyna.

Divina Lysi mía:
 perdona, si me atrevo,
à llamarte assi, quando
aun, de ser tuya, el nombre no merezco.
5 A èsto, no osadia
 es llamarte assi; puesto,
 que à ti te sobran rayos,
 si en mi pudiera aver atrevimientos.
Error es de la lengua;
10 que lo que dize Imperio
 del dueño, en el dominio,
 parezcan possessiones, en el siervo.
Mi Rey, dize el Vassallo,
 mi Carcel, dize el preso,
15 y el mas humilde Esclavo,
 sin agraviarlo, llama suyo, al dueño.
Assi, quando yo mia,
 te llamo, no pretendo,
 que juzguen, que eres mia,
20 sino solo, que yo ser tuya, quiero.
Yo te vi; pero basta,
 que à publicar incendios,
 basta apuntar la causa;
 sin añadir la culpa del efecto.
25 Que mirarte tan alta,
 no impide à mi denuedo;
 que no ay Deidad segura
 al altivo volar del pensamiento.
Y aunque otras más merezcan;
30 en distancia del Cielo,
 lo mismo dista el valle
 mas humilde, que el monte más sobervio.
En fin yo de adorarte
 el delito confiesso;
35 si quieres castigarme,
 esse mismo castigo serà premio.
 —1689

82

She expresses her loving respect, explaining what she means when she says Her Ladyship the Vicereine, Marquise de la Laguna, belongs to her[1]

My divine Lysis:
 do forgive my darling,
if so I address you,
unworthy though I am to be known as yours.
5 I cannot think it bold
to call you so, well knowing
you've ample thunderbolts
to shatter any overweening[2] of mine.
 It's the tongue that misspeaks
10 when what is called dominion—
I mean, the master's rule—
is made to seem possession by the slave.
 The vassal says: my king;
my prison, the convict says;
15 and any humble slave
will call the master his without offense.
 Thus, when I call you mine,
it's not that I expect
you'll be considered such—
20 only that I hope I may be yours.
 I saw you—need more be said?
To broadcast a fire,
telling the cause suffices—
no need to apportion blame for the effect.
25 Seeing you so exalted
does not prevent my daring;
no god is ever secure
against the lofty flight of human thought.
 There are women more deserving,
30 yet in distance from heaven
the humblest of valleys
seems no farther than the highest peak.
 In sum, I must admit
to the crime of adoring you;
35 should you wish to punish me,
the very punishment will be reward.
 —1988

[1] *She expresses … to her* These headings were included in the first editions of Sor Juana's collected works; scholars are unsure as to who wrote them.

[2] *overweening* Presumptuousness.

92

She demonstrates the inconsistency of men's wishes in blaming
women for what they themselves have caused

Silly, you men—so very adept
 at wrongly faulting womankind,
not seeing you're alone to blame
for faults you plant in woman's mind.

5 After you've won by urgent plea
the right to tarnish her good name,
you will expect her to behave—
you, that coaxed her into shame.

You batter her resistance down
10 and then, all righteousness, proclaim
that feminine frivolity,
not your persistence, is to blame.

When it comes to bravely posturing,
your witlessness must take the prize:
15 you're the child that makes a bogeyman,
and then recoils in fear and cries.

Presumptuous beyond belief,
you'd have the woman you pursue
be Thais[1] when you're courting her,
20 Lucretia[2] once she falls to you.

For plain default of common sense,
could any action be so queer
as oneself to cloud the mirror,
then complain that it's not clear?

25 Whether you're favored or disdained,
nothing can leave you satisfied.
You whimper if you're turned away,
you sneer if you've been gratified.

With you, no woman can hope to score;
30 whichever way, she's bound to lose;
spurning you, she's ungrateful;
succumbing, you call her lewd.

Your folly is always the same:
you apply a single rule

35 to the one you accuse of looseness
and the one you brand as cruel.

What happy mean could there be
for the woman who catches your eye,
if, unresponsive, she offends
40 yet whose complaisance you decry?

Still, whether it's torment or anger—
and both ways you've yourselves to blame—
God bless the woman who won't have you,
no matter how loud you complain.

45 It's your persistent entreaties
that change her from timid to bold.
Having made her thereby naughty,
you would have her good as gold.

So where does the greater guilt lie
50 for a passion that should not be:
with the man who pleads out of baseness
or the woman debased by his plea?

Or which is more to be blamed—
though both will have cause for chagrin:
55 the woman who sins for money
or the man who pays money to sin?

So why are you men all so stunned
at the thought you're all guilty alike?
Either like them for what you've made them
60 or make of them what you can like.

If you'd give up pursuing them,
you'd discover, without a doubt,
you've a stronger case to make
against those who seek you out.

65 I well know what powerful arms
you wield in pressing for evil:
your arrogance is allied
with the world, the flesh, and the devil!

—1689 (TRANSLATION 1988)

1 *Thais* Ancient Greek courtesan (c. 4th century BCE) who fol-
lowed the troops of Alexander the Great during his conquests. She
was known as a lover of one of Alexander's generals and possibly of
Alexander himself.

2 *Lucretia* Ancient Roman noblewoman (c. 6th century BCE)
who is said to have been raped by Sextus Tarquinus, the son of the
last king of Rome, and to have subsequently died by suicide.

165

Which contains a fantasy satisfied with a love befitting it

Semblance of my elusive love, hold still—
image of a bewitchment fondly cherished,
lovely fiction that robs my heart of joy,
fair mirage that makes it joy to perish.
5 Since already my breast, like willing iron,
yields to the powerful magnet of your charms,
why must you so flatteringly allure me,
then slip away and cheat my eager arms?
 Even so, you shan't boast, self-satisfied,
10 that your tyranny has triumphed over me,
evade as you will arms opening wide,
 all but encircling your phantasmal[1] form:
in vain shall you elude my fruitless clasp,
for fantasy holds you captive in its grasp.
—1692 (TRANSLATION 1988)

from the *Reply to Sor Philothea*

In November 1690, Sor Juana wrote a letter addressed
to her friend and confessor, Manuel Fernández de
Santa Cruz, Bishop of Tlaxcala, offering her com-
mentary on a sermon given in the mid-seventeenth
century by venerated Portuguese Jesuit António
Vieira. Sor Juana disagreed with Vieira on his inter-
pretation of John 13, a chapter of the New Testament
in which Christ washes the feet of his disciples and
then gives them a new commandment: "That ye love
one another; as I have loved you, that ye also love
one another." Her letter became controversial—less
so because of the unorthodoxy of her argument than
because of her boldness in daring to question the
theological arguments of a male religious superior.
 Juana's letter appeared in print in Puebla at the
end of November, published without her consent
by someone identifying as "Sor Philothea"—in real-
ity, Sor Juana's confessor Fernández. In a prefatory
"admonishment,"[2] Philothea expresses admiration
for Juana's intelligence, but nonetheless censures

what she presents as Juana's impious and unfeminine
willingness to opine on both religious and secular
subjects. A few months later, Juana published her
own reply to Philothea, excerpted here, in which she
vigorously defends her right as a woman to pursue
both worldly and spiritual knowledge.

My most illustrious Lady: …

Coming down to particulars, I confess to you,
with the ingenuousness[3] owed to you and the
truth and clarity natural and habitual with me, that
my not having written much on sacred subjects is not
from disinclination or lack of application, but from
an excess of the awe and reverence due those Sacred
Letters, for the understanding of which I acknowledge
myself so ill-equipped and which I am so unworthy
to treat. There ever resounds in my ears, with no little
dread, our Lord's threat and interdiction to sinners
like me: *Quare tu enarras iustitias meas, et assumis tes-
tamentum meum per os tuum?*[4] This question and the
awareness that even to learned men the reading of the
Canticle of Canticles[5] was forbidden until they were
over thirty, and that of Genesis as well, the latter on
account of its obscurity, the former lest the appeal of
those epithalamiums[6] give imprudent youth cause to
apply their sense to carnal affections. My great father
Saint Jerome confirms this, requiring that the former
be the last thing studied, for the same reason, *At ulti-
mum sine periculo discat Canticum Canticorum, ne si
in exordio legerit, sub carnalibus verbis spiritualium
Nuptiarum Epithalamium non intelligens, vulneretur.*[7]

1 *phantasmal* Imaginary or immaterial

2 See the website component of this anthology for selections from
the admonishment.

3 *ingenuousness* Openness; sincerity.

4 *Quare tu … os tuum?* God's words to the wicked in Psalm
50.16, quoted here from the Latin Vulgate: "What hast thou to do to
declare my statutes, or that thou shouldest take my covenant in thy
mouth?"

5 *the Canticle of Canticles* Book of the Old Testament better
known as the Song of Solomon or the Song of Songs. A poetic cel-
ebration of romantic and erotic love, it is notable for being the only
book of the Old Testament that gives virtually no explicit attention
to religious matters—though some Christian and Jewish scholars
read it as an allegory of Christ's or God's love for humanity.

6 *epithalamiums* Marriage songs.

7 *At ultimum … vulneretur* Latin: "But last of all, let her,
without risk, study the Canticle of Canticles; lest she suffer harm
by reading it at the outset without grasping the epithalamium of

And Seneca says: *Teneris in annis haut clara est fides*.[1] Then how should I dare to take this into my unworthy hands, when my sex, age, and especially my way of life all oppose it? And so I confess that many times this fear has taken the pen from my hand and caused the subject to sink back into the very mind from which it sought to emerge.

I encountered no such problem in secular subjects, since heresy against art is punished, not by the Holy Office, but by the laughter of the intelligent and the censure of the critical. The censure, *iusta vel iniusta, timenda non est*,[2] for it does not interfere with communion and attending mass, whence it concerns me little or not at all. For, in the opinion of the very people who slander me for writing, I am under no obligation to be learned nor do I possess the capacity never to err. Therefore my failure involves neither fault nor discredit: no fault since there is no chance of my not erring and *ad impossibilia nemo tenetur*.[3] And in truth I have never written except when pressured and forced to and then only to please others and even then not only without enjoyment but with actual repugnance because I have never thought of myself as possessing the intelligence and educational background required of a writer. Hence my usual reply to those who urge me on, especially where sacred matters are involved: what aptitude have I, what preparation, what subjects, what familiarity do I possess for such a task, beyond a handful of superficial sophistries?[4] Let such things be

left to those who understand them; I want no trouble with the Holy Office. I am ignorant and I shudder to think that I might utter some disreputable proposition or distort the proper understanding of some passage or other. My purpose in studying is not to write, much less to teach (this would be overbearing pride in my case), but simply to see whether studying makes me less ignorant. This is my reply and these are my feelings.

I have never written of my own accord, but only when pressured by others. I could truthfully say to them: *Vos me coegistis*.[5] What is true and I will not deny (first because it is public knowledge and then—even if this counts against me—because God, in His goodness, has favored me with a great love of the truth) is that from my first glimmers of reason, my inclination to letters was of such power and vehemence, that neither the reprimands of others—and I have received many—nor my own considerations—and there have been not a few of these—have succeeded in making me abandon this natural impulse which God has implanted in me—only His Majesty knows why and wherefore and His Majesty also knows that I have prayed to Him to extinguish the light of my mind, only leaving sufficient to keep His Law, since any more is overmuch, so some say, in a woman, and there are even those who say it is harmful. His Majesty also knows that, not succeeding in this, I have tried to inter[6] my name along with my mind and sacrifice it to Him alone who gave it to me; and that this was precisely my motivation in taking the veil, even though the exercises and shared life which a community entails were repellent to the independence and tranquillity which my inclination to study needed. And once in the community, the Lord God knows and, in the world, he knows who alone had the right to know it, how hard I tried to conceal my name, and that he did not allow this, saying that it was temptation, which no doubt it was.[7] If I could repay you some part of what I owe you, my Lady, I think I would be paying you simply by relating this, for it has never escaped

spiritual marriage beneath the carnal words" (Trueblood). The quotation is from the *Epistle to Laeta*, a letter from Saint Jerome to one of his female followers, who had sought his advice on how to raise her daughter in Rome as a virgin consecrated to Christ. The Hieronymite Order, of which Sor Juana was a member, is modeled after the life of Saint Jerome.

[1] *Teneris in … est fides* Latin: "Faith is not clearly defined in youth" (Trueblood). The quotation is from the tragedy *Octavia*, often attributed to the Roman philosopher and playwright Seneca the Younger.

[2] *iusta vel … non est* Latin: "whether deserved or not, is not to be feared" (Trueblood). This may play on a commonly quoted Latin statement that translates to "the judgment of a pastor, whether deserved or not, is to be feared." See Pope Gregory I, *Homilia in Evangelia* (591–92).

[3] *ad impossibilia nemo tenetur* Latin: "no one is obliged to attempt the impossible" (Trueblood)—a maxim capturing a principle in ancient Roman law.

[4] *sophistries* Convincing but fallacious or shallow arguments.

[5] *Vos me coegistis* Latin: "You have compelled me" (Trueblood). See 2 Corinthians 12.11: "I am become a fool in glorying; ye have compelled me: for I ought to have been commended of you: for in nothing am I behind the very chiefest apostles, though I be nothing."

[6] *inter* Bury.

[7] [Translator's note] A probable allusion to her confessor, Antonio Núñez de Miranda, S.J.

my lips before, except when addressed to one who had the right to know it. But I want you to know that, in throwing wide open to you the gates of my heart, exposing to your gaze its most tightly guarded secrets, my justification for the liberty I am taking is the great debt I owe to your venerable person and overly generous favors.

To go on with the account of this strong bent of mine, about which I want you to be fully informed, let me say that when I was not yet three, my mother sent a sister of mine, older than I, to learn to read in one of those establishments called *Amigas*,[1] at which point affection and mischievousness on my part led me to follow her. Seeing that she was being given lessons, I became so inflamed with the desire to learn to read, that I tricked the mistress—or so I thought—by telling her that my mother had directed her to give me lessons. This was not believable and she did not believe me, but falling in with my little trick, she did give me lessons. I continued attending and she went on teaching me, no longer as a joke, since the event opened her eyes. I learned to read in so short a time that I already knew how when my mother found out, for the mistress kept it from her in order to give her a pleasant surprise and receive her recompense all at one time. I kept still, since I thought I would be whipped for having acted on my own initiative. The person who taught me is still alive (may God preserve her) and can attest to this.

I remember that at this period, though I loved to eat, as children do at that age, I refrained from eating cheese, because someone had told me it made you stupid, and my urge to learn was stronger than my wish to eat, powerful as this is in children. Afterward, when I was six or seven and already knew how to read and write, along with all the sewing skills and needlework that women learn, I discovered that in the City of Mexico there was a university with schools where the different branches of learning could be studied, and as soon as I learned this I began to deluge my mother with urgent and insistent pleas to change my manner of dress and send me to stay with relatives in the City of Mexico so that I might study and take courses at the university. She refused, and rightly so; nevertheless, I found a way to read many different books my grandfather owned, notwithstanding the punishments and

reproofs this entailed, so that when I went to the City of Mexico people were astonished, not so much at my intelligence as at the memory and store of knowledge I had at an age at which it would seem I scarcely had time to learn to speak.

I began to study Latin, in which I do not believe I had twenty lessons in all, and I was so intensely studious that despite the natural concern of women—especially in the flower of their youth—with dressing their hair, I used to cut four or five fingers' width from mine, keeping track of how far it had formerly reached, and making it my rule that if by the time it grew back to that point, I did not know such-and-such a thing which I had set out to learn as it grew, I would cut it again as a penalty for my dullness. Thus it would happen that it would grow back and I still would not know what I had set myself to learn, because my hair grew rapidly, whereas I was a slow learner, and I did indeed cut it as a punishment for my slowness, for I did not consider it right that a head so bare of knowledge should be dressed with hair, knowledge being the more desirable ornament. I became a nun because, although I knew that the way of life involved much that was repellent to my nature—I refer to its incidental, not its central aspects—nevertheless, given my total disinclination to marriage, it was the least unreasonable and most becoming choice I could make to assure my ardently desired salvation. To which first consideration, as most important, all the other small frivolities of my nature yielded and gave way, such as my wish to live alone, to have no fixed occupation which might curtail my freedom to study, nor the noise of a community to interfere with the tranquil stillness of my books. This made me hesitate a little before making up my mind, until, enlightened by learned persons that hesitation was temptation, I overcame it by the grace of God and entered upon the life I now pursue so unworthily. I thought I was escaping from myself, but, alas for me, I had brought myself along. In this propensity I brought my greatest enemy, given me by Heaven whether as a boon or a punishment I cannot decide, for, far from dying out or being hindered by all the exercises religion entails, it exploded like gunpowder. *Privatio est causa appetitus*[2] had its confirmation in me.

1 *Amigas* Latin: "girls' elementary schools" (Trueblood).

2 *Privatio est causa appetitus* Latin: "Privation arouses the appetite" (Trueblood).

I went back (I misspeak: I had never stopped); I went on with the studious pursuit (in which I found relaxation during all the free time remaining from my obligations) of reading and more reading, study and more study, with no other teacher than books themselves. One can readily imagine how hard it is to study from those lifeless letters, lacking a teacher's live voice and explanations. Still I happily put up with all those drawbacks, for the sheer love of learning. Oh, if it had only been for the love of God, which would have been the sound way, what merit would have been mine! I *will* say that I tried to uplift my study as much as I could and direct it to serving Him, since the goal I aspired to was the study of theology, it seeming to me a mean sort of ineptitude for a Catholic not to know all that can be found out in this life through natural means concerning divine mysteries. I also felt that being a nun and not a lay person, I should, because of my ecclesiastical status, make a profession of letters— and furthermore that, as a daughter of Saint Jerome and Saint Paula,[1] it would be a great disservice for the daughter of such learned parents to be a fool. This is what I took upon myself, and it seemed right to do so, unless of course—and this is probably the case—it was simply a way of flattering and applauding my own natural tendency, proposing its own pleasure to it as an obligation.

In this way I went on, continually directing the course of my study, as I have said, toward the eminence of sacred theology. To reach this goal, I considered it necessary to ascend the steps of human arts and sciences, for how can one who has not mastered the style of the ancillary[2] branches of learning hope to understand that of the queen of them all? How, lacking logic, was I to understand the general and specific methodologies of which Holy Scripture is composed? How, without rhetoric, could I understand its figures, tropes, and locutions? How, without physics, all the natural questions concerning the nature of sacrificial animals, which symbolize so many things already explicated, and so many others? How, whether Saul's

being cured by the sound of David's harp[3] came about by virtue of the natural power of music, or through supernatural powers which God was pleased to bestow on David? How, lacking arithmetic, could one understand such mysterious computations of years, days, months, hours, weeks, as those of Daniel[4] and others, for the intelligence of which one needs to know the natures, concordances, and properties of numbers? How, without geometry, could one measure the sacred ark of the covenant[5] and the holy city of Jerusalem, whose mysterious measurements form a cube in all its dimensions, and the marvelous proportional distribution of all its parts?[6] How, without a knowledge of architecture, is one to understand Solomon's great temple,[7] of which God Himself was the artificer who provided the arrangement and layout, the wise king being only the overseer who carried it out? In it, no column's base was without its mystery, no column without its symbolic sense, no cornice without allusiveness, no architrave without meaning, and so on with all its parts, not even the most miniscule fillet serving solely as support or complement to the design of the whole, but rather itself symbolizing greater things. How will one understand the historical books without a full knowledge of the principles and divisions of which history consists? Those recapitulations in the narrative which postpone what actually occurred first? How will

3 *Saul's being ... David's harp* See 1 Samuel 16.23: "And it came to pass, when the evil spirit from God was upon Saul, that David took an harp, and played with his hand: so Saul was refreshed, and was well, and the evil spirit departed from him." Saul, the first king of a united Israel, was succeeded to the throne by his son-in-law David, a talented musician.

4 *Daniel* Biblical prophet. The Book of Daniel includes numerous highly specific prophecies in which the durations of events are sometimes given in exact numbers of days.

5 *ark of the covenant* Gold-plated chest said to house the stone tablets upon which the Ten Commandments are written. Its exact dimensions are specified in Genesis 6.15.

6 *the holy city ... its parts* Revelation 21 provides a detailed description of the holy city of New Jerusalem, which includes its measurements: "And the city lieth foursquare, and the length is as large as the breadth: and he measured the city with the reed, twelve thousand furlongs. The length and the breadth and the height of it are equal" (Revelation 21.16).

7 *Solomon's great temple* Holy Temple in ancient Jerusalem said to have been constructed by Solomon, king of Israel. The temple's measurements and features are outlined in 2 Chronicles 3–4.

1 *Saint Paula* Follower of Saint Jerome, who joined Jerome in Bethlehem with her two daughters and established the Hieronymite convent to which Sor Juana's convent traced its origins (347–404).

2 *ancillary* Subservient; supporting.

334 SOR JUANA INÉS DE LA CRUZ

one understand the legal books without a complete acquaintance with both codes of law? How, without a great deal of erudition, all the matters of secular history mentioned in Holy Writ, all the customs of the Gentiles, the rites of the ways of speaking? How, without many rules and much reading of the Church Fathers, will one be able to understand the prophets' obscure forms of expression? And how, unless one is thoroughly versed in music, will one understand those musical proportions, with all their fine points, found in so many passages, especially in Abraham's petitions to God for the cities, asking whether He would forgive them, providing there were fifty righteous men, from which number he went down to forty-five, which is the *sesquinone* and is as from *mi* to *re*: thence to forty, which is the *sesquioctave* and as from *re* to *mi*; thence to thirty, which is the *sesquitierce*, or the proportion of the *Diatessaron*; thence to twenty, which is the *sesquialter*, or that of the *diapente*; thence to ten, which is the *duple*, or *diapason*—and went no further, there being no other harmonic proportions.[1] Now, how is this to be understood without music? …

… I confess that I am far removed from wisdom's confines and that I have wished to pursue it, though *a longe*.[2] But the sole result has been to draw me closer to the flames of persecution, the crucible of torture, and this has even gone so far as a formal request that study be forbidden me.

This was successful in one instance involving a very holy and very ingenuous prelate who thought studying was something for the Inquisition[3] and ordered me to cease. I obeyed her (for the three months her right to

so order me lasted) as regarded not taking a book in hand, but as to ceasing study altogether, it not being in my power, I could not carry it out. For, although I did not study from books, I did from everything God has created, all of it being my letters, and all this universal chain of being my book. I saw nothing without reflecting on it; I heard nothing without wondering at it—not even the tiniest, most material thing. For, as there is no created thing, no matter how lowly, in which one cannot recognize the *me fecit Deus*,[4] there is none that does not confound the mind once it stops to consider it. Thus, I repeat, I looked and marveled at all of them, so much so that simply from the person with whom I spoke, and from what that person said to me, countless reflections arose in my mind. What could be the origin of so great a variety of characters and minds, when all belonged to one species? Which humors and hidden qualities could bring this about? If I saw a figure, I at once fell to working out the relationship of its lines, measuring it with my mind and recasting it along different ones. Sometimes I would walk back and forth across the front of a sleeping-room of ours—a very large one—and observe how, though the lines of its two sides were parallel and its ceiling horizontal, one's vision made it appear as if the lines inclined toward each other and the ceiling were lower at the far end, from which I inferred that visual lines run straight but not parallel, tending rather toward a pyramidal figure. And I asked myself whether this could be the reason the ancients questioned whether the world was spherical or not. Because, although it appears to be, this could be an optical illusion, and show concavities where there might in fact be none.

This type of observation would occur to me about everything and still does, without my having any say in the matter; indeed, it continually irritates me because it tires my mind. I thought the same thing occurred in everyone's case, and with writing verse as well, until experience proved me wrong. This turn, or habit, of mind is so strong that I can look upon nothing without reflecting on it. Two little girls were playing with a top in my presence. The moment I saw its movement and form, I began, in my crazy way, to consider the easy motion of the spherical form, and how, the impulse once given, it continued independently of its

[1] *Abraham's petitions … harmonic proportions* In Genesis 18, God declares he will destroy the cities of Sodom and Gomorrah, whose inhabitants have been sinful. Abraham petitions God to save the righteous inhabitants, asking, "Peradventure there be fifty righteous within the city: wilt thou also destroy and not spare the place for the fifty righteous that are therein?"; when God agrees, Abraham gradually lowers the number of righteous inhabitants as Sor Juana describes. Sor Juana applies Pythagorean musical theory, popularized by Italian music theorist Pietro Cerone (1566–1625), to her interpretation of the narrative.

[2] *a longe* Latin: from afar.

[3] *something for the Inquisition* I.e., a matter of concern to be brought up before the Inquisition—a group of institutions, established by the Catholic Church during the Middle Ages and greatly expanded by the seventeenth century, designed to combat various kinds of heresy.

[4] *me fecit Deus* Latin: "God made me" (Trueblood).

cause, since at a distance from the girl's hand, which originated the motion, the top went on dancing. Nor was this enough for me. I had flour brought and sifted, so as to tell, when the top danced over it, whether the circles its motion described were perfect or not. I discovered that they were simply spirals which moved farther and farther from the circular in proportion as the impulse wore down. Other girls were playing with pins—childhood's most frivolous game. I would approach and observe the shapes the pins took, and on noticing that three chanced to form a triangle, I would set about actually connecting them, recalling that this was the shape the mysterious ring of Solomon was said to have taken—that ring on which there were distant glimmerings and depictions of the Most Holy Trinity,[1] by virtue of which it worked such prodigious and marvelous things. This was also said to be the shape of David's harp, for which reason Saul was said to have been cured by its sound. The harps of our day have retained the same shape.

What could I not tell you, my Lady, of the secrets of Nature which I have discovered in cooking! That an egg hangs together and fries in fat or oil, and that, on the contrary, it disintegrates in syrup. That, to keep sugar liquid, it suffices to add the tiniest part of water in which a quince or some other tart fruit has been. That the yolk and white of the same egg are so different in nature, that when eggs are used with sugar, the yolks must be used separately from the whites, never together with them. I do not wish to tire you with such trivia, which I relate only to give you a full picture of my native turn of mind, which will, no doubt, make you laugh. But, Madam, what is there for us women to know, if not bits of kitchen philosophy? As Lupercio Leonardo said: One can perfectly well philosophize while cooking supper.[2] And I am always saying, when I observe these small details: If Aristotle[3] had been a cook, he would have written much more.

But to continue with the workings of my mind, let me say that this line of thought is so constant with me that I have no need of books. On one occasion, when, owing to some serious stomach trouble, the doctor forbade my studying, I obeyed for several days, but then I pointed out that allowing me books would be much less harmful, since my mental activity was so vigorous, so vehement, that it used up more spirits in a quarter of an hour than studying from books did in four days. So they agreed reluctantly to allow me to read. And not only that, my Lady: even my sleep was not free from this constant activity of my brain. In fact, it seems to go on during sleep with all the more freedom and lack of restraint, putting together the separate images it has carried over from waking hours with greater clarity and tranquility, debating with itself, composing verses, of which I could draw up a whole catalogue for you, including certain thoughts and subtleties I have arrived at more easily while asleep than while awake, which I won't go into, not wishing to bore you. What has been said suffices for your own acumen and high-mindedness to grasp with clarity and full understanding my native disposition of mind and the origin, methods, and present state of my studies.

Even if these studies were to be viewed, my Lady, as to one's credit (as I see they are indeed celebrated in men), none would be due me, since I pursue them involuntarily. If they are seen as reprehensible, for the same reason I do not think I should be blamed. Still, though, I am so unsure of myself, that neither in this nor in anything do I trust my own judgment. Hence I leave the decision up to your supreme talent, and will abide by whatever it decrees, with no antagonism and no reluctance, for this has been nothing more than a simple account of my inclination to letters. ...

—1691 (TRANSLATION 1988)

[1] *mysterious ring ... Most Holy Trinity* Likely a reference to the Seal of Solomon, a signet ring said to have been possessed by King Solomon, and to have given him the power to command spirits and communicate with animals; the seal is often depicted in the shape of a six-pointed star.

[2] [Translator's note] The Aragonese poet Bartolomé Leonardo de Argensola (1562–1631), not his brother Lupercio, is the source of the saying ("First Satire," lines 143–44).

[3] *Aristotle* Greek philosopher (384–322 BCE).

COTTON MATHER
1663 – 1728

Puritan minister and intellectual Cotton Mather is often vilified as a repressive fanatic responsible for the deadly moral panic known as the Salem witch trials. But the real Mather was far more complex: while he was the key spokesperson for the trials' legitimacy, his earlier work advocated the sympathetic treatment of witches; in addition to his religious studies he was a popularizer of scientific advances and, for his accomplishments in the sciences, was made a fellow of the Royal Society; he argued strenuously in support of gender hierarchy, class divisions, and slavery, but he also asserted the potential equality of all souls. Some American historians have viewed Mather's work as expressing the last gasp of Puritan dominance in New England, while others have seen him as a participant in a cultural shift, transforming older religious ideas into a form that could be carried forward into the eighteenth century.

Born in Boston, the capital of the Massachusetts Bay Colony, Cotton Mather was the son of the spiritual leader Increase Mather, and the grandson of Richard Mather and John Cotton, Puritan clerics who were instrumental in the colony's foundation. A gifted child, Mather enrolled in Harvard (where his father was president) at age eleven, the youngest person to be admitted to the college. Mather firmly believed that his parentage obliged him to accomplish great things; he also, like many Puritans, believed in the Calvinist doctrine that he—like all humans—was a depraved creature who deserved any suffering he experienced. Mather's classmates found his piety insufferable, and he was frequently subjected to physical violence from his peers. For much of his youth, Mather worked to overcome a stutter that threatened to prevent him from becoming a minister.

Mather applied himself to his studies, and he graduated from Harvard in 1678 with an education in Latin, Greek, and Hebrew, having read deeply across the sciences and humanities. He continued to expand his knowledge throughout his life; in addition to accessing his father's library and the Harvard library, he would come to own more than three thousand books, forming one of the largest personal libraries in America. Writing in an ornate, allusive writing style more common to writers of the sixteenth century, he published almost four hundred books and pamphlets over his lifetime—by some estimates, more than the output of all other New England ministers combined. Of these, his most celebrated work during his lifetime was the *Magnalia Christi Americana* (1702), a religious history of seventeenth-century New England. At the same time, he spent decades of his life working on his *Biblia Americana*, a sprawling work of biblical commentary that totaled forty-five hundred manuscript pages at the time of his death; largely because of its size and complexity, this work remained unpublished until the twenty-first century.

In 1685, Mather was ordained as pastor of North Boston Church, the same post once held by his father. Massachusetts was in the midst of major cultural and political changes: in the 1680s, the English government revoked the Massachusetts Bay Colony's charter, a move that destabilized the power of the Puritan ruling class Mather belonged to. At the same time, the dogmatically religious society that the Puritans had established was giving way to a more secular and rationalistic culture. Mather's preaching called upon individuals to deepen their relationships with God and come to see, as Mather and other Puritans did, the divine and the demonic as fully entangled with everyday life. In one typical sermon, he encouraged Christians to feel the warmth of God's love, saying, "There is nothing that will bring you so near Heaven, or help you lead a Heavenly life, as to keep alive a comfortable persuasion … that God your savior has loved you." Mather also undertook many community projects, including extensive efforts to convert the enslaved people of Boston to Christianity. He put forward his ideas regarding the importance

of good works in the widely read book *Bonifacius, or Essays to Do Good* (1710)—a work Benjamin Franklin would later satirize through his writing persona "Silence Dogood," but which he would also come to credit with inspiring his own desire to be "a useful citizen."

Mather's life took a dramatic turn in 1688, when a family was afflicted by what Boston's spiritual and medical authorities considered a case of demonic possession. After an Irish Catholic washerwoman was held responsible and executed for witchcraft, Mather took it upon himself to care for one of the affected children. He undertook a study of her symptoms and published his findings in *Memorable Providences, Relating to Witchcrafts and Possessions* (1689). Widely read in England and America, the text established Mather as an expert on witchcraft and popularized the notion that the devil was at work in Massachusetts.

In 1692, reports of witchcraft emerged from Salem Village, and a special court was established to investigate the situation. In an ambiguous letter to the judges, Mather voiced support for the trial, but also urged caution. "[I]t is necessary that all proceedings thereabout be managed with an exceeding tenderness towards those that may be complained of," his letter declared, but he appeared to contradict this warning with the closing statement that "[n]evertheless, we cannot but humbly recommend unto the government, the speedy and vigorous prosecution" of witches. Mather's letter was either disregarded or taken as an endorsement of the proceedings: nineteen people were convicted and executed on spurious evidence, and one man was crushed to death when he refused to enter a plea. Mather was not present for the trials, but he may have attended at least one execution.

After the executions were carried out, Mather composed an account of events, *Wonders of the Invisible World* (1692), with the endorsement of the lieutenant governor, William Stoughton, one of the trials' fiercest judges. Though the book expresses occasional reservations regarding the trials, its overall thrust is to justify the proceedings and vindicate the judges' decisions. *Wonders of the Invisible World* would be followed by an outpouring of oppositional tracts, the most famous of which was Robert Calef's *More Wonders of the Invisible World* (1700). Calef, who appears to have hated Mather, accused him of "carrying both fire to increase, and water to quench, the conflagration." The portrait of Mather put forward in *More Wonders* helped to shape his popular image in later centuries as a figure of oppression and superstition.

Mather studied natural phenomena with the same experimental eye he used to study witchcraft. He was one of the strongest advocates for science and modern medicine in Massachusetts. In 1721, when Boston was struck by a smallpox epidemic, Mather publicly endorsed inoculation, a practice he had learned of from the Proceedings of the Royal Society (a prestigious scientific organization of which he was a fellow) as well as from Onesimus, an enslaved man he held for many years. Smallpox inoculation had long been practiced in parts of Africa, and was already spreading among black people in America, but Mather's endorsement persuaded hundreds of white Bostonians to undergo inoculation. (Many more, however, were not persuaded, and one opponent of inoculation attempted to bomb Mather's house.)

Mather died in 1728, survived by his third wife and only two of his fifteen children. His obituaries tended to praise him effusively, glossing over his involvement in the witch trials and other controversies; according to one publication, he was "perhaps the principal ornament of this country, and the greatest scholar that was ever bred in it." But by the nineteenth and twentieth centuries, Mather's reputation was overshadowed by his association with the executions at Salem. In popular culture, he was interpreted as a villain: in a series of Marvel comics, an evil "witch-slayer" bore his name. Today, academics are more likely to recognize Mather as a complex figure attempting to respond to large-scale changes in American religious and political life. Some contemporary scholars suggest that his personal, passionate approach to faith laid the groundwork for a new religious movement that would come to exercise a profound influence upon American culture and politics: evangelicalism.

———————————

NOTE ON THE TEXT: The text presented here is based on the original 1693 edition. Spelling and punctuation have been modernized in accordance with the practices of this anthology.

⌘ ⌘ ⌘

from *The Wonders of the Invisible World*

from ENCHANTMENTS ENCOUNTERED

The New-Englanders are a people of God settled in those which were once the Devil's territories; and it may easily be supposed that the Devil was exceedingly disturbed when he perceived such a people here accomplishing the promise of old made unto our blessed Jesus that He should have the utmost[1] parts of the earth for His possession. There was not a greater uproar among the Ephesians[2] when the gospel was first brought among them than there was among the powers of the air[3] (after whom those Ephesians walked) when first the silver trumpets of the gospel here made the joyful sound. The Devil, thus irritated, immediately tried all sorts of methods to overturn this poor plantation: and so much of the church as was fled into this wilderness immediately found the Serpent cast out of his mouth a flood[4] for the carrying of it away. I believe, that never were more satanical devices used for the unsettling of any people under the sun,[5] than what have been employed for the extirpation[6] of the vine which God has here planted, casting out the heathen, and preparing a room before it, and causing it to take deep root, and fill the land; so that it sent its boughs unto the Atlantic Sea eastward, and its branches unto the Connecticut River westward, and the hills were covered with the shadows thereof.[7] But

all those attempts of hell have hitherto been abortive, many an Ebenezer[8] has been erected unto the praise of God, by His poor people here; and, having obtained help from God, we continue to this Day.

Wherefore[9] the Devil is now making one attempt more upon us; an attempt more difficult, more surprising, more snarled with unintelligible circumstances than any that we have hitherto encountered; an attempt, so critical, that if we get well through, we shall soon enjoy halcyon days[10] with all the vultures of hell trodden under our feet. He has wanted his incarnate legions to persecute us, as the people of God have in the other hemisphere been persecuted: he has therefore drawn forth his more spiritual[11] ones to make an attack upon us. We have been advised, by some credible Christians yet alive, that a malefactor accused of witchcraft as well as murder, and executed in this place more than forty years ago, did then give notice of an horrible plot against the country by witchcraft, and a foundation of witchcraft then laid, which if it were not seasonably[12] discovered would probably blow up and pull down all the churches in the country.

And we have now with horror seen the discovery of such a witchcraft! An army of devils is horribly broke in upon the place which is the center and, after a sort, the first-born of our English settlements:[13] and the houses of the good people there are filled with the doleful shrieks of their children and servants, tormented by

[1] *utmost* Most remote.

[2] *Ephesians* Residents of the Ancient Greek city of Ephesus. A riot broke out during the apostle Paul's ministry in Ephesus when he denounced the goddess Diana, whom the majority of Ephesians worshipped. See Acts 19.23–41.

[3] *powers of the air* Diabolical forces. See Ephesians 2.2: "in time past ye walked according to the course of this world, according to the prince of the power of the air, the spirit that now worketh in the children of disobedience."

[4] *the Serpent* I.e., Satan; *the Serpent ... a flood* I.e., Satan unleashed a host of maladies to destroy the Christian settlements. See Revelation 12.15.

[5] *under the sun* Phrase used frequently in Ecclesiastes to refer to the worldly realm.

[6] *extirpation* Uprooting.

[7] *vine which ... thereof* See Psalm 80.8–11: "Thou hast brought a vine out of Egypt: thou hast cast out the heathen, and planted it.

Thou preparedst room before it, and didst cause it to take deep root, and it filled the land. The hills were covered with the shadow of it, and the boughs thereof were like the goodly cedars. She sent out her boughs unto the sea, and her branches unto the river."

[8] *Ebenezer* Hebrew: Stone of help. In 1 Samuel 7.12, the Israelite prophet Samuel erects a stone by this name to commemorate God's assistance in defeating the Philistines, enemies of the Israelites.

[9] *Wherefore* For this reason.

[10] *we shall ... days* At the time of this writing, Mather believed that the Second Coming of Christ was likely to happen in 1697; *halcyon* Prosperous and happy.

[11] *spiritual* Supernatural.

[12] *seasonably* In a timely manner.

[13] *first-born of our English settlements* Mather's claim is not literally true: Jamestown, founded in 1607, was the first permanent English settlement in North America. The Salem region was, however, home to one of the first English settlements that would become a part of the Massachusetts Bay Colony.

invisible hands, with tortures altogether preternatural.[1] After the mischiefs there endeavoured,[2] and since in part conquered, the terrible plague of evil angels hath made its progress into some other places, where other persons have been in like manner diabolically handled. These our poor afflicted neighbours, quickly after they became infected and infested with these demons, arrive to a capacity of discerning those which they conceive the shapes of their troublers;[3] and notwithstanding the great and just suspicion that the demons might impose the shapes of innocent persons in their spectral exhibitions[4] upon the sufferers (which may perhaps prove no small part of the witch plot in the issue[5]), yet many of the persons thus represented,[6] being examined, several of them have been convicted of a very damnable witchcraft: yea, more than one twenty have confessed that they have signed unto a book, which the Devil showed them, and engaged in his hellish design of bewitching and ruining our land.

We know not, at least I know not, how far the delusions of Satan may be interwoven into some circumstances of the confessions; but one would think all the rules of understanding humane affairs are at an end if after so many most voluntary harmonious confessions, made by intelligent persons of all ages, in sundry towns, at several times, we must not believe the main strokes wherein those confessions all agree: especially when we have a thousand preternatural things every day before our eyes, wherein the confessors do acknowledge their concernment,[7] and give demonstration of their being so concerned. If the devils now can strike the minds of men, with any poisons of so fine a composition and operation, that scores of innocent people shall unite in confessions of a crime, which we see actually committed, it is a thing prodigious, beyond the wonders of the

former ages, and it threatens no less than a sort of a dissolution upon the world.

Now, by these confessions 'tis agreed that the Devil has made a dreadful knot[8] of witches in the country, and by the help of witches has dreadfully increased that knot; that these witches have driven a trade of commissioning their confederate spirits to do all sorts of mischiefs to the neighbours, whereupon there have ensued such mischievous consequences upon the bodies and estates of the neighbourhood, as could not otherwise be accounted for; yea, that at prodigious witch-meetings, the wretches have proceeded so far as to concert and consult the methods of rooting out the Christian religion from this country, and setting up instead of it, perhaps a more gross diabolism[9] than ever the world saw before. And yet it will be a thing little short of miracle, if in so spread a business as this, the Devil should not get in some of his juggles,[10] to confound the discovery of all the rest. …

Doubtless, the thoughts of many will receive a great scandal against New England from the number of persons that have been accused or suspected for witchcrafts in this country: But it were easy to offer many things that may answer and abate the scandal. If the Holy God should anywhere permit the devils to hook two or three wicked scholars into witchcraft, and then by their assistance to range with their poisonous insinuations among ignorant, envious, discontented people till they have cunningly decoyed them into some sudden act, whereby the toils of hell shall be perhaps inextricably cast over them: what country in the world would not afford witches, numerous to a prodigy?[11] Accordingly, the kingdoms of Sweden, Denmark, Scotland, yea, and England itself, as well as the Province of New England, have had their storms of witchcrafts breaking upon them, which have made most lamentable devastations: which also I wish may be the last. And it is not uneasy to be imagined that God has not brought out all the witchcrafts in many other lands with such a speedy, dreadful, destroying jealousy as burns forth upon such high treasons committed here in a land of uprightness. Transgressors may more quickly here than elsewhere

[1] *preternatural* Out of the ordinary, unnatural.

[2] *endeavoured* Attacked.

[3] *arrive to … their troublers* I.e., become able to identify the witches.

[4] *spectral exhibitions* Ghostly phenomena, experienced through visions.

[5] *in the issue* In the end.

[6] *represented* Portrayed by the demons seen in the accusers visions.

[7] *concernment* Involvement.

[8] *knot* Association of people.

[9] *diabolism* Devil worship.

[10] *juggles* Occult deceptions.

[11] *numerous to a prodigy* I.e., amazingly numerous.

become a prey to the vengeance of Him who has eyes like a flame of fire, and who walks in the midst of the golden candlesticks. Moreover, there are many parts of the world, who if they do upon this occasion insult over this people of God, need only to be told the story of what happened at Loim, in the Duchy of Gulic,[1] where, a popish curate, having ineffectually tried many charms to eject the Devil out of a damsel there possessed, he passionately bid the Devil to come out of her, into himself; but the Devil answered him, *Quid mihi Opus est eum tentare, quem Novissimo Die, Jure Optimo sum Possessurus?* that is, What need I meddle with one, whom I am sure to have and hold at the Last Day, as my own forever![2]

But besides all this, give me leave to add: it is to be hoped, that among the persons represented by the spectres which now afflict our neighbours, there will be found some that never explicitly contracted[3] with any of the evil angels. The witches have not only intimated, but some of them acknowledge, that they have plotted the representations of innocent persons, to cover and shelter themselves in their witchcrafts; now, although our good God has hitherto generally preserved us from the abuse therein designed by the Devils for us, yet who of us can exactly state how far our God may for our chastisement permit the Devil to proceed in such an abuse? ...

from THE TRIAL OF MARTHA CARRIER[4]

1. Martha Carrier was indicted for the bewitching of certain persons, according to the form usual in such cases. Pleading Not Guilty to her indictment, there were first brought in a considerable number of the bewitched persons, who not only made the court sensible[5] of an horrid witchcraft committed upon them,

but also deposed that it was Martha Carrier, or her shape,[6] that grievously tormented them by biting, pricking, pinching, and choking of them. It was further deposed, that while this Carrier was on her examination before the magistrates, the poor people were so tortured that everyone expected their death upon the very spot; but that upon the binding of Carrier, they were eased. Moreover the look of Carrier then laid[7] the afflicted people for dead; and her touch, if her eye at the same time were off them, raised them again. Which things were also now seen upon her trial. And it was testified, that upon the mention of some having their necks twisted almost round by the shape of this Carrier, she replied, It's no matter, though their necks had been twisted quite off.

2. Before the trial of this prisoner, several of her own children had frankly and fully confessed not only that they were witches themselves, but that this their mother had made them so. This confession they made with great shows of repentance, and with much demonstration of truth. They related place, time, occasion; they gave an account of journeys, meetings, and mischiefs by them performed; and were very credible in what they said. Nevertheless, this evidence was not produced against the prisoner at the bar,[8] inasmuch as there was other evidence enough to proceed upon.

3. Benjamin Abbot gave in his testimony that last March was a twelve month,[9] this Carrier was very angry with him upon laying out some land near her husband's. Her expressions in this anger were that she would stick as close to Abbot as the bark stuck to the tree, and that he should repent of it afore seven years came to an end, so as Doctor Prescot should[10] never cure him. These words were heard by others, besides Abbot himself; who also heard her say, She would hold his nose as close to the grindstone as ever it was held[11] since his name was Abbot. Presently after this, he was taken with a swelling in his foot, and then with a pain in his side, and exceedingly tormented. It

1 *Duchy of Gulic* State in what is now Germany.

2 *What need ... own forever* I.e., the Devil has no need to possess the cleric because, as a Catholic, the cleric is already destined for damnation.

3 *contracted* Entered into an agreement.

4 *MARTHA CARRIER* Woman born between 1643 and 1650 and hanged for witchcraft in 1692. She had been a resident of Billerica, Massachusetts, but lived in Andover, Massachusetts, by the time of her trial.

5 *sensible* Cognizant.

6 *her shape* I.e., a spectral vision of Martha Carrier.

7 *laid* Cast to the ground.

8 *at the bar* I.e., in court.

9 *a twelve month* One year prior.

10 *so as ... should* In such a way that Doctor Prescot could.

11 *hold his nose ... was held* Treat him cruelly and dominate him as much as anyone ever had.

bred unto a sore, which was lanced by Doctor Prescot, and several gallons of corruption[1] ran out of it. For six weeks it continued very bad; and then another sore bred in his groin, which was also lanced by Doctor Prescot. Another sore then bred in his groin, which was likewise cut, and put him to very great misery. He was brought unto death's door, and so remained until Carrier was taken, and carried away by the constable; from which very day, he began to mend, and so grew better every day, and is well ever since. Sarah Abbot, also his wife, testified that her Husband was not only all this while afflicted in his body, but also that strange, extraordinary and unaccountable calamities befell his cattle; their death being such as they could guess at no natural reason for.

4. Allin Toothaker[2] testified that Richard, the son of Martha Carrier, having some difference with him, pulled him down by the hair of the head. When he rose again, he was going to strike at Richard Carrier; but fell down flat on his back to the ground, and had not power to stir hand or foot, until he told Carrier he yielded; and then he saw the shape of Martha Carrier go off his breast. This Toothaker had received a wound in the wars; and he now testified that Martha Carrier told him he should never be cured. Just afore the apprehending of Carrier, he could thrust a knitting needle into his wound, four inches deep; but presently after her being seized, he was thoroughly healed. He further testified that when Carrier and he sometimes were at variance,[3] she would clap her hands at him, and say, he should get nothing by it.[4] Whereupon he several times lost his cattle by strange deaths whereof no natural causes could be given.

5. John Rogger[5] also testified that upon the threatening words of this malicious Carrier, his cattle would be strangely bewitched; as was more particularly then described.

6. Samuel Preston[6] testified, that about two years ago, having some difference with Martha Carrier, he lost a cow in a strange preternatural unusual manner; and about a month after this, the said Carrier, having again some difference with him, she told him he had lately lost a cow, and it should not be long before he lost another! Which accordingly came to pass; for he had a thriving and well-kept Cow, which without any known cause quickly fell down and Died.

7. Phebe Chandler[7] testified, that about a fortnight before the apprehension of Martha Carrier, on a Lord's Day,[8] while the psalm was singing in the Church, this Carrier then took her by the shoulder and shaking her, asked her where she lived. She made her no answer, although as Carrier, who lived next door to her father's house, could not in reason but know[9] who she was. Quickly after this, as she was at several times crossing the fields, she heard a voice that she took to be Martha Carrier's and it seemed as if it was over her head. The voice told her she should within two or three days be poisoned. Accordingly, within such a little time, one half of her right hand became greatly swollen, and very painful; as also part of her face; whereof she can give no account how it came. It continued very bad for some days; and several times since, she has had a great pain in her breast; and been so seized on her legs, that she has hardly been able to go. She added that lately, going well to the House of God,[10] Richard, the son of Martha Carrier, looked very earnestly upon her, and immediately her hand, which had formerly been poisoned, as is above said, began to pain her greatly, and she had a strange burning at her stomach; but was then struck deaf, so that she could not hear any of the prayer or singing till the two or three last words of the psalm.

8. One Foster,[11] who confessed her own share in the witchcraft for which the prisoner stood indicted, affirmed that she had seen the prisoner at some of their witch meetings, and that it was this Carrier, who persuaded her to be a witch. She confessed that the Devil

[1] *corruption* Fetid material.

[2] *Allin Toothaker* Resident (c. 1670–?) of Billerica and nephew of Martha Carrier.

[3] *at variance* In conflict.

[4] *should get nothing by it* Gain no advantage (from their quarrel).

[5] *John Rogger* John Rogers (1641–95), who had lived near Martha Carrier in Billerica.

[6] *Samuel Preston* Farmer and innkeeper (1649–1738) in Salem.

[7] *Phebe Chandler* Resident (1680–1720) of Andover.

[8] *Lord's Day* Sunday.

[9] *could not … know* I.e., must know.

[10] *House of God* Church.

[11] *Foster* Ann Foster (c. 1617–92), an Andover resident who died in prison after being accused of witchcraft.

carried them on a pole to a witch meeting, but the pole broke, and she hanging about Carrier's neck they both fell down, and she then received an hurt by the fall, whereof she was not at this very time recovered.

9. One Lacy,[1] who likewise confessed her share in this witchcraft, now testified that she and the prisoner were once bodily present at a witch meeting in Salem Village; and that she knew the prisoner to be a witch, and to have been at a diabolical sacrament,[2] and that the prisoner was the undoing of her and her children by enticing them into the snare of the Devil.

10. Another Lacy,[3] who also confessed her share in this witchcraft, now testified that the prisoner was at the witch meeting in Salem Village where they had bread and wine administered unto them.[4]

11. In the time of this prisoner's trial, one Susanna Shelden[5] in open court had her hands unaccountably tied together with a wheel-band, so fast[6] that without cutting, it could not be loosed. It was done by a spectre; and the sufferer affirmed it[7] was the prisoner's.

Memorandum. This rampant hag, Martha Carrier, was the person of whom the confessions of the witches and of her own children among the rest agreed that the Devil had promised her she should be Queen of Hell. —1693

[1] *Lacy* Mary Lacy (1652–1707), resident of Andover and daughter of Ann Foster.

[2] *diabolical sacrament* Ritual parodying the sacrament of the Lord's Supper performed by Christians.

[3] *Another Lacy* Mary Lacy Kempe (1674–1744), daughter of Mary Lacy.

[4] *had bread … unto them* I.e., held a diabolical sacrament; bread and wine are consumed during the Lord's Supper.

[5] *Susanna Shelden* One of the principal accusers (c. 1674–?) during the Salem Witch Trials.

[6] *fast* Tight.

[7] *it* I.e., the specter.

CANASSATEGO

c. 1684 – 1750

In June 1750, two Moravian Christian missionaries paid an unannounced visit to the Onondaga diplomat and orator Canassatego. The missionaries wrote that Canassatego "knew at once who we were, called us by name, and seemed very much pleased to see us. He began to laugh for joy, in his peculiar manner, and one felt and saw that we were welcome guests." The skill with which, on this occasion, Canassatego put his Euro-American visitors at ease encapsulates his adroit management, for nearly a decade, of the complex, sensitive relationship between the Haudenosaunee Confederacy, which he represented as an emissary, and the British North American colonies. Canassatego's recorded speeches provide an evocative example of how eighteenth-century Native Americans drew on and reworked their oral literary traditions as they navigated the increasing pressures of white colonial expansion. His diplomatic and rhetorical abilities also gained Canassatego a noteworthy afterlife in Euro-American culture; in particular, the famous closing words of a speech he gave to colonial delegates in Lancaster, Pennsylvania, in 1744—"We are a powerful confederacy; and by your observing the same methods our wise forefathers have taken, you will acquire fresh strength and power"—arguably influenced the movement for colonial unity that underlies the very idea of the United States itself.

Little is known about Canassatego's early life; he was "about 60 years of age" in 1744, according to one white observer. By the time he first appears in the historical record in 1742, Canassatego had become one of the "chief men" of the Onondaga nation, a founding member of the Haudenosaunee Confederacy. He seems not to have had any connections to the Onondaga's hereditary sachems, however, and apparently gained his position purely by dint of his political and rhetorical skill, charisma, and ambition.

By the 1730s, the Haudenosaunee—caught between the contending colonial empires of Britain and France, embroiled in conflict with various Indigenous rivals, and ravaged by epidemics, famine, and alcohol abuse—were in danger of losing the powerful position they had long held in the politics of northeastern North America. In an attempt to strengthen its hand, the confederacy began forging closer ties with the British colony of Pennsylvania. In 1736, in a council that Canassatego likely attended, Pennsylvania agreed to recognize Haudenosaunee supremacy over all Indigenous peoples in its region and to deal only with the Haudenosaunee when negotiating any further land acquisitions; in exchange, the Haudenosaunee would help protect Pennsylvania's borderlands and take responsibility for managing disputes between Pennsylvania and other Indigenous nations.

This 1736 agreement set the stage for Canassatego's emergence as a leading Haudenosaunee representative in their subsequent dealings with Pennsylvania and its neighboring colonies. In 1742, Canassatego served in this capacity in negotiations meant to finalize territorial acquisitions Pennsylvania had made in the previous few years from the Haudenosaunee and Lenape (Delaware). After collecting the asking price for land the Haudenosaunee had sold, Canassatego shrewdly maneuvered the Pennsylvanian delegates into making an additional payment with a speech that sharply refuted Euro-American stereotypes of Indigenous simplicity or ignorance: "We know our lands are now become more valuable; the white people think we don't know their value, but we are sensible that the land is everlasting, and the few goods we receive for it are soon worn out and gone." Canassatego also held up the Haudenosaunee side of their pact with Pennsylvania while simultaneously asserting Haudenosaunee supremacy over other Indigenous peoples with a withering address to the Lenape, who were attempting to dispute an underhanded treaty (the so-called "Walking Purchase" of 1737) that had ceded more of their territory to Pennsylvania. Canassatego told the Lenape delegates, "We conquered you, we made women of you, you know you are women, and can no more sell land than women," and demanded that they relinquish the disputed land to Pennsylvania: "Take the advice of a wise man and remove immediately."

In addition to his rhetorical dexterity, Canassatego's stature as a diplomat stemmed from his mastery of the protocols of Haudenosaunee diplomacy and his fluency with the elaborate metaphorical language that the Haudenosaunee used to describe their relations with other peoples. (Some of these metaphors, such as "burying the tomahawk," have made their way into modern American vernacular.) This fluency is particularly on display in the speeches that Canassatego gave at Lancaster in 1744, during a conference to resolve territorial disputes between the Haudenosaunee and several colonies. The Haudenosaunee were demanding compensation for land they claimed to have conquered from the Susquehannock nation, while the colonial representatives asserted that they had previously purchased the land in question from the Susquehannock and thus owed the Haudenosaunee nothing. Canassatego defended the primacy of the Haudenosaunee's territorial claims over those of the Euro-American newcomers in a series of powerful speeches, forcing the colonial delegates to acknowledge the Haudenosaunee's claims in practice, if not in theory, by paying the compensation the Haudenosaunee had demanded. (Canassatego's speeches at Lancaster, like those he gave in the other major councils in which he took part, were probably translated by Conrad Weiser, a German-born Pennsylvanian interpreter; Canassatego developed a close partnership with Weiser that further contributed to Canassatego's diplomatic successes.)

After Lancaster, Canassatego took part in at least two more Haudenosaunee–colonial conferences, at Albany, New York, in 1745 and Philadelphia in 1749, in which he continued to use all his skills to keep the Haudenosaunee both friendly with and independent of the British colonies and to derive the greatest possible material benefit to the Haudenosaunee from the sale of Indigenous land. He died in 1750. The most common explanation of his death, both at the time and today, is that he was assassinated, but whether his assassins were French agents, pro-French Haudenosaunee, or compatriots angered by a deal he had allegedly made to sell communal Haudenosaunee land (the three main prevailing theories) remains unknown.

Canassatego's diplomatic speeches were printed by Benjamin Franklin, the official publisher of the records of Pennsylvania's Indigenous treaty negotiations. These published records were widely read in both the colonies and Britain; as a result, Canassatego became, after his death, something of a transatlantic celebrity. The English author John Shebbeare, for example, made Canassatego a character in his satirical novel *Lydia, or Filial Piety* (1755), using him to critique various aspects of British society from a conventional "noble savage" perspective. Scholars have also argued that Canassatego directly influenced Franklin's political thought, and hence fundamental U.S. political ideas, by his recommendations that the disparate and sometimes fractious British colonies forge a united confederacy after the model of the Haudenosaunee—a recommendation he made most famously in his closing speech at the 1744 Lancaster conference. Canassatego's presentation of the Haudenosaunee as a model for colonial unity, it has been suggested, shaped the plan for a unified colonial government that Franklin proposed at the 1754 Albany Congress and ultimately the U.S. Constitution—another example of the way in which Canassatego's oratory, by drawing powerfully on his people's rhetorical and literary traditions, gave those traditions a compelling new form.

NOTE ON THE TEXT: The text presented here of Canassatego's 26 June 1744 speech at Lancaster is based on the version of the speech printed by Benjamin Franklin in Philadelphia in 1744. Spelling and punctuation have been modernized according to the practices of this anthology.

⌘ ⌘ ⌘

from *Speech at Lancaster, 26 June 1744*

... Brother, the Governor of Maryland,

When you mentioned the affair of the land yesterday,[1] you went back to old times, and told us, you had been in possession of the province of Maryland above one hundred years; but what is one hundred years in comparison of the length of time since our claim began—since we came out of this ground? For we must tell you, that long before one hundred years our ancestors came out of this very ground, and their children have remained here ever since. You came out of the ground in a country that lies beyond the seas; there you may have a just claim, but here you must allow us to be your elder brethren, and the lands to belong to us long before you knew anything of them. It is true, that above one hundred years ago the Dutch came here in a ship, and brought with them several goods, such as awls, knives, hatchets, guns, and many other particulars, which they gave us. And when they had taught us how to use their things, and we saw what sort of people they were, we were so well pleased with them, that we tied their ship to the bushes on the shore; and afterwards, liking them still better the longer they stayed with us, and thinking the bushes too tender, we removed the rope, and tied it to the trees; and as the trees were liable to be blown down by high winds, or to decay of themselves, we, from the affection we bore them, again removed the rope, and tied it to a strong and big rock [here the interpreter said, "They mean the Oneida[2] country"] and not content with this, for its further security we removed the rope to the big mountain [here the interpreter said, "They mean the Onondaga[3] country"] and there we tied it very fast, and rolled wampum[4] about it; and, to make it still more secure, we stood upon the wampum, and sat down upon it, to defend it, and to prevent any hurt coming to it, and did our best endeavours that it might remain uninjured forever. During all this time the newcomers, the Dutch, acknowledged our right to the lands, and solicited us, from time to time, to grant them parts of our country, and to enter into league and covenant with us, and to become one people with us.[5]

After this the English came into the country, and, as we were told, became one people with the Dutch.[6] About two years after the arrival of the English, an English governor[7] came to Albany, and finding what great friendship subsisted between us and the Dutch, he approved it mightily, and desired to make as strong a league, and to be upon as good terms with us as the Dutch were, with whom he was united, and to become one people with us. And by his further care in looking into what had passed between us, he found that the rope which tied the ship to the great mountain was only fastened with wampum, which was liable to break and rot, and to perish in a course of years; he therefore told us, he would give us a silver chain, which would be much stronger, and would last forever. This we accepted, and fastened the ship with it, and it

[1] *When you ... yesterday* Haudenosaunee diplomatic protocol dictated that responses to any major proposals or statements be delivered the day after the proposal or statement in question was made; this was a way of showing that the recipients of the proposal or statement had taken it seriously and given it respectful consideration before delivering their response.

[2] *Oneida* One of the five founding nations of the Haudenosaunee Confederacy; the name means "people of the standing stone."

[3] *Onondaga* Another of the five founding Haudenosaunee nations; the name means "hill place people." Canassatego was an Onondaga.

[4] *wampum* Belts and strings of wampum, a type of bead made from shells, are used among the Indigenous nations of eastern North America for numerous purposes, including the recording of treaties, stories, and historical events as well as ceremonial exchange, trade, and decorative art.

[5] *above one hundred ... with us* In Haudenosaunee oral tradition, the treaty the Haudenosaunee made with the Dutch (in 1613, according to the tradition) is known as the Two Row Wampum Treaty; the Haudenosaunee consider it to be the basis for all their subsequent treaties with European and Euro-American governments and to still be in effect.

[6] *After this ... the Dutch* The Dutch settlement of New Amsterdam—the nucleus of what is now New York City—was surrendered to the British in 1664; Britain took over the rest of New Netherland, the Dutch colony on the northeastern Atlantic seaboard, in 1674.

[7] *an English governor* Edmund Andros, governor of New York colony from 1674 to 1683. In 1675, Andros asked for Haudenosaunee assistance in the conflicts then engulfing many of the British North American colonies, including King Philip's War in New England and Bacon's Rebellion in Virginia. Andros's agreement with the Haudenosaunee formed the basis for the series of treaties and alliances between the Haudenosaunee and the British colonies that came to be called the Covenant Chain.

has lasted ever since. Indeed we have had some small differences with the English, and, during these misunderstandings, some of their young men would, by way of reproach, be every now and then telling us, that we should have perished if they had not come into the country and furnished us with strouds[1] and hatchets, and guns, and other things necessary for the support of life; but we always gave them to understand that they were mistaken—that we lived before they came amongst us, and as well, or better, if we may believe what our forefathers have told us. We had then room enough, and plenty of deer, which was easily caught; and though we had not knives, hatchets, or guns, such as we have now, yet we had knives of stone, and hatchets of stone, and bows and arrows, and those served our uses as well then as the English ones do now. We are now straitened,[2] and sometimes in want of deer, and liable to many other inconveniencies since the English came among us, and particularly from that pen-and-ink work that is going on at the table (pointing to the secretary), and we will give you an instance of this. Our Brother Onas,[3] a great while ago, came to Albany to buy the Susquehanna lands[4] of us, but our Brother, the Governor of New York, who, as we suppose, had not a good understanding with our Brother Onas, advised us not to sell him any land, for he would make an ill use of it. And pretending to be our good friend, he advised us, in order to prevent Onas's, or any other person's imposing upon us, and that we might always have our land when we should want it, to put it into his hands, and told us, he would keep it for our life, and never open his hands, but keep them close shut, and not part with any of it, but at our request. Accordingly we trusted him, and put our land into his hands, and charged him to keep it safe for our use; but, some time after, he went to England, and carried our land with him, and there sold it to our Brother Onas for a large sum of money. And when, at the instance of our Brother Onas, we were minded to sell him some lands, he told us, we had sold the Susquehanna lands already to the Governor of New York, and that he had bought them from him in England, though when he came to understand how the Governor of New York had deceived us, he very generously paid us for our lands over again.

Though we mention this instance of an imposition put upon us by the Governor of New York, yet we must do the English the justice to say, we have had their hearty assistances in our wars with the French, who were no sooner arrived amongst us than they began to render us uneasy, and to provoke us to war, and we have had several wars with them, during all which we constantly received assistance from the English, and, by their means, we have always been able to keep up our heads against their attacks.

We now come nearer home. We have had your deeds interpreted to us, and we acknowledge them to be good and valid, and that the Conestoga or Susquehannock Indians had a right to sell those lands to you, for they were then theirs; but since that time we have conquered them, and their country now belongs to us, and the lands we demanded satisfaction for are no part of the lands comprised in those Deeds. They are the Cohongorontas[5] lands; those, we are sure, you have not possessed one hundred years—no, nor above ten years, and we made our demands so soon as we knew your people were settled in those parts. These have never been sold, but remain still to be disposed of; and we are well pleased to hear you are provided with goods, and do assure you of our willingness to treat with you for those unpurchased lands; in confirmation whereof, we present you with this belt of wampum.

Which was received with the usual ceremonies.
—1744

[1] *strouds* Blankets made of stroud (a coarse woolen fabric) that were sold or traded to Indigenous people.

[2] *straitened* Reduced in means; impoverished.

[3] *Onas* Treaty name, meaning "quill pen," that the Haudenosaunee used for the governors of Pennsylvania Colony.

[4] *Susquehanna lands* I.e., lands in the valley of the Susquehanna River, which flows through parts of New York and Pennsylvania.

[5] [Franklin's note] I.e., Potomac. ["Cohongorontas" was the Haudenosaunee name for the Potomac River west of the Blue Ridge Mountains.]

IN CONTEXT

Indigenous–Settler Negotiations in the Mid-Eighteenth Century

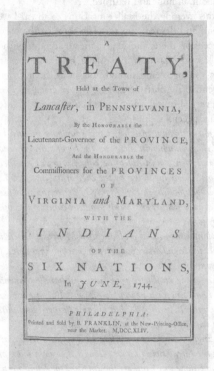

A

TREATY,

Held at the Town of

Lancaſter, in PENNSYLVANIA,

By the HONOURABLE the

Lieutenant-Governor of the PROVINCE,

And the HONOURABLE the

Commiſſioners for the PROVINCES

OF

VIRGINIA *and* MARYLAND,

WITH THE

INDIANS

OF THE

SIX NATIONS,

In *JUNE,* 1744.

PHILADELPHIA:

Printed and Sold by B. FRANKLIN, at the New-Printing-Office, near the Market. M,DCC,XLIV.

Title page of Benjamin Franklin's publication of the negotiations at Lancaster in 1744.

from George Washington, *The Journal of Major George Washington* (1754)

In the autumn of 1753, George Washington—then just 21 years old—volunteered for a diplomatic mission on behalf of the governor of Virginia to the Ohio Country, the region watered by the Ohio River and its tributaries, on the other side of the Appalachian Mountains from the British North American colonies, that was the subject of intensifying territorial disputes among the British, the French, and the Indigenous nations caught between them. Washington was tasked with carrying a letter to the French, demanding that they halt the construction of forts near the Ohio's headwaters and withdraw from the region; the French refusal to accede to these demands helped spark the French and Indian War the following year. In the course of his journey, Washington conducted numerous negotiations with not only the French but also the Indigenous peoples of the Ohio Country. The report of his travels and negotiations that Washington prepared was published by the Virginia governor in order to raise awareness of the perceived French threat; it became popular reading and was reprinted on both sides of the Atlantic.

[24 November 1753] ... As soon as I came into town, I went to Monacatoocha (as the Half-King[1] was out at his hunting-cabin on Little Beaver Creek, about 15 miles off) and informed him by John Davison, my Indian interpreter, that I was sent a messenger to the French general; and was ordered to call upon the sachems of the Six Nations, to acquaint them with it. I gave him a string of wampum,[2] and a twist of tobacco, and desired him to send for the Half-King; which he promised to do by a runner in the morning, and for other sachems. I invited him and the other great men present to my tent, where they stayed about an hour and returned. ...

25th ... About 3 o'clock this evening the Half-King came to town. I went up and invited him and Davison, privately, to my tent, and desired him to relate some of the particulars of his journey to the French commandant, and reception there; and to give me an account of the ways and distance. He told me that the nearest and levellest way was now impassable, by reason of many large miry savannas;[3] that we must be obliged to go by Venango,[4] and should not get to the near fort under 5 or 6 night's sleep, good travelling. When he went to the fort, he said he was received in a very stern manner by the late commander; who asked him very abruptly, what he had come about, and to declare his business, which he said he did in the following speech.

Fathers, I am come to tell you your own speeches; what your own mouths have declared. Fathers, you, in former days, set a silver basin before us, wherein there was the leg of a beaver, and desired of all nations to come and eat of it; to eat in peace and plenty, and not to be churlish to one another; and that if any such person should be found to be a disturber, I here lay down by the edge of the dish a rod, which you must scourge them with; and if I your father should get foolish, in my old days, I desire you may use it upon me as well as others.

Now, fathers, it is you that are the disturbers in this land, by coming and building your towns, and taking it away unknown to us, and by force.

Fathers, we kindled a fire a long time ago, at a place called Montreal, where we desired you to stay, and not to come and intrude upon our land. I now desire you may dispatch to that place; for be it known to you, fathers, that this is our land, and not yours.

Fathers, I desire you may hear me in civilness; if not, we must handle that rod which was laid down for the use of the obstreperous. If you had come in a peaceable manner, like our brothers the English, we should not have been against your trading with us, as they do; but to come, fathers, and build great houses upon our land, and to take it by force, is what we cannot submit to.

Fathers, both you and the English are white, we live in a country between; therefore the land belongs to neither one nor the other: but the Great Being above allowed it to be a place of residence for us; so fathers, I desire you to withdraw, as I have done our brothers the English; for I will keep you at arms length. I lay this down as a trial for both, to see which will have the greatest regard to it, and that side we will stand by, and

[1] *Monacatoocha* Lenape (Delaware) name for Scarouady, a chief of the Oneida nation of the Haudenosaunee; *the Half-King* I.e., Tanacharison, an adopted member of the Seneca nation of the Haudenosaunee who was, with Scarouady, one of the leaders of the Haudenosaunee and their allies and subordinates in the Ohio Country. "Half-King," the title by which he was known to Euro-Americans, reflected their perception of him as a viceroy or high-ranking delegate empowered to conduct diplomacy with Euro-Americans and other Indigenous nations on behalf of the Haudenosaunee Grand Council; however, this view may have been a misconception. Like Scarouady, Tanacharison was based at Logstown, a major multiethnic Native American community on the Ohio River near present-day Pittsburgh, Pennsylvania, that is the "town" referred to earlier in this sentence.

[2] *wampum* Belts and strings of wampum, a type of bead made from shells, are used among the Indigenous nations of eastern North America for numerous purposes, including the recording of treaties, stories, and historical events as well as ceremonial exchange, trade, and decorative art.

[3] *savannas* Wetlands.

[4] *Venango* Anglicization of an Indigenous name for what is now called French Creek, a tributary of the Allegheny River in present-day northwestern Pennsylvania that was an important link between the Great Lakes and the Ohio River in the eighteenth century.

make equal sharers with us. Our brothers the English have heard this, and I come now to tell it to you, for I am not afraid to discharge[1] you off this land.

This he said was the substance of what he said to the general, who made this reply.

Now, my child, I have heard your speech; you spoke first, but it is my time to speak now. Where is my wampum that you took away, with the marks of towns in it? This wampum I do not know, which you have discharged me off the land with; but you need not put yourself to the trouble of speaking, for I will not hear you: I am not afraid of flies, or mosquitos, for Indians are such as those; I tell you, down that river[2] I will go, and will build upon it, according to my command. If the river was blocked up, I have forces sufficient to burst it open, and tread under my feet all that stand in opposition, together with their alliances; for my force is as the sand upon the sea shore. Therefore, here is your wampum, I fling it at you. Child, you talk foolish; you say this land belongs to you, but there is not the black of my nail yours.[3] I saw that land sooner than you did, before the Shannoahs[4] and you were at war. Lead was the man that went down, and took possession of that river:[5] it is my land, and I will have it, let who will stand up for, or say against it. I'll buy and sell with the English (mockingly). If people will be ruled by me, they may expect kindness, but not else. …

26th. We met in council at the long-house, about 9 o'clock, where I spoke to them as follows,

Brothers, I have called you together in council, by order of your brother the governor of Virginia, to acquaint you that I am sent, with all possible dispatch, to visit, and deliver a letter to the French commandant, of very great importance to your brothers the English; and I dare say, to you their friends and allies.

I was desired, brothers, by your brother the governor, to call upon you, the sachems of the nations, to inform you of it, and to ask your advice and assistance to proceed the nearest and best road to the French. You see, brothers, I have got thus far on my journey.

His honour likewise desired me to apply to you for some of your young men, to conduct and provide provisions for us on our way, and be a safeguard against those French Indians who have taken up the hatchet against us. I have spoke this particularly to you, brothers, because his honour our governor treats you as good friends and allies, and holds you in great esteem. To confirm what I have said, I give you this string of wampum.

After they had considered some time on the above, the Half-King got up and spoke.

Now, my brothers, in regard to what my brother the governor has desired of me, I return you this answer.

I rely upon you as a brother ought to do, as you say we are brothers and one people: we shall put heart in hand, and speak to our fathers the French concerning the speech they made to me, and you may depend that we will endeavour to be your guard.

Brother, as you have asked my advice, I hope you will be ruled by it, and stay till I can provide a company to go with you: the French speech-belt[6] is not here, I have it to go for to my hunting cabin; likewise the people which I have ordered in are not yet come, nor cannot till the third night from this, till which time, brother, I must beg you to stay.

[1] *discharge* Send away, get rid of.

[2] *that river* I.e., the Ohio.

[3] *not the … yours* I.e., not the smallest portion of it is yours. (The expression "the black of my nail" refers to a small quantity or a slim margin.)

[4] *Shannoahs* Shawnee. The Shawnee nation was one of several Indigenous nations that fought the expanding Haudenosaunee for control of the Ohio Country in the seventeenth century.

[5] *Lead … that river* In 1749, the French Canadian officer Pierre-Joseph Céloron de Blainville led an expedition to the Ohio Country to strengthen France's claim to the region, established by explorations in the seventeenth century; news of Céloron's expedition was one of the primary instigators of Washington's own 1753 mission. During his expedition, Céloron buried several inscribed lead plates at the mouths of tributaries of the Ohio River to both announce and physically enact French possession. The French general (as reported by Tanacharison and Washington) seems here to be personifying these lead plates and blending them with Céloron himself.

[6] *the French speech-belt* I.e., the wampum belt "with the marks of towns in it" referred to in the French general's speech quoted above.

I intend to send a guard of Mingos,[1] *Shannoahs, and Delawares, that our brothers may see the love and loyalty we bear them.*

As I had orders to make all possible dispatch, and waiting here was very contrary to my inclination, I thanked him in the most suitable manner I could, and told him that my business required the greatest expedition,[2] and would not admit of that delay: he was not well pleased that I should offer to go before the time he had appointed, and told me that he could not consent to our going without a guard, for fear some accident should befall us, and draw a reflection upon him; besides, says he, this is a matter of no small moment,[3] and must not be entered into without due consideration; for now I intend to deliver up the French-speech-belt, and make the Shannoahs and Delawares do the same; and accordingly he gave orders to King Shingiss,[4] who was present, to attend on Wednesday night with the wampum, and two men of their nation to be in readiness to set out with us next morning. As I found it was impossible to get off without affronting them in the most egregious manner, I consented to stay. ...

29th. The Half-King and Monocatoocha came very early, and begged me to stay one day more, for notwithstanding they had used all the diligence in their power, the Shannoah chiefs had not brought the wampum they ordered, but would certainly be in tonight; if not, they would delay me no longer, but would send it after us as soon as they arrived. When I found them so pressing in their request, and knew that returning of wampum was the abolishing of agreements, and giving this up was shaking of all dependence upon the French, I consented to stay, as I believed an offence offered at this crisis might be attended with greater ill consequence than another day's delay. ...

6th, the Half-King came to my tent, quite sober, and insisted very much that I should stay and hear what he had to say to the French; I fain would have prevented[5] his speaking anything 'til he came to the commandant, but could not prevail. He told me that at this place a council fire was kindled, where all their business with these people was to be transacted, and that the management of the Indian affairs was left solely to Monsieur Joncaire.[6] As I was desirous of knowing the issue of this, I agreed to stay[.] ...

About 10 o'clock they met in council; the King spoke much the same as he had before done to the general, and offered the French speech-belt which had before been demanded, with the marks of four towns on it, which Monsieur Joncaire refused to receive; but desired him to carry it to the fort to the commander.[7] ...

15th, The commandant ordered a plentiful store of liquor, provision, etc. to be put on board our canoe, and appeared to be extremely complaisant,[8] though he was exerting every artifice that he could invent to set our own Indians at variance with us, to prevent their going 'til after our departure: presents, rewards,

[1] *Mingos* "Mingo," a term derived from the Lenape word mingwe (meaning treacherous or stealthy), was a name applied in the eighteenth century to Haudenosaunee who migrated to the Ohio Country from their traditional territories in what is now upstate New York.

[2] *expedition* Promptness, speed.

[3] *moment* Importance.

[4] *King Shingiss* Shingas, a leader of the Lenape in the Ohio Country, who went on to fight (reluctantly) on the French side of the ensuing French and Indian War. His title of "king" was a designation conferred by the British colonial governments, reflecting their desire to deal diplomatically with a single Indigenous leader rather than the numerous local chiefs or elders who held power in decentralized Indigenous nations like the Lenape.

[5] *fain ... prevented* Wanted to prevent.

[6] *Monsieur Joncaire* Philippe-Thomas Chabert de Joncaire (c. 1707–c. 1766), French Canadian army officer and interpreter who was a principal French diplomat to the Haudenosaunee and other Indigenous peoples of the Ohio Country. At the time of Washington's expedition, he commanded Fort d'Anjou (later renamed Fort Machault), a French military installation at the confluence of French Creek and the Allegheny River in what is now northwestern Pennsylvania.

[7] *to the fort ... commander* I.e., to Fort Le Boeuf, a French fort further up French Creek, about fifteen miles from the shores of Lake Erie. Its commander, Jacques Legardeur de Saint-Pierre (1701–55), was Joncaire's superior officer and is the "commandant" referred to in the following entry (for 15 December).

[8] *complaisant* Polite.

and everything that could be suggested by him or his officers. I can't say that ever in my life I suffered so much anxiety as I did in this affair; I saw that every stratagem that the most fruitful brain could invent was practised to win the Half-King to their interest, and that leaving him here was giving them the opportunity they aimed at. I went to the Half-King and pressed him in the strongest terms to go: he told me the commandant would not discharge him 'til the morning. I then went to the commandant and desired him to do their business, and complained of ill treatment; for keeping them, as they were part of my company, was detaining me; which he promised not to do, but to forward my journey as much as he could. He protested he did not keep them, but was ignorant of the cause of their stay; though I soon found it out: he had promised them a present of guns, etc. if they would wait 'til the morning.

As I was very much pressed by the Indians to wait this day for them, I consented, on a promise that nothing should hinder them in the morning.

16th, The French were not slack in their inventions to keep the Indians this day also; but as they were obligated, according to promise, to give the present, they then endeavoured to try the power of liquor, which I doubt not would have prevailed at any other time than this, but I urged and insisted with the King so closely upon his word that he refrained and set off with us as he had engaged. …

The Indians giving a talk to Colonel Bouquet in a conference at a council fire, near his camp on the banks of Muskingum in North America in Oct. 1764. This image—depicting negotiations between Native Americans and Colonel Henry Bouquet, a Swiss-born officer who led British troops in the Ohio Country during Pontiac's War (1763–66)—captures some of the details of how such Indigenous–colonial negotiations during this period were conducted, including the parallel use of wampum, by Indigenous people, and written manuscripts, by Euro–Americans, to memorialize the proceedings.

JONATHAN EDWARDS

1703 – 1758

On 8 July 1741, Jonathan Edwards visited the congregation of Enfield, Connecticut—one of the few communities in New England to remain unmoved by the explosion of religious enthusiasm known as the First Great Awakening. To this initially aloof crowd, Edwards delivered "Sinners in the Hands of an Angry God," an oration that would become one of the best-known sermons in American history. "O sinner! Consider the fearful danger that you are in," Edwards warned, soon eliciting outbursts of emotion from his transformed audience. "The God that holds you over the pit of hell, much as one holds a spider … abhors you." A prominent theologian and philosopher, Edwards is best known for inspiring—and then theorizing—religious revivals, first in his own congregation in the mid-1730s and then as a participant in the larger Great Awakening that swept New England in the early 1740s. His religious writings had a lasting effect upon Protestant theology in New England, and his philosophical works helped to shape American views on free will, aesthetics, and history for generations. Edwards remains an influential thinker for American Calvinists, and his work continues to be studied for its innovative fusion of Protestant Christianity and Enlightenment philosophy.

Born in East Windsor, Connecticut, in 1703, Jonathan Edwards was the fifth child of Esther Stoddard and minister Timothy Edwards. At thirteen, he enrolled at Yale, where he was shocked to discover what he described as his classmates' "monstrous impieties." A dutiful student who immersed himself in the literature of Enlightenment thinkers such as Isaac Newton and John Locke, in college Edwards struggled with his religious beliefs until he underwent a conversion experience that filled him, he would later write, with "constant delight and pleasure." In 1727, he was ordained in Northampton, Massachusetts, as an assistant pastor to his grandfather, Solomon Stoddard.

Two years later, Edwards succeeded Stoddard as the sole pastor of the Congregational Church in Northampton. In this role, he developed his characteristic style of preaching. Following in the footsteps of such Puritan ministers as William Perkins and William Ames, Edwards adopted a "plain style" of speech, which focused on making clear connections between divine wisdom and everyday life. His sermons typically derive a theme from scripture, outline theological assertions related to the theme, and then discuss some practical applications of those theological points. Edwards believed that New England was at risk of falling into depravity: taverns were becoming widespread, premarital sex was common, and young people were spending less time in prayer. "Arminianism"—a catch-all term used by strict Calvinists to refer to a range of views in which humans can play a role in their own salvation—was also growing in popularity. In response to these developments, Edwards delivered a public lecture in Boston in 1731, "God Glorified in Man's Dependence," which stirringly defended the Calvinist tenet that humankind relies completely on God.

Beginning in 1733, Edwards sought to rejuvenate his congregation's passion for Calvinist spirituality. He encouraged the town elders to persuade the younger generation to take religion more seriously. By 1735, partly due to Edwards's moving sermons, religious fervor had taken hold of the town. Hundreds of people made open professions of faith. "All the conversation in all companies and upon all occasions was upon [spiritual and eternal things] only," Edwards recalled in *A Faithful Narrative of the Surprising Work of God* (1737). "Other discourse than of the things of religion would scarcely be tolerated." The spiritual awakening came to a conclusion in early June 1735, when Edwards's uncle, overwhelmed by fear for his spiritual state, died by suicide.

The larger-scale revival of Calvinist spirituality that became known as the First Great Awakening gathered momentum in 1740. All across New England, expressions of religious ecstasy grew commonplace. Believing this to be a sign of Christianity's imminent triumph over evil, Edwards wrote and preached in support of the revival. In the process, he established himself as a leading representative of a growing community of New England ministers, known as the New Lights, who believed that the revivals represented the work of God.

During the First Great Awakening, Edwards was recognized by his fellow ministers as an exceptionally skilled author of sermons, and he was sometimes called upon to inspire spiritual awakening in disinterested congregations—most famously in the congregation of Enfield, to which he preached "Sinners in the Hands of an Angry God." Although Edwards was not a particularly passionate speaker, his words inspired many parishioners to weep and cry out so excessively that, as a member of the congregation recorded in his diary, Edwards was unable to finish the sermon. He is now best known for this undeniably provocative sermon, but it is actually an outlier; only two of his sermons focus on hell and its torments. He spoke far more frequently about God's benevolence and the beauty of God's creation.

The spiritual renewal that Edwards helped to inspire was not universally celebrated. For a faction of New England's religious establishment known as the Old Lights, the revival spirit precipitated by Edwards and other so-called "New Light" preachers was, as the Boston pastor Charles Chauncy put it, "a disease, a sort of madness" masquerading as real piety. As the Great Awakening spread through New England, Edwards frequently wrote and spoke in response to the concern that many of the converts were driven by emotional frenzy, rather than true apprehensions of divine grace. In *A Treatise Concerning Religious Affections* (1746), his most thorough work on the matter, he drew upon the philosophy of John Locke to differentiate authentic religious experiences from mere enthusiasm.

Once the fervor of the Great Awakening died out in the mid-1740s, Edwards began to lose favor with his own congregation, and in 1750 he was dismissed as pastor. He then became a missionary to the Mahican of Stockbridge, a town founded for the purpose of colonizing and converting Indigenous people through integration with settler families. Edwards believed that unconverted Mahican were in a state of sin and ignorance, and that it was the responsibility of the English to spread the gospel and give them sufficient education to read and understand the Bible: "we do no more than our duty in it," he said to his Indigenous congregation, "for it was once with our forefathers as 'tis with you. They formerly were in great darkness." While in Stockbridge, Edwards composed *Freedom of Will* (1754), a dense work of philosophy in which he considered the compatibility of divine power with human free will.

In 1758, just weeks after being appointed president of the College of New Jersey—now called Princeton—Edwards died following complications from an inoculation against smallpox. (Unlike modern vaccination, eighteenth-century inoculation carried some risk of infection with the disease.) After his death, Edwards's disciples would go on to found a theological movement known as New Divinity, in which a significant number of New England ministers would be schooled. Throughout the eighteenth and nineteenth centuries, many American authors and religious figures felt compelled either to embrace or debunk the worldview Edwards had argued for. Harriet Beecher Stowe shared Edwards's belief that the second coming of Christ would take place after the Church had overthrown the antichristian forces of evil, saved a vast number of souls, and instituted a paradisiacal global society. Edwards, however, had owned enslaved people, and, in Stowe's view, his chief failing was that he had not explicitly recognized slavery as an antichristian force. Ralph Waldo Emerson, by contrast, considered Edwards's theology to be a "disease" that prevented people from recognizing their own inherent dignity. For the United States to progress as a society, Emerson believed, it would need to leave the spirituality of Puritan-inspired thinkers such as Edwards behind.

Throughout the nineteenth century, Edwards was viewed as the culmination of the Puritan tradition that preceded him and the spiritual forefather of the evangelical movements that followed. He proved to be a significant influence upon the writers and preachers of the Second Great Awakening of the 1790s to 1830s, and his ideas shaped the theology that dominated nineteenth-century New England seminaries. By the turn of the twentieth century, however, Edwards was treated as a "Great Anachronism" for his

attachment to old-fashioned religiosity. His reputation was resurrected in the mid-twentieth century, when he was hailed by critics such as Perry Miller and Sacvan Bercovitch as one of the first figures in colonial America to be recognized as an important intellectual on both sides of the Atlantic. In the twenty-first century, Edwards's direct influence has been largely limited to Calvinist institutions, although his work continues to be widely anthologized. "It is safe to say," early Americanist Edward Gallagher suggests, "that there will never be an American literature without 'Sinners in the Hands of an Angry God.' It is simply too compelling."

NOTE ON THE TEXT: The text of "Sinners in the Hands of an Angry God" is based on the 1741 edition published in Boston by S. Kneeland and T. Green. Spelling and punctuation have been modernized in accordance with the practices of this anthology.

⌘⌘⌘

Sinners in the Hands of an Angry God

Deuteronomy 32.35[1]
—Their Foot shall slide in due Time—

In this verse is threatened the vengeance of God on the wicked unbelieving Israelites, that were God's visible people, and lived under means of grace;[2] and that, notwithstanding all God's wonderful works that he had wrought towards that people, yet remained, as is expressed (Deuteronomy 32.28) void of counsel, having no understanding in them;[3] and that, under all the cultivations of heaven, brought forth bitter and poisonous fruit; as in the two verses next preceding the text.[4]

The expression I have chosen for my text, *Their foot shall slide in due time*, seems to imply the following things relating to the punishment and destruction that these wicked Israelites were exposed to.

1. That they were *always* exposed to destruction; as one that stands or walks in slippery places is always exposed to fall. This is implied in the manner of their destruction's coming upon them, being represented by their foot sliding. The same is expressed, Psalm 73.18: *Surely thou didst set them in slippery places; thou castedst them down into destruction.*

2. It implies that they were always exposed to *sudden* unexpected destruction. As he that walks in slippery places is every moment liable to fall; he can't foresee one moment whether he shall stand or fall the next; and when he does fall, he falls at once without warning. Which is also expressed in Psalm 73.18–19: *Surely thou didst set them in slippery places; thou castedst them down into destruction: How are they brought into desolation as in a moment?*

3. Another thing implied is, that they are liable to fall *of themselves*, without being thrown down by the hand of another. As he that stands or walks on slippery ground, needs nothing but his own weight to throw him down.

4. That the reason why they are not fallen already, and do not fall now, is only that God's appointed time

[1] *Deuteronomy 32.35* "To me belongeth vengeance and recompence; their foot shall slide in due time: for the day of their calamity is at hand, and the things that shall come upon them make haste."

[2] *lived under means of grace* Lived under the terms of the covenant of grace, according to which humans cannot be saved through their own actions, but only by the grace of God.

[3] *void of … them* See Deuteronomy 32.28–29: "For they are a nation void of counsel, neither is there any understanding in them. O that they were wise, that they understood this, that they would consider their latter end!"

[4] *two verses … text* See Deuteronomy 32.32–33: "For their vine is of the vine of Sodom, and of the fields of Gomorrah: their grapes are grapes of gall, their clusters are bitter: their wine is the poison of dragons, and the cruel venom of asps." In this passage, Sodom and Gomorrah refer to two biblical cities populated by wicked people,

which God consumed with fire and brimstone in a demonstration of divine judgment.

is not come. For it is said, that when that due time, or appointed time comes, *their foot shall slide*. Then they shall be left to fall as they are inclined by their own weight. God won't hold them up in these slippery places any longer, but will let them go; and then, at that very instant, they shall fall into destruction; as he that stands in such slippery declining ground, on the edge of a pit that he can't stand alone, when he is let go he immediately falls and is lost.

The observation from the words that I would now insist upon is this: *There is nothing that keeps wicked men at any one moment out of hell, but the mere pleasure of God.* By the mere pleasure of God, I mean his sovereign pleasure, his arbitrary will, restrained by no obligation, hindered by no manner of difficulty, any more than if nothing else but God's mere will had in the least degree, or in any respect whatsoever, any hand in the preservation of wicked men one moment. The truth of this observation may appear by the following considerations.

1. There is no want[1] of *power* in God to cast wicked men into hell at any moment. Men's hands can't be strong when God rises up. The strongest have no power to resist him, nor can any deliver out of his hands. He is not only able to cast wicked men into hell, but he can most *easily* do it. Sometimes an earthly prince meets with a great deal of difficulty to subdue a rebel, that he has found means to fortify himself, and has made himself strong by the numbers of his followers. But it is not so with God. There is no fortress that is any defense from the power of God. Though hand join in hand, and vast multitudes of God's enemies combine and associate themselves, they are easily broken in pieces. They are as great heaps of light chaff before the whirlwind; or large quantities of dry stubble before devouring flames.[2] We find it easy to tread on and crush a worm that we see crawling on the earth; so 'tis easy for us to cut or singe a slender thread that anything hangs by: thus easy is it for God when he pleases to cast his enemies down to hell. What are we,

that we should think to stand before him, at whose rebuke the earth trembles, and before whom the rocks are thrown down?[3]

2. They *deserve* to be cast into hell; so that divine justice never stands in the way, it makes no objection against God's using his power at any moment to destroy them. Yea, on the contrary, justice calls aloud for an infinite punishment of their sins. Divine justice says of the tree that brings forth such grapes of Sodom, *Cut it down, why cumbereth it the ground?*, Luke 13.7. The sword of divine justice is every moment brandished over their heads, and 'tis nothing but the hand of arbitrary mercy, and God's mere will, that holds it back.

3. They are *already* under a sentence of condemnation to hell. They do not only justly deserve to be cast down thither, but the sentence of the law of God, that eternal and immutable rule of righteousness that God has fixed between him and mankind, is gone out against them, and stands against them; so that they are bound over[4] already to hell. John 3.18: *He that believeth not is condemned already.* So that every unconverted man[5] properly belongs to hell; that is his place; from thence he is. John 8.23: *Ye are from beneath.* And thither he is bound; 'tis the place that justice, and God's word, and the sentence of his unchangeable law assign to him.

4. They are now the objects of that very *same* anger and wrath of God that is expressed in the torments of hell. And the reason why they don't go down to hell at each moment, is not because God, in whose power they are, is not then very angry with them; as angry as he is with many of those miserable creatures now tormented in hell, who there feel and bear the fierceness of his wrath. Yea, God is a great deal more angry with great numbers that are now on earth. Yea, doubtless with many that are now in this congregation, that it

[1] *want* Lack.

[2] *They are … whirlwind* See Psalm 1.4: "The ungodly are not so: but are like the chaff which the wind driveth away"; *large quantities … devouring flames* See Isaiah 5.24: "Therefore as the fire devoureth the stubble, and the flame consumeth the chaff, so their root shall be as rottenness, and their blossom shall go up as dust: because they have cast away the law of the Lord of hosts, and despised the word of the Holy One of Israel."

[3] *earth trembles* See Jeremiah 10.10: "But the Lord is the true God, he is the living God, and an everlasting king: at his wrath the earth shall tremble, and the nations shall not be able to abide his indignation"; *before whom … down* See Nahum 1.6: "Who can stand before his indignation? And who can abide in the fierceness of his anger? His fury is poured out like fire and the rocks are thrown down by him."

[4] *bound over* Condemned.

[5] *unconverted man* The unconverted include not only those who have not converted to Christianity, but also those who have not publicly proclaimed a conversion experience of being personally saved by God.

may be are at ease and quiet, than he is with many of those who are now in the flames of hell.[1]

So that it is not because God is unmindful of their wickedness, and does not resent it, that he does not let loose his hand and cut them off. God is not altogether such a one as themselves, though they may imagine him to be so. The wrath of God burns against them, their damnation does not slumber; the pit is prepared, the fire is made ready, the furnace is now hot, ready to receive them, the flames do now rage and glow. The glittering sword is whet, and held over them, and the pit hath opened her mouth under them.[2]

5. The *Devil* stands ready to fall upon them, and seize them as his own, at what moment God shall permit him. They belong to him; he has their souls in his possession, and under his dominion. The scripture represents them as his goods, Luke 11.21.[3] The devils watch them; they are ever by them at their right hand; they stand waiting for them, like greedy hungry lions that see their prey,[4] and expect to have it, but are for the present kept back. If God should withdraw his hand, by which they are restrained, they would in one moment fly upon their poor souls. The old serpent[5] is gaping for them; hell opens its mouth wide to receive them; and if God should permit it, they would be hastily swallowed up and lost.

6. There are in the souls of wicked men those hellish *principles* reigning, that would presently kindle and flame out into hell fire, if it were not for God's restraints. There is laid in the very nature of carnal men, a foundation for the torments of hell. There are those corrupt principles, in reigning power in them, and in full possession of them, that are seeds of hell fire. These principles are active and powerful, exceeding violent in their nature, and if it were not for the restraining hand of God upon them, they would soon break out, they would flame out after the same manner as the same corruptions, the same enmity does in the hearts of damned souls, and would beget the same torments as they do in them.[6] The souls of the wicked are in scripture compared to the troubled sea, Isaiah 57.20.[7] For the present, God restrains their wickedness by his mighty power, as he does the raging waves of the troubled sea, saying, *Hitherto shalt thou come, but no further;*[8] but if God should withdraw that restraining power, it would soon carry all before it. Sin is the ruin and misery of the soul; it is destructive in its nature; and if God should leave it without restraint, there would need nothing else to make the soul perfectly miserable. The corruption of the heart of man is immoderate and boundless in its fury; and while wicked men live here, it is like fire pent up by God's restraints, whereas if it were let loose, it would set on fire the course of nature; and as the heart is now a sink of sin, so if sin was not restrained, it would immediately turn the soul into a fiery oven, or a furnace of fire and brimstone.

7. It is no security to wicked men for one moment, that there are no *visible means* of *death* at hand.[9] 'Tis no security to a natural man,[10] that he is now in health, and that he does not see which way he should now

1 *Yea, God … hell* Edwards alludes to the Reformed Protestant concept of "the invisible church"—the idea that there is a community of Christians, the elect, who have already received or are destined to receive salvation, and whose identities are known by God alone. Not all members of the "visible church"—the institutional communities of worship—are members of the invisible church: some apparent Christians are destined for hell.

2 *The glittering sword* See Deuteronomy 32.41: "If I whet my glittering sword, and mine hand take hold on judgment; I will render vengeance to mine enemies, and will reward them that hate me"; *pit hath … under them* See Numbers 16.30: "But if the Lord make a new thing, and the earth open her mouth, and swallow them up, with all that appertain unto them, and they go down quick into the pit; then ye shall understand that these men have provoked the Lord."

3 *Luke 11.21* In Luke 11.20–22, Jesus metaphorically describes demons as "strong men" who treat human beings as property, and describes God as an even stronger man who can take away the demons' possessions with ease.

4 *greedy hungry … their prey* See Psalm 104.21: "The young lions roar after their prey, and seek their meat from God."

5 *old serpent* Satan. See Revelation 12.9.

6 *These principles … in them* I.e., wicked people are governed by powerful forces of sin, and if God did not hold these forces in check the wicked would be just as tormented on earth as they are in hell.

7 *Isaiah 57.20* "But the wicked are like the troubled sea, when it cannot rest, whose waters cast up mire and dirt."

8 *Hitherto shalt thou … no further* See Job 38.11.

9 *It is … at hand* I.e., wicked people should not take any comfort in the fact that there may not appear to be any immediate risk of dying.

10 *natural man* Person who remains in a state of original sin. See 1 Corinthians 2.14: "But the natural man receiveth not the things of the Spirit of God: for they are foolishness unto him: neither can he know them, because they are spiritually discerned."

immediately go out of the world by any accident, and that there is no visible danger in any respect in his circumstances. The manifold[1] and continual experience of the world in all ages, shows this is no evidence that a man is not on the very brink of eternity, and that the next step will not be into another world. The unseen, unthought-of ways and means of persons going suddenly out of the world are innumerable and inconceivable. Unconverted men walk over the pit of hell on a rotten covering, and there are innumerable places in this covering so weak that they will not bear their weight, and these places are not seen. The arrows of death fly unseen at noonday;[2] the sharpest sight cannot discern them. God has so many different unsearchable ways of taking wicked men out of the world and sending them to hell, that there is nothing to make it appear that God had need to be at the expense of a miracle, or go out of the ordinary course of his providence,[3] to destroy any wicked man, at any moment. All the means that there are of sinners going out of the world, are so in God's hands, and so universally and absolutely subject to his power and determination, that it does not depend at all the less on the mere will of God whether sinners shall at any moment go to hell, than if means were never made use of or at all concerned in the case.[4]

8. Natural men's *prudence* and *care* to preserve their own *lives*, or the care of others to preserve them, do not secure them a moment.[5] To this, divine providence and universal experience do also bear testimony. There is this clear evidence that men's own wisdom is no security to them from death; that if it were otherwise we should see some difference between the wise and politic men of the world, and others, with regard to their liableness to early and unexpected death: but how

is it in fact? Ecclesiastes 2.16: *How dieth the wise man? even as the fool.*

9. All wicked men's *pains* and *contrivance*[6] which they use to escape hell, while they continue to reject Christ, and so remain wicked men, do not secure them from hell one moment. Almost every natural man that hears of hell, flatters himself that he shall escape it; he depends upon himself for his own security; he flatters himself in what he has done, in what he is now doing, or what he intends to do. Every one lays out matters in his own mind how he shall avoid damnation, and flatters himself that he contrives well for himself, and that his schemes will not fail. They hear indeed that there are but few saved, and that the greater part of men that have died heretofore are gone to hell; but each one imagines that he lays out matters better for his own escape than others have done. He does not intend to come to that place of torment; he says within himself, that he intends to take effectual care, and to order matters so for himself as not to fail.

But the foolish children of men miserably delude themselves in their own schemes, and in confidence in their own strength and wisdom; they trust to nothing but a shadow. The greater part of those who heretofore have lived under the same means of grace, and are now dead, are undoubtedly gone to hell; and it was not because they were not as wise as those who are now alive: it was not because they did not lay out matters as well for themselves to secure their own escape. If we could speak with them and inquire of them, one by one, whether they expected, when alive and when they used to hear about hell, ever to be the subjects of misery: we doubtless, should hear one and another reply, "No, I never intended to come here: I had laid out matters otherwise in my mind; I thought I should contrive well for myself; I thought my scheme good. I intended to take effectual care; but it came upon me unexpected; I did not look for it at that time, and in that manner; it came as a thief;[7] Death outwitted me: God's wrath was too quick for me. Oh, my cursed foolishness! I was flattering myself, and pleasing myself with vain dreams of what I would do hereafter;

[1] *manifold* Diverse.

[2] *The arrows ... noonday* See Psalm 91.5: "Thou shalt not be afraid for the terror by night; nor for the arrow that flieth by day."

[3] *providence* Divine foresight, power, and governance.

[4] *All the ... the case* I.e., all factors that can make a person die are ultimately controlled by God. Consequently, people's lives are just as much in God's hands as they would be if God directly caused people to die without the mediation of seemingly external factors (such as disease and war).

[5] *Natural men's ... a moment* I.e., it does not matter how much one takes care of one's health or avoids risky behaviors: anyone can die at an unexpected time.

[6] *contrivance* Scheming, clever planning.

[7] *came as a thief* See 1 Thessalonians 5.2: "the day of the Lord so cometh as a thief in the night."

and when I was saying peace and safety, then sudden destruction came upon me."[1]

10. God has laid himself under *no obligation*, by any promise to keep any natural man out of hell one moment. God certainly has made no promises either of eternal life, or of any deliverance or preservation from eternal death, but what are contained in the covenant of grace,[2] the promises that are given in Christ, in whom all the promises are yea and amen. But surely they have no interest in the promises of the covenant of grace who are not the children of the covenant, who do not believe in any of the promises, and have no interest in the Mediator[3] of the covenant.

So that, whatever some have imagined and pretended about promises made to natural men's earnest seeking and knocking,[4] 'tis plain and manifest, that whatever pains a natural man takes in religion, whatever prayers he makes, till he believes in Christ, God is under no manner of obligation to keep him a moment from eternal destruction.

So that thus it is that natural men are held in the hand of God over the pit of hell; they have deserved the fiery pit, and are already sentenced to it; and God is dreadfully provoked, his anger is as great towards them as to those that are actually suffering the executions of the fierceness of his wrath in hell, and they have done nothing in the least to appease or abate that anger, neither is God in the least bound by any promise to hold them up one moment; the devil is waiting for them, hell is gaping for them, the flames gather and flash about them, and would fain lay hold on them, and swallow them up; the fire pent up in their own hearts is struggling to break out: and they have no interest in any Mediator, there are no means within reach that can be any security to them. In short, they have no refuge, nothing to take hold of; all that preserves them every moment is the mere arbitrary will, and uncovenanted, unobliged forbearance of an incensed God.

APPLICATION

The use may be of *awakening* unconverted persons[5] in this congregation. This that you have heard is the case of every one of you that are out of Christ.[6] That world of misery, that lake of burning brimstone, is extended abroad under you. *There* is the dreadful pit of the glowing flames of the wrath of God; there is hell's wide gaping mouth open; and you have nothing to stand upon, not anything to take hold of; there is nothing between you and hell but the air; 'tis only the power and mere pleasure of God that holds you up.

You probably are not sensible of this; you find you are kept out of hell, but do not see the hand of God in it; but look at other things, as the good state of your bodily constitution, your care of your own life, and the means you use for your own preservation. But indeed these things are nothing; if God should withdraw his hand, they would avail no more to keep you from falling, than the thin air to hold up a person that is suspended in it.

Your wickedness makes you as it were heavy as lead[7] and to tend downwards with great weight and pressure towards hell; and if God should let you go, you would immediately sink and swiftly descend and plunge into the bottomless gulf, and your healthy constitution, and your own care and prudence, and best contrivance, and all your righteousness, would have no more influence to uphold you and keep you out of hell than a spider's web would have to stop a falling rock. Were it not for the sovereign pleasure of God, the earth would not bear you one moment; for you are a burden to it; the creation groans with you; the creature[8] is made subject to the bondage of your corruption, not willingly; the sun does not willingly shine upon you to give you light to serve sin and Satan; the earth does not willingly yield her increase to satisfy your lusts; nor is it willingly

1 *peace and safety … upon me* See 1 Thessalonians 5.3.

2 *God certainly … of grace* Edwards alludes to the Calvinist tenet of "limited atonement," which holds that salvation is granted only to those members of God's elect.

3 *the Mediator* I.e., Christ.

4 *seeking and knocking* See Matthew 7.7: "Ask, and it shall be given you; seek, and ye shall find; knock, and it shall be opened."

5 *unconverted persons* Parishioners who had not yet publicly proclaimed their experience of salvation, and thus had not obtained full church membership.

6 *out of Christ* Not saved, not a member of the elect.

7 *heavy as lead* See Exodus 15.10, where God is praised for drowning the Egyptians, enemies of the Israelites, in the sea: "Thou didst blow with thy wind, the sea covered them: they sank as lead in the mighty waters."

8 *creature* Thing or being created by God.

a stage for your wickedness to be acted upon; the air does not willingly serve you for breath to maintain the flame of life in your vitals, while you spend your life in the service of God's enemies. God's creatures are good, and were made for men to serve God with, and do not willingly subserve to[1] any other purpose, and groan when they are abused to purposes so directly contrary to their nature and end. And the world would spew you out, were it not for the sovereign hand of him who hath subjected it in hope.[2] There are the black clouds of God's wrath now hanging directly over your heads, full of the dreadful storm, and big with thunder; and were it not for the restraining hand of God, it would immediately burst forth upon you. The sovereign pleasure of God, for the present, stays his rough wind; otherwise it would come with fury, and your destruction would come like a whirlwind,[3] and you would be like the chaff on the summer threshing floor.

The wrath of God is like great waters that are dammed for the present; they increase more and more, and rise higher and higher, till an outlet is given; and the longer the stream is stopped, the more rapid and mighty is its course, when once it is let loose. 'Tis true, that judgment against your evil works has not been executed hitherto; the floods of God's vengeance have been withheld; but your guilt in the meantime is constantly increasing, and you are every day treasuring up more wrath; the waters are constantly rising, and waxing more and more mighty; and there is nothing but the mere pleasure of God that holds the waters back that are unwilling to be stopped and press hard to go forward. If God should only withdraw his hand from the flood-gate, it would immediately fly open, and the fiery floods of the fierceness and wrath of God, would rush forth with inconceivable fury and would come upon you with omnipotent power; and if your strength were ten thousand times greater than it is, yea, ten thousand times greater than the strength of the stoutest, sturdiest devil in hell, it would be nothing to withstand or endure it.

The bow of God's wrath is bent,[4] and the arrow made ready on the string, and justice bends the arrow at your heart, and strains the bow, and it is nothing but the mere pleasure of God, and that of an angry God, without any promise or obligation at all, that keeps the arrow one moment from being made drunk with your blood.

Thus all you that never passed under a great change of heart, by the mighty power of the Spirit of God upon your souls; all you that were never born again,[5] and made new creatures, and raised from being dead in sin, to a state of new, and before altogether unexperienced light and life, are in the hands of an angry God. However you may have reformed your life in many things, and may have had religious affections, and may keep up a form of religion in your families and closets,[6] and in the house of God, 'tis nothing but his mere pleasure that keeps you from being this moment swallowed up in everlasting destruction. However unconvinced you may now be of the truth of what you hear, by and by you will be fully convinced of it. Those that are gone from being in the like circumstances with you, see that it was so with them; for destruction came suddenly upon most of them; when they expected nothing of it, and while they were saying, Peace and safety: now they see, that those things on which they depended for peace and safety, were nothing but thin air and empty shadows.

The God that holds you over the pit of hell, much as one holds a spider, or some loathsome insect over the fire, abhors you, and is dreadfully provoked: his wrath towards you burns like fire; he looks upon you as worthy of nothing else, but to be cast into the fire; he is of purer eyes than to bear to have you in his sight; you are ten thousand times more abominable in his eyes, than the most hateful venomous serpent is in ours. You have offended him infinitely more than ever a stubborn rebel did his prince; and yet 'tis nothing but his

1 *subserve to* Serve, facilitate.

2 *him who ... in hope* See Romans 8.20: "the creature was made subject to vanity, not willingly, but by reason of him who hath subjected the same in hope."

3 *your destruction ... whirlwind* See Proverbs 1.26–27, where wisdom addresses "fools," saying "I also will laugh at your calamity; I will mock when your fear cometh; when your fear cometh as desolation, and your destruction cometh as a whirlwind."

4 *The bow ... bent* See Psalm 7.11–12: "God judgeth the righteous, and God is angry with the wicked every day. If he turn not, he will whet his sword; he hath bent his bow, and made it ready."

5 *born again* I.e., saved; spiritually reborn through faith in Christ.

6 *closets* I.e., private rooms.

hand that holds you from falling into the fire every moment. 'Tis to be ascribed to nothing else, that you did not go to hell the last night; that you was suffered to awake again in this world, after you closed your eyes to sleep. And there is no other reason to be given, why you have not dropped into hell since you arose in the morning, but that God's hand has held you up. There is no other reason to be given why you have not gone to hell, since you have sat here in the house of God, provoking his pure eyes by your sinful wicked manner of attending his solemn worship. Yea, there is nothing else that is to be given as a reason why you do not this very moment drop down into hell.

O sinner! Consider the fearful danger you are in: 'Tis a great furnace of wrath, a wide and bottomless pit, full of the fire of wrath, that you are held over in the hand of that God, whose wrath is provoked and incensed as much against you, as against many of the damned in hell. You hang by a slender thread, with the flames of divine wrath flashing about it, and ready every moment to singe it, and burn it asunder; and you have no interest in any Mediator, and nothing to lay hold of to save yourself, nothing to keep off the flames of wrath, nothing of your own, nothing that you ever have done, nothing that you can do, to induce God to spare you one moment.

And consider here more particularly several things concerning that wrath that you are in such danger of.

1. *Whose* wrath it is: it is the wrath of the infinite God. If it were only the wrath of man, though it were of the most potent prince, it would be comparatively little to be regarded. The wrath of kings is very much dreaded, especially of absolute monarchs, who have the possessions and lives of their subjects wholly in their power, to be disposed of at their mere will. Proverbs 20.2: *The fear of a king is as the roaring of a lion: Whoso provoketh him to anger, sinneth against his own soul.* The subject that very much enrages an arbitrary prince, is liable to suffer the most extreme torments that human art can invent, or human power can inflict. But the greatest earthly potentates in their greatest majesty and strength, and when clothed in their greatest terrors, are but feeble, despicable worms of the dust in comparison of the great and almighty Creator and King of heaven and earth. It is but little that they can do, when most enraged and when they have exerted the utmost of their fury. All the kings of the earth, before God, are as grasshoppers;[1] they are nothing and less than nothing: both their love and their hatred is to be despised. The wrath of the great king of kings[2] is as much more terrible than theirs, as his majesty is greater. Luke 12.4–5: *And I say unto you, my friends, Be not afraid of them that kill the body, and after that, have no more that they can do. But I will forewarn you whom you shall fear: fear him, which after he hath killed, hath power to cast into hell: yea, I say unto you, fear him.*

2. 'Tis the *fierceness* of his wrath that you are exposed to. We often read of the fury of God; as in Isaiah 59.18: *According to their deeds, accordingly he will repay fury to his adversaries.* So Isaiah 66.15: *For behold, the Lord will come with fire, and with his chariots like a whirlwind, to render his anger with fury, and his rebuke with flames of fire.* And in many other places. So, Rev. 19.15, we read of *The wine press of the fierceness and wrath of Almighty God.* The words are exceeding terrible. If it had only been said, *the wrath of God,* the words would have implied that which is infinitely dreadful: but 'tis not only said so, but *the fierceness and wrath of God.* The fury of God! The fierceness of Jehovah! Oh, how dreadful that must be! Who can utter or conceive what such expressions carry in them! But it is not only said so, but *the fierceness and wrath of almighty God.* As though there would be a very great manifestation of his almighty power in what the fierceness of his wrath should inflict, as though omnipotence should be as it were enraged and excited, as men are wont to exert their strength in the fierceness of their wrath. Oh! Then, what will be the consequence! What will become of the poor worms that shall suffer it! Whose hands can be strong? And whose heart endure? To what a dreadful, inexpressible, inconceivable depth of misery must the poor creature be sunk who shall be the subject of this!

Consider this, you that are here present, that yet remain in an unregenerate state. That God will execute the fierceness of his anger implies that he will inflict wrath without any pity. When God beholds the ineffable extremity of your case, and sees your torment to be so vastly disproportioned to your strength, and sees how your poor soul is crushed, and sinks down, as it

[1] *grasshoppers* See Isaiah 40.22: "It is he that sitteth upon the circle of the earth, and the inhabitants thereof are as grasshoppers."

[2] *king of kings* God.

were, into an infinite gloom; he will have no compassion upon you, he will not forbear the executions of his wrath, or in the least lighten his hand; there shall be no moderation or mercy, nor will God then at all stay his rough wind; he will have no regard to your welfare, nor be at all careful lest you should suffer too much in any other sense, than only that you shall not suffer beyond what strict justice requires. Nothing shall be withheld, because it's so hard for you to bear. Ezekiel 8.18: *Therefore will I also deal in fury: mine eye shall not spare, neither will I have pity; and though they cry in mine ears with a loud voice, yet I will not hear them.* Now God stands ready to pity you; this is a day of mercy; you may cry now with some encouragement of obtaining mercy. But when once the day of mercy is past, your most lamentable and dolorous[1] cries and shrieks will be in vain; you will be wholly lost and thrown away of God, as to any regard to your welfare. God will have no other use to put you to but to suffer misery; you shall be continued in being to no other end, for you will be a vessel of wrath fitted to destruction; and there will be no other use of this vessel, but to be filled full of wrath. God will be so far from pitying you when you cry to him, that 'tis said he will only *laugh and mock,* Proverbs 1.25–26, etc.

How awful[2] are those words, Isaiah 63.3, which are the words of the great God. *I will tread them in mine anger, and will trample them in my fury, and their blood shall be sprinkled upon my garments, and I will stain all my raiment.*[3] 'Tis perhaps impossible to conceive of words that carry in them greater manifestations of these three things, *viz.*[4] contempt, and hatred, and fierceness of indignation. If you cry to God to pity you, he will be so far from pitying you in your doleful case, or showing you the least regard or favour, that instead of that, he will only tread you under foot. And though he will know that you cannot bear the weight of omnipotence treading upon you, yet he will not regard that, but he will crush you under his feet without mercy; he will crush out your blood, and make it fly, and it shall be sprinkled on his garments, so as to stain all his raiment.

He will not only hate you, but he will have you in the utmost contempt: no place shall be thought fit for you, but under his feet to be trodden down as the mire of the streets.

3. The misery you are exposed to is that which God will inflict to that end, that he might *show* what that *wrath* of Jehovah is. God hath had it on his heart to show to angels and men, both how excellent his love is and also how terrible his wrath is. Sometimes earthly kings have a mind to show how terrible their wrath is by the extreme punishments they would execute on those that would provoke them. Nebuchadnezzar, that mighty and haughty monarch of the Chaldean empire, was willing to show his wrath when enraged with Shadrach, Meshach, and Abednego;[5] and accordingly gave orders that the burning fiery furnace should be heated seven times hotter than it was before; doubtless, it was raised to the utmost degree of fierceness that human art could raise it. But the great God is also willing to show his wrath, and magnify his awful majesty and mighty power in the extreme sufferings of his enemies. Romans 9.22: *What if God, willing to show his wrath, and to make his power known, endured with much long-suffering the vessels of wrath fitted to destruction?* And seeing this is his design, and what he has determined, even to show how terrible the unrestrained wrath, the fury and fierceness of Jehovah is, he will do it to effect. There will be something accomplished and brought to pass that will be dreadful with a witness. When the great and angry God hath risen up and executed his awful vengeance on the poor sinner, and the wretch is actually suffering the infinite weight and power of his indignation, then will God call upon the whole universe to behold that awful majesty and mighty power that is to be seen in it. Isaiah 33.12–14: *And the people shall be as the burnings of lime, as thorns cut up shall they be burnt in the fire. Hear ye that are far off, what I have done; and ye that are near, acknowledge my might. The sinners in Zion are afraid; fearfulness hath surprised the hypocrites,* etc.

Thus it will be with you that are in an unconverted state, if you continue in it; the infinite might, and

[1] *dolorous* Sorrowful, marked by suffering.

[2] *awful* Awe-inspiring.

[3] *raiment* Clothing.

[4] *viz.* Abbreviation of the Latin videlicet, meaning "namely," or "that is to say."

[5] *Shadrach, Meshach, and Abednego* Three Jewish youths in the book of Daniel who refused to bow before an image of Nebuchadnezzar, the king of Babylon, and were punished by being cast into a furnace. God prevented the flames from harming them. See Daniel 3.

majesty, and terribleness of the Omnipotent GOD shall be magnified upon you, in the ineffable strength of your torments. You shall be tormented in the presence of the holy angels, and in the presence of the Lamb;[1] and when you shall be in this state of suffering, the glorious inhabitants of heaven shall go forth and look on the awful spectacle, that they may see what the wrath and fierceness of the Almighty is; and when they have seen it, they will fall down and adore that great power and majesty. Isaiah 66.23–24: *And it shall come to pass, that from one new moon to another, and from one sabbath to another, shall all flesh come to worship before me, saith the Lord. And they shall go forth and look upon the carcasses of the men that have transgressed against me; for their worm shall not die, neither shall their fire be quenched, and they shall be an abhorring unto all flesh.*

4. 'Tis *everlasting* wrath. It would be dreadful to suffer this fierceness and wrath of Almighty God one moment; but you must suffer it to all eternity. There will be no end to this exquisite horrible misery. When you look forward, you shall see a long forever, a boundless duration before you, which will swallow up your thoughts, and amaze your soul; and you will absolutely despair of ever having any deliverance, any end, any mitigation, any rest at all. You will know certainly that you must wear out long ages, millions of millions of ages, in wrestling and conflicting with this almighty merciless vengeance; and then when you have so done, when so many ages have actually been spent by you in this manner, you will know that all is but a point to what remains. So that your punishment will indeed be infinite. Oh, who can express what the state of a soul in such circumstances is! All that we can possibly say about it, gives but a very feeble, faint representation of it; 'tis inexpressible and inconceivable: For *who knows the power of God's anger?*[2]

How dreadful is the state of those that are daily and hourly in the danger of this great wrath and infinite misery! But this is the dismal case of every soul in this congregation that has not been born again, however moral and strict, sober and religious, they may otherwise be. Oh that you would consider it, whether you be young or old! There is reason to think that there are many in this congregation now hearing this discourse, that will actually be the subjects of this very misery to all eternity. We know not who they are, or in what seats they sit, or what thoughts they now have. It may be they are now at ease, and hear all these things without much disturbance, and are now flattering themselves that they are not the persons, promising themselves that they shall escape. If we knew that there was one person, and but one, in the whole congregation, that was to be the subject of this misery, what an awful thing would it be to think of! If we knew who it was, what an awful sight would it be to see such a person! How might all the rest of the congregation lift up a lamentable and bitter cry over him! But, alas! instead of one, how many is it likely will remember this discourse in hell? And it would be a wonder, if some that are now present should not be in hell in a very short time, even before this year is out. And it would be no wonder if some persons, that now sit here, in some seats of this meeting-house,[3] in health, quiet and secure, should be there before tomorrow morning. Those of you that finally continue in a natural condition, that shall keep out of hell longest will be there in a little time! Your damnation does not slumber; it will come swiftly, and, in all probability, very suddenly upon many of you. You have reason to wonder that you are not already in hell. 'Tis doubtless the case of some whom you have seen and known that never deserved hell more than you, and that heretofore appeared as likely to have been now alive as you. Their case is past all hope; they are crying in extreme misery and perfect despair; but here you are in the land of the living and in the house of God, and have an opportunity to obtain salvation. What would not those poor damned hopeless souls give for one day's opportunity such as you now enjoy!

And now you have an extraordinary opportunity, a day wherein Christ has thrown the door of mercy wide open, and stands in calling and crying with a loud voice to poor sinners; a day wherein many are flocking to him, and pressing into the kingdom of God.[4] Many are daily coming from the east, west, north and south; many that were very lately in the same miserable condition that you are in, are now in a happy state, with

1 *the Lamb* Christ.

2 *who knows ... God's anger* See Psalm 90.11: "Who knoweth the power of thine anger? Even according to thy fear, so is thy wrath."

3 *meeting-house* Place of worship.

4 *And now ... of God* At the time Edwards delivered this sermon, the First Great Awakening, a surge of religious enthusiasm, was spreading across New England.

their hearts filled with love to him who has loved them, and washed them from their sins in his own blood, and rejoicing in hope of the glory of God. How awful is it to be left behind at such a day! To see so many others feasting, while you are pining and perishing! To see so many rejoicing and singing for joy of heart, while you have cause to mourn for sorrow of heart, and howl for vexation of spirit! How can you rest one moment in such a condition? Are not your souls as precious as the souls of the people at Suffield,[1] where they are flocking from day to day to Christ?

Are there not many here who have lived *long* in the world, and are not to this day born again? And so are aliens from the commonwealth of Israel,[2] and have done nothing ever since they have lived, but treasure up wrath against the day of wrath? Oh, sirs, your case, in an especial manner, is extremely dangerous. Your guilt and hardness of heart is extremely great. Do you not see how generally persons of your years are passed over and left in the present remarkable and wonderful dispensation of God's mercy? You had need to consider yourselves and awake thoroughly out of sleep. You cannot bear the fierceness and wrath of the infinite God.

And you that are *young men* and *young women*, will you neglect this precious season which you now enjoy, when so many others of your age are renouncing all youthful vanities, and flocking to Christ? You especially have now an extraordinary opportunity; but if you neglect it, it will soon be with you as with those persons who spent all the precious days of youth in sin, and are now come to such a dreadful pass in blindness and hardness.

And you, *children* that are unconverted, do not you know that you are going down to hell, to bear the dreadful wrath of that God, who is now angry with you every day and every night? Will you be content

to be the children of the devil, when so many other children in the land are converted, and are become the holy and happy children of the king of kings?

And let everyone that is yet out of Christ, and hanging over the pit of hell, whether they be old men and women, or middle aged, or young people, or little children, now hearken to the loud calls of God's word and providence. This acceptable year of the Lord, a day of such great favour to some, will doubtless be a day of as remarkable vengeance to others. Men's hearts harden, and their guilt increases apace at such a day as this, if they neglect their souls; and never was there so great danger of such persons being given up to hardness of heart and blindness of mind. God seems now to be hastily gathering in his elect in all parts of the land; and probably the greater part of adult persons that ever shall be saved will be brought in now in a little time, and that it will be as it was on the great outpouring of the Spirit upon the Jews in the apostles' days; the election will obtain, and the rest will be blinded.[3] If this should be the case with you, you will eternally curse this day, and will curse the day that ever you was born, to see such a season of the pouring out of God's Spirit, and will wish that you had died and gone to hell before you had seen it. Now undoubtedly it is, as it was in the days of John the Baptist, the axe is in an extraordinary manner laid at the root of the trees, that every tree which brings not forth good fruit, may be hewn down and cast into the fire.[4]

Therefore, let every one that is out of Christ, now awake and fly from the wrath to come. The wrath of Almighty God is now undoubtedly hanging over a great part of this congregation. Let every one fly out of Sodom: *Haste and escape for your lives, look not behind you, escape to the mountain, lest you be consumed.*[5]

—1741

1 *Suffield* A neighboring town in Massachusetts where, two days earlier, Edwards had delivered a sermon that was enthusiastically received by an audience of more than two hundred people.

2 *aliens from ... of Israel* People who are estranged from the church, i.e., are not members of the elect.

3 *the election ... be blinded* See Romans 11.7: "Israel hath not obtained that which he seeketh for; but the election hath obtained it, and the rest were blinded."

4 *the axe ... the fire* See Luke 3.9: "And now also the axe is laid unto the root of the trees: every tree therefore which bringeth not forth good fruit is hewn down, and cast into the fire."

5 *Haste and ... consumed* See Genesis 19.17, where an angel warns Lot to flee the city of Sodom before it is destroyed by God: "Escape for thy life; look not behind thee, neither stay thou in all the plain; escape to the mountain, lest thou be consumed."

IN CONTEXT

The Preaching of Jonathan Edwards

While most reports suggest that he did not speak with the dramatic enthusiasm of some Great Awakening ministers, Edwards had a reputation as an effective preacher. The first of the following selections, from the diary of Stephen Williams (1694–1782), a minister from Longmeadow, Massachusetts, offers a first-person account of the intense reaction Edwards provoked when he delivered "Sinners in the Hands of an Angry God" at Enfield. A brief, general description of Edwards's oratorical style can be found in the next selection, from *An Account of the Revival of Religion in Boston* by Great Awakening supporter Thomas Prince (1687–1758). Finally, Edwards's style is discussed more extensively in *The Life and Character of the Late Reverend Mr. Jonathan Edwards*, a biography by Edwards's friend and fellow theologian Samuel Hopkins (1721–1803).

from The diary of Stephen Williams (manuscript 1716–82)

[8 JULY 1741]

[W]ent over to Enfield where we met dear Mr. E[dwards] of N[orth] H[ampton], who ... preached a most awakening sermon from those words Deuteronomy 32.35—and before the sermon was done there was a great moaning and crying out throughout the whole house: what shall I do to be saved—oh I am going to Hell—oh what shall I do for a Christ—so that the minister was obliged to desist. [The] shrieks and cries were piercing and amazing. After some time of waiting, the congregation were still so that a prayer was made by Mr. W[illiams], and after that we descended from the pulpit and discoursed with the people—some in one place and some in another—and amazing and astonishing the power—God was seen and several souls were hopefully wrought upon that night, and oh the cheerfulness and pleasantness of their countenances that received comfort. Oh that God would strengthen and confirm. We sang an hymn and prayed and dispersed the assembly.

[9 JULY 1741]

In the morning when I awoke I had a great desire in my soul that God would give me to see at L[ong] M[eadow] what I had seen at Enfield. I seemed affected and moved—ready to dissolve in tears—but can't well tell why. ...

from Thomas Prince, *An Account of the Revival of Religion in Boston, in the years 1740–1–2–3* (1743)

A remarkable instance of conviction ... has been sometimes under the ministry of the Rev. Mr. ... Edwards of Northampton, a preacher of a low and moderate voice, a natural way of delivery, and without any agitation of body or anything else in the manner to excite attention; except his habitual and great solemnity, looking and speaking as in the presence of God, and with a weighty sense of the matter delivered. ...

from Samuel Hopkins, *The Life and Character of the Late Reverend Mr. Jonathan Edwards* (1765)

... Mr. Edwards had the most universal character of a good preacher of almost any minister in this age. There were but few that heard him, who did not call him a good preacher, however they might dislike his religious principles, and be much offended at the same truths when delivered by others: And most admired him above all that ever they heard. His eminency as a preacher seems to be owing to the following things.

First, The great pains he took in composing his sermons, especially in the first part of his life. As by his early rising, and constant attention to his study, he had more time than most others; so he spent more time in making his sermons. He wrote most of his sermons all out, for near twenty years after he first began to preach; though he did not wholly confine himself to his notes in his delivering them. ...

His appearance in the desk was with a good grace, and his delivery easy, natural and very solemn. He had not a strong, loud voice; but appeared with such gravity and solemnity, and spake with such distinctness, clearness and precision; his words were so full of ideas, set in such a plain and striking light, that few speakers have been so able to demand the attention of an audience as he. His words often discovered[1] a great degree of inward fervor, without much noise or external emotion, and fell with great weight on the minds of his hearers. He made but little motion of his head or hands in the desk, but spake so as to discover the motion of his own heart, which tended in the most natural and effectual manner to move and affect others.

As he wrote his sermons out at large for many years, and always wrote a considerable part of most of his public discourses; so he carried his notes into the desk with him, and read the most that he had wrote; yet he was not so confined to his notes, when he had wrote at large, but that, if some thoughts were suggested while he was speaking, which did not occur when writing, and appeared to him pertinent and striking, he would deliver them; and that with as great propriety and fluency, and oftener with greater pathos, and attended with a more sensible good effect on his hearers, than all he had wrote.

Though, as has been observed, he was wont to read so considerable a part of what he delivered; yet he was far from thinking this the best way of preaching in general; and looked upon his using his notes so much as he did, a deficiency and infirmity. ...

His prayers were indeed *extempore*. He was the farthest from any appearance of a form, as to his words and manner of expression, of almost any man. He was quite singular and inimitable in this, by any who have not a spirit of real and undissembled devotion. Yet he always expressed himself with decency and propriety. He appeared to have much of the grace and spirit of prayer; to pray with the spirit and with the understanding: and he performed this part of duty much to the acceptance and edification of those who joined with him. He was not wont, in ordinary cases to be long in his prayers: an error which he observed was often hurtful to public and social prayer, as it tends rather to damp than promote true devotion. ...

[1] *discovered* Revealed.

ELIZABETH ASHBRIDGE

1713 – 1755

Elizabeth Ashbridge's spiritual memoir, *Some Account of the Fore Part of the Life of Elizabeth Ashbridge* (1774), is a remarkable first-person account of the life of a non-wealthy woman living in colonial America, from a time when such voices were infrequently heard in the literary world. Born in England into a family of modest means, Ashbridge endured years of poverty and abuse in America before her struggle for moral independence and religious fulfilment brought her into the fold of the Society of Friends, otherwise known as the Quaker church. Her narrative, published by her third husband almost two decades after her death, is a fascinating example of the Quaker tradition of spiritual autobiography as well as a spirited account of Ashbridge's navigation of the many difficulties she faced in America.

Some Account is almost the only known source of factual information on the life of Ashbridge, who was born to Mary and Thomas Sampson in Cheshire, England in 1713. Mary Sampson, a devout Anglican, was a profound influence on Ashbridge, but Thomas Sampson was physically distant throughout her childhood, working frequently at sea as a ship's physician. Ashbridge was banished from the household following her elopement, at the age of fourteen, with a poor stocking weaver; she was left widowed shortly thereafter. She then moved to Ireland, and first began questioning her faith under the influence of her Catholic relatives. Before long, Ashbridge found herself "filled with the thought of coming to America." Like countless people in eighteenth- and nineteenth-century Ireland, she was lured unknowingly into signing a contract of indenture to pay for her Atlantic passage; for the following three years, she was held in an abusive position of servitude in New York. Following her release, Ashbridge briefly considered becoming an actress (a profession many in the eighteenth century considered to be immodest and associated with prostitution); she studied theater literature for a time, before marrying an itinerant schoolteacher she names only as "Sullivan."

From this point on, as the couple moved periodically between New York, New Jersey, and Pennsylvania, Ashbridge explored various Christian denominations, before finding herself drawn into the Society of Friends. Quakers, though no longer openly persecuted to the degree that they had been in the seventeenth century, remained widely ostracized (at least outside of Quaker-settled areas, most notably Pennsylvania). They were pacifists, in many cases abolitionists, and a number were vegetarians; they cultivated habits of plain dress, plain speech, and plain worship that members of many other denominations found off-putting. But in the Society of Friends Ashbridge finally found a spiritual home.

Her marriage, however, was not an easy one. Sullivan began verbally and physically abusing Ashbridge, while he himself became increasingly dependent on alcohol. But by about 1738, Ashbridge had not only converted to the Quaker faith herself but had also begun influencing the increasingly troubled Sullivan to rethink his faith; he converted shortly before his death (around 1740).

Ashbridge's narrative ends here, but we know from a scattering of historical sources, including several testimonials appended to the end of *Some Account*, that in the years following her second husband's death she became a prominent Quaker minister. Ashbridge married Pennsylvanian and fellow Quaker Aaron Ashbridge in 1746, and embarked on a ministerial tour of Ireland in 1753. She died in County Carlow two years later.

The chronology of Ashbridge's *Account* has led most scholars to agree that the text was written around 1745, not long after she received news of Sullivan's death, and before her third marriage; it is considered likely that she continued to revise the document in later years. Copies of her manuscript were in circulation within the Quaker community by 1757; the narrative was probably read by John Woolman, one of the leading Quaker figures of the eighteenth century, while he was working on his own influential *Journal of John Woolman* (1774). During the eighteenth century, autobiographical writing became an important tradition amongst Quakers; Ashbridge's narrative shares numerous traits with

other such autobiographies; it was common to provide detailed descriptions of one's early experiences of other churches prior to discovering the Quakers, and to emphasize one's outsider status as a member of a widely ostracized religious group. Yet the *Account* is also distinctive—not least of all for its substantial portion that describes Ashbridge's indenture, with impassioned accompanying condemnations of her master's moral hypocrisy.

 Some Account was first published in Ashbridge's home county of Cheshire, England in 1774, nearly two decades after her death. The first American edition was published in 1807, with a heavily revised text; this edition substantially modernized Ashbridge's original spelling, punctuation, and syntax, and also weakened and sometimes omitted her more impassioned statements, including the many references to her inner struggle against Satan. New editions of the narrative continued to be released numerous times over the following decades, with Ashbridge continuing to be seen as an important figure within the Society of Friends. Since the late-twentieth century, interest in Ashbridge has extended far beyond the Quaker community. Her *Account* continues to engage readers and to provoke conversations about indentured servitude, about religion in early America, and about gender roles and expectations in the eighteenth century.

NOTE ON THE TEXT: The full title of Elizabeth Ashbridge's narrative, as published in England in 1774, is *Some Account of the Fore Part of the Life of Elizabeth Ashbridge, who died in Truth's service at the house of Robert Lecky at Kilnock in the County of Carlow Ireland; the 16th of 5th mo. 1755. Written by her own Hand many years ago.* This edition, like all those published later in the eighteenth and nineteenth centuries, was based on one or more copies of Ashbridge's manuscript, the original of which has not survived. The text presented below is reprinted with permission from Daniel B. Shea's authoritative 1990 edition, published in the anthology *Journeys in New Worlds: Early American Women's Narratives*, edited by William L. Andrews. Spelling and punctuation have been modernized in accordance with the practices of this anthology.

⌘ ⌘ ⌘

Some Account of the Fore Part of the Life of Elizabeth Ashbridge

My life being attended with many uncommon occurrences—some of which I through disobedience brought upon myself, and others I believe were for my good—I therefore thought proper to make some remarks on the dealings of divine goodness to me, and have often had cause with David to say, "it was good for me that I have been afflicted,"[1] etc.; and most earnestly I desire that whosoever reads the following lines may take warning and shun the evils that I have through the deceitfulness of Satan been drawn into.

 To begin with my beginning. I was born in Middlewich, in Cheshire, in the year 1713, of honest parents. My father [was] a doctor of physic, or surgeon;[2] his name was Thomas Sampson. My mother's name was Mary. My father was a man that bore a good character, but not so strictly religious as my mother, who was a pattern[3] of virtue to me. I was the only child of my father but not of my mother, she being a widow when my father married her, and had two children by her former husband, a son and a daughter. Soon after my birth, my father took to the sea and followed his profession on board a ship, in many long voyages, till I arrived to the age of twelve years, and then [he] left off, so that my education lay mostly on my mother, in which she discharged[4] her duty by endeavoring to instill in me, in my tender age, the principles of virtue; for which I have since had cause to be thankful to the

[1] *it was good ... afflicted* See Psalm 119.71; the Psalms of the Old Testament are said to have been authored by the prophet King David.

[2] *doctor of physic, or surgeon* I.e., medical doctor.

[3] *pattern* Model.

[4] *discharged* Fulfilled.

Lord, and that he blessed me with such a parent whose good advice and counsel to me has been as bread cast on the waters;[1] and may all parents have the same testimony in their children's breasts. In a word, she was a good example to all about her, and beloved by most that knew her, though not of the same religious persuasion I am now of. But alas for me, as soon as the time came that she might reasonably have expected the benefit of her labours, and have had comfort in me, I left her—of which I shall speak in its place.

In my very infancy, I had an awful regard for[2] religion and a great love for religious people, particularly the ministers, and sometimes wept with sorrow that I was not a boy that I might have been one, believing them all good men and so beloved of God. Also I had a great love for the poor, remembering I had read that they were blessed of the Lord;[3] this I took to mean such as were poor in this world. I often went to their poor cottages to see them, and used to think they were better off than me, and if I had any money or anything else I would give it to them, remembering that those that gave to such lent to the Lord.[4] For I had when very young earnest desires to be beloved by him, and used to make remarks on those that pretended to religion; and when I heard the gentlemen swear it made me sorry, for my Mother told me if I used any naughty words God would not love me.

As I grew up, I took notice there were several different religious societies,[5] wherefore I often went alone and wept with desires that I might be directed to the right. Thus my young years were attended with these and such like tender desires, though I was sometimes guilty of faults incident to children, and then I always found something in me that made me sorry. From my infancy till fourteen years of age I was as innocent as most children—about which time my sorrows began, and have continued for the most part of my life ever

since, by giving way to a foolish passion in setting my affections on a young man who courted me without my parents' consent till I consented;[6] and with sorrow of heart may say I suffered[7] myself to be carried off in the night, and before my parents found me, was married. Though as soon as they missed me, all possible search was made, but all in vain till too late to recover me.

This precipitate action plunged me into a deal of sorrow. I was soon smote with remorse for thus leaving my parents, whose right it was to have disposed of me[8] to their contents, or at least to have been consulted in the affair. I was soon chastised for my disobedience—Divine Providence let me see my error. In five months, I was stripped of the darling of my soul and left a young and disconsolate widow. I had then no home to fly to. My husband was poor, had nothing but his trade, which was a stocking weaver, and my father was so displeased he would do nothing for me. My dear mother had some compassion and used to keep me amongst the neighbours. At last by her advice I went over to Dublin, to a relation of hers, in hopes that absence would regain my father's affection. But he continued inflexible, and would not send for me again, and I durst[9] not return without it.

This relation was one of the people called Quakers. His conduct was so different from the manner of my education (which was in the way of the Church of England) that it proved very disagreeable to me, for though (as I have said) I had a religious education, yet I was allowed to sing and dance, which my cousin disallowed of,[10] and I having great vivacity in my natural disposition could not bear to give way to the gloomy sense of sorrow and convictions;[11] therefore [I] let it have the wrong effect, so gave up to be more wild and airy than ever, for which he often reproved me. But I then thought (as many do now of this Society) it was

[1] *as bread ... waters* See Ecclesiastes 11.1: "Cast thy bread upon the waters: for thou shalt find it after many days."

[2] *had ... regard for* I.e., was filled with awe and respect for.

[3] *they were ... Lord* See Matthew 5.3: "Blessed are the poor in spirit: for theirs is the kingdom of heaven."

[4] *those that ... the Lord* See Proverbs 19.17: "He that hath pity upon the poor lendeth unto the Lord; and that which he hath given will he pay him again."

[5] *societies* Denominations.

[6] *consented* I.e., to marry him.

[7] *suffered* Allowed.

[8] *disposed of me* Married me off.

[9] *durst* Dared.

[10] *which ... disallowed of* Quakers during this period generally disapproved of amusements such as music, dance, and theater.

[11] *convictions* In eighteenth-century theological use, the word conviction(s) could refer to the sense that all humans are convicted as sinners.

the effect of singularity, and therefore would not bear it, nor be controlled,[1] and having a distant relation in the west of Ireland, left Dublin and went thither; and here I might take my swing, for what rendered me disagreeable to the former was quite pleasing to the latter.

Between these two relations I spent three years and three months. While I was in Ireland, I contracted an intimate acquaintance with a widow and her daughter that were Papists,[2] with whom I used to have a deal of discourse about religion, they in defence of their faith and I of mine. And though I was then wild, yet it often made me very thoughtful. The old woman would tell me of such mighty miracles done by their priests that I began to be shaken, and thought if these things were so, they must of a truth be the apostles' successors.[3]

The old woman perceived it and one day in a rapture said, "Oh! If I can under God be the happy instrument to convert you to the holy Catholic faith, all the sins that ever I committed will be forgiven." In a while it got so far that the priest came to converse with me, and I, being young and my judgment weak, was ready to believe what they said, and wild as I was, it cost me many tears with desires that I might be rightly directed; for some time I frequented their place of worship, but none of my relations knew what was my motive. At length I concluded never to be led darkly into their belief, and if their articles of faith are good, they'll not be against my knowing them. So the next time I had an opportunity with the priest, I told him I had some thoughts of becoming one of his flock but did not care to join till I knew all I must agree to; I therefore desired him to let me see their principles. He answered I must first confess my sins to him, and gave me till the next day to consider them.

I was not much against it, for thought I, "I have done nothing if all the world knew that any can hurt me for, and if what this man says be true, it will be for my good." And when he came again I told him all

that I could remember, which for my part I thought bad enough, but he thought me (as he said) the most innocent creature that ever made confession to him. When I had done, he took a book out and read it, all which I was to swear to, if I joined with them; and, though young, [I] made my remarks[4] as he went on, but I shall neither give myself the trouble of writing, nor any of reading, a deal of the ridiculous stuff it contained. But what made me sick of my new intention (I believe I should have swallowed the rest) was to swear that I believed the Pretender[5] to be the true heir to the Crown of England; and that he was King James' son, and also that whosoever died out of the pale[6] of that Church was damned.

As to the first, I did not believe it essential to salvation whether I believed it or not, and to take an oath to any such thing would be very unsafe; and the second struck directly against charity, which the Apostle preferred before all other graces;[7] and besides, I had a religious mother who was not of that opinion. I thought it therefore barbarous in me to believe she would be damned, yet concluded to take it into consideration. But before I saw him again a sudden turn took hold, which put a final end to it.

My father still keeping me at such a distance that I thought myself quite shut out of his affections, I therefore concluded since my absence was so agreeable, he should have it; and getting acquainted with a gentlewoman that then lately came from Pennsylvania (and was going back again), where I had an uncle (my mother's brother), I soon agreed[8] with her for my passage, and being ignorant of the nature of an

[1] *But I then … nor be controlled* I.e., I later understood that my increased wildness was the result of a desire to rebel (or be singular), and I therefore would neither tolerate his criticisms nor allow myself to be controlled.

[2] *Papists* Roman Catholics; the term was often used pejoratively by non-Catholics.

[3] *they must … apostles' successors* I.e., the leadership of the Catholic Church must be derived from the original apostles.

[4] *made my remarks* Thought to myself.

[5] *Pretender* One who asserts a claim to a throne. In this case, Ashbridge refers to James Stuart (1688–1766), son of the deposed King James II (1633–1701). James Stuart attempted to seize the English and Scottish thrones several times, most notably in the Jacobite rebellion of 1715; his cause was again taken up by his son Charles Edward Stuart in 1745. The Stuart claimants to the throne were Catholic, as were the majority of their Scottish and Irish supporters.

[6] *out of the pale* Outside the bounds; i.e., not a member.

[7] *charity, which … graces* See 1 Corinthians 13.13: "And now abideth faith, hope, charity, these three; but the greatest of these is charity"; 1 Corinthians is among several biblical books attributed to Paul the Apostle.

[8] *agreed* Negotiated.

indenture,[1] soon became bound, though in a private manner (for fear I should be found out), though this was repugnant to law. As soon as this was over, she invited me to go and see the vessel I was to go in, to which I readily consented, not knowing what would follow, and when I came on board, I found a young woman ([whom] I afterward understood was of a very good family and had been deluded away by this creature[2]). I was extremely pleased to think I should have such an agreeable companion, and while we were in discourse our kidnapper left us and went on shore, and when I wanted to go was not permitted.

Here I was kept near three weeks; at the end thereof the friends of the other young woman found her out and fetched her on shore; by which means mine found me, and sent the water bailiff, who took me also on shore. Our gentlewoman was forced to keep incognito or she would have been laid fast.[3]

I was kept close[4] for two weeks, but at last found means to get away, for I was so filled with the thought of coming to America that I could not give it up, and meeting with the captain, I enquired when they sailed. He told me. I got on board and came in the same ship, and have cause to believe there was a providential hand in it.

There was sixty Irish servants on board (I came now unindentured), and several English passengers, but not one of them[5] understood the Irish language but myself: I had taken no small pains to learn it. I could understand so much as to discover anything they discoursed upon, which was of great service to us all. There was

also on board the gentlewoman beforementioned and a young man, her husband's brother (twenty of those servants belonged to her). While we were on the coast of Ireland (for the wind kept us there some weeks) I overheard those creatures[6] contriving how they should be free when they came to America; to accomplish their design they concluded to rise and kill the ship's crew and all the English on board, and the abovementioned young man was to navigate the vessel. The same night I discovered[7] their barbarous design privately to the captain, who let the English know it. The next day they bore for the shore and some small distance off the Cove of Cork lowered sail and dropped anchor under pretence that the wind was not fair to stand their course. So [they] hoisted out the boat and invited the passengers to go on shore to divert[8] themselves, and among the rest the rebels' captain; he did, which was all they wanted. As soon as he was on shore the rest left him and came on board. Our captain immediately ordered to weigh anchor and hoist sail, but there were great outcries for the young man on shore. The captain told them the wind freshened up, and that he would not stay for his own son. So their treachery was betrayed in good time; and in such a manner that they did not mistrust it,[9] for it was thought most advisable to keep it private, lest any of them should do me a mischief; but at length they found out that I understood Irish, by my smiling at an Irish story they were telling, and from that time they devised many ways to hurt me, and several of them were corrected and put in irons for it.

In nine weeks from the time I left Ireland we arrived at New York, viz.[10] on the 15th of the 7th month[11] 1732, and then those to whom I had been instrumental under providence to save life proved treacherous to me:

[1] *the nature of an indenture* An indenture was a form of temporary unpaid servitude, generally lasting several years. Such arrangements were entered into by many prospective emigrants to North America in exchange for their overseas passage and at least minimal food and housing upon arrival. While indenture was itself entirely legal, it was a poorly regulated and often highly abusive system; many people from poor or otherwise marginalized communities—including a vast number of Irish immigrants—were lured into signing binding contracts of indenture without full knowledge of what they were agreeing to.

[2] *this creature* I.e., the gentlewoman.

[3] *laid fast* Arrested.

[4] *kept close* I.e., by her relatives.

[5] *them* I.e., the English passengers. (The Irish servants would have all spoken Irish, or *Gaeilge*, and in many cases might have known English only as a second language or not at all.)

[6] *those creatures* I.e., the Irish servants.

[7] *discovered* Revealed.

[8] *divert* Amuse.

[9] *mistrust it* I.e., suspect how their plot had been revealed.

[10] *viz.* Abbreviation of Latin videlicet, meaning "that is to say" or "namely."

[11] *7th month* Quakers developed a practice of calling the months of the year and the days of the week numerically, rather than using names that alluded to pagan deities. It is worth noting that the Gregorian calendar was not adopted in the British colonies (including the Americas) until 1752. According to the older Julian calendar, the new year began on 25 March—thus, *7th month* here likely means somewhere in the vicinity of our September.

I was a stranger in a strange land.[1] The captain got an indenture wrote and demanded of me to sign it, withal threatening a gaol[2] if I refused; I told him I could find means to satisfy him for my passage without becoming bound. They then told me I might take my choice either to sign that, or have [the one] that I had signed in Ireland [used] in force against me (by this time I had learned the character of the aforesaid woman, that she was a vile creature, and feared that if ever I was in her power she would use me ill on her brother's account). I therefore in a fright signed that, and though there was no magistrate present, I being ignorant in such cases, it did well enough to make me a servant four years.

In two weeks' time I was sold, and were it possible to convey in characters a sense of the sufferings of my servitude, it would make the most strong heart pity the misfortunes of a young creature as I was, who had a tender education; for though my father had no great estate, yet he lived well. I had been used to little but my school, but now it had been[3] better for me if I had been brought up to more hardship. For a while at first I was pretty well used, but in a little time the scale turned, occasioned by a difference that happened between my master and me, wherein I was innocent.[4] From that time he set himself against me and was inhuman. He would not suffer me to have clothes to be decent in, having to go barefoot in his service in the snowy weather and the meanest drudgery, wherein I suffered the utmost hardship that my body was able to bear, which, with the aforesaid troubles, had like to[5] have been my ruin to all eternity had not Almighty God in mercy interposed.

My Master would seem to be a Very Religious Man, taking the Sacrament[6] (so called), & used to Pray every Night in his family, except when his Prayer Book was

Lost, for he never Pray'd without it that I knew of. The Afforesaid Difference was of Such a kind that it made me Sick of his Religion; for tho' I had but little my Self yet I had an Idea what sort of People they should be that were so. At Length the old Enemy[7] by insinuations made me believe there was no such thing as Religion, & that the Convictions I had felt from my Infancy was no other than the prejudice of Education, which Convictions were at times so Strong that I have gone alone & fallen with my face to the Ground crying for mercy: but now I began to be hardened, and for Some months I do not Remember that I felt any such thing, so was Ready to Conclude that there was no God; that such thoughts were foolish & all but Priest Craft: and though I had a Great Veneration for that set of men in my youth, I now looked on them in another Manner: & what corroborated me in my Atheistical opinion was, my Master's house used to be a place of Great resort[8] of the Clergy, which gave me much opportunity to make my Remarks. Sometimes those that Came out of the Country lodged there & their Evening Diversion used to be Cards & Singing, & a few minutes after, Prayers and Singing Psalms to Almighty God. I used to think, if there be a God he is a pure being, & will not hear the Prayers of Polluted Lips: But he that hath in an abundant manner shewn mercy to me (as will be seen in the sequel) did not Long Suffer me to Doubt in this Matter, but in a moment, when my feet were near the Bottomless Pit, Pluckt me Back.

To one woman (and no other) I had discovered[9] the nature of the difference which two years before had happened between my master and me; by her means he heard of it, and though he knew it was true yet he sent for the town whipper to correct me. I was called in; he never asked me whether I had told any such thing but ordered me to strip, at which my heart was ready to burst—for I could as freely have given up my life as suffer such ignomi003y. I then said if there be a God, be graciously pleased to look down on one of the most unhappy creatures and plead my cause, for thou knows what I have said is the truth, and were it not for a principle more noble than he[10] was capable of I would

<div style="text-align: right; font-style: italic;">original spelling</div>

original spelling (left margin)

1 *a stranger in a strange land* Moses' description of himself in Egypt; see Exodus 2.22.

2 *gaol* Jail.

3 *had been* Would have been.

4 *a difference … innocent* Some scholars have speculated that the "difference," or dispute, between Ashbridge and her master may have been that she had resisted his unwanted sexual advances.

5 *had like to* Would almost.

6 *taking the Sacrament* I.e., partaking of the weekly ceremony of the Eucharist—consuming bread and wine (as the body and blood of Jesus Christ) during Mass. Writing as a Quaker, Ashbridge rejects ceremonies such as the Eucharist as empty rituals.

7 *old Enemy* Satan.

8 *resort* Gathering.

9 *discovered* Revealed.

10 *he* Ashbridge's master.

have told it before his wife. I then fixed my eyes on the barbarous man, and in a flood of tears said: "Sir, if you have no pity on me, yet for my father's sake spare me from this shame," for before this time he had heard of my father etc. several ways, "and if you think I deserve such punishment, do it yourself." He then took a turn over[1] the room and bid the whipper go about his business, and I came off without a blow, which I thought something remarkable. But now I began to think my credit was gone (for they said many things of me which I blessed God were not true), and here I suffer so much cruelty I cannot bear it.

The Enemy immediately came in and put me in a way how to be rid of it all, and tempted me to end my miserable life. I joined with it and for that purpose went into the garret to hang myself. Now it was I was convinced there was a God, for as my feet entered the place, horror seized [me] to that degree. I trembled much, and as I stood like one in amaze, it seemed as though I heard a voice say, "there is a Hell beyond the grave"; at which I was greatly astonished, and now convinced that there was an almighty Power, to whom I then prayed, saying, "God be merciful and enable me to bear what thou in thy providence shall bring or suffer to come upon me for my disobedience." I then went down again, but let none know what I had been about. Soon after this I had a dream, and though some make a ridicule of dreams, yet this seemed a significant one to me and therefore shall mention it. I thought somebody knocked at the door, by which when I had opened it there stood a grave woman, holding in her right hand an oil lamp burning, who with a solid countenance fixed her eyes upon me and said, "I am sent to tell thee that if thou'll return to the Lord thy God who hath created thee, he will have mercy on thee, and thy lamp shall not be put out in obscure darkness." Upon which the light flamed from the lamp in an extraordinary manner, and she left me and I awoke.

But alas! I did not give up nor comply with the heavenly vision, as I think I may call it, for after this I had like to have been caught in another snare, which if I had would probably have been my ruin, from which I was also preserved. I was counted[2] a fine singer and dancer, in which I took great delight, and once falling in with some of the playhouse company then at New

York, they took a great fancy to me, as they said, and persuaded me to become an actress amongst them, and they would find means to get me from my cruel servitude, and I should live like a lady. The proposal took with me and I used no small pains to qualify myself for it in reading their playbooks, even when I should have slept, yet was put to the demur[3] when I came to consider what my father would say—who had forgiven my disobedience in marrying and earnestly desiring to see me again had sent for me home—but my proud heart would not consent to return in so mean[4] a condition; therefore I chose bondage rather.

So when I had served near three years, I bought off the remainder of my time[5] and then took to my needle, by which I could maintain myself handsomely.[6] But, alas, I was not sufficiently punished: I had got released from one cruel servitude, and then, not contented, got into another, and this for life. A few months after, I married a young man that fell in love with me for my dancing, a poor motive for a man to choose a wife, or a woman a husband. But for my part I fell in love with nothing I saw in him, and it seems unaccountable that I who had refused several, both in this country and Ireland, at last married a man I had no value for. In a few days after we were married he took me from [New] York. Being a schoolmaster, he had hired[7] in the country to keep school; he led me to New England and there settled in a place called Westerly in Rhode Island Government. With regard to religion he was much like myself—without any—and when in drink would use the worst of oaths. I do not mention this to expose my husband, but to show the effect it had on me, for I now saw myself ruined as I thought, being joined to a man I had no love for and that was a pattern of no good to me; then I began to think what a couple we were, like two joining hands and going to destruction, and thereupon concluded if I was not forsaken of heaven to alter my course of life. But to set my affections upon the divine being and not love my husband seemed impossible: therefore I daily desired with tears that my affections

[1] *took a turn over* Walked around.

[2] *counted* Considered.

[3] *was put to the demur* Became reluctant.

[4] *mean* Lowly.

[5] *bought off ... my time* I.e., obtained freedom in exchange for payment for her remaining contracted years of servitude.

[6] *handsomely* Amply.

[7] *schoolmaster* A male teacher; *hired* Secured employment.

might be in a right manner set upon my husband, and can say in a little time my love was sincere to him.

I now resolved to do my duty to God, and expecting I must come to the knowledge of it by the scriptures, I took to reading them with a resolution to follow their directions, but the more I read the more uneasy I grew, especially about baptism. For although I had reason to believe I had been sprinkled in my infancy, because at the age of thirteen I passed under the Bishop's hands for confirmation[1] (as twas called), yet I could not find any precedent for that practice, and lighting on that place where it is said, "he that believes and is baptized,"[2] etc., here I observed belief went before baptism, which I was not capable of when sprinkled. Hence [I] grew much dissatisfied, and living in a neighbourhood that were mostly Seventh Day Baptists,[3] I conversed much with them. At length, thinking it my real duty, I was in the winter time baptised by one of their teachers, but did not join strictly with them, though I began to think the seventh day was the true Sabbath, and for some time kept it. My husband did not oppose me, for he saw I grew more affectionate to him. I did not leave off singing and dancing, so but that I could divert him when he'd ask me. But I did not find that satisfaction in what I had done as I expected.

Soon after this my husband and I concluded to go for[4] England, and for that end went to Boston and there found a ship bound for Liverpool. We agreed for[5] our passage and expected to sail in two weeks, but my time was not to go yet, for there came a gentleman who hired the ship to carry him and his attendance to Philadelphia and to take no other passengers; and there being no other ship near sailing we for that time gave it out.[6] We stayed several weeks in Boston, and I still continued dissatisfied as to religion; though I had reformed my conduct so as to be accounted by those that knew me a sober woman. Yet [I] was not content, for even then I expected to find the sweets of such a change, and though several thought me religious, I durst not think so myself, but what to do to be so was an utter stranger. I used to converse with people of all societies as opportunity offered, and like many others had got a pretty deal of head knowledge, and several societies thought me of their opinions severally.[7] But I joined strictly with none, resolving never to leave searching till I had found the truth. This was in the twenty-second year of my age.

While we were in Boston I one day went into the Quaker meeting,[8] not expecting to find what I wanted, but out of curiosity. At this meeting there was a woman Friend [who] spoke, at which I was a little surprised, for though I had heard of women's preaching I had never heard one before.[9] I looked on her with pity for her ignorance (as I thought) and contempt of her practise, saying to myself; "I am sure you are a fool, for if ever I should turn Quaker, which will never be, I would not be a preacher." In these and such like thoughts I sat while she was speaking; after she had done, there stood up a man, which I could better bear. He spoke well and I thought raised sound doctrine from good Joshua's resolution, viz., "as for me and my house we will serve the Lord,"[10] etc. After he had sat silent a while he went to prayer, which was something so awful and affecting as drew tears from my eyes, yet a[11] stranger to the cause.

1 *sprinkled* Baptized (by having water sprinkled upon one's head); *confirmation* Religious rite of passage, usually experienced between the ages of ten to thirteen, reserved for those who had previously been baptized.

2 *he that ... baptized* See Mark 16.16: "He that believeth and is baptized shall be saved; but he that believeth not shall be damned."

3 *Seventh Day Baptists* Christian denomination, whose members observe the Sabbath on Saturday (the seventh day) as opposed to Sunday.

4 *concluded to go for* Decided to travel to.

5 *agreed for* Arranged.

6 *gave it out* Gave up.

7 *severally* Each in turn.

8 *meeting* Term used by Quakers for their religious services. In the 1774 text, the capitalization of "meeting" when used in this sense is inconsistent. The editors have followed modern conventions regarding the capitalization of nouns relating to religious services.

9 *a woman Friend ... one before* Quakers (officially, The Society of Friends) were notable for their belief in the spiritual equality of men and women; both men and women were permitted to speak—give voice to their spontaneous prayers—during meetings, which were otherwise generally characterised by sustained periods of prayerful silence.

10 *as for ... Lord* See Joshua 24.15: "And if it seem evil unto you to serve the Lord, choose you this day whom ye will serve; whether the gods which your fathers served that were on the other side of the flood, or the gods of the Amorites, in whose land ye dwell: but as for me and my house, we will serve the Lord."

11 *yet a* Though I was still a.

Soon after this we left Boston, and my husband being given to ramble[1]—which was very disagreeable to me, but I must submit—we came to Rhode Island by water, from thence to the east end of Long Island, where we hired to keep school. This place was mostly settled with Presbyterians. I soon got acquainted with some of the most religious of them, for though I was poor yet [I] was favoured with reception amongst people of the best credit, and had frequent discourses with them. But the more I was acquainted, the worse I liked their opinions, so remained dissatisfied; and the old Enemy of my happiness knowing that I was resolved to abandon him and seek peace for my soul, he fresh assaults me and laid a bait, with which I had like to[2] have been caught. One day, having been abroad, at my return home I found the people at whose house we had taken a room had left some flax[3] in an apartment through which I passed to my own, at sight of which I was immediately tempted to steal to make me some thread. I went to it and took a small bunch in my hand, at which I was smote with remorse. Being of such a kind that my very nature abhorred it, I laid it down, saying, "Lord keep me from such a vile action as this." But the twisting serpent did not leave me yet, but assaulted again so strong and prevalent that I took it into my own room; but when I came there horror seized me, and bursting into tears [I] cried, "Oh thou God of mercy, enable me to resist this temptation," which he in his mercy did, and gave me power to say, "Get thee behind me Satan,[4] I'll resist till I'll die before I'll yield." And then I carried it back, and returning to my room was filled with thanksgiving to God, and wrapped in such a frame[5] as I have not words to express, neither can any guess but those who have resisted temptations: these have it in their own experience to taste the sweet peace that flows to the soul.

My husband soon hired further up the island, where we were nearer a Church of England to which I used to go, for though I disliked some of their ways, yet I liked them best. But now a fresh exercise[6] fell upon me, and of such a sort as I had never heard of any being in the like, and while under it I thought myself alone. I was in the Second Month[7] sitting by a fire in company with several, my husband also present; there arose a thunder gust, and with the noise that struck my ear a voice attended, even as the sound of a mighty trumpet, piercing through me with these words, "O! Eternity, eternity, the endless term of long eternity," at which I was exceedingly surprized, sitting speechless as in a trance, and in a moment saw myself in such a state as made me despair of ever being in a happy one. I seemed to see a long roll[8] wrote in black characters, at sight whereof I heard a voice say to me, "This is thy sins." I then saw sin to be exceeding sinful. But this was not all, for immediately followed another, saying, "and the blood of Christ is not sufficient to wash them out; this is shown thee that thou mayest confess thy damnation is just, and not in order that they should be forgiven."

All this while I sat speechless. At last I got up trembling, and threw myself on a bed; the company thought my indisposition proceeded only from a fright at the thunder, but alas, it was of another kind, and from that time for several months I was in the utmost despair, and if any time I would endeavour to hope or lay hold of any gracious promise, the old Accuser would come in, telling me it was now too late, I had withstood the day of mercy till it was over, and that I should add to my sins by praying for pardon and provoke divine vengeance to make a monument of wrath of me. I was like one already in torment; my sleep departed from me, I eat little, I became extremely melancholy, and took no delight in anything. Had all the world been mine and the glory of it, I would now have gladly given it for one glimpse of hope. My husband was shocked to see me so changed; I that once could divert him with a song (in which he greatly delighted), nay after I grew religious as to the outward could now do it no longer. My singing now was turned into mourning and my dancing into lamentations; my

1 *ramble* Wander.

2 *had like to* Would likely; was almost.

3 *flax* I.e., flax fibers, to be used for making linen fabric.

4 *Get thee ... Satan* See Matthew 16.23: "Get thee behind me, Satan: thou art an offence unto me: for thou savourest not the things that be of God, but those that be of men." The phrase is also used in Luke 4.8, in the context of the Temptation of Christ.

5 *wrapped in such a frame* Absorbed in such an emotional state.

6 *exercise* State of distress.

7 *Second Month* Roughly equivalent to April in the Gregorian calendar.

8 *roll* List.

nights and days were one continual scene of sorrows. I let none know my desperate condition. My husband used all means in his power to divert my melancholy, but in vain: the wound was too deep to be healed with anything short of the true Balm of Gilead.[1] I durst not go much alone[2] for fear of evil spirits, but when I did my husband would not suffer it, and if I took the Bible he would take it from me saying, "How you are altered; you used to be agreeable company, but now I have no comfort of you." I endeavoured to bear all with patience, expecting soon to bear more than man could inflict upon me.

At length I went to the priest to see if he could relieve me, but he was a stranger to my case; he advised me to take the sacrament and use some innocent diversions, and lent me a book of prayers, which he said was fit for my condition, but all was in vain. As to the sacrament, I thought myself in a state very unfit to receive it worthily, and could not use the prayers, for I then thought if ever my prayers would be acceptable, I should be enabled to pray without form.[3] Diversions were burdensome, for, as I said above, my husband used all means tending that way to no purpose, yet he with some others once persuaded me to go to the raising of a building[4] (where such company were collected) in expectation of alleviating my grief, but contrarywise it proved a means of adding to my sorrow; for in the meantime there came an officer to summon a jury to enquire concerning the body of a man that had hanged himself, which as soon as I understood seemed to be attended with a voice saying, "Thou shall be the next monument of such wrath, for thou art not worthy to die a natural death." And for two months I was daily tempted to destroy myself, and sometimes so strong that I could hardly resist. Through fear of that sort when I went alone I used to throw off my apron and garters, and if I had a knife cast it from me

crying, "Lord keep me from taking that life thou gave, and which thou would have made happy if I had on my part joined with the offers of thy grace, and had regarded the convictions attending me from my youth: the fault is my own, thou O Lord art clear." And yet so great was my agony that I desired death that I might know the worst of my torments, of which I had so sharp a foretaste. All this while I could not shed a tear; my heart was as hard as a stone and my life miserable, but God that's full of mercy and long forbearance in his own good time delivered my soul out of this thraldom.

For one night as I lay in bed (my husband by me asleep), bemoaning my miserable condition, I had strength to cry, "O, my God, hast thou no mercy left? Look down, I beseech thee, for Christ's sake, who has promised that all manner of sins and blasphemies shall be forgiven; Lord, if thou will graciously please to extend this promise to me, an unworthy creature trembling before thee, there is nothing thou shalt command but I will obey." In an instant my heart was tendered, and I dissolved in a flow of tears, abhorring my past offences, and admiring the mercy of God, for I now was made to hope in Christ my redeemer, and enabled to look upon him with an eye of faith and saw fulfilled what I believed when the priest lent me his book, viz., that if ever my prayers would be acceptable I should be enabled to pray without form, and so used form no more.

Nevertheless, I thought I ought to join with some religious society, but met with none I liked in everything; yet the Church of England seeming nearest, I joined with them and took the sacrament (so called), and can say in truth I did it with reverence and fear. Being now released from deep distress I seemed like another creature, and often went alone without fear, and tears abundantly flowed from my eyes, and once as I was abhorring myself in great humility of mind, I heard a gracious voice full of love, saying, "I will never leave thee, nor forsake thee, only obey what I shall make known to thee." I then entered into covenant,[5] saying, "My soul doth magnify thee the God of mercy—if thou'll vouchsafe thy grace, the rest of my days shall be devoted to thee, and if it be thy will that I beg my bread I'll be content and submit to thy providence."

[1] *Balm of Gilead* Medicinal ointment named after Gilead, where it was traditionally produced; its healing of the body is considered analogous to Christ's healing of the soul. See Jeremiah 8.22.

[2] *go much alone* I.e., leave home unaccompanied.

[3] *without form* I.e., without the guidance of established written prayers; spontaneously.

[4] *raising of a building* Community event centered on the building of a house or other structure, often accompanied by music and dance.

[5] *entered into covenant* Entered a state of full engagement with God.

I now began to think of my relations in Pennsylvania whom I had not yet seen, and having a great desire that way, got leave of my husband to go, and also a certificate from the priest on Long Island in order that if I made any stay, I might be received as a member[1] wherever I came; then setting out, my husband bore me company to the Blazing Star Ferry, saw me safe over and then returned. On the way, near a place called Maidenhead [New Jersey], I fell from my horse and I was disabled from traveling for some time. In the interval I abode at the house of an honest-like Dutchman, who with his wife were very kind to me, and though they had much trouble going to the doctor and waiting upon me (for I was several days unable to help myself), yet would have nothing for it (which I thought exceedingly kind), but charged[2] me if ever I came that way again to call and lodge there. I mention this because by and by I shall have occasion to remark this place again.

Hence I came to Trenton [New Jersey] Ferry, where I met with no small mortification upon hearing that my relations were Quakers, and, what was the worst of all, my aunt a preacher. I was sorry to hear it, for I was exceedingly prejudiced against these people and have often wondered with what face they could call themselves Christians. I repented my coming and had a mind to have turned back. At last I concluded to go and see them since I was so far on my journey, but expected little comfort from my visit. But see how God brings unforeseen things to pass, for by my going there I was brought to my knowledge of his truth. I went from Trenton to Philadelphia by water, thence to my uncle's on horseback, where I met with very kind reception; for though my uncle was dead and my aunt married again, yet both her husband and she received me in a very kind manner.

I had not been there three hours before I met with a shock, and my opinion began to alter with respect to these people. For, seeing a book lying on the table (and being much for reading), I took it up. My aunt, observing, said, "Cousin that is a Quakers' book," for perceiving I was not a Quaker, I suppose she thought I would not like it. I made her no answer, but revolving in my

mind, "What can these people write about? For I have heard that they deny the scriptures and have no other bible but George Fox's Journal,[3] and deny all the holy ordinances." So [I] resolved to read, but had not read two pages before my very heart burned within me and tears issued from my eyes, which I was afraid would be seen, therefore with the book (Samuel Crisp's Two Letters[4]) I walked into the garden, sat down, and the piece being small, read it through before I went in. But sometimes [I] was forced to stop to vent my tears, my heart as it were uttering these involuntary expressions: "My God must I (if ever I come to the true knowledge of thy truth) be of this man's opinion, who has sought thee as I have done, and join with these people that a few hours ago I preferred the Papists before? O thou, the God of my Salvation and of my Life, who hast in an abundant manner manifested thy long suffering and tender mercy, redeeming me as from the lowest hell, a monument of thy grace. Lord, my soul beseecheth thee to direct me in the right way and keep me from error, and then according to thy covenant I'll think nothing too near to part with for thy name's sake. If these things be so, oh! Happy people thus beloved of God."

After I came a little to myself again, I washed my face lest any in the house should perceive I had been weeping. But this night got but little sleep, for the old Enemy began to suggest that I was one of those that wavered and was not steadfast in the faith, advancing several texts of scripture against me and them, as, in the latter days there should be those that would deceive the very elect:[5] and these were they, and that I was in danger of being deluded. Here the subtle[6] serpent transformed himself so hiddenly that I verily believed this to be a timely caution from a good angel—so

[1] *certificate ... member* I.e., a certificate proving that she was a member of the Anglican Church and could take communion with the local congregation wherever she went.

[2] *charged* Instructed; suggested.

[3] *George Fox's Journal* Spiritual autobiography of George Fox (1624–91), founder of the Society of Friends. It was published posthumously in 1694, and was used as a guide by other Quakers.

[4] *Samuel Crisp's Two Letters* Famous Quaker conversion narrative, *Two Letters Written by Samuel Crisp, about the Year 1702, to Some of His Acquaintance, Upon His Change from a Chaplain of the Church of England, to Join with the People Called Quakers* (1722). (See the "In Context" materials below.)

[5] *there should ... very elect* See Matthew 24.24: "For there shall arise false Christs, and false prophets, and shall shew great signs and wonders; insomuch that, if it were possible, they shall deceive the very elect."

[6] *subtle* Cunning.

resolved to beware of the Deceiver, and for some weeks did not touch any of their books.

The next day being the first of the week, I wanted to have gone to Church, which was distant about four miles, but being a stranger and having nobody to go along with me was forced to give it out, and as most of the family was going to meeting, I went with them, but with a resolution not to like them, and so it was fully suffered. For as they sat in silence[1] I looked over the meeting, thinking with myself, "How like fools these people sit; how much better would it be to stay at home and read the Bible or some good book than to come here and go to sleep." For my part I was very sleepy, and thought they were no better than myself. Indeed at length I fell asleep, and had like to [have] fallen down, but this was the last time I ever fell asleep in a meeting, though often assaulted[2] with it.

Now I began to be lifted up with spiritual pride and thought myself better than they, but through mercy this did not last long, for in a little time I was brought low and saw that these were the people to whom I must join. It may seem strange that I who had lived so long with one of this Society[3] in Dublin should yet be so great a stranger to them. In answer let it be considered that during the time I was there I never read one of their books nor went to one meeting, and besides I had heard such ridiculous stories of them as made me esteem them the worst of any society of people; but God that knew the sincerity of my heart looked with pity on my weakness and soon let me see my error.

In a few weeks there was an afternoon's meeting held at my uncle's[4] to which came that servant of the Lord, William Hammans, who was made then instrumental

to the convincing me of the truth more perfectly, and helping me over some great doubts, though I believe no one did ever sit in greater opposition than I did when he first stood up. But I was soon brought down, for he preached the gospel with such power I was forced to give up and confess it was the truth. As soon as meeting ended I endeavoured to get alone, for I was not fit to be seen, I being so broken, yet afterward the restless Adversary assaulted me again, on this wise.[5] In the morning before this meeting, I had been disputing with my uncle about baptism, which was the subject this good man dwelt upon, which was handled so clearly as to answer all my scruples beyond all objection. Yet the crooked Serpent alleged that the sermon that I had heard did not proceed from divine revelation but that my uncle and aunt had acquainted the Friend of me;[6] which being strongly suggested, I fell to accusing them with it, of which they both cleared themselves saying they had not seen him since my coming into these parts until he came into the meeting. I then concluded he was a messenger sent of God to me, and with fervent cries desired I might be directed aright, and now laid aside all prejudice and set my heart open to receive the truth in the love of it. And the Lord in his own good time revealed to my soul not only the beauty there is in truth, and how those should shine that continue faithful to it, but also the emptiness of all shadows which in the day were glorious; but now he the Son of Glóry was come to put an end to them all, and to establish everlasting righteousness in the room[7] thereof, which is a work in the soul. He likewise let me see that all I had gone through was to prepare me for this day, and that the time was near that he would require me to go forth and declare to others what he the God of Mercy had done for my soul, at which I was surprized and begged to be excused for fear I should bring dishonour to the truth and cause his holy name to be evil spoken of.

All the while, I never let any know the condition I was in, nor did I appear like a Friend, and feared a discovery. I now began to think of returning to my husband but found a restraint to stay where I was. I then

[1] *sat in silence* Quaker meetings of this kind consist of unprogrammed worship, which is often predominantly silent, interrupted intermittently by impromptu vocal ministry from attendees. Those who practice this form of worship believe in each individual's ability to make direct connection with God. (Other Quakers practice programmed worship and attend meetings which are similar to the church services of other Protestant denominations.)

[2] *assaulted* Tempted.

[3] *Society* I.e., the Society of Friends.

[4] *meeting held at my uncle's* During this period Quakers often held their meetings in members' homes rather than in formal meeting houses; with the exception of Pennsylvania and certain other areas, Quakers were frequently subject to persecution.

[5] *on this wise* In this way.

[6] *acquainted … of me* I.e., had previously told the Quaker of Ashbridge's doubts.

[7] *room* Place.

hired to keep school and, hearing of a place for him, wrote desiring him to come to me, but let him know nothing how it was with me. I loved to go to meetings, but did not like to be seen to go on weekdays,[1] and therefore to shun it used to go from my school through the woods, but notwithstanding all my care the neighbours that were not Friends began to revile me, calling me Quaker, saying they supposed I intended to be a fool and turn preacher; I then received the same censure that I (a little above a year before) had passed on one of the handmaids of the Lord at Boston, and so weak was I, alas! I could not bear the reproach, and in order to change their opinions got into greater excess in apparel[2] than I had freedom to wear for some time before I came acquainted with Friends.

In this condition I continued till my husband came, and then began the trial of my faith. Before he reached me, he heard I was turned Quaker, at which he stamped, saying, "I'd rather heard she had been dead as well as I love her, for if so, all my comfort is gone." He then came to me and had not seen me before for four months. I got up and met him, saying, "My Dear, I am glad to see thee," at which he flew in a passion of anger and said, "The Devil thee thee, don't thee me."[3] I used all the mild means I could to pacify him, and at length got him fit to go and speak to my relations, but he was alarmed, and as soon as we got alone said, "So I see your Quaker relations have made you one." I told him they had not, which was true, nor had I ever told him how it was with me. But he would have it that I was one, and therefore would not let me stay among them, and having found a place to his mind, hired and came directly back to fetch me hence, and in one afternoon walked near thirty miles to keep me from meeting, the next day being First Day. And on the morrow [he] took me to the aforesaid place and hired lodgings at a churchman's house, who was one of the wardens and a bitter enemy to Friends, and used to do all he could to

irritate my husband against them, and would tell me abundance of ridiculous stuff; but my judgement was too clearly convinced to believe it.

I still did not appear like a Friend, but they all believed I was one. When my husband and he used to be making their diversion and reviling, I used to sit in silence, but now and then an involuntary sigh would break from me, at which he would tell my husband, "There, did I not tell that your wife was a Quaker? And she will be a preacher." Upon which my husband once in a great rage came up to me and, shaking his hand over me, said, "You had better be hanged in that day." I then, Peter-like,[4] in a panic, denied my being a Quaker, at which great horror seized upon me, which continued near three months, so that I again feared that by denying the Lord that bought me, the heavens were shut against me, for great darkness surrounded, and I was again plunged into despair. I used to walk much alone in the wood, where no eye saw nor ear heard, and there lament my miserable condition, and have often gone from morning till night and have not broke my fast.

Thus I was brought so low that my life was a burden to me; the Devil seemed to vaunt that though the sins of my youth were forgiven, yet now he was sure of me, for that I had committed the unpardonable sin and Hell inevitable would be my portion, and my torment would be greater than if I had hanged myself at first. In this doleful state I had none to bewail my doleful condition, and even in the night when I could not sleep under the painful distress of mind, if my husband perceived me weeping he would revile me for it. At length when he and his friends thought themselves too weak to overset me (though I feared it was already done), he went to the priest at Chester [Pennsylvania] to advise what to do with me. This man knew I was a member of the Church, for I had shown him my certificate: his advice was to take me out of Pennsylvania and find someplace where there was no Quakers, and then it would wear off. To this my husband agreed, saying he did not care where he went if he could but restore me to that liveliness of temper I was naturally of, and to that Church of which I was a member. I on my part had no spirit to oppose the proposal, neither

[1] *I loved … weekdays* Unlike the church services of more traditional Christian denominations, Quaker meetings might be held throughout the week.

[2] *got into greater excess in apparel* Started wearing more elaborate clothing. Ashbridge wished to avoid appearing like a Quaker.

[3] *The Devil … thee me."* Quakers were noted for their use of the pronouns "thee," "thou," and "thine" in everyday speech; the practice derived from an older context in which "thou" was considered an informal alternative to the plural and formal "you."

[4] *Peter-like* The apostle Peter denied his affiliation with Jesus three times before finally repenting.

much cared where I was, for I seemed to have nothing to hope for, but daily expected to be made a spectacle of divine wrath, and was possessed with a thought that it would be by thunder ere long.

The time of removal came, and I must go. I was not suffered to go to bid my relations farewell. My husband was poor and kept no horse, so I must travel on foot. We came to Wilmington [Delaware], (fifteen miles) thence to Philadelphia by water; here he took me to a tavern where I soon became the spectacle and discourse of the company. My husband told them, "My wife is a Quaker," and that he designed if possible to find out some place where there was none. "O," thought I, "I was once in a condition deserving that name, but now it is over with me. O! that I might from a true hope once more have an opportunity to confess to the truth"; though I was sure of suffering all manner of cruelties, I would not regard it.

These were my concerns while he was entertaining the company with my story, in which he told them that I had been a good dancer, but now he could get me neither to dance nor sing; upon which one of the company stands up, saying, "I'll go fetch my fiddle, and we'll have a dance," at which my husband was much pleased. The fiddle came, the sight of which put me in a sad condition for fear if I refused my husband would be in a great passion; however I took up this resolution not to comply, whatever be the consequence. He comes to me, takes me by the hand, saying, "Come my dear, shake off that gloom, and let's have a civil dance; you would now and then when you was a good churchwoman, and that's better than a stiff Quaker." I, trembling, desired to be excused, but he insisted on it, and knowing his temper to be exceeding choleric,[1] [I] durst not say much, yet did not consent. He then plucked me round the room till tears affected my eyes, at sight whereof the musician stopped and said, "I'll play no more, let your wife alone," of which I was glad.

There was also a man in company who came from Freehold in East Jersey. He said, "I see your wife is a Quaker, but if you will take my advice you need not go so far," for my husband's design was for Staten Island; "Come and live amongst us; we'll soon cure her of her Quakerism, for we want a schoolmaster and mistress too," (I followed the same business); to which

he agreed, and a happy turn it was for me, as will be seen by and by. And the wonderful turn of Providence, who had not yet abandoned me, but raised a glimmering hope, affording the answer of peace in refusing to dance, for which I was more rejoiced than to be made mistress of much riches; and in floods of tears I said, "Lord, I dread to ask and yet without thy gracious pardon I'm miserable; I therefore fall down before thy throne, imploring mercy at thine hand. O Lord, once more I beseech thee, try my obedience and then whatsoever thou commands, I will obey, and not fear to confess thee before men."

Thus was my soul engaged before God in sincerity, and he in tender mercy heard my cries, and in me has shown that he delights not in the death of a sinner,[2] for he again set my mind at liberty to praise him, and I longed for an opportunity to confess to his truth, which he showed me should come. But in what manner I did not see, but believed the word that I had heard, which in a little time was fulfilled to me. My husband, as aforesaid, agreed to go to Freehold, and in our way thither we came to Maidenhead, where I went to see the kind Dutchman before mentioned, who made us welcome and invited us to stay a day or two.

While we were here, there was held a great meeting of the Presbyterians, not only for worship but business also: for one of their preachers, being charged with drunkenness, was this day to have his trial before a great number of their priests, etc. We went to it, of which I was afterwards glad. Here I perceived great divisions among the people about who should be their shepherd: I greatly pitied their condition, for I now saw beyond the men made ministers and what they preached for, and which those at this meeting might have done had not the prejudice of education, which is very prevalent, blinded their eyes. Some insisted to have the old offender restored, some to have a young man they had upon trial some weeks, a third party was for sending for one from New England. At length stood up one and, directing himself to the chief speaker, said, "Sir, when we have been at the expense (which will be no small matter) of fetching this gentleman from New England, maybe he'll not stay with

[1] *choleric* Prone to anger.

[2] *he delights ... sinner* See Ezekiel 18.23: "Have I any pleasure at all that the wicked should die? saith the Lord God: and not that he should return from his ways, and live?"

us." *Answer,* "Don't you know how to make him stay?" *Reply,* "No Sir." "I'll tell you then," said he (to which I gave good attention). "Give him a good salary and I'll engage[1] he'll stay." "O," thought I, "these mercenary creatures: they are all actuated by one and the same thing, even the love of money, and not the regard of souls." This (called Reverend) gentleman, whom these people almost adored, to my knowledge had left his flock on Long Island and moved to Philadelphia where he could get more money. I myself have heard some of them on the island say that they almost impoverished themselves to keep him, but [they] not being able to equal Philadelphia's invitation, he left them without a shepherd. This man, therefore, knowing their ministry all proceeded from one cause, might be purchased with the same thing; surely these and such like are the shepherd that regards the fleece more than the flock, in whose mouths are lies, saying the Lord had sent them, and that they were Christ's ambassadors, whose command to those he sent was, "Freely ye have received, freely give;[2] and blessed be his holy Name." So they do to this day.

I durst not say anything to my husband of the remarks I had made, but laid them up in my heart, and they served to strengthen me in my resolution. Hence we set forward to Freehold, and coming through Stony Brook [New Jersey] my husband turned towards me tauntingly and said, "Here's one of Satan's synagogues,[3] don't you want to be in it? O I hope to see you cured of this new religion." I made no answer but went on, and in a little time, we came to a large run of water over which was no bridge, and being strangers knew no way to escape it, but through we must go: he carried over our clothes, which we had in bundles. I took off my

shoes and waded over in my stockings, which served somewhat to prevent the chill of the water, being very cold and a fall of snow in the 12th month.[4] My heart was concerned in prayer that the Lord would sanctify all my afflictions to me and give me patience to bear whatsoever should be suffered to come upon me. We walked the most part of a mile before we came to the first house, which was a sort of a tavern. My husband called for some spiritous liquors, but I got some weakened cider mulled, which when I had drank of (the cold being struck to my heart) made me extremely sick, insomuch that when we were a little past the house I expected I should have fainted, and not being able to stand, fell down under a fence. My husband, observing, tauntingly said, "What's the matter now? What, are you drunk? Where is your religion now?" He knew better and at that time I believe he pitied me, yet was suffered grievously to afflict me. In a little time I grew better, and going on we came to another tavern, where we lodged. The next day I was indifferent[5] well, so proceeded, and as we journeyed a young man driving an empty cart overtook us. I desired my husband to ask the young man to let us ride; he did, [and] it was readily granted.

I now thought myself well off, and took it as a great favour, for my proud heart was humbled, and I did not regard the looks of it, though the time had been that I would not have been seen in one.[6] This cart belonged to a man at Shrewsbury [New Jersey], and was to go through the place we designed for,[7] so we rode on (but soon had the care of the team to ourselves from a failure in the driver) to the place where I was intended to be made a prey of; but see how unforeseen things are brought to pass by a Providential hand. 'Tis said and answered, "Shall we do evil that good may come?" God forbid—yet hence good came to me. Here my husband would have had me stay while we went to see the team safe at home I told him "no," since he had led me through the country like a vagabond, I would not stay behind him, so went on, and lodged that night

[1] *engage* Guarantee.

[2] *Freely … give* See Matthew 10.8.

[3] *Satan's synagogues* See Revelations 2.9: "I know thy works, and tribulation, and poverty, (but thou art rich) and I know the blasphemy of them which say they are Jews, and are not, but are the synagogue of Satan." The meaning of this passage has been much discussed by biblical scholars and is not entirely clear; what is clear, however, is that this and other passages in Revelations have been cited over many centuries by those seeking to find biblical support for anti-Semitic prejudice, by way of suggesting that all Jewish places of worship are associated with Satan. (There were very few Jews in New Jersey in the eighteenth century, so it is unlikely that the couple was in fact passing a synagogue.)

[4] *12th month* Approximately February according to the Gregorian calendar.

[5] *indifferent* Tolerably.

[6] *the time had … one* I.e., there was a time when I would not have been seen in a cart such as this.

[7] *designed for* Were headed toward.

at the man's house who owned the team. Next morning, in our return to Freehold, we met a man riding on full speed, who, stopping, said to my husband, "Sir, are you a schoolmaster?" *Answer,* "Yes." "I came to tell you," replied the stranger, "of two new schoolhouses, and want a master in each, and are two miles apart." How this stranger came to hear of us, who came but the night before, I never knew, but I was glad he was not one called a Quaker, lest my husband might have thought it had been a plot; and then turning to my husband I said, "My dear, look on me with pity; if thou has any affections left for me—which I hope thou hast, for I am not conscious of having done anything to alienate them—here is," continued I, "an opportunity to settle us both, for I am willing to do all in my power towards getting an honest livelihood."

My expressions took place, and after a little pause he consented, took the young man's directions, and made towards the place, and in our way came to the house of a worthy Friend, whose wife was a preacher, though we did not know it. I was surprized to see the people so kind to us that were strangers; we had not been long in the house till we were invited to lodge there that night, [it] being the last in the week. I said nothing, but waited to hear my master speak; he soon consented, saying, "My wife has had a tedious travel and I pity her"; at which kind expression I was affected, for they were now very seldom used to me. The Friends' kindness could not proceed from my appearing in the garb of a Quaker, for I had not yet altered my dress. The woman of the house, after we had concluded to stay, fixed her eyes upon me and said, "I believe thou hast met with a deal of trouble," to which I made but little answer. My husband, observing they were of that sort of people he had so much endeavoured to shun, would give us no opportunity for any discourse that night, but the next morning I let the Friend know a little how it was with me. Meeting time came, to which I longed to go, but durst not ask my husband leave for fear of disturbing him, till we were settled; and then thought I, "If ever I am favoured to be in this place, come life or death, I'll fight through, for my salvation is at stake." The Friend, getting ready for meeting, asked my husband if he would go, saying they knew who were to be his employers, and if they were at meeting would speak to them. He then consented to go; then said

the woman Friend, "And wilt thou let thy wife go?" which he denied, making several objections, all which she answered so prudently that he could not be angry, and at last consented. And with joy I went, for I had not been at one for near four months, and a heavenly meeting this was. I now renewed my covenant and saw the word of the Lord made good, that I should have another opportunity to confess his name, for which my spirit did rejoice in the God of my salvation, who had brought strange things to pass. May I ever be preserved in humility, never forgetting his tender mercies to me.

Here, according to my desire, we settled; my husband got one school and I the other, and [we] took a room at a Friend's house a mile from each school and eight miles from the meeting House. Before next First Day we were got to our new settlement, and [I] now concluded to let my husband to see I was determined to join with Friends. When First Day came, I directed myself to him in this manner: "My dear, art thou willing to let me go to a meeting?" At which he flew into a rage, saying, "No you shan't." I then drew up my resolution and told him, as a dutiful wife ought, so I was ready to obey all his lawful commands, but where they imposed upon my conscience, I no longer durst. For I had already done it too long, and wronged myself by it, and though he was near and I loved him as a wife ought, yet God was nearer than all the world to me, and had made me sensible this was the way I ought to go. The which, I assured him, was no small cross to my own will, yet [I] had given up my heart, and hoped that he that called for it would enable me the residue[1] of my life to keep it steadily devoted to him, whatever I suffered for it, adding I hoped not to make him[2] any the worse wife for it. But all I could say was in vain; he was inflexible and would not consent.

I had now put my hand to the plough, and resolved not to look back, so went without leave; but expected to be immediately followed and forced back, but he did not. I went to one of the neighbours and got a girl to show me the way, then went on rejoicing and praising God in my heart, who had thus far given me power and another opportunity to confess to his truth. Thus for some time I had to go eight miles on foot to meetings, which I never thought hard; my husband

1 *residue* Remainder.

2 *him* I.e., her husband.

soon bought a horse, but would not let me ride him, neither when my shoes were worn out would he let me have a new pair, thinking by that means to keep me from going to meetings, but this did not hinder me, for I have taken strings and tied round to keep them on.

He, finding no hard usage could alter my resolution, neither threatening to beat me, nor doing it—for he several times struck me with sore blows which I endeavoured to bear with patience, believing the time would come when he would see I was in the right (which he accordingly did)—he once came up to me and took out his pen knife saying, "If you offer[1] to go to meeting tomorrow, with this knife I'll cripple you, for you shall not be a Quaker." I made him no answer, but when morning came, set out as usual and he was not suffered to hurt me. In despair of recovering me himself; he now flew to the priest for help and told him I had been a very religious woman in the way of the Church of England, was a member of it, and had a good certificate from Long Island, but now was bewitched and turned Quaker, which almost broke his heart. He therefore desired, as he[2] was one who had the care of souls, [that] he would come and pay me a visit and use his endeavours to reclaim me, and hoped by the blessing of God it would be done. The priest consented to come; the time was set, which was to be that day [in] two weeks, for he said he could not come sooner. My husband came home extremely pleased, and told me of it, at which I smiled, saying, "I hope to be enabled to give him a reason for the hope that is in me," at the same time believing the priest would never trouble me (nor ever did).

Before his appointed time came it was required of me in a more public manner to confess to the world what I was and to give up in prayer in a meeting, the sight[3] of which and the power that attended it made me tremble, and I could not hold myself still. I now again desired death and would have freely given up my natural life a ransom; and what made it harder to me, I was not yet taken under the care of Friends, and what kept me from requesting it was for fear I might be overcome and bring a scandal on the Society. I begged

to be excused till I was joined to Friends,[4] and then I would give up freely, to which I received this answer, as though I had heard a distinct voice: "I am a covenant-keeping God, and the word that I spoke to thee when I found thee in distress, even that I would never leave thee nor forsake thee if thou would be obedient to what I should make known to thee, I will assuredly make good: but if thou refuse, my spirit shall not always strive; fear not, I will make way for thee through all thy difficulties, which shall be many for my name's sake, but be thou faithful and I will give thee a crown of life."[5] I, being then sure it was God that spoke, said, "Thy will, God, be done, I am in thy hand; do with me according to thy Word," and gave up.[6] But after it was over the enemy came in like a flood, telling me I had done what I ought not, and should now bring dishonour to this people. This gave me a little shock, but it did not at this time last long.

This day as usual I had gone on foot. My husband (as he afterwards told me) lying on the bed at home, these words ran through him: "Lord, where shall I fly to shun thee[7] etc.?" upon which he arose and, seeing it rain, got his horse and came to fetch me; and coming just as the meeting broke up, I got on horseback as quick as possible, lest he should hear what had happened. Nevertheless, he heard of it, and as soon as we were got into the woods he began, saying, "What do you mean thus to make my life unhappy? What, could you not be a Quaker without turning fool after this manner?" I answered in tears, saying, "My dear, look on me with pity, if thou hast any. Canst thou think that I, in the bloom of my days, would bear all that thou knowest of and a great deal more that thou knowest not of if I did not believe it to be my duty?" This took hold of him, and taking my hand he said, "Well, I'll even give you up, for I see it don't avail to strive. If it be of God I can't overthrow it, and if it be of yourself

[1] *usage* Treatment; *offer* Attempt.

[2] *he* I.e., the priest.

[3] *give up in prayer* I.e., pray aloud before the meeting; *sight* Thought.

[4] *joined to Friends* I.e., made an official member of the Society of Friends.

[5] *crown of life* See James 1.12: "Blessed is the man that endureth temptation: for when he is tried, he shall receive the crown of life, which the Lord hath promised to them that love him"; see also Revelations 2.10.

[6] *and gave up* I.e., spoke before the meeting.

[7] *Lord, where … shun thee* See Psalms 139.7: "Whither shall I go from thy spirit? or wither shall I flee from thy presence?"

it will soon fall." I saw tears stand in his eyes, at which my heart was overcome with joy, and I would not have changed conditions with a queen.

I already began to reap the fruits of my obedience, but my trial ended not here, the time being up that the priest was to come; but no priest appeared. My husband went to fetch him, but he would not come, saying he was busy, which so displeased my husband that he'd never go to hear him more, and for some time went to no place of worship. Now the unwearied Adversary found out another scheme, and with it wrought so strong that I thought all I had gone through but a little to this. It came upon me in such an unexpected manner, in hearing a woman relate a book she had read in which it was asserted that Christ was not the son of God. As soon as she had spoke these words—if a man had spoke I could not have more distinctly heard these words—"No more he is, it's all a fancy and the contrivance of men," and an horror of great darkness fell upon me, which continued for three weeks.

The exercise I was under I am not able to express, neither durst I let any know how it was with me. I again sought desolate places where I might make my moan, and have lain whole nights and don't know that my eyes were shut to sleep. I again thought myself alone, but would not let go my faith in Him,[1] often saying in my heart, "I'll believe till I die," and kept a hope that he that had delivered me out of the paw of the bear and out of the jaws of the devouring lion[2] would in his own time deliver me out of his temptation also—which he in mercy did, and let me see that this was for my good, in order to prepare me for future service which he had for me to do, and that it was necessary his ministers should be dipped into all states, that thereby they might be able to speak to all conditions, for which my soul was thankful to him, the God of mercies, who had at several times redeemed me from great distress. And I found the truth of his words, that all things should work together for good to those

that loved and feared him, which I did with my whole heart, and hope ever shall while I have a being. This happened just after my first appearance, and Friends had not been to talk with me, nor did they know well what to do till I had appeared again, which was not for some time, when the monthly meeting appointed four Friends to give me a visit, which I was glad of; and gave them such satisfaction that they left me well satisfied. I then joined with Friends.

My husband still went to no place of worship. One day he said, "I'd go to meeting, only I am afraid I shall hear you clack,[3] which I cannot bear." I used no persuasions, yet when meeting time came, he got the horse, took me behind him, and went to meeting: but for several months if he saw me offer to rise,[4] he would go out, till once I got up before he was aware and then (as he afterwards said) he was ashamed to go, and from that time never did, nor hindered me from going to meetings. And though he (poor man) did not take up the cross, yet his judgement was convinced, and sometimes in a flood of tears would say, "My dear, I have seen the beauty there is in the truth, and that thou art in the right, and I pray God preserve thee in it. But as for me the cross is too heavy, I cannot bear it." I told him I hoped he that had given me strength would also favour him. "O!" said he, "I can't bear the reproach thou dost, to be called turncoat and to become a laughing stock to the world, but I'll no longer hinder thee," which I looked on as a great favour, that my way was thus far made easy, and a little hope remained that my prayers would be heard on his account.

In this place he had got linked in with some that he was afraid would make game of him, which indeed they already did, asking him when he designed to commence preacher, for that they saw he intended to turn Quaker, and seemed to love his wife better since she did than before (we were now got to a little house by ourselves which, though mean,[5] and little to put in it, our bed no better than chaff,[6] yet I was truly content and did not envy the rich their riches; the only desire I had now was my own preservation, and to be blessed

[1] *Him* In the 1774 text, the pronouns "he" and "him" when referring to God are normally not capitalized; inconsistencies such as this one have, however, been retained here.

[2] *he that had … lion* When offering to face Goliath, the Philistine champion, David, a shepherd who in the past had slain both a lion and a bear to defend his flock, declared, "The Lord that delivered me out of the paw of the lion, and out of the paw of the bear, he will deliver me out of the hand of this Philistine"; see 1 Samuel 17.37.

[3] *clack* Speak.

[4] *offer to rise* Break the silence of the meeting with vocal ministry.

[5] *mean* Humble; lowly.

[6] *bed no better than chaff* I.e., the mattress was comprised only of corn husks, hay, or other similar materials.

with the reformation of my husband). These men used to come to our house and there provoke my husband to sit up and drink, sometimes till near day, while I have been sorrowing in a stable. As I once sat in this condition I heard my husband say to his company, "I can't bear any longer to afflict my poor wife in this manner, for whatever you may think of her, I do believe she is a good woman," upon which he came to me and said, "Come in, my dear; God has given thee a deal of patience. I'll put an end to this practice"; and so he did, for this was the last time they sat up at night.

My husband now thought that if he was in any place where it was not known that he'd been so bitter against Friends, he could do better than here. But I was much against his moving, fearing it would tend to his hurt, having been for some months much altered for the better, and would often in a broken and affectionate manner condemn his bad usage to me. I told him I hoped it had been for my good, even to the better establishing me in the truth, and therefore would not have him to be afflicted about it, and according to the measure of grace received did what I could both by example and advice for his good: and my advice was for him to fight through here, fearing he would grow weaker and the Enemy gain advantage over him if he thus fled. But all I could say did not prevail against his moving, and hearing of a place at Bordentown [New Jersey], [he] went there, but that did not suit; he then moved to Mount Holly [New Jersey], and there we settled. He got a good school and so did I.

Here we might have done very well; we soon got our house prettily furnished for poor folks; I now began to think I wanted but one thing to complete my happiness, *viz.* the reformation of my husband, which, alas! I had too much reason to doubt; for it fell out according to my fears, and he grew worse here, and took much to drinking, so that it seemed as if my life was to be a continual scene of sorrows, and most earnestly I prayed to Almighty God to endue[1] me with patience to bear my afflictions and submit to his providence, which I can say in truth I did without murmuring or ever uttering an unsavoury expression to the best of my knowledge. Except once, my husband coming home a little in drink (in which frame he was very fractious) and finding me at work by a candle, came to me, put

it out, and fetching me a box on the ear,[2] said, "You don't earn your light"; on which unkind usage (for he had not struck me for two years so it went hard with me) I uttered these rash expressions: "Thou art a vile man," and I was a little angry, but soon recovered and was sorry for it. He struck me again, which I received without so much as a word in return, and that likewise displeased him; so he went on in a distracted[3] like manner, uttering several expressions that bespoke despair, as that he now believed that he was predestinated to damnation, and he did not care how soon God would strike him dead, and the like. I durst say but little; at length, in the bitterness of my soul, I broke out in these words: "Lord, look down on mine afflictions and deliver me by some means or other." I was answered, I should soon be, and so I was, but in such a manner as I verily thought it would have killed me. In a little time he went to Burlington, where he got in drink, and enlisted himself to go a common soldier to Cuba, *anno* 1740.[4]

I had drank many bitter cups—but this seemed to exceed them all, for indeed my very senses seemed shaken; I now a thousand times blamed myself for making such an unadvised request, fearing I had displeased God in it, and [that] though he had granted it, it was in displeasure, and suffered to be in this manner to punish me; though I can truly say I never desired his death, no more than my own, nay not so much. I have since had cause to believe his mind was benefitted by the undertaking (which hope makes up for all I have suffered from him), being informed he did in the army what he could not do at home, *viz.*, suffered for the testimony of truth. When they came to prepare for an engagement, he refused to fight,[5] for which he was whipped and brought before the general, who asked him why he enlisted if he would not fight. "I did it," said he, "in a drunken frolic, when the Devil had

[1] *endue* Endow.

[2] *fetching me a box on the ear* Striking me in the side of the head.

[3] *distracted* Distressed.

[4] *Cuba ... 1740* During the eighteenth century the British made various attempts to wrest Cuba from Spanish control; they captured Guantanamo Bay in 1741. Britain succeeded in capturing all of Cuba in 1762, but under the terms of the Treaty of Paris a year later they exchanged the island of Cuba for the colony of Florida.

[5] *he refused to fight* Quakers are pacifists; Ashbridge takes her husband's refusal to fight as a sign that he has turned Quaker.

the better of me, but my judgment is convinced that I ought not, neither will I, whatever I suffer; I have but one life, and you may take that if you please, but I'll never take up arms." They used[1] him with much cruelty to make him yield, but could not, by means whereof he was so disabled that the general sent him to the hospital at Chelsea,[2] where in nine months' time he died. And I hope [he] made a good end, for which I prayed both night and day till I heard of his death.

Thus I thought it my duty to say what I could in his favour, as I have been obliged to say so much of his hard usage to me, all which I hope did me good; and although he was so bad, yet had several good properties, and I never thought him the worst of men. He was one I loved, and had he let religion have its perfect work, I should have thought myself happy in the lowest state of life. And I've cause to bless God, who enabled me in the station of a wife to do my duty, and now a widow to submit to his will, always believing everything he doeth to be right. May he in all stations of life so preserve me, by the arm of divine power, that I may never forget his tender mercies to me, the remembrance whereof doth often bow my soul in humility before his throne, saying, "Lord, what was I that thou should have revealed to me the knowledge of thy truth, and done so much for me, who deserved thy displeasure rather? But in me hast thou shown thy long suffering and tender mercy; may thou O God be glorified and I abased, for it is thy own works that praise thee, and of a truth to the humble soul thou makest every bitter thing sweet. The End.

THUS FAR WAS HER OWN WRITING THE OTHER SIDE WROTE BY HER HUSBAND AND SENT WITH HERS[3]

Here ends what was perfected by her pen before she left home which was the 11th 5th month 1753, though she had made some beginning and several times expressed to me a desire to commemorate the further gracious dealings of Divine Providence with her and leave some hints of her experience for the service of such as should think worthwhile to read what she wrote; but a concern for visiting the churches abroad prevailing so weightily on her mind took the place of all other concerns.

Her husband[4] had been gone some two or three years before she had a certain account of his death; he left her near £80 in debt, for which by law she was not answerable, because without effects.[5] Yet as there were many creditors who complained, saying they would not have trusted him if it had not been for his wife's sake—she therefore (that truth might not suffer) engaged to pay them all as fast as she could, and as soon as ability was afforded, settled to school keeping, whereby with her needle she maintained herself handsomely and by degrees paid off near all the said debts in the time of her widowhood, in which time she also traveled considerably in the service of truth.

In the 9th month 1746 we were married at Burlington (West Jersey) in endeared affections, and the sense of truth greatly prevailing at the time, which blessing, through mercy continuing, made our company mutual, dear and agreeable, even to a wish, yet we must part. Sufficiently convinced that her Lord and Master called for her service abroad, my heart was prepared and made willing to resign a darling and worthy object indeed of my love and delight, and though it hath pleased the Lord (who is above all worthy) to remove her without indulging my longing desires of once more rejoicing with her in time, yet being fully satisfied that she is taken from the troubles thereof to a happy eternity, I feel a good degree of comfortable composure and resignation to the Divine Will; believing, as she did, that whatsoever He doth is right; never having once repented my giving her up to the service of truth, in which she died as aforesaid.

AARON ASHBRIDGE

—1990, 1774 (WRITTEN C. 1745)

[1] *used* Treated.

[2] *Chelsea* District of southwestern London.

[3] This is the first of several appendices included in the 1774 printing of Ashbridge's *Account*. It is followed there by a "lament" by Aaron Ashbridge on having learned of his wife's death abroad, by a brief account of her illness and death by John Gough, and by the testimony of a member of the Waterford Quaker community affirming Ashbridge's talent as a minister.

[4] *Her husband* I.e., Sullivan.

[5] *without effects* I.e., she (as a woman) owned no property.

In Context

Quaker Conversion Narratives

Ashbridge recounts the extraordinary influence exerted on her by the experience of reading Samuel Crisp's *Two Letters Written by Samuel Crisp, about the Year 1702, to Some of His Acquaintance, Upon His Change from a Chaplain of the Church of England, to Join with the People Called Quakers*. Crisp's account was one of the most popular of Quaker conversion narratives; first published in 1722, it was published in many editions over the course of the eighteenth century. The pages that follow are reproduced from the tenth edition (1778).

[9]

may not be the least thought, word, motion, gesture, or action, but what is exactly agreeable to his most holy will, as if I saw him standing before me, and as if I were to be judged by him for the thought of my heart next moment ? O divine life ! O seraphic soul ! O that I could always stand here ! for here is no reflection, no sorrow, no repentance ; but at God's right hand there is perfect peace, and a river of unspeakable joy. O that we might imitate the life of Jesus, and be thoroughly furnished unto every good word and work !

This was the frequent breathing of my soul to God, when I was in the country ; but more especially after I had left my new preferment of a chaplain, and took private lodgings in London : in this retirement, I hope I may say, without boasting, that I was very devout and religious, and I found great comfort and refreshment in it from the Lord, who let me see the beauty of holiness ; and the sweetness that arises from an humbled, mortified life, was then very pleasant to my taste, and I
B rejoiced

[10]

rejoiced in it more than in all the delights and pleasures of the world.

And now it pleased God to shew me, that if I would indeed live strictly and holily, as becomes the gospel, then I must leave the communion of the church of England ; but I knew not yet which way to determine myself, nor to what body of men I should join, who were more orthodox and more regular in their lives. As for the Quakers, so called, I was so great a stranger to them, that I had never read any of their books, nor do I remember, that ever I conversed with any one man of that communion in my whole life : I think there was one in Foxley, while I was curate there, but I never saw the man, though I went several times to his house on purpose to talk with him, and to bring him off from his mad and wild enthusiasm, as I then ignorantly thought it to be : as for that way, I knew it was every where spoken against ; he that had a mind to appear more witty and ingenious than the rest, would chuse this for the subject of his profane jests and drollery ; with this he makes sport, and diverts
the

[11]

the company ; for a Quaker is but another name for a fool or a mad-man, and was scarce ever mentioned, but with scorn and contempt. As for drollery, I confess, I was never any great friend to it ; but indeed, if all was true that was laid to the Quakers charge, I thought that they were some of the worst people that ever appeared in the world ; and wondered with what face they could call themselves Christians, since I was told they denied the fundamental articles of the holy faith, to which I ever bore the highest veneration and esteem : and notwithstanding I had always lived at the greatest distance from that people, and was very zealous in the worship of the church of England, and upon all occasions would speak very honourably of it ; moreover, was content to suffer some few inconveniences upon that account, as thou very well knowest, yet my father still looked upon me as inclining to the Quakers ; and some years ago signified to a friend, he was afraid I would become an enthusiast ; and, whilst I was at Bungan school, he sent me two books to read that were written against the Quakers, B 2 one

[12]

one of which was John Faldo's, who hath been sufficiently exposed for it by William Penn.

Whilst I lived in London, in that private retired manner, I was just now speaking of, walking very humbly in the sight of God, and having opportunity to reflect upon my past life ; as I had occasion to be one day at a bookseller's shop, I happened to cast my eye on Barclay's works ; and having heard in the country, that he was a man of great account amongst the Quakers, I had a mind to see what their principles were, and what defence they could make for themselves ; for sure, thought I, these people are not so silly and ridiculous, nor maintainers of such horrid opinions, as the author of the Snake, and some others, would make us believe. I took Barclay home with me, and I read him through in a week's time, save a little treatise at the end, which finding it to be very philosophical, I omitted ; but, however, I soon read enough to convince me of my own blindness and ignorance of the things of God ; there I found a light to break in upon my mind,

[13]

mind, which did mightily refresh and comfort me in that poor, low, and humble state, in which I then was ; for indeed I was, and had been for a considerable time before, very hungry and thirsty after righteousness, and therefore I received the truth with all readiness of mind : it was like balm to my soul, and as showers of rain to the thirsty earth, which is parched with heat and drought. This author laid things down so plainly, and proved them with such ingenuity and dexterity of learning, and opened the scriptures so clearly to me, that, without standing to cavil, dispute, raise argument or objection, or consulting with flesh and blood, I presently resigned myself to God, and weeping for joy that I had found so great a treasure, I often thanked him with tears in my eyes for so kind a visitation of his love, that he was graciously pleased to look toward me when my soul cried after him ; so that, though before I was in great doubt and trouble of mind, not knowing which way to determine myself, yet now the sun breaking out so powerfully upon me, the clouds were scattered ; I was now fully satisfied in my own mind which

[14]

which way I ought to go, and to what body of people I should join myself.

So I immediately left the communion of the church of England, and went to Grace-church-street meeting. After I had read Barclay, I read some other books of that kind, among which was an excellent piece, though in a small volume, called, No Cross, no Crown. Thus I continued reading, and frequenting meetings for several weeks together, but did not let any one soul know what I was about : the first man I conversed with was George Whitehead, and this was several weeks after I began to read Barclay, and frequent their meetings : by him I was introduced into more acquaintance, and still the farther I went, the more I liked their plainness, and the decency and simplicity of their conversation : they do not use the ceremonies and salutations of the church of England, but shake hands freely, and converse together as brothers and sisters that are sprung of the same royal seed, and made kings and priests unto God. O ! the love, the sweetness and tenderness of affection I have seen among this people !

Flusht with Conceit (whichshe ŷ Spirit calls)
Upon a Tub see how Dame Silence bawls
Whilst Dunghill Cocks in a most pious strain
Listen to heare the Cackling of the Hen

The Quakers
Meeting

In publick who can beare a Female tattle
Let me in Bed heare my kinde Mistreß prattle
For ŷ their Preaching edifies the Nation
It must be by an use of Application

Anonymous (possibly Marcellus Laroon the elder) after Egbert van Heemskerck, *The Quaker Meeting*, date unknown. In the late seventeenth century, London-based Dutch painter Egbert van Heemskerck produced a series of paintings depicting Quaker meetings. Art and religious historians are in disagreement about the degree to which these paintings were intended as satire or as accurate representations of Quaker worship, but certainly they inspired numerous prints whose satirical qualities are more clearly evident, such as the one reproduced here. Many of these prints were accompanied by poems that lampooned Quaker forms of worship, often by emphasizing the leading roles that women took in these meetings. Although this print is separated from Ashbridge's Quaker experience by an ocean and several decades, it is nevertheless representative of the sorts of derision female Quakers like Ashbridge were often subject to in America.

The text of the poem at the bottom reads: "Flusht with Conceit (which she it Spirit calls) / Upon a Tub see how Dame Silence bawls / Whilst Dunghill Cocks in a most pious strain / Listen to heare the Cackling of the hen. / In publick who can beare a Female tattle / Let me in Bed heare my kinde Mistress prattle / For if their Preaching edifies the Nation / It must be by an use of Application."

LUCY TERRY
c. 1724/30 – 1821

Lucy Terry is celebrated as the author of the first known work of literature by an African American. That work, the short occasional poem "Bars Fight," was transmitted orally by her community members for decades after its composition circa 1746, before being published in the mid-nineteenth century.

Terry (whose birth name is unknown), is thought by several scholars to have been born around 1730 (though some others have argued that she was born as early as 1724), probably in West Africa. She was brought enslaved to Rhode Island in early childhood; her name was likely given her by the slaveholder who first purchased her, Samuel Terry. She grew up in Deerfield, Massachusetts—then a frontier settlement that was home to a significant number of enslaved individuals—as the legal property of Ebenezer and Abigail Wells. She was baptized in 1735 and admitted into full church communion in 1744. In Deerfield, Terry developed a reputation as a compelling storyteller, reportedly attracting enthusiastic audiences at the local tavern. Josiah Holland's *History of Western Massachussetts* describes her as follows:

> One of the most noteworthy characters in the early history of Deerfield was a colored woman, known as "Luce Bijah."[1] She was … known for her wit and shrewdness. Her house was the constant resort of the boys, to hear her talk. She removed with her husband and children to Vermont, and purchased a tract of land, the title to which proved imperfect. A suit was brought to dispossess her, and she argued her case against Stephen R. Bradley and Royal Tyler (afterwards, Chief Justice of Vermont). Judge Chase, who held the court, said that Luce made a better argument than he had heard at the bar of Vermont. Luce was a poetess, and commemorated in verse the end of the "Bars Fight."

The "Bars fight" itself occurred on 25 August 1746. A group of approximately fifty Abenaki warriors, under the command of the French army, launched an attack, targeting a field known locally as "the Bars" where a group of (largely or entirely white) villagers had gathered to begin their haymaking. The villagers were unaware of the recent capture of Fort Massachusetts by the French army and their Indigenous allies, a small part of the mounting hostilities that would lead to the French and Indian War in the following decade. The attack led to the deaths of five villagers, with one young girl, Eunice Allen, surviving a severe head injury, and her younger brother, Samuel Allen, taken captive. Much of what is known today of this incident is owed to Terry's poem, which was presumably composed not long after the attack, and which nineteenth-century historian George Sheldon would later describe as "the fullest contemporary account of that bloody tragedy which has been preserved."

Stylistically the poem is a striking mix, with some elements suggestive of the ballad form (often the means of memorializing local history), some suggestive of other verse forms—and with interesting differences between the stylistic features of the first eighteen lines and those of the last ten. Clearly the poem (which may well have been intended to be sung) struck a chord; through one means or another it was preserved orally for decades. Its first appearance in print was on the front page of the *Springfield Republican* on 20 November 1854, shortly prior to its inclusion in Holland's two-volume work.

In May 1756, Terry married Abijah Prince, a free African American. Not long thereafter, she was freed from slavery, possibly through purchase by her husband; the couple's six children—two of whom likely fought for the American army during the Revolutionary War—would all be born into freedom. The family eventually settled in Vermont in the 1770s, where they came to own a substantial amount of property and to hold positions of considerable respect in the community. That said, the Princes remained

[1] Though she is most often referred to as "Lucy Terry," various records refer to her as "Bijah's Luce," "Lucy Abijah," and "Luce Bijah" (after the name of her husband, Abijah Prince).

subject to racial prejudice; the continual violence and harassment of one neighbor who sought to drive them off their land led to the court case Holland refers to, in which Terry successfully petitioned for legal protection. (Numerous other accounts exist of Terry defending herself and her family in court, though most of these have not been substantiated by surviving court documents.)

Terry died in 1821, likely in her nineties. Her funeral was attended by the well-known African American minister and writer Lemuel Haynes, who composed an antislavery poem to be read at the occasion. A long obituary in the *Vermont Gazette* foregrounded her respectability and religiosity as well as her intelligence and narrative talents, claiming that "the fluency of her speech captivated all around her, and was not destitute of instruction and edification."

"Bars Fight" remains Terry's only known composition. Though dismissed by some scholars in the twentieth century as "doggerel," the poem is highly valued today—as a historical document recounting one part of the struggle between white settlers and the Indigenous peoples of early America; as a work revealing the talents and the sympathies of a young African American woman in the mid-eighteenth century; and as an important text in the ongoing exploration of the liminal space between the cultures of orality and those of the written word.

NOTE ON THE TEXT: The text presented below is based on that printed as part of the history of Deerfield, in Volume Two of Josiah Holland's *History of Western Massachusetts* (1855). Spelling and punctuation have been modernized in accordance with the practices of this anthology.

⌘ ⌘ ⌘

Bars[1] Fight

August 'twas the twenty-fifth,
Seventeen hundred forty-six;
The Indians did in ambush lay,
Some very valiant men to slay,
5 The names of whom I'll not leave out.
Samuel Allen like a hero fought.
And though he was so brave and bold,
His face no more shall we behold.
Eleazer Hawks was killed outright,
10 Before he had time to fight—
Before he did the Indians see,
Was shot and killed immediately.
Oliver Amsden he was slain,
Which caused his friends much grief and pain.
15 Simeon Amsden they found dead,
Not many rods[2] distant from his head.
Adonijah Gillett we do hear

Did lose his life which was so dear.
John Sadler fled across the water,
20 And thus escaped the dreadful slaughter.
Eunice Allen see the Indians coming,
And hopes to save herself by running,
And had not her petticoats stopped her,
The awful creatures had not catched her,
25 Nor tommy hawked her on the head,
And left her on the ground for dead.[3]
Young Samuel Allen, Oh lack-a-day!
Was taken and carried to Canada.[4]
—1855 (COMPOSED C. 1746)

[1] *Bars* Local name for a meadow outside Deerfield, Massachusetts.

[2] *rods* Units of measurement, equalling approximately five and a half yards.

[3] *Eunice Allen ... for dead* Eunice Allen, who was thirteen at the time of the attack, survived her injuries, reportedly living to over eighty years of age.

[4] *Young Samuel ... to Canada* The eight-year-old son of the Samuel Allen whose death is noted earlier in the poem, young Samuel Allen was taken captive by the attackers and held for ransom for a year and nine months, during which period he was said to have assimilated into Abenaki society; contemporary reports suggest that he was reluctant to return to his previous Massachusetts life. It is with reference to these concluding lines and the story of Samuel Allen that some scholars have drawn connections between Terry's poem and the captivity narrative tradition within American literature.

SAGOYEWATHA

c. 1758 – 1830

Popularly known as Red Jacket, Sagoyewatha was a Seneca chief and orator. Renowned for his powers of persuasion in Indigenous councils—and for his ability to adapt Haudenosaunee rhetoric to the persuasion of settler audiences—he often spoke on behalf of the Seneca at treaty councils from the 1780s to the 1820s, articulating the positions that Seneca leaders had collectively agreed upon. He sought peace whenever possible, as the diplomatic tradition of the Haudenosaunee dictated, while also defending Seneca land and culture, often with an ironic wit. He is best known for his rhetorically powerful speeches in defense of Indigenous land rights and religious practices, and for his diplomatic efforts on behalf of the Haudenosaunee—efforts that Haudenosaunee negotiators continue to build on in the present day.

Sagoyewatha was most likely born in Canoga, New York (the exact location of his birthplace is unclear); his father was Cayuga, and his mother was a member of an influential Senecan family that included other important figures such as the war chief Cornplanter and the religious leader Handsome Lake. The Seneca are a matrilineal society, and Sagoyewatha was born into his mother's clan, the Wolf clan. In childhood he received the name Otetiani ("Always Ready"). Legend has it that early in his life he attended an important council of Indigenous leaders on the Shenandoah river, where he heard Logan the Orator—a war leader of the Haudenosaunee—speak. This experience sparked an ambition, and it is said that the young Sagoyewatha would spend a great deal of time alone in the forest "playing Logan": practicing his skills of persuasion. He also served as a runner, a messenger tasked with accurately recounting council proceedings to other communities.

The role of diplomat and peacemaker is vitally important in Haudenosaunee culture, the orator acting as a steward for the Great Law of Peace of the People of the Longhouse.[1] Sagoyewatha's ambition was to join the long history of respected Indigenous orators, including Garangula, Hendrick, Skenandoah, Adario, and Logan. In the 1770s, the young Otetiani was given a new name, Sagoyewatha, often translated as "the keeper awake" and considered a tribute to his rhetorical power to captivate his audience. (Recently, it has been suggested that the name may simply mean "he wakes them up early," with no particular reference to Sagoyewatha's oratorical gifts.)

During the American Revolutionary War the Seneca generally supported a neutral position, but most eventually sided with the British. While Sagoyewatha was not a successful soldier—in fact, accusations of cowardice from his political rivals would follow him for the rest of his life—he was more successful in his diplomatic role as a runner, and British officers gave him a British military jacket in recognition of his services. He wore such a jacket from then on, embracing the name of "Red Jacket." The British government did not, however, prove to be a reliable ally to the Seneca: as part of the treaty that ended the war, Britain gave America large portions of land that earlier agreements had recognized as belonging to Indigenous peoples. Many Seneca migrated to Canada as a result, but Sagoyewatha stayed in the Genesee River Valley in New York and became a key negotiator representing the Seneca who remained to the American government.

President Washington requested a meeting with Sagoyewatha in 1792, in an effort to convince the Seneca chiefs to support efforts to contain wars with Indigenous peoples in the West. Sagoyewatha's speech on the historical context of the wars impressed Washington so greatly that he gave the chief a

[1] An oral constitution of the Haudenosaunee, or Six Nations (originally Five Nations), the Great Law of Peace enshrines individual rights and creates a consensus-based federation among the nations.

silver "peace medal." Sagoyewatha was also influential in the negotiation of the Treaty of Canandaigua in 1794—the "peace and friendship" treaty between the Six Nations of the Iroquois and the new government of the United States. The treaty, to which Sagoyewatha was a signatory, did not secure as much land as he had wanted for the Seneca, but it did acknowledge the right of Indigenous nations to negotiate directly with the American government. While the federal government did not consistently adhere to the terms of the treaty, it remains in force in the twenty-first century and is still the legal basis for the sovereignty of Haudenosaunee nations.

In 1805, Sagoyewatha gave the speech for which he is most famous, his "Reply to Jacob Cram," sometimes titled "Religion for the White Man and the Red," or "We Never Quarrel about Religion." In this speech, Sagoyewatha explains Haudenosaunee leadership's refusal to allow missionaries to establish churches on Seneca reservations. By 1807, however, he faced opposition from those within his own community who had converted to Christianity, and this schism among the people deepened, becoming a crisis in 1826 when Christian Seneca sold land to the Ogden company—a private land developer— against the wishes of those chiefs who followed the traditional religion. When Sagoyewatha and thirty or forty other leaders from the "Pagan party" protested this sale, which had been obtained through bribery and threats, the agreement was not ratified. The Ogden company ignored this, however, and succeeded in buying, under extortionate terms, almost all of the Seneca reservation in Western New York. Sagoyewatha was for a time deposed from his leadership role, probably as a result of this controversy and certainly on account of his continued resistance to Christianity. He did, however, regain his position before his death. His later years were shadowed by alcoholism, by the deaths of his children, and by a period of separation from his wife following her conversion to Christianity. He died of cholera in 1830.

As an orator whose speeches were delivered in Seneca but recorded in English translation, Sagoyewatha left behind a written record that at best only partially captures his achievements. His work, however, is far better documented than is typical for a Native American orator of this period; many of his most important speeches took place on occasions that were facilitated by first-rate interpreters and thoroughly recorded, and much (though by no means all) of the writing attributed to him has a consistency of tone and style that suggests a certain degree of accuracy. Beginning in the mid-1810s, Seneca leadership began consciously to harness the reach of print media, and it appears that many of Sagoyewatha's speeches from this point onward were intended not only for performance but also for transcription in newspapers and pamphlets.

By the time of his death, Sagoyewatha's reputation was such that, a decade later, his biographer could write that "[t]he name of Red-Jacket, the great orator of the Six Nations, is among those most familiar to the American ear." Several biographies were written about Sagoyewatha in the nineteenth and twentieth centuries, and his speeches were frequently distributed in pamphlets and schoolbooks. Competing narratives of his life, however, have long circulated. One such image, promulgated by his political opponents, emphasized his military failures and his alcoholism, portraying him as a self-serving coward. Another, at least as false, romanticized his wisdom and eloquence and eulogized him as the "last of the Senecas"—invoking the common stereotype of the vanishing "noble savage" who is worthy of respect but whose era has sadly passed. In recent decades, scholarship has focused on Sagoyewatha as a major contributor to an ongoing tradition of Haudenosaunee diplomacy. Scholars have analyzed his speeches with reference to Haudenosaunee rhetoric and ideology, and have emphasized the foundation he helped to lay for later generations of Indigenous resistance.

NOTE ON THE TEXT: This text is based on the first printing of the speech in the *Monthly Anthology and Boston Review*, April 1809; additions made by the *Monthly Anthology* appear in square brackets below. The history of the transmission of this speech is somewhat unclear; it was published almost three years after it was delivered, and scholars believe that the council probably took place in November rather than, as the *Monthly Anthology* suggests, in the summer. Sagoyewatha kept track of what was published about him, however, and there is no evidence that he disputed the text's accuracy.

⌘⌘⌘

[*Reply to the Missionary Jacob Cram*][1]

[In the summer of 1805, a number of the principal Chiefs and Warriors of the Six Nations of Indians,[2] principally Senecas, assembled at Buffalo Creek, in the State of New York, at the particular request of a gentle-man Missionary from the State of Massachusetts.[3] The Missionary being furnished with an Interpreter, and accompanied by the Agent of the United States for Indian affairs,[4] met the Indians in Council, when the following talk took place.]

FIRST, BY THE AGENT.

Brothers of the Six Nations; I rejoice to meet you at this time, and thank the Great Spirit, that he has preserved you in health, and given me another opportunity of taking you by the hand.

Brothers; The person who sits by me is a friend who has come a great distance to hold a talk with you. He will inform you what his business is, and it is my request that you would listen with attention to his words.

MISSIONARY. *My Friends*; I am thankful for the opportunity afforded us of uniting together at this time. I had a great desire to see you, and inquire into your state and welfare; for this purpose I have travelled a great distance, being sent by your old friends, the Boston Missionary Society. You will recollect they formerly sent missionaries among you, to instruct you in religion, and labour for your good. Although they have not heard from you for a long time, yet they have not forgotten their brothers the Six Nations, and are still anxious to do you good.

Brothers; I have not come to get your lands or your money, but to enlighten your minds, and to instruct you how to worship the Great Spirit agreeably to his mind and will, and to preach to you the gospel of his son Jesus Christ. There is but one religion, and but one way to serve God, and if you do not embrace the right way, you cannot be happy hereafter. You have never worshipped the Great Spirit in a manner acceptable to him; but have, all your lives, been in great errors and darkness. To endeavour to remove these errors, and open your eyes, so that you might see clearly, is my business with you.

Brothers; I wish to talk with you as one friend talks with another; and, if you have any objections to receive the religion which I preach, I wish you to state them; and I will endeavour to satisfy your minds, and remove the objections.

Brothers; I want you to speak your minds freely; for I wish to reason with you on the subject, and, if possible, remove all doubts, if there be any on your minds. The subject is an important one, and it is of consequence that you give it an early attention while the offer is made you. Your friends, the Boston Missionary Society, will continue to send you good and faithful ministers, to instruct and strengthen you in religion, if, on your part, you are willing to receive them.

Brothers; Since I have been in this part of the country, I have visited some of your small villages, and talked with your people. They appear willing to receive instruction, but, as they look up to you as their older brothers in council, they want first to know your opinion on the subject.

You have now heard what I have to propose at present. I hope you will take it into consideration, and give me an answer before we part.

[1] Originally published under the title Indian Speech; *Jacob Cram* New England missionary and author of *Journal of a Missionary Tour* (1808).

[2] *Six Nations of Indians* Also known as the Haudenosaunee Confederacy or Iroquois Confederacy, this alliance of Iroquoian-speaking nations—including the Mohawk, Onondaga, Oneida, Cayuga, Seneca, and later the Tuscarora—constituted a powerful political and trading community in Northeastern North America from the seventeenth to nineteenth centuries. The Haudenosaunee Confederacy, though now much reduced in population, continues to advocate for its sovereign communities in both the United States and Canada.

[3] [Note from the *Monthly Anthology*] Rev. Mr. Cram.

[4] *Agent of the United States for Indian affairs* Person authorized by the U.S. government to act on its behalf during negotiations with Indigenous peoples. Agents oversaw trade, distributed annual payments to the sachems, attempted to manage conflicts, and enacted the forced removal of Indigenous peoples from their land and onto reservations. This role was largely unsupervised and involved the handling of a great deal of money and trade goods; while some agents were honest, many were corrupt and self-serving, inflicting untold damage on the Indigenous communities.

[After about two hours consultation amongst themselves, the Chief commonly called, by the white people, Red Jacket,[1] rose and spoke as follows:]

Friend and Brother; It was the will of the Great Spirit that we should meet together this day. He orders all things, and has given us a fine day for our Council. He has taken his garment from before the sun, and caused it to shine with brightness upon us. Our eyes are opened, that we see clearly; our ears are unstopped, that we have been able to hear distinctly the words you have spoken. For all these favours we thank the Great Spirit; and Him *only*.

Brother; This council fire was kindled by you. It was at your request that we came together at this time. We have listened with attention to what you have said. You requested us to speak our minds freely. This gives us great joy; for we now consider that we stand upright before you, and can speak what we think. All have heard your voice, and all speak to you now as one man. Our minds are agreed.

Brother; You say you want an answer to your talk before you leave this place. It is right you should have one, as you are a great distance from home, and we do not wish to detain you. But we will first look back a little, and tell you what our fathers have told us, and what we have heard from the white people.

Brother; Listen to what we say.

There was a time when our forefathers owned this great island. Their seats[2] extended from the rising to the setting sun. The Great Spirit had made it for the use of Indians. He had created the buffalo, the deer, and other animals for food. He had made the bear and the beaver. Their skins served us for clothing. He had scattered them over the country, and taught us how to take them. He had caused the earth to produce corn for bread. All this He had done for his red children, because He loved them. If we had some disputes about our hunting ground, they were generally settled without the shedding of much blood. But an evil day came upon us. Your forefathers crossed the great water, and landed on this island. Their numbers were small. They found friends and not enemies. They told us they had

fled from their own country for fear of wicked men, and had come here to enjoy their religion. They asked for a small seat. We took pity on them, granted their request; and they sat down amongst us. We gave them corn and meat, they gave us poison [alluding, it is supposed, to ardent spirits[3]] in return.

The white people had now found our country. Tidings were carried back, and more came amongst us. Yet we did not fear them. We took them to be friends. They called us brothers. We believed them, and gave them a larger seat. At length their numbers had greatly increased. They wanted more land; they wanted our country. Our eyes were opened, and our minds became uneasy. Wars took place. Indians were hired to fight against Indians, and many of our people were destroyed. They also brought strong liquor amongst us. It was strong and powerful, and has slain thousands.

Brother; Our seats were once large and yours were small. You have now become a great people, and we have scarcely a place left to spread our blankets. You have got our country, but are not satisfied; you want to force your religion upon us.

Brother; Continue to listen.

You say that you are sent to instruct us how to worship the Great Spirit agreeably to his mind, and, if we do not take hold of the religion which you white people teach, we shall be unhappy hereafter. You say that you are right and we are lost. How do we know this to be true? We understand that your religion is written in a book. If it was intended for us as well as you, why has not the Great Spirit given to us, and not only to us, but why did he not give to our forefathers the knowledge of that book, with the means of understanding it rightly? We only know what you tell us about it. How shall we know when to believe, being so often deceived by the white people?

Brother; You say there is but one way to worship and serve the Great Spirit. If there is but one religion; why do you white people differ so much about it? Why not all agreed, as you can all read the book?

Brother; We do not understand these things.

We are told that your religion was given to your forefathers, and has been handed down from father to son. We also have a religion, which was given to our

1 [Note from the *Monthly Anthology*] His Indian name is, Sagu-yu-whàt-hah; which interpreted is, *Keeper-awake.*

2 *seats* Lands.

3 *ardent spirits* I.e., alcohol. It is also possible that Sagoyewatha uses "poison" here to refer to disease rather than to alcohol.

forefathers, and has been handed down to us their children. We worship in that way. It teaches us to be thankful for all the favours we receive; to love each other, and to be united. We never quarrel about religion.

Brother; The Great Spirit has made us all, but he has made a great difference between his white and red children. He has given us different complexions and different customs. To you He has given the arts. To these He has not opened our eyes. We know these things to be true. Since He has made so great a difference between us in other things; why may we not conclude that He has given us a different religion according to our understanding? The Great Spirit does right. He knows what is best for his children; we are satisfied.

Brother; We do not wish to destroy your religion, or take it from you. We only want to enjoy our own.

Brother; We are told that you have been preaching to the white people in this place. These people are our neighbours. We are acquainted with them. We will wait a little while, and see what effect your preaching has upon them. If we find it does them good, makes them honest, and less disposed to cheat Indians; we will then consider again of what you have said.

Brother; You have now heard our answer to your talk, and this is all we have to say at present.

As we are going to part, we will come and take you by the hand, and hope the Great Spirit will protect you on your journey, and return you safe to your friends.

As the Indians began to approach the missionary, he rose hastily from his seat and replied, that he could not take them by the hand; that there was no fellowship between the religion of God and the works of the devil.

This being interpreted to the Indians, they smiled, and retired in a peaceable manner.

It being afterwards suggested to the missionary that his reply to the Indians was rather indiscreet;[1] he observed, that he supposed the ceremony of shaking hands would be received by them as a token that he assented to what they had said. Being otherwise informed, he said he was sorry for the expressions.

—1805 (PUBLISHED 1809)

1 *indiscreet* Inconsiderate, rude.

Benjamin Franklin

1706 – 1790

Benjamin Franklin, though best known as one of the founders of the United States, played staggeringly diverse roles in the course of his transatlantic career: diplomat, political theorist, inventor, scientist, entrepreneur, humorist, and autobiographer. He is often put forward—and in many ways put himself forward—as an exemplar of the mythical "self-made man," the ambitious yet unpretentious person whose success relies on nothing but his own hard work and perhaps a touch of shrewd talent.

Though he spent decades of his life in England, and his politics, values, and prose style were in many ways shaped by European influences, Franklin repurposed these influences for an American context; his contributions to the ideological and intellectual traditions of the United States have ensured his enduring reputation as an exemplary figure of American culture.

Franklin was born in Boston in 1706, the youngest son of seventeen children raised in the household of Josiah Franklin—who had left England as a Calvinist dissident in the previous century—and his second wife Abiah Folger. Josiah initially intended Benjamin for the ministry, but removed him from the necessary grammar school after only two years, likely for financial reasons. After a short period working in his father's soap and candle making business, Benjamin was apprenticed to his brother James, who was soon to found the innovative, satirical, and frequently controversial newspaper *The New-England Courant*.

Although he would later describe James as a "harsh and tyrannical" master, the printing trade suited Franklin well, not least because the work exposed him to reading material beyond that of his father's religious library. In particular, Franklin became a dedicated student of pre-Enlightenment philosophers such as John Locke and Francis Bacon; essayists Daniel Defoe, Joseph Addison, and Richard Steele; and classical Greek and Roman philosophers.

In 1722, Franklin secretly submitted the first in a series of fourteen satirical letters to the *Courant* under the pseudonym "Silence Dogood," the purported widow of a country minister. Like much of Franklin's later writing, the Dogood letters blend lighthearted humor with genuine social commentary; they poke fun at contemporary fashions and also address subjects from religious hypocrisy to the poor education of women. The revelation that James's sixteen-year-old brother was the true author of these remarkably popular—and frequently provocative—letters caused a significant rift in an already strained relationship, as did James's subsequent imprisonment for publishing articles that were critical of the religious and political authorities. In 1723, Franklin moved to Pennsylvania—a Quaker-led state, and hence more progressive than Puritan Boston—to begin establishing an independent career. This decision to strike out on his own became an integral part of Franklin's legend of self-made success.

In Philadelphia, Franklin found brief employment at a printing house; he then traveled to London, England, where he worked as a typesetter and frequented coffeehouses, participating in London's intellectual scene. While in England, he published *A Dissertation on Liberty and Necessity, Pleasure and Pain* (1725), a pamphlet in which he concluded that traditional religion was useless and illogical. (In later years, Franklin regretted this argument and burned all extant copies of the pamphlet he could find.) In 1729, having returned to Philadelphia, he partnered with fellow-printer Hugh Meredith to purchase the *Pennsylvania Gazette*, which soon became the most successful newspaper in the colonies and a leader in the burgeoning field of American news publishing. On occasion, Franklin wrote for the paper himself.

In the meantime, he also engaged with his "Junto," an intellectual club formed of likeminded friends who gathered regularly to share essays and discuss ideas. In 1730 he entered a common-law marriage with Deborah Read, a love interest from his youth who had been abandoned by her first husband; Read would later manage Franklin's businesses while he was living in England. The couple had two children, and also raised the future Loyalist leader William Franklin, Franklin's illegitimate son whose mother's identity he never revealed.

The year 1732 saw the launch of *Poor Richard's Almanack*, Franklin's most ambitious project yet and for many years his best-known achievement. Annual almanacs were staples of nearly all colonial homes, providing weather forecasts, astronomical and astrological predictions, and bits of entertainment and advice suitable for general readers—the latter of which Franklin's almanac took to remarkable heights. In the persona of poor country man Richard Saunders, Franklin filled the almanac with countless catchy proverbs and aphorisms, many of which, as Franklin openly acknowledged, were adaptations of well-known European proverbs. As Saunders, Franklin espoused what many have come to think of as quintessential values of modern capitalism: thrift, industriousness, productivity, and painstaking self-improvement. The *Almanack* was extraordinarily successful, selling upwards of 10,000 copies in one year. Many of the *Poor Richard* maxims—particularly those that Franklin compiled in "The Way to Wealth," an essay he wrote as part of the preface to the final issue of the almanac published under his supervision in 1758—have become almost inescapably ingrained in the American vernacular.

Franklin continued to publish essays over the course of the following decades, though from the late 1740s onwards his time was increasingly devoted to research into natural phenomena such as electricity, as well as to civic and political pursuits. (Franklin is credited with several inventions, including the lightning rod; his findings regarding electricity were initially ridiculed but eventually earned him the prestigious Copley Medal.) Franklin was elected to the Pennsylvania Assembly in 1751, and from 1757 to 1775 worked as a colonial representative in London. During this time, he became agent to the Crown for several of the Thirteen Colonies and published writing in support of colonial interests. Once a steadfast loyalist, by the outbreak of the American Revolution Franklin was a reluctant revolutionary, and in 1776 he was invited to join the committee responsible for drafting the Declaration of Independence; some of the document's most famous lines, including the line beginning "We hold these truths to be self-evident," were refined by him. In addition to signing the Declaration, he was among the signatories to the Treaty of Paris (1783) that ended the Revolutionary War and to the U.S. Constitution (1787).

Franklin first began composing what came to be known as his *Autobiography* (1791) in 1771, at the age of sixty-five. While incomplete, the memoir remains his most renowned literary creation. Franklin himself never used the term "autobiography," but the text is considered a foundational work of the genre, blending the common "confessional" mode often associated with religious writers with a more secular mode focused at least as much on his public as his private affairs. The *Autobiography* is often considered Franklin's fullest exploration of what it means to live virtuously; it recounts, as he writes in Part Two, his "bold and arduous project of arriving at moral perfection." The carefully selected, self-consciously crafted chronicle of Franklin's life was quickly interpreted as a prototypical American narrative; as his friend Benjamin Vaughan asserted in a letter of 1783, "All that has happened to you is also connected with the detail of the manners and situation of a rising people."

After the Revolutionary War, Franklin continued to work on his political writings. His 1784 pamphlet "Information to Those Who Would Remove to America," directed at prospective immigrants, influentially characterized the United States as a "land of labor," a country of opportunity for those ambitious enough to pursue it. In "Remarks Concerning the Savages" (1784), Franklin commented directly on the country's racial politics, criticizing American mistreatment of Indigenous cultures. In a later pamphlet, "On the Slave Trade" (1790), he continued his critique of racial injustice, this time focusing on the hypocrisy of slave ownership. Like many well-off white Americans throughout the eighteenth century, Franklin owned enslaved people for much of his adulthood; later in life, he became increasingly skeptical of the ethics of the slave trade, and was elected president of the country's first abolitionist society in 1787.

Franklin's funeral in 1790 was attended by about 20,000 people. By the time of his death, he had witnessed and taken an active part in the most dramatic social and political transformations America

had experienced since the earliest years of colonialism. His personal myth has since become so strongly entwined with mainstream ideas of American national character that he has often been embraced or rejected on this basis, even as his writings have remained widely read and broadly influential. The Transcendentalists of the early nineteenth century tended to feel that, as Emerson phrased it, "Franklin's man is a frugal, inoffensive, thrifty citizen, but savors of nothing heroic"—a position that anticipates the censure of later critics such as D.H. Lawrence. Franklin's fierce independence, entrepreneurial innovation, and sense of social responsibility, however, have been cited as inspiration by industrialists from Andrew Carnegie to Elon Musk, even as scholars—perhaps most influentially, Max Weber in his 1905 work *The Protestant Ethic and the Spirit of Capitalism*—have criticized Franklin as an advocate of damaging capitalistic values. Yet Franklin's body of work and achievements are more varied and complex than any of these assessments suggests, and as his biographer Walter Isaacson notes, his multifaceted image is continually reinterpreted "to reflect, or refract, the attitudes of each succeeding era."

NOTE ON THE TEXTS: The texts of "Remarks Concerning the Savages of North America" and "On the Slave Trade" presented below are based on the versions that appear in Albert Henry Smyth's *The Writings of Benjamin Franklin* (ten volumes, 1905–07). The spelling and punctuation of these texts have been modernized in accordance with the practices of this anthology. The text of Franklin's *Autobiography* (Parts One and Two of which are presented below, with the full text appearing in the website component) is based on that published in J.A. Leo Lemay's *Benjamin Franklin: Writings* (1987). This edition provides a clean edition of the "genetic text" first prepared by Lemay and Paul M. Zall for the University of Tennessee Press in 1981, which is in turn based on Franklin's original, unpublished manuscript. The spelling and punctuation of the *Autobiography* have not been modernized here, with the exception of Franklin's superscript abbreviations (for example, *corr*g for *correcting*, or *4*to for *quarto*), which have been modernized throughout. A fully modernized version of the text is included in the website component of this anthology.

⌘ ⌘ ⌘

Remarks Concerning the Savages of North America

Savages we call them, because their manners differ from ours, which we think the perfection of civility; they think the same of theirs.

Perhaps, if we could examine the manners of different nations with impartiality, we should find no people so rude,[1] as to be without any rules of politeness; nor any so polite, as not to have some remains of rudeness.

The Indian men, when young, are hunters and warriors; when old, counsellors; for all their government is by counsel of the sages; there is no force, there are no prisons, no officers to compel obedience, or inflict punishment. Hence they generally study oratory, the best speaker having the most influence. The Indian women till the ground, dress the food, nurse and bring up the children, and preserve and hand down to posterity the memory of public transactions. These employments of men and women are accounted as natural and honourable. Having few artificial wants, they have abundance of leisure for improvement by conversation. Our laborious manner of life, compared with theirs, they esteem slavish and base; and the learning, on which we value ourselves, they regard as frivolous and useless. An instance of this occurred at the Treaty of Lancaster,[2] in Pennsylvania, *anno* 1744, between the Government of Virginia and the Six Nations. After the principal business was settled, the commissioners from Virginia acquainted the Indians, by a speech, that there was at Williamsburg a college, with a fund for

[1] *rude* Uncivilized.

[2] *Treaty of Lancaster* Treaty in which the Six Nations Confederacy (also known as the Iroquois or Haudenosaunee) ceded their lands in the Shenandoah Valley to the British.

educating Indian youth;[1] and that, if the Six Nations would send down half a dozen of their young lads to that college, the government would take care that they should be well provided for, and instructed in all the learning of the white people. It is one of the Indian rules of politeness not to answer a public proposition the same day that it is made; they think it would be treating it as a light matter, and that they show it respect by taking time to consider it, as of a matter important. They therefore deferred their answer till the day following; when their speaker began, by expressing their deep sense of the kindness of the Virginia government, in making them that offer; "for we know," says he, "that you highly esteem the kind of learning taught in those colleges, and that the maintenance of our young men, while with you, would be very expensive to you. We are convinced, therefore, that you mean to do us good by your proposal; and we thank you heartily. But you, who are wise, must know that different nations have different conceptions of things; and you will therefore not take it amiss, if our ideas of this kind of education happen not to be the same with yours. We have had some experience of it; several of our young people were formerly brought up at the colleges of the northern provinces; they were instructed in all your sciences; but, when they came back to us, they were bad runners, ignorant of every means of living in the woods, unable to bear either cold or hunger, knew neither how to build a cabin, take a deer, or kill an enemy, spoke our language imperfectly, were therefore neither fit for hunters, warriors, nor counsellors; they were totally good for nothing. We are however not the less obliged by your kind offer, though we decline accepting it; and, to show our grateful sense of it, if the gentlemen of Virginia will send us a dozen of their sons, we will take great care of their education, instruct them in all we know, and make *men* of them."

Having frequent occasions to hold public councils, they have acquired great order and decency in conducting them. The old men sit in the foremost ranks, the warriors in the next, and the women and children in the hindmost. The business of the women is to take exact notice of what passes, imprint it in their memories (for they have no writing), and communicate it to their children. They are the records of the council, and they preserve traditions of the stipulations in treaties 100 years back; which, when we compare with our writings, we always find exact. He that would speak, rises. The rest observe a profound silence. When he has finished and sits down, they leave him 5 or 6 minutes to recollect, that, if he has omitted anything he intended to say, or has anything to add, he may rise again and deliver it. To interrupt another, even in common conversation, is reckoned highly indecent. How different this is from the conduct of a polite British House of Commons, where scarce a day passes without some confusion, that makes the Speaker hoarse in calling *to order*; and how different from the mode of conversation in many polite companies of Europe, where, if you do not deliver your sentence with great rapidity, you are cut off in the middle of it by the impatient loquacity of those you converse with, and never suffered to finish it!

The politeness of these savages in conversation is indeed carried to excess, since it does not permit them to contradict or deny the truth of what is asserted in their presence. By this means they indeed avoid disputes; but then it becomes difficult to know their minds, or what impression you make upon them. The missionaries who have attempted to convert them to Christianity, all complain of this as one of the great difficulties of their mission. The Indians hear with patience the truths of the Gospel explained to them, and give their usual tokens of assent and approbation; you would think they were convinced. No such matter. It is mere civility.

A Swedish minister, having assembled the chiefs of the Susquehanah Indians, made a sermon to them, acquainting them with the principal historical facts on which our religion is founded; such as the fall of our first parents by eating an apple, the coming of Christ to repair the mischief, his miracles and suffering, etc. When he had finished, an Indian orator stood up to thank him. "What you have told us," says he, "is all very good. It is indeed bad to eat apples. It is better to make them all into cider. We are much obliged by your kindness in coming so far, to tell us these things which you have heard from your mothers. In return, I will tell you some of those we have heard from ours. In the

[1] *at Williamsburg ... Indian youth* In its early years, the College of William and Mary, established in 1693, was conceived of in part as a place of higher education for Indigenous men.

beginning, our fathers had only the flesh of animals to subsist on; and if their hunting was unsuccessful, they were starving. Two of our young hunters, having killed a deer, made a fire in the woods to broil some part of it. When they were about to satisfy their hunger, they beheld a beautiful young woman descend from the clouds, and seat herself on that hill, which you see yonder among the blue mountains. They said to each other, it is a spirit that has smelled our broiling venison, and wishes to eat of it; let us offer some to her. They presented her with the tongue; she was pleased with the taste of it, and said, 'Your kindness shall be rewarded; come to this place after thirteen moons, and you shall find something that will be of great benefit in nourishing you and your children to the latest generations.' They did so, and, to their surprise, found plants they had never seen before; but which, from that ancient time, have been constantly cultivated among us, to our great advantage. Where her right hand had touched the ground, they found maize; where her left hand had touched it, they found kidney beans; and where her backside had sat on it, they found tobacco." The good missionary, disgusted with this idle tale, said, "What I delivered to you were sacred truths; but what you tell me is mere fable, fiction, and falsehood." The Indian, offended, replied, "My brother, it seems your friends have not done you justice in your education; they have not well instructed you in the rules of common civility. You saw that we, who understand and practise those rules, believed all your stories; why do you refuse to believe ours?"

When any of them come into our towns, our people are apt to crowd round them, gaze upon them, and incommode them, where they desire to be private; this they esteem great rudeness, and the effect of the want[1] of instruction in the rules of civility and good manners. "We have," say they, "as much curiosity as you, and when you come into our towns, we wish for opportunities of looking at you; but for this purpose we hide ourselves behind bushes, where you are to pass, and never intrude ourselves into your company."

Their manner of entering one another's village has likewise its rules. It is reckoned uncivil in travelling strangers to enter a village abruptly, without giving notice of their approach. Therefore, as soon as they arrive within hearing, they stop and hollow,[2] remaining there till invited to enter. Two old men usually come out to them, and lead them in. There is in every village a vacant dwelling, called *the Strangers' House*. Here they are placed, while the old men go round from hut to hut, acquainting the inhabitants, that strangers are arrived, who are probably hungry and weary; and everyone sends them what he can spare of victuals,[3] and skins to repose on. When the strangers are refreshed, pipes and tobacco are brought; and then, but not before, conversation begins, with enquiries who they are, whither bound, what news, etc.; and it usually ends with offers of service, if the strangers have occasion[4] of guides, or any necessaries for continuing their journey; and nothing is exacted for the entertainment.

The same hospitality, esteemed among them as a principal virtue, is practised by private persons; of which Conrad Weiser,[5] our interpreter, gave me the following instance. He had been naturalized among the Six Nations, and spoke well the Mohock[6] language. In going through the Indian country, to carry a message from our Governor to the council at Onondaga, he called at the habitation of Canassatego,[7] an old acquaintance, who embraced him, spread furs for him to sit on, placed before him some boiled beans and venison, and mixed some rum and water for his drink. When he was well refreshed, and had lit his pipe, Canassatego began to converse with him; asked how he had fared the many years since they had seen each other; whence he then came; what occasioned the journey, etc. Conrad answered all his questions; and when the discourse began to flag, the Indian, to continue it, said, "Conrad, you have lived long among the white people, and know something of their customs; I have been sometimes

[1] *want* Lack.

[2] *hollow* I.e., holler; shout.

[3] *victuals* Food.

[4] *occasion* Need.

[5] *Conrad Weiser* Pennsylvanian diplomat (1696–1760) who worked as an interpreter between the Pennsylvania Colony and various local Indigenous groups.

[6] *Mohock* I.e., Mohawk, the Iroquoian language spoken by the Mohawk people (who are members of the Six Nations Confederacy).

[7] *Canassatego* Onondaga political leader and diplomat for the Six Nations (c. 1684–1750), renowned for his oratorical abilities; Franklin oversaw the printing of several of Canassatego's speeches, including two excerpted elsewhere in this volume (see both the bound book and online components).

at Albany, and have observed, that once in seven days they shut up their shops, and assemble all in the great house; tell me what it is for? What do they do there?" "They meet there," says Conrad, "to hear and learn *good things*." "I do not doubt," says the Indian, "that they tell you so; they have told me the same; but I doubt the truth of what they say, and I will tell you my reasons. I went lately to Albany to sell my skins and buy blankets, knives, powder, rum, etc. You know I used generally to deal with Hans Hanson; but I was a little inclined this time to try some other merchant. However, I called first upon Hans, and asked him what he would give for beaver. He said he could not give any more than four shillings a pound; 'but,' says he, 'I cannot talk on business now; this is the day when we meet together to learn *good things*, and I am going to the meeting.' So I thought to myself, 'Since we cannot do any business today, I may as well go to the meeting too,' and I went with him. There stood up a man in black, and began to talk to the people very angrily. I did not understand what he said; but, perceiving that he looked much at me and at Hanson, I imagined he was angry at seeing me there; so I went out, sat down near the house, struck fire, and lit my pipe, waiting till the meeting should break up. I thought too, that the man had mentioned something of beaver, and I suspected it might be the subject of their meeting. So, when they came out, I accosted my merchant. 'Well, Hans,' says I, 'I hope you have agreed to give more than four shillings a pound.' 'No,' says he, 'I cannot give so much; I cannot give more than three shillings and sixpence.' I then spoke to several other dealers, but they all sung the same song—three and sixpence—three and sixpence. This made it clear to me, that my suspicion was right; and, that whatever they pretended of meeting to learn *good things*, the real purpose was to consult how to cheat Indians in the price of beaver. Consider but a little, Conrad, and you must be of my opinion. If they met so often to learn *good things*, they would certainly have learnt some before this time. But they are still ignorant. You know our practice. If a white man, in travelling through our country, enters one of our cabins, we all treat him as I treat you; we dry him if he is wet, we warm him if he is cold, we give him meat and drink, that he may allay his thirst and hunger; and we spread soft furs for him to rest and sleep on; we demand nothing in return. But, if I go into a white

man's house at Albany, and ask for victuals and drink, they say, 'Where is your money?' and if I have none, they say, 'Get out, you Indian dog.' You see they have not yet learned those little *good things*, that we need no meetings to be instructed in, because our mothers taught them to us when we were children; and therefore it is impossible their meetings should be, as they say, for any such purpose, or have any such effect; they are only to contrive *the cheating of Indians in the price of beaver.*"[1]
—c. 1783–84

On the Slave Trade

This letter is Franklin's last known work, published in *The Federal Gazette* on 25 March 1790, less than a month before his death. An example of Franklin's many literary hoaxes, the piece claims to present a speech by Algerian political leader Sidi Mehemet Ibrahim, in defense of the trade in Christian slaves; in reality, both Ibrahim and his speech are inventions of Franklin's.

TO THE EDITOR OF THE *FEDERAL GAZETTE*

March 23d, 1790

Sir,

Reading last night in your excellent paper the speech of Mr. Jackson[2] in Congress against their meddling with the affair of slavery, or attempting to mend

[1] [Franklin's note] It is remarkable that in all ages and countries hospitality has been allowed as the virtue of those whom the civilized were pleased to call barbarians. The Greeks celebrated the Scythians for it. The Saracens possessed it eminently, and it is to this day the reigning virtue of the wild Arabs. St. Paul, too, in the relation of his voyage and shipwreck on the island of Melita says the barbarous people showed us no little kindness; for they kindled a fire, and received us every one, because of the present rain, and because of the cold.—F. [*Scythians* Nomadic people who flourished in parts of Eastern Europe and Central Asia in the first millennium BCE; *Saracens* Medieval term used to denote Muslim Arabs; *St. Paul … Melita* See Acts 27–28; "Melita" here refers to the island of Malta.]

[2] *Mr. Jackson* Georgia politician James Jackson (1757–1806), who opposed the abolition of slavery.

the condition of the slaves, it put me in mind of a simi-
lar one made about 100 years since by Sidi Mehemet
Ibrahim, a member of the Divan of Algiers,[1] which may
be seen in Martin's Account of his Consulship, anno
1687.[2] It was against granting the petition of the sect
called *Erika*, or Purists, who prayed for the abolition
of piracy and slavery as being unjust. Mr. Jackson does
not quote it; perhaps he has not seen it. If, therefore,
some of its reasonings are to be found in his eloquent
speech, it may only show that men's interests and intel-
lects operate and are operated on with surprising simi-
larity in all countries and climates, when under similar
circumstances. The African's speech, as translated, is as
follows.

*"Allah Bismillah, etc. God is great, and Mahomet is his
Prophet."*

Have these *Erika* considered the consequences of
granting their petition? If we cease our cruises against
the Christians, how shall we be furnished with the
commodities their countries produce, and which are
so necessary for us? If we forbear to make slaves of
their people, who in this hot climate are to cultivate
our lands? Who are to perform the common labours
of our city, and in our families? Must we not then
be our own slaves? And is there not more compas-
sion and more favour due to us as Mussulmen,[3] than
to these Christian dogs? We have now above 50,000
slaves in and near Algiers. This number, if not kept up
by fresh supplies, will soon diminish, and be gradually
annihilated. If we then cease taking and plundering
the infidel ships, and making slaves of the seamen
and passengers, our lands will become of no value for
want of cultivation; the rents of houses in the city will
sink one half; and the revenues of government arising
from its share of prizes be totally destroyed! And for
what? To gratify the whims of a whimsical sect, who
would have us, not only forbear making more slaves,
but even to manumit those we have.

But who is to indemnify[4] their masters for the loss?
Will the state do it? Is our treasury sufficient? Will the

Erika do it? Can they do it? Or would they, to do what
they think justice to the slaves, do a greater injustice
to the owners? And if we set our slaves free, what is to
be done with them? Few of them will return to their
countries; they know too well the greater hardships
they must there be subject to; they will not embrace
our holy religion; they will not adopt our manners;
our people will not pollute themselves by intermarry-
ing with them. Must we maintain them as beggars in
our streets, or suffer our properties to be the prey of
their pillage? For Men long accustomed to slavery will
not work for a livelihood when not compelled. And
what is there so pitiable in their present condition?
Were they not slaves in their own countries?

Are not Spain, Portugal, France, and the Italian
states governed by despots, who hold all their sub-
jects in slavery, without exception? Even England
treats its sailors as slaves; for they are, whenever the
government pleases, seized, and confined in ships of
war, condemned not only to work, but to fight, for
small wages, or a mere subsistence, not better than
our slaves are allowed by us. Is their condition then
made worse by their falling into our hands? No; they
have only exchanged one slavery for another, and I
may say a better; for here they are brought into a land
where the sun of Islamism gives forth its light, and
shines in full splendor, and they have an opportunity
of making themselves acquainted with the true doc-
trine, and thereby saving their immortal souls. Those
who remain at home have not that happiness. Sending
the slaves home then would be sending them out of
light into darkness.

I repeat the question, What is to be done with
them? I have heard it suggested that they may be
planted in the wilderness, where there is plenty of
land for them to subsist on, and where they may
flourish as a free state; but they are, I doubt, too little
disposed to labour without compulsion, as well as too
ignorant to establish a good government, and the wild
Arabs would soon molest and destroy or again enslave
them. While serving us, we take care to provide them
with everything, and they are treated with humanity.
The labourers in their own country are, as I am well
informed, worse fed, lodged, and clothed. The con-
dition of most of them is therefore already mended,
and requires no further improvement. Here their lives
are in safety. They are not liable to be impressed for
soldiers,[5] and forced to cut one another's Christian

[1] *Divan of Algiers* Council of senior officials of the Regency
of Algiers, the term for Algeria when it was under the rule of the
Ottoman Empire.

[2] *Martin's Account ... 1687* A fictional account.

[3] *Mussulmen* I.e., Muslims.

[4] *indemnify* Compensate.

[5] *impressed for soldiers* Forced into military service, often by
means of a "press gang" who would seize men without notice.

throats, as in the wars of their own countries. If some of the religious mad bigots, who now tease[1] us with their silly petitions, have in a fit of blind zeal freed their slaves, it was not generosity, it was not humanity, that moved them to the action; it was from the conscious burden of a load of sins, and hope, from the supposed merits of so good a work, to be excused damnation.

How grossly are they mistaken in imagining slavery to be disallowed by the Alcoran![2] Are not the two precepts, to quote no more, "*Masters, treat your slaves with kindness; slaves, serve your masters with cheerfulness and fidelity,*" clear proofs to the contrary? Nor can the plundering of infidels be in that sacred book forbidden, since it is well known from it, that God has given the world, and all that it contains, to his faithful Mussulmen, who are to enjoy it of right as fast as they conquer it. Let us then hear no more of this detestable proposition, the manumission of Christian slaves, the adoption of which would, by depreciating our lands and houses, and thereby depriving so many good citizens of their properties, create universal discontent, and provoke insurrections, to the endangering of government and producing general confusion. I have therefore no doubt, but this wise council will prefer the comfort and happiness of a whole nation of true believers to the whim of a few *Erika*, and dismiss their petition.

The result was, as Martin tells us, that the Divan came to this resolution; "The doctrine, that plundering and enslaving the Christians is unjust, is at best *problematical*; but that it is the interest of this state to continue the practice is clear; therefore let the petition be rejected."

And it was rejected accordingly.

And since like motives are apt to produce in the minds of men like opinions and resolutions, may we not, Mr. Brown,[3] venture to predict, from this account, that the petitions to the Parliament of England for abolishing the slave trade, to say nothing of other legislatures, and the debates upon them,

will have a similar conclusion? I am, Sir, your constant reader and humble servant,

HISTORICUS

—1790

from the *Autobiography*

The work known today as the *Autobiography* of Benjamin Franklin has complicated origins, both in its composition and its publication history. Franklin worked on the manuscript over the course of four distinct periods of his life, beginning it in 1771 as a letter to his son William Franklin, and leaving it unfinished upon his death in April 1790, nearly twenty years later. Despite its incomplete state—the narrative ends with Franklin's arrival in London in 1757—the work quickly achieved international renown, and was by the mid-1800s considered a seminal work of American literature.

Several copies of Franklin's original manuscript came to be circulated in North America and Europe shortly after his death. This led to the first publication of the *Autobiography* in France in 1791, titled *Mémoirs de la vie privée de Benjamin Franklin* (*Memoirs of the Private Life of Benjamin Franklin*). This translated text, based on a flawed copy that included only Part 1, nevertheless became the basis for subsequent publications of the work, including English versions re-translated from the French. Franklin's grandson William Temple Franklin published a more accurate edition that included Parts 1, 2, and 3 in 1817, but this version was nevertheless heavily edited. In the 1860s, Franklin's original manuscript made its way into the hands of American diplomat John Bigelow, who proceeded to edit and publish the first version of the work to include all four parts in 1868.

In 1981, Franklin scholars J.A. Leo Lemay and Paul M. Zall published *The Autobiography of Benjamin Franklin: A Genetic Text*, the first version to reproduce all of Franklin's copious revisions and amendments to the manuscript. The text presented below is based on the version published in Lemay's *Benjamin Franklin: Writings* (1987), which is a revised "clear text" based on the genetic text. Spelling and punctuation have not been modernized.

[1] *tease* Irritate.

[2] *the Alcoran* The Qur'an; the notable 1647 translation of the Qur'an into French, in turn translated into English in 1649, was titled *L'Alcoran de Mahomet.*

[3] *Mr. Brown* Andrew Brown (c. 1744–97), editor of the *Federal Gazette.*

PART 1

Twyford, at the Bishop of St Asaph's[1]
1771.

Dear Son,

I have ever had a Pleasure in obtaining any little Anecdotes of my Ancestors. You may remember the Enquiries I made among the Remains of my Relations when you were with me in England;[2] and the Journey I took for that purpose. Now imagining it may be equally agreeable to you to know the Circumstances of *my* Life, many of which you are yet unacquainted with; and expecting a Weeks uninterrupted Leisure in my present Country Retirement, I sit down to write them for you. To which I have besides some other Inducements. Having emerg'd from the Poverty & Obscurity in which I was born & bred, to a State of Affluence & some Degree of Reputation in the World, and having gone so far thro' Life with a considerable Share of Felicity, the conducing Means I made use of, which, with the Blessing of God, so well succeeded, my Posterity may like to know, as they may find some of them suitable to their own Situations, & therefore fit to be imitated.—That Felicity, when I reflected on it, has induc'd me sometimes to say, that were it offer'd to my Choice, I should have no Objection to a Repetition of the same Life from its Beginning, only asking the Advantage Authors have in a second Edition to correct some Faults of the first. So would I if I might, besides correcting the Faults, change some sinister Accidents & Events of it for others more favourable, but tho' this were deny'd, I should still accept the Offer. However, since such a Repetition is not to be expected, the Thing most like living one's Life over again, seems to be a *Recollection*

of that Life; and to make that Recollection as durable as possible, the putting it down in Writing.—Hereby, too, I shall indulge the Inclination so natural in old Men, to be talking of themselves and their own past Actions, and I shall indulge it, without being tiresome to others who thro' respect to Age might think themselves oblig'd to give me a Hearing, since this may be read or not as any one pleases. And lastly, (I may as well confess it, since my Denial of it will be believ'd by no body) perhaps I shall a good deal gratify my own *Vanity*. Indeed, I scarce ever heard or saw the introductory Words, *Without Vanity I may say*, &c. but some vain thing immediately follow'd. Most People dislike Vanity in others whatever Share they have of it themselves, but I give it fair Quarter wherever I meet with it, being persuaded that it is often productive of Good to the Possessor & to others that are within his Sphere of Action: And therefore in many Cases it would not be quite absurd if a Man were to thank God for his Vanity among the other Comforts of Life.—

And now I speak of thanking God, I desire with all Humility to acknowledge, that I owe the mention'd Happiness of my past Life to his kind Providence, which lead me to the Means I us'd & gave them Success.—My Belief of This, induces me to *hope*, tho' I must not *presume*, that the same Goodness will still be exercis'd towards me in continuing that Happiness, or in enabling me to bear a fatal Reverso,[3] which I may experience as others have done, the Complexion of my future Fortune being known to him only: and in whose Power it is to bless to us even our Afflictions.

The Notes one of my Uncles (who had the same kind of Curiosity in collecting Family Anecdotes) once put into my Hands, furnish'd me with several Particulars, relating to our Ancestors. From those Notes I learnt that the Family had liv'd in the same Village, Ecton in Northamptonshire, for 300 Years, & how much longer he knew not, (perhaps from the Time when the Name *Franklin* that before was the Name of an Order of People, was assum'd by them for a Surname, when others took Surnames all over

[1] *Twyford ... St Asaph's* At the time he began writing his memoirs, Franklin was living with his friend Jonathan Shipley, the Bishop of St. Asaph (1714–88), at his home in Twyford, near London. In the years leading up to the American Revolution, Shipley became a vocal opponent of George III's management of the American colonies.

[2] *You may remember ... England* In 1757, Franklin traveled with his son William to London on a political appointment. While there, in July 1758, the two of them visited their ancestral homes in Ecton and Banbury. The diplomatic proceedings of this trip to England are described in Part Four of Franklin's *Autobiography*, included in the website component of this anthology.

[3] *Reverso* Latin: Return; i.e., reversal of fortunes. Franklin may also have in mind the dueling technique of "riverso," a backhanded cut.

the Kingdom.—[1]) on a Freehold of about 30 Acres, aided by the Smith's Business which had continued in the Family till his Time, the eldest Son being always bred to that Business. A Custom which he & my Father both followed as to their eldest Sons.—When I search'd the Register at Ecton, I found an Account of their Births, Marriages and Burials, from the Year 1555 only, there being no Register kept in that Parish at any time preceding.—By that Register I perceiv'd that I was the youngest Son of the youngest Son for 5 Generations back. My Grandfather Thomas, who was born in 1598, lived at Ecton till he grew too old to follow Business longer, when he went to live with his Son John, a Dyer at Banbury in Oxfordshire, with whom my Father serv'd an Apprenticeship. There my Grandfather died and lies buried. We saw his Gravestone in 1758. His eldest Son Thomas liv'd in the House at Ecton, and left it with the Land to his only Child, a Daughter, who with her Husband, one Fisher of Wellingborough sold it to Mr Isted, now Lord of the Manor there. My Grandfather had

4 Sons that grew up, viz. Thomas, John, Benjamin and Josiah. I will give you what Account I can of them at this distance from my Papers, and if those are not lost in my Absence, you will among them find many more Particulars. Thomas was bred a Smith under his Father, but being ingenious, and encourag'd in Learning (as all his Brothers like wise werre,) by an Esquire Palmer then the principal Gentleman in that Parish, he qualify'd himself for the Business of Scrivener,[2] became a considerable Man in the County Affairs, was a chief Mover[3] of all publick Spirited Undertakings, for the County or Town of Northampton & his own Village, of which many Instances were told us at Ecton, and he was much taken Notice of and patroniz'd by the then Lord Halifax. He died in 1702 Jan. 6. old Stile,[4] just 4 Years to a Day before I was born. The Account we receiv'd of his Life & Character from some old People at Ecton, I remember struck you as something extraordinary from its Similarity to what you knew of mine. Had he died on the same Day, you said one might have suppos'd a Transmigration.[5]—John was bred a Dyer, I believe of Woollens. Benjamin, was bred a Silk Dyer, serving an Apprenticeship at London. He was an ingenious Man, I remember him well, for when I was a Boy he came over to my Father in Boston, and lived in the House with us some Years. He lived to a great Age. His Grandson Samuel Franklin[6] now lives in Boston. He left behind him two Quarto Volumes, M.S. of his own Poetry, consisting of little occasional Pieces[7] address'd to his Friends and Relations, of which the following sent to me, is a Specimen.

1 [Franklin's note] As a proof that Franklin was anciently the common name of an order or rank in England, see Judge Fortescue, *De laudibus Legum Angliae*, written about the year 1412, in which is the following passage, to show that good juries might easily be formed in any part of England.

"Regio etiam illa, ita respersa refertaque est *possessoribus terrarum* et agrorum, quod in ea, villula tam parva reperiri non poterit, in qua non est *miles*, *armiger*, vel pater-familias, quails ibidem *Franklin* vulgariter nuncupatur, magnis ditatus possessionibus, nec non libere tenentes et alii *valecti* plurimi, suis patrimoniis sufficientes ad faciendum juratum, in forma praenotata."

"Moreover, the same country is so filled and replenished with landed menne, that therein so small a Thorpe cannot be found werein dweleth not a knight, an esquire, or such a householder, as is there commonly called a *Franklin*, enriched with great possessions; and also other freeholders and many yeomen able for their livelihoods to make a jury in form aforementioned."—(*Old Translation*.)

Chaucer too calls his Country Gentleman, a *Franklin*, and after describing his good housekeeping thus characterises him:

"This worthy Franklin bore a purse of silk,
Fix'd to his girdle, white as morning milk.
Knight of the Shire, first Justice at th' Assize,
To help all the poor, the doubtful to advise.
In all employments, generous, just, he proved;
Renown'd for courtesy, by all beloved."

[*Chaucer* English poet Geoffrey Chaucer (c. 1340–1400); Franklin provides a loose paraphrase of several lines in Chaucer's *Canterbury Tales*.]

2 *Scrivener* One who writes or copies documents, especially legal documents, professionally; scribe.

3 *Mover* I.e., one who brings actions or ideas into motion.

4 *old Stile* I.e., according to the Julian calendar, which was in use in Britain and its colonies until 1752. By the Gregorian calendar, Benjamin Franklin was born 17 January 1706.

5 *Transmigration* I.e., transferral of a deceased person's soul into another's body.

6 *Samuel Franklin* Benjamin Franklin's cousin, a cutler by trade.

7 *Quarto* Book format which employs large sheets of paper folded to produce four pages each; *M.S.* Manuscript; *occasional Pieces* I.e., poems written in honor of specific occasions.

Sent to My Name upon a Report
of his Inclination to Martial affaires
7 July 1710

Beleeve me Ben. It is a Dangerous Trade
The Sword has Many Marr'd as well as Made
By it doe many fall Not Many Rise
Makes Many poor few Rich and fewer Wise
Fills Towns with Ruin, fields with blood beside
Tis Sloths Maintainer, And the Shield of pride
Fair Citties Rich to Day, in plenty flow
War fills with want, Tomorrow, & with woe
Ruin'd Estates, The Nurse of Vice, broke limbs
& scars
 Are the Effects of Desolating Warrs

Sent to B. F. in N. E.[1] 15 July 1710

B e to thy parents an Obedient Son
E ach Day let Duty constantly be Done
N ever give Way to sloth or lust or pride
I f free you'd be from Thousand Ills beside
A bove all Ills be sure Avoide the shelfe[2]
M ans Danger lyes in Satan sin and selfe
I n vertue Learning Wisdome progress Make
N ere shrink at Suffering for thy saviours sake
F raud and all Falsehood in thy Dealings Flee
R eligious Always in thy station be
A dore the Maker of thy Inward part
N ow's the Accepted time, Give him thy Heart
K eep a Good Conscience 'tis a constant Frind
L ike Judge and Witness This Thy Acts Attend
I n Heart with bended knee Alone Adore
N one but the Three in One forevermore.

He had form'd a Shorthand of his own, which he taught me, but never practising it I have now forgot it. I was nam'd after this Uncle, there being a particular Affection between him and my Father. He was very pious, a great Attender of Sermons of the best Preachers, which he took down in his Shorthand and had with him many Volumes of them.—He was also much of a Politician, too much perhaps for his Station. There fell lately into my Hands in London a Collection he had made of all the principal Pamphlets relating to Publick

Affairs from 1641 to 1717. Many of the Volumes are wanting,[3] as appears by the Numbering, but there still remains 8 Vols. Folio, and 24 in quarto & octavo.[4]—A Dealer in old Books met with them, and knowing me by my sometimes buying of him, he brought them to me. It seems my Uncle must have left them here when he went to America, which was about 50 Years since. There are many of his Notes in the Margins.—

This obscure Family of ours was early in the Reformation, and continu'd Protestants thro' the Reign of Queen Mary, when they were sometimes in Danger of Trouble on Account of their Zeal against Popery.[5] They had got an English Bible,[6] & to conceal & secure it, it was fastned open with Tapes under & within the Frame of a Joint Stool. When my Great Great Grandfather read in it to his Family, he turn'd up the Joint Stool upon his Knees, turning over the Leaves then under the Tapes. One of the Children stood at the Door to give Notice if he saw the Apparitor coming, who was an Officer of the Spiritual Court. In that Case the Stool was turn'd down again upon its feet, when the Bible remain'd conceal'd under it as before. This Anecdote I had from my Uncle Benjamin.—The Family continu'd all of the Church of England till about the End of Charles the Second's Reign,[7] when some of the Ministers that had been outed for Nonconformity, holding Conventicles[8] in Northamptonshire,

1 *N. E.* New England.

2 *the shelfe* Uselessness (referring to the phrase "on the shelf," designating something that is out of the way or inactive).

3 *wanting* Missing.

4 *Folio* Book format involving single large sheets of paper folded once; *octavo* Book format produced by folding a standard-sized printing sheet three times to form eight leaves.

5 *early in the Reformation* I.e., early supporters of the Protestant Reformation, a sixteenth-century religious movement that sought to reform the Catholic Church and ultimately established the Protestant form of Christianity. The Protestant Church of England was established under Henry VIII's reign in 1534; *continu'd Protestants … Queen Mary* The Catholic Church was re-established in England under the reign of Mary I (1553–58), initiating a brief period of severe persecution of dissenters; *Popery* Derogatory term for Catholicism.

6 *English Bible* The translation of the Bible into vernacular languages was a central element of the Protestant Reformation; the reference here is likely to the Geneva Bible, the favored translation of the Puritans, so named because of its creation by English dissenters who fled to Switzerland during Mary I's reign.

7 *the End … Reign* 1685.

8 *Conventicles* Meetings held by nonconformists to the Church of England; such dissension was outlawed by the Conventicle Act of 1664.

Benjamin & Josiah adher'd to them, and so continu'd all their Lives. The rest of the Family remain'd with the Episcopal Church.[1]

Josiah, my Father, married young, and carried his Wife[2] with three Children unto New England, about 1682. The Conventicles having been forbidden by Law, & frequently disturbed, induced some considerable Men of his Acquaintance to remove to that Country, and he was prevail'd with to accompany them thither, where they expected to enjoy their Mode of Religion with Freedom.—By the same Wife he had 4 Children more born there, and by a second Wife ten more, in all 17, of which I remember 13 sitting at one time at his Table, who all grew up to be Men & Women, and married;—I was the youngest Son and the youngest Child but two, & was born in Boston, N. England.

My Mother the second Wife was Abiah Folger, a Daughter of Peter Folger, one of the first Settlers of New England, of whom honourable mention is made by Cotton Mather,[3] in his Church History of that Country, (entitled Magnalia Christi Americana) as a *godly learned Englishman*, if I remember the Words rightly.—I have heard that he wrote sundry small occasional Pieces, but only one of them was printed which I saw now many Years since. It was written in 1675, in the homespun Verse of that Time & People, and address'd to those then concern'd in the Government there. It was in favour of Liberty of Conscience, & in behalf of the Baptists, Quakers, & other Sectaries, that had been under Persecution; ascribing the Indian Wars[4] & other Distresses, that had befallen the Country to that Persecution, as so many Judgments of God, to punish so heinous an Offence; and exhorting a Repeal of those uncharitable Laws. The whole appear'd to me as written with a good deal of Decent Plainness & manly Freedom. The six concluding Lines I remember, tho'

I have forgotten the two first of the Stanza, but the Purport of them was that his Censures proceeded from *Goodwill*, & therefore he would be known as the Author,

> because to be a Libeller, (says he)
> I hate it with my Heart.
> From Sherburne Town[5] where now I dwell,
> My Name I do put here,
> Without Offence, your real Friend,
> It is Peter Folgier.

My elder Brothers were all put Apprentices to different Trades. I was put to the Grammar School at Eight Years of Age, my Father intending to devote me as the Tithe of his Sons[6] to the Service of the Church. My early Readiness in learning to read (which must have been very early, as I do not remember when I could not read) and the Opinion of all his Friends that I should certainly make a good Scholar, encourag'd him in this Purpose of his. My Uncle Benjamin too approv'd of it, and propos'd to give me all his Shorthand Volumes of Sermons I suppose as a Stock to set up with, if I would learn his Character.[7] I continu'd however at the Grammar School not quite one Year, tho' in that time I had risen gradually from the Middle of the Class of that Year to be the Head of it, and farther was remov'd into the next Class above it, in order to go with that into the third at the End of the Year. But my Father in the mean time, from a View of the Expence of a College Education which, having so large a Family, he could not well afford, and the mean Living many so educated were afterwards able to obtain, Reasons that he gave to his Friends in my Hearing, altered his first Intention, took me from the Grammar School, and sent me to a School for Writing & Arithmetic kept by a then famous Man, Mr Geo. Brownell, very successful in his Profession generally, and that by mild encouraging Methods. Under him I acquired fair Writing pretty soon, but I fail'd in the Arithmetic, & made no Progress in it.—At Ten Years old, I was taken home to assist

[1] *Episcopal Church* American branch of the Anglican Church.

[2] *his Wife* Josiah Franklin's first wife was Anne Child, who died in 1689 of complications from childbirth.

[3] *Cotton Mather* Colonial religious leader and historian; his *Magnalia Christi Americana* was published in 1702 and tells of various significant events in the history of New England.

[4] *the Indian Wars* The most serious seventeenth-century conflict between the New England colonies and Indigenous peoples (in this case the Wampanoag and several allied nations), known in English as King Philip's War, broke out in 1675, the same year that Folger's poem was written.

[5] [Franklin's note] In the Island of Nantucket.

[6] *the Tithe of his Sons* Traditionally, a tithe is one-tenth of one's earnings, given annually to the Church; the implication here is that Franklin's father intended his youngest son to enter into the ministry, in place of the traditional tithe.

[7] *his Character* I.e., his method of shorthand.

my Father in his Business, which was that of a Tallow Chandler and Sope-Boiler.[1] A Business he was not bred to, but had assumed on his Arrival in New England & on finding his Dying Trade[2] would not maintain his Family, being in little Request. Accordingly I was employed in cutting Wick for the Candles, filling the Dipping Mold, & the Molds for cast Candles, attending the Shop, going of Errands, &c.—I dislik'd the Trade and had a strong Inclination for the Sea; but my Father declar'd against it; however, living near the Water, I was much in and about it, learnt early to swim well, & to manage Boats, and when in a Boat or Canoe with other Boys I was commonly allow'd to govern,[3] especially in any case of Difficulty; and upon other Occasions I was generally a Leader among the Boys, and sometimes led them into Scrapes, of which I will mention one Instance, as it shows an early projecting public Spirit, tho' not then justly conducted. There was a Salt Marsh that bounded part of the Mill Pond, on the Edge of which at Highwater, we us'd to stand to fish for Minews.[4] By much Trampling, we had made it a mere Quagmire. My Proposal was to build a Wharf there fit for us to stand upon, and I show'd my Comrades a large Heap of Stones which were intended for a new House near the Marsh, and which would very well suit our Purpose. Accordingly in the Evening when the Workmen were gone, I assembled a Number of my Playfellows, and working with them diligently like so many Emmets,[5] sometimes two or three to a Stone, we brought them all away and built our little Wharff.—The next Morning the Workmen were surpriz'd at Missing the Stones; which were found in our Wharff; Enquiry was made after the Removers; we were discovered & complain'd of; several of us were corrected by our Fathers; and tho' I pleaded the Usefulness of the Work, mine convinc'd me that nothing was useful which was not honest.—

I think you may like to know something of his Person[6] & Character. He had an excellent Constitution of Body, was of middle Stature, but well set and very strong. He was ingenious, could draw prettily, was skill'd a little in Music and had a clear pleasing Voice, so that when he play'd Psalm Tunes on his Violin & sung withal as he some times did in an Evening after the Business of the Day was over, it was extreamly agreeable to hear. He had a mechanical Genius too, and on occasion was very handy in the Use of other Tradesmen's Tools. But his great Excellence lay in a sound Understanding, and solid Judgment in prudential Matters, both in private & publick Affairs. In the latter indeed he was never employed, the numerous Family he had to educate & the Straitness of his Circumstances, keeping him close to his Trade, but I remember well his being frequently visited by leading People, who consulted him for his Opinion on Affairs of the Town or of the Church he belong'd to & show'd a good deal of Respect for his Judgment and Advice. He was also much consulted by private Persons about their Affairs when any Difficulty occur'd, & frequently chosen an Arbitrator between contending Parties.—At his Table he lik'd to have as often as he could, some sensible Friend or Neighbour, to converse with, and always took care to start some ingenious or useful Topic for Discourse, which might tend to improve the Minds of his Children. By this means he turn'd our Attention to what was good, just, & prudent in the Conduct of Life; and little or no Notice was ever taken of what related to the Victuals on the Table, whether it was well or ill drest, in or out of season, of good or bad flavour, preferable or inferior to this or that other thing of the kind; so that I was bro't up in such a perfect Inattention to those Matters as to be quite Indifferent what kind of Food was set before me; and so unobservant of it, that to this Day, if I am ask'd I can scarce tell, a few Hours after dinner, what I din'd upon.—This has been a Convenience to me in travelling, where my Companions have been sometimes very unhappy for want of a suitable Gratification of their more delicate because better instructed Tastes and Appetites.—

My Mother had likewise an excellent Constitution. She suckled all her 10 Children. I never knew either my Father or Mother to have any Sickness but that of

[1] *Tallow Chandler and Sope-Boiler* Manufacturer of candles (made of tallow, a cheap preparation of animal fats) and soap.

[2] *Dying Trade* I.e., his work as a dyer. (During this period, the vast majority of textiles used in the English colonies were imported from England, which may help explain the lack of business opportunities for a dyer in New England.)

[3] *govern* I.e., steer the boat.

[4] *Minews* Minnows.

[5] *Emmets* Ants.

[6] *Person* I.e., physical appearance.

which they dy'd, he at 89 & she at 85 Years of age. They lie buried together at Boston, where I some Years since plac'd a Marble over their Grave with this Inscription

<div align="center">

Josiah Franklin
And Abiah his Wife
Lie here interred.
They lived lovingly together in Wedlock
Fifty-five Years.—
Without an Estate or any gainful Employment,
By constant Labour and Industry,
With God's Blessing,
They maintained a large Family
Comfortably;
And brought up thirteen Children,
And seven Grandchildren
Reputably.
From this Instance, Reader,
Be encouraged to Diligence in thy Calling,
And distrust not Providence.
He was a pious & prudent Man,
She a discreet and virtuous Woman.
Their youngest Son,
In filial Regard to their Memory,
Places this Stone.
J. F. born 1655—Died 1744. Ætat[1] 89
A. F. born 1667—died 1752 —— 85.

</div>

By my rambling Digressions I perceive my self to be grown old. I us'd to write more methodically.—But one does not dress for private Company as for a publick Ball. 'Tis perhaps only Negligence.—

To return. I continu'd thus employ'd in my Father's Business for two Years, that is till I was 12 Years old; and my Brother John, who was bred to that Business having left my Father, married and set up for himself at Rhodeisland, there was all Appearance that I was destin'd to supply his Place and be a Tallow Chandler. But my Dislike to the Trade continuing, my Father was under Apprehensions that if he did not find one for me more agreable, I should break away and get to Sea, as his Son Josiah had done to his great Vexation. He therefore sometimes took me to walk with him,

and see Joiners, Bricklayers, Turners, Braziers,[2] &c. at their Work, that he might observe my Inclination, & endeavour to fix it on some Trade or other on Land.— It has ever since been a Pleasure to me to see good Workmen handle their Tools; and it has been useful to me, having learnt so much by it, as to be able to do little Jobs my self in my House, when a Workman could not readily be got; & to construct little Machines for my Experiments while the Intention of making the Experiment was fresh & warm in my Mind. My Father at last fix'd upon the Cutler's[3] Trade, and my Uncle Benjamin's Son Samuel who was bred to that Business in London being about that time establish'd in Boston, I was sent to be with him some time on liking. But his Expectations of a Fee with me displeasing my Father, I was taken home again.

From a Child I was fond of Reading, and all the little Money that came into my Hands was ever laid out in Books. Pleas'd with the Pilgrim's Progress,[4] my first Collection was of John Bunyan's Works, in separate little Volumes. I afterwards sold them to enable me to buy R. Burton's[5] Historical Collections; they were small Chapmen's Books[6] and cheap, 40 or 50 in all.— My Father's little Library consisted chiefly of Books in polemic Divinity,[7] most of which I read, and have since often regretted, that at a time when I had such a Thirst for Knowledge, more proper Books had not fallen in my Way, since it was now resolv'd I should not be a Clergyman. Plutarch's Lives[8] there was, in which I read abundantly, and I still think that time spent to great Advantage. There was also a Book of Defoe's

1 *Ætat* Abbreviation for the Latin aetatis, meaning "aged."

2 *Joiners* Woodworkers, especially of ornamental or small pieces; *Turners* Those who manufacture objects on a lathe; *Braziers* Makers of brass objects.

3 *Cutler* Maker of cutlery.

4 *the Pilgrim's Progress* Christian allegorical novel (1678) by English Puritan John Bunyan; in the eighteenth century it was among the most widely read works of fiction in the English language.

5 *R. Burton* Robert or Richard Burton, pseudonym of English writer and bookseller Nathaniel Crouch (born 1632); his popular historical works consisted primarily of material rewritten on the basis of other historians' work.

6 *Chapmen's Books* Chapbooks; small, cheaply bound booklets.

7 *polemic Divinity* I.e., argumentative works on theological questions.

8 *Plutarch's Lives* Collection of biographical writings on important historical figures by ancient Greek writer Plutarch (46 CE–c. 120 CE).

called an Essay on Projects and another of Dr Mather's call'd Essays to do Good,[1] which perhaps gave me a Turn of Thinking that had an Influence on some of the principal future Events of my Life.

This Bookish Inclination at length determin'd my Father to make me a Printer, tho' he had already one Son, (James) of that Profession. In 1717 my Brother James return'd from England with a Press & Letters[2] to set up his Business in Boston. I lik'd it much better than that of my Father, but still had a Hankering for the Sea.—To prevent the apprehended Effect of such an Inclination, my Father was impatient to have me bound[3] to my Brother. I stood out some time, but at last was persuaded and signed the Indentures,[4] when I was yet but 12 Years old.—I was to serve as an Apprentice till I was 21 Years of Age, only I was to be allow'd Journeyman's Wages during the last Year. In a little time I made great Proficiency in the Business, and became a useful Hand to my Brother. I now had Access to better Books. An Acquaintance with the Apprentices of Booksellers, enabled me sometimes to borrow a small one, which I was careful to return soon & clean. Often I sat up in my Room reading the greatest Part of the Night, when the Book was borrow'd in the Evening & to be return'd early in the Morning lest it should be miss'd or wanted.—And after some time an ingenious Tradesman[5] who had a pretty[6] Collection of Books, & who frequented our Printing House, took Notice of me, invited me to his Library, & very kindly lent me such Books as I chose to read. I now took a Fancy to Poetry, and made some little Pieces. My Brother, thinking it might turn to account encourag'd me, & put me on composing two occasional Ballads. One was called the *Light House Tragedy*, & contain'd an Account of the drowning of Capt. Worthilake with

his Two Daughters; the other was a Sailor Song on the Taking of *Teach* or Blackbeard the Pirate.[7] They were wretched Stuff, in the Grubstreet Ballad Stile,[8] and when they were printed he sent me about the Town to sell them. The first sold wonderfully, the Event being recent, having made a great Noise. This flatter'd my Vanity. But my Father discourag'd me, by ridiculing my Performances, and telling me Verse-makers were generally Beggars; so I escap'd being a Poet, most probably a very bad one. But as Prose Writing has been of great Use to me in the Course of my Life, and was a principal Means of my Advancement, I shall tell you how in such a Situation I acquir'd what little Ability I have in that Way.

There was another Bookish Lad in the Town, John Collins by Name, with whom I was intimately acquainted. We sometimes disputed, and very fond we were of Argument, & very desirous of confuting one another. Which disputatious Turn, by the way, is apt to become a very bad Habit, making People often extreamly disagreable in Company, by the Contradiction that is necessary to bring it into Practice, & thence, besides souring & spoiling the Conversation, is productive of Disgusts & perhaps Enmities where you may have occasion for Friendship. I had caught it by reading my Father's Books of Dispute about Religion. Persons of good Sense, I have since observ'd, seldom fall into it, except Lawyers, University Men, and Men of all Sorts that have been bred at Edinborough.[9] A Question was once some how or other started between Collins & me, of the Propriety of educating the Female Sex in Learning, & their Abilities for Study. He was of Opinion that it was improper; & that they were naturally unequal to it. I took the contrary Side, perhaps

[1] *Essay on Projects* 1697 prose work by English writer Daniel Defoe, discussing subjects such as banking, economic development, and women's education; *Essays to do Good* Mather's 1710 collection of essays on morality and religious piety.

[2] *Letters* I.e., type for printing.

[3] *bound* Apprenticed.

[4] *Indentures* Contract of indentured apprenticeship, by which one was obliged to work, generally without any pay, for a set period of years.

[5] [Franklin's note] Mr Matthew Adams.

[6] *pretty* Commendable, admirable.

[7] *the drowning … Two Daughters* The Boston lighthouse keeper George Worthylake was drowned on 3 November 1718 along with his wife, daughters, a friend, a servant, and an enslaved man; *Taking of … the Pirate* The famous English pirate Edward Teach—better known as Blackbeard—was killed in a battle with the Royal Navy on 22 November 1718.

[8] *Grubstreet Ballad Stile* Grub Street was an impoverished area of London known for its proliferation of hack writers who sold cheap, hastily written pamphlets and ballads on current subjects of interest.

[9] *Men of … at Edinborough* Franklin alludes generally to contemporary stereotypes about Scottish people, including the idea that they are prone to argumentation; in a 1766 letter to Benjamin Rush and Jonathan Potts, Franklin describes the people of Edinburgh as being "very shrewd and observing."

a little for Dispute sake. He was naturally more eloquent, had a ready Plenty of Words, and sometimes as I thought bore me down more by his Fluency than by the Strength of his Reasons. As we parted without settling the Point, & were not to see one another again for some time, I sat down to put my Arguments in Writing, which I copied fair & sent to him. He answer'd & I reply'd. Three or four Letters of a Side had pass'd, when my Father happen'd to find my Papers, and read them. Without entring into the Discussion, he took occasion to talk to me about the Manner of my Writing, observ'd that tho' I had the Advantage of my Antagonist in correct Spelling & pointing[1] (which I ow'd to the Printing House) I fell far short in elegance of Expression, in Method and in Perspicuity, of which he convinc'd me by several Instances. I saw the Justice of his Remarks, & thence grew more attentive to the *Manner* in Writing, and determin'd to endeavour at Improvement.—

About this time I met with an odd Volume of the Spectator.[2] I had never before seen any of them. I bought it, read it over and over, and was much delighted with it. I thought the Writing excellent, & wish'd if possible to imitate it. With that View, I took some of the Papers, & making short Hints of the Sentiment in each Sentence, laid them by a few Days, and then without looking at the Book, try'd to compleat the Papers again, by expressing each hinted Sentiment at length & as fully as it had been express'd before, in any suitable Words that should come to hand.

Then I compar'd my Spectator with the Original, discover'd some of my Faults & corrected them. But I found I wanted[3] a Stock of Words or a Readiness in recollecting & using them, which I thought I should have acquir'd before that time, if I had gone on making Verses, since the continual Occasion for Words of the same Import but of different Length, to suit the Measure, or of different Sound for the Rhyme, would have laid me under a constant Necessity of searching

for Variety, and also have tended to fix that Variety in my Mind, & make me Master of it. Therefore I took some of the Tales & turn'd them into Verse: And after a time, when I had pretty well forgotten the Prose, turn'd them back again. I also sometimes jumbled my Collections of Hints into Confusion, and after some Weeks endeavour'd to reduce them into the best Order, before I began to form the full Sentences & compleat the Paper. This was to teach me Method in the Arrangement of Thoughts. By comparing my Work afterwards with the original, I discover'd many faults and amended them; but I sometimes had the Pleasure of Fancying that in certain Particulars of small Import, I had been lucky enough to improve the Method or the Language and this encourag'd me to think I might possibly in time come to be a tolerable English Writer, of which I was extreamly ambitious.

My Time for these Exercises & for Reading, was at Night after Work, or before Work began in the Morning; or on Sundays, when I contrived to be in the Printing House alone, evading as much as I could the common Attendance on publick Worship, which my Father used to exact of me when I was under his Care:—And which indeed I still thought a Duty; tho' I could not, as it seemed to me, afford the Time to practise it.

When about 16 Years of Age I happen'd to meet with a Book written by one Tryon,[4] recommending a Vegetable Diet. I determined to go into it. My Brother being yet unmarried, did not keep House, but boarded himself & his Apprentices in another Family. My refusing to eat Flesh occasioned an Inconveniency, and I was frequently chid for my singularity.[5] I made my self acquainted with Tryon's Manner of preparing some of his Dishes, such as Boiling Potatoes, or Rice, making Hasty Pudding,[6] & a few others, and then propos'd to my Brother, that if he would give me Weekly half the Money he paid for my Board, I would board my self. He instantly agreed to it, and I presently found that I could save half what he paid me. This was an additional Fund for buying Books: But I had another

1 *pointing* Punctuation.

2 *the Spectator* Short-lived but highly influential London periodical published daily by Joseph Addison and Richard Steele from 1711 to 1712, and by Addison alone for several months in 1714; its essays discussed morality, manners, and literature, all with a distinctively witty prose style.

3 *wanted* Lacked; needed.

4 *Tryon* English writer Thomas Tryon, whose 1691 *A Way to Health* recommended vegetarianism as a healthful diet and advocated for better treatment of animals.

5 *singularity* Unusualness.

6 *Hasty Pudding* Quick porridge made of grains or cornmeal.

Advantage in it. My Brother and the rest going from the Printing House to their Meals, I remain'd there alone, and dispatching presently my light Repast, (which often was no more than a Bisket or a Slice of Bread, a Handful of Raisins or a Tart from the Pastry Cook's, and a Glass of Water) had the rest of the Time till their Return, for Study, in which I made the greater Progress from that greater Clearness of Head & quicker Apprehension which usually attend Temperance in Eating & Drinking. And now it was that being on some Occasion made asham'd of my Ignorance in Figures, which I had twice fail'd in learning when at School, I took Cocker's[1] Book of Arithmetick, & went thro' the whole by my self with great Ease.—I also read Seller's & Sturmy's[2] Books of Navigation, & became acquainted with the little Geometry they contain, but never proceeded far in that Science.—And I read about this Time Locke On Human Understanding and the Art of Thinking by Messrs du Port Royal.[3]

While I was intent on improving my Language, I met with an English Grammar (I think it was Greenwood's[4]) at the End of which there were two little Sketches of the Arts of Rhetoric and Logic, the latter finishing with a Specimen of a Dispute in the Socratic Method.[5] And soon after I procur'd Xenophon's[6] Memorable Things of Socrates, wherein there are many Instances of the same Method. I was charm'd with it, adopted it, dropt my abrupt Contradiction, and positive Argumentation, and put on the humble Enquirer & Doubter. And being then, from reading Shaftsbury

& Collins,[7] become a real Doubter in many Points of our Religious Doctrine, I found this Method safest for my self & very embarrassing to those against whom I used it, therefore I took a Delight in it, practis'd it continually & grew very artful & expert in drawing People even of superior Knowledge into Concessions the Consequences of which they did not foresee, entangling them in Difficulties out of which they could not extricate themselves, and so obtaining Victories that neither my self nor my Cause always deserved.—I continu'd this Method some few Years, but gradually left it, retaining only the Habit of expressing my self in Terms of modest Diffidence, never using when I advance any thing that may possibly be disputed, the Words, *Certainly*, *undoubtedly*, or any others that give the Air of Positiveness to an Opinion; but rather say, *I conceive*, or *I apprehend* a Thing to be so or so, *It appears to me*, or *I should think it so or so for such & such Reasons*, or *I imagine* it to be so, or *it is so* if *I am not mistaken*.—This Habit I believe has been of great Advantage to me, when I have had occasion to inculcate my Opinions & persuade Men into Measures that I have been from time to time engag'd in promoting.— And as the chief Ends of Conversation are to *inform*, or to be *informed*, to *please* or to *persuade*, I wish well meaning sensible Men would not lessen their Power of doing Good by a Positive assuming Manner that seldom fails to disgust, tends to create Opposition, and to defeat every one of those Purposes for which Speech was given us, to wit, giving or receiving Information, or Pleasure: For If you would *inform*, a positive dogmatical Manner in advancing your Sentiments, may provoke Contradiction & prevent a candid Attention. If you wish Information & Improvement from the Knowledge of others and yet at the same time express your self as firmly fix'd in your present Opinions, modest sensible Men, who do not love Disputation, will probably leave you undisturb'd in the Possession of your Error; and by such a Manner you can seldom

[1] *Cocker* English engraver Edward Cocker, credited as the author of the popular 1677 textbook *Cocker's Arithmetick*.

[2] *Seller's & Sturmy's* John Seller (1632–97) and Samuel Sturmy (1633–69), popular English writers on marine navigation.

[3] *Locke On Human Understanding* John Locke's influential philosophical work *An Essay on Human Understanding* (1689); *Art of . . . Port Royal* 1662 treatise on logic by French philosophers Antoine Arnauld and Pierre Nicole.

[4] *Greenwood* English grammarian James Greenwood, author of *An Essay Towards a Practical English Grammar* (1711).

[5] *Socratic Method* Common term for the method of philosophical discourse exemplified by the Greek philosopher Socrates (c. 470–399 BCE), characterized by the continual asking of probing questions rather than making definitive statements.

[6] *Xenophon* Greek historian and philosopher (c. 430–354 BCE), a friend and disciple of Socrates's who defended the controversial elder philosopher in numerous works.

[7] *Shaftsbury & Collins* Anthony Ashley Cooper, 1st Earl of Shaftesbury (1621–83), politician who supported religious freedom (within the bounds of Protestantism), and Anthony Collins (1676–1729), freethinker and religious skeptic.

hope to recommend your self in *pleasing* your Hearers, or to persuade those whose Concurrence you desire.—Pope[1] says, judiciously,

> Men should be taught as if you taught them not,
> And things unknown propos'd as things forgot,—

farther recommending it to us,

> To speak tho' sure, with seeming Diffidence.

And he might have couple'd with this Line that which he has coupled with another, I think less properly,

> For want of Modesty is want of Sense.[2]

If you ask why *less properly*, I must repeat the Lines;

> "Immodest Words admit of *no* Defence;
> "*For* Want of Modesty is Want of Sense."

Now is not *Want of Sense*, (where a Man is so unfortunate as to want it) some Apology for his *Want of Modesty*? and would not the Lines stand more justly thus?

> Immodest Words admit *but this* Defence,
> That Want of Modesty is Want of Sense.

This however I should submit to better Judgments.—

My Brother had in 1720 or 21, begun to print a Newspaper. It was the second that appear'd in America,[3] & was called *The New England Courant*. The only one before it, was *the Boston News Letter*. I remember his being dissuaded by some of his Friends from the Undertaking, as not likely to succeed, one Newspaper being in their Judgment enough for America.—At this time 1771 there are not less than five & twenty.—He went on however with the Undertaking, and after having work'd in composing the Types & printing off the Sheets I was employ'd to carry the Papers thro' the Streets to the Customers.—He had some ingenious Men among his Friends who amus'd themselves by writing little Pieces for this Paper, which gain'd it Credit, & made it more in Demand; and these Gentlemen often visited us.—Hearing their Conversations, and their Accounts of the Approbation their Papers were receiv'd with, I was excited to try my Hand among them. But being still a Boy, & suspecting that my Brother would object to printing any Thing of mine in his Paper if he knew it to be mine, I contriv'd to disguise my Hand, & writing an anonymous Paper[4] I put it in at Night under the Door of the Printing House. It was found in the Morning & communicated to his Writing Friends when they call'd in as Usual. They read it, commented on it in my Hearing, and I had the exquisite Pleasure, of finding it met with their Approbation, and that, in their different Guesses at the Author none were named but Men of some Character among us for Learning & Ingenuity.—I suppose now that I was rather lucky in my Judges: And that perhaps they were not really so very good ones as I then esteem'd them. Encourag'd however by this, I wrote and convey'd in the same Way to the Press several more Papers, which were equally approv'd, and I kept my Secret till my small Fund of Sense for such Performances was pretty well exhausted, & then I discovered[5] it; when I began to be considered a little more by my Brother's Acquaintance, and in a manner that did not quite please him, as he thought, probably with reason, that it tended to make me too vain. And perhaps this might be one Occasion of the Differences that we began to have about this Time. Tho' a Brother, he considered himself as my Master, & me as his Apprentice; and accordingly expected the same Services from me as he would from another; while I thought he demean'd me too much in some he requir'd of me, who from a Brother expected more Indulgence. Our Disputes were often brought before our Father, and I fancy I was either generally in the right, or else a better Pleader, because the Judgment was generally in my favour. But my Brother was passionate & had often

[1] *Pope* English poet Alexander Pope (1688–1744); Franklin quotes (loosely) below from his *An Essay on Criticism*, lines 576–77 and 569.

[2] *For want ... of Sense* This line is in fact a misquotation from Wentworth Dillon's *Essay on Translated Verse* (1684).

[3] *It was ... in America* James Franklin's newspaper was in fact the fifth newspaper to be printed in America.

[4] *an anonymous Paper* Franklin refers here to his "Silence Dogood" papers, a series of letters purported to be written by the widow Silence Dogood, published between 12 April and 8 October 1722. Letters 1, 2, and 5 are included in the online component of this anthology.

[5] *discovered* Revealed.

beaten me, which I took extreamly amiss;[1] and thinking my Apprenticeship very tedious, I was continually wishing for some Opportunity of shortening it, which at length offered in a manner unexpected.

One of the Pieces in our News-Paper, on some political Point which I have now forgotten, gave Offence to the Assembly.[2] He was taken up, censur'd and imprison'd for a Month by the Speaker's Warrant, I suppose because he would not discover his Author.[3] I too was taken up & examin'd before the Council; but tho' I did not give them any Satisfaction, they contented themselves with admonishing me, and dismiss'd me; considering me perhaps as an Apprentice who was bound to keep his Master's Secrets. During my Brother's Confinement, which I resented a good deal, notwithstanding our private Differences, I had the Management of the Paper; and I made bold to give our Rulers some Rubs[4] in it, which my Brother took very kindly, while others began to consider me in an unfavourable Light, as a young Genius that had a Turn for Libelling & Satyr.[5] My Brother's Discharge was accompany'd with an Order of the House, (a very odd one) *that James Franklin should no longer print the Paper called the New England Courant.* There was a Consultation held in our Printing House among his Friends what he should do in this Case. Some propos'd to evade the Order by changing the Name of the Paper; but my Brother seeing Inconveniences in that, it was finally concluded on as a better Way, to let it be printed for the future under the Name of *Benjamin Franklin.* And to avoid the Censure of the Assembly that might fall on him, as still printing it by his Apprentice, the Contrivance was, that my old Indenture should be return'd to me with a full Discharge on the Back of it, to be shown on Occasion;[6] but to secure to him the Benefit of my Service I was to sign new Indentures for the Remainder of the Term, which were to be kept private. A very flimsy Scheme it was, but however it was immediately executed, and the Paper went on accordingly under my Name for several Months. At length a fresh Difference[7] arising between my Brother and me, I took upon me to assert my Freedom, presuming that he would not venture to produce the new Indentures. It was not fair in me to take this Advantage, and this I therefore reckon one of the first Errata[8] of my Life: But the Unfairness of it weigh'd little with me, when under the Impressions of Resentment, for the Blows[9] his Passion too often urg'd him to bestow upon me. Tho' He was otherwise not an ill-natur'd Man: Perhaps I was too saucy & provoking.—

When he found I would leave him, he took care to prevent my getting Employment in any other Printing-House of the Town, by going round & speaking to every Master, who accordingly refus'd to give me Work. I then thought of going to New York as the nearest Place where there was a Printer: and I was the rather inclin'd to leave Boston, when I reflected that I had already made my self a little obnoxious, to the governing Party; & from the arbitrary Proceedings of the Assembly in my Brother's Case it was likely I might if I stay'd soon bring my self into Scrapes; and farther that my indiscrete Disputations about Religion began to make me pointed at with Horror by good People, as an Infidel or Atheist; I determin'd on the Point: but my Father now siding with my Brother, I was sensible that if I attempted to go openly, Means would be used to prevent me. My Friend Collins therefore undertook to manage a little for me. He agreed with the Captain of a New York Sloop[10] for my Passage, under the Notion of my being a young Acquaintance of his that had got a naughty Girl with Child, whose Friends would compel me to marry her, and therefore I could not appear or come away publickly. So I sold some of my Books to raise a little Money, Was taken on board privately, and as we had a fair Wind, in three Days I found my self in New York near 300 Miles from home, a Boy of but 17,

1 [Franklin's note] I fancy his harsh & tyrannical Treatment of me, might be a means of impressing me with that Aversion to arbitrary Power that has stuck to me thro' my whole Life.

2 *One of … the Assembly* The article in question suggested that certain public figures in Boston had connections to local piracy.

3 *discover his Author* I.e., reveal who had written the controversial article.

4 *Rubs* Criticisms.

5 *Satyr* I.e., satire.

6 *my old Indenture … Occasion* I.e., Franklin was to be freed of his prior indenture, and given papers of discharge to display to the authorities if need be.

7 *Difference* Conflict.

8 *Errata* Errors in a printed book, marked out for correction in the second edition.

9 *Blows* Beatings.

10 *Sloop* Small, single-masted sailing vessel.

without the least Recommendation to or Knowledge of any Person in the Place, and with very little Money in my Pocket.—

My Inclinations for the Sea, were by this time worne out, or I might now have gratify'd them.—But having a Trade, & supposing my self a pretty good Workman, I offer'd my Service to the Printer of the Place, old Mr William Bradford.[1]—He could give me no Employment, having little to do, and Help enough already: But, says he, my Son at Philadelphia has lately lost his principal Hand, Aquila Rose, by Death. If you go thither I believe he may employ you.—Philadelphia was 100 Miles farther. I set out, however, in a Boat for Amboy;[2] leaving my Chest and Things to follow me round by Sea. In crossing the Bay we met with a Squall that tore our rotten Sails to pieces, prevented our getting into the Kill,[3] and drove us upon Long Island. In our Way a drunken Dutchman, who was a Passenger too, fell over board; when he was sinking I reach'd thro' the Water to his shock Pate[4] & drew him up so that we got him in again.—His Ducking sober'd him a little, & he went to sleep, taking first out of his Pocket a Book which he desir'd I would dry for him. It prov'd to be my old favourite Author Bunyan's Pilgrim's Progress in Dutch, finely printed on good Paper with copper Cuts,[5] a Dress better than I had ever seen it wear in its own Language. I have since found that it has been translated into most of the Languages of Europe, and suppose it has been more generally read than any other Book except perhaps the Bible.—Honest John[6] was the first that I know of who mix'd Narration & Dialogue, a Method of Writing very engaging to the Reader, who in the most interesting Parts finds himself as it were brought into the Company, & present at the Discourse. De foe in his Cruso, his Moll Flanders, Religious Courtship, Family Instructor,[7] & other Pieces, has imitated it with Success. And Richardson has done the same in his Pamela,[8] &.—

When we drew near the Island[9] we found it was at a Place where there could be no Landing, there being a great Surff on the stony Beach. So we dropt Anchor & swung round towards the Shore. Some People came down to the Water Edge & hallow'd to us, as we did to them. But the Wind was so high & the Surff so loud, that we could not hear so as to understand each other. There were Canoes on the Shore, & we made Signs & hallow'd that they should fetch us, but they either did not understand us, or thought it impracticable. So they went away, and Night coming on, we had no Remedy but to wait till the Wind should abate, and in the mean time the Boatman & I concluded to sleep if we could, and so crouded into the Scuttle[10] with the Dutchman who was still wet, and the Spray beating over the Head of our Boat, leak'd thro' to us, so that we were soon almost as wet as he. In this Manner we lay all Night with very little Rest. But the Wind abating the next Day, we made a Shift to reach Amboy before Night, having been 30 Hours on the Water without Victuals, or any Drink but a Bottle of filthy Rum:—The Water we sail'd on being salt.—

In the Evening I found my self very feverish, & went ill to Bed. But having read somewhere that cold Water drank plentifully was good for a Fever, I follow'd the Prescription, sweat plentifully most of the Night, my Fever left me, and in the Morning crossing the Ferry, proceeded on my Journey, on foot, having 50 Miles to Burlington,[11] where I was told I should find Boats that would carry me the rest of the Way to Philadelphia.

[1] *William Bradford* William Bradford (1660–1752), English-born printer who pioneered the American printing trade.

[2] *Amboy* Perth Amboy, New Jersey, located just across from the southern point of Staten Island.

[3] *the Kill* Narrow body of water separating northern Staten Island from New Jersey, known as Kill van Kull; the Kill branches west off the Upper New York Bay, which divides Long Island from New Jersey.

[4] *shock Pate* Head covered with rough, shaggy hair.

[5] *copper Cuts* Copper-plate engravings.

[6] *John* I.e., John Bunyan. (*The Pilgrim's Progress* is often considered one of the first novels in the English language.)

[7] *Cruso … Family Instructor* List of works by Daniel Defoe; today, *Robinson Crusoe* (1719) and *Moll Flanders* (1722) are considered novels, while *Religious Courtship* (1722) and *The Family Instructor* (1715) are considered nonfiction conduct manuals.

[8] *Pamela* 1740 epistolary novel by Samuel Richardson.

[9] *the Island* I.e., Staten Island.

[10] *Scuttle* Covered square hole that is a means of moving between decks.

[11] *Burlington* City in New Jersey, on the bank of the Delaware River, which forms the border between New Jersey and Pennsylvania.

It rain'd very hard all the Day, I was thoroughly soak'd, and by Noon a good deal tir'd, so I stopt at a poor Inn, where I staid all Night, beginning now to wish that I had never left home. I cut so miserable a Figure too, that I found by the Questions ask'd me I was suspected to be some runaway Servant, and in danger of being taken up on that Suspicion.—However, I proceeded the next Day, and got in the Evening to an Inn within 8 or 10 Miles of Burlington, kept by one Dr Brown.—

He entred into Conversation with me while I took some Refreshment, and finding I had read a little, became very sociable and friendly. Our Acquaintance continu'd as long as he liv'd. He had been, I imagine, an itinerant Doctor, for there was no Town in England, or Country in Europe, of which he could not give a very particular Account. He had some Letters,[1] & was ingenious, but much of an Unbeliever, & wickedly undertook some Years after to travesty the Bible in doggrel Verse as Cotton had done Virgil.[2]—By this means he set many of the Facts in a very ridiculous Light, & might have hurt weak minds if his Work had been publish'd:—but it never was.—At his House I lay that Night, and the next Morning reach'd Burlington.—But had the Mortification to find that the regular Boats were gone, a little before my coming, and no other expected to go till Tuesday, this being Saturday. Wherefore I return'd to an old Woman in the Town of whom I had bought Gingerbread to eat on the Water, & ask'd her Advice; she invited me to lodge at her House till a Passage by Water should offer; & being tired with my foot Travelling, I accepted the Invitation. She understanding I was a Printer, would have had me stay at that Town & follow my Business, being ignorant of the Stock necessary to begin with. She was very hospitable, gave me a Dinner of Ox Cheek with great Goodwill, accepting only of a Pot of Ale in return. And I tho't my self fix'd till Tuesday should come. However walking in the Evening by the Side of the River a Boat came by, which I found was going towards Philadelphia, with several People in her. They took me in, and as there was no Wind, we row'd all the Way; and about Midnight, not having yet seen the City, some of the Company were confident we must have pass'd it, and would row no farther, the others knew not where we were, so we put towards the Shore, got into a Creek, landed near an old Fence with the Rails of which we made a Fire, the Night being cold, in October, and there we remain'd till Daylight. Then one of the Company knew the Place to be Cooper's Creek a little above Philadelphia, which we saw as soon as we got out of the Creek, and arriv'd there about 8 or 9 a Clock, on the Sunday morning, and landed at the Market street Wharff.—

I have been the more particular in this Description of my Journey, & shall be so of my first Entry into that City, that you may in your Mind compare such unlikely Beginning with the Figure I have since made there. I was in my working Dress, my best Cloaths being to come round by Sea. I was dirty from my Journey; my Pockets were stuff'd out with Shirts & Stockings; I knew no Soul, nor where to look for Lodging. I was fatigu'd with Travelling, Rowing & Want of Rest. I was very hungry; and my whole Stock of Cash consisted of a Dutch Dollar[3] and about a Shilling in Copper. The latter I gave the People of the Boat for my Passage, who at first refus'd it on Account of my Rowing; but I insisted on their taking it, a Man being sometimes more generous when he has but a little Money than when he has plenty, perhaps thro' Fear of being thought to have but little. Then I walk'd up the Street, gazing about, till near the Market House I met a Boy with Bread. I had made many a Meal on Bread, & inquiring where he got it, I went immediately to the Baker's he directed me to in second Street; and ask'd for Bisket, intending such as we had in Boston, but they it seems, were not made in Philadelphia, then I ask'd for a threepenny Loaf, and was told they had none such: so not considering or knowing the Difference of Money & the greater Cheapness nor the Names of his Bread, I bad him give me three pennyworth of any sort. He gave me accordingly three great Puffy Rolls. I was surpriz'd at the Quantity, but took it, and having no Room in my Pockets, walk'd off, with a Roll under each Arm, & eating the other. Thus I went up Market Street as far as fourth Street, passing by the Door of Mr Read, my future Wife's Father, when she standing at the Door

1 *Letters* I.e., academic or literary education.

2 *as Cotton ... Virgil* Reference to *Scarronides: or, Virgil travestie* (1664–70), English writer Charles Cotton's notoriously vulgar parody of the *Aeneid* (29–19 BCE) by the Roman poet Virgil.

3 *Dutch Dollar* Also known as the guilder, a Dutch coin that was circulated in colonial America.

saw me, & thought I made as I certainly did a most awkward ridiculous Appearance. Then I turn'd and went down Chestnut Street and part of Walnut Street, eating my Roll all the Way, and coming round found my self again at Market street Wharff, near the Boat I came in, to which I went for a Draught of the River Water, and being fill'd with one of my Rolls, gave the other two to a Woman & her Child that came down the River in the Boat with us and were waiting to go farther. Thus refresh'd I walk'd again up the Street, which by this time had many clean dress'd People in it who were all walking the same Way; I join'd them, and thereby was led into the great Meeting House of the Quakers[1] near the Market. I sat down among them, and after looking round a while & hearing nothing said, being very drowzy thro' Labour & want of Rest the preceding Night, I fell fast asleep, and continu'd so till the Meeting broke up, when one was kind enough to rouse me. This was therefore the first House I was in or slept in, in Philadelphia.—

Walking down again towards the River, & looking in the Faces of People, I met a young Quaker Man whose Countenance I lik'd, and accosting him requested he would tell me where a Stranger could get Lodging. We were then near the Sign of the Three Mariners. Here, says he, is one Place that entertains Strangers, but it is not a reputable House; if thee[2] wilt walk with me, I'll show thee a better. He brought me to the Crooked Billet in Water-Street. Here I got a Dinner. And while I was eating it, several sly Questions were ask'd me, as it seem'd to be suspected from my youth & Appearance, that I might be some Runaway. After Dinner my Sleepiness return'd: and being shown to a Bed, I lay down without undressing, and slept till Six in the Evening; was call'd to Supper; went to Bed again very early and slept soundly till the next Morning. Then I made my self as tidy as I could, and went to Andrew Bradford the Printer's.—I found in the Shop the old Man his Father, whom I had seen at New York, and who travelling on horse back had got to Philadelphia

before me.—He introduc'd me to his Son, who receiv'd me civilly, gave me a Breakfast, but told me he did not at present want a Hand, being lately supply'd with one. But there was another Printer in town lately set up, one Keimer,[3] who perhaps might employ me; if not, I should be welcome to lodge at his House, & he would give me a little Work to do now & then till fuller Business should offer.

The old Gentleman said, he would go with me to the new Printer: And when we found him, Neighbour, says Bradford, I have brought to see you a young Man of your Business, perhaps you may want such a One. He ask'd me a few Questions, put a Composing Stick[4] in my Hand to see how I work'd, and then said he would employ me soon, tho' he had just then nothing for me to do. And taking old Bradford whom he had never seen before, to be one of the Towns People that had a Good Will for him, enter'd into a Conversation on his present Undertaking & Prospects; while Bradford not discovering[5] that he was the other Printer's Father; on Keimer's Saying he expected soon to get the greatest Part of the Business into his own Hands, drew him on by artful Questions and starting little Doubts, to explain all his Views, what Interest he rely'd on, & in what manner he intended to proceed.—I who stood by & heard all, saw immediately that one of them was a crafty old Sophister,[6] and the other a mere Novice. Bradford left me with Keimer, who was greatly surpriz'd when I told him who the old Man was.

Keimer's Printing House I found, consisted of an old shatter'd Press, and one small worn-out Fount[7] of English, which he was then using himself, composing in it an Elegy on Aquila Rose before-mentioned, an ingenious young Man of excellent Character much respected in the Town, Clerk of the Assembly, & a pretty[8] Poet. Keimer made Verses, too, but very indif-

[1] *Quakers* Members of the religious denomination formally known as the Society of Friends; the group had a significant presence in Pennsylvania, which had been founded by the Quaker William Penn in 1681.

[2] *thee* Quakers were known for their use of the pronouns "thee" and "thou" and related turns of phrase that were otherwise considered outdated in everyday speech by the eighteenth-century.

[3] *Keimer* English-born printer Samuel Keimer, who had emigrated to Pennsylvania after a stint in debtors' prison shortly before Franklin's arrival.

[4] *Composing Stick* Printing tool on which one arranges pieces of movable type into lines, and which is then set into a printing galley.

[5] *discovering* Revealing.

[6] *Sophister* Clever and conniving person.

[7] *Fount* Assemblage of type in a given size and style.

[8] *pretty* I.e., skillful, talented.

ferently.[1]—He could not be said to write them, for his Manner was to compose them in the Types directly out of his Head; so there being no Copy, but one Pair of Cases, and the Elegy likely to require all the Letter, no one could help him.—I endeavour'd to put his Press (which he had not yet us'd, & of which he understood nothing) into Order fit to be work'd with; & promising to come & print off his Elegy as soon as he should have got it ready, I return'd to Bradford's, who gave me a little Job to do for the present, & there I lodged & dieted. A few Days after Keimer sent for me to print off the Elegy. And now he had got another Pair of Cases, and a Pamphlet to reprint, on which he set me to work.—

These two Printers I found poorly qualified for their Business. Bradford had not been bred to it, & was very illiterate; and Keimer tho' something of a Scholar, was a mere Compositor, knowing nothing of Presswork.[2] He had been one of the French Prophets[3] and could act their enthusiastic Agitations. At this time he did not profess any particular Religion, but something of all on occasion; was very ignorant of the World, & had, as I afterwards found, a good deal of the Knave in his Composition. He did not like my Lodging at Bradford's while I work'd with him. He had a House indeed, but without Furniture, so he could not lodge me; But he got me a Lodging at Mr Read's beforementioned, who was the Owner of his House. And my Chest & Clothes being come by this time, I made rather a more respectable Appearance in the Eyes of Miss Read, than I had done when she first happen'd to see me eating my Roll in the Street.—

I began now to have some Acquaintance among the young People of the Town, that were Lovers of Reading with whom I spent my Evenings very pleasantly and gaining Money by my Industry & Frugality, I lived very agreeably, forgetting Boston as much as I could, and not desiring that any there should know where I resided except my Friend Collins who was in my Secret, & kept it when I wrote to him.—At length an Incident happened that sent me back again much sooner than I had intended.—

I had a Brother-in-law, Robert Holmes, Master of a Sloop, that traded between Boston and Delaware. He being at New Castle,[4] 40 Miles below Philadelphia, heard there of me, and wrote me a Letter, mentioning the Concern of my Friends in Boston at my abrupt Departure, assuring me of their Goodwill to me, and that every thing would be accommodated to my Mind if I would return, to which he exhorted me very earnestly.—I wrote an Answer to his Letter, thank'd him for his Advice, but stated my Reasons for quitting Boston fully, & in such a Light as to convince him I was not so wrong as he had apprehended.—Sir William Keith[5] Governor of the Province, was then at New Castle, and Capt. Holmes happening to be in Company with him when my Letter came to hand, spoke to him of me, and show'd him the Letter. The Governor read it, and seem'd surpriz'd when he was told my Age. He said I appear'd a young Man of promising Parts, and therefore should be encouraged: The Printers at Philadelphia were wretched ones, and if I would set up there, he made no doubt I should succeed; for his Part, he would procure me the publick Business, & do me every other Service in his Power. This my Brother-in-Law afterwards told me in Boston. But I knew as yet nothing of it; when one Day Keimer and I being at Work together near the Window, we saw the Governor and another Gentleman (which prov'd to be Col. French, of New Castle) finely dress'd, come directly across the Street to our House, & heard them at the Door. Keimer ran down immediately, thinking it a Visit to him. But the Governor enquir'd for me, came up, & with a Condescension[6] & Politeness I had been quite unus'd to, made me many Compliments, desired to be acquainted with me, blam'd me kindly for not having made my self known to him when I first came to the Place, and would have me away with him to the Tavern where he was going with Col. French to taste

1 *indifferently* In inferior quality.

2 *a mere Compositor … Presswork* I.e., familiar with the work of setting type (composing) but not with operating the printing press.

3 *French Prophets* Millenarian group originating in the Protestant Camisard sect of early-eighteenth-century France; following a period of violent persecution under the Catholic Louis XIV between 1702 and 1715, a small group of Camisards emigrated to London, where they and their followers became known as the French Prophets. The Prophets became infamous for undergoing wild, violent fits during meetings.

4 *New Castle* Town in Delaware.

5 *William Keith* The Scottish-born Sir William Keith served as Governor of Pennsylvania and Delaware from 1717 to 1726.

6 *Condescension* Gracious behavior shown to a social inferior.

as he said some excellent Madeira.[1] I was not a little surpriz'd, and Keimer star'd like a Pig poison'd. I went however with the Governor & Col. French, to a Tavern the Corner of Third Street, and over the Madeira he propos'd my Setting up my Business, laid beforre me the Probabilities of Success, & both he & Col French, assur'd me I should have their Interest & Influence in procuring the Publick Business of both Governments. On my doubting whether my Father would assist me in it, Sir William said he would give me a Letter to him, in which he would state the Advantages,—and he did not doubt of prevailing with him. So it was concluded I should return to Boston in the first Vessel with the Governor's Letter recommending me to my Father. In the mean time the Intention was to be kept secret, and I went on working with Keimer as usual, the Governor sending for me now & then to dine with him, a very great Honour I thought it, and convers-ing with me in the most affable, familiar, & friendly manner imaginable. About the End of April 1724. a little Vessel offer'd for Boston. I took Leave of Keimer as going to see my Friends. The Governor gave me an ample Letter, saying many flattering things of me to my Father, and strongly recommending the Project of my setting up at Philadelphia, as a Thing that must make my Fortune.—We struck on a Shoal in going down the Bay & sprung a Leak, we had a blustring time at Sea, and were oblig'd to pump almost continually, at which I took my Turn.—We arriv'd safe however at Boston in about a Fortnight.—I had been absent Seven Months and my Friends had heard nothing of me, for my Br. Holmes was not yet return'd; and had not writ-ten about me. My unexpected Appearance surpriz'd the Family; all were however very glad to see me and made me Welcome, except my Brother. I went to see him at his Printing-House: I was better dress'd than ever while in his Service, having a genteel new Suit from Head to foot, a Watch, and my Pockets lin'd with near Five Pounds Sterling in Silver. He receiv'd me not very frankly,[2] look'd me all over, and turn'd to his Work again. The Journey-Men were inquisitive where I had been, what sort of a Country it was, and how I lik'd it? I prais'd it much, & the happy Life I led in it; express-ing strongly my Intention of returning to it; and one

of them asking what kind of Money we had there, I produc'd a handful of Silver, and spread it before them, which was a kind of Raree-Show[3] they had not been us'd to, Paper being the Money of Boston.[4] Then I took an Opportunity of letting them see my Watch: and lastly, (my Brother still grum & sullen) I gave them a Piece of Eight[5] to drink & took my Leave.—This Visit of mine offended him extreamly. For when my Mother some time after spoke to him of a Reconciliation, & of her Wishes to see us on good Terms together, & that we might live for the future as Brothers, he said, I had insulted him in such a Manner before his People that he could never forget or forgive it.—In this however he was mistaken.—

My Father receiv'd the Governor's Letter with some apparent Surprize; but said little of it to me for some Days; when Capt. Holmes returning, he show'd it to him, ask'd if he knew Keith, and what kind of a Man he was: Adding his Opinion that he must be of small Discretion,[6] to think of setting a Boy up in Business who wanted yet 3 Years of being at Man's Estate.[7] Ho[l]mes said what he could in favor of the Project; but my Father was clear in the Impropriety of it; and at last gave a flat Denial to it. Then he wrote a civil Letter to Sir William thanking him for the Patronage he had so kindly offered me, but declining to assist me as yet in Setting up, I being in his Opinion too young to be trusted with the Management of a Business so important; & for which the Preparation must be so expensive.—

My friend & Companion Collins, who was a Clerk at the Post-Office, pleas'd with the Account I gave him of my new Country, determin'd to go thither also:— And while I waited for my Fathers Determination, he set out before me by Land to Rhodeisland, leaving his Books which were a pretty Collection of Mathematicks

1 *Madeira* Portuguese fortified wine.

2 *frankly* I.e., openly or warmly.

3 *Raree-Show* Peep show.

4 *Paper being the Money of Boston* Paper money had only been introduced in Pennsylvania in the previous year.

5 *Piece of Eight* Spanish dollar (a common form of currency in the colonies).

6 *small Discretion* Poor judgment.

7 *wanted yet ... Man's Estate* I.e., was still three years short of being considered a grown man. (Franklin was at this time eighteen years old.)

& Natural Philosophy,[1] to come with mine & me to New York where he propos'd to wait for me. My Father, tho' he did not approve Sir William's Proposition was yet pleas'd that I had been able to obtain so advantageous a Character from a Person of such Note where I had resided, and that I had been so industrious & careful as to equip my self so handsomely in so short a time: therefore seeing no Prospect of an Accommodation between my Brother & me, he gave his Consent to my Returning again to Philadelphia, advis'd me to behave respectfully to the People there, endeavour to obtain the general Esteem, & avoid lampooning & libelling to which he thought I had too much Inclination;—telling me, that by steady Industry and a prudent Parsimony,[2] I might save enough by the time I was One and Twenty to set me up, & that if I came near the Matter, he would help me out with the Rest.—This was all I could obtain, except some small Gifts as Tokens of his & my Mother's Love, when I embark'd again for New-York, now with their Approbation & their Blessing.—

The Sloop putting in at Newport, Rhodeisland, I visited my Brother John, who had been married & settled there some Years. He received me very affectionately, for he always lov'd me.—A Friend of his, one Vernon, having some Money due to him in Pensilvania, about 35 Pounds Currency, desired I would receive it for him, and keep it till I had his Directions what to remit it in. Accordingly he gave me an Order.—This afterwards occasion'd me a good deal of Uneasiness.—At Newport we took in a Number of Passengers for New York: Among which were two young Women, Companions, and a grave, sensible Matron-like Quaker-Woman with her Attendants.—I had shown an obliging Readiness to do her some little Services which impress'd her I suppose with a degree of Good-will towards me.— Therefore when she saw a daily growing Familiarity between me & the two Young Women, which they appear'd to encourage, she took me aside & said, Young Man, I am concern'd for thee, as thou hast no Friend with thee, and seems not to know much of the World, or of the Snares Youth is expos'd to; depend upon it those are very bad Women, I can see it in all their Actions, and if thee art not upon thy Guard, they

will draw thee into some Danger: they are Strangers to thee,—and I advise thee in a friendly Concern for thy Welfare, to have no Acquaintance with them.—As I seem'd at first not to think so ill of them as she did, she mention'd some Things she had observ'd & heard that had escap'd my Notice; but now convinc'd me she was right. I thank'd her for her kind Advice, and promis'd to follow it.—When we arriv'd at New York, they told me where they liv'd, & invited me to come and see them: but I avoided it. And it was well I did: For the next Day, the Captain miss'd a Silver Spoon & some other Things that had been taken out of his Cabbin, and knowing that these were a Couple of Strumpets,[3] he got a Warrant to search their Lodgings, found the stolen Goods, and had the Thieves punish'd.—So tho' we had escap'd a sunken Rock which we scrap'd upon in the Passage, I thought this Escape of rather more Importance to me. At New York I found my Friend Collins, who had arriv'd there some Time before me. We had been intimate from Children, and had read the same Books together. But he had the Advantage of more time for Reading, & Studying and a wonderful Genius for Mathematical Learning in which he far outstript me. While I liv'd in Boston most of my Hours of Leisure for Conversation were spent with him, & he continu'd a sober as well as an industrious Lad; was much respected for his Learning by several of the Clergy & other Gentlemen, & seem'd to promise making a good Figure in Life: but during my Absence he had acquir'd a Habit of Sotting with Brandy; and I found by his own Account & what I heard from others, that he had been drunk every day since his Arrival at New York, & behav'd very oddly. He had gam'd too and lost his Money, so that I was oblig'd to discharge his Lodgings,[4] & defray his Expences to and at Philadelphia:—Which prov'd extreamly inconvenient to me.—The then Governor of N York, Burnet,[5] Son of Bishop Burnet hearing from the Captain that a young Man, one of his Passengers, had a great many Books, desired he would bring me to see him. I waited

[3] *Strumpets* Derogatory term for prostitutes.

[4] *discharge his Lodgings* I.e., pay the remainder of his rent.

[5] *Burnet* William Burnet, English-born governor of New York and New Jersey from 1720 to 1728, and of Massachusetts and New Hampshire from 1728 to 1729. His father was the Scottish philosopher Gilbert Burnet, Bishop of Salisbury.

[1] *Determination* Decision; *Natural Philosophy* Branch of study which would today broadly be termed "science."

[2] *Parsimony* Thriftiness.

upon him accordingly, and should have taken Collins with me but that he was not sober. The Governor treated me with great Civility, show'd me his Library, which was a very large one, & we had a good deal of Conversation about Books & Authors. This was the second Governor who had done me the Honour to take Notice of me, which to a poor Boy like me was very pleasing.—We proceeded to Philadelphia. I received on the Way Vernon's Money, without which we could hardly have finish'd our Journey.—Collins wish'd to be employ'd in some Counting House; but whether they discover'd his Dramming[1] by his Breath, or by his Behaviour, tho' he had some Recommendations, he met with no Success in any Application, and continu'd Lodging & Boarding at the same House with me & at my Expence. Knowing I had that Money of Vernon's he was continually borrowing of me, still promising Repayment as soon as he should be in Business. At length he had got so much of it, that I was distress'd to think what I should do, in case of being call'd on to remit it.—His Drinking continu'd, about which we sometimes quarrel'd, for when a little intoxicated he was very fractious. Once in a Boat on the Delaware with some other young Men, he refused to row in his Turn: I will be row'd home, says he. We will not row you, says I. You must says he, or stay all Night on the Water, just as you please. The others said, Let us row; What signifies it? But my Mind being soured with his other Conduct, I continu'd to refuse. So he swore he would make me row, or throw me overboard; and coming along stepping on the Thwarts[2] towards me, when he came up & struck at me, I clapt my Hand under his Crutch, and rising pitch'd him head-fore-most into the River. I knew he was a good Swimmer, and so was under little Concern about him; but before he could get round to lay hold of the Boat, we had with a few Strokes pull'd her out of his Reach.—And ever when he drew near the Boat, we ask'd if he would row, striking a few Strokes to slide her away from him.—He was ready to die with Vexation, & obstinately would not promise to row; however seeing him at last beginning to tire, we lifted him in; and brought him home dripping wet in the Evening. We hardly exchang'd a civil Word afterwards; and a West India Captain who

had a Commission to procure a Tutor for the Sons of a Gentleman at Barbadoes, happening to meet with him, agreed to carry him thither. He left me then, promising to remit me the first Money he should receive in order to discharge the Debt. But I never heard of him after.—The Breaking into this Money of Vernon's was one of the first great Errata of my Life. And this Affair show'd that my Father was not much out in his Judgment when he suppos'd me too Young to manage Business of Importance. But Sir William, on reading his Letter, said he was too prudent. There was great Difference in Persons, and Discretion did not always accompany Years, nor was Youth always without it. And since he will not set you up, says he, I will do it my self. Give me an Inventory of the Things necessary to be had from England, and I will send for them. You shall repay me when you are able; I am resolv'd to have a good Printer here, and I am sure you must succeed. This was spoken with such an Appearance of Cordiality, that I had not the least doubt of his meaning what he said.—I had hitherto kept the Proposition of my Setting up a Secret in Philadelphia, & I still kept it. Had it been known that I depended on the Governor, probably some Friend that knew him better would have advis'd me not to rely on him, as I afterwards heard it as his known Character to be liberal of Promises which he never meant to keep.—Yet unsolicited as he was by me, how could I think his generous Offers insincere? I believ'd him one of the best Men in the World.—

I presented him an Inventory of a little Printing House, amounting by my Computation to about 100£ Sterling. He lik'd it, but ask'd me if my being on the Spot in England to chuse the Types & see that every thing was good of the kind, might not be of some Advantage. Then, says he, when there, you may make Acquaintances & establish Correspondencies in the Bookselling, & Stationery Way. I agreed that this might be advantageous. Then says he, get yourself ready to go with Annis;[3] which was the annual Ship, and the only one at that Time usually passing between London and Philadelphia. But it would be some Months before Annis sail'd, so I continu'd working with Keimer, fretting about the Money Collins had got from me, and in

[1] *Dramming* Drinking.

[2] *Thwarts* Rower's seat on a boat.

[3] *Annis* I.e., Thomas Annis, captain of the packet *London Hope*.

daily Apprehensions of being call'd upon by Vernon, which however did not happen for some Years after.—

I believe I have omitted mentioning that in my first Voyage from Boston, being becalm'd off Block Island,[1] our People set about catching Cod & hawl'd up a great many. Hitherto I had stuck to my Resolution of not eating animal Food; and on this Occasion, I consider'd with my Master Tryon the taking every Fish as a kind of unprovok'd Murder, since none of them had or ever could do us any Injury that might justify the Slaughter.—All this seem'd very reasonable.—But I had formerly been a great Lover of Fish, & when this came hot out of the Frying Pan, it smelt admirably well. I balanc'd some time between Principle & Inclination: till I recollected, that when the Fish were opened, I saw smaller Fish taken out of their Stomachs:—Then, thought I, if you eat one another, I don't see why we mayn't eat you. So I din'd upon Cod very heartily and continu'd to eat with other People, returning only now & then occasionally to a vegetable Diet. So convenient a thing is it to be a *reasonable Creature*, since it enables one to find or make a Reason for every thing one has a mind to do.—

Keimer & and I liv'd on a pretty good familiar Footing & agreed tolerably well: for he suspected nothing of my Setting up. He retain'd a great deal of his old Enthusiasms, and lov'd an Argumentation. We therefore had many Disputations. I us'd to work him so with my Socratic Method, and had trapann'd[2] him so often by Questions apparently so distant from any Point we had in hand, and yet by degrees led to the Point, and brought him into Difficulties & Contradictions, that at last he grew ridiculously cautious, and would hardly answer me the most common Question, without asking first, *What do you intend to infer from that?* However it gave him so high an Opinion of my Abilities in the Confuting Way, that he seriously propos'd my being his Colleague in a Project he had of setting up a new Sect. He was to preach the Doctrines, and I was to confound all Opponents. When he came to explain with me upon the Doctrines, I found several Conundrums which I objected to, unless I might have my Way a little too, and introduce some of mine. Keimer wore his

Beard at full Length, because somewhere in the Mosaic Law it is said, *thou shalt not mar the Corners of thy Beard.*[3] He likewise kept the seventh day Sabbath;[4] and these two Points were Essentials with him.—I dislik'd both, but agreed to admit them upon Condition of his adopting the Doctrine of using no animal Food. I doubt,[5] says he, my Constitution will not bear that. I assur'd him it would, & that he would be the better for it. He was usually a great Glutton, and I promis'd my self some Diversion in half-starving him. He agreed to try the Practice if I would keep him Company. I did so and we held it for three Months. We had our Victuals dress'd and brought to us regularly by a Woman in the Neighbourhood, who had from me a List of 40 Dishes to be prepar'd for us at different times, in all which there was neither Fish Flesh nor Fowl, and the Whim suited me the better at this time from the Cheapness of it, not costing us above 18d[6] Sterling each, per Week.—I have since kept several Lents[7] most strictly, Leaving the common Diet for that, and that for the common, abruptly, without the least Inconvenience: So that I think there is little in the Advice of making those Changes by easy Gradations.—I went on pleasantly, but Poor Keimer suffer'd grievously, tir'd of the Project, long'd for the Flesh Pots of Egypt,[8] and order'd a roast Pig; He invited me & two Women Friends to dine with him, but it being brought too soon upon table, he could not resist the Temptation, and ate it all up before we came.—

[1] *Block Island* About thirty miles northeast of the tip of Long Island, part of Rhode Island.

[2] *trapann'd* Ensnared.

[3] *Mosaic Law* Series of strictures laid down in the Torah, or the first five books of the Hebrew Bible (the Old Testament); *thou shalt ... thy Beard* See Leviticus 19.27. Wearing a long beard was considered unusual by western eighteenth-century standards of grooming.

[4] *seventh day Sabbath* I.e., observance of the Sabbath, or day of rest, on Saturday rather than Sunday. The practice is upheld by numerous Christian denominations as well as within Judaism.

[5] *doubt* Fear; suspect.

[6] *18d* Eighteen pence.

[7] *Lents* The Christian observance of Lent, the forty-day period preceding Easter, traditionally involves various forms of fasting, often including abstaining from meat.

[8] *long'd for ... Egypt* Common expression referring to a longing for indulgent bodily pleasures; see Exodus 16.3: "And the children of Israel said unto them, Would to God we had died by the hand of the Lord in the land of Egypt, when we sat by the flesh pots, and when we did eat bread to the full; for ye have brought us forth into this wilderness, to kill this whole assembly with hunger."

I had made some Courtship during this time to Miss Read, I had a great Respect & Affection for her, and had some Reason to believe she had the same for me: but as I was about to take a long Voyage, and we were both very young, only a little above 18. it was thought most prudent by her Mother to prevent our going too far at present, as a Marriage if it was to take place would be more convenient after my Return, when I should be as I expected set up in my Business. Perhaps too she thought my Expectations not so well founded as I imagined them to be.—

My chief Acquaintances at this time were, Charles Osborne, Joseph Watson, & James Ralph; All Lovers of Reading. The two first were Clerks to an eminent Scrivener or Conveyancer[1] in the Town, Charles Brogden; the other was Clerk to a Merchant. Watson was a pious sensible young Man, of great Integrity.— The others rather more lax in their Principles of Religion, particularly Ralph, who as well as Collins had been unsettled by me, for which they both made me suffer.—Osborne was sensible, candid, frank, sincere, and affectionate to his Friends; but in litterary Matters too fond of Criticising. Ralph, was ingenious, genteel in his Manners, & extreamly eloquent; I think I never knew a prettier Talker.—Both of them were great Admirers of Poetry, and began to try their Hands in little Pieces. Many pleasant Walks we four had together, on Sundays into the Woods near Skuylkill,[2] where we read to one another & conferr'd on what we read. Ralph was inclin'd to pursue the Study of Poetry, not doubting but he might become eminent in it and make his Fortune by it, alleging that the best Poets must when they first began to write, make as many Faults as he did.—Osborne dissuaded him, assur'd him he had no Genius for Poetry, & advis'd him to think of nothing beyond the Business he was bred to; that in the mercantile way tho' he had no Stock, he might by his Diligence & Punctuality recommend himself to Employment as a Factor,[3] and in time acquire wherewith to trade on his own Account. I approv'd the amusing one's Self with Poetry now & then, so far as to improve one's Language, but no farther. On this it was

propos'd that we should each of us at our next Meeting produce a Piece of our own Composing, in order to improve by our mutual Observations, Criticisms & Corrections. As Language & Expression were what we had in View, we excluded all Considerations of Invention, by agreeing that the Task should be a Version of the 18th Psalm,[4] which describes the Descent of a Deity. When the Time of our Meeting drew nigh, Ralph call'd on me first, & let me know his Piece was ready. I told him I had been busy, & having little Inclination had done nothing.—He then show'd me his Piece for my Opinion; and I much approv'd it, as it appear'd to me to have great Merit. Now, says he, Osborne never will allow the least Merit in any thing of mine, but makes 1000 Criticisms out of mere Envy. He is not so jealous of you. I wish therefore you would take this Piece, & produce it as yours. I will pretend not to have had time, & so produce nothing: We shall then see what he will say to it.—It was agreed, and I immediately transcrib'd it that it might appear in my own hand. We met. Watson's Performance was read: there were some Beauties in it: but many Defects. Osborne's was read: It was much better. Ralph did it Justice, remark'd some Faults, but applauded the Beauties. He himself had nothing to produce. I was backward,[5] seem'd desirous of being excus'd, had not had sufficient Time to correct, &c. but no Excuse could be admitted, produce I must. It was read and repeated; Watson and Osborne gave up the Contest; and join'd in applauding it immoderately. Ralph only made some Criticisms & propos'd some Amendments, but I defended my Text. Osborne was against Ralph, & told him he was no better a Critic than Poet; so he dropt the Argument. As they two went home together, Osborne express'd himself still more strongly in favour of what he thought my Production, having restrain'd himself before as he said, lest I should think

[1] *Conveyancer* Lawyer who specializes in drafting property deeds.

[2] *Skuylkill* Main river running through Philadelphia.

[3] *Factor* Agent.

[4] *18th Psalm* See Psalm 18.6–10: "In my distress I called upon the Lord, and cried unto my God: he heard my voice out of his temple, and my cry came before him, even into his ears. Then the earth shook and trembled; the foundations also of the hills moved and were shaken, because he was wroth. There went up a smoke out of his nostrils, and fire out of his mouth devoured: coals were kindled by it. He bowed the heavens also, and came down: and darkness was under his feet. And he rode upon a cherub, and did fly: yea, he did fly upon the wings of the wind."

[5] *backward* I.e., reluctant.

it Flattery. But who would have imagin'd, says he, that Franklin had been capable of such a Performance; such Painting, such Force! such Fire! he has even improv'd the Original! In his common Conversation, he seems to have no Choice of Words; he hesitates and blunders; and yet, good God, how he writes!—When we next met, Ralph discover'd the Trick we had plaid him, and Osborne was a little laught at. This Transaction fix'd Ralph in his Resolution of becoming a Poet. I did all I could to dissuade him from it, but He continued scribbling Verses, till *Pope*[1] cur'd him.—He became however a pretty good Prose Writer. More of him hereafter. But as I may not have occasion again to mention the other two, I shall just remark here, that Watson died in my Arms a few Years after, much lamented, being the best of our Set. Osborne went to the West Indies, where he became an eminent Lawyer & made Money, but died young. He and I had made a serious Agreement, that the one who happen'd first to die, should if possible make a friendly Visit to the other, and acquaint him how he found things in that separate State. But he never fulfill'd his Promise.

The Governor, seeming to like my Company, had me frequently to his House; & his Setting me up was always mention'd as a fix'd thing. I was to take with me Letters recommendatory to a Number of his Friends, besides the Letter of Credit, to furnish me with the necessary Money for purchasing the Press & Types, Paper, &c. For these Letters I was appointed to call at different times, when they were to be ready, but a future time was still named.—Thus he went on till the Ship whose Departure too had been several times postponed was on the Point of sailing. Then when I call'd to take my Leave & receive the Letters, his Secretary, Dr Bard, came out to me and said the Governor was extreamly busy, in writing, but would be down at Newcastle before the Ship, & there the Letters would be delivered to me.

Ralph, tho' married & having one Child, had determined to accompany me in this Voyage. It was thought he intended to establish a Correspondence, & obtain Goods to sell on Commission. But I found afterwards, that thro' some Discontent with his Wifes Relations, he purposed to leave her on their Hands, & never return again.—Having taken leave of my Friends, & interchang'd some Promises with Miss Read, I left Philadelphia in the Ship, which anchor'd at Newcastle. The Governor was there. But when I went to his Lodging, the Secretary came to me from him with the civillest Message in the World, that he could not then see me being engag'd in Business of the utmost Importance, but should send the Letters to me on board, wish'd me heartily a good Voyage and a speedy Return, &c. I return'd on board, a little puzzled, but still not doubting.—

Mr Andrew Hamilton, a famous Lawyer of Philadelphia, had taken Passage in the same Ship for himself and Son: and with Mr Denham a Quaker Merchant, & Messrs Onion & Russel Masters of an Iron Work in Maryland, had engag'd the Great Cabin; so that Ralph and I were forc'd to take up with a Birth in the Steerage:[2]—And none on board knowing us, were considered as ordinary Persons.—But Mr Hamilton & his Son (it was James, since Governor)[3] return'd from New Castle to Philadelphia, the Father being recall'd by a great Fee to plead for a seized Ship.—And just before we sail'd Col. French coming on board, & showing me great Respect, I was more taken Notice of, and, with my Friend Ralph invited by the other Gentlemen to come into the Cabin, there being now Room. Accordingly we remov'd thither.

Understanding that Col. French had brought on board the Governor's Dispatches,[4] I ask'd the Captain for those Letters that were to be under my Care. He said all were put into the Bag together; and he could not then come at them; but before we landed in England, I should have an Opportunity of picking them out. So I was satisfy'd for the present, and we proceeded on our Voyage. We had a sociable Company in the Cabin, and lived uncommonly well, having the Addition of all Mr Hamilton's Stores, who had laid in plentifully. In this Passage Mr Denham contracted a

[1] *Pope* Alexander Pope (1688–1744), who was during the eighteenth century widely considered an exemplary poet. Ralph's work would later be parodied in Pope's *Dunciad* (1728–43), which satirizes the hack writers of contemporary England.

[2] *Birth* I.e., berth; lodging on board a ship; *Steerage* Lower cargo deck, often the cheapest and most unpleasant place of accommodation.

[3] *James, since Governor* James Hamilton, who served as governor of Pennsylvania from 1748 to 1754 and from 1759 to 1763.

[4] *Dispatches* Letters and other communications.

Friendship for me that continued during his Life. The Voyage was otherwise not a pleasant one, as we had a great deal of bad Weather.—

When we came into the Channel,[1] the Captain kept his Word with me, & gave me an Opportunity of examining the Bag for the Governor's Letters. I found none upon which my Name was put, as under my Care; I pick'd out 6 or 7 that by the Handwriting I thought might be the promis'd Letters, especially as one of them was directed to Basket the King's Printer, and another to some Stationer.[2] We arriv'd in London the 24th of December, 1724.—I waited upon the Stationer who came first in my Way, delivering the Letter as from Governor Keith. I don't know such a Person, says he: but opening the Letter, O, this is from Riddlesden; I have lately found him to be a compleat Rascal, and I will have nothing to do with him, nor receive any Letters from him. So, putting the Letter into my Hand, he turn'd on his Heel & left me to serve some Customer.—I was surprized to find these were not the Governor's Letters. And after recollecting and comparing Circumstances, I began to doubt his Sincerity. I found my Friend Denham, and opened the whole Affair to him. He let me into Keith's Character; told me there was not the least Probability that he had written any Letters for me, that no one who knew him had the smallest Dependence on him, and he laught at the Notion of the Governor's giving me a Letter of Credit, having as he said no Credit to give.—On my expressing some Concern about what I should do: He advis'd me to endeavour getting some Employment in the Way of my Business. Among the Printers here, says he, you will improve yourself; and when you return to America, you will set up to greater Advantage.

We both of us happen'd to know, as well as the Stationer, that Riddlesden the Attorney, was a very Knave. He had half ruin'd Miss Read's Father by persuading him to be bound for him.[3] By his Letter it appear'd, there was a secret Scheme on foot to the Prejudice of Hamilton, (Suppos'd to be then coming over with us,) and that Keith was concern'd in it with Riddlesden. Denham, who was a Friend of Hamilton's, thought he ought to be acquainted with it. So when he arriv'd in England, which was soon after, partly from Resentment & Ill-Will to Keith & Riddlesden, & partly from Good Will to him: I waited on him, and gave him the Letter. He thank'd me cordially, the Information being of Importance to him. And from that time he became my Friend, greatly to my Advantage afterwards on many Occasions.

But what shall we think of a Governor's playing such pitiful Tricks, & imposing so grossly on a poor ignorant Boy! It was a Habit he had acquired. He wish'd to please every body; and having little to give, he gave Expectations.—He was otherwise an ingenious sensible Man, a pretty good Writer, & a good Governor for the People, tho' not for his Constituents the Proprietaries,[4] whose Instructions he sometimes disregarded.—Several of our best Laws were of his Planning, and pass'd during his Administration.—

Ralph and I were inseparable Companions. We took Lodgings together in Little Britain[5] at 3/6[6] per Week, as much as we could then afford.—He found some Relations, but they were poor & unable to assist him. He now let me know his Intentions of remaining in London, and that he never meant to return to Philadelphia—He had brought no Money with him, the whole he could muster having been expended in paying his Passage.—I had 15 Pistoles:[7] So he borrowed occasionally of me, to subsist while he was looking out for Business.—He first endeavoured to get into the Playhouse, believing himself qualify'd for an Actor; but Wilkes,[8] to whom he apply'd, advis'd him candidly not to think of that Employment, as it was impossible he should succeed in it. Then he propos'd to Roberts,

[1] *the Channel* I.e., the English Channel, body of water separating England from the European continent.

[2] *Basket* John Baskett (c. 1665–1742); *Stationer* Seller of books and stationery.

[3] *bound for him* Legally responsible for paying his debts.

[4] *his Constituents the Proprietaries* As a proprietary colony, the land of Pennsylvania was legally owned by its proprietaries (William Penn and his descendants), who continued to reside in England. In the coming decades conflicts of interest would frequently arise between Pennsylvania's proprietaries and the political leaders who resided in the colony.

[5] *Little Britain* Small district of London, known for its many booksellers.

[6] *3/6* Three shillings and sixpence.

[7] *Pistoles* Gold coins used as currency internationally.

[8] *Wilkes* Irish-born actor and prominent theater manager Robert Wilks (c. 1665–1732).

a Publisher in Paternoster Row,[1] to write for him a Weekly Paper like the Spectator, on certain Conditions, which Roberts did not approve. Then he endeavour'd to get Employment as a Hackney Writer to copy for the Stationers & Lawyers about the Temple:[2] but could find no Vacancy.—

I immediately got into Work at Palmer's then a famous Printing House in Bartholomew Close;[3] and here I continu'd near a Year. I was pretty diligent; but spent with Ralph a good deal of my Earnings in going to Plays & other Places of Amusement. We had together consum'd all my Pistoles, and now just rubb'd on from hand to mouth. He seem'd quite to forget his Wife & Child, and I by degrees my Engagements with Miss Read, to whom I never wrote more than one Letter, & that was to let her know I was not likely soon to return. This was another of the great Errata of my Life, which I should wish to correct if I were to live it over again.—In fact, by our Expences, I was constantly kept unable to pay my Passage.

At Palmer's I was employ'd in Composing for the second Edition of Woollaston's Religion of Nature.[4] Some of his Reasonings not appearing to me well-founded, I wrote a little metaphysical Piece, in which I made Remarks on them. It was entitled, *A Dissertation on Liberty & Necessity, Pleasure and Pain.*[5]—I inscrib'd it to my Friend Ralph.—I printed a small Number. It occasion'd my being more consider'd by Mr Palmer, as a young Man of some Ingenuity, tho' he seriously expostulated with me upon the Principles of my Pamphlet which to him appear'd abominable. My printing this Pamphlet was another Erratum.

While I lodg'd in Little Britain I made an Acquaintance with one Wilcox a Bookseller, whose Shop was at the next Door. He had an immense Collection of second-hand Books. Circulating Libraries were not then in Use; but we agreed that on certain reasonable Terms which I have now forgotten, I might take, read & return any of his Books. This I esteem'd a great Advantage, & I made as much Use of it as I could.—

My Pamphlet by some means falling into the Hands of one Lyons, a Surgeon, Author of a Book intituled *The Infallibility of Human Judgment*, it occasioned an Acquaintance between us; he took great Notice of me, call'd on me often, to converse on those Subjects, carried me to the Horns a pale Ale-House in [blank] Lane, Cheapside, and introduc'd me to Dr Mandevile, Author of the Fable of the Bees[6] who had a Club there, of which he was the Soul, being a most facetious[7] entertaining Companion. Lyons too introduc'd me to Dr Pemberton, at Batson's Coffee House, who promis'd to give me an Opportunity some time or other of seeing Sir Isaac Newton,[8] of which I was extreamly desirous; but this never happened.

I had brought over a few Curiosities among which the principal was a Purse made of the Asbestos, which purifies by Fire.[9] Sir Hans Sloane[10] heard of it, came to see me, and invited me to his House in Bloomsbury Square; where he show'd me all his Curiosities, and

[1] *Paternoster Row* Street near Little Britain, known as a center of the book and printing trade.

[2] *about the Temple* Around the notable central London legal district known as the Temple.

[3] *Bartholomew Close* Near Little Britain.

[4] *Woollaston's Religion of Nature* 1722 philosophical work by Anglican priest William Woolaston, which proposed a system of morality that could be discerned directly from "nature" rather than from religious doctrine; the work had a substantial influence on the development of Deism later in the eighteenth century.

[5] *A Dissertation … and Pain* Franklin's pamphlet argues against commonplace conceptions of free will and morality, to the point of claiming that virtue and vice are nonexistent. He later destroyed all copies of the work that he could find, though a few have survived to the twenty-first century.

[6] *the Fable of the Bees* 1714 work by Dutch-born philosopher Bernard Mandeville, which proposes, through an allegory depicting a hive of bees, that social cohesion and economic prosperity are ultimately the result of the individual pursuit of personal gain, rather than of virtuous action or generosity.

[7] *facetious* Elegantly amusing and agreeable.

[8] *Dr Pemberton* English physician and mathematician Henry Pemberton (1694–1771); *Sir Isaac Newton* English physicist and mathematician (1642–1727) who formulated a number of revolutionary theories about the physical world, including the law of gravity; he was a friend of Pemberton's.

[9] *a Purse … by Fire* The mineral asbestos—widely known as an effective fire retardant—is formed of thin fibrous crystals, which can be spun and woven into a coarse sort of cloth—though this product never came into widespread use.

[10] *Sir Hans Sloane* Anglo-Irish naturalist and collector (1660–1753), whose collections would form the basis of the British Museum and the Natural History Museum; Franklin's asbestos purse remains part of the Natural History Museum's collection.

persuaded me to let him add that to the Number, for which he paid me handsomely.—

In our House there lodg'd a young Woman; a Millener,[1] who I think had a Shop in the Cloisters. She had been genteelly bred; was sensible & lively, and of most pleasing Conversation.—Ralph read Plays to her in the Evenings, they grew intimate, she took another Lodging, and he follow'd her. They liv'd together some time, but he being still out of Business, & her Income not sufficient to maintain them with her Child, he took a Resolution of going from London, to try for a Country School, which he thought himself well qualify'd to undertake, as he wrote an excellent Hand, & was a Master of Arithmetic & Accounts.—This however he deem'd a Business below him, & confident of future better Fortune when he should be unwilling to have it known that he once was so meanly employ'd, he chang'd his Name, & did me the Honour to assume mine.—For I soon after had a Letter from him, acquainting me, that he was settled in a small Village in Berkshire, I think it was, where he taught reading & writing to 10 or a dozen Boys at 6 pence each per Week, recommending Mrs T. to my Care, and desiring me to write to him directing for Mr Franklin Schoolmaster at such a Place. He continu'd to write frequently, sending me large Specimens of an Epic Poem, which he was then composing, and desiring my Remarks & Corrections.—These I gave him from time to time, but endeavour'd rather to discourage his Proceeding. One of Young's[2] Satires was then just publish'd. I copy'd & sent him a great Part of it, which set in a strong Light the Folly of pursuing the Muses[3] with any Hope of Advancement by them. All was in vain. Sheets of the Poem continu'd to come by every Post. In the mean time Mrs T. having on his Account lost her Friends & Business, was often in Distresses, & us'd to send for me, and borrow what I could spare to help her out of them. I grew fond of her Company, and being at that time under no Religious Restraint, & presuming on my Importance to her, I attempted Familiarities, (another Erratum) which she repuls'd with a proper

Resentment, and acquainted him with my Behaviour. This made a Breach between us, & when he return'd again to London, he let me know he thought I had cancel'd all the Obligations he had been under to me.—So I found I was never to expect his Repaying me what I lent to him or advanc'd for him. This was however not then of much Consequence, as he was totally unable.—And in the Loss of his Friendship I found my self reliev'd from a Burthen. I now began to think of getting a little Money beforehand; and expecting better Work, I left Palmer's to work at Watts's near Lincoln's Inn Fields, a still greater Printing House. Here I continu'd all the rest of my Stay in London.

At my first Admission into this Printing House, I took to working at Press, imagining I felt a Want of the Bodily Exercise I had been us'd to in America, where Presswork is mix'd with Composing.[4] I drank only Water; the other Workmen, near 50 in Number, were great Guzzlers of Beer. On occasion I carried up & down Stairs a large Form of Types in each hand, when others carried but one in both Hands. They wonder'd to see from this & several Instances that the Water-American as they call'd me was *stronger* than themselves who drunk *strong* Beer. We had an Alehouse Boy who attended always in the House to supply the Workmen. My Companion at the Press, drank every day a Pint before Breakfast, a Pint at Breakfast with his Bread and Cheese; a Pint between Breakfast and Dinner; a Pint at Dinner; a Pint in the Afternoon about Six o'clock, and another when he had done his Day's-Work. I thought it a detestable Custom.—But it was necessary, he suppos'd, to drink *strong* Beer that he might be *strong* to labour. I endeavour'd to convince him that the Bodily Strength afforded by Beer could only be in proportion to the Grain or Flour of the Barley dissolved in the Water of which it was made; that there was more Flour in a Pennyworth of Bread, and therefore if he would eat that with a Pint of Water, it would give him more Strength than a Quart of Beer.—He drank on however, & had 4 or 5 Shillings to pay out of his Wages every Saturday Night for that muddling Liquor; an Expence

[1] *Millener* Milliner; purveyor of hats and other accessories.

[2] *Young* English poet Edward Young, who published a series of satirical works between 1725 and 1728.

[3] *the Muses* I.e., an artistic or literary career; the Muses are Greek mythological figures representing the arts.

[4] *where Presswork … with Composing* I.e., where the task of setting type is done by the same workers as the more physically active task of working the printing press.

I was free from.—And thus these poor Devils keep themselves always under.[1]

Watts after some Weeks desiring to have me in the Composing-Room, I left the Pressmen. A new *Bienvenu* or Sum for Drink, being 5/, was demanded of me by the Compostors. I thought it an Imposition, as I had paid below.[2] The Master thought so too, and forbad my Paying it. I stood out two or three Weeks, was accordingly considered as an Excommunicate, and had so many little Pieces of private Mischief done me, by mixing my Sorts, transposing my Pages, breaking my Matter,[3] &c. &c. if I were ever so little out of the Room, & all ascrib'd to the Chapel Ghost, which they said ever haunted those not regularly admitted, that notwithstanding the Master's Protection, I found myself oblig'd to comply and pay the Money; convinc'd of the Folly of being on ill Terms with those one is to live with continually. I was now on a fair Footing with them, and soon acquir'd considerable Influence. I propos'd some reasonable Alterations in their[4] Chapel Laws, and carried them against all Opposition. From my Example a great Part of them, left their muddling Breakfast of Beer & Bread & Cheese, finding they could with me be supply'd from a neighbouring House with a large Porringer[5] of hot Water-gruel, sprinkled with Pepper, crumb'd with Bread, & a Bit of Butter in it, for the Price of a Pint of Beer, viz, three half-pence. This was a more comfortable as well as cheaper Breakfast, & kept their Heads clearer.—Those who continu'd sotting with Beer all day, were often, by not paying, out of Credit at the Alehouse, and us'd to make Interest with me to get Beer, *their Light*, as they phras'd it, *being out*. I watch'd the Pay table on Saturday Night, & collected what I stood engag'd for them, having to pay some times near Thirty Shillings a Week

on their Accounts.—This, and my being esteem'd a pretty good Riggite, that is a jocular verbal Satyrist, supported my Consequence in the Society.—My constant Attendance, (I never making a St. Monday[6]), recommended me to the Master; and my uncommon Quickness at Composing, occasion'd my being put upon all Work of Dispatch[7] which was generally better paid. So I went on now very agreably.—

My Lodging in Little Britain being too remote, I found another in Duke-street opposite to the Romish[8] Chapel. It was two pair of Stairs backwards at an Italian Warehouse. A Widow Lady kept the House; she had a Daughter & a Maid Servant, and a Journey-man who attended the Warehouse, but lodg'd abroad.— After sending to enquire my Character at the House where I last lodg'd, she agreed to take me in at the same Rate 3/6[9] per Week, cheaper as she said from the Protection she expected in having a Man lodge in the House. She was a Widow, an elderly Woman, had been bred a Protestant, being a Clergyman's Daughter, but was converted to the Catholic Religion by her Husband, whose Memory she much revered, had lived much among People of Distinction, and knew a 1000 Anecdotes of them as far back as the Times of Charles the second.[10] She was lame in her Knees with the Gout, and therefore seldom stirr'd out of her Room, so sometimes wanted Company; and hers was so highly amusing to me; that I was sure to spend an Evening with her whenever she desired it. Our Supper was only half an Anchovy each, on a very little Strip of Bread & Butter, and half a Pint of Ale between us.—But the Entertainment was in her Conversation. My always keeping good Hours, and giving little Trouble in the Family, made her unwilling to part with me; so that, when I talk'd of a Lodging I had heard of, nearer my Business, for 2/[11] a Week, which, intent as I now was

[1] *under* I.e., poor.

[2] *A new Bienvenu … below* I.e., because Franklin was employed in a new position, the "compostors" or typesetters demanded of him the fee ordinarily exacted of new employees, despite the fact that he had already paid that same fee when he began his previous job as a pressman; *5/* Five shillings.

[3] *Sorts* Individual pieces of type; *Matter* Types arranged and ready for printing.

[4] [Franklin's note] A Printing House is always called a Chappel by the Workmen.—

[5] *Porringer* Small, handled bowl for soups and porridges.

[6] *making a St. Monday* Treating Monday as a holiday (presumably implying missing or being late for work due to the previous night's merriment).

[7] *Work of Dispatch* I.e., work that needs to be completed promptly.

[8] *Romish* Roman Catholic.

[9] *3/6* Three shillings and sixpence.

[10] *Charles the second* King of England, Scotland, and Ireland from 1660 to 1685.

[11] *2/* Two shillings.

on saving Money, made some Difference; she bid me not think of it, for she would abate me two Shillings a Week for the future, so I remain'd with her at 1/6¹ as long as I staid in London.—

In a Garret of her House there lived a Maiden Lady of 70 in the most retired² Manner, of whom my Landlady gave me this Account, that she was a Roman-Catholic, had been sent abroad when young & lodg'd in a Nunnery with an Intent of becoming a Nun: but the Country not agreeing with her, she return'd to England, where there being no Nunnery, she had vow'd to lead the Life of a Nun as near as might be done in those Circumstances: Accordingly She had given all her Estate to charitable Uses, reserving only Twelve Pounds a Year to live on, and out of this Sum she still gave a great deal in Charity, living her self on Watergruel only, & using no Fire but to boil it.—She had lived many Years in that Garret, being permitted to remain there gratis by successive catholic Tenants of the House below, as they deem'd it a Blessing to have her there. A Priest visited her, to confess her every Day. I have ask'd her, says my Landlady, how she, as she liv'd, could possibly find so much Employment for a Confessor? O, says she, it is impossible to avoid *vain Thoughts*. I was permitted once to visit her: She was chearful & polite, & convers'd pleasantly. The Room was clean, but had no other Furniture than a Matras, a Table with a Crucifix & Book, a Stool, which she gave me to sit on, and a Picture over the Chimney of St. *Veronica*, displaying her Handkerchief with the miraculous Figure of Christ's bleeding Face on it,³ which she explain'd to me with great Seriousness. She look'd pale, but was never sick, and I give it as another Instance on how small an Income Life & Health may be supported.—

At Watts's Printinghouse I contracted an Acquaintance with an ingenious young Man, one Wygate, who having wealthy Relations, had been better educated than most

Printers, was a tolerable Latinist, spoke French, & lov'd Reading. I taught him, & a Friend of his, to swim, at twice going into the River, & they soon became good Swimmers. They introduc'd me to some Gentlemen from the Country who went to Chelsea by Water to see the College and Don Saltero's Curiosities.⁴ In our Return, at the Request of the Company, whose Curiosity Wygate had excited, I stript & leapt into the River, & swam from near Chelsea to Blackfryars,⁵ performing on the Way many Feats of Activity both upon & under Water, that surpriz'd & pleas'd those to whom they were Novelties.—I had from a Child been ever delighted with this Exercise, had studied & practis'd all Thevenot's⁶ Motions & Positions, added some of my own, aiming at the graceful & easy, as well as the Useful.—All these I took this Occasion of exhibiting to the Company, & was much flatter'd by their Admiration.—And Wygate, who was desirous of becoming a Master, grew more & more attach'd to me on that account, as well as from the Similarity of our Studies. He at length propos'd to me travelling all over Europe together, supporting ourselves every where by working at our Business. I was once inclin'd to it. But mentioning it to my good Friend Mr Denham, with whom I often spent an Hour, when I had Leisure. He dissuaded me from it; advising me to think only of returning to Pensilvania, which he was now about to do.—

I must record one Trait of this good Man's Character. He had formerly been in Business at Bristol, but fail'd in Debt to a Number of People, compounded⁷ and went to America. There, by a close Application to Business as a Merchant, he acquir'd a plentiful Fortune in a few Years. Returning to England in the Ship with

¹ *1/6* One shilling and sixpence.

² *retired* Reclusive.

³ *St. Veronica … on it* Saint Veronica is said to have witnessed Christ on his journey to his execution at Calvary, and to have been moved by his suffering to offer him her veil to wipe his bleeding head. According to Christian legend, an image of Christ's face was then imprinted upon the veil, which became known as the Veil of Veronica, a sacred relic in Catholic worship and a common subject of Catholic artwork.

⁴ *Chelsea … Don Saltero's Curiosities* Don Saltero's was a well-known coffeehouse in the riverside district of Chelsea, founded in 1695 by a former servant of Hans Sloane and remarkable for its housing of many artifacts and curiosities. The College Franklin refers to is in fact the Chelsea Hospital, founded in 1682 on the former site of the Chelsea theological college.

⁵ *Blackfryars* District of central London, approximately four miles downriver from Chelsea.

⁶ *Thevenot* Melchisédech Thévenot, French scientist, cartographer, and diplomat whose *The Art of Swimming* (1696) was among the first published works to discuss swimming and give instruction on swimming techniques.

⁷ *compounded* Made an agreement for paying only part of his debts.

me, He invited his old Creditors to an Entertainment, at which he thank'd them for the easy Composition[1] they had favour'd him with, & when they expected nothing but the Treat, every Man at the first Remove,[2] found under his Plate an Order on a Banker for the full Amount of the unpaid Remainder with Interest.

He now told me he was about to return to Philadelphia, and should carry over a great Quantity of Goods in order to open a Store there: He propos'd to take me over as his Clerk, to keep his Books (in which he would instruct me) copy his Letters, and attend the Store. He added, that as soon as I should be acquainted with mercantile Business he would promote me by sending me with a Cargo of Flour & Bread &c to the West Indies, and procure me Commissions from others; which would be profitable, & if I manag'd well, would establish me handsomely. The Thing pleas'd me, for I was grown tired of London, remember'd with Pleasure the happy Months I had spent in Pennsylvania, and wish'd again to see it. Therefore I immediately agreed, on the Terms of Fifty Pounds a Year Pensylvania Money; less indeed than my present Gettings as a Compostor, but affording a better Prospect.—

I now took Leave of Printing, as I thought for ever, and was daily employ'd in my new Business; going about with Mr Denham among the Tradesmen, to purchase various Articles, & see them pack'd up, doing Errands, calling upon Workmen to dispatch, &c. and when all was on board, I had a few Days Leisure. On one of these Days I was to my Surprize sent for by a great Man I knew only by Name, a Sir William Wyndham[3] and I waited upon him. He had heard by some means or other of my Swimming from Chelsey to Blackfryars, and of my teaching Wygate and another young Man to swim in a few Hours. He had two Sons about to set out on their Travels;[4] he wish'd to have them first taught Swimming; and propos'd to gratify me handsomely if I

would teach them.—They were not yet come to Town and my Stay was uncertain, so I could not undertake it. But from this Incident I thought it likely, that if I were to remain in England and open a Swimming School, I might get a good deal of Money.—And it struck me so strongly, that had the Overture been sooner made me, probably I should not so soon have returned to America.—After Many Years, you & I had something of more Importance to do with one of these Sons of Sir William Wyndham, become Earl of Egremont, which I shall mention in its Place.[5]—

Thus I spent about 18 Months in London. Most Part of the Time, I work'd hard at my Business, & spent but little upon my self except in seeing Plays, & in Books.—My Friend Ralph had kept me poor. He owed me about 27 Pounds; which I was now never likely to receive; a great Sum out of my small Earnings. I lov'd him notwithstanding, for he had many amiable Qualities.—tho' I had by no means improv'd my Fortune.—But I had pick'd up some very ingenious Acquaintance whose Conversation was of great Advantage to me, and I had read considerably.

We sail'd from Gravesend on the 23[d] of July 1726.— For The Incidents of the Voyage, I refer you to my Journal, where you will find them all minutely related. Perhaps the most important Part of that Journal is the *Plan*[6] to be found in it which I formed at Sea, for regulating my future Conduct in Life. It is the more remarkable, as being form'd when I was so young, and yet being pretty faithfully adhered to quite thro' to old Age.—We landed in Philadelphia the 11th of October, where I found sundry Alterations. Keith was no longer Governor, being superseded by Major Gordon:[7] I met him walking the Streets as a common Citizen. He seem'd a little asham'd at seeing me, but pass'd without saying any thing. I should have been as much asham'd

[1] *Composition* I.e., the settlement of his debts.

[2] *Remove* I.e., of plates.

[3] *Sir William Wyndham* English politician (c. 1688–1740) who during this period was serving as leader of the Tory opposition in the House of Commons.

[4] *their Travels* Throughout the eighteenth century (and well into the nineteenth) it was common for young British men of means to travel the European continent upon the completion of their formal education.

[5] *something of … its Place* The son referred to is Charles Wyndham, 2nd Earl of Egremont, who as Secretary of State for the Southern Department (1761–63) in the British Cabinet had oversight of the American colonies. Franklin does not in fact return to this subject in the *Autobiography*.

[6] *my Journal … the Plan* This plan seems to have been lost, not appearing in the version of the journal that survives; a small segment Franklin referred to as "the preamble and heads of it" has survived through a 1785 copy by his friend William Rawle.

[7] *Major Gordon* Patrick Gordon, a military veteran who served as Pennsylvania's governor from 1726 to 1736.

at seeing Miss Read, had not her Friends despairing with Reason of my Return, after the Receipt of my Letter, persuaded her to marry another, one Rogers, a Potter, which was done in my Absence. With him however she was never happy, and soon parted from him, refusing to cohabit with him, or bear his Name It being now said that he had another Wife. He was a worthless Fellow tho' an excellent Workman which was the Temptation to her Friends. He got into Debt, ran away in 1727 or 28, went to the West Indies, and died there. Keimer had got a better House, a Shop well supply'd with Stationary, plenty of new Types, a number of Hands tho' none good, and seem'd to have a great deal of Business.

Mr Denham took a Store in Water Street, where we open'd our Goods. I attended the Business diligently, studied Accounts, and grew in a little Time expert at selling.—We lodg'd and boarded together, he counsell'd me as a Father, having a sincere Regard for me: I respected & lov'd him: and we might have gone on together very happily: But in the Beginning of February 1726/7[1] when I had just pass'd my 21st Year, we both were taken ill. My Distemper was a Pleurisy,[2] which very nearly carried me off:—I suffered a good deal, gave up the Point in my own mind, & was rather disappointed when I found my self recovering; regretting in some degree that I must now sometime or other have all that disagreeable Work to do over again.—I forget what his Distemper was. It held him a long time, and at length carried him off. He left me a small Legacy in a nuncupative[3] Will, as a Token of his Kindness for me, and he left me once more to the wide World. For the Store was taken into the Care of his Executors, and my Employment under him ended:—My Brother-in-law Homes, being now at Philadelphia, advis'd my Return to my Business. And Keimer tempted me with an Offer of large Wages by the Year to come & take the Management of his Printing-House that he might better attend his Stationer's Shop.—I had heard a bad Character of him in London, from his Wife & her Friends, & was not fond of having any more to do with him. I try'd for farther Employment as a Merchant's Clerk; but not readily meeting with any, I clos'd again with Keimer.—

I found in *his* House these Hands; Hugh Meredith a Welsh-Pensilvanian, 30 Years of Age, bred to Country Work: honest, sensible, had a great deal of solid Observation, was something of a Reader, but given to drink:—Stephen Potts, a young Country Man of full Age, bred to the Same:—of uncommon natural Parts, & great Wit & Humour, but a little idle.— These he had agreed with at extream low Wages, per Week, to be rais'd a Shilling every 3 Months, as they would deserve by improving in their Business, & the Expectation of these high Wages to come on hereafter was what he had drawn them in with.—Meredith was to work at Press, Potts at Bookbinding, which he by Agreement, was to teach them, tho' he knew neither one nor t'other. John —— a wild Irishman brought up to no Business, whose Service for 4 Years Keimer had purchas'd from the Captain of a Ship. He too was to be made a Pressman. George Webb, an Oxford Scholar, whose Time for 4 Years he had likewise bought, intending him for a Compositor: of whom more presently. And David Harry, a Country Boy, whom he had taken Apprentice. I soon perceiv'd that the Intention of engaging me at Wages so much higher than he had been us'd to give, was to have these raw cheap Hands form'd thro' me, and as soon as I had instructed them, then, they being all articled to him, he should be able to do without me.—I went on however, very cheerfully; put his Printing House in Order, which had been in great Confusion, and brought his Hands by degrees to mind their Business and to do it better.

It was an odd Thing to find an Oxford Scholar in the Situation of a bought Servant. He was not more than 18 Years of Age, & gave me this Account of himself; that he was born in Gloucester, educated at a Grammar School there, had been distinguish'd among the Scholars for some apparent Superiority in performing his Part when they exhibited Plays; belong'd to the Witty Club there, and had written some Pieces in Prose & Verse which were printed in the Gloucester Newspapers.—Thence he was sent to Oxford; where

[1] *February 1726/7* According to the Gregorian calendar, the year of Franklin's and Denham's illnesses was 1727. Franklin here employs the practice of dual dating, which accounts for the fact that the date of the beginning of the new year varied among countries still using the Julian calendar, such as Britain and its colonies, where the new year was marked on 25 March.

[2] *Pleurisy* Painful inflammation of the lungs.

[3] *nuncupative* Given orally rather than written down.

he continu'd about a Year, but not well-satisfy'd, wishing of all things to see London & become a Player.[1] At length receiving his Quarterly Allowance of 15 Guineas, instead of discharging his Debts, he walk'd out of Town, hid his Gown in a Furz[2] Bush, and footed it to London, where having no Friend to advise him, he fell into bad Company, soon spent his Guineas, found no means of being introduc'd among the Players, grew necessitous, pawn'd his Cloaths & wanted Bread. Walking the Street very hungry, & not knowing what to do with himself, a Crimp's Bill[3] was put into his Hand, offering immediate Entertainment & Encouragement to such as would bind themselves to serve in America. He went directly, sign'd the Indentures, was put into the Ship & came over; never writing a Line to acquaint his Friends what was become of him. He was lively, witty, good-natur'd and a pleasant Companion; but idle, thoughtless & imprudent to the last Degree.

John the Irishman soon ran away. With the rest I began to live very agreeably; for they all respected me, the more as they found Keimer incapable of instructing them, and that from me they learnt something daily. We never work'd on Saturday, that being Keimer's Sabbath. So I had two Days for Reading. My Acquaintance with ingenious People in the Town, increased. Keimer himself treated me with great Civility & apparent Regard; and nothing now made me uneasy but my Debt to Vernon, which I was yet unable to pay being hitherto but a poor Oeconomist.[4]—He however kindly made no Demand of it.

Our Printing House often wanted Sorts, and there was no Letter Founder[5] in America. I had seen Types cast at James's in London, but without much Attention to the Manner: However I now contriv'd a Mould, made use of the Letters we had, as Puncheons, struck

the Matrices[6] in Lead, and thus supply'd in a pretty tolerable way all Deficiencies. I also engrav'd several Things on occasion. I made the Ink, I was Warehouseman & every thing, in short quite a Factotum.[7]—

But however serviceable I might be, I found that my Services became every Day of less Importance, as the other Hands improv'd in the Business. And when Keimer paid my second Quarter's Wages, he let me know that he felt them too heavy, and thought I should make an Abatement. He grew by degrees less civil, put on more of the Master, frequently found Fault, was captious[8] and seem'd ready for an Out-breaking. I went on nevertheless with a good deal of Patience, thinking that his incumber'd Circumstances were partly the Cause. At length a Trifle snapt our Connexion. For a great Noise happening near the Courthouse, I put my Head out of the Window to see what was the Matter. Keimer being in the Street look'd up & saw me, call'd out to me in a loud Voice and angry Tone to mind my Business, adding some reproachful Words, that nettled me the more for their Publicity, all the Neighbours who were looking out on the same Occasion being Witnesses how I was treated. He came up immediately into the Printing-House, continu'd the Quarrel, high Words pass'd on both Sides, he gave me the Quarter's Warning[9] we had stipulated, expressing a Wish that he had not been oblig'd to so long a Warning: I told him his Wish was unnecessary for I would leave him that Instant; and so taking my Hat walk'd out of Doors; desiring Meredith whom I saw below to take care of some Things I left, & bring them to my Lodging.—

Meredith came accordingly in the Evening, when we talk'd my Affair over. He had conceiv'd a great Regard for me, & was very unwilling that I should leave the House while he remain'd in it. He dissuaded me from returning to my native Country which I began to think of. He reminded me that Keimer was in debt for all he possess'd, that his Creditors began to be uneasy, that he kept his Shop miserably, sold often without Profit for ready Money, and often trusted without keeping Accounts. That he must therefore fail; which

[1] *Player* Actor.

[2] *Gown* Scholar's robes; *Furz* Furze, thorny shrub common throughout England, also known as gorse.

[3] *Crimp's Bill* A "crimp" is an agent for a shipping company, especially one who procures or impresses workers. Here, the "crimp's bill" is presumably an advertisement for a position of indentured servitude in the colonies.

[4] *Oeconomist* Economist; manager of one's finances.

[5] *Letter Founder* One who casts metal into types.

[6] *Puncheons* Stamps; *Matrices* Molds.

[7] *Factotum* Person who does all manner of work.

[8] *captious* Inclined to criticize or find fault.

[9] *Quarter's Warning* I.e., notice of dismissal, to be given a quarter-year in advance.

would make a Vacancy I might profit of.—I objected my Want of Money. He then let me know, that his Father had a high Opinion of me, and from some Discourse that had pass'd between them, he was sure would advance Money to set us up, if I would enter into Partnership with him.—My Time, says he, will be out with Keimer in the Spring. By that time we may have our Press & Types in from London:—I am sensible I am no Workman. If you like it, Your Skill in the Business shall be set against the Stock I furnish; and we will share the Profits equally.—The Proposal was agreable, and I consented. His Father was in Town, and approv'd of it, the more as he saw I had great Influence with his Son, had prevail'd on him to abstain long from Dramdrinking, and he hop'd might break him of that wretched Habit entirely, when we came to be so closely connected. I gave an Inventory to the Father, who carry'd it to a Merchant; the Things were sent for; the Secret was to be kept till they should arrive, and in the mean time I was to get Work if I could at the other Printing House.—But I found no Vacancy there, and so remain'd idle a few Days, when Keimer, on a Prospect of being employ'd to print some Paper-money, in New Jersey, which would require Cuts & various Types that I only could supply, and apprehending Bradford might engage me & get the Jobb from him, sent me a very civil Message, that old Friends should not part for a few Words the Effect of sudden Passion, and wishing me to return. Meredith persuaded me to comply, as it would give more Opportunity for his Improvement under my daily Instructions.—So I return'd, and we went on more smoothly than for some time before.— The New Jersey Jobb was obtain'd. I contriv'd a Copper-Plate Press for it, the first that had been seen in the Country.—I cut several Ornaments and Checks for the Bills.[1] We went together to Burlington, where I executed the Whole to Satisfaction, & he received so large a Sum for the Work, as to be enabled thereby to keep his Head much longer above Water.—

At Burlington I made an Acquaintance with many principal People of the Province. Several of them had been appointed by the Assembly a Committee to attend the Press, and take Care that no more Bills were printed than the Law directed. They were therefore by Turns constantly with us, and generally he who attended brought with him a Friend or two for Company. My Mind having been much more improv'd by Reading than Keimer's, I suppose it was for that Reason my Conversation seem'd to be more valu'd. They had me to their Houses, introduc'd me to their Friends and show'd me much Civility, while he, tho' the Master, was a little neglected. In truth he was an odd Fish, ignorant of common Life, fond of rudely opposing receiv'd Opinions, slovenly to extream dirtiness, enthusiastic in some Points of Religion, and a little Knavish withal. We continu'd there near 3 Months, and by that time I could reckon among my acquired Friends, Judge Allen, Samuel Bustill, the Secretary of the Province, Isaac Pearson, Joseph Cooper & several of the Smiths, Members of Assembly, and Isaac Decow the Surveyor General. The latter was a shrewd sagacious old Man, who told me that he began for himself when young by wheeling Clay for the Brickmakers, learnt to write after he was of Age, cary'd the Chain[2] for Surveyors, who taught him Surveying, and he had now by his Industry acquir'd a good Estate; and says he, I foresee, that you will soon work this Man out of his Business & make a Fortune in it at Philadelphia. He had not then the least Intimation of my Intention to set up there or any where.—These Friends were afterwards of great Use to me, as I occasionally was to some of them.—They all continued their Regard for me as long as they lived.—

Before I enter upon my public Appearance in Business, it may be well to let you know the then State of my Mind, with regard to my Principles and Morals, that you may see how far those influenc'd the future Events of my Life. My Parent's had early given me religious Impressions, and brought me through my Childhood piously in the Dissenting Way.[3] But I was scarce 15 when, after doubting by turns of several Points as I found them disputed in the different Books I read, I began to doubt of Revelation[4] it self. Some Books

[1] *cut several … the Bills* I.e., made engravings for the ornamental designs and checked patterns for the paper money.

[2] *Chain* Surveying tool used for measuring distance; the length of one chain is sixty-six feet.

[3] *in the Dissenting Way* I.e., as a Congregationalist rather than an Episcopalian (Anglican).

[4] *Revelation* I.e., the idea that the Bible is the word of God revealed to humanity.

against Deism[1] fell into my Hands; they were said to be the Substance of Sermons preached at Boyle's[2] Lectures. It happened that they wrought an Effect on me quite contrary to what was intended by them: For the Arguments of the Deists which were quoted to be refuted, appeared to me much Stronger than the Refutations. In short I soon became a thorough Deist. My Arguments perverted some others, particularly Collins & Ralph: but each of them having afterwards wrong'd me greatly without the least Compunction, and recollecting Keith's Conduct towards me, (who was another Freethinker) and my own towards Vernon & Miss Read which at Times gave me great Trouble, I began to suspect that this Doctrine tho' it might be true, was not very useful.—My London Pamphlet, which had for its Motto those Lines of Dryden

> ——Whatever is, is right
> Tho' purblind Man / Sees but a Part of
> The Chain, the nearest Link,
> His Eyes not carrying to the equal Beam,
> That poizes all above.[3]

And from the Attributes of God, his infinite Wisdom, Goodness & Power concluded that nothing could possibly be wrong in the World, & that Vice & Virtue were empty Distinctions, no such Things existing: appear'd now not so clever a Performance as I once thought it; and I doubted whether some Error had not insinuated itself unperceiv'd, into my Argument, so as to infect all that follow'd, as is common in metaphysical Reasonings.—I grew convinc'd that *Truth, Sincerity & Integrity* in Dealings between Man & Man, were

of the utmost Importance to the Felicity of Life, and I form'd written Resolutions, (wh^ch. still remain in my Journal Book) to practise them ever while I lived. Revelation had indeed no weight with me as such; but I entertain'd an Opinion, that tho' certain Actions might not be bad *because* they were forbidden by it, or good *because* it commanded them; yet probably those Actions might be forbidden *because* they were bad for us, or commanded *because* they were beneficial to us, in their own Natures, all the Circumstances of things considered. And this Persuasion, with the kind hand of Providence, or some guardian Angel, or accidental favourable Circumstances & Situations, or all together, preserved me (thro' this dangerous Time of Youth & the hazardous Situations I was sometimes in among Strangers, remote from the Eye & Advice of my Father,) without any *wilful* gross Immorality or Injustice that might have been expected from my Want of Religion.—I say *wilful*, because the Instances I have mentioned, had something of *Necessity* in them, from my Youth, Inexperience, & the Knavery of others.—I had therefore a tolerable Character to begin the World with, I valued it properly, & determin'd to preserve it.—

We had not been long return'd to Philadelphia, before the New Types arriv'd from London.—We settled with Keimer, & left him by his Consent before he heard of it.—We found a House to hire near the Market, and took it. To lessen the Rent, (which was then but 24£ a Year tho' I have since known it to let for 70) We took in Thomas Godfrey a Glazier, & his Family, who were to pay a considerable Part of it to us, and we to board with them. We had scarce opened our Letters & put our Press in Order, before George House, an Acquaintance of mine, brought a Countryman to us; whom he had met in the Street enquiring for a Printer. All our Cash was now expended in the Variety of Particulars we had been obliged to procure, & this Countryman's Five Shillings, being our First Fruits & coming so seasonably, gave me more Pleasure than any Crown[4] I have since earn'd; and the Gratitude I felt towards House, has made me often more ready than perhaps I should otherwise have been to assist young Beginners.—

[1] *Deism* School of religious and philosophical thought that grew to prominence during the Enlightenment, proposing that God exists only as the creator of the universe, and has had little or no influence on the world since creation; more generally, Deists deny the literal truth or importance of the Bible and other teachings of formal religion.

[2] *Boyle* English chemist and Anglican priest Robert Boyle (1627–91), who lectured against Deism and other forms of religious skepticism.

[3] *Whatever is … all above* Franklin's quotation and attribution is slightly mistaken. The first line is in fact from Alexander Pope's *An Essay on Man* (1733–34), the final line of Epistle I—though it bears a resemblance to a line from John Dryden's 1679 play *Oedipus*: "What ever is, is in its causes just" (3.1.243). The remainder of the quotation is from Dryden's *Oedipus*, 3.1.245–48.

[4] *Crown* Five-shilling coin.

There are Croakers[1] in every Country always boding its Ruin. Such a one then lived in Philadelphia, a Person of Note, an elderly Man, with a wise Look and very grave Manner of Speaking. His Name was Samuel Mickle. This Gentleman, a Stranger to me, stopt one Day at my Door, and ask'd me if I was the young Man who had lately opened a new Printing-house: Being answer'd in the Affirmative; He said he was sorry for me; because it was an expensive Undertaking, & the Expence would be lost, for Philadelphia was a sinking Place, the People already half Bankrupts or near being so; all Appearances to the contrary such as new Buildings & the Rise of Rents, being to his certain Knowledge fallacious; for they were in fact among the Things that would soon ruin us. And he gave me such a Detail of Misfortunes now existing or that were soon to exist, that he left me half-melancholy. Had I known him before I engag'd in this Business, probably I never should have done it.—This Man continu'd to live in this decaying Place, & to declaim[2] in the same Strain, refusing for many Years to buy a House there, because all was going to Destruction, and at last I had the Pleasure of seeing him give five times as much for one as he might have bought it for when he first began his Croaking.—

I should have mention'd before, that in the Autumn of the preceding Year, I had form'd most of my ingenious Acquaintance into a Club, for mutual Improvement, which we call'd the Junto.[3] We met on Friday Evenings. The Rules I drew up, requir'd that every Member in his Turn should produce one or more Queries on any Point of Morals, Politics or Natural Philosophy, to be discuss'd by the Company, and once in three Months produce and read an Essay of his own Writing on any Subject he pleased. Our Debates were to be under the Direction of a President, and to be conducted in the sincere Spirit of Enquiry after Truth, without fondness for Dispute, or Desire of Victory; and to prevent Warmth,[4] all Expressions of Positiveness in Opinions, or of direct Contradiction, were after some time made

contraband & prohibited under small pecuniary Penalties. The first Members were, Joseph Brientnal, a Copyer of Deeds for the Scriveners; a good-natur'd friendly middle-ag'd Man, a great Lover of Poetry, reading all he could meet with, & writing some that was tolerable; very ingenious in many little Nicknackeries, & of sensible Conversation. Thomas Godfrey, a self-taught Mathematician, great in his Way, & afterwards Inventor of what is now call'd Hadley's Quadrant.[5] But he knew little out of his way, and was not a pleasing Companion, as like most Great Mathematicians I have met with, he expected unusual Precision in every thing said, or was forever denying or distinguishing upon Trifles,[6] to the Disturbance of all Conversation.—He soon left us.—Nicholas Scull, a Surveyor, afterwards Surveyor-General, Who lov'd Books, & sometimes made a few Verses. William Parsons, bred a Shoemaker, but loving Reading, had acquir'd a considerable Share of Mathematics, which he first studied with a View to Astrology that he afterwards laught at. He also became Surveyor General.—William Maugridge, a Joiner, & a most exquisite Mechanic, & a solid sensible Man. Hugh Meredith, Stephen Potts, & George Webb, I have Characteris'd before. Robert Grace, a young Gentleman of some Fortune, generous, lively & witty, a Lover of Punning and of his Friends. And William Coleman, then a Merchant's Clerk, about my Age, who had the coolest clearest Head, the best Heart, and the exactest Morals, of almost any Man I ever met with. He became afterwards a Merchant of great Note, and one of our Provincial Judges: Our Friendship continued without Interruption to his Death, upwards of 40 Years. And the Club continu'd almost as long and was the best School of Philosophy, Morals & Politics that then existed in the Province; for our Queries which were read the Week preceding their Discussion, put us on reading with Attention upon the several Subjects, that we might speak more to the purpose: and here too we acquired better Habits of Conversation, every thing being studied in our Rules which might

[1] *Croakers* Those who speak prophesies of doom.

[2] *declaim* Recite passionately.

[3] *Junto* In its origins, the term refers to a small committee who gather together for the advancement of mutual political goals or of the public interest.

[4] *Warmth* Passionate debate; anger.

[5] *Hadley's Quadrant* Navigational tool better known today as the octant; similar devices were invented around the same time, independently, by both Thomas Godfrey and the English mathematician John Hadley (1682–1744).

[6] *distinguishing upon Trifles* I.e., drawing attention to minute or petty distinctions between things.

prevent our disgusting each other. From hence the long Continuance of the Club, which I shall have frequent Occasion to speak farther of hereafter; But my giving this Account of it here, is to show something of the Interest I had, every one of these exerting themselves in recommending Business to us.—Brientnal particularly procur'd us from the Quakers, the Printing 40 Sheets of their History, the rest being to be done by Keimer: and upon this we work'd exceeding hard, for the Price was low. It was a Folio, Pro Patria Size, in Pica with Long Primer Notes.[1] I compos'd of it a Sheet a Day, and Meredith work'd it off at Press. It was often 11 at Night and sometimes later, before I had finish'd my Distribution for the next days Work: For the little Jobbs sent in by our other Friends now & then put us back. But so determin'd I was to continue doing a Sheet a Day of the Folio, that one Night when having impos'd my Forms, I thought my Days Work over, one of them by accident was broken and two Pages reduc'd to Pie,[2] I immediately distributed & compos'd it over again before I went to bed. And this Industry visible to our Neighbours began to give us Character and Credit; particularly I was told, that mention being made of the new Printing Office at the Merchants Every-night-Club, the general Opinion was that it must fail, there being already two Printers in the Place, Keimer & Bradford; but Doctor Baird (whom you and I saw many Years after at his native Place, St. Andrews in Scotland) gave a contrary Opinion; for the Industry of that Franklin, says he, is superior to any thing I ever saw of the kind: I see him still at work when I go home from Club; and he is at Work again before his Neighbours are out of bed. This struck the rest, and we soon after had Offers from one of them to supply us with Stationary. But as yet we did not chuse to engage in Shop Business.

I mention this Industry the more particularly and the more freely, tho' it seems to be talking in my own Praise, that those of my Posterity who shall read it, may know the Use of that Virtue, when they see its Effects in my Favour throughout this Relation.—

George Webb, who had found a Friend that lent him wherewith to purchase his Time of Keimer,[3] now came to offer himself as a Journeyman to us. We could not then imploy him, but I foolishly let him know, as a Secret, that I soon intended to begin a Newspaper, & might then have Work for him.—My Hopes of Success as I told him were founded on this, that the then only Newspaper,[4] printed by Bradford, was a paltry thing, wretchedly manag'd, no way entertaining; and yet was profitable to him.—I therefore thought a good Paper could scarcely fail of good Encouragement I requested Webb not to mention it, but he told it to Keimer, who immediately, to be beforehand with[5] me, published Proposals for Printing one himself,—on which Webb was to be employ'd.—I resented this, and to counteract them, as I could not yet begin our Paper, I wrote several Pieces of Entertainment for Bradford's Paper, under the Title of the Busy Body which Brientnal continu'd some Months.[6] By this means the Attention of the Publick was fix'd on that Paper, & Keimers Proposals which we burlesqu'd and ridicul'd, were disregarded. He began his Paper however, and after carrying it on three Quarters of a Year, with at most only 90 Subscribers, he offer'd it to me for a Trifle, & I having been ready some time to go on with it, took it in hand directly and it prov'd in a few Years extreamly profitable to me.[7]—

I perceive that I am apt to speak in the singular Number, though our Partnership still continu'd. The Reason may be, that in fact the whole Management of the Business lay upon me. Meredith was no Compostor, a poor Pressman, & seldom sober. My Friends lamented my Connection with him, but I was to make the best of it.

[1] *Pro Patria Size* According to Frank Woodworth Pine's 1916 edition of the *Autobiography*, this term refers to "A sheet 8-½ by 13-½ inches, having the words *pro patria* [Latin: for the fatherland] in translucent letters in the body of the paper"; *in Pica with Long Primer Notes* I.e., the main text is in pica (the font size today standardized as size 12), with footnotes in size 10.

[2] *Pie* Printer's term for a confused jumble of types.

[3] *wherewith to … of Keimer* Money to pay Keimer for his remaining years of servitude and thereby be released from his contract of indenture.

[4] *then only Newspaper* Andrew Bradford's *The American Weekly Mercury* was published from 1719 to 1749.

[5] *be beforehand with* I.e., get ahead of.

[6] *several Pieces … some Months* Thirty-two of these letters were published in the *Mercury* over the course of 1729.

[7] *his Paper … to me* This was the paper that later became known as the *Pennsylvania Gazette*, which under Franklin's ownership (1729–48) became one of the most prominent newspapers in the North American colonies.

Our first Papers made a quite different Appearance from any before in the Province, a better Type & better printed: but some spirited Remarks[1] of my Writing on the Dispute then going on between Governor Burnet and the Massachusetts Assembly, struck the principal People, occasion'd the Paper & the Manager of it to be much talk'd of, & in a few Weeks brought them all to be our Subscribers. Their Example was follow'd by many, and our Number went on growing continually.—This was one of the first good Effects of my having learnt a little to scribble.—Another was, that the leading Men, seeing a News Paper now in the hands of one who could also handle a Pen, thought it convenient to oblige & encourage me.—Bradford still printed the Votes & Laws & other Publick Business. He had printed an Address of the House[2] to the Governor in a coarse blundering manner; We reprinted it elegantly & correctly, and sent one to every Member. They were sensible of the Difference, it strengthen'd the Hands of our Friends in the House, and they voted us their Printers for the Year ensuing.

Among my Friends in the House I must not forget Mr Hamilton before mentioned, who was then returned from England & had a Seat in it. He interested himself for me strongly in that Instance, as he did in many others afterwards, continuing his Patronage till his Death.[3] Mr Vernon about this time put me in mind of the Debt I ow'd him:—but did not press me.—I wrote him an ingenuous Letter of Acknowledgments, crav'd his Forbearance a little longer which he allow'd me, & as soon as I was able I paid the Principal with Interest & many Thanks.—So that *Erratum* was in some degree corrected.—

But now another Difficulty came upon me, which I had never the least Reason to expect. Mr. Meredith's Father, who was to have paid for our Printing House according to the Expectations given me, was able to advance only one Hundred Pounds, Currency, which had been paid, & a Hundred more was due to the Merchant; who grew impatient & su'd us all. We gave Bail, but saw that if the Money could not be rais'd in time, the Suit must come to a Judgment & Execution, & our hopeful Prospects must with us be ruined, as the Press & Letters must be sold for Payment, perhaps at half-Price.—In this Distress two true Friends whose Kindness I have never forgotten nor ever shall forget while I can remember any thing, came to me separately unknown to each other, and without any Application from me, offering each of them to advance me all the Money that should be necessary to enable me to take the whole Business upon my self, if that should be practicable, but they did not like my continuing the Partnership with Meredith, who as they said was often seen drunk in the Streets, & playing at low Games in Alehouses, much to our Discredit. These two Friends were *William Coleman* & *Robert Grace*. I told them I could not propose a Separation while any Prospect remain'd of the Merediths fulfilling their Part of our Agreement. Because I thought my self under great Obligations to them for what they had done & would do if they could. But if they finally fail'd in their Performance, & our Partnership must be dissolv'd, I should then think myself at Liberty to accept the Assistance of my Friends. Thus the matter rested for some time. When I said to my Partner, perhaps your Father is dissatisfied at the Part you have undertaken in this Affair of ours, and is unwilling to advance for you & me what he would for you alone: If that is the Case, tell me, and I will resign the whole to you & go about my Business. No—says he, my Father has really been disappointed[4] and is really unable; and I am unwilling to distress him farther. I see this is a Business I am not fit for. I was bred a Farmer, and it was a Folly in me to come to Town & put my self at 30 Years of Age an Apprentice to learn a new Trade. Many of our Welsh People are going to settle in North

[1] A long footnote in Franklin's original manuscript reprints the text of these "Remarks," which was published in the *Gazette* on 9 October 1729; that footnote has been omitted here in the interest of clarity and brevity. The dispute referred to centered on Governor Burnet's demands, supported by the Board of Trade in England, to receive a fixed salary from the Massachusetts Assembly, when it had previously been the practice of the Assembly to simply reward the governor with periodic grants "according to their sense of his merit and services." Burnet remained rigidly attached to his demand until his death, as did his successors, until the matter was put to rest in favor of the Assembly during the governorship of Jonathan Belcher (1730–41).

[2] *the House* I.e., the Assembly.

[3] [Franklin's note] I got his Son once 500£.

[4] *disappointed* I.e., in financial matters.

Carolina[1] where Land is cheap: I am inclin'd to go with them, & follow my old Employment. You may find Friends to assist you. If you will take the Debts of the Company upon you, return to my Father the hundred Pound he has advanc'd, pay my little personal Debts, and give me Thirty Pounds & a new Saddle, I will relinquish the Partnership & leave the whole in your Hands. I agreed to this Proposal. It was drawn up in Writing, sign'd & seal'd immediately. I gave him what he demanded & he went soon after to Carolina; from whence he sent me next Year two long Letters, containing the best Account that had been given of that Country, the Climate, Soil, Husbandry, &c. for in those Matters he was very judicious. I printed them in the Papers, and they gave grate Satisfaction to the Publick.

As soon as he was gone, I recurr'd to my two Friends; and because I would not give an unkind Preference to either, I took half what each had offered & I wanted, of one, & half of the other; paid off the Company Debts, and went on with the Business in my own Name, advertising that the Partnership was dissolved. I think this was in or about the Year 1729.[2]—

About this Time there was a Cry among the People for more Paper-Money, only 15,000£ being extant in the Province & that soon to be sunk. The wealthy Inhabitants oppos'd any Addition, being against all Paper Currency, from an Apprehension that it would depreciate as it had done in New England to the Prejudice of all Creditors.[3]—We had discuss'd this Point in our Junto, where I was on the Side of an Addition, being persuaded that the first small Sum

struck in 1723 had done much good, by increasing the Trade Employment, & Number of Inhabitants in the Province, since I now saw all the old Houses inhabited, & many new ones building, where as I remember'd well, that when I first walk'd about the Streets of Philadelphia, eating my Roll, I saw most of the Houses in Walnut street between Second & Front streets with Bills on their Doors, to be let; and many likewise in Chestnut Street, & other Streets; which made me then think the Inhabitants of the City were one after another deserting it.—Our Debates possess'd me so fully of the Subject, that I wrote and printed an anonymous Pamphlet on it, entituled, *The Nature & Necessity of a Paper Currency*. It was well receiv'd by the common People in general; but the Rich Men dislik'd it; for it increas'd and strengthen'd the Clamour for more Money; and they happening to have no Writers among them that were able to answer it, their Opposition slacken'd, & the Point was carried by a Majority in the House. My Friends there, who conceiv'd I had been of some Service, thought fit to reward me, by employing me in printing the Money, a very profitable Jobb, and a great Help to me.—This was another Advantage gain'd by my being able to write. The Utility of this Currency became by Time and Experience so evident, as never afterwards to be much disputed, so that it grew soon to 55,000£ and in 1739 to 80,000£ since which it arose during War to upwards of 350,000£. Trade, Building & Inhabitants all the while increasing. Tho' I now think there are Limits beyond which the Quantity may be hurtful.—

I soon after obtain'd, thro' my Friend Hamilton, the Printing of the NewCastle[4] Paper Money, another profitable Jobb, as I then thought it; small Things appearing great to those in small Circumstances. And these to me were really great Advantages, as they were great Encouragements.—He procured me also the Printing of the Laws and Votes of that Government which continu'd in my Hands as long as I follow'd the Business.—

I now open'd a little Stationer's Shop. I had in it Blanks[5] of all Sorts the correctest that ever appear'd

[1] *Welsh People … North Carolina* The royal colony of North Carolina was founded in 1729; many of its earliest European settlers were Welsh Presbyterians, who settled in Cape Fear in an area eventually known as the Welsh Tract.

[2] *I think … 1729* In fact, Franklin's partnership with Meredith was dissolved in July 1730, and officially announced in 1732, once he had paid off all the company debts.

[3] *About this … all Creditors* Pennsylvania's first paper currency had been issued in a fixed installment in 1723. Paper money was at this period still a relatively new and ill-defined concept in the colonies, with paper bills having no intrinsic value but acting instead as "bills of credit," backed by real estate collateral and intended to be eventually redeemed and retired (or "sunk") by the colonial government. Poor management of the issuing of paper currency had led to extreme inflation in New England and South Carolina, which had most negatively affected wealthy creditors in the colony.

[4] *NewCastle* Political center of Delaware, which was owned by the same proprietaries as Pennsylvania.

[5] *Blanks* I.e., documents with blank spaces, designed for various purposes.

among us, being assisted in that by my Friend Brientnal; I had also Paper, Parchment, Chapmen's Books, &c. One Whitemash a Compositor I had known in London, an excellent Workman now came to me & work'd with me constantly & diligently, and I took an Apprentice the Son of Aquila Rose. I began now gradually to pay off the Debt I was under for the Printing-House.—In order to secure my Credit and Character as a Tradesmen, I took care not only to be in *Reality* Industrious & frugal, but to avoid all *Appearances* of the Contrary. I drest plainly; I was seen at no Places of idle Diversion; I never went out a-fishing or shooting; a Book, indeed, sometimes debauch'd me from my Work; but that was seldom, snug,[1] & gave no Scandal: and to show that I was not above my Business, I sometimes brought home the Paper I purchas'd at the Stores, thro' the Streets on a Wheelbarrow. Thus being esteem'd an industrious thriving young Man, and paying duly for what I bought, the Merchants who imported Stationary solicited my Custom, others propos'd supplying me with Books, & I went on swimmingly.—In the mean time, Keimer's Credit & Business declining daily, he was at last forc'd to sell his Printing-house to satisfy his Creditors. He went to Barbadoes, & there lived some Years, in very poor Circumstances.

His Apprentice David Harry, whom I had instructed while I work'd with him, set up in his Place at Philadelphia having bought his Materials. I was at first apprehensive of a powerful Rival in Harry, as his Friends were very able, & had a good deal of Interest. I therefore propos'd a Partnership to him; which he, fortunately for me, rejected with Scorn. He was very proud, dress'd like a Gentleman, liv'd expensively, took much Diversion & Pleasure abroad, ran in debt, & neglected his Business, upon which all Business left him; and finding nothing to do, he follow'd Keimer to Barbadoes; taking the Printinghouse with him. There this Apprentice employ'd his former Master as a Journeyman. They quarrel'd often. Harry went continually behind-hand, and at length was forc'd to sell his Types, and return to his Country Work in Pensilvania. The Person that bought them, employ'd Keimer to use them, but in a few years he died. There remain'd now no Competitor with me at Philadelphia, but the old one, Bradford, who was rich & easy, did a

little Printing now & then by straggling Hands, but was not very anxious about the Business. However, as he kept the Post Office, it was imagined he had better Opportunities of obtaining News, his Paper was thought a better Distributer of Advertisements than mine, & therefore had many more, which was a profitable thing to him & a Disadvantage to me. For tho' I did indeed receive & send Papers by the Post, yet the publick Opinion was otherwise; for what I did send was by Bribing the Riders[2] who took them privately: Bradford being unkind enough to forbid it: which occasion'd some Resentment on my Part; and I thought so meanly of him for it, that when I afterwards came into his Situation, I took care never to imitate it.

I had hitherto continu'd to board with Godfrey who lived in Part of my House with his Wife & Children, & had one Side of the Shop for his Glazier's Business, tho' he work'd little, being always absorb'd in his Mathematics.—Mrs Godfrey projected a Match for me with a Relation's Daughter, took Opportunities of bringing us often together, till a serious Courtship on my part ensu'd the Girl being in herself very deserving. The old Folks encourag'd me by continual Invitations to Supper, & by leaving us together, till at length it was time to explain. Mrs Godfrey manag'd our little Treaty. I let her know that I expected as much Money with their Daughter as would pay off my Remaining Debt for the Printing-house, which I believe was not then above a Hundred Pounds.[3] She brought me Word they had no such Sum to spare. I said they might mortgage their House in the Loan Office.—The Answer to this after some Days was, that they did not approve the Match; that on Enquiry of Bradford they had been inform'd the Printing Business was not a profitable one, the Types would soon be worn out & more wanted, that S. Keimer & D. Harry had fail'd one after the other, and I should probably soon follow them; and therefore I was forbidden the House, & the Daughter shut up.—Whether this was a real Change of Sentiment, or only Artifice, on a Supposition of our being too far engag'd in Affection to retract, & therefore that we

1 *snug* Unseen; private.

2 *Riders* Postal delivery workers.

3 *I let her know ... Pounds* Such financial settlements were commonly involved in drawing up marriage contracts in the eighteenth century.

should steal a Marriage,[1] which would leave them at Liberty to give or withhold what they pleas'd, I know not: But I suspected the latter, resented it, and went no more. Mrs Godfrey brought me afterwards some more favourable Accounts of their Disposition, & would have drawn me on again: But I declared absolutely my Resolution to have nothing more to do with that Family. This was resented by the Godfreys, we differ'd, and they removed, leaving me the whole House, and I resolved to take no more Inmates. But this Affair having turn'd my Thoughts to Marriage, I look'd round me, and made Overtures of Acquaintance in other Places; but soon found that the Business of a Printer being generally thought a poor one, I was not to expect Money with a Wife unless with such a one, as I should not otherwise think agreable.—In the mean time that hard-to-be-govern'd Passion of Youth, had hurried me frequently into Intrigues with low Women that fell in my Way, which were attended with some Expence & great Inconvenience, besides a continual Risque to my Health by a Distemper which of all Things I dreaded,[2] tho' by great good Luck I escaped it.—

A friendly Correspondence as Neighbours & old Acquaintances, had continued between me & Mrs Read's Family who all had a Regard for me from the time of my first Lodging in their House. I was often invited and consulted in their Affairs, wherein I sometimes was of Service.—I pity'd poor Miss Read's unfortunate Situation, who was generally dejected, seldom chearful, and avoided Company. I consider'd my Giddiness & Inconstancy when in London as in a great degree the Cause of her Unhappiness; tho' the Mother was good enough to think the Fault more her own than mine, as she had prevented our Marrying before I went thither, and persuaded the other Match in my Absence. Our mutual Affection was revived, but there were now great Objections to our Union. That Match was indeed look'd upon as invalid, a preceding Wife being said to be living in England; but this could not easily be prov'd, because of the Distance &c. And tho' there was a Report of his Death, it was not certain. Then, tho' it should be true, he had left many Debts which his Successor might be call'd upon to pay. We ventured however, over all these Difficulties, and I took her to Wife[3] Sept. 1. 1730. None of the Inconveniencies happened that we had apprehended, she prov'd a good & faithful Helpmate, assisted me much by attending the Shop, we throve together, and have ever mutually endeavour'd to make each other happy.—Thus I corrected that great *Erratum* as well as I could.

About this Time our Club meeting, not at a Tavern, but in a little Room of Mr Grace's set apart for that Purpose; a Proposition was made by me, that since our Books were often referr'd to in our Disquisitions upon the Queries, it might be convenient to us to have them all together where we met, that upon Occasion they might be consulted; and By thus clubbing our Books to a common Library, we should, while we lik'd to keep them together, have each of us the Advantage of using the Books of all the other Members, which would be nearly as beneficial as if each owned the whole. It was lik'd and agreed to, & we fill'd one End of the Room with such Books as we could best spare. The Number was not so great as we expected; and tho' they had been of great Use, yet some Inconveniencies occurring for want of due Care of them, the Collection after about a Year was separated, & each took his Books home again.

And now I set on foot my first Project of a public Nature, that for a Subscription Library. I drew up the Proposals, got them put into Form by our great Scrivener Brockden, and by the help of my Friends in the Junto, procur'd Fifty Subscribers of 40/[4] each to begin with & 10/ a Year for 50 Years, the Term our Company was to continue. We afterwards obtain'd a Charter, the Company being increas'd to 100. This was the Mother of all the N American Subscription Libraries now so numerous. It is become a great thing itself, & continually increasing.—These Libraries have improv'd the general Conversation of the Americans, made the common Tradesmen & Farmers as intelligent as most Gentlemen from other Countries, and perhaps have contributed in some degree to the Stand so generally made throughout the Colonies in Defence of their Privileges.—

1 *steal a Marriage* I.e., elope.

2 *a Distemper … I dreaded* I.e., syphilis.

3 *took her to Wife* Due to the uncertainty regarding Read's first husband, her marriage to Franklin was never considered legal; their union was nevertheless considered legitimate and acceptable by most within the community, and they referred to one another as husband and wife.

4 *40/* Forty shillings.

Memorandum

Thus far was written with the Intention express'd in the Beginning and therefore contains several little family Anecdotes of no Importance to others. What follows was written many Years after in compliance with the Advice contain'd in these Letters, and accordingly intended for the Publick. The Affairs of the Revolution occasion'd the Interruption.[1]

PART 2

Letter from Mr. Abel James,[2] with Notes on my Life, (received in Paris.)

My dear & honored Friend.

I have often been desirous of writing to thee, but could not be reconciled to the Thought that the Letter might fall into the Hands of the British, lest some Printer or busy Body should publish some Part of the Contents & give our Friends Pain & myself Censure.

Some Time since there fell into my Hands to my great Joy about 23 Sheets in thy own hand-writing containing an Account of the Parentage & Life of thyself, directed to thy Son ending in the Year 1730 with which there were Notes likewise in thy writing, a Copy of which I inclose in Hopes it may be a means if thou continuedst it up to a later period, that the first & latter part may be put together; & if it is not yet continued, I hope thou wilt not delay it, Life is uncertain as the Preacher tells us,[3] and what will the World say if kind, humane & benevolent Ben Franklin should leave his Friends & the World deprived of so pleasing & profitable a Work, a Work which would be useful & entertaining not only to a few, but to millions.

The Influence Writings under that Class have on the Minds of Youth is very great, and has no where appeared so plain as in our public Friends' Journals. It almost insensibly leads the Youth into the Resolution of endeavouring to become as good and as eminent as the Journalist. Should thine for Instance when published, and I think it could not fail of it, lead the Youth to equal the Industry & Temperance of thy early Youth, what a Blessing with that Class would such a Work be. I know of no Character living nor many of them put together, who has so much in his Power as Thyself to promote a greater Spirit of Industry & early Attention to Business, Frugality and Temperance with the American Youth. Not that I think the Work would have no other Merit & Use in the World, far from it, but the first is of such vast Importance, that I know nothing that can equal it.

The foregoing letter and the minutes accompanying it being shewn to a friend, I received from him the following:

LETTER FROM MR. BENJAMIN VAUGHAN.[4]
Paris, January 31, 1783.

MY DEAREST SIR,

When I had read over your sheets of minutes of the principal incidents of your life, recovered for you by your Quaker acquaintance; I told you I would send you a letter expressing my reasons why I thought it would be useful to complete and publish it as he desired. Various concerns have for some time past prevented this letter being written, and I do not know whether it was worth any expectation: happening to be at leisure however at present, I shall by writing at least interest and instruct myself; but as the terms I am inclined to use may tend to offend a person of your manners, I shall only tell you how I would address any other person, who was as good and as great as yourself, but less diffident. I would say to him, Sir, I *solicit* the history of your life from the following motives.

Your history is so remarkable, that if you do not give it, somebody else will certainly give it; and perhaps so as nearly to do as much harm, as your own management of the thing might do good.

It will moreover present a table of the internal circumstances of your country, which will very much

[1] *Thus far ... the Interruption* Part One of the *Autobiography* was written in 1771; Franklin began Part Two while working as the U.S. Minister to France in 1784.

[2] *Abel James* A Quaker merchant friend from Philadelphia. This letter was written in 1782.

[3] *Life is ... tells us* The uncertainty of life and death is a major theme of the Book of Ecclesiastes, whose wisdom-dispensing narrator, Kohelet, is often referred to as simply "the Preacher."

[4] *BENJAMIN VAUGHAN* British politician (1751–1835) who supported the American Revolution. He later became a member of the American Philosophical Society founded by Franklin and his associates.

tend to invite to it settlers of virtuous and manly minds. And considering the eagerness with which such information is sought by them, and the extent of your reputation, I do not know of a more efficacious advertisement than your Biography would give.

All that has happened to you is also connected with the detail of the manners and situation of *a rising* people; and in this respect I do not think that the writings of Caesar and Tacitus[1] can be more interesting to a true judge of human nature and society.

But these, Sir, are small reasons in my opinion, compared with the chance which your life will give for the forming of future great men; and in conjunction with your *Art of Virtue*,[2] (which you design to publish) of improving the features of private character, and consequently of aiding all happiness both public and domestic.

The two works I allude to, Sir, will in particular give a noble rule and example of *self-education*. School and other education constantly proceed upon false principles, and shew a clumsy apparatus pointed at a false mark; but your apparatus is simple, and the mark a true one; and while parents and young persons are left destitute of other just means of estimating and becoming prepared for a reasonable course in life, your discovery that the thing is in many a man's private power, will be invaluable!

Influence upon the private character late in life, is not only an influence late in life, but a weak influence. It is in *youth* that we plant our chief habits and prejudices; it is in youth that we take our party as to profession, pursuits, and matrimony. In youth therefore the turn is given; in youth the education even of the next generation is given; in youth the private and public character is determined; and the term of life extending but from youth to age, life ought to begin well from youth; and more especially *before* we take our party as to our principal objects.

But your Biography will not merely teach self-education, but the education of *a wise man*; and the wisest man will receive lights and improve his progress, by seeing detailed the conduct of another wise man. And why are weaker men to be deprived of such helps, when we see our race has been blundering on in the dark, almost without a guide in this particular, from the farthest trace of time. Shew then, Sir, how much is to be done, *both to sons and fathers*; and invite all wise men to become like yourself; and other men to become wise.

When we see how cruel statesmen and warriors can be to the humble race, and how absurd distinguished men can be to their acquaintance, it will be instructive to observe the instances multiply of pacific acquiescing manners; and to find how compatible it is to be great and *domestic*; enviable and yet *good-humoured*.

The little private incidents which you will also have to relate, will have considerable use, as we want above all things, *rules of prudence in ordinary affairs*; and it will be curious to see how you have acted in these. It will be so far a sort of key to life, and explain many things that all men ought to have once explained to them, to give them a chance of becoming wise by foresight.

The nearest thing to having experience of one's own, is to have other people's affairs brought before us in a shape that is interesting; this is sure to happen from your pen. Your affairs and management will have an air of simplicity or importance that will not fail to strike; and I am convinced you have conducted them with as much originality as if you had been conducting discussions in politics or philosophy; and what more worthy of experiments and system, (its importance and its errors considered) than human life!

Some men have been virtuous blindly, others have speculated fantastically, and others have been shrewd to bad purposes; but you, Sir, I am sure, will give under your hand, nothing but what is at the same moment, wise, practical, and good.

Your account of yourself (for I suppose the parallel I am drawing for Dr. Franklin, will hold not only in point of character but of private history), will shew that you are ashamed of no origin; a thing the more important, as you prove how little necessary all origin is to happiness, virtue, or greatness.

[1] *Caesar and Tacitus* Roman military leader and dictator Gaius Julius Caesar (100–44 BCE), who wrote two memoirs of his experience of the Gallic Wars, and Roman historian Publius Cornelius Tacitus (c. 56–c. 120 CE).

[2] *Art of Virtue* Franklin appears to have first proposed this work in a 1760 letter to the Scottish philosopher Henry Home, Lord Kames (1696–1782). This distinct work was never begun, though Part Two of the *Autobiography* is generally considered to have been written with some of its ambitions in mind.

As no end likewise happens without a means, so we shall find, Sir, that even you yourself framed a plan by which you became considerable; but at the same time we may see that though the event is flattering, the means are as simple as wisdom could make them; that is depending upon nature, virtue, thought, and habit.

Another thing demonstrated will be the propriety of every man's waiting for his time for appearing upon the stage of the world. Our sensations being very much fixed to the moment, we are apt to forget that more moments are to follow the first, and consequently that man should arrange his conduct so as to suit the *whole* of a life. Your attribution appears to have been applied to your *life*, and the passing moments of it have been enlivened with content and enjoyment, instead of being tormented with foolish impatience or regrets. Such a conduct is easy for those who make virtue and themselves their standard, and who try to keep themselves in countenance by examples of other truly great men, of whom patience is so often the characteristic.

Your Quaker correspondent, Sir, (for here again I will suppose the subject of my letter resembling Dr. Franklin,) praised your frugality, diligence, and temperance, which he considered as a pattern for all youth; but it is singular that he should have forgotten your modesty, and your disinterestedness,[1] without which you never could have waited for your advancement, or found your situation in the mean time comfortable; which is a strong lesson to shew the poverty of glory, and the importance of regulating our minds.

If this correspondent had known the nature of your reputation as well as I do, he would have said; your former writings and measures would secure attention to your Biography, and Art of Virtue; and your Biography and Art of Virtue, in return, would secure attention to them. This is an advantage attendant upon a various character,[2] and which brings all that belongs to it into greater play; and it is the more useful, as perhaps more persons are at a loss for the *means* of improving their minds and characters, than they are for the time or the inclination to do it.

But there is one concluding reflection, Sir, that will shew the use of your life as a mere piece of biography. This style of writing seems a little gone out of vogue, and yet it is a very useful one; and your specimen of it may be particularly serviceable, as it will make a subject of comparison with the lives of various public cut-throats and intriguers, and with absurd monastic self-tormentors, or vain literary triflers. If it encourages more writings of the same kind with your own, and induces more men to spend lives fit to be written; it will be worth all Plutarch's Lives put together.

But being tired of figuring to myself a character of which every feature suits only one man in the world, without giving him the praise of it; I shall end my letter, my dear Dr. Franklin, with a personal application to your proper self.

I am earnestly desirous then, my dear Sir, that you should let the world into the traits of your genuine character, as civil broils[3] may otherwise tend to disguise or traduce it. Considering your great age, the caution of your character, and your peculiar style of thinking, it is not likely that any one besides yourself can be sufficiently master of the facts of your life, or the intentions of your mind.

Besides all this, the immense revolution of the present period, will necessarily turn our attention towards the author of it; and when virtuous principles have been pretended in it, it will be highly important to shew that such have really influenced; and, as your own character will be the principal one to receive a scrutiny, it is proper (even for its effects upon your vast and rising country, as well as upon England and upon Europe), that it should stand respectable and eternal. For the furtherance of human happiness, I have always maintained that it is necessary to prove that man is not even at present a vicious and detestable animal; and still more to prove that good management may greatly amend him; and it is for much the same reason, that I am anxious to see the opinion established, that there are fair characters existing among the individuals of the race; for the moment that all men, without exception, shall be conceived abandoned,[4] good people will cease efforts deemed to be hopeless, and perhaps think of

[1] *singular* Strange; *disinterestedness* I.e., impartiality, lack of prejudice.

[2] *a various character* I.e., a person of varied abilities, interests, and achievements.

[3] *broils* Conflicts.

[4] *abandoned* Unrestrained; immoral.

taking their share in the scramble of life, or at least of making it comfortable principally for themselves.

Take then, my dear Sir, this work most speedily into hand: shew yourself good as you are good, temperate as you are temperate; and above all things, prove yourself as one who from your infancy have loved justice, liberty, and concord, in a way that has made it natural and consistent for you to have acted, as we have seen you act in the last seventeen years of your life. Let Englishmen be made not only to respect, but even to love you. When they think well of individuals in your native country, they will go nearer to thinking well of your country; and when your countrymen see themselves well thought of by Englishmen, they will go nearer to thinking well of England. Extend your views even further; do not stop at those who speak the English tongue, but after having settled so many points in nature and politics, think of bettering the whole race of men.

As I have not read any part of the life in question, but know only the character that lived it, I write somewhat at hazard.[1] I am sure however, that the life, and the treatise I allude to (on the *Art of Virtue*), will necessarily fulfil the chief of my expectations; and still more so if you take up the measure of suiting these performances to the several views above stated. Should they even prove unsuccessful in all that a sanguine admirer of yours hopes from them, you will at least have framed pieces to interest the human mind; and whoever gives a feeling of pleasure that is innocent to man, has added so much to the fair side of a life otherwise too much darkened by anxiety, and too much injured by pain.

In the hope therefore that you will listen to the prayer addressed to you in this letter, I beg to subscribe myself, my dearest Sir, &c. &c.
Signed BENJ. VAUGHAN.

Continuation of the Account of my Life.
Begun at Passy[2] 1784

It is some time since I receiv'd the above Letters, but I have been too busy till now to think of complying with the Request they contain. It might too be much better done if I were at home among my Papers, which would aid my Memory, & help to ascertain Dates. But my Return being uncertain, and having just now a little Leisure, I will endeavour to recollect & write what I can; If I live to get home, it may there be corrected and improv'd.

Not having any Copy here of what is already written, I know not whether an Account is given of the means I used to establish the Philadelphia publick Library, which, from a small Beginning is now become so considerable, though I remember to have come down to near the Time of that Transaction, 1730. I will therefore begin here, with an Account of it, which may be struck out if found to have been already given.—

At the time I establish'd my self in Pensylvania, there was not a good Bookseller's Shop in any of the Colonies to the Southward of Boston. In New-York & Philadelphia the Printers were indeed Stationers, they sold only Paper, &c. Almanacks,[3] Ballads, and a few common School Books. Those who lov'd Reading were oblig'd to send for their Books from England.—The Members of the Junto had each a few. We had left the Alehouse where we first met, and hired a Room to hold our Club in. I propos'd that we should all of us bring our Books to that Room, where they would not only be ready to consult in our Conferences, but become a common Benefit, each of us being at Liberty to borrow such as he wish'd to read at home. This was accordingly done, and for some time contented us. Finding the Advantage of this little Collection, I propos'd to render the Benefit from Books more common by commencing a Public Subscription Library. I drew a Sketch of the Plan and Rules that would be necessary, and got a skilful Conveyancer Mr Charles Brockden to put the whole in Form of Articles of Agreement to be subscribed, by which each Subscriber engag'd to pay a certain Sum down for the first Purchase of Books and an annual Contribution for encreasing them.—So few were the Readers at that time in Philadelphia, and the Majority of us so poor, that I was not able with great Industry to find more than Fifty Persons, mostly young Tradesmen, willing to pay down for this purpose Forty shillings each, & Ten Shillings per Annum. On this

[1] *at hazard* I.e., running the risk of being mistaken in his assumptions about the *Autobiography*.

[2] *Passy* Wealthy suburb of Paris in which Franklin and his grandson resided while he was working as U.S. Minister to France.

[3] *Almanacks* Annual publications including calendars and predictions for the agricultural year.

little Fund we began. The Books were imported. The Library was opened one Day in the Week for lending to the Subscribers, on their Promisory Notes to pay Double the Value if not duly returned. The Institution soon manifested its Utility, was imitated by other Towns and in other Provinces, the Librarys were augmented by Donations, Reading became fashionable, and our People having no publick Amusements to divert their Attention from Study became better acquainted with Books, and in a few Years were observ'd by Strangers to be better instructed & more intelligent than People of the same Rank generally are in other Countries.—

When we were about to sign the above-mentioned Articles, which were to be binding on us, our Heirs, &c for fifty Years, Mr Brockden, the Scrivener, said to us, "You are young Men, but it is scarce probable that any of you will live to see the Expiration of the Term fix'd in this Instrument." A Number of us, however, are yet living: But the Instrument was after a few Years rendred null by a Charter that incorporated & gave Perpetuity to the Company.—

The Objections, & Reluctances I met with in Soliciting the Subscriptions, made me soon feel the Impropriety of presenting one's self as the Proposer of any useful Project that might be suppos'd to raise one's Reputation in the smallest degree above that of one's Neighbours, when one has need of their Assistance to accomplish that Project. I therefore put my self as much as I could out of sight, and stated it as a Scheme of *a Number of Friends*, who had requested me to go about and propose it to such as they thought Lovers of Reading. In this way my Affair went on more smoothly, and I ever after practis'd it on such Occasions; and, from my frequent Successes, can heartily recommend it. The present little Sacrifice of your Vanity will afterwards be amply repaid. If it remains a while uncertain to whom the Merit belongs, some one more vain than yourself will be encourag'd to claim it, and then even Envy will be dispos'd to do you Justice, by plucking those assum'd Feathers, & restoring them to their right Owner.

This Library afforded me the Means of Improvement by constant Study, for which I set apart an Hour or two each Day; and thus repair'd in some Degree the Loss of the Learned Education my Father once intended for me. Reading was the only Amusement I allow'd my

self. I spent no time in Taverns, Games, or Frolicks of any kind. And my Industry in my Business continu'd as indefatigable as it was necessary. I was in debt for my Printing-house, I had a young Family[1] coming on to be educated, and I had to contend with for Business two Printers who were establish'd in the Place before me. My Circumstances however grew daily easier: my original Habits of Frugality continuing. And My Father having among his Instructions to me when a Boy, frequently repeated a Proverb of Solomon, "*Seest thou a Man diligent in his Calling, he shall stand before Kings, he shall not stand before mean Men.*"[2] I from thence consider'd Industry as a Means of obtaining Wealth and Distinction, which encourag'd me; tho' I did not think that I should ever literally stand before Kings, which however has since happened.—for I have stood before five,[3] & even had the honour of sitting down with one, the King of Denmark, to Dinner.

We have an English Proverb that says,

He that would thrive
Must ask his Wife;

it was lucky for me that I had one as much dispos'd to Industry & Frugality as my self. She assisted me chearfully in my Business, folding & stitching Pamphlets, tending Shop, purchasing old Linen Rags for the Paper-makers, &c &c. We kept no idle Servants, our Table was plain & simple, our Furniture of the cheapest. For instance my Breakfast was a long time Bread & Milk, (no Tea,) and I ate it out of a twopenny earthen Porringer with a Pewter Spoon. But mark how Luxury will enter Families, and make a Progress, in Spite of Principle. Being Call'd one Morning to Breakfast, I found it in a China Bowl with a Spoon of Silver. They had been bought for me without my Knowledge by my Wife, and had cost her the enormous Sum of three and

[1] *a young Family* Franklin's first son, William Franklin, was born in 1730 to an unknown mother, and raised by Franklin and Read together. The couple had two more children: Francis Folger (1732–36), and Sarah (1743–1808).

[2] *Seest thou … mean Men* See Proverbs 22.29.

[3] *I have stood before five* Franklin met kings Louis XV (r. 1715–74) and Louis XVI (r. 1774–92) of France, George II (r. 1727–60) and George III (r. 1760–1820) of the United Kingdom, and Christian VII of Denmark and Norway (r. 1766–1808), who invited Franklin for dinner when both men were in London in 1768.

twenty Shillings, for which she had no other Excuse or Apology to make, but that she thought *her* Husband deserv'd a Silver Spoon & China Bowl as well as any of his Neighbours. This was the first Appearance of Plate[1] & China in our House, which afterwards in a Course of Years as our Wealth encreas'd, augmented gradually to several Hundred Pounds in Value.—

I had been religiously educated as a Presbyterian; and tho' some of the Dogmas of that Persuasion, such as the Eternal Decrees of God, Election, Reprobation,[2] &c. appear'd to me unintelligible, others doubtful, & I early absented myself from the Public Assemblies of the Sect, Sunday being my Studying-Day, I never was without some religious Principles; I never doubted, for instance, the Existence of the Deity, that he made the World, & govern'd it by his Providence; that the most acceptable Service of God was the doing Good to Man; that our Souls are immortal; and that all Crime will be punished & Virtue rewarded either here or hereafter; these I esteem'd the Essentials of every Religion, and being to be found in all the Religions we had in our Country I respected them all, tho' with different degrees of Respect as I found them more or less mix'd with other Articles which without any Tendency to inspire, promote or confirm Morality, serv'd principally to divide us & make us unfriendly to one another.— This Respect to all, with an Opinion that the worst had some good Effects, induc'd me to avoid all Discourse that might tend to lessen the good Opinion another might have of his own Religion; and as our Province increas'd in People and new Places of worship were continually wanted, & generally erected by voluntary Contribution, my Mite[3] for such purpose, whatever might be the Sect, was never refused.—

Tho' I seldom attended any Public Worship, I had still an Opinion of its Propriety, and of its Utility when rightly conducted, and I regularly paid my annual Subscription for the Support of the only Presbyterian Minister or Meeting we had in Philadelphia. He us'd to visit me sometimes as a Friend, and admonish me to attend his Administrations, and I was now and then prevail'd on to do so, once for five Sundays successively. Had he been, *in my Opinion*, a good Preacher perhaps I might have continued, notwithstanding the occasion I had for the Sunday's Leisure in my Course of Study: But his Discourses were chiefly either polemic Arguments, or Explications of the peculiar Doctrines of our Sect, and were all to me very dry, uninteresting and unedifying, since not a single moral Principle was inculcated or enforc'd, their Aim seeming to be rather to make us Presbyterians than good Citizens. At length he took for his Text that Verse of the 4th Chapter of Philippians, *Finally, Brethren, Whatsoever Things are true, honest, just, pure, lovely, or of good report, if there be any virtue, or any praise, think on these Things*; & I imagin'd in a Sermon on such a Text, we could not miss of having some Morality: But he confin'd himself to five Points only as meant by the Apostle,[4] viz. 1. Keeping holy the Sabbath Day. 2. Being diligent in Reading the Holy Scriptures. 3. Attending duly the Publick Worship. 4. Partaking of the Sacrament.[5] 5. Paying a due Respect to God's Ministers.—These might be all good Things, but as they were not the kind of good Things that I expected from that Text, I despaired of ever meeting with them from any other, was disgusted, and attended his Preaching no more.— I had some Years before compos'd a little Liturgy or Form of Prayer for my own private Use, viz, in 1728. entitled, *Articles of Belief & Acts of Religion.*[6] I return'd to the Use of this, and went no more to the public Assemblies.—My Conduct might be blameable, but I leave it without attempting farther to excuse it, my present purpose being to relate Facts, and not to make Apologies for them.—

It was about this time I conceiv'd the bold and arduous Project of arriving at moral Perfection. I wish'd to live without committing any Fault at any time; I would conquer all that either Natural Inclination,

[1] *Plate* I.e., silverware.

[2] *Eternal Decrees of God* God's eternal plan for and sovereign control over the universe; *Election* The Calvinist doctrine that God has predetermined the members of the "elect" (those whose souls will be saved upon death), without any reference to their earthly actions; *Reprobation* Eternal damnation.

[3] *Mite* Small donation.

[4] *the Apostle* The Apostle Paul, said to be the author of the Epistle to the Philippians.

[5] *Partaking of the Sacrament* I.e., participating in the ceremony of the Eucharist, the consuming of the bread and wine that are believed to be spiritual representations of the body and blood of Christ.

[6] *Articles of ... Religion* Much of this private liturgy has survived in manuscript form.

Custom, or Company might lead me into. As I knew, or thought I knew, what was right and wrong, I did not see why I might not *always* do the one and avoid the other. But I soon found I had undertaken a Task of more Difficulty than I had imagined: While my Care was employ'd in guarding against one Fault, I was often surpriz'd by another. Habit took the Advantage of Inattention. Inclination was sometimes too strong for Reason. I concluded at length, that the mere speculative Conviction that it was our Interest to be compleatly virtuous, was not sufficient to prevent our Slipping, and that the contrary Habits must be broken and good Ones acquired and established, before we can have any Dependance on a steady uniform Rectitude of Conduct. For this purpose I therefore contriv'd the following Method.—

In the various Enumerations of the moral Virtues I had met with in my Reading, I found the Catalogue more or less numerous, as different Writers included more or fewer Ideas under the same Name. Temperance, for Example, was by some confin'd to Eating & Drinking, while by others it was extended to mean the moderating every other Pleasure, Appetite, Inclination or Passion, bodily or mental, even to our Avarice & Ambition. I propos'd to myself, for the sake of Clearness, to use rather more Names with fewer Ideas annex'd to each, than a few Names with more Ideas; and I included under Thirteen Names of Virtues all that at that time occurr'd to me as necessary or desirable, and annex'd to each a short Precept, which fully express'd the Extent I gave to its Meaning.—

These Names of Virtues with their Precepts were

1. TEMPERANCE.
Eat not to Dulness.
Drink not to Elevation.

2. SILENCE.
Speak not but what may benefit others or your self. Avoid trifling Conversation.

3. ORDER.
Let all your Things have their Places. Let each Part of your Business have its Time.

4. RESOLUTION.
Resolve to perform what you ought. Perform without fail what you resolve.

5. FRUGALITY.
Make no Expence but to do good to others or yourself: i.e. Waste nothing.

6. INDUSTRY.
Lose no Time.—Be always employ'd in something useful.—Cut off all unnecessary Actions.—

7. SINCERITY.
Use no hurtful Deceit. Think innocently and justly; and, if you speak; speak accordingly.

8. JUSTICE.
Wrong none, by doing Injuries or omitting the Benefits that are your Duty.

9. MODERATION.
Avoid Extreams. Forbear resenting Injuries so much as you think they deserve.

10. CLEANLINESS.
Tolerate no Uncleanness in Body, Cloaths or Habitation.—

11. TRANQUILITY.
Be not disturbed at Trifles, or at Accidents common or unavoidable.

12. CHASTITY.
Rarely use Venery[1] but for Health or Offspring; Never to Dulness, Weakness, or the Injury of your own or another's Peace or Reputation.—

13. HUMILITY.
Imitate Jesus and Socrates.—

My intention being to acquire the *Habitude* of all these Virtues, I judg'd it would be well not to distract my Attention by attempting the whole at once, but to fix it on one of them at a time, and when I should be Master of that, then to proceed to another, and so on till I should have gone thro' the thirteen. And as the previous Acquisition of some might facilitate the Acquisition of certain others, I arrang'd them with that View as they stand above. *Temperance* first, as it tends to procure that Coolness & Clearness of Head, which is so necessary where constant Vigilance was to be kept up, and Guard maintained, against the unremitting Attraction of ancient Habits, and the Force of perpetual Temptations. This being acquir'd & establish'd, *Silence* would be more easy, and my Desire being to gain Knowledge at the same

[1] *use Venery* Have sex.

time that I improv'd in Virtue, and considering that in Conversation it was obtain'd rather by the Use of the Ears than of the Tongue, & therefore wishing to break a Habit I was getting into of Prattling, Punning, & Joking, which only made me acceptable to trifling Company, I gave *Silence* the second Place. This and the next, *Order*, I expected would allow me more Time for attending to my Project and my Studies; RESOLUTION once become habitual, would keep me firm in my Endeavours to obtain all the subsequent Virtues; *Frugality* & *Industry*, by freeing me from my remaining Debt, & producing Affluence & Independance would make more easy the Practice of *Sincerity* and *Justice*, &c. &c. Conceiving then that agreeable to the Advice of Pythagoras in his Golden Verses,[1] daily Examination would be necessary, I contriv'd the following Method for conducting that Examination.

I made a little Book in which I allotted a Page for each of the Virtues. I rul'd each Page with red Ink so as to have seven Columns, one for each Day of the Week, marking each Column with a Letter for the Day. I cross'd these Columns with thirteen red Lines, marking the Beginning of each Line with the first Letter of one of the Virtues, on which Line & in its proper Column I might mark by a little black Spot every Fault I found upon Examination, to have been committed respecting that Virtue upon that Day.

[1] [Franklin's note] *Let not the stealing God of Sleep surprize,*
Nor creep in Slumbers on thy weary Eyes,
Ere ev'ry Action of the former Day,
Strictly *thou dost, and* righteously *survey.*
With Rev'rence at thy own Tribunal stand,
And answer justly to thy own Demand.
Where have I been? In what have I transgrest?
What Good or Ill has this Day's Life exprest?
Where have I fail'd in what I ought to do?
In what to GOD, *to Man, or to myself I owe?*
Inquire severe whate'er from first to last,
From Morning's Dawn till Ev'nings Gloom has past.
If Evil were thy Deeds, repenting mourn,
And let thy Soul with strong Remorse be torn:
If Good, the Good with Peace of Mind repay,
And to thy secret Self with Pleasure say, }
Rejoice, my Heart, for all went well to Day.
[The "Golden Verses" to which Franklin refers are a work of uncertain origin most famously published in Latin in 1494 by the Greek scholar Constantine Lascaris and attributed to the ancient Greek philosopher Pythagoras (c. 570–c. 495 BCE); the lines included here are Franklin's own translation.]

Form of the pages.

	S.	M.	T.	W.	T.	F.	S.
TEMPERANCE.							
EAT NOT TO DULLNESS; DRINK NOT TO ELEVATION.							
T.							
S.	*	*		*		*	
O.	* *	*	*		*	*	*
R.			*			*	
F.		*			*		
I.			*				
S.							
J.							
M.							
C.							
T.							
C.							
H.							

I determined to give a Week's strict Attention to each of the Virtues successively. Thus in the first Week my great Guard was to avoid every the least Offence against Temperance, leaving the other Virtues to their ordinary Chance, only marking every Evening the Faults of the Day. Thus if in the first Week I could keep my first Line marked T clear of Spots, I suppos'd the Habit of that Virtue so much strengthen'd and its opposite weaken'd, that I might venture extending my Attention to include the next, and for the following Week keep both Lines clear of Spots. Proceeding thus to the last, I could go thro' a Course compleat in Thirteen Weeks, and four Courses in a Year.—And like him who having a Garden to weed, does not attempt to eradicate all the bad Herbs at once, which would exceed his Reach and his Strength, but works on one of the Beds at a time, & having accomplish'd the first proceeds to a second; so I should have, (I hoped) the encouraging Pleasure of seeing on my Pages the Progress I made in Virtue, by clearing successively my Lines of their Spots, till in the End by a Number of Courses, I should be happy in viewing a clean Book after a thirteen Weeks daily Examination.

This my little Book had for its Motto these Lines from *Addison's Cato*;

Here will I hold: If there is a Pow'r above us,
(And that there is, all Nature cries aloud
Thro' all her Works) he must delight in Virtue,
And that which he delights in must be happy.[1]

Another from *Cicero*.

*O Vitæ Philosophia Dux! O Virtutum indagatrix, expul-
trixque vitiorum! Unus dies bene, & ex preceptis tuis
actus, peccanti immortalitati est anteponendus.*[2]

Another from the Proverbs of Solomon speaking of
Wisdom or Virtue;

Length of Days is in her right hand, and in her Left
Hand Riches and Honours; Her Ways are Ways of
Pleasantness, and all her Paths are Peace.[3] III, 16, 17.

And conceiving God to be the Fountain of Wisdom,
I thought it right and necessary to solicit his Assistance
for obtaining it; to this End I form'd the following little
Prayer, which was prefix'd to my Tables of Examination;
for daily Use.

*O powerful Goodness! bountiful Father! merciful Guide!
Increase in me that Wisdom which discovers my truest
Interests; Strengthen my Resolutions to perform what
that Wisdom dictates. Accept my kind Offices to thy other
Children, as the only Return in my Power for thy con-
tinual Favours to me.*

I us'd also sometimes a little Prayer which I took
from *Thomson's* Poems. viz

*Father of Light and Life, thou Good supreme,
O teach me what is good, teach me thy self!
Save me from Folly, Vanity and Vice,
From every low Pursuit, and fill my Soul*

With Knowledge, conscious Peace, & Virtue pure,
Sacred, substantial, neverfading Bliss!*[4]

The Precept of *Order* requiring that *every Part of
my Business should have its allotted Time*, one Page
in my little Book contain'd the following Scheme of
Employment for the Twenty-four Hours of a natural
Day,

THE MORNING. *Question.* What good shall I do this day?	5 6 7	Rise, wash, and ad- dress *Powerful Goodness!* Contrive day's business, and take the resolution of the day; prosecute the present study, and break- fast.
	8 9 10 11	Work.
NOON.	12 1	Read, or overlook my accounts, and dine.
	2 3 4 5	Work.
EVENING. *Question.* What good have I have done to-day?	6 7 8 9	Put things in their places. Supper. Music or diversion, or conversa- tion. Examination of the day.
NIGHT,	10 11 12 1 2 3 4	Sleep.

I enter'd upon the Execution of this Plan for Self
Examination, and continu'd it with occasional
Intermissions for some time. I was surpriz'd to find
myself so much fuller of Faults than I had imagined,
but I had the Satisfaction of seeing them diminish. To
avoid the Trouble of renewing now & then my little
Book, which by scraping out the Marks on the Paper
of old Faults to make room for new Ones in a new
Course, became full of Holes: I transferr'd my Tables
& Precepts to the Ivory Leaves of a Memorandum
Book, on which the Lines were drawn with red Ink
that made a durable Stain, and on those Lines I mark'd
my Faults with a black Lead Pencil, which Marks I
could easily wipe out with a wet Sponge. After a while
I went thro' one Course only in a Year, and afterwards
only one in several Years; till at length I omitted them
entirely, being employ'd in Voyages & Business abroad
with a Multiplicity of Affairs, that interfered. But I

1 *Here will … be happy* See Joseph Addison's 1713 play *Cato, A
Tragedy*, 5.1.15–18.

2 *O Vitæ … est anteponendus* Latin: O philosophy, guide of life!
O searcher out of virtue and exterminator of vice! One day spent
well and in accordance with thy precepts is worth an immortality
of sin; partial quotation from Roman philosopher Marcus Tullius
Cicero's *Tusculan Disputations* (c. 45 BCE), translated here by Frank
Woodworth Pine (1916).

3 *Length of … are Peace* See Proverbs 3.16–17; the Book of
Proverbs is traditionally attributed to King Solomon.

4 *Father of … neverfading Bliss!* See James Thomson's 1726 poem
The Seasons, "Winter," lines 218–23.

always carried my little Book with me. My Scheme of ORDER, gave me the most Trouble, and I found, that tho' it might be practicable where a Man's Business was such as to leave him the Disposition of his Time, that of a Journey-man Printer for instance, it was not possible to be exactly observ'd by a Master, who must mix with the World, and often receive People of Business at their own Hours.—*Order* too, with regard to Places for Things, Papers, &c. I found extreamly difficult to acquire. I had not been early accustomed to it, & having an exceeding good Memory, I was not so sensible of the Inconvenience attending Want of Method. This Article therefore cost me so much painful Attention & my Faults in it vex'd me so much, and I made so little Progress in Amendment, & had such frequent Relapses, that I was almost ready to give up the Attempt, and content my self with a faulty Character in that respect. Like the Man who in buying an Ax of a Smith my Neighbour, desired to have the whole of its Surface as bright as the Edge; the Smith consented to grind it bright for him if he would turn the Wheel. He turn'd while the Smith press'd the broad Face of the Ax hard & heavily on the Stone, which made the Turning of it very fatiguing. The Man came every now & then from the Wheel to see how the Work went on; and at length would take his Ax as it was without farther Grinding. No, said the Smith, Turn on, turn on; we shall have it bright by and by; as yet 'tis only speckled. Yes, says the Man; but—*I think I like a speckled Ax best.*—And I believe this may have been the Case with many who having for want of some such Means as I employ'd found the Difficulty of obtaining good, & breaking bad Habits, in other Points of Vice & Virtue, have given up the Struggle, & concluded that *a speckled Ax was best.* For something, that pretended to be Reason was every now and then suggesting to me, that such extream Nicety as I exacted of my self might be a kind of Foppery[1] in Morals, which, if it were known would make me ridiculous; that a perfect Character might be attended with the Inconvenience of being envied and hated; and that a benevolent Man should allow a few Faults in himself, to keep his Friends in Countenance. In Truth I found myself incorrigible with respect to *Order*; and now I am grown old, and

my Memory bad, I feel very sensibly[2] the want of it. But on the whole, tho' I never arrived at the Perfection I had been so ambitious of obtaining, but fell far short of it, yet I was by the Endeavour made a better and a happier Man than I otherwise should have been, if I had not attempted it; As those who aim at perfect Writing by imitating the engraved Copies, tho' they never reach the wish'd for Excellence of those Copies, their Hand[3] is mended by the Endeavour, and is tolerable while it continues fair & legible.—

And it may be well my Posterity should be informed, that to this little Artifice, with the Blessing of God, their Ancestor ow'd the constant Felicity of his Life down to his 79th Year in which this is written. What Reverses may attend the Remainder is in the Hand of Providence: But if they arrive the Reflection on past Happiness enjoy'd ought to help his Bearing them with more Resignation. To *Temperance* he ascribes his long-continu'd Health, & what is still left to him of a good Constitution; to *Industry* and *Frugality* the early Easiness of his Circumstances, & Acquisition of his Fortune, with all that Knowledge that enabled him to be a useful Citizen, and obtain'd for him some Degree of Reputation among the Learned. To *Sincerity* & *Justice* the Confidence of his Country, and the honourable Employs it conferr'd upon him. And to the joint Influence of the whole Mass of the Virtues, even in the imperfect State he was able to acquire them, all that Evenness of Temper, & that Chearfulness in Conversation which makes his Company still sought for, & agreable even to his younger Acquaintance. I hope therefore that some of my Descendants may follow the Example & reap the Benefit.—

It will be remark'd that, tho' my Scheme was not wholly without Religion there was in it no Mark of any of the distinguishing Tenets of any particular Sect.—I had purposely avoided them; for being fully persuaded of the Utility and Excellency of my Method, and that it might be serviceable to People in all Religions, and intending some time or other to publish it, I would not have any thing in it that should prejudice any one of any Sect against it.—I purposed writing a little Comment on each Virtue, in which I would have shown the Advantages of possessing it, & the Mischiefs attending

[1] *Nicety* Fastidiousness; *Foppery* Excessive vanity or affectation.

[2] *sensibly* Strongly.

[3] *Hand* I.e., handwriting.

its opposite Vice; and I should have called my Book the ART *of Virtue*, because it would have shown the *Means & Manner* of obtaining Virtue; which would have distinguish'd it from the mere Exhortation to be good, that does not instruct & indicate the Means; but is like the Apostle's Man of verbal Charity, who only, without showing to the Naked & the Hungry *how* or where they might get Cloaths or Victuals, exhorted them to be fed & clothed.[1] *James* II, 15, 16.—

But it so happened that my Intention of writing & publishing this Comment was never fulfilled. I did indeed, from time to time put down short Hints of the Sentiments, Reasonings, &c. to be made use of in it; some of which I have still by me: But the necessary close Attention to private Business in the earlier part of my Life, and public Business since, have occasioned my postponing it. For it being connected in my Mind with a *great and extensive Project* that required the whole Man to execute, and which an unforeseen Succession of Employs prevented my attending to, it has hitherto remain'd unfinish'd.—

In this Piece it was my Design to explain and enforce this Doctrine, that vicious Actions are not hurtful because they are forbidden, but forbidden because they are hurtful, the Nature of Man alone consider'd: That it was therefore every ones Interest to be virtuous, who wish'd to be happy even in this World. And I should from this Circumstance, there being always in the World a Number of rich Merchants, Nobility, States and Princes, who have need of honest Instruments for the Management of their Affairs, and such being so rare, have endeavoured to convince young Persons, that no Qualities were so likely to make a poor Man's Fortune as those of Probity & Integrity.

My List of Virtues contain'd at first but twelve: But a Quaker Friend having kindly inform'd me that I was generally thought proud; that my Pride show'd itself frequently in Conversation; that I was not content with being in the right when discussing any Point, but was overbearing & rather insolent; of which he convinc'd me by mentioning several Instances;—I determined endeavouring to cure myself if I could

of this Vice or Folly among the rest, and I added *Humility* to my List, giving an extensive Meaning to the Word.—I cannot boast of much Success in acquiring the *Reality* of this Virtue; but I had a good deal with regard to the *Appearance* of it.—I made it a Rule to forbear all direct Contradiction to the Sentiments of others, and all positive Assertion of my own. I even forbid myself agreable to the old Laws of our Junto, the Use of every Word or Expression in the Language that imported a fix'd Opinion; such as *certainly*, *undoubtedly*, &c. and I adopted instead of them, *I conceive*, *I apprehend*, or *I imagine* a thing to be so or so, or it so appears to me at present.—When another asserted something that I thought an Error, I deny'd my self the Pleasure of contradicting him abruptly, and of showing immediately some Absurdity in his Proposition; and in answering I began by observing that in certain Cases or Circumstances his Opinion would be right, but that in the present case there *appear'd* or *seem'd* to me some Difference, &c. I soon found the Advantage of this Change in my Manners. The Conversations I engag'd in went on more pleasantly. The modest way in which I propos'd my Opinions, procur'd them a readier Reception and less Contradiction; I had less Mortification when I was found to be in the wrong, and I more easily prevail'd with others to give up their Mistakes & join with me when I happen'd to be in the right. And this Mode, which I at first put on, with some violence to natural Inclination, became at length so easy & so habitual to me, that perhaps for these Fifty Years past no one has ever heard a dogmatical Expression escape me. And to this Habit (after my Character of Integrity) I think it principally owing, that I had early so much Weight with my Fellow Citizens, when I proposed new Institutions, or Alterations in the old; and so much Influence in public Councils when I became a Member. For I was but a bad Speaker, never eloquent, subject to much Hesitation in my choice of Words, hardly correct in Language, and yet I generally carried my Points.[2]—

In reality there is perhaps no one of our natural Passions so hard to subdue as *Pride*. Disguise it, struggle with it, beat it down, stifle it, mortify it as much as one pleases, it is still alive, and will every now and then peep out and show itself. You will see it perhaps often

1 *the Apostle's … clothed* See James 2.15–16: "If a brother or sister be naked, and destitute of daily food, And one of you say unto them, Depart in peace, be ye warmed and filled; notwithstanding ye give them not those things which are needful to the body; what doth it profit?"

2 *carried my Points* Was successful in my arguments.

in this History. For even if I could conceive that I had compleatly overcome it, I should probably be proud of my Humility.—

Thus far written at Passy 1784
—1987 (WRITTEN 1771–90)

[The full text of Benjamin Franklin's *Autobiography* is included in the website component of this anthology.]

IN CONTEXT

Portraits of Benjamin Franklin

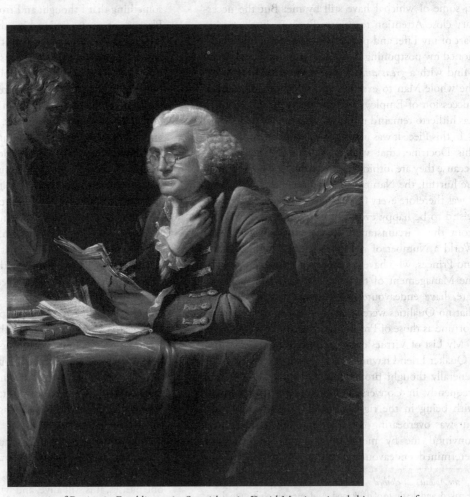

David Martin, portrait of Benjamin Franklin, 1767. Scottish artist David Martin painted this portrait of Franklin while he was in London protesting British taxation of the colonies. Franklin is overlooked by a bust of Isaac Newton (1643–1727), the famed English mathematician and physicist.

Line engraving by Augustin de Saint-Aubin, after Charles Nicolas Cochin, 1777. The caption under his name reads, "Born in Boston, in New England, on 17 January 1706."

Joseph Siffred Duplessis, portrait of Benjamin Franklin, c. 1785. Likely the most famous portrait of Franklin, this was painted by the well-known French portrait artist Duplessis while Franklin was living in Passy, shortly before his replacement as minister plenipotentiary to France by Thomas Jefferson.

MIRABEAU ARRIVE AUX CHAMPS ÉLISÉES.

Louis Joseph Masquelier, *Mirabeau Arrive Aux Champs Élisées* ("Mirabeau Arrives at the Elysian Fields"), 1792. This remarkable engraving depicts the recently deceased French revolutionary politician the Comte de Mirabeau, who had eulogized Franklin in June 1790, arriving at the Elysian Fields, the location of the afterlife for virtuous and heroic individuals in Greek mythology. Benjamin Franklin offers Mirabeau a crown of laurels; they are surrounded by other eminent men of the eighteenth century, including French philosophers Jean-Jacques Rousseau and Voltaire.

Benjamin West, *Benjamin Franklin Drawing Electricity from the Sky*, c. 1816. This posthumous portrait commemorates Franklin's famous 1753 kite experiment, in which he proved that lightning is derived from electricity. Franklin is surrounded by *putti*: symbolic figures, commonly found in European art from the Renaissance to the nineteenth century, that can represent various passions, states of being, or mental faculties. West (who had been a friend of Franklin's) is also known for his historical paintings depicting events such as the 1759 Battle of Quebec, and political paintings such as that commemorating the signing of the Treaty of Paris in 1783.

Samson Occom

1723 – 1792

Today, the Mohegan minister Samson Occom is best known for his autobiographical narrative, a rhetorically powerful account of his life as an Indigenous leader skilled in the language, and following the religion, of the English settlers. In his own lifetime, he was a famous and admired preacher whose books were popular and influential across racial and cultural lines. He was also an accomplished community leader, forming diplomatic connections between tribes and using his knowledge of settler legal and political systems to preserve the independence and land rights of Native Americans.

Samson Occom was born in 1723 in Ben's Town, Connecticut, to Joshua Occom, a prominent Mohegan, and Sarah Samson, a descendant of Pequot leaders. Occom was educated in the skills of hunting and fishing, as well as in the arts, particularly oratory and the interpretation of wampum.[1] He also taught himself to read and write in English. Occom was raised with traditional Mohegan spiritual beliefs, but the evangelical movement known as the Great Awakening brought changes to his family's religious life. His mother converted to Christianity in 1739, and Occom had his own conversion experience at eighteen, when he heard the preaching of Great Awakening radical John Davenport.

In 1742, Occom joined the Mohegan Tribal Council, and, in an effort to become a more effective advocate for his people, he sought further education. He approached the white minister Eleazar Wheelock, who taught Occom higher skills in English, as well as Greek, Latin, and Hebrew. Occom's success inspired Wheelock to found Moor's Indian Charity School, whose curriculum included Bible study and writing skills in classical languages as well as English. Occom helped to recruit Indigenous students for the new school, but difficulties with his eyesight prevented him from attending Yale as planned.

In 1749, Occom established himself as a schoolteacher in Montauk, Long Island, where he also served the Montaukett people in various ways: as a minister; as a healer practicing local Indigenous medicine; and as a judge and counselor resolving community disputes. At first he received no compensation for this work, and later he was given a salary far below what would have been offered to a white minister in the same position. While Great Awakening theology presented black and Indigenous people as the spiritual equals of white people, this view was largely not upheld in practice by the movement's white leadership, many of whom felt that, as Wheelock claimed, "an Indian Missionary may be supported with less than half the expense, that will be necessary to support an Englishman." To supplement his paltry missionary income, Occom labored as a woodworker, bookbinder, farmer, hunter, and fisher.

The financial pressures on Occom increased after he married Mary Fowler, a woman from a powerful Montaukett family, in 1751; the couple would eventually have twelve children. Through his marriage, Occom joined the Montaukett community, and he described some of their cultural practices in "An Account of the Montauk Indians, on Long-Island" (1761, published 1809). Although he lived among the Montaukett, Occom maintained his leadership role as a Mohegan. In particular, he was for decades an important player in the Mason Case, a drawn-out and controversial legal battle against the Connecticut Colony regarding the sale of Mohegan territory to settlers. Occom, like many other Mohegan, objected to settler encroachment on communal lands, arguing that pre-existing treaties and deeds made the sales

[1] Wampum, shell beads, are used for many purposes including trade and record keeping. The white and purple beads are arranged in belts or strands to form patterns that can be interpreted by an expert reader.

illegal. The dispute lasted for much of the eighteenth century, and was, in the end, decided in favor of the colony.

At Wheelock's urging, in 1765 Occom undertook a two-year trip to Britain to raise funds for the Indian Charity School. The decision to send him was controversial, with white religious leaders either questioning Occom's authenticity as an example of a converted "heathen" or claiming he did not really have the skills of a minister: as Occom phrased it in a letter to Wheelock, "some say I can't talk Indian, others say I can't read." In response to these accusations, Occom produced "The True Account of My Education," the first draft of his famous autobiographical narrative. His career remained a subject of controversy, however, and two years later he felt compelled to write a significantly expanded version of the autobiography.

During his preaching tour of Britain, Occom was treated, he later wrote, as a "gazing stock" for curious audiences—but his oratorical skill made his trip an unqualified success. He met prominent religious and political figures including the king, rejected an invitation from the archbishop of Canterbury to join the Anglican Church, and befriended the influential Great Awakening evangelist George Whitefield. He returned to America having raised a remarkable twelve thousand pounds for the Charity School—only to discover that Wheelock instead planned to spend the money on the foundation of Dartmouth College, which would, almost exclusively, serve white students. Meanwhile, Wheelock had not followed through on his promise to look after Occom's family, who were destitute and starving. Disillusioned, Occom left the missionary society and cut his ties to Wheelock.

As an independent traveling preacher, Occom continued to develop his oratorical style. While his sermons of the 1750s and 60s tend to offer straightforward explication of Bible verses, his later sermons expand their interpretive scope, moving beyond individual moral applications to touch on wider cultural and political issues. This more sophisticated approach is exemplified in Occom's *A Sermon, Preached at the Execution of Moses Paul, an Indian* (1772). The occasion for the sermon was the execution of a Mohegan man, Moses Paul, for murder; Paul, who claimed that he had been sentenced by a racist court for a killing made in self-defense, had invited Occom to speak. Occom, preaching on the idea that "the wages of sin is death" (Romans 6.23), asked all the attending audience to consider their own imminent demise and punishment, urged Paul to accept salvation before his execution, and concluded by exhorting the Indigenous audience members in particular to forsake alcohol, which had been involved in the incident.

A Sermon, Preached at the Execution of Moses Paul was a significant event in both its oral and written forms. An impressive crowd of black, Indigenous, and white listeners gathered, according to the Hartford *Courant*, "as much excited to hear Mr. Occum preach, as to see the execution." The sermon was revised and published in book form—the only one of Occom's sermons to appear in print during his lifetime—and was among the most popular works of the decade, issued in nineteen editions. The work made Occom famous in New England; by 1773 he found he had "continual calls to preach both by the English and the Indians."

Occom followed his sermon with another, perhaps equally influential publication: *A Choice Collection of Hymns and Spiritual Songs* (1774). The collection of over 100 hymns featured work by prominent English writers such as Isaac Watts and John and Charles Wesley, selected from a substantial personal hymnal library Occom had gathered while in Britain. Alongside these appeared previously unpublished American hymns collected by Occom during his years of itinerant preaching; the book also includes hymns written by Occom himself. According to its subtitle, the hymnal was "Intended for the Edification of Sincere Christians, of All Denominations," and it helped establish a pattern for the nascent genre of interdenominational hymnals in America. The collection remained popular across the colonies into the nineteenth century, and "Throughout the Saviour's Life We Trace," one of Occom's own contributions, remains a standard in many hymnals.

Also in the early 1770s, Occom began to work with his brother-in-law David Fowler to establish a new settlement, where Indigenous Christians from across New England could practice their religion and culture with minimal interference from Anglo-Americans. They negotiated a land grant from the Oneida in the colony of New York, and in the 1780s Occom and his family were among

the hundreds of Indigenous Christians who emigrated to the new community, called Brotherton or Eeyamequittoowauconnuck. As a resident, he continued to advocate on behalf of the settlement, at one point successfully petitioning the government to restore two thousand acres that had been illegally leased to white occupants. In the nineteenth century, Brotherton was relocated to Wisconsin, where it remains a distinct Indigenous community.

Occom moved to New Stockbridge, near Brotherton, less than a year before his death in 1792. He maintained his status as a community leader up to the end of his life, preaching to both white and Indigenous audiences multiple times a week, and hundreds of people attended his funeral. The extent of his literary importance, however, was not widely recognized until the late twentieth century. In the 1980s, Bernd Peyer rediscovered Occom's autobiographical narrative and published it for the first time, presenting him as "the 'father' of modern Native American literature"; later in the century, LaVonne Brown Ruoff identified *A Sermon, Preached at the Execution of Moses Paul* as the first bestseller by an Indigenous American. Since then, scholarship has often focused on Occom's status as a cross-cultural figure; while some critics interpret his adoption of Christianity and English literary arts as a loss of his own Indigenous culture, others admire what they see as his savvy deployment of Anglo-American ideas and rhetorical strategies in defense of Indigenous communities and ways of life.

NOTE ON THE TEXTS: The text of the autobiographical narrative, unpublished in Occom's lifetime, is based upon the original manuscript, scans of which are available online at The Occom Circle. Selections from *A Sermon, Preached at the Execution of Moses Paul, an Indian* are based on the first edition of that text (1772), while the text of "The Sufferings of Christ" is based upon that appearing in the first edition of *A Choice Collection of Hymns and Spiritual Songs* (1774). The text of "The Most Remarkable and Strange State, Situation, and Appearance of Indian Tribes in This Great Continent," also unpublished during Occom's life, is based upon the version appearing in Joanna Brooks's 2006 work *The Collected Writings of Samson Occom*. Spelling and punctuation have been modernized according to the practices of this anthology.

⌘⌘⌘

 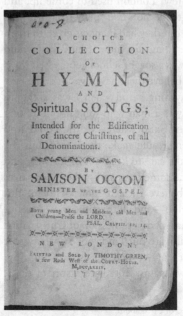

Title pages of *A Sermon Preached at the Execution of Moses Paul* (fourth edition, 1772) and *A Choice Collection of Hymns and Spiritual Songs* (third edition, 1774).

[*Autobiographical Narrative*]

Having seen and heard several representations, in England and Scotland, made by some gentlemen in America, concerning me, and finding many gross mistakes in their account—I thought it my duty to give a short plain and honest account of myself, that those who may hereafter see it, may know the truth concerning me.

FROM MY BIRTH TILL I RECEIVED THE CHRISTIAN RELIGION

I was born a heathen and brought up in heathenism, till I was between 16 and 17 years of age, at a place called Mohegan, in New London, Connecticut, in New England. My parents lived a wandering life, as did all the Indians at Mohegan; they chiefly depended upon hunting, fishing, and fowling for their living and had no connection with the English, excepting to [traffic] with them in their small trifles—and they strictly maintained and followed their heathenish ways, customs and religion—though there was some preaching among them. Once a fortnight, in the summer season, a minister from N[ew] London used to come up, and the Indians to attend; not that they regarded[1] the Christian religion, but they had blankets given to them every fall of the year, and for these things they would attend. And there was a sort of school kept, when I was quite young, but I believe there never was one that ever learned to read anything.[2] And when I was about 10 years of age there was a man who went about among the Indian wigwams, and where ever he could find the Indian children, would make them read; but the children used to take care to keep out of his way; and he used to catch me sometimes and make me say over my letters; and I believe I learnt some of them. But this was soon over too—and all this time there was not one amongst us, that made a profession of Christianity. Neither did we cultivate our land, nor kept any sort of creatures except dogs, which we used in hunting; and we dwelt in wigwams. These are a sort of tents, covered with mats made of flags.[3] And to this time we were unacquainted with the English tongue in general, though there were a few, who understood a little of it.

FROM THE TIME OF OUR REFORMATION TILL I LEFT MR. WHEELOCK[4]

When I was 16 years of age, we heard a strange rumor among the English, that there were extraordinary ministers preaching from place to place and a strange concern among the white people. This was in the spring of the year. But we saw nothing of these things, till some time in the summer, when some ministers began to visit us and preach the word of god; and the common people also came frequently and exhorted us to the things of god. Which it pleased the lord, as I humbly hope, to bless and accompany with divine influence to the conviction and saving conversion of a number of us; amongst whom I was one that was impressed with the things we had heard. These preachers did not only come to us, but we frequently went to their meetings and churches. Constantly, after I was awakened and converted, I went to all the meetings I could come at; and continued under trouble of mind about 6 months; at which time I began to learn the English letters; got me a primer and used to go to my English neighbours frequently for assistance in reading, but went to no school. And when I was 17 years of age, I had, as I trust, a discovery of the way of salvation through Jesus, and was enabled to put my trust in him alone for life and salvation. From this time the distress and burden of my mind was removed, and I found serenity and pleasure of soul, in serving god. By this time I just began to read in the New Testament without spelling[5]—and I had a stronger desire still to learn to read the word of god, and at the same time had an uncommon pity and compassion to my poor brethren according to the flesh. I used to wish I was capable of instructing my poor kindred. I used to think, if I could once learn to read I would instruct the poor children in reading—and used frequently to talk with our Indians concerning

1 *regarded* Respected or cared about.

2 *there never … anything* I.e., no one who attended the school learned to read.

3 *flags* Rushes, or grasslike plants.

4 *MR. WHEELOCK* Eleazar Wheelock (1711–79), Connecticut minister and educator.

5 *without spelling* I.e., easily; without having to pronounce the individual letters.

religion. Thus I continued till I was in my 19th year: by this time I could read a little in the Bible. At this time my poor mother was going to Lebanon, and having had some knowledge of Mr. Wheelock and hearing he had a number of English youth under his tuition, I had a great inclination to go to him and be with him a week or a fortnight,[1] and desired my mother to ask Mr. Wheelock whether he would take me a little while to instruct me in reading. Mother did so, and when she came back, she said Mr. Wheelock wanted to see me as soon as possible. So I went up, thinking I should be back again in a few days; when I got up there, he received me with kindness and compassion and in stead of staying a fortnight or 3 weeks, I spent 4 years with him.

After I had been with him some time, he began to acquaint his friends of my being with him, and of his intentions of educating me, and my circumstances. And the good people began to give some assistance to Mr. Wheelock, and gave me some old and some new clothes. Then he represented the case to the honorable commissioners at Boston, who were commissioned by the Honorable Society in London for Propagating the Gospel among the Indians in New England and parts adjacent, and they allowed him 60£ in old tenor,[2] which was about 6£ sterling, and they continued it 2 or 3 years, I can't tell exactly. While I was at Mr. Wheelock's, I was very weakly and my health much impaired, and at the end of 4 years, I over strained my eyes to [such a] degree, I could not pursue my studies any longer; and out of these 4 years I lost just about one year—and was obliged to quit my studies.

From the Time I Left Mr. Wheelock till I Went to Europe

As soon as I left Mr. Wheelock, I endeavoured to find some employ among the Indians; went to Nahantuck,[3] thinking they may want a school master, but they had one; then went to Narraganset,[4] and they were indifferent about school, and went back to Mohegan, and heard a number of our Indians were going to Montauk, on Long Island, and I went with them. And the Indians there were very desirous to have me keep a school amongst them, and I consented, and went back a while to Mohegan; and some[time] in November I went on the island, I think it is 17 years ago last November. I agreed to keep school with them half a year, and left it with them to give me what they pleased; and they took turns to provide food for me. I had near 30 scholars this winter; I had evening school too for those that could not attend the day school— and began to carry on their meetings, though they had a minister, one Mr. Horton, the Scotch Society's[5] missionary; but he spent, I think, two thirds of his time at Shenecock, 30 miles from Montauk. We met together 3 times for divine worship every sabbath and once on every Wednesday evening. I read the scriptures to them and used to expound upon some particular passages in my own tongue;[6] visited the sick and attended their burials. When the half year expired, they desired me to continue with them, which I complied with, for another half year. When I had fulfilled that, they were urgent to have me stay longer, so I continued till I was married, which was about 2 years after I went there.

And continued to instruct them in the same manner as I did before. After I was married a while, I found there was need of a support more than I needed while I was single—and I made my case known to Mr. Buell and to Mr. Wheelock, and also the needy circumstances and the desires of these Indians of my continuing amongst them, and the commissioners were so good as to grant £15 per an. sterling—and I kept on in my service as usual, yea I had additional service. I kept school as I did before and carried on the religious meetings as often as ever, and attended the sick and their funerals, and did what writings they wanted, and often sat as a judge to reconcile and decide their matters between them, and had visitors of Indians from

[1] *a fortnight* Two weeks.

[2] *old tenor* I.e., Connecticut currency, which was worth much less than the British pound sterling; both types of money circulated in the colony.

[3] *Nahantuck* Also called Niantic, territory of the Niantic people on the Connecticut coast.

[4] *Narraganset* Territory of the Narragansett people on the coast of Rhode Island.

[5] *Scotch Society* The Scottish Society for the Propagation of Christian Knowledge, a missionary society.

[6] *my own tongue* Mohegan-Pequot, a language closely related to Montauk.

all quarters; and, as our custom is, we freely entertain all visitors. And was fetched often from my tribe and from others to see into their affairs both religious [and] temporal—besides my domestic concerns—and it pleased the Lord to increase my family fast. And soon after I was married, Mr. Horton left these Indians and the Shenecock Indians, and after this I was licenced to p[reach] and then I had the whole care of these Indians at Montauk, and visited the Shenecock Indians often. Used to set out Saturdays towards night and come back again Mondays. I have been obliged to set out from home after sun set, and ride 30 miles in the night, to preach to these Indians. And some Indians at Shenecock sent their children to my school at Montauk, I kept one of them some time, and had a young man a half year from Mohegan, a lad from Nahantuck, who was with me almost a year; and had little or nothing for keeping them.

My method in the school was, as soon as the children got together, and took their proper seats, I prayed with them, then began to hear them.[1] I generally began (after some of them could spell and read) with those that were yet in their alphabets, so around, as they were properly seated, till I got through, and I obliged them to study their books, and to help one another. When they could not make out a hard word they brought [it] to me—and I usually heard them, in the summer season 8 times a day, 4 in the morning, and in the afternoon. In the winter season 6 times a day, as soon as they could spell, they were obliged to spell when ever they wanted to go out. I concluded with prayer; I generally heard my evening scholars 3 times round, and as they go out the school, everyone that can spell is obliged to spell a word, and to go out leisurely one after another. I catechised[2] 3 or 4 times a week according to the assembly's shorter catechism, and many times proposed questions of my own, and in my own tongue. I found difficulty with some children, who were somewhat dull; most of these can soon learn to say over their letters, they distinguish the sounds by the ear, but their eyes can't distinguish the letters, and the way I took to cure them was by making an alphabet on small bits of paper, and glued them on small chips of cedar after this manner: A, B, etc. I put these on letters in order on a bench then point to one letter and bid a child to take notice of it, and then I order the child to fetch me the letter from the bench; if it brings the letter, it is well, if not it must go again and again till it brings the right letter. When they can bring any letters this way, then I just jumble them together, and bid them to set them in alphabetical order, and it is a pleasure to them; and they soon learn their letters this way.

I frequently discussed or exhorted my scholars, in religious matters. My method in our religious meetings was this: sabbath morning we assemble together about 10 o'c[lock] and begin with singing; we generally sung Dr. Watts's[3] psalms or hymns. I distinctly read the psalm or hymn first, and then gave the meaning of it to them, after that sing, then pray, and sing again after prayer. Then proceed to read some suitable portion of scripture, and so just give the plain sense of it in familiar discourse and apply it to them, so conclude with prayer and singing. In the after noon and evening we proceed in the same manner, and so in Wednesday evening. Some time after Mr. Horton left these Indians, there was a remarkable revival of religion among these Indians and many were hopefully converted to the saving knowledge of god in Jesus. It is to be observed before Mr. Horton left these Indians they had some prejudices infused in their minds, by some enthusiastical exhorters from New England, against Mr. Horton, and many of them had left him; by this means he was discouraged, and sued a dismission[4] and was dismissed from these Indians. And being acquainted with the enthusiasts in New England and the make and the disposition of the Indians, [I] took a mild way to reclaim them. I opposed them not openly but let them go on in their way, and whenever I had an opportunity, I would read such passages of the scriptures, and I thought would confound their notions, and I would come to them with all authority, saying, "thus saith the Lord"; and by this means, the Lord was pleased to bless my poor endeavours, and they were reclaimed, and brought to hear almost any of the ministers.

[1] *hear them* I.e., hear them read or recite their lessons.

[2] *catechised* Taught the fundamentals of religious belief, especially by questioning students with reference to a catechism, a book summarizing a religion's official theology.

[3] *Dr. Watts* Isaac Watts (1674–1748), English minister best known as the author of numerous hymns.

[4] *sued a dismission* Asked to be released from his post.

I am now to give an account of my circumstances and manner of living. I dwelt in a wigwam, a small hut with small poles and covered with mats made of flags, and I was obliged to move twice a year, about 2 miles distance, by reason of the scarcity of wood, for in one neck of land they planted their corn, and in another, they had their wood, and I was obliged to have my corn carted and my hay also—and I got my ground plowed every year, which cost me about 12 s[hillings] an acre; and I kept a cow and a horse, for which I paid 21 shillings every year York currency,[1] and went 18 miles to mill for every dust of meal we used in my family. I hired or joined with my neighbours to go to mill, with a horse or ox cart, or on horseback, and sometimes went myself. My family increasing fast, and my visitors also, I was obliged to contrive every way to support my family; I took all opportunities, to get something to feed my family daily. I planted my own corn, potatoes, and beans; I used to be out hoeing my corn sometimes before sun rise and after my school is dismissed, and by this means I was able to raise my own pork, for I was allowed to keep 5 swine. Some mornings and evenings I would be out with my hook and line to catch fish, and in the fall of year and in the spring, I used my gun, for we lived very handy for fowl, and I was very expert with [a] gun, and fed my family with fowl. I could more than pay for my powder and shot with feathers. At other times I bound old books for Easthampton people, made wooden spoons and ladles, stocked guns, and worked on cedar to make pails, piggins,[2] and churns etc. Besides all these difficulties I met with adverse providence: I bought a mare, had it but little while, and she fell into the quick sands and died. After a while bought another, I kept her about half year, and she was gone, and I never heard nor seen her from that day to this; it was supposed some rogue stole her. I got another and [it] died with a distemper, and last of all I bought a young mare, and kept her till she had one colt, and she broke her leg and died, and presently after the colt died also. In the whole I lost 5 horse kind; all these losses helped to pull me down; and by this time I got greatly in debt, and acquainted my circumstances to some of my friends, and they represented my case to the commissioners of Boston, and

interceded with them for me, and they were pleased to vote [£]15 for my help, and soon after sent a letter to my good friend at N[ew] London, acquainting him that they had superseded[3] their vote; and my friends were so good as to represent my needy circumstances still to them, and they were so good at last, as to vote £15 and sent it, for which I am very thankful. And the Reverend Mr. Buell was so kind as to write in my behalf to the gentlemen of Boston; and he told me they were much displeased with him, and heard also once and again that they blamed me for being extravagant. I can't conceive how these gentlemen would have me live. I am ready to impute [it] to their ignorance, and I would wish they had changed circumstances with me but one month, that they may know by experience what my case really was; but I am now fully convinced, that it was not ignorance, for I believe it can be proved to the world that these same gentlemen gave a young missionary, a single man, *one hundred pounds* for one year, and fifty pounds for an interpreter, and thirty pounds for an introducer; so it cost them one hundred and eighty pounds in one single year, and they sent too where there was no need of a missionary.

Now you see what difference they made between me and other missionaries; they gave me 180 pounds for 12 years service, which they gave for one year's service in another mission. In my service (I speak like a fool,[4] but I am constrained) I was my own interpreter. I was both a school master and minister to the Indians, yea I was their ear, eye and hand, as well as mouth. I leave it with the world, as wicked as it is, to judge whether I ought not to have had half as much, they gave a young man just mentioned, which would have been but £50 a year; and if they ought to have given me that, I am not under obligations to them, I owe them nothing at all. What can be the reason that they used me after this manner? I can't think of anything, but this as a poor Indian boy said, who was bound out to an English family, and he used to drive plow for a young man, and he whipped and beat him almost every day, and the young man found fault with him, and complained of him to his master and the poor boy was called to

[1] *York currency* Money printed by the colony of New York.

[2] *piggins* Small buckets or deep ladles.

[3] *superseded* Suspended or retracted.

[4] *I speak like a fool* See 2 Corinthians 11.23: "Are they ministers of Christ? (I speak as a fool) I am more; in labours more abundant, in stripes above measure, in prisons more frequent, in deaths oft."

answer for himself before his master, and he was asked, what it was he did, that he was so complained of and beat almost every day. He said, he did not know, but he supposed it was because he could not drive any better; but says he, I drive as well as I know how; and at other times he beats me, because he is of a mind to beat me; but says he, I believe he beats [me] for the most of the time because I am an Indian.

So I am ready to say, they have used [me] thus, because I can't instruct the Indians so well as other missionaries; but I can assure *them* I have endeavoured to teach them as well as I [know] how—but I must say, I believe it is because I am a poor Indian. I can't help that god has made me so; I did not make my self so.—
—1982 (WRITTEN 1765, 1768)

from *A Sermon, Preached at the Execution of Moses Paul, an Indian*

INTRODUCTION

By the melancholy providence of God, and at the earnest desire and invitation of the poor condemned Criminal, I am here before this great concourse of people at this time, to give the last discourse to the poor miserable object who is to be executed this day before your eyes, for the due reward of his folly and madness, and enormous wickedness. It is an unwelcome task to me to speak upon such an occasion; but since it is the desire of the poor man himself, who is to die a shameful death this day, in conscience I cannot deny him; I must endeavor to do the great work the dying man requests.

I conclude that this great concourse of people have come together to see the execution of justice upon this poor Indian; and I suppose the biggest part of you look upon yourselves Christians, and as such, I hope you will demean yourselves;[1] and that you will have suitable commiseration towards this poor object. Though you can't in justice pray for his life to be continued in this world, yet you can pray earnestly for the salvation of his poor soul, consistently with the mind of God. Let this be therefore, the fervent exercise of our souls: for

this is the last day we have to pray for him. As for you that don't regard religion, it cannot be expected, that you will put up one petition for this miserable creature: yet I would entreat you seriously to consider the frailty of corrupt nature, and behave yourselves as becomes rational creatures.

And in a word, Let us all be suitably affected with the melancholy occasion of the day; knowing that we are all dying creatures, and accountable unto God. Though this poor condemned creature will in a few minutes know more than all of us, either in unutterable joy, or in inconceivable woe, yet we shall certainly know as much as he in a few days.[2]

The sacred words that I have chosen to speak from, upon this undesirable occasion, are found written in the Epistle of St. Paul to the

ROMANS 6.23
For the wages of sin is death, but the gift of God is eternal life through Jesus Christ our Lord.

Death is called the king of terrors, and it ought to be the subject of every man and woman's thoughts daily; because it is that unto which they are liable every moment of their lives: And therefore it cannot be unseasonable to think, speak and hear of it at any time, and especially on this mournful occasion; for we must all come to it, how soon we cannot tell; whether we are prepared or not prepared, ready or not ready, whether death is welcome or not welcome, we must feel the force of it: whether we concern ourselves with death or not, it will concern itself with us. Seeing that this is the case with every one of us, what manner of persons ought we to be in all holy conversation and godliness; how ought men to exert themselves in preparation for death continually; for they know not what a day or an hour may bring forth, with respect to them. But, alas! according to the appearance of mankind in general, death is the least thought of. They go on from day to day, as if they were to live here forever, as if this was the only life. They contrive, rack their inventions, disturb their rest, and even hazard their lives in all manner of dangers, both by sea and land; yea, they leave no stone unturned that they may live in

[1] *demean yourselves* Conduct yourselves.

[2] *in a few days* See Job 14.1: "Man that is born of a woman is of few days and full of trouble."

the world, and at the same time have little or no con-trivance to die well. God and their souls are neglected, and heaven and eternal happiness are disregarded; Christ and his religion are despised—yet most of these very men intend to be happy when they come to die, not considering that there must be great preparation in order to die well. Yea there is none so fit to live as those that are fit to die; those that are not fit to die are not fit to live. …

I have now gone through what I proposed from my text. And I shall now make some application of the whole.

First to the criminal in particular; and then to the auditory[1] in general.

My poor unhappy Brother MOSES;

As it was your own desire that I should preach to you this last discourse, so I shall speak plainly to you. You are the bone of my bone, and flesh of my flesh.[2] You are an Indian, a despised creature; but you have despised yourself; yea you have despised God more; you have trodden under foot his authority; you have despised his commands and precepts; And now, as God says, be sure your sins will find you out.[3] And now, poor Moses, your sins have found you out, and they have overtaken you this day; the day of your death is now come; the king of terrors is at hand; you have but a very few moments to breathe in this world. The just law of man, and the holy law of Jehovah, call aloud for the destruction of your mortal life; God says, "Whoso sheddeth man's blood, by man shall his blood be shed."[4] This is the ancient decree of heaven, and it is to be executed by man; nor have you the least gleam of hope of escape, for the unalterable sentence is passed; the terrible day of execution is come; the unwelcome guard is about you; and the fatal instruments of death are now made ready; your coffin and your grave, your last lodging, are open ready to receive you.

Alas! poor Moses, now you know by sad, by woeful experience, the living truth of our text, that the wages of sin is death. You have been already dead; yea twice dead: by nature spiritually dead. And since the awful sentence of death has been passed upon you, you have been dead to all the pleasures of this life; or all the pleasures, lawful or unlawful, have been dead to you: And death, which is the wages of sin, is standing even on this side of your grave ready to put a final period to your mortal life; and just beyond the grave, eternal death awaits your poor soul, and devils are ready to drag your miserable soul down to their bottomless den, where everlasting woe and horror reigns; the place is filled with doleful shrieks, howls and groans of the damned. Oh! to what a miserable, forlorn, and wretched condition has your extravagance folly and wickedness brought you! i.e. if you die in your sins. And O! what manner of repentance ought you to manifest! How ought your heart to bleed for what you have done! How ought you to prostrate your soul before a bleeding God! And under self-condemna-tion, cry out, Ah Lord, ah Lord, what have I done! Whatever partiality, injustice and error there may be among the judges of the earth, remember that you have deserved a thousand deaths, and a thousand hells, by reason of your sins, at the hands of a holy God. Should God come out against you in strict jus-tice, alas! what could you say for yourself? for you have been brought up under the bright sun-shine, and plain, and loud sound of the gospel; and you have had a good education; you can read and write well; and God has given you a good natural understanding: And therefore your sins are so much more aggravated. You have not sinned in such an ignorant manner as others have done; but you have sinned with both your eyes open as it were, under the light even the glori-ous light of the gospel of the Lord Jesus Christ. You have sinned against the light of your own conscience, against your knowledge and understanding; you have sinned against the pure and holy laws of God, the just laws of men; you have sinned against heaven and earth; you have sinned against all the mercies and goodness of God; you have sinned against the whole Bible, against the old and new-testament; you have sinned against the blood of Christ, which is the blood of the everlasting covenant. O poor Moses, see what you have done! And now repent, repent, I say again repent; see how the blood you shed cries against you,

[1] *auditory* Listeners.

[2] *bone of … my flesh* See Genesis 2.23.

[3] *be sure … you out* See Numbers 32.23.

[4] *Whoso … be shed* See Genesis 9.6.

and the Avenger of Blood[1] is at your heels. O fly, fly, to the blood of the Lamb of God[2] for the pardon of all your aggravated sins.

But let us now turn to a more pleasant theme. Though you have been a great sinner, a heaven daring sinner; yet hark and hear the joyful sound from heaven, even from the King of kings, and Lord of lords; that the gift of God is eternal life, through Jesus Christ our Lord. It is a free gift, and offered to the greatest sinners, and upon their true repentance towards God and faith in the Lord Jesus Christ, they shall be welcome to the life they have spoken of; it is offered upon free terms. He that hath no money may come; he that hath no righteousness, no goodness, may come, the call is to poor undone sinners; the call is not to the righteous, but sinners calling them to repentance. Hear the voice of the Son of the most high God, Come unto me, all [ye] that labour and are heavy laden, and I will give you rest.[3] This is a call, a gracious call to you, poor Moses, under your present burden and distresses. ... O Moses! this is good news to you in this last day of your life; here is a crucified Saviour at hand for your sins; his blessed hands are out-stretched, all in a gore of blood for you. This is the only Saviour, an Almighty Saviour, just such as you stand in infinite and perishing need of. O, poor Moses! hear the dying prayer of a gracious Saviour on the accursed tree[4]—Father forgive them for they know not what they do.[5] This was a prayer for his enemies and murderers; and it is for you, if you will now only repent and believe in him. ... O, poor Moses, now believe on the Lord Jesus Christ with all your heart, and thou shalt be saved eternally. Come just as you are, with all your sins and abominations, with all your filthiness, with all your blood-guiltiness, with all your condemnation, and lay hold of the hope set before you this day. This is the last day of salvation with

your soul; you will be beyond the bounds of mercy in a few minutes more. O what a joyful day would it be if you would now openly believe in and receive the Lord Jesus Christ; it would be the beginning of heavenly days with your poor soul; instead of a melancholy day, it would be a wedding day to your soul: It would cause the very angels in heaven to rejoice, and the saints on earth to be glad; it would cause the angels to come down from the realms above, and wait hovering about your gallows, ready to convey your soul to the heavenly mansions, there to take the possession of eternal glory and happiness, and join the heavenly choirs in singing the songs of Moses and the Lamb: There to set down forever with Abraham, Isaac and Jacob[6] in the kingdom of God's glory; and your shame and guilt shall be forever banished from the place, and all sorrow and fear forever fly away, and tears be wiped from your face; and there shall you forever admire the astonishing and amazing and infinite mercy of God in Christ Jesus, in pardoning such a monstrous sinner as you have been; there you will claim the highest note of praise, for the riches of free grace in Christ Jesus. But if you will not accept of a Saviour so freely offered to you this last day of your life, you must this very day bid a farewell to God the Father, Son and Holy Ghost, to heaven and all the saints and angels that are there; and you must bid all the saints in this lower world an eternal farewell, and even the whole world. And so I must leave you in the hands of God; and I must turn to the whole auditory.

Sirs, We may plainly see, from what we have heard, and from the miserable object before us, into what a doleful condition sin has brought mankind, even into a state of death and misery. We are by nature as certainly under the sentence of death from God, as this miserable man is by the just determination of man; and we are all dying creatures, and we are, or ought to be sensible of it: and this is the dreadful fruit of sin. O! let us then fly from all appearance of sin; let us fight against it with all our might; let us repent and turn to our God, and believe on the Lord Jesus Christ, that we may live forever; let us all prepare for death, for we know not how soon, nor how suddenly we may be called out of the world. ...

1 *Avenger of Blood* See Deuteronomy 19.4–12, which recommends no capital punishment for accidental killings but states that a person who kills deliberately out of hatred should be delivered "into the hand of the avenger of blood, that he may die."

2 *Lamb of God* Jesus, especially when considered as a sacrifice for the atonement of humankind's sin. See John 1.29 and Revelation 22.3.

3 *Come unto ... you rest* See Matthew 11.28.

4 *tree* Cross.

5 *Father ... they do* See Luke 23.34.

6 *Abraham, Isaac and Jacob* Biblical patriarchs.

I shall now address myself to the Indians, my brethren and kindred according to the flesh.

My poor kindred,

You see the woeful consequences of sin, by seeing this our poor miserable countryman now before us, who is to die this day for his sins and great wickedness. And it was the sin of drunkenness that has brought this destruction and untimely death upon him. There is a dreadful woe denounced from the Almighty against drunkards; and it is this sin, this abominable, this beastly and accursed sin of drunkenness, that has stripped us of every desirable comfort in this life; by this we are poor, miserable and wretched; by this sin we have no name nor credit in the world among polite nations; for this sin we are despised in the world, and it is all right and just, for we despised ourselves more; and if we don't regard ourselves, who will regard us? And it is for our sins, and especially for that accursed, that most devilish sin of drunkenness that we suffer every day. For the love of strong drink we spend all that we have, and everything we can get. By this sin we can't have comfortable houses, nor anything comfortable in our houses; neither food nor raiment, nor decent utensils. We are obliged to put up any sort of shelter just to screen us from the severity of the weather, and we go about with very mean, ragged and dirty clothes, almost naked. And we are half-starved, for the most of the time obliged to pick up anything to eat. And our poor children are suffering every day for want of the necessaries of life; they are very often crying for want of food, and we have nothing to give them; and in the cold weather they are shivering and crying, being pinched with cold—All this is for the love of strong drink. And this is not all the misery and evil we bring on ourselves in this world; but when we are intoxicated with strong drink we drown our rational powers, by which we are distinguished from the brutal creation;[1] we unman ourselves, and bring ourselves not only level with the beasts of the field, but seven degrees beneath them; yea we bring ourselves level with the devils; I don't know but we make ourselves worse than devils, for I never heard of drunken devils.

My poor kindred, do consider what a dreadful abominable sin drunkenness is. God made us men, and we choose to be beast and devils; God made us rational creatures, and we choose to be fools. Do consider further, and behold a drunkard and see how he looks, when he has drowned his reason; how deformed and shameful does he appear? He disfigures every part of him, both soul and body, which was made after the image of God. He appears with awful deformity, and his whole visage[2] is disfigured; if he attempts to speak he cannot bring out his words distinct, so as to be understood; if he walks he reels and staggers to and fro, and tumbles down. And see how he behaves, he is now laughing, and then he is crying; he is singing and the next minute he is mourning; and is all love to every one, and anon he is raging, and for fighting, and killing all before him, even the nearest and dearest relations and friends: Yea nothing is too bad for a drunken man to do. He will do that which he would not do for the world, in his right mind; he may lie with his own sister or daughter as Lot did.[3]

Further, when a person is drunk, he is just good for nothing in the world; he is of no service to himself, to his family, to his neighbours, or his country; and how much more unfit is he to serve God: yet he is just fit for the service of the devil.

Again, a man in drunkenness is in all manner of dangers, he may be killed by his fellow-men, by wild beasts, and tame beasts; he may fall into the fire, into the water, or into a ditch; or he may fall down as he walks along, and break his bones or his neck; and he may cut himself with edge-tools. Further, if he has any money or anything valuable, he may lose it all, or may be robbed, or he may make a foolish bargain, and be cheated out of all he has.

I believe you know the truth of what I have just now said, many of you, by sad experience; yet you will go on still in your drunkenness. Though you have been cheated over and over again, and you have lost your substance by drunkenness, yet you will venture to go on in this most destructive sin. O fools when will ye be wise? We all know the truth of what I have been saying, by what we have seen and heard of drunken deaths. How many have been drowned in our rivers, and how many frozen to death in the winter season! yet drunkards go on without fear and consideration: alas,

[1] *the brutal creation* I.e., non-human animals.

[2] *visage* Face.

[3] *may lie … Lot did* In Genesis 19.30–38, Lot's daughters get him drunk and then rape him so that they can conceive children.

alas! What will become of all such drunkards? Without doubt they must all go to hell, except they truly repent and turn to God. Drunkenness is so common amongst us, that even our young men and young women are not ashamed to get drunk. Our young men will get drunk as soon as they will eat when they are hungry. It is generally esteemed among men, more abominable for a woman to be drunk, than a man; and yet there is nothing more common amongst us than female drunkards. Women ought to be more modest than men; the holy scriptures recommend modesty to women in particular—but drunken women have no modesty at all. It is more intolerable for a woman to get drunk, if we consider further, that she is in great danger of falling into the hands of the sons of Belial,[1] or wicked men, and being shamefully treated by them.

And here I cannot but observe, we find in sacred writ, a woe denounced against men, who put their bottles to their neighbors mouth to make them drunk, that they may see their nakedness:[2] And no doubt there are such devilish men now in our days, as there were in the days of old.

And to conclude, consider my poor kindred, you that are drunkards, into what a miserable condition you have brought yourselves. There is a dreadful woe thundering against you every day, and the Lord says, That drunkards shall not inherit the kingdom of God.[3]

And now let me exhort you all to break off from your drunkenness, by a gospel repentance, and believe on the Lord Jesus and you shall be saved. Take warning by this doleful sight before us, and by all the dreadful judgments that have befallen poor drunkards. O let us reform our lives, and live as becomes dying creatures, in time to come. Let us be persuaded that we are accountable creatures to God, and we must be called to an account in a few days. You that have been careless all your days, now awake to righteousness, and be concerned for your poor and never dying souls. Fight against all sins, and especially the sin that easily besets

you, and behave in time to come as becomes rational creatures; and above all things, receive and believe on the Lord Jesus Christ, and you shall have eternal life; and when you come to die, your souls will be received into heaven, there to be with the Lord Jesus in eternal happiness, with all the saints in glory; which, God of his infinite mercy grant, through Jesus Christ our Lord. Amen.

—1772

The Sufferings of Christ

1

Throughout the Saviour's life we trace,
 Nothing but shame and deep disgrace,
No period else is seen;
 Till he a spotless victim fell,
5 Tasting in soul a painful Hell,
 Caused by the creature's sin.[4]

2

On the cold ground methinks I see
My Jesus kneel, and pray for me;
 For this I him adore;
10 Seized with a chilly sweat throughout,
 Blood-drops did force their passage out
 Through ev'ry opened pore.

3

A pricking thorn his temples bore;
His back with lashes all was tore,
15 Till one the bones might see;
 Mocking, they pushed him here and there,
 Marking his way with blood and tear,
Pressed by the heavy tree.° cross

4

Thus up the hill he painful came,
20 Round him they mock, and make their game,
 At length his cross they rear;

[1] sons of Belial See Judges 19, in which a horde of men, described as "sons of Belial," demand to be allowed to rape a man who is staying in the city as a guest. The man gives them his concubine instead, and they rape her until she dies.

[2] woe denounced ... nakedness See Habakkuk 2.15.

[3] That drunkards ... of God See 1 Corinthians 6.10: "Nor thieves, nor covetous, nor drunkards, nor revilers, nor extortioners, shall inherit the kingdom of God."

[4] the creature's sin The sin of created beings. According to most Christian theology, Jesus' crucifixion was a sacrifice made necessary by the sin committed by the first humans, Adam and Eve.

And can you see the mighty God,
Cry out beneath sin's heavy load,
Without one thankful tear?

5

25 Thus veiled in humanity,
He dies in anguish on the tree;
What tongue his grief can tell?
The shudd'ring rocks their heads recline,
The mourning sun refuse to shine,
30 When the creator fell.

6

Shout, brethren, shout in songs divine,
He drank the gall, to give us wine,[1]
To quench our parching thirst;
Seraphs° advance your voices higher; angels
35 Bride of the Lamb,[2] unite the choir,
And laud thy precious Christ.
—1774

The Most Remarkable and Strange State, Situation, and Appearance of Indian Tribes in This Great Continent

Sometimes I am ready to conclude that they are under great curse from God. But when I come to look and view the nations of the world, I can't see that they are under greater curse than other nations. There are the poor Negroes; how long have they been in wretched and most cruel slavery—thousands and millions of 'em? And when I come to consider and see the conduct of the most learned, polite, and rich nations of the world, I find them to be the most tyrannical, cruel, and inhuman oppressors of their fellow creatures in the world; these make all the confusions and distractions among the nations of the whole world.

They are the nations that enslave the poor Negroes in such barbarous manner as outdo the savage Indians in North America, and these are called Christian nations. You may see Mr. John Wesley's account of [the] Slave Trade.[3] Now let's [query]—Who is under the greatest curse: he that [inclines] to such hardness of heart, as to exercise the utmost cruelty upon their fellow creatures,[4] or they that are thus tormented? As for my part I cannot see so far as to determine who are under the greatest curse of all nations; I believe all Adamites[5] are under a curse. As for this life, it is as nothing, it is altogether uncertain.

Shall now take notice of things peculiar to the Natives of this country. Indians, so called, in this most extensive continent, are universally poor, they have no notion of laying up much for the future, they all live from hand to mouth, as the common saying is, chiefly by hunting, fishing, and fowling. The women raise little corn, beans, and pumpkins, and pick wild fruits, and do other drudgery. Those that live among or near the white people have learned, some of them, to live a little in imitation of them, but very poor still. They are good servants to themselves, they have no economy[6] to live; wasteful and imprudent, both of time and substance, they will worry and toil all day to lose two shillings and gain six pence, they have no patience nor ambition to appear great in the world, they have no notion of much learning, them that have had some learning made little or no good use of it. Many have lost all their learning. They learn no trades; if any of them have learned, they follow it not. They have no laws or regulations neither; every one does what is right in his own eyes. Yet in general they [are] kind to one another, and are not given to lying, cheating, and stealing much; what [they do] this way is trifling. But they are much for drinking strong drink, yet I can't think that it is more natural to them than other n[ations] their manner.[7]
—2006 (WRITTEN 1783)

1 *drank the gall* See Matthew 27.34, in which the soldiers supervising Jesus' crucifixion give him "vinegar to drink mixed with gall"; *give us wine* In John 2.1–11, Jesus miraculously transforms water into wine.

2 *the Lamb* Jesus. The phrase "the bride, the Lamb's wife" appears in Revelation 21.9 and has been interpreted to refer to the city of heaven, to the soul, or to the Christian church as a whole.

3 *Mr. John … Slave Trade* English Methodist leader John Wesley's antislavery pamphlet *Thoughts upon Slavery* (1774).

4 *creatures* Beings created by God.

5 *Adamites* Humans, who, according to the Bible, are descended from the first people, Adam and Eve.

6 *economy* Prudent management of household resources, including money and food.

7 *than other … manner* Than it is to other nations.

Elm Bark Box

Samson Occom sent this decorated box, made from elm bark, to his sister Lucy in Mohegan; it is possible that he carved the box himself. The box documents his journey to Brotherton, a pantribal separatist community he was instrumental in helping to establish on former Oneida territory in the colony of New York. The pattern on the side of the box is called the "Trail of Life" or "Path of the Sun," reflecting both the cycle of life from birth to death and the course of the sun, from sunrise in the east to sunset in the west. The journey from Mohegan to Brotherton was also, literally, a movement westward, from Connecticut to New York. Markings on the top of the box represent each of the tribes from which the migrants to Brotherton originated.

—C. 1780S–1790S

J. Hector St. John de Crèvecoeur

1735 – 1813

At once intimately familiar with and yet in ways an outsider to American culture, French-born J. Hector St. John de Crèvecoeur earned renown in his life as an authority on Americanness, during the very years when the nation's political character was being challenged and defined. His *Letters from an American Farmer* (1782) vividly brought both the successes and the failures of American society to life for European audiences, and earned him a smaller but still substantial reputation in the country they depicted. Long interpreted as the literal thoughts of their creator, the *Letters*, written in the persona of Pennsylvania-born "Farmer James," have a complex reception history that has been shaped by changing tastes and political currents, and complicated by the fact that different and sometimes conflicting versions of the text were published during Crèvecoeur's lifetime. For over two centuries readers have struggled to reconcile the different sides of "Farmer James," who writes that America is "the most perfect society now existing in the world," but who concludes, upon witnessing the horrors of American slavery, that Americans "certainly are not that class of beings which we vainly think ourselves to be."

Born to members of the petty nobility in Normandy in 1735, Michel-Guillaume Jean de Crèvecoeur received an austere classical education under the tutorship of Catholic Jesuits in Caen, before moving to England in 1754 to live with distant relatives. He moved to French Canada the following year, after the untimely death of his English fiancée, and was employed by the French militia as a surveyor and map-maker during the French and Indian War. He became widely commended for his skills as a cartographer, but a battle wound and his subsequent disgrace after an undisclosed controversy led Crèvecoeur to again seek a different life. By late 1759 Crèvecoeur was making his way southwards to the British colonies, intent on making a living as an American farmer.

Though he did not settle immediately—spending approximately a decade working on an itinerant basis as a tradesperson and surveyor throughout New York, New England, and the Great Lakes region—by 1769 Crèvecoeur had become a British subject, had changed his name to James Hector St. John, and had purchased a large tract of land in Orange County, New York. It was shortly after his marriage to the Protestant Mehitable Tippett that Crèvecoeur began his work on a series of pieces reflecting upon the burgeoning American culture he now found himself a part of. When the American Revolution broke out in 1776, Crèvecoeur was conflicted; his wife's family were staunch Loyalists, but many of his other acquaintances supported the colonial rebels. Crèvecoeur himself decided to evade the conflict by heading back to France with his son in 1780, ostensibly with the aim of securing his children's inheritance—though he was hindered in his efforts by a few months' stint as British prisoner of war, on suspicion of being a Patriot spy.

Having eventually reached England, Crèvecoeur sought a publisher for his now-complete series of literary pieces in the popular eighteenth-century genre of epistolary writing. The collection aroused the interest of publisher Thomas Davies (a friend of Samuel Johnson), and *Letters from an American Farmer; Describing Certain Provincial Situations, Manners, and Customs Not Generally Known; and Conveying Some Idea of the Late and Present Interior Circumstances of the British Colonies in North America* was printed in London in 1782. The letters are narrated by the self-described "humble American Planter" Farmer James—a farmer in Pennsylvania rather than New York—and addressed to a "Mr. F.B.," a refined Englishman who is described as having visited Farmer James and his wife on their homestead, and who is said to be still curious about the state of affairs in the colonies. They describe a good deal of the culture, industry, geography, and politics of early America—and convey too a good deal of emotional content,

as Mr. F.B. is said in Letter 2 to have requested: "... you used, in your refined style, to denominate me the farmer of feelings. How rude must those feelings be in him who daily holds the ax or the plough! ... Those feelings, however, I will delineate as well as I can, agreeably to your earnest request."

With peace negotiations now well under way between Britain and the United States, Davies advertised the work as the unvarnished truth, asserting that the letters contained "much authentic information, little known on this side the Atlantic. They cannot, therefore, fail of being highly interesting, to the people of England, at a time when everybody's attention is directed toward the affairs of America." The collection was an immediate success in England. The *Letters*'s blend of sentimentality, romanticism, and Enlightenment political values rendered them highly interesting to a wide variety of audiences; a second edition was soon printed in London, and translations into Dutch and German ensued. Crèvecoeur's narrator both praises America as a farmer's paradise (and cultural melting pot) and condemns it as a place of horrendous enslavement and violent warfare, but many readers appeared to pay attention primarily to the more optimistic opening letters; indeed, the collection received some criticism on both sides of the Atlantic for what George Washington, otherwise an admirer of the work, described as a "too flattering" portrait of the nation.

Crèvecoeur soon returned to France, where he found himself a celebrity and began associating with members of the Parisian intellectual elite, while also working on a substantially altered French version of the *Lettres d'un Cultivateur Américain* (1784; 1787). Though he had appeared to harbor a degree of Loyalist sympathy while living in the rebelling colonies, here Crèvecoeur was embraced by the French as a specimen of an American Patriot, an image underscored by the intensely anti-British stance taken by many of the letters in the French-language edition. Largely abandoning the framing conceit of Farmer James, the French text provides a more explicitly philosophical exploration of Crèvecoeur's themes; the influence of French *philosophes* such as Rousseau and Voltaire is evident.

The growing tension between Crèvecoeur's French and American identities only increased when he was sent to the United States as a consul by the French government in 1783. Crèvecoeur's return to New York late that year was marked by tragedy: he found that his wife had been killed, his homestead destroyed in a raid, and that his two other children had barely escaped death themselves, and been taken in by strangers in Boston. After several politically successful but emotionally exhausting years working in the United States, Crèvecoeur eventually resigned from his French governmental position. He returned to France permanently in 1790.

The timing of his return was unfortunate. Once again, the pacifist Crèvecoeur was surrounded by political turmoil as the French Revolution took hold; many of his acquaintances were executed or sent into exile during the Reign of Terror in 1793–94. Crèvecoeur himself fled Paris for Germany. Later in the decade he supported himself by writing agricultural pamphlets in Normandy. His last major work, *Voyage dans la Haute-Pennsylvanie et dans l'état de New-York* (1801), was virtually ignored upon publication; some found the work's philosophical ambitiousness to be at odds with their vision of the quaint, artless sentimentality of Farmer James. Crèvecoeur died of heart complications in 1813.

In the decades following his death, *Letters from an American Farmer* fell into obscurity, remaining out of print for many decades. Some nineteenth-century critics admired it as a quaint historical curiosity; the 1856 *Cyclopaedia of American Literature* describes the text as "pleasing and agreeable" but "all sentiment and susceptibility ... looking at homely American life in the Claude Lorraine glass of fanciful enthusiasm." New editions published in 1904 and 1912 signaled a revival of scholarly interest; still, the *Letters* were read primarily as interesting sociological documents rather than as literary works—although D.H. Lawrence in his 1923 *Studies in Classic American Literature* acknowledged Crèvecoeur as the emotional "prototype of the American." That year also saw the publication of *Sketches of Eighteenth Century America*, a collection of letters that had not made it into Crèvecoeur's original collection, though some of them had provided the basis for portions of the French *Lettres*.

It was only in the latter half of the twentieth century that literary scholars began to read the *Letters* with a view to their almost novelistic quality, acknowledging Crèvecoeur's Farmer James as a literary creation rather than as simply a version of his author, and taking into fuller consideration the thematic progression of the twelve letters considered as a whole. Interest among historians increased as well, as

scholars came to see Crèvecoeur's influence on contemporary works such as Thomas Jefferson's *Notes on the State of Virginia* (1787), as well as on early sociological writings such as Alexis de Tocqueville's monumental *Democracy in America* (1835–40). In the twenty-first century scholarly interest has grown further, particularly in the wake of Dennis D. Moore's edition (2013), which brings together the twelve *Letters* with more than a dozen other essays by Crèvecoeur.

———————

NOTE ON THE TEXT: The text presented below is based on the two earliest London editions of *Letters from an American Farmer; Describing Certain Provincial Situations, Manners, and Customs, Not Generally Known; and Conveying Some Idea of the Late and Present Interior Circumstances of the British Colonies in North America* (1782 and 1783); the 1783 edition includes numerous corrections made by the author. Various modern editions—notably Dennis D. Moore's *Letters from an American Farmer and Other Essays* (2013)—have also been consulted. Spelling and punctuation have been modernized in accordance with the practices of this anthology.

⌘⌘⌘

LETTERS

FROM AN

AMERICAN FARMER;

DESCRIBING

CERTAIN PROVINCIAL SITUATIONS,
MANNERS, AND CUSTOMS,

NOT GENERALLY KNOWN;

AND CONVEYING

SOME IDEA OF THE LATE AND PRESENT
INTERIOR CIRCUMSTANCES

OF THE

BRITISH COLONIES

IN

NORTH AMERICA.

WRITTEN FOR THE INFORMATION OF A FRIEND
IN ENGLAND,

By J. HECTOR ST. JOHN,
A FARMER IN PENNSYLVANIA.

LONDON,
PRINTED FOR THOMAS DAVIES IN RUSSEL STREET COVENT-
GARDEN, AND LOCKYER DAVIS IN HOLBORN.
M DCC LXXXII.

from *Letters from an American Farmer*

from Letter 2
On the Situation, Feelings, and Pleasures
of an American Farmer

As you are the first enlightened European I have ever had the pleasure of being acquainted with, you will not be surprised that I should, according to your earnest desire and my promise, appear anxious of preserving your friendship and correspondence. By your accounts, I observe [that] a material difference subsists between your husbandry, modes, and customs, and ours. Everything is local. Could we enjoy the advantages of the English farmer, we should be much happier, indeed; but this wish, like many others, implies a contradiction; and could the English farmer have some of those privileges we possess, they would be the first[1] of their class in the world. Good and evil, I see, are to be found in all societies, and it is in vain to seek for any spot where those ingredients are not mixed. I therefore rest satisfied, and thank God that my lot is to be an American farmer, instead of a Russian boor, or a Hungarian peasant. I thank you kindly for the idea, however dreadful, which you have given me of their lot and condition; your observations have confirmed me in the justness of my ideas, and I am happier now than I thought myself before. It is strange that misery, when viewed in others, should become to us a sort of real good, though I am far from rejoicing to hear that there are in the world men so thoroughly wretched. They are no doubt as harmless, industrious, and willing to work as we are. Hard is their fate to be thus condemned to a slavery worse than that of our negroes. Yet, when young, I entertained some thoughts of selling my farm. I thought it afforded but a dull repetition of the same labours and pleasures. I thought the former tedious and heavy, the latter few and insipid. But when I came to consider myself as divested of my farm, I then found the world so wide, and every place so full, that I began to fear lest there would be no room for me. My farm, my house, my barn, presented to my imagination objects from which I adduced quite new ideas; they were more forcible than before. Why should

not I find myself happy, said I, where my father was before? He left me no good books it is true; he gave me no other education than the art of reading and writing: but he left me a good farm, and his experience; he left me free from debts, and no kind of difficulties to struggle with. I married, and this perfectly reconciled me to my situation. My wife rendered my house all at once cheerful and pleasing; it no longer appeared gloomy and solitary as before. When I went to work in my fields, I worked with more alacrity and sprightliness. I felt that I did not work for myself alone, and this encouraged me much. My wife would often come with her knitting in her hand, and sit under the shady trees, praising the straightness of my furrows and the docility of my horses. This swelled my heart and made everything light and pleasant, and I regretted that I had not married before. I felt myself happy in my new situation, and where is that station which can confer a more substantial system of felicity than that of an American farmer, possessing freedom of action, freedom of thoughts, ruled by a mode of government which requires but little from us? I owe nothing but a peppercorn[2] to my country, a small tribute to my king, with loyalty and due respect. I know no other landlord than the Lord of all land, to whom I owe the most sincere gratitude. My father left me three hundred and seventy-one acres of land, forty-seven of which are good timothy[3] meadow, an excellent orchard, a good house, and a substantial barn. It is my duty to think how happy I am that he lived to build and to pay for all these improvements. What are the labours which I have to undergo? What are my fatigues, when compared to his, who had everything to do, from the first tree he felled to the finishing of his house? Every year I kill from 1,500 to 2,000 weight of pork, 1,200 of beef, half a dozen of good wethers[4] in harvest; of fowls my wife has always a great stock: what can I wish more? My negroes[5] are tolerably faithful and healthy. By a

[1] *first* Most well off.

[2] *peppercorn* Small, insignificant amount (in this case, a small tithe or amount of tax).

[3] *timothy* Type of grass, commonly used to graze cattle and horses or to make hay.

[4] *wethers* Male sheep.

[5] *My negroes* Farmer James uses the expression "my negroes" again in Letter 12 (included as part of the website component of this anthology), when he makes this declaration: "I intend to say to

long series of industry and honest dealings, my father left behind him the name of a good man. I have but to tread his paths to be happy and a good man like him. I know enough of the law to regulate my little concerns with propriety, nor do I dread its power. These are the grand outlines of my situation; but as I can feel much more than I am able to express, I hardly know how to proceed. When my first son was born, the whole train of my ideas was suddenly altered. Never was there a charm that acted so quickly and powerfully. I ceased to ramble in imagination through the wide world. My excursions, since, have not exceeded the bounds of my farm, and all my principal pleasures are now centered within its scanty limits: but, at the same time, there is not an operation belonging to it in which I do not find some food for useful reflections. This is the reason, I suppose, that when you were here, you used, in your refined style, to denominate me the farmer of feelings. How rude[1] must those feelings be in him who daily holds the ax or the plough! How much more refined, on the contrary, those of the European, whose mind is improved by education, example, books, and by every acquired advantage! Those feelings, however, I will delineate as well as I can, agreeably to your earnest request. When I contemplate my wife, by my fireside, while she either spins, knits, darns, or suckles our child, I cannot describe the various emotions of love, of gratitude, of conscious pride, which thrill in my heart, and often overflow in involuntary tears. I feel the necessity, the sweet pleasure, of acting my part, the part of an husband and father, with an attention and propriety which may entitle me to my good fortune. It is true these pleasing images vanish with the smoke of my pipe, but, though they disappear from my mind, the impression they have made on my heart is indelible. When I play with the infant, my warm imagination runs forward, and eagerly anticipates his future temper and constitution. I would willingly open the book of fate, and know in which page his destiny is delineated.

my negroes—In the name of God, be free, my honest lads, I thank you for your past services; go, from henceforth, and work for yourselves; look on me as your old friend, and fellow labourer." In 1780, Pennsylvania (the state in which Farmer James resides) became the first state to begin to abolish slavery, though the gradual approach to emancipation meant that many people remained enslaved well into the 1800s.

[1] *rude* Uncultivated.

Alas! where is the father who, in those moments of paternal ecstasy, can delineate one half of the thoughts which dilate his heart? I am sure I cannot. Then again I fear for the health of those who are become so dear to me, and, in their sicknesses, I severely pay for the joys I experienced while they were well. Whenever I go abroad it is always involuntary. I never return home without feeling some pleasing emotion, which I often suppress as useless and foolish. The instant I enter on my own land, the bright idea of property, of exclusive right, of independence, exalt my mind. Precious soil, I say to myself, by what singular custom of law is it that thou wast made to constitute the riches of the free-holder? What should we American farmers be without the distinct possession of that soil? It feeds, it clothes us; from it we draw even a great exuberancy, our best meat, our richest drink; the very honey of our bees comes from this privileged spot. No wonder we should thus cherish its possession; no wonder that so many Europeans, who have never been able to say that such portion of land was theirs, cross the Atlantic to realize that happiness! This formerly rude soil has been converted by my father into a pleasant farm, and, in return it has established all our rights. On it is founded our rank, our freedom, our power as citizens; our importance as inhabitants of such a district. These images, I must confess, I always behold with pleasure, and extend them as far as my imagination can reach: for this is what may be called the true and the only philosophy of an American farmer. Pray do not laugh in thus seeing an artless countryman tracing himself through the simple modifications of his life. Remember that you have required it, therefore, with candor, though with diffidence, I endeavour to follow the thread of my feelings, but I cannot tell you all. Often, when I plough my low ground, I place my little boy on a chair which screws to the beam of the plough. Its motion and that of the horses please him; he is perfectly happy, and begins to chat. As I lean over the handle, various are the thoughts which crowd into my mind. I am now doing for him, I say, what my father formerly did for me; may God enable him to live that he may perform the same operations for the same purposes when I am worn out and old! I relieve his mother of some trouble while I have him with me; the odoriferous furrow exhilarates his spirits, and seems to do the

child a great deal of good, for he looks more blooming since I have adopted that practice. Can more pleasure, more dignity, be added to that primary occupation? The father, thus ploughing with his child, and to feed his family, is inferior only to the emperor of China ploughing as an example to his kingdom. In the evening, when I return home through my low grounds, I am astonished at the myriads of insects which I perceive dancing in the beams of the setting sun. I was before scarcely acquainted with their existence; they are so small that it is difficult to distinguish them; they are carefully improving this short evening space, not daring to expose themselves to the blaze of our meridian sun. I never see an egg brought on my table but I feel penetrated with the wonderful change it would have undergone but for my gluttony. It might have been a gentle useful hen leading her chickens with a care and vigilance which speaks shame to many women. A cock, perhaps, arrayed with the most majestic plumes, tender to its mate, bold, courageous, endowed with an astonishing instinct, with thoughts, with memory, and every distinguishing characteristic of the reason of man! I never see my trees drop their leaves and their fruit in the autumn, and bud again in the spring, without wonder. The sagacity of those animals, which have long been the tenants of my farm, astonish me: some of them seem to surpass even men in memory and sagacity. I could tell you singular instances of that kind. What then is this instinct which we so debase, and of which we are taught to entertain so diminutive an idea? My bees, above any other tenants of my farm, attract my attention and respect. I am astonished to see that nothing exists but what has its enemy; one species pursue and live upon the other. Unfortunately, our kingbirds are the destroyers of those industrious insects; but, on the other hand, these birds preserve our fields from the depredation of crows which they pursue on the wing with great vigilance and astonishing dexterity. Thus divided by two interested motives, I have long resisted the desire I had to kill them, until last year, when I thought they[1] increased too much, and my indulgence had been carried too far. It was at the time of swarming, when they all came and fixed themselves on the neighbouring trees, whence they caught those that returned loaded from the fields.[2] This made me resolve to kill as many as I could, and I was just ready to fire, when a bunch of bees as big as my fist issued from one of the hives, rushed on one of the birds, and probably stung him, for he instantly screamed, and flew, not as before in an irregular manner, but in a direct line. He was followed by the same bold phalanx,[3] at a considerable distance, which unfortunately becoming too sure of victory, quitted their military array and disbanded themselves. By this inconsiderate step they lost all that aggregate of force which had made the bird fly off. Perceiving their disorder, he immediately returned and snapped as many as he wanted; nay, he had even the impudence to alight on the very twig from which the bees had driven him. I killed him and immediately opened his craw, from which I took 171 bees. I laid them all on a blanket in the sun, and, to my great surprise, 54 returned to life, licked themselves clean, and joyfully went back to the hive, where they probably informed their companions of such an adventure and escape as I believe had never happened before to American bees! I draw a great fund of pleasure from the quails which inhabit my farm; they abundantly repay me, by their various notes and peculiar tameness, for the inviolable hospitality I constantly show them in the winter. Instead of perfidiously taking advantage of their great and affecting distress, when nature offers nothing but a barren universal bed of snow, when irresistible necessity forces them to my barn doors, I permit them to feed unmolested; and it is not the least agreeable spectacle which that dreary season presents, when I see those beautiful birds, tamed by hunger, intermingling with all my cattle and sheep, seeking in security for the poor scanty grain which but for them would be useless and lost. Often, in the angles of the fences, where the motion of the wind prevents the snow from settling, I carry them both chaff[4] and grain; the one to feed them, the other to prevent their tender feet from freezing fast to the earth, as I have frequently observed them to do. I do not know an instance in which the singular barbarity of man is so strongly delineated, as in the catching and murdering those harmless birds, at that cruel season of the year. …

1 *they* I.e., the kingbirds.

2 *those … fields* I.e., the bees.

3 *phalanx* Small, compact body of soldiers.

4 *chaff* Husks of grains or of corn.

from LETTER 3
WHAT IS AN AMERICAN?

I wish I could be acquainted with the feelings and thoughts which must agitate the heart and present themselves to the mind of an enlightened Englishman when he first lands on this continent. He must greatly rejoice that he lived at a time to see this fair country discovered and settled; he must necessarily feel a share of national pride, when he views the chain of settlements which embellishes these extended shores. When he says to himself, "This is the work of my countrymen, who, when convulsed by factions,[1] afflicted by a variety of miseries and wants, restless and impatient, took refuge here. They brought along with them their national genius,[2] to which they principally owe what liberty they enjoy, and what substance they possess." Here he sees the industry of his native country displayed in a new manner, and traces in their works the embryos of all the arts, sciences, and ingenuity which flourish in Europe. Here he beholds fair cities, substantial villages, extensive fields, an immense country filled with decent houses, good roads, orchards, meadows, and bridges, where an hundred years ago all was wild, woody and uncultivated! What a train of pleasing ideas this fair spectacle must suggest; it is a prospect which must inspire a good citizen with the most heartfelt pleasure. The difficulty consists in the manner of viewing so extensive a scene. He is arrived on a new continent; a modern society offers itself to his contemplation, different from what he had hitherto seen. It is not composed, as in Europe, of great lords who possess everything, and of a herd of people who have nothing. Here are no aristocratical families, no courts, no kings, no bishops, no ecclesiastical dominion, no invisible power giving to a few a very visible one; no great manufacturers employing thousands, no great refinements of luxury. The rich and the poor are not so far removed from each other as they are in Europe. Some few towns excepted, we are all tillers of the earth, from Nova Scotia to West Florida. We are a people of cultivators, scattered over an immense territory, communicating with each other by means of good roads and navigable rivers, united by the silken bands of mild government, all respecting the laws, without dreading their power, because they are equitable. We are all animated with the spirit of an industry which is unfettered and unrestrained, because each person works for himself. If he travels through our rural districts he views not the hostile castle, and the haughty mansion, contrasted with the clay-built hut and miserable cabin, where cattle and men help to keep each other warm, and dwell in meanness, smoke, and indigence.[3] A pleasing uniformity of decent competence appears throughout our habitations. The meanest of our log-houses is a dry and comfortable habitation. Lawyer or merchant are the fairest titles our towns afford; that of a farmer is the only appellation of the rural inhabitants of our country. It must take some time ere he can reconcile himself to our dictionary, which is but short in words of dignity, and names of honour. There, on a Sunday, he sees a congregation of respectable farmers and their wives, all clad in neat homespun,[4] well mounted, or riding in their own humble wagons. There is not among them an esquire, saving the unlettered[5] magistrate. There he sees a parson as simple as his flock, a farmer who does not riot[6] on the labour of others. We have no princes for whom we toil, starve, and bleed; we are the most perfect society now existing in the world. Here man is free as he ought to be; nor is this pleasing equality so transitory as many others are. Many ages will not see the shores of our great lakes replenished with inland nations, nor the unknown bounds of North America entirely peopled. Who can tell how far it extends? Who can tell the millions of men whom it will feed and contain? For no European foot has as yet travelled half the extent of this mighty continent!

The next wish of this traveller will be to know whence came all these people. They are a mixture of English, Scotch, Irish, French, Dutch, Germans, and Swedes. From this promiscuous[7] breed, that race now called Americans have arisen. The eastern provinces[8] must

1 *convulsed by factions* I.e., distressed or agitated by disputes.

2 *national genius* I.e., the distinctive spirit and qualities of their respective nations.

3 *meanness* Shabbiness or squalor; *indigence* Poverty.

4 *homespun* Clothing made from yarn or thread spun at home.

5 *saving* Except for; *unlettered* Unsophisticated; having a limited education.

6 *riot* Make merry; live indulgently.

7 *promiscuous* Varied; mixed.

8 *eastern provinces* I.e., New England.

indeed be excepted, as being the unmixed descendants of Englishmen. I have heard many wish that they had been more intermixed also: for my part, I am no wisher, and think it much better as it has happened. They exhibit a most conspicuous figure in this great and variegated picture; they too enter for a great share in the pleasing perspective displayed in these thirteen provinces. I know it is fashionable to reflect on[1] them, but I respect them for what they have done; for the accuracy and wisdom with which they have settled their territory; for the decency of their manners; for their early love of letters;[2] their ancient college,[3] the first in this hemisphere; for their industry,[4] which to me who am but a farmer, is the criterion of everything. There never was a people, situated as they are, who with so ungrateful a soil have done more in so short a time. Do you think that the monarchical ingredients, which are more prevalent in other governments, have purged them from all foul stains? Their histories assert the contrary.

In this great American asylum,[5] the poor of Europe have by some means met together, and in consequence of various causes; to what purpose should they ask one another what countrymen they are? Alas, two thirds of them had no country. Can a wretch who wanders about, who works and starves, whose life is a continual scene of sore affliction or pinching penury;[6] can that man call England or any other kingdom his country? A country that had no bread for him, whose fields procured him no harvest, who met with nothing but the frowns of the rich, the severity of the laws, with jails and punishments; who owned not a single foot of the extensive surface of this planet? No! urged by a variety of motives, here they came. Everything has tended to regenerate them: new laws, a new mode of living, a new social system. Here they are become men; in Europe they were as so many useless plants, wanting vegetative mould,[7] and refreshing showers. They withered, and were mowed down by want, hunger, and war; but now by the power of transplantation, like all other plants they have taken root and flourished! Formerly they were not numbered in any civil lists[8] of their country, except in those of the poor; here they rank as citizens. By what invisible power has this surprising metamorphosis been performed? By that of the laws and that of their industry. The laws, the indulgent[9] laws, protect them as they arrive, stamping on them the symbol of adoption; they receive ample rewards for their labours; these accumulated rewards procure them lands; those lands confer on them the title of freemen, and to that title every benefit is affixed which men can possibly require. This is the great operation daily performed by our laws. From whence proceed these laws? From our government. Whence the government? It is derived from the original genius and strong desire of the people ratified and confirmed by the crown. This is the great chain which links us all, this is the picture which every province exhibits, Nova Scotia excepted.[10] There the crown has done all; either there were no people who had genius, or it was not much attended to: the consequence is, that the province is very thinly inhabited indeed; the power of the crown in conjunction with the musketos[11] has prevented men from settling there. Yet some parts of it flourished once, and it contained a mild, harmless set of people. But for the fault of a few leaders, the whole were banished. The greatest political error the crown ever committed in America, was to cut off men from a country which wanted nothing but men!

What attachment can a poor European emigrant have for a country where he had nothing? The knowledge of the language, the love of a few kindred as poor as himself, were the only cords that tied him: his country

[1] *reflect on* Criticize or portray negatively.

[2] *letters* Learning.

[3] *ancient college* Harvard College in Massachusetts, established in 1636.

[4] *industry* Industriousness.

[5] *asylum* Place of shelter or sanctuary.

[6] *pinching penury* Biting poverty.

[7] *wanting vegetative mould* I.e., lacking fertilizer.

[8] *civil lists* Government records of significant members of a society.

[9] *indulgent* Tolerant.

[10] *Nova Scotia excepted* Reference to the 1755 Expulsion of the Acadians, which occurred in the wake of the French and Indian War, when longtime French Acadian settlers were forcibly removed from Nova Scotia by the British government for refusing to sign an oath of allegiance.

[11] *musketos* Mosquitos.

is now that which gives him land, bread, protection, and consequence; *Ubi panis ibi patria*,[1] is the motto of all emigrants. What then is the American, this new man? He is either an European, or the descendant of an European, hence that strange mixture of blood, which you will find in no other country. I could point out to you a family whose grandfather was an Englishman, whose wife was Dutch, whose son married a French woman, and whose present four sons have now four wives of different nations. *He* is an American, who leaving behind him all his ancient prejudices and manners, receives new ones from the new mode of life he has embraced, the new government he obeys, and the new rank he holds. He becomes an American by being received in the broad lap of our great *Alma Mater*.[2] Here individuals of all nations are melted into a new race of men, whose labours and posterity will one day cause great changes in the world. Americans are the western pilgrims, who are carrying along with them that great mass of arts, sciences, vigour, and industry which began long since in the east; they will finish the great circle. The Americans were once scattered all over Europe; here they are incorporated into one of the finest systems of population which has ever appeared, and which will hereafter become distinct by the power of the different climates they inhabit. The American ought therefore to love this country much better than that wherein either he or his forefathers were born. Here the rewards of his industry follow with equal steps the progress of his labour; his labour is founded on the basis of nature, *self-interest*; can it want a stronger allurement? Wives and children, who before in vain demanded of him a morsel of bread, now, fat and frolicksome, gladly help their father to clear those fields whence exuberant crops are to arise to feed and to clothe them all; without any part being claimed, either by a despotic prince, a rich abbot, or a mighty lord. Here religion demands but little of him; a small voluntary salary to the minister,[3] and gratitude to God; can

he refuse these? The American is a new man, who acts upon new principles; he must therefore entertain new ideas, and form new opinions. From involuntary idleness, servile dependence, penury, and useless labour, he has passed to toils of a very different nature, rewarded by ample subsistence. This is an American.

British America is divided into many provinces, forming a large association, scattered along a coast 1,500 miles extent and about 200 wide. This society I would fain examine, at least such as it appears in the middle provinces; if it does not afford that variety of tinges and gradations which may be observed in Europe, we have colours peculiar to ourselves. For instance, it is natural to conceive that those who live near the sea must be very different from those who live in the woods; the intermediate space will afford a separate and distinct class.

Men are like plants; the goodness and flavour of the fruit proceeds from the peculiar soil and exposition in which they grow. We are nothing but what we derive from the air we breathe, the climate we inhabit, the government we obey, the system of religion we profess, and the nature of our employment. Here you will find but few crimes; these have acquired as yet no root among us. I wish I were able to trace all my ideas; if my ignorance prevents me from describing them properly, I hope I shall be able to delineate a few of the outlines, which are all I propose.

Those who live near the sea, feed more on fish than on flesh, and often encounter that boisterous element. This renders them more bold and enterprising; this leads them to neglect the confined occupations of the land. They see and converse with a variety of people; their intercourse[4] with mankind becomes extensive. The sea inspires them with a love of traffic,[5] a desire of transporting produce from one place to another; and leads them to a variety of resources which supply the place of labour. Those who inhabit the middle settlements, by far the most numerous, must be very different; the simple cultivation of the earth purifies them, but the indulgences of the government, the soft remonstrances of religion, the rank of independent freeholders,[6] must necessarily inspire them with senti-

[1] *Ubi panis ibi patria* Latin: Where there is bread, there is my homeland.

[2] *Alma Mater* Latin: Bountiful Mother.

[3] *voluntary … minister* In parts of Europe, payment of tithes to the established church—which funded the salaries of the clergy—was compulsory, even for those who did not belong to the established church.

[4] *intercourse* Interactions.

[5] *traffic* Trade.

[6] *freeholders* Landowners.

ments very little known in Europe among people of the same class. What do I say? Europe has no such class of men; the early knowledge they acquire, the early bargains they make, give them a great degree of sagacity. As freemen they will be litigious; pride and obstinacy are often the cause of lawsuits; the nature of our laws and governments may be another. As citizens it is easy to imagine that they will carefully read the newspapers, enter into every political disquisition, freely blame or censure governors and others. As farmers they will be careful and anxious to get as much as they can, because what they get is their own. As northern men they will love the cheerful cup. As Christians, religion curbs them not in their opinions; the general indulgence leaves everyone to think for themselves in spiritual matters; the laws inspect our actions, our thoughts are left to God. Industry, good living, selfishness, litigiousness, country politics, the pride of freemen, religious indifference, are their characteristics. If you recede still farther from the sea, you will come into more modern settlements; they exhibit the same strong lineaments, in a ruder[1] appearance. Religion seems to have still less influence, and their manners are less improved.

Now we arrive near the great woods, near the last inhabited districts;[2] there men seem to be placed still farther beyond the reach of government, which in some measure leaves them to themselves. How can it pervade every corner? As they were driven there by misfortunes, necessity of beginnings, desire of acquiring large tracks of land, idleness, frequent want of economy,[3] ancient debts; the reunion of such people does not afford a very pleasing spectacle. When discord, want of unity and friendship; when either drunkenness or idleness prevail in such remote districts, contention, inactivity, and wretchedness must ensue. There are not the same remedies to these evils as in a long-established community. The few magistrates they have are in general little better than the rest; they are often in a perfect state of war; that of man against man, sometimes decided by blows, sometimes by means of the law; that of man against every wild inhabitant of these venerable woods, of which they are come to dispossess them. There men

appear to be no better than carnivorous animals of a superior rank, living on the flesh of wild animals when they can catch them, and when they are not able, they subsist on grain. He who would wish to see America in its proper light, and have a true idea of its feeble beginnings and barbarous rudiments, must visit our extended line of frontiers where the last settlers dwell, and where he may see the first labours of settlement, the mode of clearing the earth, in their different appearances; where men are wholly left dependent on their native tempers, and on the spur of uncertain industry, which often fails when not sanctified by the efficacy of a few moral rules. There, remote from the power of example, and check of shame,[4] many families exhibit the most hideous parts of our society. They are a kind of forlorn hope, preceding by ten or twelve years the most respectable army of veterans[5] which come after them. In that space, prosperity will polish some, vice and the law will drive off the rest, who uniting again with others like themselves will recede still farther; making room for more industrious people, who will finish their improvements, convert the log house into a convenient habitation, and rejoicing that the first heavy labours are finished, will change in a few years that hitherto barbarous country into a fine, fertile, well-regulated district. Such is our progress, such is the march of the Europeans toward the interior parts of this continent. In all societies there are off-casts; this impure part serves as our precursors or pioneers; my father himself was one of that class,[6] but he came upon honest principles, and was therefore one of the few who held fast; by good conduct and temperance he transmitted to me his fair inheritance, when not above one in fourteen of his contemporaries had the same good fortune.

Forty years ago this smiling country was thus inhabited; it is now purged, a general decency of manners prevails throughout, and such has been the fate of our best countries.

Exclusive of those general characteristics, each province has its own, founded on the government,

[1] *ruder* Less refined.

[2] *last inhabited districts* I.e., the "frontier" regions beyond the borders of the Thirteen Colonies.

[3] *want of economy* Poor management of personal finances.

[4] *check of shame* I.e., the power of shame to change or restrain one's behavior.

[5] *veterans* Experienced settlers.

[6] *my father ... that class* Crèvecoeur's own father was a country gentleman in France who never visited America.

climate, mode of husbandry,[1] customs, and peculiarity of circumstances. Europeans submit insensibly to these great powers, and become, in the course of a few generations, not only Americans in general, but either Pennsylvanians, Virginians, or provincials under some other name. Whoever traverses the continent must easily observe those strong differences, which will grow more evident in time. The inhabitants of Canada, Massachusetts, the middle provinces, the southern ones will be as different as their climates; their only points of unity will be those of religion and language.

As I have endeavoured to show you how Europeans become Americans, it may not be disagreeable to show you likewise how the various Christian sects introduced wear out, and how religious indifference becomes prevalent. When any considerable number of a particular sect happen to dwell contiguous to each other, they immediately erect a temple, and there worship the Divinity agreeably to their own peculiar ideas. Nobody disturbs them. If any new sect springs up in Europe, it may happen that many of its professors[2] will come and settle in America. As they bring their zeal with them, they are at liberty to make proselytes if they can, and to build a meeting and to follow the dictates of their consciences; for neither the government nor any other power interferes. If they are peaceable subjects, and are industrious, what is it to their neighbours how and in what manner they think fit to address their prayers to the Supreme Being? But if the sectaries are not settled close together, if they are mixed with other denominations, their zeal will cool for want of fuel, and will be extinguished in a little time. Then the Americans become as to religion, what they are as to country, allied to all. In them the name of Englishman, Frenchman, and European is lost, and in like manner, the strict modes of Christianity as practised in Europe are lost also. This effect will extend itself still farther hereafter, and though this may appear to you as a strange idea, yet it is a very true one. I shall be able perhaps hereafter to explain myself better; in the meanwhile, let the following example serve as my first justification.

Let us suppose you and I to be travelling. We observe that in this house, to the right, lives a Catholic, who prays to God as he has been taught, and believes in transubstantiation;[3] he works and raises wheat, he has a large family of children, all hale and robust; his belief, his prayers offend nobody. About one mile farther on the same road, his next neighbour may be a good honest plodding German Lutheran, who addresses himself to the same God, the God of all, agreeably to the modes he has been educated in, and believes in consubstantiation;[4] by so doing he scandalizes nobody; he also works in his fields, embellishes the earth, clears swamps, etc. What has the world to do with his Lutheran principles? He persecutes nobody, and nobody persecutes him; he visits his neighbours, and his neighbours visit him. Next to him lives a seceder,[5] the most enthusiastic of all sectaries; his zeal is hot and fiery, but separated as he is from others of the same complexion, he has no congregation of his own to resort to, where he might cabal[6] and mingle religious pride with worldly obstinacy. He likewise raises good crops, his house is handsomely painted, his orchard is one of the fairest in the neighbourhood. How does it concern the welfare of the country, or of the province at large, what this man's religious sentiments are, or really whether he has any at all? He is a good farmer, he is a sober, peaceable, good citizen. … This is the visible character; the invisible one is only guessed at, and is nobody's business. … Each of these people instruct their children as well as they can, but these instructions are feeble compared to those which are given to the youth of the poorest class in Europe. Their children will therefore grow up less zealous and more indifferent in matters of religion than their parents. The foolish vanity, or rather the fury of making proselytes, is unknown here; they have no time, the seasons call for all their attention, and thus in a few years, this mixed neighbourhood will exhibit a strange religious medley, that will be neither pure Catholicism

1 *husbandry* Farming.

2 *professors* Followers.

3 *transubstantiation* Central belief of Catholicism that the bread and wine consumed during the ritual of the Eucharist literally transform into the body and blood of Christ.

4 *consubstantiation* As opposed to transubstantiation, this doctrine holds that the bread and wine taken at communion represent the spiritual presence of Christ, but are not actually transformed into his body and blood.

5 *seceder* One who has withdrawn participation from any formal religious organization.

6 *cabal* Conspire with others; mingle dangerously.

nor pure Calvinism.[1] A very perceptible indifference, even in the first generation, will become apparent; and it may happen that the daughter of the Catholic will marry the son of the seceder, and settle by themselves at a distance from their parents. What religious education will they give their children? A very imperfect one. If there happens to be in the neighbourhood any place of worship—we will suppose a Quaker's meeting—rather than not show their fine clothes,[2] they will go to it, and some of them may perhaps attach themselves to that society. Others will remain in a perfect state of indifference; the children of these zealous parents will not be able to tell what their religious principles are, and their grandchildren still less. ... Thus all sects are mixed as well as all nations; thus religious indifference is imperceptibly disseminated from one end of the continent to the other; which is at present one of the strongest characteristics of the Americans. Where this will reach no one can tell; perhaps it may leave a vacuum fit to receive other systems. Persecution, religious pride, the love of contradiction, are the food of what the world commonly calls religion. These motives have ceased here. Zeal in Europe is confined; here it evaporates in the great distance it has to travel. There it is a grain of powder enclosed;[3] here it burns away in the open air, and consumes without effect.

But to return to our back settlers. I must tell you that there is something in the proximity of the woods which is very singular. It is with men as it is with the plants and animals that grow and live in the forests; they are entirely different from those that live in the plains. I will candidly tell you all my thoughts, but you are not to expect that I shall advance any reasons. By living in or near the woods, their actions are regulated by the wildness of the neighbourhood. The deer often come to eat their grain, the wolves to destroy their sheep, the bears to kill their hogs, the foxes to catch their poultry. This surrounding hostility immediately puts the gun into their hands; they watch these animals, they kill some; and thus by defending their property, they

soon become professed hunters; this is the progress; once hunters, farewell to the plough. The chase renders them ferocious, gloomy, and unsociable; a hunter wants no neighbour, he rather hates them, because he dreads the competition. In a little time their success in the woods makes them neglect their tillage. They trust to the natural fecundity of the earth, and therefore do little; carelessness in fencing often exposes what little they sow to destruction; they are not at home to watch; in order therefore to make up the deficiency, they go oftener to the woods. That new mode of life brings along with it a new set of manners, which I cannot easily describe. These new manners, being grafted on the old stock, produce a strange sort of lawless profligacy, the impressions of which are indelible. The manners of the Indian natives are respectable, compared with this European medley. Their wives and children live in sloth and inactivity; and having no proper pursuits, you may judge what education the latter receive. Their tender minds have nothing else to contemplate but the example of their parents; like them they grow up a mongrel breed, half civilized, half savage, except nature stamps on them some constitutional propensities. That rich, that voluptuous sentiment is gone which struck them so forcibly; the possession of their freeholds no longer conveys to their minds the same pleasure and pride. To all these reasons you must add, their lonely[4] situation, and you cannot imagine what an effect on manners the great distances they live from each other has! Consider one of the last settlements in its first view: of what is it composed? Europeans who have not that sufficient share of knowledge they ought to have, in order to prosper; people who have suddenly passed from oppression, dread of government, and fear of laws, into the unlimited freedom of the woods. This sudden change must have a very great effect on most men, and on that class particularly. Eating of wild meat, whatever you may think, tends to alter their temper; though all the proof I can adduce is that I have seen it: and having no place of worship to resort to, what little society this might afford is denied them. ... Thus our bad people are those who are half cultivators and half hunters; and the worst of them are those who have degenerated altogether into the hunting state. As old ploughmen and new men of the woods, as Europeans

[1] *Calvinism* Branch of Protestant belief based on the teachings of French dissenter John Calvin (1509–64), presented here as diametrically opposed to Catholicism.

[2] *Quaker's meeting ... fine clothes* Quakers were known for their adherence to principles of plain dress.

[3] *powder enclosed* I.e., as gunpowder is enclosed in a gun.

[4] *lonely* I.e., remote and unpopulated.

and new-made Indians, they contract the vices of both; they adopt the moroseness and ferocity of a native, without his mildness, or even his industry at home. If manners are not refined, at least they are rendered simple and inoffensive by tilling the earth; all our wants are supplied by it, our time is divided between labour and rest, and leaves none for the commission of great misdeeds. As hunters it is divided between the toil of the chase, the idleness of repose, or the indulgence of inebriation. Hunting is but a licentious idle life, and if it does not always pervert good dispositions; yet, when it is united with bad luck, it leads to want: want stimulates that propensity to rapacity and injustice, too natural to needy men, which is the fatal gradation. After this explanation of the effects which follow by living in the woods, shall we yet vainly flatter ourselves with the hope of converting the Indians? We should rather begin with converting our back-settlers; and now if I dare mention the name of religion, its sweet accents would be lost in the immensity of these woods. Men thus placed, are not fit either to receive or remember its mild instructions; they want temples and ministers, but as soon as men cease to remain at home, and begin to lead an erratic life, let them be either tawny or white, they cease to be its disciples. …

Europe contains hardly any other distinctions but lords and tenants; this fair country alone is settled by freeholders, the possessors of the soil they cultivate, members of the government they obey, and the framers of their own laws, by means of their representatives. This is a thought which you have taught me to cherish; our distance from Europe, far from diminishing, rather adds to our usefulness and consequence as men and subjects. Had our forefathers remained there, they would only have crouded it, and perhaps prolonged those convulsions which had shook it so long. Every industrious European who transports himself here, may be compared to a sprout growing at the foot of a great tree; it enjoys and draws but a little portion of sap; wrench it from the parent roots, transplant it, and it will become a tree bearing fruit also. Colonists are therefore intitled to the consideration due to the most useful subjects; a hundred families barely existing in some parts of Scotland, will here in six years, case an annual exportation of 10,000 bushels of wheat: 100 bushels being but a common quantity for an

industrious family to sell, if they cultivate good land. It is here then that the idle may be employed, the useless become useful, and the poor become rich; but by riches I do not mean gold and silver, we have but little of those metals; I mean a better sort of wealth, cleared lands, cattle, good houses, good cloaths, and an increase of people to enjoy them.

There is no wonder that this country has so many charms, and presents to Europeans so many temptations to remain in it. A traveller in Europe becomes a stranger as soon as he quits his own kingdom; but it is otherwise here. We know, properly speaking, no strangers; this is every person's country; the variety of our soils, situations, climates, governments, and produce, hath something which must please every body. No sooner does an European arrive, no matter of what condition, than his eyes are opened upon the fair prospect; he hears his language spoke, he retraces many of his own country manners, he perpetually hears the names of families and towns with which he is acquainted; he sees happiness and prosperity in all places disseminated; he meets with hospitality, kindness, and plenty every where; he beholds hardly any poor, he seldom hears of punishments and executions; and he wonders at the elegance of our towns, those miracles of industry and freedom. He cannot admire enough our rural districts, our convenient roads, good taverns, and our many accommodations; he involuntarily loves a country where every thing is so lovely. When in England, he was a mere Englishman; here he stands on a larger portion of the globe, not less than its fourth part, and may see the productions of the north, in iron and naval stores; the provisions of Ireland, the grain of Egypt, the indigo, the rice of China. He does not find, as in Europe, a crouded society, where every place is over-stocked; he does not feel that perpetual collision of parties, that difficulty of beginning, that contention which oversets so many. There is room for every body in America; has he any particular talent, or industry? he exerts it in order to procure a livelihood, and it succeeds. Is he a merchant? the avenues of trade are infinite; is he eminent in any respect? he will be employed and respected. Does he love a country life? pleasant farms present themselves; he may purchase what he wants, and thereby become an American farmer. Is he a labourer, sober and industrious? he

need not go many miles, nor receive many informations before he will be hired, well fed at the table of his employer, and paid four or five times more than he can get in Europe. Does he want uncultivated lands? thousands of acres present themselves, which he may purchase cheap. Whatever be his talents or inclinations, if they are moderate, he may satisfy them. I do not mean that every one who comes will grow rich in a little time; no, but he may procure an easy, decent maintenance, by his industry. Instead of starving he will be fed, instead of being idle he will have employment; and these are riches enough for such men as come over here. The rich stay in Europe, it is only the middling and poor that emigrate. Would you wish to travel in independent idleness, from north to south, you will find easy access, and the most chearful reception at every house; society without ostentation, good cheer without pride, and every decent diversion which the country affords, with little expense. It is no wonder that the European who has lived here a few years, is desirous to remain; Europe with all its pomp, is not to be compared to this continent, for men of middle stations, or labourers.

An European, when he first arrives, seems limited in his intentions, as well as in his views; but he very suddenly alters his scale; two hundred miles formerly appeared a very great distance, it is now but a trifle; he no sooner breathes our air than he forms schemes, and embarks in designs he never would have thought of in his own country. There the plenitude of society confines many useful ideas, and often extinguishes the most laudable schemes which here ripen into maturity. Thus Europeans become Americans. ...

... It is of very little importance how, and in what manner an indigent man arrives; for if he is but sober, honest, and industrious, he has nothing more to ask of heaven. Let him go to work, he will have opportunities enough to earn a comfortable support, and even the means of procuring some land; which ought to be the utmost wish of every person who has health and hands to work. I knew a man who came to this country, in the literal sense of the expression, stark naked; I think he was a Frenchman, and a sailor on board an English man-of-war.[1] Being discontented, he had stripped himself and swam ashore; where finding

clothes and friends, he settled afterwards at Maraneck, in the county of Chester, in the province of New-York: he married and left a good farm to each of his sons. I knew another person who was but twelve years old when he was taken on the frontiers of Canada by the Indians; at his arrival at Albany he was purchased by a gentleman, who generously bound him apprentice to a tailor. He lived to the age of ninety, and left behind him a fine estate and a numerous family, all well settled; many of them I am acquainted with. Where is then the industrious European who ought to despair?

After a foreigner from any part of Europe is arrived, and become a citizen, let him devoutly listen to the voice of our great parent, which says to him, "Welcome to my shores, distressed European; bless the hour in which thou didst see my verdant fields, my fair navigable rivers, and my green mountains! If thou wilt work, I have bread for thee;[2] if thou wilt be honest, sober, and industrious, I have greater rewards to confer on thee—ease and independence. I will give thee fields to feed and clothe thee; a comfortable fireside to sit by, and tell thy children by what means thou hast prospered; and a decent bed to repose on. I shall endow thee beside with the immunities of a freeman.[3] If thou wilt carefully educate thy children, teach them gratitude to God, and reverence to that government, that philanthropic government, which has collected here so many men and made them happy. I will also provide for thy progeny; and to every good man this ought to be the most holy, the most powerful, the most earnest wish he can possibly form, as well as the most consolatory prospect when he dies. Go thou and work and till; thou shalt prosper, provided thou be just, grateful and industrious." ... In the year 1770, I purchased some lands in the county of ——, which I intended for one of my sons; and was obliged to go there in order to see them properly surveyed and marked out: the soil is good, but the country has a very wild aspect. However, I observed with pleasure that land sells very fast; and I am in hopes when the lad gets a wife, it

[1] *man-of-war* Large warship.

[2] *thee* In late eighteenth-century America, the use of *thee* and *thou* as second person singular pronouns was often a sign of membership of the Society of Friends (the Quakers), who had been the first European settlers in Pennsylvania. Farmer James and (especially) his wife use these pronouns with some frequency in certain of the *Letters*.

[3] *immunities of a freeman* Rights of a free person.

will be a well-settled decent country. Agreeable to our customs, which indeed are those of nature, it is our duty to provide for our eldest children while we live, in order that our homesteads may be left to the youngest, who are the most helpless. Some people are apt to regard the portions given to daughters as so much lost to the family; but this is selfish, and is not agreeable to my way of thinking; they cannot work as men do; they marry young: I have given an honest European a farm to till for himself, rent free, provided he clears an acre of swamp every year, and that he quits it whenever my daughter shall marry. It will procure her a substantial husband, a good farmer—and that is all my ambition.

Whilst I was in the woods I met with a party of Indians; I shook hands with them, and I perceived they had killed a cub; I had a little Peack brandy, they perceived it also, we therefore joined company, kindled a large fire, and ate an hearty supper. I made their hearts glad, and we all reposed on good beds of leaves. Soon after dark, I was surprised to hear a prodigious hooting through the woods; the Indians laughed heartily. One of them, more skillful than the rest, mimicked the owls so exactly, that a very large one perched on a high tree over our fire. We soon brought him down; he measured five feet seven inches from one extremity of the wings to the other. By Captain —— I have sent you the talons, on which I have had the heads of small candlesticks fixed. Pray keep them on the table of your study for my sake. …

<div style="text-align:center">from LETTER 9</div>

DESCRIPTION OF CHARLES-TOWN;[1] THOUGHTS ON SLAVERY; ON PHYSICAL EVIL; A MELANCHOLY SCENE

Charles-Town is, in the north, what Lima is in the south; both are capitals of the richest provinces of their respective hemispheres: you may therefore conjecture that both cities must exhibit the appearances necessarily resulting from riches. Peru abounding in gold, Lima is filled with inhabitants who enjoy all those gradations of pleasure, refinement, and luxury, which proceed from wealth. Carolina produces commodities more valuable perhaps than gold, because they are gained by greater industry; it exhibits also on our northern stage a display of riches and luxury, inferior indeed to the former, but far superior to what are to be seen in our northern towns. Its situation is admirable, being built at the confluence of two large rivers, which receive in their course a great number of inferior streams; all navigable in the spring, for flat boats. Here the produce of this extensive territory concentres; here therefore is the seat of the most valuable exportation; their wharfs, their docks, their magazines,[2] are extremely convenient to facilitate this great commercial business. The inhabitants are the gayest in America; it is called the centre of our beau monde, and is always filled with the richest planters of the province, who resort hither in quest of health and pleasure. Here are always to be seen a great number of valetudinarians from the West Indies, seeking for the renovation of health, exhausted by the debilitating nature of their sun, air, and modes of living. Many of these West Indians have I seen, at thirty, loaded with the infirmities of old age; for nothing is more common in those countries of wealth, than for persons to lose the abilities of enjoying the comforts of life, at a time when we northern men just begin to taste the fruits of our labour and prudence. The round of pleasure, and the expenses of those citizens' tables, are much superior to what you would imagine: indeed the growth of this town and province have been astonishingly rapid. It is pity that the narrowness of the neck on which it stands prevents it from increasing; and which is the reason why houses are so dear. The heat of the climate, which is sometimes very great in the interior parts of the country, is always temperate in Charles-Town; though sometimes when they have no sea breezes the sun is too powerful. The climate renders excesses of all kinds very dangerous, particularly those of the table; and yet, insensible or fearless of danger, they live on, and enjoy a short and a merry life: the rays of their sun seem to urge them irresistibly to dissipation and pleasure: on the contrary, the women, from being abstemious,[3] reach to a longer period of life, and seldom die without having had several husbands. An European at his first arrival must be greatly surprised when he sees the elegance of their houses, their sumptuous furniture, as well as the

[1] DESCRIPTION OF CHARLES-TOWN It is likely that Crèvecoeur himself never traveled to South Carolina, and that what knowledge he had of the region was second-hand.

[2] *magazines* Storehouses.

[3] *abstemious* Moderate in their habits.

magnificence of their tables; can he imagine himself in a country, the establishment of which is so recent?

The three principal classes of inhabitants are lawyers, planters, and merchants; this is the province which has afforded to the first the richest spoils, for nothing can exceed their wealth, their power, and their influence. They have reached the *ne plus ultra*[1] of worldly felicity; no plantation is secured, no title is good, no will is valid, but what they dictate, regulate, and approve. The whole mass of provincial property is become tributary to this society—which, far above priests and bishops, disdain to be satisfied with the poor Mosaical portion of the tenth.[2] I appeal to the many inhabitants, who, while contending perhaps for their right to a few hundred acres, have lost by the mazes of the law their whole patrimony. These men are more properly law givers than interpreters of the law; and have united here, as well as in most other provinces, the skill and dexterity of the scribe with the power and ambition of the prince: who can tell where this may lead in a future day? The nature of our laws, and the spirit of freedom, which often tends to make us litigious,[3] must necessarily throw the greatest part of the property of the colonies into the hands of these gentlemen. In another century, the law will possess in the north, what now the church possesses in Peru and Mexico.

While all is joy, festivity, and happiness in Charles-Town, would you imagine that scenes of misery overspread in the country? Their ears by habit are become deaf, their hearts are hardened; they neither see, hear, nor feel for the woes of their poor slaves, from whose painful labours all their wealth proceeds. Here the horrors of slavery, the hardship of incessant toils, are unseen; and no one thinks with compassion of those showers of sweat and tears which from the bodies of Africans daily drop, and moisten the ground they till. The cracks of the whip urging these miserable beings to excessive labour, are far too distant from the gay Capital to be heard. The chosen race eat, drink, and live happy, while the unfortunate one grubs up the ground,

raises indigo, or husks the rice; exposed to a sun full as scorching as their native one; without the support of good food, without the cordials of any cheering liquor. This great contrast has often afforded me subjects of the most afflicting meditation. On the one side, behold a people enjoying all that life affords most bewitching and pleasurable, without labour, without fatigue, hardly subjected to the trouble of wishing. With gold, dug from Peruvian mountains, they order vessels to the coasts of Guinea; by virtue of that gold, wars, murders, and devastations are committed in some harmless, peaceable African neighbourhood, where dwelt innocent people, who even knew not but that all men were black.[4] The daughter torn from her weeping mother, the child from the wretched parents, the wife from the loving husband; whole families swept away and brought through storms and tempests to this rich metropolis! There, arranged like horses at a fair, they are branded like cattle, and then driven to toil, to starve, and to languish for a few years on the different plantations of these citizens. And for whom must they work? For persons they know not, and who have no other power over them than that of violence; no other right than what this accursed metal has given them! Strange order of things! Oh, Nature, where art thou? Are not these blacks thy children as well as we? On the other side, nothing is to be seen but the most diffusive misery and wretchedness, unrelieved even in thought or wish! Day after day they drudge on without any prospect of ever reaping for themselves; they are obliged to devote their lives, their limbs, their will, and every vital exertion to swell the wealth of masters; who look not upon them with half the kindness and affection with which they consider their dogs and horses. Kindness and affection are not the portion of those who till the earth, who carry burdens, who convert the logs into useful boards. This reward, simple and natural as one would conceive it, would border on humanity; and planters must have none of it!

If negroes are permitted to become fathers, this fatal indulgence only tends to increase their misery: the poor companions of their scanty pleasures are likewise the companions of their labours; and when at some critical seasons they could wish to see them relieved, with

[1] *ne plus ultra* Highest point; pinnacle.

[2] *the poor ... tenth* I.e., tithes, taxes paid to the church equivalent to one-tenth of one's annual earnings. Tithe laws are set out in the Old Testament or the Torah as part of what is called Mosaic Law.

[3] *litigious* Inclined towards having disputes, particularly legal disputes.

[4] *who even ... black* I.e., who did not even know that not all men are black.

tears in their eyes they behold them perhaps doubly oppressed, obliged to bear the burden of nature—a fatal present—as well as that of unabated tasks. How many have I seen cursing the irresistible propensity, and regretting that, by having tasted of those harmless joys, they had become the authors of double misery to their wives. Like their masters, they are not permitted to partake of those ineffable sensations with which nature inspires the hearts of fathers and mothers; they must repel them all, and become callous and passive. This unnatural state often occasions the most acute, the most pungent of their afflictions; they have no time, like us, tenderly to rear their helpless offspring, to nurse them on their knees, to enjoy the delight of being parents. Their paternal fondness is embittered by considering that, if their children live, they must live to be slaves like themselves; no time is allowed them to exercise their pious office.[1] The mothers must fasten them on their backs, and, with this double load, follow their husbands in the fields, where they too often hear no other sound than that of the voice or whip of the task-master, and the cries of their infants, broiling in the sun. These unfortunate creatures cry and weep like their parents, without a possibility of relief; the very instinct of the brute, so laudable, so irresistible, runs counter here to their master's interest; and to that god all the laws of nature must give way. Thus planters get rich; so raw, so unexperienced am I in this mode of life, that were I to be possessed of a plantation, and my slaves treated as in general they are here, never could I rest in peace; my sleep would be perpetually disturbed by a retrospect of the frauds committed in Africa, in order to entrap them; frauds surpassing in enormity everything which a common mind can possibly conceive. I should be thinking of the barbarous treatment they meet with on shipboard; of their anguish, of the despair necessarily inspired by their situation, when torn from their friends and relations; when delivered into the hands of a people differently coloured, whom they cannot understand; carried in a strange machine over an ever agitated element, which they had never seen before; and finally delivered over to the severities of the whippers, and the excessive labours of the field. Can it be possible that the force of custom should ever make me deaf to all these reflections, and as insensible

to the injustice of that trade, and to their miseries, as the rich inhabitants of this town seem to be? What then is man; this being who boasts so much of the excellence and dignity of his nature, among that variety of inscrutable mysteries, of unsolvable problems with which he is surrounded? The reason why man has been thus created is not the least astonishing! It is said, I know, that they are much happier here than in the West-Indies; because land being cheaper upon this continent than in those islands, the fields allowed them to raise their subsistence from are in general more extensive. The only possible chance of any alleviation depends on the humour of the planters, who, bred in the midst of slaves, learn from the example of their parents to despise them; and seldom conceive either from religion or philosophy any ideas that tend to make their fate less calamitous; except[2] some strong native tenderness of heart, some rays of philanthropy, overcome the obduracy[3] contracted by habit.

I have not resided here long enough to become insensible of pain for the objects which I every day behold. In the choice of my friends and acquaintance, I always endeavour to find out those whose dispositions are somewhat congenial with my own. We have slaves likewise in our northern provinces;[4] I hope the time draws near when they will be all emancipated: but how different their lot, how different their situation, in every possible respect! They enjoy as much liberty as their masters, they are as well clad, and as well fed; in health and sickness they are tenderly taken care of; they live under the same roof, and are, truly speaking, a part of our families. Many of them are taught to read and write, and are well instructed in the principles of religion; they are the companions of our labours, and treated as such; they enjoy many perquisites,[5] many established holidays, and are not obliged to work more than white people. They marry where inclination leads

[1] *office* Role; duty.

[2] *except* Unless.

[3] *obduracy* Inability to be moved by pity; hard-heartedness.

[4] *We have ... northern provinces* Pennsylvania (the home state of Farmer James) began a process of gradual abolition in 1780; New York State (Crèvecoeur's residence while he was writing the bulk of the *Letters*) did likewise in 1799. The last enslaved people in New York State were not freed until 1827.

[5] *enjoy many perquisites* I.e., receive many rewards or forms of compensation for their labor.

them; visit their wives every week; are as decently clad as the common people; they are indulged in educating, cherishing, and chastising their children, who are taught subordination to them as to their lawful parents. In short, they participate in many of the benefits of our society, without being obliged to bear any of its burdens. They are fat, healthy, and hearty, and far from repining at their fate; they think themselves happier than many of the lower class whites: they share with their masters the wheat and meat provision they help to raise; many of those whom the good Quakers have emancipated have received that great benefit with tears of regret, and have never quitted, though free, their former masters and benefactors.

But is it really true, as I have heard it asserted here, that those blacks are incapable of feeling the spurs of emulation,[1] and the cheerful sound of encouragement? By no means; there are a thousand proofs existing of their gratitude and fidelity: those hearts in which such noble dispositions can grow, are then like ours, they are susceptible of every generous sentiment, of every useful motive of action; they are capable of receiving lights, of imbibing ideas that would greatly alleviate the weight of their miseries. But what methods have in general been made use of to obtain so desirable an end? None; the day in which they arrive and are sold, is the first of their labours; labours, which from that hour admit of no respite; for though indulged by law with relaxation on Sundays, they are obliged to employ that time which is intended for rest, to till their little plantations.[2] What can be expected from wretches in such circumstances? Forced from their native country, cruelly treated when on board, and not less so on the plantations to which they are driven; is there anything in this treatment but what must kindle all the passions, sow the seeds of inveterate resentment, and nourish a wish of perpetual revenge? They are left to the irresistible effects of those strong and natural propensities; the blows they receive, are they conducive to extinguish them, or to win their

affections? They are neither soothed by the hopes that their slavery will ever terminate but with their lives; [n]or yet encouraged by the goodness of their food, or the mildness of their treatment. The very hopes held out to mankind by religion, that consolatory system so useful to the miserable, are never presented to them; neither moral nor physical means are made use of to soften their chains; they are left in their original and untutored state, that very state wherein the natural propensities of revenge and warm passions are so soon kindled. Cheered by no one single motive that can impel the will, or excite their efforts, nothing but terrors and punishments are presented to them; death is denounced[3] if they run away; horrid dilaceration[4] if they speak with their native freedom; perpetually awed by the terrible cracks of whips, or by the fear of capital punishments, while even those punishments often fail of their purpose.

A clergyman settled a few years ago at George-Town, and feeling as I do now, warmly recommended to the planters, from the pulpit, a relaxation of severity; he introduced the benignity of Christianity, and pathetically made use of the admirable precepts of that system to melt the hearts of his congregation into a greater degree of compassion toward their slaves than had been hitherto customary; "Sir (said one of his hearers) we pay you a genteel salary to read to us the prayers of the liturgy, and to explain to us such parts of the Gospel as the rule of the church directs; but we do not want you to teach us what we are to do with our blacks." The clergyman found it prudent to withhold any farther admonition. Whence this astonishing right, or rather this barbarous custom, for most certainly we have no kind of right beyond that of force? We are told, it is true, that slavery cannot be so repugnant to human nature as we at first imagine, because it has been practised in all ages, and in all nations: the Lacedemonians themselves, those great assertors of liberty, conquered the Helotes with the design of making them their slaves;[5] the Romans, whom we consider as

[1] *emulation* Ambition.

[2] *indulged by law ... plantations* In many areas, enslaved people were legally required to be given "leisure time" from their ordinary labor on Sundays, a fact held up by many enslavers as proof that American slavery was not as cruel as their opponents claimed; however, as the narrator here points out, enslaved individuals generally had to use this time for the tending of their own small vegetable allotments and for other tasks required for their sustenance.

[3] *denounced* Threatened.

[4] *dilaceration* Tearing of the body; i.e., severe physical abuse.

[5] *Lacedemonians ... their slaves* The Helots were a class of people subjugated by the Lacedemonians (or the Spartans) in the ancient world. Historians have long debated whether the Helots were truly members of an enslaved class or whether their status was something between that of enslaved and free.

our masters in civil and military policy, lived in the exercise of the most horrid oppression; they conquered to plunder and to enslave. What a hideous aspect the face of the earth must then have exhibited! Provinces, towns, districts, often depopulated; their inhabitants driven to Rome, the greatest market in the world, and there sold by thousands! The Roman dominions were tilled by the hands of unfortunate people, who had once been, like their victors free, rich, and possessed of every benefit society can confer; until they became subject to the cruel right of war, and to lawless force. Is there then no superintending power who conducts the moral operations of the world, as well as the physical? The same sublime hand which guides the planets round the sun with so much exactness, which preserves the arrangement of the whole with such exalted wisdom and paternal care, and prevents the vast system from falling into confusion; doth it abandon mankind to all the errors, the follies, and the miseries, which their most frantic rage, and their most dangerous vices and passions can produce?

The history of the earth! doth it present anything but crimes of the most heinous nature, committed from one end of the world to the other? We observe avarice, rapine,[1] and murder, equally prevailing in all parts. History perpetually tells us of millions of people abandoned to the caprice of the maddest princes, and of whole nations devoted to the blind fury of tyrants. Countries destroyed; nations alternately buried in ruins by other nations; some parts of the world beautifully cultivated, returned again to the pristine state; the fruits of ages of industry, the toil of thousands in a short time destroyed by few! If one corner breathes in peace for a few years, it is, in turn subjected, torn, and levelled; one would almost believe the principles of action in man, considered as the first agent of this planet, to be poisoned in their most essential parts. We certainly are not that class of beings which we vainly think ourselves to be; man an animal of prey, seems to have rapine and the love of bloodshed implanted in his heart; nay, to hold it the most honourable occupation in society: we never speak of a hero of mathematics, a hero of knowledge or humanity; no, this illustrious appellation is reserved for the most successful butchers of the world. If Nature has given us a fruitful soil to

inhabit, she has refused us such inclinations and propensities as would afford us the full enjoyment of it. Extensive as the surface of this planet is, not one half of it is yet cultivated, not half replenished; she created man, and placed him either in the woods or plains, and provided him with passions which must forever oppose his happiness: everything is submitted to the power of the strongest; men, like the elements, are always at war; the weakest yield to the most potent; force, subtilty, and malice, always triumph over unguarded honesty, and simplicity. Benignity, moderation, and justice, are virtues adapted only to the humble paths of life: we love to talk of virtue and to admire its beauty, while in the shade of solitude, and retirement; but when we step forth into active life, if it happen to be in competition with any passion or desire, do we observe it to prevail? Hence so many religious impostors have triumphed over the credulity of mankind, and have rendered their frauds the creeds of succeeding generations, during the course of many ages; until worn away by time, they have been replaced by new ones. Hence the most unjust war, if supported by the greatest force, always succeeds; hence the most just ones, when supported only by their justice, as often fail. Such is the ascendancy of power; the supreme arbiter of all the revolutions which we observe in this planet: so irresistible is power, that it often thwarts the tendency of the most forcible causes, and prevents their subsequent salutary effects, though ordained for the good of man by the Governor of the universe. Such is the perverseness of human nature; who can describe it in all its latitude?

In the moments of our philanthropy we often talk of an indulgent nature, a kind parent, who for the benefit of mankind has taken singular pains to vary the genera of plants, fruits, grain, and the different productions of the earth, and has spread peculiar blessings in each climate. This is undoubtedly an object of contemplation which calls forth our warmest gratitude; for so singularly benevolent have those parental intentions been, that where barrenness of soil or severity of climate prevail, there she has implanted in the heart of man sentiments which overbalance every misery, and supply the place of every want. She has given to the inhabitants of these regions an attachment to their savage rocks and wild shores, unknown to those who inhabit the fertile fields of the temperate zone. Yet if we attentively view

[1] *rapine* Plunder.

this globe, will it not appear rather a place of punishment than of delight? And what misfortune! that those punishments should fall on the innocent, and its few delights be enjoyed by the most unworthy. Famine, diseases, elementary convulsions, human feuds, dissensions, etc., are the produce of every climate; each climate produces, besides, vices and miseries peculiar to its latitude. View the frigid sterility of the north, whose famished inhabitants, hardly acquainted with the sun, live and fare worse than the bears they hunt—and to which they are superior only in the faculty of speaking. View the arctic and antarctic regions, those huge voids where nothing lives; regions of eternal snow; where winter in all his horrors has established his throne, and arrested every creative power of nature. Will you call the miserable stragglers in these countries by the name of men? Now contrast this frigid power of the north and south with that of the sun; examine the parched lands of the torrid zone, replete with sulphureous exhalations; view those countries of Asia subject to pestilential infections which lay nature waste; view this globe often convulsed both from within and without; pouring forth from several mouths, rivers of boiling matter, which are imperceptibly leaving immense subterranean graves, wherein millions will one day perish! Look at the poisonous soil of the equator, at those putrid slimy tracks, teeming with horrid monsters, the enemies of the human race; look next at the sandy continent, scorched perhaps by the fatal approach of some ancient comet, now the abode of desolation. Examine the rains, the convulsive storms of those climates, where masses of sulphur, bitumen, and electrical fire, combining their dreadful powers, are incessantly hovering and bursting over a globe threatened with dissolution. On this little shell, how very few are the spots where man can live and flourish! Even under those mild climates which seem to breathe peace and happiness, the poison of slavery, the fury of despotism, and the rage of superstition, are all combined against man! There only the few live and rule, whilst the many starve and utter ineffectual complaints: there, human nature appears more debased perhaps than in the less favoured climates. The fertile plains of Asia, the rich low lands of Egypt and of Diarbeck,[1] the fruitful fields border-

ing on the Tigris and the Euphrates,[2] the extensive country of the East Indies in all its separate districts; all these must to the geographical eye seem as if intended for terrestrial paradises: but though surrounded with the spontaneous riches of nature, though her kindest favours seem to be shed on those beautiful regions with the most profuse hand, yet there in general we find the most wretched people in the world. Almost everywhere, liberty, so natural to mankind, is refused, or rather enjoyed but by their tyrants; the word slave is the appellation of every rank, who adore as a divinity a being worse than themselves; subject to every caprice, and to every lawless rage which unrestrained power can give. Tears are shed, perpetual groans are heard, where only the accents of peace, alacrity, and gratitude should resound. There the very delirium of tyranny tramples on the best gifts of nature, and sports with the fate, the happiness, the lives of millions: there the extreme fertility of the ground always indicates the extreme misery of the inhabitants!

Everywhere one part of the human species are taught the art of shedding the blood of the other; of setting fire to their dwellings; of levelling the works of their industry: half of the existence of nations regularly employed in destroying other nations. What little political felicity is to be met with here and there has cost oceans of blood to purchase; as if good was never to be the portion of unhappy man. Republics, kingdoms, monarchies, founded either on fraud or successful violence, increase by pursuing the steps of the same policy, until they are destroyed in their turn, either by the influence of their own crimes, or by more successful but equally criminal enemies.

If from this general review of human nature, we descend to the examination of what is called civilized society; there the combination of every natural and artificial want, makes us pay very dear for what little share of political felicity we enjoy. It is a strange heterogeneous assemblage of vices and virtues, and of a variety of other principles, forever at war, forever jarring, forever producing some dangerous, some distressing extreme. Where do you conceive then that nature intended we should be happy? Would you prefer the state of men in the woods, to that of men in a more

[1] *Diarbeck* Diyarbakir, significant city in Turkey.

[2] *Tigris and the Euphrates* River system in western Asia; part of a historically significant region known as the Fertile Crescent.

improved situation? Evil preponderates in both; in the first they often eat each other for want of food, and in the other they often starve each other for want of room. For my part, I think the vices and miseries to be found in the latter, exceed those of the former; in which real evil is more scarce, more supportable, and less enormous. Yet we wish to see the earth peopled; to accomplish the happiness of kingdoms, which is said to consist in numbers. Gracious God! to what end is the introduction of so many beings into a mode of existence in which they must grope amidst as many errors, commit as many crimes, and meet with as many diseases, wants, and sufferings!

The following scene will I hope account for these melancholy reflections, and apologize for the gloomy thoughts with which I have filled this letter: my mind is, and always has been, oppressed since I became a witness to it. I was not long since invited to dine with a planter who lived three miles from ———, where he then resided. In order to avoid the heat of the sun, I resolved to go on foot, sheltered in a small path, leading through a pleasant wood. I was leisurely travelling along, attentively examining some peculiar plants which I had collected, when all at once I felt the air strongly agitated; though the day was perfectly calm and sultry. I immediately cast my eyes toward the cleared ground, from which I was but at a small distance, in order to see whether it was not occasioned by a sudden shower; when at that instant a sound resembling a deep rough voice, uttered, as I thought, a few inarticulate monosyllables. Alarmed and surprized, I precipitately looked all round, when I perceived at about six rods distance[1] something resembling a cage, suspended to the limbs of a tree; all the branches of which appeared covered with large birds of prey, fluttering about, and anxiously endeavouring to perch on the cage. Actuated by an involuntary motion of my hands more than by any design of my mind, I fired at them; they all flew to a short distance, with a most hideous noise: when, horrid to think and painful to repeat, I perceived a negro, suspended in the cage, and left there to expire! I shudder when I recollect that the birds had already picked out his eyes; his cheek bones were bare; his arms had been attacked in several places, and his body seemed covered with a multitude of wounds. From the edges of the hollow sockets and from the lacerations with which he was disfigured, the blood slowly dropped, and tinged the ground beneath. No sooner were the birds flown, than swarms of insects covered the whole body of this unfortunate wretch, eager to feed on his mangled flesh and to drink his blood. I found myself suddenly arrested by the power of affright and terror; my nerves were convulsed; I trembled, I stood motionless, involuntarily contemplating the fate of this negro, in all its dismal latitude. The living spectre, though deprived of his eyes, could still distinctly hear, and in his uncouth dialect begged me to give him some water to allay his thirst. Humanity herself would have recoiled back with horror; she would have balanced whether to lessen such reliefless distress, or mercifully with one blow to end this dreadful scene of agonizing torture! Had I had a ball in my gun, I certainly should have dispatched[2] him; but finding myself unable to perform so kind an office, I sought, though trembling, to relieve him as well as I could. A shell ready fixed to a pole, which had been used by some negroes, presented itself to me; filled it with water, and with trembling hands I guided it to the quivering lips of the wretched sufferer. Urged by the irresistible power of thirst, he endeavoured to meet it, as he instinctively guessed its approach by the noise it made in passing through the bars of the cage. "Tankè, you whitè man, tankè you, puté somè poyson and givè me." How long have you been hanging there? I asked him. "Two days, and me no die; the birds, the birds; aaah me!" Oppressed with the reflections which this shocking spectacle afforded me, I mustered strength enough to walk away, and soon reached the house at which I intended to dine. There I heard that the reason for this slave being thus punished, was on account of his having killed the overseer of the plantation. They told me that the laws of self-preservation rendered such executions necessary; and supported the doctrine of slavery with the arguments generally made use of to justify the practice; with the repetition of which I shall not trouble you at present.

Adieu.

[1] *at about ... rods distance* About thirty yards away.

[2] *dispatched* Killed.

from Letter 10
On Snakes; and on the Hummingbird

Why would you prescribe this talk; you know that what we take up ourselves seems always lighter than what is imposed on us by others. You insist on my saying something about our snakes; and in relating what I know concerning them, were it not for two singularities, the one of which I saw, and the other I received from an eye-witness, I should have but very little to observe. The southern provinces are the countries where nature has formed the greatest variety of alligators, snakes, serpents; and scorpions, from the smallest size, up to the *pine barren*, the largest species known here. We have but two, whose stings are mortal, which deserve to be mentioned; as for the black one, it is remarkable for nothing but its industry, agility, beauty, and the art of enticing birds by the power of its eyes. I admire it much, and never kill it, though its formidable length and appearance often get the better of the philosophy of some people, particularly of Europeans. The most dangerous one is the *pilot*, or *copperhead*; for the poison of which no remedy has yet been discovered. It bears the first name because it always precedes the rattlesnake; that is, quits its state of torpidity in the spring a week before the other. It bears the second name on account of its head being adorned with many copper-coloured spots. It lurks in rocks near the water, and is extremely active and dangerous. Let man beware of it! I have heard only of one person who was stung by a copperhead in this country. The poor wretch instantly swelled in a most dreadful manner; a multitude of spots of different hues alternately appeared and vanished, on different parts of his body: his eyes were filled with madness and rage, he cast them on all present with the most vindictive looks: he thrust out his tongue as the snakes do; he hissed through his teeth with inconceivable strength, and became an object of terror to all bystanders. To the lividness of a corpse he united the desperate force of a maniac; they hardly were able to fasten him, so as to guard themselves from his attacks; when in the space of two hours death relieved the poor wretch from his struggles, and the spectators from their apprehensions. ...

One anecdote I must relate, the circumstances of which are as true as they are singular.[1] One of my constant walks when I am at leisure, is in my lowlands, where I have the pleasure of seeing my cattle, horses, and colts. ... From this simple grove I have amused myself an hundred times in observing the great number of hummingbirds with which our country abounds: the wild blossoms everywhere attract the attention of these birds, which like bees subsist by suction. From this retreat I distinctly watch them in all their various attitudes; but their flight is so rapid that you cannot distinguish the motion of their wings. On this little bird nature has profusely lavished her most splendid colours; the most perfect azure, the most beautiful gold, the most dazzling red, are forever in contrast, and help to embellish the plumes of his majestic head. The richest pallet of the most luxuriant painter could never invent anything to be compared to the variegated tints with which this insect bird is arrayed. Its bill is as long and as sharp as a coarse sewing needle; like the bee, nature has taught it to find out in the calix of flowers and blossoms, those mellifluous[2] particles that serve it for sufficient food; and yet it seems to leave them untouched, undeprived of anything that our eyes can possibly distinguish. When it feeds, it appears as if immoveable, though continually on the wing; and sometimes, from what motives I know not, it will tear and lacerate flowers into a hundred pieces: for, strange to tell, they are the most irascible of the feathered tribe. Where do passions find room in so diminutive a body? They often fight with the fury of lions, until one of the combatants falls a sacrifice and dies. When fatigued, it has often perched within a few feet of me, and on such favourable opportunities I have surveyed it with the most minute attention. Its little eyes appear like diamonds, reflecting light on every side: most elegantly finished in all parts it is a miniature work of our great parent; who seems to have formed it the smallest, and at the same time the most beautiful of the winged species.

As I was one day sitting solitary and pensive in my primitive arbour, my attention was engaged by a strange sort of rustling noise at some paces distance. I looked all around without distinguishing anything,

[1] *singular* Unusual.

[2] *mellifluous* Honey-like.

until I climbed one of my great hemp stalks; when to my astonishment, I beheld two snakes of considerable length, the one pursuing the other with great celerity through a hemp stubble field. The aggressor was of the black kind, six feet long; the fugitive was a water snake, nearly of equal dimensions. They soon met, and in the fury of their first encounter, they appeared in an instant firmly twisted together; and whilst their united tails beat the ground, they mutually tried with open jaws to lacerate each other. What a fell aspect[1] did they present! Their heads were compressed to a very small size, their eyes flashed fire; and after this conflict had lasted about five minutes, the second found means to disengage itself from the first, and hurried toward the ditch. Its antagonist instantly assumed a new posture, and half creeping and half erect, with a majestic mien, overtook and attacked the other again, which placed itself in the same attitude, and prepared to resist. The scene was uncommon and beautiful, for thus opposed they fought with their jaws, biting each other with the utmost rage; but notwithstanding this appearance of mutual courage and fury, the water snake still seemed desirous of retreating toward the ditch, its natural element. This was no sooner perceived by the keen-eyed black one, than twisting its tail twice round a stalk of hemp, and seizing its adversary by the throat, not by means of its jaws, but by twisting its own neck twice round that of the water snake, pulled it back from the ditch. To prevent a defeat the latter took hold likewise of a stalk on the bank, and by the acquisition of that point of resistance became a match for its fierce antagonist. Strange was this to behold; two great snakes strongly adhering to the ground, mutually fastened together by means of the writhings which lashed them to each other, and stretched at their full length, they pulled but pulled in vain; and in the moments of greatest exertions that part of their bodies which was entwined, seemed extremely small, while the rest appeared inflated, and now and then convulsed with strong undulations, rapidly following each other. Their eyes seemed on fire, and ready to start out of their heads; at one time the conflict seemed decided; the water-snake bent itself into two great folds, and by that operation rendered the other more than commonly outstretched; the next minute the new struggles of the black one gained an unexpected superiority, it acquired two great folds likewise, which necessarily extended the body of its adversary in proportion as it had contracted its own. These efforts were alternate; victory seemed doubtful, inclining sometimes to the one side and sometimes to the other; until at last the stalk to which the black snake fastened, suddenly gave way, and in consequence of this accident they both plunged into the ditch. The water did not extinguish their vindictive rage; for by their agitations I could trace, though not distinguish, their mutual attacks. They soon re-appeared on the surface twisted together, as in their first onset; but the black snake seemed to retain its wonted[2] superiority, for its head was exactly fixed above that of the other, which it incessantly pressed down under the water, until it was stifled, and sunk. The victor no sooner perceived its enemy incapable of farther resistance, than abandoning it to the current, it returned on shore and disappeared.

—1782, 1783

[1] *fell aspect* Dreadful appearance.

[2] *wonted* Usual.

In Context

Nantucket and Charles-Town

Nantucket and its environs and Charles-Town and its environs present contrasting faces of America to Crèvecoeur's Farmer James. Images of both are provided here. (For Crèvecoeur's account of Nantucket, see the excerpt from Letter 4 included in the anthology's website component.)

The Town of Sherbourne on the Island of Nantucket.

"The inhabitants are the gayest in America; [Charles-Town] is called the centre of our beau monde," wrote Crèvecoeur in the late eighteenth century. Many of the buildings from that era are still standing—including the building now known as "the Pink House," which dates from 1712 and which served as a tavern for much of the eighteenth century. Photograph by Brian Stansberry, 2010. (Licensed under CC BY 3.0.)

Indigo Processing, St Stephen's Parish [approximately 30 miles north of Charlestown], 1762.

John Adams
1735 – 1826

Abigail Adams
1744 – 1818

The letters of John and Abigail Adams to one another have long been valued for their emotional depth as well as for the information they disclose about the public and private lives of some of the leading figures of early America. Over the course of their fifty-four-year marriage—much of which was spent living apart—the Adamses exchanged well over 1,000 letters, almost half of them sent during the Revolutionary War. Taken together, these letters are expressive both of the optimism and of the many anxieties that characterized the political upheavals of the 1770s and 80s. Abigail's correspondence is expressive too of the changing place of women in eighteenth-century America; in her writing we can see clearly how the familiar letter provided an important space in which women could make their voices heard.

Abigail Smith was born in Weymouth, Massachusetts in 1744 to William Smith, a Congregational minister, and Elizabeth Quincy Smith, a descendant of the influential Quincy family. Abigail did not receive a formal education, but she was taught to read and write at home and was encouraged to make use of the relatively substantial family library. John Adams was born eight years earlier in Braintree, Massachusetts, also into a locally prominent family, and began practicing the law in the late 1750s. The two met in 1759, when Abigail was fifteen years old, though they did not begin a courtship until three years later. They married in 1764; over the next eight years they would have five children, including future President John Quincy Adams.

In the years following their marriage, John Adams became increasingly involved in colonial politics, and by the early 1770s he had developed a reputation as an outspoken proponent of complete independence. John's new involvement in national politics initiated his first extended absence from Abigail; in 1774 he was invited to join the First Continental Congress in Philadelphia. He left Abigail in Braintree to raise their children and manage the family farm, and John and Abigail saw very little of one another over the next ten years. While John participated in events such as the drafting of the Declaration of Independence—where he was a strong supporter of the work of young lawyer and pamphleteer Thomas Jefferson—Abigail more keenly felt the more immediate effects of the War, including the violence of nearby battles and the rapid spread of diseases such as smallpox and dysentery, which ravaged the family in the autumn of 1775.

John's persistent absence was hard on the family, to whom Abigail often read his letters aloud. Such sharing of correspondence among family and friends was typical of the era, when letter-writing flourished as a literary form, thereby straddling the line between the public and the private. As postal services improved and literacy became more widespread, the consequent increase in correspondence was accompanied by a plethora of new writing manuals aimed specifically at letter writers; epistolary writing became more and more established as a distinct genre. It came as well to be seen by many as a form in which accomplished women could—and even should—excel (unlike other literary forms, to which women's access was still largely restricted). Letter-writing became for many women a newly accessible platform for intellectual exchange; this can be seen in Abigail Adams's exchanges with female friends such as poet, playwright, historian, and political writer Mercy Otis Warren, as well as in her exchanges with her husband. Abigail's most famous letter has often been referred to by its well-known remonstrance to

John to "Remember the Ladies" when drafting the laws of the new nation. The letter has been celebrated by generations of readers as an eloquent declaration of the rights of women—though some have rightly cautioned against reading Abigail as a feminist in the modern sense, and have drawn attention to John's less-than-supportive written response. Apparently disappointed with her husband's dismissal of her ideas, Abigail later copied her "Remember the Ladies" letter to Warren, writing: "So I have help'd the Sex abundantly, but I will tell [John] I have only been making trial of the Disintrestedness of his Virtue, and when weigh'd in the balance have found it wanting."

The Adams letters cease after 1801, when John finished his four-year term as President; he had previously spent two terms as George Washington's Vice President, and before that had lived for an extended period as a diplomat in France, the Netherlands, and England, visited for short periods in London and The Hague by Abigail.

John's friendship with Thomas Jefferson—who had served as Adams's Vice President—had deteriorated late in the century, as their political opinions began to diverge. Though they never saw one another again after Jefferson was elected President in 1801, they revived their correspondence around 1812; these letters too have become famous. They continue to fascinate readers both for what they reveal of the relationship between the two men, and for the ways in which they express differing political and philosophical ideals of the early nineteenth century. (Selections from the correspondence between Adams and Jefferson are included in the website component of this anthology.)

John Adams and Jefferson died on the same day in 1826, on the fiftieth anniversary of the Revolution; Abigail had died eight years earlier, in 1818.

John had first begun copying out his letters to Abigail in 1776 to ensure their preservation; he insisted that she do the same, writing: "I really think your Letters are much better worth preserving than mine." Abigail, for her part, often expressed anxiety about her writing, and even asked that John burn her letters. Many later readers, however, have agreed with John that Abigail was the better and more interesting writer. The first published edition of their correspondence was *Letters of Mrs. Adams, the Wife of John Adams*, published by their grandson Charles Francis Adams in 1840. Only later was it followed by a collection culled from both sets of letters. *Letters of Mrs. Adams* was immediately successful, going through four large printings in its first eight years. C.F. Adams, who claimed that neither correspondent "ever dreamed that [their letters] might ultimately be shown to the world," asserted that the correspondence was a rare and invaluable representation of the private impact of the American Revolution. Interest has not waned significantly since the 1800s, and editions of the Adams and Adams-Jefferson letters have continued to be released well into the twenty-first century.

NOTE ON THE TEXTS: The texts of the letters between John and Abigail Adams are with three exceptions based on those appearing in Volumes 1 and 2 of *The Adams Family Correspondence* (1963), edited by L.H. Butterfield, Wendell D. Garrett, and Marjorie Sprague and part of *The Adams Papers* series; other editions have also been consulted—most notably those edited by Charles Francis Adams (*The Letters of Mrs. Adams, the Wife of John Adams* [1840], and *The Letters of John Adams* [1841]), the earliest published editions. For the Abigail Adams letter of 19 August 1774, the text provided in the Charles Francis Adams edition has been used as the base text; for the John Adams letter of 3 July 1776, the text found in the Charles Francis Adams edition has been used as the base text. Spelling and punctuation have been modernized in accordance with the practices of this anthology.

⌘ ⌘ ⌘

from ABIGAIL ADAMS TO JOHN ADAMS

Braintree, 19 August, 1774

The great distance between us makes the time appear very long to me. It seems already a month since you left me.[1] The great anxiety I feel for my country, for you, and for our family, renders the day tedious, and the night unpleasant. The rocks and quicksands appear upon every side. What course you can or will take is all wrapped in the bosom of futurity. Uncertainty and expectation leave the mind great scope. Did ever any kingdom or state regain its liberty, when once it was invaded, without bloodshed? I cannot think of it without horror. …

I want much to hear from you. I long impatiently to have you upon the stage of action. The first of September, or the month of September, perhaps, may be of as much importance to Great Britain, as the Ides of March[2] were to Caesar. I wish you every public, as well as private blessing, and that wisdom which is profitable both for instruction and edification, to conduct you in this difficult day. The little flock remember papa, and kindly wish to see him; so does your most affectionate

Abigail Adams

ABIGAIL ADAMS TO JOHN ADAMS

November 27, 1775

'Tis a fortnight tonight since I wrote you a line, during which I have been confined with the jaundice, rheumatism and a most violent cold; I yesterday took a puke which has relieved me, and I feel much better today. Many, very many people who have had the dysentery, are now afflicted both with the jaundice and rheumatism; some it has left in hectics, some in dropsies.[3]

The great and incessant rains we have had this fall (the like cannot be recollected) may have occasioned some of the present disorders. The jaundice is very prevalent in the camp. We have lately had a week of very cold weather, as cold as January, and a flight of snow, which I hope will purify the air of some of the noxious vapours. It has spoiled many hundreds of bushels of apples, which were designed for cider, and which the great rains had prevented people from making up. Suppose we have lost 5 barrels by it.

Colonel Warren[4] returned last week to Plymouth, so that I shall not hear anything from you till he goes back again which will not be till the last of this month.

He damped my spirits greatly by telling me that the Court had prolonged your stay another month.[5] I was pleasing myself with the thoughts that you would soon be upon your return. 'Tis in vain to repine. I hope the public will reap what I sacrifice.

I wish I knew what mighty things were fabricating. If a form of government is to be established here, what one will be assumed? Will it be left to our assemblies to choose one? and will not many men have many minds? and shall we not run into dissentions among ourselves?

I am more and more convinced that Man is a dangerous creature, and that power, whether vested in many or a few, is ever grasping, and like the grave cries "give, give." The great fish swallow up the small, and he who is most strenuous for the rights of the people, when vested with power, is as eager after the prerogatives of government. You tell me of degrees of perfection to which human nature is capable of arriving, and I believe it, but at the same time lament that our admiration should arise from the scarcity of the instances.

The building up a great empire, which was only hinted at by my correspondent, may now I suppose be realized even by the unbelievers. Yet will not ten

[1] *It seems … left me* John Adams had departed Braintree to attend the First Continental Congress in Philadelphia on 10 August.

[2] *Ides of March* Date of the assassination of Julius Caesar, which occurred on the fifteenth, or "Ides," of March.

[3] *hectics* Fever; *dropsies* Swelling caused by abnormal fluid retention.

[4] *Colonel Warren* James Warren (1726–1808), Massachusetts politician and Paymaster General of the Continental Army; Warren and his wife Mercy Otis Warren (1728–1814) were close friends of the Adamses until they cut ties over political disagreements in the 1780s.

[5] *the Court … another month* Adams's commission as a delegate in the Second Continental Congress, which had originally been planned to end in December, had been extended until the end of January, due in large part to the inability of the House of Representatives to agree on new delegates for the year 1776.

thousand difficulties arise in the formation of it? The reins of government have been so long slackened, that I fear the people will not quietly submit to those restraints which are necessary for the peace, and security, of the community; if we separate from Britain, what code of laws will be established? How shall we be governed so as to retain our liberties? Can any government be free which is not administered by general stated laws? Who shall frame these laws? Who will give them force and energy? 'Tis true your resolution[s] as a body have hitherto had the force of laws. But will they continue to have?

When I consider these things, and the prejudices of people in favour of ancient customs and regulations, I feel anxious for the fate of our monarchy or democracy or whatever is to take place. I soon get lost in a labyrinth of perplexities, but whatever occurs, may justice and righteousness be the stability of our times, and order arise out of confusion. Great difficulties may be surmounted by patience and perseverance.

I believe I have tired you with politics. As to news we have not any at all. I shudder at the approach of winter when I think I am to remain desolate.[1] Suppose your weather is warm yet. Mr. Mason and Thaxter[2] live with me, and render some part of my time less disconsolate. Mr. Mason is a youth who will please you, he has spirit, taste and sense. His application to his studies is constant and I am much mistaken if he does not make a very good figure in his profession.

I have with me now the only daughter of your brother; I feel a tenderer affection for her as she has lost a kind parent.[3] Though too young to be sensible[4] of her own loss, I can pity her. She appears to be a child of a very good disposition—only wants to be a little used to company.[5]

Our little ones send duty[6] to pappa and want much to see him. Tom says he won't come home till the battle is over—some strange notion he has got into his head. He has got a political creed to say to him when he returns.

I must bid you good night. 'Tis late for one who am much of an invalid.[7] I was disappointed last week in receiving a packet by the post, and upon unsealing it found only four newspapers. I think you are more cautious than you need be. All letters I believe have come safe to hand. I have sixteen from you, and wish I had as many more. Adieu. Yours.

ABIGAIL ADAMS TO JOHN ADAMS

Braintree, March 31, 1776

I wish you would ever write me a letter half as long as I write you; and tell me if you may where your fleet are gone? What sort of defence Virginia can make against our common enemy? Whether it is so situated as to make an able defence? Are not the gentry, lords, and the common people vassals;[8] are they not like the uncivilized natives Britain represents us to be? I hope their rifle men, who have shown themselves very savage and even bloodthirsty, are not a specimen of the generality of the people.

I am willing to allow the colony great merit for having produced a Washington, but they have been shamefully duped by a Dunmore.[9]

I have sometimes been ready to think that the passion for liberty cannot be equally strong in the breasts of those who have been accustomed to deprive their fellow creatures of theirs. Of this I am certain: that it is not founded upon that generous and Christian

1 *desolate* I.e., alone; lonely.

2 *Mr. Mason and Thaxter* Jonathan Mason (1756–1831), a lawyer acquaintance, and John Thaxter Jr. (1755–91), Abigail's cousin and occasional tutor to her son, John Quincy Adams.

3 *daughter … kind parent* John Adams's niece Susanna Adams (1766–1826), whose father had died in August 1775.

4 *sensible* Aware; conscious.

5 *wants … company* I.e., needs to become accustomed to having company.

6 *send duty* I.e., send their regards.

7 *much of an invalid* I.e., still weak from her recent illness.

8 *Are not … people vassals* Adams compares the current social structure in Virginia to that of feudalism, in which only the wealthy and well-born were landowners, and the common people were merely tenants and servants.

9 *the colony … Dunmore* Virginia was the birthplace of both George Washington and John Murray, Lord Dunmore, the Virginian governor who took numerous actions, including proclaiming martial law, in order to suppress the revolution.

principal of doing to others as we would that others should do unto us.

Do not you want to see Boston? I am fearful of the smallpox, or I should have been in before this time. I got Mr. Crane[1] to go to our house[2] and see what state it was in. I find it has been occupied by one of the doctors of a regiment, very dirty, but no other damage has been done to it. The few things which were left in it are all gone. Cranch[3] has the key which he never delivered up. I have wrote to him for it and am determined to get it cleaned as soon as possible and shut it up. I look upon it a new acquisition of property, a property which one month ago I did not value at a single shilling, and could with pleasure have seen it in flames.

The town in general is left in a better state than we expected, more owing to a precipitate flight[4] than any regard to the inhabitants, though some individuals discovered a sense of honour and justice and have left the rent of the houses in which they were, for the owners and the furniture unhurt, or if damaged sufficient to make it good.

Others have committed abominable ravages. The mansion house of your President[5] is safe and the furniture unhurt whilst both the house and furniture of the Solicitor General[6] have fallen a prey to their own merciless party. Surely the very fiends feel a reverential awe for virtue and patriotism, whilst they detest the parricide[7] and traitor.

I feel very differently at the approach of spring to what I did a month ago. We knew not then whether we could plant or sow with safety, whether when we had toiled we could reap the fruits of our own industry, whether we could rest in our own cottages, or whether we should not be driven from the sea coasts to seek shelter in the wilderness, but now we feel as if we might sit under our own vine and eat the good of the land.

I feel a *gaieté de coeur*[8] to which before I was a stranger. I think the sun looks brighter, the birds sing more melodiously, and Nature puts on a more cheerful countenance. We feel a temporary peace, and the poor fugitives are returning to their deserted habitations.

Tho we felicitate ourselves, we sympathize with those who are trembling least the Lot of Boston should be theirs. But they cannot be in similar circumstances unless pusilanimity and cowardise should take possession of them. They have time and warning given them to see the Evil and shun it.—I long to hear that you have declared an independency—and by the way in the new Code of Laws which I suppose it will be necessary for you to make I desire you would Remember the Ladies, and be more generous and favourable to them than your ancestors. Do not put such unlimited power into the hands of the Husbands. Remember all Men would be tyrants if they could. If perticuliar care and attention is not paid to the Laidies we are determined to foment a Rebelion, and will not hold ourselves bound by any Laws in which we have no voice, or Representation.

That your sex are naturally tyrannical is a truth so thoroughly established as to admit of no dispute, but such of you as wish to be happy willingly give up the harsh title of Master for the more tender and endearing one of Friend. Why, then, not put it out of the power of the vicious and the lawless to use us with cruelty and indignity with impunity? Men of sense in all ages abhor those customs which treat us only as the vassals of your sex. Regard us then as beings placed by providence under your protection and in imitation of the Supreme Being make use of that power only for our happiness.

original spelling

[1] *Mr. Crane* Presumably the Adams's agent; little else is known about this name.

[2] *our house* The family's Boston residence.

[3] *Cranch* While Abigail Adams did have a brother-in-law named Richard Cranch, it seems more likely, given the context here, that this is a misspelling of "Crane," the agent referred to above.

[4] *precipitate flight* Adams refers to the British army's withdrawal from Boston on 17 March 1776 at the end of the eleven-month-long Siege of Boston.

[5] *your President* John Hancock (1737–93), wealthy merchant and president of the Second Continental Congress. His family home, Hancock Manor, was considered one of the finest buildings in Massachusetts.

[6] *Solicitor General* Samuel Quincy (1735–89), attorney and relative of John Adams.

[7] *parricide* Literally, someone who murders his or her father; figuratively, a traitor to one's ruler or country.

[8] *gaieté de coeur* French: cheerfulness of heart.

from John Adams to Abigail Adams

Philadelphia, 3 July, 1776[1]

Your favor of 17 June, dated at Plymouth, was handed me by yesterday's post. I was much pleased to find that you had taken a journey to Plymouth, to see your friends, in the long absence of one whom you may wish to see. The excursion will be an amusement, and will serve your health. How happy would it have made me to have taken this journey with you! ...

Yesterday, the greatest question was decided, which ever was debated in America,[2] and a greater, perhaps, never was nor will be decided among men. A Resolution was passed without one dissenting Colony "that these United States are, and of right ought to be, free and independent States, and as such they have, and of right ought to have, full power to make war, conclude peace, establish commerce and to do all other acts and things which other States may rightfully do." You will see, in a few days, a Declaration setting forth the causes which have impelled us to this mighty revolution, and the reasons which will justify it in the sight of God and man. A plan of confederation will be taken up in a few days. ...

... I am surprised at the suddenness as well as greatness of this revolution. Britain has been filled with folly, and America with wisdom; at least, this is my judgment. Time must determine. It is the will of Heaven that the two countries should be sundered forever. It may be the will of Heaven that America shall suffer calamities still more wasting, and distresses yet more dreadful. If this is to be the case, it will have this good effect at least. It will inspire us with many virtues, which we have not, and correct many errors, follies and vices which threaten to disturb, dishonor, and destroy us. The furnace of affliction produces refinement in states as well as individuals. And the new Governments we are assuming in every part will require a purification from our vices, and an augmentation of our

virtues, or they will be no blessings. The people will have unbounded power, and the people are extremely addicted to corruption and venality,[3] as well as the great. But I must submit all my hopes and fears to an overruling providence, in which, unfashionable as the faith may be, I firmly believe.

John Adams to Abigail Adams

Philadelphia, July 3rd, 1776

Had a Declaration of Independency been made seven months ago, it would have been attended with many great and glorious effects[4] We might before this hour, have formed alliances with foreign states. We should have mastered Quebec and been in possession of Canada[5] You will perhaps wonder how such a Declaration would have influenced our affairs in Canada, but if I could write with freedom I could easily convince you that it would, and explain to you the manner how. Many gentlemen in high stations and of great influence have been duped by the ministerial bubble of commissioners to treat[6] And in real, sincere expectation of this event, which they so fondly wished, they have been slow and languid, in promoting measures for the reduction[7] of that province. Others there are in the colonies who really wished that our enterprise in Canada would be defeated, that the colonies might be brought into danger and distress between two fires, and be thus induced to submit. Others really wished to defeat the expedition to Canada, lest the conquest of it should elevate the minds of the people too much to hearken to those terms of reconciliation which they believed would be offered us. These jarring

[1] *Philadelphia ... 1776* John Adams wrote two letters to Abigail on this date, both of which are included here.

[2] *Yesterday ... in America* The independence of the United States was formally declared by the Second Continental Congress on the second of July, 1776; the final wording of the Declaration of Independence was approved two days later.

[3] *venality* The state of being overly mercenary—too willing to act for the sake of financial or other worldly rewards.

[4] *effects* The ellipses here are all in the original text; they do not indicate any excerpting on the part of the editors of this anthology.

[5] *mastered Quebec ... Canada* Here and throughout this paragraph, Adams refers to the failed invasion of Canada that began in June 1775, in which the Continental Army hoped to capture British territory in Quebec and convince French Canadians to join the revolutionary cause.

[6] *treat* Negotiate.

[7] *reduction* Capture.

views, wishes and designs, occasioned an opposition to many salutary measures which were proposed for the support of that expedition, and caused obstructions, embarrassments and studied delays, which have finally lost us the province.

All these causes however in conjunction would not have disappointed us, if it had not been for a misfortune, which could not be foreseen, and perhaps could not have been prevented, I mean the prevalence of the smallpox among our troops This fatal pestilence completed our destruction. It is a frown of Providence upon us, which we ought to lay to heart.

But on the other hand, the delay of this declaration to this time has many great advantages attending it. The hopes of reconciliation, which were fondly entertained by multitudes of honest and well meaning though weak and mistaken people, have been gradually and at last totally extinguished. Time has been given for the whole people maturely to consider the great question of independence and to ripen their judgments, dissipate their fears, and allure their hopes, by discussing it in newspapers and pamphlets, by debating it, in assemblies, conventions, committees of safety and inspection, in town and county meetings, as well

as in private conversations, so that the whole people in every colony of the 13 have now adopted it as their own Act. This will cement the Union, and avoid those heats and perhaps convulsions which might have been occasioned by such a Declaration six months ago.

But the day is past. The second day of July 1776 will be the most memorable epoch in the history of America. I am apt to believe that it will be celebrated, by succeeding generations, as the great anniversary festival. It ought to be commemorated as the Day of Deliverance by solemn acts of devotion to God Almighty. It ought to be solemnized with pomp and parade, with shows, games, sports, guns, bells, bonfires and illuminations[1] from one end of this continent to the other from this time forward forever more.

You will think me transported[2] with enthusiasm but I am not. I am well aware of the toil and blood and treasure that it will cost us to maintain this Declaration, and support and defend these States. Yet through all the gloom I can see the rays of ravishing light and glory. I can see that the end is more than worth all the means. And that posterity will triumph in that day's transaction, even although we should rue it,[3] which I trust in God we shall not.

[1] *illuminations* I.e., decorating a place or building with lights.

[2] *transported* Carried away.

[3] *even ... rue it* I.e., even if we ourselves lament having to take part in it.

THOMAS PAINE
1737 – 1809

Born in obscurity and buried in ignominy 72 years later, Thomas Paine nevertheless played a signifi-cant role in the histories of three nations. After failing in numerous early careers, Paine became an overnight success with the publication of his first pamphlet in the American colonies, *Common Sense* (1776), and his talent for political rhetoric and persuasion made him an important influence in the Revolutionary War effort in America, in the drafting of Jefferson's Declaration of Independence, and in the formation of the French National Assembly.

Paine was born in the town of Thetford in Norfolk, England, the only son of a Quaker couple, Joseph Pain (a shopkeeper of modest means who made and sold "stays" or corsets) and his wife Frances (Cocke) Pain.[1] Thomas spent several years at the local grammar school before beginning an appren-ticeship with his father. At sixteen he ran away from home and briefly signed on with a privateer before returning to Thetford. Three years later he is reported to have worked for a time in London for "a very noted stay-maker," but the next year he again signed on with a privateer—this time for six months. On his return he moved to Dover, where he took up the stay-maker's trade once more. In 1759 he borrowed ten pounds to finance his own stay-making shop in the nearby town of Sandwich; here he met and married Mary Lambert, a maid in a local shopkeeper's household, whose father worked for the Customs and Excise Service. But Paine was unable to make a living for himself in the stay-making business; his shop failed, and at about the same time—in 1760—Mary died in childbirth, together with the infant.

Between 1756 and 1774 Paine lived several times for brief periods in London, where in his spare time he attended lectures and met several leading intellectual figures of the day—among them the astronomer John Bevis, the mathematician (and Commissioner of the Board of Excise) George Lewis Scott, and the renowned scientist and intellectual Benjamin Franklin.

Paine continued to live a peripatetic life through his twenties and thirties, working for varying lengths of time as a tobacco-shop proprietor, a grocer, a teacher, and an exciseman (a traveling tax collector)—a profession that he may have become interested in through the influence of Mary's father. Though twice dismissed from excise positions, he had something of an impact on that profession, agitat-ing for better pay and working conditions for excisemen, and publishing in 1772 a pamphlet arguing these points, *The Case of the Officers of Excise*. During the years 1768 to 1774 Paine lived in Lewes, Sussex (a town that had suffered from economic hardship and that had something of a tradition of radical politi-cal activity); here he joined the White Hart Inn's debating club, and became politically active. In 1771 he married Elizabeth Ollive, the daughter of a prominent Lewes shopkeeper. In 1774, however, his life fell apart again; he was dismissed for the second time as an excise officer, the shop he had inherited from Elizabeth's father failed, and he was threatened with debtor's prison. He and Elizabeth formally separated, and Paine moved to London.

In London he was befriended by Franklin; when Paine decided to emigrate, Franklin provided him with letters of introduction. Paine arrived in Philadelphia in November 1774 in very poor health, but by the following spring he had been hired by printer Robert Aiken to edit a new publication, the *Pennsylvania Magazine*. Paine had finally found his calling; under his editorship the magazine's circula-tion rose to over 1,500 (said by some to have been higher than any other American magazine of its day).

1 At some point before 1769 Paine added an "e" to his surname.

Paine began to contribute pieces to the magazine himself, beginning in March 1775 with an essay on "African Slavery in America" in which he argued that those who had been enslaved had "a natural, perfect right" to freedom. The essay led to the formation the following month of the Society for the Relief of Free Negroes, Unlawfully Held in Bondage (America's earliest known antislavery society); Paine would later play a significant role in the drafting of the 1780 legislation that initiated the gradual abolition of slavery in Pennsylvania.

As hostilities between Britain and its American colonies were escalating in December 1775, Paine was able to put his writing skills to further use when he was commissed by Franklin and other prominent figures to write a pamphlet; on 9 January 1776 he issued *Common Sense*, one of the first publications to argue that America should immediately declare full independence from Britain. The pamphlet was an extraordinary success; even scholars such as Trish Loughran who have helpfully called into question a number of unverifiable claims concerning the number of copies circulated have affirmed that it was "immensely popular." In plain and forceful language, Paine called on ordinary people to give their energy to a higher purpose—the creation of America. His accessible prose, compelling logic, and gift for dismissing opposing arguments made him for a time the American Revolution's most adept promoter.

Dubbing Britain a "tyrannical oppressor," *Common Sense* argues that government, at best "a necessary evil," should serve to protect its citizens and preserve their freedom. A subsequent series of letters, entitled *The American Crisis* (1776–83), continued to muster support for the revolution in the face of military setbacks and public fear and despondency. One such letter's rousing and powerful rhetoric—"These are times that try men's souls…"—was read to George Washington's troops on Christmas Eve in an effort to boost their morale.

After the Revolutionary War ended, Paine spent considerable time in Britain and France. The publication of Edmund Burke's conservative pamphlet attacking the French Revolution, *Reflections on the Revolution in France* (1790), spurred him to publish a rebuttal, based largely on the account of the Revolution he had been working on at the time. Part 1 of Paine's *Rights of Man* (1791) came in the midst of a pamphlet storm of replies to Burke (among them Mary Wollstonecraft's *A Vindication of the Rights of Men*). Demonstrating once again his powers of persuasion, and leaning on the weight of his experience in the American Revolution (the work was dedicated to George Washington), Paine challenged Burke's view of the French Revolution. *Rights of Man* insists that each generation, rather than being ruled by preceding generations, "must be as free to act for itself, in all cases, as the ages and generations which preceded it." Paine argues that men have certain natural rights, existent from birth and given by their creator, which society is formed to protect and to enforce through the provision of civil rights. Part 2 of *Rights of Man* (1792) went further, arguing that American independence had set in motion the changes that would bring down the tyranny of hereditary government in Europe. This attack on the monarchy and aristocracy saw Paine charged with treason in England; he took refuge in France, where he had been made an honorary citizen.

Paine was in 1792 elected to the French National Assembly, and the following year he was appointed to a committee that had been tasked with the job of drafting a new French constitution. With the coming to power of the Jacobin government of Maximilien Robespierre, however, Paine fell from favor; he was imprisoned during the Reign of Terror (1793–94), and narrowly avoided the guillotine. Paine (who blamed George Washington for not having secured his release from prison earlier) was finally freed following Robespierre's execution in 1794. Paine—whose opinionated nature, disdain for social convention, and carefree habits of spending and of borrowing had cost him many friends and supporters—once more found himself at the center of controversy, this time for his last major work, *The Age of Reason* (1794–95). This deist denunciation of the Bible and of organized Christianity (along with religious institutions of all denominations) met with widespread hostility; Paine, who returned to America in 1802, was labeled an infidel and an atheist. Ostracised, he spent the final years of his life in poverty. When he died Paine was buried on his farm in New Rochelle, under a tombstone stating simply—at his request—"The author of Common Sense"; his request to be buried in a Quaker graveyard had been refused. A decade later the famed radical writer and politician William Cobbett arranged for his remains to be exhumed, with

the intent of according Paine a more honored burial place in Britain. Cobbett's plans were frustrated, however, and the whereabouts of Paine's remains has been unknown ever since.

If Paine's reputation had its ups and downs during his lifetime, so too has his posthumous reputation. The disgrace he had suffered following the publication of *The Age of Reason* lingered in many minds long after his death, and disapproval of Paine's character continued to color many discussions of his writings. Thus, for example, an 1851 article in the Philadelphia magazine *Arthur's Home Gazette* by Arthur J. Stanbury attacked Paine as "an infidel, a debauchee, a drunkard, a liar, a blasphemer, and a profane swearer." An answering opinion piece in William Lloyd Garrison's newspaper *The Liberator* offered a defense that ridiculed Stanbury's *ad hominem* reasoning, as well as its hypocrisy: "Paine was a drunkard, and therefore his opinions were detestable. [Famous American statesman Daniel] Webster was a drunkard, but his opinions are worthy of all deference. Paine was licentious, and therefore unfit to receive distinguished consideration; Webster is licentious, but is worthy of the highest national honor." (The *Liberator* piece ended on a note of optimism: "the good shall yet triumph," it predicted, in the ways that Paine had striven for.)

Paine was celebrated by many (Walt Whitman among them) in the late nineteenth and early twentieth centuries, but he continued to be disparaged as well (particularly by those of a conservative bent); one 1924 history of American literature dismisses him in a couple of lines as "an obscure Englishman of whiggish temper [who became] the fiercest advocate of American independence." And some twentieth-century anthologists and literary historians ignore him altogether; Barrett Wendell's 1925 literary history of America makes no more mention of Paine than does Samuel Knapp's 1829 overview. But for the most part Paine's positive contribution to American literature was, by the early twentieth century, at least grudgingly recognized—as, for example, William P. Trent's 1903 literary history acknowledges it: "Time has not made more palatable [the] vulgarity [of Paine's writings], but it has made us see that even if the man never ceased to be a philistine, he was of greater service to his race than most children of 'sweetness and light' are wont to be."

By mid century writers were no longer judged so harshly on grounds such as "vulgarity" and "philistinism," and the acknowledgments of Paine's importance ceased to be grudging. Throughout the later decades of the twentieth century and the early decades of this century Paine's centrality both to the history of America and to its literature has been universally recognized. Included in every major anthology of American literature, his writing has been lauded not only for its rhetorical power and persuasiveness but also for helping to shape a plain style of American prose writing.

NOTE ON THE TEXTS: The early publishing history of *Common Sense* is a tangled one. When printer Robert Bell's first printing of 1,000 copies of the 47-page pamphlet quickly sold out, Bell ordered a second printing—but without having paid Paine, as had earlier been agreed, half the profits from the first printing. Paine then contracted a new edition with another printer (Thomas and William Bradford), while Bell himself also issued further editions (adding the phrase "by an Englishman" to the title page). Paine and the Bradfords arranged to price their edition of the pamphlet significantly lower than Bell had priced his, and the Bradford edition substantially outsold Bell's. The Bradford version included a new introduction and (as it declared on the title page) "several additions in the body of the work," as well as "an appendix; together with an address to the people called Quakers." The additions to "the body of the work" were primarily charts and tables; most of the text was unrevised. Nevertheless, it was the text of this second edition (and that of the near-identical third edition) which reached the greatest number of Americans in 1776; for that reason, it is the second rather than the first edition that we have used as a base text here.

Paine issued three editions of "The American Crisis" in late 1776; the text excerpted here is that issued third (dated 23 December). The base text for the excerpts from *The Age of Reason* (available in the anthology's website component) is that of the original 1794 edition (though the chapter divisions added in later editions are indicated in the notes).

Except where otherwise noted, spelling and punctuation have been modernized according to the practices of this anthology.

⌘ ⌘ ⌘

COMMON SENSE;

ADDRESSED TO THE

INHABITANTS

OF

AMERICA,

On the following interesting

SUBJECTS.

I. Of the Origin and Design of Government in general,
with concise Remarks on the English Constitution.

II. Of Monarchy and Hereditary Succession.

III. Thoughts on the present State of American Affairs.

IV. Of the present Ability of America, with some mis-
cellaneous Reflections.

Man knows no Master save creating HEAVEN,
Or those whom choice and common good ordain.
 THOMSON.

PHILADELPHIA;

Printed, and Sold, by R. BELL, in Third-Street.

MDCCLXXVI.

Title page of the first edition of Paine's pamphlet, showing its full, 52-word title: *Common Sense: addressed to the inhabitants of America, on the following interesting subjects. I. Of the origin and design of government in general, with concise remarks on the English Constitution. II. Of monarchy and hereditary succession. III. Thoughts on the present state of American affairs. IV. Of the present ability of America, with some miscellaneous reflections.* The quotation ("Man knows no master save creating Heaven, / Or those whom choice and common good ordain") is from Part 4: Britain of James Thomson's long poem *Liberty* (1736). The context is a passage discussing the history of the early Britons—"sons of nature," as Thomson presents them— who were "unsubdued" by either "tyrant force" or "tyrant custom." It is from their experience that the general moral is drawn that humankind is not to be ruled except by "creating Heaven" or, alternatively, by such principles as our own choices and the interests of the common good command us to follow.

from *Common Sense*

INTRODUCTION

Perhaps the sentiments contained in the following pages, are not yet sufficiently fashionable to procure them general favor; a long habit of not thinking a thing *wrong*, gives it a superficial appearance of being right, and raises at first a formidable outcry in defense of custom. But the tumult soon subsides. Time makes more converts than reason.

As a long and violent abuse of power, is generally the Means of calling the right of it in question (and in Matters too which might never have been thought of, had not the Sufferers been aggravated into the inquiry) and as the King of England hath undertaken in his own Right, to support the Parliament in what he calls Theirs, and as the good people of this country are grievously oppressed by the combination, they have an undoubted privilege to inquire into the pretensions of both, and equally to reject the usurpation of either.

In the following sheets, the author hath studiously avoided every thing which is personal among ourselves. Compliments as well as censure to individuals make no part thereof. The wise, and the worthy, need not the triumph of a pamphlet; and those whose sentiments are injudicious, or unfriendly, will cease of themselves unless too much pains are bestowed upon their conversion.

The cause of America is in a great measure the cause of all mankind. Many circumstances hath, and will arise, which are not local, but universal, and through which the principles of all Lovers of Mankind are affected, and in the Event of which, their Affections are interested. The laying a Country desolate with Fire and Sword, declaring War against the natural rights of all Mankind, and extirpating the Defenders thereof from the Face of the Earth, is the Concern of every Man to whom Nature hath given the Power of feeling; of which Class, regardless of Party Censure, is the
AUTHOR.

P.S. The Publication of this new Edition hath been delayed, with a View of taking notice (had it been necessary) of any Attempt to refute the Doctrine of Independance: As no Answer hath yet appeared, it is now presumed that none will, the Time needful for getting such a Performance ready for the Public being considerably past.

Who the Author of this Production is, is wholly unnecessary to the Public, as the Object for Attention is the *Doctrine* itself, not the Man. Yet it may not be unnecessary to say, That he is unconnected with any Party, and under no sort of Influence public or private, but the influence of reason and principle.

Philadelphia, February 14, 1776

from OF THE ORIGIN AND DESIGN OF GOVERNMENT IN GENERAL, WITH CONCISE REMARKS ON THE ENGLISH CONSTITUTION

Some writers have so confounded society with government as to leave little or no distinction between them; whereas they are not only different, but have different origins. Society is produced by our wants, and government by our wickedness; the former promotes our happiness positively by uniting our affections, the latter negatively by restraining our vices. The one encourages intercourse, the other creates distinctions. The first is a patron, the last a punisher.

Society in every state is a blessing, but government even in its best state is but a necessary evil; in its worst state an intolerable one; for when we suffer, or are exposed to the same miseries *by a government*, which we might expect in a country *without government*, our calamity is heightened by reflecting that we furnish the means by which we suffer. Government, like dress, is the badge of lost innocence; the palaces of kings are built on the ruins of the bowers of paradise. For were the impulses of conscience clear, uniform, and irresistibly obeyed, man would need no other lawgiver; but that not being the case, he finds it necessary to surrender up a part of his property to furnish means for the protection of the rest; and this he is induced to do by the same prudence which in every other case advises him out of two evils to choose the least. *Wherefore*, security being the true design and end of government, it unanswerably follows that whatever *form* thereof appears most likely to ensure it to us, with the least expense and greatest benefit, is preferable to all others.

original spelling

In order to gain a clear and just idea of the design and end of government, let us suppose a small number of persons settled in some sequestered part of the earth, unconnected with the rest; they will then represent the first peopling of any country, or of the world. In this state of natural liberty, society will be their first thought. A thousand motives will excite them thereto; the strength of one man is so unequal to his wants, and his mind so unfitted for perpetual solitude, that he is soon obliged to seek assistance and relief of another, who in his turn requires the same. Four or five united would be able to raise a tolerable dwelling in the midst of a wilderness, but one man might labour out of the common period of life without accomplishing anything; when he had felled his timber he could not remove it, nor erect it after it was removed; hunger in the meantime would urge him from his work, and every different want would call him a different way. Disease, nay even misfortune would be death, for though neither might be mortal, yet either would disable him from living, and reduce him to a state in which he might rather be said to perish than to die.

Thus necessity, like a gravitating power, would soon form our newly arrived emigrants into society, the reciprocal blessings of which would supersede, and render the obligations of law and government unnecessary, while they remained perfectly just to each other; but as nothing but heaven is impregnable to vice, it will unavoidably happen that, in proportion as they surmount the first difficulties of emigration, which bound them together in a common cause, they will begin to relax in their duty and attachment to each other; and this remissness will point out the necessity of establishing some form of government to supply the defect of moral virtue. ...

Here then is the origin and rise of government—namely, a mode rendered necessary by the inability of moral virtue to govern the world; here too is the design and end of government, viz.[1] freedom and security. And, however our eyes may be dazzled with show, or our ears deceived by sound; however prejudice may warp our wills, or interest darken our understanding, the simple voice of nature and of reason will say, it is right.

I draw my idea of the form of government from a principle in nature, which no art can overturn, viz. that the more simple anything is, the less liable it is to be disordered; and the easier repaired when disordered; and with this maxim in view, I offer a few remarks on the so much boasted constitution of England.[2] That it was noble for the dark and slavish times in which it was erected, is granted. When the world was overrun with tyranny, the least remove therefrom was a glorious rescue. But that it is imperfect, subject to convulsions, and incapable of producing what it seems to promise, is easily demonstrated.

Absolute governments (though the disgrace of human nature) have this advantage with them, that they are simple; if the people suffer, they know the head from which their suffering springs, know likewise the remedy, and are not bewildered by a variety of causes and cures. But the constitution of England is so exceedingly complex that the nation may suffer for years together without being able to discover in which part the fault lies; some will say in one and some in another, and every political physician will advise a different medicine.

I know it is difficult to get over local or long-standing prejudices, yet if we will suffer ourselves to examine the component parts of the English constitution, we shall find them to be the base remains of two ancient tyrannies, compounded with some new republican materials.

First—The remains of monarchical tyranny in the person of the king.

Secondly—The remains of aristocratical tyranny in the persons of the peers.

Thirdly—The new republican materials, in the persons of the commons,[3] on whose virtue depends the freedom of England.

1 *viz.* Short for the Latin videlicet, meaning "namely" or "that is to say."

2 *constitution of England* Whereas the American Constitution is a document (with later amendments) that declares itself to be exactly that, earlier constitutions such as that of Britain were not codified into any single document. They were instead based on convention—comprised of shared understandings founded on a number of background documents (such as the Magna Carta of 1215 and the Declaration of Rights of 1688), together with the history of their interpretation by the monarch, by the courts, and by Parliament. It is thus appropriate to refer to the English (or British) constitution with a lower-case "c."

3 *the commons* I.e., the members of the House of Commons.

The two first, by being hereditary, are independent of the people; wherefore in a constitutional sense they contribute nothing towards the freedom of the state.

To say that the constitution of England is a union of three powers reciprocally checking each other, is farcical, either the words have no meaning, or they are flat contradictions.

To say that the Commons is a check upon the king, presupposes two things:

First—That the king is not to be trusted without being looked after, or in other words, that a thirst for absolute power is the natural disease of monarchy.

Secondly—That the Commons, by being appointed for that purpose, are either wiser or more worthy of confidence than the crown.

But as the same constitution which gives the Commons a power to check the king by withholding the supplies, gives afterwards the king a power to check the Commons, by empowering him to reject their other bills; it again supposes that the king is wiser than those whom it has already supposed to be wiser than him. A mere absurdity!

There is something exceedingly ridiculous in the composition of monarchy; it first excludes a man from the means of information, yet empowers him to act in cases where the highest judgment is required. The state of a king shuts him from the world, yet the business of a king requires him to know it thoroughly; wherefore the different parts, by unnaturally opposing and destroying each other, prove the whole character to be absurd and useless.

Some writers have explained the English constitution thus; the king, say they, is one, the people another; the peers are an house in behalf of the king; the Commons in behalf of the people; but this hath all the distinctions of a house divided against itself; and though the expressions be pleasantly arranged, yet when examined they appear idle and ambiguous; and it will always happen, that the nicest[1] construction that words are capable of, when applied to the description of some thing which either cannot exist, or is too incomprehensible to be within the compass of description, will be words of sound only, and though they may amuse the ear, they cannot inform the mind, for this explanation includes a previous question, viz. *How came the king by a power which the people are afraid to trust, and always obliged to check?* Such a power could not be the gift of a wise people; neither can any power, *which needs checking*, be from God. Yet the provision which the constitution makes supposes such a power to exist.

But the provision is unequal to the task; the means either cannot or will not accomplish the end, and the whole affair is a *felo de se*;[2] for as the greater weight will always carry up the less, and as all the wheels of a machine are put in motion by one, it only remains to know which power in the constitution has the most weight, for that will govern; and though the others, or a part of them, may clog, or, as the phrase is, check the rapidity of its motion, yet so long as they cannot stop it, their endeavors will be ineffectual; the first moving power will at last have its way, and what it wants[3] in speed is supplied by time.

That the crown is this overbearing part in the English constitution needs not be mentioned, and that it derives its whole consequence merely from being the giver of places and pensions is self-evident, wherefore, though we have been wise enough to shut and lock a door against absolute monarchy, we at the same time have been foolish enough to put the crown in possession of the key.

The prejudice of Englishmen in favour of their own government by king, lords, and commons, arises as much or more from national pride than reason. Individuals are undoubtedly safer in England than in some other countries, but the *will* of the king is as much the *law* of the land in Britain as in France, with this difference, that instead of proceeding directly from his mouth, it is handed to the people under the more formidable shape of an act of parliament. ...

from OF MONARCHY AND HEREDITARY SUCCESSION

Mankind being originally equals in the order of creation, the equality could only be destroyed by some subsequent circumstance; the distinctions of rich, and poor, may in a great measure be accounted for, and that without having recourse to the harsh, ill sounding names of oppression and avarice. Oppression is

[1] *nicest* Most carefully worded.

[2] *felo de se* Latin: suicide or self-murder; here, negating contradictions, and so absurdities.

[3] *wants* Lacks.

often the *consequence*, but seldom or never the *means* of riches; and though avarice will preserve a man from being necessitously poor, it generally makes him too timorous to be wealthy.

But there is another and greater distinction for which no truly natural or religious reason can be assigned, and that is, the distinction of men into kings and subjects. Male and female are the distinctions of nature, good and bad the distinctions of heaven; but how a race of men came into the world so exalted above the rest, and distinguished like some new species, is worth enquiring into, and whether they are the means of happiness or of misery to mankind.

In the early ages of the world, according to the scripture chronology, there were no kings; the consequence of which was there were no wars; it is the pride of kings which throws mankind into confusion. …

Government by kings was first introduced into the world by the Heathens, from whom the children of Israel copied the custom. It was the most prosperous invention the Devil ever set on foot for the promotion of idolatry. The Heathens paid divine honors to their deceased kings, and the Christian world hath improved on the plan by doing the same to their living ones. …

To the evil of monarchy we have added that of hereditary succession; and as the first is a degradation and lessening of ourselves, so the second, claimed as a matter of right, is an insult and an imposition on posterity. For all men being originally equals, no one by birth could have a right to set up his own family in perpetual preference to all others for ever, and though himself might deserve some decent degree of honors of his contemporaries, yet his descendants might be far too unworthy to inherit them. One of the strongest natural proofs of the folly of hereditary right in kings, is, that nature disapproves it; otherwise she would not so frequently turn it into ridicule by giving mankind *an ass for a lion*.[1] …

England, since the conquest,[2] hath known some few good monarchs, but groaned beneath a much larger number of bad ones; yet no man in his senses can say that their claim under William the Conqueror is a very honorable one. A French bastard landing with an armed banditti, and establishing himself king of England against the consent of the natives, is in plain terms a very paltry rascally original—it certainly hath no divinity in it. However, it is needless to spend much time in exposing the folly of hereditary right; if there are any so weak as to believe it, let them promiscuously worship the ass and lion, and welcome. I shall neither copy their humility, nor disturb their devotion. …

But it is not so much the absurdity as the evil of hereditary succession which concerns mankind. Did it ensure a race of good and wise men it would have the seal of divine authority, but as it opens a door to the foolish, the wicked, and the improper, it hath in it the nature of oppression. Men who look upon themselves [as] born to reign, and others to obey, soon grow insolent; selected from the rest of mankind, their minds are early poisoned by importance; and the world they act in differs so materially from the world at large, that they have but little opportunity of knowing its true interests, and when they succeed to the government are frequently the most ignorant and unfit of any throughout the dominions.

Another evil which attends hereditary succession is that the throne is subject to be possessed by a minor at any age; all which time the regency, acting under the cover of a king, have every opportunity and inducement to betray their trust. The same national misfortune happens when a king, worn out with age and infirmity, enters the last stage of human weakness. In both these cases the public becomes a prey to every miscreant who can tamper successfully with the follies either of age or infancy.

The most plausible plea which hath ever been offered in favour of hereditary succession is that it preserves a nation from civil wars; and were this true, it would be weighty; whereas, it is the most barefaced falsity ever imposed upon mankind. The whole history of England disowns the fact. Thirty kings and two minors

[1] *an ass for a lion* The lion is symbolic of the monarchy; Paine is suggesting that the hereditary system often results in a person with few kingly qualities assuming the crown. (The reference may be in part prompted by Aesop's fable "The Ass in the Lion's Skin," in which a lonely ass discovers a lion's skin and puts it on; through this means he pretends to be a lion and terrorizes other animals. The ass's owner eventually recognizes the ass by his ears, and beats him.)

[2] *the conquest* I.e., the Norman Conquest of 1066, under William I (1021–87), "the Conqueror."

have reigned in that distracted[1] kingdom since the conquest, in which time there have been (including the Revolution[2]) no less than eight civil wars and nineteen rebellions. Wherefore instead of making for peace, it makes against it, and destroys the very foundation it seems to stand on. ...

In short, monarchy and succession have laid (not this or that kingdom only) but the world in blood and ashes. 'Tis a form of government which the word of God bears testimony against, and blood will attend it. ...

In England a king hath little more to do than to make war and give away places; which in plain terms, is to impoverish the nation and set it together by the ears. A pretty business indeed for a man to be allowed eight hundred thousand sterling a year for, and worshipped into the bargain! Of more worth is one honest man to society and in the sight of God, than all the crowned ruffians that ever lived.

THOUGHTS ON THE PRESENT STATE OF AMERICAN AFFAIRS

In the following pages I offer nothing more than simple facts, plain arguments, and common sense; and have no other preliminaries to settle with the reader, than that he will divest himself of prejudice and prepossession, and suffer his reason and his feelings to determine for themselves; that he will put *on*, or rather that he will not put *off*, the true character of a man, and generously enlarge his views beyond the present day.

Volumes have been written on the subject of the struggle between England and America. Men of all ranks have embarked in the controversy, from different motives, and with various designs; but all have been ineffectual, and the period of debate is closed. Arms, as the last resource, decide the contest; the appeal was the choice of the king, and the continent hath accepted the challenge.

It hath been reported of the late Mr. Pelham[3] (who, though an able minister, was not without his faults) that on his being attacked in the House of Commons, on the score that his measures were only of a temporary kind, replied "they will last my time." Should a thought so fatal and unmanly possess the colonies in the present contest, the name of ancestors will be remembered by future generations with detestation.

The sun never shined on a cause of greater worth. 'Tis not the affair of a city, a country, a province, or a kingdom, but of a continent—of at least one eighth part of the habitable globe. 'Tis not the concern of a day, a year, or an age; posterity are virtually involved in the contest, and will be more or less affected, even to the end of time, by the proceedings now. Now is the seed time of continental union, faith and honor. The least fracture now will be like a name engraved with the point of a pin on the tender rind of a young oak; the wound will enlarge with the tree, and posterity read it in full grown characters.

By referring the matter from argument to arms, a new era for politics is struck; a new method of thinking hath arisen. All plans, proposals, etc. prior to the nineteenth of April, i.e., to the commencement of hostilities,[4] are like the almanacs of the last year; which, though proper then, are superseded and useless now. Whatever was advanced by the advocates on either side of the question then, terminated in one and the same point, viz. a union with Great Britain; the only difference between the parties was the method of effecting it; the one proposing force, the other friendship; but it hath so far happened that the first hath failed, and the second hath withdrawn her influence.

As much hath been said of the advantages of reconciliation, which, like an agreeable dream, hath passed away and left us as we were, it is but right, that we should examine the contrary side of the argument, and inquire into some of the many material injuries which these colonies sustain, and always will sustain, by being connected with, and dependant on Great Britain. To

1 *distracted* Divided; disunified.

2 *Revolution* A long period of revolution and civil war in England began in 1642 and lasted until 1660, when the monarchy was restored. The term "revolution" is also used in British history with reference to the overthrow of James II in 1688 (the so-called "Glorious Revolution").

3 *Mr. Pelham* Henry Pelham (1694–1754), English prime minister from 1743 until his death.

4 *commencement of hostilities* On 19 April 1775, fifteen months before the Declaration of Independence, British and American forces clashed at Lexington, Massachusetts, in what is often thought of as the first battle of the American Revolution.

examine that connection and dependence, on the principles of nature and common sense, to see what we have to trust to, if separated, and what we are to expect, if dependant.

I have heard it asserted by some, that as America hath flourished under her former connection with Great Britain, that the same connection is necessary towards her future happiness, and will always have the same effect. Nothing can be more fallacious than this kind of argument. We may as well assert that because a child has thrived upon milk, that it is never to have meat, or that the first twenty years of our lives is to become a precedent for the next twenty. But even this is admitting more than is true, for I answer roundly, that America would have flourished as much, and probably much more, had no European power had anything to do with her. The commerce by which she hath enriched herself are the necessaries of life, and will always have a market while eating is the custom of Europe.

But she has protected us, say some. That she has engrossed[1] us is true, and defended the continent at our expense as well as her own is admitted—and she would have defended Turkey from the same motive, viz. the sake of trade and dominion.

Alas, we have been long led away by ancient prejudices, and made large sacrifices to superstition. We have boasted the protection of Great Britain, without considering, that her motive was interest, not attachment; that she did not protect us from our enemies on our account, but from her enemies on her own account, from those who had no quarrel with us on any other account, and who will always be our enemies on the same account. Let Britain wave her pretensions to the continent, or the continent throw off the dependence, and we should be at peace with France and Spain were they at war with Britain. The miseries of Hanover's last war ought to warn us against connections.[2]

It has lately been asserted in parliament that the colonies have no relation to each other but through the parent country—i.e., that Pennsylvania and the Jerseys,[3] and so on for the rest, are sister colonies by the way of England; this is certainly a very roundabout way of proving relationship, but it is the nearest and only true way of proving enemyship, if I may so call it. France and Spain never were, nor perhaps ever will be our enemies as Americans, but as our being the *subjects of Great-Britain*.

But Britain is the parent country, say some. Then the more shame upon her conduct. Even brutes do not devour their young, nor savages make war upon their families; wherefore the assertion, if true, turns to her reproach. But it happens not to be true, or only partly so, and the phrase *parent* or *mother country* hath been jesuitically[4] adopted by the king and his parasites, with a low papistical[5] design of gaining an unfair bias on the credulous weakness of our minds. Europe, and not England, is the parent country of America. This new world hath been the asylum for the persecuted lovers of civil and religious liberty from *every part* of Europe. Hither have they fled, not from the tender embraces of the mother, but from the cruelty of the monster; and it is so far true of England, that the same tyranny which drove the first emigrants from home, pursues their descendants still.

In this extensive quarter of the globe, we forget the narrow limits of three hundred and sixty miles (the extent of England) and carry our friendship on a larger scale; we claim brotherhood with every European Christian, and triumph in the generosity of the sentiment.

It is pleasant to observe by what regular gradations we surmount the force of local prejudice, as we enlarge

1 *engrossed* Dominated.

2 *The miseries ... connections* Paine here refers to the Seven Years' War (1756–63), a major military conflict that involved a number of European powers, including Britain and France. Though Britain was eventually largely successful militarily, success did not come easily; heavy losses were suffered (not least of all in the American colonies), and Britain doubled its national debt in order to finance the war. The British monarchs during this period—George II and then George III—were both of the House of Hanover.

3 *Jerseys* Between 1674 and 1702 New Jersey was divided into East and West Jersey.

4 *jesuitically* Paine is here partaking in a long tradition of anti-Catholic prejudice. The Jesuits—a Catholic religious order—were known for the rigorous training in logic and argumentation that they provided in their schools. Non-Catholics often disparaged Jesuitical practices of argumentation as conniving and deceitful.

5 *papistical* Of a sort that one would expect from the pope and his followers. It was a common slur among the English (and among many Protestants elsewhere) to suggest that the Pope and, more generally, the Catholic church exercised undue influence over its credulous followers.

our acquaintance with the world. A man born in any town in England divided into parishes, will naturally associate most with his fellow parishioners (because their interests in many cases will be common) and distinguish him by the name of neighbour; if he meet him but a few miles from home, he drops the narrow idea of a street, and salutes him by the name of townsman; if he travel out of the county, and meet him in any other, he forgets the minor divisions of street and town, and calls him countryman, i.e. county-man; but if in their foreign excursions they should associate in France or any other part of Europe, their local remembrance would be enlarged into that of Englishmen. And by a just parity of reasoning, all Europeans meeting in America, or any other quarter of the globe, are countrymen; for England, Holland, Germany, or Sweden, when compared with the whole, stand in the same places on the larger scale which the divisions of street, town, and county do on the smaller ones; distinctions too limited for continental minds. Not one third of the inhabitants, even of this province,[1] are of English descent. Wherefore I reprobate the phrase of parent or mother country applied to England only, as being false, selfish, narrow, and ungenerous.

But admitting that we were all of English descent—what does it amount to? Nothing. Britain, being now an open enemy, extinguishes every other name and title: And to say that reconciliation is our duty, is truly farcical. The first king of England, of the present line (William the Conqueror) was a Frenchman, and half the peers of England[2] are descendants from the same country; wherefore, by the same method of reasoning, England ought to be governed by France.

Much hath been said of the united strength of Britain and the colonies, that in conjunction they might bid defiance to the world. But this is mere presumption; the fate of war is uncertain, neither do the expressions mean anything; for this continent would never suffer itself to be drained of inhabitants to support the British arms in either Asia, Africa, or Europe.

Besides, what have we to do with setting the world at defiance? Our plan is commerce, and that, well attended to, will secure us the peace and friendship of all Europe; because, it is the interest of all Europe to have America a free port. Her trade will always be a protection, and her barrenness of gold and silver secure her from invaders.

I challenge the warmest advocate for reconciliation to show a single advantage that this continent can reap by being connected with Great Britain. I repeat the challenge; not a single advantage is derived. Our corn[3] will fetch its price in any market in Europe, and our imported goods must be paid for, buy them where we will.

But the injuries and disadvantages which we sustain by that connection are without number; and our duty to mankind at large, as well as to ourselves, instruct us to renounce the alliance, because any submission to, or dependence on Great Britain tends directly to involve this continent in European wars and quarrels; and sets us at variance with nations who would otherwise seek our friendship, and against whom we have neither anger nor complaint. As Europe is our market for trade, we ought to form no partial connection with any part of it. It is the true interest of America to steer clear of European contentions, which she never can do while, by her dependence on Britain, she is made the make-weight in the scale of British politics.

Europe is too thickly planted with kingdoms to be long at peace, and whenever a war breaks out between England and any foreign power, the trade of America goes to ruin because of her connection with Britain. The next war may not turn out like the last,[4] and should it not, the advocates for reconciliation now will be wishing for separation then, because neutrality, in that case, would be a safer convoy than a man-of-war.[5] Every thing that is right or natural pleads for separation. The blood of the slain, the weeping voice of Nature cries, "'Tis time to part." Even the distance at which the Almighty hath placed England and America is a strong and natural proof that the authority of the one, over the other, was never the design of Heaven. The time likewise at which the continent was discovered adds weight to the argument, and the manner in which it

1 *this province* Pennsylvania.

2 *peers of England* Members of the upper house of the British parliament, the House of Lords, who were at the time all members of the English nobility.

3 *corn* Grain.

4 *may not ... like the last* I.e., may not end with Britain as the victor (as did the Seven Years' War).

5 *man-of-war* Large, heavily armed naval warship.

was peopled increases the force of it. The Reformation[1] was preceded by the discovery of America, as if the Almighty graciously meant to open a sanctuary to the persecuted in future years, when home should afford neither friendship nor safety.

The authority of Great Britain over this continent is a form of government which sooner or later must have an end. And a serious mind can draw no true pleasure by looking forward, under the painful and positive conviction that what he calls "the present constitution" is merely temporary. As parents, we can have no joy, knowing that this government is not sufficiently lasting to ensure anything which we may bequeath to posterity. And by a plain method of argument, as we are running the next generation into debt, we ought to do the work of it; otherwise we use them meanly[2] and pitifully. In order to discover the line of our duty rightly, we should take our children in our hand, and fix our station a few years farther into life; that eminence will present a prospect which a few present fears and prejudices conceal from our sight.

Though I would carefully avoid giving unnecessary offence, yet I am inclined to believe that all those who espouse the doctrine of reconciliation may be included within the following descriptions: interested men,[3] who are not to be trusted; weak men, who cannot see; prejudiced men, who *will not* see; and a certain set of moderate men, who think better of the European world than it deserves; and this last class, by an ill-judged deliberation, will be the cause of more calamities to this continent, than all the other three.

It is the good fortune of many to live distant from the scene of sorrow; the evil is not sufficiently brought to their doors to make them feel the precariousness with which all American property is possessed. But let our imaginations transport us for a few moments to Boston; that seat of wretchedness[4] will teach us wisdom, and instruct us for ever to renounce a power in whom we can have no trust. The inhabitants of that unfortunate city, who but a few months ago were in ease and affluence, have now, no other alternative than to stay and starve, or turn out to beg. Endangered by the fire of their friends if they continue within the city, and plundered by the soldiery if they leave it, in their present condition they are prisoners without the hope of redemption, and in a general attack for their relief, they would be exposed to the fury of both armies.

Men of passive tempers look somewhat lightly over the offences of Britain, and, still hoping for the best, are apt to call out, "Come, come, we shall be friends again, for all this." But examine the passions and feelings of mankind, bring the doctrine of reconciliation to the touchstone of nature, and then tell me whether you can hereafter love, honour, and faithfully serve the power that hath carried fire and sword into your land? If you cannot do all these, then are you only deceiving yourselves, and by your delay bringing ruin upon posterity. Your future connection with Britain, whom you can neither love nor honour, will be forced and unnatural, and, being formed only on the plan of present convenience, will in a little time fall into a relapse more wretched than the first. But if, you say, you can still pass the violations over, then I ask, Hath your house been burnt? Hath your property been destroyed before your face? Are your wife and children destitute of a bed to lie on, or bread to live on? Have you lost a parent or a child by their hands, and yourself the ruined and wretched survivor? If you have not, then are you not a judge[5] of those who have. But if you have, and still can shake hands with the murderers, then are you unworthy[6] of the name of husband, father, friend, or lover, and whatever may be your rank or title in life; you have the heart of a coward, and the spirit of a sycophant.

This is not inflaming or exaggerating matters, but trying them by those feelings and affections which nature justifies, and without which we should be incapable of discharging the social duties of life, or enjoying the felicities of it. I mean not to exhibit horror for the purpose of provoking revenge, but to awaken us from fatal and unmanly slumbers, that we may pursue determinately some fixed object. It is not in the power

[1] *The Reformation* I.e., the emergence of Protestantism in Europe, which in its early years (and in areas where Catholicism remained the dominant religion) led to the persecution of many dissenters by the Catholic Church.

[2] *meanly* Stingily.

[3] *interested men* I.e., people who have a financial interest or some other personal involvement in a particular matter.

[4] *Boston … wretchedness* At the time Paine was writing, Boston was blockaded and occupied by the British military.

[5] *then are you not a judge* I.e., then it is not your place to judge.

[6] *are you unworthy* You are unworthy.

of Britain or of Europe to conquer America, if she do not conquer herself by delay and timidity. The present winter is worth an age if rightly employed, but if lost or neglected, the whole continent will partake of the misfortune; and there is no punishment which that man will not deserve, be he who, or what, or where he will, that may be the means of sacrificing a season so precious and useful.

It is repugnant to reason, to the universal order of things, to all examples from former ages, to suppose that this continent can longer remain subject to any external power. The most sanguine in Britain does not think so. The utmost stretch of human wisdom cannot, at this time, compass a plan short of separation which can promise the continent even a year's security. Reconciliation is now a fallacious dream. Nature hath deserted the connection, and Art cannot supply her place. For, as Milton wisely expresses, "never can true reconcilement grow where wounds of deadly hate have pierced so deep."[1] ...

As to government matters, it is not in the power of Britain to do this continent justice; the business of it will soon be too weighty and intricate to be managed with any tolerable degree of convenience by a power so distant from us, and so very ignorant of us—for if they cannot conquer us, they cannot govern us. To be always running three or four thousand miles with a tale or a petition, waiting four or five months for an answer (which, when obtained, requires five or six more to explain it in), will in a few years be looked upon as folly and childishness. There was a time when it was proper, and there is a proper time for it to cease.

Small islands not capable of protecting themselves are the proper objects for kingdoms to take under their care; but there is something very absurd in supposing a continent to be perpetually governed by an island. In no instance hath nature made the satellite larger than its primary planet, and as England and America, with respect to each other, reverses the common order of nature, it is evident they belong to different systems: England to Europe, America to itself.

I am not induced by motives of pride, party, or resentment to espouse the doctrine of separation and independence; I am clearly, positively, and conscientiously

persuaded that it is the true interest of this continent to be so; that everything short of that is mere patchwork, that it can afford no lasting felicity—that it is leaving the sword to our children, and shrinking back at a time when a little more, a little farther, would have rendered this continent the glory of the earth. ...

But where, says some, is the King of America? I'll tell you, Friend; he reigns above, and doth not make havoc of mankind like the Royal Brute of Britain. Yet, that we may not appear to be defective even in earthly honors, let a day be solemnly set apart for proclaiming the charter; let it be brought forth placed on the divine law, the word of God; let a crown be placed thereon, by which the world may know, that, so far as we approve of monarchy, that in America the law is king. For, as in absolute governments the King is law, so in free countries the law ought to be King; and there ought to be no other. But, lest any ill use should afterwards arise, let the crown at the conclusion of the ceremony be demolished, and scattered among the people whose right it is.

A government of our own is our natural right. And when a man seriously reflects on the precariousness of human affairs, he will become convinced that it is infinitely wiser and safer to form a constitution of our own in a cool deliberate manner, while we have it in our power, than to *trust* such an interesting event to time and chance. If we omit it now,[2] some Massanello[3] may hereafter arise who, laying hold of popular disquietudes, may collect together the desperate and the discontented, and by assuming to themselves the powers of government, may sweep away the liberties of the continent like a deluge. Should the government of America return again into the hands of Britain, the tottering situation of things will be a temptation for some desperate adventurer to try his fortune; and in such a case, what relief can Britain give? Ere she could hear the news, the fatal business might be done; and ourselves suffering like the wretched Britons under the oppression of the Conqueror. Ye that oppose independence

[1] *never can ... so deep* See John Milton's 1667 poem *Paradise Lost*, 4.98–99. (Ironically, the words are spoken by Lucifer.)

[2] *omit it now* Neglect to do it now.

[3] [Paine's note] Thomas Anello, otherwise Massanello, a fisherman of Naples who, after spiriting up his countrymen in the public marketplace, against the oppression of the Spaniards, to whom the place was then subject, prompted them to revolt, and in the space of a day became king. [The rebel leader is more commonly referred to as Tommaso Aniello (1620–47).]

now, ye know not what ye do; ye are opening a door to eternal tyranny by keeping vacant the seat of government. There are thousands, and tens of thousands, who would think it glorious to expel from the continent that barbarous and hellish power which hath stirred up the Indians and Negroes to destroy us. The cruelty hath a double guilt; it is dealing brutally by us, and treacherously by them.

To talk of friendship with those in whom our reason forbids us to have faith, and our affections wounded through a thousand pores instruct us to detest, is madness and folly. Every day wears out the little remains of kindred between us and them, and can there be any reason to hope that, as the relationship expires, the affection will increase; or that we shall agree better, when we have ten times more and greater concerns to quarrel over than ever?

Ye that tell us of harmony and reconciliation, can ye restore to us the time that is past? Can ye give to prostitution its former innocence? Neither can ye reconcile Britain and America. The last cord now is broken; the people of England are presenting addresses against us.[1]

There are injuries which Nature cannot forgive; she would cease to be Nature if she did. As well can the lover forgive the ravisher of his mistress, as the continent forgive the murders of Britain. The Almighty hath implanted in us these unextinguishable feelings for good and wise purposes. They are the guardians of His image in our hearts. They distinguish us from the herd of common animals. The social compact would dissolve, and justice be extirpated the earth (or have only a casual existence) were we callous to the touches of affection. The robber and the murderer would often escape unpunished, did not the injuries which our tempers sustain provoke us into justice.

O ye that love mankind! Ye that dare oppose, not only the tyranny, but the tyrant, stand forth! Every spot of the old world is overrun with oppression. Freedom hath been hunted round the globe. Asia and Africa have long expelled her. Europe regards her like a stranger, and England hath given her warning to depart. O! receive the fugitive, and prepare in time an asylum for mankind. ...

—1776

IN CONTEXT

A Response to *Common Sense*

<hr />

1 *presenting addresses against us* Initiating conflict with us.

from Charles Inglis, *The Deceiver Unmasked; or, Loyalty and Interest United in Answer to a Pamphlet Entitled* Common Sense (1776)

Charles Inglis (1734–1816) emigrated to the American colonies in 1755; he worked for some years as a priest in Delaware before being appointed to Trinity Church in New York. Vehemently opposed to Paine's suggestion that the colonies declare independence from Britain, Inglis was one of several loyalists who issued pamphlets in response to Paine's *Common Sense*. When Inglis first issued his pamphlet under the provocative title *The Deceiver Unmasked* (in an edition printed by Samuel Loudon), it met with a violent reaction from the Sons of Liberty group—as Hugh Hughes described in a 31 March letter to John Adams:

> There has been a Pamphlet written and published here against our natural rights and "Common Sense." It has met with its demerit. Some of our sturdy Sons seized between 1,500 and 2,000 of them at Sam Loudon's, and consigned them to the flames. This has given great umbrage to several of our pretended friends, but they are forced to pocket the affront.

Following this act of vandalism, Inglis re-issued the pamphlet with a different printer under a less incendiary title: *The True Interest of America Impartially Stated, in Certain Strictures on a Pamphlet Entitled Common Sense* (1776).

In the face of the success of the Revolution, Inglis returned to England (in 1783), but in 1787 he emigrated again to the British colonies—this time to Nova Scotia, where he became the Anglican Church's first bishop to be based in North America.

Preface

The following pages contain an answer to one of the most artful, insidious, and pernicious pamphlets I have ever met with. It is addressed to the passions of the populace, at a time when their passions are much inflamed. At such juncture, cool reason and judgement are too apt to sleep: the mind is easily imposed on. ...

The author of *Common Sense* has availed himself of all these circumstances. Under the mask of friendship to America, in the present calamitous situation of affairs, he gives vent to his own private resentment and ambition, and recommends a scheme which must infallibly prove ruinous. He proposes that we should renounce our allegiance to the sovereign, break off all connection with Great Britain, and set up an independent empire of the republican kind. Sensible that such a proposal must, even at this time, be shocking to the ears of Americans, he insinuates that the novelty of his sentiments is the only obstacle to their success. ...

I find no common sense in this pamphlet, but much uncommon frenzy. It is an outrageous insult on the common sense of Americans—an insidious attempt to poison their minds and seduce them from their loyalty and truest interest. The principles of government laid down in it are not only false, but too absurd to have ever entered the head of a crazy politician before. ...

The author calls himself an Englishman, but whether he is a native of Old England or new England is a thing I neither know nor care about. I am only to know him by the features he hath here exhibited of himself, which are those of an avowed republican, utterly averse and unfriendly to the English constitution. ...

From our former connection with Great Britain we have already derived numberless advantages and benefits; from a closer union with her, on proper principles, we may derive still greater benefits in future. Duty, gratitude, interest, nay, providence, by its all-wise dispensations, loudly call on both countries to unite, and would join them together; and may infamy be the portion of that wretch who would put them asunder.

February 16, 1776

Consider this matter as you will, view the Declaration of Independency[1] in what light you please; the ruin of America must be the inevitable consequence. Our author's earnestness and zeal, therefore, that we should declare ourselves independent, serves only to prove that he himself is desperate, and that he would gladly bring his whole continent into the same situation. ...

For my part, I look upon this pamphlet to be the most injurious, in every respect, to America, of any that has appeared since these troubles began. Its natural and necessary tendency is to produce jealousy, dissention, and disunion among us. The Continental Congress, the several provincial congresses and assemblies, have all unanimously and in the strongest terms disclaimed every idea of independency. They have repeatedly declared their abhorrence of such a step; they have as often declared their firm attachment to our sovereign and the parent state. They have declared that placing them in the same situation they were [in] at the close of the last war was their only object—that when this was done, by repealing the obnoxious acts,[2] our former harmony and friendship would be restored. I appeal to the reader whether all this had not been done from one end of the continent to the other. ...

... I have now considered everything in this Incendiary's pamphlet, that deserves notice. If some things are passed over, it is not because they are unanswerable; but because they are not worthy of an answer. I have on purpose omitted every subject, the discussion of which might tend to raise jealousy among the colonists; such as religion, the claims of some colonies on others, besides many more of the same kind. But it was more difficult to avoid speaking of these, than to point out what prolific sources of animosity, bitterness and bloody contests they must infallibly prove, were America to become independent. The whole is freely submitted to their reader's candid, dispassionate judgement.

The author of *Common Sense* may probably call me "a disguised tory, a prejudiced man," or what in his estimation "will be productive of more calamities to this continent than all others—a moderate man." But I am too conscious of the sincerity of my own heart, and of the rectitude of my intentions, to pay any regard to whatever he is pleased to call me. Who indeed would be ambitious of his approbation, when he expressly reprobates moderation—that offspring of true wisdom and sound judgement? The welfare of America is what I wish for above any earthly thing. I am fully, firmly and conscientiously persuaded that our author's scheme of independency and republicanism is big with ruin—with inevitable ruin to America. Against this scheme therefore, which totally changes the ground we set out on, as an honest man, as a friend to human nature, I must and will bear testimony.

Let the spirit, design and motives which are undeniably evident in our respective pamphlets, decide which should be attended to most.

The author of *Common Sense* is a violent stickler for democracy or republicanism only—every other species of government is reprobated by him as tyrannical. I plead for that constitution which has been formed by the wisdom of ages—is the admiration of mankind—is best adapted to the genius of Britons, and is most friendly toward liberty.

He takes pleasure in aggravating every circumstance of our unhappy dispute—would inspire others with the same rage that instigates himself and would set his fellow subjects to cutting each other's throats. *I* would most gladly, were it in my power, draw a veil of eternal oblivion over any errors which Great Britain or the colonies may have fallen into; I would willingly persuade them to mutual harmony and union, since on these their mutual happiness and interest depend.

He is evidently goaded on by ambition and resentment, to seek for the gratification of those passions in an independent republic here; which would reduce America to the same desperate state with himself. *I*

[1] *view the Declaration of Independency* I.e., view the prospect of a Declaration of Independence. Inglis's pamphlet appeared in March; Jefferson's Declaration of Independence was not issued until August.

[2] *obnoxious acts* The series of 1774 measures known in Britain as the "Coercive Acts" and in the American colonies as the "Intolerable Acts" (or, as here, the "obnoxious acts") included the following: an act authorizing the blockading of Boston harbor so as to ensure that British authorities controlled trade; an act authorizing British officials to replace the elected Massachusetts Council with Crown appointees; an act authorizing trials to be moved from the colonies to Britain if the British authorities judged it advisable to do so; and an act allowing British army officials to insist upon better accommodation for their colonial troops.

have no interest to serve but what is common to my countrymen—but what every American of property is concerned in equally with me.

He places himself at the head of a party; and spurns from him with the utmost contempt and indignation, all who will not enlist under his banner. *I* am of no party, but so far the welfare of America is aimed at; and I believe there are many who aim at this in every party. I have not learnt to pace with such entire acquiescence in the trammels of any party, as not to desert it, the moment it deserts the interest of my country.

He recommends a new, untried, romantic scheme, at which we would at first have shuddered—which is big with inevitable ruin and is the last stage of political frenzy. *I* am for pursuing the same object and acting on the same principles and plan with which we set out, when this contest began, and of whose success there is a moral certainty.

This, as far as I can know or see, is the true state of our case—let Heaven and Earth judge between us.

America is far from being yet in a desperate situation. I am confident she may obtain honourable and advantageous terms from Great Britain. A few years of peace will soon retrieve all her losses. She will rapidly advance to a state of maturity, whereby she may not only repay the parent state amply for all past benefits; but also lay under the greatest obligations. America, till very lately, has been the happiest country in the universe. Blessed with all that nature could bestow with profusest bounty, she enjoyed besides, more liberty, greater privileges than any other land. How painful is it to reflect on these things, and to look forward to the gloomy prospects now before us! But it is not too late to hope that matters may mend. By prudent management, her former happiness may again return, and continue to increase for ages to come, in a union with the parent state.

However distant humanity may wish the period; yet, in the rotation of human affairs, a period may arrive, when (both countries being prepared for it) some terrible disaster, some dreadful convulsion in Great Britain, may transfer the seat of empire to this western hemisphere—where the British constitution, like the phoenix from its parent's ashes, shall rise with youthful vigor and shine with doubled splendor.

But if America should now mistake her real interest—if her sons, infatuated with romantic notions of conquest and empire, ere things are ripe, should adopt this republican's scheme—they will infallibly destroy this smiling prospect. They will dismember this happy country—make it a scene of blood and slaughter and entail wretchedness and misery on millions yet unborn.

Quod Deus a nobis procul avertae.[1]

from *The American Crisis*[2]

These are the times that try men's souls. The summer soldier and the sunshine patriot will, in this crisis, shrink from the service of their country; but he that stands it now[3] deserves the love and thanks of man and woman. Tyranny, like hell, is not easily conquered; yet we have this consolation with us, that the harder the conflict, the more glorious the triumph. What we obtain too cheap, we esteem too lightly: it is dearness[4] only that gives every thing its value. Heaven knows how to put a proper price upon its goods; and it would be strange indeed if so celestial an article as freedom should not be highly rated. Britain, with an army to enforce her tyranny, has declared that she has a right (not only to tax) but "to bind us in all cases

1 *Quod ... avertae* Latin: Which [thing] may God keep far away from us; May God keep this prospect far in the distance.

2 This was the first in a series of "Crisis" pamphlets that Paine issued between December 1776 and December 1783.

3 *stands it now* Endures the crisis now.

4 *dearness* Great expense.

whatsoever,"[1] and if being bound in that manner is not slavery, then is there not such a thing as slavery upon earth. Even the expression is impious; for so unlimited a power can belong only to God.

Whether the independence of the continent was declared too soon, or delayed too long, I will not now enter into as an argument; my own simple opinion is, that had it been eight months earlier, it would have been much better. We did not make a proper use of last winter; neither could we, while we were in a dependent state. However, the fault, if it were one, was all our own;[2] we have none to blame but ourselves. But no great deal is lost yet. All that Howe[3] has been doing for this month past, is rather a ravage than a conquest, which the spirit of the Jerseys,[4] a year ago, would have quickly repulsed, and which time and a little resolution will soon recover.

I have as little superstition in me as any man living, but my secret opinion has ever been, and still is, that God Almighty will not give up a people to military destruction, or leave them unsupportedly to perish, who have so earnestly and so repeatedly sought to avoid the calamities of war, by every decent method which wisdom could invent. Neither have I so much of the infidel in me as to suppose that He has relinquished the government of the world, and given us up to the care of devils; and as I do not, I cannot see on what grounds the king of Britain can look up to heaven for help against us; a common murderer, a highwayman, or a house-breaker, has as good a pretence as he. ...

—1776

[1] *to bind ... whatsoever* Reference to a statement made in the Declaratory Act (1766): "[the British government] had, hath, and of right ought to have, full power and authority to make laws and statutes of sufficient force and validity to bind the colonies and people of America, subjects of the crown of great Britain, in all cases whatsoever."

[2] [Paine's note] The present winter is worth an age, if rightly employed; but, if lost or neglected, the whole continent will partake of the evil; and there is no punishment that man does not deserve, be he who, or what, or where he will, that may be the means of sacrificing a season so precious and useful. [Paine is here quoting from *Common Sense*.]

[3] *Howe* Sir William Howe (1729–1814), commander of the British forces during the Revolutionary War.

[4] *the Jerseys* East New Jersey and West New Jersey; Paine is referring to Washington's successful surprise attack on Christmas Day of the previous year.

Thomas Jefferson
1743 – 1826

From his own time through to the twenty-first century, Thomas Jefferson has remained one of the most admired figures in American history. Yet his legacy is extraordinarily complex and, in many ways, controversial; it has been interpreted and re-interpreted in myriad ways since his death. As the primary author of the Declaration of Independence, Jefferson penned some of the most cherished and quintessentially American phrases in the nation's history, setting out the ideals of democracy, equality, and religious freedom that remain close to its political heart. Yet many historians have seen Jefferson's position as an advocate of freedom and equality as deeply conflicted, given his status as a lifelong slaveholder and his troubling comments on natural racial difference. Jefferson embodies the profound contradictions at the heart of America's political and cultural history.

Jefferson was born into relative privilege in Shadwell, Virginia, the son of well-to-do plantation owner Peter Jefferson and his wife Jane Randolph Jefferson. He inherited the plantation—and its numerous enslaved people—upon the death of his father in 1757. Jefferson was educated privately for several years; at the age of sixteen he entered William and Mary College in Williamsburg, where he became immersed in the study of ethics, law, history, and natural philosophy. After leaving the college in 1762, Jefferson pursued further study of the law, and continued to work in the legal profession until the end of the decade, when he was elected to the colonial legislature of Virginia. In 1772 Jefferson married Martha Wayles, who brought well over one hundred enslaved people into the marriage upon her father's death; the couple would go on to have six children, though only two would live into adulthood.

Among the notable efforts of Jefferson's early political career was a failed attempt to repeal the 1691 legislation that effectively made manumission illegal in Virginia. In later years, he would reflect bitterly on the rejection of his proposed bill, writing that, "indeed, during the regal government, nothing liberal could expect success. Our minds were circumscribed within narrow limits, by an habitual belief that it was our duty to be subordinate to the mother country in all matters of government." As tensions between America and the "mother country" increased, so did Jefferson's prominence as a political figure and writer of political documents. In 1774, in response to the political unrest following the Boston Tea Party, Jefferson was called upon to draft the *Summary View of the Rights of British America*, arguably the strongest written expression of antipathy against British rule published in the American colonies up to that point. While it did not expressly support separation from the Crown, the article contained many ideas that anticipated those expressed two years later in the Declaration of Independence; the *Summary View* argued that the British monarch had no legitimate right to impose laws on the colonists without their consent, and that to do so was an infringement upon their God-given rights. The document was controversial, and was not officially adopted by the First Virginia Convention of 1774; nevertheless, it was widely circulated as a pamphlet among patriotically inclined readers, and its ideas soon became central to the philosophy of what was increasingly appearing to be an inevitable war.

In 1776, Jefferson became the unofficial leader of a committee of five chosen by the Second Continental Congress to draft a Declaration of Independence. The influence of John Locke's *Two Treatises* (in which the British philosopher argues that the authority of monarchs is founded on the consent of the people) on the Declaration has long been recognized, but Jefferson's approach may have owed at least as much to the influence of other thinkers, especially to Scottish Enlightenment philosophers such as Francis Hutcheson (1694–1746), who contributed significantly to developing the idea of natural,

"unalienable" rights. The now-famous phrasings of the Declaration were refined through numerous revisions, some of which were highly significant. In his *Autobiography*, Jefferson emphasises his role as the document's primary author while drawing attention to the differences between the draft he presented before the Congress and the edited version that would become the official document of the Revolution; the passages removed by the Congress include some of Jefferson's strongest indictments of the British King, as well as a vehement and controversial passage censuring Britain for its role in the "execrable commerce" of the slave trade. The final work was approved on the fourth of July, though it was not in fact signed until August.

Jefferson returned to Virginia after the Declaration was signed; he was elected to the House of Delegates in September 1776 and to the position of Governor in 1779. His time in state politics was marked by the introduction of a number of rejected bills, including a bill for providing free public education for both boys and girls, and "A Bill for Establishing Religious Freedom," which became the basis for the Virginia Statute for Religious Freedom in 1786; Jefferson later considered this last to be among his greatest achievements.

Shortly after the end of his second term as Virginia's governor, Jefferson began working on *Notes on the State of Virginia* (1787), the only book he published during his lifetime. It was prompted by a questionnaire sent him and other state representatives in 1780 by French diplomat François Marbois, as part of an endeavor by France to learn more about its new allies (France, too, was then at war with the British). In answering Marbois's twenty-two queries about Virginia's laws, geographical features, economy, Indigenous population, and other matters, Jefferson, who had long been a keen historian and collector of historical documents, took the endeavor far more seriously than any of the other delegates, only a handful of whom had responded with even brief replies. Over the following two years, Jefferson expanded his initial response—to which Marbois had responded with delight in December 1781—into a multifaceted examination of the political, social, and economic constitution of the emerging United States, as seen through the lens of the state of Virginia. The text's meticulous collation of information, as well as its blending of areas of study that might today be seen as disparate, reflects Enlightenment-era ideas about the interconnectedness of rational knowledge. Many parts of the text are direct responses to the ideas and writings of contemporary European thinkers, most notably those of French naturalist the Comte de Buffon, whose theories about the physical inferiority of American species Jefferson takes pains to refute. Interspersed through Jefferson's recitals of facts are many passages expressing his views on matters such as emigration, religion, slavery, and race. His reflections on the latter two subjects are of particular interest to modern readers. At the time of the text's publication, Jefferson expressed fears that his condemnation of slavery would prove controversial; today, it is the apparently incongruous racism expressed throughout the text (especially in Query 14, where he offers some deeply disturbing opinions about the intellectual inferiority of African Americans, as well as in his less pejorative but still troubling comments about Indigenous Americans) that prompts in many readers disconcerted questions about Jefferson's intellectual legacy.

Jefferson did not initially intend his *Notes* for broad circulation, and it was not until 1787 that he succumbed to increasing public demand and arranged for the general publication of the text in London. Though his contemporary readers were generally enthusiastic, Jefferson himself often dismissed the work as a mere collection of notes. Many nineteenth-century readers likewise criticized the text's heterogeneity; today, however, *Notes on the State of Virginia* is widely acknowledged to be among the most important American books of the eighteenth century.

When *Notes* was published, Jefferson was himself living in Paris, where he had been appointed in 1785 to take over Benjamin Franklin's position as U.S. Minister to France. (Here he struck up an acquaintance with the Comte de Buffon, to whom he presented both a cougar skin and a stuffed moose as proof of the great size of American species.) Jefferson returned to America in 1790, after which he served in a string of increasingly powerful political roles: Secretary of State, Vice President to John Adams, and eventually—though it was not a role he much desired—President. His Presidency was marked by, among many things, an emphasis on states' rights and on Western expansion. Through the 1803 purchase of the Louisiana Territory from France, Jefferson's government almost doubled the geographical size

of the young republic, acquiring undisputed control of the strategically and commercially important New Orleans and the Mississippi River—and also acquiring nominal control over vast areas occupied by Native Americans. The purchase seems an extraordinary bargain in hindsight; the Americans had been willing to pay $10 million for New Orleans and its environs alone, and were astonished to find the French, who were preoccupied both with war in Europe and with the unexpected strength of rebel forces in their Caribbean colony of Saint-Domingue, willing to part with the entire territory for $15 million (well under $1 billion in today's money). Yet the transaction was highly controversial at the time, with many Americans opposing the purchase on the grounds that it could unnecessarily involve the republic in European quarrels—and could worsen divisions between North and South over slavery. Notably, Jefferson made no move to limit the expansion of slavery into the new territory. He was, however, responsible for enacting the 1808 Act Prohibiting the Importation of Slaves, a small step toward abolition that was celebrated by many abolitionists at the time.

Jefferson retired from public life in 1809, after two terms as President, and spent his last years embracing life as an agriculturalist at his now-famous plantation, Monticello. He began writing his memoirs in 1821 after many requests from friends and admirers; though today known generally as *The Autobiography of Thomas Jefferson*, this short text was first published only as part of the collected *Papers of Thomas Jefferson*, released posthumously in 1829. In a coincidence that has now reached the status of myth, Jefferson died on the fourth of July on the fiftieth anniversary of the Declaration of Independence, just hours before the death of his friend, adversary, and fellow Declaration drafter John Adams. After his death, the vast majority of Jefferson's enslaved people were sent to the auction block.

In recent years, one of the most controversial aspects of Jefferson's life has been his long-term sexual relationship with Sally Hemings, an enslaved mixed-race woman approximately thirty years his junior. The relationship likely began soon after Martha Jefferson's 1782 death. Rumors of the relationship were first made public in 1802 by newspaper scandalmonger James T. Callender, and they surfaced repeatedly in the following decades (perhaps most famously in William Wells Brown's 1853 novel *Clotel; or, The President's Daughter*). Until the late twentieth century, however, the vast majority of historians and scholars dismissed the allegation that Jefferson had fathered several children with Hemings; it was only in the 1990s that an increasing willingness to accept the oral testimonies that had been given by Hemings's descendants since the 1800s—together with DNA testing—finally persuaded mainstream historians to accept the reality of the relationship. This aspect of Jefferson's life—along with the fact that, of the approximately six hundred enslaved people he owned throughout his life, Jefferson freed only nine—continues to complicate the reputation of a figure who prided himself on his lifelong opposition to slavery as an industry, and who wrote with such memorable eloquence about the fundamental rights and equality of all people.

NOTE ON THE TEXTS: The excerpt from Thomas Jefferson's *Autobiography*, which includes the Declaration of Independence, has been taken from the A.A. Lipscomb and A.E. Bergh's 1903 edition of *The Writings of Thomas Jefferson*. As is now standard practice in anthologies of this sort, the differences between Jefferson's original version of the Declaration and that finally adopted by the Second Continental Congress are indicated, here with the omitted text underlined, and text added by the Congress placed in square brackets. The text of *Notes on the State of Virginia* is taken from the London edition of 1787. Except in the Declaration, spelling and punctuation have been modernized in accordance with the practices of this anthology.

⌘⌘⌘

from *The Autobiography of Thomas Jefferson*

Congress proceeded the same day[1] to consider the Declaration of Independence, which had been reported and lain on the table the Friday preceding, and on Monday referred to a committee of the whole. The pusillanimous idea that we had friends in England worth keeping terms with still haunted the minds of many. For this reason, those passages which conveyed censures on the people of England were struck out, lest they should give them offence. The clause, too, reprobating the enslaving the inhabitants of Africa, was struck out in complaisance to South Carolina and Georgia, who had never attempted to restrain the importation of slaves, and who, on the contrary, still wished to continue it. Our northern brethren also, I believe, felt a little tender under those censures; for though their people had very few slaves themselves, yet they had been pretty considerably carriers of them to others. The debates, having taken up the greater parts of the 2nd, 3rd, and 4th days of July, were, on the evening of the last, closed; the Declaration was reported by the committee, agreed to by the House, and signed by every member present, except Mr. Dickinson.[2] As the sentiments of men are known not only by what they receive, but what they reject also, I will state the form of the Declaration as originally reported. The parts struck out by Congress shall be distinguished by a black line drawn under them; and those inserted by them shall be placed in the margin, or in a concurrent column.[3]

A DECLARATION BY THE REPRESENTATIVES OF THE UNITED STATES OF AMERICA, IN GENERAL CONGRESS ASSEMBLED

When, in the course of human events, it becomes necessary for one people to dissolve the political bands which have connected them with another, and to assume among the powers of the earth the separate and equal station to which the laws of nature and of nature's God entitle them, a decent respect to the opinions of mankind requires that they should declare the causes which impel them to the separation.

We hold these truths to be self evident:[4] that all men are created equal; that they are endowed by their Creator with [certain] inherent and inalienable rights;[5] that among these are life, liberty, and the pursuit of happiness;[6] that to secure these rights, governments are instituted among men, deriving their just powers from the consent of the governed; that whenever any form of government becomes destructive of these ends, it is the right of the people to alter or to abolish it, and to institute new government, laying its foundation on such principles, and organizing its powers in such form, as to them shall seem most likely to effect their safety and happiness. Prudence, indeed, will dictate that governments long established should not be changed for light and transient causes; and accordingly all experience hath shown that mankind are more disposed to suffer while evils are sufferable, than to right themselves by abolishing the forms to which they are accustomed. But when a long train of abuses and usurpations, begun at a distinguished[7] period and pursuing invariably the same object, evinces a design to reduce them under absolute despotism, it is their right, it is their duty to throw off such government, and to provide new guards for their future security. Such has been the patient sufferance of these colonies; and such is not the necessity

[1] *the same day* 1 July 1776.

[2] *Mr. Dickinson* John Dickinson (1732–1808), the representative from Pennsylvania. He was generally resistant to the idea of violent revolution, and believed that declaring independence was inadvisable until the colonies had finished drafting the Articles of Confederation and established foreign allies.

[3] *those inserted ... column* In this reproduction of the Declaration, text added by the committee has been indicated with square brackets.

[4] *self evident* An earlier draft of the text had the words "sacred and undeniable" here.

[5] *inalienable rights* The idea of "unalienable rights" has been traced by some to Scottish philosopher Francis Hutcheson's *Inquiry into the Original of Our Ideas of Beauty and Virtue* (1726), which was widely influential in eighteenth-century America.

[6] *life ... happiness* Compare with John Locke's *Two Treatises of Government* (1689), where it is argued that "man" has a natural right to preserve his "life, liberty, and estate [property]."

[7] *distinguished* Distinct; particular.

which constrains them to <u>expunge</u> [alter] their former systems of government. The history of the present king of Great Britain[1] is a history of <u>unremitting</u> injuries and usurpations, <u>among which appears no solitary fact to contradict the uniform tenor of the rest, but all have</u> [all having] in direct object the establishment of an absolute tyranny over these states. To prove this, let facts be submitted to a candid world <u>for the truth of which we pledge a faith yet unsullied by falsehood</u>.

He has refused his assent to laws the most wholesome and necessary for the public good.

He has forbidden his governors to pass laws of immediate and pressing importance, unless suspended in their operation till his assent should be obtained; and, when so suspended, he has utterly neglected to attend to them.

He has refused to pass other laws for the accommodation of large districts of people, unless those people would relinquish the right of representation in the legislature, a right inestimable to them, and formidable to tyrants only.

He has called together legislative bodies at places unusual, uncomfortable, and distant from the depository of their public records, for the sole purpose of fatiguing them into compliance with his measures.

He has dissolved representative houses repeatedly <u>and continually</u> for opposing with manly firmness his invasions on the rights of the people.

He has refused for a long time after such dissolutions to cause others to be elected, whereby the legislative powers, incapable of annihilation, have returned to the people at large for their exercise, the state remaining, in the meantime, exposed to all the dangers of invasion from without and convulsions within.

He has endeavored to prevent the population of these states; for that purpose obstructing the laws for naturalization of foreigners, refusing to pass others to encourage their migrations hither, and raising the conditions of new appropriations of lands.

He has <u>suffered</u> [obstructed] the administration of justice <u>totally to cease in some of these states</u> [by] refusing his assent to laws for establishing judiciary powers.

He has made <u>our</u> judges dependent on his will alone for the tenure of their offices, and the amount and payment of their salaries.

He has erected a multitude of new offices, <u>by a self-assumed power</u> and sent hither swarms of new officers to harass our people and eat out their substance.[2]

He has kept among us in times of peace standing armies <u>and ships of war</u> without the consent of our legislatures.

He has affected to render the military independent of, and superior to, the civil power.

He has combined with others to subject us to a jurisdiction foreign to our constitutions and unacknowledged by our laws, giving his assent to their acts of pretended legislation for quartering large bodies of armed troops among us; for protecting them by a mock trial from punishment for any murders which they should commit on the inhabitants of these states; for cutting off our trade with all parts of the world; for imposing taxes on us without our consent; for depriving us [in many cases] of the benefits of trial by jury; for transporting us beyond seas to be tried for pretended offences; for abolishing the free system of English laws in a neighboring province, establishing therein an arbitrary government, and enlarging its boundaries,[3] so as to render it at once an example and fit instrument for introducing the same absolute rule into these <u>states</u> [colonies]; for taking away our charters, abolishing our most valuable laws, and altering fundamentally the forms of our governments; for suspending our own legislatures, and declaring themselves invested with power to legislate for us in all cases whatsoever.

He has abdicated government here <u>withdrawing his governors, and declaring us out of his allegiance and protection</u> [by declaring us out of his protection, and waging war against us].

He has plundered our seas, ravaged our coasts, burnt our towns, and destroyed the lives of our people.

[1] *present king of Great Britain* George III (r. 1760–1820).

[2] *eat out their substance* Consume their food and produce.

[3] *for abolishing … boundaries* The reference is to the Quebec Act of 1774, a controversial act of British Parliament granting numerous special rights to the French inhabitants of the Province of Quebec, which territory Britain had recently acquired from France following the Seven Years' War. The Act extended the province's borders significantly and gave its French inhabitants the right to practice Catholicism, among other things. This was seen by many in the Thirteen Colonies as a threat to Protestantism, as an unjust concession to the French designed to placate them, and moreover as a show of Britain's arbitrary power; it was often referred to as one of the "Intolerable Acts" instigating the American Revolution.

He is at this time transporting large armies of foreign mercenaries[1] to complete the works of death, desolation and tyranny already begun with circumstances of cruelty and perfidy [scarcely paralleled in the most barbarous ages, and totally] unworthy the head of a civilized nation.

He has constrained our fellow citizens taken captive on the high seas, to bear arms against their country, to become the executioners of their friends and brethren, or to fall themselves by their hands.

He has [excited domestic insurrection among us, and has] endeavored to bring on the inhabitants of our frontiers, the merciless Indian savages, whose known rule of warfare is an undistinguished destruction of all ages, sexes and conditions of existence.

He has incited treasonable insurrections of our fellow citizens, with the allurements of forfeiture and confiscation of our property.

He has waged cruel war against human nature itself, violating its most sacred rights of life and liberty in the persons of a distant people who never offended him, captivating and carrying them into slavery in another hemisphere, or to incur miserable death in their transportation thither. This piratical warfare, the opprobrium of INFIDEL powers, is the warfare of the CHRISTIAN king of Great Britain. Determined to keep open a market where MEN should be bought and sold, he has prostituted his negative[2] for suppressing every legislative attempt to prohibit or to restrain this execrable commerce. And that this assemblage of horrors might want no fact of distinguished die,[3] he is now exciting those very people to rise in arms among us, and to purchase that liberty of which he has deprived them,[4] by murdering the people on whom he also obtruded them: thus paying off former crimes committed against the LIBERTIES of one people, with crimes which he urges them to commit against the LIVES of another.

In every stage of these oppressions we have petitioned for redress in the most humble terms: our repeated petitions have been answered only by repeated injuries.

A prince whose character is thus marked by every act which may define a tyrant is unfit to be the ruler of a [free] people who mean to be free. Future ages will scarcely believe that the hardiness of one man adventured, within the short compass of twelve years only, to lay a foundation so broad and so undisguised for tyranny over a people fostered and fixed in principles of freedom.

Nor have we been wanting in attentions to our British brethren. We have warned them from time to time of attempts by their legislature to extend a [an unwarrantable] jurisdiction over these our states [us]. We have reminded them of the circumstances of our emigration and settlement here, no one of which could warrant so strange a pretension: that these were effected at the expense of our own blood and treasure, unassisted by the wealth or the strength of Great Britain: that in constituting indeed our several forms of government, we had adopted one common king, thereby laying a foundation for perpetual league and amity with them: but that submission to their parliament was no part of our constitution, nor ever in idea, if history may be credited: and, we [have] appealed to their native justice and magnanimity as well as to [and we have conjured them by] the ties of our common kindred to disavow these usurpations which were likely to [would inevitably] interrupt our connection and correspondence. They too have been deaf to the voice of justice and of consanguinity, and when occasions have been given them, by the regular course of their laws, of removing from their councils the disturbers of our harmony, they have, by their free election, re-established them in power. At this very time too, they are permitting their chief magistrate to send over not only soldiers of our common blood, but Scotch and foreign mercenaries to

[1] *foreign mercenaries* As the revolutionary conflict mounted, Britain entered into treaties with a number of small German states, primarily Hesse-Kassel and Hesse-Hanau, and hired their troops for support in the coming war. These German soldiers—who were not, technically, mercenaries—were referred to as Hessians and came to be known for their brutality and penchant for plundering.

[2] *negative* Right of veto.

[3] *that this ... die* The meaning here is unclear, though a variety of possible interpretations have been put forward. One possible reading might be: "And that this list of horrors might lack no distinctive fact," with "die" possibly being a variant spelling of "dye." Others have put forward that "fact" is a misprint for "facet," with the meaning thus being: "in order that this horrific combination [of evils] might lack nothing in completeness [like a six-sided die with distinct markings on all six sides]."

[4] *exciting those ... deprived them* Lord Dunmore's 1775 Proclamation promised freedom to any enslaved persons who would join the Loyalist army.

invade and destroy us. These facts have given the last stab to agonizing affection, and manly spirit bids us to renounce forever these unfeeling brethren. We must endeavor to forget our former love for them, and hold them as we hold the rest of mankind, enemies in war, in peace friends. We might have been a free and a great people together; but a communication of grandeur and of freedom, it seems, is below their dignity. Be it so, since they will have it. The road to happiness and to glory is open to us, too. We will tread it apart from them, and [We must therefore] acquiesce in the necessity which denounces our eternal separation [and hold them as we hold the rest of mankind, enemies in war, in peace friends]!

[Draft version][1]

We therefore the representatives of the United States of America in General Congress assembled, do in the name, and by the authority of these states reject and renounce all allegiance and subjection to the kings of Great Britain and all others who may hereafter claim by, through or under them; we utterly dissolve all political connection which may heretofore have subsisted between us and the people or parliament of Great Britain: and finally we do assert and declare these colonies to be free and independent states, and that as free and independent states, they have full power to levy war, conclude peace, contract alliances, establish commerce, and to do all other acts and things which independent states may of right do.

And for the support of this declaration, we mutually pledge to each other our lives, our fortunes, and our sacred honor.

[End of facing-column]

The Declaration thus signed on the 4th, on paper was engrossed[2] on parchment, & signed again on the 2d. of August.

—1829 (WRITTEN 1821; DECLARATION WRITTEN 1776)

[Final Version]

We, therefore, the representatives of the United States of America in General Congress assembled, appealing to the supreme judge of the world for the rectitude of our intentions, do in the name, and by the authority of the good people of these colonies, solemnly publish and declare, that these united colonies are, and of right ought to be free and independent states; that they are absolved from all allegiance to the British crown, and that all political connection between them and the state of Great Britain is, and ought to be, totally dissolved; and that as free and independent states, they have full power to levy war, conclude peace, contract alliances, establish commerce, and to do all other acts and things which independent states may of right do.

And for the support of this declaration, with a firm reliance on the protection of divine providence, we mutually pledge to each other our lives, our fortunes, and our sacred honor.

[1] To show the substantial revisions made to these closing paragraphs, the editors here follow the standard practice of presenting them in facing-column format, with Jefferson's original (deletions underlined) in the left-hand column and the final text in the right-hand column.

[2] *engrossed* Written out in clear, formal handwriting.

IN CONTEXT

British and American Reactions to the Declaration of Independence

Throughout the summer of 1776, most Americans first encountered the Declaration of Independence through public readings or through broadsides posted about towns. On 6 July 1776, *The Pennsylvania Evening Post* was the first newspaper to print the text of the Declaration in full, though without comment; other papers throughout the newly formed United States followed suit in the coming days and weeks, some with brief descriptions of local responses to the news. To a large extent, many saw the Declaration as merely an official statement of ideas that had already been shared throughout the colonies in the years leading up to the war; to others, however, that statement fundamentally changed the nature and meaning of the conflict. In a letter on 10 September 1776, American diplomat William Lee wrote that "The Declaration of Independence on the part of America has totally changed the nature of the contest between that country and Great Britain. It is now on the part of Great Britain a scheme of conquest, which few imagine can succeed."

The text of the Declaration first reached Britain in early August. Historians are uncertain which British newspaper was the very first to print the text, but the August edition of *The Scots Magazine* was among the earliest; the document was there accompanied by two substantial footnotes (by a contributor identified only as "an Englishman") commenting derisively on two of the Declaration's most famous statements: that "all men are created equal" and that "they are endowed by their Creator with certain unalienable Rights, that among these are Life, Liberty and the pursuit of Happiness." Not all British newspapers were hostile to the Declaration, however. One contributor to *The Gentleman's Magazine* responded to the sentiments of the "Englishman" with disdain and with implied support for the American cause; the radical, anti-monarchical, pro-American newspaper *The Crisis* printed the document with a preamble praising "the Declaration of INDEPENDENCE of the BRAVE, FREE, and VIRTUOUS Americans, against the most dastardly, slavish, and vicious TYRANT, that ever disgraced a Nation, whose savage cruelties are covered under a mask of Religion."

Thomas Jefferson's involvement in drafting the text was largely overlooked in early accounts of the process. The first printed work to explicitly reference Jefferson as the primary author of the Declaration of Independence was Ezra Stiles's sermon "The United States Elevated to Glory and Honor" (1783), where it was claimed that Jefferson had "poured the soul of the continent into the monumental act of independence." Even still, this attribution did not become commonplace until much later. In the first volume of David Ramsay's *History of the American Revolution* (1789), one of the earliest histories of the period, Jefferson is mentioned only once, in the list of signatories to the Declaration.

from the *New-York Journal* (11 July 1776)

On Wednesday last [the Declaration of Independence] was read at the head of each brigade of the Continental Army, posted at and near New York, and everywhere received with loud huzzahs and the utmost demonstrations of joy.

The same evening the equestrian statue of George III, which Tory pride and folly raised in the year 1770, was by the Sons of Freedom laid prostrate in the dirt, the just desert of an ungrateful tyrant! The

lead wherewith this monument was made is to be run into bullets, to assimilate with the brain of our infatuated[1] adversaries, who to gain a peppercorn,[2] have lost an empire.

Quos Deus vult perdere, prius dementat.[3]

from *The Virginia Gazette* (10 August 1776)

On Monday last, being court day, the DECLARATION of INDEPENDENCE was publicly proclaimed in the town of Richmond, before a large concourse of respectable freeholders of Henrico county, and upwards of 100 of the militia, who assembled on that grand occasion. It was received with universal shouts of joy, and re-echoed by three volleys of small arms.[4] The same evening the town was illuminated, and the members of the committee held a club, when many patriotic toasts were drank. Although there were near 1000 people present, the whole was conducted with the utmost decorum, and the satisfaction visible in every countenance sufficiently evinces their determination to support it with their lives and fortunes.

from *The Scots Magazine* (August 1776)[5]

In what are [men] created equal? Is it in size, strength, understanding, figure, moral or civil accomplishments, or situation of life? Every ploughman knows that they are not created equal in any of them. All men, it is true, are equally created: but what is this in the purpose? It certainly is no reason why the Americans should turn rebels, because the people of G. Britain are their fellow-creatures, *i.e.* are created as well as themselves. It may be a reason why they should not rebel, but most indisputably is none why they should. They therefore have introduced their self-evident truth, either through ignorance, or by design, with a self-evident falsehood; since I will defy any American rebel, or any of their patriotic retainers here in England, to point out to me any two men throughout the whole world of whom it may with truth be said, that they are created equal.

The meaning of these words the Congress appear not at all to understand: "among which are life, liberty, and the pursuit of happiness." Let us put some of these words together. All men are endowed by their Creator with the unalienable right of life. How far they may be endowed with this unalienable right I do not yet say, but, sure I am, these gentry[6] assume to themselves an unalienable right of talking nonsense. Was it ever heard since the introduction of blunders into the world, that life was a man's right? Life or animation is of the essence of human nature, and is that without which one is not a man; and therefore to call life a right, is to betray a total ignorance of the meaning of words. A living man, *i.e.* a man with life, hath a right to a great many things; but to say that a man with life hath a right to be a man with life, is so purely American, that I believe the texture of no other brain upon the face of the earth will admit the idea. Whatever it may be, I have tried to make an idea out of it, but own[7] I am unable. Prior to my having any right at all as a man, it is certain *I* must be a man, and such a man *I* certainly cannot be if I have no life; and therefore if it be said that *I* have a right to life, then the word

[1] *infatuated* Filled with foolishness.

[2] *peppercorn* Something small and insignificant; a trifle.

[3] *Quos Deus … dementat* Latin: Those whom God wishes to destroy, he first deprives of reason. This Latin phrase was frequently quoted in the eighteenth century, though its origins are unclear.

[4] *small arms* Handheld firearms.

[5] The excerpts presented here were originally included as footnotes to the text of the Declaration, whose author was identified only as "an Englishman."

[6] *gentry* In the eighteenth century this term (then and now in general use as a term used to refer to those of high social status) was often used playfully or sarcastically to refer to any group of people, or the people in general—"folks."

[7] *own* Admit that.

"I" must signify something without life; and, consequently, something without life must be supposed to have a property, which without life it is not possible it can have.

Well, but they say, all men have not only a right to life, but an unalienable right. The word *unalienable* signifies that which is not alienable, and that which is not alienable is what cannot be transferred so as to become another's, so that their unalienable right is a right which they cannot transfer to a broomstick or a cabbage-stalk; and because they cannot transfer their own lives from themselves to a cabbage-stalk, therefore they think it absolutely necessary that they should rebel; and, out of a decent respect to the opinions of mankind, allege this as one of the causes which impels them to separate themselves from those to whom they owe obedience.

The next assigned cause and ground of their rebellion is, that every man hath an unalienable right to liberty: and here the words, as it happens, are not nonsense; but then they are not true: slaves there are in America; and where there are slaves, their liberty is alienated.

If the Creator hath endowed man with an unalienable right to liberty, no reason in the world will justify the abridgement of that liberty, and a man hath a right to do everything that he thinks proper without control or restraint; and upon the same principle, there can be no such things as servants, subjects, or governments of any kind whatsoever. In a word, every law that hath been in the world since the formation of Adam gives the lie to this self-evident truth (as they are pleased to term it): because every law, divine or human, that is or hath been in the world, is an abridgement of man's liberty.

Their next self-evident truth and ground of rebellion is, that they have an unalienable right to the pursuit of happiness. The pursuit of happiness an unalienable right! This surely is outdoing everything that went before. Put it into English: The pursuit of happiness is a right with which the Creator hath endowed me, and which can neither be taken from me, nor can I transfer it to another. Did ever any mortal alive hear of taking a pursuit of happiness from a man? What they possibly can mean by these words, I own, is beyond my comprehension. A man may take from me a horse or a cow, or I may alienate either of them from myself, as I may likewise anything that I have; but how that can be taken from me, or alienated, which I have not, must be left for the solution of some unborn Oedipus.[1]

from *The Gentleman's Magazine* (October 1776)

Mr. Urban,[2]

In your last magazine[3] you have inserted some thoughts on the late declaration of the American congress: the thoughts of a gentleman who does himself the honour to call himself an Englishman. But whether he will pardon me or no, I must take the liberty to say, I am ashamed to own him for a fellow-citizen. An Englishman hath advantages beyond other men for acquiring generous sentiments: when anyone, therefore, in writing or conversation, is guilty of meanness[4] and insolence, whatever he says of himself, no man will give him credit by assuming the honourable appellation of ENGLISHMAN.

[1] *Oedipus* Figure in Greek mythology, most famous for the tragic circumstances whereby he unknowingly killed his father and married his mother, but also known for having defeated the monstrous Sphinx by solving a difficult riddle.

[2] *Mr. Urban* Edward Cave, who went by the pseudonym "Sylvanus Urban," was the original editor of *The Gentleman's Magazine*. Even after Cave's death in 1754, letters submitted to the magazine were often addressed to "Mr. Urban."

[3] *In your last magazine* The "Englishman" footnotes to the *Scots Magazine* printing of the Declaration were reprinted as a separate article in the September issue of *The Gentleman's Magazine*, under the title "Thoughts on the Late Declaration of the American Congress."

[4] *meanness* Lowliness or smallness of mind.

No man, Mr. Urban, can betray meanness to a greater degree, than by totally disregarding his own natural rights, nor greater insolence, than by charging others with ignorance in subjects which they understand much better than himself.

I think it may fairly be presumed that the gentleman upon whose strictures I am animadverting sets no very high value on his own natural rights, because he does what he can to destroy them. He would prove, if he could, that men are not created equal, and enquires, "Is it in size, strength, understanding, figure, moral or civil accomplishments? Every ploughman," says he, "knows that they are not created equal in any of these." But I ask, whoever affirmed they were? Nevertheless, as, originally, any one man had as much right to reign and rule over another man, as that other man had to reign and rule over him, it is certainly in this sense (the sense of the declaration) a self-evident TRUTH, that all men were created equal; though this gentleman has the MODESTY to pronounce it a self-evident FALSEHOOD.

He would prove too, if he could, that men have no right to life, liberty, and the pursuit of happiness. Let him not therefore complain, nor make resistance, should anyone attempt to deprive him of life or liberty; and should his task-master command him to hew wood and draw water, let him not murmur, for, according to his notion, no man has a right to pursue his own plan of happiness.

This gentleman, I presume, can demonstrate, that, since the world was made, there never existed any such thing as oppression among mankind. Indeed, if his arguments are good, he has already done it: for certainly there can be no oppression where there are no natural rights. True it is, the phrase used in the declaration is *unalienable* rights; and surely unalienable rights they are, if natural—rights which men have received from God, together with their nature, are inseparable from it.

But the congress are such fools they do not understand the meaning of the words "unalienable rights." *Unalienable* means, according to this witty gentleman, that which cannot be transferred to another. If he had been wise, he would have known, that to *alienate*, strictly speaking, signifies to *estrange from* or to *take away*: and that certainly a thing may be taken away from a man, which yet cannot be transferred to another. Very unfortunately, indeed, this meaning interferes a little with the gentleman's wit; for he doubtless imagined himself to be very witty when he talked of the Americans' rights being transferred to a broomstick or a cabbage-stalk. But he is more than a wit, he is a metaphysician.[1] Hear him: "Life or animation is of the essence of human nature, and is that without which one is not a man: and therefore to call life a right is to betray a total ignorance of the meaning of words." And now please to take notice, while, like a consummate logician, he adds, "To say that a man with life hath a right to be a man with life, is so purely American, that I believe the texture of no other brain upon the face of the earth will admit the idea." In reply I will only observe, that as, according to his account, a man with life has no *right* to be a man with life; if, at any time, a highwayman should happen to pistol this gentleman, in so doing, by his way of reasoning, the highwayman will do him no *wrong*.

To prove that mankind have no unalienable right to enjoy liberty, this gentleman argues: "Slaves there are in America; and where there are slaves, there liberty is alienated." But, surely, though I should ever be so unhappy as to lose my liberty, it will not follow that I have no right to it. Does not all the world know that great numbers have a right to enjoy what is yet with-holden from them? It cannot be doubted, however, that this gentleman has more penetration than all the world beside!

Further, to prove the matter more fully, he affirms that every law which has been in the world since the formation of Adam gives the lie to this self-evident truth, as the congress are pleased to term it (viz.[2] that every man has an unalienable right to liberty) because, says he, "every law, divine or human, that is or hath been in the world, is an abridgement of liberty." Divine laws have nothing to do here. As for human laws, if they take away *liberty*, they neither do nor can take away the *right* to it. Nothing, however, can be more certain than that, if the existence of human laws will prove that mankind have no right to liberty, this gentleman (clever as he is) will be a little puzzled to show any reason why he ought not to be a slave;

[1] *metaphysician* I.e., philosopher who examines subjects such as the nature of reality, the relationship between the human mind and body, and the degree to which free will may exist.

[2] *viz.* Abbreviation for the Latin videlicet, meaning "namely" or "that is to say."

and, indeed, if he were, seeing he is so zealous an advocate for slavery, in my judgment, he would derive as little pity as any other slave.

The declaration asserts that mankind have an unalienable right to the pursuit of happiness. The gentleman pretends not to dispute this point, but exclaims, "Did ever any mortal alive hear of taking a pursuit of happiness from a man? What they possibly can mean by these words, I own, is beyond my comprehension." But who can help it, if the gentleman's brain is of such a texture that he cannot comprehend the difference between a *house* and a *right* to possess that house?

If, after all, he will needs be a metaphysician, it will not misbecome him to be a little more modest; and before he again affects to display his *wit*, let him *endeavour* at least to fill up the void in his *judgment*.

Yours, etc.

PHILANDER[1]

from David Ramsay, *History of the American Revolution* (1789)

The motion for declaring the colonies free and independent, was first made in Congress, by Richard Henry Lee, of Virginia. ... When the time for taking the subject under consideration arrived, much knowledge, ingenuity and eloquence were displayed on both sides of the question. The debates were continued for some time, and with great animation. In these, John Adams, and John Dickinson, took leading and opposite parts. The former ... strongly urged the immediate dissolution of all political connection of the colonies with Great Britain, from the voice of the people, from the necessity of the measure in order to obtain foreign assistance, from a regard to consistency, and from the prospects of glory and happiness, which opened beyond the war, to a free and independent people. Mr. Dickinson replied to this speech. ... He then urged that the present time was improper for the declaration of independence, that the war might be conducted with equal vigour without it, that it would divide the Americans, and unite the people of Great Britain against them. ...

After a full discussion, the measure of declaring the colonies free and independent was approved, by nearly an unanimous vote. The anniversary of the day on which this great event took place, has ever since been consecrated by the Americans to religious gratitude, and social pleasures. It is considered by them as the birth day of their freedom.

The act of the united colonies for separating themselves from the government of Great Britain, and declaring their independence, was expressed in the following words. [Here the text of the Declaration of Independence is printed.] ...

The declaration of independence read publicly in all the states, and was welcomed with many demonstrations of joy. The people were encouraged by it to bear up under the calamities of war, and viewed the evils they suffered, only as the thorn that ever accompanies the rose. The army received it with particular satisfaction. As far as it had validity, so far it secured them from suffering as rebels, and held out to their view an object, the attainment of which would be an adequate recompense for the toils and dangers of war. They were animated by the consideration that they were no longer to risk their lives for the trifling purpose of procuring a repeal of a few oppressive acts of parliament, but for a new organization of government, that would forever put it out of the power of Great Britain to oppress them. The flattering prospects of an extensive commerce, freed from British restrictions, and the honours and emoluments of office in independent states now began to glitter before the eyes of the colonists, and reconciled them to the difficulties of their situation. What was supposed in Great Britain to be their primary object, had only a secondary influence. While they were charged with aiming at independence from the impulse of avarice and ambition, they were ardently wishing for a reconciliation. But, after they had been compelled to adopt that measure, these powerful principles of human action opposed its retraction and stimulated to its support. That separation which the colonists at first dreaded as an evil, they soon gloried in as a national blessing. ...

[1] *PHILANDER* Like many of those who wrote for periodicals during this period, the author of this piece chose to use a pseudonym.

from *Notes on the State of Virginia*

from QUERY 6
A NOTICE OF THE MINES AND
OTHER SUBTERRANEOUS RICHES;
ITS TREES, PLANTS, FRUITS, ETC.

... Of the Indian of South America I know nothing, for I would not honor with the appellation of knowledge what I derive from the fables published of them. These I believe to be just as true as the fables of Aesop. This belief is founded on what I have seen of man, white, red, and black, and what has been written of him by authors, enlightened themselves, and writing amidst an enlightened people. The Indian of North America being more within our reach, I can speak of him somewhat from my own knowledge, but more from the information of others better acquainted with him, and on whose truth and judgment I can rely. From these sources I am able to say, in contradiction to this representation,[1] that he is neither more defective in ardor, nor more impotent with his female, than the white reduced to the same diet and exercise; that he is brave, when an enterprise depends on bravery; education with him making the point of honor consist in the destruction of an enemy by stratagem,[2] and in the preservation of his own person free from injury; or perhaps this is nature, while it is education which teaches us to honor force more than finesse; that he will defend himself against an host of enemies, always choosing to be killed, rather than to surrender, [even] though it be to the whites, who he knows will treat him well; that in other situations also he meets death with more deliberation, and endures tortures with a firmness unknown almost to religious enthusiasm with us; that he is affectionate to his children, careful of them, and indulgent in the extreme; that his affections comprehend his other connections, weakening, as with us, from circle to circle, as they recede from the center; that his friendships are strong and faithful to the uttermost extremity; that his sensibility[3] is keen, even the warriors weeping most bitterly on the loss of their children, though in general they endeavour to appear superior to human events; that his vivacity and activity of mind is equal to ours in the same situation—hence his eagerness for hunting, and for games of chance. The women are submitted to unjust drudgery. This I believe is the case with every barbarous people. With such, force is law. The stronger sex therefore imposes on the weaker. It is civilization alone which replaces women in the enjoyment of their natural equality. That first teaches us to subdue the selfish passions, and to respect those rights in others which we value in ourselves. Were we in equal barbarism, our females would be equal drudges. The man with them is less strong than with us, but their woman stronger than ours, and both for the same obvious reason: because our man and their woman is habituated to labour, and formed by it. With both races the sex which is indulged with ease is least athletic. An Indian man is small in the hand and wrist for the same reason for which a sailor is large and strong in the arms and shoulders, and a porter in the legs and thighs. They raise fewer children than we do. The causes of this are to be found not in a difference of nature, but of circumstance. The women very frequently attending the men in their parties of war and of hunting, childbearing becomes extremely inconvenient to them. It is said, therefore, that they have learnt the practice of procuring abortion by the use of some vegetable, and that it even extends to prevent conception for a considerable time after. During these parties they are exposed to numerous hazards, to excessive exertions, to the greatest extremities of hunger. Even at their homes the nation depends for food, through a certain part of every year, on the gleanings of the forest—that is, they experience a famine once in every year. With all animals, if the female be badly fed, or not fed at all, her young

[1] *this representation* In this segment, as in many parts of the *Notes*, Jefferson is directly refuting the theories (or "representations") of the French naturalist Comte de Buffon (1707–88). Buffon theorized in his *Histoire Naturelle* that American flora and fauna were naturally inferior in a variety of ways to those native to Europe, Asia, and Africa. According to Buffon, this theory of "degeneracy," as it has come to be called, also applied to the Indigenous people of the Americas.

[2] *point of honor ... stratagem* Like many colonial Americans of the time, Jefferson privileges European forms of warfare, which often involved open shows of military strength, over the more subtle and strategic forms practiced by many Indigenous peoples.

[3] *sensibility* I.e., sensitivity; the capacity for strong emotional responses. (Eighteenth-century philosophy and aesthetic theory was particularly interested in the contrast between sense, or reason, and sensibility.)

perish; and if both male and female be reduced to like want,[1] generation becomes less active, less productive. To the obstacles then of want and hazard, which nature has opposed to the multiplication of wild animals for the purpose of restraining their numbers within certain bounds, those of labour and of voluntary abortion are added with the Indian. No wonder then if they multiply less than we do. Where food is regularly supplied, a single farm will show more of cattle than a whole country of forests can of buffaloes. The same Indian women, when married to white traders who feed them and their children plentifully and regularly, who exempt them from excessive drudgery, who keep them stationary and unexposed to accident, produce and raise as many children as the white women. Instances are known, under these circumstances, of their rearing a dozen children. An inhuman practice once prevailed in this country of making slaves of the Indians. It is a fact well known with us that the Indian women so enslaved produced and raised as numerous families as either the whites or blacks among whom they lived. …

… But if cold and moisture be the agents of nature for diminishing the races of animals,[2] how comes she all at once to suspend their operation as to the physical man of the new world, whom the Count acknowledges to be "*à peu près de même stature que l'homme de notre monde*,"[3] and to let loose their influence on his moral faculties? How has this "combination of the elements and other physical causes, so contrary to the enlargement of animal nature in this new world, these obstacles to the development and formation of great germs,"[4] been arrested and suspended, so as to permit the human body to acquire its just[5] dimensions, and by what inconceivable process has their action been directed on his mind alone? To judge of the truth of this, to form a just estimate of their genius and mental powers, more facts are wanting, and great allowance to be made for those circumstances of their situation which call for a display of particular

talents only. This done, we shall probably find that they are formed in mind as well as in body, on the same module with the "*Homo sapiens Europaeus*."[6] The principles of their society forbidding all compulsion, they are to be led to duty and to enterprise by personal influence and persuasion. Hence eloquence in council, bravery and address in war, become the foundations of all consequence with them. To these acquirements all their faculties are directed. Of their bravery and address[7] in war we have multiplied proofs, because we have been the subjects on which they were exercised. Of their eminence in oratory we have fewer examples, because it is displayed chiefly in their own councils. Some, however, we have of very superior lustre. I may challenge the whole orations of Demosthenes and Cicero,[8] and of any more eminent orator, if Europe has furnished more eminent, to produce a single passage, superior to the speech of Logan, a Mingo chief,[9] to Lord Dunmore when governor of this state. And, as a testimony of their talents in this line, I beg leave to introduce it, first stating the incidents necessary for understanding it.

In the spring of the year 1774, a robbery and murder were committed on an inhabitant of the frontiers of Virginia, by two Indians of the Shawnee tribe. The neighbouring whites, according to their custom, undertook to punish this outrage in a summary way. Colonel Cresap,[10] a man infamous for the many murders he had committed on those much-injured people, collected a

[1] *like want* The same state of lack (i.e., of food).

[2] *But if … of animals* Buffon posited that the degeneracy of American species was a result of the continent's comparatively cold and wet climate.

[3] *à peu … notre monde* French: approximately the same size as the man in our [part of the] world.

[4] *great germs* Organisms capable of developing impressively.

[5] *just* Proper.

[6] *Homo sapiens Europaeus* Swedish taxonomist Carl Linnaeus (1707–78), who invented the name *homo sapiens*, further categorized human beings into four racialized subspecies—*Americanus*, *Afer*, *Europaeus*, and *Asiaticus*. These categories influenced the study of human genetics for years to come.

[7] *address* Skill.

[8] *Demosthenes and Cicero* Highly respected politicians and orators from ancient Greece and Rome, respectively.

[9] *Logan, a Mingo chief* Logan (c. 1723–80) was a member of the Cayuga, one of the Six Nations of the Iroquois Confederacy, though he later became affiliated with the Mingo, a group composed of Iroquois people who had moved to the western region of Ohio County.

[10] *Colonel Cresap* Michael Cresap (1742–75), a trader and land developer who participated in numerous raids against Native Americans in Ohio County. Though Logan himself identifies Cresap as the murderer of his family members in the following speech, scholars today generally agree that the perpetrator of what is now known as the Yellow Creek Massacre was in fact Daniel Greathouse (c. 1752–75).

party, and proceeded down the Kanhaway[1] in quest of vengeance. Unfortunately a canoe of women and children, with one man only, was seen coming from the opposite shore, unarmed, and unsuspecting an hostile attack from the whites. Cresap and his party concealed themselves on the bank of the river, and the moment the canoe reached the shore, singled out their objects, and, at one fire, killed every person in it. This happened to be the family of Logan, who had long been distinguished as a friend of the whites. This unworthy return provoked his vengeance. He accordingly signalized himself in the war which ensued.[2] In the autumn of the same year, a decisive battle was fought at the mouth of the Great Kanhaway, between the collected forces of the Shawanees, Mingoes, and Delawares, and a detachment of the Virginia militia. The Indians were defeated, and sued for peace. Logan however disdained to be seen among the suppliants. But, lest the sincerity of a treaty should be distrusted, from which so distinguished a chief absented himself, he sent by a messenger the following speech to be delivered to Lord Dunmore.[3]

[1] *the Kanhaway* I.e., the Kanawha River, a tributary of the Ohio.

[2] *the war which ensued* Known as Lord Dunmore's War, after the Virginian governor who instigated it, in an endeavor—which was ultimately successful—to claim Shawnee and Mingo land for the colonies.

[3] *he sent … Lord Dunmore* In a later edition of the *Notes*, Jefferson provides a substantial appendix in which he further explains the circumstances by which he had come to know this version of Logan's speech, which had been widely circulated in American newspapers in the 1770s:

> I remembered, however, that Gen. Gibson was still living, and knew that he had been the translator of the speech. I wrote to him immediately. He, in answer, declared to me, that he was the very person sent by Lord Dunmore to the Indian town; that, after he had delivered his message there, Logan took him out to a neighboring wood; sat down with him and, rehearsing, with tears, the catastrophe of his family, gave him that speech for Lord Dunmore; that he carried it to Lord Dunmore; translated it for him; has turned to it in the Encyclopedia, as taken from the Notes on Virginia, and finds that it was his translation I had used, with only two or three verbal variations of no importance. These, I suppose, had arisen in the course of successive copies.

Jefferson also cites the following letter from Kentucky judge Harry Innes, dated 2 March 1799:

I appeal to any white man to say, if ever he entered Logan's cabin hungry, and he gave him not meat; if ever he came cold and naked, and he clothed him not. During the course of the last long and bloody war,[4] Logan remained idle in his cabin, an advocate for peace. Such was my love for the whites, that my countrymen pointed as they passed, and said, "Logan is the friend of white men." I had even thought to have lived with you, but for the injuries of one man. Colonel Cresap, the last spring, in cold blood, and unprovoked, murdered all the relations of Logan, not sparing even my women and children. There runs not a drop of my blood in the veins of any living creature. This called on me for revenge. I have sought it; I have killed many; I have fully glutted my vengeance. For my country, I rejoice at the beams of peace. But do not harbour a thought that mine is the joy of fear. Logan never felt fear. He will not turn on his heel to save his life. Who is there to mourn for Logan?—Not one.

...

> In 1774 I lived in Fincastle county, now divided into Washington, Montgomery and part of Wythe. Being intimate in Colonel Preston's family, I happened in July to be at his house, when an express was sent to him, as the County Lieutenant, requesting a guard of the militia to be ordered out for the protection of the inhabitants residing low down on the north fork of Holston River. The express brought with him a war club, and a note which was left tied to it at the house of one Robertson, whose family were cut off by the Indians, and gave rise for the application to Colonel Preston, of which the following is a copy, then taken by me in my memorandum book.
>
> Captain Cresap,
>
> What did you kill my people on Yellow Creek for? The white people killed my kin, at Conestoga, a great while ago; and I thought nothing of that. But you killed my kin again on Yellow Creek, and took my Cousin Prisoner. Then I thought I must kill too; and I have been three times to war since; but the Indians are not angry: only myself.
>
> Captain JOHN LOGAN

[4] *last … bloody war* I.e., the French and Indian War (1754–63), during which many Indigenous peoples allied with the French.

from QUERY 11
A DESCRIPTION OF THE INDIANS
ESTABLISHED IN THAT STATE?

When the first effectual settlement of our colony was made, which was in 1607,[1] the country from the sea-coast to the mountains, and from Patowmac to the most southern waters of James River, was occupied by upwards of forty different tribes of Indians. Of these the *Powhatans*, the *Mannahoacs*, and *Monacans*, were the most powerful. Those between the sea-coast and falls of the rivers were in amity with one another, and attached to the *Powhatans* as their link of union. Those between the falls of the rivers and the mountains were divided into two confederacies; the tribes inhabiting the head waters of Patowmac and Rappahanoc being attached to the *Mannahoacs*; and those on the upper parts of James River to the *Monacans*. But the *Monacans* and their friends were in amity with the *Mannahoacs* and their friends, and waged joint and perpetual war against the *Powhatans*. We are told that the *Powhatans*, *Mannahoacs*, and *Monacans* spoke languages so radically different, that interpreters were necessary when they transacted business.[2] Hence we may conjecture that this was not the case between all the tribes, and probably that each spoke the language of the nation to which it was attached, which we know to have been the case in many particular instances. Very possibly there may have been anciently three different stocks, each of which, multiplying in a long course of time, had separated into so many little societies. This practice results from the circumstance of their having never submitted themselves to any laws, any coercive power, any shadow of government. Their only controls are their manners, and that moral sense of right and wrong, which, like the sense of tasting and feeling, in every man makes a part of his nature. An offence against these is punished by contempt, by exclusion from society, or, where the case is serious, as that of murder, by the individuals whom it concerns. Imperfect as this species of coercion may seem, crimes are very rare among them; insomuch that were it made a question, whether no law, as among the savage Americans, or too much law, as among the civilized Europeans, submits man to the greatest evil, one who has seen both conditions of existence would pronounce it to be the last, and that the sheep are happier of themselves, than under care of the wolves. It will be said that great societies cannot exist without government. The Savages therefore break them into small ones. …

… What would be the melancholy sequel of their history may, however, be augured from the census of 1669, by which we discover that the tribes therein enumerated were, in the space of 62 years, reduced to about one-third of their former numbers. Spirituous liquors, the smallpox, war, and an abridgment of territory, to a people who lived principally on the spontaneous productions of nature, had committed terrible havoc among them, which generation, under the obstacles opposed to it among them, was not likely to make good. That the lands of this country were taken from them by conquest is not so general a truth as is supposed. I find in our historians and records repeated proofs of purchase, which cover a considerable part of the lower country; and many more would doubtless be found on further search.[3] The upper country we know has been acquired altogether by purchases made in the most unexceptionable form. …

I know of no such thing existing as an Indian monument; for I would not honour with that name arrow points, stone hatchets, stone pipes, and half-shapen images. Of labour on the large scale, I think there is no remain[4] as respectable as would be a common ditch for the draining of lands, unless indeed it be the barrows,[5] of which many are to be found all over this country. These are of different sizes, some of them constructed of earth, and some of loose stones. That they were repositories of the dead, has been obvious to all; but on what particular occasion constructed, was matter of doubt. Some have thought they covered the bones

[1] *1607* Year in which the Virginia Company arrived on the shores of Virginia, on land occupied by the Powhatan Confederacy, and established Jamestown.

[2] *We are told … transacted business* While the Manahoac and the Monacan languages are Siouan, the Powhatan language is of the Algonquian group.

[3] *further search* Jefferson's original manuscript contains here the following comment, which was later crossed out: "It is true that these purchases were sometimes made with the price in one hand and the sword in the other."

[4] *no remain* I.e., no surviving structure.

[5] *barrows* Large grave mounds and other earthworks.

of those who have fallen in battles fought on the spot of interment. Some ascribed them to the custom, said to prevail among the Indians, of collecting, at certain periods, the bones of all their dead, wheresoever deposited at the time of death. Others again supposed them the general sepulchres for towns, conjectured to have been on or near these grounds; and this opinion was supported by the quality of the lands in which they are found (those constructed of earth being generally in the softest and most fertile meadow-grounds on riversides) and by a tradition, said to be handed down from the Aboriginal Indians, that, when they settled in a town, the first person who died was placed erect, and earth put about him, so as to cover and support him; that, when another died, a narrow passage was dug to the first, the second reclined against him, and the cover of earth replaced, and so on. There being one of these in my neighbourhood, I wished to satisfy myself whether any, and which of these opinions were just. For this purpose I determined to open and examine it thoroughly. It was situated on the low grounds of the Rivanna, about two miles above its principal fork, and opposite to some hills, on which had been an Indian town. It was of a spheroidical form, of about 40 feet diameter at the base, and had been of about twelve feet altitude, though now reduced by the plough to seven and a half, having been under cultivation about a dozen years. Before this it was covered with trees of twelve inches diameter, and round the base was an excavation of five feet depth and width, from whence the earth had been taken of which the hillock was formed. I first dug superficially in several parts of it, and came to collections of human bones, at different depths, from six inches to three feet below the surface. These were lying in the utmost confusion, some vertical, some oblique, some horizontal, and directed to every point of the compass, entangled, and held together in clusters by the earth. Bones of the most distant parts were found together, as, for instance, the small bones of the foot in the hollow of a skull; many skulls would sometimes be in contact, lying on the face, on the side, on the back, top or bottom, so as, on the whole, to give the idea of bones emptied promiscuously from a bag or basket, and covered over with earth, without any attention to their order. The bones of which the greatest numbers remained were skulls, jaw-bones, teeth, the bones of the arms, thighs, legs, feet, and hands. A few ribs remained, some vertebrae of the neck and spine without their processes,[1] and one instance only of the[2] bone which serves as a base to the vertebral column. The skulls were so tender, that they generally fell to pieces on being touched. The other bones were stronger. There were some teeth which were judged to be smaller than those of an adult; a skull which, on a slight view, appeared to be that of an infant, but it fell to pieces on being taken out, so as to prevent satisfactory examination; a rib, and a fragment of the under-jaw of a person about half grown; another rib of an infant; and part of the jaw of a child, which had not yet cut its teeth. This last furnishing the most decisive proof of the burial of children here, I was particular in my attention to it. It was part of the right half of the under-jaw. The processes by which it was articulated[3] to the temporal bones were entire; and the bone itself firm to where it had been broken off, which, as nearly as I could judge, was about the place of the eyetooth.[4] Its upper edge, wherein would have been the sockets of the teeth, was perfectly smooth. Measuring it with that of an adult, by placing their hinder processes together, its broken end extended to the penultimate grinder of the adult. This bone was white, all the others of a sand colour. The bones of infants being soft, they probably decay sooner, which might be the cause so few were found here.

I proceeded then to make a perpendicular cut through the body of the barrow, that I might examine its internal structure. This passed about three feet from its center, was opened to the former surface of the earth, and was wide enough for a man to walk through and examine its sides. At the bottom, that is, on the level of the circumjacent plain, I found bones; above these a few stones, brought from a cliff a quarter of a mile off, and from the river one-eighth of a mile off; then a large interval of earth, then a stratum of bones, and so on. At one end of the section were four strata of bones plainly distinguishable; at the other, three; the strata in one part not ranging with those in another. The bones nearest the surface were least decayed. No holes were discovered in any of them, as if made with bullets, arrows, or

[1] *without their processes* I.e., not attached to one another to form a row.

[2] [Jefferson's note] The os sacrum.

[3] *articulated* Attached.

[4] *eyetooth* Canine tooth.

other weapons. I conjectured that in this barrow might have been a thousand skeletons. Everyone will readily seize the circumstances above related, which militate against the opinion that it covered the bones only of persons fallen in battle; and against the tradition also, which would make it the common sepulchre of a town, in which the bodies were placed upright, and touching each other. Appearances certainly indicate that it has derived both origin and growth from the accustomary collection of bones, and deposition of them together; that the first collection had been deposited on the common surface of the earth, a few stones put over it, and then a covering of earth, that the second had been laid on this, had covered more or less of it in proportion to the number of bones, and was then also covered with earth; and so on. The following are the particular circumstances which give it this aspect. 1. The number of bones. 2. Their confused position. 3. Their being in different strata. 4. The strata in one part having no correspondence with those in another. 5. The different states of decay in these strata, which seem to indicate a difference in the time of inhumation. 6. The existence of infant bones among them. But on whatever occasion they may have been made, they are of considerable notoriety among the Indians: for a party passing, about thirty years ago, through the part of the country where this barrow is, went through the woods directly to it, without any instructions or enquiry, and having staid about it some time, with expressions which were construed to be those of sorrow, they returned to the high road, which they had left about half a dozen miles to pay this visit, and pursued their journey. There is another barrow, much resembling this in the low grounds of the South branch of Shenandoah, where it is crossed by the road leading from the Rock-fish gap to Staunton. Both of these have, within these dozen years, been cleared of their trees and put under cultivation, are much reduced in their height, and spread in width, by the plough, and will probably disappear in time. There is another on a hill in the Blue ridge of mountains, a few miles North of Wood's gap, which is made up of small stones thrown together. This has been opened and found to contain human bones, as the others do. There are also many others in other parts of the country.

Great question has arisen from whence came those aboriginal inhabitants of America? Discoveries, long

ago made, were sufficient to shew that a passage from Europe to America was always practicable, even to the imperfect navigation of ancient times. In going from Norway to Iceland, from Iceland to Groenland, from Groenland to Labrador, the first traject is the widest: and this having been practised from the earliest times of which we have any account of that part of the earth, it is not difficult to suppose that the subsequent trajects may have been sometimes passed. Again, the late discoveries of Captain Cook, coasting from Kamschatka[1] to California, have proved that, if the two continents of Asia and America be separated at all, it is only by a narrow streight. So that from this side also, inhabitants may have passed into America: and the resemblance between the Indians of America and the eastern inhabitants of Asia, would induce us to conjecture, that the former are the descendants of the latter, or the latter of the former: excepting indeed the Eskimaux, who, from the same circumstance of resemblance, and from identity of language, must be derived from the Groenlanders, and these probably from some of the northern parts of the old continent.[2] A knowledge of their several languages would be the most certain evidence of their derivation which could be produced. In fact, it is the best proof of the affinity of nations which ever can be referred to. How many ages have elapsed since the English, the Dutch, the Germans, the Swiss, the Norwegians, Danes and Swedes have separated from their common stock? Yet how many more must elapse before the proofs of their common origin, which exist in their several languages, will disappear? It is to be lamented then, very much to be lamented, that we have suffered so many of the Indian tribes already to extinguish, without our having previously collected and deposited in the records of literature, the general rudiments at least of the languages they spoke. Were vocabularies formed of all the languages spoken in North and South America, preserving their appellations of the most common objects in nature, of those

[1] *late* Recent; *Captain Cook* James Cook (1728–79), English explorer and cartographer of the Pacific; *Kamschatka* The Kamchatka Peninsula in far-eastern Russia. In fact, Cook himself never made it to Kamchatka; his colleague Charles Clerke led the voyage there after Cook was killed on the island of Hawaii.

[2] *the Eskimaux … old continent* The ancestors of various Eskimo/Inuit peoples, including the Greenlandic Inuit, are the Thule, who originated in Alaska circa 1000 CE.

—original spelling —

which must be present to every nation barbarous or civilized, with the inflections of their nouns and verbs, their principles of regimen and concord, and these deposited in all the public libraries, it would furnish opportunities to those skilled in the languages of the old world to compare them with these, now, or at any future time, and hence to construct the best evidence of the derivation of this part of the human race.

But imperfect as is our knowledge of the tongues spoken in America, it suffices to discover the following remarkable fact. Arranging them under the radical[1] ones to which they may be palpably traced, and doing the same by those of the red men of Asia, there will be found probably twenty in America, for one in Asia, of those radical languages, so called because, if they were ever the same, they have lost all resemblance to one another. A separation into dialects may be the work of a few ages only, but for two dialects to recede from one another till they have lost all vestiges of their common origin, must require an immense course of time; perhaps not less than many people give to the age of the earth. A greater number of those radical changes of language having taken place among the red men of America, proves them of greater antiquity than those of Asia. ...

from QUERY 14
THE ADMINISTRATION OF JUSTICE AND
DESCRIPTION OF THE LAWS?

... The following variations from the British model[2] are perhaps worthy of being specified.

Debtors unable to pay their debts, and making faithful delivery of their whole effects,[3] are released from confinement, and their persons forever discharged from restraint for such previous debts; but any property they may afterwards acquire will be subject to their creditors.

The poor, unable to support themselves, are maintained by an assessment on the titheable persons in their parish. This assessment is levied and administered by twelve persons in each parish, called vestrymen, originally chosen by the housekeepers of the parish, but afterwards filling vacancies in their own body by their own choice. These are usually the most discreet[4] farmers, so distributed through their parish that every part of it may be under the immediate eye of some one of them. They are well acquainted with the details and economy[5] of private life, and they find sufficient inducements to execute their charge[6] well, in their philanthropy, in the approbation of their neighbours, and the distinction which that gives them. The poor who have neither property, friends, nor strength to labour, are boarded in the houses of good farmers, to whom a stipulated sum is annually paid. To those who are able to help themselves a little, or have friends from whom they derive some succours, inadequate however to their full maintenance, supplementary aids are given, which enable them to live comfortably in their own houses, or in the houses of their friends. Vagabonds, without visible property or vocation, are placed in workhouses, where they are well clothed, fed, lodged, and made to labour. Nearly the same method of providing for the poor prevails through all our states; and from Savannah to Portsmouth you will seldom meet a beggar. In the larger towns indeed they sometimes present themselves. These are usually foreigners, who have never obtained a settlement in any parish. I never yet saw a native American[7] begging in the streets or highways. A subsistence is easily gained here; and if, by misfortunes, they are thrown on the charities of the world, those provided by their own country are so comfortable and so certain, that they never think of relinquishing them to become strolling beggars. Their situation too, when sick, in the family of a good farmer, where every member is emulous[8] to do them kind offices, where they are visited by all the neighbours, who bring them the little rarities which their sickly appetites may crave, and who take by rotation the nightly watch over them, when their condition requires it, is without comparison better than in a general hospital, where the sick,

[1] radical Original, foundational.

[2] British model I.e., British parliamentary law, which Jefferson discusses in the preceding paragraphs; here he contrasts this system with certain laws adopted in the United States.

[3] effects Property.

[4] discreet Prudent; trustworthy.

[5] economy Management (especially of household affairs).

[6] charge Duty.

[7] native American I.e., a person of European descent born and raised in America.

[8] emulous Desirous (especially in a competitive manner).

the dying, and the dead are crammed together, in the same rooms, and often in the same beds. The disadvantages inseparable from general hospitals are such as can never be counterpoised by all the regularities of medicine and regimen. Nature and kind nursing save a much greater proportion in our plain way, at a smaller expense, and with less abuse. One branch only of hospital institution is wanting with us; that is, a general establishment for those labouring under difficult cases of chirurgery.[1] The aids of this art are not equivocal. But an able chirurgeon cannot be had in every parish. Such a receptacle should therefore be provided for those patients; but no others should be admitted.

Marriages must be solemnized either on special licence, granted by the first magistrate of the county, on proof of the consent of the parent or guardian of either party under age, or after solemn publication, on three several[2] Sundays, at some place of religious worship in the parishes where the parties reside. The act of solemnization may be by the minister of any society of Christians, who shall have been previously licensed for this purpose by the court of the county. Quakers and Menonists[3] however are exempted from all these conditions, and marriage among them is to be solemnized by the society itself.

A foreigner of any nation not in open war with us becomes naturalized by removing to the state to reside, and taking an oath of fidelity, and thereupon acquires every right of a native citizen; and citizens may divest themselves of that character by declaring, by solemn deed or in open court, that they mean to expatriate themselves, and no longer to be citizens of this state.

Conveyances of land must be registered in the court of the county wherein they lie, or in the general court, or they are void, as to creditors, and subsequent purchasers.

Slaves pass by descent and dower[4] as lands do. Where the descent is from a parent, the heir is bound to pay an equal share of their value in money to each of his brothers and sisters.

Slaves, as well as lands, were entailable[5] during the monarchy; but, by an act of the first republican assembly, all donees in tail,[6] present and future, were vested with the absolute dominion of the entailed subject.

Bills of exchange, being protested, carry 10 per cent interest from their date.

No person is allowed, in any other case, to take more than five per cent per annum simple interest for the loan of monies.

Gaming debts are made void, and monies actually paid to discharge such debts (if they exceeded 40 shillings) may be recovered by the payer within three months, or by any other person afterwards.

Tobacco, flour, beef, pork, tar, pitch, and turpentine, must be inspected by persons publicly appointed, before they can be exported. …

Many of the laws which were in force during the monarchy being relative merely to that form of government, or inculcating principles inconsistent with republicanism, the first assembly which met after the establishment of the commonwealth appointed a committee to revise the whole code, to reduce it into proper form and volume, and report it to the assembly. This work has been executed by three gentlemen,[7] and reported, but probably will not be taken up till a restoration of peace shall leave to the legislature leisure to go through such a work.

The plan of the revisal was this. The common law of England—by which is meant, that part of the English law which was anterior to the date of the oldest statutes extant—is made the basis of the work. It was thought dangerous to attempt to reduce it to a text; it was therefore left to be collected from the usual monuments of it. Necessary alterations in that, and so much of the whole body of the British statutes, and of acts of assembly, as were thought proper to be retained, were digested into 126 new acts, in which simplicity of style

1 *chirurgery* Surgery.

2 *several* Successive.

3 *Menonists* Mennonites.

4 *dower* I.e., the property inherited by a widow upon the death of her husband.

5 *entailable* An entail was a rule of settlement limiting who could inherit one's property in successive generations, legally preventing future owners from bequeathing any of the inherited estate to any person at will.

6 *donees in tail* Those in possession of a previously entailed property.

7 *three gentlemen* The three revisors Jefferson refers to are himself, George Wythe (1726–1806), and Edmund Pendleton (1721–1803).

was aimed at, as far as was safe. The following are the most remarkable alterations proposed:

To change the rules of descent, so as that the lands of any person dying intestate[1] shall be divisible equally among all his children, or other representatives, in equal degree.

To make slaves distributable among the next of kin, as other moveables.

To have all public expenses, whether of the general treasury, or of a parish or county (as for the maintenance of the poor, building bridges, courthouses, etc.), supplied by assessments on the citizens, in proportion to their property.

To hire undertakers for keeping the public roads in repair, and indemnify individuals through whose lands new roads shall be opened.

To define with precision the rules whereby aliens should become citizens, and citizens make themselves aliens.

To establish religious freedom on the broadest bottom.

To emancipate all slaves born after passing the act. The bill reported by the revisors does not itself contain this proposition; but an amendment containing it was prepared, to be offered to the legislature whenever the bill should be taken up, and further directing that they should continue with their parents to a certain age, then be brought up, at the public expense, to tillage, arts or sciences, according to their geniuses,[2] till the females should be eighteen, and the males twenty-one years of age, when they should be colonized to such place as the circumstances of the time should render most proper, sending them out with arms,[3] implements of household and of the handicraft arts, seeds, pairs of the useful domestic animals, etc.; to declare them a free and independent people, and extend to them our alliance and protection, till they have acquired strength; and to send vessels at the same time to other parts of the world for an equal number of white inhabitants, to induce whom to migrate hither, proper encouragements were to be proposed. It will probably be asked, Why not retain and incorporate the blacks into the state, and thus save the expense of supplying, by importation of white settlers, the vacancies they will leave? Deep rooted prejudices entertained by the whites; ten thousand recollections, by the blacks, of the injuries they have sustained; new provocations; the real distinctions which nature has made; and many other circumstances, will divide us into parties, and produce convulsions which will probably never end but in the extermination of the one or the other race. To these objections, which are political, may be added others, which are physical and moral. The first difference which strikes us is that of colour. Whether the black of the negro resides in the reticular membrane between the skin and scarf-skin,[4] or in the scarf-skin itself; whether it proceeds from the colour of the blood, the colour of the bile, or from that of some other secretion—the difference is fixed in nature, and is as real as if its seat and cause were better known to us. And is this difference of no importance? Is it not the foundation of a greater or less share of beauty in the two races? Are not the fine mixtures of red and white, the expressions of every passion by greater or less suffusions of colour in the one, preferable to that eternal monotony, which reigns in the countenances, that immoveable veil of black which covers all the emotions of the other race? Add to these, flowing hair, a more elegant symmetry of form, their own judgment in favour of the whites, declared by their preference of them, as uniformly as is the preference of the Oranootan[5] for the black women over those of his own species. The circumstance of superior beauty is thought worthy attention in the propagation of our horses, dogs, and other domestic animals; why not in that of man? Besides those of colour, figure, and hair, there are other physical distinctions proving a difference of race. They have less hair on the face and body. They secrete less by the kidneys, and more by the glands of the skin, which gives them a very strong and disagreeable odour. This greater degree of transpiration renders them more tolerant of heat, and less so of cold, than the whites. Perhaps too a difference of structure in the pulmonary apparatus, which a late ingenious[6] experimentalist has discovered to be the

[1] *intestate* Not having left a will.

[2] *geniuses* Particular skills or inclinations.

[3] *arms* Weapons.

[4] *scarf-skin* Epidermis, or outermost layer of skin.

[5] *Oranootan* Orangutan.

[6] [Jefferson's note] Crawford. [Adair Crawford (1748–95), English physicist and chemist who studied the relationship between heat and respiration.]

principal regulator of animal heat, may have disabled them from extricating, in the act of inspiration, so much of that fluid from the outer air, or obliged them in expiration, to part with more of it. They seem to require less sleep. A black, after hard labour through the day, will be induced by the slightest amusements to sit up till midnight or later, though knowing he must be out with the first dawn of the morning. They are at least as brave, and more adventuresome. But this may perhaps proceed from a want of forethought, which prevents their seeing a danger till it be present. When present, they do not go through it with more coolness or steadiness than the whites. They are more ardent after their female, but love seems with them to be more an eager desire, than a tender delicate mixture of sentiment and sensation. Their griefs are transient. Those numberless afflictions, which render it doubtful whether heaven has given life to us in mercy or in wrath, are less felt, and sooner forgotten with them. In general, their existence appears to participate more of sensation than reflection. To this must be ascribed their disposition to sleep when abstracted from their diversions, and unemployed in labour. An animal whose body is at rest, and who does not reflect, must be disposed to sleep of course. Comparing them by their faculties of memory, reason, and imagination, it appears to me, that in memory they are equal to the whites; in reason much inferior, as I think one could scarcely be found capable of tracing and comprehending the investigations of Euclid;[1] and that in imagination they are dull, tasteless, and anomalous. It would be unfair to follow them to Africa for this investigation. We will consider them here, on the same stage with the whites, and where the facts are not apocryphal on which a judgment is to be formed. It will be right to make great allowances for the difference of condition, of education, of conversation, of the sphere in which they move. Many millions of them have been brought to, and born in, America. Most of them indeed have been confined to tillage, to their own homes, and their own society; yet many have been so situated, that they might have availed themselves of the conversation of their masters; many have been

brought up to the handicraft arts, from that circumstance have always been associated with the whites. Some have been liberally educated, and all have lived in countries where the arts and sciences are cultivated to a considerable degree, and have had before their eyes samples of the best works from abroad. The Indians, with no advantages of this kind, will often carve figures on their pipes not destitute of design and merit. They will crayon[2] out an animal, a plant, or a country, so as to prove the existence of a germ[3] in their minds which only wants cultivation. They astonish you with strokes of the most sublime oratory, such as prove their reason and sentiment strong, their imagination glowing and elevated. But never yet could I find that a black had uttered a thought above the level of plain narration; never see even an elementary trait of painting or sculpture. In music they are more generally gifted than the whites with accurate ears for tune and time, and they have been found capable of imagining a small catch.[4] Whether they will be equal to the composition of a more extensive run of melody, or of complicated harmony, is yet to be proved. Misery is often the parent of the most affecting touches in poetry. Among the blacks is misery enough, God knows, but no poetry. Love is the peculiar *œstrum*[5] of the poet. Their love is ardent, but it kindles the senses only, not the imagination. Religion indeed has produced a Phyllis Whately;[6] but it could not produce a poet. The compositions published under her name are below the

[1] *Euclid* Ancient Greek mathematician (c. 300 BCE), whose *Elements* was frequently used for the teaching of mathematics during this period.

[2] *crayon* Sketch.

[3] *germ* Seed.

[4] [Jefferson's note] The instrument proper to them is the Banjar, which they brought hither from Africa, and which is the original of the guitar, its chords being precisely the four lower chords of the guitar. [The banjo originated in enslaved communities in the Caribbean and American colonies, and can possibly trace its roots to a number of West African musical instruments. The origin of the guitar, however, is unrelated to either the banjo or its West African ancestors. *catch* Short, simple tune.]

[5] *œstrum* Something, especially a kind of passion, which incites a given activity.

[6] *Phyllis Whately* Phillis Wheatley, an enslaved, West African-born woman whose *Poems on Various Subjects, Religious and Moral* (1773) was the first book of poetry to be published by an African American woman. It brought her a great deal of fame on both sides of the Atlantic; Wheatley was emancipated shortly after the volume's publication. A great many of her poems centered on religious (especially Methodist) themes.

dignity of criticism. The heroes of the *Dunciad* are to her, as Hercules to the author of that poem.[1] Ignatius Sancho[2] has approached nearer to merit in composition; yet his letters do more honour to the heart than the head. They breathe the purest effusions of friendship and general philanthropy, and show how great a degree of the latter may be compounded with strong religious zeal. He is often happy in the turn of his compliments, and his style is easy and familiar, except when he affects a Shandean[3] fabrication of words. But his imagination is wild and extravagant, escapes incessantly from every restraint of reason and taste, and, in the course of its vagaries, leaves a tract of thought as incoherent and eccentric, as is the course of a meteor through the sky. His subjects should often have led him to a process of sober reasoning, yet we find him always substituting sentiment for demonstration. Upon the whole, though we admit him to the first place among those of his own colour who have presented themselves to the public judgment, yet when we compare him with the writers of the race among whom he lived, and particularly with the epistolary class, in which he has taken his own stand, we are compelled to enroll him at the bottom of the column. This criticism supposes the letters published under his name to be genuine, and to have received amendment from no other hand—points which would not be of easy investigation.

The improvement of the blacks in body and mind, in the first instance of their mixture with the whites, has been observed by everyone, and proves that their inferiority is not the effect merely of their condition of life. We know that among the Romans, about the Augustan age[4] especially, the condition of their slaves was much more deplorable than that of the blacks on the continent of America. The two sexes were confined in separate apartments, because to raise a child cost the master more than to buy one. Cato,[5] for a very restricted indulgence to his slaves in this particular, took from them a certain price. But in this country the slaves multiply as fast as the free inhabitants. Their situation and manners place the commerce between the two sexes almost without restraint. The same Cato, on a principle of economy, always sold his sick and superannuated slaves. He gives it as a standing precept to a master visiting his farm, to sell his old oxen, old waggons, old tools, old and diseased servants, and everything else become useless. ... The American slaves cannot enumerate this among the injuries and insults they receive. It was the common practice to expose in the island of Aesculapius, in the Tyber,[6] diseased slaves, whose cure was like to become tedious. The Emperor Claudius,[7] by an edict, gave freedom to such of them as should recover, and first declared, that if any person chose to kill rather than to expose them, it should be deemed homicide. The exposing them is a crime of which no instance has existed with us; and were it to be followed by death, it would be punished capitally. We are told of a certain Vedius Pollio, who, in the presence of Augustus, would have given a slave as food to his fish, for having broken a glass.[8] With the Romans, the regular method of taking the evidence of their slaves was under torture. Here it has been thought better never to resort to their evidence. When a master was murdered, all his slaves, in the same house, or within hearing, were condemned to death. Here punishment falls on the guilty only, and as precise proof is required

1 *The heroes ... that poem* The *Dunciad* (1728–43) is a mock-heroic epic poem written by English satirical poet Alexander Pope. Jefferson's comparison of Pope to Hercules is meant to allude to Pope's short and disfigured stature, caused by a number of childhood illnesses.

2 *Ignatius Sancho* British African author, composer, and actor born into slavery in 1729. His *Letters of the Late Ignatius Sancho, an African* were published posthumously in 1782, and included extensive commentary on political, domestic, and artistic life in eighteenth-century England, as well as on his early period of enslavement.

3 *Shandean* Allusion to Laurence Sterne's 1759–67 novel *The Life and Opinions of Tristram Shandy*, known for its imaginative use of language. Ignatius Sancho famously wrote to Sterne in 1766 to ask that he more strongly publicize his antislavery opinions.

4 *Augustan age* Period of the reign of Augustus, first emperor of the Roman Empire (r. 27 BCE–14 CE).

5 *Cato* Cato the Elder (234–149 BCE), Roman politician and historian. Below, Jefferson cites Cato's writings on slavery from *De Re Rusticâ* or *De Agri Cultura* (*On Agriculture*).

6 *expose* Leave to die; *Aesculapius, in the Tyber* Tiber Island, named after the river which flows through Rome, was then the site of a temple to Aesculapius, the god of medicine and healing.

7 *Emperor Claudius* Emperor of Rome from 41 to 54 CE.

8 *Vedius Pollio ... a glass* Pollio was notorious even during his lifetime for his luxurious tastes and excessive cruelty. It is indeed said that he regularly punished those he enslaved by feeding them to his eels.

against him as against a freeman. Yet notwithstanding these and other discouraging circumstances among the Romans, their slaves were often their rarest artists. They excelled too in science, insomuch as to be usually employed as tutors to their master's children. Epictetus, Terence, and Phaedrus[1] were slaves. But they were of the race of whites. It is not their condition then, but nature, which has produced the distinction. Whether further observation will or will not verify the conjecture that nature has been less bountiful to them in the endowments of the head, I believe that in those of the heart she will be found to have done them justice. That disposition to theft with which they have been branded, must be ascribed to their situation, and not to any depravity of the moral sense. The man in whose favour no laws of property exist, probably feels himself less bound to respect those made in favour of others. When arguing for ourselves, we lay it down as a fundamental that laws, to be just, must give a reciprocation of right—that, without this, they are mere arbitrary rules of conduct, founded in force, and not in conscience; and it is a problem which I give to the master to solve, whether the religious precepts against the violation of property were not framed for him as well as his slave? And whether the slave may not as justifiably take a little from one who has taken all from him, as he may slay one who would slay him? That a change in the relations in which a man is placed should change his ideas of moral right and wrong, is neither new, nor peculiar to the colour of the blacks. Homer tells us it was so 2600 years ago.

Ημισυ, γαζ τ᾽ ἀρετῆς ἀποαίννυιαι ευρύθπα Ζευς
Ανερς, ευτ᾽ ἀν μιν κατά δθλιον ἡμαζ ἑλησιν.
Od. 17. 323.

… Jove fix'd it certain, that whatever day
Makes man a slave, takes half his worth away.[2]

[1] *Epictetus* Greek-Roman Stoic philosopher (c. 55–135 CE); *Terence* Roman playwright (c. 190–c. 159 BCE); *Phaedrus* Roman fabulist from the first century CE.

[2] *Jove … worth away* Jefferson quotes from Book 17 of Alexander Pope's translation of *The Odyssey of Homer* (1715–20); *Jove* Roman name for the Greek god Zeus.

But the slaves of which Homer speaks were whites. Notwithstanding these considerations which must weaken their respect for the laws of property, we find among them numerous instances of the most rigid integrity, and as many as among their better instructed masters, of benevolence, gratitude, and unshaken fidelity. The opinion that they are inferior in the faculties of reason and imagination, must be hazarded with great diffidence. To justify a general conclusion requires many observations, even where the subject may be submitted to the anatomical knife, to optical glasses,[3] to analysis by fire, or by solvents. How much more then where it is a faculty, not a substance, we are examining; where it eludes the research of all the senses; where the conditions of its existence are various and variously combined; where the effects of those which are present or absent bid defiance to calculation; let me add too, as a circumstance of great tenderness, where our conclusion would degrade a whole race of men from the rank in the scale of beings which their Creator may perhaps have given them. To our reproach it must be said, that though for a century and a half we have had under our eyes the races of black and of red men, they have never yet been viewed by us as subjects of natural history. I advance it therefore as a suspicion only, that the blacks, whether originally a distinct race, or made distinct by time and circumstances, are inferior to the whites in the endowments both of body and mind. It is not against experience to suppose that different species of the same genus, or varieties of the same species, may posses different qualifications. Will not a lover of natural history then, one who views the gradations in all the races of animals with the eye of philosophy, excuse an effort to keep those in the department of man as distinct as nature has formed them? This unfortunate difference of colour, and perhaps of faculty, is a powerful obstacle to the emancipation of these people. Many of their advocates, while they wish to vindicate the liberty of human nature, are anxious also to preserve its dignity and beauty. Some of these, embarrassed by the question "What further is to be done with them?" join themselves in opposition with those who are actuated by sordid avarice only. Among the Romans emancipation required but one effort. The slave, when made free, might mix with, without staining, the blood of his

[3] *optical glasses* I.e., microscopes or magnifying glasses.

master. But with us a second is necessary, unknown to history. When freed, he is to be removed beyond the reach of mixture. ...

QUERY 18
THE *PARTICULAR* CUSTOMS AND MANNERS THAT MAY HAPPEN TO BE RECEIVED IN THAT STATE?

It is difficult to determine on the standard by which the manners of a nation may be tried, whether *catholic*,[1] or *particular*. It is more difficult for a native to bring to that standard the manners of his own nation, familiarized to him by habit. There must doubtless be an unhappy influence on the manners of our people produced by the existence of slavery among us. The whole commerce between master and slave is a perpetual exercise of the most boisterous passions, the most unremitting despotism on the one part, and degrading submissions on the other. Our children see this, and learn to imitate it; for man is an imitative animal. This quality is the germ of all education in him. From his cradle to his grave he is learning to do what he sees others do. If a parent could find no motive either in his philanthropy or his self-love, for restraining the intemperance of passion towards his slave, it should always be a sufficient one that his child is present. But generally it is not sufficient. The parent storms, the child looks on, catches the lineaments of wrath, puts on the same airs in the circle of smaller slaves, gives a loose to his worst of passions, and thus nursed, educated, and daily exercised in tyranny, cannot but be stamped by it with odious peculiarities. The man must be a prodigy who can retain his manners and morals undepraved by such circumstances. And with what execration[2] should the statesman be loaded who, permitting one half the citizens thus to trample on the rights of the other, transforms those into despots, and these into enemies, destroys the morals of the one part, and the *amor patriæ*[3] of the other. For if a slave can have a country in this world, it must be any other in preference to that in which he is born to live and labour for another, in which he must lock up the faculties of his nature, contribute as far as depends on his individual endeavours to the evanishment of the human race, or entail his own miserable condition on the endless generations proceeding from him. With the morals of the people, their industry also is destroyed. For in a warm climate, no man will labour for himself who can make another labour for him. This is so true, that of the proprietors of slaves a very small proportion indeed are even seen to labour. And can the liberties of a nation be thought secure when we have removed their only firm basis, a conviction in the minds of the people that these liberties are of the gift of God? That they are not to be violated but with his wrath? Indeed I tremble for my country when I reflect that God is just; that his justice cannot sleep forever; that considering numbers, nature and natural means only, a revolution of the wheel of fortune, an exchange of situation, is among possible events; that it may become probable by supernatural interference! The Almighty has no attribute which can take side with us in such a contest. But it is impossible to be temperate and to pursue this subject through the various considerations of policy, of morals, of history natural and civil. We must be contented to hope they will force their way into everyone's mind. I think a change already perceptible, since the origin of the present revolution. The spirit of the master is abating, that of the slave rising from the dust, his condition mollifying, the way I hope preparing, under the auspices of heaven, for a total emancipation, and that this is disposed, in the order of events, to be with the consent of the masters, rather than by their extirpation.
—1787

[1] *catholic* Universal.

[2] *execration* Curse.

[3] *amor patriæ* Latin: love of one's country.

IN CONTEXT

Responses to Jefferson's *Notes on the State of Virginia*

from review of "*Observations sur la Virginie*, par M.J.,[1] traduites de l'Anglais," *Mercure de France* (2 June 1787)

Following the private circulation of the first edition of Jefferson's *Notes on the State of Virginia* among his acquaintances in Paris—and the subsequent threat of pirated editions and unauthorized translations—Jefferson reluctantly assented to the publication in 1786 of a French edition, translated (and substantially reorganized) by French Enlightenment *philosophe* Abbé Morellet. Jefferson was reportedly unhappy with the resulting text, favoring a far more straightforward and literal approach than Morellet had taken. Nevertheless, the anonymous review reproduced below, from the prestigious Paris literary and cultural journal *Mercure de France*, shows the enthusiastic response *Observations sur la Virginie* elicited among French intellectuals.

... [T]here is a] certain class of men who have regarded those whom we call the *Philosophes* as incapable of treating with and of conducting public affairs. We might defend philosophy in two ways. First, by stating that there are no good administrators who became as such without a great deal of philosophy; second, that it is no less true that many good philosophers were once excellent administrators. ...

Those who are familiar with the author of the work that we announce here—who did not wish to be named at the beginning of his book—will undoubtedly add his example [of someone able to combine the talents of a philosopher with those of an administrator] to that of his illustrious compatriot;[2] and those readers will not be slow to recognize, in the *Observations sur la Virginie*, this happy reunion of knowledge that tends towards the same purpose—the happiness of men—by the two paths that lead there, the study of nature and that of man in society.

This work is one of few that we can call truly instructive. A great number of well-observed facts, and of useful truths competently discussed; a great simplicity; a species of eloquence that naturally attends the subject; a sense of the rights of man; the calm of conviction with the warmth that inspires the love of truth—these are the characteristics of the *Notes on Virginia*, *Observations sur la Virginie*, a title which we find very modest, having seen all of the interesting information which the author has scattered throughout. ...

The author reveals an interesting result[3] that may confirm the general opinion that climates change gradually as a result of the progress of culture and population. By the reports of elderly people, the warm [periods], as well as the cold [periods] are less intense in Virginia than they were at previous times, the snows less frequent, less abundant, and less long lasting, the rivers freeze less frequently: a truth soft and flattering to the man who sees himself as sharing with nature the domain of the earth, and who changes and renews its entire surface in order to beautify his home. ...

[1] *M.J.* I.e., Monsieur J.; Jefferson wished to remain unnamed on the title page of the French translation, though his authorship was widely known among the intellectual community.

[2] *his illustrious compatriot* The reviewer here refers to Benjamin Franklin, who is discussed in a previous paragraph; Franklin had preceded Jefferson as United States Minister to France, serving from 1779 to 1785.

[3] *an interesting result* I.e., of his meteorological studies. Starting in the mid-1770s, Jefferson kept a meticulous meteorological diary, and also sought to collect climate data for previous decades through interviews with a number of older Virginians. These observations are recorded in Query 7, "Climate." Jefferson there suggests (though without terms as strong as those of this reviewer) that the gradual warming of the Virginian climate has been beneficial to the state's inhabitants, especially to its farmers.

We see here a plan for gradually granting freedom to the blacks, the author finding, with reason, serious inconveniences and great difficulties in enfranchising them all at once in the midst of the European race, who are lesser in number, and whose form and color would rapidly be altered by the intermixture. He proposes to raise black children at the public expense, girls up to the age of eighteen, and males up to the age of twenty-one; to give them land in the interior parts of the country, and means of cultivating it; to declare them free and independent; and to protect them until they have gained sufficient ability to support themselves.

We have fought too long against the enslavement of the Negroes—this horrible practice, the shame of humanity—without having provided the means to end it. We love to see sentiment and love of the good as clear and as precise in their measurements here as cold reason.

We must praise the author all the more for his zeal for the enfranchising of the blacks, for, unlike others who have pleaded the cause of this unhappy race, he truly believes them to be inferior to the whites. The reasons behind his opinion are clear. We may therein recognize the distinction of the philosopher who is wise as well as human, who can disentangle the good that is possible from that which is not, and who can recognize the limits of such truths as are incessantly repeated by declaimers.

… [In] discussing the population of the United States and the means by which it might be increased, the author states that the government should not endeavor to hasten its growth through the forced importation of foreigners; this precept is very wise, but I am not quite convinced by the reasons he gives, namely *the belief that foreigners will bring over from Europe their vices, their prejudices, and their habits of servility*. I believe too strongly in the influence of good laws and good government over the spirit and character of men to fear that Europeans would retain in America the errors and the vices that they have brought from our continent. No matter how many Europeans might go to this new country, they will be forced to disperse and to mingle with long-time residents, and they will necessarily become assimilated with the people amongst whom they have come to reside. The spirit of superstition and of servitude will not germinate or take root in a land of light and liberty. The author supports his fears with a hypothetical example in which several million Americans are thrown all at once into a European state, with various inconveniences arising from this emigration; aside from the fact that several million people would never be thrown into a country all at once, there is another significant difference between the two situations. Americans who have moved to Europe would have a hard time submitting to so many oppressive and vicious laws—the yoke of which only habituation could support—and would thus disturb the peace, or, if you wish, the system of public bondage. But the coarsest European, who would not himself understand the value of equality or liberty, will, having disembarked in Philadelphia or Boston, quickly become familiar with the mores and laws of the country he has chosen as an asylum, and will see therein a more powerful means of attaining happiness.

from James McCune Smith, "On the Fourteenth Query of Thomas Jefferson's *Notes on Virginia*," *The Anglo-African Magazine* (August 1859)

James McCune Smith (1813–65) was a physician, writer, and public intellectual; he was also the first African American to receive a medical degree, having studied at the University of Glasgow after being rejected from a number of American universities. Born into slavery in New York City, he was among the last enslaved people to be freed by the state's gradual abolition act, whose final stage came to pass in 1827. Smith used his background in medicine as a position from which to challenge prevailing theories about the inferiority of African Americans, many of which were based in phrenology and other dubious outlets for scientific racism. It is from this standpoint that much of the following discussion of Jefferson's "Query 14" is written; in some ways, the article below is a testament to the continuing influence of Jefferson's writings—including his writings on race and slavery—on American society and culture in the nineteenth century.

"What further is to be done with them?"[1] enquired Thomas Jefferson in 1787. "What, then, *is* to be done?"[2] is demanded of Dr. Dewey fifty-seven years afterwards. These questions relate to the colored population of these United States. "What further is to be done with them?" "What is to be done with them?" Can they be elevated to the same rank with the white citizens of this great Republic? This question involves another: Is the standard occupied by the whites really elevated above that occupied by the black population? What is the standard of mind—of excellence? Is it ingenuity in constructing machinery? Is it in morals? Is it in physical courage? Or is it to be measured by the tone of a "shop-keeping gentility"? The standard of excellence is not fixed. The question of elevation must therefore be an undeterminate question. It is hard to say who is more elevated—the master, learned, acute, ingenious, the constructor of splendid machinery, the framer of laws, the successful financier, the acute philosopher—the one master of all this, with a slave-whip in his hand—or, the poor Christian slave, his breast heaving, his eyes raining tears, his flesh rooted up, quivering beneath the lash, whilst he prays God to soften the heart of the accomplished torturer—who is the more elevated?

It is better to lay aside, then, this word "*elevation*," because it is uncertain in its meaning. Let us put the same question in another form: Can the black and the white live together in harmony under American institutions, each contributing to the peace and prosperity of the country, and to the development of the problem of self-government involved in American institutions? ...

Mr. Jefferson contends that there are physical and mental distinctions between the negro and the white man—distinctions which must ever prevent them from an equal and harmonious participation in the blessings of democratic freedom.

This constitutes the main proposition in his fourteenth query. In support of this proposition he produces certain views, speculations, and reasonings, which many writers since his day, including De Tocqueville[3] and Dr. Dewey, have admitted without questioning, and have urged as quite unanswerable. In fact, the only stain upon the literary merit of De Tocqueville's great work consists in this: he gives Mr. Jefferson's views as if they were De Tocqueville's views, and gives them in Mr. Jefferson's own words—thus, not only committing unpardonable plagiarism, but also adding the apparently independent and calm opinion of a foreign observer in favor of the perpetuation of American Slavery. ...

On the 268th page of his Notes on Virginia, Mr. Jefferson asks: "Why not retain and incorporate the blacks into the State," etc. He answers, on the next page, "Deep-rooted prejudices entertained by the whites; ten thousand recollections by the blacks of the injuries they have sustained; new provocations; the real distinctions which nature has made; and many other circumstances, will divide us into parties, and produce convulsions which will probably never end but in the extermination of the one or the other race. To these objections, which are political, may be added others which are physical and moral," etc.

Mr. Jefferson then states the physical and mental differences which exist, and which, in his opinion, will forever prevent the incorporation of the blacks into the State. His arrangement of these views is so mixed and confused that we must depart from it, and consider, *first*, the physical, *secondly*, the mental differences between the races.

First, in regard to the physical differences between the races. ...

[1] [Smith's note] Jefferson's Notes, Fourteenth Query, p. 202. Edit. 1801. Philad.

[2] [Smith's note] A Discourse on Slavery and the Annexation of Texas, by Orville Dewey. New York: C.S. Francis. 1844. [Orville Dewey (1794–1882) was a lecturer and Unitarian minister. In the document referred to here, Dewey strongly condemns the evils of slavery, but simultaneously defends the notion that Africans are an inferior race who require white European guidance to become valuable members of American society. In arguing this latter point, Dewey refers the reader to the "evidence" of African inferiority provided in Jefferson's fourteenth query.]

[3] *De Tocqueville* French historian and political philosopher Alexis de Tocqueville, whose 1831 tour of the United States with his colleague Gustave de Beaumont led to the publication of *Democracy in America* (1835, 1840), his famous and influential study of American society, politics, and culture. De Tocqueville was opposed to slavery, but modern scholars disagree about whether or not he genuinely supported the idea of racial equality.

The physical differences which are urged as existing between whites and blacks are, *first*, those which relate to the bones of the body; *secondly*, those which relate to the muscles; *thirdly*, those which relate to the texture of the hair; and *fourthly*, the color of the skin. …

THE COLOR OF THEIR SKIN

is, in the opinion of Thomas Jefferson and his followers, another objection to incorporating the blacks into the American Republic. This may be called the "physical distinction" upon which the question is made to rest by the opponents of the black man in this Republic.

Mr. Jefferson asks, with an air of triumph, "Is this difference of no importance? Is it not the foundation of a greater or less share of beauty in the two races? Are not the fine mixtures of red and white, the expressions of every passion by greater or less suffusions of color in the one, preferable to that eternal monotony which reigns in the countenances, that immovable veil of black which covers all the emotions of the other race?" We regret that a sense of propriety prohibits us from finishing this quotation, for the argument against the part which must be omitted is full and conclusive.[1] …

… Mr. Jefferson himself, if we may credit the statement of Dr. Bacon,[2] in his account of the colored Virginians who are now living in Liberia—Mr. Jefferson himself has left living testimony against his own expressions above quoted—testimony whose close resemblances to himself, and partial inheritance of his talents, should forever close the mouths of men who refer to Jefferson's Notes on Virginia as proof of the impossibility of incorporating the colored race into the State. "That testimony," says Dr. Bacon, "is a colored grand-daughter of Thomas Jefferson."[3] Those who are anxious to examine this matter will find the statements alluded to in the *Wanderings on the Seas and Shores of Africa*, by Dr. F.R. Bacon. …

We have now arrived at a resting place in this tedious array of facts. We have carefully examined into the principal physical differences, which are alleged to constitute a bar in the way of incorporating the black men into the American State.

Do these differences in reality constitute such a bar? "Words," said Mirabeau, "are things."[4] The history of words would be one of the most interesting of all histories. You may have observed that we use the word black, as distinguishing the class whom we have under consideration. This word "black," and the other word "negro," were the common, the usual, term used for this class at the time Mr. Jefferson wrote. That is more than fifty years ago. The newspapers, sure indices[5] of public opinion, now call this same class *"colored people."* The class is the same, the name is changed; they are no longer blacks, bordering on beastiality; they are "colored," and they are a "people." I will not stop to enquire whether the word "colored" be used as a euphony for black, nor whether it marks the fact of an already perceptible change in the hue of the skin of this class. It answers our argument if it shows, and it does show, a lessening of the

[1] *We regret … conclusive* Smith refers here to Jefferson's assertion that African Americans show a natural sexual "preference" for white people, "as uniformly as is the preference of the Oranootan [Orangutan] for the black women over those of his own species. The circumstance of superior beauty is thought worthy attention in the propagation of our horses, dogs, and other domestic animals; why not in that of man?"

[2] *Dr. Bacon* David Francis Bacon (1813–65), member of the American Colonization Society. Bacon spent several months working as a physician in Liberia, the African-American colony established by the ACS; his account was published in 1843.

[3] *a colored … Jefferson* That Jefferson had a long-term sexual relationship with Sally Hemings, a woman he enslaved, was disputed for almost two hundred years, beginning with rumors in the early 1800s. In 1998, however, the results of DNA tests put the matter beyond reasonable doubt. Jefferson likely fathered all six of Hemings's children, though evidence for the idea that some descendants may have emigrated to Liberia is scant.

[4] *Words … things* Honoré Gabriel Riqueti, comte de Mirabeau (1749–91), was a leader of the French Revolution. The statement "words are things" was used by Lord Byron in his epic poem *Don Juan* (1819) and attributed by him to Mirabeau, but the attribution appears to be an error.

[5] *indices* Indicators.

distance—a step towards harmony and reciprocal kindness between man and his fellow man—between the black and the white man in this Republic.

The question is already partly answered; the physical differences do not constitute a permanent bar, because the public voice has already softened the terms which denote those differences.

Then there is that other word, "people." What does it mean? Tell us, poor, cringing sycophant, thou who are fearful that the two races can only live together as master and slave, what does this word "people" mean? In Thomas Jefferson's time, "we, the people," meant men endowed with certain inalienable rights; men exercising those rights, the noblest of which was the great, the God-like right of governing themselves! There was then, in that word "people," a profound, a sublime import. It meant men who were part and parcel of—were the great sires and the great inheritors of this "Fair broad Empire, State with State,"[1] which their prowess in war had snatched from tyrannical hands—which their wisdom in peace had erected into a magnificent fabric, capable of holding within its ample dome the majestic presence of Liberty! …

The question asked by Mr. Jefferson in his fourteenth query would never have been propounded had he been acquainted with the philosophy of human progress. Instead of asking, "How shall we get rid of them?"—instead of affirming that they could never be safely incorporated in the State—had he possessed the insight or sagacity for which he is so celebrated, he would have welcomed their presence as one of the positive elements of natural progress. Why this is so we have endeavored to show in the first number of this magazine, in the article on "Civilization," etc. That essay, written in 1844, was slightly amended when published in 1859. Its views are mainly the same with those of Mr. Buckle,[2] in his work on "Civilization in England," and receive support from the higher authority of Mr. Mill,[3] in his remarkable work on "Liberty," published recently in London. Mr. Mill says, (p. 129): "The modern *regime* of public opinion is, in an unorganized form, what the Chinese educational and political systems are in an organized; and unless individuality shall be able successfully to assert itself against this yoke, Europe, notwithstanding its noble antecedents and its professed Christianity, will tend to become another China. What is it that has hitherto preserved Europe from this lot? What has made the European family of nations an improving instead of a stationary portion of mankind? Not any superior excellence in them, which, when it exists, exists as an effect, not as a cause; but their remarkable diversity of character and culture. Individuals, classes, and nations have been extremely unlike one another; they have struck out a great variety of paths, each leading to something valuable, and although at every period those who traveled in different paths have been intolerant of one another, each has in time endured to receive the good which the others have offered." …

Whilst Jefferson [and] Dewey … raise their impotent voices to exclude the blacks from the United States, Henry Ward Beecher[4] exclaims from his pulpit, with higher instincts and keener insight, "What! drive out the colored people from among us? I would as soon, with these two hands, undertake to uproot and cast out every shrub, bush, and tree that grows between this and the Rocky Mountains!"

[1] *Fair broad … with State* See "Washington" (1848) by American poet William Cullen Bryant.

[2] *Mr. Buckle* English historian Henry Thomas Buckle (1821–62).

[3] *Mr. Mill* John Stuart Mill (1806–73), English philosopher and politician. *On Liberty* is among his most famous and influential works.

[4] *Henry Ward Beecher* Clergyman and abolitionist (1813–87).

THE FEDERALIST

During and immediately after the American Revolution (1776–83), the thirteen former colonies which had become the first thirteen states of the United States had been governed by the Articles of Confederation, which was presented to Congress in 1776 and ratified in 1781. In the wake of the Revolutionary War, however, the political context shifted, and the Articles were not proving sufficient to meet new challenges. Political factions and protest movements began to cause civil unrest, and in 1787 twelve states sent delegates to Philadelphia to revise the Articles. The delegates decided that the revisions needed were so extensive that it would be better to draft a new Constitution. Once the Constitution was written, each state was to hold a convention and either ratify or reject it, setting up one of the stormiest political debates in American history. On one side were the Federalists—who urged ratification—and on the other were the Anti-Federalists, who worried that the Constitution would impinge on individual freedom. It was out of this debate that the eighty-five essays that comprise *The Federalist* were born.

The Federalist essays were published in the pages of several New York newspapers from 27 October 1787 to 28 May 1788, in an effort to sway the delegates of New York state to support ratification. They were originally published under the pen name "Publius" in honor of Roman consul Publius Valerius Publicola (d. 503 BCE), whose surname means "friend of the people." They were actually written by three men: Alexander Hamilton (1757–1804), James Madison (1751–1836), and John Jay (1745–1829). Each of these authors was a prominent lawmaker, and each made significant contributions to the United States in its infancy: Hamilton was the first Secretary of the Treasury, Madison the fourth President of the United States, and Jay the first Chief Justice of the Supreme Court.

In 1787 prominent Anti-Federalists, using the pen names "Cato," "Centinel," and "Brutus," began publishing letters and essays in newspapers, arguing against the proposed Constitution. In October 1787, Cato wrote that the Constitution's "principles, and the exercise of them will be dangerous to your liberty and happiness"; earlier in the same month, Centinel claimed that the Constitution was "the most daring attempt to establish a despotic aristocracy among freemen, that the world has ever witnessed." Hamilton, Madison, and Jay responded by writing in support of the Constitution, detailing how checks and balances were built in to divide power and protect the rights of the states and the citizens. In "The Federalist No. 1," Hamilton wrote that the series of essays would "endeavour to give a satisfactory answer to all the objections which shall have made their appearance, that may seem to have any claim to your attention." And *The Federalist* does cover a great deal of ground, including the military, international relations, economic issues, taxation, and executive power. Its central argument, however, is that a strong federal union would be far more beneficial for the growing nation, economically and politically, than a looser collection of independent states. The authors warn against the oppressive powers of sectarianism and advocate a strong constitutional union to protect individuals.

Although the authorship of a few essays is still debated, it is generally accepted that, of the 85 essays, Hamilton wrote 51, Madison 29, and Jay 5. Madison later explained that "though carried on in concert, the writers are not mutually answerable for all the ideas of each other, there being seldom time for even a perusal of the pieces by any but the writer before they were wanted at the press." The pace of writing was indeed swift—all 85 of the papers were written within six months, and sometimes three or four articles would appear within a single week. New York ratified the Constitution on 26 July 1788, and the main object of *The Federalist* was achieved. Government under the new constitution was scheduled to begin on 4 March 1789.

The Anti-Federalists, however, also achieved some of their aims, most notably the addition of a Bill of Rights, designed to secure individual freedoms and to prevent a strong central government from devolving into tyranny. James Madison wrote twelve amendments for the Constitution that would address the Anti-Federalist concerns and limit the power of government. Madison argued that these

should be incorporated into the Constitution, but instead they were adopted as codicils. Ten of the amendments were ratified in 1790, forming the American Bill of Rights.

As works of persuasive writing, *The Federalist* papers have been the subject of much analysis in regard to their rhetorical style, and in regard to the perceived similarities and differences between the styles of their three authors. Madison's contributions have been seen by many as the most carefully intellectual of the three. Although the *Papers* were intended as persuasive commentary on a pertinent contemporary matter, they were immediately recognized for their wider significance as outstanding contributions to Western political thought. George Washington wrote to Hamilton that he believed the essays would "merit the notice of posterity" even after the "transient circumstances" of their conception were over; and in a letter to Madison, Thomas Jefferson wrote that *The Federalist* comprised "the best commentary on the principles of government which ever was written." Today *The Federalist* is acknowledged as vitally important for interpreting the provisions of the American constitution; the essays continue to be cited as touchstones by the Supreme Court of the United States in rendering decisions, and by leading politicians and political writers in discussing current political issues.

NOTE ON THE TEXTS: The texts presented here are based on the original newspaper printings: for *The Federalist* No. 1, this was the version printed in *The Independent Journal* on 27 October 1787; for *The Federalist* No. 10, this was the version printed in *The Daily Advertiser* on 22 November 1787. Jacob Cooke's 1961 edition, *The Federalist*, was also consulted.

⌘ ⌘ ⌘

from *The Federalist*

NO. 1 [ALEXANDER HAMILTON]

October 27, 1787

To the People of the State of New York.

AFTER an unequivocal experience of the inefficiency of the subsisting[1] Federal Government, you are called upon to deliberate on a new Constitution for the United States of America. The subject speaks its own importance; comprehending in its consequences, nothing less than the existence of the UNION, the safety and welfare of the parts of which it is composed, the fate of an empire, in many respects, the most interesting in the world. It has been frequently remarked, that it seems to have been reserved to the people of this country, by their conduct and example, to decide the important question, whether societies of men are really capable or not of establishing good government from reflection and choice, or whether they are forever destined to depend, for their political constitutions, on accident and force. If there be any truth in the remark, the crisis at which we are arrived may with propriety be regarded as the era in which that decision is to be made; and a wrong election[2] of the part we shall act, may, in this view, deserve to be considered as the general misfortune of mankind.

This idea will add the inducements of philanthropy to those of patriotism to heighten the solicitude which all considerate and good men must feel for the event. Happy will it be if our choice should be directed by a judicious estimate of our true interests, unperplexed and unbiased by considerations not connected with the public good. But this is a thing more ardently to be wished, than seriously to be expected. The plan offered to our deliberations affects too many particular interests, innovates upon too many local institutions, not to involve in its discussion a variety of objects foreign to its merits, and of views, passions and prejudices little favourable to the discovery of truth.

1 *subsisting* Existing, current.

2 *election* Choice.

Among the most formidable of the obstacles which the new Constitution will have to encounter may readily be distinguished the obvious interest of a certain class of men in every State to resist all changes which may hazard a diminution of the power, emolument[1] and consequence of the offices they hold under the State-establishments—and the perverted[2] ambition of another class of men, who will either hope to aggrandize themselves by the confusions of their country, or will flatter themselves with fairer prospects of elevation from the subdivision of the empire into several partial confederacies, than from its union under one government.

It is not, however, my design to dwell upon observations of this nature. I am well aware that it would be disingenuous to resolve indiscriminately the opposition of any set of men (merely because their situations might subject them to suspicion) into interested or ambitious views. Candour will oblige us to admit that even such men may be actuated by upright intentions; and it cannot be doubted that much of the opposition which has made its appearance, or may hereafter make its appearance, will spring from sources, blameless at least, if not respectable, the honest errors of minds led astray by preconceived jealousies and fears. So numerous indeed and so powerful are the causes, which serve to give a false bias to the judgment, that we, upon many occasions, see wise and good men on the wrong as well as on the right side of questions, of the first magnitude to society. This circumstance, if duly attended to, would furnish a lesson of moderation to those, who are ever so much persuaded of their being in the right, in any controversy. And a further reason for caution, in this respect, might be drawn from the reflection, that we are not always sure, that those who advocate the truth are influenced by purer principles than their antagonists. Ambition, avarice, personal animosity, party opposition, and many other motives not more laudable than these, are apt to operate as well upon those who support as upon those who oppose the right side of a question. Were there not even these inducements to moderation, nothing could be more ill-judged than that intolerant spirit which has, at all times, characterised political parties. For, in politics as in religion, it is equally absurd to aim at making proselytes by fire and sword. Heresies in either can rarely be cured by persecution.

And yet however just these sentiments will be allowed to be, we have already sufficient indications, that it will happen in this as in all former cases of great national discussion. A torrent of angry and malignant passions will be let loose. To judge from the conduct of the opposite parties, we shall be led to conclude, that they will mutually hope to evince the justness of their opinions, and to increase the number of their converts by the loudness of their declamations, and by the bitterness of their invectives. An enlightened zeal for the energy and efficiency of government will be stigmatized, as the offspring of a temper fond of despotic power and hostile to the principles of liberty. An overscrupulous jealousy[3] of danger to the rights of the people, which is more commonly the fault of the head than of the heart, will be represented as mere pretence and artifice; the bait for popularity at the expense of public good. It will be forgotten, on the one hand, that jealousy is the usual concomitant of violent love, and that the noble enthusiasm of liberty is too apt to be infected with a spirit of narrow and illiberal distrust. On the other hand, it will be equally forgotten, that the vigour of government is essential to the security of liberty; that, in the contemplation of a sound and well-informed judgment, their interest can never be separated; and that a dangerous ambition more often lurks behind the specious mask of zeal for the rights of the people, than under the forbidding appearance of zeal for the firmness and efficiency of government. History will teach us, that the former has been found a much more certain road to the introduction of despotism, than the latter, and that of those men who have overturned the liberties of republics the greatest number have begun their career, by paying an obsequious court to the people,[4] commencing Demagogues and ending Tyrants.

In the course of the preceding observations I have had an eye, my Fellow Citizens, to putting you upon your guard against all attempts, from whatever quarter, to influence your decision in a matter of the utmost

[1] *emolument* Profit.

[2] *perverted* Misguided.

[3] *jealousy* Fear or suspicion.

[4] *paying an obsequious ... people* I.e., being overly eager to gratify popular demands.

moment to your welfare by any impressions other than those which may result from the evidence of truth. You will, no doubt, at the same time, have collected from the general scope of them that they proceed from a source not unfriendly to the new Constitution. Yes, my Countrymen, I own to you, that, after having given it an attentive consideration, I am clearly of opinion, it is your interest to adopt it. I am convinced, that this is the safest course for your liberty, your dignity, and your happiness. I effect not reserves,[1] which I do not feel. I will not amuse you with an appearance of deliberation, when I have decided. I frankly acknowledge to you my convictions, and I will freely lay before you the reasons on which they are founded. The consciousness of good intentions disdains ambiguity. I shall not however multiply professions on this head. My motives must remain in the depository of my own breast: my arguments will be open to all, and may be judged of by all. They shall at least be offered in a spirit, which will not disgrace the cause of truth.

I propose in a series of papers to discuss the following interesting particulars—*The utility of the* UNION *to your political prosperity*—*The insufficiency of the present Confederation to preserve that Union*—*The necessity of a government at least equally energetic with the one proposed to the attainment of this object*—*The conformity of the proposed constitution to the true principles of republican government*—*Its analogy to your own state constitution*—and lastly, *The additional security, which its adoption will afford to the preservation of that species of government, to liberty and to property.*

In the progress of this discussion I shall endeavour to give a satisfactory answer to all the objections which shall have made their appearance that may seem to have any claim to your attention.

It may perhaps be thought superfluous to offer arguments to prove the utility of the UNION, a point, no doubt, deeply engraved on the hearts of the great body of the people in every state, and one, which it may be imagined has no adversaries. But the fact is, that we already hear it whispered in the private circles of those who oppose the new constitution, that the Thirteen States are of too great extent for any general system, and that we must of necessity resort to separate confederacies of distinct portions of the whole.[2] This doctrine will, in all probability, be gradually propagated, till it has votaries enough to countenance an open avowal of it. For nothing can be more evident, to those who are able to take an enlarged view of the subject, than the alternative of an adoption of the new Constitution, or a dismemberment of the Union. It will therefore be of use to begin by examining the advantages of that Union, the certain evils and the probable dangers, to which every State will be exposed from its dissolution. This shall accordingly constitute the subject of my next address.

PUBLIUS.

No. 10 [JAMES MADISON]

November 22, 1787

To the People of the State of New York.

AMONG the numerous advantages promised by a well-constructed Union, none deserves to be more accurately developed[3] than its tendency to break and control the violence of faction.[4] The friend of popular[5] governments, never finds himself so much alarmed for their character and fate, as when he contemplates their propensity to this dangerous vice. He will not fail therefore to set a due value on any plan which, without violating the principles to which he is attached, provides a proper cure for it. The instability, injustice and confusion introduced into the public councils, have in truth been the mortal diseases under which popular governments have everywhere perished; as they continue to be the favorite and fruitful topics from which the adversaries to liberty derive their most specious declamations.[6] The valuable improvements made by the American constitutions on the popular models, both ancient and modern, cannot certainly

[1] *effect not reserves* Will not pretend to have reservations.

[2] [Hamilton's note] The same idea, tracing the arguments to their consequences, is held out in several of the late publications against the New Constitution. (Publius)

[3] *developed* Discussed, explained.

[4] *faction* Conflicting interest groups or political parties.

[5] *popular* I.e., democratic.

[6] *specious* Attractive, but false; *declamations* Public rhetoric.

be too much admired; but it would be an unwarrantable partiality, to contend that they have as effectually obviated[1] the danger on this side as was wished and expected. Complaints are everywhere heard from our most considerate and virtuous citizens, equally the friends of public and private faith, and of public and personal liberty; that our governments are too unstable; that the public good is disregarded in the conflicts of rival parties; and that measures are too often decided, not according to the rules of justice, and the rights of the minor party; but by the superior force of an interested[2] and overbearing majority. However anxiously we may wish that these complaints had no foundation, the evidence of known facts will not permit us to deny that they are in some degree true. It will be found indeed, on a candid review of our situation, that some of the distresses under which we labor, have been erroneously charged on the operation of our governments; but it will be found, at the same time, that other causes will not alone account for many of our heaviest misfortunes; and particularly, for that prevailing and increasing distrust of public engagements, and alarm for private rights, which are echoed from one end of the continent to the other. These must be chiefly, if not wholly, effects of the unsteadiness and injustice, with which a factious spirit has tainted our public administrations.

By a faction I understand a number of citizens, whether amounting to a majority or minority of the whole, who are united and actuated by some common impulse of passion, or of interest, adverse to the rights of other citizens, or to the permanent and aggregate interests of the community.

There are two methods of curing the mischiefs of faction: the one, by removing its causes; the other, by controlling its effects.

There are again two methods of removing the causes of faction: the one by destroying the liberty which is essential to its existence; the other, by giving to every citizen the same opinions, the same passions, and the same interests.

It could never be more truly said than of the first remedy, that it is worse than the disease. Liberty is to faction, what air is to fire, an aliment[3] without which it instantly expires. But it could not be a less folly to abolish liberty, which is essential to political life, because it nourishes faction, than it would be to wish the annihilation of air, which is essential to animal life, because it imparts to fire its destructive agency. The second expedient is as impracticable, as the first would be unwise. As long as the reason of man continues fallible, and he is at liberty to exercise it, different opinions will be formed. As long as the connection subsists between his reason and his self-love, his opinions and his passions will have a reciprocal influence on each other; and the former will be objects to which the latter will attach themselves. The diversity in the faculties of men from which the rights of property originate, is not less an insuperable obstacle to a uniformity of interests. The protection of these faculties is the first object of government. From the protection of different and unequal faculties of acquiring property, the possession of different degrees and kinds of property immediately results: and from the influence of these on the sentiments and views of the respective proprietors, ensues a division of the society into different interests and parties.

The latent causes of faction are thus sown in the nature of man; and we see them everywhere brought into different degrees of activity, according to the different circumstances of civil society. A zeal for different opinions concerning religion, concerning government and many other points, as well of speculation as of practice; an attachment to different leaders ambitiously contending for pre-eminence and power; or to persons of other descriptions whose fortunes have been interesting to the human passions, have in turn divided mankind into parties, inflamed them with mutual animosity, and rendered them much more disposed to vex and oppress each other, than to cooperate for their common good. So strong is this propensity of mankind to fall into mutual animosities, that where no substantial occasion presents itself, the most frivolous and fanciful distinctions have been sufficient to kindle their unfriendly passions, and excite their most violent conflicts. But the most common and durable source of factions, has been the various and unequal distribution of property. Those who hold, and those who are without property, have ever formed distinct interests

[1] *obviated* Avoided.

[2] *interested* Concerned with private advantage.

[3] *aliment* Nourishment.

in society. Those who are creditors, and those who are debtors, fall under a like discrimination. A landed[1] interest, a manufacturing interest, a mercantile interest, a monied interest, with many lesser interests, grow up of necessity in civilized nations, and divide them into different classes, actuated by different sentiments and views. The regulation of these various and interfering interests forms the principal task of modern legislation, and involves the spirit of party and faction in the necessary and ordinary operations of government.

No man is allowed to be a judge in his own cause; because his interest would certainly bias his judgment, and, not improbably, corrupt his integrity. With equal, nay with greater reason, a body of men, are unfit to be both judges and parties, at the same time; yet, what are many of the most important acts of legislation, but so many judicial determinations, not indeed concerning the rights of single persons, but concerning the rights of large bodies of citizens; and what are the different classes of legislators, but advocates and parties to the causes which they determine? Is a law proposed concerning private debts? It is a question to which the creditors are parties on one side, and the debtors on the other. Justice ought to hold the balance between them. Yet the parties are and must be themselves the judges; and the most numerous party, or, in other words, the most powerful faction must be expected to prevail. Shall domestic manufactures be encouraged, and in what degree, by restrictions on foreign manufactures? are questions which would be differently decided by the landed and the manufacturing classes; and probably by neither, with a sole regard to justice and the public good. The apportionment of taxes on the various descriptions of property, is an act which seems to require the most exact impartiality; yet, there is perhaps no legislative act in which greater opportunity and temptation are given to a predominant party, to trample on the rules of justice. Every shilling[2] with which they overburden the inferior number, is a shilling saved to their own pockets.

It is in vain to say, that enlightened statesmen will be able to adjust these clashing interests, and render them all subservient to the public good. Enlightened statesmen will not always be at the helm: nor, in many cases, can such an adjustment be made at all, without taking into view indirect and remote considerations, which will rarely prevail over the immediate interest which one party may find in disregarding the rights of another, or the good of the whole.

The inference to which we are brought, is, that the *causes* of faction cannot be removed; and that relief is only to be sought in the means of controlling its *effects*.

If a faction consists of less than a majority, relief is supplied by the republican principle, which enables the majority to defeat its sinister views by regular vote. It may clog the administration, it may convulse the society; but it will be unable to execute and mask its violence under the forms of the Constitution. When a majority is included in a faction, the form of popular government on the other hand enables it to sacrifice to its ruling passion or interest, both the public good and the rights of other citizens. To secure the public good, and private rights, against the danger of such a faction, and at the same time to preserve the spirit and the form of popular government, is then the great object to which our enquiries are directed. Let me add that it is the great desideratum,[3] by which alone this form of government can be rescued from the opprobrium[4] under which it has so long labored, and be recommended to the esteem and adoption of mankind.

By what means is this object attainable? Evidently by one of two only. Either the existence of the same passion or interest in a majority at the same time, must be prevented; or the majority, having such co-existent passion or interest, must be rendered, by their number and local situation, unable to concert and carry into effect schemes of oppression. If the impulse and the opportunity be suffered[5] to coincide, we well know that neither moral nor religious motives can be relied on as an adequate control. They are not found to be such on the injustice and violence of individuals, and lose their efficacy in proportion to the number combined together; that is, in proportion as their efficacy becomes needful.

From this view of the subject, it may be concluded, that a pure democracy,[6] by which I mean, a society,

[1] *landed* Relating to the class of people who own land.

[2] *shilling* Coin worth twelve pennies.

[3] *desideratum* Latin: thing which is desired.

[4] *opprobrium* Reproach.

[5] *suffered* Permitted.

[6] *pure democracy* Also known as direct democracy.

consisting of a small number of citizens, who assemble and administer the government in person, can admit of no cure for the mischiefs of faction. A common passion or interest will, in almost every case, be felt by a majority of the whole; a communication and concert[1] results from the form of government itself; and there is nothing to check the inducements to sacrifice the weaker party, or an obnoxious[2] individual. Hence it is, that such democracies have ever been spectacles of turbulence and contention; have ever been found incompatible with personal security, or the rights of property; and have in general been as short in their lives, as they have been violent in their deaths. Theoretic politicians, who have patronized[3] this species of government, have erroneously supposed, that by reducing mankind to a perfect equality in their political rights, they would, at the same time, be perfectly equalized and assimilated in their possessions, their opinions, and their passions.

A republic, by which I mean a government in which the scheme of representation takes place, opens a different prospect, and promises the cure for which we are seeking. Let us examine the points in which it varies from pure democracy, and we shall comprehend both the nature of the cure, and the efficacy which it must derive from the Union.

The two great points of difference between a democracy and a republic are, first, the delegation of the government, in the latter, to a small number of citizens elected by the rest: secondly, the greater number of citizens, and greater sphere of country, over which the latter may be extended.

The effect of the first difference is, on the one hand to refine and enlarge the public views, by passing them through the medium of a chosen body of citizens, whose wisdom may best discern the true interest of their country, and whose patriotism and love of justice, will be least likely to sacrifice it to temporary or partial considerations. Under such a regulation, it may well happen that the public voice pronounced by the representatives of the people, will be more consonant to the public good, than if pronounced by the people themselves convened for the purpose. On the other hand, the effect may be inverted. Men of factious tempers, of local prejudices, or of sinister designs, may by intrigue, by corruption or by other means, first obtain the suffrages,[4] and then betray the interests of the people. The question resulting is, whether small or extensive republics are most favorable to the election of proper guardians of the public weal:[5] and it is clearly decided in favor of the latter by two obvious considerations.

In the first place it is to be remarked that however small the republic may be, the representatives must be raised to a certain number, in order to guard against the cabals[6] of a few; and that however large it may be, they must be limited to a certain number, in order to guard against the confusion of a multitude. Hence the number of representatives in the two cases, not being in proportion to that of the constituents, and being proportionally greatest in the small republic, it follows, that if the proportion of fit characters, be not less, in the large than in the small republic, the former will present a greater option, and consequently a greater probability of a fit choice.

In the next place, as each representative will be chosen by a greater number of citizens in the large than in the small republic, it will be more difficult for unworthy candidates to practice with success the vicious arts, by which elections are too often carried; and the suffrages of the people being more free, will be more likely to center on men who possess the most attractive merit, and the most diffusive[7] and established characters.

It must be confessed, that in this, as in most other cases, there is a mean, on both sides of which inconveniencies will be found to lie. By enlarging too much the number of electors, you render the representative too little acquainted with all their local circumstances and lesser interests; as by reducing it too much, you render him unduly attached to these, and too little fit to comprehend and pursue great and national objects. The federal Constitution forms a happy combination in this respect; the great and aggregate interests being referred to the national, the local and particular, to the state legislatures.

The other point of difference is, the greater number of citizens and extent of territory which may be brought

1 *concert* Agreement.

2 *obnoxious* Vulnerable.

3 *patronized* Supported.

4 *suffrages* Votes.

5 *weal* Wellbeing.

6 *cabals* Intrigues.

7 *diffusive* Generous and broad-minded.

within the compass of Republican, than of Democratic Government; and it is this circumstance principally which renders factious combinations less to be dreaded in the former, than in the latter. The smaller the society, the fewer probably will be the distinct parties and interests composing it; the fewer the distinct parties and interests, the more frequently will a majority be found of the same party; and the smaller the number of individuals composing a majority, and the smaller the compass within which they are placed, the more easily will they concert and execute their plans of oppression. Extend the sphere, and you take in a greater variety of parties and interests; you make it less probable that a majority of the whole will have a common motive to invade the rights of other citizens; or if such a common motive exists, it will be more difficult for all who feel it to discover their own strength, and to act in unison with each other. Besides other impediments, it may be remarked, that where there is a consciousness of unjust or dishonorable purposes, communication is always checked by distrust, in proportion to the number whose concurrence is necessary.

Hence it clearly appears, that the same advantage, which a republic has over a democracy, in controlling the effects of faction, is enjoyed by a large over a small republic—is enjoyed by the Union over the states composing it. Does this advantage consist in the substitution of representatives, whose enlightened views and virtuous sentiments render them superior to local prejudices, and to schemes of injustice? It will not be denied, that the representation of the Union will be most likely to possess these requisite endowments. Does it consist in the greater security afforded by a greater variety of parties, against the event of any one party being able to outnumber and oppress the rest? In an equal degree does the increased variety of parties, comprised within the Union, increase this security? Does it, in fine,[1] consist in the greater obstacles opposed to the concert and accomplishment of the secret wishes of an unjust and interested majority? Here, again, the extent of the Union gives it the most palpable advantage.

The influence of factious leaders may kindle a flame within their particular states, but will be unable to spread a general conflagration through the other states: a religious sect, may degenerate into a political faction in a part of the confederacy; but the variety of sects dispersed over the entire face of it, must secure the national councils against any danger from that source: a rage for paper money,[2] for an abolition of debts, for an equal division of property, or for any other improper or wicked project, will be less apt to pervade the whole body of the Union, than a particular member of it; in the same proportion as such a malady is more likely to taint a particular county or district, than an entire state.

In the extent and proper structure of the Union, therefore, we behold a republican remedy for the diseases most incident to republican government. And according to the degree of pleasure and pride, we feel in being republicans, ought to be our zeal in cherishing the spirit, and supporting the character of Federalists.

PUBLIUS.

—1787

[1] *in fine* In conclusion.

[2] *rage for paper money* Coin money was often in short supply in colonial America, leading to various experiments with paper money (still a novel and ill-defined concept at this time) starting in the late 1600s; waves of inflation and depreciation of currency persisted well into the 1700s, resulting in Parliamentary acts that limited the issuing of paper currency.

Venture Smith

c. 1729 – 1805

When he dictated the story of his life to an amanuensis in the late 1790s, Venture Smith was a prosperous farmer, sailor, and landowner, and in many ways a respected member of his Connecticut community. Yet Smith was, as the title of his autobiography describes him, "A Native of Africa," and had experienced the cruelties of American slavery firsthand, having spent twenty-six years of his life enslaved. The text that resulted from his narration, *A Narrative of the Life and Adventures of Venture, A Native of Africa* (1798), is among the most distinctive memoirs of slavery published before the Civil War, both for its literary qualities and for its subject's unique path to self-made freedom. Advertised upon publication as a lesson in morality for both black and white audiences, the *Narrative* demonstrates the diversity of early African American literature, and contributes today to our understanding of the complexity of race relations in eighteenth-century America.

The *Narrative* describes Smith's remarkable journey from princedom in West Africa to enslavement in colonial New England, and ultimately to freedom and financial prosperity in Connecticut. Named Broteer Furro at birth, Smith's father was Saungm Furro, prince of what the *Narrative* refers to as the Tribe of Dukandarra. Kidnapped as a child by African slave traders under the command of "some white nation," Broteer was forced to witness the brutal murder of his father before being trafficked to the coast of what is now Ghana, where he was purchased by Rhode Island farmer Robinson Mumford, who proceeded to give him the name "Venture" (because he was purchased with Mumford's "own private venture"). After enduring the harrowing ordeal of the Middle Passage aboard Mumford's ship, the *Charming Susannah* (during which many of the enslaved people died of smallpox), most of Venture's fellow Africans were sold into plantation slavery in the Barbados—a near death sentence, due to the extraordinarily harsh conditions they were subjected to there.

Venture, however, was taken back with Mumford to his property in Rhode Island, where he was trained into household slavery. His enslavement would continue for the next two-and-a-half decades in various locations in colonial Rhode Island, Long Island, and Connecticut, during which he married Marget, a fellow enslaved person, joined a failed escape attempt, and was himself sold to different enslavers three further times, resulting in a temporary separation from his wife and their youngest daughter. It was under his fourth and final enslaver, Colonel Oliver Smith, that Venture undertook the drawn-out task of "redeeming" himself—purchasing his own way out of slavery—by selling his labor during his spare hours. Venture took his new last name from Colonel Smith—who had priced Venture's freedom at the exorbitant fee of seventy-two pounds. Over the course of the next two decades, Smith worked tirelessly, primarily as a woodcutter, eventually securing the freedom of his two children, his pregnant wife, and several other enslaved men.

By the time of his *Narrative*'s publication, Smith was a landowner of above-average means, owning well over 100 acres of land in Connecticut. Despite his apparent social respectability, however, it is worth noting that Smith was repeatedly cheated in his business endeavors, and that he was often prevented on account of his race from seeking full reparations for these losses, a fact he occasionally reflects upon in his *Narrative* with bitterness. It is unclear what exactly motivated Smith, at the age of nearly seventy, to have his autobiography recorded and published, though it appears he was encouraged in the endeavor by several community and family members. Most scholars today accept the local tradition that his amanuensis was Elisa Niles, a white Connecticut schoolteacher and Revolutionary War veteran; nothing more is known about Niles's relationship to Smith.

A Narrative of the Life and Adventures of Venture, A Native of Africa, was published in Connecticut in 1798 by Charles Holt, publisher of the *New London Bee*, where he promoted Smith as "a negro remarkable for size, strength, industry, fidelity, and frugality." Holt may have seen Smith's story of self-made

success as fitting into his own moral publishing agenda; among the works he wrote and printed were numerous tracts on temperance and industry, and his 1798 printings also included an edition of *The Life of Dr. Benjamin Franklin*. We do not know for certain the degree to which either Smith, Niles, or Holt were familiar with the developing tradition of the slave narrative, or with other autobiographical texts by African and African American authors—such as those by Olaudah Equiano and John Marrant—but certainly Smith's own *Narrative* occupies a distinctive place in that genre. Most notably, Smith's *Narrative* is almost (though not entirely) void of Christian religious references; in a burgeoning literary tradition saturated with many deeply spiritual texts, this was a significant absence.

Smith's *Narrative* was never a best seller, and was out of print even in Connecticut for a good deal of the nineteenth century. Yet aspects of Venture Smith's story appear to have remained alive in his community long after his death. In 1896—almost 100 years after its original publication—a new edition of the *Narrative* was published with an appendix entitled "Traditions of Venture!" Quite aside from being a model of frugal morality or indeed a representative of antislavery resistance, Smith had become, according to this appendix, a figure of local legend. The appendix collects numerous folkloric stories regarding Smith's large stature and impressive physical feats, as well as descriptions of his numerous descendants; it does not comment on Smith's enslavement, aside from remarking that Colonel Oliver Smith "generously permitted" Venture to purchase his freedom.

Smith died in 1805, at the age of approximately seventy-seven. An account of his burial is given in the 1896 edition of the *Narrative*: "His heavy body was conveyed … to the cemetery adjoining the First Congregational Church in East Haddam, for burial, by four strong men fittingly chosen. The two in front were white, proving the respect he had won, while two of his own race assisted in the rear." Smith was seldom mentioned in studies of slavery or of the abolitionist movement until late in the twentieth century. Since at least 2006, when the graves of Smith and Marget were excavated as part of a heavily publicized project led by their descendants, his *Narrative* has come to be seen by many as a challenging but essential text in the canon of black eighteenth-century literature.

NOTE ON THE TEXT: The text of the work presented here is based on the first edition of *A Narrative of the Life and Adventures of Venture, A Native of Africa: But resident above sixty years in the United States of America*, printed by Charles Holt in New London in 1798. Spelling and punctuation have been modernized in accordance with the practices of this anthology.

⌘ ⌘ ⌘

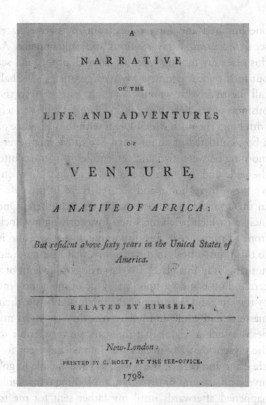

A Narrative of the Life and Adventures of Venture, A Native of Africa: But resident above sixty years in the United States of America

PREFACE

The following account of the life of Venture, is a relation of simple facts, in which nothing is added in substance to what he related himself. Many other interesting and curious passages of his life might have been inserted; but on account of the bulk to which they must necessarily have swelled this narrative, they were omitted. If any should suspect the truth of what is here related, they are referred to people now living who are acquainted with most of the facts mentioned in the narrative.

The reader is here presented with an account, not of a renowned politician or warrior, but of an untutored African slave, brought into this Christian country at eight years of age, wholly destitute of all education but what he received in common with other domesticated animals, enjoying no advantages that could lead him to suppose himself superior to the beasts, his fellow servants. And if he[1] shall derive no other advantage from perusing this narrative, he may experience those sensations of shame and indignation, that will prove him to be not wholly destitute of every noble and generous feeling.

The subject of the following pages, had he received only a common education, might have been a man of high respectability and usefulness; and had his education been suited to his genius, he might have been an ornament and an honor to human nature. It may perhaps, not be unpleasing to see the efforts of a great mind wholly uncultivated, enfeebled and depressed by slavery, and struggling under every disadvantage. The reader may here see a Franklin and a Washington, in a state of nature, or rather in a state of slavery.[2] Destitute as he is of all education, and broken by hardships and infirmities of age, he still exhibits striking traces of native ingenuity and good sense.

This narrative exhibits a pattern of honesty, prudence and industry, to people of his own colour; and perhaps some white people would not find themselves degraded by imitating such an example.

The following account is published in compliance with the earnest desire of the subject of it, and likewise a number of respectable persons who are acquainted with him.

A narrative of the life, etc.

CHAPTER I
CONTAINING AN ACCOUNT OF HIS LIFE, FROM HIS BIRTH TO THE TIME OF HIS LEAVING HIS NATIVE COUNTRY.

I was born at Dukandarra, in Guinea,[3] about the year 1729. My father's name was Saungm Furro, Prince of the Tribe of Dukandarra. My father had three wives.

[1] *he* I.e., the reader.

[2] *see a ... slavery* I.e., see American founders Benjamin Franklin and George Washington as they might have been had they been born into slavery.

[3] *Guinea* In the 1700s this term referred to a large portion of West Africa.

Polygamy was not uncommon in that country, especially among the rich, as every man was allowed to keep as many wives as he could maintain. By his first wife he had three children. The eldest of them was myself, named by my father, Broteer. The other two were named Cundazo and Soozaduka. My father had two children by his second wife, and one by his third. I descended from a very large, tall and stout[1] race of beings, much larger than the generality of people in other parts of the globe, being commonly considerable above six feet in height, and every way well proportioned.

The first thing worthy of notice which I remember was, a contention between my father and mother, on account of my father's marrying his third wife without the consent of his first and eldest, which was contrary to the custom generally observed among my countrymen. In consequence of this rupture, my mother left her husband and country, and travelled away with her three children to the eastward. I was then five years old. She took not the least sustenance along with her, to support either herself or children. I was able to travel along by her side; the other two of her offspring she carried one on her back, and the other being a sucking child,[2] in her arms. When we became hungry, my mother used to set us down on the ground, and gather some of the fruits which grew spontaneously in that climate. These served us for food on the way. At night we all lay down together in the most secure place we could find, and reposed ourselves until morning. Though there were many noxious[3] animals there; yet so kind was our Almighty protector, that none of them were ever permitted to hurt or molest us. Thus we went on our journey until the second day after our departure from Dukandarra, when we came to the entrance of a great desert. During our travel in that we were often affrighted with the doleful howlings and yellings of wolves, lions, and other animals. After five days' travel we came to the end of this desert, and immediately entered into a beautiful and extensive interval country. Here my mother was pleased to stop and seek a refuge for me. She left me at the house of a very rich farmer. I was then, as I should judge, not less than

one hundred and forty miles from my native place, separated from all my relations and acquaintance. At this place my mother took her farewell of me, and set out for her own country. My new guardian, as I shall call the man with whom I was left, put me into the business of tending sheep, immediately after I was left with him. The flock which I kept with the assistance of a boy, consisted of about forty. We drove them every morning between two and three miles to pasture, into the wide and delightful plains. When night drew on, we drove them home and secured them in the cote.[4] In this round I continued during my stay there. One incident which befell me when I was driving my flock from pasture, was so dreadful to me in that age, and is to this time so fresh in my memory, that I cannot help noticing[5] it in this place. Two large dogs sallied out of a certain house and set upon me. One of them took me by the arm, and the other by the thigh, and before their master could come and relieve me, they lacerated my flesh to such a degree that the scars are very visible to the present day. My master was immediately sent for. He came and carried me home, as I was unable to go[6] myself on account of my wounds. Nothing remarkable happened afterwards until my father sent for me to return home.

Before I dismiss[7] this country, I must just inform my reader what I remember concerning this place. A large river runs through this country in a westerly course. The land for a great way on each side is flat and level, hedged in by a considerable rise of the country at a great distance from it. It scarce ever rains there, yet the land is fertile; great dews fall in the night, which refresh the soil. About the latter end of June or first of July, the river begins to rise, and gradually increases until it has inundated the country for a great distance, to the height of seven or eight feet. This brings on a slime which enriches the land surprisingly. When the river has subsided, the natives begin to sow and plant, and the vegetation is exceeding rapid. Near this rich river my guardian's land lay. He possessed, I cannot exactly tell how much, yet this I am certain of respecting it, that he owned an immense tract. He possessed likewise

[1] *stout* Powerfully built.

[2] *sucking child* I.e., a breastfeeding infant.

[3] *noxious* Dangerous.

[4] *cote* Shelter for animals.

[5] *noticing* I.e., making note of; mentioning.

[6] *go* Walk.

[7] *dismiss* Stop writing about.

a great many cattle and goats. During my stay with him I was kindly used, and with as much tenderness, for what I saw, as [though I was] his only son, although I was an entire stranger to him, remote from friends and relations. The principal occupations of the inhabitants there were the cultivation of the soil and the care of their flocks. They were a people pretty similar in every respect to that of mine, except in their persons, which were not so tall and stout. They appeared to be very kind and friendly. I will now return to my departure from that place.

My father sent a man and horse after me. After settling with my guardian for keeping me, he took me away and went for home. It was then about one year since my mother brought me here. Nothing remarkable occurred to us on our journey until we arrived safe home.

I found then that the difference[1] between my parents had been made up previous to their sending for me. On my return, I was received both by my father and mother with great joy and affection, and was once more restored to my paternal dwelling in peace and happiness. I was then about six years old.

Not more than six weeks had passed after my return, before a message was brought by an inhabitant of the place where I lived the preceding year to my father, that that place had been invaded by a numerous army, from a nation not far distant, furnished with musical instruments, and all kinds of arms[2] then in use; that they were instigated by some white nation who equipped and sent them to subdue and possess the country; that his nation[3] had made no preparation for war, having been for a long time in profound peace, that they could not defend themselves against such a formidable train of invaders, and must therefore necessarily evacuate their lands to the fierce enemy, and fly to the protection of some chief; and that if he[4] would permit them they should come under his rule and protection when they had to retreat from their own possessions. He was a kind and merciful prince, and therefore consented to these proposals.

[1] *difference* Dispute.

[2] *arms* Weapons.

[3] *his nation* I.e., the nation among whom Smith had lived in the previous year.

[4] *he* I.e., Smith's father.

He had scarcely returned to his nation with the message, before the whole of his people were obliged to retreat from their country, and come to my father's dominions.

He gave them every privilege and all the protection his government could afford. But they had not been there longer than four days before news came to them that the invaders had laid waste their country, and were coming speedily to destroy them in my father's territories. This affrighted them, and therefore they immediately pushed off to the southward, into the unknown countries there, and were never more heard of.

Two days after their retreat, the report turned out to be but too true. A detachment from the enemy came to my father and informed him, that the whole army was encamped not far out of his dominions, and would invade the territory and deprive his people of their liberties and rights, if he did not comply with the following terms. These were to pay them a large sum of money, three hundred fat cattle, and a great number of goats, sheep, asses, etc.

My father told the messenger he would comply rather than [accept] that his subjects should be deprived of their rights and privileges, which he was not then in circumstances to defend from so sudden an invasion. Upon turning out those articles, the enemy pledged their faith and honor that they would not attack him. On these he relied and therefore thought it unnecessary to be on his guard against the enemy. But their pledges of faith and honor proved no better than those of other unprincipled hostile nations; for, a few days after[wards], a certain relation of the king came and informed him that the enemy who sent terms of accommodation to him and received tribute to their satisfaction, yet meditated an attack upon his subjects by surprise, and that probably they would commence their attack in less than one day; and concluded with advising him, as he was not prepared for war, to order a speedy retreat of his family and subjects. He complied with this advice.

The same night which was fixed upon to retreat, my father and his family set off about break of day. The king and his two younger wives went in one company, and my mother and her children in another. We left our dwellings in succession, and my father's company went on first. We directed our course for a large shrub

plain, some distance off, where we intended to conceal ourselves from the approaching enemy, until we could refresh and rest ourselves a little. But we presently found that our retreat was not secure. For having struck up a little fire for the purpose of cooking victuals,[1] the enemy, who happened to be encamped a little distance off, had sent out a scouting party who discovered us by the smoke of the fire, just as we were extinguishing it, and about to eat. As soon as we had finished eating, my father discovered the party, and immediately began to discharge arrows at them. This was what I first saw, and it alarmed both me and the women, who being unable to make any resistance, immediately betook ourselves to the tall thick reeds not far off, and left the old king to fight alone. For some time I beheld him from the reeds defending himself with great courage and firmness, till at last he was obliged to surrender himself into their hands.

They then came to us in the reeds, and the very first salute I had from them was a violent blow on the head with the fore part of a gun, and at the same time a grasp round the neck. I then had a rope put about my neck, as had all the women in the thicket with me, and were immediately led to my father, who was likewise pinioned[2] and haltered for leading. In this condition we were all led to the camp. The women and myself being pretty submissive, had tolerable treatment from the enemy, while my father was closely interrogated respecting his money, which they knew he must have. But as he gave them no account of it, he was instantly cut and pounded on his body with great inhumanity, [so] that he might be induced by the torture he suffered to make the discovery.[3] All this availed not in the least to make him give up his money, but he despised[4] all the tortures which they inflicted, until the continued exercise and increase of torment, obliged him to sink and expire. He thus died without informing his enemies of the place where his money lay. I saw him while he was thus tortured to death. The shocking scene is to this day fresh in my mind, and I have often been overcome while thinking on it. He was a man of remarkable stature. I should judge as much as six

feet and six or seven inches high, two feet across his shoulders, and every way well proportioned. He was a man of remarkable strength and resolution, affable, kind and gentle, ruling with equity and moderation.

The army of the enemy was large, I should suppose consisting of about six thousand men. Their leader was called Baukurre. After destroying the old prince, they decamped and immediately marched towards the sea, lying to the west, taking with them myself and the women prisoners. In the march a scouting party was detached from the main army. To the leader of this party I was made waiter, having to carry his gun, etc. As we were a-scouting we came across a herd of fat cattle, consisting of about thirty in number. These we set upon, and immediately wrested from their keepers, and afterwards converted them into food for the army. The enemy had remarkable success in destroying the country wherever they went. For as far as they had penetrated, they laid the habitations waste and captured the people. The distance they had now brought me was about four hundred miles. All the march I had very hard tasks imposed on me, which I [was told I] must perform on pain of punishment. I was obliged to carry on my head a large flat stone used for grinding our corn, weighing, as I should suppose, as much as 25 pounds; besides victuals, mat and cooking utensils. Though I was pretty large and stout of my age, yet these burdens were very grievous to me, being only about six years and an half old.

We were then come to a place called Malagasco. When we entered the place we could not see the least appearance of either houses or inhabitants, but upon stricter search found, that instead of houses above ground they had dens in the sides of hillocks, contiguous to ponds and streams of water. In these we perceived they had all hid themselves, as I suppose they usually did upon such occasions. In order to compel them to surrender, the enemy contrived to smoke them out with faggots.[5] These they put to the entrance of the caves and set them on fire. While they were engaged in this business, to their great surprise some of them were desperately wounded with arrows which fell from above on them. This mystery they soon found

1 *victuals* Food.

2 *pinioned* Bound by the arms.

3 *make the discovery* Reveal to them (where the money was).

4 *despised* Defied; was dismissive of.

5 *faggots* Bundles of kindling.

out. They perceived that the enemy[1] discharged these arrows through holes on the top of the dens directly into the air. Their weight brought them back, point downwards, on their enemies'[2] heads, whilst they were smoking the inhabitants out. The points of their arrows were poisoned, but their enemy had an antidote for it, which they instantly applied to the wounded part. The smoke at last obliged the people to give themselves up. They came out of their caves, first spatting[3] the palms of their hands together, and immediately after extended their arms, crossed at their wrists, ready to be bound and pinioned. I should judge that the dens above mentioned were extended about eight feet horizontally into the earth, six feet in height and as many wide. They were arched overhead and lined with earth, which was of the clay kind, and made the surface of their walls firm and smooth.

The invaders then pinioned the prisoners of all ages and sexes indiscriminately, took their flocks and all their effects, and moved on their way towards the sea. On the march the prisoners were treated with clemency, on account of their being submissive and humble. Having come to the next tribe, the enemy laid siege and immediately took men, women, children, flocks, and all their valuable effects. They then went on to the next district, which was contiguous to the sea, called in Africa, Anamaboo.[4] The enemy's provisions were then almost spent, as well as their strength. The inhabitants knowing what conduct they had pursued, and what were their present intentions, improved the favorable opportunity, attacked them, and took enemy, prisoners, flocks and all their effects. I was then taken a second time. All of us were then put into the castle,[5] and kept for market. On a certain time I and other prisoners were put on board a canoe, under our master, and rowed away to a vessel belonging to Rhode Island, commanded by Capt. Collingwood, and the mate Thomas Mumford. While we were going

to the vessel, our master told us all to appear to the best possible advantage for sale. I was bought on board by one Robertson[6] Mumford, steward of said vessel, for four gallons of rum, and a piece of calico, and called VENTURE, on account of his having purchased me with his own private venture. Thus I came by my name. All the slaves that were bought for that vessel's cargo were two hundred and sixty.

Chapter 2
Containing an account of his life, from the time of his leaving Africa, to that of his becoming free.

After all the business was ended on the coast of Africa, the ship sailed from thence to Barbadoes. After an ordinary passage, except great mortality by the smallpox, which broke out on board, we arrived at the island of Barbadoes: but when we reached it, there were found out of the two hundred and sixty that [had] sailed from Africa, not more than two hundred alive. These were all sold, except myself and three more, to the planters there.

The vessel then sailed for Rhode Island, and arrived there after a comfortable passage. Here my master sent me to live with one of his sisters, until he could carry me to Fisher's Island, the place of his residence. I had then completed my eighth year. After staying with his sister some time I was taken to my master's place to live.

When we arrived at Narraganset, my master went ashore in order to return a part of the way by land, and gave me the charge of the keys of his trunks on board the vessel, and charged me not to deliver them up to anybody, not even to his father, without his orders. To his directions I promised faithfully to conform. When I arrived with my master's articles at his house, my master's father asked me for his son's keys, as he wanted to see what his trunks contained. I told him that my master [had] intrusted me with the care of them until he should return, and that I had given him my word to be faithful to the trust, and could not therefore give him or any other person the keys without my master's directions. He insisted that I should deliver to him the keys, threatening to punish me if I did not. But I let him know that he should not have them let him say

[1] *the enemy* I.e., the people hiding in the caves.

[2] *their enemies* I.e., the invading slavers.

[3] *spatting* Clapping.

[4] *Anamaboo* Town on the coast of present-day Ghana, an important center of the transatlantic slave trade on the Gold Coast.

[5] *the castle* One of the many coastal slave-trading fortresses controlled by the British; scholars are unsure in which particular castle Smith was held captive.

[6] *Robertson* An error on the part of either Smith or his amanuensis; Mumford's given name was Robinson.

what he would. He then laid aside trying to get them. But notwithstanding he appeared to give up trying to obtain them from me, yet I mistrusted that he would take some time when I was off my guard, either in the daytime or at night to get them. Therefore I slung them round my neck, and in the daytime concealed them in my bosom, and at night I always lay with them under me, that no person might take them from me without being apprized of it. Thus I kept the keys from everybody until my master came home. When he returned he asked where Venture was. As I was then within hearing, I came, and said, here sir, at your service. He asked me for his keys, and I immediately took them off my neck and reached them out to him. He took them, stroked my hair, and commended me, saying in presence of his father that his young Venture was so faithful that he never would have been able to have taken the keys from him but by violence; that he should not fear to trust him with his whole fortune, for that he[1] had been in his native place so habituated to keeping his word that he would sacrifice even his life to maintain it.

The first of the time of living at my master's own place, I was pretty much employed in the house at carding wool[2] and other household business. In this situation I continued for some years, after which my master put me to work out of doors. After many proofs of my faithfulness and honesty, my master began to put great confidence in me. My behavior to him had as yet been submissive and obedient. I then began to have hard tasks imposed on me. Some of these were to pound four bushels of ears of corn every night in a barrel for the poultry, or be rigorously punished. At other seasons of the year I had to card wool until a very late hour. These tasks I had to perform when I was about nine years old.

Some time after I had another difficulty and oppression which was greater than any I had ever experienced since I came into this country. This was to serve two masters.[3] James Mumford, my master's son, when his father had gone from home in the morning, and given me a stint to perform that day, would order me to do *this* and *that* business different from what my master directed me. One day in particular, the authority which my master's son had set up had like to have produced melancholy effects. For my master having set me off my business to perform that day and then left me to perform it, his son came up to me in the course of the day, big with authority, and commanded me very arrogantly to quit my present business and go directly about what he should order me. I replied to him that my master had given me so much to perform that day, and that I must therefore faithfully complete it in that time. He then broke out into a great rage, snatched a pitchfork and went to lay[4] me over the head therewith; but I as soon got another and defended myself with it, or otherwise he might have murdered me in his outrage. He immediately called some people who were within hearing at work for him, and ordered them to take his hair rope and come and bind me with it. They all tried to bind me but in vain, though there were three assistants in number. My upstart master then desisted, put his pocket handkerchief before his eyes and went home with a design to tell his mother of the struggle with young Venture. He told her that their young Venture had become so stubborn that he could not control him, and asked her what he should do with him. In the meantime I recovered my temper, voluntarily caused myself to be bound by the same men who [had] tried in vain before, and [was] carried before my young master, that he might do what he pleased with me. He took me to a gallows made for the purpose of hanging cattle on, and suspended me on it. Afterwards he ordered one of his hands to go to the peach orchard and cut him three dozen of whips to punish me with. These were brought to him, and that was all that was done with them, as I was released and went to work after hanging on the gallows about an hour.

After I had lived with my master thirteen years, being then about twenty-two years old, I married Meg, a slave of his who was about my age. My master owned a certain Irishman,[5] named Heddy, who about that

[1] *he* I.e., Venture.

[2] *carding wool* Cleaning and detangling raw wool in preparation for spinning.

[3] *to serve two masters* See Matthew 6.24: "No man can serve two masters: for either he will hate the one, and love the other; or else he will hold to the one, and despise the other."

[4] *lay* Strike.

[5] *owned a certain Irishman* I.e., held him as an indentured servant. Indentured servants would be held by their masters for a predetermined number of years, usually seven or ten. Though indentured

time formed a plan of secretly leaving his master. After he had long had this plan in meditation he suggested it to me. At first I cast a deaf ear to it, and rebuked Heddy for harboring in his mind such a rash undertaking. But after he had persuaded and much enchanted me with the prospect of gaining my freedom by such a method, I at length agreed to accompany him. Heddy next inveigled two of his fellow servants to accompany us. The place to which we designed[1] to go was the Mississippi. Our next business was to lay in a sufficient store of provisions for our voyage. We privately collected out of our master's store six great old cheeses, two firkins[2] of butter, and one whole batch of new bread. When we had gathered all our own clothes and some more, we took them all about midnight, and went to the water side. We stole our master's boat, embarked, and then directed our course for the Mississippi River.

We mutually confederated not to betray or desert one another on pain of death. We first steered our course for Montauk Point, the east end of Long Island. After our arrival there we landed, and Heddy and I made an incursion into the island after fresh water, while our two comrades were left at a little distance from the boat, employed at cooking. When Heddy and I had sought some time for water, he returned to our companions, and I continued on looking for my object. When Heddy had performed his business with our companions who were engaged in cooking, he went directly to the boat, stole all the clothes in it, and then travelled away for East Hampton, as I was informed. I returned to my fellows not long after. They informed me that our clothes were stolen, but could not determine who was the thief, yet they suspected Heddy as he was missing. After reproving my two comrades for not taking care of our things which were in the boat, I advertised Heddy and sent two men in search of him. They pursued and overtook him at Southampton and returned him to the boat. I then thought it might afford some chance for my freedom, or at least a palliation for my running away, to return Heddy immediately to his master, and inform him that I was induced to go away

by Heddy's address. Accordingly I set off with him and the rest of my companions for our master's, and arrived there without any difficulty. I informed my master that Heddy was the ringleader of our revolt, and that he had used us ill. He immediately put Heddy into custody, and myself and companions were well received and went to work as usual.

Not a long time passed after that, before Heddy was sent by my master to New London gaol. At the close of that year I was sold to a Thomas Stanton, and had to be separated from my wife and one daughter, who was about one month old. He resided at Stonington Point. To this place I brought with me from my late master's, two johannes,[3] three old Spanish dollars, and two thousand of coppers, besides five pounds of my wife's money. This money I got by cleaning gentlemen's shoes and drawing[4] boots, by catching muskrats and minks, raising potatoes and carrots, etc. and by fishing in the night, and at odd spells.

All this money, amounting to near twenty-one pounds York currency,[5] my master's brother, Robert Stanton, hired of me, for which he gave me his note.[6] About one year and a half after that time, my master purchased my wife and her child for seven hundred pounds old tenor.[7] One time my master sent me two miles after a barrel of molasses, and ordered me to carry it on my shoulders. I made out to carry it all the way to my master's house. When I lived with Captain George Mumford, only to try my strength, I took up on my knees a tierce of salt containing seven bushels, and carried it two or three rods.[8] Of this fact there are several eye witnesses now living.

servants—especially those from Ireland—might in some cases have been treated very poorly by their masters, they were not considered chattel in the way enslaved persons were.

[1] *designed* Planned.

[2] *firkins* Small casks.

[3] *johannes* Portuguese gold coins, worth approximately 36 shillings.

[4] *drawing* Mending.

[5] *York currency* I.e., paper money printed in the colony of New York.

[6] *hired of ... his note* I.e., Stanton borrowed the twenty-one pounds from Smith, giving him a promissory note stating he would return the money.

[7] *old tenor* Paper money issued in Massachusetts or Rhode Island before 1741, after which it was replaced by a new currency.

[8] *tierce ... seven bushels* Cask of salt weighing approximately 450 pounds; *rods* Units of measure equalling about five and a half yards.

Towards the close of the time that I resided with this master, I had a falling out with my mistress. This happened one time when my master was gone to Long Island a gunning. At first the quarrel began between my wife and her mistress. I was then at work in the barn, and hearing a racket in the house, induced me to run there and see what had broken out. When I entered the house, I found my mistress in a violent passion with my wife, for what she informed me was a mere trifle; such a small affair that I forbear to put my mistress to the shame of having it known. I earnestly requested my wife to beg pardon of her mistress for the sake of peace, even if she had given no just occasion for offence. But whilst I was thus saying, my mistress turned the blows which she was repeating on my wife to me. She took down her horse-whip, and while she was glutting her fury with it, I reached out my great black hand, raised it up and received the blows of the whip on it which were designed for my head. Then I immediately committed the whip to the devouring fire.

When my master returned from the island, his wife told him of the affair, but for the present he seemed to take no notice of it, and mentioned not a word about it to me. Some days after his return, in the morning as I was putting on a log in the fireplace, not suspecting harm from anyone, I received a most violent stroke on the crown of my head with a club two feet long and as large round as a chair-post. This blow very badly wounded my head, and the scar of it remains to this day. The first blow made me have my wits about me you may suppose, for as soon as he went to renew it, I snatched the club out of his hands and dragged him out of the door. He then sent for his brother to come and assist him, but I presently left my master, took the club he wounded me with, carried it to a neighboring Justice of the Peace, and complained of my master. He finally advised me to return to my master, and live contented with him till he abused me again, and then complain. I consented to do accordingly. But before I set out for my master's, up he come and his brother Robert after me. The Justice improved[1] this convenient opportunity to caution my master. He asked him for what he treated his slave thus hastily and unjustly, and told him what would be the consequence if he

continued the same treatment towards me.[2] After the Justice had ended his discourse with my master, he and his brother set out with me for home, one before and the other behind me. When they had come to a bye place,[3] they both dismounted their respective horses, and fell to beating me with great violence. I became enraged at this and immediately turned them both under me, laid one of them across the other, and stamped both with my feet what I would.

This occasioned my master's brother to advise him to put me off. A short time after this I was taken by a constable and two men. They carried me to a blacksmith's shop and had me handcuffed. When I returned home my mistress enquired much of her waiters,[4] whether Venture was handcuffed. When she was informed that I was, she appeared to be very contented and was much transported with the news. In the midst of this content and joy, I presented myself before my mistress, showed her my handcuffs, and gave her thanks for my gold rings. For this my master commanded a negro of his to fetch him a large ox chain. This my master locked on my legs with two padlocks. I continued to wear the chain peaceably for two or three days, when my master asked me with contemptuous hard names whether I had not better be freed from my chains and go to work. I answered him, No. Well then, said he, I will send you to the West Indies[5] or banish you, for I am resolved not to keep you. I answered him I crossed the waters to come here, and I am willing to cross them to return.

For a day or two after this not anyone said much to me, until one Hempsted Miner, of Stonington, asked

[1] *improved* I.e., made use of.

[2] *carried it … towards me* In appealing to the law for protection from his enslaver, Smith may have been inspired by the recent story of Sharper, an enslaved ten-year-old boy who had approached a justice of the peace in New London on 9 September 1753, having suffered astonishing physical abuse at the hands of his enslaver, James Rogers. The case was brought to court in 1755, with the jury ultimately siding with Sharper and two others who had been cruelly abused by Rogers; the three enslaved plaintiffs were not freed, but were rather sent to live in new households. The story was widely publicized in local newspapers at the time.

[3] *bye place* Hidden or unfrequented area.

[4] *enquired … waiters* I.e., kept asking those attending her.

[5] *send you … West Indies* A severe threat, given the exceptionally harsh conditions of slavery on the sugar plantations of the West Indies.

me if I would live with him. I answered him that I would. He then requested me to make myself discontented and to appear as unreconciled to my master as I could before that he bargained with him for me; and that in return he would give me a good chance to gain my freedom when I came to live with him. I did as he requested me. Not long after Hempsted Miner purchased me of my master for fifty-six pounds lawful. He took the chain and padlocks from off me immediately after.

It may here be remembered that I related a few pages back that I hired out a sum of money to Mr. Robert Stanton, and took his note for it. In the fray between my master Stanton and myself, he broke open my chest containing his brother's note to me, and destroyed it. Immediately after my present master bought me, he determined to sell me at Hartford. As soon as I became apprized of it, I bethought myself that I would secure a certain sum of money which lay by me, safer than to hire it out to a Stanton. Accordingly I buried it in the earth, a little distance from Thomas Stanton's, in the road over which he passed daily. A short time after my master carried me to Hartford, and first proposed to sell me to one William Hooker of that place. Hooker asked whether I would go to the German Flats[1] with him. I answered, No. He said I should, if not by fair means I should by foul. If you will go by no other measures, I will tie you down in my sleigh. I replied to him, that if he carried me in that manner, no person would purchase me, for it would be thought that he had a murderer for sale. After this he tried no more, and said he would not have me as a gift.

My master next offered me to Daniel Edwards, Esq. of Hartford, for sale. But not purchasing me, my master pawned me to him for ten pounds, and returned to Stonington. After some trial of my honesty, Mr. Edwards placed considerable trust and confidence in me. He put me to serve as his cup-bearer and waiter. When there was company at his house, he would send me into his cellar and other parts of his house to fetch wine and other articles occasionally for them. When I had been with him some time, he asked me why my master wished to part with such an honest negro, and why he did not keep me himself. I

replied that I could not give him the reason, unless it was to convert me into cash, and speculate with me as with other commodities. I hope that he can never justly say it was on account of my ill conduct that he did not keep me himself. Mr. Edwards told me that he should be very willing to keep me himself, and that he would never let me go from him to live, if it was not unreasonable and inconvenient for me to be parted from my wife and children; therefore he would furnish me with a horse to return to Stonington, if I had a mind for it. As Miner did not appear to redeem me I went, and called at my old master Stanton's first to see my wife, who was then owned by him. As my old master appeared much ruffled at my being there, I left my wife before I had spent any considerable time with her, and went to Colonel O. Smith's. Miner had not as yet wholly settled with Stanton for me, and had before my return from Hartford given Col. Smith a bill of sale of me. These men once met to determine which of them should hold me, and upon my expressing a desire to be owned by Col. Smith, and upon my master's settling the remainder of the money which was due to Stanton for me, it was agreed that I should live with Col. Smith. This was the third time of my being sold, and I was then thirty-one years old. As I never had an opportunity of redeeming myself whilst I was owned by Miner, though he promised to give me a chance, I was then very ambitious of obtaining it. I asked my master one time if he would consent to have me purchase my freedom. He replied that he would. I was then very happy, knowing that I was at that time able to pay part of the purchase money, by means of the money which I some time since buried. This I took out of the earth and tendered to my master, having previously engaged a free negro man to take his security for it, as I was the property of my master, and therefore could not safely take his obligation myself. What was wanting[2] in redeeming myself, my master agreed to wait on me for, until I could procure it for him. I still continued to work for Col. Smith. There was continually some interest accruing on my master's note to my friend the free negro man above named, which I received, and with some besides which I got by fishing, I laid out in land adjoining my old master Stanton's. By cultivating this land with the

[1] *German Flats* Town in New York.

[2] *wanting* Lacking.

greatest diligence and economy, at times when my master did not require my labor,[1] in two years I laid up ten pounds. This my friend tendered my master for myself, and received his note for it.

Being encouraged by the success which I had met in redeeming myself, I again solicited my master for a further chance of completing it. The chance for which I solicited him was that of going out to work the ensuing winter. He agreed to this on condition that I would give him one quarter of my earnings. On these terms I worked the following winter, and earned four pounds sixteen shillings, one quarter of which went to my master for the privilege, and the rest was paid him on my own account. This, added to the other payments, made up forty-four pounds, eight shillings, which I had paid on my own account. I was then about thirty-five years old.

The next summer I again desired he would give me a chance of going out to work. But he refused and answered that he must have my labor this summer, as he did not have it the past winter. I replied that I considered it as hard that I could not have a chance to work out when the season became advantageous, and that I must only be permitted to hire myself out in the poorest season of the year. He asked me after this what I would give him for the privilege per month. I replied that I would leave it wholly with his own generosity to determine what I should return him a month. Well then, said he, if so two pounds a month. I answered him that if that was the least he would take I would be contented.

Accordingly I hired myself out at Fisher's Island, and earned twenty pounds, thirteen pounds six shillings of which my master drew for the privilege, and the remainder I paid him for my freedom. This made fifty-one pounds two shillings which I paid him. In October following I went and wrought[2] six months at Long Island. In that six month's time I cut and

corded four hundred cords[3] of wood, besides threshing out seventy-five bushels of grain, and received of my wages down only twenty pounds, which left remaining a larger sum. Whilst I was out that time, I took up on my wages only one pair of shoes. At night I lay on the hearth, with one coverlet over and another under me. I returned to my master and gave him what I received of my six months labor. This left only thirteen pounds eighteen shillings to make up the full sum for my redemption. My master liberated me, saying that I might pay what was behind if I could ever make it convenient, otherwise it would be well. The amount of the money which I had paid my master towards redeeming my time was seventy-one pounds two shillings. The reason of my master for asking such an unreasonable price was, he said, to secure himself in case I should ever come to want. Being thirty-six years old, I left Col. Smith once for all. I had already been sold three different times, made considerable money with seemingly nothing to derive it from, been cheated out of a large sum of money, lost much by misfortunes, and paid an enormous sum for my freedom.

CHAPTER 3
CONTAINING AN ACCOUNT OF HIS LIFE, FROM THE TIME OF HIS PURCHASING HIS FREEDOM TO THE PRESENT DAY.

My wife and children were yet in bondage to Mr. Thomas Stanton. About this time I lost a chest containing, besides clothing, about thirty-eight pounds in paper money. It was burnt by accident. A short time after I sold all my possessions at Stonington, consisting of a pretty piece of land and one dwelling house thereon, and went to reside at Long Island. For the first four years of my residence there, I spent my time in working for various people on that and at the neighboring islands. In the space of six months I cut and corded upwards of four hundred cords of wood. Many other singular and wonderful labors I performed in cutting wood there, which would not be inferior to those just recited, but for brevity sake I must omit them. In the aforementioned four years,

[1] *labor* This word is spelled in this fashion six times in the original 1798 publication, and spelled *labour* three times. The policy of this anthology is to retain British spellings in early American works wherever they are consistently used. In cases such as this one, however, where it is not entirely clear if either spelling was preferred, the inconsistency has been retained.

[2] *wrought* Worked.

[3] *cords* Large piles of firewood, measuring about eight by four by four feet.

what wood I cut at Long Island amounted to several thousand cords, and the money which I earned thereby amounted to two hundred and seven pounds ten shillings. This money I laid up carefully by me. Perhaps some may enquire what maintained me all the time I was laying up money. I would inform them that I bought nothing which I did not absolutely want.[1] All fine clothes I despised in comparison with my interest, and never kept but just what clothes were comfortable for common days, and perhaps I would have a garment or two which I did not have on at all times, but as for superfluous finery I never thought it to be compared with a decent homespun dress,[2] a good supply of money and prudence. Expensive gatherings of my mates I commonly shunned, and all kinds of luxuries I was perfectly a stranger to; and during the time I was employed in cutting the aforementioned quantity of wood, I never was at the expense of six-pence worth of spirits.[3] Being after this labour forty years of age, I worked at various places, and in particular on Ram Island, where I purchased Solomon and Cuff, two sons of mine, for two hundred dollars each.

It will here be remembered how much money I earned by cutting wood in four years. Besides this I had considerable money, amounting in all to near three hundred pounds. When I had purchased my two sons, I had then left more than one hundred pounds. After this I purchased a negro man, for no other reason than to oblige him, and gave for him sixty pounds. But in a short time after he run away from me, and I thereby lost all that I gave for him, except twenty pounds which he paid me previous to his absconding.[4] The rest of my money I laid out in land, in addition to a farm which I owned before, and a dwelling house thereon. Forty-four years had then completed their revolution since my entrance into this existence of servitude and misfortune. Solomon, my eldest son, being then in his seventeenth year, and all my hope and dependence for help, I hired him out to one Charles Church of Rhode Island for one year, on consideration of his giving him twelve pounds and an opportunity of acquiring some learning. In the course of the year, Church fitted out a vessel for a whaling voyage, and being in want of hands to man her, he induced my son to go, with the promise of giving him on his return a pair of silver buckles, besides his wages. As soon as I heard of his going to sea, I immediately set out to go and prevent it if possible. But on my arrival at Church's, to my great grief, I could only see the vessel my son was in almost out of sight going to sea. My son died of the scurvy in this voyage, and Church has never yet paid me the least of his wages. In my son, besides the loss of his life, I lost equal to seventy-five pounds.

My other son being but a youth, still lived with me. About this time I chartered a sloop of about thirty tons burden,[5] and hired men to assist me in navigating her. I employed her mostly in the wood trade to Rhode Island, and made clear of all expenses above one hundred dollars with her in better than one year. I had then become something forehanded,[6] and being in my forty-fourth year, I purchased my wife Meg, and thereby prevented having another child to buy, as she was then pregnant. I gave forty pounds for her.

During my residence at Long Island, I raised one year with another, ten cartloads of watermelons, and lost a great many every year besides by the thievishness of the sailors. What I made by the watermelons I sold there, amounted to nearly five hundred dollars. Various other methods I pursued in order to enable me to redeem my family. In the night time I fished with set-nets and pots for eels and lobsters, and shortly after went [on] a whaling voyage in the service of Col. Smith. After being out seven months, the vessel returned, laden with four hundred barrels of oil.[7] About this time, I become possessed of another dwelling-house, and my temporal affairs were in a pretty prosperous condition. This and my industry was what alone saved me from being expelled [from] that part of the island in which I resided, as an act was passed by the select-men of the place, that all negroes residing there should be expelled.

[1] *want* Need.

[2] *decent homespun dress* Decent homemade clothing.

[3] *spirits* I.e., hard alcohol.

[4] *I purchased ... absconding* It seems that the man was purchased with the intention that he pay Smith back in full before properly claiming his freedom.

[5] *burden* Carrying capacity of a ship.

[6] *forehanded* Financially stable; having money set aside for the future.

[7] *oil* Whale oil (at the time the most widely used fuel for lamps).

Next after my wife, I purchased a negro man for four hundred dollars. But he having an inclination to return to his old master, I therefore let him go. Shortly after I purchased another negro man for twenty-five pounds, whom I parted with shortly after.

Being about forty-six years old, I bought my oldest child Hannah of[1] Ray Mumford, for forty-four pounds, and she still resided with him. I had already redeemed from slavery myself, my wife and three children, besides three negro men.

About the forty-seventh year of my life, I disposed of all my property at Long Island, and came from thence into East Haddam. I hired myself out at first to Timothy Chapman for five weeks, the earnings of which time I put up carefully by me. After this I wrought for Abel Bingham about six weeks. I then put my money together and purchased of said Bingham ten acres of land, lying at Haddam Neck,[2] where I now reside. On this land I labored with great diligence for two years, and shortly after purchased six acres more of land contiguous to my other. One year from that time I purchased seventy acres more of the same man, and paid for it mostly with the produce of my other land. Soon after I bought this last lot of land, I set up a comfortable dwelling house on my farm, and built it from the produce thereof. Shortly after I had much trouble and expense with my daughter Hannah, whose name has before been mentioned in this account. She was married soon after I redeemed her, to one Isaac, a free negro, and shortly after her marriage fell sick of a mortal disease; her husband, a dissolute and abandoned[3] wretch, paid but little attention to her in her illness. I therefore thought it best to bring her to my house and nurse her there. I procured her all the aid mortals could afford, but notwithstanding this she fell a prey to her disease, after a lingering and painful endurance of it.

The physician's bills for attending her during her illness amounted to forty pounds. Having reached my fifty-fourth year, I hired two negro men, one named William Jacklin, and the other Mingo. Mingo lived with me one year, and having received his wages, run

in debt to me eight dollars, for which he gave me his note. Presently after he tried to run away from me without troubling himself to pay up his note. I procured a warrant, took him, and requested him to go to Justice Throop's of his own accord, but he refusing, I took him on my shoulders, and carried him there, distant about two miles. The justice, asking me if I had my prisoner's note with me, and replying that I had not, he told me that I must return with him and get it. Accordingly I carried Mingo back on my shoulders, but before we arrived at my dwelling, he complained of being hurt, and asked me if this was not a hard way of treating our fellow creatures. I answered him that it would be hard thus to treat our honest fellow creatures. He then told me that if I would let him off my shoulders, he had a pair of silver shoe-buckles, one shirt and a pocket handkerchief, which he would turn out to me. I agreed, and let him return home with me on foot; but the very following night, he slipped from me, stole my horse and has never paid me even his note. The other negro man, Jacklin, being a comb-maker by trade, he requested me to set him up, and promised to reward me well with his labor. Accordingly I bought him a set of tools for making combs, and procured him stock. He worked at my house about one year, and then run away from me with all his combs, and owed me for all his board.

Since my residence at Haddam Neck, I have owned of boats, canoes and sail vessels, not less than twenty. These I mostly employed in the fishing and trafficking[4] business, and in these occupations I have been cheated out of considerable money by people whom I traded with taking advantage of my ignorance of numbers.

About twelve years ago, I hired a whale-boat and four black men, and proceeded to Long Island after a load of round clams. Having arrived there, I first purchased of James Webb, son of Orange Webb, six hundred and sixty clams, and afterwards, with the help of my men, finished loading my boat. The same evening, however, this Webb stole my boat, and went in her to Connecticut River, and sold her cargo for his own benefit. I thereupon pursued him, and at length, after an additional expense of nine crowns, recovered the boat;

1 *of* From.

2 *Haddam Neck* In Connecticut.

3 *abandoned* Given to abandoning himself to uncontrolled impulses; unrestrained.

4 *trafficking* Transport.

but for the proceeds of her cargo I never could obtain any compensation.

Four years after, I met with another loss, far superior to this in value, and I think by no less wicked means. Being going to New London with a grandchild, I took passage in an Indian's boat, and went there with him. On our return, the Indian took on board two hogs-heads[1] of molasses, one of which belonged to Capt. Elisha Hart, of Saybrook, to be delivered on his wharf. When we arrived there, and while I was gone, at the request of the Indian, to inform Captain Hart of his arrival, and receive the freight for him, one hogshead of the molasses had been lost overboard by the people in attempting to land it on the wharf. Although I was absent at the time, and had no concern whatever in the business, as was known to a number of respect-able witnesses, I was nevertheless prosecuted by this conscientious gentleman (the Indian not being able to pay for it) and obliged to pay upwards of ten pounds lawful money, with all the costs of court. I applied to several gentlemen for counsel in this affair, and they advised me, as my adversary was rich, and threatened to carry the matter from court to court till it would cost me more than the first damages would be to pay the sum and submit to the injury; which I accord-ing did, and he has often since insultingly taunted me with my unmerited misfortune. Such a proceeding as this, committed on a defenceless stranger, almost worn out in the hard service of the world, without any foundation in reason or justice, whatever it may be called in a Christian land, would in my native country have been branded as a crime equal to highway rob-bery. But Captain Hart was a *white gentleman*, and I a *poor African; therefore it was all right, and good enough for the black dog.*

I am now sixty-nine years old. Though once straight and tall, measuring without shoes six feet one inch and an half, and every way well proportioned, I am now bowed down with age and hardship. My strength, which was once equal if not superior to any man whom I have ever seen, is now enfeebled so that life is a burden, and it is with fatigue that I can walk a couple of miles, stooping over my staff. Other griefs are still behind, on account of which some aged people, at least, will pity me. My eyesight has

gradually failed, till I am almost blind, and whenever I go abroad[2] one of my grandchildren must direct my way; besides for many years I have been much pained and troubled with an ulcer on one of my legs. But amidst all my griefs and pains, I have many consola-tions; Meg, the wife of my youth, whom I married for love, and bought with my money, is still alive. My freedom is a privilege which nothing else can equal. Notwithstanding all the losses I have suffered by fire, by the injustice of knaves, by the cruelty and oppres-sion of false hearted friends, and the perfidy of my own countrymen whom I have assisted and redeemed from bondage, I am now possessed of more than one hundred acres of land, and three habitable dwelling houses. It gives me joy to think that I have and that I *deserve* so good a character, especially for *truth* and *integrity*. While I am now looking to the grave as my home, my joy for this world would be full—IF my children, Cuff for whom I paid two hundred dollars when a boy, and Solomon[3] who was born soon after I purchased his mother—If Cuff and Solomon—O! that they had walked in the way of their father. But a father's lips are closed in silence and in grief!—Vanity[4] of vanities, all is vanity!

FINIS.

2 *abroad* Outside the home.

3 *Solomon* Smith had two sons named Solomon; the younger, born in 1774, was named after the elder Solomon who had died the year before. While some scholars have interpreted this lament as an implicit criticism of the elder Solomon's pursuit of riches—includ-ing the promised "silver buckles"—at sea, a note in the 1896 edition of the text suggests that it is the younger Solomon who is being referred to here. That note reads: "The closing words … were omit-ted in the later editions. It is probable that both [sons] improved later, especially so in the case of Solomon, who is well spoken of by elderly men now living, as having maintained a good character." A second note further reads: "Venture in the closing words of his auto-biography disparages his sons Cuff and Solomon. The compiler, on inquiry among the elderly people who remembered them well, fails to find sufficient warrant for the language of criticism. Evidently, if any youthful foibles early appeared, they were soon overcome."

4 *Vanity* In this context, the quality of being without substance or significance—as various forms of Christianity teach is true of all worldly things. See Ecclesiastes 1.2–4: "Vanity of vanities, saith the Preacher, vanity of vanities; all is vanity. What profit hath a man of all his labour which he taketh under the sun? One generation passeth away, and another generation cometh: but the earth abideth for ever."

1 *hogsheads* Large casks.

CERTIFICATE

Stonington, *November* 3, 1798

THESE certify, that Venture, a free negro man, aged about 69 years, and was, as we have ever understood, a native of Africa, and formerly a slave to Mr. James Mumford, of Fisher's Island, in the state of New York; who sold him to Mr. Thomas Stanton, 2d, of Stonington, in the state of Connecticut, and said Stanton sold said Venture to Col. Oliver Smith, of the aforesaid place. That said Venture hath sustained the character of a faithful servant, and that of a temperate, honest and industrious man, and being ever intent on obtaining his freedom, he was indulged by his masters after the ordinary labour on the days of his servitude, to improve the nights in fishing and other employments to his own emolument, in which time he procured so much money as to purchase his freedom from his late master Col. Smith; after which he took upon himself the name of Venture Smith, and has, since his freedom, purchased a negro woman, called Meg, to whom he was previously married, and also his children who were slaves, and said Venture has since removed himself and family to the town of East-Haddam, in this state, where he hath purchased lands on which he hath built a house, and there taken up his abode.

NATHANIEL MINOR, Esq.
ELIJAH PALMER, Esq.
Capt. AMOS PALMER
ACORS SHEFFIELD
EDWARD SMITH[1]
—1798

[1] *EDWARD SMITH* Son of Colonel Oliver Smith.

SLAVERY AND RESISTANCE
CONTEXTS

From the moment Europeans began to colonize the Americas in the 1490s, slavery played an essential role in the process. The first people European settlers enslaved in North America were Indigenous inhabitants of the Caribbean, especially the Taíno people, whom Spanish colonizers abused with extraordinary violence. Hearing reports of the suffering and destruction, the Spanish government struggled to balance what it saw as a moral imperative to care for its new Indigenous subjects with its desire to maintain cheap labor in its colonies. Spain outlawed the enslavement of Indigenous people in 1542, but the laws contained so many loopholes and were so poorly enforced that they only slightly improved the situation in practice.

In English colonies in the seventeenth and eighteenth centuries, the enslavement of Indigenous people was typically framed as a form of punishment. Settlers enslaved whole communities after defeating them in war,[1] and from the 1670s onward forced servitude (including lifetime enslavement) was commonly inflicted on Indigenous people as a punishment for unpaid debt and other crimes. Because Indigenous slavery took so many different forms across America—many of them extralegal—it was difficult to stamp out by legal means and, on a smaller scale, continued in some places into the twentieth century. In part because of its dubious legal status, Indigenous slavery was not nearly as thoroughly documented or frequently discussed in writing as the enslavement of Africans, but this relative absence from the written record belies its economic and human significance: an estimated 2.5 to 5 million Indigenous people were enslaved or forced into servitude in North America in the four hundred years following Columbus's first voyage.

The history of black slavery in North America also begins with the first European colony, Hispaniola, where Africans were forcibly transported at least as early as 1501. Some Spanish authorities—many of whom considered themselves humanitarians—suggested that enslaved Africans should replace enslaved Indigenous people as a primary source of manual labor, believing that Africans (who had previous exposure to smallpox and other diseases common in Europe) were better suited to survive the hardships. A slave trade between Europe and Africa, originally dominated by Portuguese traders, pre-existed colonization of the Americas, but as profit-seeking settler-colonists seized land to mine or to cultivate in the "New World," the demand for labor fostered the growth of the trade into a much larger, crueler, and more formalized operation. In the English colonies, an important turning point was 1619, the date of the first recorded sale of enslaved Africans in British North America. Gradually, African slavery's scale and economic impact eclipsed Indigenous slavery in North America, with the plantation-based economies of the American South and the West Indies especially becoming dependent on the labor and expertise of enslaved black people.

For black people in North America in the seventeenth century, experiences of enslavement could be profoundly brutal everywhere but also differed dramatically by region and personal circumstance. For those captured in Africa, the "middle passage," the months-long journey from Africa to the Americas, was unspeakably horrific: captives were underfed, abused cruelly by the crew, and packed so closely together in such unsanitary conditions that between a tenth and a fifth of them usually died.[2] On the Southern plantations, enslavers imposed order through violence, dehumanization, and the deliberate suppression of enslaved people's cultures of origin—even as they often relied on the agricultural knowledge of

[1] See "In Context: Mapping Colonial Conflict" and "In Context: Indigenous Experiences of Metacom's War," both included elsewhere in this volume, for materials relating to the Pequot War (1636–38) and King Philip's War (1675–78), both of which involved mass enslavements.

[2] Mortality rates tended to be much higher earlier in the trade and substantially lower later on, for a variety of reasons including the length of the journey.

the people they enslaved. A class hierarchy developed within black populations, as a small number of enslaved people—most often those born into slavery in North America—acquired highly valued skills that empowered them to negotiate with their enslavers and, in some cases, enabled them to purchase their own freedom. Particularly in the North, work of all kinds was far less racially segregated than it would be in the nineteenth century, and initially many enslaved black people worked with, socialized with, and had children with free and especially indentured white people. This fluidity was deeply troubling to white authorities, and colonies passed laws forbidding mixed-race marriage and codifying slavery in increasingly restrictive ways. These laws helped to foster across classes a gradual increase in social segregation and in white people's belief in their racial superiority.

Enslaved Africans resisted their oppression in large and small ways. On slave ships, revolts were relatively common, and many individuals escaped their situation by suicide. Once in America, enslaved people resisted by running away, and by sabotaging or deliberately slowing the pace of their work. There were some attempts at violent rebellion, but these were much less frequent and on a smaller scale than in the colonies of the West Indies, where a much higher percentage of the population was enslaved and rebellion appeared more likely to effect change.[1] Toward the end of the eighteenth century, black Americans began in significant numbers to incorporate rhetoric into their activism, using sermons and speeches, court petitions, and autobiographical narratives, among other genres, to argue for slavery's abolition.

Antislavery writings from this period often invoke Christian arguments, especially the view, popularized during the Great Awakening beginning in the 1730s, that human souls are equal in the eyes of God. Many enslaved people's religious practice combined elements of the religions brought from Africa—which included Islam, a wide range of polytheistic religions, and to a lesser extent Christianity—but interest in Christianity among enslaved people intensified dramatically with the advent of the Great Awakening. Revivals held obvious appeal for enslaved and free black audiences: they were held before racially mixed congregations, they encouraged spiritual ecstasy in a way that reflected the influence of black Americans' rituals, and they articulated an inspiring vision of heaven as an end to suffering and of salvation as equally open to everyone regardless of class or race. As the century progressed, black church leaders began to found independent congregations and, in the North, to form charitable groups known as African Societies; both types of institution played a role in opposing slavery and ameliorating its effects. White abolitionists, too, were often motivated by Protestant religious fervor, and many were Methodists or Quakers. But Christian arguments were also made by proslavery writers and speakers, who quoted Bible verses endorsing slavery and emphasized the importance of accepting the will of God.

In the last decades of the eighteenth century, abolitionist writers frequently drew on the same ideals of freedom and political equality that had been used to justify the American Revolution. Such arguments struck a chord with many white enslavers who were caught up in revolutionary fervor, and some did free the people they had enslaved in the period surrounding the Revolution. In New England, laws that opposed slavery—usually by instituting gradual emancipation—were passed during this period. But ironies and inconsistencies abounded. The majority of the nation's founders held enslaved people, but many were also opposed to slavery in principle—though even this opposition was informed by a racist desire to cultivate a white-dominated population. After the Revolution, the new government followed a course of economic and political expediency and did little to disturb the system of slavery in the South, or the plantation economy that continued to rely on it. There was a resurgence of hope among abolitionists around 1808, when the United States outlawed American involvement in the African slave trade, but this soon proved a woefully insufficient measure, as America itself had a growing enslaved population that facilitated a lively trade between states. As slavery decreased in the North and continued in the South, the decades following the American Revolution set the stage for the growing division between free and unfree states that would later motivate the Civil War.

⌘ ⌘ ⌘

[1] Most rebellions ended in mass executions of enslaved people; one exception, the Haitian Revolution, is discussed in the section on "Rebellions and Revolutions" elsewhere in this volume.

from King Alfonso I (Nzinga Mbemba) of Kongo, letter to King João III of Portugal, 18 October 1526[1]

Kongo and Portugal established diplomatic relations in the 1480s, and King Alfonso I of Kongo (r. 1509–c. 1542) is known for his selective adoption of Portuguese cultural practices, especially Catholicism, which he strove to foster among his own people. In the letter excerpted below, addressed to the king of Portugal, Alfonso I laments the effects of the slave trade on his nation. Despite the vehemence of his statements, it is important to note that Alfonso I did not oppose the trade altogether, but wanted it to be more effectively regulated. His letter was in part a request that Portugal stop providing aid to the kingdom of Ndongo (now Angola), which was ostensibly subordinate to Kongo but had been capturing Alfonso's people with Portugal's support.

Sir, Your Highness should know how our kingdom is being lost in so many ways that it is convenient to provide for the necessary remedy, since this is caused by the excessive freedom given by your agents and officials to the men and merchants who are allowed to come to this kingdom to set up shops with goods and many things which have been prohibited by us, and which they spread through our kingdoms and domains in such an abundance that many of our vassals,[2] whom we had in obedience, do not comply because they have the things in greater abundance than we ourselves; and it was with these things that we had them content and subjected under our vassalage and jurisdiction, so it is doing a great harm not only to the service of God, but to the security and peace of our kingdoms and state as well.

And we cannot reckon how great the damage is, since the mentioned merchants are taking every day our natives, sons of the land and the sons of our noblemen and vassals and our relatives, because the thieves and men of bad conscience grab them wishing to have the things and wares of this kingdom which they are ambitious of. They grab them and get them to be sold;

and so great, Sir, is the corruption and licentiousness that our country is being completely depopulated, and Your Highness should not agree with this nor accept it as in your service. ...

from Bartolomé de las Casas, *History of the Indies*[3] (1561)

Spanish priest and political figure Bartolomé de las Casas argued against the enslavement of Indigenous people and documented its cruelties in a number of works. In the passage excerpted below from his extensive *History of the Indies*, he discusses the enslavement of Indigenous Bahamians to work the mines of Hispaniola in the early sixteenth century. For more substantial selections from Las Casas's works, see the "Civilizations in Contact" section elsewhere in this anthology.

Those Spaniards who were exhausting the Indians in the gold mines [of Hispaniola] and in other forms of killing labor saw that their numbers dwindled every day and that they were dying out. Having no thought beyond their own material interests and the loss that the disappearance of the Indians might cause them, they hit on the idea of bringing in people from other islands to take the place of those who perished here, in order to keep the mines and other business enterprises going. To this end ... they persuaded the King that the Lucayas or Yucayas Islands[4] were full of people who lived in unprofitable idleness and who, left to themselves, would never become Christians. They asked the King to authorize Spanish residents in this island to fit out ships to bring those people here, so that they could be converted, and also make themselves useful in the gold mines. This, they said, would be profitable and greatly to His Highness' advantage. ...

When [the Indians] arrived, mostly at Puerto de Plata and Puerto Real on the north coast opposite the Lucayas, they were disembarked and divided into lots,

[1] Translated by B. Davidson, 1967.

[2] *vassals* I.e., subordinate kingdoms.

[3] Translated from the Spanish by John H. Parry and Robert J. Keith, 1984.

[4] *Lucayas ... Islands* I.e., the Bahamas.

according to the size of the investment that each of the adventurers had made: the old with the young, the sick with the healthy (for many fell sick at sea, and even died of hunger, thirst, and close confinement below decks in that hot climate). In the lots, no attempt was made to keep together wives and husbands, nor parents and children; for no more account was made of them than if they had been indeed the lowest of animals. …

from Bernardino de Manzanedo, dispatch to King Charles I of Spain, 1518[1]

From the beginnings of North American colonization, the Spanish government was deeply conflicted about Spanish exploitation of the Indigenous inhabitants of the land it colonized. Bernardino de Manzanedo was one of three religious officials sent in 1516 to the Indies to observe the way Indigenous people in the colonies were treated and to consider reforms to the system. In his report to the king, Manzanedo discusses several possible approaches, from improving the regulation of the system of forced labor already in place to freeing the Indigenous communities entirely. The excerpts below include his arguments in favor of the latter, as well as his suggestion—made by many Spanish officials during the period—that enslaved Africans could replace the Indigenous labor force, especially for the most strenuous jobs.

It seems, from what I have seen of them, that the Indians of Hispaniola and San Juan[2] are perfectly capable of governing themselves in their own traditional fashion; but they have neither the knowledge nor the ability to organize a community according to our laws and customs, and will not do so unless the Spaniards put pressure on them. Further, it appears that they have no enthusiasm for our holy faith and will not embrace it unless they are compelled. If they are allowed to live according to their own desire, few of them will be saved. They are more likely, I fear, to cling to their ancient rites and ceremonies than to turn to the worship of God.

In view of what has happened in the past, and of the ill-treatment that these Indians have suffered and still suffer, I greatly fear that if they are placed in the power of the Spaniards, whatever form their subjection may take, they will be ill-treated and their number will decline. It would seem to me best, therefore, that they should not be placed in the care of the Spaniards, if a way can be found of avoiding it, due consideration being given to other legitimate local interests. Personal opinions are unreliable, however, and I may be wrong; so I will outline two or three suggested ways of dealing with these Indians and remit them to Your Royal conscience, so that Your Highness may consider them and decide which policy would be most pleasing to God.

Felipe Guamán Poma de Ayala, "Negroes: How they have so much patience," *The First New Chronicle and Good Government,* c. 1615. Felipe Guamán Poma de Ayala, a member of the Quechuan nobility in Peru, sent to King Philip III of Spain an extensive manuscript critiquing the actions of the Spanish government in his homeland; most of the manuscript focuses on the mistreatment of Indigenous people, but a small portion of the text depicts the enslavement of black people. This illustration's caption translates to "good blacks endure the abuses of their master with patience and the love of Christ."

1 Translated by John H. Parry and Robert J. Keith, 1984.

2 *San Juan* Spanish colony in what is now Puerto Rico.

Some say that Your Highness should command all the Indians of this island to be set free entirely, so that no Spaniard might employ their labor except by their own free will. Their welfare should be entrusted to religious persons who would instruct them in our holy Catholic faith and teach them to live according to our customs. It is said that Your Highness is bound in conscience to do this; partly because of the concession made by the Pope to the Crown of Castile,[1] which states that they are to be converted to Christianity by the most effective means; partly to render satisfaction to God for the murders and robberies wickedly committed against these Indians, and for past neglect of their salvation and welfare. This policy would also bring great gains, because the Indian population would, within a few years, be greatly increased; and since they would be Christians, and better instructed in our customs than they are at present, they would be more valuable subjects of Your Highness and Your descendants. If this policy is not followed, on the other hand, they will die out, and this will be a serious loss to Your Highness, to say nothing of the inhumanity of leaving Your vassals to die. There can be no doubt that this is what will happen; the present daily decline in numbers is an unmistakable warning.

The objections raised to this policy are that royal revenue would be lost and the settlers ruined; and that the Indians would rebel and return to their idolatry and their vicious habits. The proponents of this policy reply that Your Highness should encourage settlement (as other princes have done in less promising territories than these) and should assist the settlers so that they can support themselves and strike roots here; and that if this is done, the Indians will not rebel, nor will they return to their bad habits, because the religious will so work among them that, with God's help, in a short time they will be Christian and peaceful; nor will the royal revenue be lost if Your Highness can help the settlers to import slaves and other necessities; and even if there should be some loss of revenue, that is preferable to a bad conscience. …

Many people think that the best way to improve the condition of the Indians would be to remove them from the gold workings. They are people of weak constitution; they drink nothing but water, and their diet of cassava bread contains very little nourishment. Gold production requires hard manual labor, and this is thought to be the cause of the death of many of them. Initially Your Highness's revenues would be reduced; but they would soon increase rapidly, because the Indians so released could be employed in farming, and so the land would be cultivated and settled as it is not now, for our people are so obsessed with gold that no one will spare a single Indian from the mines to till the soil. I shall have more to say about this later. If my suggestion does not find favor, at least Your Highness should order that the pick-and-shovel work be done by Negro slaves, or by some other strong slaves, and not by Indians, because it is too arduous for them. …

All the settlers of Hispaniola beg Your Highness to give them permission to import Negro slaves, because they say that the Indians do not provide them with enough labor to be able to support themselves there. The fathers[2] and I spoke with Your Highness's officials, the judges, and with some of the councilmen of Santo Domingo about this article and, seeing the need of this island, it seemed to all of us that it would be good for them to be imported, on condition that there be as many or more women as men and that they are brought straight from Africa, rather than being raised in Castile or other places because those who are turn out great rogues. This will be a great benefit for Your Highness's revenues, which will otherwise decrease steadily, and it will relieve the Indians of much of their labor if they remain in *encomiendas*;[3] also, the settlers will be more firmly rooted when they find that they have their own property, which cannot be taken away from them. If Your Highness decides that this should be conceded, it should be commanded that the blacks be brought from certain lands where their customs and conditions are known to be better and not from others where they are usually bad. …

[1] *the concession … of Castile* In 1493 the Pope decreed that the Spanish monarchy (Isabella I of Castile and Ferdinand II of Aragon) had the right to a vast swath of the western hemisphere. The decree charged the monarchs to ensure that "the Catholic faith and the Christian religion be exalted and be everywhere increased and spread."

[2] *The fathers* I.e., the other religious officials Manzanedo traveled with.

[3] *encomiendas* Estates granted to Spanish colonists along with the authority to tax Indigenous inhabitants or demand labor in lieu of taxes.

from John Rolfe, letter to Sir Edwin Sandys, January 1620[1]

English colonist John Rolfe is best known for his marriage to the Powhatan woman Matoaka, more commonly referred to as Pocahontas, and his role in the development of commercial tobacco production in Virginia. The brief passage excerpted below—from a letter addressed to Edward Sandys, treasurer of the Virginia Company overseeing the colony—is the first written record of the sale of enslaved black people in British North America. The enslaved people Rolfe mentions were probably Kimbundu speakers from the kingdom of Ndongo who had been sold to Portuguese enslavers; on its way to the Americas the Portuguese slave ship was captured by English privateers who seized the enslaved people as loot.

... About the latter end of August, a Dutch man of war[2] of the burden[3] of a 160 tons arrived at Point-Comfort,[4] the commander's name Capt. Jope, his pilot for the West Indies one Mr. Marmaduke, an Englishman. They met with the treasurer in the West Indies, and determined to hold consort ship hitherward,[5] but in their passage lost one the other. He[6] brought not anything but 20 and odd Negroes, which the governor and cape merchant[7] bought for victuals[8] (whereof he was in great need as he pretended[9]) at the best and easiest rates they could. He had a large and ample commission from his Excellency to range and to take purchase in the West Indies. ...

[1] In preparing this text, the editors consulted the version of Rolfe's letter transcribed in *The Records of the Virginia Company of London, Volume 3* (1933).

[2] *Dutch man of war* A man of war is a large warship; the ship Rolfe describes, *The White Lion*, traveled under a Dutch flag but had a British crew.

[3] *burden* Carrying capacity.

[4] *Point-Comfort* Now called Fort Monroe, on the southern part of the Virginia coast.

[5] *hold consort ship hitherward* I.e., travel together in this direction.

[6] *He* I.e., Captain Jope.

[7] *cape merchant* Merchant in charge of a trading post.

[8] *bought for victuals* Purchased in exchange for provisions.

[9] *pretended* Claimed.

from Edward Waterhouse, "A Declaration of the State of the Colony and Affairs in Virginia" (1622)

In 1622, losing more and more of their most fertile land to settlers' tobacco fields, Powhatan warriors carried out a surprise attack on the colony of Jamestown, killing about a quarter of the population in a single day. Colonial official Edward Waterhouse, writing on behalf of the Virginia Company, discussed the attack in "A Declaration of the State of the Colony and Affairs in Virginia, with a Relation of the Barbarous Massacre in the Time of Peace and League, Treacherously Executed by the Native Infidels upon the English." In his report, which was printed in England, Waterhouse argues that the surprise attack gives the colonists moral license to "punish" the Powhatan with all manner of violence, including enslavement. As Waterhouse predicted, settlers did exact violent revenge on the Powhatan, burning numerous villages; when a Powhatan delegation came to discuss the terms of a peace agreement, the settlers poisoned them. As the century progressed, Indigenous enslavement came to play a key role in the Virginia economy—though by 1700 its economic importance was overwhelmingly eclipsed by the enslavement of Africans.

Tobacco paper, seventeenth century. Tobacco papers such as this, used to package tobacco for sale in England, often featured images of black or Indigenous people.

... [O]ur hands, which before were tied with gentleness and fair usage, are now set at liberty by the treacherous violence of the savages, not untying the knot, but cutting it: So that we—who hitherto have had possession of no more ground than their waste,[1] and our purchase at a valuable consideration to their own contentment, gained—may now by right of war, and law of nations, invade the country and destroy them who sought to destroy us: whereby we shall enjoy their cultivated places, turning the laborious mattock[2] into the victorious sword (wherein there is more both ease, benefit, and glory) and possessing the fruits of others' labours. Now their cleared grounds in all their villages (which are situate in the fruitfullest places of the land) shall be inhabited by us, whereas heretofore the grubbing[3] of woods was the greatest labour. ...

... [T]he Indians, who before were used as friends, may now most justly be compelled to servitude and drudgery, and supply the room[4] of men that labour, whereby even the meanest[5] of the plantation[6] may employ themselves more entirely in their arts and occupations, which are more generous, whilst Savages perform their inferior works of digging in mines, and the like, of whom also some may be sent for the service of the Summer Islands.[7]

John Saffin, "The Negroes Character" (1701)

John Saffin and Samuel Sewall, two Massachusetts judges, engaged in a pamphlet debate over slavery that was prompted by Saffin's attempt to enslave his black indentured servant, Adam, after the term of indenture expired. (The courts found in favor of Adam.) Sewall's antislavery pamphlet, *The Selling of Joseph* (1700), is excerpted in this anthology's website component. Saffin's proslavery response,

A Brief and Candid Answer (1701), included the following viciously racist poem—a relatively early example of the sort of vitriol that would be invoked often by proponents of slavery over the coming centuries.

Cowardly and cruel are those Blacks innate,
Prone to revenge, imp° of *offspring*
 inveterate° hate, *longstanding*
He that exasperates them, soon espies
Mischief and murder in their very eyes.
5 Libidinous,° deceitful, false and rude, *lustful*
The spume° issue[8] of ingratitude. *frothy*
The premises considered, all may tell,
How near good Joseph[9] they are parallel.

anonymous, letter to the *South Carolina Gazette*, 14 October 1732

The labor performed by enslaved people on South Carolina's rice plantations was among the most grueling in North America. Enslaved people used creative ways to limit the excessive demands their enslavers placed on them; often, resistance took the form of working more slowly, breaking tools, or otherwise interfering with production in a way that enslavers could not be certain was deliberate but that drew attention to the plantation's dependence on its enslaved population. One larger-scale resistance method was the burning of barns—a serious financial blow that could easily befall a plantation accidentally, but that also seemed suspiciously common when the barns were full of rice.

1 *waste* Wilderness.

2 *mattock* Tool used to dig up roots and stones and prepare hard soil for planting.

3 *grubbing* Clearing land of stumps and rocks.

4 *the room* I.e., a sufficient supply.

5 *meanest* Poorest; of the lowest status.

6 *plantation* Colony.

7 *Summer Islands* Bermuda.

8 *issue* Outflow, offspring, or result. Elsewhere in *A Brief and Candid Answer*, Saffin discusses the commonly held racist belief that Africans were the descendants of Ham, whose son Canaan was cursed by God because Ham disrespected his father, Noah; see Genesis 9.22–27.

9 *Joseph* Biblical figure who is wrongfully sold into slavery; see Genesis 37. Sewall's tract interprets Joseph's story as evidence that the Bible condemns slavery.

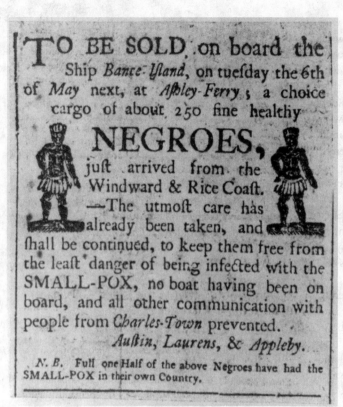

Poster advertising the sale of enslaved people in Charleston, 1760. People forcibly taken from the West African "Windward" or "Rice Coast," extending from present-day Senegal to Sierra Leone and Liberia, were especially valuable to South Carolina and Georgia plantation owners because of their expertise in the cultivation of rice and other crops. Enslaved people from West Africa brought with them knowledge of irrigation methods and other technologies that became broadly used in Southern rice and, later, indigo production. Because the enslaved population of South Carolina and Georgia was so large and so strongly linked to the "Rice Coast," it developed a distinct culture with its own language, Gullah, combining influences from English and from the numerous cultures and languages of the "Rice Coast," especially from Sierra Leone.

I have taken notice for several years past, that there has not one winter elapsed without one or more barns being burnt, and two winters since,[1] there was no less than five. Whether it is owing to accident, carelessness, or severity, I will not pretend to determine, but am afraid chiefly to the latter. I desire therefore, as a friend of the planters,[2] that you'll insert the following account from Pon Pon,[3] which, I hope, will forewarn the planters of their danger, and make them for the future more careful and human.

"About 3 weeks since, Mr. James Gray worked his negroes late in his barn at night, and the next morning before day hurried them out again, and when they came to it, found it burnt down to the ground, and all that was in it."

[1] *two winters since* Two winters before.

[2] *planters* Plantation owners.

[3] *Pon Pon* The Pon Pon River, now also called the South Edisto River, in South Carolina. Rice plantations were frequently established near rivers.

from John Woolman, *Some Considerations on the Keeping of Negroes* (1754)

One of the first prominent Quakers to publicly oppose slavery, John Woolman was influential in increasing antislavery sentiment among Quakers, who came to play a significant role in the abolition movement on both sides of the Atlantic. Born in New Jersey, he traveled throughout the colonies and eventually to England, preaching and publishing on slavery and other political and ethical issues; the antislavery essay excerpted below was published in Philadelphia. Woolman was personally steadfast in his abolitionist principles, abstaining from the use of sugar, dyed clothing, and other products of slavery.

"Forasmuch as ye did it to the least of these my brethren, ye did it unto me."

—Matthew 25.40

As many times there are different motives to the same action, and one does that from a generous heart which another does for selfish ends: the like may be said in this case.

There are various circumstances among those that keep negroes, and different ways by which they fall under their care; and I doubt not, there are many well disposed persons amongst them who desire rather to manage wisely and justly in this difficult matter, than to make gain of it.

But the general disadvantage which these poor negroes lie under in an enlightened Christian country having often filled me with real sadness, I now think it my duty, through divine aid, to offer some thoughts thereon to the consideration of others.

When we remember that all nations are of one blood (Genesis 3.20), that in this world we are but sojourners, that we are subject to the like afflictions and infirmities of body, the like disorders and frailties in mind, the like temptations, the same death, and the same judgment, and that the All-wise Being is Judge and Lord over us all, it seems to raise an idea of general brotherhood, and a disposition easy to be touched with a feeling of each other's afflictions; but when we forget those things and look chiefly at our outward circumstances, in this and some ages past, constantly retaining in our minds the distinction betwixt us and them, with respect to our knowledge and improvement in things divine, natural and artificial, our breasts being apt to be filled with fond[1] notions of superiority, there is danger of erring in our conduct toward them.

We allow them to be of the same species with ourselves; the odds is, we are in a higher station, and enjoy greater favour than they. And when it is thus that our heavenly Father endoweth some of his children with distinguished gifts, they are intended for good ends; but if those thus gifted are thereby lifted up above their brethren, not considering themselves as debtors to the weak, nor behaving themselves as faithful stewards, none who judge impartially can suppose them free from ingratitude. ...

To consider mankind otherwise than brethren, to think favours are peculiar[2] to one nation, and exclude others, plainly supposes a darkness in the understanding: for as God's love is universal, so where the mind is sufficiently influenced by it, it begets a likeness of itself, and the heart is enlarged toward all men. Again, to conclude a people froward,[3] perverse, and worse by nature than others (who ungratefully receive favours and apply them to bad ends): this will excite a behaviour toward them unbecoming the excellence of true religion.

To prevent such error, let us calmly consider their circumstance; and the better to do it, make their case ours. Suppose, then, that our ancestors and we had been exposed to constant servitude in the more servile and inferior employments of life; that we had been destitute of the help of reading and good company; that amongst ourselves we had had but few wise and pious instructors; that the religious amongst our superiors seldom took notice of us; that while others, in ease, have plentifully heaped up the fruit of our labour, we had received barely enough to relieve nature; and being wholly at the command of others, had generally been treated as a contemptible, ignorant part of mankind. Should we, in that case, be less abject than they now are? Again, if oppression be so hard to bear that, a wise man is made mad by it (Ecclesiastes 7.7), then a series of oppressions altering the behaviour and manners of a people is what may reasonably be expected.

When our property is taken contrary to our mind, by means appearing to us unjust, it is only through divine influence, and the enlargement of heart from thence proceeding, that we can love our reputed oppressors. If the negroes fall short in this, an uneasy, if not a disconsolate disposition will be awakened, and remain like seeds in their minds, producing sloth and many other habits appearing odious to us, with which being free men, they, perhaps, had not been chargeable.[4] These and other circumstances, rightly considered, will lessen the too great disparity which some make between us and them. ...

When self-love presides in our minds, our opinions are biased in our own favour; in this condition, being concerned with a people so situated that they have no voice to plead their own cause, there is danger of using ourselves to an undisturbed partiality, till, by long

1 *fond* Foolish.

2 *peculiar* Specific.

3 *froward* Headstrong and obstinate.

4 *with which ... chargeable* I.e., if they had been free they might not have developed such habits.

custom, the mind becomes reconciled with it, and the judgment itself infected.

To humbly apply to God for wisdom, that we may thereby be enabled to see things as they are, and ought to be, is very needful; hereby the hidden things of darkness may be brought to light, and the judgment made clear. We shall then consider mankind as brethren; though different degrees and a variety of qualifications and abilities, one dependant on another, be admitted, yet high thoughts will be laid aside, and all men treated as becometh the sons of one father, agreeable to the doctrine of Christ Jesus.

He hath laid down the best criterion by which mankind ought to judge of their own conduct, and others judge for them of theirs, one towards another, *viz.*[1] "Whatsoever ye would that men should do unto you, do ye even so to them." I take it that all men by nature are equally entitled to the equity of this rule, and under the indispensable obligations of it. One man ought not to look upon another man or society of men as so far beneath him that he should not put himself in their place, in all his actions towards them, and bring all to this test, viz. How should I approve of this conduct, were I in their circumstance, and they in mine?[2] ...

It may be objected that there is the cost of purchase, and risk of their lives to them who possess [enslaved people], and therefore [it is] needful that they make the best use of their time. In a practice just and reasonable, such objections may have weight; but if the work be wrong from the beginning, there is little or no force in them. If I purchase a man who has never forfeited his liberty, the natural right of freedom is in him; and shall I keep him and his posterity in servitude and ignorance?

How should I approve of this conduct, were I in his circumstances, and he in mine? ...

[1] *viz.* Abbreviation of the Latin videlicet, meaning "namely," or "that is to say."

[2] *He hath ... in mine* From Alexander Arscott, *Some Considerations Relating to the Present State of Christian Religion* (1731), a tract that was widely read in the eighteenth century.

from James Grainger, *The Sugar-Cane* (1764)

James Grainger, an English-born doctor and manager of his family's sugarcane plantation on the Caribbean island of St. Kitts, is best-remembered for his long poem *The Sugar-Cane* (1764), which was frequently reprinted in the eighteenth and early nineteenth centuries. It was received by English readers as a substantial literary achievement; Samuel Johnson, for example, wrote of Grainger that "we have been destitute till now of an American poet, that could bear any degree of competition." Grainger described his poem as a "West-India georgic"; the georgic genre, named for the Roman poet Virgil's *Georgics* (c. 29 BCE), typically addresses agriculture or other rural matters, often with instructional intent. The first three books of *The Sugar-Cane* describe the landscape of the Caribbean and the cultivation and harvesting of sugarcane, while the last offers a guide to purchasing and overseeing enslaved people. This final book, excerpted below, evokes the third book of Virgil's *Georgics*, which discusses the care of livestock. Grainger is more moderate than many of his peers in the treatment he suggests enslaved people should receive, but Johnson nonetheless reflected that in this last portion of the book "that tenderness and humanity, with which the former part of the poem seems replete, is, in some measure, forgotten."

from BOOK 4

In mind, and aptitude for useful toil,
... The negroes differ: muse that difference sing.

Whether to wield the hoe, or guide the plane;[3]
Or for domestic uses thou intend'st
5 The sunny Libyan: from what clime they spring,
It not imports;[4] if strength and youth be theirs.

[3] *plane* Tool used to smooth a wooden surface.

[4] *It not imports* It is of no importance.

Yet those from Congo's wide-extended plains,
Through which the long Zaire[1] winds with crystal
 stream,
Where lavish Nature sends indulgent forth
10 Fruits of high flavour, and spontaneous seeds
Of bland nutritious quality, ill bear
The toilsome field; but boast a docile mind,
And happiness of features. These, with care,
Be taught each nice° mechanic art: or trained *precise*
15 To household offices: their ductile souls
Will all thy care, and all thy gold repay.

But, if the labours of the field demand
Thy chief attention; and the ambrosial cane
Thou long'st to see, with spiry frequence, shade
20 Many an acre: planter, choose the slave,
Who sails from barren climes; where art alone,
Offspring of rude[2] necessity, compels
The sturdy native or° to plant the soil, *either*
Or stem vast rivers for his daily food.

25 Such are the children of the Golden Coast;[3]
Such the Papaws,[4] of negroes far the best:
And such the numerous tribes that skirt the shore,
From rapid Volta to the distant Rey.[5]

But, planter, from what coast soe'er they sail,
30 Buy not the old: they ever sullen prove;
With heart-felt anguish, they lament their home;
They will not, cannot work; they never learn
Thy native language; they are prone to ails;
And oft by suicide their being end.

35 Must thou from Africk reinforce thy gang?
Let health and youth their every sinew firm;
Clear roll their ample eye; their tongue be red;
Broad swell their chest; their shoulders wide expand;

Not prominent their belly; clean and strong
40 Their thighs and legs, in just proportion rise.
Such soon will brave the fervours of the clime;
And free from ails, that kill thy negro-train,
A useful servitude will long support.

Yet, if thine own, thy children's life, be dear;
45 Buy not a Cormantee,[6] though healthy, young.
Of breed too generous for the servile field;
They, born to freedom in their native land,
Choose death before dishonourable bonds:
Or, fired with vengeance, at the midnight hour,
50 Sudden they seize thine unsuspecting watch,[7]
And thine own poinard° bury in thy breast. ... *dagger*

When first your Blacks are novel to the hoe;
Study their humours: some, soft-soothing words;
Some, presents; and some, menaces subdue;
55 And some I've known, so stubborn is their kind,
Whom blows, alas! could win alone to toil.

Yet, planter, let humanity prevail.
Perhaps thy negro, in his native land,
Possesed large fertile plains, and slaves, and herds:
60 Perhaps, whene'er he deigned to walk abroad,
The richest silks, from where the Indus rolls,[8]
His limbs invested in their gorgeous pleats:
Perhaps he wails° his wife, his children, left *mourns for*
To struggle with adversity: perhaps
65 Fortune, in battle for his country fought,
Gave him a captive to his deadliest foe:
Perhaps, incautious, in his native fields,
(On pleasurable scenes his mind intent)
All as he wandered; from the neighbouring grove,
70 Fell° ambush dragged him to the hated *cruel*
 main.° *ocean*
Were they even sold for crimes; ye polished, say!
Ye, to whom Learning opes her amplest page!
Ye, whom the knowledge of a living God
Should lead to virtue! Are ye free from crimes?

1 *long Zaire* Zaire River, now known as the Congo River; the second-longest river in Africa.

2 *rude* Harsh; uncivilized.

3 *Golden Coast* I.e., Gold Coast, now Ghana.

4 *Papaws* Popos, a Portuguese term for the Xlwa people of present-day Benin.

5 *rapid Volta ... Rey* The Volta and Rey are bodies of water that empty into the Gulf of Guinea, almost a thousand miles apart; the Volta River is in Ghana, and the Rio del Rey estuary is in Cameroon.

6 *Cormantee* European word applied to enslaved people from a number of different Gold Coast kingdoms; many shared a common language, Akan, but they were otherwise culturally distinct.

7 *watch* I.e., night watch.

8 *where the Indus rolls* The Indus river flows through China, India, and Pakistan.

75 Ah pity, then, these uninstructed swains;[1]
 And still let mercy soften the decrees
 Of rigid justice, with her lenient hand.

 Oh, did the tender muse possess the power,
 Which monarchs have, and monarchs oft abuse:

80 'Twould be the fond ambition of her soul,
 To quell tyrannic sway; knock off the chains
 Of heart-debasing slavery; give to man,
 Of every colour and of every clime,
 Freedom, which stamps him image of his God.
85 Then laws, Oppression's scourge, fair Virtue's prop,
 Offspring of Wisdom! should impartial reign,
 To knit the whole in well-accorded strife:
 Servants, not slaves; of choice, and not compelled;
 The Blacks should cultivate the Cane-land Isles. …

Belinda Sutton, "The Petition of Belinda, an African"[2] (1782)

After Isaac Royall, a member of a wealthy family with Loyalist ties, fled America during the Revolutionary War, his assets were seized by the government and the people he had enslaved were freed. One of these, Belinda (later Belinda Sutton), petitioned the General Court of Massachusetts to receive a pension from the Royall estate. She was granted a sum of fifteen pounds and twelve shillings per year, but several further petitions show that she only received her pension a handful of times. Nonetheless, her petition is celebrated both as an autobiographical work—one that may have been authored in collaboration with the prominent abolitionist Prince Hall—and for its outcome, which some consider the first court-ordered payment of reparations for slavery.

To the honourable the senate and house of representatives, in general court assembled:
 The petition of Belinda, an African, humbly shows,

[1] *swains* Rural people, especially agricultural workers; the term is often used in pastoral poetry in reference to young rural men in love.

[2] The present text is based upon the original manuscript of the petition.

That seventy years have rolled away, since she, on the banks of the Rio de Valta,[3] received her existence. The mountains covered with spicy forests, the valleys loaded with the richest fruits, spontaneously produced, joined to that happy temperature of air which excludes excess, would have yielded her the most complete felicity, had not her mind received early impressions of the cruelty of men, whose faces were like the moon, and whose bows and arrows were like the thunder and the lightning of the clouds. The idea of these, the most dreadful of all enemies, filled her infant slumbers with horror, and her noon-tide moments with cruel apprehensions! But her affrighted imagination, in its most alarming extension, never represented distresses equal to what she hath since really experienced. For before she had twelve years enjoyed the fragrance of her native groves, and ere she had realized that Europeans placed their happiness in the yellow dust[4] which she carelessly marked with her infant foot-steps—even when she, in a sacred grove, with each hand in that of a tender parent, was paying her devotion to the great Orisa,[5] who made all things—an armed band of white men, driving many of her countrymen in chains, rushed into the hallowed shades! Could the tears, the sighs, and supplications, bursting from the tortured parental affection, have blunted the keen edge of avarice, she might have been rescued from agony, which many of her country's children have felt, but which none have ever yet described. In vain she lifted her supplicating voice to an insulted father, and her guiltless hands to a dishonoured deity! She was ravished[6] from the bosom of her country, from the arms of her friends, while the advanced age of her parents, rendering them unfit for servitude, cruelly separated them from her forever!

 Scenes which her imagination had never conceived of—a floating world—the sporting monsters of the deep—and the familiar meeting of billows[7] and clouds strove, but in vain, to divert her melancholy attention

[3] *Rio de Valta* Volta River in what is now Ghana, in West Africa.

[4] *yellow dust* I.e., gold.

[5] *Orisa* Yoruba: Spirit or deity. This word is not part of any languages traditionally spoken in the part of Ghana where Belinda was kidnapped, though some Ewe-speakers of the region have a similar concept.

[6] *ravished* Violently abducted.

[7] *billows* Waves.

from three hundred Africans in chains, suffering the most excruciating torments; and some of them rejoicing that the pangs of death came like a balm to their wounds.

Once more her eyes were blessed with a continent: but alas! how unlike the land where she received her being! Here all things appeared unpropitious. She learned to catch the ideas marked by the sounds of language, only to know that her doom was slavery, from which death alone was to emancipate her. What did it avail her, that the walls of her lord were hung with splendor, and that the dust trodden under foot in her native country crowded his gates with sordid worshippers? The laws had rendered her incapable of receiving property—and though she was a free moral agent, accountable for her actions, yet she never had a moment at her own disposal! Fifty years her faithful hands have been compelled to ignoble servitude for the benefit of an Isaac Royall, until—as if nations must be agitated, and the world convulsed, for the preservation of that freedom which the Almighty Father intended for *all* the human race—the present war[1] was commenced. The terrors of men armed in the cause of freedom compelled her master to fly—and to breathe away his life in a land where lawless domination sits enthroned, pouring bloody outrage and cruelty on all who dare to be free.[2]

The face of your petitioner is now marked with the furrows of time, and her frame feebly bending under the oppression of years, while she, by the laws of the land, is denied the enjoyment of one morsel of that immense wealth, a part whereof hath been accumulated by her own industry, and the whole augmented by her servitude.

Wherefore, casting herself at the feet of your honours, as to a body of men formed for the extirpation of vassalage, for the reward of virtue, and the just returns of honest industry—she prays that such allowance may be made her, out of the estate of colonel Royall, as will prevent her, and her more infirm daughter, from misery in the greatest extreme, and scatter comfort over the short and downward path of their lives—and she will ever pray.

Boston 13th February 1783

[X] the mark of Belinda

[1] *present war* I.e., the American Revolutionary War (1775–83).

[2] *The terrors … to be free* Royall fled to the British colony of Nova Scotia and subsequently to England.

from "Old Elizabeth," *Memoir of Old Elizabeth, a Coloured Woman* (1863)

> Born to enslaved Methodist parents in 1766, the woman known as Old Elizabeth obtained her freedom at the age of thirty and spent much of her life as a traveling preacher. She traveled to places where she risked re-enslavement, and, as both a woman and a black person, she faced significant persecution everywhere from those who felt she had no right to preach; nonetheless, she had a remarkably successful, long career. Her short memoir, dictated a few years before her death in 1866, was published by Quakers in Philadelphia. The following passage describes her experience of religion under slavery in the eighteenth century.

In the following Narrative of "OLD ELIZABETH," which was taken mainly from her own lips in her 97th year, her simple language has been adhered to as strictly as was consistent with perspicuity and propriety.

I was born in Maryland in the year 1766. My parents were slaves. Both my father and mother were religious people, and belonged to the Methodist Society. It was my father's practice to read in the Bible aloud to his children every Sabbath morning. At these seasons, when I was but five years old, I often felt the overshadowing of the Lord's Spirit, without at all understanding what it meant; and these incomes and influences[3] continued to attend me until I was eleven years old, particularly when I was alone, by which I was preserved from doing anything that I thought was wrong.

In the eleventh year of my age, my master sent me to another farm, several miles from my parents, brothers, and sisters, which was a great trouble to me. At last I grew so lonely and sad I thought I should die if I did not see my mother. I asked the overseer if I might go, but being positively denied, I concluded to go without his knowledge. When I reached home my mother was away. I set off and walked twenty miles before I found her. I stayed with her for several days, and we returned together. Next day I was sent back to my new place, which renewed my sorrow. At parting, my mother told me that I had, "nobody in the wide world to look to

[3] *incomes and influences* I.e., infusions of divine will and power.

but God." These words fell upon my heart with ponderous weight, and seemed to add to my grief. I went back repeating as I went, "none but God in the wide world." On reaching the farm, I found the overseer was displeased at me for going without his liberty. He tied me with a rope, and gave me some stripes of which I carried the marks for weeks.

After this time, finding as my mother said, I had none in the world to look to but God, I betook myself to prayer, and in every lonely place I found an altar. I mourned sore like a dove and chattered forth my sorrow, moaning in the corners of the field, and under the fences.

I continued in this state for about six months, feeling as though my head were waters,[1] and I could do nothing but weep. I lost my appetite, and not being able to take enough food to sustain nature, I became so weak I had but little strength to work; still I was required to do all my duty. One evening, after the duties of the day were ended, I thought I could not live over the night, so threw myself on a bench, expecting to die, and without being prepared to meet my Maker; and my spirit cried within me, "must I die in this state, and be banished from Thy presence forever? I own I am a sinner in Thy sight, and not fit to live where thou art." Still it was my fervent desire that the Lord would pardon me. Just at this season,[2] I saw with my spiritual eye an awful gulf of misery. As I thought I was about to plunge into it, I heard a voice saying, "rise up and pray," which strengthened me. I fell on my knees and prayed the best I could the Lord's Prayer.[3] Knowing no more to say, I halted, but continued on my knees. My spirit was then taught to pray, "Lord, have mercy on me—Christ save me." Immediately there appeared a director, clothed in white raiment. I thought he took me by the hand and said, "come with me." He led me down a long journey to a fiery gulf, and left me standing upon the brink of this awful pit. I began to scream for mercy, thinking I was about to be plunged to the belly of hell, and believed I should sink

to endless ruin. Although I prayed and wrestled with all my might, it seemed in vain. Still, I felt all the while that I was sustained by some invisible power. At this solemn moment, I thought I saw a hand from which hung, as it were, a silver hair, and a voice told me that all the hope I had of being saved was no more than a hair; still, pray, and it will be sufficient. I then renewed my struggle, crying for mercy and salvation, until I found that every cry raised me higher and higher, and my head was quite above the fiery pillars. Then I thought I was permitted to look straight forward, and saw the Saviour standing with His hand stretched out to receive me. An indescribably glorious light was in Him, and He said, "Peace, peace, come unto me." At this moment I felt that my sins were forgiven me, and the time of my deliverance was at hand. I sprang forward and fell at his feet, giving Him all the thanks and highest praises, crying, "Thou hast redeemed me— Thou hast redeemed me to thyself." I felt filled with light and love. At this moment I thought my former guide took me again by the hand and led me upward, till I came to the celestial world and to heaven's door, which I saw was open, and while I stood there, a power surrounded me which drew me in, and I saw millions of glorified spirits in white robes. After I had this view, I thought I heard a voice saying, "Art thou willing to be saved?" I said, "Yes Lord." Again I was asked, "Art thou willing to be saved in my way?" I stood speechless until he asked me again, "Art thou willing to be saved in my way?" Then I heard a whispering voice say, "If thou art not saved in the Lord's way, thou canst not be saved at all," at which I exclaimed, "Yes Lord, in thy own way." Immediately a light fell upon my head, and I was filled with light, and I was shown the world lying in wickedness, and was told I must go there, and call the people to repentance, for the day of the Lord was at hand; and this message was as a heavy yoke upon me,[4] so that I wept bitterly at the thought of what I should have to pass through. While I wept, I heard a voice say, "Weep not; some will laugh at thee, some will scoff at thee, and the dogs will bark at thee, but while thou doest my will, I will be with thee to the ends of the earth."

[1] *my head were waters* See Jeremiah 9.1: "Oh that my head were waters, and mine eyes a fountain of tears, that I might weep day and night for the slain of the daughter of my people!"

[2] *season* Time.

[3] *Lord's Prayer* Commonly recited Christian prayer; see Matthew 6.9–13 and Luke 11.2–4.

[4] *this message ... upon me* See Matthew 11.29–30, where Jesus instructs his followers, "Take my yoke upon you, and learn of me; for I am meek and lowly in heart: and ye shall find rest unto your souls. For my yoke is easy, and my burden is light."

I was at this time not yet thirteen years old. The next day, when I had come to myself, I felt like a new creature in Christ, and all my desire was to see the Saviour.

I lived in a place where there was no preaching, and no religious instruction; but every day I went out amongst the haystacks, where the presence of the Lord overshadowed me, and I was filled with sweetness and joy, and was as a vessel filled with holy oil.[1] In this way I continued for about a year; many times while my hands were at my work, my spirit was carried away to spiritual things. One day as I was going to my old place behind the haystacks to pray, I was assailed with this language: "Are you going there to weep and pray? What a fool! There are older professors[2] than you are, and they do not take that way to get to heaven. People whose sins are forgiven ought to be joyful and lively, and not be struggling and praying." With this I halted and concluded I would not go, but do as other professors did, and so went off to play; but at this moment the light that was in me became darkened, and the peace and joy that I once had departed from me.

About this time I was moved back to the farm where my mother lived, and then sold to a stranger. Here I had deep sorrows and plungings, not having experienced a return of that sweet evidence and light with which I had been favoured formerly; but by watching unto prayer, and wrestling mightily with the Lord, my peace gradually returned, and with it a great exercise and weight upon my heart for the salvation of my fellow creatures; and I was often carried to distant lands and shown places where I should have to travel and deliver the Lord's message. Years afterwards, I found myself visiting those towns and countries that I had seen in the light as I sat at home at my sewing—places of which I had never heard.

Some years from this time I was sold to a Presbyterian for a term of years, as he did not think it right to hold slaves for life. Having served him faithfully my time out, he gave me my liberty, which was about the thirtieth year of my age. ...

[1] *a vessel filled with holy oil* See 2 Kings 4.17, in which a woman is saved from selling her sons into servitude to pay her debts; her container of oil miraculously fills a large number of vessels without emptying, and she sells the oil instead of her sons.

[2] *professors* People who openly state their beliefs, especially their faith in Christianity.

from Jupiter Hammon, *An Address to the Negroes in the State of New York* (1787)

Though he was born into slavery and remained enslaved until his death, Jupiter Hammon achieved prominence as a preacher and religious poet, becoming the first African American writer to publish his poetry in America. Hammon grew up in Long Island, where his enslaver, Henry Lloyd, allowed him to receive an education, and where his worldview was strongly influenced by the Christian principles of the Great Awakening. After Lloyd's death, Hammon remained enslaved by the family and moved to Connecticut with Lloyd's son, where he became involved in the abolitionist movement. The pamphlet excerpted here is based on his sermon delivered to the African Society of New York City in September 1786.

R especting obedience to masters. Now ... whether it is right, and lawful, in the sight of God, for them to make slaves of us or not, I am certain that while we are slaves, it is our duty to obey our masters, in all their lawful commands, and mind them unless we are bid to do that which we know to be sin, or forbidden in God's word. The apostle Paul says, "Servants be obedient to them that are your masters according to the flesh, with fear and trembling in singleness in your heart as unto Christ: Not with eye service, as men pleasers, but as the servants of Christ doing the will of God from the heart: With good will doing service to the Lord, and not to men: Knowing that whatever thing a man doeth the same shall he receive of the Lord, whether he be bond or free."[3] Here is a plain command of God for us to obey our masters. It may seem hard for us, if we think our masters wrong in holding us slaves, to obey in all things, but who of us dare dispute with God! He has commanded us to obey, and we ought to do it cheerfully, and freely.

This should be done by us, not only because God commands, but because our own peace and comfort depend upon it. As we depend upon our masters for what we eat and drink and wear, and for all our comfortable things in this world, we cannot be happy, unless we please them. This we cannot do without

[3] *Servants ... or free* See Ephesians 6.5–8.

obeying them freely, without muttering or finding fault. If a servant strives to please his master and studies and takes pains to do it, I believe there are but few masters who would use such a servant cruelly. Good servants frequently make good masters. If your master is really hard, unreasonable and cruel, there is no way so likely for you to convince him of it, as always to obey his commands, and try to serve him, and take care of his interest, and try to promote it all in your power. If you are proud and stubborn and always finding fault, your master will think the fault lies wholly on your side, but if you are humble, and meek, and bear all things patiently, your master may think he is wrong. If he does not, his neighbors will be apt to see it, and will befriend you, and try to alter his conduct. If this does not do, you must cry to him, who has the hearts of all men in his hands, and turneth them as the rivers of waters are turned.[1] …

Now I acknowledge that liberty is a great thing, and worth seeking for, if we can get it honestly, and by our good conduct, prevail on our masters to set us free: Though for my own part I do not wish to be free, yet I should be glad if others, especially the young negroes, were to be free, for many of us, who are grown up slaves, and have always had masters to take care of us, should hardly know how to take care of ourselves; and it may be more for our own comfort to remain as we are. That liberty is a great thing we may know from our own feelings, and we may likewise judge so from the conduct of the white-people, in the late war.[2] How much money has been spent, and how many lives had been lost, to defend their liberty. I must say that I have hoped that God would open their eyes, when they were so much engaged for liberty, to think of the state of the poor blacks, and to pity us. He has done it in some measure, and has raised us up many friends, for which we have reason to be thankful, and to hope in his mercy. What may be done further, he only knows, for *known unto God are all his ways from the beginning.*[3] But this my dear brethren is by no means the greatest

thing we have to be concerned about. Getting our liberty in this world is nothing to our having the liberty of the children of God. … There are but two places where all go after death, white and black, rich and poor; those places are Heaven and Hell. …

Those of you who can read I must beg you to read the Bible, and whenever you can get time, study the Bible, and if you can get no other time, spare some of your time from sleep, and learn what the mind and will of God is. But what shall I say to them who cannot read. This lay with great weight on my mind, when I thought of writing to my poor brethren, but I hope that those who can read will take pity on them and read what I have to say to them. In hopes of this I will beg of you to spare no pains in trying to learn to read. If you are once engaged you may learn. Let all the time you can get be spent in trying to learn to read. Get those who can read to learn[4] you, but remember, that what you learn for, is to read the Bible. If there was no Bible, it would be no matter whether you could read or not. Reading other books would do you no good. But the Bible is the word of God, and tells you what you must do to please God; it tells you how you may escape misery, and be happy for ever. …

Benjamin Banneker, letter to Thomas Jefferson, 19 August 1791

> Born free in Maryland and largely self-educated, Benjamin Banneker was frequently held up by abolitionists as evidence against the belief, common among white people, that black people were intellectually inferior to other races—and as an illustration of what black Americans might achieve if not oppressed by slavery. Banneker's numerous accomplishments included a role in the surveying of the District of Columbia, as well as the publication of a series of almanacs based on his own astronomical calculations. He sent the manuscript of one such almanac along with the following letter to Thomas Jefferson. The letter was published with Jefferson's response and widely circulated; the following version is from a 1792 Philadelphia printing titled *Copy of a Letter from Benjamin Banneker to the Secretary of State, with His Answer.*

[1] *the hearts … turned* See Proverbs 21.1: "The king's heart is in the hand of the Lord, as the rivers of water: he turneth it whithersoever he will."

[2] *the late war* I.e., the American Revolutionary War (1775–83).

[3] *known unto … beginning* See Acts 15.18: "Known unto God are all his works from the beginning of the world."

[4] *learn* Teach.

S̱ir,

I am fully sensible of the greatness of that freedom which I take with you on the present occasion; a liberty which seemed to me scarcely allowable when I reflected on that distinguished and dignified station in which you stand,[1] and the almost general prejudice and prepossession which is so prevalent in the world against those of my complexion.

I suppose it is a truth too well attested to you to need a proof here, that we are a race of beings who have long laboured under the abuse and censure of the world; that we have long been looked upon with an eye of contempt; and that we have long been considered rather as brutish than human, and scarcely capable of mental endowments.

Sir, I hope I may safely admit, in consequence of that report which hath reached me, that you are a man far less inflexible in sentiments of this nature than many others, that you are measurably friendly and well disposed toward us, and that you are willing and ready to lend your aid and assistance to our relief from those many distresses and numerous calamities to which we are reduced.

Now, Sir, if this is founded in truth, I apprehend you will readily embrace every opportunity to eradicate that train of absurd and false ideas and opinions which so generally prevails with respect to us; and that your sentiments are concurrent with mine; which are that one universal Father hath given being to us all; and that he hath not only made us all of one flesh, but that he hath also, without partiality, afforded us all the same sensations, and endued us all with the same faculties; and that however variable we may be in society or religion, however diversified in situation or colour, we are all of the same family, and stand in the same relation to him.

Sir, if these are sentiments of which you are fully persuaded, I hope you cannot but acknowledge that it is the indispensable duty of those who maintain for themselves the rights of human nature, and who profess[2] the obligations of Christianity, to extend their power and influence to the relief of every part of the human race, from whatever burden or oppression they may unjustly labour under; and this, I apprehend, a full conviction of the truth and obligation of these principles should lead all to.

Sir, I have long been convinced that if your love for yourselves, and for those inestimable laws which preserved to you the rights of human nature, was founded on sincerity; you could not but be solicitous that every individual, of whatsoever rank or distinction, might with you equally enjoy the blessings thereof; neither could you rest satisfied short of the most active diffusion of your exertions in order to their promotion from any state of degradation to which the unjustifiable cruelty and barbarism of men may have reduced them.

Sir, I freely and cheerfully acknowledge that I am of the African race, and in that colour which is natural to them, of the deepest dye;[3] and it is under a sense of the most profound gratitude to the Supreme Ruler of the universe that I now confess to you that I am not under that state of tyrannical thraldom, and inhuman captivity, to which too many of my brethren are doomed; but that I have abundantly tasted of the fruition of those blessings which proceed from that free and unequalled liberty with which you are favoured; and which, I hope, you will willingly allow you have received from the immediate hand of that Being from whom proceedeth every good and perfect gift.

Sir, suffer[4] me to recall to your mind that time in which the arms and tyranny of the British Crown were exerted, with every powerful effort, in order to reduce you to a state of servitude. Look back, I entreat you, on the variety of dangers to which you were exposed; reflect on that time in which every human aid appeared unavailable, and in which even hope and fortitude wore the aspect of inability to the conflict; and you cannot but be led to a serious and grateful sense of your miraculous and providential preservation; you cannot but acknowledge that the present freedom and tranquility which you enjoy you have mercifully received, and that it is the peculiar[5] blessing of Heaven.

This, Sir, was a time in which you clearly saw into the injustice of a state of slavery, and in which you had just apprehensions of the horrors of its condition. It

1 *that distinguished ... stand* Jefferson was at this time Secretary of State.

2 *profess* Claim; declare faith in.

3 [Banneker's note] My father was brought here a s[lav]e from Africa.

4 *suffer* Allow.

5 *peculiar* Particular.

was now that your abhorrence thereof was so excited, that you publicly held forth this true and invaluable doctrine, which is worthy to be recorded and remembered in all succeeding ages. "We hold these truths to be self-evident: that all men are created equal, and that they are endowed by their Creator with certain unalienable rights, and that among these are life, liberty, and the pursuit of happiness."[1]

Here was a time in which your tender feelings for yourselves had engaged you thus to declare; you were then impressed with proper ideas of the great valuation of liberty, and the free possession of those blessings to which you were entitled by nature. But, Sir, how pitiable is it to reflect that although you were so fully convinced of the benevolence of the Father of mankind, and of his equal and impartial distribution of these rights and privileges which he had conferred upon them, that you should at the same time counteract his mercies in detaining by fraud and violence so numerous a part of my brethren, under groaning captivity and cruel oppression? that you should at the same time be found guilty of that most criminal act, which you professedly detested in others, with respect to yourselves?

I suppose that your knowledge of the situation of my brethren is too extensive to need a recital here; neither shall I presume to prescribe methods by which they may be relieved; otherwise than by recommending to you and all others to wean yourselves from these narrow prejudices which you have imbibed with respect to them, and as Job proposed to his friends, "put your soul in their souls' stead."[2] Thus shall your hearts be enlarged with kindness and benevolence toward them, and thus shall you need neither the direction of myself or others in what manner to proceed herein.

And now, Sir, although my sympathy and affection for my brethren hath caused my enlargement[3] thus far, I ardently hope that your candour and generosity will plead with you in my behalf when I make known to you that it was not originally my design; but having taken up my pen in order to direct to you, as a present, a copy of an almanac which I have calculated for the succeeding year, I was unexpectedly and unavoidably led thereto.

This calculation is the production of my arduous study in this my advanced stage of life; for having long had unbounded desires to become acquainted with the secrets of nature, I have had to gratify my curiosity herein through my own assiduous application to astronomical study, in which I need not to recount to you the many difficulties and disadvantages which I have had to encounter.

And although I had almost declined to make my calculation for the ensuing year; in consequence of that time which I had allotted therefore being taken up at the Federal Territory, by the request of Mr. Andrew Ellicott;[4] yet finding myself under several engagements to printers of this state, to whom I had communicated my design, on my return to my place of residence, I industriously applied myself thereto; which I hope I have accomplished with correctness and accuracy, a copy of which I have taken the liberty to direct to you, and which I humbly request you will favourably receive. And although you may have the opportunity of perusing it after its publication; yet I chose to send it to you in manuscript previous thereto, that thereby you might not only have an earlier inspection, but that you might also view it in my own hand writing.

And now, Sir, I shall conclude and subscribe my self with the most profound respect,

Your most obedient humble servant,

Benjamin Banneker

from Peter Williams Jr., "An Oration on the Abolition of the Slave Trade," 1 January 1808

Born in New Jersey, Peter Williams Jr. attended the African Free School for black students in New York and, like many of the school's alumni, became a prominent member of New York's African American community. He founded a

[1] *We hold ... happiness* From the Declaration of Independence, which Jefferson drafted.

[2] *as Job ... stead* Job, whose faith is tested by a series of great misfortunes, is told by his friends that his suffering is his own fault. He says to them, "I also could speak as ye do: if your soul were in my soul's stead, I could heap up words against you, and shake mine head at you" (Job 16.4).

[3] *enlargement* Abundance of speech or writing.

[4] *Andrew Ellicott* American land surveyor with whom Banneker worked on the survey that established the boundaries of the District of Columbia (here called the "Federal Territory").

predominantly African American Episcopalian church in the city and was eventually ordained as a priest; he was also a leader in several abolitionist and charity organizations and co-founder of the newspaper *Freedom's Journal*. Williams delivered the speech excerpted here on the day the act abolishing the importation of enslaved people into the United States took effect. The act's passage was an important achievement and a moment of optimism for the abolition movement, but it did nothing to prevent a thriving trade in enslaved people within the United States—and a substantial transatlantic trade persisted illegally for some time after the act's passage.

Fathers, brethren, and fellow citizens:
At this auspicious moment, I felicitate you on the abolition of the slave trade. This inhuman branch of commerce, which, for some centuries past, has been carried on to a considerable extent, is, by the singular interposition of Divine Providence, this day extinguished. An event so important, so pregnant with happy consequences, must be extremely consonant to every philanthropic heart.

But to us, Africans, and descendants of Africans, this period is deeply interesting. We have felt, sensibly felt, the sad effects of this abominable traffic. It has made, if not ourselves, our forefathers and kinsmen its unhappy victims, and pronounced on them, and their posterity, the sentence of perpetual slavery. But benevolent men have voluntarily stepped forward to obviate the consequences of this injustice and barbarity. They have striven, assiduously, to restore our natural rights; to guaranty[1] them from fresh innovations; to furnish us with necessary information; and to stop the source from whence our evils have flowed.

The fruits of these laudable endeavors have long been visible; each moment they appear more conspicuous, and this day has produced an event which shall ever be memorable and glorious in the annals of history. We are now assembled to celebrate this momentous era; to recognize the beneficial influences of humane exertions; and by suitable demonstrations of joy, thanksgiving, and gratitude, to return to our heavenly Father, and to our earthly benefactors, our sincere acknowledgments.

Review, for a moment, my brethren, the history of the slave trade. Engendered in the foul recesses of the sordid mind, the unnatural monster inflicted gross evils on the human race. Its baneful footsteps are marked with blood; its infectious breath spreads war and desolation; and its train is composed of the complicated miseries of cruel and unceasing bondage.

Before the enterprising spirit of European genius explored the western coast of Africa, the state of our forefathers was a state of simplicity, innocence, and contentment. Unskilled in the arts of dissimulation, their bosoms were the seats of confidence, and their lips were the organs of truth. Strangers to the refinements of civilized society, they followed with implicit obedience the (simple) dictates of nature. Peculiarly observant of hospitality, they offered a place of refreshment to the weary, and an asylum to the unfortunate. Ardent in their affections, their minds were susceptible of the warmest emotions of love, friendship, and gratitude.

Although unacquainted with the diversified luxuries and amusements of civilized nations, they enjoyed some singular advantages, from the bountiful hand of nature and from their own innocent and amiable manners, which rendered them a happy people. But, alas! this delightful picture has long since vanished; the angel of bliss has deserted their dwelling; and the demon of indescribable misery has rioted, uncontrolled, on the fair fields of our ancestors.

After Columbus unfolded to civilized man the vast treasures of this western world, the desire of gain, which had chiefly induced the first colonists of America to cross the waters of the Atlantic, surpassing the bounds of reasonable acquisition, violated the sacred injunctions of the gospel, frustrated the designs of the pious and humane, and enslaving the harmless aborigines, compelled them to drudge in the mines.

The severities of this employment was so insupportable to men who were unaccustomed to fatigue that, according to Robertson's "History of America,"[2] upwards of nine hundred thousand were destroyed in

[1] *guaranty* Safeguard.

[2] *Robertson's ... America* Scottish historian William Robertson's *History of America* (1777).

the space of fifteen years on the island of Hispaniola.[1] A consumption so rapid must, in a short period, have deprived them of the instruments of labor, had not the same genius which first produced it found out another method to obtain them. This was no other than the importation of slaves from the coast of Africa.

The Genoese made the first regular importation, in the year 1517, by virtue of a patent granted by Charles of Austria[2] to a Flemish favorite; since which, this commerce has increased to an astonishing and almost incredible degree.

After the manner of ancient piracy, descents were first made on the African coast; the towns bordering on the ocean were surprised, and a number of the inhabitants carried into slavery.

Alarmed at these depredations, the natives fled to the interior, and there united to secure themselves from the common foe. But the subtle invaders were not easily deterred from their purpose. Their experience, corroborated by historical testimony, convinced them that this spirit of unity would baffle every violent attempt; and that the most powerful method to dissolve it would be to diffuse in them the same avaricious disposition which they themselves possessed; and to afford them the means of gratifying it, by ruining each other. Fatal engine; fatal thou hast proved to man in all ages; where the greatest violence has proved ineffectual, their undermining principles have wrought destruction. By thy deadly power, the strong Grecian arm, which bid the world defiance, fell nerveless; by thy potent attacks, the solid pillars of Roman grandeur shook to their base; and, Oh! Africans! by this parent of the slave trade, this grandsire of misery, the mortal blow was struck which crushed the peace and happiness of our country. Affairs now assumed a different aspect: the appearances of war were changed into the most amicable pretensions, presents apparently inestimable were made, and all the bewitching and alluring wiles of the seducer were practiced. The harmless African, taught to believe a friendly countenance,[3] the sure token of a corresponding heart, soon disbanded his fears and evinced a favorable disposition towards his flattering enemies.

Thus the foe, obtaining an intercourse by a dazzling display of European finery, bewildered their simple understandings and corrupted their morals. Mutual agreements were then made; the Europeans were to supply the Africans with those gaudy trifles which so strongly affected them, and the Africans in return were to grant the Europeans their prisoners of war, and convicts, as slaves. These stipulations, naturally tending to delude the mind, answered the twofold purpose of enlarging their criminal code and of exciting incessant war at the same time that it furnished a specious pretext for the prosecution of this inhuman traffic. Bad as this may appear, had it prescribed the bounds of injustice, millions of unhappy victims might have still been spared. But, extending widely beyond measure and without control, large additions of slaves were made by kidnapping and the most unpalliated[4] seizures.

Trace the past scenes of Africa and you will manifestly perceive these flagrant violations of human rights. The prince who once delighted in the happiness of his people, who felt himself bound by a sacred contract to defend their persons and property, was turned into their tyrant and scourge: he, who once strove to preserve peace and good understanding with the different nations, who never unsheathed his sword but in the cause of justice, at the signal of a slave ship assembled his warriors and rushed furiously upon his unsuspecting friends. What a scene does that town now present, which a few moments past was the abode of tranquility. At the approach of the foe, alarm and confusion pervade every part; horror and dismay are depicted on every countenance; the aged chief, starting from his couch, calls forth his men to repulse the hostile invader. All ages obey the summons; feeble youth and decrepit age join the standard;[5] while the foe, to effect his purpose, fires[6] the town.

[1] *Hispaniola* Now Haiti and the Dominican Republic, Hispaniola was the site of Spain's first major colonization effort in the Americas.

[2] *Charles of Austria* Charles V (1500–58), who held various ruling titles including Holy Roman Emperor, Archduke of Austria, and King of Spain. Before Charles V authorized the transport of thousands of enslaved people directly from Africa into the Americas, the transatlantic trade was largely limited to enslaved people born in Spain.

[3] *countenance* Facial expression.

[4] *unpalliated* Uncloaked; blatant.

[5] *join the standard* I.e., join the military force.

[6] *fires* Sets fire to.

Now, with unimaginable terror the battle commences: hear now the shrieks of the women, the cries of the children, the shouts of the warriors, and the groans of the dying. See with what desperation the inhabitants fight in defense of their darling joys. But, alas! overpowered by a superior foe, their force is broken; their ablest warriors fall; and the wretched remnant are taken captives.

Where are now those pleasant dwellings, where peace and harmony reigned incessant? where those beautiful fields, whose smiling crops and enchanting verdure enlivened the heart of every beholder? Alas! those tenements are now enveloped in destructive flames; those fair fields are now bedewed with blood and covered with mangled carcasses. Where are now those sounds of mirth and gladness, which loudly rang throughout the village? where those darling youth, those venerable aged, who mutually animated the festive throng? Alas! those exhilarating peals are now changed into the dismal groans of inconceivable distress: the survivors of those happy people are now carried into cruel captivity. Ah! driven from their native soil, they cast their languishing eyes behind, and with aching hearts bid adieu to every prospect of joy and comfort.

A spectacle so truly distressing is sufficient to blow into a blaze the most latent spark of humanity; but, the adamantine[1] heart of avarice, dead to every sensation of pity, regards not the voice of the sufferers, but hastily drives them to market for sale.

Oh, Africa, Africa! to what horrid inhumanities have thy shores been witness; thy shores, which were once the garden of the world, the seat of almost paradisiacal joys, have been transformed into regions of woe; thy sons, who were once the happiest of mortals, are reduced to slavery, and bound in weighty shackles now fill the trader's ship. But, though defeated in the contest for liberty, their magnanimous souls scorn the gross indignity, and choose death in preference to slavery. Painful; Ah! painful must be that existence which the rational mind can deliberately doom to self-destruction. Thus, the poor Africans, robbed of every joy, while they see not the most transient, glimmering, ray of hope to cheer their saddened hearts, sink into the abyss of consummate misery. Their lives, embittered by

reflection, anticipation, and present sorrows, they feel burdensome; and death (whose dreary mansions appall the stoutest hearts) they view as their only shelter.

You, my brethren, beloved Africans, who had passed the days of infancy when you left your country, you best can tell the aggravated sufferings of our unfortunate race; your memories can bring to view these scenes of bitter grief. What, my brethren, when dragged from your native land on board the slave ship, what was the anguish which you saw, which you felt? what the pain, what the dreadful forebodings which filled your throbbing bosoms?

But you, my brethren, descendants of African forefathers, I call upon you to view a scene of unfathomable distress. Let your imagination carry you back to former days. Behold a vessel, bearing our forefathers and brethren from the place of their nativity to a distant and inhospitable clime; behold their dejected countenances, their streaming eyes, their fettered limbs; hear them, with piercing cries, and pitiful moans, deploring their wretched fate. After their arrival in port, see them separated without regard to the ties of blood or friendship: husband from wife; parent from child; brother from sister; friend from friend. See the parting tear rolling down their fallen cheeks; hear the parting sigh die on their quivering lips.

But let us no longer pursue a theme of boundless affliction. An enchanting sound now demands your attention. Hail! hail! glorious day, whose resplendent rising disperseth the clouds which have hovered with destruction over the land of Africa, and illumines it by the most brilliant rays of future prosperity. Rejoice, Oh! Africans! No longer shall tyranny, war, and injustice, with irresistible sway, desolate your native country; no longer shall torrents of human blood deluge its delightful plains; no longer shall it witness your countrymen wielding among each other the instruments of death; nor the insidious kidnapper, darting from his midnight haunt, on the feeble and unprotected; no longer shall its shores resound with the awful howlings of infatuated warriors, the deathlike groans of vanquished innocents, nor the clanking fetters of woe-doomed captives. Rejoice, Oh, ye descendants of Africans! No longer shall the United States of America, nor the extensive colonies of Great Britain, admit the degrading commerce of the human species: no longer shall

[1] *adamantine* Extraordinarily hard.

they swell the tide of African misery by the importation of slaves. Rejoice, my brethren, that the channels are obstructed through which slavery, and its direful concomitants, have been entailed on the African race. But let incessant strains of gratitude be mingled with your expressions of joy. Through the infinite mercy of the great Jehovah,[1] this day announces the abolition of the slave trade. Let, therefore, the heart that is warmed by the smallest drop of African blood glow in grateful transports,[2] and cause the lofty arches of the sky to reverberate eternal praise to his boundless goodness. ...

from Boyrereau Brinch, *The Blind African Slave, or Memoirs of Boyrereau Brinch, Nick-named Jeffrey Brace* (1810)

Boyrereau Brinch's memoir suggests that he experienced a happy childhood in West Africa in a place he called Bow-woo (probably in what is now Mali) before his abduction into slavery. After a brief period as an enslaved sailor, Brinch was taken to Connecticut and sold numerous times before eventually obtaining his freedom by serving in the Revolutionary War (1775–83). He moved to Vermont, where he became a farmer and prominent abolitionist. Brinch, though literate, was blind in the last decades of his life, and he dictated his biography to Benjamin Prentiss, a white lawyer who acted as both his editor and scribe, and who appears to have been at least as close to poverty as Brinch himself. Prentiss and Brinch hoped to earn some money from their venture as well as to increase awareness of the harms of slavery, but their book garnered almost no interest; by the 1810s the abolitionist movement had focused its attention on the South and was far less interested in the stories of enslaved people in the North. Twenty-first-century readers, however, have found much of historical and literary interest in Brinch's vivid and penetrating descriptions of places and events from his West African homeland to the battles of the American Revolution. The following excerpts begin with the infamous Middle Passage and the process of "slave-breaking" that enslaved people often endured before they were considered

fit for sale. The selection concludes with a brief account of some of the people Brinch was sold to in Connecticut, providing some sense of the range of experiences that enslaved people might have in the North.

from CHAPTER 4

... As soon as we had fairly got under way, and about bidding adieu to the African coast forever, the captain and many of the officers made choice of such of the young women as they chose to sleep with them in their hammocks, whom they liberated from chains and introduced into their several[3] apartments. After the officers had provided themselves with mistresses of color, they made arrangements for the keeping and feeding the slaves. We were fastened in rows, as before observed, so that we could set upon our rumps or lie upon our backs, as was most convenient, and as our exercises were not much, we, it was concluded, could do with little food; our allowance was put at two scanty meals per day, which consisted of about six ounces of boiled rice and Indian corn each meal, with the addition of about one gill of fresh water. While in this situation, the ship's crew had been butchering a goat, and threw some meat, which fell near me, but a boy caught [it] too quick for me, and swallowed it as soon as a hound would have done. I thought it was my right as it fell before me, and therefore clenched him, but one of my comrades interfered and, admonishing us, said it was extremely wrong for us to contend, as we had no parents or friends to take our parts, and could only bring disgrace upon ourselves. We desisted and mutually exchanged forgiveness. ...

In this situation upon the boisterous deep, where each gale wafted us to a returnless distance from our families and friends, almost famished with hunger and thirst, to add horror to the scene, the sailors who were not provided with mistresses would force[4] the women before the eyes of their husbands. A sailor one day forced the wife of a slave by the name of Blay, before his face. Blay, whose blood boiled with wrath and indignation, said to his comrades in chains, "Let us rise

[1] *Jehovah* God.

[2] *transports* Bursts of joy.

[3] *several* Various.

[4] *force* Rape.

and take them, and force them to conduct us back to our native country again; there is more of us than of them, and who is there among us who had not rather die honorably than live ignominious slaves?" The interpreter happened to overhear him, and gave information against him. Poor Blay was taken to the gunwale and received 80 lashes, and was then put in chains with a double weight of iron. At this treatment, well may we cry out with Ezekiel—"Behold their abomination in the sight of the Lord."[1]

After a voyage of about five months, the vessel arrived at Barbados, in the West Indies, in the year of our Lord, one thousand seven hundred and fifty-nine, or one thousand seven hundred and sixty, with the slaves who had not either died with disease, mourned themselves to death, or starved. Many of the children actually died with hunger, pent up in the same ship where midnight and beastly intoxication bloated the miserable owner. The cries of the innocent African boy, destitute of the protection of a parent, if they reached the ears, could not penetrate the heart of a christian so as to cause him to bestow a morsel of bread upon his infant captive, even enough to save his life.

The slaves, consisting of about three hundred in number, including women and children, were carefully taken out of the ship and put into a large prison, or rather house of subjection. In this house we were all, above twelve years of age, chained together, and sat in large circles round the room, and put to picking oakum.[2] A slave by the name of Syneyo, from the town of Yellow-Bonga,[3] taken in the manner formerly described, and who was one of the judges in that place,[4] refused to work. He rose up, and in his native language, made the following speech to the captain, which was repeated to him by the interpreter:

"Sir, we will sooner suffer death than submit to such abominable degradation. The brow of our great father, the sun, frowns with indignation on beholding the majesty of human nature abused, as we are, and rendered more brutal than the ravenous wild beasts, as ye are. Feel like mortal man, and what I say may prevent your spirit from being blotted out forever. You came to our country; you and your friends were treated with hospitality; we washed and anointed your feet; we gave you the best of our wines to drink, our most delicious food to eat; we entertained you with every amusement our country could afford. We prayed for you, burnt incense and offered up sacrifices for you; we gave you presents of gold, ivory, corn[5] and rice, with many other valuable things; and what return did you make us? You invited us to see your ship; we were credulous, even vigilance was asleep; you traitorously gave us opiates, which caused us to sleep; you bound us captives and bore us away to this place; you and your myrmidons[6] ravished our wives and daughters, whipped us with many stripes, starved our children to death, and suffered[7] others to die unnoticed. And now you hold us in bondage and oblige us to work unceasingly. Is this the reward of friendship, hospitality and protection? Are you a christian people? Then do unto us as we have done unto you; strip us of these chains, and conduct us back to our own shores. If christianity will not move you to perform so just an act, look at those little fatherless children, whom you kidnapped from their parents—hear their cries, behold their sufferings, think of the bewailing of their bereft parents, look across the great waters to that village where you were almost idolized—view the distresses your conduct has brought upon it, and if you have one spark of human sensibility, or even the least shade of humanity, if you are what you profess to be, a christian; repent and let us, whom you call heathens, return to our once happy shores; thereby, if you cannot obliterate, heal as much as possible the wounds you have made."

On the close of this speech, all was silent for a few minutes; but the captain in his turn made a speech more to the purpose. With a countenance that would terrify a crocodile and a voice like the braying of a jackass, he said:

[1] *Behold their … the Lord* See Ezekiel 8, in which Ezekiel is shown a vision of the people of Israel committing a series of "abominations."

[2] *picking oakum* Unraveling old tarry ropes to extricate oakum, a tarred fiber used largely as a sealant for wooden ships. Picking oakum was a tedious, painful task often assigned to prisoners as a form of punishment.

[3] *Yellow-Bonga* Town Brinch describes as being about 280 miles south of his home, Bow-woo.

[4] *in that place* I.e., in his home of Yellow-Bonga.

[5] *corn* Grain.

[6] *myrmidons* Subordinates who follow commands—especially unethical commands—without question.

[7] *suffered* Allowed.

DESCRIPTION OF A SLAVE SHIP.

Illustration of a slave ship, 1789. This image, showing how enslaved people were held on the British slave ship *Brooks*, was widely circulated by abolitionists; this particular version appeared in a London broadside. The accompanying description noted that, without sufficient room to lie on their backs, "the men … were placed, as is usual in full ships, on their sides, or on each other."

"Oh you impudent, rebellious, treasonable, cowardly, saucy, low, black slave, I will teach you discipline, obedience, and submission, and what is more, I will learn[1] you your duty. You seem to speak as though you thought yourself equal to white people, you Ethiopian black brute, you shall have but twelve kernels of corn per day—your breakfast shall be fifty stripes—and if your work is not done, I leave you to the care of this my overseer, who will deal with you as you deserve."

This order was strictly complied with. From Monday until Wednesday following, no one received any other allowance, except water, which we were driven to, in drove,[2] and obliged to lie down and drink.

From Wednesday until Saturday, we had each one ounce of biscuit in addition. All began to be subdued and to work according to their strength and abilities.

[1] *learn* Teach.

[2] *drove* Herd.

from CHAPTER 5

… We … suffered for food in a manner and to a degree of which even a faint description would be considered as fabulous, therefore I forbear to disclose it. Thus I remained for about three months from the time I was taken from the ship, starved, whipped and tortured in the most shameful manner, obliged to work unceasingly, in order I suppose that the clement, benevolent and charitable white man should be satisfied that the heathen spirit of an African boy of noble birth should be sufficiently subdued, rendered tame, docile and submissive; and all for my good that I should thereby become a tame, profitable and honest slave. The natural man must be obliterated and degraded, that even the thought of liberty must never be suffered to contaminate itself in a negro's mind; and the odious thing, equality, should be taught by European discipline never to raise its head. …

[Brinch is sold to a frigate captain and forced to fight in the Seven Years' War (1756–63); he is then taken to Connecticut and sold again, to a profoundly cruel Puritan living in Milford, a small town near New Haven. This new enslaver is so abusive that another Milford resident, Samuel Eells, feels compelled to rescue Brinch and give him an opportunity to recover from the starvation and physical injury he has been subjected to.]

from CHAPTER 8

… Mr. Samuel Eals used me very well while I remained with him; but as soon as I was able to work, I was sold to one Peter Pridon, son of the old priest Pridon, of Old Milford. I lived with him about two months and got five severe whippings for crying nights. From Pridon I was bartered away for some old horses to one Gibbs, who was a man of very inferior talents, possessing great pride and ostentation, always at work and in a hurry. He had the longest nose and chin I ever saw attached to a man's face, thin lips, and a voice that was less pleasing than the ravens. With this man I stayed about three months, and to describe the particular management of his family would only mortify those who live in the same way at the present time. I have thought he took a peculiar delight in whipping me, as I uniformly received about four whippings per day. If I was awkward, cried too much, or was lazy, it was sure to purchase me a good drubbing.[1] Sometimes I got a flogging for freezing my feet while I was foddering[2] and cutting the ice out of the watering place. And one day, while I was getting corn up stairs, I designedly pushed his boy downstairs, for while I had the basket upon my shoulder he began whipping me & chirping to me, as would a driver to his horse. For this I was knocked downstairs, basket, corn and all shared the same fate; and to complete my punishment, the next morning I received fifty lashes with a horse-whip. Next I was sold to Phineas Baldwin of the town of Old Milford. I continued with him until summer, or rather spring, when I went to live with his son Phineas, who had two small children to tend. In his nursery I was engaged until the last of May, when I was sold to Jones Green, of the same place. Green did not whip me but about twice in a week, except now and then a kicking. From Green I was transferred to one Murrier, a tanner, where I remained until September, at which time the widow Mary Stiles, of Woodbury, Connecticut, bought me. This was a glorious era in my life, as widow Stiles was one of the finest women in the world; she possessed every christian virtue. …

When this lady died I descended like real estate, in fee simple[3] to her son Benjamin Stiles, Esq. About four years after her death, her two sons, Benjamin and David, were drafted to fight in the revolution. I also entered the banners of freedom. Alas! Poor African slave, to liberate freemen, my tyrants. …

[1] *drubbing* Beating.

[2] *foddering* Feeding animals.

[3] *fee simple* Term usually used in reference to land; it indicates that the land's owner possesses it entirely (as opposed to, for example, leasing it) and can sell or use it as desired.

Olaudah Equiano or Gustavus Vassa

c. 1745 – 1797

Olaudah Equiano's *The Interesting Narrative of the Life of Olaudah Equiano* was one of the first slave narratives written in English, and is now universally acknowledged to be among the most significant and influential of all eighteenth-century texts. His narrative was a document of central importance for the abolitionist movement, showing readers the horrors of slavery while also demonstrating the eloquence of a native-born African who had been educated in the Western tradition, and displaying to the devout that black people were as capable of spiritual enlightenment as were whites.

Until the beginning of this century Equiano's account of his early years was generally taken entirely at face value: it was accepted that he had been born in what is now southern Nigeria, into the Igbo nation; that he had been kidnaped at the age of eleven and enslaved for some time in Africa; and that he was eventually brought across the Atlantic in slavery. In a 1999 article and then in his 2005 biography of Equiano, historian Vincent Carretta challenged his account, citing two documents suggesting that Equiano had been born not in Africa, but in Carolina. The issue remains disputed and may never be entirely resolved. It is significant, however, that neither Carretta nor other scholars have challenged the authenticity of the information Equiano provides about life in Africa, the passage across the Atlantic, and so on; if Equiano himself was indeed born into American slavery, he would have obtained such information directly from enslaved Africans he knew. At issue, then, is not the fundamental reality of the account Equiano provides, but only whether the early part of his narrative represents a first-hand account or an act of creative imagination based on first-hand research.

Equiano's account of his life following his purchase in Virginia by the British naval captain Michael Henry Pascal is not in dispute. While enslaved by Pascal (who renamed him "Gustavus Vassa") Equiano began his career as a mariner. For the next ten or eleven years, Equiano traveled widely around the Mediterranean, Europe, and the Americas with a series of enslavers; he was engaged in several battles during the Seven Years' War (1756–63), including the 1758 siege of Louisbourg in what is now Nova Scotia. He was sold in May of 1763 for £40 to Robert King, a Philadelphia Quaker who owned property on the Caribbean island of Monserrat and had various shipping interests. After working for King for approximately three years, Equiano was by 1766 able to purchase his freedom.

After securing his freedom, Equiano settled in England. (While slavery was still permitted in England's overseas colonies, it had no legal standing in England itself, where there was a relatively large population of free blacks.) From time to time he earned his living there—working for some time as a hairdresser, for example—but for many years he kept returning to the sea to earn a living, working on vessels traveling not only to American ports such as Savannah and Charleston but also to Turkey, to the Caribbean, and to South America. In 1773 he served on a scientific expedition to the Arctic, and in 1775–76 he was hired to assist in the setting up of a plantation colony in Central America, where his duties included acting as an overseer of enslaved workers.

He had been taught to read and write while still enslaved and in the 1780s Equiano began to use these skills to draw attention to the plight of enslaved people and to petition for the abolition of slavery. He played a key role in helping to bring to the attention of the public the 1781 case of the slave ship *Zong*, from which 132 enslaved people had been thrown overboard; he was a founder (together with Ottobah Cugoano and others) of the Sons of Africa, which became an influential abolitionist group; he worked closely over many years with prominent white abolitionists (including Granville Sharpe, Thomas Clarkson, and William Wilberforce); his narrative made a deep impression on John Wesley, the Methodist leader (Equiano himself became a Methodist, as he recounts in his narrative); and it made an impression too on the hundreds of influential Britons whose support Equiano enlisted when he published his *Interesting Narrative* in 1789. By that time Equiano was himself a leader of the campaign against the slave

trade, and he was as tireless—and as effective—in promoting the book after it had been published as he had been in soliciting support beforehand.

When in 1792 he married Susannah Cullen, a woman he had met while promoting his book in Cambridge, the occasion was considered worthy of notice in the provincial press as well as in London. The *Derby Mercury* was among the newspapers reporting on the event:

> On the 9th instant was married at Soham, in Cambridgeshire, Gustavus Vassa, the African, well known in England as the champion and advocate for procuring a suppression of the slave trade, to Miss Cullen, daughter of Mr. Cullen, of Ely. A vast number of people were assembled on the occasion.

The change in Equiano's circumstances occasioned only a brief pause in Equiano's efforts on behalf of the abolitionist cause: "when I have given her eight or ten days comfort," he wrote a friend, "I mean directly to go to Scotland and sell my fifth editions."

The *Interesting Narrative* went through several more English editions in Equiano's lifetime, and he appears to have become quite well-to-do in his later years, both from the proceeds of book sales and from other ventures (including as a money-lender to some of his influential London contacts). He and Susannah had two children—both daughters. He died in London of unknown causes, on the 31st of March 1797.

The reception history of the *Interesting Narrative* in America differs strikingly from that in Britain. When the book was first published in London in 1789, it was prefaced by a letter addressed jointly to the British Houses of Parliament and accompanied by a list of 311 subscribers, including not only prominent names associated with the British abolitionist movement but also many names from the highest ranks of British society (among them the Prince of Wales, the Duke of York, and the Bishop of London). The book was widely reviewed in Britain, and widely read; several other editions followed, typically including the names of additional influential subscribers, together with fresh testimonials. Reviewers' discussions of the book typically focused on those aspects of the *Interesting Narrative* to which Equiano had drawn attention in his letter to Parliament, and treated the book as a whole as "an instrument" that aimed to bring change to Equiano's "suffering countrymen" who had been enslaved: "may the God of heaven inspire benevolence on that important day when the question of Abolition is to be discussed," Equiano implored the members of the House of Lords and House of Commons.

The circumstances were quite different when the book was published in the United States in 1791. The book was published by a New York printer largely known for publishing religious books. It included a list of just 113 subscribers, none of them particularly prominent in society and none of them especially notable as abolitionists. Indeed (as the research of Akiyo Ito has revealed), the American subscribers were very largely of the artisan class—"bakers, grocers, cartmen, cabinetmakers, carpenters, tailors, watchmakers, blacksmiths" and so on, many of whom owned enslaved people. Ito persuasively suggests that these early American readers may have valued Equiano's narrative less as an antislavery tract than as a travel and adventure narrative. Interestingly, even when Equiano's *Interesting Narrative* was re-issued in America (some thirty years after its initial edition had received so little attention), this aspect of the book seems to have been emphasized; a bookseller's 1837 description that was published more than once in William Lloyd Garrison's antislavery newspaper *The Liberator* mentions that Equiano had "lived as a slave," but places more emphasis on the book's "great variety of wonderful scenes, which give his narrative an interest scarcely surpassed by Robinson Crusoe."

It is perhaps unsurprising that, as an abolitionist text, the *Interesting Narrative* exerted far less influence in America than in Britain. For one thing, Equiano himself declared a strong connection to "old England," and little if any to America; for another, relatively little of the time that Equiano had spent enslaved had been in any part of what later became the United States. The text nevertheless has a good deal to say about slavery in the continental American colonies; the various encounters that Equiano reports (in Chapters 6, 7, and 8) having experienced in Savannah alone provide a searing indictment of the institution as it existed in the Thirteen Colonies.

Interest in Equiano's narrative—along with interest in slave narratives generally—dropped off in the late nineteenth and early twentieth centuries, and it was not until the latter part of the twentieth century that the *Interesting Narrative* began to be again widely read and widely studied. By the early twenty-first century, however, it had become one of the most widely taught texts in the canons of British and American literature—and in the newly formed canon of transatlantic literature. For the most part it has been studied fruitfully as an abolitionist text; an awareness of the book's early American reception history is a reminder that the *Interesting Narrative* can also be appreciated from numerous other angles as well. It is among other things a lively adventure narrative, a Christian conversion narrative, a remarkable tour of the transatlantic economic world—and a richly layered portrait of a man of extraordinary and sometimes contradictory character. Curious about all manner of things, blessed with seemingly boundless entrepreneurial energy, and blessed as well with keen descriptive and storytelling powers, Equiano reveals himself to be a highly talented self-fashioner. He is by turns boastful and self-deprecating; deeply religious and highly worldly. An impassioned and effective opponent of slavery, he was also an apologist for the slave trade within Africa, and a man who allowed himself to be employed for a time as an overseer of enslaved people. "My life and fortune have been extremely chequered, and my adventures various," Equiano declares near the end of the *Interesting Life*. His narrative has often been read, in the words of Joanna Brooks, as "a collective autobiography for millions who survived the slave trade," and unquestionably the text has much to tell us of that collective experience. But—as its earliest American readers appear to have recognized—it has much to tell us too of one of the most extraordinary individuals of his time.

NOTE ON THE TEXT: The texts of the various editions of the *Interesting Narrative* do not vary greatly; the changes Equiano made for the later British editions very largely involved the addition of testimonials and quotations from favorable reviews of the book. The American edition carried a different title page and subscriber list, but the text itself closely followed that of the first two London editions. The first edition, published in 1789, has here been used as a base text. Some paragraph breaks have been added, and spelling and punctuation have been modernized in accordance with the practices of this anthology.

⌘ ⌘ ⌘

Frontispiece and title page of the first American edition of Equiano's *Interesting Narrative*, 1791.

from *The Interesting Narrative of the Life of Olaudah Equiano or Gustavus Vassa, the African. Written by Himself*

from CHAPTER I[1]

The author's account of his country, and their manners and customs—Administration of justice—Embrenche—Marriage ceremony, and public entertainments—Mode of living—Dress—Manufactures—Buildings—Commerce—Agriculture—War and religion—Superstition of the natives—Funeral ceremonies of the priests or magicians—Curious mode of discovering poison—Some hints concerning the origin of the author's countrymen, with the opinions of different writers on that subject.

I believe it is difficult for those who publish their own memoirs to escape the imputation of vanity; nor is this the only disadvantage under which they labour: it is also their misfortune that what is uncommon is rarely, if ever, believed, and what is obvious we are apt to turn from with disgust, and to charge the writer with impertinence. People generally think those memoirs only worthy to be read or remembered which abound in great or striking events, those, in short, which in a high degree excite either admiration or pity: all others they consign to contempt and oblivion. It is therefore, I confess, not a little hazardous in a private and obscure individual, and a stranger too, thus to solicit the indulgent attention of the public; especially when I own[2] I offer here the history of neither a saint, a hero, nor a tyrant. I believe there are few events in my life which have not happened to many: it is true the incidents of it are numerous; and, did I consider myself an European, I might say my sufferings were great: but when I compare my lot with that of most of my countrymen, I regard myself as a particular favourite of Heaven, and acknowledge the mercies of Providence in every occurrence of my life. If then the following narrative does not appear sufficiently interesting to engage general attention, let my motive be some excuse for its publication. I am not so foolishly vain as to expect from it either immortality or literary reputation. If it affords any satisfaction to my numerous friends, at whose request it has been written, or in the smallest degree promotes the interests of humanity, the ends for which it was undertaken will be fully attained, and every wish of my heart gratified. Let it therefore be remembered that, in wishing to avoid censure, I do not aspire to praise.

That part of Africa, known by the name of Guinea, to which the trade for slaves is carried on, extends along the coast above 3400 miles, from the Senegal to Angola, and includes a variety of kingdoms. Of these the most considerable is the kingdom of Benin,[3] both as to extent and wealth, the richness and cultivation of the soil, the power of its king, and the number and warlike disposition of the inhabitants. It is situated nearly under the line,[4] and extends along the coast about 170 miles, but runs back into the interior part of Africa to a distance hitherto I believe unexplored by any traveller; and seems only terminated at length by the empire of Abyssinia, near 1500 miles from its beginning. This kingdom is divided into many provinces or districts: in one of the most remote and fertile of which, called Eboe, I was born, in the year 1745, in a charming fruitful vale named Essaka. The distance of this province from the capital of Benin and the sea coast must be very considerable; for I had never heard of white men or Europeans, nor of the sea. And our subjection to the king of Benin was little more than nominal, for every transaction of the government, as far as my slender observation extended, was conducted by the chiefs or elders of the place. The manners and government of a people who have little commerce with other countries are generally very simple, and the history of what passes in one family or village may serve as a specimen of a nation. My father was one of those elders or chiefs I have spoken of, and was styled Embrenche; a term, as I remember, importing the highest distinction, and signifying in our language a *mark* of grandeur. This mark is conferred on the person

[1] The entire first chapter is included in the website component of this anthology.

[2] *own* Admit.

[3] *kingdom of Benin* This kingdom extended over part of present-day Nigeria as well as present-day Benin.

[4] *under the line* South of the equator.

entitled to it by cutting the skin across at the top of the forehead, and drawing it down to the eyebrows; and while it is in this situation applying a warm hand, and rubbing it until it shrinks up into a thick weal[1] across the lower part of the forehead. Most of the judges and senators were thus marked; my father had long borne it. I had seen it conferred on one of my brothers, and I was also *destined* to receive it by my parents. Those Embrenche, or chief men, decided disputes and punished crimes, for which purpose they always assembled together. The proceedings were generally short, and in most cases the law of retaliation prevailed. I remember a man was brought before my father and the other judges for kidnapping a boy; and, although he was the son of a chief or senator, he was condemned to make recompense by a man or woman slave. Adultery, however, was sometimes punished with slavery or death, a punishment which I believe is inflicted on it throughout most of the nations of Africa, so sacred among them is the honour of the marriage bed, and so jealous are they of the fidelity of their wives. Of this I recollect an instance: a woman was convicted before the judges of adultery, and delivered over, as the custom was, to her husband to be punished. Accordingly he determined to put her to death; but it being found, just before her execution, that she had an infant at her breast; and no woman being prevailed on to perform the part of a nurse, she was spared on account of the child. The men, however, do not preserve the same constancy to their wives which they expect from them; for they indulge in a plurality, though seldom in more than two. Their mode of marriage is thus: both parties are usually betrothed when young by their parents (though I have known the males to betroth themselves). On this occasion a feast is prepared, and the bride and bridegroom stand up in the midst of all their friends, who are assembled for the purpose, while he declares she is thenceforth to be looked upon as his wife, and that no other person is to pay any addresses to her. This is also immediately proclaimed in the vicinity, on which the bride retires from the assembly. Some time after she is brought home to her husband, and then another feast is made, to which the relations of both parties are invited. Her parents then deliver her to the bridegroom, accompanied with a number of blessings, and at the same time they tie round her waist a cotton string of the thickness of a goose-quill, which none but married women are permitted to wear: she is now considered as completely his wife; and at this time the dowry is given to the new married pair, which generally consists of portions of land, slaves, and cattle, household goods, and implements of husbandry. These are offered by the friends of both parties; besides which the parents of the bridegroom present gifts to those of the bride, whose property she is looked upon before marriage; but after it she is esteemed the sole property of her husband. The ceremony being now ended, the festival begins, which is celebrated with bonfires, and loud acclamations of joy, accompanied with music and dancing.

We are almost a nation of dancers, musicians, and poets. Thus every great event, such as a triumphant return from battle or other cause of public rejoicing, is celebrated in public dances, which are accompanied with songs and music suited to the occasion. The assembly is separated into four divisions which dance either apart or in succession, and each with a character peculiar to itself. The first division contains the married men, who in their dances frequently exhibit feats of arms, and the representation of a battle. To these succeed the married women, who dance in the second division. The young men occupy the third; and the maidens the fourth. Each represents some interesting scene of real life, such as a great achievement, domestic employment, a pathetic[2] story, or some rural sport; and as the subject is generally founded on some recent event, it is therefore ever new. This gives our dances a spirit and variety which I have scarcely seen elsewhere.[3] We have many musical instruments, particularly drums of different kinds, a piece of music which resembles a guitar, and another much like a stickado.[4] These last are chiefly used by betrothed virgins, who play on them on all grand festivals.

As our manners are simple, our luxuries are few. The dress of both sexes is nearly the same. It generally consists of a long piece of calico, or muslin, wrapped loosely round the body, somewhat in the form of a highland

[1] *weal* Mark; welt.

[2] *pathetic* Conveying a sense of pathos; emotionally affecting.

[3] [Equiano's note] When I was in Smyrna I have frequently seen the Greeks dance after this manner.

[4] *stickado* Musical instrument similar to a xylophone.

plaid. This is usually dyed blue, which is our favourite colour. It is extracted from a berry, and is brighter and richer than any I have seen in Europe. Besides this, our women of distinction wear golden ornaments; which they dispose with some profusion on their arms and legs. When our women are not employed with the men in tillage, their usual occupation is spinning and weaving cotton, which they afterwards dye and make it into garments. They also manufacture earthen vessels, of which we have many kinds. Among the rest tobacco pipes, made after the same fashion, and used in the same manner, as those in Turkey.[1]

Our manner of living is entirely plain; for as yet the natives are unacquainted with those refinements in cookery which debauch the taste: bullocks, goats, and poultry supply the greatest part of their food. These constitute likewise the principal wealth of the country, and the chief articles of its commerce. ...

As we live in a country where nature is prodigal of her favours, our wants are few and easily supplied; of course, we have few manufactures. They consist for the most part of calicoes, earthen ware, ornaments, and instruments of war and husbandry. But these make no part of our commerce, the principal articles of which, as I have observed, are provisions. In such a state money is of little use; however, we have some small pieces of coin, if I may call them such. They are made something like an anchor, but I do not remember either their value or denomination. We have also markets, at which I have been frequently with my mother. These are sometimes visited by stout mahogany-coloured men from the south west of us: we call them Oye-Eboe, which term signifies "red men living at a distance." They generally bring us firearms, gunpowder, hats, beads, and dried fish. The last we esteemed a great rarity, as our waters were only brooks and springs. These articles they barter with us for odoriferous woods and earth, and our salt of wood ashes. They always carry slaves through our land; but the strictest account is exacted of their manner of procuring them before they are suffered to pass. Sometimes indeed we sold slaves to them, but they were only prisoners of war, or such among us

as had been convicted of kidnapping, or adultery, and some other crimes which we esteemed heinous. ...

As to religion, the natives believe that there is one Creator of all things,[2] and that he lives in the sun and is girded round with a belt; that he may never eat or drink; but, according to some, he smokes a pipe, which is our own favourite luxury. They believe he governs events, especially our deaths or captivity; but, as for the doctrine of eternity, I do not remember to have ever heard of it: some however believe in the transmigration of souls in a certain degree. Those spirits which are not transmigrated, such as our dear friends or relations, they believe always attend them and guard them from the bad spirits or their foes. For this reason they always before eating, as I have observed, put some small portion of the meat, and pour some of their drink, on the ground for them; and they often make oblations of the blood of beasts or fowls at their graves. I was very fond of my mother, and almost constantly with her. When she went to make these oblations at her mother's tomb, which was a kind of small solitary thatched house, I sometimes attended her. There she made her libations and spent most of the night in cries and lamentations. I have been often extremely terrified on these occasions. The loneliness of the place, the darkness of the night, and the ceremony of libation, naturally awful and gloomy, were heightened by my mother's lamentations; and these, concurring with the cries of doleful birds by which these places were frequented, gave an inexpressible terror to the scene.

We compute the year from the day on which the sun crosses the line, and on its setting that evening there is a general shout throughout the land—at least, I can speak from my own knowledge, throughout our vicinity. The people at the same time make a great noise with rattles, not unlike the basket rattles used by children here, though much larger, and hold up their hands to heaven for a blessing. It is then the greatest offerings are made, and those children whom our wise men foretell will be fortunate are then presented to different people. I remember many used to come to see me, and I was carried about to others for that purpose. ...

[1] [Equiano's note] The bowl is earthen, curiously figured, to which a long reed is fixed as a tube. This tube is sometimes so long as to be borne by one, and frequently out of grandeur by two boys.

[2] *believe ... things* For an interesting comparison, see the discussion of Theism and of Atheism in Gronniosaw's *Narrative* (included in the website component of this anthology).

CHAPTER 2

The author's birth and parentage—His being kid-
napped with his sister—Their separation—Surprise
at meeting again—Are finally separated—Account
of the different places and incidents the author met
with till his arrival on the coast—The effect the
sight of a slave ship had on him—He sails for the
West Indies—Horrors of a slave ship—Arrives at
Barbadoes, where the cargo is sold and dispersed.

I hope the reader will not think I have trespassed on
his patience in introducing myself to him with some
account of the manners and customs of my country.[1]
They had been implanted in me with great care, and
made an impression on my mind which time could
not erase, and which all the adversity and variety of
fortune I have since experienced served only to rivet
and record; for, whether the love of one's country be
real or imaginary, or a lesson of reason, or an instinct of
nature, I still look back with pleasure on the first scenes
of my life, though that pleasure has been for the most
part mingled with sorrow.

I have already acquainted the reader with the time
and place of my birth. My father, besides many slaves,
had a numerous family, of which seven lived to grow
up, including myself and a sister, who was the only
daughter. As I was the youngest of the sons, I became,
of course, the greatest favourite with my mother, and
was always with her; and she used to take particular
pains to form my mind. I was trained up from my ear-
liest years in the art of war; my daily exercise was shoot-
ing and throwing javelins, and my mother adorned me
with emblems after the manner of our greatest war-
riors. In this way I grew up till I was turned the age of
eleven, when an end was put to my happiness in the
following manner. Generally, when the grown people
in the neighbourhood were gone far in the fields to
labour, the children assembled together in some of the
neighbours' premises to play; and commonly some of
us used to get up a tree to look out for any assailant or
kidnapper that might come upon us; for they some-
times took those opportunities of our parents' absence
to attack and carry off as many as they could seize. One

day, as I was watching at the top of a tree in our yard,
I saw one of those people come into the yard of our
next neighbour but one, to kidnap, there being many
stout[2] young people in it. Immediately on this I gave
the alarm of the rogue, and he was surrounded by the
stoutest of them, who entangled him with cords, so
that he could not escape till some of the grown people
came and secured him. But alas! ere long it was my fate
to be thus attacked, and to be carried off, when none
of the grown people were nigh. One day, when all our
people were gone out to their works as usual, and only
I and my dear sister were left to mind the house, two
men and a woman got over our walls and in a moment
seized us both, and, without giving us time to cry out
or make resistance, they stopped our mouths and ran
off with us into the nearest wood. Here they tied our
hands and continued to carry us as far as they could,
till night came on, when we reached a small house
where the robbers halted for refreshment and spent the
night. We were then unbound, but were unable to take
any food; and, being quite overpowered by fatigue and
grief, our only relief was some sleep, which allayed our
misfortune for a short time.

The next morning we left the house and continued
travelling all the day. For a long time we had kept
the woods, but at last we came into a road, which I
believed I knew. I had now some hopes of being deliv-
ered, for we had advanced but a little way before I dis-
covered some people at a distance, on which I began to
cry out for their assistance. But my cries had no other
effect than to make them tie me faster and stop my
mouth, and then they put me into a large sack. They
also stopped my sister's mouth and tied her hands, and
in this manner we proceeded till we were out of the
sight of these people. When we went to rest the follow-
ing night they offered us some victuals, but we refused
it, and the only comfort we had was in being in one
another's arms all that night, and bathing each other
with our tears. But alas! we were soon deprived of even
the small comfort of weeping together. The next day
proved a day of greater sorrow than I had yet experi-
enced, for my sister and I were then separated while we
lay clasped in each other's arms. It was in vain that we
besought them not to part us; she was torn from me
and immediately carried away, while I was left in a state

1 *my country* Equiano says he was born in Essaka, a country
located in the interior of present-day Nigeria.

2 *stout* Sturdily built; strong.

of distraction not to be described. I cried and grieved continually, and for several days I did not eat anything but what they forced into my mouth.

At length, after many days travelling, during which I had often changed masters, I got into the hands of a chieftain in a very pleasant country. This man had two wives and some children, and they all used[1] me extremely well, and did all they could to comfort me—particularly the first wife, who was something like my mother. Although I was a great many days' journey from my father's house, yet these people spoke exactly the same language with us. This first master of mine, as I may call him, was a smith,[2] and my principal employment was working his bellows, which were the same kind as I had seen in my vicinity. They were in some respects not unlike the stoves here in gentlemen's kitchens, and were covered over with leather; and in the middle of that leather a stick was fixed, and a person stood up and worked it in the same manner as is done to pump water out of a cask with a hand pump. I believe it was gold he worked, for it was of a lovely bright yellow colour, and was worn by the women on their wrists and ankles.

I was there I suppose about a month, and they at last used to trust me some little distance from the house. This liberty I used in embracing every opportunity to inquire the way to my own home; and I also sometimes, for the same purpose, went with the maidens in the cool of the evenings to bring pitchers of water from the springs for the use of the house. I had also remarked where the sun rose in the morning and set in the evening as I had travelled along, and I had observed that my father's house was towards the rising of the sun. I therefore determined to seize the first opportunity of making my escape, and to shape my course for that quarter; for I was quite oppressed and weighed down by grief after my mother and friends; and my love of liberty, ever great, was strengthened by the mortifying circumstance of not daring to eat with the free-born children, although I was mostly their companion.

While I was projecting my escape, one day an unlucky event happened which quite disconcerted my plan and put an end to my hopes. I used to be sometimes employed in assisting an elderly woman slave to cook and take care of the poultry, and one morning while I was feeding some chickens, I happened to toss a small pebble at one of them, which hit it on the middle and directly killed it. The old slave, having soon after missed the chicken, inquired after it; and on my relating the accident (for I told her the truth, because my mother would never suffer me to tell a lie), she flew into a violent passion, threatened that I should suffer for it, and, my master being out, she immediately went and told her mistress what I had done. This alarmed me very much, and I expected an instant flogging, which to me was uncommonly dreadful, for I had seldom been beaten at home. I therefore resolved to fly, and accordingly I ran into a thicket that was hard by and hid myself in the bushes. Soon afterwards my mistress and the slave returned, and, not seeing me, they searched all the house; but, not finding me, and I not making answer when they called to me, they thought I had run away, and the whole neighbourhood was raised in the pursuit of me. In that part of the country (as in ours) the houses and villages were skirted with woods, or shrubberies, and the bushes were so thick that a man could readily conceal himself in them so as to elude the strictest search. The neighbours continued the whole day looking for me, and several times many of them came within a few yards of the place where I lay hid. I then gave myself up for lost entirely and expected every moment, when I heard a rustling among the trees, to be found out and punished by my master. But they never discovered me, though they were often so near that I even heard their conjectures as they were looking about for me; and I now learned from them that any attempt to return home would be hopeless. Most of them supposed I had fled towards home, but the distance was so great, and the way so intricate, that they thought I could never reach it, and that I should be lost in the woods. When I heard this I was seized with a violent panic and abandoned myself to despair. Night too began to approach, and aggravated all my fears. I had before entertained hopes of getting home, and I had determined when it should be dark to make the attempt; but I was now convinced it was fruitless, and I began to consider that, if possibly I could escape all other animals, I could not those of the human kind, and that, not knowing the way, I must perish in the woods. Thus was I like the hunted deer:

[1] *used* Treated.

[2] *smith* One who works with metals.

Ev'ry leaf and ev'ry whisp'ring breath
Conveyed a foe, and ev'ry foe a death.[1]

I heard frequent rustlings among the leaves, and, being pretty sure they were snakes, I expected every instant to be stung by them. This increased my anguish, and the horror of my situation became now quite insupportable. I at length quitted the thicket, very faint and hungry, for I had not eaten or drank anything all the day, and crept to my master's kitchen, from whence I set out at first, and which was an open shed, and laid myself down in the ashes with an anxious wish for death to relieve me from all my pains. I was scarcely awake in the morning when the old woman slave, who was the first up, came to light the fire and saw me in the fireplace. She was very much surprised to see me, and could scarcely believe her own eyes. She now promised to intercede for me, and went for her master, who soon after came and, having slightly reprimanded me, ordered me to be taken care of and not to be ill-treated.

Soon after this my master's only daughter, and child by his first wife, sickened and died, which affected him so much that for some time he was almost frantic, and really would have killed himself, had he not been watched and prevented. However, in a small time afterwards he recovered, and I was again sold. I was now carried to the left of the sun's rising, through many different countries and a number of large woods. The people I was sold to used to carry me very often, when I was tired, either on their shoulders or on their backs. I saw many convenient, well built sheds along the roads, at proper distances to accommodate the merchants and travellers, who lay in those buildings along with their wives, who often accompany them; and they always go well armed.

From the time I left my own nation, I always found somebody that understood me, till I came to the sea coast. The languages of different nations did not totally differ,[2] nor were they so copious as those of the Europeans, particularly the English. They were therefore easily learned, and while I was journeying thus through Africa I acquired two or three different tongues. In this manner I had been travelling for a considerable time when one evening, to my great surprise, whom should I see brought to the house where I was but my dear sister! As soon as she saw me she gave a loud shriek and ran into my arms. I was quite overpowered: neither of us could speak, but for a considerable time clung to each other in mutual embraces, unable to do any thing but weep. Our meeting affected all who saw us; and indeed I must acknowledge, in honour of those sable[3] destroyers of human rights, that I never met with any ill treatment, or saw any offered to their slaves, except tying them when necessary, to keep them from running away. When these people knew we were brother and sister they indulged us together, and the man to whom I supposed we belonged lay with us, he in the middle, while she and I held one another by the hands across his breast all night; and thus for a while we forgot our misfortunes in the joy of being together. But even this small comfort was soon to have an end, for scarcely had the fatal morning appeared when she was again torn from me forever! I was now more miserable, if possible, than before. The small relief which her presence gave me from pain was gone, and the wretchedness of my situation was redoubled by my anxiety after her fate and my apprehensions lest her sufferings should be greater than mine, when I could not be with her to alleviate them. Yes, thou dear partner of all my childish sports! thou sharer of my joys and sorrows! happy should I have ever esteemed myself to encounter every misery for you, and to procure your freedom by the sacrifice of my own. Though you were early forced from my arms, your image has been always riveted in my heart, from which neither time nor fortune have been able to remove it; so that, while the thoughts of your sufferings have damped my prosperity, they have mingled with adversity and increased its bitterness. To that Heaven which protects the weak from the strong, I commit the care of your innocence and virtues, if they have not already received their full reward, and if your youth and delicacy have not long since fallen victims to the violence of the African trader, the pestilential stench of a Guinea ship,[4] the seasoning in the

[1] *Ev'ry … death* See lines 287–88 of John Denham's "Cooper's Hill": "Now every leaf, and every moving breath / Presents a foe, and every foe a death."

[2] *languages … differ* The Igbo languages and other languages in the Niger-Congo language family share many features not only with each other but also with many Bantu languages.

[3] *sable* Dark skinned.

[4] *Guinea ship* Slave ship from Guinea.

European colonies, or the lash and lust of a brutal and unrelenting overseer.

I did not long remain after my sister. I was again sold and carried through a number of places, till, after travelling a considerable time, I came to a town called Tinmah, in the most beautiful country I had yet seen in Africa. It was extremely rich, and there were many rivulets which flowed through it and supplied a large pond in the centre of the town, where the people washed. Here I first saw and tasted cocoanuts, which I thought superior to any nuts I had ever tasted before; and the trees, which were loaded, were also interspersed amongst the houses, which had commodious shades adjoining and were in the same manner as ours, the insides being neatly plastered and whitewashed. Here I also saw and tasted for the first time sugar cane. Their money consisted of little white shells the size of the fingernail. I was sold here for one hundred and seventy-two of them by a merchant who lived, and brought me, there. I had been about two or three days at his house when a wealthy widow, a neighbour of his, came there one evening and brought with her an only son, a young gentleman about my own age and size. Here they saw me; and, having taken a fancy to me, I was bought of the merchant and went home with them. Her house and premises were situated close to one of those rivulets I have mentioned, and were the finest I ever saw in Africa: they were very extensive, and she had a number of slaves to attend her. The next day I was washed and perfumed, and when mealtime came I was led into the presence of my mistress, and ate and drank before her with her son. This filled me with astonishment, and I could scarce help expressing my surprise that the young gentleman should suffer[1] me, who was bound, to eat with him, who was free; and not only so, but that he would not at any time either eat or drink till I had taken first, because I was the eldest (which was agreeable to our custom). Indeed, everything here, and all their treatment of me, made me forget that I was a slave. The language of these people resembled ours so nearly that we understood each other perfectly. They had also the very same customs as we. There were likewise slaves daily to attend us, while my young master and I with other boys sported with our darts and bows and arrows, as I had been used to do at home. In this resemblance to my former happy state I passed about two months; and I now began to think I was to be adopted into the family, and was beginning to be reconciled to my situation and to forget by degrees my misfortunes, when all at once the delusion vanished; for, without the least previous knowledge, one morning early, while my dear master and companion was still asleep, I was wakened out of my reverie to fresh sorrow, and hurried away even amongst the uncircumcised.[2]

Thus at the very moment I dreamed of the greatest happiness I found myself most miserable, and it seemed as if fortune wished to give me this taste of joy only to render the reverse more poignant. The change I now experienced was as painful as it was sudden and unexpected. It was a change indeed from a state of bliss to a scene which is inexpressible by me, as it discovered[3] to me an element I had never before beheld, and till then had no idea of, and wherein such instances of hardship and cruelty continually occurred, as I can never reflect on but with horror.

All the nations and people I had hitherto passed through resembled our own in their manners, customs, and language, but I came at length to a country, the inhabitants of which differed from us in all those particulars. I was very much struck with this difference, especially when I came among a people who did not circumcise, and ate without washing their hands. They cooked also in iron pots, and had European cutlasses and cross bows, which were unknown to us, and fought with their fists amongst themselves. Their women were not so modest as ours, for they ate and drank and slept with their men. But, above all, I was amazed to see no sacrifices or offerings among them. In some of those places the people ornamented themselves with scars, and likewise filed their teeth very sharp. They wanted sometimes to ornament me in the same manner, but I would not suffer them, hoping that I might sometime be among a people who did not thus disfigure themselves, as I thought they did. At last I came to the banks of a large river which was covered with canoes, in which the people appeared to live with their household utensils and provisions of all kinds. I was beyond measure astonished at this, as I had never before seen

[1] *suffer* Permit.

[2] *uncircumcised* I.e., heathens, foreigners.

[3] *discovered* Revealed.

any water larger than a pond or a rivulet, and my surprise was mingled with no small fear when I was put into one of these canoes and we began to paddle and move along the river. We continued going on thus till night; and when we came to land and made fires on the banks, each family by themselves, some dragged their canoes on shore, others stayed and cooked in theirs and laid in them all night. Those on the land had mats, of which they made tents, some in the shape of little houses. In these we slept, and after the morning meal we embarked again and proceeded as before. I was often very much astonished to see some of the women, as well as the men, jump into the water, dive to the bottom, come up again, and swim about.

Thus I continued to travel, sometimes by land, sometimes by water, through different countries and various nations, till, at the end of six or seven months after I had been kidnapped, I arrived at the seacoast. It would be tedious and uninteresting to relate all the incidents which befell me during this journey, and which I have not yet forgotten; of the various hands I passed through, and the manners and customs of all the different people among whom I lived. I shall therefore only observe that in all the places where I was the soil was exceedingly rich; the pumpkins, eadas,[1] plantains, yams, etc., etc., were in great abundance, and of incredible size. There were also vast quantities of different gums, though not used for any purpose, and everywhere a great deal of tobacco. The cotton even grew quite wild, and there was plenty of redwood. I saw no mechanics[2] whatever in all the way, except such as I have mentioned. The chief employment in all these countries was agriculture, and both the males and females, as with us, were brought up to it, and trained in the arts of war.

The first object which saluted my eyes when I arrived on the coast was the sea, and a slave ship, which was then riding at anchor and waiting for its cargo. These filled me with astonishment, which was soon converted into terror when I was carried on board. I was immediately handled and tossed up, to see if I were sound, by some of the crew; and I was now persuaded that I had gotten into a world of bad spirits, and that they were going to kill me. Their complexions, too, differing so

much from ours, their long hair, and the language they spoke (which was very different from any I had ever heard) united to confirm me in this belief. Indeed, such were the horrors of my views and fears at the moment that, if ten thousand worlds had been my own, I would have freely parted with them all to have exchanged my condition with that of the meanest[3] slave in my own country. When I looked round the ship, too, and saw a large furnace of copper boiling, and a multitude of black people of every description chained together, every one of their countenances expressing dejection and sorrow, I no longer doubted of my fate; and, quite overpowered with horror and anguish, I fell motionless on the deck and fainted. When I recovered a little I found some black people about me who I believed were some of those who brought me on board and had been receiving their pay; they talked to me in order to cheer me, but all in vain. I asked them if we were not to be eaten by those white men with horrible looks, red faces, and loose hair. They told me I was not, and one of the crew brought me a small portion of spirituous liquor in a wine glass; but, being afraid of him, I would not take it out of his hand. One of the blacks therefore took it from him and gave it to me, and I took a little down my palate, which, instead of reviving me as they thought it would, threw me into the greatest consternation at the strange feeling it produced, having never tasted any such liquor before.

Soon after this the blacks who brought me on board went off, and left me abandoned to despair. I now saw myself deprived of all chance of returning to my native country, or even the least glimpse of hope of gaining the shore, which I now considered as friendly; and I even wished for my former slavery in preference to my present situation, which was filled with horrors of every kind, still heightened by my ignorance of what I was to undergo. I was not long suffered to indulge my grief; I was soon put down under the decks, and there I received such a salutation in my nostrils as I had never experienced in my life; so that, with the loathsomeness of the stench and crying together, I became so sick and low that I was not able to eat, nor had I the least desire to taste anything. I now wished for the last friend, death, to relieve me; but soon, to my grief, two of the white men offered me eatables; and, on my refusing to

[1] *eadas* Eddoes (a variety of tropical vegetable).

[2] *mechanics* Artisans.

[3] *meanest* Most lowly; worst treated.

eat, one of them held me fast by the hands and laid me across, I think, the windlass,[1] and tied my feet while the other flogged me severely. I had never experienced anything of this kind before; and although, not being used to the water, I naturally feared that element the first time I saw it, yet nevertheless, could I have got over the nettings, I would have jumped over the side. But I could not, and besides, the crew used to watch us very closely who were not chained down to the decks, lest we should leap into the water, and I have seen some of these poor African prisoners most severely cut for attempting to do so, and hourly whipped for not eating. This indeed was often the case with myself.

In a little time after, amongst the poor chained men I found some of my own nation, which in a small degree gave ease to my mind. I inquired of these what was to be done with us; they gave me to understand we were to be carried to these white people's country to work for them. I then was a little revived and thought, if it were no worse than working, my situation was not so desperate. But still I feared I should be put to death; the white people looked and acted, as I thought, in so savage a manner—for I had never seen among any people such instances of brutal cruelty, and this not only shown towards us blacks, but also to some of the whites themselves. One white man in particular I saw, when we were permitted to be on deck, flogged so unmercifully with a large rope near the foremast that he died in consequence of it, and they tossed him over the side as they would have done a brute.[2] This made me fear these people the more, and I expected nothing less than to be treated in the same manner. I could not help expressing my fears and apprehensions to some of my countrymen. I asked them if these people had no country, but lived in this hollow place (the ship). They told me they did not, but came from a distant one. "Then," said I, "how comes it in all our country we never heard of them?" They told me because they lived so very far off. I then asked, where were their women? had they any like themselves? I was told they had. "And why," said I, "do we not see them?" They answered, because they were left behind. I asked how the vessel could go. They told me they could not tell, but that

there were cloths put upon the masts by the help of the ropes I saw, and then the vessel went on; and the white men had some spell or magic they put in the water when they liked in order to stop the vessel. I was exceedingly amazed at this account, and really thought they were spirits. I therefore wished much to be from amongst them,[3] for I expected they would sacrifice me. But my wishes were vain, for we were so quartered that it was impossible for any of us to make our escape.

While we stayed on the coast I was mostly on deck, and one day, to my great astonishment, I saw one of these vessels coming in with the sails up. As soon as the whites saw it, they gave a great shout, at which we were amazed; and the more so as the vessel appeared larger by approaching nearer. At last she came to an anchor in my sight, and when the anchor was let go I and my countrymen who saw it were lost in astonishment to observe the vessel stop, and were now convinced it was done by magic. Soon after this the other ship got her boats out, and they came on board of us, and the people of both ships seemed very glad to see each other. Several of the strangers also shook hands with us black people and made motions with their hands, signifying, I suppose, we were to go to their country; but we did not understand them.

At last, when the ship we were in had got in all her cargo, they made ready with many fearful noises, and we were all put under deck, so that we could not see how they managed the vessel. But this disappointment was the least of my sorrow. The stench of the hold while we were on the coast was so intolerably loathsome that it was dangerous to remain there for any time, and some of us had been permitted to stay on the deck for the fresh air, but now that the whole ship's cargo were confined together, it became absolutely pestilential. The closeness of the place and the heat of the climate, added to the number in the ship, which was so crowded that each had scarcely room to turn himself, almost suffocated us. This produced copious perspirations, so that the air soon became unfit for respiration from a variety of loathsome smells, and brought on a sickness among the slaves, of which many died, thus falling victims to the improvident avarice, as I may call it, of their purchasers. This wretched situation was again aggravated

[1] *windlass* On board ship, a mechanical contrivance used for winding ropes or chains.

[2] *brute* Non-human animal.

[3] *from amongst them* Away from them.

by the galling[1] of the chains, now become insupportable, and the filth of the necessary tubs,[2] into which the children often fell, and were almost suffocated. The shrieks of the women and the groans of the dying rendered the whole a scene of horror almost inconceivable. Happily perhaps for myself, I was soon reduced so low here that it was thought necessary to keep me almost always on deck; and from my extreme youth I was not put in fetters. In this situation I expected every hour to share the fate of my companions, some of whom were almost daily brought upon deck at the point of death, which I began to hope would soon put an end to my miseries. Often did I think many of the inhabitants of the deep much more happy than myself. I envied them the freedom they enjoyed, and as often wished I could change my condition for theirs. Every circumstance I met with served only to render my state more painful and heighten my apprehensions and my opinion of the cruelty of the whites.

One day they had taken a number of fishes; and when they had killed and satisfied themselves with as many as they thought fit, to our astonishment who were on the deck, rather than give any of them to us to eat as we expected, they tossed the remaining fish into the sea again, although we begged and prayed for some as well as we could, but in vain; and some of my countrymen, being pressed by hunger, took an opportunity, when they thought no one saw them, of trying to get a little privately; but they were discovered, and the attempt procured them some very severe floggings.

One day, when we had a smooth sea and moderate wind, two of my wearied countrymen who were chained together (I was near them at the time), preferring death to such a life of misery, somehow made through the nettings and jumped into the sea. Immediately another quite dejected fellow, who, on account of his illness, was suffered to be out of irons, also followed their example; and I believe many more would very soon have done the same if they had not been prevented by the ship's crew, who were instantly alarmed. Those of us that were the most active were in a moment put down under the deck, and there was such a noise and confusion amongst the people of the ship as I never heard before, to stop her and get the boat out to go after the slaves. However, two of the wretches were drowned; but they got the other, and afterwards flogged him unmercifully for thus attempting to prefer death to slavery.

In this manner we continued to undergo more hardships than I can now relate, hardships which are inseparable from this accursed trade. Many a time we were near suffocation from the want of fresh air, which we were often without for whole days together. This, and the stench of the necessary tubs, carried off many.

During our passage I first saw flying fishes, which surprised me very much: they used frequently to fly across the ship, and many of them fell on the deck. I also now first saw the use of the quadrant;[3] I had often with astonishment seen the mariners make observations with it, and I could not think what it meant. They at last took notice of my surprise, and one of them, willing to increase it, as well as to gratify my curiosity, made me one day look through it. The clouds appeared to me to be land, which disappeared as they passed along. This heightened my wonder, and I was now more persuaded than ever that I was in another world, and that everything about me was magic.

At last we came in sight of the island of Barbados, at which the whites on board gave a great shout and made many signs of joy to us. We did not know what to think of this, but as the vessel drew nearer we plainly saw the harbour and other ships of different kinds and sizes, and we soon anchored amongst them off Bridgetown. Many merchants and planters now came on board, though it was in the evening. They put us in separate parcels[4] and examined us attentively. They also made us jump, and pointed to the land, signifying we were to go there. We thought by this we should be eaten by these ugly men, as they appeared to us; and, when soon after we were all put down under the deck again, there was much dread and trembling among us, and nothing but bitter cries to be heard all the night from these apprehensions, insomuch that at last the white people got some old slaves from the land to pacify us. They told us we were not to be eaten, but to work, and were soon to go on land, where we should see many of our country people. This report eased us much; and

[1] *galling* Chafing.

[2] *necessary tubs* Containers for human excrement.

[3] *quadrant* Instrument used for taking altitudes.

[4] *parcels* Groups.

sure enough, soon after we were landed, there came to us Africans of all languages.

We were conducted immediately to the merchant's yard, where we were all pent up together like so many sheep in a fold, without regard to sex or age. As every object was new to me, everything I saw filled me with surprise. What struck me first was that the houses were built with stories, and in every other respect different from those in Africa. But I was still more astonished on seeing people on horseback. I did not know what this could mean, and indeed I thought these people were full of nothing but magical arts. While I was in this astonishment, one of my fellow prisoners spoke to a countryman of his about the horses, who said they were the same kind they had in their country. I understood them, though they were from a distant part of Africa, and I thought it odd I had not seen any horses there; but afterwards, when I came to converse with different Africans, I found they had many horses amongst them, and much larger than those I then saw.

We were not many days in the merchant's custody before we were sold after their usual manner, which is this: on a signal given (as the beat of a drum), the buyers rush at once into the yard where the slaves are confined, and make choice of that parcel they like best. The noise and clamour with which this is attended, and the eagerness visible in the countenances of the buyers, serve not a little to increase the apprehensions of the terrified Africans, who may well be supposed to consider them as the ministers of that destruction to which they think themselves devoted. In this manner, without scruple, are relations and friends separated, most of them never to see each other again. I remember in the vessel in which I was brought over, in the men's apartment there were several brothers who, in the sale, were sold in different lots; and it was very moving on this occasion to see and hear their cries at parting. O ye nominal Christians![1] Might not an African ask you, "Learned you this from your God, who says unto you, 'Do unto all men as you would men should do unto you'? Is it not enough that we are torn from our country and friends to toil for your luxury and lust of gain?[2] Must every tender feeling be likewise sacrificed to your avarice? Are the dearest friends and relations, now rendered more dear by their separation from their kindred, still to be parted from each other, and thus prevented from cheering the gloom of slavery with the small comfort of being together and mingling their sufferings and sorrows? Why are parents to lose their children, brothers their sisters, or husbands their wives?" Surely this is a new refinement in cruelty, which, while it has no advantage to atone for it, thus aggravates distress and adds fresh horrors even to the wretchedness of slavery.

from CHAPTER 3[3]

The author is carried to Virginia—His distress—Surprise at seeing a picture and a watch—Is bought by Captain Pascal, and sets out for England—His terror during the voyage—Arrives in England—His wonder at a fall of snow—Is sent to Guernsey, and in some time goes on board a ship of war with his master—Some account of the expedition against Louisbourg under the command of Admiral Boscawen, in 1758.

I now totally lost the small remains of comfort I had enjoyed in conversing with my countrymen; the women too, who used to wash and take care of me, were all gone different ways, and I never saw one of them afterwards.

I stayed in this island for a few days; I believe it could not be above a fortnight; when I and some few more slaves, that were not saleable amongst the rest, from very much fretting, were shipped off in a sloop for North America. On the passage we were better treated than when we were coming from Africa, and we had plenty of rice and fat pork. We were landed up a river a good way from the sea, about Virginia county, where we saw few or none of our native Africans, and not one soul who could talk to me. I was a few weeks weeding grass, and gathering stones in a plantation; and at last all my companions were distributed different ways, and only myself was left. I was now exceedingly miserable, and thought myself worse off than any of the rest of my companions; for they could talk to each other, but I had no person to speak to that I could understand.

[1] *nominal Christians* So-called Christians.

[2] *lust of gain* Desire for riches.

[3] A longer selection of excerpts from this chapter is included as part of the website component of this anthology.

In this state I was constantly grieving and pining,[1] and wishing for death rather than anything else.

While I was in this plantation the gentleman, to whom I suppose the estate belonged, being unwell, I was one day sent for to his dwelling house to fan him; when I came into the room where he was I was very much affrighted at some things I saw, and the more so as I had seen a black woman slave as I came through the house, who was cooking the dinner, and the poor creature was cruelly loaded with various kinds of iron machines; she had one particularly on her head, which locked her mouth so fast that she could scarcely speak; and could not eat nor drink. I was much astonished and shocked at this contrivance, which I afterward learned was called the iron muzzle. Soon after I had a fan put into my hand, to fan the gentleman while he slept; and so I did indeed with great fear. While he was fast asleep, I indulged myself a great deal in looking about the room, which to me appeared very fine and curious. The first object that engaged my attention was a watch which hung on the chimney, and was going. I was quite surprised at the noise it made and was afraid it would tell the gentleman anything I might do amiss: and when I immediately after observed a picture hanging in the room, which appeared constantly to look at me, I was still more affrighted, having never seen such things as these before. At one time I thought it was something relative to magic; and not seeing it move I thought it might be some way the whites had to keep their great men when they died, and offer them libation as we used to do to our friendly spirits. In this state of anxiety I remained till my master awoke, when I was dismissed out of the room, to my no small satisfaction and relief; for I thought that these people were all made up of wonders. In this place I was called Jacob; but on board the *African Snow* I was called Michael.

I had been some time in this miserable, forlorn, and much dejected state, without having anyone to talk to, which made my life a burden, when the kind and unknown hand of the Creator (who in very deed leads the blind in a way they know not) now began to appear, to my comfort; for one day the captain of a merchant ship, called the *Industrious Bee*, came on some business to my master's house. This gentleman, whose name was Michael Henry Pascal, was a lieutenant in the royal navy, but now commanded this trading ship, which was somewhere in the confines of the county many miles off. While he was at my master's house it happened that he saw me, and liked me so well that he made a purchase of me. I think I have often heard him say he gave thirty or forty pounds sterling for me; but I do not now remember which. However, he meant me for a present to some of his friends in England: and I was sent accordingly from the house of my then master, one Mr. Campbell, to the place where the ship lay; I was conducted on horseback by an elderly black man (a mode of travelling which appeared very odd to me). When I arrived I was carried on board a fine large ship, loaded with tobacco, etc. and just ready to sail for England. I now thought my condition much mended; I had sails to lie on, and plenty of good vitals[2] to eat; and everybody on board used me very kindly, quite contrary to what I had seen of any white people before; I therefore began to think that they were not all of the same disposition. A few days after I was on board we sailed for England.

I was still at a loss to conjecture my destiny. By this time, however, I could smatter a little imp'rfect English; and I wanted to know as well as I could where we were going. Some of the people of the ship used to tell me they were going to carry me back to my own country, and this made me very happy. I was quite rejoiced at the sound of going back; and thought if I should get home what wonders I should have to tell. But I was reserved for another fate, and was soon undeceived when we came within sight of the English coast. While I was on board this ship, my captain and master named me Gustavus Vassa.[3] I at that time began to understand him a little, and refused to be called so, and told him as well as I could that I would be called Jacob; but he said I should not, and still called me Gustavus; and when I refused to answer to my new name, which at first I did, it gained me many a cuff; so at length I submitted, and was obliged to bear the present name, by which I have been known ever since.

1 *pining* Becoming exhausted with mental suffering.

2 *vitals* Nutritious foods.

3 *Gustavus Vassa* The sixteenth-century Swedish monarch Gustav Vasa was widely regarded as a hero to his people; a 1739 play by Henry Brooke, *Gustavus Vasa, the Deliverer of His Country*, helped to make Vasa well-known in the English-speaking world.

The ship had a very long passage; and on that account we had very short allowance of provisions. Towards the last we had only one pound and a half of bread per week, and about the same quantity of meat, and one quart of water a day. We spoke with only one vessel the whole time we were at sea, and but once we caught a few fishes. In our extremities the captain and people told me in jest they would kill and eat me; but I thought them in earnest, and was depressed beyond measure, expecting every moment to be my last. While I was in this situation one evening they caught with a good deal of trouble, a large shark, and got it on board. This gladdened my poor heart exceedingly, as I thought it would serve the people to eat instead of their eating me; but very soon, to my astonishment, they cut off a small part of the tail, and tossed the rest over the side. This renewed my consternation; and I did not know what to think of these white people, though I very much feared they would kill and eat me.

There was on board the ship a young lad who had never been at sea before, about four or five years older than myself: his name was Richard Baker. He was a native of America, had received an excellent education, and was of a most amiable temper. Soon after I went on board he shewed me a great deal of partiality and attention, and in return I grew extremely fond of him. We at length became inseparable; and, for the space of two years, he was of very great use to me, and was my constant companion and instructor. Although this dear youth had many slaves of his own, yet he and I have gone through many sufferings together on shipboard; and we have many nights lain in each other's bosoms when we were in great distress. Thus such a friendship was cemented between us as we cherished till his death, which, to my very great sorrow, happened in the year 1759, when he was up the Archipelago, on board his majesty's ship the *Preston*: an event which I have never ceased to regret, as I lost at once a kind interpreter, an agreeable companion, and a faithful friend; who, at the age of fifteen, discovered a mind superior to prejudice; and who was not ashamed to notice, to associate with, and to be the friend and instructor of one who was ignorant, a stranger, of a different complexion, and a slave! My master had lodged in his mother's house in America: he respected him very much, and made him always eat with him in the cabin. He used often to tell

him jocularly that he would kill me to eat. Sometimes he would say to me the black people were not good to eat, and would ask me if we did not eat people in my country. I said, No: then he said he would kill Dick (as he always called him) first, and afterwards me. Though this hearing relieved my mind a little as to myself, I was alarmed for Dick and whenever he was called I used to be very much afraid he was to be killed; and I would peep and watch to see if they were going to kill him: nor was I free from this consternation till we made the land.

One night we lost a man overboard; and the cries and noise were so great and confused in stopping the ship, that I, who did not know what was the matter, began, as usual, to be very much afraid, and to think they were going to make an offering with me, and perform some magic; which I still believed they dealt in. As the waves were very high, I thought the ruler of the seas was angry, and I expected to be offered up to appease him. This filled my mind with agony, and I could not any more that night close my eyes again to rest. However, when daylight appeared I was a little eased in my mind; but still every time I was called, I used to think it was to be killed.

Sometime after this we saw some very large fish, which I afterwards found were called grampusses.[1] They looked to me extremely terrible, and made their appearance just at dusk and were so near as to blow the water on the ship's deck. I believed them to be the rulers of the sea; and, as the white people did not make any offerings at anytime, I thought they were angry with them: and, at last, what confirmed my belief was, the wind just then died away, and a calm ensued, and in consequence of it the ship stopped going. I supposed that the fish had performed this, and I hid myself in the fore part of the ship, through fear of being offered up to appease them, every minute peeping and quaking: but my good friend Dick came shortly towards me, and I took an opportunity to ask him, as well as I could, what these fish were. Not being able to talk much English, I could but just make him understand my question; and not at all, when I asked him if any offerings were to be made to them: however, he told me these fish would swallow anybody; which

[1] *grampusses* The name "grampus" is applied to several species of whale and dolphin.

sufficiently alarmed me. Here he was called away by the captain, who was leaning over the quarter-deck railing and looking at the fish; and most of the people were busied in getting a barrel of pitch to light, for them to play with. The captain now called me to him, having learned some of my apprehensions from Dick; and having diverted himself and others for some time with my fears, which appeared ludicrous enough in my crying and trembling, he dismissed me. The barrel of pitch was now lighted and put over the side into the water: by this time it was just dark, and the fish went after it; and, to my great joy, I saw them no more.

However, all my alarms began to subside when we got sight of land; and at last the ship arrived at Falmouth, after a passage of thirteen weeks. Every heart on board seemed gladdened on our reaching the shore, and none more than mine. The captain immediately went on shore, and sent on board some fresh provisions, which we wanted very much: we made good use of them, and our famine was soon turned into feasting, almost without ending. It was about the beginning of the spring 1757 when I arrived in England; and I was nearly twelve years of age at that time. I was very much struck with the buildings and the pavement of the streets in Falmouth; and, indeed, any object I saw filled me with new surprise. One morning when I got upon deck, I saw it covered all over with the snow that fell overnight: as I had never seen anything of the kind before, I thought it was salt; so I immediately ran down to the mate and desired him, as well as I could, to come and see how somebody in the night had thrown salt all over the deck. He, knowing what it was, desired me to bring some of it down to him: accordingly I took up a handful of it, which I found very cold indeed; and when I brought it to him he desired me to taste it. I did so, and I was surprised beyond measure. I then asked him what it was; he told me it was snow: but I could not in anywise understand him. He asked me if we had no such thing in my country; and I told him, No. I then asked him the use of it, and who made it; he told me a great man in the heavens, called God: but here again I was to all intents and purposes at a loss to understand him; and the more so when a little after I saw the air filled with it, in a heavy shower, which fell down on the same day. After this I went to church; and having never been at such a place before, I was again

amazed at seeing and hearing the service. I asked all I could about it; and they gave me to understand it was worshipping God, who made us and all things. I was still at a great loss, and soon got into an endless field of inquiries, as well as I was able to speak and ask about things. However, my little friend Dick used to be my best interpreter; for I could make free with him, and he always instructed me with pleasure: and from what I could understand by him of this God, and in seeing these white people did not sell one another, as we did, I was much pleased; and in this I thought they were much happier than we Africans. I was astonished at the wisdom of the white people in all things I saw; but was amazed at their not sacrificing, or making any offerings, and eating with unwashed hands, and touching the dead. I likewise could not help remarking the particular slenderness of their women, which I did not at first like; and I thought they were not so modest and shamefaced as the African women.

I had often seen my master and Dick employed in reading; and I had a great curiosity to talk to the books, as I thought they did; and so to learn how all things had a beginning: for that purpose I have often taken up a book, and have talked to it, and then put my ears to it, when alone, in hopes it would answer me; and I have been very much concerned when I found it remained silent.[1] ...

[1] *I had often ... remained silent* A similar episode is recounted in James Albert Ukawsaw Gronniosaw's 1772 *A Narrative of the Most Remarkable Particulars in the Life of James Albert Ukawsaw Gronniosaw, an African Prince, as Related by Himself* (excerpts from which are included as part of the website component of this anthology). Before he learned to read, Gronniosaw reports that he believed that books could talk:

> I was never so surprised in my whole life as when I saw the book talk to my master, for I thought it did, as I observed him to look upon it and move his lips. I wished it would do so to me. As soon as my master had done reading, I followed him to the place where he put the book, being mightily delighted with it, and when nobody saw me, I opened it and put my ear down close upon it in great hope that it would say something to me, but was very sorry and greatly disappointed when I found it would not speak.

As Henry Louis Gates has noted, the "trope of the talking book" appears in at least five slave narratives between 1770 and 1815 (those of Gronniosaw, Equiano, John Marant [1785], Ottobah Cuguano [1787], and John Jea [1811]).

from CHAPTER 4

The author is baptized—Narrowly escapes drowning—Goes on an expedition to the Mediterranean—Incidents he met with there—Is witness to an engagement between some English and French ships—A particular account of the celebrated engagement between Admiral Boscawen and Mons. Le Clue, off Cape Logas, in August 1759—Dreadful explosion of a French ship—The author sails for England—His master appointed to the command of a fire-ship—Meets a negro boy, from whom he experiences much benevolence—Prepares for an expedition against Belle-Isle—A remarkable story of a disaster which befell his ship—Arrives at Belle-Isle—Operations of the landing

It was now between two and three years since I first came to England, a great part of which I had spent at sea; so that I became inured to that service,[1] and began to consider myself as happily situated; for my master treated me always extremely well; and my attachment and gratitude to him were very great. From the various scenes I had beheld on ship-board, I soon grew a stranger to terror of every kind, and was, in that respect at least, almost an Englishman. I have often reflected with surprise that I never felt half the alarm at any of the numerous dangers I have been in, that I was filled with at the first sight of the Europeans, and at every act of theirs, even the most trifling, when I first came among them, and for some time afterwards. That fear, however, which was the effect of my ignorance, wore away as I began to know them. I could now speak English tolerably well, and I perfectly understood everything that was said. I now not only felt myself quite easy with these new countrymen, but relished their society and manners. I no longer looked upon them as spirits, but as men superior to us; and therefore I had the stronger desire to resemble them; to imbibe their spirit, and imitate their manners; I therefore embraced every occasion of improvement; and every new thing that I observed I treasured up in my memory. I had long wished to be able to read and write; and for this purpose I took every opportunity to gain instruction, but had made as yet very little progress.

However, when I went to London with my master, I had soon an opportunity of improving myself, which I gladly embraced. Shortly after my arrival, he sent me to wait upon the Miss Guerins,[2] who had treated me with much kindness when I was there before; and they sent me to school.

While I was attending these ladies their servants told me I could not go to Heaven unless I was baptized. This made me very uneasy; for I had now some faint idea of a future state: accordingly I communicated my anxiety to the eldest Miss Guerin, with whom I was become a favourite, and pressed her to have me baptized; when to my great joy she told me I should. She had formerly asked my master to let me be baptized, but he had refused; however she now insisted on it; and he being under some obligation to her brother complied with her request; so I was baptized in St. Margaret's Church, Westminster, in February 1759, by my present name. The clergyman, at the same time, gave me a book, called *A Guide to the Indians*,[3] written by the Bishop of Sodor and Man. On this occasion Miss Guerin did me the honour to stand as godmother, and afterwards gave me a treat. I used to attend these ladies about the town, in which service I was extremely happy; as I had thus many opportunities of seeing London, which I desired of all things. I was sometimes, however, with my master at his rendezvous house, which was at the foot of Westminster Bridge. Here I used to enjoy myself in playing about the bridge stairs, and often in the watermen's wherries,[4] with other boys. On one of these occasions there was another boy with me in a wherry, and we went out into the current of the river: while we were there two more stout boys came to us in another wherry, and, abusing us for taking the boat, desired me to get into the other wherry-boat. Accordingly I went to get out of the wherry I was in; but just as I had got one of my feet into the other boat the boys shoved it off, so that I fell into the Thames; and, not being able to swim, I should unavoidably have been

[1] *became inured to that service* Grew accustomed to life at sea.

[2] *the Miss Guerins* Elizabeth Martha Guerin and Mary Guerin, cousins of Michael Henry Pascal.

[3] *A Guide to the Indians* Bishop Thomas Wilson's *An Essay Towards an Instruction for the Indians* was published in London in 1740; this is likely the book Equiano is thinking of.

[4] *watermen's wherries* Small boats belonging to those offering ferry services on the river.

drowned, but for the assistance of some watermen who providentially came to my relief.

The *Namur* being again got ready for sea, my master, with his gang,[1] was ordered on board; and, to my no small grief I was obliged to leave my school-master, whom I liked very much, and always attended[2] while I stayed in London, to repair on board with my master. Nor did I leave my kind patronesses, the Miss Guerins, without uneasiness and regret. They often used to teach me to read, and took great pains to instruct me in the principles of religion and the knowledge of God. I therefore parted from those amiable ladies with reluctance; after receiving from them many friendly cautions how to conduct myself, and some valuable presents.

When I came to Spithead, I found we were destined for the Mediterranean, with a large fleet, which was now ready to put to sea. We only waited for the arrival of the admiral, who soon came on board; and about the beginning of the spring, 1759, having weighed anchor and got under way, sailed for the Mediterranean; and in eleven days from the Land's End, we got to Gibraltar. While we were here I used to be often on shore, and got various fruits in great plenty, and very cheap.

I had frequently told several people, in my excursions on shore, the story of my being kidnapped with my sister, and of our being separated, as I have related before; and I had as often expressed my anxiety for her fate, and my sorrow at having never met her again. One day, when I was on shore, and mentioning these circumstances to some persons, one of them told me he knew where my sister was, and, if I would accompany him, he would bring me to her. Improbable as this story was I believed it immediately, and agreed to go with him, while my heart leaped for joy: and, indeed, he conducted me to a black young woman, who was so like my sister that at first sight I really thought it was her: but I was quickly undeceived; and, on talking to her, I found her to be of another nation.

While we lay here the *Preston* came in from the Levant. As soon as she arrived, my master told me I should now see my old companion, Dick, who had gone in her when she sailed for Turkey. I was much rejoiced at this news, and expected every minute to embrace him; and when the captain came on board of our ship, which he did immediately after, I ran to inquire after my friend; but, with inexpressible sorrow, I learned from the boat's crew that the dear youth was dead! and that they had brought his chest, and all his other things, to my master. These he afterwards gave to me, and I regarded them as a memorial of my friend, whom I loved, and grieved for as a brother.

While we were at Gibraltar, I saw a soldier hanging by his heels, at one of the moles:[3] I thought this a strange sight, as I had seen a man hanged in London by his neck. At another time I saw the master of a frigate towed to shore on a grating, by several of the men-of-war boats, and discharged the fleet, which I understood was a mark of disgrace for cowardice. On board the same ship there was also a sailor hung up at the yard-arm. ...

After the taking of this island [Belle-Isle] our ships, with some others commanded by Commodore Stanhope in the *Swiftsure*, went to Basse-road, where we blocked up a French fleet. Our ships were there from June till February following; and in that time I saw a great many scenes of war, and stratagems on both sides to destroy each other's fleet. Sometimes we would attack the French with some ships of the line; at other times with boats; and frequently we made prizes.[4] Once or twice the French attacked us by throwing shells with their bomb-vessels: and one day as a French vessel was throwing shells at our ships she broke from her springs, behind the isle of I de Re: the tide being complicated, she came within a gun shot of the *Nassau* but the *Nassau* could not bring a gun to bear upon her, and thereby the Frenchman got off. We were twice attacked by their fire-floats, which they chained together, and then let them float down with the tide; but each time we sent boats with graplings, and towed them safe out of the fleet.

We had different commanders while we were at this place, Commodores Stanhope, Dennis, Lord Howe, etc. From hence, before the Spanish war began, our ship and the *Wasp* sloop were sent to St. Sebastian in Spain, by Commodore Stanhope; and Commodore Dennis afterwards sent our ship as a cartel to Bayonne in France, after which we went in February in 1762 to

1 *gang* Crew.

2 *attended* Called on; was friendly towards.

3 *moles* Stone structures forming breakwaters or piers.

4 *made prizes* Captured enemy ships with valuable cargo aboard.

Belle-Isle, and there stayed till the summer, when we left it, and returned to Portsmouth.

After our ship was fitted out again for service, in September she went to Guernsey, where I was very glad to see my old hostess, who was now a widow, and my former little charming companion, her daughter. I spent some time here very happily with them, till October, when we had orders to repair to Portsmouth. We parted from each other with a great deal of affection; and I promised to return soon, and see them again, not knowing what all-powerful fate had determined for me. Our ship having arrived at Portsmouth, we went into the harbour, and remained there till the latter end of November, when we heard great talk about a peace;[1] and, to our very great joy, in the beginning of December we had orders to go up to London with our ship to be paid off. We received this news with loud huzzas, and every other demonstration of gladness; and nothing but mirth was to be seen throughout every part of the ship. I too was not without my share of the general joy on this occasion. I thought now of nothing but being freed, and working for myself and thereby getting money to enable me to get a good education; for I always had a great desire to be able at least to read and write; and while I was on ship-board I had endeavoured to improve myself in both. While I was in the *Aetna* particularly, the captain's clerk taught me to write, and gave me a smattering of arithmetic as far as the rule of three.[2] There was also one Daniel Queen, about forty years of age, a man very well educated, who messed with me on board this ship, and he likewise dressed and attended the captain.

Fortunately, this man soon became very much attached to me, and took very great pains to instruct me in many things. He taught me to shave and dress hair a little, and also to read in the Bible, explaining many passages to me, which I did not comprehend. I was wonderfully surprised to see the laws and rules of my country written almost exactly here; a circumstance which I believe tended to impress our manners and customs more deeply on my memory. I used to tell him of this resemblance; and many a time we have

sat up the whole night together at this employment. In short, he was like a father to me; and some even used to call me after his name; they also styled me the black Christian. Indeed, I almost loved him with the affection of a son. Many things I have denied myself that he might have them; and when I used to play at marbles or any other game, and won a few halfpence, or got any little money, which I sometimes did, for shaving any one, I used to buy him a little sugar or tobacco, as far as my stock of money would go. He used to say, that he and I never should part; and that when our ship was paid off, as I was as free as himself or any other man on board, he would instruct me in his business, by which I might gain a good livelihood. This gave me new life and spirits and my heart burned within me, while I thought the time long till I obtained my freedom. For though my master had not promised it to me, yet, besides the assurances I had received that he had no right to detain me, he always treated me with the greatest kindness, and reposed in me an unbounded confidence; he even paid attention to my morals; and would never suffer me to deceive him, or tell lies, of which he used to tell me the consequences; and that if I did so God would not love me; so that, from all this tenderness, I had never once supposed, in all my dreams of freedom, that he would think of detaining me any longer than I wished.

In pursuance of our orders, we sailed from Portsmouth for the Thames, and arrived at Deptford the 10th of December, where we cast anchor just as it was high water. The ship was up about half an hour, when my master ordered the barge to be manned; and all in an instant, without having before given me the least reason to suspect anything of the matter, he forced me into the barge; saying, I was going to leave him, but he would take care I should not. I was so struck with the unexpectedness of this proceeding, that for some time I did not make a reply, only I made an offer to go for my books and chest of clothes, but he swore I should not move out of his sight; and if I did, he would cut my throat, at the same time taking his hanger.[3] I began, however, to collect myself and, plucking up courage, I told him I was free, and he could not by law serve[4] me so. But this only enraged him the

[1] *a peace* The Seven Years' War ended in February of 1763 with the signing of the Treaty of Paris.

[2] *the rule of three* Method for discovering a fourth number in a series involving proportions, once the first three are known.

[3] *hanger* Short, curved sword.

[4] *serve* Treat.

more; and he continued to swear, and said he would soon let me know whether he would or not, and at that instant sprung himself into the barge from the ship, to the astonishment and sorrow of all on board. The tide, rather unluckily for me, had just turned downward, so that we quickly fell down the river along with it, till we came among some outward-bound West Indiamen; for he was resolved to put me on board the first vessel he could get to receive me. The boat's crew, who pulled against their will, became quite faint different times, and would have gone ashore; but he would not let them. Some of them strove them to cheer me, and told me he could not sell me, and that they would stand by me, which revived me a little; and I still entertained hopes; for as they pulled along he asked some vessels to receive me, but they could not. But, just as we had got a little below Gravesend, we came alongside of a ship which was going away the next tide for the West Indies; her name was the *Charming Sally*, Captain James Doran; and my master went on board and agreed with him for me; and in a little time I was sent for into the cabin.

When I came there, Captain Doran asked me if I knew him; I answered that I did not; "Then," said he, "you are now my slave." I told him my master could not sell me to him, nor to anyone else. "Why," said he, "did not your master buy you?" I confessed he did. "But I have served him," said I, "many years, and he has taken all my wages and prize-money,[1] for I only got one sixpence during the war; besides this I have been baptized; and by the laws of the land no man has a right to sell me." And I added, that I had heard a lawyer and others at different times tell my master so. They both then said that those people who told me so were not my friends; but I replied, it was very extraordinary that other people did not know the law as well as they. Upon this Captain Doran said I talked too much English; and if I did not behave myself well, and be quiet, he had a method on board to make me. I was too well convinced of his power over me to doubt what he said; and, my former sufferings in the slave ship presenting themselves to my mind, the recollection of them made me shudder. However, before I retired I told them that as I could not get any right

among men here I hoped I should hereafter in Heaven; and I immediately left the cabin, filled with resentment and sorrow. The only coat I had with me my master took away with him, and said if my prize-money had been £10,000 he had a right to it all, and would have taken it. I had about nine guineas, which, during my long sea-faring life, I had scraped together from trifling perquisites and little ventures; and I hid it that instant, lest my master should take that from me likewise, still hoping that by some means or other I should make my escape to the shore; and indeed some of my old shipmates told me not to despair, for they would get me back again; and that, as soon as they could get their pay, they would immediately come to Portsmouth to me, where this ship was going. But, alas! all my hopes were baffled, and the hour of my deliverance was yet far off. My master, having soon concluded his bargain with the captain, came out of the cabin, and he and his people got into the boat and put off; I followed them with aching eyes as long as I could, and when they were out of sight I threw myself on the deck, while my heart was ready to burst with sorrow and anguish.

from CHAPTER 5[2]

The author's reflections on his situation—Is deceived by a promise of being delivered—His despair at sailing for the West Indies—Arrives at Montserrat, where he is sold to Mr. King—Various interesting instances of oppression, cruelty, and extortion, which the author saw practiced upon the slaves in the West Indies during his captivity from the year 1763 to 1766—Address on it to the planters.

Thus, at the moment I expected all my toils to end, was I plunged, as I supposed, in a new slavery;[3] in

1 *prize-money* Share of the valuables seized when capturing other vessels.

2 The entire fifth chapter is included in the website component of this anthology.

3 *Thus ... slavery* Equiano was sold to Captain James Doran in December 1762. The sale came as a shock, as Equiano had expected to become a free man at the conclusion of the Seven Years' War, in which he had served as a sailor. Given the somewhat ambiguous legal status of slavery in England at the time—enslaved people were typically but unofficially held to be freemen upon arrival in England—Michael Pascal, the British Royal Navy Lieutenant who had bought Equiano on his arrival in Virginia, had a difficult time finding a new enslaver for Equiano. Eventually, he contacted Doran,

comparison to which all my service hitherto had been "perfect freedom"; and whose horrors, always present to my mind, now rushed on it with tenfold aggravation. I wept very bitterly for some time: and began to think that I must have done something to displease the Lord, that he thus punished me so severely. This filled me with painful reflections on my past conduct; I recollected that on the morning of our arrival at Deptford[1] I had rashly sworn that as soon as we reached London I would spend the day in rambling and sport. My conscience smote me for this unguarded expression: I felt that the Lord was able to disappoint me in all things, and immediately considered my present situation as a judgment of Heaven on account of my presumption in swearing: I therefore, with contrition of heart, acknowledged my transgression to God, and poured out my soul before him with unfeigned repentance, and with earnest supplications I besought him not to abandon me in my distress, nor cast me from his mercy for ever. In a little time my grief, spent with its own violence, began to subside; and after the first confusion of my thoughts was over I reflected with more calmness on my present condition: I considered that trials and disappointments are sometimes for our good, and I thought God might perhaps have permitted this in order to teach me wisdom and resignation; for he had hitherto shadowed me with the wings of his mercy, and by his invisible but powerful hand brought me the way I knew not. These reflections gave me a little comfort, and I rose at last from the deck with dejection and sorrow in my countenance, yet mixed with some faint hope that the *Lord would appear* for my deliverance. ...

... On the 13th of February 1763, from the masthead, we descried our destined island Montserrat; and soon after I beheld those

> Regions of sorrow, doleful shades, where peace
> And rest can rarely dwell. Hope never comes

That comes to all, but torture without end
Still urges.[2]

At the sight of this land of bondage,[3] a fresh horror ran through all my frame, and chilled me to the heart. My former slavery now rose in dreadful review to my mind, and displayed nothing but misery, stripes, and chains; and, in the first paroxysm of my grief, I called upon God's thunder, and his avenging power, to direct the stroke of death to me, rather than permit me to become a slave, and be sold from lord to lord.

In this state of my mind our ship came to an anchor, and soon after discharged her cargo. I now knew what it was to work hard; I was made to help to unload and load the ship. And, to comfort me in my distress in that time, two of the sailors robbed me of all my money, and ran away from the ship. I had been so long used to an European climate that at first I felt the scorching West India sun very painful, while the dashing surf would toss the boat and the people in it frequently above high water mark. Sometimes our limbs were broken with this, or even attended with instant death, and I was day by day mangled and torn.

About the middle of May, when the ship was got ready to sail for England, I all the time believing that Fate's blackest clouds were gathering over my head, and expecting their bursting would mix me with the dead, Captain Doran sent for me ashore one morning, and I was told by the messenger that my fate was then determined. With trembling steps and fluttering heart I came to the captain, and found with him one Mr. Robert King, a Quaker,[4] and the first merchant in the place. The captain then told me my former master had sent me there to be sold; but that he had desired him to get me the best master he could, as he told him I was a very deserving boy, which Captain Doran said

captain of the merchant ship *Charming Sally*, who agreed to act as agent, transporting Equiano to be sold in Montserrat, in the West Indies.

[1] *Deptford* Southeast London area on the River Thames's south bank. Equiano arrived at Deptford on 10 December 1762.

[2] *Regions of sorrow ... Still urges* Cf. John Milton, *Paradise Lost* (1.65–68). This verse offers the poem's first view of hell, but Equiano somewhat mitigates the bleaker meaning of Milton's lines, changing "rest can never dwell" to "rest can rarely dwell."

[3] *land of bondage* Phrase often used in reference to Egypt as the site of the Israelites' captivity and slavery in the Old Testament.

[4] *Quaker* The Quakers (formally known as the Society of Friends) are a Protestant sect that was and is committed to pacifism, equality of the sexes, and social reform. They typically sought to avoid worldly vanities, adhering to customs of plain dress, and using an old-fashioned diction (employing the pronouns thee and thou for example).

he found to be true; and if he were to stay in the West Indies he would be glad to keep me himself; but he could not venture to take me to London, for he was very sure that when I came there I would leave him. I at that instant burst out a crying, and begged much of him to take me to England with him, but all to no purpose. He told me he had got me the very best master in the whole island, with whom I should be as happy as if I were in England, and for that reason he chose to let him have me, though he could sell me to his own brother-in-law for a great deal more money than what he got from this gentleman. Mr. King, my new master, then made a reply, and said the reason he had bought me was on account of my good character; and, as he had not the least doubt of my good behaviour, I should be very well off with him. He also told me he did not live in the West Indies, but at Philadelphia, where he was going soon; and, as I understood something of the rules of arithmetic, when we got there he would put me to school, and fit me for a clerk. This conversation relieved my mind a little, and I left those gentlemen considerably more at ease in myself than when I came to them; and I was very grateful to Captain Doran, and even to my old master, for the character they had given me; a character which I afterward found of infinite service to me. I went on board again, and took leave of all my shipmates; and the next day the ship sailed. When she weighed anchor I went to the waterside and looked at her with a very wishful and aching heart, and followed her with my eyes and tears until she was totally out of sight. I was so bowed down with grief that I could not hold up my head for many months; and if my new master had not been kind to me I believe I should have died under it at last. And indeed I soon found that he fully deserved the good character which Captain Doran had given me of him; for he possessed a most amiable disposition and temper, and was very charitable and humane. If any of his slaves behaved amiss he did not beat or use them ill, but parted with them. This made them afraid of disobliging him; and as he treated his slaves better than any other man on the island, so he was better and more faithfully served by them in return. By this kind treatment I did at last endeavour to compose myself; and with fortitude, though moneyless, determined to face whatever fate had decreed for me. Mr. King soon asked me what I

could do; and at the same time said he did not mean to treat me as a common slave. I told him I knew something of seamanship, and could shave and dress hair pretty well; and I could refine wines, which I had learned on shipboard, where I had often done it; and that I could write, and understood arithmetic tolerably well as far as the Rule of Three. He then asked me if I knew anything of gauging;[1] and, on my answering that I did not, he said one of his clerks should teach me to gauge.

Mr. King dealt in all manner of merchandise, and kept from one to six clerks. He loaded many vessels in a year; particularly to Philadelphia, where he was born, and was connected with a great mercantile house in that city. He had besides many vessels and droggers,[2] of different sizes, which used to go about the island; and others to collect rum, sugar, and other goods. I understood pulling and managing those boats very well; and this hard work, which was the first that he set me to, in the sugar seasons used to be my constant employment. I have rowed the boat, and slaved at the oars, from one hour to sixteen in the twenty-four; during which I had fifteen pence sterling per day to live on, though sometimes only ten pence. However this was considerably more than was allowed to other slaves that used to work with me, and belonged to other gentlemen on the island: those poor souls had never more than nine pence per day, and seldom more than six pence, from their masters or owners, though they earned them three or four pisterines:[3] for it is a common practice in the West Indies for men to purchase slaves though they have not plantations themselves, in order to let them out to planters and merchants at so much a piece by the day, and they give what allowance they choose out of this produce of their daily work to their slaves for subsistence; this allowance is often very scanty. My master often gave the owners of these slaves two and a half of these pieces per day, and found the poor fellows in victuals[4] himself, because he thought the owners did not feed them well enough according to the work

1 *gauging* Calculating the holding capacity or contents of a ship or other container.

2 *drogger* Slow, awkward coasting vessel used in the West Indies.

3 [Equiano's note] These pisterines are of the value of a shilling [twelve pence].

4 *found ... victuals* I.e., gave them food.

they did. The slaves used to like this very well; and, as they knew my master to be a man of feeling, they were always glad to work for him in preference to any other gentleman: some of whom, after they had been paid for these poor people's labours, would not give them their allowance out of it. Many times have I even seen these unfortunate wretches beaten for asking for their pay; and often severely flogged by their owners if they did not bring them their daily or weekly money exactly to the time; though the poor creatures were obliged to wait on the gentlemen they had worked for sometimes for more than half the day before they could get their pay; and this generally on Sundays, when they wanted the time for themselves. In particular, I knew a countryman of mine who once did not bring the weekly money directly that it was earned; and though he brought it the same day to his master, yet he was staked to the ground for this pretended negligence, and was just going to receive a hundred lashes, but for a gentleman who begged him off fifty. …

Once, for a few days, I was let out to fit a vessel, and I had no victuals allowed me by either party; at last I told my master of this treatment, and he took me away from it. In many of the estates, on the different islands where I used to be sent for rum or sugar, they would not deliver it to me, or any other negro; he was therefore obliged to send a white man along with me to those places; and then he used to pay him six to ten pisterines a day. From being thus employed, during the time I served Mr. King, in going about the different estates on the island, I had all the opportunity I could wish for to see the dreadful usage of the poor men; usage that reconciled me to my situation, and made me bless God for the hands into which I had fallen.

I had the good fortune to please my master in every department in which he employed me; and there was scarcely any part of his business, or household affairs, in which I was not occasionally engaged. I often supplied the place of a clerk,[1] in receiving and delivering cargoes to the ships, in tending stores, and delivering goods: and, besides this, I used to shave and dress my master when convenient, and take care of his horse; and when it was necessary, which was very often, I worked likewise on board of different vessels of his. By these means I became very useful to my master; and

saved him, as he used to acknowledge, above a hundred pounds a year. Nor did he scruple to say I was of more advantage to him than any of his clerks; though their usual wages in the West Indies are from sixty to a hundred pounds current[2] a year.

I have sometimes heard it asserted that a negro cannot earn his master the first cost;[3] but nothing can be further from the truth. I suppose nine tenths of the mechanics throughout the West Indies are negro slaves; and I well know the coopers[4] among them earn two dollars a day; the carpenters the same, and oftentimes more; as also the masons, smiths, and fishermen, etc. and I have known many slaves whose masters would not take a thousand pounds current for them. But surely this assertion refutes itself; for, if it be true, why do the planters and merchants pay such a price for slaves? And, above all, why do those who make this assertion exclaim the most loudly against the abolition of the slave trade? So much are men blinded, and to such inconsistent arguments are they driven by mistaken interest! I grant, indeed, that slaves are sometimes, by half-feeding, half-clothing, over-working and stripes,[5] reduced so low, that they are turned out as unfit for service, and left to perish in the woods, or expire on a dunghill.

My master was several times offered by different gentlemen one hundred guineas for me; but he always told them he would not sell me, to my great joy: and I used to double my diligence and care for fear of getting into the hands of those men who did not allow a valuable slave the common support of life. Many of them even used to find fault with my master for feeding his slaves so well as he did; although I often went hungry, and an Englishman might think my fare very indifferent; but he used to tell them he always would do it, because the slaves thereby looked better and did more work.

While I was thus employed by my master I was often witness to cruelties of every kind, which were exercised on my unhappy fellow slaves. I used frequently to have different cargoes of new negroes in my care for sale; and it was almost a constant practice with our clerks, and

[1] *supplied the place of a clerk* Filled the position of clerk.

[2] *current* Currency.

[3] *first cost* Price paid for an enslaved person.

[4] *coopers* Makers of wooden casks, barrels, and other vessels for storing goods.

[5] *stripes* Whip lashes.

other whites, to commit violent depredations on the chastity of the female slaves; and these I was, though with reluctance, obliged to submit to at all times, being unable to help them. When we have had some of these slaves on board my master's vessels to carry them to other islands, or to America, I have known our mates to commit these acts most shamefully, to the disgrace, not of Christians only, but of men. I have even known them gratify their brutal passion with females not ten years old; and these abominations some of them practised to such scandalous excess, that one of our captains discharged the mate and others on that account. And yet in Montserrat I have seen a negro-man staked to the ground, and cut most shockingly,[1] and then his ears cut off bit by bit, because he had been connected with a white woman who was a common prostitute: as if it were no crime in the whites to rob an innocent African girl of her virtue; but most heinous in a black man only to gratify a passion of nature, where the temptation was offered by one of a different colour, though the most abandoned woman of her species.[2]

Another negro man was half-hanged, and then burnt, for attempting to poison a cruel overseer. Thus by repeated cruelties are the wretched first urged to despair, and then murdered, because they still retain so much of human nature about them as to wish to put an end to their misery, and retaliate on their tyrants! These overseers are indeed for the most part persons of the worst character of any denomination of men in the West Indies. Unfortunately, many humane gentlemen, by not residing on their estates, are obliged to leave the management of them in the hands of these human butchers, who cut and mangle the slaves in a shocking manner on the most trifling occasions, and altogether treat them in every respect like brutes. They

pay no regard to the situation of pregnant women, nor the least attention to the lodging of the field negroes. Their huts, which ought to be well covered, and the place dry where they take their little repose, are often open sheds, built in damp places; so that, when the poor creatures return tired from the toil of the field, they contract many disorders, from being exposed to the damp air in this uncomfortable state, while they are heated, and their pores are open. This neglect certainly conspires with many others to cause a decrease in the births as well as in the lives of the grown negroes. I can quote many instances of gentlemen who reside on their estates in the West Indies, and then the scene is quite changed; the negroes are treated with lenity and proper care, by which their lives are prolonged, and their masters are profited. To the honour of humanity, I knew several gentlemen who managed their estates in this manner; and they found that benevolence was their true interest. And, among many I could mention in several of the islands, I knew one in Montserrat[3] whose slaves looked remarkably well, and never needed any fresh supplies of negroes; and there are many other estates, especially in Barbadoes, which, from such judicious treatment, need no fresh stock of negroes at any time. I have the honour of knowing a most worthy and humane gentleman, who is a native of Barbadoes, and has estates there.[4] This gentleman has written a treatise on the usage of his own slaves. He allows them two hours for refreshment at mid-day; and many other indulgencies and comforts, particularly in their lying; and, besides this, he raises more provisions on his estate than they can destroy; so that by these attentions he saves the lives of his negroes, and keeps them healthy, and as happy as the condition of slavery can admit. I myself, as shall appear in the sequel,[5] managed an estate, where, by those attentions, the negroes were uncommonly cheerful and healthy, and did more work by half than by the common mode of treatment they usually do. For want,[6] therefore, of such care and

1 *cut most shockingly* The likely punishment implied here is castration.

2 The following paragraph was added here by Equiano in some later editions: "One Mr. D[rummond] told me that he had sold 41,000 negroes, and that he once cut off a negro-man's leg for running away.—I asked him if the man had died in the operation, how he, as a Christian, could answer for the horrid act before God? and he told me, answering was a thing of another world, but what he thought and did were policy. I told him that the Christian doctrine taught us to do unto others as we would that others should do unto us. He then said that his scheme had the desired effect—it cured that man and some others of running away."

3 [Equiano's note] Mr. Dubury, and many others, Montserrat.

4 [Equiano's note] Sir Philip Bibbes, Baronet, Barbadoes.

5 *in the sequel* Hereafter. The first three editions of *The Interesting Narrative* were published in two volumes, with Chapters 1–6 included in the first volume and Chapters 7–12 in the second. See Chapter 11 for Equiano's account of his time spent as an overseer.

6 *want* Lack.

attention to the poor negroes, and otherwise oppressed as they are, it is no wonder that the decrease should require 20,000 new negroes annually to fill up the vacant places of the dead.

Even in Barbadoes, notwithstanding those humane exceptions which I have mentioned, and others I am acquainted with, which justly make it quoted as a place where slaves meet with the best treatment, and need fewest recruits of any in the West Indies, yet this island requires 1000 negroes annually to keep up the original stock, which is only 80,000. So that the whole term of a negro's life may be said to be there but sixteen years![1] And yet the climate here is in every respect the same as that from which they are taken, except in being more wholesome. Do the British colonies decrease in this manner? And yet what a prodigious difference is there between an English and West India climate?

While I was in Montserrat I knew a negro man, named Emanuel Sankey, who endeavoured to escape from his miserable bondage, by concealing himself on board of a London ship: but fate did not favour the poor oppressed man; for, being discovered when the vessel was under sail, he was delivered up again to his master. This *Christian master* immediately pinned the wretch down to the ground at each wrist and ankle, and then took some sticks of sealing wax, and lighted them, and dropped it all over his back. There was another master who was noted for cruelty; and I believe he had not a slave but what had been cut, and had pieces fairly taken out of the flesh: and, after they had been punished thus, he used to make them get into a long wooden box or case he had for that purpose, in which he shut them up during pleasure.[2] It was just about the height and breadth of a man; and the poor wretches had no room, when in the case, to move.

It was very common in several of the islands, particularly in St. Kitt's, for the slaves to be branded with the initial letters of their master's name; and a load of heavy iron hooks hung about their necks. Indeed on the most trifling occasions they were loaded with chains; and often instruments of torture were added. The iron muzzle, thumb-screws, etc. are so well known, as not to need a description, and were sometimes applied for the slightest faults. I have seen a negro beaten till some

of his bones were broken, for even letting a pot boil over.[3] ...

from CHAPTER 6[4]

Some account of Brimstone-Hill in Montserrat—Favourable change in the author's situation—He commences merchant with three pence—His various success in dealing in the different islands, and America, and the impositions he meets with in his transactions with Europeans—A curious imposition on human nature—Danger of the surfs in the West Indies—Remarkable instance of kidnapping a free mulatto—The author is nearly murdered by Doctor Perkins in Savannah.

In the preceding chapter I have set before the reader a few of those many instances of oppression, extortion, and cruelty, which I have been a witness to in the West Indies: but, were I to enumerate them all, the catalogue would be tedious and disgusting. The punishments of the slaves on every trifling occasion are so frequent, and so well known, together with the different instruments with which they are tortured, that it cannot any longer afford novelty to recite them; and they are too shocking to yield delight either to the writer or the reader. I shall therefore hereafter only mention such as incidentally befell myself in the course of my adventures. ...

Some time in the year 1763 kind Providence seemed to appear rather more favourable to me. One of my master's vessels, a Bermudas sloop, about sixty tons, was commanded by one Captain Thomas Farmer, an Englishman, a very alert and active man, who gained my master a great deal of money by his good

[1] [Equiano's note] Benezet's "Account of Guinea," p. 16.

[2] *during pleasure* At discretion.

[3] The following lines appear in some later editions: "It is not uncommon after a flogging, to make slaves go on their knees, and thank their owners, and pray, or rather say, God bless them. I have often asked many of the men slaves (who used to go several miles to their wives, and late in the night, after having been wearied with a hard day's labour) why they went so far for wives, and why they did not take them of their own master's negro women, and particularly those who lived together as household slaves? Their answers have ever been—'Because when the master or mistress choose to punish the women, they make the husbands flog their own wives, and that they could not bear to do.'"

[4] A longer selection of excerpts is included in the website component of this anthology.

management in carrying passengers from one island to another; but very often his sailors used to get drunk and run away from the vessel, which hindered him in his business very much. This man had taken a liking to me; and many different times begged of my master to let me go a trip with him as a sailor; but he would tell him he could not spare me, though the vessel sometimes could not go for want of hands, for sailors were generally very scarce in the island. However, at last, from necessity or force, my master was prevailed on, though very reluctantly, to let me go with this captain; but he gave great charge to him to take care that I did not run away, for if I did he would make him pay for me. This being the case, the captain had for some time a sharp eye upon me whenever the vessel anchored; and as soon as she returned I was sent for on shore again. Thus was I slaving as it were for life, sometimes at one thing, and sometimes at another; so that the captain and I were nearly the most useful men in my master's employment. I also became so useful to the captain on shipboard, that many times, when he used to ask for me to go with him, though it should be but for twenty-four hours, to some of the islands near us, my master would answer he could not spare me, at which the captain would swear, and would not go the trip; and tell my master I was better to him on board than any three white men he had; for they used to behave ill in many respects, particularly in getting drunk; and then they frequently got the boat stove,[1] so as to hinder the vessel from coming back as soon as she might have done. This my master knew very well; and at last, by the captain's constant entreaties, after I had been several times with him, one day, to my great joy, my master told me the captain would not let him rest, and asked me whether I would go aboard as a sailor, or stay on shore and mind the stores, for he could not bear any longer to be plagued in this manner. I was very happy at this proposal, for I immediately thought I might in time stand some chance by being on board to get a little money, or possibly make my escape if I should be used ill: I also expected to get better food, and in greater abundance; for I had felt much hunger oftentimes, though my master treated his slaves, as I have observed, uncommonly well. I therefore, without hesitation, answered him, that I would go and be

a sailor if he pleased. Accordingly, I was ordered on board directly. Nevertheless, between the vessel and the shore, when she was in port, I had little or no rest, as my master always wished to have me along with him. Indeed, he was a very pleasant gentleman, and but for my expectations on shipboard I should not have thought of leaving him. But the captain liked me also very much, and I was entirely his right-hand man. I did all I could to deserve his favour, and in return I received better treatment from him than any other I believe ever met with in the West Indies in my situation.

After I had been sailing for some time with this captain, at length I endeavoured to try my luck and commence merchant. I had but a very small capital to begin with; for one single half bit, which is equal to three pence in England,[2] made up my whole stock. However I trusted to the Lord to be with me; and at one of our trips to St. Eustatia, a Dutch island, I bought a glass tumbler with my half bit, and when I came to Montserrat I sold it for a bit, or sixpence. Luckily we made several successive trips to St. Eustatia (which was a general mart for the West Indies, about twenty leagues from Montserrat); and in our next, finding my tumbler so profitable, with this one bit I bought two tumblers more; and when I came back I sold them for two bits, equal to a shilling sterling. When we went again, I bought with these two bits four more of these glasses, which I sold for four bits on our return to Montserrat; and in our next voyage to St. Eustatia I bought two glasses with one bit, and with the other three I bought a jug of Geneva,[3] nearly about three pints in measure. When we came to Montserrat I sold the gin for eight bits, and the tumblers for two, so that my capital now amounted in all to a dollar, well husbanded[4] and acquired in the space of a month or six weeks, when I blessed the Lord that I was so rich. As we sailed to different islands, I laid this money out in various things occasionally, and it used to turn out to very good account, especially when we went

[1] *got the boat stove* Stove the boat in; made a hole in the boat.

[2] *single half bit … England* A half bit was a unit of Spanish currency; three English pence would be the equivalent of perhaps a couple of American dollars today in purchasing power.

[3] *Geneva* Geneva gin (in the late eighteenth century a very inexpensive and widely available type of liquor).

[4] *well husbanded* Carefully managed.

to Guadaloupe, Grenada, and the rest of the French islands.

Thus was I going all about the islands upwards of four years, and ever trading as I went, during which I experienced many instances of ill usage, and have seen many injuries done to other negroes in our dealings with Europeans: and, amidst our recreations, when we have been dancing and merry-making, they, without cause, have molested and insulted us. Indeed, I was more than once obliged to look up to God on high, as I had advised the poor fisherman some time before. And I had not been long trading for myself in the manner I have related above, when I experienced the like trial in company with him as follows: This man being used to the water, was upon an emergency put on board of us by his master to work as another hand, on a voyage to Santa Cruz; and at our sailing he had brought his little all for a venture, which consisted of six bits' worth of limes and oranges in a bag; I had also my whole stock, which was about twelve bits' worth of the same kind of goods, separate in two bags; for we had heard these fruits sold well in that island. When we came there, in some little convenient time he and I went ashore with our fruits to sell them; but we had scarcely landed when we were met by two white men, who presently took our three bags from us. We could not at first guess what they meant to do; and for some time we thought they were jesting with us; but they too soon let us know otherwise, for they took our ventures immediately to a house hard by, and adjoining the fort, while we followed all the way begging of them to give us our fruits, but in vain. They not only refused to return them, but swore at us, and threatened if we did not immediately depart they would flog us well. We told them these three bags were all we were worth in the world, and that we brought them with us to sell when we came from Montserrat, and shewed them the vessel. But this was rather against us, as they now saw we were strangers as well as slaves. They still therefore swore, and desired us to be gone, and even took sticks to beat us; while we, seeing they meant what they said, went off in the greatest confusion and despair. Thus, in the very minute of gaining more by three times than I ever did by any venture in my life before, was I deprived of every farthing I was worth. An insupportable misfortune! But how to help ourselves we knew not.

In our consternation we went to the commanding officer of the fort and told him how we had been served[1] by some of his people; but we obtained not the least redress: he answered our complaints only by a volley of imprecations against us, and immediately took a horse-whip, in order to chastise us, so that we were obliged to turn out much faster than we came in. I now, in the agony of distress and indignation, wished that the ire of God in his forked lightning might transfix these cruel oppressors among the dead.

Still however we persevered; went back again to the house, and begged and besought them again and again for our fruits, till at last some other people that were in the house asked if we would be contented if they kept one bag and gave us the other two. We, seeing no remedy whatever, consented to this; and they, observing one bag to have both kinds of fruit in it, which belonged to my companion, kept that; and the other two, which were mine, they gave us back. As soon as I got them, I ran as fast as I could, and got the first negro man I could to help me off; my companion, however, stayed a little longer to plead; he told them the bag they had was his, and likewise all that he was worth in the world; but this was of no avail, and he was obliged to return without it. The poor old man, wringing his hands, cried bitterly for his loss; and, indeed, he then did look up to God on high, which so moved me with pity for him, that I gave him nearly one third of my fruits. We then proceeded to the markets to sell them; and Providence was more favourable to us than we could have expected, for we sold our fruits uncommonly well; I got for mine about thirty-seven bits. Such a surprising reverse of fortune in so short a space of time seemed like a dream to me, and proved no small encouragement for me to trust the Lord in any situation. My captain afterwards frequently used to take my part, and get me my right, when I have been plundered or used ill by these tender Christian depredators; among whom I have shuddered to observe the unceasing blasphemous execrations which are wantonly thrown out by persons of all ages and conditions, not only without occasion, but even as if they were indulgences and pleasure.

At one of our trips to St. Kitt's I had eleven bits of my own; and my friendly captain lent me five bits

1 *served* Treated.

more, with which I bought a Bible. I was very glad to get this book, which I scarcely could meet with anywhere. I think there was none sold in Montserrat; and, much to my grief, from being forced out of the *Aetna* in the manner I have related, my Bible, and the Guide to the Indians, the two books I loved above all others, were left behind.

While I was in this place, St. Kitt's, a very curious imposition on human nature took place. A white man wanted to marry in the church a free black woman that had land and slaves in Montserrat: but the clergyman told him it was against the law of the place to marry a white and a black in the church. The man then asked to be married on the water, to which the parson consented, and the two lovers went in one boat, and the parson and clerk in another, and thus the ceremony was performed. After this the loving pair came on board our vessel, and my captain treated them extremely well, and brought them safe to Montserrat.

The reader cannot but judge of the irksomeness of this situation to a mind like mine, in being daily exposed to new hardships and impositions, after having seen many better days, and having been as it were in a state of freedom and plenty; added to which, every part of the world I had hitherto been in seemed to me a paradise in comparison of the West Indies. My mind was therefore hourly replete with inventions and thoughts of being freed, and, if possible, by honest and honourable means; for I always remembered the old adage; and I trust it has ever been my ruling principle, that honesty is the best policy; and likewise that other golden precept—to do unto all men as I would they should do unto me. However, as I was from early years a predestinarian,[1] I thought whatever fate had determined must ever come to pass; and therefore, if ever it were my lot to be freed nothing could prevent me, although I should at present see no means or hope to obtain my freedom; on the other hand, if it were my fate not to be freed, I never should be so, and all my endeavours for that purpose would be fruitless.

In the midst of these thoughts, I therefore looked up with prayers anxiously to God for my liberty; and at the same time I used every honest means, and endeavoured all that was possible on my part to obtain it. In process of time I became master of a few pounds, and in a fair way of[2] making more, which my friendly captain knew very well; this occasioned him sometimes to take liberties with me: but whenever he treated me waspishly I used plainly to tell him my mind, and that I would die before I would be imposed on as other negroes were, and that to me life had lost its relish when liberty was gone. This I said although I foresaw my then well-being or future hopes of freedom (humanly speaking) depended on this man. However, as he could not bear the thoughts of my not sailing with him, he always became mild on my threats. I therefore continued with him; and, from my great attention to his orders and his business, I gained him credit, and through his kindness to me I at last procured my liberty. While I thus went on, filled with the thoughts of freedom, and resisting oppression as well as I was able, my life hung daily in suspense, particularly in the surfs I have formerly mentioned, as I could not swim. These are extremely violent throughout the West Indies, and I was ever exposed to their howling rage and devouring fury in all the islands. I have seen them strike and toss a boat right up an end, and maim several on board. Once in the Grenada islands, when I and about eight others were pulling a large boat with two puncheons[3] of water in it, a surf struck us, and drove the boat and all in it about half a stone's throw, among some trees, and above the high-water mark. We were obliged to get all the assistance we could from the nearest estate to mend the boat, and launch it into the water again. At Montserrat one night, in pressing hard to get off the shore on board, the punt[4] was overset with us four times; the first time I was very near being drowned; however the jacket I had on kept me up above water a little space of time, while I called on a man near me who was a good swimmer, and told him I could not swim; he then made haste to me, and, just as I was sinking, he caught hold of me, and brought me to sounding,[5] and then he went and brought the punt also. As soon as we had turned the water out of her, lest we should

[1] *predestinarian* One who believes that all that occurs is predestined by God. (The question of to what degree human events are predestined was the subject of heated dispute at the time within the Methodist church, which Equiano joined in 1774.)

[2] *in a fair way of* On the way to.

[3] *puncheons* Barrels.

[4] *punt* Small boat.

[5] *to sounding* To where one could find sound footing underwater.

be used ill for being absent, we attempted again three times more, and as often the horrid surfs served us as at first; but at last, the fifth time we attempted, we gained our point, at the imminent hazard of our lives.

One day also, at Old Road in Montserrat, our captain, and three men besides myself, were going in a large canoe in quest of rum and sugar, when a single surf tossed the canoe an amazing distance from the water, and some of us even a stone's throw from each other: most of us were very much bruised; so that I and many more often said, and really thought, that there was not such another place under the heavens as this. I longed therefore much to leave it, and daily wished to see my master's promise performed of going to Philadelphia. While we lay in this place a very cruel thing happened on board of our sloop which filled me with horror; though I found afterwards such practices were frequent. There was a very clever and decent free young mulatto-man who sailed a long time with us: he had a free woman for his wife, by whom he had a child; and she was then living on shore, and all very happy. Our captain and mate, and other people on board, and several elsewhere, even the natives of Bermudas, all knew this young man from a child that he was always free, and no one had ever claimed him as their property: however, as might too often overcomes right in these parts, it happened that a Bermudas captain, whose vessel lay there for a few days in the road, came on board of us, and seeing the mulatto-man, whose name was Joseph Clipson, he told him he was not free, and that he had orders from his master to bring him to Bermudas. The poor man could not believe the captain to be in earnest; but he was very soon undeceived, his men laying violent hands on him: and although he shewed a certificate of his being born free in St. Kitt's, and most people on board knew that he served his time to boat building,[1] and always passed for a free man, yet he was taken forcibly out of our vessel. He then asked to be carried ashore before the secretary or magistrates, and these infernal invaders of human rights promised him he should; but, instead of that, they carried him on board of the other vessel: and the next day, without giving the poor man any hearing on shore, or suffering him even to see his wife or child, he was carried away,

and probably doomed never more in this world to see them again.

Nor was this the only instance of this kind of barbarity I was a witness to. I have since often seen in Jamaica and other islands free men, whom I have known in America, thus villainously trepanned[2] and held in bondage. I have heard of two similar practices even in Philadelphia—and, were it not for the benevolence of the Quakers in that city, many of the sable[3] race, who now breathe the air of liberty, would, I believe, be groaning indeed under some planter's chains. These things opened my mind to a new scene of horror to which I had been before a stranger. Hitherto I had thought only slavery dreadful; but the state of a free negro appeared to me now equally so at least, and in some respects even worse, for they live in constant alarm for their liberty; and even this is but nominal, for they are universally insulted and plundered without the possibility of redress; for such is the equity of the West Indian laws, that no free negro's evidence will be admitted in their courts of justice. In this situation, is it surprising that slaves, when mildly treated, should prefer even the misery of slavery to such a mockery of freedom? I was now completely disgusted with the West Indies, and thought I never should be entirely free until I had left them. ...

About the latter end of the year 1764 my master bought a larger sloop, called the *Providence*, about seventy or eighty tons, of which my captain had the command. I went with him into this vessel, and we took a load of new slaves for Georgia and Charlestown.[4] My master now left me entirely to the captain, though he still wished for me to be with him; but I, who always much wished to lose sight of the West Indies, was not a little rejoiced at the thoughts of seeing any other country. Therefore, relying on the goodness of my captain, I got ready all the little venture I could; and, when the vessel was ready, we sailed, to my great joy. When we got to our destined places, Georgia and Charlestown, I expected I should have an opportunity of selling my little property to advantage: but here, particularly in Charlestown, I met with buyers, white men, who imposed on me as in other places. Notwithstanding, I

[1] *served his time to boat building* Was apprenticed as a boat builder.

[2] *trepanned* Taken by force.

[3] *sable* Dark skinned.

[4] *Charlestown* Charleston, South Carolina.

was resolved to have fortitude; thinking no lot or trial is too hard when kind Heaven is the rewarder.

We soon got loaded again, and returned to Montserrat; and there, amongst the rest of the islands, I sold my goods well; and in this manner I continued trading during the year 1764; meeting with various scenes of imposition, as usual.

After this, my master fitted out his vessel for Philadelphia, in the year 1765; and during the time we were loading her, and getting ready for the voyage, I worked with redoubled alacrity, from the hope of getting money enough by these voyages to buy my freedom in time, if it should please God; and also to see the town of Philadelphia, which I had heard a great deal about for some years past; besides which, I had always longed to prove my master's promise the first day I came to him. In the midst of these elevated ideas, and while I was about getting my little merchandize in readiness, one Sunday my master sent for me to his house. When I came there, I found him and the captain together; and, on my going in, I was struck with astonishment at his telling me he heard that I meant to run away from him when I got to Philadelphia: "And therefore," said he, "I must sell you again: you cost me a great deal of money, no less than forty pounds sterling; and it will not do to lose so much. You are a valuable fellow," continued he; "and I can get any day for you one hundred guineas, from many gentlemen in this island." And then he told me of Captain Doran's brother-in-law, a severe master, who ever wanted to buy me to make me his overseer. My captain also said he could get much more than a hundred guineas for me in Carolina. This I knew to be a fact; for the gentleman that wanted to buy me came off several times on board of us, and spoke to me to live with him, and said he would use me well.

When I asked what work he would put me to he said, as I was a sailor, he would make me a captain of one of his rice vessels. But I refused: and fearing, at the same time, by a sudden turn I saw in the captain's temper, he might mean to sell me, I told the gentleman I would not live with him on any condition, and that I certainly would run away with his vessel: but he said he did not fear that, as he would catch me again; and then he told me how cruelly he would serve me if I should do so. My captain, however, gave him to understand that I knew something of navigation, so he thought better of it; and, to my great joy, he went away. I now told my master I did not say I would run away in Philadelphia; neither did I mean it, as he did not use me ill, nor yet the captain: for if they did I certainly would have made some attempts before now; but as I thought that if it were God's will I ever should be freed it would be so, and, on the contrary, if it was not his will it would not happen; so I hoped, if ever I were freed, whilst I was used well, it should be by honest means; but, as I could not help myself, he must do as he pleased; I could only hope and trust to the God of Heaven; and at that instant my mind was big with inventions and full of schemes to escape. I then appealed to the captain whether he ever saw any sign of my making the least attempt to run away; and asked him if I did not always come on board according to the time for which he gave me liberty; and, more particularly, when all our men left us at Gaurdeloupe and went on board of the French fleet, and advised me to go with them, whether I might not, and that he could not have got me again. To my no small surprise, and very great joy, the captain confirmed every syllable that I had said: and even more; for he said he had tried different times to see if I would make any attempt of this kind, both at St. Eustatia and in America, and he never found that I made the smallest; but, on the contrary, I always came on board according to his orders; and he did really believe, if I ever meant to run away, that, as I could never have had a better opportunity, I would have done it the night the mate and all the people left our vessel at Gaurdeloupe.

The captain then informed my master, who had been thus imposed on by our mate, though I did not know who was my enemy, the reason the mate had for imposing this lie upon him; which was, because I had acquainted the captain of the provisions the mate had given away or taken out of the vessel. This speech of the captain was like life to the dead to me, and instantly my soul glorified God; and still more so on hearing my master immediately say that I was a sensible fellow, and he never did intend to use me as a common slave; and that but for the entreaties of the captain, and his character of me, he would not have let me go from the stores about as I had done; that also, in so doing, he thought by carrying one little thing or other to

different places to sell I might make money. That he also intended to encourage me in this by crediting me with half a puncheon of rum and half a hogshead of sugar at a time; so that, from being careful, I might have money enough, in some time, to purchase my freedom; and, when that was the case, I might depend upon it he would let me have it for forty pounds sterling money, which was only the same price he gave for me. This sound gladdened my poor heart beyond measure; though indeed it was no more than the very idea I had formed in my mind of my master long before, and I immediately made him this reply: "Sir, I always had that very thought of you, indeed I had, and that made me so diligent in serving you." He then gave me a large piece of silver coin, such as I never had seen or had before, and told me to get ready for the voyage, and he would credit me with a tierce[1] of sugar, and another of rum; he also said that he had two amiable sisters in Philadelphia, from whom I might get some necessary things. Upon this my noble captain desired me to go aboard; and, knowing the African metal,[2] he charged me not to say anything of this matter to anybody; and he promised that the lying mate should not go with him any more. This was a change indeed; in the same hour to feel the most exquisite pain, and in the turn of a moment the fullest joy. It caused in me such sensations as I was only able to express in my looks; my heart was so overpowered with gratitude that I could have kissed both of their feet. When I left the room I immediately went, or rather flew, to the vessel, which being loaded, my master, as good as his word, trusted me with a tierce of rum, and another of sugar, when we sailed, and arrived safe at the elegant town of Philadelphia. I soon sold my goods here pretty well; and in this charming place I found everything plentiful and cheap.

While I was in this place a very extraordinary occurrence befell me. I had been told one evening of a wise woman, a Mrs. Davis, who revealed secrets, foretold events, etc. I put little faith in this story at first, as I could not conceive that any mortal could foresee the future disposals[3] of Providence, nor did I believe in any other revelation than that of the Holy Scriptures;

however, I was greatly astonished at seeing this woman in a dream that night, though a person I never before beheld in my life; this made such an impression on me that I could not get the idea the next day out of my mind, and I then became as anxious to see her as I was before indifferent; accordingly in the evening, after we left off working, I inquired where she lived, and being directed to her, to my inexpressible surprise, beheld the very woman in the very same dress she appeared to me to wear in the vision. She immediately told me I had dreamed of her the preceding night; related to me many things that had happened with a correctness that astonished me; and finally told me I should not be long a slave: this was the more agreeable news, as I believed it the more readily from her having so faithfully related the past incidents of my life. She said I should be twice in very great danger of my life within eighteen months, which, if I escaped, I should afterwards go on well; so, giving me her blessing, we parted. After staying here some time till our vessel was loaded, and I had bought in my little traffic, we sailed from this agreeable spot for Montserrat, once more to encounter the raging surfs.

We arrived safe at Montserrat, where we discharged our cargo; and soon after that we took slaves on board for St. Eustatia, and from thence to Georgia. I had always exerted myself and did double work, in order to make our voyages as short as possible; and from thus overworking myself while we were at Georgia I caught a fever and ague. I was very ill for eleven days and near dying; eternity was now exceedingly impressed on my mind, and I feared very much that awful event. I prayed the Lord therefore to spare me; and I made a promise in my mind to God, that I would be good if ever I should recover. At length, from having an eminent doctor to attend me, I was restored again to health; and soon after we got the vessel loaded, and set off for Montserrat. During the passage, as I was perfectly restored, and had much business of the vessel to mind, all my endeavours to keep up my integrity, and perform my promise to God, began to fail; and, in spite of all I could do, as we drew nearer and nearer to the islands, my resolutions more and more declined, as if the very air of that country or climate seemed fatal to piety. When we were safe arrived at Montserrat, and I had got ashore, I forgot my former resolutions. Alas! How prone is the heart to leave that God it wishes

1 *a tierce* One third of a barrel.

2 *metal* Character.

3 *disposals* Arrangements.

to love! and how strongly do the things of this world strike the senses and captivate the soul!

After our vessel was discharged, we soon got her ready, and took in, as usual, some of the poor oppressed natives of Africa, and other negroes; we then set off again for Georgia and Charlestown. We arrived at Georgia, and, having landed part of our cargo, proceeded to Charlestown with the remainder. While we were there, I saw the town illuminated; the guns were fired, and bonfires and other demonstrations of joy shown, on account of the repeal of the Stamp Act.[1]

Here I disposed of some goods on my own account; the white men buying them with smooth promises and fair words, giving me however but very indifferent payment. ...

We soon came to Georgia, where we were to complete our lading; and here worse fate than ever attended me: for one Sunday night, as I was with some negroes in their master's yard in the town of Savannah, it happened that their master, one Doctor Perkins, who was a very severe and cruel man, came in drunk; and, not liking to see any strange negroes in his yard, he and a ruffian of a white man he had in his service beset me in an instant, and both of them struck me with the first weapons they could get hold of. I cried out as long as I could for help and mercy; but, though I gave a good account of myself, and he knew my captain, who lodged hard by him, it was to no purpose. They beat and mangled me in a shameful manner, leaving me near dead. I lost so much blood from the wounds I received that I lay quite motionless, and was so benumbed that I could not feel anything for many hours. Early in the morning they took me away to the jail. As I did not return to the ship all night, my captain, not knowing where I was, and being uneasy that I did not then make my appearance, he made inquiry after me; and, having found where I was, immediately came to me. As soon as the good man saw me so cut and mangled, he could not forbear weeping; he soon got me out of jail to his lodgings, and immediately sent for the best doctors in the place, who at first declared it as their opinion that I could not recover. My captain

on this went to all the lawyers in the town for their advice, but they told him they could do nothing for me as I was a negro. He then went to Doctor Perkins, the hero who had vanquished me, and menaced him, swearing he would be revenged of him, and challenged him to fight. But cowardice is ever the companion of cruelty—and the Doctor refused.

However, by the skilfulness of one Doctor Brady of that place, I began at last to mend; but, although I was so sore and bad with the wounds I had all over me that I could not rest in any posture, yet I was in more pain on account of the captain's uneasiness about me than I otherwise should have been. The worthy man nursed and watched me all the hours of the night; and I was, through his attention and that of the doctor, able to get out of bed in about sixteen or eighteen days. All this time I was very much wanted on board, as I used frequently to go up and down the river for rafts, and other parts of our cargo, and stow them when the mate was sick or absent.

In about four weeks I was able to go on duty; and in a fortnight after, having got in all our lading, our vessel set sail for Montserrat; and in less than three weeks we arrived there safe towards the end of the year. This ended my adventures in 1764 [1765]; for I did not leave Montserrat again till the beginning of the following year.

END OF THE FIRST VOLUME

from CHAPTER 7[2]

The author's disgust at the West Indies—Forms schemes to obtain his freedom—Ludicrous disappointment he and his Captain meet with in Georgia—At last, by several successful voyages, he acquires a sum of money sufficient to purchase it—Applies to his master, who accepts it, and grants his manumission, to his great joy—He afterwards enters as a freeman on board one of Mr. King's ships, and sails for Georgia—Impositions on free negroes as usual—His venture of turkeys—Sails for Montserrat, and on his passage his friend, the Captain, falls ill and dies.

[1] Stamp Act The 1765 Stamp Act (requiring that various printed papers be produced on stamped paper of English manufacture) was a form of tax imposed on the American colonies by the British colonial government. The Stamp Act inspired outrage in the colonies, and was repealed the following year.

[2] This chapter is included in its entirety in the website component of this anthology.

Every day now brought me nearer my freedom, and I was impatient till we proceeded again to sea, that I might have an opportunity of getting a sum large enough to purchase it. I was not long ungratified; for, in the beginning of the year 1766, my master bought another sloop, named the *Nancy*, the largest I had ever seen. She was partly laden, and was to proceed to Philadelphia; our Captain had his choice of three, and I was well pleased he chose this, which was the largest; for, from his having a large vessel, I had more room, and could carry a larger quantity of goods with me. Accordingly, when we had delivered our old vessel, the *Prudence*, and completed the lading of the *Nancy*, having made near three hundred per cent, by four barrels of pork I brought from Charlestown, I laid in as large a cargo as I could, trusting to God's providence to prosper my undertaking.

With these views I sailed for Philadelphia. On our passage, when we drew near the land, I was for the first time surprised at the sight of some whales, having never seen any such large sea monsters before; and as we sailed by the land one morning I saw a puppy whale close by the vessel; it was about the length of a wherry boat, and it followed us all the day till we got within the Capes.[1] We arrived safe and in good time at Philadelphia, and I sold my goods there chiefly to the Quakers. They always appeared to be a very honest discreet sort of people, and never attempted to impose on me;[2] I therefore liked them, and ever after chose to deal with them in preference to any others.

One Sunday morning while I was here, as I was going to church, I chanced to pass a meeting-house.[3] The doors being open, and the house full of people, it excited my curiosity to go in. When I entered the house, to my great surprise, I saw a very tall woman standing in the midst of them, speaking in an audible voice something which I could not understand. Having never seen anything of this kind before, I stood and stared about me for some time, wondering at this odd scene. As soon as it was over I took an opportunity to make inquiry about the place and people, when I was informed they were called Quakers. I particularly asked what that woman I saw in the midst of them had said, but none of them were pleased to satisfy me; so I quitted them, and soon after, as I was returning, I came to a church crowded with people; the church-yard was full likewise, and a number of people were even mounted on ladders, looking in at the windows. I thought this a strange sight, as I had never seen churches, either in England or the West Indies, crowded in this manner before. I therefore made bold to ask some people the meaning of all this, and they told me the Rev. Mr. George Whitfield[4] was preaching. I had often heard of this gentleman, and had wished to see and hear him; but I had never before had an opportunity. I now therefore resolved to gratify myself with the sight, and I pressed in amidst the multitude. When I got into the church, I saw this pious man exhorting the people with the greatest fervour and earnestness, and sweating as much as I ever did while in slavery on Montserrat beach. I was very much struck and impressed with this; I thought it strange I had never seen divines exert themselves in this manner before, and I was no longer at a loss to account for the thin congregations they preached to.

When we had discharged our cargo here, and were loaded again, we left this fruitful land once more, and set sail for Montserrat. My traffic had hitherto succeeded so well with me, that I thought, by selling my goods when we arrived at Montserrat, I should have enough to purchase my freedom. But, as soon as our vessel arrived there, my master came on board, and gave orders for us to go to St. Eustatia, and discharge our cargo there, and from thence proceed for Georgia. I was much disappointed at this; but thinking, as usual, it was of no use to encounter with the decrees of fate, I submitted without repining, and we went to St. Eustatia. After we had discharged our cargo there we took in a live cargo, as we call a cargo of slaves. Here I sold my goods tolerably well; but, not being able to lay out all my money in this small island to as much advantage as in many other places, I laid out

1 *got within the Capes* Delaware Bay (which leads to the Delaware river and the city of Philadelphia) is entered as one passes between Cape May to the north and Cape Henlopen to the south.

2 *impose on me* Treat me unfairly or dishonestly.

3 *meeting-house* In early America churches were often referred to as meeting houses.

4 *Rev. Mr. George Whitfield* Whitfield (also spelled Whitefield) (1714–70) was originally an Anglican minister; renowned for his charismatic preaching, he became one of the founders of Methodism and one of the leaders of the Great Awakening of the 1730s and 1740s.

only part, and the remainder I brought away with me net.[1] We sailed from hence for Georgia, and I was glad when we got there, though I had not much reason to like the place from my last adventure in Savannah; but I longed to get back to Montserrat and procure my freedom, which I expected to be able to purchase when I returned. …

We set sail once more for Montserrat, and arrived there safe; but much out of humour with our friend the silversmith. When we had unladen the vessel, and I had sold my venture, finding myself master of about forty-seven pounds, I consulted my true friend, the Captain, how I should proceed in offering my master the money for my freedom. He told me to come on a certain morning, when he and my master would be at breakfast together. Accordingly, on that morning I went, and met the Captain there, as he had appointed. When I went in, I made my obeisance to my master, and with my money in my hand, and many fears in my heart, I prayed him to be as good as his offer to me, when he was pleased to promise me my freedom as soon as I could purchase it. This speech seemed to confound him; he began to recoil: and my heart that instant sunk within me. "What," said he, "give you your freedom? Why, where did you get the money? Have you got forty pounds sterling?" "Yes, sir," I answered. "How did you get it?" replied he. I told him, very honestly. The Captain then said he knew I got the money very honestly and with much industry, and that I was particularly careful. On which my master replied, I got money much faster than he did; and said he would not have made me the promise he did if he had thought I should have got money so soon. "Come, come," said my worthy Captain, clapping my master on the back, "Come, Robert, (which was his name) I think you must let him have his freedom; you have laid your money out very well; you have received good interest for it all this time, and here is now the principal at last. I know Gustavus has earned you more than an hundred a-year, and he will still save you money, as he will not leave you—Come, Robert, take the money." My master then said he would not be worse than his promise; and, taking the money, told me to go to the Secretary at the Register Office, and get my manumission[2] drawn up.

These words of my master were like a voice from heaven to me: in an instant all my trepidation was turned into unutterable bliss; and I most reverently bowed myself with gratitude, unable to express my feelings, but by the overflowing of my eyes, while my true and worthy friend, the Captain, congratulated us both with a peculiar degree of heartfelt pleasure.

As soon as the first transports of my joy were over, and that I had expressed my thanks to these my worthy friends in the best manner I was able, I rose with a heart full of affection and reverence, and left the room, in order to obey my master's joyful mandate of going to the Register Office. As I was leaving the house I called to mind the words of the Psalmist, in the 126th Psalm, and like him, "I glorified God in my heart, in whom I trusted."[3] These words had been impressed on my mind from the very day I was forced from Deptford to the present hour, and I now saw them, as I thought, fulfilled and verified. My imagination was all rapture as I flew to the Register Office, and, in this respect, like the apostle Peter,[4] (whose deliverance from prison was so sudden and extraordinary, that he thought he was in a vision) I could scarcely believe I was awake. Heavens! who could do justice to my feelings at this moment! Not conquering heroes themselves, in the midst of a triumph—Not the tender mother who has just regained her long-lost infant, and presses it to her heart—Not the weary hungry mariner, at the sight of the desired friendly port—Not the lover, when he once more embraces his beloved mistress, after she had been ravished from his arms!—All within my breast was tumult, wildness, and delirium! My feet scarcely touched the ground, for they were winged with joy, and, like Elijah, as he rose to heaven,[5] they "were with lightning sped as I went on." Every one I met I told of my happiness, and blazed about the virtue of my amiable master and captain.

1 *net* Without having made any additional payments.

2 *manumission* Release from enslavement.

3 *the Psalmist … trusted* The words quoted by Equiano do not appear in this psalm; it is not entirely clear what passage he may have had in mind—possibly Psalm 28.

4 [Equiano's note] Acts, Ch. 12, verse 9.

5 *rose to heaven* See 2 Kings 2.1–18.

When I got to the office and acquainted the Register with my errand he congratulated me on the occasion, and told me he would draw up my manumission for half price, which was a guinea. I thanked him for his kindness; and, having received it and paid him, I hastened to my master to get him to sign it, that I might be fully released. Accordingly, he signed the manumission that day, so that, before night, I who had been a slave in the morning, trembling at the will of another, was become my own master, and completely free. I thought this was the happiest day I had ever experienced; and my joy was still heightened by the blessings and prayers of the sable race, particularly the aged, to whom my heart had ever been attached with reverence.

As the form of my manumission has something peculiar in it, and expresses the absolute power and dominion one man claims over his fellow, I shall beg leave to present it before my readers at full length:

Montserrat—To all men unto whom these presents shall come:[1] I Robert King, of the parish of St. Anthony in the said island, merchant, send greeting: Know ye, that I, the aforesaid Robert King, for and in consideration of the sum of seventy pounds current money of the said island, to me in hand paid, and to the intent that a negro man-slave, named Gustavus Vassa, shall and may become free, have manumitted, emancipated, enfranchised, and set free, and by these presents do manumit, emancipate, enfranchise, and set free, the aforesaid negro man-slave, named Gustavus Vassa, for ever, hereby giving, granting, and releasing unto him, the said Gustavus Vassa, all right, title, dominion, sovereignty, and property, which, as lord and master over the aforesaid Gustavus Vassa, I had, or now I have, or by any means whatsoever I may or can hereafter possibly have over him the aforesaid negro, for ever. In witness whereof I the abovesaid Robert King have unto these presents set my hand and seal, this tenth day of July, in the year of our Lord one thousand seven hundred and sixty-six.
Robert King

Signed, sealed, and delivered in the presence of Terrylegay, Montserrat.

Registered the within manumission at full length, this eleventh day of July, 1766, in liber[2]
D. Terrylegay, Register.

———

In short, the fair as well as black people immediately styled me by a new appellation, to me the most desirable in the world, which was Freeman, and at the dances I gave,[3] my Georgia superfine blue clothes made no indifferent appearance, as I thought. Some of the sable females, who formerly stood aloof, now began to relax and appear less coy; but my heart was still fixed on London, where I hoped to be ere long. So that my worthy captain and his owner, my late master, finding that the bent of my mind was towards London, said to me, "We hope you won't leave us, but that you will still be with the vessels." Here gratitude bowed me down; and none but the generous mind can judge of my feelings, struggling between inclination and duty. However, notwithstanding my wish to be in London, I obediently answered my benefactors that I would go in the vessel, and not leave them; and from that day I was entered on board as an able-bodied sailor, at thirty-six shillings per month, besides what perquisites I could make. My intention was to make a voyage or two, entirely to please these my honoured patrons; but I determined that the year following, if it pleased God, I would see Old England once more, and surprise my old master, Capt. Pascal, who was hourly in my mind; for I still loved him, notwithstanding his usage of me, and I pleased myself with thinking of what he would say when he saw what the Lord had done for me in so short a time, instead of being, as he might perhaps suppose, under the cruel yoke of some planter.

With these kind of reveries, I used often to entertain myself, and shorten the time till my return; and now, being as in my original free African state, I embarked on board the *Nancy*, after having got all things ready for our voyage. In this state of serenity, we sailed for St. Eustatia; and, having smooth seas and calm weather, we soon arrived there: after taking our cargo on board, we proceeded to Savannah in Georgia, in August, 1766. ...

———

1 *these presents shall come* The present words shall be shown.

2 *liber* Latin: book.

3 *gave* Attended.

from Chapter 8

The author, to oblige Mr. King, once more embarks for Georgia in one of his vessels—A new captain is appointed—They sail, and steer a new course—Three remarkable dreams—The vessel is shipwrecked on the Bahama bank, but the crew are preserved, principally by means of the author—He sets out from the island with the captain, in a small boat, in quest of a ship—Their distress—Meet with a wrecker—Sail for Providence—Are overtaken again by a terrible storm, and are all near perishing—Arrive at New Providence—The author, after some time, sails from thence to Georgia—Meets with another storm, and is obliged to put back and refit—Arrives at Georgia—Meets new impositions—Two white men attempt to kidnap him—Officiates as a parson at a funeral ceremony—Bids adieu to Georgia, and sails for Martinico.

… We stayed in New Providence[1] about seventeen or eighteen days; during which time I met with many friends, who gave me encouragement to stay there with them: but I declined it; though, had not my heart been fixed on England, I should have stayed, as I liked the place extremely, and there were some free black people here who were very happy, and we passed our time pleasantly together, with the melodious sound of the catguts,[2] under the lime and lemon trees. At length Captain Phillips hired a sloop to carry him and some of the slaves that he could not sell to Georgia; and I agreed to go with him in this vessel, meaning now to take my farewell of that place. When the vessel was ready, we all embarked; and I took my leave of New Providence, not without regret. We sailed about four o'clock in the morning, with a fair wind, for Georgia; and about eleven o'clock the same morning a short and sudden gale sprung up and blew away most of our sails; and, as we were still amongst the keys, in a very few minutes it dashed the sloop against the rocks. Luckily for us the water was deep; and the sea was not so angry but that, after having for some time laboured hard, and being many in number, we were saved through God's

mercy; and, by using our greatest exertions, we got the vessel off. The next day we returned to Providence, where we soon got her again refitted. Some of the people swore that we had spells set upon us by somebody in Montserrat; and others that we had witches and wizards amongst the poor helpless slaves; and that we never should arrive safe at Georgia. But these things did not deter me; I said, "Let us again face the winds and seas, and swear not, but trust to God, and he will deliver us." We therefore once more set sail; and, with hard labour, in seven days' time arrived safe at Georgia.

After our arrival we went up to the town of Savannah; and the same evening I went to a friend's house to lodge, whose name was Mosa, a black man. We were very happy at meeting each other; and after supper we had a light till it was between nine and ten o'clock at night. About that time the watch or patrol came by; and, discerning a light in the house, they knocked at the door: we opened it; and they came in and sat down, and drank some punch with us: they also begged some limes of me, as they understood I had some, which I readily gave them. A little after this they told me I must go to the watch-house with them: this surprised me a good deal, after our kindness to them; and I asked them, why so? They said that all negroes who had light in their houses after nine o'clock were to be taken into custody, and either pay some dollars or be flogged. Some of those people knew that I was a free man; but, as the man of the house was not free, and had his master to protect him, they did not take the same liberty with him they did with me. I told them that I was a free man, and just arrived from Providence; that we were not making any noise, and that I was not a stranger in that place, but was very well known there: "Besides," said I, "what will you do with me?"—"That you shall see," replied they, "but you must go to the watch-house with us." Now whether they meant to get money from me or not I was at a loss to know; but I thought immediately of the oranges and limes at Santa Cruz: and seeing that nothing would pacify them I went with them to the watch-house, where I remained during the night. Early the next morning these imposing ruffians flogged a negro man and woman that they had in the watch-house, and then they told me that I must be flogged too. I asked why? and if there was no law for free men? And told them if there was I would

1 *New Providence* The largest of the Bahama Islands.

2 *the melodious sound of the catguts* Catgut was commonly used to make strings for stringed instruments (such as fiddles).

have it put in force against them. But this only exasperated them the more; and instantly they swore they would serve[1] me as Doctor Perkins had done; and they were going to lay violent hands on me; when one of them, more humane than the rest, said that as I was a free man they could not justify stripping me by law. I then immediately sent for Doctor Brady, who was known to be an honest and worthy man; and on his coming to my assistance they let me go.

This was not the only disagreeable incident I met with while I was in this place; for, one day, while I was a little way out of the town of Savannah, I was beset by two white men, who meant to play their usual tricks with me in the way of kidnapping. As soon as these men accosted me, one of them said to the other, "This is the very fellow we are looking for that you lost": and the other swore immediately that I was the identical person. On this they made up to me, and were about to handle me; but I told them to be still and keep off; for I had seen those kind of tricks played upon other free blacks, and they must not think to serve me so. At this they paused a little, and one said to the other—it will not do; and the other answered that I talked too good English. I replied, I believed I did; and I had also with me a revengeful stick equal to the occasion; and my mind was likewise good. Happily however it was not used; and, after we had talked together a little in this manner, the rogues left me. I stayed in Savannah some time, anxiously trying to get to Montserrat once more to see Mr. King, my old master, and then to take a final farewell of the American quarter of the globe. At last I met with a sloop called the *Speedwell*, Captain John Bunton, which belonged to Grenada, and was bound to Martinico, a French island, with a cargo of rice, and I shipped myself on board of her. Before I left Georgia a black woman, who had a child lying dead, being very tenacious of the church burial service,[2] and not able to get any white person to perform it, applied to me for that purpose. I told her I was no parson; and besides, that the service over the dead did not affect the soul. This, however, did not satisfy her; she still urged me very hard: I therefore complied with her earnest entreaties, and at last consented to act the parson for

the first time in my life. As she was much respected, there was a great company both of white and black people at the grave. I then accordingly assumed my new vocation, and performed the funeral ceremony to the satisfaction of all present; after which I bade adieu to Georgia, and sailed for Martinico.

from CHAPTER 9[3]

The author arrives at Martinico—Meets with new difficulties—Gets to Montserrat, where he takes leave of his old master, and sails for England—Meets Capt. Pascal—Learns the French horn—Hires himself with Doctor Irving, where he learns to freshen sea water—Leaves the doctor, and goes a voyage to Turkey and Portugal; and afterwards goes a voyage to Grenada, and another to Jamaica—Returns to the Doctor, and they embark together on a voyage to the North Pole, with the Hon. Capt. Phipps—Some account of that voyage, and the dangers the author was in—He returns to England.

I thus took a final leave of Georgia; for the treatment I had received in it disgusted me very much against the place; and when I left it and sailed for Martinico I determined never more to revisit it. My new captain conducted his vessel safer than my former one; and, after an agreeable voyage, we got safe to our intended port. While I was on this island I went about a good deal, and found it very pleasant: in particular I admired the town of St. Pierre, which is the principal one in the island, and built more like an European town than any I had seen in the West Indies. In general also, slaves were better treated, had more holidays, and looked better than those in the English islands. After we had done our business here, I wanted my discharge, which was necessary; for it was then the month of May, and I wished much to be at Montserrat to bid farewell to Mr. King, and all my other friends there, in time to sail for Old England in the July fleet. ...

We had a most prosperous voyage, and, at the end of seven weeks, arrived at Cherry-Garden stairs.[4] Thus

[1] *serve* Treat.

[2] *very tenacious of the church burial service* Determined to have a church burial service for her child.

[3] A longer selection of excerpts from this chapter is included as part of the website component of this anthology.

[4] *Cherry-Garden stairs* Landing area on the Thames, in London's east end.

were my longing eyes once more gratified with a sight of London, after having been absent from it above four years. I immediately received my wages, and I never had earned seven guineas so quick in my life before; I had thirty-seven guineas in all, when I got cleared of the ship. I now entered upon a scene, quite new to me, but full of hope.

In this situation my first thoughts were to look out for some of my former friends, and amongst the first of those were the Miss Guerins. As soon, therefore, as I had regaled myself I went in quest of those kind ladies, whom I was very impatient to see; and with some difficulty and perseverance, I found them at May's-hill, Greenwich. They were most agreeably surprised to see me, and I quite overjoyed at meeting with them. I told them my history, at which they expressed great wonder, and freely acknowledged it did their cousin, Capt. Pascal, no honour. He then visited there frequently; and I met him four or five days after in Greenwich Park. When he saw me he appeared a good deal surprised, and asked me how I came back? I answered, "In a ship." To which he replied dryly, "I suppose you did not walk back to London on the water." As I saw, by his manner, that he did not seem to be sorry for his behaviour to me, and that I had not much reason to expect any favour from him, I told him that he had used me very ill, after I had been such a faithful servant to him for so many years; on which, without saying any more, he turned about and went away. A few days after this I met Capt. Pascal at Miss Guerin's house, and asked him for my prize-money.[1] He said there was none due to me; for, if my prize-money had been £.10,000, he had a right to it all. I told him I was informed otherwise; on which he bade me defiance; and, in a bantering tone, desired me to commence a lawsuit against him for it: "There are lawyers enough," said he, "that will take the cause in hand, and you had better try it." I told him then that I would try it, which enraged him very much; however, out of regard to the ladies, I remained still, and never made any farther demand of my right.

Some time afterwards these friendly ladies asked me what I meant to do with myself, and how they could assist me. I thanked them, and said, if they pleased, I would be their servant; but if not, as I had thirty-seven guineas, which would support me for some time, I would be much obliged to them to recommend me to some person who would teach me a business whereby I might earn my living. They answered me very politely, that they were sorry it did not suit them to take me as their servant, and asked me what business I should like to learn? I said, hair-dressing. They then promised to assist me in this; and soon after they recommended me to a gentleman whom I had known before, one Capt. O'Hara, who treated me with much kindness, and procured me a master, a hair-dresser, in Coventry-court, Haymarket, with whom he placed me. I was with this man from September till the February following.

In that time we had a neighbour in the same court who taught the French horn. He used to blow it so well that I was charmed with it, and agreed with him to teach me to blow it. Accordingly he took me in hand, and began to instruct me, and I soon learned all the three parts. I took great delight in blowing on this instrument, the evenings being long; and besides that, I was fond of it. I did not like to be idle, and it filled up my vacant hours innocently.

At this time also I agreed with the Rev. Mr. Gregory, who lived in the same court, where he kept an academy and an evening-school, to improve me in arithmetic. This he did as far as barter and alligation; so that all the time I was there I was entirely employed. In February 1768 I hired myself to Dr. Charles Irving, in Pall Mall, so celebrated for his successful experiments in making sea water fresh; and here I had plenty of hair-dressing to improve my hand. This gentleman was an excellent master; he was exceedingly kind and good tempered; and allowed me in the evenings to attend my schools, which I esteemed a great blessing; therefore I thanked God and him for it, and used all my diligence to improve the opportunity.

This diligence and attention recommended me to the notice and care of my three preceptors, who on their parts bestowed a great deal of pains in my instruction, and besides were all very kind to me. My wages, however, which were by two thirds less than I ever had in my life (for I had only £.12 per annum) I soon found would not be sufficient to defray this extraordinary expense of masters, and my own necessary expenses; my old thirty-seven guineas had by this time worn all

1 *prize-money* Share of the valuables seized when capturing other vessels.

away to one. I thought it best, therefore, to try the sea again in quest of more money, as I had been bred to it, and had hitherto found the profession of it successful. I had also a very great desire to see Turkey, and I now determined to gratify it. Accordingly, in the month of May, 1768, I told the doctor my wish to go to sea again, to which he made no opposition; and we parted on friendly terms.

The same day I went into the city in quest of a master. I was extremely fortunate in my inquiry; for I soon heard of a gentleman who had a ship going to Italy and Turkey, and he wanted a man who could dress hair well. I was overjoyed at this, and went immediately on board of his ship, as I had been directed, which I found to be fitted up with great taste, and I already foreboded no small pleasure in sailing in her. Not finding the gentleman on board, I was directed to his lodgings, where I met with him the next day, and gave him a specimen of my dressing. He liked it so well that he hired me immediately, so that I was perfectly happy; for the ship, master, and voyage, were entirely to my mind. The ship was called the *Delawar*, and my master's name was John Jolly, a neat smart good-humoured man, just such a one as I wished to serve. We sailed from England in July following, and our voyage was extremely pleasant. We went to Villa Franca, Nice, and Leghorn;[1] and in all these places I was charmed with the richness and beauty of the countries, and struck with the elegant buildings with which they abound. We had always in them plenty of extraordinary good wines and rich fruits, which I was very fond of; and I had frequent occasions of gratifying both my taste and curiosity; for my captain always lodged on shore in those places, which afforded me opportunities to see the country around. I also learned navigation of the mate, which I was very fond of. When we left Italy we had delightful sailing among the Archipelago islands, and from thence to Smyrna in Turkey. This is a very ancient city; the houses are built of stone, and most of them have graves adjoining to them; so that they sometimes present the appearance of church-yards. Provisions are very plentiful in this city, and good wine less than a penny a pint. The grapes, pomegranates, and many other fruits, were also the richest and largest I ever tasted. The natives are well looking and strong

made, and treated me always with great civility. In general, I believe they are fond of black people; and several of them gave me pressing invitations to stay amongst them, although they keep the franks, or Christians,[2] separate, and do not suffer them to dwell immediately amongst them. I was astonished in not seeing women in any of their shops, and very rarely any in the streets; and whenever I did they were covered with a veil from head to foot, so that I could not see their faces, except when any of them out of curiosity uncovered them to look at me, which they sometimes did. I was surprised to see how the Greeks are, in some measure, kept under by the Turks,[3] as the negroes are in the West Indies by the white people. The less refined Greeks, as I have already hinted, dance here in the same manner as we do in my nation. On the whole, during our stay here, which was about five months, I liked the place and the Turks extremely well. I could not help observing one very remarkable circumstance there: the tails of the sheep are flat, and so very large, that I have known the tail even of a lamb to weigh from eleven to thirteen pounds. The fat of them is very white and rich, and is excellent in puddings, for which it is much used. Our ship being at length richly loaded with silk, and other articles, we sailed for England.

In May 1769, soon after our return from Turkey, our ship made a delightful voyage to Oporto in Portugal, where we arrived at the time of the carnival.[4] On our arrival, there were sent on board to us thirty-six articles to observe, with very heavy penalties if we should break any of them; and none of us even dared to go on board any other vessel or on shore till the Inquisition had sent on board and searched for every thing illegal, especially bibles.[5] Such as were produced, and

[2] *franks, or Christians* "Frank," originally a term for members of the ancient tribes that inhabited what is now France, came in medieval times to be widely used in the Middle East as a term for Western European Christians; this usage persisted into the eighteenth century and beyond.

[3] *the Greeks ... the Turks* Greece was under the control of the Turkish Ottoman Empire from late medieval times until Greek independence was declared in 1832.

[4] *the carnival* Probably the festival of São João (St. John), a major celebration held in Porto in June.

[5] *Inquisition ... bibles* From the thirteenth until the early nineteenth centuries the Roman Catholic church operated a set of institutions known collectively as the "Holy Inquisition," the purpose of which was to combat heresy. Roman Catholic [continued ...]

[1] *Leghorn* Livorno (a seaport in northwest Italy).

certain other things, were sent on shore till the ships were going away; and any person in whose custody a bible was found concealed was to be imprisoned and flogged, and sent into slavery for ten years. I saw here many very magnificent sights, particularly the garden of Eden, where many of the clergy and laity went in procession in their several orders with the Host,[1] and sung Te Deum.[2] I had a great curiosity to go into some of their churches, but could not gain admittance without using the necessary sprinkling of holy water at my entrance. From curiosity, and a wish to be holy, I therefore complied with this ceremony, but its virtues were lost on me, for I found myself nothing the better for it. This place abounds with plenty of all kinds of provisions. The town is well built and pretty, and commands a fine prospect. Our ship having taken in a load of wine, and other commodities, we sailed for London, and arrived in July following. Our next voyage was to the Mediterranean. The ship was again got ready, and we sailed in September for Genoa. This is one of the finest cities I ever saw; some of the edifices were of beautiful marble, and made a most noble appearance; and many had very curious fountains before them. The churches were rich and magnificent, and curiously adorned both in the inside and out. But all this grandeur was in my eyes disgraced by the galley slaves,[3] whose condition both there and in other parts of Italy is truly piteous and wretched. After we had stayed there some weeks, during which we bought many different things which we wanted, and got them very cheap, we sailed to Naples, a charming city, and remarkably clean. The bay is the most beautiful I ever saw; the moles[4] for shipping are excellent. I thought it extraordinary to see grand operas acted here on Sunday nights, and even attended by their majesties. I too, like these great ones, went to those sights, and vainly served God in the day while I thus served mammon effectually at night. While we remained here there happened an eruption of Mount Vesuvius, of which I had a perfect view. It was extremely awful; and we were so near that the ashes from it used to be thick on our deck.

After we had transacted our business at Naples we sailed with a fair wind once more for Smyrna, where we arrived in December. A seraskier[5] or officer took a liking to me here, and wanted me to stay, and offered me two wives; however I refused the temptation. The merchants here travel in caravans or large companies. I have seen many caravans from India, with some hundreds of camels, laden with different goods. The people of these caravans are quite brown. Among other articles, they brought with them a great quantity of locusts,[6] which are a kind of pulse, sweet and pleasant to the palate, and in shape resembling French beans, but longer. Each kind of goods is sold in a street by itself, and I always found the Turks very honest in their dealings. They let no Christians into their mosques or churches, for which I was very sorry; as I was always fond of going to see the different modes of worship of the people wherever I went. The plague broke out while we were in Smyrna, and we stopped taking goods into the ship till it was over. She was then richly laden, and we sailed in about March 1770 for England. One day in our passage we met with an accident which was near burning the ship. A black cook, in melting some fat, overset the pan into the fire under the deck, which immediately began to blaze, and the flame went up very high under the foretop. With the fright the poor cook became almost white, and altogether speechless. Happily however we got the fire out without doing much mischief. After various delays in this passage, which was tedious, we arrived in Standgate Creek[7] in July; and, at the latter end of the year, some new event occurred, so that my noble captain, the ship, and I all separated.

In April 1771 I shipped myself as a steward with Capt. Wm. Robertson of the ship *Grenada Planter*,

practice did not encourage private study of the Bible by individuals; preferred practice was for the clergy to interpret the Bible to the laity. (Protestant denominations, in contrast, encouraged individuals to read and study the Bible on their own.)

[1] *the Host* Communion wafers.

[2] *Te Deum* Latin: To God. The *Te Deum* prayer is recited or sung during Catholic services.

[3] *galley slaves* Galleys were ships propelled either by sail or by oars—with the rowing done by enslaved people (generally, war captives).

[4] *moles* Stone structures forming breakwaters or piers.

[5] *seraskier* High-ranking military official.

[6] *locusts* Locust beans (also known as iru beans), legumes from a tree common in much of West Africa.

[7] *Standgate Creek* Harbor located near the mouth of the Thames in southeast England.

once more to try my fortune in the West Indies; and we sailed from London for Madeira, Barbadoes, and the Grenades. ...

[At the end of the voyage] we arrived in England, and I got clear of this ship. But, being still of a roving disposition, and desirous of seeing as many different parts of the world as I could, I shipped myself soon after, in the same year, as steward on board of a fine large ship, called the *Jamaica*, Captain David Watt; and we sailed from England in December 1771 for Nevis and Jamaica. I found Jamaica to be a very fine large island, well peopled, and the most considerable of the West India islands. There was a vast number of negroes here, whom I found as usual exceedingly imposed upon by the white people, and the slaves punished as in the other islands. There are negroes whose business it is to flog slaves; they go about to different people for employment, and the usual pay is from one to four bits. I saw many cruel punishments inflicted on the slaves in the short time I stayed here. In particular I was present when a poor fellow was tied up and kept hanging by the wrists at some distance from the ground, and then some half hundred weights were fixed to his ancles, in which posture he was flogged most unmercifully. There were also, as I heard, two different masters noted for cruelty on the island, who had staked up two negroes naked, and in two hours the vermin stung them to death. I heard a gentleman I well knew tell my captain that he passed sentence on a negro man to be burnt alive for attempting to poison an overseer. I pass over numerous other instances, in order to relieve the reader by a milder scene of roguery.

Before I had been long on the island, one Mr. Smith at Port Morant bought goods of me to the amount of twenty-five pounds sterling; but when I demanded payment from him, he was going each time to beat me, and threatened that he would put me in jail. One time he would say I was going to set his house on fire, at another he would swear I was going to run away with his slaves. I was astonished at this usage from a person who was in the situation of a gentleman, but I had no alternative; I was therefore obliged to submit. When I came to Kingston, I was surprised to see the number of Africans who were assembled together on Sundays; particularly at a large commodious place, called Spring Path. Here each different nation of Africa meet and dance after the manner of their own country. They still retain most of their native customs: they bury their dead, and put victuals, pipes and tobacco, and other things, in the grave with the corpse, in the same manner as in Africa. Our ship having got her loading we sailed for London, where we arrived in the August following. On my return to London, I waited on my old and good master, Dr. Irving, who made me an offer of his service again. Being now tired of the sea I gladly accepted it. I was very happy in living with this gentleman once more; during which time we were daily employed in reducing old Neptune's dominions by purifying the briny element and making it fresh. Thus I went on till May 1773, when I was roused by the sound of fame, to seek new adventures, and to find, towards the North Pole, what our Creator never intended we should, a passage to India. ...

—1789

IN CONTEXT

Equiano's Narrative as a Philadelphia Abolitionist Pamphlet

The first illustrated edition of any part of Equiano's *Interesting Narrative* seems to have been a 36-page pamphlet largely made up of excerpts from Equiano's work. The pamphlet was issued in 1829 in Philadelphia by Samuel Wood, a Quaker printer who had been publishing abolitionist broadsides and pamphlets since the early years of the century. As illustrations, Wood included several woodcuts (several of which had appeared in his earlier publications and were now re-purposed); he also appended to the Equiano material "the following *Remarks upon the Slave Trade*," which Wood had originally published in 1807 as a reprint of "a pamphlet lately published by a society at Plymouth, in Great Britain, from which the Philadelphia Society for Promoting the Abolition of Slavery have taken the following extracts, and have added a copy of the plate, which accompanied it." The plate (shown right) bears a close resemblance to Thomas Clarkson's 1787 diagram of the hold of the slave ship *Brooks*, which had been widely reprinted and was credited with helping significantly to spur abolitionist sentiment.

Title page and illustration, *The Life and Adventures of Olaudah Equiano* (1829).

IN CONTEXT

Reactions to Olaudah Equiano's Work

from *The Analytic Review* (May 1789)[1]

The life of an African, written by himself, is certainly a curiosity, as it has been a favourite philosophic whim to degrade the numerous nations, on whom the sun-beams more directly dart, below the common level of humanity, and hastily to conclude that nature, by making them inferior to the rest of the human race, designed to stamp them with a mark of slavery. ... If these volumes do not exhibit extraordinary intellectual powers, sufficient to wipe off the stigma, yet the activity and ingenuity, which conspicuously appear in the character of Gustavus, place him on a par with the general mass of men, who fill the subordinate stations in a more civilized society than that which he was thrown into at his birth.

from *The Monthly Review* (June 1789)

We entertain no doubt of the general authenticity of this very intelligent African's story; though it is not improbable that some English writer has assisted him in the compilement, or, at least, the correction of his book; for it is sufficiently well-written. The Narrative wears an honest face; and we have conceived a good opinion of the man, from the artless manner in which he has detailed the variety of adventures and vicissitudes which have fallen to his lot. His publication appears very seasonable, at a time when negro-slavery is the subject of public investigation; and it seems calculated to increase the odium that has been excited against the West-India planters, on account of the cruelties that some are said to have exercised on their slaves, many instances of which are here detailed.

from "Descriptive Catalogue of Anti-Slavery Works for Sale by Isaac Knaap, at the Depository, No. 25, Cornhill," published in *The Liberator*, 27 October 1837, and again 17 November 1837.

> In all, Knapp's list includes 68 works; among the more notable listed ahead of Equiano's *Interesting Narrative* are "Mrs. Child's Appeal" (Lydia Child's *An Appeal in Favor of That Class of Americans Called Africans*), listed at number 2; Archy Moore's *The Slave*, listed at number 4; Charles Ball's *A Narrative of the Life and Adventures of Charles Ball*, listed at number 5; Phillis Wheatley's *Memoir and Poems*, listed at number 18; Whittier's *Poems*, listed at number 20; and a collection of Lemuel Haynes's writings, listed at number 30.

36. GUSTAVUS VASSA. 294 pp. 12 mo. Cloth 62 1-2-

The life of Olaudah Equiano, or Gustavus Vassa, the African, written by himself. With two lithographic Prints.

This is the life of a native African, of powerful intellect, who was 'stolen out of his own land,' lived as a slave in Pennsylvania, went several voyages to the West Indies, and to several ports in Europe, narrowly escaped death several times, and passed through a great variety of wonderful scenes, which give his narrative an interest scarcely surpassed by Robinson Crusoe.

[1] Though published anonymously, this review is now known to have been written by Mary Wollstonecraft.

ABSALOM JONES
1746 – 1818

Priest, pamphleteer, and social activist Absalom Jones was among the most influential African American religious leaders of the late eighteenth and early nineteenth centuries. In the years following the passage of Pennsylvania's pivotal—yet far from radical—Gradual Abolition Act (1780), Jones played an important part in advocating for the place of free African Americans in Philadelphia's public sphere, both through his community and religious work and through his writings. His written works—which include petitions, a sermon, a brief autobiographical text, and a co-authored pamphlet—provide a unique perspective on the social and racial climate of the nation's first capital, and present a powerful voice dedicated to the promotion of Christian morality and to the uplift of both enslaved and free African Americans.

Jones was born into bondage in Sussex, Delaware on 6 November 1746, enslaved first as a field hand and then as a house servant. Though he was not permitted to receive formal schooling, Jones taught himself to read by buying books with the small change he received from the "ladies and gentlemen" who visited his enslaver's household from time to time. Among the first books he purchased was a copy of the New Testament. At the age of sixteen, Jones was taken to Philadelphia with his enslaver to work in a store, while his mother and siblings were all sold into a new household. The hope of being able to continue to correspond with his family motivated Jones to learn to write (it is unclear whether any of his family members also had some degree of literacy). Eventually, Jones was granted permission to attend, for a single term, a Quaker-run night school for African Americans.

In 1770, Jones married an enslaved woman named Mary King, and—while he was himself still enslaved—purchased her freedom with money loaned from the Quaker community. Thereafter he began a long and arduous pursuit of his own manumission, which his enslaver repeatedly refused to grant him. The couple were permitted to move into a private residence on a small plot of land, but lived in the perpetual knowledge that the property could be legally seized at any moment by Jones's enslaver. In 1780, four years after the Declaration of Independence, Pennsylvania passed a Gradual Abolition Act; this did not change the status of those already living in slavery, and even those born after 1780 to enslaved people were legally bound to twenty-eight years of indentured servitude. Nevertheless, the Act did bring change; by 1790 almost 90 percent of Philadelphia's black population were free. Jones was officially granted his freedom in 1784, after which he worked several years more under his former enslaver, for "good wages," as he puts it in an autobiographical sketch.

By 1787 Jones was preaching at the St. George Methodist Church, where he met fellow lay minister Richard Allen, also a formerly enslaved man who would later become a significant black religious leader in his own right. Together, Jones and Allen formed the Free African Society, an initially non-sectarian association aimed at promoting black welfare and education. Members paid a shilling to the Society every month, and the pool of funds was used to benefit widows, orphans, and the poor—though only those whose poverty had not, as the Society's mission statement declared, been "brought on them by their own imprudence." The Society would admit "no drunkard[s] nor disorderly person[s]."

Over time, Jones's evangelism in the community brought more and more African Americans into the congregation at St. George's, a fact which began to discomfit many of the church's white members. In 1792, shortly after the Free African Society had donated a substantial amount of money to refurbishing the building, church leaders unexpectedly demanded that the black and white worshippers be segregated, with blacks relegated to the seats at the back in the gallery. It was in response to this humiliation that Jones

led a walkout from St. George's, and went on to found what he initially called the First African Church. Two years later, the church gained official recognition from the Episcopal Diocese of Philadelphia, and became the African Episcopal Church of St. Thomas.

Jones's community leadership was dramatically tested in 1793; in the autumn of that year, Philadelphia was struck by a vicious outbreak of yellow fever, which would ultimately kill about a tenth of its population. Jones, Richard Allen, and the members of the Free African Society provided crucial aid to the disease's victims and their families, working alongside prominent white physician Benjamin Rush to treat patients, transport the bodies of the dead, and organize burials. The disaster led to Jones's first published work, a pamphlet co-authored with Allen that defended the conduct of the African American community throughout the epidemic; a more substantial account of that event, along with an excerpt of Jones and Allen's *A Narrative of the Proceedings of the Black People, During the Late Awful Calamity in Philadelphia* (1794), is included in the website component of this anthology.

Jones continued through the 1790s and early 1800s to defend the rights and the reputations of free African Americans and to advocate for the emancipation of the enslaved. He often collaborated with others; his 1799 "Petition of the People of Colour," calling on the United States to end the external and internal slave trade, was signed by 73 supporters. On 1 January 1808 he gave what would become his most famous sermon (today referred to as the "Thanksgiving Sermon"), praising the United States for abolishing the transatlantic slave trade. Today, the sermon's call on free African Americans to be grateful to their white "benefactors" and to conduct themselves "in such a manner as to furnish no cause of regret to the deliverers of our nation for their kindness to us" may strike readers as oddly conciliatory; such cautiousness shows a leader working hard to navigate the ambiguities of black peoples' social status in the developing Republic.

Jones died in 1818, well before the explosion of abolitionist culture among white Americans and decades before the institution of slavery was finally ended in the United States. His work has been acknowledged by later black activists and writers such as W.E.B. Du Bois, and he continues to fascinate readers and scholars concerned with the nature and possibility of African American citizenship in the early nation.

NOTE ON THE TEXT: The text of "The Petition of the People of Colour" is taken from the version printed in John Parrish's 1806 *Remarks on the Slavery of Black People*. Spelling and punctuation have been modernized in accordance with the practices of this anthology.

⌘ ⌘ ⌘

The Petition of the People of Colour

To the President, Senate, and House of Representatives

The Petition of the People of Colour, free men, within the city and suburbs of Philadelphia, humbly showeth,

That, thankful to God, our Creator, and to the Government under which we live for the blessings and benefits granted to us in the enjoyment of our natural right to liberty, and the protection of our persons and property from the oppression and violence which so great a number of like colour and national descent are subject to, we feel ourselves bound, from a sense of these blessings, to continue in our respective allotments,[1] and to lead honest and peaceable lives, rendering due submission unto the laws, and exciting and encouraging each other thereto, agreeable to the uniform advice of our friends of every denomination.

1 *allotments* I.e., social positions.

Yet[1] Providential favour we ourselves enjoy, we cannot be insensible of the condition of our afflicted brethren, suffering under various circumstances, in different parts of these states; but deeply sympathizing with them, [we] are incited by a sense of social duty, and humbly conceive ourselves authorized to address and petition you on their behalf, believing them to be objects of your representation in your public councils, in common with ourselves and every other class of citizen within the jurisdiction of the United States, according to the design of the present Constitution, formed by the General Convention, and ratified in the different states, as set forth in the preamble thereto in the following words, viz.[2] "We, the people of the United States, in order to form a more perfect union, establish justice, insure domestic tranquillity, provide for the common defence, and to secure the blessings of liberty to ourselves and posterity, do ordain, etc."[3] We apprehend this solemn compact is violated by a trade carried on in a clandestine manner to the coast of Guinea,[4] and another equally wicked [trade] practised openly by citizens of some of the southern states, upon the waters of Maryland and Delaware. Men sufficiently callous to qualify them for the brutal purpose are employed in kidnapping those of our brethren that are free, and purchasing others of such as claim a property in them; thus, those poor helpless victims, like droves of cattle, are seized, fettered, and hurried into places provided for this most horrid traffic, such as dark cellars and garrets, as is notorious at Northwest-fork, Chestertown, Eastown, and diverse[5] other places. After a sufficient number is obtained, they are forced on board vessels, crowded under hatches, without the least commiseration, left to deplore the sad separation of the dearest ties in nature—husband from wife, and parents from children; thus packed together, they are transported to Georgia and other places, and there inhumanly exposed to sale. Can any commerce, trade, or transaction, so detestably shock the feeling of man, or degrade the dignity of his nature, equal to[6] this? And how increasingly is the evil aggravated, when practised in a land high in profession of the benign doctrines of our Blessed Lord, who taught his followers to do unto others as they would they should do unto them. Your petitioners desire not to enlarge,[7] though volumes might be filled with the sufferings of this grossly abused part of the human species, seven hundred thousand of whom, it is said, are now in unconditional bondage in these states; but conscious of the rectitude of our motives in a concern so nearly affecting us, and so effectually interesting to the welfare of this country, we cannot but address you as guardians of our rights, and patrons of equal and national liberties, hoping you will view the subject in an impartial, unprejudiced light. We do not ask for an immediate emancipation of all, knowing that the degraded state of many, and their want[8] of education, would greatly disqualify [them] for such a change; yet, [we] humbly desire you may exert every means in your power to undo the heavy burdens, and prepare the way for the oppressed to go free, that every yoke may be broken. The law not long since[9] enacted by Congress, called the Fugitive Bill,[10] is in its execution found to be attended with circumstances peculiarly hard and distressing; for many of our afflicted brethren, in order to avoid the barbarities wantonly exercised upon them, or through fear of being carried off by those men-stealers, being forced to seek refuge by flight, they are then, by armed men, under colour of this law, cruelly treated, or brought back in chains to those that have no claim upon them. In the Constitution

[1] *Yet* Despite the.

[2] *viz.* Abbreviation for the Latin videlicet, meaning "namely" or "that is to say."

[3] *We, the people ... etc.* Preamble to the Constitution of the United States (1789).

[4] *Guinea* At the time, this term referred to a large portion of West Africa, the starting point of the transatlantic slave trade.

[5] *Northwest-fork, Chestertown, Eastown* Towns in Delaware, Maryland, and Pennsylvania which were strongholds of the internal slave trade; *diverse* Various.

[6] *equal to* I.e., as much as.

[7] *enlarge* Exaggerate.

[8] *want* Lack.

[9] *since* Ago.

[10] *Fugitive Bill* Jones refers to the Fugitive Slave Act of 1793, which enabled slaveholders, their agents, and their attorneys to pursue enslaved people who had run away, capture them, and return them to slavery, regardless of what state or territory they were apprehended in. Aside from making escapes from slavery even more difficult than before, this act also enabled the capture and enslavement of free African Americans, who, if accused of being runaways, would have no chance of a fair trial.

and the Fugitive Bill, no mention is made of black people, or slaves; therefore, if the Bill of Rights, or the Declaration of Congress[1] are of any validity, we beseech that as we are men, we may be admitted to partake of the liberties and unalienable rights therein held forth; firmly believing that the extending of justice and equity to all classes, would be a means of drawing down the blessing of Heaven upon this land, for the peace and prosperity of which, and the real happiness of every member of the community, we fervently pray. Philadelphia, 30th of December, 1799.

Absalom Jones and others, 73 subscribers[2]

—1799

The handwritten text of the petition, as it is preserved in the Records of the U.S. House of Representatives.

[1] *Declaration of Congress* I.e., the Declaration of Independence.

[2] *subscribers* I.e., signatories.

Rebellions and Revolutions
Contexts

The late eighteenth and early nineteenth centuries were a time of great change and turmoil, both in the Americas and in Britain and Europe. Enlightenment philosophers such as Voltaire, John Locke, Jean-Jacques Rousseau, and Thomas Paine had set forth powerful ideas about the natural rights of individuals. These rights, they argued, existed regardless of social class; the old hierarchal institutions that had long structured European society—the monarchy, the aristocracy, and the church—came to be seen by many as upholding a system that benefitted the few while depriving the many of their rights and livelihoods. The Enlightenment voices that called for throwing off the yokes of absolute monarchy and state religion resonated strongly in Europe, and also in the European colonies, including in North America. White settler colonists grew increasingly enraged at being controlled by an overseas power even as they largely saw freedom in terms that excluded people of other races. Meanwhile, for some enslaved and Indigenous people in the European colonies, the new rhetoric of freedom and equality provided useful terms to make their own struggles for emancipation—which long pre-dated these Enlightenment-era revolutions—legible on the world stage.

The different revolutions, then, saw issues of rights and of freedoms from different perspectives. In America the right to hold private property ranked high—and, much as the "founding fathers" did not wish to replicate the hierarchies of England, nor did they wish to embrace unfettered democracy, which they associated with mob rule. The revolutionaries in France in 1789–90, on the other hand, placed far more emphasis on equality—and far less on private property rights. The same was true, at least initially, in Haiti (though the early ideals of both the Haitian and French Revolutions were widely betrayed later during periods of horrific violence). In the United States, opinion was divided with regard to the French Revolution. Most white Americans were dismayed by the Haitian Revolution (even half a century later, the prospect of "a negro nation, a sort of Hayti on the continent" being formed in the United States—or in Texas—was deployed to inspire racist and reactionary fears among America's white population), but the Haitian Revolution offered a vision of hope to black Americans, both enslaved and free. The Haitian Revolution affected mainland North America in other ways too; not least of all, in imposing such military and financial costs on Napoleon's France that he sold the territory of Louisiana, the vast majority of it still inhabited and controlled by Native Americans, to the United States for a bargain price. The conflicts that resulted from these passionate strivings for different freedoms were manifold, complex, and interwoven.

The following selections may be read alongside the many other materials in this anthology that relate to the themes of freedom and revolution. The period introduction to this volume offers an overview of the revolutionary period, from its beginnings in Indigenous uprisings such as Pontiac's War (1763) to the American, Haitian, and French Revolutions that followed. The section elsewhere in this volume entitled "Contexts: Slavery and Resistance" offers further readings on enslaved people's struggle for freedom in the Americas and Caribbean. And many relevant texts also appear under various author entries, both within this volume and in the website component—including those of Benjamin Franklin, John and Abigail Adams, Thomas Jefferson, Thomas Paine, Philip Freneau, Phillis Wheatley, Susanna Rowson, Royall Tyler, and Lemuel Haynes.

⌘⌘⌘

"Pontiac's War"

from anonymous [believed to be Robert Navarre], *Journal of the Pontiac Conspiracy* (1763) [1]

At the conclusion of the Seven Years' War in 1763, the French ceded their territory in North America to the British (with the exception of Louisiana, which was ceded to Spain). To the Indigenous tribes of the Ohio Valley and Great Lakes, the departure of the French and arrival of the British was viewed with alarm. Many of the peoples from this area, known as the upper country or *pays-d'en-haut*, had built trusted trade relationships with the French and believed that the British were comparatively treacherous and disrespectful. And, more broadly, the defeat of the French in North America left a power vacuum; in a variety of earlier conflicts, Indigenous peoples had often been able to use the power struggle between the English and the French to their advantage, shifting allegiances according to which power offered them better protection.

Throughout the British colonies, the encroachment of white settlers on land occupied by Indigenous peoples (and in many cases supposedly protected by treaty rights) was an ongoing issue. Pontiac, an Odawa war chief, drew on the visions of the Lenape prophet Neolin to gather an armed force to resist this encroachment. Pontiac drew on several of Neolin's ideas, including his vision of a shared identity among the various tribes of Indigenous peoples, and his conviction that there should be a return to pre-contact ways of life. Neolin's religious prophecies also include a clear divine instruction to drive the British off Indigenous lands. Pontiac successfully amplified Neolin's message in his speeches to Indigenous councils, and, in 1763, an attack was launched on Fort Detroit, marking the beginning of the war that the British termed "Pontiac's Rebellion" (though it involved a large coalition of Indigenous groups, and Pontiac was only one leader among many).

The war lasted until 1766; over the course of it, the Indigenous coalition captured several British forts and killed hundreds of white settlers, prompting a violent British response.

The rebellion's consequences were far-reaching. An increased sense among Indigenous peoples of a "pan-Indian" identity was one important consequence. Another was the British decision during the war to issue the Proclamation of 1763, under the terms of which lands west of the Appalachian Mountains were declared to be reserved for Indigenous peoples, and sales of Indigenous land to private individuals were to be prohibited. The British authorities proved unable (or in some cases unwilling) to enforce these new regulations, however. Settlers, infuriated by these restrictions, largely ignored them. One further consequence, then, was a fraying of relations between American colonists and British authorities. All in all, the rebellion of 1763 helped set the stage for the complicated era historians often call the "age of revolutions," beginning with the American Revolution (1775–83) and ending with the European Revolutions of the mid-nineteenth century.

The excerpts that follow are drawn from *Journal of the Pontiac Conspiracy* (1763), which is usually attributed to Robert Navarre. Navarre was in charge of mediating land and property disputes for the French authorities in Detroit, and he continued to work as a translator and interpreter after the British took over (he could speak several Indigenous languages). As an eyewitness of the events leading up to Pontiac's Rebellion, Navarre provides valuable, detailed accounts of Neolin's visions and of Pontiac's speeches; it is important to be aware, however, that Navarre's relation of these events is mediated by his own Eurocentric perspective.

... The council of the three nations, Ottawas, Pottawattamies, and the bad Huron band,[2]

[1] The text presented here is based on the 1912 Burton edition, translated from the French by R.C. Ford.

[2] *Ottawas, Pottawattamies ... Huron band* These tribes all became involved in Pontiac's War. Of those mentioned here, the Odawa and Pottawatomi were members of the alliance of the Council of Three Fires (along with the Ojibwe). Most of the Wendat (Huron) groups living in the area had built longstanding alliances with the French.

took place and was presided over by Pontiac in his capacity of head chief of all the northern nations. He made a speech, and as a reason for his action exhibited war-belts which he claimed he had received from his Great Father, the King of France, to induce him to attack the English. …

They listened to him as chief, and in order to flatter his vanity and excite his pride they promised to do whatever he wished. Delighted to find so much loyalty among the three nations which numbered four hundred and sixty men, he craftily made use of their weakness to get complete control over them. To accomplish this he related in the council the story of a Wolf (Delaware) Indian,[1] who had journeyed to Heaven and talked with the Master of Life.[2] He spoke with so much eloquence that his narrative had just the effect upon them that he desired.

This story deserves a place here since it contains in blackest aspect the reason of the attack upon the English, and upon the French too, perhaps, if God in His mercy had not disposed differently. It is as follows:

An Indian of the Wolf nation, eager to make the acquaintance of the Master of Life—this is the name for God among all the Indians—resolved to undertake the journey to Paradise, where he knew He resided, without the knowledge of any of his tribe or village. But the question was how to succeed in his purpose and find the way thither. Not knowing anyone who had been there and was thus able to teach him the road, he had recourse to incantation in the hope of deriving some good augury from his trance. As a rule all the Indians, even those who are enlightened, are subject to superstition, and put a good deal of credence in their dreams and those things which one has a good deal of trouble to wean them from. This episode will be proof of what I say.

This Wolf Indian in his dream imagined that he had only to set out and by dint of travelling would arrive at the celestial dwelling. This he did the next day. Early in the morning he arose and equipped himself for a hunting journey, not forgetting to take provisions and

ammunition, and a big kettle. Behold him then setting out like that on his journey to Heaven to see the Master of Life.

The first seven days of his journey were quite favorable to his plans; he walked on without growing discouraged, always with a firm belief that he would arrive at his destination, and eight days went by without his encountering anything which could hinder him in his desire. On the evening of the eighth day he halted at sunset as usual, at the opening to a little prairie upon the bank of a stream which seemed to him a suitable camping place. As he was preparing his shelter for the night he beheld at the other end of this prairie where he camped, three roads, wide and plainly marked. … [After false starts down two of the roads, he took] the third road which he followed for a day without discovering anything. Suddenly he saw before him what appeared to be a mountain of marvelous whiteness and he stopped, overcome with astonishment. Nevertheless, he again advanced, firmly determined to see what this mountain could be, but when he arrived at the foot of it he no longer saw any road and was sad. At this juncture, not knowing what to do to continue his way, he looked around in all directions and finally saw a woman of this mountain, of radiant beauty, whose garments dimmed the whiteness of the snow. And she was seated.

This woman addressed him in his own tongue: "Thou appearest to me surprised not to find any road to lead thee where thou wishest to go. I know that for a long while thou hast been desirous of seeing the Master of Life and of speaking with him; that is why thou hast undertaken this journey to see him. The road which leads to his abode is over the mountain, and to ascend it thou must forsake all that thou hast with thee, and disrobe completely, and leave all thy trappings and clothing at the foot of the mountain. No one shall harm thee; go and bathe thyself in a river which I shall show thee, and then thou shalt ascend."

The Wolf was careful to obey the words of the woman, but one difficulty yet confronted him, namely, to know how to reach the top of the mountain which was perpendicular, pathless, and smooth as ice. He questioned this woman how one should go about climbing up, and she replied that if he was really anxious to see the Master of Life he would have to ascend,

[1] *Wolf (Delaware) Indian* Neolin, who is being referred to here, was a member of the Wolf clan of the Lenape people, an Indigenous tribe of the Northeastern Woodlands.

[2] *Master of Life* Another name for the Indigenous concept of the Great Spirit or primary life force.

helping himself only with his hand and his left foot. This appeared to him impossible, but encouraged by the woman he set about it and succeeded by dint of effort. ...

Here he saw the Master of Life who took him by the hand and gave him a hat all bordered with gold to sit down upon. The Wolf hesitated to do this for fear of spoiling the hat, but he was ordered to do so, and obeyed without reply.

After the Indian was seated the Lord said to him: "I am the Master of Life, and since I know what thou desirest to know, and to whom thou wishest to speak, listen well to what I am going to say to thee and to all the Indians:

"I am He who hath created the heavens and the earth, the trees, lakes, rivers, all men, and all that thou seest and hast seen upon the earth. Because I love you, ye must do what I say and love, and not do what I hate. I do not love that ye should drink to the point of madness, as ye do; and I do not like that ye should fight one another. Ye take two wives, or run after the wives of others; ye do not well, and I hate that. Ye ought to have but one wife, and keep her till death. When ye wish to go to war, ye conjure and resort to the medicine dance, believing that ye speak to me; ye are mistaken—it is to Manitou that ye speak, an evil spirit who prompts you to nothing but wrong, and who listens to you out of ignorance of me.

"This land where ye dwell I have made for you and not for others. Whence comes it that ye permit the Whites upon your lands? Can ye not live without them? I know that those whom ye call the children of your Great Father[1] supply your needs, but if ye were not evil, as ye are, ye could surely do without them. Ye could live as ye did live before knowing them—before those whom ye call your brothers had come upon your lands. Did ye not live by the bow and arrow? Ye had no need of gun or powder, ... I do not forbid you to permit among you the children of your Father;[2] I love them. They know me and pray to me, and I supply their wants and all they give you. But as to those who

come to trouble your lands[3]—drive them out, make war upon them. I do not love them at all; they know me not, and are my enemies, and the enemies of your brothers. Send them back to the lands which I have created for them and let them stay there. Here is a prayer which I give thee in writing to learn by heart and to teach to the Indians and their children."

The Wolf replied that he did not know how to read. He was told that when he should have returned to earth he would have only to give the prayer to the chief of his village who would read it and teach him and all the Indians to know it by heart; and he must say it night and morning without fail, and do what he has just been told to do. ...

The Wolf promised to do faithfully what the Master of Life told him, and that he would recommend it well to the Indians, and that the Master of Life would be pleased with them. ...

This adventure was soon noised about among the people of the whole village who came to hear the message of the Master of Life, and then went to carry it to the neighboring villages. The members of these villages came to see the pretended traveller, and the news was spread from village to village and finally reached Pontiac. He believed all this, as we believe an article of faith, and instilled it into the minds of all those in his council. They listened to him as to an oracle, and told him that he had only to speak and they were all ready to do what he demanded of them.

Pontiac, delighted at the success of his harangue, told the Hurons and Pottawattamies to return to their villages, and that in four days he would go to the Fort[4] with his young men for the peace-pipe dance,[5] and that while the dancers were engaged some other young men would roam around in the Fort to spy out all that was being done, the number of men the English had in the garrison, the number of traders, and the houses they occupied. All of this happened as he had said. ...

[1] *children of your Great Father* Colonial authorities often referred to their monarchs as the "Great Father" or "Great Mother" in their treaties with Indigenous peoples; in this context, the king of France, Louis XV, is being referenced.

[2] *children of your Father* The French.

[3] *those ... lands* The English.

[4] *Fort* Fort Detroit, a French stronghold that had been taken over by the British in 1760.

[5] *peace-pipe dance* Ceremonial dance involving smoking sacred pipes. Europeans often referred to ceremonial pipe-smoking as "peace-pipes," because such smoking took place at treaty agreements; pipes were smoked, however, for many other sacred and political decision-making ceremonies, including that of going to war.

Pontiac, wholly occupied with his project and nourishing in his heart a poison which was to be fateful for the English, and perhaps for the French, sent runners the following day, Monday, the 2nd of May, to each of the Huron and Pottawattamy villages to discover the real feeling of each of these two nations, for he feared to be crossed in his plans. These emissaries had orders to notify these nations for him that Thursday, the 5th of May, at mid-day, a grand council would be held in the Pottawattamy village which was situated between two and three miles below the Fort toward the southwest, and that the three nations should meet there and that no woman should be allowed to attend for fear of betraying their plans.

When the appointed day had come all the Ottawas with Pontiac at their head, and the bad band of the Hurons in [the] charge of Takay,[1] repaired to the Pottawattamy village where the expected council was to be held. Care had been taken to send the women out of the village so that they might not hear anything of what should be decided. Pontiac ordered sentinels to be placed around the village in order not to be disturbed in their council. When all these precautions had been taken each Indian seated himself in the circle according to rank, and Pontiac at the head, as great chief of all, began to speak. He said:

"It is important for us, my brothers, that we exterminate from our lands this nation which seeks only to destroy us. You see as well as I that we can no longer supply our needs, as we have done, from our brothers, the French. The English sell us goods twice as dear as the French do, and their goods do not last. Scarcely have we bought a blanket or something else to cover ourselves with before we must think of getting another; and when we wish to set out for our winter camps they do not want to give us any credit as our brothers, the French, do.

"When I go to see the English commander and say to him that some of our comrades are dead, instead of bewailing their death, as our French brothers do, he laughs at me and at you. If I ask anything for our sick, he refuses with the reply that he has no use for us. From all this you can well see that they are seeking our ruin. Therefore, my brothers, we must all swear their

destruction and wait no longer. Nothing prevents us; they are few in numbers, and we can accomplish it. All the nations who are our brothers attack them—why should we not attack? Are we not men like them? Have I not shown you the wampum belts[2] which I received from our Great Father, the Frenchman? He tells us to strike them—why do we not listen to his words? What do we fear? It is time. Do we fear that our brothers, the French, who are here among us will prevent us? They do not know our plans, and they could not hinder anyway, if they would. You all know as well as I that when the English came upon our lands to drive out our Father, Belestre,[3] they took away all the Frenchmen's guns and that they now have no arms to protect themselves with. Therefore, it is time for us to strike. If there are any French who side with them, let us strike them as well as the English. Remember what the Master of Life told our brother, the Wolf, to do. That concerns us all as well as others. I have sent wampum belts and messengers to our brothers, the Chippewas of Saginaw, and to our brothers, the Ottawas of Michillimackinac, and to those of the Thames River to join us. They will not be slow in coming, but while we wait let us strike anyway. There is no more time to lose. When the English are defeated we shall then see what there is left to do, and we shall stop up the ways hither so that they may never come again upon our lands."

The speech, which Pontiac delivered in such an energetic tone, produced its desired effect upon the members of the council, and they all swore with one accord the complete destruction of the English. …

from George III, The Royal Proclamation of 1763

Responding to the outbreak of Pontiac's War (see above), King George III issued the following Proclamation, which sets out rules for future land settlement in British North America. Pontiac's War had shown Britain

[1] *Takay* Chief of the people the French called the Huron, but who call themselves the Wendat or Wyandot people.

[2] *wampum belts* Belts of shell beads used by Indigenous peoples for numerous purposes, including sending messages, record-keeping, and trade.

[3] *Belestre* François Marie Picote, Sieur de Bellestre was the commander of Fort Detroit until he surrendered in the autumn of 1760.

that the Indigenous peoples would not accept the theft of their lands passively, and the Proclamation attempted to quell rebellion by asserting Indigenous rights and the legitimacy of Indigenous land titles, as well as by creating a land barrier between settler and Indigenous populations. All territory west of the Appalachians was deemed an Indigenous reserve, and any land purchased by settlers to the east had to be first bought by the Crown from the Indigenous people. Any European-settled land held in contradiction to these rules was required to be vacated immediately. These restrictions, as outlined in the Proclamation below, became a source of significant tension between settlers and the British authorities in the years leading up to the American Revolutionary War. As the British did not uphold the promises made to Indigenous peoples in this Proclamation, the document did little in the long run to secure their goodwill.

The Royal Proclamation of 1763.

And whereas it is just and reasonable, and ... essential to our interest, and the security of our colonies, that the several nations or tribes of Indians with whom we are connected, and who live under our protection, should not be molested or disturbed in the possession of such parts of our dominions and territories as, not having been ceded to or purchased by us, are reserved to them, or any of them, as their hunting grounds—We do therefore, with the advice of our Privy Council, declare it to be our royal will and pleasure, that no Governor or Commander in Chief in any of our colonies of Quebec, East Florida, or West Florida, do presume, upon any pretence whatever, to grant warrants of survey, or pass any patents for lands beyond the bounds of their respective governments, as described in their commissions: as also that no Governor or Commander in Chief in any of our other colonies or plantations in America do presume for the present, and until our further pleasure be known, to grant warrants of survey, or pass patents for any lands beyond the heads or sources of any of the rivers which fall into the Atlantic ocean from the West and North West, or upon any lands whatever, which, not having been ceded to or purchased by us as aforesaid, are reserved to the said Indians, or any of them.

And we do further declare it to be our royal will and pleasure, for the present as aforesaid, to reserve under our sovereignty, protection, and dominion, for the use of the said Indians, all the lands and territories not included within the limits of our said three new governments, or within the limits of the territory granted to the Hudson's Bay Company, as also all the lands and territories lying to the westward of the sources of the rivers which fall into the sea from the West and North West as aforesaid.

And we do hereby strictly forbid, on pain of our displeasure, all our loving subjects from making any purchases or settlements whatever, or taking possession of any of the lands above reserved, without our especial leave and licence for that purpose first obtained.

And we do further strictly enjoin and require all persons whatever who have either wilfully or inadvertently seated themselves upon any lands within the countries above described, or upon any other lands which, not having been ceded to or purchased by us,

are still reserved to the said Indians as aforesaid, forthwith to remove themselves from such settlements.

And whereas great frauds and abuses have been committed in purchasing lands of the Indians, to the great prejudice of our interests, and to the great dissatisfaction of the said Indians: In order, therefore, to prevent such irregularities for the future, and to the end that the Indians may be convinced of our justice and determined resolution to remove all reasonable cause of discontent, we do, with the advice of our Privy Council strictly enjoin and require, that no private person do presume to make any purchase from the said Indians of any lands reserved to the said Indians, within those parts of our colonies where we have thought proper to allow settlement: but that, if at any time any of the said Indians should be inclined to dispose of the said lands, the same shall be purchased only for us, in our name, at some public meeting or assembly of the said Indians, to be held for that purpose by the Governor or Commander in Chief of our colony respectively within which they shall lie: and in case they shall lie within the limits of any proprietary government, they shall be purchased only for the use and in the name of such proprietaries, conformable to such directions and instructions as we or they shall think proper to give for that purpose:

Given at our Court at St. James's the 7th Day of October 1763, in the third year of our reign.

GOD SAVE THE KING

The Revolutionary War

from George III, Speech to Parliament, 30 November 1774

> At the end of the year 1774, tensions between Britain and the American colonists were at a high pitch. Britain, with the intention of quelling rebellion in America in the wake of the Boston Tea Party, had passed the Coercive Acts (more widely known as the Intolerable Acts), which effectively placed Boston harbor under martial law. In response, the Continental Congress met in Philadelphia that September, and they drafted a list of grievances for the king; they also passed

> a resolution that, if the Intolerable Acts were not repealed by 1 December 1774, the colonies would begin to boycott British imports. The Acts were not repealed. George III delivered the following speech in the British Parliament the day before the colonial resolution was to take effect; the excerpts below include a response from the British House of Commons, underscoring Parliament's support for the king.

> As with all news in this period, word of this speech took some time to cross the Atlantic. The text of the full speech, together with relevant speeches made in Parliament, was printed as a broadside in Boston, 31 January 1775.

My Lords and Gentlemen,

It gives me much concern, that I am obliged, at the opening of this Parliament, to inform you, that a most daring spirit of resistance and disobedience to the law still unhappily prevails in the province of the Massachusetts Bay, and has in diverse[1] parts of it broke forth in fresh violences of a very criminal nature. These proceedings have been countenanced and encouraged in other of my colonies and unwarrantable attempts have been made to obstruct the commerce of this kingdom, by unlawful combinations. I have taken such measures, and given such orders, as I judged most proper and effectual for carrying into execution the laws which were passed in the last session of the late Parliament,[2] for the protection and security of the commerce of my subjects, and for the restoring and preserving peace, order, and good government, in the province of the Massachusetts Bay; and you may depend upon my firm and steadfast resolution to withstand every attempt to weaken or impair the supreme authority of this legislature over all the dominions of my Crown; the maintenance of which I consider as essential to the dignity, the safety, and the welfare, of the British empire; assuring myself, that, while I act upon these principles, I shall never fail to receive your assistance and support. ...

[1] *diverse* Several.

[2] *laws ... Parliament* I.e., the Intolerable Acts. See headnote, above.

from Response of the House of Commons,
8 December 1774

The House of Commons Address of Thanks to his Majesty, for his most gracious Speech from the Throne, is as follows:

Most gracious Sovereign,

We, your Majesty's most dutiful and loyal subjects, the Commons of Great Britain in Parliament assembled, return your Majesty our humble thanks for your most gracious speech from the throne.

Permit us to assure your Majesty, that we receive with the highest sense of your Majesty's goodness the early information which you have been pleased to give us, of the state of the province of the Massachusetts Bay.

We feel the most sincere concern, that a spirit of disobedience and resistance to the law should still unhappily prevail in that province, and that it has broke forth in fresh violences of a most criminal nature; and we cannot but lament that such proceedings should have been countenanced and encouraged in any other of your Majesty's colonies; and that any of your subjects should have been so far deluded and misled, as to make rash and unwarrantable attempts to obstruct the commerce of your Majesty's kingdoms by unlawful combinations.[1]

We beg leave to present our most dutiful thanks to your Majesty, for having taken such measures as your Majesty judged most proper and effectual, for carrying into execution the laws which were passed in the last session of the late Parliament, for the protection and security of the commerce of your Majesty's subjects, and for restoring and preserving peace, order, and good government, in the province of the Massachusetts Bay.

The Able Doctor, or America Swallowing the Bitter Draught, 1774. This political cartoon originally appeared in Britain in *London Magazine*. In it, Lord North, Britain's prime minister, is forcing the Intolerable Acts—pictured as tea—down the throat of a woman who, the caption tells us, is "America." The Intolerable Acts (officially known as the Coercive Acts) imposed taxes on the American colonies for tea and other goods, and placed Boston harbor under martial law.

[1] *combinations* Conspiracies.

Your faithful Commons, animated by your Majesty's gracious assurances, will use every means in their power to assist your Majesty in maintaining entire and inviolate the supreme authority of this legislature over all the dominions of your Crown; being truly sensible that we should betray the trust reposed in us, and be wanting in every duty which we owe to your Majesty and to our fellow subjects, if we failed to give our most zealous support to those great constitutional principles which govern your Majesty's conduct in this important business, and which is so essential to the dignity, safety, and welfare of the British empire. ...

We assure your Majesty, that we will, with the utmost cheerfulness, grant to your Majesty every necessary supply; and that we consider ourselves bound by gratitude, as well as duty, to give every proof of our most affectionate attachment to a prince,[1] who, during the whole course of his reign, has made the happiness of his people the object of all his views, and the rule of all his actions.

from William Wirt, *Sketches of the Life and Character of Patrick Henry* (1817)

Virginia lawyer Patrick Henry (later to become governor) first attracted notice for his impassioned resistance to the Stamp Act. He gained attention again as a delegate to the First Continental Congress in 1774, when he called for voting by the colonies to be tied to population, with each colony's delegates casting a number of votes proportionate to that colony's white population. No colony's votes should be weighted more heavily than others, argued Henry: "the distinction between Virginians, Pennsylvanians, New Yorkers, and New Englanders is no more. I am not a Virginian but an American."

Early 1775 brought word to the American colonies of the resolve of George III and the British government to take a firm stand against the "daring spirit of resistance and disobedience to the laws, which so strongly prevails in the province of the Massachusetts Bay" (see above). The Continental Congress had sent the

king a petition setting out its grievances; Britain had been increasing its military presence in the American colonies. In various states, conventions were held to discuss the next course of action; the Second Virginia Convention brought together 120 delegates (among them George Washington, Thomas Jefferson, and Patrick Henry).

Henry's famous "Give Me Liberty or Give Me Death" speech was delivered to the convention on March 23. No written text of the speech has survived; the only versions we have are based on the one reconstructed by biographer William Wirt over thirty years later, relying on the memories of those who had heard the speech. (Had any of them taken notes? Even that is unclear.) Notwithstanding the doubts over the accuracy of the version that has come down to us, Henry's speech has become a foundational text of American history and oratory; it remains interesting as an example not only of impassioned speech-making but also of martial argumentation—and the entire episode remains interesting for the light it sheds on differences of opinion in the Revolutionary era (differences of opinion not only between Virginia and Britain and among the Virginians themselves, but also between colonial Virginians and colonial Jamaicans).

Frontispiece, William Wirt, *Sketches of the Life and Character of Patrick Henry*, 1817.

[1] *prince* I.e., leader.

from Section 4

On Monday, the 20th of March, 1775, the convention of delegates from the several counties and corporations of Virginia, met for the second time. This assembly was held in the old church in the town of Richmond. Mr. Henry was a member of that body also. The reader will bear in mind the tone of the instructions given by the convention of the preceding year to their deputies in congress. He will remember, that while they recite with great feeling, the series of grievances under which the colonies had laboured, and insist with firmness on their constitutional rights, they give nevertheless, the most explicit and solemn pledge of their faith and true allegiance to his majesty King George the III and avow their determination to support him with their lives and fortunes, in the legal exercise of all his just rights and prerogatives. He will remember, that these instructions contain, also, an expression of their sincere approbation of a connection with Great Britain, and of their ardent wishes for a return of that friendly intercourse, from which this country had derived so much prosperity and happiness. These sentiments still influenced many of the leading members of the convention of 1775. They could not part with the fond hope, that those peaceful days would again return, which had shed so much light and warmth over the land; and the report of the king's gracious reception of the petition from Congress, tended to cherish and foster that hope, and to render them averse to any measure of violence. But Mr. Henry saw things with a steadier eye and a deeper insight. His judgment was too solid to be duped by appearances; and his heart too firm and manly to be amused by false and flattering hopes. He had long since read the true character of the British Court; and saw that no alternative remained for his country but abject submission or heroic resistance. It was not for a soul like Henry's to hesitate between these courses. He had offered upon the altar of liberty no divided heart. The gulf of war which yawned before him, was indeed fiery and fearful; but he saw that the awful plunge was inevitable. The body of the convention however, hesitated. They cast around "a longing lingering look"[1] on those flowery fields, on

which peace, and ease, and joy, were still sporting; and it required all the energies of a mentor like Henry, to push them from the precipice, and conduct them over the stormy sea of the revolution, to liberty and glory.

The convention being formed and organized for business, proceeded, in the first place, to express their unqualified approbation of the measures of Congress, and to declare, that they considered "this whole continent as under the highest obligations to that respectable body, for the wisdom of their counsels, and their unremitted endeavours to maintain and preserve inviolate the just rights and liberties of his majesty's dutiful and loyal subjects in America."

They next resolve, that "the warmest thanks of the convention, and of all the inhabitants of this colony, were due, and that this just tribute of applause be presented to the worthy delegates, deputed by a former convention, to represent this colony in general congress, for their cheerful undertaking and faithful discharge of the very important trust reposed in them."

The morning of the 23d March was opened, by reading a petition and memorial from the assembly of Jamaica[2] to the king's most excellent majesty: whereupon it was "resolved, that the unfeigned thanks and most grateful acknowledgments of the convention be presented to that very respectable assembly, for the exceeding generous and affectionate part they have so nobly taken, in the unhappy contest between Great Britain and her colonies; and for their truly patriotic endeavours to fix the just claims of the colonists upon the most permanent constitutional principles: that the assembly be assured, that it is the most ardent wish of this colony (and they were persuaded of the whole continent of North America) to see a speedy return of those halcyon days, when we lived a free and happy people."

These proceedings were not adapted to the taste of Mr. Henry; on the contrary, they were "gall and wormwood"[3] to him. The house required to be wrought

[1] *a longing lingering look* See Thomas Gray's "An Elegy Written in a Country Churchyard" (1751), line 81.

[2] *petition ... of Jamaica* Reference to *The Humble Petition and Memorial of the Assembly of Jamaica*, 28 December 1774. The Jamaican colonists petitioned the king to respect the constitutional rights of settlers throughout the empire, while simultaneously assuring the king of their own unwavering loyalty.

[3] *gall and wormwood* See Lamentations 3.19: "Remembering mine affliction and my misery, the wormwood and the gall"; *gall* Bile; *wormwood* Bitter herb.

up to a bolder tone. He rose, therefore, and moved the following manly resolutions:

"Resolved, That a well-regulated militia, composed of gentlemen and yeomen,[1] is the natural strength and only security of a free government; that such a militia in this colony, would forever render it unnecessary for the mother country to keep among us for the purpose of our defence, any standing army of mercenary soldiers, always subversive of the quiet, and dangerous to the liberties of the people, and would obviate the pretext of taxing us for their support.

"That the establishment of such a militia is, *at this time*, peculiarly necessary, by the state of our laws, for the protection and defence of the country, some of which are already expired, and others will shortly be so; and that the known remissness of government in calling us together in legislative capacity, renders it too insecure, in this time of danger and distress, to rely that opportunity will be given of renewing them, in general assembly, *or making any provision to secure our inestimable rights and liberties, from those further violations with which they are threatened.*

"Resolved, therefore, That this colony be immediately put into a state of defence, and that [there] be a committee to prepare a plan for embodying, arming, and disciplining such a number of men, as may be sufficient for that purpose."

The alarm which such a proposition must have given to those who had contemplated no resistance of a character more serious than petition, non-importation,[2] and passive fortitude, and who still hung with suppliant tenderness on the skirts of Britain, will be readily conceived by the reflecting reader. The shock was painful. It was almost general. The resolutions were opposed as not only rash in policy, but as harsh and well-nigh impious in point of feeling. Some of the warmest patriots of the convention opposed them. Richard Bland, Benjamin Harrison, and Edmund Pendleton, who had so lately drunk of the fountain of patriotism in the continental congress, and Robert C. Nicholas, one of the best as well as ablest men and patriots in the state, resisted them with all their influence and abilities.

They urged the late gracious reception of the Congressional petition[3] by the throne. They insisted that national comity, and much more filial respect, demanded the exercise of a more dignified patience. That the sympathies of the parent country were now on our side. That the friends of American liberty in parliament, were still with us, and had, as yet, had no cause to blush for our indiscretion. That the manufacturing interests of Great Britain, already smarting under the effects of our non-importation, co-operated powerfully towards our relief. That the sovereign himself had relented, and showed that he looked upon our sufferings with an eye of pity. "Was this a moment," they asked, "to disgust our friends, to extinguish all the conspiring sympathies which were working in our favour; to turn their friendship into hatred, their pity into revenge? And what was there, they asked, in the situation of the colony, to tempt us to this? Were we a great military people? Were we ready for war? Where were our stores—where were our arms—where our soldiers—where our generals—where our money, the sinews of war? They were nowhere to be found. In truth, we were poor—we were naked—we were defenceless. …

These arguments and topics of persuasion, were so well justified by the appearance of things, and were moreover so entirely in unison with that love of ease and quiet which is natural to man, and that disposition to hope for happier times, even under the most forbidding circumstances, that an ordinary man, in Mr. Henry's situation, would have been glad to compound with the displeasure of the house, by being permitted to withdraw his resolutions in silence.

Not so, Mr. Henry. His was a spirit fitted to raise the whirlwind, as well as to ride in it. His was that comprehensive view, that unerring prescience, that perfect command over the actions of men, which qualified him not merely to guide, but almost to create the destinies of nations.

[1] *yeomen* Respectable small landowners that nonetheless rank under gentlemen.

[2] *non-importation* I.e., a boycott of British goods.

[3] *Congressional petition* On 24 October 1774, the First Continental Congress sent a petition, written by John Dickinson, to George III protesting the Intolerable Acts. The petition asserted that the colonists would remain loyal if the Acts were repealed and other grievances were addressed.

He rose at this time with a majesty unusual to him in an exordium,[1] and with all that self-possession by which he was so invariably distinguished. "No man," he said, "thought more highly than he did, of the patriotism, as well as abilities, of the very worthy gentlemen who had just addressed the house. But different men often saw the same subject in different lights; and therefore, he hoped it would not be thought disrespectful to those gentlemen, if, entertaining as he did, opinions of a character very opposite to theirs, should speak forth his sentiments freely, and without reserve. This," he said, "was no time for ceremony. The question before the house was one of awful moment to this country. For his own part, he considered it as nothing less than a question of freedom or slavery. And in proportion to the magnitude of the subject, ought to be the freedom of the debate. It was only in this way that they could hope to arrive at truth, and fulfil the great responsibility which they held to God and their country. Should he keep back his opinions, at such a time, through fear of giving offence, he should consider himself as guilty of treason towards his country, and of an act of disloyalty toward the majesty of Heaven, which he revered above all earthly kings."

"Mr. President,"[2] said he, "it is natural to man to indulge in the illusions of hope. We are apt to shut our eyes against a painful truth—and listen to the song of that siren, till she transforms us into beasts.[3] Is it," he asked, "the part of wise men, engaged in a great and arduous struggle for liberty? Were we disposed to be of the number of those, who having eyes, see not, and having ears, hear not, the things which so nearly concern their temporal salvation? For his part, whatever anguish of spirit it might cost, he was willing to know the whole truth to know the worst, and to provide for it."

"He had," he said, "but one lamp by which his feet were guided: and that was the lamp of experience. He knew of no way of judging of the future, but by the past. And judging by the past, he wished to know what there had been in the conduct of the British ministry for the last ten years, to justify those hopes with which gentlemen had been pleased to solace themselves and the house? Is it that insidious smile with which our petition has been lately received? Trust it not, sir; it will prove a snare to your feet.[4] Suffer not yourselves to be betrayed with a kiss.[5] Ask yourselves how this gracious reception of our petition, comports with those warlike preparations which cover our waters and darken our land? Are fleets and armies necessary to a work of love and reconciliation? Have we shown ourselves so unwilling to be reconciled, that force must be called in to win back our love? Let us not deceive ourselves, sir. These are the implements of war and subjugation—the last arguments to which kings resort. I ask gentlemen, sir, what means this martial array, if its purpose be not to force us to submission? Can gentlemen assign any other possible motive for it? Has Great Britain any enemy in this quarter of the world, to call for all this accumulation of navies and armies? No, sir: she has none. They are meant for us: they can be meant for no other. They are sent over to bind and rivet upon us those chains, which the British ministry have been so long forging. And what have we to oppose to them? Shall we try argument? Sir, we have been trying that for the last ten years. Have we anything new to offer upon the subject? Nothing. We have held the subject up in every light of which it is capable; but it has been all in vain. Shall we resort to entreaty and humble supplication? What terms shall we find, which have not been already exhausted? Let us not, I beseech you, sir, deceive ourselves longer. Sir, we have done everything that could be done, to avert the storm which is now coming on. We have petitioned—we have remonstrated—we have supplicated—we have prostrated ourselves before the throne, and have implored its interposition to arrest the tyrannical hands of the ministry and parliament. Our petitions have been slighted; our remonstrances have produced additional violence and insult; our supplications have been disregarded; and we have been spurned, with contempt, from the foot of the throne.

1 *exordium* The beginning of a speech.

2 *Mr. President* The presiding officer of the First Congressional Congress, Peyton Randolph (1721–75).

3 *siren ... beasts* This is a conflation of two of the many dangers that Odysseus uses his wits to escape in Homer's *Odyssey*: the Sirens are creatures whose song can enchant sailors to their deaths by shipwreck, and Circe is a sorceress who turns men into beasts.

4 *snare ... feet* See Job 18.8: "For he is cast into a net by his own feet, and he walketh upon a snare."

5 *betrayed with a kiss* Judas marks his betrayal of Christ with a kiss. See Matthew 26.47–49.

In vain, after these things, may we indulge the fond hope of peace and reconciliation. There is no longer any room for hope. If we wish to be free—if we mean to preserve inviolate those inestimable privileges for which we have been so long contending—if we mean not basely to abandon the noble struggle in which we have been so long engaged, and which we have pledged ourselves never to abandon, until the glorious object of our contest shall be obtained—we must fight!—I repeat it, sir; we must fight!! An appeal to arms and to the God of Hosts, is all that is left us!"[1]

"They tell us, sir," continued Mr. Henry, "that we are weak—unable to cope with so formidable an adversary. But when shall we be stronger? Will it be the next week, or the next year? Will it be when we are totally disarmed; and when a British guard shall be stationed in every house? Shall we gather strength by irresolution and inaction? Shall we acquire the means of effectual resistance, by lying supinely on our back, and hugging the delusive phantom of hope, until our enemies shall have bound us, hand and foot? Sir, we are not weak, if we make a proper use of those means which the God of nature hath placed in our power. Three millions of people, armed in the holy cause of liberty, and in such a country as that which we possess, are invincible by any force which our enemy can send against us. Besides, sir, we shall not fight our battles alone. There is a just God who presides over the destinies of nations; and who will raise up friends to fight our battles for us. The battle, sir, is not to the strong alone; it is to the vigilant, the active, the brave. Besides, sir, we have no election.[2] If we were base enough to desire it, it is now too late to retire from the contest. There is no retreat, but in submission and slavery! Our chains are forged. Their clanking may be heard on the plains of Boston! The war is inevitable—and let it come!! I repeat it, sir; let it come!!!

"It is in vain, sir, to extenuate the matter. Gentlemen may cry, peace, peace—but there is no peace. The war is actually begun! The next gale that sweeps from the north, will bring to our ears the clash of resounding arms! Our brethren are already in the field! Why stand we here idle? What is it that gentlemen wish? What would they have? Is life so dear; or peace so sweet, as to be purchased at the price of chains, and slavery? Forbid it, Almighty God!—I know not what course others may take; but as for me," cried he, with both his arms extended aloft, his brows knit, every feature marked with the resolute purpose of his soul, and his voice swelled to its boldest note of exclamation—"give me liberty, or give me death!"

He took his seat. No murmur of applause was heard. The effect was too deep. After the trance of a moment, several members started from their seats. The cry, "to arms," seemed to quiver on every lip, and gleam from every eye! Richard H. Lee[3] arose and supported Mr. Henry, with his usual spirit and elegance. But his melody was lost amidst the agitations of that ocean, which the master spirit of the storm had lifted up on high. That supernatural voice still sounded in their ears, and shivered along their arteries. They heard, in every pause, the cry of liberty or death. They became impatient of speech—their souls were on fire for action. ...

[1] [Wirt's note] "Imagine to yourself," says my correspondent, (judge Tucker), "this sentence delivered with all the calm dignity of Cato, of Utica; imagine to yourself the Roman senate, assembled in the capitol, when it was entered by the profane Gauls, who, at first, were awed by their presence, as if they had entered an assembly of the gods! Imagine that you heard that Cato addressing such a senate—imagine that you saw the hand-writing on the wall of Belshazzar's palace—imagine you heard a voice as from heaven uttering the words, 'We must fight,' as the doom of fate, and you may have some idea of the speaker, the assembly to whom he addressed himself, and the auditory, of which I was one." [*Cato* Cato the Younger (95–46 BCE) was a Roman senator famous for his integrity; he died by suicide rather than accept Julius Caesar's dictatorship; *hand-writing … Belshazzar* In Daniel 5, a disembodied hand writes King Belshazzar's fate on the wall; no astrologer or fortuneteller in the land could decipher it, but the prophet Daniel is called, and he tells Belshazzar that his ungodly ways have been weighed in the balance and found wanting, and that his kingdom will fall.]

[2] *election* Choice.

[3] *Richard H. Lee* Politician from Virginia, best known for the Lee Resolution of 1776, which called for American independence from Great Britain.

Benjamin Franklin, "What Would Satisfy the Americans?" (1775); "Join, or Die" (1754)

Benjamin Franklin played an important role over several decades in the events that led to the formation of the American republic. One early contribution was his publication of the "Join, or Die" image in the 9 May 1754 issue of his *Pennsylvania Gazette*. It is the earliest extant image depicting the concept of the unification of the British colonies of eastern North America, but it was not conceived of with a view to the unification of the colonies as an independent nation. The intent was rather to encourage the formation of a united front against the French and the Indigenous peoples who were allied to them. The French, in Franklin's view (as he put it in the editorial accompanying the drawing), intended to "establish themselves, settle their Indians, … kill, seize, and imprison our traders … , murder and scalp our farmers, with their wives and children, and take an easy possession of such parts of British territory as they find most convenient for them." The image was later repurposed by others in a variety of ways. During the 1765 Stamp Act controversy it was used as part of an effort to unify the colonies against the imposition by Britain of what were seen to be unfair taxes, and it was repurposed again during the American Revolution, when Paul Revere and others used the image as a way of visualizing the imperative for uniting in the effort to win independence.

Franklin continued to participate in American affairs of the utmost gravity until a few years before his death (see his author entry elsewhere in this volume), but he was always capable of a light-hearted take on even the most serious of circumstances—as the anecdote below from 1775 illustrates. (At the time Franklin was nearing the end of the almost two decades he spent in London.)

"WHAT WOULD SATISFY THE AMERICANS?"

Doctor Franklin, being in England in the Year 1775 was asked by a Nobleman, what would satisfy the Americans? Answered, That it might easily be comprised in a few Re's

Which he immediately wrote on a piece of Paper Thus,

Re {
call your Forces,
store Castle William,
pair the Damage done to Boston,
peal your unconstitutional Acts,
nounce your pretentions to Tax us,
fund the duties you have extorted; after this
quire, and
ceive payment for the destroyed Tea,[1] with the voluntary grants of the Colonies, And then
joice in a happy
conciliation.

"JOIN, OR DIE"

[1] *destroyed Tea* During the Boston Tea Party uprising against the British imposition of the Tea Tax, the American colonists threw 92,000 pounds of tea belonging to the East India Company into Boston harbor.

In 1782, twenty-one-year-old Deborah Sampson joined the 4th Massachusetts Regiment under the name Robert Shurtliff. Sampson fought under this disguise in a number of skirmishes over the course of seventeen months, and was promoted to the status of an orderly before an injury led to the discovery of her biological sex and she was honorably discharged. Though Sampson is far from the only "female soldier" known to have fought for the Continental Army, her story reached a wider audience than most, and eventually became the basis for Herman Mann's (heavily embellished) 1797 biography *The Female Review*, which he wrote based on interviews he had conducted with Sampson. While some readers balked at Sampson's rejection of traditional gender roles, most found reason to praise the patriotic sentiment that had prompted this course of action. The portrait reproduced here was painted from life in 1797 by Joseph Stone, and likely commissioned by Mann; a version of the portrait was used as the frontispiece to *The Female Review*. Substantial excerpts from that work are included in the author entry for Mann/Sampson in the website component of this anthology.

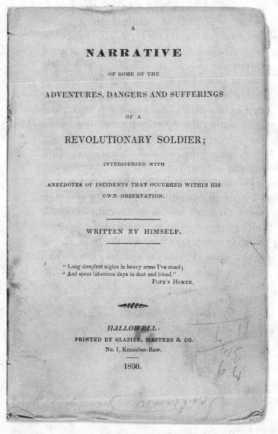

Title page, Joseph Plumb Martin, *A Narrative of Some of the Adventures, Dangers, and Sufferings of a Revolutionary Soldier; Interspersed with Anecdotes of Incidents that Occurred within His Own Observation*, 1830. Though not published until several decades after the war, the narrative by Joseph Plumb Martin (1760–1850) of his years as a soldier is arguably the best record we have of the experience of ordinary soldiers during the Revolutionary War. With a wealth of anecdotes, Martin (who was an enlisted soldier from 1776 to 1783) provides a vivid sense of the hardships endured by enlisted men, and of the poor treatment they received not only during the course of the war but also after it was over. Substantial excerpts from his narrative are included in the website component of this anthology.

Poems and Songs

During the Revolutionary War and the decades preceding it, patriotic songs and poems flourished in American oral and print culture. These popular tunes were important propaganda tools for stirring the emotions—both on the revolutionaries' side and among those who supported the British. As one Revolutionary army chaplain put it at the beginning of the war, "One good song is worth a dozen addresses or proclamations."

anonymous ("A Son of Liberty"), "A New Song, Addressed to the Sons of Liberty, on the Continent of America; Particularly to the Illustrious, Glorious and Never to Be Forgotten Ninety-two of Boston," *The Pennsylvania Journal*, 1768

Before war broke out between the American colonists and the British, resistance to British colonial administration was coordinated by various branches of an underground organization known as the Sons of Liberty, a largely working-class political group whose mission was to resist taxation and to promote the rights and freedoms of the American colonists, particularly the rights of the laboring classes. In 1765 the group strongly resisted the Stamp Act, a tax imposed on the American colonies by Britain to help pay for the British troops stationed in the colonies. The British repealed the act on 18 March 1766, but new taxes were imposed with the Townshend Acts in 1767–68, which levied fees on a range of goods, including tea, china, lead, paper, and paint. Samuel Adams, thought to be the leader of the Sons of Liberty, wrote a letter in 1768 calling for a concerted resistance to the Townshend Acts. The letter was approved by the General Court of Massachusetts, which then circulated it throughout the colonies. The British authorities demanded the letter be rescinded, but the Massachusetts assemblymen—the "glorious ninety-two"—refused. A popular toast in Boston at the time was to "the glorious ninety-two, who defended the Rights of America, uninfluenced by the Mandates of

a minister, and undaunted by the Threats of a Governor."

The Sons of Liberty continued their political actions through to the beginning of the Revolutionary War; their most famous protest was the Boston Tea Party in 1773.

"The Americans are the Sons, not the Bastards of England; the Commons of America, represented in their several assemblies, have ever been in possession of the exercise of this their Constitutional Right, of giving and granting their own money; they would have been slaves, if they had not enjoyed it."—Mr. Pitt's speech[1]

Tune—"Come Jolly Bacchus" or "Glorious First of August"

Come jolly sons of liberty—
Come all with hearts united,
Our motto is "We Dare to be Free"
Not easily affrighted!
5 Oppression's band we must subdue,
Now is the time, or never;
Let each man prove this motto true.
And slavery from him sever.

Pale visag'd° fear, let none possess! faced
10 Or terrors e'er perplex him,
Posterity will ever bless,
And nought hereafter vex him;
To freedom's banner, let's repair;° return
When e're we see occasion—
15 Nor wives nor children, tho' most dear,
E're stop to look, or gaze on.

In freedom's cause, the slavish knave,° villain
'Twere better his condition,
(That might his country's ruin save!)
20 To sink into perdition;
Chain'd to a galley, groan his days,
And never be forgotten,

[1] *Mr. Pitt's speech* This quotation is drawn from British politician William Pitt's speech on the Stamp Act, which he delivered to the British Parliament in January 1766. Pitt was a consistent advocate for a more conciliatory approach toward the American colonies.

While furies[1] croak his bondage lays,[2]
After he's dead and rotten.

25 Once should this precedent take place!
Tell, what you call your own sir!
Magna Charta[3] in disgrace!
Your substance now, all flown sir!
No more shall peers now try your cause![4]
30 That time is now all over!
What need have we pray now of laws?
Now right is wrong in Trover![5]

See liberty high poised in air,
Her free born sons commanding,
35 Come on, my sons, without all fear;
Your nat'ral rights demanding!
Your cause, the Gods proclaim, is just,
Can tamely, you, be fetter'd?
In which, disturb your Fathers dust!
40 With S, be ever letter'd![6]

Obey, my brothers, nature's call,
Your country too demands it!
Let liberty ne'er have a fall!
'Tis freedom that commands it.
45 The ax, now to the root is laid.
Will you be, or bond or free?
No time to pause—then "Whose afraid?"
Live, or die in liberty!

1 *furies* In Greek mythology, creatures that pursue the guilty and exact retribution.

2 *bondage lays* Songs of slavery.

3 *Magna Charta* The Magna Carta, the charter of rights granted to the English nobles by King John in 1215, widely revered in the United States as well as in Britain as one of the documents that provided the basis for individual rights, popular sovereignty, and constitutional government.

4 *peers … cause* Clause 39 of the Magna Carta outlines, among other rights, the right to trial by one's peers (a trial by jury): "No free man shall be captured, and or imprisoned, or disseized of his freehold, and or of his liberties, or of his free customs, or be outlawed, or exiled, or in any way destroyed, nor will we proceed against him by force or proceed against him by arms, but by the lawful judgment of his peers, and or by the law of the land" (1852 translation from the Latin by Lysander Spooner).

5 *Trover* Type of lawsuit used for the recovery of damages when property is illegally taken.

6 *S … letter'd* Be marked by the letter "S," standing for "slave."

Attributed to Philip Dawe, *The Bostonians Paying the Excise-man, or Tarring and Feathering*, 1774. This image shows five Patriots tarring, feathering, and forcing tea down the throat of John Malcolm, a Loyalist and the Commissioner of Customs, who was in charge of collecting the taxes imposed by the British. In the background, the Boston Tea Party is taking place, an event which in fact occurred a month earlier than the tarring and feathering of John Malcolm on 5 January 1774.

anonymous ("A Young Woman of Virginia"), "Virginia Banishing Tea" (1774)

In protest against various British tax measures, and against the Tea Act (which granted a monopoly on tea sales in the colonies to the British East India Company, thereby making illegal the sale of the less expensive teas imported from other sources, which the colonists had grown accustomed to drinking), colonists were

encouraged to boycott tea and to consume locally made herbal teas instead. In Virginia, more active measures were also taken, including the Yorktown Tea Party on 1 November 1774, in which two half-chests of tea were thrown overboard. Although far less tea was destroyed than in the Boston Tea Party, the Yorktown protest convinced many merchants in Virginia to sign on to the Continental Association, which had been formed for the express purpose of boycotting British goods. The following poem was written by an anonymous young woman, about whom nothing is known except that she was "a native of Virginia, endowed with all the graces of a cultivated mind, pleasant external qualities, and a model of patriotism worthy the emulation of many more conspicuous."

Begone, pernicious baneful tea,
 With all Pandora's ills,[1] possessed;
Hyson,[2] no more beguiled by thee,
 My noble sons shall be oppressed.

5 To Britain fly; where gold enslaves
 And venal men their birth-right sell:
Tell North[3] and his bribed clan of knaves
 Their bloody acts were made in hell.

In Henry's reign those acts began,[4]
10 Which sacred rules of justice broke;
North now pursues the hellish plan,
 To fix on us his slavish yoke.

But we oppose, and will be free,
15 This great good cause we will defend;

Nor bribe, nor Gage,[5] nor North's decree,
 Shall make us "at his feet to bend."[6]

From Anglia's[7] ancient sons we came,
 Those heroes who for freedom fought;
20 In Freedom's cause we'll match their fame,
 By their example greatly taught.

Our king we love, but North we hate,[8]
 Nor will to him submission own;
If death's our doom, we'll brave our fate,
25 But pay allegiance to the throne.

Then rouse, my sons; from slavery; free
 Your suffering homes from God's high wrath!
Gird on your steel:[9] give liberty
 To all who follow in our path!

from Lemuel Haynes, "The Battle of Lexington" (1775)

Lemuel Haynes (1753–1833) was a black writer, clergyman, and poet. Abandoned shortly after birth, he grew up as an indentured servant in the Rose family in Connecticut, where he was encouraged to pursue an independent course of reading and religious study. He became a minuteman in 1774 and fought in the early battles of the American Revolution. After the war, he studied theology and Classics with Congregationalist clergymen in Connecticut, becoming a minister himself in 1785. He wrote significant works on abolition, including "Liberty Further Extended" (1776) and *The Nature and Importance of True Republicanism* (1801). The following patriotic

1 *Pandora's ills* In Greek mythology, Pandora is given a box containing all the sorrows of mortality and is told not to open it, but her curiosity gets the better of her; she opens the box, and the sorrows are unleashed on the world.

2 *Hyson* Brand of green tea.

3 *North* Frederick North, 2nd Earl of Guilford, better known as Lord North, who served as Britain's prime minister from 1770 to 1782.

4 *Henry's reign … began* King Henry VIII (r. 1509–47) made increased use of the Star Chamber, a court that came to be considered an oppressive tool used to override Parliament and enforce the king's proclamations.

5 *Gage* General Thomas Gage served as commander-in-chief of the British forces in North America from 1763 to 1775.

6 *at his feet to bend* Phrase from "To His Excellency Governor Belcher, on the Death of His Lady," a poem by the American poet Mather Byles (1706–88); Byles was a firm Royalist.

7 *Anglia* Latin name for England.

8 *king … hate* Power to impose taxation in Britain lay with Parliament—of which Lord North was the leader—not with the king.

9 *Gird … steel* Buckle on your swords.

ballad commemorates the first battles of the Revolutionary War in Lexington and Concord, which took place on 19 April 1775. (See also the Lemuel Haynes author entry elsewhere in this volume.)

A poem on the inhuman tragedy perpetrated on the 19th of April 1775 by a number of the British troops under the command of Thomas Gage,[1] which parricides and ravages are shocking displays of ministerial & tyrannic vengeance composed by Lemuel a young mulatto[2] who obtained what little knowledge he possesses, by his own application to letters.

…

The nineteenth day of April last
We ever shall retain
As monumental of the past
most bloody shocking scene

5 Then tyrants filled with horrid rage
A fatal journey went
& unmolested to engage
And slay the innocent …

At Lexington they did appear
10 Arrayed in hostile form
And though our friends were peaceful there
Yet on them fell the storm

Eight most unhappy victims fell
Into the arms of death
15 unpitied by those tribes of hell
who cursed them with their breath

The savage band still march along
For Concord they were bound
while oaths & curses from their tongue
20 Accent with hellish sound

To prosecute their fell° desire villainous
At Concord they unite

Two sons of freedom there expire
By their tyrannic spite
25 Thus did our friends endure their rage
without a murm'ring word
Till die they must or else engage
and join with one accord

Such pity did their breath inspire
30 That long they bore the rod[3]
And with reluctance they conspire
to shed the human blood

But pity could no longer sway
Tho' 't is a pow'rful band
35 For liberty now bleeding lay
And called them to withstand

The awful conflict now begun
To rage with furious pride
And blood in great effusion run
40 From many a wounded side

For liberty, each freedman strives
As it's a gift of God
And for it willing yield their lives
And seal it with their blood

45 Thrice happy they who thus resign
Into the peaceful grave
Much better there, in death confined
Than a surviving slave …

Although our numbers were but few
50 And they a num'rous throng
Yet we their armies do pursue
And drive their hosts along

One son of freedom could annoy
A thousand tyrant fiends
55 And their despotic tribe destroy
And chase them to their dens

Thus did the sons of Britain's king
Receive a sore disgrace

[1] *Thomas Gage* General Thomas Gage served as commander-in-chief of the British forces in North America from 1763 to 1775.

[2] *mulatto* Term, now considered offensive, for a person of both black and white ancestry.

[3] *bore the rod* Endured the burden of tyranny.

Whilst sons of freedom join to sing
60 The vict'ry they embrace

Oh! Britain how art thou become
Infamous in our eye
Nearly allied to ancient Rome
That seat of popery[1]

65 Our fathers, though a feeble band
Did leave their native place
Exiled to a desert land
This howling wilderness

A num'rous train of savage brood
70 Did then attack them round
But still they trusted in their God
Who did their foes confound

Our fathers' blood did freely flow
To buy our freedom here
75 Nor will we let our freedom go
The price was much too dear ...

Ruth Bryant, "The American Maid's Choice: An Extempore" (1776)

The following poem is drawn from Ruth Bryant's manuscript booklet from the Revolutionary era, which was brought to light in 2010 by historian Rachel Hope Cleves. Bryant (1760–83), who was just fifteen when she composed the earliest of the poems, was the daughter of middle-class parents in North Bridgewater, Massachusetts (her parents kept a small farm, and her father was also a doctor). She had seven siblings, four of whom are known to have also written poetry; William Cullen Bryant, the well-known nineteenth-century poet and abolitionist, was the son of Ruth's brother Peter. As Cleves has written, the poems are interesting both in themselves and in demonstrating that "being banned from fighting" did not prevent young women such as Bryant from "vicarious involvement in the war."

A second poem from the booklet appears in the website component of this anthology. The manuscript booklet was transcribed by Cleves for her article "'Heedless Youth': The Revolutionary War Poetry of Ruth Bryant" (2010).

Better is he that ruleth his spirit than He that taketh a city—Solomon[2]—

I choose the gallant warrior brave
Who ne'er will yield to be a slave;
5 Good government he will maintain
But nobly spurns the galling chain.

His steady spirit's always free
From each fell passion's tyranny;
He wields his sword with martial skill
10 And lays internal rebels still.

Then fortifies on every side,
Nor fears the force of wind and tide;
He keeps his guards and sentries out
And puts insulting foes to rout.

15 He to his country turns his views;
The meanest place he'll not refuse
If so he can advance the cause,
And keep the God of Nature's laws.

True courage doth his mind inspire,
20 Tempered with virtue's heavenly fire;
He burns within with ardent zeal—
Not vainly blazes—for our weal.° well-being

Convinced that justice prompts our wars,
He boldly seeks the field of Mars;[3]
25 Calm and serene he meets the foe,
Resolved to give, or take the blow.
He is determined to be free,
He'll risk his life for liberty,

1 *popery* A pejorative term for Roman Catholicism.

2 *Better is he ... Solomon* See Proverbs 16.32 (traditionally considered to be written by the prophet King Solomon): "He that is slow to anger is better than the mighty; and he that ruleth his spirit than he that taketh a city."

3 *Mars* In Roman mythology, the god of war.

Of moral worth and mind serene,
30 Polite, and of engaging mien.° manner

This noble patriot I admire
Who glows with such heroic fire;
This is the man that I approve
If he and I agree in love.

Hannah Griffitts, "Upon Reading a Book Entitled *Common Sense*" (1776)

Writing poems under the name "Fidelia," meaning "Faithful," Quaker poet Hannah Griffitts (1727–1817) composed over sixty poems that she circulated among her friends and family (many of whom were supportive of the American colonists' struggle against the British). As a Quaker pacifist, however, Griffitts could not support the war. She viewed the writer Thomas Paine, who supported revolution in his pamphlet *Common Sense* (1775–76), as incendiary, and wished that more moderate voices would prevail and find a peaceful solution to the conflict.

The vizard° dropped, see subtlety prevail, mask
Thro' ev'ry page of this fallacious tale,
Sylvania° let it not unanswered pass, Pennsylvania
But heed the well guess'd snake beneath the grass,[1]
5 A deeper wound at freedom ne'er was made,
Then by this Oliverian[2] is displayed.
Orders confounded—Dignities thrown down,
Charters degraded equal with the Crown,
The impartial press, most partially maintained
10 Freedom infringed & conscience is restrained,
The moderate man is held to public view,
"The friend of tyranny & foe to you,"
Denied the common right to represent
Forbid to give his reasons for dissent,

[1] *snake … grass* Common saying that can be traced back to the Roman poet Virgil's (70–19 BCE) *Eclogues*; the idea is that beneath a fair exterior something dangerous lurks.

[2] *Oliverian* Similar to Oliver Cromwell, the British politician who led the parliamentary revolt against King Charles I and ruled England as Lord Protector from 1653 to 1658. Cromwell persecuted Catholics and any Protestant sect that he didn't approve of, including Quakers (which is why Griffitts, in particular, would view him as a tyrant).

15 Whilst base informers (owned° a acknowledged
 public pest)
Are round the land encouraged & caressed
Our representatives the people's choice
Are held contemptuous by this daring voice.
Persons are seized & posts monopolized
20 And all our form of government despised
Then from this "specimen of rule" beware,
Behold the serpent & avoid his snare.
'Tis not in names, our present danger lies
Sixty as well as one can tyrannize,
25 Ah! then awake Sylvania & beware,
The fatal danger of this subtle snare,
Hold fast your own, your charter'd rights maintain
Nor let them weave the snare into the chain,
And whilst firm union stands° the British withstands
 foes,
30 Let not the native hand your date of freedom close.

Joseph Stansbury

Joseph Stansbury (1742–1809) moved to Philadelphia from England in 1767 and opened a china shop; he also built a reputation for his satirical poems and songs. Stansbury sympathized with the Americans but opposed the colonies' separation from England. His Loyalist position led to a brief imprisonment in 1776; he managed to stay in Philadelphia until 1780, but in that year he was arrested for treason on account of his political leanings. Upon his release he moved frequently—to Nova Scotia, to England, and back to Philadelphia, before eventually settling in New York City. Stansbury's poems reveal the dismay that a good many Americans felt at the prospect of armed rebellion against "the mother country."

"VERSES TO THE TORIES"[3] (C. 1776)

Come, ye brave, by fortune wounded
More than by the vaunting foe,
Cheer your hearts, ne'er be confounded;
Trials all must undergo.
5 Though without rhyme or reason

[3] *TORIES* American colonists loyal to Britain.

Hurried back through wilds unknown,
Virtue's smiles can make a prison
Far more charming than a throne.
Think not, though wretched, poor, or naked,
10 Your breast alone the load sustains:
Sympathizing hearts partake it—
Britain's monarch shares your pains.
This night of pride and folly over,
A dawn of hope will soon appear.
15 In its light you shall discover
Your triumphant day is near.

"The United States"[1] (c. 1783)

Now this war at length is o'er;
 Let us think of it no more.
Every party[2] lie or name,
Cancel as our mutual shame.
5 Bid each wound of faction[3] close,
Blushing we were ever foes.

Now restored to peace again,
Active commerce ploughs the main;° *sea*
All the arts of civil life
10 Swift succeed to martial strife;
Britain now allows their claim,
Rising empire, wealth, and fame.

Francis Hopkinson, "A Camp Ballad"[4] (1778)

American politician, judge, composer, designer,
and writer Francis Hopkinson (1737–91) was
widely known for his poems, songs, and satires,
which were considered vital contributions to
the patriotic literature of the day. Hopkinson
was born into Pennsylvania's cultured political
class, and after studying law took up various
posts, moving eventually to New Jersey, where
he became a representative in the Continental
Congress of 1776. A firm supporter of the
Revolution and signee of the Declaration of
Independence, Hopkinson continued serv-
ing as a judge and, by the 1880s, had secured
a reputation as one of the early republic's most
prominent literary figures.

Make room, oh! ye kingdoms in hist'ry renowned
 Whose arms have in battle with glory been
 crowned,
Make room for America, another great nation,
Arises to claim in your council a station.

5 Her sons fought for freedom, and by their own brav'ry
Have rescued themselves from the shackles of slav'ry.
America's free, and though Britain abhorred it,
Yet fame a new volume prepares to record it.

Fair freedom in Briton her throne had erected,
10 But her sons growing venal,° and she *corrupt*
 disrespected;
The goddess offended forsook the base nation,
And fixed on our mountains a more honoured
 station.

With glory immortal she here sits enthroned,
Nor fears the vain vengeance of Britain disowned,
15 Whilst Washington guards her with heroes surrounded,
Her foes shall with shameful defeat be confounded.

To arms then, to arms, 'tis fair freedom invites us;
The trumpet shrill sounding to battle excites us;
The banners of virtue unfurled,[5] shall wave o'er us,
20 Our hero lead on, and the foe fly before us.

[1] In his 1860 collection, *The Loyal Verses of Joseph Stansbury and
Doctor Jonathan Odell*, Winthrop Sargent comments: "These lines,
by Mr. Stansbury, are written on the back of his God Save the King
[England's national anthem]. Their date is probably about that of the
recognition by England of our [American] independence."

[2] *party* A group on one side of a conflict.

[3] *faction* Division.

[4] *A Camp Ballad* During the winter of 1777–78, George Wash-
ington set up camp with the Continental Army at Valley Forge,
Pennsylvania. While at this camp and despite its harsh conditions,
the army recovered from a series of defeats and engaged in military
training that resulted in the Continental Army becoming a far more
powerful force capable of defeating the British.

[5] *banners ... unfurled* Hopkinson was a member of the commit-
tee in charge of creating a design for the flag of the United States
in 1776; in 1777, the committee adopted the Stars and Stripes.
Hopkinson is credited as the designer of this flag, as well as of the
flag for the U.S. Navy.

On Heav'n and Washington placing reliance,
We'll meet the bold Briton, and bid him defiance:
Our cause we'll support, for 'tis just and 'tis glorious
When men fight for freedom they must be victorious.

Jonathan Odell, "The Old Year and the New: A Prophecy" (1779)

> Loyalist poet and minister Jonathan Odell (1737–1818) became well-known for his poetry in support of the British monarchy and in opposition to the Revolution. He came before the New Jersey Provincial Congress on account of his Loyalist writing, where he was forced to swear loyalty to America; he soon left for New York to continue his Loyalist work. After the war, Odell left the United States for New Brunswick, then part of the British colony of Nova Scotia.
>
> So convinced was Odell in 1779 that the British would finally subdue the American rebellion that he wrote the following optimistic song to ring in the New Year of 1780. Moses Colt Tyler first ascribed authorship of this poem to Odell in 1897, and it has since generally been accepted to be his work.

What though last year he past and gone,
 Why should we grieve or mourn about it?
As good a year is now begun,
And better too—let no one doubt it.

5 'Tis New Year's morn; why should we part?
 Why not enjoy what heaven has sent us?
 Let wine expand the social heart,
 Let friends, and mirth, and wine content us.

War's rude alarms disturbed last year;
10 Our country bled and wept around us;
 But this each honest heart shall cheer,
 And peace and plenty shall surround us.

Last year "King Congo,"[1] through the land,

Displayed his thirteen stripes[2] to fright us;
15 But George's[3] power, in Clinton's[4] hand,
 In this New Year shall surely right us.

Last year saw many honest men
 Torn from each dear and sweet connection;
 But this° shall see them home again, *this year*
20 And happy in their king's protection.

Last year vain Frenchmen braved our coasts,
 And baffled Howe,[5] and 'scaped from Byron;[6]
 But this shall bring their vanquished hosts
 To crouch beneath the British lion.

25 Last year rebellion proudly stood,
 Elate, in her meridian glory;
 But this shall quench her pride in blood—
 George shall avenge each martyred Tory.[7]

Then bring us wine, full bumpers° bring; *glasses*
30 Hail this New Year in joyful chorus;
 God bless great George our gracious king,
 And crush rebellion down before us!

 'Tis New Year's morn; why should we part?
 Why not enjoy what heaven has sent us?
35 Let wine expand the social heart,
 Let friends, and mirth, and wine content us.

of central Africa that now bears its name but rather to the black Chinese tea known as Congou or, more commonly, Congo, which was among the most popular varieties of tea at the time; the epithet is thus in all probability a reference to the Americans' determination to retain control of their tea supply.

[2] *thirteen stripes* American flag; the thirteen stripes represent the thirteen colonies.

[3] *George* King George III of Great Britain and Ireland (r. 1760–1820).

[4] *Clinton* General Sir Henry Clinton served from 1778 to 1782 as the British army's commander-in-chief in North America.

[5] *Howe* William Howe served as commander-in-chief of the British land forces in North America from 1775 to 1778.

[6] *Byron* John Byron, also known as "Foul-Weather Jack," served as a vice-admiral in the British Navy. He unsuccessfully attacked a French fleet in July 1779.

[7] *Tory* American loyal to Britain.

[1] *King Congo* Dismissive term for the American Continental Congress. In late eighteenth-century America (as in Britain), the word "Congo" was generally understood to refer not to the region

Margaretta Faugères, "A Salute to the Fourteenth Anniversary of American Independence" (1791)

Daughter of poet Ann Eliza Bleecker, Margaretta Faugères (1771–1801) was born into a privileged New York family. Her life was deeply affected by her mother's early death and depression (Bleecker suffered from a series of bereavements that took place during the turmoil of the revolution). Early in life, Faugères showed poetic talent, and she also dedicated herself to radical politics: she was a committed abolitionist and a supporter of the aims of the American and French Revolutions; she criticized Thomas Jefferson for his claims regarding the supposed inferiority of black people, and she supported the abolition of capital punishment. In 1792 she married Peter Faugères, who treated her cruelly; her sufferings in the marriage contributed to her weak health and early death at the age of thirty.

In 1793, Faugères collected her mother's unpublished poems and stories and released them in a book entitled *The Posthumous Works of Ann Eliza Bleecker, in Prose and Verse* (1793). The book included not only her mother's work, but also a selection of her own, including the poem below.

A ll hail to thy return,
O! ever blest auspicious morn,
By mercy's author[1] giv'n:
See! to greet the happy day
5 Sol° expands his brightest ray, *the sun*
And not a cloud obscures his way,
Nor shades the face of heav'n.
More sweet *this* day, the cannons martial roar,
Than all the dulcet° sounds which music's *sweet*
 soul can pour;
10 For ev'ry gale that o'er Columbia° flies *America*
Bids on its balmy wings some Paean[2] rise,
Some song of Liberty;
And ev'ry peal that mounts the skies,
In solemn tones of grandeur cries,
15 "AMERICA IS FREE!"

Sound, O Fame! thy clarion° strong, *trumpet*
Bear the golden notes along,
Let *Gallia*[3] hear the song;
Beat each heart with pleasure high,
20 Flush each cheek with purest joy,
Let rapture glitter in each eye,
And tune each grateful tongue.
Hail! O land! long may old time behold
Freedom o'er thee her standard wide unfold,
25 While ages shall roll on,
'Till to a chaos sinks again this ball,
'Till worlds to primogenial[4] nothing fall,
And quenched thy blaze, O sun!

from Dunmore's Proclamation, 1775

In the spring of 1775, the governor of the colony of Virginia, John Murray, the 4th Earl of Dunmore, became increasingly alarmed at reports of an impending attack by American Patriots on the state capitol of Williamsburg. Tensions continued to build, and in November of the same year Dunmore issued a proclamation that offered freedom to the enslaved and indentured male population in the state, on the condition that those freed join the British army to help stifle the rebellion. While the Proclamation secured Dunmore's immediate goal—within a month, 800 new soldiers had joined the British—in the longer term, the threat the Proclamation presented to the slave system alienated the Southern colonies even further from Britain. Patriot and Loyalist slaveholders alike were alarmed by the Proclamation, as it stirred long-held fears of a slave revolt and threatened slaveholders' economic interests. While Dunmore's Proclamation did not secure British victory in the Revolutionary War, it was never revoked by Britain: over the course of the war thousands of enslaved people joined the British army. The British public's sympathy with the plight of the enslaved grew over the course of the conflict, and many historians view Dunmore's Proclamation as a key step on

[1] *mercy's author* God.

[2] *Paean* Song of praise.

[3] *Gallia* France.

[4] *primogenial* Primordial, original.

the way to the eventual abolition of slavery in the British Empire (1833–34).

A PROCLAMATION

As I have ever entertained hopes that an accommodation might have taken place between Great Britain and this colony, without being compelled by my duty to this most disagreeable but now absolutely necessary step, rendered so by a body of armed men unlawfully assembled, … and the formation of an army, and that army now on their march to attack His Majesty's troops and destroy the well-disposed[1] subjects of this colony. To defeat such unreasonable purposes, and [so] that all such traitors and their abettors may be brought to justice, and that the peace and good order of this colony may be again restored, which the ordinary course of the civil law is unable to effect; I have thought fit to issue this, my proclamation, hereby declaring that until the aforesaid good purposes can be obtained, I do in virtue of the power and authority to me given, by His Majesty, determine to execute martial law, and cause the same to be executed throughout this colony. … And I do hereby further declare all indentured servants, negroes, or others, (appertaining to rebels,) free that are able and willing to bear arms, they joining His Majesty's troops as soon as may be, for the more speedily reducing this colony to a proper sense of their duty[,] … till such time as peace may again be restored to this at present most unhappy country. …

Given under my Hand on board the ship *William*, off Norfolk, the 7th day of November, in the sixteenth year of His Majesty's reign.

Dunmore

(God save the king.)

from Edward Rutledge, letter to Ralph Izard, 8 December 1775

The following excerpt from American politician Edward Rutledge's letter reveals that Dunmore's Proclamation (see above) was received by slaveholding Americans as yet another British abuse: "our slaves emancipated for the express purpose of massacring their masters." Rutledge represented South Carolina in the Continental Congress (1774–76) and signed the Declaration of Independence; he also owned over 50 enslaved people. The recipient of this letter, Ralph Izard, was a large landowner from South Carolina who was living in England at the time; he was thus in a position to report on British sentiment regarding the conflict. Izard was an American politician and loyal to the Revolutionary cause, and he acted as a diplomat and raised funds for the Revolution while living abroad. Izard owned at least 602 enslaved people on his 2,353-acre plantation in South Carolina; after the Revolutionary War he became one of the first South Carolina senators elected to Congress.

You will receive by this conveyance a proclamation issued by Lord Dunmore—tending, in my judgement, more effectively to work an eternal separation between Great Britain and the Colonies than any other expedience which could possibly have been thought of.

Tell me then, I beseech you (before it is too late) what are the sentiments of the English nation—are the people of that country determined to force us into independence? Or do they really imagine that we are so insensitive to the calls of reason to every injury? Do they expect that after our towns have been destroyed, our liberties repeatedly invaded, our women and children driven from their habitations, our nearest relatives sacrificed, our slaves emancipated for the express purpose of massacring their masters—can they, I say, after all their injuries, expect that we shall return to our former connection with a forgiving and a cordial disposition? …

[1] *well-disposed* I.e., loyal to Britain.

Declaration by the Representatives of the People of the Colony and Dominion of Virginia, Assembled in General Convention, 14 December 1775

> Shaken by the prospect of a widespread slave revolt that would swell the army of the British, the Virginia Congress responded to Dunmore's Proclamation (see above) with a threatening reminder that enslaved people who took up arms to free themselves were subject to the death penalty in Virginia; the Declaration simultaneously suggested that those who returned to enslavement might be pardoned.

By the Representatives of the People of the Colony and Dominion of VIRGINIA, assembled in GENERAL CONVENTION

A DECLARATION

Whereas lord Dunmore, by his proclamation, dated on board the ship *William*, off Norfolk, the 7th day of November 1775, hath offered freedom to such able-bodied slaves as are willing to join him, and take up arms, against the good people of this colony, giving thereby encouragement to a general insurrection, which may induce a necessity of inflicting the severest punishments upon those unhappy people, already deluded by his base and insidious arts; and whereas, by an act of the General Assembly now in force in this colony, it is enacted, that all negro or other slaves, conspiring to rebel or make insurrection, shall suffer death, and be excluded all benefit of clergy:[1] We think it proper to declare, that all slaves who have been, or shall be seduced, by his lordship's proclamation, or other arts, to desert their masters' service, and take up arms against the inhabitants of this colony, shall be liable to such punishment as shall hereafter be directed by the General Convention. And to that end all such, who have taken this unlawful and wicked step, may return in safety to their duty, and escape the punishment due to their crimes, we hereby promise pardon to them, they surrendering themselves to Col. William Woodford, or any other commander of our troops, and not appearing in arms after the publication hereof. And we do farther earnestly recommend it to all humane and benevolent persons in this colony to explain and make known this our offer of mercy to those unfortunate people.

EDMUND PENDLETON, president.

from Reverend John Lindsay, letter to Dr. William Robertson, 6 August 1776 [On the influence of "the American rebellion" on Jamaica]

> Over the course of the seventeenth and eighteenth centuries, slave rebellions in the British colony of Jamaica occurred frequently, more than in any other colonized part of the Americas (excepting perhaps Brazil). While the Jamaica House of Assembly issued a statement in support of the American Revolution, the enslaved population of Jamaica found inspiration in the same ideals of freedom. In the summer of 1776, when the island had fewer British soldiers to police it on account of a military unit having been sent to America, a rebellion began in Hanover, Jamaica, causing martial law to be instituted across the island.
>
> The writer of the letter excerpted below, John Lindsay, was the rector of the parish of St. Catherine and Spanish Town in Jamaica; the recipient, William Robertson, was the principal of Edinburgh University and a well-known historian.

In our constant disputes, at our tables (where by the by every person has his own waiting man[2] behind him), we have I am afraid been too careless of expressions, especially when the topic of the American rebellion has been by the disaffected amongst us dwelt upon and brandished of with strains of virtuous heroism. ... And here I give data to the first seeds of this present

[1] *benefit of clergy* In British and American law, the benefit of the clergy was a means of avoiding the death penalty by petitioning for a lesser punishment. In this context, the crime of inciting or participating in insurrection was punishable by death with no possibility of avoiding the sentence.

[2] *waiting man* I.e., enslaved servant.

conspiracy.[1] For what mind of a slave will not recoil and burn into resentment, when he shall have been the frequent witness of sedition and ingratitude in the conduct of his master—when he shall hear the obligation of a subject to his lord spurned at; the blood spilt by rebels extolled as precious drops of record;[2] obedience to laws and authority upon all these occasions mentioned with a strong idea of slavery; and men toasted into immortal honours for encountering death in every form, rather than submit to slavery, let its chains be ever so gilded. [The expression] Dear Liberty has rung in the heart of every house-bred slave, in one form or another, for these ten years past. ... Such has been the seeds sown in the mind of our domestics by our wise-acre Patriots.[3] ...

from Mercy Otis Warren, *History of the Rise, Progress, and Termination of the American Revolution* (1805)

> Mercy Otis Warren (1728–1814), one of the leading intellectual figures of her day, wrote successfully in a wide variety of genres. Her *History of the Rise, Progress, and Termination of the American Revolution* (completed in the early 1790s, but not published until 1805) is striking both for the lucid quality of its prose and for its fair-mindedness. Warren was an early and vigorous supporter of the revolutionary cause, but she did not hesitate to praise the principles and eloquence of those who did not share her views. (David Ramsay, the other major contemporary historian of the revolution, whose two-volume *History of the American Revolution* appeared in 1789, was considerably less even-handed.)

John Singleton Copley, *Mrs. James Warren* [Mercy Otis Warren], c. 1763.

from AN ADDRESS TO THE INHABITANTS OF THE UNITED STATES[4]

The solemnity that covered every countenance
... when contemplating the sword uplifted, and the horrors of civil war rushing to habitations not inured to scenes of rapine[5] and misery; even to the quiet cottage, where only concord and affection had reigned; stimulated to observation a mind that had not yielded to the assertion that all political attentions lay out of the road of female life.

It is true there are certain appropriate duties assigned to each sex; and doubtless it is the more peculiar province of masculine strength not only to repel the bold invader of the rights of his country and of mankind, but in the nervous[6] style of manly eloquence to describe the blood-stained field, and relate the story of slaughtered armies.

Sensible of this, the trembling heart has recoiled at the magnitude of the undertaking, and the hand often shrunk back from the task. Yet, recollecting that every domestic enjoyment depends on the unimpaired possession of civil and religious liberty, that a concern for the welfare of society ought equally to glow in every

[1] *present conspiracy* A slave revolt, which was feared to be island wide, that started in Hanover, Jamaica, in July 1776.

[2] *record* Evidence, memorial; in this context, it is suggested that the blood spilt constitutes a monument (to liberty).

[3] *wise-acre Patriots* Supporters of the American Revolution who think themselves wise but are actually undermining their own affairs.

[4] The address was printed as a preface to the history.

[5] *rapine* Forcible seizing of property.

[6] *nervous* Muscular, strong.

human breast, the work was not relinquished. The most interesting circumstances were collected, active characters portrayed, the principles of the times developed, and the changes marked; nor need it cause a blush to acknowledge, a detail was preserved with a view of transmitting it to the rising youth of my country, some of them in infancy, others in the European world, while the most interesting events lowered over their native land. ...

from Chapter 9

... The commissioners who had been announced as the messengers of peace, were now hourly expected; but the dubious aspect of their mission, and the equivocal character in which they were about to appear, was far from lulling to inattention the guardians of the cause of America. Their errand was ostensibly to restore peace to the colonies; but many circumstances combined to evince that the design was, in reality, to furnish new pretexts for the prosecution of the war, with redoubled vigor. Thus was the Continental Congress[1] fully convinced of the impropriety of longer holding themselves in suspense by delusory hopes, or the uncertain termination of their expectations or their fears. They were sensible the step they were about to take would either set their country on the pinnacle of human glory, or plunge it in the abject state into which turbulent and conquered colonies have been generally reduced. Yet they wisely judged that this was a proper period to break the shackles, and renounce all political union with the parent state by a free and bold declaration of the independence of the American States. This measure had been contemplated by some gentlemen in the several colonies, some months before it took place. They had communicated their sentiments to the individual members of congress, but that body had been apprehensive, that the people at large were not prepared to unite in a step so replete with important consequences. But the moment of decision had now arrived, when both the congress and the inhabitants of the colonies advanced too far to recede.

Richard Henry Lee, Esq., a delegate from the state of Virginia, a gentleman of distinguished abilities, uniform patriotism, and unshaken firmness and integrity, was the first who dared explicitly to propose that this decided measure, on which hung such mighty consequences, should no longer be delayed. This public and unequivocal proposal from a man of his virtue and shining qualities appeared to spread a kind of sudden dismay. A silent astonishment for a few minutes seemed to pervade the whole assembly; this was soon succeeded by a long debate, and a considerable division of sentiment on the important question.

After the short silence just observed, the measure proposed by Mr. Lee was advocated with peculiar zeal by John Adams, Esq., of the Massachusetts Bay. He rose with a face of intrepidity and the voice of energy, and invoked the god of eloquence to enable him to do justice to the cause of his country, and to enforce this important step in such a manner as might silence all opposition, and convince every one of the necessity of an immediate declaration of the independence of the United States of America.

Mr. John Dickinson, of Pennsylvania, took the lead in opposition to the boldness and danger of this decided measure. He had drawn [up] the petition to the king[2] forwarded by Mr. Penn, and though no man was more strenuous in support of the rights of the colonies, he had always been averse to a separation from Britain, and shuddered at the idea of an avowed revolt of the American colonies. He arose on this occasion with no less solemnity than Mr. Adams had recently done, and with equal pathos of expression, and more brilliance of epithet, he invoked the Great Governor of the Universe to animate him with powers of language sufficient to exhibit a view of the dread consequences to both countries, that such a hasty dismemberment of the empire might produce. He descanted largely on the happy effects that might probably ensue from more patient and conciliatory dispositions, and urged at least a temporary suspension of a step, that could never be revoked. He declared that it was his opinion, that even policy forbade the precipitation of this measure, and

[1] *Continental Congress* The Continental Congress was the legislative body for the thirteen American colonies, first called together in 1774 to respond to British taxation. Warren is here referring to the Second Continental Congress, which was called in 1775 and served until 1781.

[2] *petition to the king* Petition sent by the First Continental Congress to King George III in 1775; it called for the repealing of the punitive laws passed by British Parliament in response to the defiance displayed by Massachusetts protestors at the Boston Tea Party.

that humanity more strongly dictated that they ought to wait longer the success of petitions and negotiations before they formally renounced their allegiance to the king of Great Britain, broke off all connection with England, plunged alone into an unequal war, and rushed without allies into the unforeseen and inevitable dangers that attended it.

The consequences of such a solemn act of separation were indeed of serious and extensive magnitude. The energy of brilliant talents, and great strength of argument, were displayed by both parties on this weighty occasion. The reasons urging the necessity of decision, and the indubitable danger of delay, were clear and cogent; the objections, plausible, humane, and important: but after a fair discussion of the question, an accurate statement of the reasons for adopting the measure, and a candid scrutiny of the objections against it, grounded either on policy or humanity, a large majority of the members of Congress appeared in favor of an immediate renunciation of allegiance to the crown, or any future subjugation to the king of Great Britain.

A declaration of the independence of America, and the sovereignty of the United States, was drawn by the ingenious and philosophic pen of Thomas Jefferson, Esq.,[1] a delegate from the state of Virginia. The delegates from twelve[2] of the American States, agreed almost unanimously to this declaration; the language, the principles, and the spirit of which, were equally honorable to themselves and their country. It was signed by John Hancock, then president of Congress, on the fourth of July, one thousand seven hundred and seventy-six.

The allegiance of thirteen states at once, withdrawn by a solemn declaration from a government towards which they had looked with the highest veneration—whose authority they had acknowledged, whose laws they had obeyed, whose protection they had claimed for more than a century and a half—was a consideration of solemnity, a bold resolution, an experiment of

hazard,[3] especially when the infancy of the colonies as a nation, without wealth, resources, or allies, was contrasted with the strength, riches, and power of Great Britain. The timid trembled at the ideas of final separation; the disciples of passive obedience were shocked by a reflection of a breach of faith to their ancient sovereign; and the enemies to the general freedom of mankind, were incensed to madness, or involved in despair. But these classes bore a small proportion to those who resented the rejection of their petitions, and coolly surveyed the impending dangers, that threatened themselves and their children, which rendered it clear to their apprehension, that this step was necessary to their political salvation. They considered themselves no longer bound by any moral tie, to render fealty to a sovereign thus disposed to encroach on their civil freedom, which they could now secure only by a social compact[4] among themselves, and which they determined to maintain, or perish in the attempt.

By the declaration of independence, dreaded by the foes, and for a time doubtfully viewed by many of the friends of America, everything stood on a new and more respectable footing, both with regard to the operations of war, or negotiations with foreign powers. Americans could now no more be considered as rebels, in their proposals for treaties of peace and conciliation with Britain; they were a distinct people who claimed the rights, the usages, the faith, and the respect of nations, uncontrolled by any foreign power. The colonies thus irretrievably lost to Great Britain, a new face appeared on all affairs, both at home and abroad.

America had been little known among the kingdoms of Europe; she was considered only as an appendage to the power of Britain: the principles of her sons were in some respects dissimilar, and their manners not yet wrought up to the standard of refinement reigning in ancient courts: her statesmen in general were unacquainted with the intrigues necessary for negotiation, and the finesse usually hackneyed in and about

[1] [Warren's note] This wise and patriotic statesman was afterwards appointed ambassador to the court of France. On the adoption of the present constitution of government, he was appointed secretary for foreign affairs, was chosen vice-president, and afterwards president of the United States of America.

[2] [Warren's note] The members from Maryland seceded, but in a short time after joined the confederation.

[3] *hazard* Chance, risk.

[4] *social compact* Term from political philosophy referring to the implied agreement that citizens of a society make in order to ensure social benefits and security; such an agreement usually involves a sacrifice of some personal freedom in exchange for the protection of the state.

the cabinets of princes.[1] She now appeared in their eyes, a new theatre, pregnant with events that might be interesting to the civil and political institutions of nations, that had never before paid much attention to the growth, population, and importance of an immense territory beyond the Atlantic. ...

from CHAPTER 30

... America has fought for the boon of liberty. She has successfully and honorably obtained it: she has now a rank among the nations. It was now the duty of the wise and patriotic characters who had by inconceivable labor and exertion obtained the prize to guard on every side that it might not be sported away by the folly of the people or the intrigue or deception of their rulers. They had to watch at all points that her dignity was not endangered nor her independence renounced by too servilely copying either the fashionable vices or the political errors of those countries where the inhabitants are become unfit for any character but that of master and slave.

Thus, after the dissolution of the American army, the withdrawing of the French troops, the retirement of General Washington, and the retreat of the fleets and armies of the king of Great Britain, a solemnity and stillness appeared which was like the general pause of nature before the concussion of an earthquake. The state of men's minds seemed for a short time to be palsied[2] by the retrospect of dangers encountered to break off the fetters and the hazards surmounted to sweep away the claims and cut the leading strings[3] in which they had been held by the crown of Britain.

But though the connection was now dissolved and the Gordian knot[4] of union between Great Britain and America cut in sunder, though the independence of the United States was by the treaty clearly established on the broad basis of liberty, yet the Americans felt themselves in such a state of infancy that as a child just learning to walk, they were afraid of their own movements. Their debts were unpaid, their governments unsettled, and the people out of breath by their long struggle for the freedom and independence of their country. They were become poor from the loss of trade, the neglect of their usual occupations, and the drains from every quarter for the support of a long and expensive war. ...

It is indeed true that from a general attention to early education, the people of the United States were better informed in many branches of literature than the common classes of men in most other countries. Yet many of them had but a superficial knowledge of mankind. They were ignorant of the intrigues of courts, and though convinced of the necessity of government, did not fully understand its nature or origin. They had generally supposed there was little to do but to shake off the yoke of foreign domination and annihilate the name of king. ...

[F]ew had yet formed any adequate ideas and fewer indeed were sensible that though the name of liberty delights the ear and tickles the fond pride of man, it is a jewel much oftener the plaything of his imagination than a possession of real stability. It may be acquired today in all the triumph of independent feelings, but perhaps tomorrow the world may be convinced that mankind know not how to make a proper use of the prize, generally bartered in a short time as a useless bauble to the first officious master that will take the burden from the mind by laying another on the shoulders of tenfold weight. ...

The generous and disinterested of all nations must, however, wish to see the American republic fixed on such a stable basis as to become the admiration of the world. Future generations will then look back with gratitude on the era which wafted their ancestors from the European shores. They will never forget the energetic struggles of their fathers to secure the natural rights of men.[5] ...

[1] *princes* Rulers.

[2] *palsied* Paralyzed.

[3] *leading strings* Strings that caregivers used to help guide children when they learn to walk.

[4] *Gordian knot* Complex knot tied by Gordius, king of Gordium in ancient Phyrgia. An oracle predicted that whoever undid it would rule Asia, a feat accomplished by Alexander the Great when he cut through the knot with his sword.

[5] *natural rights of men* According to the philosopher John Locke, who was a central influence on Thomas Jefferson when he drafted the Declaration of Independence, the natural rights of humankind are "life, liberty, and property."

The French Revolution, and the Revolutionary Call for Women's Rights

The Enlightenment ideal of liberty that had fueled the American Revolution resonated powerfully in France, and the Americans' success in defeating the British and in creating a republic based on the rights and liberties of the citizenry (at least of the white male citizenry) inspired the French. Beginning in 1789, the French began the process of overthrowing and replacing their monarchy and much of their hierarchical social structure; many hoped to create a republic based on equal rights for all citizens. Many Americans responded at first with enthusiasm to the French Revolution; the French had been their allies against the British, and the American people were largely sympathetic to an ideology that seemed so similar to their own. But as the French Revolution grew more violent—and as the depth of the French Revolution's commitment to equality became fully apparent (in 1794 France proclaimed the freedom of all enslaved people in its colonies[1])—Americans became more divided in their response. Thomas Jefferson and the Republican party remained supportive (albeit with reservations), while Alexander Hamilton and the Federalists became increasingly hostile to the Revolution. Officially, the Americans maintained neutrality as Britain and Spain opposed the new French regime in a series of wars that lasted until 1802.

The Declaration of the Rights of Man and of the Citizen was produced by France's National Constituent Assembly in 1789; it was written by the Marquis de Lafayette, working closely with Thomas Jefferson. The Declaration is the central document outlining the core values of the French Revolution, and it had a significant impact on framing the conversation around democracy and human rights worldwide. As with the American Declaration of Independence, however, it had limitations—rights were only accorded to male citizens, despite some voices petitioning at the time to include women and people of color. (Nicolas de Condorcet, for example, put the matter quite simply: "he who votes against the right of another, whatever the religion, color, or sex of that other, has henceforth abjured his own.")

The French Revolution was also a watershed moment in the history of women's rights; writers such as Olympe de Gouges and Mary Wollstonecraft broke new ground in arguing for women's equality.

Declaration of the Rights of Man and of the Citizen (1789)[2]

Approved by the National Assembly of France, August 26, 1789

The representatives of the French people, organized as a National Assembly, believing that the ignorance, neglect, or contempt of the rights of man are the sole cause of public calamities and of the corruption of governments, have determined to set forth in a solemn declaration the natural, unalienable, and sacred rights of man, in order that this declaration, being constantly before all the members of the social body, shall remind them continually of their rights and duties; in order that the acts of the legislative power, as well as those of the executive power, may be compared at any moment with the objects and purposes of all political institutions and may thus be more respected, and, lastly, in order that the grievances of the citizens, based hereafter upon simple and incontestable principles, shall tend to the maintenance of the constitution and redound to the happiness of all. Therefore the National Assembly recognizes and proclaims, in the presence and under the auspices of the Supreme Being, the following rights of man and of the citizen:

Articles:

1. Men are born and remain free and equal in rights. Social distinctions may be founded only upon the general good.

[1] Emancipation in France's colonies was short-lived; Napoleon Bonaparte reinstated slavery in 1802.

[2] Translation from "The French Revolution, 1789–1791," ed. James Harvey Robinson, in *Translations and Reprints from the Original Sources of European History*, 1894.

2. The aim of all political association is the preservation of the natural and imprescriptible rights of man. These rights are liberty, property, security, and resistance to oppression.

3. The principle of all sovereignty resides essentially in the nation. No body nor individual may exercise any authority which does not proceed directly from the nation.

4. Liberty consists in the freedom to do everything which injures no one else; hence the exercise of the natural rights of each man has no limits except those which assure to the other members of the society the enjoyment of the same rights. These limits can only be determined by law.

5. Law can only prohibit such actions as are hurtful to society. Nothing may be prevented which is not forbidden by law, and no one may be forced to do anything not provided for by law.

6. Law is the expression of the general will. Every citizen has a right to participate personally, or through his representative, in its foundation. It must be the same for all, whether it protects or punishes. All citizens, being equal in the eyes of the law, are equally eligible to all dignities and to all public positions and occupations, according to their abilities, and without distinction except that of their virtues and talents.

7. No person shall be accused, arrested, or imprisoned except in the cases and according to the forms prescribed by law. Anyone soliciting, transmitting, executing, or causing to be executed, any arbitrary order, shall be punished. But any citizen summoned or arrested in virtue of the law shall submit without delay, as resistance constitutes an offense.

8. The law shall provide for such punishments only as are strictly and obviously necessary, and no one shall suffer punishment except it be legally inflicted in virtue of a law passed and promulgated before the commission of the offense.

9. As all persons are held innocent until they shall have been declared guilty, if arrest shall be deemed indispensable, all harshness not essential to the securing of the prisoner's person shall be severely repressed by law.

10. No one shall be disquieted on account of his opinions, including his religious views, provided their manifestation does not disturb the public order established by law.

11. The free communication of ideas and opinions is one of the most precious of the rights of man. Every citizen may, accordingly, speak, write, and print with freedom, but shall be responsible for such abuses of this freedom as shall be defined by law.

12. The security of the rights of man and of the citizen requires public military forces. These forces are, therefore, established for the good of all and not for the personal advantage of those to whom they shall be intrusted.

13. A common contribution is essential for the maintenance of the public forces and for the cost of administration. This should be equitably distributed among all the citizens in proportion to their means.

14. All the citizens have a right to decide, either personally or by their representatives, as to the necessity of the public contribution; to grant this freely; to know to what uses it is put; and to fix the proportion, the mode of assessment and of collection and the duration of the taxes.

15. Society has the right to require of every public agent an account of his administration.

16. A society in which the observance of the law is not assured, nor the separation of powers defined, has no constitution at all.

17. Since property is an inviolable and sacred right, no one shall be deprived thereof except where public necessity, legally determined, shall clearly demand it, and then only on condition that the owner shall have been previously and equitably indemnified.

"The Rights of Woman" in America

Though it was in London that the "bluestockings" became famous in the 1790s, the early response to the ideas put forward in Olympe de Gouges's 1791 "Declaration of the Rights of Woman" and Mary Wollstonecraft's 1792 *A Vindication of the Rights of Woman* may well have been (as political historian Eileen Hunt Botting has suggested) more positive in the United States than it was in Britain. The first American edition of Wollstonecraft's book was published in 1792, and by 1794 three more editions had appeared, the *Lady's Magazine* in Philadelphia had published substantial excerpts from the book, and Wollstonecraft's ideas had been widely discussed in newspapers. The impact of these ideas in 1790s America is shown here in excerpts from a 1792 letter by Annis Boudinot Stockton (an accomplished poet and a strong supporter of the American Revolution) and from an anonymous 1795 poem "by a lady" published in a Philadelphia weekly newspaper.

By century's end, however, American opinion had become less receptive to the ideas of writers such as de Gouges and Wollstonecraft. Wollstonecraft died in 1797 and her reputation suffered because her husband, William Godwin, published a scandalous biography about her private life. The reaction against Jacobin excesses in France following The Terror made revolutionary ideas in general suspect in many quarters, while revolutionary ideas about gender were to a large extent being damped down by a growing cult of sentiment. It would not be until much later in the nineteenth century that Wollstonecraft's ideas would inspire significant numbers of American women, including literary giant Margaret Fuller, to begin to press for revolutionary change.

from ANNIS BOUDINOT STOCKTON, LETTER TO
HER DAUGHTER [JULIA STOCKTON RUSH],
22 MARCH 1793

My dear Julia,
I have been engaged these two days with reading the rights of women, which I never could procure before, though it has been much longer in the neighborhood.

I have been musing upon the subject over my solitary fire till I took up the resolution to give you my sentiments upon it though I suppose it is an old thing with you—I wonder you never sent me your critique—I am much pleased with her strength of reasoning, and her sentiment in general—but think that she like many other great geniuses—establish an hypothesis and lay such weight upon it as to cause the superstructure to destroy the foundation. ... I have always contended that the education of women was not made a matter of that importance, which it ought to be—but we see that error daily correcting—and in this country, the empire of reason is not monopolized by men; there is great pains taken to improve our sex, and store their minds with that knowledge best adapted to make them useful in the situation that their creator has placed them—and we do not often see those efforts opposed by the other sex, but rather disposed to assist them by every means in their power, and men of sense generally prefer such women, as Companions through life—The state of society may be different in Europe from what it is here in America—but from the observation I have been able to make in my own country, I do not think any of that slavish obedience exists, that she talks so much of—I think the women have their equal right of everything, Latin and Greek excepted. And I believe women of the most exalted minds, and the most improved understanding, will be most likely to practice that conciliating mode of conduct, which she seems to condemn, as blind obedience, and slavish submission, to the caprice of an arbitrary tyrant, which character she seems to apply to men as a sex ... you know that it is a favourite tenet with me, that there is no sex in soul—I believe it as firmly as I do my existence—but at the same time I do not think that the sexes were made to be independent of each other—I believe that our creator intended us for different walks in life—and that it takes equal powers of mind, and understanding, properly to fulfil the duties that he has marked out for us—as it does for the other sex, to gain knowledge of the arts and sciences, and if our education was the same, our improvement would be the same—but there is no occasion for exactly the same education. I think we may draw the conclusion that there is no sex in soul, from the following illustrations—that there are many men, that have been taught, and have *not* obtained any great degree of knowledge in the

circle of the sciences—and that there *have* been women who have excelled in every branch, when they have had an opportunity of instruction, and I have no doubt if those advantages were oftener to occur, we should see more instances. ...

[S]ome of her expressions are by far, too strong for my ideas—but *she* writes like a philosopher, and *I* think as a novice—yet to sum up my poor judgement upon this wonderful book, I do really think a great deal of instruction may be gathered from it—and I am sure that no one can read it, but they may find something or other, that will correct their conduct and enlarge their ideas. ...

Adieu my love, may heaven bless you and yours and protect you this night, prays your ever affectionate
　　mother A Stockton—

from ANONYMOUS ("A LADY"), *THE PHILADELPHIA MINERVA* (17 OCTOBER 1795)

Man boasts the noble cause
　　Nor yields supine to laws
Tyrants ordain;
Let woman have a sphere
5　Nor yield to slavish fear,
Her equal rights declare,
And well maintain.
...

Let snarling critics frown,
10　Their maxims I disown,
Their ways detest;
By man, your tyrant lord,
Females, no more be awed.
Let freedom's sacred word
15　Inspire your breast.

The Haitian Revolution

The latter half of the eighteenth century saw numerous slave insurrections in colonial holdings throughout the West Indies and South America, notably in Panama, Jamaica, Surinam, and Guyana. But the only successful revolution took place in Saint-Domingue, the French colony that would later become Haiti. Beginning in 1791 and ending in 1804, the Haitian Revolution spanned thirteen years and led to the foundation of a black state free from slavery. In America, the Haitian Revolution divided opinion sharply. For a majority of white Americans the revolution was a source of considerable concern. Southern enslavers and their supporters feared that similar events would occur on their plantations—and many whites who had no fondness for slavery shared to some degree a fear of the instability that inevitably accompanied revolutionary change. As former plantation owners fled Haiti for the United States, they fanned the flames of fear. During the early stages of the revolution, American governments provided hundreds of thousands of dollars in assistance to the Haitian plantation owners as they tried to quell the rebellion, and to white Haitians who fled the island to take refuge in the United States. The American government also sought to undermine the new nation of Haiti after the revolution had finally succeeded; with the support of Congress, the Jefferson administration refused to grant diplomatic recognition to the Haitian government, and in 1806 they placed a trade embargo on Haiti.

Black Americans, on the other hand, together with many white abolitionists, were supportive and saw the conflict as further proof that societies built on slavery were inherently unstable. Haiti became a source of hope to enslaved people across the world, and to black resistance in America particularly. It continued to be a source of inspiration throughout the nineteenth century. As Frederick Douglass said in 1893, "Until [Haiti] spoke no Christian nation had abolished Negro slavery. Until she spoke no Christian nation had given to the world an organized effort to abolish slavery. Until she spoke the slave ship, followed by hungry sharks, greedy to devour the dead and dying slaves

flung overboard to feed them, ploughed in peace the South Atlantic, painting the sea with the Negro's blood."

The history of the Haitian Revolution between 1791 and 1804 is full of often-confusing twists and turns—as is the subsequent nineteenth-century history of Haiti. The set of materials provided here focuses largely on the reactions that events in Haiti provoked in the United States; a wider selection of the various proclamations and declarations that were issued by the revolutionaries themselves is included in the website component of this anthology.

Toussaint Louverture, Proclamation, 29 August 1793

Beginning in the autumn of 1791, a leader of the rebel army named Toussaint Bréda started living in the mountains on the west coast of Saint-Domingue among a group of formerly enslaved soldiers leagued with the Spanish and waging a guerilla war against the French colonial authorities and slaveholders. On 29 August 1793 at a fortification named Camp Turel, Bréda announced himself to the world under a different name, Toussaint Louverture, declaring at the same time his determination to free the enslaved people of Saint-Domingue. Scholars believe that Louverture had had advance knowledge of the intention of the French representative Léger Félicité Sonthonax to announce the abolition of slavery in Saint-Domingue on that very same day (see Sonthonax's Proclamation in the website portion of this anthology). Most historians believe that Louverture intended this brief statement to deflect support away from Sonthonax—a white newcomer from France—and instead to Louverture himself, a black leader who shared their interests.

Brothers and friends, I am Toussaint Louverture; perhaps my name has made itself known to you. I have undertaken vengeance. I want Liberty and Equality to reign in St Domingue. I am working to make that happen. Unite yourselves to us, brothers, and fight with us for the same cause.

Your very humble and obedient servant, Toussaint Louverture,

General of the armies of the king,[1] for the public good

Thomas Jefferson on the Haitian Revolution

As secretary of state from 22 March 1790 to 31 December 1793, Thomas Jefferson was a key shaper of American foreign policy during the early stages of the Haitian Revolution—as he was as president (from 4 March 1801 to 4 March 1809) during the period when Haitian independence was achieved.

from LETTER TO MARTHA JEFFERSON RANDOLPH, 24 MARCH 1791

[France's] islands, but most particularly St. Domingue and Martinique, are involved in a horrid civil war. Nothing can be more distressing than the situation of the inhabitants, as their slaves have been called into action, and are a terrible engine, absolutely ungovernable. ... An army and fleet from France are expected every hour to quell the disorders. ...

from LETTER TO MARTHA JEFFERSON RANDOLPH, 13 NOVEMBER 1791

... [T]he affairs of the French West Indies are in a desperate state. A second set of deputies has arrived here[2] to ask succours.[3] Abundance of women and children come here to avoid danger. The men are not permitted to come. I should not wonder to see some of your friends among them. ...

1 *king* Likely a reference to the Spanish king Charles IV (r. 1788–1808); the rebel fighters were allied with the Spanish at this point in the Revolution.

2 *here* I.e., the United States.

3 *ask succours* Ask for help.

from LETTER TO WILLIAM SHORT,
24 NOVEMBER 1791

... When the insurrection of their Negroes assumed a very threatening appearance, the [Haitian colonial] assembly sent a deputy here to ask assistance of military stores and provisions. He addressed himself to M. de Ternant,[1] who (the President being then in Virginia, as I was also) applied to the Secretaries of the Treasury and at War.[2] They furnished 1,000 stand of arms,[3] other military stores, and placed 40,000 dollars in the Treasury subject to the order of M. de Ternant, to be laid out in provisions, or otherwise, as he should think best. He sent the arms and other military stores. ...

... I expressed to them freely my opinion that [independence for Haiti] was neither desirable on their part nor attainable: that as to ourselves there was one case which would be peculiarly alarming to us, to wit, were there a danger of their falling under any other power, that we conceived it to be strongly our interests that they should retain their connection with the mother country;[4] that we had a common interest with them in furnishing them the necessaries of life in exchange for sugar and coffee for our own consumption, but that I thought we might rely on the justice of the mother country towards them, for their obtaining this privilege: and on the whole let them see that nothing was to be done but with the consent of the minister of France. ...

from LETTER TO WILLIAM SHORT, 5 JANUARY 1792

... We receive with deep regret daily information of the progress of insurrection and devastation in St. Domingo. Nothing indicates as yet that the evil is at its height. ...

from LETTER TO GOUVERNEUR MORRIS,[5]
10 MARCH 1792

... [O]ur wishes are cordial to the reestablishment of peace and commerce in those colonies, and to give such proofs of our good faith both to them and the mother country, as to suppress all that jealousy which might oppose itself to the free exchange of *our mutual productions*, so essential to the prosperity of those colonies and to the preservation of our *agricultural interests*. This is our true interest and our true object, and we have no reason to conceal views so justifiable, though the expression of them may require that the occasions be proper and the terms chosen with delicacy. ...

from LETTER TO DAVID HUMPHREYS, 9 APRIL 1792

... The troubles in the French island continue extreme. We have as yet heard of the arrival but of a few troops. There begins to be reason to apprehend the negroes will perhaps never be entirely reduced.[6] ...

from LETTER TO DAVID HUMPHREYS, 2 JANUARY 1793

... The French West Indies become more and more dependent on us for subsistence. There is at present some glimmering of hope that the efforts of the free inhabitants will be directed with more efficacy to the reduction[7] of the common enemy. However, we are far from certainty on that subject. ...

from LETTER TO JAMES MONROE, 14 JULY 1793

... The situation of the St. Domingo fugitives[8] (aristocrats as they are) calls aloud for pity and charity. Never was so deep a tragedy presented to the feelings of man. I deny the power of the general

[1] *M. de Ternant* Jean Baptiste de Ternant, at the time the representative in the United States of the government of France.

[2] *Secretaries ... at War* The Secretary of the Treasury and (to use the modern term) the Secretary of Defense.

[3] *stand of arms* Complete set of weapons for each soldier, including a bayonet, musket, and ammunition.

[4] *the mother country* I.e., France (the colonial power).

[5] *GOUVERNEUR MORRIS* The author of the preamble to the American Constitution, Gouvernor Morris (1752–1816) was Minister to France for the United States, 1792–94.

[6] *reduced* Brought under control.

[7] *reduction* Subjugation.

[8] *St. Domingo fugitives* I.e., white French plantation owners who had fled the island.

government to apply money to such a purpose, but I deny it with a bleeding heart.[1] It belongs to the state governments. Pray urge ours to be liberal.[2] ... I become daily more and more convinced that all the West India islands will remain in the hands of the people of colour, and a total expulsion of the whites sooner or later take place. It is high time we should foresee the bloody scenes which our children certainly, and possibly ourselves (South of Potomac[3]) have to wade through, and try to avert them. ...

from LETTER TO MARTHA JEFFERSON RANDOLPH, 1 DECEMBER 1793

... St. Domingo has expelled all its whites, has given freedom to all its blacks, has established a regular government of the blacks and coloured people, and seems now to have taken its ultimate form, and that to which all of the West India islands must come. ...

The Haitian Revolution in American Newspapers

from THE *MARYLAND GAZETTE* (ANNAPOLIS, MARYLAND, 17 NOVEMBER 1791)

By accounts from Cape-François[4] we learn that Mr. Bourne, who was appointed consul of the United States for St. Domingo, has been after some difficulty admitted provisionally to execute the duties of consul in the three ports of St. Domingo, called the ports of entry, and not elsewhere.

Extract of a letter from Cape-François, dated October 6: "The damage sustained in the province is moderately[5] estimated at 500 millions currency, besides the coffee estates, the number of which cannot be ascertained, two hundred and twenty sugar plantations have been destroyed. We now have some hope of an accommodation with the blacks, on condition of a general amnesty."

from THE *KENTUCKY GAZETTE* (LEXINGTON, KENTUCKY, 26 MAY 1792)

The ravages and havoc of the insurgents in St. Domingo have raised sugar to such an enormous price in France that mobs throughout Paris have been the consequence; who, at least, make this the ostensible cause of their riots. ...

from THE *INDEPENDENT GAZETEER* (PHILADELPHIA, PENNSYLVANIA, 10 AUGUST 1793)

The melancholy fate of Cape-François,[6] with the situation of the other settlements in St Domingo, must excite compassion in every human breast. The humane attentions of our brethren in the middle states[7] to the suffering inhabitants who have been fortunate enough to escape with their lives deserve ... the applause of all good men.

As the American trade to the French islands must receive a considerable check by the present troubles, it may not be amiss to show the importance of that trade to this country. ... [From these numbers], the immense importance of the West India trade to the United States will appear in a strong light. ... This statement likewise exhibits the magnitude of the commerce of St. Domingo compared with the other islands—it being nearly three fourths of all the trade of the French islands. The island of Hispaniola is larger than the four New England states, and one of the most fertile of all the West India islands. A part of it is under the dominion of Spain, but the largest and best portion

[1] *I deny ... bleeding heart* I.e., I maintain that providing financial assistance to [the white settlers] is not a federal responsibility, but I regret having to say that [because of my strong sympathy with those affected].

[2] *liberal* Generous.

[3] *South of Potomac* I.e., in the Southern states (south of the Potomac River).

[4] *Cape-François* Now Cap-Haïtien, this was the main city on the north coast of St. Domingue and the capital of the French colony from 1711 to 1770.

[5] *moderately* Conservatively.

[6] *fate of Cape-François* The city had been burned and pillaged during the Battle of Cap-Français on 20–22 June 1793. Most white inhabitants of the city fled to ships moored in the harbor and left the island.

[7] *middle states* Collective term for the states located between New England and the South; though there has been some variation in the precise list of states denoted by the term, Pennsylvania has always been understood by those using the term to be among "the middle states."

belongs to the French, and is exceedingly productive. The consequences of the present insurrections and disputes in the island cannot be predicted. Heaven is just, and perhaps the signal vengeance inflicted on the French settlements is the reward of the infamous traffic in human bodies, and a prelude to further and more extensive depredations[1] in the West Indies.

from *The Philadelphia Inquirer* (29 January 1794) [reprinted from the *Connecticut Courant*]

An act has been passed this session to prevent the migration of free negroes and mulattoes into the commonwealth.[2] The policy of this act is to arrest the farther propagation of St Domingo principles, and to suppress those already disseminated as soon as possible.

from Abraham Bishop, "The Rights of Black Men" (1791)

Abraham Bishop (1763–1844) had in 1791 recently returned to America from France. A farmer who often spoke out in support of the interests of the common people, he was at this time a supporter of Thomas Jefferson on many issues; later he would become an influential figure in Connecticut political circles. In arguing strenuously that America should support the Haitian Revolution, Abraham Bishop was in disagreement with Jefferson—and very much in a minority among white Americans.

"The Rights of Black Men" appeared in three separate issues (22 November, 25 November, and 6 December) of a Boston newspaper, the *Argus*.[3]

[from 22 November issue]

If freedom depends upon colour, and if the blacks were born for slaves, those in the West India islands may be called insurgents and murderers. ... But the enlightened mind of Americans will not receive such ideas. We believe that Freedom is the natural right of all rational beings, and we know that the blacks have never voluntarily resigned that freedom. Then is not their cause as just as ours? We fought with bravery, and prayed earnestly for success upon our righteous cause when we drew the sword and shed the blood of Englishmen—for what? Not to gain freedom, for we were never slaves; but to rid ourselves of taxes, imposed without our consent, and from the growing evils of usurpation. Believing our cause to have been just, I firmly believe that the cause of the blacks is just. They are asserting those rights by the sword which it is impossible to secure by mild measures. ... Let us be consistent Americans, and if we justify our own conduct in the late, glorious Revolution, let us also justify those who, in a cause like ours, fight with equal bravery.

We may feel in the cause of humanity, and may lament that the blood of white men is spilling. It would be happy indeed if the rights of man could in all countries be asserted as coolly and judiciously as they have been in France; but in the French West-India islands this could not have been done. The efforts of blacks for a peaceable assertion would have cost them their lives. Arms gave them courage in a common cause. ...

[from 25 November issue]

... Zealous in the theory of liberty, we talked in high strains about the equal rights of man, and formed ourselves into societies for the abolition of slavery. The policy of some of the states has, to their honor, reduced[4] this theory to practice. In other states, liberty and property clashed, and the last, as usual, gained the victory. The blacks are still enslaved within the United States. The Indians are driven into the society of savage beasts, and we glory in the equal rights of men, provided that *we white men can enjoy the whole of them*. ...

1 *depredations* Ravages, destructive ruinations.

2 *act ... commonwealth* On 12 December 1793, the Commonwealth of Virginia passed a law making it illegal for "any free negro or mulatto to migrate into this commonwealth" and mandating that any free African American that does arrive in the state "shall be exported to the place from whence he or she came."

3 The text of all three pieces is also made available as an appendix to Tim Mattewson's article, "'The Rights of Black Men' and the American Reaction to the Haitian Revolution," *The Journal of Negro History*, vol. 67, no. 2 (1982).

4 *reduced* Applied or adapted.

... [H]ave we forgotten the animating sound, *Liberty or Death*?[1] That sound has gone out into the world, and is rapidly expanding to the ends of the earth. From various parts of Europe we have already heard the echo, *Liberty or Death*; we have firmly asserted that *all men are free*. Yet as soon as the poor blacks ... echoed *Liberty or Death*, we have been the first to assist in riveting their chains! They are pursuing the principles which we had taught them, and are now sealing with their blood, the rights of men; yet Americans are sending assistance to their enemies. ... Vessel loads of military stores and provisions have been sent. ...

Toussaint Louverture displaying a copy of the Haitian Constitution, 1801 (with the apparent blessing of the Catholic Church). The document was in many ways paradoxical; Louverture proclaimed a Constitution framed as if Haiti were an independent state, even though it was officially still a colony of France; the Constitution abolished slavery, but required that farmhands not leave their domicile in search of employment elsewhere; it purportedly guaranteed freedom and security for all, but its provisions left almost all power ultimately in the hands of the governor—"Citizen Toussaint Louverture."

[1] *Liberty or Death* See Wirt's account of Patrick Henry's "Liberty or Death" speech, above.

Every public transaction, and most private conversations have evinced a great zeal in favour of the whites. ...

The blacks are entitled to freedom, for we did not say all *white men* are free but *all men* are free. ... The blacks took up arms to rid themselves of slavery. Arms were their only resource. ... They look to the liberating societies for that aid and support which they were taught to expect. It is cruelty, then, to withhold such aid and support—worse than cruelty to assist their enemies. ...

from Jean-Jacques Dessalines, "Liberty or Death. Proclamation. Jean-Jacques Dessalines, Governor General, to the People of Hayti"[2] (1804)

When Haiti became an independent country, Jean-Jacques Dessalines (1758–1806) declared himself the state's governor general-for-life; he then ruled as emperor of Haiti until his assassination in 1806. One of the earliest state documents printed by the new country was his "Liberty or Death" speech, excerpted below. In part, the speech is offered as a justification for a series of massacres of the remaining white population of Haiti that Dessalines had ordered in the early months of 1804.

Crimes, the most atrocious, such as were until then unheard of, and would cause nature to shudder, have been perpetrated. The measure was overheaped. At length the hour of vengeance has arrived, and the implacable enemies of the rights of man have suffered the punishment due to their crimes.

My arm, raised over their heads, has too long delayed to strike. At that signal, which the justice of God has urged, your hands, righteously armed, have brought the axe upon the ancient tree of slavery and prejudices. In vain had time, and more especially the infernal politics of Europeans, surrounded it with triple brass; you have stripped it of its armour; you

[2] This anonymous translation from the French appeared in 1804 in several American papers; it appears here as it did in the *Connecticut Herald*. See Writ's account of Patrick Henry's "Liberty or Death" speech, above.

have placed it upon your hearts, that you may become (like your natural enemies) cruel and merciless. Like an overflowing mighty torrent that tears down all opposition, your vengeful fury has carried away everything in its impetuous course. Thus perish all tyrants over innocence, all oppressors of mankind!

What then? bent for many ages under an iron yoke; the sport of the passions of men, of their injustice, and of the caprice of fortune; mutilated victims of the cupidity of white Frenchmen? after having fattened with our toils these insatiate blood-suckers, with a patience and resignation unexampled, we should again have seen that sacrilegious horde make an attempt upon our destruction, without any distinction of sex or age; and we, men without energy, of no virtue, or no delicate sensibility, should not we have plunged in their breast the dagger of desperation? Where is that vile Haytian, so unworthy of his regeneration, who thinks he has not accomplished the decrees of the Eternal, by exterminating these bloody thirsty tigers! If there is one, let him fly; indignant nature discards him from our bosom; let him hide his shame far from hence; the air we breathe is not suited to his gross organs; it is the pure air of Liberty, august and triumphant.

Yes, we have rendered to these true cannibals war for war, crime for crime, outrage for outrage.

Yes, I have saved my country—I have avenged America.[1] The avowal I make of it in the face of earth and heaven, constitutes my pride and my glory. Of what consequence to me is the opinion which contemporary and future generations will pronounce upon my conduct? I have performed my duty; I enjoy my own approbation; for me that is sufficient. But what do I say? The preservation of my unfortunate brothers, the testimony of my own conscience are not my only recompence: I have seen two classes of men, born to cherish, assist and succour one another—mixed, in a word, and blended together—crying for vengeance, and disputing the honour of the first blow. ...

[S]ooner or later Divine Justice will unchain on earth some mighty winds, above the weakness of the vulgar, for the destruction and terror of the wicked; tremble, tyrants, usurpers, scourges of the new world! our daggers are sharpened; your punishment is ready!

sixty thousand men, equipped, inured to war, obedient to my orders, burn to offer a new sacrifice to the manes of their assassinated brothers. Let that nation come who may be mad and daring enough to attack me. Already at its approach, the irritated genius[2] of Hayti, rising out of the bosom of the ocean, appears; his menacing aspect throws the waves into commotion, excites tempests, and with his mighty hand disperses ships, or dashes them in pieces; to his formidable voice the laws of nature pay obedience; diseases, plague, famine, conflagration, poison, are his constant attendants. But why calculate on the assistance of the climate and of the elements? Have I forgot that I command a people of no common cast, brought up in adversity, whose audacious daring frowns at the obstacles and increases by dangers? Let them come, then, these homicidal Cohorts! I wait for them with firmness and with a steady eye. I abandon to them freely the sea-shore, and the places where cities have existed; but woe to those who may approach too near the mountains! It were better for them that the sea received them into its profound abyss, than to be devoured by the anger of the children of Hayti.

"War and Death to Tyrants!" this is my motto; "Liberty! Independence!" this is our rallying cry

Generals, officers, soldiers, a little unlike him who has preceded me, the ex-general Toussaint Louverture, I have been faithful to the promise which I made to you when I took up arms against tyranny, and whilst the last spark of life remains in me I shall keep my oath. Never again shall a colonist or an European set his foot upon this territory with the title of master or proprietor. This resolution shall henceforward form the fundamental basis of our constitution.

Should other chiefs, after me, by pursuing a conduct diametrically opposite to mine, dig their own graves and those of their species, you will have to accuse only the law of destiny which shall have taken me away from the happiness and welfare of my fellow-citizens. May my successors follow the path I shall have traced out for them! It is the system best adapted for consolidating their power; it is the highest homage they can render to my memory.

[1] *America* Dessalines is referring to all the colonies in the Americas (North, South, and Central).

[2] *genius* Guardian spirit.

As it is derogatory to my character and my dignity to punish the innocent for the crimes of the guilty, a handful of whites, commendable by the religion they have always professed, and who have besides taken the oath to live with us in the woods, have experienced my clemency. I order that the sword respect them, and that they be unmolested.

I recommend anew and order to all the generals of department, etc. to grant succours, encouragement, and protection, to all neutral and friendly nations who may wish to establish commercial relations in this island.

The Governor-General
(Signed) Dessalines
A true Copy. The Sec'y-General
Juste Chanlatte

from Leonora Sansay, *Secret History, Or, the Horrors of St. Domingo, in a Series of Letters, Written by a Lady at Cape François,*[1] *to Col. Aaron Burr, Late Vice-President of the United States, Principally during the Command of General Rochambeau*[2] (1808)

Leonora Sansay was the daughter of an innkeeper in Philadelphia. Little is known about her outside the letters of Aaron Burr, who became the third vice president of the United States. Sansay was Burr's friend and perhaps his mistress, and she is mentioned as a captivating and beautiful woman by many powerful men at the time, including by her eventual husband, Louis Sansay, a plantation owner from Saint-Domingue who fled to America during the Haitian Revolution.

In 1802, Sansay sailed to Saint-Domingue with her husband, who wished to reclaim his property on the island. While there, Sansay corresponded at length with Burr, and these letters provide the framework for her novel, *Secret History*. Sansay's book, with its cosmopolitan scope and epistolary form, reveals the complex intersection of revolutionary and Enlightenment ideals as they clash against the inequities of race, gender, and class in the violence-torn island of Saint-Domingue in 1802–03. The following excerpt describes the protagonist's arrival to the island, which took place shortly after the rebel forces burned Cape François rather than allow the invading French forces to take the city.

from LETTER I

Cape François

We arrived safely here, my dear friend, after a passage of forty days, during which I suffered horribly from sea-sickness, heat and confinement; but the society of my fellow-passengers was so agreeable that I often forgot the inconvenience to which I was exposed. It consisted of five or six French families who, having left St. Domingo at the beginning of the revolution, were now returning[3] full of joy at the idea of again possessing the estates from which they had been driven by their revolted slaves. Buoyed by their newly awakened hopes they were all delightful anticipation. There is an elasticity in the French character which repels misfortune. They have an inexhaustible flow of spirits that bears them lightly through the ills of life.

Towards the end of the voyage, when I was well enough to go on deck, I was delighted with the profound tranquillity of the ocean, the uninterrupted view, the beautiful horizon, and wished, since fate has separated me from those I love, that I could build a dwelling on the bosom of the waters, where, sheltered from the storms that agitate mankind, I should be exposed to those of heaven only. But a truce to melancholy reflections, for here I am in St. Domingo, with a new world opening to my view.

[1] *Cape François* Now Cap-Haïtien, this was the main city on the north coast of Saint-Domingue and the capital of the French colony from 1711 to 1770 (after which the capital was moved to Port-au-Prince).

[2] *General Rochambeau* In 1802, Donatien-Marie-Joseph de Vimeur, vicomte de Rochambeau was sent by Napoleon to reclaim Saint-Domingue by whatever means necessary; Rochambeau was replacing General Leclerc, who had died of yellow fever while in Saint-Domingue. Rochambeau is infamous for his brutality and genocidal war crimes; his extreme tactics are viewed by historians, however, as instrumental in bringing together the rebel army and the free people of color in Saint-Domingue to create a united force that would defeat the French in 1803.

[3] *now returning* In 1801–02, Napoleon sent a large force to retake Saint-Domingue, prompting French plantation owners to hope that they could reclaim their property (Napoleon also planned to reinstitute slavery, which had been abolished in 1794).

Incendie du Cap.

Révolte générale des Nègres. Massacre des Blancs.

Frontispiece, *Saint-Domingue, ou Histoire de Ses Révolutions* (*Saint-Domingue, or the History of Their Revolutions*), c. 1815. The caption translates as "General Revolt of the Blacks. Massacre of the Whites," while the heading above the picture translates as "Conflagration of the Cape" (a reference to the Battle of Cape François that took place in June 1793).

My sister, whose fortunes, you know, I was obliged to follow, repents every day having so precipitately chosen a husband:[1] it is impossible for two creatures to be more different, and I foresee that she will be wretched.

On landing, we found the town a heap of ruins. A more terrible picture of desolation cannot be imagined. Passing through streets choked with rubbish, we reached with difficulty a house which had escaped the general fate. The people live in tents, or make a kind of shelter, by laying a few boards across the half-consumed beams; for the buildings being here of hewn stone, with walls three feet thick, only the roofs and floors have been destroyed. But to hear of the distress which these unfortunate people have suffered, would fill with horror the stoutest heart, and make the most obdurate melt with pity.

When the French fleet appeared before the mouth of the harbour, Christophe,[2] the Black general, who commanded at the Cape, rode through the town, ordering all the women to leave their houses—the men had been taken to the plain the day before, for he was going to set fire to the place, which he did with his own hand.

The ladies, bearing their children in their arms, or supporting the trembling steps of their aged mothers,

[1] *My sister ... husband* The fictional writer of this letter is Mary, whose sister Clara is married to a jealous and abusive husband named St. Louis. Later in the novel, there are letters by both sisters.

[2] *Christophe* General Christophe was one of the leaders of the rebel forces (along with Toussaint Louverture and Jean-Jacques Dessalines); on Louverture's orders, Christophe set fire to Cape François on 4 February 1802, two days before the French forces, led by Napoleon's brother-in-law Charles Leclerc, arrived to suppress the revolution.

ascended in crowds the mountain which rises behind the town. Climbing over rocks covered with brambles, where no path had been ever beat, their feet were torn to pieces and their steps marked with blood. Here they suffered all the pains of hunger and thirst; the most terrible apprehensions for their fathers, husbands, brothers and sons; to which was added the sight of the town in flames: and even these horrors were increased by the explosion of the powder magazine. Large masses of rock were detached by the shock, which, rolling down the sides of the mountain, many of these hapless[1] fugitives were killed. Others still more unfortunate, had their limbs broken or sadly bruised, whilst their wretched companions could offer them nothing but unavailing sympathy and impotent regret.

On the third day the negroes evacuated the place, and the fleet entered the harbour. Two gentlemen, who had been concealed by a faithful slave, went in a canoe to meet the admiral's vessel, and arrived in time to prevent a dreadful catastrophe. The general, seeing numbers of people descending the mountain, thought they were the negroes coming to oppose his landing and was preparing to fire on them, when these gentlemen informed him that they were the white inhabitants, and thus prevented a mistake too shocking to be thought of.

The men now entered from the plain and sought among the smoking ruins the objects of their affectionate solicitude. To paint these heart-rending scenes of tenderness and woe, description has no powers. The imagination itself shrinks from the task.

Three months after this period we arrived and have now been a month here, the town is rapidly rebuilding, but it is extremely difficult to find a lodging. The heat is intolerable and the season so unhealthy that the people die in incredible numbers. On the night of our arrival, Toussaint the general in chief of the negroes, was seized at the Gonaives[2] and embarked for France. This event caused great rejoicing. A short time before he was taken, he had his treasure buried in the woods, and at the return of the negroes he employed on the expedition, they were shot without being suffered to utter a word. ...

[1] *hapless* Unlucky.

[2] *Gonaives* City in northwest Haiti.

from William Wells Brown, *St. Domingo: Its Revolutions and Its Patriots, a Lecture Delivered before the Metropolitan Athenaeum, London, May 16, and at St Thomas' Church, Philadelphia, December 20, 1854* (1855)

In 1854, the novelist and orator William Wells Brown delivered one of his most significant speeches, an account of the Haitian Revolution in which he sought to honor the history of black leadership in Haiti, and to give voice to his own growing conviction that slavery in the United States might never be abolished without bloodshed. In his summary of the historical developments, Brown drew on John R. Beard's 1853 biography of the black leader Toussaint Louverture; his lecture also harkened back to the American abolitionist Maria Weston Chapman, who had years before expressed her conviction that the history of Haiti should teach America that enslaved people might in time rise up violently against the system of chattel slavery. By contextualizing the Haitian conflict within the long history of European colonial oppression, and by connecting Haitian resistance to the abolitionist cause in America, Brown made clear just how fierce and how prolonged efforts to end slavery in America might have to be.

Brown's lecture provided a much-needed corrective to the way in which historians and journalists—particularly in the United States—had generally portrayed the black leaders of the Haitian Revolution. Where many previous commentators had downplayed the achievements of Toussaint Louverture, for example, Brown presented him as a military hero on a par with—and in his motives surpassing—both Napoleon and George Washington.

After the return of Columbus to Spain, ... Dovadillo,[3] his successor, began a system of unmitigated oppression towards the Caribbeans,

[3] *Dovadillo* Likely a reference to Francisco Fernández de Bobadilla (c. 1448–1502), a Spanish official who was tasked with investigating Christopher Columbus's administration of Hispaniola (the Spanish settlement on what is now the island of Haiti and the Dominican Republic). Bobadilla arrested Columbus and took over as governor of the island from 1500 to 1502.

and eventually reduced the whole of the inhabitants to slavery; and thus commenced that hateful sin in the New World. As fresh adventurers arrived in the island,[1] the Spanish power became more consolidated and more oppressive. The natives were made to toil in the gold mines without compensation, and in many instances without any regard whatever to the preservation of human life; so much so, that in 1507 the number of natives had, by hunger, toil, and the sword, been reduced from a million to sixty thousand. Thus, in the short space of *fifteen years*, more than *nine hundred thousand* persons perished under the iron hand of slavery in the island of St. Domingo.

The most important town built by the Spaniards was Santo Domingo, situated on the south side of the island. The island was too valuable not to attract other adventurers, and, in a short period after its discovery, the French planted a colony on the north-west side of the island, which in a few years surpassed the Spanish portion in the elements of social well-being, and in commerce and agriculture.

St. Domingo suffered much from the loss of its original inhabitants; and the want of laborers to till the soil and to work in the mines first suggested the idea of importing slaves from the coast of Africa. The slave trade was soon commenced and carried on with great rapidity. Before the Africans were shipped, the name of the owner and the plantation on which they were to toil was stamped on their shoulders with a burning iron. For a number of years St. Domingo opened its markets annually to more than 20,000 newly-imported slaves. With the advance of commerce and agriculture, opulence spread in all parts of the island, and poured untold treasures into France and Spain. In a similar proportion the population increased, so that, at the beginning of the French Revolution, in 1789, there were 900,000 souls on the island. Of these, 700,000 were Africans, 60,000 men of mixed blood, and the remainder were whites and Caribbeans. ...

Many of the mulattoes[2] having received their education in Paris, where prejudice against color was unknown,[3] experienced great dissatisfaction at their proscription[4] on their return to St. Domingo. White enough to make them hopeful and aspiring, many of them possessed wealth enough to make them influential. Aware by their education of the principles of freedom that were being advocated in Europe and the United States, they were also ever on the watch to seize opportunities to better their social and political condition. In the French part of the island alone, 20,000 whites lived in the midst of 30,000 free mulattoes and 500,000 slaves. In the Spanish portion the odds were still greater in favor of the slaves. Thus the advantage of numbers and physical strength was on the side of the oppressed. Right is the most dangerous of weapons— woe to him who leaves it to his enemies!

In England, Wilberforce, Sharpe, and Clarkson[5] were using their great talents to abolish the African slave trade, and to emancipate the slaves in the English colonies. The principles which they advocated were taken up by the friends of the blacks in Paris, and a society was formed, with Gregoire, Raynal, Barnave, Brissot, Condorcet, and Lafayette[6] at its head. The English philanthropists issued their publications in London; they found their way to Paris, and thence to St. Domingo. These made the blacks aware of their rights, as well as of their strength. The island had already assumed the name of *Hayti*. The French nation, after suffering for centuries under the misrule of its profligate princes, arose *en masse* to throw off their yoke, and the news of the oath of the Tennis Court and the taking of the Bastille[7] was received with the wildest enthusiasm by

[1] *the island* Saint-Domingue (now Haiti).

[2] *mulattoes* Term, now considered offensive, for people of both black and white ancestry.

[3] *Paris … unknown* Black people living in France, and in Paris in particular, experienced less virulent racism than in other European countries, though it is not correct to say that racism was unknown there. Most black people in Paris were servants; during the French Revolution, however, black youths were sent from French colonies—particularly from Saint-Domingue—to be educated in France. Toussaint Louverture sent both of his sons to Paris for their educations.

[4] *proscription* Exclusion from society.

[5] *Wilberforce, Sharpe, and Clarkson* Prominent English abolitionists.

[6] *Gregoire … and Lafayette* Prominent French abolitionists and philosophers.

[7] *taking of the Bastille* Allusion to the July 1789 storming of the Bastille, an important political prison in Paris, by civil insurgents; this event is often viewed as marking the beginning of the French Revolution.

the mulattoes in Hayti. The announcement of these events was hailed with delight by both the white planters and the mulattoes; the former, because they thought that they saw in the dim distance the independence of the colony; the latter, because they viewed it as a movement that would secure to them equal rights with the whites. And even the slaves regarded it as a precursor to their own emancipation.

However, the general excitement which the revolution in Paris created amongst the mulattoes soon satisfied the planters that they could not retain their power without the aid of France. ...

The struggle in St. Domingo was watched with intense interest by the friends of the blacks, both in Paris and in London, and all appeared to look with hope to the rising up of a black chief, who should prove himself adequate to the emergency. Nor did they look in vain. In the midst of the disorders that threatened on all sides, the negro chief made his appearance in the form of an old slave named Toussaint.[1] This man was the grandson of the king of Arradas, one of the most wealthy, powerful, and influential monarchs on the west coast of Africa. Toussaint was a man of prepossessing appearance, of middle stature, and possessed an iron frame. His dignified, calm, and unaffected features, and broad and well-developed forehead, would cause him to be selected, in any company of men, as one who was born for a leader. By his energy and perseverance he had learned to read and write, and had carefully studied the works of Raynal,[2] and a few others who had written in behalf of human freedom. This class of literature, no doubt, had great influence over the mind of Toussaint, and did much to give him the power that he afterwards exercised in the island. His private virtues were many, and he had a deep and pervading sense of religion, and, in the camp,[3] carried it even as far as Oliver Cromwell.[4] It might be said that

an inward and prophetic genius revealed to him the omnipotence of a firm and unwearied adherence to a principle. He was not only loved by his fellow-slaves, but the planters held him in high consideration. ...

The black general [Toussaint] then issued a proclamation[5] to the people of Hayti, in which he said, "You are going to fight against enemies who have neither faith, law nor religion; they promise you liberty[6]—they intend your servitude. Why have so many ships traversed the ocean, if not to throw you again into chains? During the last ten years what have you not endured for liberty? The French do not come here to fight for their country, or for liberty, but for slavery. Let us resolve that these troops shall never leave our shores. Fortune seems to have delivered them as victims into our hands. Those whom our swords spare will be struck dead by an avenging climate; their bones will be scattered among these mountains and rocks, and tossed about by the waves of our sea. Never more will they behold their native land; never more will they be received by their mothers, their wives and their sisters; but liberty will reign over their tomb."

"To arms! to arms!" was the cry all over the island, until everyone who could use even the lightest instrument of death, was under arms. ...

We cannot close without once more reviewing the character of Toussaint. Of all the great men of St. Domingo, the first place must be given to him. He laid the foundation for the emancipation of his race and the independence of the island. He fought her battles, and at last died in a cold prison[7] for her sake and his fidelity to the cause of freedom. As an officer in battle

[1] *Toussaint* Toussaint Louverture (1743–1803), a leader of the Haitian Revolution.

[2] *Raynal* Guillaume Thomas François Raynal (1713–96) was a French Enlightenment writer whose six-volume work *Histoire des Deux Indes* (1770) was fierce in its denunciation of European colonialism and of the practice of slavery.

[3] *in the camp* During military campaigns (in military encampments).

[4] *Oliver Cromwell* Cromwell (1599–1658) was an English Puritan who led the uprising to overthrow King Charles I; he eventually

established himself as Lord Protector of the nation, ruling for five years. He is a controversial figure, considered a violent, military dictator by some and a revolutionary hero by others; his religious zeal was a motivating force in all his political and military decisions.

[5] *proclamation* Toussaint Louverture's 1793 Proclamation is included in this anthology (see above).

[6] *they ... liberty* See the 1793 Proclamation by French Civil Commissioner Léger-Félicité Sonthonax (included in the website portion of this anthology). In it, Sonthonax proclaims the end of slavery in Saint-Domingue; he is widely presumed to have done so largely out of a desire to persuade Toussaint Louverture to form an alliance with France instead of Spain.

[7] *died in a cold prison* Toussaint Louverture was captured by an army sent by Napoleon in 1802; Louverture was then deported to France, where he was imprisoned at Fort de Joux. He died of illness and malnutrition on 7 April 1803.

he had no superior in Hayti. He defeated the French in several pitched battles, drove the English from the island, and refused a crown when it was offered to him. When his friends advised him to be on his guard against the treachery of Leclerc,[1] he replied, "For one to expose one's life for one's country when in danger is a sacred duty; but to arouse one's country in order to save one's life is inglorious." From ignorance he became educated by his own exertions. From a slave he rose to be a soldier, a general, and a governor, and might have been a king. He possessed a rare genius, which showed itself in the private circle, in the council-chamber, and on the field of battle. His very name became a tower of strength to his friends and a terror to his foes.

The history of Toussaint, placed by the side of that of Napoleon, presents many striking parallels. Both born in a humble position, they raised themselves to the height of power by the force of their character. Both gained renown in legislation and government, as well as in war. Both fell the moment they had attained supreme authority. Both finished their career on a barren rock.[2]

The parallels, however, have their contrast. Toussaint fought for liberty; Napoleon fought for himself. Toussaint gained fame by leading an oppressed and injured race to the successful vindication of their rights, Napoleon made himself a name and acquired a sceptre by supplanting liberty and destroying nationalities, in order to substitute his own illegitimate despotism. Napoleon transferred Toussaint from the warm and sunny climate of the West Indies to the cold climate of the north of France; the English transferred Napoleon from the cold climate of France to the warm climate of St. Helena.

This was indeed retribution; for the man of the cold regions died in the tropics, to atone for his crime in having caused the man of the tropics to end his days in the cold regions. While Toussaint's memory will be revered by all lovers of freedom, Napoleon's will be detested.

And, lastly, Toussaint's career as a Christian, a statesman, and a general, will lose nothing by a comparison with that of Washington. Each was the leader of an oppressed and outraged people, each had a powerful enemy to contend with, and each succeeded in founding a government in the New World. Toussaint's government made liberty its watchword, incorporated it in its constitution, abolished the slave trade, and made freedom universal amongst the people. Washington's government incorporated slavery and the slave trade, and enacted laws by which chains were fastened upon the limbs of millions of people. Toussaint liberated his countrymen; Washington enslaved a portion of his, and aided in giving strength and vitality to an institution that will one day rend asunder the Union that he helped to form. Already the slave in his chains, in the rice swamps of Carolina and the cotton fields of Mississippi, burns for revenge.

In contemplating the fact that the slave would rise and vindicate his right to freedom by physical force, Jefferson said:

> Indeed, I tremble for my country when I reflect that God is just; that his justice cannot sleep forever; that, considering numbers, nature, and natural means only, a revolution of the wheel of fortune, an exchange of situation, is among possible events; that it may become probable by supernatural interference! The Almighty has no attribute which can take side with us in such a contest.
>
> What an incomprehensible machine is man! who can endure toil, famine, stripes,[3] imprisonment, and death itself, in vindication of his own liberty, and the next moment be deaf to all those motives whose power supported him through his trial, and inflict on his fellow-men a bondage, one hour of which is fraught with more misery than ages of that which he rose in rebellion to oppose.[4]

And, should such a contest take place, the God of Justice will be on the side of the oppressed blacks.

[1] *Leclerc* Charles Victoire Emmanuel Leclerc (1772–1802) was Napoleon's brother-in-law; he was sent in 1802 to reclaim Saint-Domingue by force and to capture the black officers in charge of the revolution, including Louverture.

[2] *Both ... barren rock* As noted above, Louverture died in a French prison in 1803. After losing the Battle of Waterloo, Napoleon was exiled to the rocky island of St. Helena, where he died in 1821.

[3] *stripes* Marks left on the skin by a whip.

[4] *Indeed ... oppose* This quotation is from "Query 18: Manners" in Thomas Jefferson's *Notes on the State of Virginia* (1785).

The exasperated genius[1] of Africa would rise from the depths of the ocean, and show its threatening form; and war against the tyrants would be the rallying cry. The indignation of the slaves of the south would kindle a fire so hot that it would melt their chains, drop by drop, until not a single link would remain; and the revolution that was commenced in 1776 would then be finished, and the glorious sentiments of the Declaration of Independence, "That all men are created equal, and endowed by their Creator with certain inalienable rights, among which are life, liberty, and the pursuit of happiness," would be realized, and our government would no longer be the scorn and contempt of the friends of freedom in other lands, but would really be the LAND OF THE FREE AND HOME OF THE BRAVE.

Gabriel's Rebellion and Other Rebellions by Enslaved Americans

If the American and French Revolutions helped inspire the Haitian Revolution, so too did the Haitian Revolution help inspire rebellions and revolutions elsewhere—including revolutions in Mexico (1810–21) and other Spanish-controlled territories, and several rebellions by enslaved blacks in the United States—perhaps most notably Gabriel's Rebellion in Virginia in 1800. Gabriel and his fellow rebels—including his brother Solomon, who like Gabriel was an enslaved blacksmith—worked with others enslaved in and around the state capital, Richmond, to formulate a plan of rebellion; their hope was that if they could capture the state's governor, James Monroe, they would be able to demand the abolition of slavery in return for their hostage. The plan was discovered before they could put it into effect; Gabriel and 25 others were hanged.

Newspaper Reports

The newspaper reports below give a sense of the ways in which Gabriel's Rebellion and other rebellions of enslaved blacks in the newly formed United States were seen as linked to Toussaint Louverture and the Haitian Revolution, as well as to the French Revolution (and, by extension, Frenchmen).

from THE VIRGINIA ARGUS
(RICHMOND, VIRGINIA, 3 OCTOBER 1800)

Was not the slave *Gabriel* of Virginia, as fit an object for negociation, and as fit for command as *Toussaint*—unhappily it is only the difference of situation which entitles Toussaint to a present of *three carriages* from a British agent in Philadelphia, and marks the slave of Prosser, an object for the gibbet.

from THE FEDERAL GALAXY
(BRATTLEBORO, VERMONT, 11 OCTOBER 1800)

Fredericksburg, Sept. 23
Extract of a letter to the Editor

"I left Richmond yesterday morning, all was confusion and alarm. The minutiae of the conspiracy which has been detected have not been detailed to the public, and perhaps, through a mistaken notion of prudence and policy, will not be detailed in the Richmond papers. Indeed, fear seems to have put an imprimateur[2] on the press.

"But as I conceive it a matter of great moment that the origin of this evil should be known, I now communicate to you such circumstances as I was enabled, by much industry, to collect from the most authentic sources.

"On the Saturday night when the deluge of rain fell, the plot was to have been carried into execution. One thousand negroes were to have entered the town in

1 *genius* Guardian spirit.

2 *imprimateur* Usually refers to an official license to print; here, it suggests "seal."

three directions with fire and sword. The penitentiary house, which the executive had made a magazine[1] of a few days before, and of which the conspirators were apprized, was to have been seized on in the first place, then the treasury, then the mills, and then the bridge across James river. The first would have supplied them arms and ammunition for many thousand men, the second with money, the third with bread, and the fourth would have enabled them to let in their friends and keep out their enemies from the south side of James river.

"The metropolis being in their possession, which in a few hours would have been the case, a proclamation was to have been issued, by which the negroes from the country and the southern states would have been invited to rally round their standard. In less than one week they might have calculated on 50,000 men in arms. For in addition to friends of their colour, they expected that every Frenchman would join them, every negro and mulatto,[2] and many of the most redoubtable democrats in the state. It came out in evidence on the trial of the six who were condemned on Thursday, that in the general massacre of the white males which was determined on, not a Frenchman was to be touched. It also appeared on the trial, that two Frenchmen had planned the plot, and that the General Gabriel, who is not yet caught had procured it from them. The names of those Frenchmen were not known, when I left town, but it is probable that the criminals will make some further discoveries[3] under the gallows, and that such information may be at length obtained as will enable us to drag forth those diabolical monsters from their lurking places, and bring them to condign[4] punishment. …"

October 1
Letters are received in town from Richmond which mention new discoveries relative to the intended revolt of the negroes. A plan was systemically laid for a general insurrection throughout the state, and the most brutal acts were to have been perpetrated. Several respectable characters, obnoxious to these wretches, were to be singled out for their barbarity in the massacre. Two of the most distinguished beauties of Richmond were to be devoted to the filthy embraces of the commander in chief, Gabriel, and the white women generally were to be preserved for rewards to his followers. …

from Robert Sutcliff, *Travels in Some Parts of North America in the Years 1804, 1805, and 1806* (1815)

This report of a statement given c. 1804 to a lawyer (who in turn reported it to an English traveler) by one of those accused of plotting a rebellion has often been quoted without attribution in connection with Gabriel's Rebellion of 1800. That it in fact dates from a few years later does not make it any less notable as a statement of principle.

I pursued my way to Richmond [Virginia] in the mail stage,[5] through a beautiful country, but clouded and debased by negro slavery. At the house where I breakfasted, which is called the Bowling Green, I was told that the owner had in his possession 200 slaves. In one field near the house, planted with tobacco, I counted nearly 20 women and children, picking grubs from the plants. In the afternoon I passed by a field in which several poor slaves had lately been executed, on the charge of having an intention to rise against their masters. A lawyer who was present at their trials at Richmond informed me that, on one of them being asked what he had to say to the court in his defence, he replied in a manly tone of voice, "I have nothing more than what General Washington would have had to offer, had he been taken by the British and put to trial by them. I have adventured my life in endeavoring to obtain the liberty of my countrymen, and I beg, as a favour, that I may be immediately led to execution. I know that you have pre-determined to shed my blood; why then all this mockery of a trial?"

[1] *magazine* Storehouse where ammunition and weaponry are kept.

[2] *mulatto* Term, now considered offensive, for people of both black and white ancestry.

[3] *make … discoveries* Give up some more information.

[4] *condign* Deserved, appropriate.

[5] *mail stage* Stage coach carrying mail as well as passengers.

JUDITH SARGENT MURRAY
1751 – 1820

"I think," writes Judith Sargent Murray in her first published essay on female education, "to teach young minds to aspire, ought to be the ground work of education[.] … Ambition is a noble principle, which properly directed, may be productive of the most valuable consequences." At a time when such aspirations, especially among women, were more likely to be seen as vices than as positive attributes, Murray boldly pronounced them to be laudable, encouraging girls and women to embrace ambitions beyond those of marriage and feminine domesticity, and to have pride in themselves and their mental capabilities. Aside from her essays, which comprise her most enduring work, Murray was also a poet, playwright, and religious writer. Her 1790 essay "On the Equality of the Sexes" (which preceded both Olympe de Gouges's *Declaration of the Rights of Woman and the Female Citizen* and Mary Wollstonecraft's *A Vindication of the Rights of Woman*) broke new ground by extending the Enlightenment hope for a rational society, and the American hope for an equal one, into the sphere of gender.

Born in Gloucester, Massachusetts, in 1751, Judith Sargent was the eldest child of Winthrop Sargent and Judith Saunders Sargent. The family belonged to the merchant class; their wealth stemmed from the marine trade. Judith showed exceptional intellectual promise from a young age, and while it was not possible at the time for girls to receive a formal education equivalent to that of boys, her parents ensured that she and her brother (who was preparing for Harvard) received the same level of home tutorship in subjects such as Latin and Greek. Beyond this she studied voraciously on her own, and became exceptionally well-read; nevertheless, she always regretted her lack of a formal education. As she later lamented in a letter, "It was the mode to confine the female intellect within the narrowest bounds."

At the age of eighteen, Judith married John Stevens, a prosperous sea merchant. The marriage was not founded on love; in her future writings, Murray would press for the broadening of respectable women's options beyond marriage and the raising of a family.

Murray began composing poems with some degree of seriousness in her early twenties, submitting them for publication in Boston's *The Gentleman's and Lady's Town and Country Magazine* in the 1780s. In 1782 she also wrote a catechism for Universalism, the religion to which she and her parents had (somewhat controversially) converted in the previous decade, and to which she became highly devoted. With the heightening of the American Revolutionary War, Murray became invested in the dominant spirit of liberation, and highly interested in issues related to independence and human rights. Her first secular prose publication was an essay on female education entitled "Desultory Thoughts upon the Utility of Encouraging a Degree of Self-Complacency, Especially in Female Bosoms" (1784), which was published under the pen name "Constantia." (The use of pen names was very common at the time, especially among women, who, if they published, rarely did so under their own names.) Here Murray laid the groundwork on which her future career would be built, embracing the principle of intellectual equality of the sexes, and drawing attention to the need for women to be educated and taught to value their selves.

In 1786, John Stevens died in disgrace in the West Indies (having gone there to escape debtor's prison); Judith resolved to remain unmarried and to commit the rest of her life to the Universalist church. Two years later, she married John Murray, the minister who had established the first Universalist congregation in Gloucester. Unlike her first marriage, her union with Murray was based firmly on love and mutual intellectual admiration.

In 1789, Murray submitted a poem, "Lines Occasioned by the Death of an Infant," to *The Massachusetts Magazine*, a work occasioned by her grief over the miscarriage of her son and the painful illness she suffered thereafter. The following year saw the publication of "On the Equality of the Sexes" (which she had first drafted over a decade previously) in the same magazine. The piece is in many ways a natural development of Enlightenment ideas concerning the seat of reason in the soul, the division of body and soul, and the pre-eminence of the latter over the former. Murray argued against the then-common view that women were by nature intellectually inferior to men, and therefore best-suited only to helpful domesticity and frivolous amusements. She was highly gratified when Wollstonecraft's *Vindication*, which expressed similar ideas, was released two years later. In 1792 Murray took on a new pen name, "The Gleaner," under which she published many more essays on politics and literary criticism, two plays, and the serialized novel *The Story of Margaretta*, which appeared in 1798. In that same year she acknowledged the work of "The Gleaner" to be that of "Constantia."

The Murrays had one daughter, Julia Maria, to whom they endeavored to give the best education possible. Murray published little after 1798, focusing most of her efforts on caring for her husband and editing his writings, which she helped complete and publish after his death in 1815. Julia married a Southern landowner, Adam Bingaman, and in 1818 Murray joined them on Bingaman's Natchez, Mississippi plantation, where she died two years later. For many generations after her death Murray was almost entirely forgotten. The multi-volume *American Cyclopedia* of 1866 devotes a half-page to her husband ("the father of Universalism in America") but makes no mention of her—and the same is true of histories and anthologies of American literature of the early and mid-twentieth century. Only in the 1970s, with the rise of feminist scholarship, did her ground-breaking contributions begin to be again acknowledged. As Murray's personal correspondence makes clear, she equivocated over the issue of whether or not the principle of human equality should apply to races other than her own, or even to white women of the laboring class; her limited vision in matters such as these inevitably colors the way we read her work today. But Murray remains a figure of vital importance to the spreading of the idea that women are equal to men, and deserving of the same education and the same opportunities.

NOTE ON THE TEXTS: The text of "On the Equality of the Sexes" is based on the first version printed in *The Massachusetts Magazine, or, Monthly Museum of Knowledge and Rational Entertainment* for March–April 1790. The text of "The Gleaner Contemplates the Future Prospects of Women in This 'Enlightened Age'" is taken from that found in the 1798 compilation *The Gleaner: A Miscellaneous Production*, by "Constantia," where it appears as essay number 88. Spelling and punctuation have been modernized in accordance with the practices of this anthology.

⌘ ⌘ ⌘

On the Equality of the Sexes

PART I

That minds are not alike, full well I know,
This truth each day's experience will show;
To heights surprising some great spirits soar,
With inborn strength mysterious depths explore;
5 Their eager gaze surveys the path of light,
Confessed it stood to Newton's[1] piercing sight.

Deep science, like a bashful maid retires,
And but° the *ardent* breast her worth inspires; *only*
By perseverance the coy fair is won,
10 And Genius, led by Study, wears the crown.
But some there are who wish not to improve,
Who never can the path of knowledge love,
Whose souls almost with the dull body one,
With anxious care each mental pleasure shun;
15 Weak is the leveled, enervated mind,
And but while here to vegetate designed.
The torpid spirit mingling with its clod,
Can scarcely boast its origin from God;

[1] *Newton* Sir Isaac Newton (1642–1727), English mathematician and physicist who experimented with the refraction of light.

Stupidly dull—they move progressing on—
20 They eat, and drink, and all their work is done.
While others, emulous of sweet applause,
Industrious seek for each event a cause,
Tracing the hidden springs whence knowledge flows,
Which nature all in beauteous order shows.
25 Yet cannot I their sentiments imbibe,[1]
Who this distinction to the sex ascribe,
As if a woman's form must needs enroll° incorporate
A weak, a servile, an inferior soul;
And that the guise of man must still proclaim,
30 Greatness of mind, and him, to be the same.
Yet as the hours revolve fair proofs arise,
Which the bright wreath of growing fame supplies;
And in past times some men have *sunk* so *low*,
That female records nothing *less* can show.
35 But imbecility is still confined,
And by the lordly sex to us consigned;
They rob us of the power t'improve,
And then declare we only trifles love;
Yet haste the era, when the world shall know
40 That such distinctions only dwell below;
The soul unfettered, to no sex confined,
Was for the abodes of cloudless day designed.
 Meantime we emulate their manly fires,
Though erudition all their thoughts inspires,
45 Yet nature with *equality* imparts,
And *noble passions*, swell e'en *female hearts*.

Is it upon mature consideration we adopt the idea that nature is thus partial[2] in her distributions? Is it indeed a fact that she hath yielded to one half of the human species so unquestionable a mental superiority? I know that to both sexes elevated understandings, and the reverse, are common. But, suffer[3] me to ask, in what the minds of females are so notoriously deficient, or unequal. May not the intellectual powers be ranged under these four heads—imagination, reason, memory and judgment? The province of imagination hath long since been surrendered up to us, and we have been crowned undoubted sovereigns of the regions of fancy.[4] Invention is perhaps the most arduous effort of the mind; this branch of imagination hath been particularly ceded to us, and we have been time out of mind invested with that creative faculty. Observe the variety of fashions (here I bar the contemptuous smile) which distinguish and adorn the female world; how continually are they changing, insomuch that they almost render the wise man's assertion problematical, and we are ready to say, *there is something new under the sun.*[5] Now what a playfulness, what an exuberance of fancy, what strength of inventive imagination, doth this continual variation discover? Again, it hath been observed, that if the turpitude[6] of the conduct of our sex hath been ever so enormous, so extremely ready are we, that the very first thought presents us with an apology so plausible as to produce our actions even in an amiable light. Another instance of our creative powers is our talent for slander; how ingenious are we at inventive scandal? What a formidable story can we in a moment fabricate merely from the force of a prolific imagination? How many reputations, in the fertile brain of a female, have been utterly despoiled? How industrious are we at improving[7] a hint? Suspicion how easily do we convert into conviction, and conviction, embellished by the power of eloquence, stalks abroad to the surprise and confusion of unsuspecting innocence. Perhaps it will be asked if I furnish these facts as instances of excellency in our sex. Certainly not; but as proofs of a creative faculty, of a lively imagination. Assuredly great activity of mind is thereby discovered, and was this activity properly directed, what beneficial effects would follow.

Is the needle and kitchen sufficient to employ the operations of a soul thus organized? I should conceive not. Nay, it is a truth that those very departments leave the intelligent principle vacant, and at liberty for speculation. Are we deficient in reason? We can only reason from what we know, and if an opportunity of acquiring knowledge hath been denied us, the inferiority of our sex cannot fairly be deduced from thence. Memory, I believe, will be allowed us in common, since everyone's experience must testify that a loquacious old woman is as frequently met with as a communicative old man;

1 *imbibe* Swallow; accept.

2 *partial* Biased.

3 *suffer* Allow.

4 *fancy* Imagination; fancifulness.

5 *there is … the sun* See Ecclesiastes 1.9: "and there is no new thing under the sun."

6 *turpitude* Baseness.

7 *improving* Intensifying or exaggerating.

their subjects are alike drawn from the fund of other times, and the transactions of their youth, or of maturer life, entertain, or perhaps fatigue you, in the evening of their lives. "But our judgment is not so strong—we do not distinguish so well." Yet it may be questioned, from what doth this superiority, in this determining faculty of the soul, proceed? May we not trace its source in the difference of education, and continued advantages? Will it be said that the judgment of a male of two years old is more sage[1] than that of a female's of the same age? I believe the reverse is generally observed to be true. But from that period what partiality! How is the one exalted, and the other depressed, by the contrary modes of education which are adopted! The one is taught to aspire, and the other is early confined and limited. As their years increase, the sister must be wholly domesticated, while the brother is led by the hand through all the flowery paths of science. Grant that their minds are by nature equal, yet who shall wonder at the *apparent* superiority, if indeed custom becomes *second nature*; nay if it taketh place of nature, and that it doth the experience of each day will evince.

At length arrived at womanhood, the uncultivated fair one feels a void which the employments allotted her are by no means capable of filling. What can she do? To books she may not apply; or if she doth, *to those only of the novel kind*,[2] lest she merit the appellation of a *learned lady*; and what ideas have been affixed to this term, the observation of many can testify. Fashion, scandal, and sometimes what is still more reprehensible, are then called in to her relief; and who can say to what lengths the liberties she takes may proceed? Meantime she herself is most unhappy; she feels the want[3] of a cultivated mind. Is she single, she in vain seeks to fill up time from sexual[4] employments or amusements. Is she united to a person whose soul nature made equal to her own? Education hath set him so far above her that in those entertainments which are productive of such rational felicity, she is not qualified to accompany him. She experiences a mortifying consciousness of inferiority which embitters every enjoyment. Doth the person to whom her adverse fate hath consigned her possess a mind incapable of improvement, she is equally wretched in being so closely connected with an individual whom she cannot but despise.

Now, was she[5] permitted the same instructors as her brother (with an eye however to their particular departments), for the employment of a rational mind an ample field would be opened. In astronomy she might catch a glimpse of the immensity of the Deity, and thence she would form amazing conceptions of the august and supreme Intelligence. In geography she would admire Jehovah in the midst of his benevolence; thus adapting this globe to the various wants and amusements of its inhabitants. In natural philosophy[6] she would adore the infinite majesty of heaven, clothed in condescension;[7] and as she traversed the reptile world, she would hail the goodness of a creating God. A mind, thus filled, would have little room for the trifles with which our sex are, with too much justice, accused of amusing themselves, and they would thus be rendered fit companions for those who should one day wear them as their crown.[8] Fashions, in their variety, would then give place to conjectures, which might perhaps conduce to the improvement of the literary world; and there would be no leisure for slander or detraction. Reputation would not then be blasted, but serious speculations would occupy the lively imaginations of the sex. Unnecessary visits would be precluded, and that custom would only be indulged by way of relaxation, or to answer the demands of consanguinity and friendship. Females would become discreet,[9] their judgments would be invigorated, and their partners for life being circumspectly chosen, an unhappy Hymen[10] would then be as rare as is now the reverse.

1 *sage* Wise.

2 *those ... novel kind* Throughout much of the eighteenth and early nineteenth centuries, novels were considered by many to be light and unserious in nature, appropriate only for women readers; moreover, many criticized novels as indulgent and morally unsound escapism.

3 *want* Lack.

4 *sexual* I.e., appropriate to her sex; feminine.

5 *was she* If she were.

6 *natural philosophy* I.e., the sciences.

7 *condescension* Indifference toward one's own superiority.

8 *those who ... their crown* See Proverbs 12.4: "A virtuous woman is a crown to her husband." The phrase was used in a contemporary illustration which advised women on their duties, and to "keep within compass"; see the color plates in this anthology.

9 *discreet* Prudent.

10 *Hymen* In Greek mythology, the god of marriage; thus, marriage itself.

Will it be urged that those acquirements would supersede our domestic duties? I answer that every requisite in female economy[1] is easily attained; and with truth I can add that, when once attained, they require no further *mental attention*. Nay, while we are pursuing the needle, or the superintendency of the family, I repeat, that our minds are at full liberty for reflection; that imagination may exert itself in full vigor; and that if a just foundation is early laid, our ideas will then be worthy of rational beings. If we were industrious we might easily find time to arrange them upon paper, or should avocations[2] press too hard for such an indulgence, the hours allotted for conversation would at least become more refined and rational. Should it still be vociferated, "Your domestic employments are sufficient"—I would calmly ask, is it reasonable that a candidate for immortality, for the joys of heaven, an intelligent being who is to spend an eternity in contemplating the works of Deity, should at present be so degraded as to be allowed no other ideas than those which are suggested by the mechanism of a pudding, or the sewing the seams of a garment? Pity that all such censurers of female improvement do not go one step further and deny their future existence; to be consistent they surely ought.

Yes, ye lordly, ye haughty sex, our souls are by nature *equal* to yours; the same breath of God animates, enlivens, and invigorates us; and that we are not fallen lower than yourselves, let those witness who have greatly towered above the various discouragements by which they have been so heavily oppressed; and though I am unacquainted with the list of celebrated characters on either side, yet from the observations I have made in the contracted circle in which I have moved, I dare confidently believe that, from the commencement of time to the present day, there hath been as many females as males who, by the *mere force of natural powers*, have merited the crown of applause; who, *thus unassisted*, have seized the wreath of fame. I know there are [those] who assert that, as the animal[3] powers of the one sex are superior, of course their mental faculties also must be stronger (thus attributing strength of mind to the transient organization of this earth-born

tenement[4]). But if this reasoning is just, man must be content to yield the palm[5] [to] many of the brute creation,[6] since by not a few of his brethren of the field he is far surpassed in bodily strength. Moreover, was this argument admitted, it would prove too much, for ocular demonstration evinceth that there are many robust masculine ladies and effeminate gentlemen. Yet I fancy that Mr. Pope,[7] though clogged with an enervated body, and distinguished by a diminutive stature, could nevertheless lay claim to greatness of soul; and perhaps there are many other instances which might be adduced to combat so unphilosophical an opinion. Do we not often see that when the clay-built tabernacle[8] is well nigh dissolved, when it is just ready to mingle with the parent soil, the immortal inhabitant aspires to and even attaineth heights the most sublime, and which were before wholly unexplored? Besides, were we to grant that animal strength proved anything, taking into consideration the accustomed impartiality of Nature, we should be induced to imagine that she had invested the female mind with superior strength as an equivalent for the bodily powers of man. But waiving this however palpable advantage, for *equality only* we wish to contend.

PART 2

I am aware that there are many passages in the sacred oracles which seem to give the advantage to the other sex, but I consider all these as wholly metaphorical. Thus David was a man after God's own heart,[9] yet see him enervated by his licentious passions! Behold him

1 *economy* Household management.

2 *avocations* Employments.

3 *animal* I.e., physical.

4 *this earth-born tenement* I.e., the body.

5 *palm* Honor.

6 *the brute creation* I.e., the realm of non-human animals.

7 *Mr. Pope* Alexander Pope (1688–1744), English poet, highly regarded throughout the eighteenth century; Pope had a spinal deformity that was likely caused by a form of spinal tuberculosis, and also suffered numerous chronic illnesses as an adult.

8 *tabernacle* House or dwelling-place; in other words, the body, as the dwelling-place of the soul.

9 *Thus David ... own heart* See 1 Samuel 13.14: "The Lord hath sought him a man after his own heart." David was the second king of Israel, portrayed in the Old Testament.

following Uriah to the death,[1] and show me wherein could consist the immaculate Being's complacency. Listen to the curses which Job bestoweth upon the day of his nativity,[2] and tell me where is his perfection, where his patience—*literally* it existed not. David and Job were types[3] of him who was to come; and the superiority of man, as exhibited in scripture, being also emblematical, all arguments deduced from thence of course fall to the ground. The exquisite delicacy of the female mind proclaimeth the exactness of its texture, while its nice[4] sense of honor announceth its innate, its native grandeur. And indeed, in one respect, the preeminence seems to be tacitly allowed us, for after an education which limits and confines, and employments and recreations which naturally tend to enervate the body and debilitate the mind; after we have from early youth been adorned with ribbons and other gewgaws,[5] dressed out like the ancient victims previous to a sacrifice, being taught by the care of our parents in collecting the most showy materials that the ornamenting our exterior ought to be the principal object of our attention; after, I say, fifteen years thus spent, we are introduced into the world,[6] amid the united adulation of every beholder. Praise is sweet to the soul; we are immediately intoxicated by large draughts of flattery which, being plentifully administered, is to the pride of our hearts the most acceptable incense. It is expected that with the other sex we should commence immediate war, and that we should triumph over the machinations of the most artful. We must be constantly upon our guard; prudence and discretion must be our characteristics; and we must rise superior to, and obtain a complete victory over those who have been long adding

to the native strength of their minds by an unremitted study of men and books, and who have, moreover, conceived from the loose characters which they have seen portrayed in the extensive variety of their reading a most contemptible opinion of the sex.

Thus unequal, we are, notwithstanding, forced to the combat, and the infamy which is consequent upon the smallest deviation in our conduct proclaims the high idea which was formed of our native strength; and thus, indirectly at least, is the preference acknowledged to be our due. And if we are allowed an equality of acquirement, let serious studies equally employ our minds, and we will bid our souls arise to equal strength. We will meet upon even ground, the despot man; we will rush with alacrity to the combat, and, crowned by success, we shall then answer the exalted expectations which are formed. Though sensibility,[7] soft compassion, and gentle commiseration are inmates in the female bosom, yet against every deep laid art, altogether fearless of the event, we will set them in array; for assuredly the wreath of victory will encircle the spotless brow. If we meet an equal, a sensible friend, we will reward him with the hand of amity, and through life we will be assiduous to promote his happiness; but from every deep laid scheme for our ruin, retiring into ourselves, amid the flowery paths of science, we will indulge in all the refined and sentimental pleasures of contemplation. And should it still be urged that the studies thus insisted upon would interfere with our more peculiar department,[8] I must further reply that *early hours*, and close application, will do wonders; and to her who is from the first dawn of reason taught to fill up time rationally, both the requisites will be easy.

I grant that niggard[9] fortune is too generally unfriendly to the mind; and that much of that valuable treasure, time, is necessarily expended upon the wants of the body; but it should be remembered that in embarrassed[10] circumstances our companions[11] have as little leisure for literary improvement as is afforded to us; for most certainly their provident care is at least

[1] *Behold him ... the death* David arranged the death of Uriah the Hittite, so that he could marry Uriah's wife Bathsheba. See 2 Samuel 11.2–27.

[2] *the curses ... his nativity* Job endured many earthly punishments at the hands of God, as a trial of his faith; though he remained faithful at the end, Job in his suffering cursed the day he was born. See Job 3; *nativity* Birth.

[3] *types* Prefigurations, i.e., of Christ in the New Testament.

[4] *nice* Virtuous.

[5] *gewgaws* Ornaments.

[6] *introduced into the world* In polite society of the time, for a girl to be "brought out," usually in her late teens, meant she was considered to be marriageable and allowed to engage in social affairs, such as balls.

[7] *sensibility* Heightened emotional or aesthetic awareness.

[8] *our more peculiar department* I.e., the duties particular to female life.

[9] *niggard* Stingy.

[10] *embarrassed* Difficult.

[11] *our companions* I.e., men.

as requisite as our exertions. Nay, we have even more leisure for sedentary pleasures, as our avocations are more retired, much less laborious, and, as hath been observed, by no means require that avidity of attention which is proper to the employments of the other sex. In high life, or, in other words, where the parties are in possession of affluence, the objection respecting time is wholly obviated,[1] and of course falls to the ground; and it may also be repeated that many of those hours which are at present swallowed up in fashion and scandal might be redeemed, were we habituated to useful reflections. But in one respect, O ye arbiters of our fate! we confess that the superiority is indubitably yours; you are by nature formed for our protectors; we pretend not to vie with you in bodily strength; upon this point we will never contend for victory. Shield us then, we beseech you, from external evils, and in return *we* will transact *your* domestic affairs. Yes, *your,* for are you not equally interested in those matters with ourselves? Is not the elegancy of neatness as agreeable to your sight as to ours? Is not the well-flavored viand[2] equally delightful to your taste? And doth not your sense of hearing suffer as much from the discordant sounds prevalent in an ill-regulated family, produced by the voices of children and many *et ceteras?*

CONSTANTIA

By way of supplement to the foregoing pages, I subjoin the following extract from a letter, wrote to a friend in the December of 1780.

And now assist me, O thou genius of my sex, while I undertake the arduous task of endeavouring to combat that vulgar, that almost universal errour, which hath, it seems, enlisted even Mr. P—— under its banners. The superiority of your sex hath, I grant, been time out of mind esteemed a truth incontrovertible; in consequence of which persuasion, every plan of education hath been calculated to establish this favourite tenet. Not long since;[3] weak and presuming as I was, I amused myself with selecting some arguments from nature, reason, and experience, against this so generally received idea. I confess that to sacred testimonies I had

not recourse. I held them to be merely metaphorical, and thus regarding them, I could not persuade myself that there was any propriety in bringing them to decide in this *very important debate.* However, as you, sir, confine yourself entirely to the sacred oracles, I mean to bend the whole of my artillery against those supposed proofs which you have from thence provided, and from which you have formed an intrenchment *apparently* so invulnerable. And first, to begin with our great progenitors;[4] but here, suffer me to premise, that it is for mental strength I mean to contend, for with respect to animal powers, I yield them undisputed to that sex which enjoys them in common with the lion, the tyger, and many other beasts of prey; therefore your observations respecting the *rib under the arm,*[5] *at a distance from the head,* &c. &c. in no sort militate against my view. Well, but the woman was first in the transgression.[6] Strange how blind *self love* renders you men; were you not wholly absorbed in a partial[7] admiration of your own abilities, you would long since have acknowledged the force of what I am now going to urge. It is true some ignoramuses have absurdly enough informed us that the beauteous fair of paradise,[8] was seduced from her obedience, by a malignant demon, *in the guise of a baleful serpent;* but we, who are better informed, know that the fallen spirit presented himself to her view, *a shining angel still;* for thus, saith the criticks in the Hebrew tongue, ought the word to be rendered.[9] Let us examine her motive— Hark! the seraph[10] declares that she shall attain a perfection of knowledge; for is there aught which is not comprehended under one or other of the terms *good*

1 *obviated* Made irrelevant.

2 *viand* Meal.

3 *since* Ago.

4 *our great progenitors* Adam and Eve.

5 *the rib … the arm* See Genesis 2.22: "And the rib, which the Lord God had taken from man, made he a woman, and brought unto the man."

6 *the transgression* I.e., eating the fruit of the tree of knowledge of good and evil, which was forbidden.

7 *partial* Biased.

8 *the beauteous fair of paradise* I.e., Eve.

9 *the fallen spirit … rendered* The appropriate translation of *nachash,* the word used to describe what is generally referred to as the serpent in Genesis, has been much debated by biblical scholars; one possible translation is "shining one." The serpent is often understood to be Satan or Lucifer, who was once an angel; the name Lucifer, in Latin, means "light bringer."

10 *seraph* Angel.

and *evil.* It doth not appear that she was governed by any one sensual appetite, but merely by a desire of adorning her mind; a laudable ambition fired her soul, and a thirst for knowledge impelled the predilection so fatal in its consequences. Adam could not plead the same deception; assuredly he was not deceived; nor ought we to admire his superior strength, or wonder at his sagacity, when we so often confess that example is much more influential than precept. His gentle partner stood before him, a melancholy instance of the direful effects of disobedience; he saw her not possessed of that wisdom which she had fondly hoped to obtain, but he beheld the once blooming female, disrobed of that innocence which had heretofore rendered her so lovely. To him, then, deception became impossible, as he had proof positive of the fallacy of the argument which the deceiver had suggested. What then could be his inducement to burst the barriers, and to fly directly in the face of that command, which *immediately* from the mouth of deity *he* had received, since, I say, he could not plead that fascinating stimulus, the accumulation of knowledge, as indisputable conviction was so visibly portrayed before him. What mighty cause impelled him to sacrifice myriads of beings yet unborn, and by one impious act, which *he saw* would be productive of such fatal effects, entail undistinguished ruin upon a race of beings which he was yet to produce? Blush, ye vaunters of fortitude, ye boasters of resolution, ye haughty lords of the creation; blush when ye remember that he was influenced by no other motive than a bare pusillanimous attachment to a woman! By sentiments so exquisitely soft that all his sons have, from that period, when they have designed to degrade them, described as highly feminine. Thus it should seem that all the arts of the grand deceiver (since means adequate to the purpose are, I conceive, invariably pursued) were requisite to mislead our general mother, while the father of mankind forfeited his own, and relinquished the happiness of posterity, merely in compliance with the blandishments of a female. The subsequent subjection the apostle Paul explains as a figure; after enlarging upon the subject, he adds, "*This is a great mystery; but I speak concerning Christ and the church.*"[1] Now we know with what consummate wisdom the unerring father of eternity hath formed his plans; all the types which he

hath displayed, he hath permitted *materially* to fail, in the very virtue for which *they* were famed. The reason for this is obvious; we might otherwise mistake his economy,[2] and render that honor to the creature which is due only to the creator. I know that Adam was a figure of him who was to come.[3] The grace contained in this figure is the reason of my rejoicing, and while I am very far from prostrating before the shadow, I yield joyfully in all things the preeminence to the second federal head.[4] Confiding faith is prefigured by Abraham, yet he exhibits a contrast to affiance when he says of his fair companion, she is my sister.[5] Gentleness was the characteristic of Moses, yet he hesitated not to reply to Jehovah himself. With unsaintlike tongue he murmured at the waters of strife,[6] and with rash hands he break the tables which were inscribed by the finger of divinity.[7] David, dignified with the title of the man after God's own heart, and yet how stained was his life. Solomon[8] was celebrated for wisdom, but folly is wrote in legible characters upon his almost every action. Lastly, let us turn our eyes to man in the aggregate. He is manifested as the figure of strength, but that we may not regard him as anything more than a figure, his soul is formed in no sort superior, but every way equal to the mind of her who is the emblem of weakness, and whom he hails the gentle companion of his better days.

—1790

[1] *This is … the church* See Ephesians 5.32.

[2] *economy* Management (of his created world).

[3] *him who … to come* Jesus.

[4] *second federal head* Jesus. Both Adam and Jesus are considered "federal heads" in Christian theology, meaning they represent humanity in a covenant with God; Jesus is the second, because Adam broke his covenant with God.

[5] *Confiding faith … my sister* Upon entering Egypt, Abraham fears that the Egyptians will kill him in order to abduct his wife Sarah, so he asks that Sarah say she is his sister. See Genesis 12.11–13; *affiance* Faith, trust; also, marriage.

[6] *With unsaintlike … of strife* See Exodus 17: the Israelites become angry with Moses for bringing them into a land where there is no water; in fear of their discontent, Moses confronts God, who commands Moses to strike his rod upon a rock out of which water then flows. Moses calls this water Meribah, or "strife."

[7] *Gentleness was … of divinity* Moses, leader of the Israelites who received the Ten Commandments from God, is described as very meek. In a moment of anger, he breaks one of the "tables" or stone tablets upon which the Ten Commandments are written.

[8] *Solomon* Successor to David, King Solomon was considered to be very wise, but committed sins such as idolatry.

from *The Gleaner Contemplates the Future Prospects of Women in This "Enlightened Age"*[1]

Amid the blaze of this auspicious day,
When science points the broad refulgent[2] way,
Her iron sceptre prejudice resigns,
And sovereign reason all resplendent shines.

The reader is requested to consider the four succeeding numbers[3] as supplementary to an essay which made its appearance, some years since,[4] in a periodical publication of a miscellaneous nature. The particular paper to which I advert was entitled "The Equality of the Sexes"; and however well I may think of that composition, as I do not conceive that the subject is exhausted, I have thought proper, treading in the same path, to set about collecting a few hints which may serve as additional, illustrative, or ornamental.

And, first, by way of exordium,[5] I take leave to congratulate my fair countrywomen on the happy revolution which the few past years has made in their favour; that in these infant republics, where, within my remembrance, the use of the needle was the principal attainment which was thought *necessary* for a woman, the lovely proficient is now permitted to appropriate a moiety[6] of her time to studies of a more elevated and elevating nature. Female academies are everywhere establishing, and right pleasant is the appellation to my ear.

Yes, in this younger world, "the Rights of Women" begin to be understood; we seem, at length, determined to do justice to the sex; and, improving on the opinions of a Wollstonecraft,[7] we are ready to contend for the *quantity*, as well as *quality*, of mind. The younger part of the female world have now an inestimable prize put into their hands; and it depends on the rising generation to refute a sentiment which, still retaining its advocates, grounds its arguments on the incompatibility of the present enlarged plan of female education with those necessary occupations that must ever be considered as proper to the department and comprised in the duties of a judiciously instructed and elegant woman; and, if our daughters will combine their efforts, converts to the new regulations will every day multiply among us. To argue against facts is indeed contending with both wind and tide; and, borne down by accumulating examples, conviction of the utility of the present plans will pervade the public mind, and not a dissenting voice will be heard.

I may be accused of enthusiasm; but such is my confidence in the sex that I expect to see our young women forming a new era in female history. They will oppose themselves to every trivial and unworthy monopolizer of time; and it will be apparent that the adorning their persons is not with them a primary object. They will know how to appreciate personal advantages;[8] and, considering them as bestowed by Nature, or Nature's God, they will hold them in due estimation: yet, conscious that they confer no *intrinsic* excellence on the *temporary* possessor, their admeasurement of *real virtue* will be entirely divested of all those *prepossessing ideas* which originate in a beautiful exterior. The noble expansion conferred by a liberal education will teach them *humility*; for it will give them a glance of those vast tracts of knowledge which they can never explore, until they are accommodated with far other powers than those at present assigned them; and they will contemplate their removal to a higher order of beings as a desirable event.

Mild benignity, with all the modest virtues, and every sexual[9] grace—these they will carefully cultivate;

[1] The four-part series of essays, "Observations on Women's Abilities," of which this essay is the first, was written by Murray later in the 1790s to further support her arguments in "On the Equality of the Sexes."

[2] *refulgent* Shining.

[3] *four succeeding numbers* I.e., this essay and the following three in the series.

[4] *since* Ago.

[5] *exordium* Introduction.

[6] *proficient* Expert; *moiety* Small portion.

[7] *Wollstonecraft* Mary Wollstonecraft (1759–97), important early feminist best known for her *Vindication of the Rights of Woman* (1792). In it, she argued that women and men are naturally equal, but that women have been made inferior to men as a result of inferior education.

[8] *personal advantages* Natural physical beauty.

[9] *sexual* I.e., particular to the female sex; feminine.

for they will have *learned* that in no character they can so effectually charm as in that in which nature designed them the *pre-eminence*. They will accustom themselves to reflection; they will investigate accurately, and reason will point their conclusions. Yet they will not be assuming; the characteristic trait will still remain; and retiring sweetness will insure them that consideration and respect which they do not presume to demand. Thinking justly will not only enlarge their minds and refine their ideas, but it will correct their dispositions, humanize their feelings, and present them the *friends of their species*. The beauteous bosom will no more become a lurking-place for invidious and rancorous passions; but the mild temperature of the soul will be evinced by the benign and equal tenor of their lives. Their manners will be unembarrassed; and, studious to shun even the *semblance of pedantry*, they will be careful to give to their most systematic arguments and deductions an unaffected and natural appearance. They will rather *question* than *assert*; and they will make their communications on a supposition that the point in discussion has rather *escaped the memory* of those with whom they converse, *than that it was never imprinted there*.

It is true that every faculty of their minds will be occasionally engrossed by the most momentous concerns; but as often as *necessity* or *propriety* shall render it incumbent on them, they will *cheerfully* accommodate themselves to the *more humble* duties which their situation imposes. When their sphere of action is enlarged, when they become wives and mothers, they will fill with honour the parts allotted them. Acquainted, theoretically, with the nature of their species, and experimentally[1] with themselves, they will not expect to meet in wedlock with those faultless beings who so frequently issue, armed at all points, from the teeming brain of the novelist. They will learn properly to estimate; they will look, with pity's softest eye, on the natural frailties of those whom they elect partners for life; and they will regard their virtues with that sweet complacency which is ever an attendant on a predilection founded on love, and happily combining esteem. As mothers, they will assume with alacrity their arduous employment, and they will cheerfully bend to its various departments.

They will be primarily solicitous to fulfil, in *every instance*, whatever can *justly* be denominated *duty*; and those intervals which have heretofore been devoted to frivolity will be appropriated to pursuits calculated to inform, enlarge, and sublime the soul—to contemplations which will ameliorate the heart, unfold and illumine the understanding, and gradually render the human being an eligible candidate for the society of angels.

Such, I predict, will be the daughters of Columbia;[2] and my gladdened spirit rejoices in the prospect. A sensible and informed woman—companionable and serious—possessing also a facility of temper, and united to a congenial mind—blessed with competency—and rearing to maturity a promising family of children—surely, the wide globe cannot produce a scene more truly interesting. See! the virtues are embodied—the domestic duties appear in their place, and they are all fulfilled—morality is systematized by religion, and sublimed by devotion—every movement is the offspring of elegance, and their manners have received the highest polish. A reciprocation of good offices, and a mutual desire to please, uniformly distinguishes the individuals of this enchanting society—their conversation, refined and elevated, partakes the fire of genius, while it is pointed by information; and they are ambitious of selecting subjects which, by throwing around humanity, *in its connection*, additional lustre, may implant a new motive for gratitude and teach them to anticipate the rich fruition of that immortality which they boast. Such is the family of reason—of reason, cultivated and adorned by literature.

The idea of the incapability of women is, we conceive, in this *enlightened age*, totally *inadmissible*; and we have concluded that establishing the *expediency* of admitting them to share the blessings of equality will remove every obstacle to their advancement. In proportion as nations have progressed in the arts of civilization, the value of the sex hath been understood, their rank in the scale of being ascertained, and their consequence in society acknowledged. ...

—1798

[1] *experimentally* I.e., through experience. [2] *Columbia* Female personification of America.

Briton Hammon

fl. c. 1760

On Christmas Day 1747, Massachusetts "servant" Briton Hammon embarked, with the permission of his "Master" John Winslow, on a sea voyage to Jamaica, little knowing that what should have been a half-year engagement would turn into thirteen years of captivity and displacement on both sides of the Atlantic before he could return to his home in the British colonies. Within a month of Hammon's homecoming, a pamphlet titled *A Narrative of the Uncommon Sufferings and Surprising Deliverance of Briton Hammon, A Negro Man* (1760) appeared in Boston. It purported to be a dramatic account of faith, divine Providence, and the "barbarous" savagery of Hammon's Indigenous captors. Yet to modern readers, this text is far more than a conventional—and conventionally xenophobic—captivity narrative. As the first black-authored text published in North America, and thus the first published written work in the canon of African American literature, Briton Hammon's *Narrative* is a work of unquestionable historical importance. It is also a work of very considerable interest as literature. Hammon's ambiguous social status, and his confession that the text omits "a great many things," complicate matters considerably—as do the ways in which race was constructed in the early Atlantic world. These factors call into question any simple or literal interpretations of Hammon's account of captivity, or of his "deliverance."

In June 1748, following a successful harvest in the Caribbean, the ship on which Hammon was employed was cast away off the coast of Florida, where the entire crew—aside from Hammon himself—were subsequently killed by a group of Indigenous Floridians. (Though Hammon's *Narrative* does not attempt to specify this group, some modern historians have speculated that they were of the Calusa people, whose population had, by the 1700s, been severely depleted through slaving raids encouraged by the English.) The *Narrative* goes on to describe Hammon's series of sufferings as a captive first of the Floridians and next of the Spanish in colonial Cuba; it recounts as well his later years aboard a number of English trading vessels and Royal Navy warships during the Seven Years' War, before his eventual reunion with John Winslow in London.

The account of these events in the *Narrative* is the only record we have of Hammon's life, though various conjectures have been made in recent decades on the basis of a handful of documents and census records in which his name appears. The *Narrative* itself tells us remarkably little about Hammon's life or status before and after his Atlantic adventures. Most notably, it is left unclear whether Hammon—whose race is only mentioned in the title of the work—was an enslaved person, an indentured servant, or a free employee to John Winslow. (The loose usage of the terms "master" and "servant" during the eighteenth century does not rule out any of these possibilities.) While there is increasing historical consensus that Hammon was probably enslaved (with some historians pointing out that the unambiguous term "slave" was often evaded in the slaveholding North), there continues to be disagreement as to the circumstances that led Winslow to allow Hammon to temporarily leave his service in the first place.

Likewise, the circumstances surrounding the creation and publication of Hammon's *Narrative* are almost completely obscure. Readers have generally assumed that the text, like the texts of many African American captivity narratives later in the century, would have been written by a white amanuensis based on Hammon's retelling, though again, this is conjecture. What we do know is that Hammon's *Narrative* was printed by eminent Boston publishers John Green and Joseph Russell in 1760, and that earlier that year another text had been printed by Green & Russell's frequent associates Fowle & Draper, bearing a remarkably similar title: *A Plain Narrative of the Uncommon Sufferings, and Remarkable Deliverance of Thomas Brown, of Charlestown, in New England*.

These and other circumstances surrounding Hammon's text bring to the fore questions about literary genre in the eighteenth-century literary world, as well as questions about interpretation and about black literary history as a whole. It seems at times clear that the *Narrative* falls into the genre of the

captivity narrative, an extraordinarily popular and also highly homogeneous genre in both Britain and the colonial Americas; captivity narratives were often deeply spiritual in tone and almost always centered on the literal and psychological resistance of the (usually white) captives to the culture of their Indigenous captors. Throughout his own tale, the Protestant Hammon emphasizes God's role in saving him from both the pagan Native Americans and the Catholic Spanish, and the text ends with impassioned praise of God's Providence in finally reuniting him with his "good Master" Winslow. Yet the degree to which the *Narrative*'s language reflects Hammon's private experience, rather than simply reflecting the literary and social conventions of the era, remains in doubt. Can Hammon's *Narrative* be considered a captivity narrative in the traditional sense, if he was never free to begin with? To what degree might the captivity narrative genre have provided Hammon with a language for thinking through enslavement? If Hammon's exact status is unclear, to what degree does that fact complicate the relationship of this text to earlier and later texts in the literature of slavery? Readers have been wrestling with such questions since Hammon's text was rediscovered by African American bibliographer Dorothy Porter in the mid-twentieth century; there is scant evidence for a wide readership of the text before this point.

It is accepted that in 1762 Hammon married Hannah, an African American woman and member of Plymouth's First Church, with whom he had one child. For many years this was all that was known of Hammon's life after his return to New England. More recent research, however, has revealed that Hammon probably changed his name to Nichols some time in the late 1770s, after the family with whom he and his master were living when Winslow died in 1774. Briton Nichols is listed as having fought for the Continental Army in the American Revolutionary War, as did many members of the white Nichols family (Winslow's surviving descendants remained staunch Loyalists). In later census records, Briton Nichols is described as a free husband and father. This information may further complicate interpretations of an intriguing text that provides a unique perspective on the lives of enslaved and free people of African descent in eighteenth-century America.

––––––––––

NOTE ON THE TEXT: The text of the work presented below is based on the 1760 edition of *A Narrative of the Uncommon Sufferings and Surprizing Deliverance of Briton Hamon, A Negro Man,—Servant to General Winslow, of Marshfield, in New-England; Who returned to* Boston, *after having been absent almost Thirteen Years.* Spelling and punctuation have been modernized in accordance with the practices of this anthology.

⌘ ⌘ ⌘

A Narrative of the Uncommon Sufferings and Surprising Deliverance of Briton Hammon, A Negro Man

To the reader,

As my capacities and condition of life are very low, it cannot be expected that I should make those remarks on the sufferings I have met with, or the kind Providence of a good God for my preservation, as one in a higher station; but shall leave that to the reader as he goes along, and so I shall only relate matters of fact as they occur to my mind.

On Monday, 25th day of December, 1747, with the leave of my Master, I went from Marshfield,[1] with an intention to go a voyage to sea, and the next day, the 26th, got to Plymouth, where I immediately shipped myself on board of a sloop,[2] Capt. John Howland, Master,[3] bound to Jamaica and the Bay.[4] We sailed from Plymouth in a short time, and after a pleasant passage of about thirty days arrived at Jamaica. We was

––––––––––

[1] *Marshfield* Town in Plymouth County, Massachusetts.

[2] *sloop* Small sailing ship.

[3] *Capt. John Howland, Master* Throughout the text Hammon frequently follows the mention of a ship with the name of its captain, common practice in writing of this era.

[4] *the Bay* The Bay of Capeche, in the Gulf of Mexico.

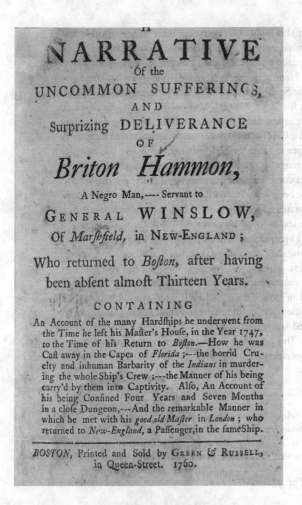

NARRATIVE
Of the
UNCOMMON SUFFERINGS,
AND
Surprizing DELIVERANCE
OF
Briton Hammon,
A Negro Man,---- Servant to
GENERAL WINSLOW,
Of *Marshfield*, in NEW-ENGLAND;

Who returned to *Boston*, after having
been absent almost Thirteen Years.

CONTAINING

An Account of the many Hardships he underwent from
the Time he left his Master's House, in the Year 1747,
to the Time of his Return to *Boston*.—How he was
Cast away in the Capes of *Florida* ;---the horrid Cru-
elty and inhuman Barbarity of the *Indians* in murder-
ing the whole Ship's Crew ;---the Manner of his being
carry'd by them into Captivity. Also, An Account of
his being Confined Four Years and Seven Months
in a close Dungeon,---And the remarkable Manner in
which he met with his *good old Master* in *London* ; who
returned to *New-England*, a Passenger, in the same Ship.

BOSTON, Printed and Sold by GREEN & RUSSELL,
in Queen-Street. 1760.

his own life, as well as the lives of the mate and nine hands,[3] as I shall presently relate.

After being upon this reef two days, the Captain ordered the boat[4] to be hoisted out, and then asked who were willing to tarry[5] on board? The whole crew was for going on shore at this time, but as the boat would not carry twelve persons at once, and to prevent any uneasiness, the Captain, a passenger, and one hand tarried on board, while the mate, with seven hands besides myself, were ordered to go on shore in the boat, which as soon as we had reached, one half were to be landed, and the other four to return to the sloop, to fetch the Captain and the others on shore. The Captain ordered us to take with us our arms,[6] ammunition, provisions and necessaries for cooking, as also a sail to make a tent of, to shelter us from the weather. After having left the sloop, we stood towards the shore, and being within two leagues of the same, we espied a number of canoes, which we at first took to be rocks, but soon found our mistake, for we perceived they moved towards us. We presently saw an English colour[7] hoisted in one of the canoes, at the sight of which we were not a little rejoiced, but on our advancing yet nearer, we found them, to our very great surprise, to be Indians, of which there were sixty. Being now so near them [that] we could not possibly make our escape, they soon came up with and boarded us, took away all our arms, ammunition, and provision. The whole number of canoes (being about twenty) then made for the sloop, except two which they left to guard us, who ordered us to follow on with them; the eighteen which made for the sloop went so much faster than we that they got on board above three hours before we came alongside, and had killed Captain Howland, the passenger and the other hand. We came to the larboard[8] side of the sloop, and they ordered us round to the starboard, and as we were passing round

detained at Jamaica only five days, from whence we sailed for the Bay, where we arrived safe in ten days. We loaded our vessel with logwood,[1] and sailed from the Bay the 25th day of May following, and the 15th day of June, we were cast away[2] on Cape Florida, about five leagues from the shore. Being now destitute of every help, we knew not what to do or what course to take in this our sad condition. The Captain was advised, intreated, and begged on, by every person on board, to heave over[board] but only twenty ton of the wood, and we should get clear—which if he had done, might have saved his vessel and cargo, and not only so, but

1 *logwood* Tree native to Mexico and Central America, exten-
sively harvested during this period for its use as a dye.

2 *cast away* Ran aground.

3 *hands* Members of the ship's crew.

4 *boat* I.e., the lifeboat.

5 *tarry* Wait.

6 *arms* Weapons.

7 *colour* Flag.

8 *larboard* Port or left side of a ship; the right side is known as
the starboard.

the bow,[1] we saw the whole number of Indians advancing forward and loading their guns, upon which the mate said, "*my lads, we are all dead men*," and before we had got round, they discharged their small arms upon us, and killed three of our hands, viz.[2] Reuben Young of Cape Cod, Mate; Joseph Little; and Lemuel Doty of Plymouth, upon which I immediately jumped overboard, choosing rather to be drowned than to be killed by those barbarous and inhuman savages. In three or four minutes after, I heard another volley, which dispatched[3] the other five, viz. John Nowland, and Nathaniel Rich, both belonging to Plymouth; and Elkanah Collymore, and James Webb, strangers;[4] and Moses Newmock, Mulatto.[5] As soon as they had killed the whole of the people, one of the canoes paddled after me, and soon came up with me, hauled me into the canoe, and beat me most terribly with a cutlass. After that they tied me down; then this canoe stood for[6] the sloop again and as soon as she came alongside, the Indians on board the sloop betook themselves to their canoes, then set the vessel on fire, making a prodigious shouting and hallowing[7] like so many devils. As soon as the vessel was burnt down to the water's edge, the Indians stood for the shore, together with our boat, on board of which they put five hands. After we came to the shore, they led me to their huts, where I expected nothing but immediate death, and as they spoke broken English, were often telling me, while coming from the sloop to the shore, that they intended to roast me alive. But the Providence of God ordered it otherwise, for He appeared for my help in this mount of difficulty, and they were better to me than my fears, and soon unbound me, but set a guard

over me every night. They kept me with them about five weeks, during which time they used me pretty well, and gave me boiled corn, which was what they often eat themselves.

The Way I made my Escape from these Villains was this; A Spanish Schooner arriving there from St. Augustine,[8] the Master of which, whose Name was Romond, asked the Indians to let me go on board his Vessel, which they granted, and the Captain[9] knowing me very well, weigh'd Anchor and carry'd me off to the Havanna,[10] and after being there four Days the Indians came after me, and insisted on having me again, as I was their Prisoner;—They made Application to the Governor,[11] and demanded me again from him; in answer to which the Governor told them, that as they had put the whole Crew to Death, they should not have me again, and so paid them Ten Dollars for me, adding, that he would not have them kill any Person hereafter, but take as many of them as they could, of those that should be cast away, and bring them to him, for which he would pay them Ten Dollars a-head. At the Havanna I lived with the Governor in the Castle about a Twelve-month, Where I was walking thro' the Street, I met with a Press-Gang[12] who immediately prest me, and put me into Goal,[13] and with a Number of others I was confin'd till next Morning, when we were all brought out, and ask'd who would go on board the King's Ships, four of which having been lately built, were bound to Old-Spain, and on my refusing to serve on board, they put me in a close[14] Dungeon, where I was confin'd *Four Years and seven months*; during which

[1] *bow* Front end of a ship.

[2] *viz.* Abbreviation of the Latin videlicet, meaning "namely," or "that is to say."

[3] *dispatched* Killed.

[4] *strangers* Foreigners.

[5] *Mulatto* Term, now considered offensive, that was commonly used in the eighteenth century in Britain and North America to classify individuals of mixed racial background; while "mulatto" generally meant a person with one white and one black parent, the term was often used rather loosely and might refer more to a person's physical appearance than to his or her actual known ancestry.

[6] *stood for* Steered towards.

[7] *hallowing* Hallooing; shouting.

[8] *St. Augustine* Then the capital of Spanish Florida.

[9] [Hammon's note] The way I came to know this gentleman was, by his being taken last war by an English privateer, and brought into Jamaica, while I was there. [*last war* The War of Jenkins' Ear (1739–48), a conflict between Britain and Spain fought primarily in the Caribbean. Hammon's master, John Winslow, had led an attack on Cartagena in 1740.]

[10] *the Havanna* Capital of Spanish Cuba.

[11] *the Governor* I.e., the Governor of Cuba, Francisco Cajigal de la Vega (1691–1777).

[12] *Press-Gang* Group authorized to seize men (generally, though not always, those appearing to be of "seafaring habits") off the streets and force them into military or naval service; *Press* Impress; compel into service.

[13] *Goal* Gaol; jail.

[14] *close* Narrow; enclosed.

original spelling

time I often made application to the Governor, by Persons who came to see the Prisoners, but they never acquainted him with it, nor did he know all this Time what became of me, which was the means of[1] my being confin'd there so long. But kind Providence so order'd it, that after I had been in this Place so long as the Time mention'd above the Captain of a Merchantman,[2] belonging to Boston, having sprung a Leak was obliged to put into the Havanna to refit, and while he was at Dinner at Mrs. Betty Howard's, she told the Captain of my deplorable Condition, and said she would be glad, if he could by some means or other relieve me; The Captain told Mrs. Howard he would use his best Endeavours for my Relief and Enlargement.[3]

Accordingly, after dinner, [the Captain] came to the prison and asked the keeper if he might see me; upon his request I was brought out of the dungeon, and after the Captain had interrogated me, [he] told me he would intercede with the Governor for my relief out of that miserable place, which he did, and the next day the Governor sent an order to release me. I lived with the Governor about a year after I was delivered from the dungeon, in which time I endeavoured three times to make my escape, the last of which proved effectual. The first time I got on board of Captain Marsh, an English twenty-gun ship, with a number of others, and lay on board concealed that night; and the next day the ship being under sail, I thought myself safe, and so made my appearance upon deck, but as soon as we were discovered the Captain ordered the boat out, and sent us all on shore. I entreated the Captain to let me, in particular,[4] tarry on board, begging and crying to him to commiserate my unhappy condition, and added that I had been confined almost five years in a close dungeon, but the Captain would not hearken to any entreaties, for fear of having the Governor's displeasure, and so I was obliged to go on shore.

After being on shore another twelvemonth, I endeavoured to make my escape the second time by trying to get on board of a sloop bound to Jamaica, and as I was going from the city to the sloop, was unhappily taken by the guard, and ordered back to the castle, and there

confined. However, in a short time I was set at liberty, and ordered with a number of others to carry the[5] Bishop from the castle through the country to confirm the old people,[6] baptize children, etc., for which he receives large sums of money. I was employed in this service about seven months, during which time I lived very well, and then returned to the castle again, where I had my liberty to walk about the city, and do work for myself. The *Beaver*, an English Man of War,[7] then lay in the harbour, and having been informed by some of the ship's crew that she was to sail in a few days, I had nothing now to do but to seek an opportunity how I should make my escape.

Accordingly, one Sunday night the Lieutenant of the ship with a number of the barge crew were in a tavern, and Mrs. Howard, who had before been a friend to me, interceded with the Lieutenant to carry me on board. The Lieutenant said he would with all his heart, and immediately I went on board in the barge. The next day the Spaniards came alongside the *Beaver* and demanded me again, with a number of others who had made their escape from them and got on board the ship, but just before I did; but the Captain, who was a true Englishman, refused them, and said he could not answer it, to deliver up any Englishmen under English colours. In a few days we set sail for Jamaica, where we arrived safe, after a short and pleasant passage.

After being at Jamaica a short time we sailed for London, as convoy to a fleet of merchantmen, who all arrived safe in the Downs.[8] I was turned over to another ship, the *Arcenceil*, and there remained about a month. From this ship I went on board the *Sandwich* of 90 guns; on board the *Sandwich* I tarried six weeks, and then was ordered on board the *Hercules*, Capt. John Porter, a 74-gun ship. We sailed on a cruise, and met with a French 84-gun ship, and had a very smart

1 *means of* Reason for.

2 *Merchantman* Merchant vessel.

3 *Enlargement* Release.

4 *in particular* I.e., as an exception from the others.

5 [Hammon's note] He is carried (by way of respect) in a large two-arm chair; the chair is lined with crimson velvet, and supported by eight persons.

6 *confirm the old people* I.e., administer the Catholic sacrament of confirmation. (It is usually administered around the age of thirteen; it is unclear whether "old" here refers to young people who have come of age, or older Catholics who never received the rite during their youth.)

7 *Man of War* Warship.

8 *the Downs* Anchorage off the coast of Kent in the English Channel.

engagement[1] in which about seventy of our hands were killed and wounded. The Captain lost his leg in the engagement, and I was wounded in the head by a small shot. We should have[2] taken this ship, if they had not cut away the most of our rigging; however, in about three hours after, a 64-gun ship came up with and took her. I was discharged from the *Hercules* the 12th day of May 1759 (having been on board of that ship three months), on account of my being disabled in the arm and rendered incapable of service, after being honourably paid the wages due to me. I was put into the Greenwich Hospital, where I stayed and soon recovered. I then shipped myself a cook[3] on board *Captain Martyn*, an armed ship in the King's service. I was on board this ship almost two months, and after being paid my wages was discharged in the month of October. After my discharge from *Captain Martyn*, I was taken sick in London of a fever, and was confined about six weeks, where I expended all my money and [was] left in very poor circumstances; and unhappy for me I knew nothing of my good Master's[4] being in London at this my very difficult time. After I got well of my sickness, I shipped myself on board of a large ship bound to Guinea,[5] and being in a public house[6] one evening, I overheard a number of persons talking about rigging a vessel bound to New England. I asked them to what part of New England this vessel was bound? [and] they told me, to Boston; and having asked them who was Commander? they told me, Captain Watt. In a few minutes after this the mate of the ship came in, and I asked him if Captain Watt did not want a cook, who told me he did, and that the Captain would be in in a few minutes; and in about half an hour the Captain came in, and then I shipped myself at once, after begging off from the ship bound to Guinea. I worked on board Captain Watt's ship

almost three months before she sailed, and one day, being at work in the hold,[7] I overheard some persons on board mention the name of Winslow, at the name of which I was very inquisitive, and having asked what Winslow they were talking about, they told me it was General Winslow, and that he was one of the passengers. I asked them what General Winslow? for I never knew my good Master by that title before; but after enquiring more particularly I found it must be Master, and in a few days' time the truth was joyfully verified by a happy sight of his person, which so overcome me that I could not speak to him for some time. My good Master was exceeding glad to see me, telling me that I was like one arose from the dead, for he thought I had been dead a great many years, having heard nothing of me for almost thirteen years.

I think I have not deviated from truth, in any particular of this my narrative, and though I have omitted a great many things, yet what is wrote may suffice to convince the reader, that I have been most grievously afflicted, and yet through the Divine Goodness, as miraculously preserved, and delivered out of many dangers; of which I desire to retain a grateful remembrance, as long as I live in the world.

And now, that in the Providence of that God who delivered his servant David out of the paw of the lion and out of the paw of the bear,[8] I am freed from a long and dreadful captivity, among worse savages than they; and am returned to my own native land, to show how great things the Lord hath done for me. I would call upon all men, and say, O Magnify the Lord with me, and let us exalt his name together! O that men would praise the Lord for His goodness, and for his wonderful works to the children of men![9]

—1760

[1] [Hammon's note] A particular account of this engagement has been published in the Boston newspapers. [*smart engagement* Fierce battle.]

[2] *should have* Would have.

[3] *shipped myself a cook* I.e., was hired as a ship's cook.

[4] *my good Master* I.e., John Winslow.

[5] *Guinea* At this period the name Guinea was often used to refer to West Africa as a whole; in this instance, the ship was probably headed there to buy enslaved people for trade.

[6] *public house* Pub.

[7] *hold* Inner chamber of a ship in which cargo is held.

[8] *who delivered ... bear* See 1 Samuel 17.37: "David said moreover, The Lord that delivered me out of the paw of the lion, and out of the paw of the bear, he will deliver me out of the hand of this Philistine."

[9] *children of men* See Psalm 90.3: "Thou turnest man to destruction; and sayest, Return, ye children of men."

Philip Freneau

1752 – 1832

Once widely considered to be the "first genuine American poet," Philip Freneau was also long dismissed as more a political propagandist than a poet, important at most as a minor forerunner to the Romanticism that blossomed in America in the nineteenth century. His place in American literary history continues to be debated, but the central facts are not in dispute; through both his poetry and his journalism, Freneau threw himself energetically into the partisan politics of the post-Revolutionary era, earning him a longstanding reputation as "the Poet of the American Revolution." He was a prolific writer in several genres, and his work encompassed a remarkably wide variety of subjects (among them history, politics, religion, and the beauties of nature).

Freneau was born into an affluent New York City merchant family in 1752 and enjoyed the advantages of wealth throughout his youth. He entered the College of New Jersey (now Princeton University) at the age of fifteen; here he was able to cultivate distinguished friendships, most notably with future president James Madison. While at college, Freneau developed a reputation for his wit and writing skills; the American Whig Society, a student club, provided him with a venue to hone these skills as well as to develop his democratic political viewpoints.

In his final year, Freneau collaborated with another classmate, future novelist Hugh Henry Brackenridge, on "A Poem on the Rising Glory of America," a long work extoling British colonial history in the Americas, ruminating on the history and supposed origins of North American Indigenous peoples (then a popular subject of speculation among Europeans and Euro-Americans), and envisioning an idealized future America. The poem was delivered as a commencement address in 1771, and published the following year.

Having laid the groundwork for a prominent literary career, Freneau continued to write poetry throughout the 1770s, publishing in a variety of newspapers and turning increasingly to political subjects as the American Revolution approached. Writing, however, was not a well-paid profession; there would be little in the way of a market in America for domestic literature until well into the 1800s. To earn an income, Freneau worked as a schoolteacher and toyed with the idea of studying theology and becoming a minister (an idea he quickly rejected). By the outbreak of the Revolutionary War in 1775, Freneau was already known for his fervidly democratic, patriotic poems, but he did not feel that his place was in the battlefield. Around 1776, he sailed to the West Indies, obtaining a secretarial position on a plantation in Saint Croix. Freneau was no stranger to slavery, having grown up in a household that had included a number of enslaved servants, but he was struck in the Caribbean by the extent and systemic nature of its cruelties, especially as its horrors contrasted with the luxurious and paradisiacal natural environment he encountered. Poems such as "To Sir Toby" (1792), an exposé of the misery behind the slave economy, and "The Wild Honey Suckle" (1786), a meditation on natural beauty and mortality, were both inspired by these experiences.

When Freneau returned to America near the end of the decade, the Revolutionary War was still underway, and he joined the patriot effort by working on merchant blockade runners, conveying supplies to blockaded ports. In 1780 he was aboard the ship *Aurora* when it was captured by the British *Scorpion*. Despite asserting that he was only a civilian passenger, Freneau was taken prisoner and spent several miserable weeks held below deck with hundreds of other prisoners, many of whom died of malnutrition and disease during the ordeal. His long poem about the experience, "The British Prison Ship" (1781), was published shortly after his release.

Toward the end of the war, while living in Philadelphia, Freneau wrote prolifically of America's triumphs and heroes for the *Freeman's Journal*. Throughout the 1780s he continued to write poetry on various subjects, often reworking individual poems as both the political landscape and his personal interests evolved; most of his poems were printed in newspapers before being published in collections.

In 1790 Freneau married Eleanor Forman. The following year he took up work as a political journalist and became deeply embroiled (on the Jeffersonian side) in the conflict between Thomas Jefferson's Democratic-Republicans and Alexander Hamilton's Federalists; under Freneau's editorship, the Philadelphia-based *National Gazette* became the most important mouthpiece of the Democratic-Republican Party. To Freneau and his frequent colleague Madison, President George Washington and the Federalist Party members who supported him represented a worryingly aristocratic, tyrannical interpretation of the U.S. Constitution. His fervidly partisan output during this period, in both journalism and poetry, bolstered his reputation in his own day as an important and influential writer but led many in later generations to disparage him as a mere polemicist. His partisanship also earned him a reputation as a "rascal" and a "wretched and insolent dog" (as Washington, who was among his political opponents, put it).

Following Jefferson's election to the Presidency in 1801, Freneau withdrew from politics and public life and retired to his family's plantation in New Jersey, Mount Pleasant. Freneau benefited from the labor of a considerable number of enslaved people, but he was an inexperienced farmer himself and was unable to make a success of the plantation. When the farm failed to produce a sufficient income, he sold the land piece by piece. He continued to write periodically, publishing a collection that included some new poems in 1815. Taking occasional work at sea and doing odd jobs around town, he spent his final years in poverty. Alone and largely forgotten, Freneau was caught in a snowstorm and froze to death at the age of eighty.

Despite his inauspicious final years, Freneau continued to be well-respected in the decades following his death, both as a writer and as a defender of the principles of liberty. More recently, critics have drawn attention to the ways in which his poetry incorporates elements of both the formal neoclassicism of the Enlightenment and the Romanticism of the later eighteenth and early nineteenth centuries. Freneau has thus often been classified as a "transitional" poet, of some historical importance but unworthy of much attention as a serious writer in his own right. Literary scholars have read poems such as "The Wild Honey Suckle," for example, largely as forerunners of William Cullen Bryant's poetry of the 1810s and of the slightly later Transcendentalist school, and have seen "The House of Night" (1779) as anticipating the work of later gothic writers such as Edgar Allan Poe.

Increasingly, however, literary scholars in this century have focused on Freneau in the context of his own time. As they have recognized, his political poems—together with visionary poems such as "On the Rising Glory of America"—powerfully express the concerns of the era and paint a vivid picture of the rapidly developing political climate of pre- and post-Revolutionary America.

NOTE ON THE TEXTS: The texts of "The Hurricane," "On Mr. Paine's *Rights of Man*," "To Sir Toby," and "The Wild Honey Suckle" are based on those printed in *Poems Written and Published during the American Revolutionary War* (1809), while that of "On the Religion of Nature" is based on that printed in *A Collection of Poems on American Affairs and a Variety of Other Subjects, Chiefly Moral and Political* (1815). The text of "The Indian Burying Ground" is based on that printed in Fred Lewis Pattee's *The Poems of Philip Freneau*, Volume 2 (1903). Spelling and punctuation have been modernized in accordance with the practices of this anthology.

⌘ ⌘ ⌘

The Hurricane[1]

Happy the man who, safe on shore,
　Now trims, at home, his evening fire;
Unmoved, he hears the tempests roar,
　That on the tufted groves expire:
5　　Alas! on us they doubly fall,
　　Our feeble bark° must bear them all. *small ship*

Now to their haunts the birds retreat,
　The squirrel seeks his hollow tree,
Wolves in their shaded caverns meet,
10　All, all are blest but wretched we—
　　Foredoomed a stranger to repose,
　　No rest the unsettled ocean knows.

While o'er the dark abyss we roam,
　Perhaps, with last departing gleam,
15　We saw the sun descend in gloom,
　No more to see his morning beam;
　　But buried low, by far too deep,
　　On coral beds, unpitied, sleep!

But what a strange, uncoasted strand
20　Is that, where fate permits no day—
　No charts have we to mark that land,
　No compass to direct that way—
　　What pilot shall explore that realm,
　　What new Columbus take the helm!

25　While death and darkness both surround,
　And tempests rage with lawless power,
Of friendship's voice I hear no sound,
　No comfort in this dreadful hour—
　　What friendship can in tempests be,
30　　What comforts on this raging sea?

The bark, accustomed to obey,
　No more the trembling pilots guide:
Alone she gropes her trackless way,
　While mountains burst on either side—
35　　Thus, skill and science both must fall;
　　And ruin is the lot of all.
　　　　—1785

The Wild Honey Suckle

Fair flower, that dost so comely grow,
　Hid in this silent, dull retreat,
Untouched thy honied blossoms blow,° *bloom*
　Unseen thy little branches greet:
5　　No roving foot shall crush thee here,
　　No busy hand provoke a tear.

By Nature's self in white arrayed,
　She bade thee shun the vulgar eye,
And planted here the guardian shade,
10　And sent soft waters murmuring by;
　　Thus quietly thy summer goes,
　　Thy days declining to repose.

Smit with those charms, that must decay,
　I grieve to see your future doom;
15　They died—nor were those flowers more gay,
　The flowers that did in Eden bloom;
　　Unpitying frosts, and Autumn's power
　　Shall leave no vestige of this flower.

From morning suns and evening dews
20　At first thy little being came:
If nothing once, you nothing lose,
　For when you die you are the same;
　　The space between, is but an hour,
　　The frail duration of a flower.
　　　　—1786, 1809

The Indian Burying Ground[2]

In spite of all the learned have said,
　I still my old opinion keep;
The posture, that we give the dead,
　Points out the soul's eternal sleep.

5　Not so the ancients of these lands—
　The Indian, when from life released,

[1] [Freneau's note] Near the east end of Jamaica, July 30, 1784.

[2] The version of this poem that was first published in 1787 is titled "Lines Occasioned by a Visit to an Old Indian Burying Ground."

Again is seated with his friends,
 And shares again the joyous feast.[1]

His imaged birds, and painted bowl,
10 And venison, for a journey dressed,
Bespeak the nature of the soul,
 Activity, that knows no rest.

His bow, for action ready bent,
 And arrows, with a head of stone,
15 Can only mean that life is spent,
 And not the old ideas gone.

Thou, stranger, that shalt come this way,
 No fraud° upon the dead commit— *theft*
Observe the swelling turf, and say
20 They do not lie, but here they sit.

Here still a lofty rock remains,
 On which the curious eye may trace
(Now wasted, half, by wearing rains)
 The fancies of a ruder[2] race.

25 Here still an aged elm aspires,
 Beneath whose far-projecting shade
(And which the shepherd still admires)
 The children of the forest played!

There oft a restless Indian queen
30 (Pale Shebah,[3] with her braided hair)
And many a barbarous form is seen
 To chide the man that lingers there.

By midnight moons, o'er moistening dews;
 In habit° for the chase arrayed, *clothing*
35 The hunter still the deer pursues,
 The hunter and the deer, a shade!° *ghost*

And long shall timorous fancy see
 The painted chief, and pointed spear,

And Reason's self shall bow the knee
40 To shadows and delusions here.
—1787

On Mr. Paine's Rights of Man[4]

Thus briefly sketched the sacred RIGHTS OF MAN,
 How inconsistent with the ROYAL PLAN!
Which for itself exclusive honour craves,
Where some are masters born, and millions slaves.
5 With what contempt must every eye look down
On that base, childish bauble called a *crown*,
The gilded bait, that lures the crowd, to come,
Bow down their necks, and meet a slavish doom;
The source of half the miseries men endure,
10 The quack that kills them, while it seems to cure.
 Roused by the Reason of his manly page,
Once more shall Paine a listening world engage:
From Reason's source, a bold reform he brings,
In raising up *mankind*, he pulls down *kings*,
15 Who, source of discord, patrons of all wrong,
On blood and murder have been fed too long:
Hid from the world, and tutored to be base,
The curse, the scourge, the ruin of our race,
Theirs was the task, a dull designing° few, *scheming*
20 To shackle beings that they scarcely knew,
Who made this globe the residence of slaves,
And built their thrones on systems formed by knaves
—Advance, bright years, to work their final fall,
And haste the period that shall crush them all.
25 Who, that has read and scanned the historic page
But glows, at every line, with kindling rage,
To see by them the rights of man aspersed,° *injured*
Freedom restrained, and Nature's law reversed,
Men, ranked with beasts, by monarchs *willed* away;
30 And bound young fools, or madmen to obey:
Now driven to wars, and now oppressed at home,
Compelled in crowds o'er distant seas to roam,
From India's climes the plundered prize to bring

1 [Freneau's note] The North American Indians bury their dead in a sitting posture; decorating the corpse with wampum, the images of birds, quadrupeds, etc: And (if that of a warrior) with bows, arrows, tomahawks, and other military weapons.

2 *fancies* Imaginings; *ruder* Simpler; uncivilized.

3 *Shebah* Biblical queen renowned for her beauty. See 1 Kings 10.

4 *Mr. Paine's Rights of Man* Thomas Paine's 1791 *Rights of Man* is a vigorous defense of the French Revolution, which had broken out in 1789 and was in many ways inspired by the principles of the American Revolution. The English-born Paine had emigrated to the American colonies in 1774 and had in 1776 published the extraordinarily influential pamphlet *Common Sense*.

To glad the strumpet,[1] or to glut the king.
35 Columbia,[2] hail! immortal be thy reign:
Without a king, we till the smiling plain;
Without a king, we trace the unbounded sea,
And traffic° round the globe, through each degree; *trade*
Each foreign clime our honored flag reveres,
40 Which asks no monarch to support the stars:
Without a *king*, the laws maintain their sway,
While honour bids each generous heart obey.
Be ours the task the ambitious to restrain,
And this great lesson teach—that kings are vain;° *worthless*
45 That warring realms to certain ruin haste,
That kings subsist by war, and wars are waste:
So shall our nation, formed on Virtue's plan,
Remain the guardian of the Rights of Man,
A vast Republic, famed through every clime,
50 Without a king, to see the end of time.
—1792

To Sir Toby[3]

A sugar planter in the interior parts of Jamaica, near the City of San Jago de la Vega (Spanish Town), 1784

The motions of his spirit are black as night,
And his affections dark as Erebus.[4]
—Shakespeare

If there exists a hell—the case is clear—
Sir Toby's slaves enjoy that portion here:
Here are no blazing brimstone lakes—'tis true;
But kindled rum too often burns as blue;
5 In which some fiend, whom nature must detest,

Steeps Toby's brand, and marks poor Cudjoe's breast.[5]
Here whips on whips excite perpetual fears,
And mingled howlings vibrate on my ears:
Here nature's plagues abound, to fret and tease,
10 Snakes, scorpions, despots, lizards, centipees°— *centipedes*
No art, no care escapes the busy lash;
All have their dues—and all are paid in cash—
The eternal driver keeps a steady eye
On a black herd, who would his vengeance fly,
15 But chained, imprisoned, on a burning soil,
For the mean avarice of a tyrant, toil![6]
The lengthy cart-whip guards this monster's reign—
And cracks, like pistols, from the fields of cane.
Ye powers! who formed these wretched tribes, relate,
20 What had they done, to merit such a fate!
Why were they brought from Eboe's[7] sultry waste,
To see that plenty which they must not taste—
Food, which they cannot buy, and dare not steal;
Yams and potatoes—many a scanty meal!
25 One, with a gibbet[8] wakes his negro's fears,
One to the windmill nails him by the ears;
One keeps his slave in darkened dens, unfed,
One puts the wretch in pickle ere he's dead:[9]
This, from a tree suspends him by the thumbs,
30 That, from his table grudges even the crumbs!
O'er yond' rough hills a tribe of females go,
Each with her gourd,[10] her infant, and her hoe;
Scorched by a sun that has no mercy here,
Driven by a devil, whom men call overseer—

1 *strumpet* Derogatory word for a female prostitute or a sexually licentious woman; here, intended more broadly to refer to a woman seen as vain or immoral.

2 *Columbia* Common personification of America, popularized in the post-Revolutionary era.

3 Originally published in *The National Gazette* in 1792 as "The Island Field Hand," this poem was entitled "The Island Field Negro" in some subsequent versions. The present text, from the 1809 edition, contains minor variations from the edition of 1795.

4 *The motions ... Erebus* See *The Merchant of Venice* 5.1.79. Freneau quotes "dull as night" incorrectly, writing "black as night." "Erebus" is a primordial deity of darkness in Greek mythology.

5 [Freneau's note] This passage has a reference to the West India custom (sanctioned by law) of branding a newly imported slave on the breast, with a red hot iron, as an evidence of the purchaser's property. [*Cudjoe* Common male name originating in the Ghanaian Akan language, which came into widespread use among white Americans to signify an enslaved man.]

6 *The eternal driver ... toil* These four lines did not appear in the 1792 version.

7 [Freneau's note] A small negro kingdom near the river Senegal. [The Eboe people—now spelled Ibo or Igbo—are in fact inhabitants of what is now southeastern Nigeria, near the mouth of the Niger River.]

8 *gibbet* This term can refer to a variety of instruments for torture or execution, including implements for displaying corpses of those who had been executed as a warning to others.

9 *One puts ... dead* This is probably a reference to the practice of flogging an enslaved person and rubbing salt and vinegar into the wounds ("pickling"); severe floggings could often lead to death.

10 *gourd* Water vessel, made of a hollowed-out gourd.

35 In chains, twelve wretches to their labours haste;
 Twice twelve I saw, with iron collars graced!
 Are such the fruits that spring from vast domains?
 Is wealth, thus got, Sir Toby, worth your pains!
 Who would your wealth on terms, like these, possess,
40 Where all we see is pregnant with distress—
 Angola's[1] natives scourged by ruffian hands,
 And toil's hard product shipped to foreign lands.
 Talk not of blossoms, and your endless spring;
 What joy, what smile, can scenes of misery bring?
45 Though nature, here, has every blessing spread,
 Poor is the labourer—and how meanly fed!

 Here Stygian[2] paintings light and shade renew,
 Pictures of hell, that Virgil's pencil drew:[3]
 Here, surly Charons[4] make their annual trip,
50 And ghosts arrive in every Guinea ship,[5]
 To find what beasts these western isles afford,
 Plutonian[6] scourges, and despotic lords:
 Here, they, of stuff determined to be free,
 Must climb the rude cliffs of the Liguanee;[7]
55 Beyond the clouds, in skulking haste repair,
 And hardly safe from brother traitors[8] there.
 —1792, 1809

[2] *Stygian* In Greek mythology the river Styx separated the world of the living from that of the dead; the region on the far side was often portrayed in ways similar to that in which Hell was later portrayed by Christians.

[3] *Here ... pencil drew* I.e., Here it is as if the light and shade paint pictures similar to the hellish scenes described by the Roman poet Virgil (70–19 BCE) in his epic the *Aeneid*.

[4] *Charons* In Greek mythology, Charon ferries the dead over the river Styx into Hades.

[5] *Guinea ship* Ship carrying enslaved captives from Guinea in West Africa.

[6] *Plutonian* Hellish; Pluto is the god of the underworld in Roman mythology.

[7] [Freneau's note] The mountains northward of Kingston.

[8] [Freneau's note] Alluding to the *Independent* Negroes in the blue mountains, who for a stipulated reward, deliver up every fugitive that falls into their hands to the English Government. [Freneau refers to the Maroons of Jamaica, descendants of enslaved Africans who had in the seventeenth century escaped slavery and formed independent communities in the Blue Mountains region; their numbers continued to be augmented over the decades as others escaped slavery to join them. War broke out between the Maroons and the British colonial government in 1720; the terms of the Peace Treaty of 1739 included that while those living in established Maroon communities should retain their independence, any further fugitives from slavery who tried to join them should be returned to their British enslavers.]

[1] *Angola* During this period, a Portuguese colony from which many people were captured and enslaved.

IN CONTEXT

Slavery in the Caribbean

William A.V. Clark, "Cutting the Sugar Cane," from *Ten Views in the Island of Antigua*, 1823. Although the various sugar-producing Caribbean islands were controlled by different colonial powers, there were many similarities. The plantations were large and highly profitable, conditions for the enslaved were typically brutal, and the enslaved population often outnumbered the white colonial population by a factor of 10–1 or more. Such was the case in Saint Croix, the Danish colony where Freneau worked as a secretary, just as it was 250 miles to the east, in the British colony of Antigua.

Adolphe Duperly, *The Destruction of Roehampton Estate in the parish of St. James's in January 1832 the property of J. Baillie Esq.*, 1833. This lithograph depicts part of what is often called the Baptist War, an 1831–32 uprising of enslaved people in Jamaica. Led primarily by black Baptist minister Samuel Sharpe, the rebellion mobilized tens of thousands of enslaved people. It was quickly suppressed by the British, with hundreds of the insurgents killed during the rebellion and in its aftermath, but many managed to flee the colony. All the remaining enslaved people were freed following the passage by the British Parliament of the 1833 Slavery Abolition Act.

On the Religion of Nature

The power, that gives with liberal hand
 The blessings man enjoys, while here,
And scatters through smiling land
 The abundant products of the year;
5 That power of nature, ever blessed,
 Bestowed religion with the rest.

Born with ourselves, her early sway
 Inclines the tender mind to take
The path of right, fair virtue's way
10 Its own felicity to make.
 This universally extends
 And leads to no mysterious ends.

Religion, such as nature taught,
 With all divine perfection suits;
15 Had all mankind the system sought

Sophists[1] would cease their vain° disputes, *useless*
 And from this source would nations know
 All that can make their heaven below.

This deals not curses to mankind,
20 Or dooms them to perpetual grief,
If from its aid no joys they find,
 It damns them not for unbelief;
 Upon a more exalted plan
 Creatress nature dealt with man—

25 Joy to the day, when all agree
 On such grand systems to proceed,
From fraud, design, and error free,
 And which to truth and goodness lead:
 Then persecution will retreat
30 And man's religion be complete.
—1795, 1815

1 *Sophists* In ancient Greece, paid teachers of philosophy and rhetoric; "sophistry" later became a term denoting clever but deceptive or insubstantial argument.

PHILLIS WHEATLEY
1753? – 1784

Phillis Wheatley was the first author of African descent to publish a book of poetry in English, *Poems on Various Subjects, Religious and Moral* (London, 1773). During her life she gained an international readership on both sides of the Atlantic. Born in Africa and kidnapped by slave traders when she was six or seven years old, Wheatley was purchased by an evangelical family in Boston who taught her to read. She immersed herself in biblical and classical traditions and soon taught herself to write, publishing her first poem in a Rhode Island newspaper when she was a young teenager. A deeply religious poet who drew on John Milton and Alexander Pope, Wheatley was praised in her time by Voltaire, Benjamin Franklin, and George Washington. She is best known for writing about her experience of slavery and the slave trade, including the controversial poem "On Being Brought from Africa to America." More recently, scholars have come to recognize and appreciate the wide diversity of Wheatley's work, including elegies, lyrics, hymns, and narrative poems inspired by the Old Testament and Ovid's *Metamorphoses*. Long recognized as the founding author of the African American literary tradition, she is now also considered one of the most important poets of colonial North America.

Wheatley was probably born in 1753 near the West coast of sub-Saharan Africa, although the precise place and date of her birth are unknown. She was brought to Boston in 1761 on the slave ship *Phillis*, after which her new enslavers, John and Susanna Wheatley, saw fit to name her. She first became famous in 1770 after the transatlantic reprinting of her elegy for George Whitefield, a founder of Methodism who preached frequently in North America and believed in the spiritual equality of Africans. Wheatley soon advertised in Boston for subscriptions to a book of twenty-eight poems but was unable to gather enough support for publication; Great Britain, however, proved friendlier ground. While visiting London with her enslavers' son, Nathaniel, in the summer of 1773, Wheatley helped arrange for her book's publication under the patronage of Selina Hastings, the Countess of Huntingdon, a Methodist leader to whom Whitefield had been personal chaplain. Wheatley was celebrated in London by many prominent historical figures, including Benjamin Franklin, Granville Sharp (the famous abolitionist), the Earl of Dartmouth (for whom Dartmouth College had been named), and Sir Brook Watson, eventual Lord Mayor of London. She wrote effusively of how she had been welcomed: "I was received in England with such kindness, complaisance, and so many marks of esteem and real friendship as astonishes me on the reflection." Wheatley soon returned to Boston, however, to care for the ailing Susanna.

As a poet, Wheatley was particularly adept at the heroic couplet, the dominant poetic form of the eighteenth century. Her devotion to Protestant Christianity is revealed in elegies that exhort surviving relatives to seek comfort in the glory of salvation. As with Milton before her, Wheatley mingled biblical references with frequent allusions to Greek and Roman myth, often invoking the Muses to her aid. A few meditative poems explore the workings of the mind ("On Recollection," "On Imagination"), while more explicitly political poems such as "To the Right Honourable William, Earl of Dartmouth" display her commitment to freedom and equality. Wheatley's letters to prominent individuals and personal friends —including Obour Tanner, an enslaved black woman living in Newport, Rhode Island—address her religious faith, her transatlantic travels, the sale of her book of poems, and her strident antislavery beliefs.

Wheatley's poetry challenged Western culture's racist belief—evidenced in the writings of David Hume, Immanuel Kant, and Thomas Jefferson—that people of African descent were inferior to

whites—even that Africans were less than fully human. Her patrons and publishers rightly assumed that many readers would be incredulous that an enslaved woman and native of Africa could have written a volume of poetry. *Poems on Various Subjects* thus includes a preface by Wheatley's enslaver verifying her authorship, and an attestation of her poetic abilities signed by eighteen prominent Bostonians, including Thomas Hutchison, Governor of Massachusetts, and John Hancock, future signer of the Declaration of Independence. Her poetic achievement remained an important touchstone in debates about race and slavery well into the nineteenth century.

Immediately after *Poems on Various Subjects* was published, many readers expressed outrage that such an accomplished poet was still enslaved. Responding to this pressure, John Wheatley manumitted Phillis in 1773. Throughout the period of the American Revolution she continued to write and publish poems—among them a panegyric to George Washington. The war disrupted the transatlantic network of Methodist patrons that had supported her early career, however, and she never garnered enough support to publish a second book. She married John Peters, a free black man, in 1778. Wheatley took her husband's last name as her own, thereafter publishing poetry and signing letters as Phillis Peters. The Peters were ambitious and resourceful, but the couple faced serious misfortune; it is likely they had at least one child who died in infancy, and John Peters was in prison for debt when Wheatley Peters herself died in 1784. The unpublished work she left behind does not survive, but *Poems on Various Subjects* received renewed attention beginning in the mid-nineteenth century, when Wheatley was adopted as an icon of the American antislavery movement.

NOTE ON THE TEXTS: Unless otherwise noted, the texts of the poems presented here are from the 1773 first London edition of *Poems on Various Subjects, Religious and Moral*. Some of Wheatley's poems from that volume also exist in other versions; as an example, we have presented "On the Death of the Rev. Mr. George Whitefield" in facing column format, with a broadside version first published in Boston in 1770 alongside the 1773 version. We also include a poem that dates from later than 1773 and a number of Wheatley's letters; information on those texts is provided in footnotes. Spelling and punctuation have been modernized in accordance with the practices of this anthology.

⌘ ⌘ ⌘

To Maecenas[1]

Maecenas, you, beneath the myrtle shade,
Read o'er what poets sung, and shepherds played.
What felt those poets but you feel the same?
Does not your soul possess the sacred flame?
5 Their noble strains° your equal genius shares *verses*
In softer language, and diviner airs.

 While Homer[2] paints lo! circumfused° *dispersed*
 in air,
Celestial Gods in mortal forms appear;
Swift as they move hear each recess rebound,
10 Heav'n quakes, earth trembles, and the shores resound.

Great Sire of verse, before my mortal eyes,
The lightnings blaze across the vaulted skies,
And, as the thunder shakes the heav'nly plains,
A deep-felt horror thrills through all my veins.
15 Where gentler strains demand thy graceful song,
The length'ning line moves languishing along.
When great Patroclus[3] courts Achilles' aid,
The grateful tribute of my tears is paid;
Prone on the shore he feels the pangs of love,
20 And stern Pelides[4] tend'rest passions move.

 Great Maro's[5] strain in heav'nly numbers flows,
The Nine[6] inspire, and all the bosom glows.

[1] *Maecenas* Wealthy Roman patron (d. 8 BCE) and the dedicatee of poems by Horace (56–8 BCE) and Virgil (70–19 BCE), including *The Georgics* (36–29 BCE).

[2] *Homer* Ancient Greek poet, traditionally believed to be the author of the *Iliad* and *Odyssey*. Wheatley read Homer in a popular English translation by Alexander Pope (1688–1744).

[3] *Patroclus* In the *Iliad*, the character who pleads with *Achilles*, the great Greek warrior, to return to battle.

[4] *Pelides* Another name in the *Iliad* for Achilles, the son of Peleus.

[5] *Maro* Common name for Virgil.

[6] *Nine* The Muses, nine goddesses who preside over the arts.

O could I rival thine and Virgil's page,
Or claim the Muses with the Mantuan Sage;[1]
25 Soon the same beauties should my mind adorn,
And the same ardors in my soul should burn:
Then should my song in bolder notes arise,
And all my numbers pleasingly surprize;
But here I sit, and mourn a grov'ling mind,
30 That fain would mount, and ride upon the wind.

Not you, my friend, these plaintive strains become,
Not you, whose bosom is the Muses home;
When they from tow'ring Helicon[2] retire,
They fan in you the bright immortal fire,
35 But I less happy, cannot raise the song,
The fault'ring music dies upon my tongue.

The happier Terence[3] all the choir inspir'd,
His soul replenished, and his bosom fir'd;
But say, ye Muses, why this partial grace,
40 To one alone of Afric's sable race;
From age to age transmitting thus his name
With the first glory in the rolls of fame?

Thy virtues, great Maecenas! shall be sung
In praise of Him, from those virtues sprung:
45 While blooming wreaths around thy temples spread,
I'll snatch a laurel from thine honoured head,
While you indulgent smile upon the deed.

As long as Thames[4] in streams majestic flows,
Or Naiads[5] in their oozy beds repose,
50 While Phoebus[6] reigns above the starry train,
While bright Aurora[7] purples o'er the main,
So long, great Sir, the muse thy praise shall sing,
So long thy praise shall make Parnassus[8] ring:

Then grant, Maecenas, thy paternal rays,
55 Hear me propitious,° and defend my lays. *with favor*
—1773

To the University of Cambridge,[9] in New-England

While an intrinsic ardor prompts to write,
The muses promise to assist my pen;
'Twas not long since I left my native shore
The land of errors, and Egyptian[10] gloom:
5 Father of mercy, 'twas thy gracious hand
Brought me in safety from those dark abodes.

Students, to you 'tis giv'n to scan the heights
Above, to traverse the ethereal space,
And mark the systems of revolving worlds.
10 Still more, ye sons of science ye receive
The blissful news by messengers from heav'n,
How Jesus' blood for your redemption flows.
See him with hands out-stretched upon the cross;
Immense compassion in his bosom glows;
15 He hears revilers, nor resents their scorn:
What matchless mercy in the Son of God!
When the whole human race by sin had fall'n,
He deigned to die that they might rise again,
And share with him in the sublimest skies,
20 Life without death, and glory without end.

Improve your privileges while they stay,
Ye pupils, and each hour redeem, that bears
Or good or bad report of you to heav'n.
Let sin, that baneful evil to the soul,
25 By you be shunned, nor once remit your guard;
Suppress the deadly serpent in its egg.
Ye blooming plants of human race divine,
An Ethiop[11] tells you 'tis your greatest foe;
Its transient sweetness turns to endless pain,
30 And in immense perdition sinks the soul.
—1773 (WRITTEN 1767)

1 *Mantuan Sage* Another name for Virgil, born in Mantua.

2 *Helicon* Mountain sacred to the Muses.

3 [Wheatley's note] He was an African by birth. [Terence was a dramatist (d. c. 159 BCE) born in Carthage, in North Africa, who lived for a time as an enslaved person in Rome.]

4 *Thames* The great river that flows through London.

5 *Naiads* Nymphs dwelling in springs and rivers.

6 *Phoebus* Apollo, god of the sun.

7 *Aurora* Goddess of the dawn.

8 *Parnassus* Sacred mountain in Greece associated with Apollo and the Muses.

9 *University of Cambridge* Harvard University, in Cambridge, Massachusetts.

10 *Egyptian* Egypt was often substituted as a name for the entire continent of Africa.

11 *Ethiop* Ethiopian; i.e., African. Like Egypt, Ethiopia was often substituted as a name for Africa.

To the King's Most Excellent Majesty[1]

Your subjects hope, dread Sire—
 The crown upon your brows may flourish long,
And that your arm may in your God be strong!
O may your sceptre num'rous nations sway,
5 And all with love and readiness obey!

 But how shall we the British king reward!
Rule thou in peace, our father, and our lord!
Midst the remembrance of thy favours past,
The meanest peasants most admire the last.[2]
10 May George, belov'd by all the nations round,
Live with heav'ns choicest constant blessings crown'd!

Great God, direct, and guard him from on high,
And from his head let ev'ry evil fly!
And may each clime with equal gladness see
15 A monarch's smile can set his subjects free!
 —1773 (WRITTEN 1768)

On Being Brought from Africa to America

'Twas mercy brought me from my Pagan land,
 Taught my benighted soul to understand
That there's a God, that there's a Saviour too:
Once I redemption neither sought nor knew.
5 Some view our sable race with scornful eye,
"Their colour is a diabolic die."
Remember, *Christians*, *Negros*, black as Cain,[3]
May be refined and join th' angelic train.
 —1773

1 As Wheatley's note to line 9 indicates, this poem, addressed to King George III (1738–1820), celebrates the repeal of the Stamp Act, a controversial measure that taxed printed material (such as newspapers and legal documents) throughout the American colonies. It was repealed in 1766.

2 [Wheatley's note] The Repeal of the Stamp Act.

3 *Cain* The oldest son of Adam and Eve, who kills his younger brother, Abel, in Genesis 4. As punishment, God exiles Cain from Eden and sets a mark of sin upon him. Some in Wheatley's time believed this mark took the form of dark skin, and attempted to justify slavery on the grounds that Africans were descended from Cain.

On Imagination

Thy various works, imperial queen, we see,
 How bright their forms! how decked with pomp
 by thee!
Thy wond'rous acts in beauteous order stand,
And all attest how potent is thine hand.

5 From Helicon's[4] refulgent° heights attend; *radiant*
Ye sacred choir, and my attempts befriend:
To tell her glories with a faithful tongue,
Ye blooming graces, triumph in my song.

Now here, now there, the roving Fancy flies,
10 Till some loved object strikes her wand'ring eyes,
Whose silken fetters all the senses bind,
And soft captivity involves the mind.

Imagination! who can sing thy force?
Or who describe the swiftness of thy course?
15 Soaring through air to find the bright abode,
Th' empyreal° palace of the thund'ring God, *heavenly*
We on thy pinions° can surpass the wind, *wings*
And leave the rolling universe behind:
From star to star the mental optics rove,
20 Measure the skies, and range the realms above.
There in one view we grasp the mighty whole,
Or with new worlds amaze th' unbounded soul.

 Though Winter frowns to Fancy's raptured eyes
The fields may flourish, and gay scenes arise;
25 The frozen deeps° may break their iron bands, *seas*
And bid their waters murmur o'er the sands.
Fair Flora[5] may resume her fragrant reign,
And with her flow'ry riches deck the plain;
Sylvanus[6] may diffuse his honours round,
30 And all the forest may with leaves be crowned;
Show'rs may descend, and dews their gems disclose,
And nectar sparkle on the blooming rose.

 Such is thy pow'r, nor are thine orders vain,
O thou the leader of the mental train:

4 *Helicon* Mountain sacred to the Muses.

5 *Flora* Roman goddess of spring.

6 *Sylvanus* Roman god of the forest.

35 In full perfection all thy works are wrought,
 And thine the sceptre o'er the realms of thought.
 Before thy throne the subject-passions bow,
 Of subject-passions sov'reign ruler thou;
 At thy command joy rushes on the heart,
40 And through the glowing veins the spirits dart.

 Fancy might now her silken pinions° try *wings*
 To rise from earth, and sweep th' expanse on high;
 From Tithon's[1] bed now might Aurora rise,
 Her cheeks all glowing with celestial dies,° *colors*
45 While a pure stream of light o'erflows the skies.
 The monarch of the day I might behold,
 And all the mountains tipt with radiant gold,
 But I reluctant leave the pleasing views,
 Which Fancy dresses to delight the Muse;
50 Winter austere forbids me to aspire,
 And northern tempests damp the rising fire;
 They chill the tides of Fancy's flowing sea,
 Cease then, my song, cease the unequal lay.
 —1773

To the Right Honourable William, Earl of Dartmouth, His Majesty's Principal Secretary of State for North-America[2]

Hail, happy day, when, smiling like the morn,
Fair Freedom rose, New-England to adorn:
The northern clime beneath her genial ray,
Dartmouth, congratulates thy blissful sway:
5 Elate with hope her race no longer mourns,
Each soul expands, each grateful bosom burns,

1 *Tithon* Trojan prince, mortal lover of Aurora, goddess of the dawn.

2 *William ... North-America* William Legge (1731–1801), Second Earl of Dartmouth, in 1772 appointed Secretary of State for the Colonies by Lord North (1732–92). Dartmouth's support for the repeal of the Stamp Act in 1766 had earned him a favorable reputation among colonists angered by British taxation policies; expectations upon his appointment were therefore high. Wheatley initially wrote this poem at the instigation of Thomas Wooldridge, who suggested Dartmouth's appointment as a subject when he visited the Wheatleys in Boston in October 1772. Wheatley revised the poem for its inclusion in *Poems on Various Subjects*; that is the version printed here.

While in thine hand with pleasure we behold
The silken reins, and Freedom's charms unfold.
Long lost to realms beneath the northern skies
10 She shines supreme, while hated faction dies:
Soon as appeared the Goddess° long desired, *freedom*
Sick at the view, she° languished and expired; *faction*
Thus from the splendors of the morning light
The owl in sadness seeks the caves of night.

15 No more, America, in mournful strain
Of wrongs, and grievance unredressed complain,
No longer shall thou dread the iron chain,
Which wanton Tyranny with lawless hand
Had made, and with it meant t' enslave the land.

20 Should you, my lord, while you peruse my song,
Wonder from whence my love of freedom sprung,
Whence flow these wishes for the common good,
By feeling hearts alone best understood,
I, young in life, by seeming cruel fate
25 Was snatch'd from Afric's fancy'd happy seat:
What pangs excruciating must molest,° *disturb*
What sorrows labour in my parent's breast?
Steeled° was that soul and by no misery moved *hardened*
That from a father seized his babe belov'd:
30 Such, such my case.[3] And can I then but pray
Others may never feel tyrannic sway?

 For favours past, great Sir, our thanks are due,
And thee we ask thy favours to renew,
Since in thy pow'r, as in thy will before,
35 To soothe the griefs, which thou did'st once deplore.
May heav'nly grace the sacred sanction° give *blessing*
To all thy works, and thou forever live
Not only on the wings of fleeting fame,
Though praise immortal crowns the patriot's name,
40 But to conduct to heav'ns refulgent° *radiant*
 fane,° *temple*
May fiery coursers° sweep th' ethereal plain, *horses*
And bear thee upwards to that blest abode,
Where, like the prophet, thou shalt find thy God.
 —1773

3 *Steeled ... my case* Wheatley references being stolen from her father's arms by a slave trader unmoved by his abominable task.

To S.M.,[1] a Young African Painter, on Seeing His Works

To show the lab'ring bosom's deep intent,
And thought in living characters to paint,
When first thy pencil did those beauties give,
And breathing figures learnt from thee to live,
5 How did those prospects give my soul delight,
A new creation rushing on my sight?
Still, wond'rous youth! each noble path pursue,
On deathless glories fix thine ardent view:
Still may the painter's and the poet's fire
10 To aid thy pencil, and thy verse conspire!
And may the charms of each seraphic[2] theme
Conduct thy footsteps to immortal fame!
High to the blissful wonders of the skies
Elate thy soul, and raise thy wishful eyes.
15 Thrice happy, when exalted to survey
That splendid city, crowned with endless day,
Whose twice fix gates on radiant hinges ring:
Celestial Salem blooms in endless spring.[3]

Calm and serene thy moments glide along,
20 And may the muse inspire each future song!
Still, with the sweets of contemplation bless'd,
May peace with balmy wings your soul invest!
But when these shades of time are chased away,
And darkness ends in everlasting day,
25 On what seraphi pinions° wings
 shall we move,
And view the landscapes in the realms above?
There shall thy tongue in heav'nly murmurs flow,

And there my muse with heav'nly transport glow:
No more to tell of Damon's[4] tender sighs,
30 Or rising radiance of Aurora's[5] eyes,
For nobler themes demand a nobler strain,
And purer language on th'ethereal plain.
Cease, gentle muse! the solemn gloom of night
Now seals the fair creation from my sight.
—1773

A Farewell to America. To Mrs. S.W.[6]

1

Adieu, New-England's smiling meads,° meadows
 Adieu, the flow'ry plain:
I leave thine op'ning charms, O spring,
 And tempt the roaring main.° sea

2

5 In vain for me the flow'rets rise,
 And boast their gaudy pride,
While here beneath the northern skies
 I mourn for health denied.

3

Celestial maid of rosy hue,[7]
10 O let me feel thy reign!
I languish till thy face I view,
 Thy vanish'd joys regain.

4

Susanna mourns, nor can I bear
 To see the crystal show'r,
15 Or mark the tender falling tear
 At sad departure's hour;

1 *S.M.* The painter Scipio Moorhead (fl. 1773), a person enslaved by John Moorhead of Boston. The engraving of Wheatley's reproduced in this anthology is copied from a portrait that some scholars attribute to this artist.

2 *seraphic* Angelic, heavenly; the angels surrounding God's throne are referred to as seraphim.

3 *That splendid ... endless spring* Reference to "new Jerusalem," an earthly paradise that, according to Revelation 21, will descend from heaven after the end times. This city experiences no night and is surrounded by twelve gates, each named for one of the twelve tribes of Israel; *Salem* Another name for Jerusalem.

4 *Damon* Generic name in pastoral poetry for a farmer, dating back to Virgil.

5 *Aurora* Goddess of the dawn.

6 *S.W.* Susanna Wheatley, the poet's mistress. This poem commemorates Wheatley's transatlantic voyage to London, where she traveled both for her health and to oversee the publication of *Poems on Various Subjects*, in which this poem was printed. Susanna Wheatley stayed behind in Boston.

7 *Celestial ... hue* The New England sun.

5

Not unregarding can I see
 Her soul with grief opprest:
But let no sighs, no groans for me,
20 Steal from her pensive breast.

6

In vain the feather'd warblers sing,
 In vain the garden blooms,
And on the bosom of the spring
 Breathes out her sweet perfumes

7

25 While for Britannia's° distant shore *Great Britain's*
 We sweep the liquid plain,
And with astonish'd eyes explore
 The wide-extended main.

8

Lo! Health appears! celestial dame!
30 Complacent and serene,
With Hebe's[1] mantle o'er her Frame,
 With soul-delighting mein.° *strength*

9

To mark the vale where London lies
 With misty vapours crown'd,

35 Which cloud Aurora's[2] thousand dyes,° *colors*
 And veil her charms around,

10

Why, Phoebus,[3] moves thy car so slow?
 So slow thy rising ray?
Give us the famous town to view,
40 Thou glorious king of day!

11

For thee, Britannia, I resign
 New-England's smiling fields
To view again her charms divine,
 What joy the prospect yields!

12

45 But thou! Temptation hence away,
 With all thy fatal train° *consequences*
Nor once seduce my soul away,
 By thine enchanting strain.° *music*

13

Thrice happy they, whose heav'nly shield
50 Secures their souls from harms,
And fell temptation on the field
 Of all its pow'r disarms!
—1773

1 *Hebe* Greek goddess of youth.

2 *Aurora* Goddess of the dawn.
3 *Phoebus* Apollo, god of the sun.

To His Excellency General Washington[1]

The following letter and verses were written by the famous Phillis Wheatley, the African Poetess, and presented to his Excellency Gen. Washington.[2]

Sir,

I have taken the freedom to address your Excellency in the enclosed poem, and entreat your acceptance, though I am not insensible of its inaccuracies. Your being appointed by the Grand Continental Congress to be Generalissimo of the armies of North America, together with the fame of your virtues, excite sensations not easy to suppress. Your generosity, therefore, I presume, will pardon the attempt. Wishing your Excellency all possible success in the great cause you are so generously engaged in. I am,

Your Excellency's most obedient humble servant,
Phillis Wheatley.

Celestial choir! enthroned in realms of light,
Columbia's[3] scenes of glorious toils I write.
While freedom's cause her anxious breast alarms,
She flashes dreadful in refulgent° arms. radiant
5 See mother earth her offspring's fate bemoan,
And nations gaze at scenes before unknown!
See the bright beams of heaven's revolving light
Involved in sorrows and the veil of night!

The goddess comes, she moves divinely fair,
10 Olive and laurel binds her golden hair:
Wherever shines this native of the skies,
Unnumbered charms and recent graces rise.
Muse! Bow propitious° while my pen relates favorably
How pour her armies through a thousand gates,
15 As when Eolus[4] heaven's fair face deforms,
Enwrapped in tempest and a night of storms;
Astonished ocean feels the wild uproar,
The refluent° surges beat the sounding shore; flowing
Or thick as leaves in Autumn's golden reign,
20 Such, and so many, moves the warrior's train.
In bright array they seek the work of war,
Where high unfurled the ensign° waves in air. flag
Shall I to Washington their praise recite?
Enough thou know'st them in the fields of fight.
25 Thee, first in peace and honors—we demand
The grace and glory of thy martial band.
Famed for thy valour, for thy virtues more,
Hear every tongue thy guardian aid implore!
One century scarce performed its destined round,
30 When Gallic° powers Columbia's fury found;[5] French
And so may you, whoever dares disgrace
The land of freedom's heaven-defended race!
Fix'd are the eyes of nations on the scales,
For in their hopes Columbia's arm prevails.
35 Anon Britannia° droops the pensive head, Great Britain
While round increase the rising hills of dead.
Ah! cruel blindness to Columbia's state!
Lament thy thirst of boundless power too late.
Proceed, great chief, with virtue on thy side,
40 Thy ev'ry action let the goddess guide.
A crown, a mansion, and a throne that shine,
With gold unfading, Washington! Be thine.

—1775

1 Wheatley sent this poem to George Washington on 26 October 1775. At the time she was in Providence, Rhode Island, having fled there with the Wheatleys during the British Occupation of Boston, and Washington was in Cambridge, Massachusetts, commanding the troops of the colonial army. Washington replied on 28 February 1776, writing, "I thank you most sincerely for your polite notice of me, in the elegant lines you enclosed; and however underserving I may be of such encomium and panegyrick, the style and manner exhibit a striking proof of your poetical talents." The poem was first published in the *Virginia Gazette* on 20 March 1776.

2 *The following ... Gen. Washington* The poem appears here as it was published in the *Pennsylvania Magazine*, edited by Thomas Paine (1763–1809)—together with this headnote and Wheatley's letter.

3 *Columbia* The personification of America, a term derived from Christopher Columbus. Columbia is the "Goddess" referenced throughout the poem (see line 9).

4 *Eolus* Aeolus, god of the wind.

5 *Gallic ... found* Wheatley references the French and Indian War (1754–63), which pitted Anglo-Americans against France and their Native American allies. It was during this war that Washington initially made his reputation as a military commander.

On the Death of the Rev. Mr. George Whitefield

Phillis Wheatley revised her poems throughout her career and especially for her 1773 book *Poems on Various Subjects, Religious and Moral*. Many important poems exist in earlier versions, including "To the Right Honourable William, Earl of Dartmouth" and "Farewell to America." Wheatley significantly revised the poem that first brought her transatlantic fame, her elegy for George Whitefield, the Methodist minister. Whitefield toured the American colonies multiple times, delivering sermons outdoors to thousands of people during the Great Awakening of the 1730s and 1740s. He was well known as a philanthropist and advocate for the spiritual equality of black people, although, notably, he was not an abolitionist. Wheatley's elegy circulated as a broadside and was reprinted widely in Britain and North America. Included here are two versions: the first published within weeks of Whitefield's death in 1770, and the later version published in *Poems on Various Subjects*. In the book version, Wheatley's poem is divorced from its initial context to fit with the other poems in the collection: the long headnote from the broadside, included here, was replaced in the book with a brief title and the date of its original publication. Wheatley also shortened the poem by over a dozen lines; made many subtle changes to her language ("Inflame the soul" in line 8, for example, becomes "Inflame the heart"); and cut a passage about the Boston Massacre.

On the Death of the Rev. Mr. George Whitefield

[Broadside version (1770)]

An elegiac poem, on the death of that celebrated divine, and eminent servant of Jesus Christ, the late Reverend, and pious George Whitefield, Chaplain to the Right Honorable the Countess of Huntingdon,[1] &c. &c., who made his exit from this transitory state, to dwell in the celestial realms of bliss, on Lord's Day, 30th of September, 1770, when he was seized with a fit of the asthma, at Newbury-Port, near Boston, in New England. In which is a condolatory address to his truly noble benefactress, the worthy and pious Lady Huntingdon—and the Orphan-Children in Georgia;[2] who, with many thousands, are left, by the death of this great man, to lament the loss of a father, friend, and benefactor.

On the Death of the Rev. Mr. George Whitefield

[Poems on Various Subjects *version (1773)*]

[1] *Countess of Huntingdon* Selina Hastings (1707–91), an evangelical who founded the "Huntingdon Connexion," a group of radical Methodists who broke from the Church of England in 1782. Whitefield was her personal Chaplain at the time of his death.

[2] *Orphan-Children in Georgia* Whitefield founded an orphanage in Bethesda, Georgia, in 1738, and throughout his career solicited funds for its upkeep.

By Phillis, a servant girl[1] of 17 years of age, belonging to Mr.
J. Wheatley, of Boston:—and has been but 9 years in this
country from Africa.

Hail happy saint on thy immortal throne!
To thee complaints of grievance are unknown;
We hear no more the music of thy tongue,
Thy wonted° auditories° cease to throng. *usual / audiences*
5 Thy lessons in unequalled° accents flowed! *unparalleled*
While emulation in each bosom glowed;
Thou didst, in strains of eloquence refined,
Inflame the soul, and captivate the mind.
Unhappy we, the setting sun deplore!
10 Which once was splendid, but it shines no more.
He leaves this earth for Heaven's unmeasured height:
And worlds unknown, receive him from our fight;
There Whitefield wings, with rapid course his way,
And sails to Zion,[2] through vast seas of day.

15 When his Americans were burdened sore,[3]
When streets were crimsoned with their guiltless gore![4]
Unrivaled friendship in his breast now strove:
The fruit thereof was charity and love
Towards America—couldst thou do more
20 Than leave thy native home, the British shore,
To cross the great Atlantic's wat'ry road,
To see America's distressed abode?
Thy prayers, great saint, and thy incessant cries,
Have pierced the bosom of thy native skies!
25 Thou moon hast seen, and ye bright stars of light
Have witness been of his requests by night!
He prayed that grace in every heart might dwell:
He longed to see America excel;
He charged its youth to let the grace divine
30 Arise, and in their future actions shine;
He offered that he did himself receive,

Hail, happy saint, on thine immortal throne,
Possesed of glory, life, and bliss unknown;
We hear no more the music of thy tongue,
Thy wonted° auditories° cease to throng. *usual / audiences*
5 Thy sermons in unequalled° accents flowed, *unparalleled*
And ev'ry bosom with devotion glowed;
Thou didst in strains of eloquence refined
Inflame the heart, and captivate the mind.
Unhappy we the setting sun deplore,
10 So glorious once, but ah! it shines no more.

 Behold the prophet in his tow'ring flight!
He leaves the earth for heav'n's unmeasured height,
And worlds unknown recieve him from our fight.
There Whitefield wings with rapid course his way,
15 And sails to Zion through vast seas of day.

Thy prayers, great saint, and thine incessant cries
Have peirced the bosom of thy native skies.
Thou moon hast seen, and all the stars of light,
How he has wrestled with his God by night.
20 He prayed that grace in ev'ry heart might dwell,
He longed to see America excel;
He charged its youth that ev'ry grace divine
Should with full lustre in their conduct shine;
That Saviour, which his soul did first receive,

1 *servant girl* In Boston at this time "servant" was a common
euphemism for "slave."

2 *Zion* Heaven, or the promised land.

3 *burdened sore* Burdened with much suffering.

4 *streets ... gore* Reference to the Boston Massacre on 5 March
1770, which Whitefield condemned. British troops fired without
orders into a group of civilians, killing three and setting off a fire-
storm of anti-British sentiment in the colonies.

[*Broadside version* (1770) *cont'd*]

A greater gift not God himself can give:
He urged the need of Him to every one;
It was no less than God's co-equal Son!
35 Take Him ye wretched for your only good;
Take Him ye starving souls to be your food.
Ye thirsty, come to this life giving stream:
Ye preachers, take him for your joyful theme:
Take Him, "my dear Americans," he said,
40 Be your complaints in his kind bosom laid:
Take Him ye Africans, he longs for you;
Impartial Saviour, is his title due;
If you will choose to walk in grace's road,
You shall be sons, and kings, and priests to God.

45 Great Countess! We Americans revere
Thy name, and thus condole[1] thy grief sincere:
We mourn with thee, that tomb obscurely placed,
In which thy Chaplain undisturbed doth rest.
New England sure, doth feel the orphan's smart;[2]
50 Reveals the true sensations of his heart:
Since this fair Sun, withdraws his golden rays,
No more to brighten these distressful days!
His lonely Tabernacle, sees no more
A Whitefield landing on the British shore:
55 Then let us view him in yon azure skies:
Let every mind with this loved object rise.
No more can he exert his lab'ring breath,
Seized by the cruel messenger of death.
What can his dear America return?
60 But drop a tear upon his happy urn,
Thou tomb, shalt safe retain thy sacred trust,
Till life divine re-animate his dust.
—1770

[*Poems on Various Subjects version* (1773) *cont'd*]

25 The greatest gift that ev'n a God can give,
He freely offered to the num'rous throng,
That on his lips with list'ning pleasure hung.

"Take him, ye wretched, for your only good,
Take him ye starving sinners, for your food;
30 Ye thirsty, come to this life-giving stream,
Ye preachers, take him for your joyful theme;
Take him my dear Americans, he said,
Be your complaints on his kind bosom laid:
Take him, ye Africans, he longs for you,
35 Impartial Saviour is his title due:
Washed in the fountain of redeeming blood,
You shall be sons, and kings, and priests to God."

 Great Countess,[3] we Americans revere
Thy name, and mingle in thy grief sincere;
40 New England deeply feels, the Orphans mourn,
Their more than father will no more return.

But, though arrested by the hand of death,
Whitefield no more exerts his lab'ring breath,
Yet let us view him in th' eternal skies,
45 Let ev'ry heart to this bright vision rise;
While the tomb safe retains its sacred trust,
Till life divine re-animates his dust.
—1773

1 *condole* Sympathize with.

2 *smart* Suffering. A reference to the orphanage Whitefield supported in Georgia.

3 [Wheatley's note] The Countess of Huntingdon, to whom Mr. Whitefield was Chaplain.

Selected Letters

Phillis Wheatley wrote dozens of letters to friends and acquaintances in New England and abroad. Her correspondents included prominent individuals such as George Washington and Selina Hastings, the Countess of Huntingdon, as well as Obour Tanner, an enslaved African woman who lived in Newport, Rhode Island, and Samson Occom, the Mohegan minister.

TO OBOUR TANNER, IN NEW-PORT [RHODE ISLAND]
19 May 1772
Boston

Dear Sister

I received your favour of February 6th for which I give you my sincere thanks. I greatly rejoice with you in that realizing view, and I hope experience, of the saving change which you so emphatically describe. Happy were it for us if we could arrive to that evangelical repentance, and the true holiness of heart which you mention. Inexpressibly happy should we be could we have a due sense of beauties and excellence of the crucified Saviour. In his crucifixion may be seen marvelous displays of grace and love, sufficient to draw and invite us to the rich and endless treasures of his mercy; let us rejoice in and adore the wonders of God's infinite love in bringing us from a land semblant of[1] darkness itself, and where the divine light of revelation (being obscured) is as darkness.[2] Here, the knowledge of the true God and eternal life are made manifest; but there, profound ignorance overshadows the land. Your observation is true, namely, that there was nothing in us to recommend us to God. Many of our fellow creatures are passed by, when the bowels of divine love expanded towards us. May this goodness & long suffering of God lead us to unfeigned repentance.

It gives me very great pleasure to hear of so many of my nation,[3] seeking with eagerness the way to true felicity. O may we all meet at length in that happy

[1] *semblant of* Resembling.

[2] *is as darkness* Here Wheatley touches on the irony that her enslavement has also provided access to Christian revelation. See also her poem "On Being Brought from Africa to America."

[3] *of my nation* Of African descent.

mansion. I hope the correspondence between us will continue, (my being much indisposed this winter past was the reason of my not answering yours before now) which correspondence I hope may have the happy effect of improving our mutual friendship. Till we meet in the regions of consummate blessedness, let us endeavor by the assistance of divine grace, to live the life, and we shall die the death of the righteous. May this be our happy case and of those who are travelling to the region of felicity,[4] is the earnest request of your affectionate

Friend and humble servant, Phillis Wheatley

TO SELINA HASTINGS, COUNTESS OF HUNTINGDON[5]
27 June 1773
London

It is with pleasure I acquaint your Ladyship of my safe arrival in London after a fine passage of five weeks, in the ship London with my young master (advised by my physicians for my health) have brought a letter from Richard Carey,[6] Esquire, but was disappointed by your absence of the honour of waiting upon your Ladyship with it. I would have enclosed it, but was doubtful of the safety of the conveyance.

I should think myself very happy in seeing your Ladyship, and if you was so desirous of the image of the author as to propose it for a frontispiece I flatter myself that you would accept the reality.[7]

[4] *the region of felicity* Heaven.

[5] *SELINA HASTINGS ... HUNTINGDON* Selina Hastings (1707–91), an evangelical who founded the "Huntingdon Connexion," a group of radical Methodists who broke from the Church of England in 1782. Wheatley wrote this letter soon after she arrived in London, where she had traveled for her health and to oversee the publication of *Poems on Various Subjects*.

[6] *Richard Carey* An acquaintance of the Wheatley family and correspondent of the Countess of Huntingdon who wrote a letter of introduction for the poet.

[7] *image ... the reality* The Countess of Huntingdon had herself suggested that an engraved image of the author appear as the frontispiece to *Poems on Various Subjects*. Wheatley left Great Britain before the two had a chance to meet in person.

I conclude with thanking your ladyship for permitting the dedication[1] of my poems to you; and am not insensible, that, under the patronage of your Ladyship, not more eminent in the station of life than in your exemplary piety and virtue, my feeble efforts will be shielded from the severe trials of unpitying criticism and, being encouraged by your Ladyship's indulgence, I the more freely resign to the world these juvenile productions, and am Madam, with greatest humility, your dutiful humble servant,

Phillis Wheatley

TO COLONEL DAVID WOOSTER,[2]
NEW HAVEN, CONNECTICUT
18 October 1773
Boston

Sir,

... I take the freedom to transmit to you, a short sketch of my voyage and return from London where I went for the recovery of my health as advised by my physician. I was received in England with such kindness, complaisance,[3] and so many marks of esteem and real friendship as astonishes me on the reflection, for I was no more than 6 weeks there.—Was introduced to Lord Dartmouth and had near half an hour conversation with his Lordship, with whom was Alderman Kirkman.[4]—Then to Lord Lincoln, who visited me at my own Lodgings with the famous Dr. Solander,[5] who accompanied Mr. Banks in his late expedition around the world.

Then to Lady Cavendish, and Lady Carteret Webb, —Mrs. Palmer a poetess, an accomplished Lady.—Dr. Thos. Gibbons, Rhetoric Professor, To Israel Maudit, Esquire, Benjamin Franklin, Esquire, F.R.S., Granville Sharp,[6] Esquire, who attended me to the Tower[7] and showed the lions, panthers, tigers, etc., the horse armoury, small armoury, the crowns, sceptres, diadems, the font for Christening the royal family. Saw Westminster Abbey, British Museum, Cox's Museum, Saddler's Wells, Greenwich Hospital, Park and Chapel, the royal observatory at Greenwich, etc., etc., too many things and places to trouble you with in a letter.—The Earl of Dartmouth made me a compliment[8] of 5 guineas, and desired me to get the whole of Mr. Pope's[9] Works, as the best he could recommend to my perusal, this I did, also got Hudibras, Don Quixote, and Gay's Fables[10]—was presented with a folio edition of Milton's Paradise Lost,[11] printed on a silver type, so called from its elegance, (I suppose) by Mr. Brook Watson,[12] whose coat of arms is prefixed.—Since my return to America my master, has at the desire of my friends in England given me my freedom. The instrument[13] is drawn, so as to secure me and my property from the hands of

[1] *the dedication* In agreeing to have *Poems on Various Subjects* dedicated to her, the Countess of Huntingdon publically endorsed Wheatley as a poet.

[2] *DAVID WOOSTER* An army general (1711–77) who fought for the British in the French and Indian War (1754–63) and then for the United States in the Revolution. He died in battle in 1777; see Wheatley's poem "On the Death of General Wooster" in the website component of this anthology.

[3] *complaisance* Politeness.

[4] *Lord Dartmouth* William Legge (1731–1801), Second Earl of Dartmouth, in 1772 appointed Secretary of State for the Colonies by Lord North (1732–92); see Wheatley's poem addressed to him, above; *Alderman Kirkman* John Kirckman (1741–80), an alderman of the city of London.

[5] *Dr. Solander* Daniel Solander (1736–82), a botanist who accompanied Joseph Banks (1743–1820) on a voyage to the South Pacific.

[6] *Mrs. Palmer* Mary Reynolds Palmer (1716–96), sister of Sir Joshua Reynolds (1723–92); *Israel Maudit* (1708–87), an agent in London for the State of Massachusetts; *Benjamin Franklin* North American politician (1706–90) and at the time an agent for the colonies in Britain; *F.R.S.* Fellow of the Royal Society; *Granville Sharp* British abolitionist (1735–1813).

[7] *the Tower* The Tower of London, medieval castle of the kings of England. By the eighteenth century it had acquired its modern function as a public museum. The other places mentioned in the letter were popular tourist sites at the time.

[8] *compliment* Gift.

[9] *Mr. Pope* Alexander Pope (1688–1744), eighteenth-century British poet. Pope's work was an important influence on Wheatley long before it was recommended that she purchase this complete edition of his works for herself.

[10] *Hudibras* A poem by Samuel Butler (1612–80); *Don Quixote* The novel by Miguel de Cervantes (1605–15); *Gay's Fables* Poems for children by John Gay (1685–1732).

[11] *Paradise Lost* Epic poem by John Milton (1608–74), originally published in 1667. A "folio edition" was a large-format, expensive publication.

[12] *Brook Watson* A merchant (1735–1807) and eventual Lord Mayor of London (1796–97).

[13] *instrument* Manumission paper guaranteeing Wheatley's freedom.

executors, administrators, etc., of my master,[1] and secure whatsoever should be given me as my own. A copy is sent to Israel Maudit, Esquire, F.R.S.

I expect my books[2] which are published in London in Capt. Hall,[3] who will be here I believe in 8 or 10 days. I beg the favour that you would honor the enclosed proposals,[4] and use your interest with gentleman and ladies of your acquaintance to subscribe also, for the more subscribers there are, the more it will be for my advantage, as I am to have half the sale of the books.[5] This I am the more solicitous for, as I am now upon my own footing and whatever I get by this is entirely mine, and it is the chief I have to depend upon.[6] I must also request you would desire the printers in New Haven not to reprint that book, as it will be a great hurt to me, preventing any further benefit that I might receive from the sale of my copies from England.[7] The price is 2/6d [two shillings, six pence] bound or 2 [shillings]/ Sterling sewed.[8] If any should be so ungenerous as to reprint them the genuine copy may be known, for it is signed and in my own handwriting.[9] My dutiful respects attend your Lady and children and I am

ever respectfully your obliged humble servant,
Phillis Wheatley

[1] *secure ... my master* Wheatley is careful to document and secure her freedom in case her status is questioned after John Wheatley's death. Enslaved people were at the mercy of their enslavers' heirs or executors and were often sold for profit or to settle debts.

[2] *my books* The volume *Poems on Various Subjects, Religious and Moral*, published by Archibald Bell in 1773.

[3] *in Capt. Hall* I.e., the ship commanded by Captain Hall, in which Wheatley expected her poems to be delivered across the Atlantic.

[4] *proposals* Advertisements encouraging buyers to "subscribe," i.e., pay a deposit ahead of time, for the book.

[5] *sale of the books* Profit from the sale of the books.

[6] *depend upon* Now, as a free woman, Wheatley supported herself partly through her writing.

[7] *copies from England* Colonial printers commonly issued unauthorized reprints of books published originally in Britain. Wheatley here pleads with Col. Wooster to help prevent such piracy in New Haven.

[8] *bound ... sewed* Two ways in which books were prepared for purchase; books bought "sewed" were often subsequently bound by their owners.

[9] *handwriting* Wheatley apparently signed each authorized copy of her book to distinguish it from pirated texts. *Poems on Various Subjects* was not reprinted in North America until 1786, two years after Wheatley's death.

TO OBOUR TANNER, IN NEW-PORT [RHODE ISLAND]
30 October 1773
Boston

Dear Obour,

I received your most kind epistles of August 27th and October 13th by a young man of your acquaintance, for which I am obliged to you. I hear of your welfare with pleasure; but this acquaints[10] you that I am at present indisposed by a cold, and since my arrival[11] have been visited by the asthma.

Your observations on our dependence on the Deity, and your hopes that my wants will be supplied from his fullness which is in Christ Jesus, is truly worthy of yourself.—I can't say but my voyage to England has conduced to[12] the recovery (in a great measure) of my health. The friends I found there among the nobility and the gentry, their benevolent conduct towards me, the unexpected, and unmerited civility and complaisance[13] with which I was treated by all, fills me with astonishment. I can scarcely realize[14] it.—This I humbly hope has the happy effect of lessening me in my own esteem. Your reflections on the sufferings of the Son of God, and the inestimable price of our immortal souls, plainly demonstrate the sensations of a soul united to Jesus. What you observe of Esau[15] is true of all mankind, who, (left to themselves) would sell their heavenly birthrights for a few moments of sensual pleasure whose wages at last (dreadful wages!) is eternal condemnation. Dear Obour let us not sell our birthright for a thousand worlds, which indeed would be as dust upon the balance.—The God of the seas and dry land, has graciously brought me home in safety. Join with me in thanks to him for so great a mercy, and that it may excite me to praise him with cheerfulness, to preserve in grace and faith, and in the knowledge of our Creator and Redeemer,—that my heart may be filled with gratitude. ...

most affectionately ever yours,
Phillis Wheatley

[10] *acquaints* Informs.

[11] *arrival* Return from London in September 1773.

[12] *conduced to* Aided in.

[13] *complaisance* Politeness.

[14] *realize* Believe in the reality of.

[15] *Esau* In Genesis 25.29–34, Esau sold his birthright to his brother Jacob for bread and pottage.

TO SAMSON OCCOM

Samson Occom (1723–92) was a Mohegan and an
ordained clergy member who toured North America
preaching with George Whitefield. He often lodged
with the Wheatleys during visits to Boston. In the
1760s Occom traveled to Great Britain and like
Wheatley was patronized by Selina Hastings (1707–
91), the Countess of Huntingdon. During his life,
Occom published a sermon and a book of hymns
and also wrote an autobiography that was pub-
lished after his death. A frequent correspondent of
the Wheatley family, including Phillis, Occom also
helped sell Wheatley's book of poems in 1773. The
letter below from Wheatley to Occom is her most
direct condemnation of the institution of slavery
in the name of natural rights and liberty. It was
reprinted in newspapers throughout New England
(and is reprinted here with the headnote that accom-
panied it in such publications).

The following is an extract of a letter from Phillis, a
Negro Girl of Mr. Wheatley's,[1] in Boston, to the Rev.
Samson Occom, which we are desired to insert as a
specimen of her ingenuity.—It is dated 11th Feb., 1774.

Revered and honored Sir,

I have this day received your obliging kind epistle,
and am greatly satisfied with your reasons respecting
the Negroes, and think highly reasonable what you
offer in vindication of their natural rights: Those that
invade them cannot be insensible that the divine light
is chasing away the thick darkness which broods over
the land of Africa; and the chaos which has reigned
so long, is converting into beautiful order, and reveals
more and more clearly, the glorious dispensation of
civil and religious liberty, which are so inseparably
united, that there is little or no enjoyment of one with-
out the other: otherwise, perhaps, the Israelites had
been less solicitous for their freedom from Egyptian
slavery;[2] I don't say they would have been contented
without it, by no means, for in every human breast,
God has implanted a principle, which we call love of
freedom; it is impatient of oppression, and pants for
deliverance; and by the leave of our modern Egyptians[3]
I will assert, that the same principle lives in us. God
grant deliverance in his own way and time, and get
him honour upon all those whose avarice impels them
to countenance and help forward the calamities of
their fellow creatures. This I desire not for their hurt,
but to convince them of the strange absurdity of their
conduct whose words and actions are so diametrically
opposite. How well the cry for liberty, and the reverse
disposition for the exercise of oppressive power over
others agree,—I humbly think it does not require the
penetration of a philosopher to determine.—

[1] *Negro Girl of Mr. Wheatley's* This description implies that
Phillis was still enslaved, but in fact she had been granted her free-
dom months earlier.

[2] *Egyptian slavery* A reference to the book of Exodus, in which
Moses liberates the Israelites from slavery in Egypt.

[3] *modern Egyptians* White enslavers. Wheatley is comparing
Americans who enslave Africans to Egyptians who enslaved the
Israelites in the Bible.

In Context

Preface to Phillis Wheatley's *Poems on Various Subjects, Religious and Moral* (1773)

Phillis Wheatley's publishers included extensive introductory material to convince readers that she was in fact the author of the poems that followed. Such material included a letter from John Wheatley, her enslaver, and an attestation signed by more than a dozen prominent citizens of Boston. Prefaces like this were not unusual for texts written by unlikely authors; when *Poems, on Several Occasions* (1785) appeared, by Wheatley's contemporary Anne Yearsley, a poor "milkwoman," the volume featured a preface by Hannah More. Nevertheless, the stakes were different for black authors who faced a predominantly racist society who thought them unequal to the task of expressing imaginative thoughts in writing. More than half a century later, this practice still continued; Frederick Douglass's *Narrative* (1845) featured two prefaces by white patrons and sponsors, the abolitionists William Lloyd Garrison and Wendell Phillips.

The following is a Copy of a Letter sent by the Author's Master to the Publisher.

Phillis was brought from Africa to America, in the Year 1761, between seven and eight years of age. Without any assistance from school education, and by only what she was taught in the family, she, in sixteen months' time from her arrival, attained the English language, to which she was an utter stranger before, to such a degree, as to read any, the most difficult parts of the sacred writings, to the great astonishment of all who heard her.

As to her writing, her own curiosity led her to it; and this she learnt in so short a time, that in the year 1765, she wrote a letter to the Rev. Mr. Occom,[1] the Indian minister, while in England.

She has a great inclination to learn the Latin tongue, and has made some progress in it. This relation is given by her master who bought her and with whom she now lives.

<div align="right">

John Wheatley
Boston, 14 November, 1772

</div>

To the Public

As it has been repeatedly suggested to the publisher, by persons, who have seen the manuscript, that numbers would be ready to suspect they were not really the writings of Phillis, he has procured the following attestation, from the most respectable characters in Boston, that none might have the least ground for disputing their original.

We whose names are under-written, do assure the world, that the poems specified in the following Page,[2] were (as we verily believe) written by Phillis, a young Negro girl, who was but a few years since, brought an uncultivated barbarian[3] from Africa, as has ever since been, and now is, under the disadvantage of

[1] *Mr. Occom* Samson Occom (1723–92), Mohegan minister, who toured England as a minister in the 1760s. This early letter does not survive.

[2] [original note] The words "following page" allude to the contents of the manuscript copy, which are wrote at the back of the above attestation.

[3] *uncultivated barbarian* Uncivilized and uncultured, without the connotation of rudeness or violence (as in modern usage).

serving as a slave in a family in this town. She has been examined by some of the best judges,[1] and is thought qualified to write them.

His Excellency THOMAS HUTCHINSON, Governor,
The Hon. ANDREW OLIVER, Lieutenant-Governor.

The Hon. Thomas Hubbard,	The Rev. Charles Cheuney, D.D.[2]
The Hon. John Erving,	The Rev. Mather Byles, D.D.
The Hon. James Pitts,	The Rev. Ed. Pemberton, D.D.
The Hon. Harrison Gray,	The Rev. Andrew Elliot, D.D.
The Hon. James Bowdoin,	The Rev. Samuel Cooper, D.D.
John Hancock, Esq;	The Rev. Samuel Mather, D.D.
Joseph Green, Esq;	The Rev. Mr. John Moorhead,
Richard Carey, Esq;	Mr. John Wheatley, her Master.

N.B. The original attestation, signed by the above gentlemen, may be seen by applying to Archibald Bell, Bookseller, No. 8, Aldgate-Street.

On the Death of a Young Lady of Five Years of Age

From dark abodes to fair ethereal° light *heavenly*
Th' enraptured innocent has winged her flight;
On the kind bosom of eternal love
She finds unknown beatitude above.
5 This know, ye parents, nor her loss deplore,
She feels the iron hand of pain no more;
The dispensations of unerring grace,
Should turn your sorrows into grateful praise;
Let then no tears for her henceforward flow,
10 No more distressed in our dark vale below.

Her morning sun, which rose divinely bright,
Was quickly mantled with the gloom of night;
But hear in heav'n's blest bow'rs your Nancy fair,
And learn to imitate her language there.
15 "Thou, Lord, whom I behold with glory crowned,

By what sweet name, and in what tuneful sound
Wilt thou be praised? Seraphic° pow'rs are faint *angelic*
Infinite love and majesty to paint.
To thee let all their grateful voices raise,
20 And saints and angels join their songs of praise."

Perfect in bliss she from her heav'nly home
Looks down, and smiling beckons you to come;
Why then, fond parents, why these fruitless groans?
Restrain your tears, and cease your plaintive moans.
25 Freed from a world of sin, and snares, and pain,
Why would you wish your daughter back again?
No—bow resigned. Let home your grief control,
And check the rising tumult of the soul.
Calm in the prosperous, and adverse day,
30 Adore the God who gives and takes away;
Eye him in all, his holy name revere,
Upright your actions, and your hearts sincere,
Till having sailed through life's tempestuous sea,

1 *examined ... judges* Most notable among the signatories are: Thomas Hutchinson (1711–80), current Governor of Massachusetts; Andrew Oliver (1706–74), Lieutenant Governor; Thomas Hubbard (1702–73), at the time treasurer of Harvard College; James Bowdoin (1726–90), future Governor of Massachusetts for whom Bowdoin college would be named; John Hancock (1737–93), famous signatory of the Declaration of Independence; Samuel Cooper (1725–83), minister of the Brattle Street Congregational Church; Samuel Mather (1706–85), son of Cotton Mather (1663–28), prominent Puritan minister; and John Moorhead (1703–73), enslaver of Scipio Moorhead, the African painter to whom Wheatley addressed a poem in 1772 (see above).

2 *D.D.* Doctor of Divinity.

And from its rocks, and boist'rous billows free,
35 Yourselves, safe landed on the blissful shore,
Shall join your happy babe to part no more.
—1773

On the Death of a Young Gentleman

Who taught thee conflict with the pow'rs of night,
 To vanquish Satan in the fields of fight?
Who strung thy feeble arms with might unknown,
How great thy conquest, and how bright thy crown!
5 War with each princedom, throne, and pow'r is o'er,
The scene is ended to return no more.
O could my muse thy seat on high behold,
How decked with laurel, how enriched with gold!
O could she hear what praise thine harp employs,
10 How sweet thine anthems, how divine thy joys!
What heav'nly grandeur should exalt her strain!° song
What holy raptures in her numbers reign!
To soothe the troubles of the mind to peace,
To still the tumult of life's tossing seas,
15 To ease the anguish of the parent's heart,
What shall my sympathizing verse impart?
Where is the balm to heal so deep a wound?
Where shall a sov'reign remedy be found?
Look, gracious Spirit, from thine heav'nly bow'r,
20 And thy full joys into their bosoms pour;
The raging tempest of their grief control,
And spread the dawn of glory through the soul,
To eye the path the saint departed trod,
And trace him to the bosom of his God.
—1773

An Hymn to the Morning

Attend my lays, ye ever honour'd nine,[1]
 Assist my labours, and my strains° refine; verses
In smoothest numbers pour the notes along,
For bright Aurora[2] now demands my song.

Aurora hail, and all the thousands dies;° colors
Which deck thy progress through the vaulted skies:
The morn awakes, and wide extends her rays,
On ev'ry leaf the gentle zephyr plays;
Harmonious lays the feather'd race[3] resume,
10 Dart the bright eye, and shake the painted plume.

Ye shady groves, your verdant gloom display
To shield your poet from the burning day
Calliope[4] awake the sacred lyre,
While thy fair sisters fan the pleasing fire:
15 The bow'rs, the gales, the variegated skies
In all their pleasures in my bosom rise.

See in the east th' illustrious king of day!
His rising radiance drives the shades away—
But Oh! I feel his fervid beams too strong,
20 And scarce begun, concludes th' abortive song.
—1773

On Recollection

Mneme[5] begin. Inspire, ye sacred nine,[6]
 Your vent'rous Afric in her great design.
Mneme, immortal pow'r, I trace thy spring:
Assist my strains, while I thy glories sing:
5 The acts of long departed years, by thee
Recover'd, in due order ranged we see:
Thy pow'r the long-forgotten calls from night,
That sweetly plays before the fancy's sight.
 Mneme in our nocturnal visions pours
10 The ample treasure of her secret stores;° materials
Swift from above she wings her silent flight
Through Phoebe's[7] realms, fair regent of the night;
And, in her pomp of images displayed,
To the high-raptured poet gives her aid,
15 Through the unbounded regions of the mind,
Diffusing light celestial and refined.

3 *feather'd race* Birds.

4 *Calliope* The Muse specifically devoted to epic poetry.

5 *Mneme* Mnemosyne, mother of the classical Muses and the personification of memory.

6 *nine* The Muses, nine goddesses who preside over the arts.

7 *Phoebe* The moon.

1 *nine* Muses, the goddesses who inspire the arts.

2 *Aurora* Goddess of the dawn.

The heav'nly phantom paints the actions done
By ev'ry tribe beneath the rolling sun.

Mneme, enthroned within the human breast,
20 Has vice condemned, and ev'ry virtue blest.
How sweet the sound when we her plaudit° applause
 hear?
Sweeter than music to the ravished ear,
Sweeter than Maro's[1] entertaining strains° verses
Resounding through the groves, and hills, and plains.
25 But how is Mneme dreaded by the race,[2]
Who scorn her warnings, and despise her grace?
By her unveiled each horrid crime appears,
Her awful hand a cup of wormwood° bears. bitterness
Days, years mispent, O what a hell of woe!
30 Hers the worst tortures that our souls can know.

Now eighteen years[3] their destined course have run,
In fast succession round the central sun.
How did the follies of that period pass

Unnoticed, but behold them writ in brass!
35 In Recollection see them fresh return,
And sure 'tis mine to be ashamed, and mourn.

O Virtue, smiling in immortal green,
Do thou exert thy pow'r, and change the scene;
Be thine employ to guide my future days,
40 And mine to pay the tribute of my praise.

Of Recollection such the pow'r enthroned
In ev'ry breast, and thus her pow'r is owned.
The wretch, who dared the vengeance of the skies,[4]
At last awakes in horror and surprize,
45 By her alarmed, he sees impending fate,
He howls in anguish, and repents too late.
But O! what peace, what joys are hers t' impart
To ev'ry holy, ev'ry upright heart!
Thrice blest the man, who, in her sacred shrine,
50 Feels himself sheltered from the wrath divine!
—1773

[1] *Maro* During the Middle ages, a common name for Virgil
(70–19 BCE).

[2] *the race* I.e., people of a certain nature.

[3] *eighteen years* Wheatley's approximate age at the time she wrote
the poem.

[4] *dared ... skies* Dared to sin, prompting God's wrath.

LEMUEL HAYNES

1753 – 1833

Lemuel Haynes occupied an unusual position throughout his career as an African American minister who preached to predominantly white congregations. A prolific writer and a powerful speaker, Haynes was widely known during his life and celebrated in the decades following his death, both for the depth of his contributions to religious thought and for his apparent transcendence of the racial prejudices that dominated American life in the early republic. As more of Haynes's writings have been discovered since the late twentieth century, the breadth of his intellectual engagement with some of the crucial themes of the Revolutionary and early abolitionist era has become clear, confirming that, for Haynes as for many early abolitionists, matters of divine law could not be separated from matters of human rights and liberty.

Haynes was born in Connecticut in 1753 to a white mother and a black father, both of whose identities remain unclear to historians. At the age of five months he was abandoned and taken to Massachusetts to live with the Roses, a pious white farming family. They took him in to become an indentured servant, a position which remained a common lot for orphaned children well into the nineteenth century (especially for children of African or Native American descent). The social and familial position occupied by such children varied dramatically from situation to situation, but it appears in Haynes's case that he was treated unusually well; in a later autobiographical sketch, Haynes recollects that Mrs. Rose treated him "as though [he] was her own child." David Rose, a deacon in the Congregational Church, allowed Haynes to attend a district school, while also encouraging him in the study of Calvinist theology. Despite the school's limited annual schedule and Haynes's frequent inability to attend classes due to his farm work, he quickly became a dedicated scholar as well as a passionate Calvinist.

Haynes was freed from his indenture at the age of twenty-one. Swept up in the period's revolutionary spirit, he enlisted as a minuteman in 1774, and in 1776 as a soldier in the Continental Army, though that service was cut short by a bout of typhus fever. Upon his return to the Rose farm in the autumn of 1776, Haynes resumed his scholarly pursuits, taking on private lessons in Latin and Greek. By 1780, having developed a local reputation as a powerful preacher, Haynes was licensed as a lay preacher in the Congregational Church. In 1783 he accepted a proposal of marriage from white schoolteacher Elizabeth Babbit, whose conversion experience had been directly influenced by Haynes's preaching; the two went on to have ten children.

Haynes was ordained as a minister in 1785, and three years later began his thirty-year ministerial role in Rutland, Vermont. In a religious climate increasingly rent by doctrinal dissent—Calvinism being beset by the perceived threats of Universalism and deism—Haynes became widely known for his passionate upholding of conservative Calvinist theology. He also wrote prolifically, and in the 1790s he began to publish essays, sermons, and poems on both religious and political matters, including his opposition to the War of 1812. Haynes's eminence continued to grow in the early 1800s, and he was granted an honorary master's degree from Middlebury College in 1804. The following year, Haynes cemented his fame among the New England Calvinist community with "Universal Salvation," one of the most popular sermons of that era. This bitingly satirical sermon was delivered in direct response to the Universalist teachings of Hosea Ballou, who had spoke out against the doctrine of eternal damnation and asserted that all souls, even those of the most sinful, would eventually receive the grace of God. "Universal Salvation" was published at the urging of Haynes's congregation in 1806; at least forty editions were printed over the following several decades, appearing as far away as Pennsylvania and Ohio.

Haynes's position as an African American ministering to predominantly white congregations made him a focus of the era's pervasive racism. Even whites who accepted him as their minister were evidently sometimes in denial on this point; one unnamed sermon attendee is recorded as having said that Haynes was "the whitest man [he] ever saw." The tide turned against Haynes in 1818, when a number of changing social factors in rural Vermont—not the least of which was an increase in racism among the white community—led to Haynes's dismissal from his ministerial position. He spent the remainder of his life as an itinerant preacher, moving between Vermont and New York, where he died in 1833. Despite the controversies that had affected his later career, Haynes's reputation grew in the years following his death. In 1837, an article in *The Colored American* described Haynes as "the only man of known African descent" to have "ever succeeded in overpowering the system of American caste." That same year saw the release of Timothy Mathew Cooley's *Sketches of the Life and Character of the Rev. Lemuel Haynes*, which included a number of previously unpublished sermons.

Among the many of Haynes's works that were published posthumously, "Liberty Further Extended: Or Free Thoughts on the Illegality of Slave-Keeping" holds a special place. Likely written shortly after the Declaration of Independence, the essay remained unknown until 1983, when it was rediscovered by scholar Ruth Bogin. The manuscript appears to be a near-final draft, but ends mid-sentence; whether the remaining material has been lost, or whether the project was abandoned by Haynes remains unclear. Regardless, the document overturns a longstanding assumption about Haynes—that he had not participated in the conversation over slavery in the eighteenth century. It had been on the basis of this assumption that Vernon Loggins, in his 1931 literary history *The Negro Author*, lamented that Haynes had "turned his back on the sufferings of the blacks in America," and that consequently "his career must be looked upon as a sort of tragedy." Composed very early in his career, "Liberty Further Extended" displays Haynes's extensive biblical knowledge as he engages with the arguments of various eighteenth-century tracts on the slave trade as well as with late-eighteenth-century philosophical conversations about freedom and natural rights. Scholarship on Haynes has increased significantly since the publication of this piece, re-establishing him as a central figure of early African American intellectual life.

NOTE ON THE TEXT: The text of "Liberty Further Extended: Or Free Thoughts on the Illegality of Slave-Keeping" is based on the original 1776 manuscript rediscovered by Ruth Bogin and reproduced in the 1983 article "'Liberty Further Extended': A 1776 Antislavery Manuscript by Lemuel Haynes" in *The William and Mary Quarterly*. Spelling and punctuation have been modernized in accordance with the practices of this anthology.

⌘ ⌘ ⌘

from *Liberty Further Extended: Or Free Thoughts on the Illegality of Slave-Keeping*

We hold these truths to be self-evident, that all men are created equal, that they are endowed by their creator with certain unalienable rights, that among these are life, liberty, and the pursuit of happiness.

Congress

The Preface.[1] As tyranny had its origin from the infernal regions, so it is the duty and honor of every son of freedom to repel her first motions. But while we are engaged in the important struggle, it cannot be thought impertinent for us to turn one eye into our own breast, for a little moment, and see whether, through some inadvertency, or a self-contracted spirit, we do not find the monster lurking in our own bosom; that now while we are inspired with so noble a spirit and becoming zeal, we may be disposed

[1] *The Preface* This is the only such heading included in the handwritten document; it is not clear where Haynes intended the preface to be concluded and the body of the piece to begin.

to tear her from us. If the following would produce such an effect, the author should rejoice.

It is evident by ocular demonstration that man, by his depravity, hath procured many corrupt habits which are detrimental to society. And although there is a way prescribed whereby man may be re-instated into the favour of God,[1] yet these corrupt habits are not extirpated, nor can the subject of renovation boast of perfection, 'till he leaps into a state of immortal existence.[2] Yet it hath pleased the majesty of Heaven to exhibit His will to men, and endow them with an intellect which is susceptible of speculation;[3] yet, as I observed before, man, in consequence of the fall,[4] is liable to digressions. But to proceed:

Liberty (and freedom) is an innate principle which is unmoveably placed in the human species, and to see a man aspire after it is not enigmatical, seeing he acts no ways incompatible with his own nature; consequently, he that would infringe upon a man's liberty may reasonably expect to meet with opposition, seeing the defendant cannot comply to non-resistance, unless he counteracts the very laws of nature.

Liberty is a jewel which was handed down to man from the cabinet of heaven, and is coeval with[5] his existence. And as it proceeds from the Supreme Legislature of the universe, so it is He which hath a sole right to take away; therefore, he that would take away a man's liberty assumes a prerogative that belongs to another, and acts out of his own domain.

One man may boast a superiority above another in point of natural privilege; yet if he can produce no convincive arguments in vindication of this pre-eminence, his hypothesis is to be suspected. To affirm that an Englishman[6] has a right to his liberty is a truth

which has been so clearly evinced, especially of late, that to spend time in illustrating this would be but superfluous tautology. But I query whether liberty is so contracted a principle as to be confined to any nation under Heaven; nay, I think it not hyperbolical to affirm that even an African has equally as good a right to his liberty in common with Englishmen.

I know that those that are concerned in the Slave-trade, Do pretend to Bring arguments in vindication of their practise; yet if we give them a candid Examination, we shall find them (Even those of the most cogent kind) to be Essentially Deficient. We live in a day wherein *Liberty* & *freedom* is the subject of many millions Concern; and the important Struggle hath already caused great Effusion of Blood; men seem to manifest the most sanguine resolution not to Let their natural rights go without[7] their Lives go with them; a resolution, one would think Every one that has the Least Love to his country, or futer posterity, would fully confide in, yet while we are so zelous to maintain, and foster our own invaded rights, it cannot be tho't impertinent for us Candidly to reflect on our own conduct, and I doubt not But that we shall find that subsisting in the midst of us, that may with propriety be stiled[8] *Opression*, nay, much greater opression, than that which Englishmen seem so much to spurn at. I mean an oppression which they, themselves, impose upon others.

It is not my business to enquire into every particular practise that is practised in this land that may come under this odious character; but what I have in view is humbly to offer some free thoughts on the practise of *slave-keeping*. Oppression is not spoken of, nor ranked, in the sacred oracles among the least of those sins that are the procuring cause of those signal judgments which God is pleased to bring upon the children of men. Therefore let us attend. I mean to write[9] with freedom, yet with the greatest submission.

And the main proposition which I intend for some brief illustration is this, namely, that an *African*, or,

original spelling

[1] *God* This word, as well as the pronouns "he" and "his" when referring to God, are inconsistently capitalized in Haynes's original manuscript. The editors have capitalized all occurrences of these terms, in keeping with modern practice.

[2] *nor can ... immortal existence* I.e., a person cannot experience full spiritual rebirth and the cleansing of their sins until they have begun the afterlife.

[3] *susceptible of speculation* Able to see and understand evident truths; perceptive.

[4] *the fall* I.e., the fall from the Garden of Eden; original sin.

[5] *is coeval with* Has existed as long as.

[6] *Englishman* By this term Haynes evidently includes whites living in the Thirteen Colonies as well as those on the other side

of the Atlantic; this piece was written after independence had been declared, but before the independent states of the United States of America had been firmly established.

[7] *without* Unless.

[8] *stiled* Called.

[9] *write* The handwritten manuscript here has *white* for *write*.

in other terms, *that a Negro may justly challenge, and has an undeniable right to his liberty; consequently, the practise of slave-keeping, which so much abounds in this land, is illicit.*

Every privilege that mankind enjoys [has its] origin from God; and whatever acts are passed in any earthly court which are derogatory to those edicts that are passed in the court of Heaven, the act is *void*. If I have a particular privilege granted to me by God, and the act is not revoked nor the power that granted the benefit vacated (as it is impossible but that God should ever remain immutable[1]), then he that would infringe upon my benefit assumes an unreasonable and tyrannic power.

It hath pleased god to "make of one blood all nations of men, for to dwell upon the face of the Earth." Acts 17.26. And as all are of one species, so there are the same laws and aspiring principles placed in all nations; and the effects that these laws will produce are similar to each other. Consequently, we may suppose that what is precious to one man is precious to another, and what is irksome or intolerable to one man is so to another, considered in a law of nature. Therefore we may reasonably conclude that liberty is equally as precious to a *black man* as it is to a *white one*, and bondage equally as intolerable to the one as it is to the other. Seeing it affects the laws of nature equally as much in the one as it does in the other. But, as I observed before, those privileges that are granted to us by the Divine Being, no one has the least right to take them from us without our consent; and there is not the least precept or practise in the sacred scriptures that constitutes a black man a slave, any more than a white one.

Shall a man's color be the decisive criterion whereby to judge of his natural right? Or because a man is not of the same colour with his neighbour, shall he be deprived of those things that distinguisheth him from the beasts of the field?

I would ask, whence is it that an Englishman is so far distinguished from an African in point of natural privilege? Did he receive it in his original constitution? Or by some subsequent grant? Or does he boast of some higher descent that gives him this pre-eminence? For my part, I can find no such revelation. It is a lamentable consequence of the fall that mankind have an insatiable thirst after superiority one over another; so that however common or prevalent the practise may be, it does not amount even to a circumstance that the practise is warrantable.

God has been pleased to distinguish some men from others as to natural abilities, but not as to natural *right*, as they came out of His hands.

But sometimes men by their flagitious practise[2] forfeit their liberty into the hands of men, by becoming unfit for society; but have the *Africans* ever, as a nation, forfeited their liberty in this manner? Whatever individuals have done, yet I believe no such challenge can be made upon them as a body. As there should be some rule whereby to govern the conduct of men, so it is the duty and interest of a community to form a system of law that is calculated to promote the commercial interest of each other; and so long as it produces so blessed an effect, it should be maintained. But when, instead of contributing to the well-being of the community, it proves baneful to its subjects over whom it extends, then it is high time to call it in question. Should any ask where shall we find any system of law whereby to regulate our moral conduct? I think there is none so explicit and indefinite, as that which was given by the Blessed Saviour of the world: "As you would that men should do unto you, do you even so to them."[3] One would think that the mention of the precept would strike conviction to the heart of these slave-traders, unless an avaricious disposition governs the laws of humanity.

If we strictly adhere to the rule, we shall not impose anything upon others but what we should be willing should be imposed upon us were we in their condition.

I shall now go on to consider the manner in which the slave-trade is carried on, by which it will plainly appear that the practise is vile and atrocious, as well as the most inhuman. … [Haynes here quotes from several eighteenth-century accounts.]

But I need not stand painting the dreary scene. Let me rather appeal to tender parents, whether this is exaggerating matters? Let me ask them what would be their distress, should one of their dearest children be snatched from them, in a clandestine manner, and

[1] *as it is … immutable* I.e., as is impossible, since God and his laws do not change.

[2] *flagitious practise* I.e., crimes or sins.

[3] *As you … to them* See Matthew 7.12, often known as the "Golden Rule," from Christ's Sermon on the Mount.

carried to Africa, or some other foreign land, to be under the most abject slavery for life, among a strange people? Would it not embitter all your domestic comforts? Would he not be ever upon your mind? Nay, doth not nature even recoil at the reflection?

And is not there many ready to say (unless void of natural affections) that it would not fail to bring them down with sorrow to the grave? And surely, this has been the awful fate of some of those Negroes that have been brought into these plantations; which is not to be wondered at, unless we suppose them to be without natural affections—which is to rank them below the very beasts of the field. …

I shall now go on to take under consideration some of those arguments which those that are concerned in the slave-trade do use in vindication of their practise; which arguments, I shall endeavour to show, are lame and defective.

The first argument that I shall take notice of is this, *viz.*,[1] that in all probability the Negroes are of Canaan's posterity, which were destined by the Almighty to slavery: therefore the practise is warrantable.[2] To which I answer: Whether the Negroes are of Canaan's posterity or not, perhaps is not known by any mortal under Heaven. But allowing they were actually of Canaan's posterity, yet we have no reason to think that this curse lasted any longer than the coming of Christ: when that Son of righteousness arose this wall of partition was broken down.[3] Under the Law,[4] there were

many external ceremonies that were typical of spiritual things, or which shadowed forth the purity and perfection of the Gospel. As corporeal blemishes, spurious birth, flagitious practises, debarred them from the congregation of the Lord, thereby showing the intrinsic purity of heart that a concealed Gospel required as the pre-requisite for heaven, and as Ham uncovered his father's nakedness, that is, did not endeavour to conceal it, but gazed perhaps with a lascivious eye, which was repugnant to the Law which was afterwards given to the Children of Israel. So it was most necessary that God should manifest His signal disapprobation of this heinous sin, by making him[5] and his posterity a public example to the world, that thereby they might be set apart, and separated from the people of God as unclean. And we find it was a privilege granted to God's people of old that they might enslave the heathen, and the stranger that were in the land, thereby to show the superior privileges God's people enjoyed above the rest of the world. So that we, Gentiles, were then subject to slavery, being then heathen; so that if they will keep close to the letter they must own themselves yet subject to the yoke, unless we suppose them *free* by being brought into the same place, or having the same privileges with the Jews—then it follows that we may enslave all nations, be they white or black, that are heathens, which they themselves will not allow. We find, under that dispensation, God declaring that he would *visit the iniquity of the fathers upon the children, unto the third, and fourth generation,*[6] etc. And we find it so in the case of *Ham*, as well as many others, their posterity being extrinsically unclean.

But now our glorious high priest[7] hath visibly appeared in the flesh, and hath established a more glorious economy.[8] He hath not only visibly broken down that wall of partition that interposed between the offended majesty of Heaven and rebellious sinners and removed those tedious forms under the Law

[1] *viz.* Abbreviation for the Latin videlicet, meaning "namely" or "that is to say."

[2] *the Negroes … warrantable* The Curse of Canaan (also known as the Curse of Ham, after the father of Canaan) was an Old Testament story used by some proponents of slavery to justify the enslavement of Africans. As the story is told in Genesis 9.20–27, Noah fell into a drunken stupor and was then seen naked by his son Ham; Noah was angered by this, and thereafter cursed Ham's son Canaan, declaring that "a servant of servants shall he be unto his brethren." Those who used this as a defense of slavery claimed that Africans were the descendants of Canaan and were thus cursed to the same servitude (despite the fact that the curse was made by Noah, and apparently not sanctioned by God).

[3] *when that … broken down* Haynes refers to the Christian understanding (adopted by eighteenth-century abolitionists) that the New Covenant brought by Jesus supersedes any covenants established between God and the Israelites in the Old Testament.

[4] *the Law* I.e., the codes of laws set forth in the Old Testament, including Mosaic and Levitical Law.

[5] *him* I.e., Ham.

[6] *visit … generation* See Exodus 20.5: "Thou shalt not bow down thyself to them, nor serve them: for I the Lord thy God am a jealous God, visiting the iniquity of the fathers upon the children unto the third and fourth generation of them that hate me." Similar language is used in several other passages of the Old Testament.

[7] *our glorious high priest* I.e., Jesus Christ.

[8] *economy* System.

which savoured so much of servitude, and which *could never make the comers thereunto perfect*,[1] by rendering them obsolete. But he has removed those many embarrassments and distinctions that they were incident to under so contracted a dispensation. …

But you will say that slave-keeping was practised even under the Gospel, for we find Paul and the other apostles exhorting *servants to be obedient to their masters*,[2] to which I reply that it might be they were speaking to servants in *minority* in general. But doubtless it was practised in the days of the Apostles from what St. Paul says, 1 Corinthians 7.21: "Art thou called, being a servant? Care not for it; but if thou mayest be made free, use it rather." So that the Apostle seems to recommend freedom if attainable, q.[e.]d.[3]—"if it is thy unhappy lot to be a slave, yet if thou art spiritually free let the former appear so minute a thing when compared with the latter that it is comparatively unworthy of notice; yet since freedom is so excellent a jewel which none have a right to extirpate, and if there is any hope of attaining it, use all lawful measures for that purpose." So that however extant or prevalent it might be in that or this age, yet it does not in the least reverse the unchangeable laws of God, or of nature, or make that become lawful which is in itself unlawful; neither is it strange if we consider the moral depravity of man's nature, throughout all ages of the world, that mankind should deviate from the unerring rules of Heaven. …

But I shall take notice of one argument more which these slave-traders use, and it is this, *viz.*, that those Negroes that are emigrated into these colonies are brought out of a land of darkness under the meridian light[4] of the Gospel; and so it is a great blessing instead of a curse. But I would ask, who is this that darkeneth counsel by words without knowledge?[5] Let us attend to the great apostle[6] speaking to us in Romans 3.8., where he reproves some slanderers who told it as a maxim preached by the apostles that they said "Let us do evil that good may come," whose damnation the inspired penman pronounces with an emphasis to be just. And again Chapter 6 verse 1, where by way of interrogation he asks, "Shall we continue in sin that grace may abound?" The answer is obvious: "God forbid." But that those slave-merchants that trade upon the coasts of Africa do not aim at the spiritual good of their slaves is evident by their behaviour towards them; if they had their spiritual good at heart, we should expect that those slave-merchants that trade upon their coasts would, instead of causing quarrellings and bloodshed among them, which is repugnant to Christianity and below the character of humanity, be solicitous to demean exemplary among them, that by their wholesome conduct those heathen might be induced to entertain high and admiring thoughts of our holy religion. Those slaves in these colonies are generally kept under the greatest ignorance and blindness, and they are scarcely ever told by their white masters whether there is a Supreme Being that governs the universe, or whether there is any reward or punishments beyond the grave. Nay such are those restrictions that they are kept under that they scarcely know that they have a right to be free, or if they do they are not allowed to speak in their defence. Such is their abject condition, that that genius[7] that is peculiar to the human race cannot have that cultivation that the polite world is favoured with, and therefore they are styled the ignorant part of the world; whereas were they under the same advantages to get knowledge with them, perhaps their progress in arts would not be inferior.

But should we give ourselves the trouble to enquire into the grand motive that indulges men to concern themselves in a trade so vile and abandoned,[8] we shall find it to be this, namely, to stimulate their carnal avarice, and to maintain men in pride, luxury, and idleness. And how much it hath subserved to this vile purpose I leave the candid[9] public to judge; I speak it

1 *could never … perfect* See Hebrews 10.1: "For the law having a shadow of good things to come, and not the very image of the things, can never with those sacrifices which they offered year by year continually make the comers thereunto perfect."

2 *exhorting servants … masters* See Titus 2.9; the Epistle to Titus is one of the many books of the New Testament attributed to the Apostle Paul, a first-century CE minister in Rome.

3 *q.[e.]d.* Quod erat demonstrandum (Latin: thus it is demonstrated).

4 *meridian light* I.e., light as powerful as the sun at its meridian.

5 *who is this … knowledge?* See Job 38.2, in which God speaks to the suffering Job about the inability of humans to attain true divine understanding.

6 *the great apostle* I.e., Paul, the author of the Epistle to the Romans in the New Testament.

7 *genius* Particular spirit.

8 *abandoned* Uninhibitedly evil.

9 *candid* Unbiased.

with reverence, yet I think all must give in that it hath such a tendency.

But although God is of long patience, yet it does not last always; nay, he has *whet his glittering sword, and his hand hath already taken hold on judgement;*[1] for who knows how far that the unjust oppression which hath abounded in this land may be the procuring cause of this very judgement that now impends, which so much portends slavery?

For this is God's way of working. Often He brings the same judgements or evils upon men as they unrighteously bring upon others. As is plain from Judges 1[2] and on:

> But Adonibezek fled, and they pursued after him, and caught him, and cut off his thumbs, and his great toes.

> And Adonibezek said, threescore and ten kings having their thumbs and their great toes cut off gathered their meat under my table: as I have done, so god hath requited me.

And as wicked Ahab and Jezebel, to gratify their covetousness, caused Naboth to be put to death,[3] and as dogs licked the blood of Naboth, the word of the Lord was, by the prophet, "Elijah, thus saith the Lord, in the place where dogs licked the blood of Naboth, shall dogs lick thy blood even thine." See 1 Kings 21.19. "And of Jezebel also spake the Lord, saying, The dogs shall eat Jezebel by the walls of Jezreel." Verse 23.

And we find the judgement actually accomplished upon Ahab in the 22nd Chapter and 38th verse.

And upon Jezebel in the 9th Chapter 2 of Kings.

Again Revelations 16.6., "For they have shed the blood of saints and prophets, and thou hast given them blood to drink; for they are worthy." And chapter 18.6. "Reward her even as she rewarded you." I say this is often God's way of dealing, by retaliating back upon men the same evils that they unjustly bring upon others. I don't say that we have reason to think that oppression is the alone cause of this judgement that God is pleased to bring upon this land, nay, but we have the greatest reason to think that this is not one of the least. And whatever some may think that I am instigated by a false zeal, and all that I have said upon the subject is mere novelty: yet I am not afraid to appeal to the conscience of any rational and honest man, as to the truth of what I have just hinted at. And if any will not confide in what I have humbly offered, I am persuaded it must be such short-sighted persons whose contracted eyes never penetrate through the narrow confines of self, and are mere vassals to filthy Lucre.[4] …

—1983 (WRITTEN 1776)

[1] *whet his … judgement* See Deuteronomy 32.41.

[2] *Judges 1* The passages quoted below tell of the Canaanite king Adonibezek, who used to cut off the thumbs and toes of the kings he conquered; he is then defeated by Judah, God's chosen champion for the Israelites, and has his thumbs and toes cut off in the same way.

[3] *And as wicked Ahab … death* Ahab and Jezebel are presented in the Book of Kings as wicked rulers, who, during their reign over Israel, attempt to replace Yahweh with the false god Baal. Ahab is also described as coveting the vineyard of the commoner Naboth; to gain it for her husband, Jezebel falsely accuses Naboth of blasphemy, causing him to be stoned to death.

[4] *Lucre* Wealth (especially in a negative sense).

Susanna Haswell Rowson

c. 1762 – 1824

Susanna Rowson was the author of America's first bestselling sentimental romance, *Charlotte Temple*, but her prolific transatlantic career spanned many genres and roles. In addition to influencing the history of the American novel with her prose fiction, she was a well-known actor and playwright, and, later in life, she founded a successful school for girls and became a respected educator. An early professional writer who judiciously crafted her own celebrity, she described herself as an "Englishwoman" but wrote about the new nation of America with fierce patriotism—and with particular attention to the trials and virtues of American womanhood. Though she approached this last subject with varying degrees of radicalism and conservatism during her long career, her novels and plays consistently explore feminist themes. This made her a controversial figure, derided as "the American Sappho" but also praised for "elevat[ing] the moral character of her own sex."

Rowson was born Susanna Haswell in Portsmouth, England, into an educated, military family. Her father was a naval officer; her mother died of complications from childbirth when Susanna was ten days old. Rowson spent a happy childhood in Massachusetts, where her father was stationed, and she was educated at home. She became well-read in contemporary literature and philosophy, aided in part by her family's friendship with the activist James Otis (1725–83), who took an interest in her education and was an early influence. Famous for coining the phrase "Taxation without Representation is tyranny," Otis was an advocate of colonial rights and of African American rights, and his dedication to Enlightenment ideals of freedom and equality had a deep and lasting effect on Rowson.

The Revolutionary War changed things for Rowson's loyalist family, as they were interned in 1775. The family was then freed by means of a prisoner exchange, and they returned to England in 1778. Much later, in a defense of her own patriotism, she would describe herself as "equally attached to either country":

> the unhappy dissentions affected me in the same manner as a person may be imagined to feel, who having a tender lover, and an affectionate brother who are equally dear to her heart, and by whom she is equally beloved, sees them engaged in a quarrel with, and fighting against each other, when, let whichsoever party conquer, she cannot be supposed insensible to the fate of the vanquished.

The family's property in America was confiscated, and they lived in England in straitened circumstances, selling Rowson's inheritance to support themselves. She also took a position as governess to contribute to the family income.

Rowson began her writing career in 1786, publishing *Victoria. A Novel in Two Volumes*. In the same year she married William Rowson, a struggling businessperson with a passion for the theater. He was supportive of Susanna's writing—in part because the couple needed the money she earned—and shortly after her marriage Susanna became increasingly involved in the theater herself, publishing an anonymous satirical critique of the London scene, *A Trip to Parnassus* (1788). She also continued to produce novels, including *The Inquisitor or Invisible Rambler* (1788), a series of vignettes inspired by Laurence Sterne's *A Sentimental Journey* (1768). A moralistic romance, *Mary, or the Test of Honour*, followed in 1789, and in 1791 she published *Mentoria*, a collection of dialogues and tales, as well as the sentimental novel *Charlotte Temple* (under the title *Charlotte, A Tale of Truth*).

Charlotte Temple was a modest success in England, but its sales were not substantial enough to offset the failure of William Rowson's hardware business, and the couple moved to Edinburgh to join a theater company in 1791. They did well as actors, and in 1793 they traveled to Philadelphia to join the New Theater Company. In America, Susanna kept up an intense working life, acting at night and writing by day. On 30 June 1794, she premiered her first full-length comic opera, *Slaves in Algiers; or A Struggle for Freedom.* Like many of Rowson's later plays, *Slaves in Algiers* focuses on its female characters and expresses a conservative feminism strongly influenced by Mary Wollstonecraft's *A Vindication of the Rights of Woman*, which had been published in Philadelphia in 1792. The often-quoted couplet from the epilogue of *Slaves in Algiers*—"Women were born for universal sway; / Men to adore, be silent, and obey"—is likely intended somewhat ironically, but it does reflect the expansion of social and economic opportunities for American women in the Revolutionary period.

In 1794, Rowson arranged to have *Charlotte Temple* published in the United States. A cautionary tale of a young Englishwoman seduced and brought to New York, abandoned by her seducer, and left to die in childbirth, the novel became a sensation and would be issued in over 225 editions, staying in print through to the end of the nineteenth century. Its popularity inaugurated a significant trend in sentimental fiction—and in novels by women—on the American literary scene. Now famous, Rowson continued to write plays at a fast pace, including *The Female Patriot. A Farce* (1794), *The Volunteers. A Farce* (1795), and *Americans in England. A Comedy* (1795). In the same span of years she released American editions of some of her earlier English books, as well as the new novel *Trials of the Human Heart* (1795). None of these approached the success of *Charlotte Temple*, though *Rebecca; or, The Fille de Chambre* (English edition 1792, American edition 1794) was her second-most popular work.

Rowson retired from the stage in 1797 and opened "Mrs. Rowson's Academy for Young Ladies" in Boston. As headmistress, she taught the daughters of upper-class New England families and wrote textbooks and histories, including *Rowson's Abridgement of Universal Geography* (1805) and *Youth's First Steps in Geography* (1811). During the decades she spent running the Academy, her commitment to gender equality diminished; in her 1804 poem "Rights of Woman," she declares that women should enjoy self-respect and freedom to run their households, but that they should not "interfere / With politics, divinity, or law." Yet she continued to assert women's potential to "attain the goal of perfection as well as the other sex" in arts and literature, and her 1822 textbook *Exercises in History* offers biographies of great women, including queens and other political leaders, presented as models for her students. While headmistress, she continued to write and publish novels, as well as poetry and periodical literature. She taught at her school until 1822 and died two years later.

Rowson's literary reputation rested for a long time on the success of *Charlotte Temple*, which was generally dismissed by modernist literary critics as a work of sentimental fiction. Mid-twentieth-century critic Leslie Fiedler, for example, called her a "third-rate sentimentalist," and assessments such as these sidelined her writing until the late twentieth century. Since then, as popular and sentimental novels have received more scholarly attention, *Charlotte Temple* has once again become a canonical text, with critics tracing the novel's influence to important later writers such as Rebecca Harding Davis and Harriet Beecher Stowe. More recent critics have also appreciated Rowson's larger body of work, particularly the plays and textbooks, and have highlighted her contributions to the early national culture of the United States. The complexity of her approach to issues such as slavery and women's rights makes her an illuminating voice in the Revolutionary-era debate concerning who should constitute the "people" of America.

NOTE ON THE TEXT: The text of the play is based on the 1794 edition, printed in Philadelphia by Wrigley and Berriman. Spelling and punctuation have been modernized in accordance with the practices of this anthology.

Slaves in Algiers; or, A Struggle for Freedom: A Play, Interspersed with Songs, in Three Acts

When Susanna Rowson published *Slaves in Algiers* in 1794, she dedicated it to the "Citizens of the United States of North America" and stated that her chief aim was "to place the social virtues [of the United States] in the fairest point of view, and hold up, to merited contempt and ridicule, their opposite vices." Set in an Algerian harem, the play extols the Enlightenment ideals of liberty and equality and censures Algerian culture, which Rowson stereotypes as hierarchical, lawless, and tyrannical toward women and enslaved people.

With its fervent nationalism, the play capitalized on current events: the capture and enslavement of Americans on the coast of North Africa was an ongoing problem, and anxiety about it united Americans. Following Independence, when American trade ships were no longer protected by the British Navy, "Barbary" pirates from Northern African states—what are now Algeria, Morocco, Libya, and Tunisia— intensified their attacks on American ships in the Mediterranean Sea, demanding tribute payments. If refused, they would pillage the ships and press Americans into slavery, holding them for ransom. The spectacle of white slavery and the high cost of tribute—by 1797 the U.S. government was giving a fifth of its annual budget to the Barbary states—incensed Americans and would in time lead to the establishment of the U.S. Navy. When Rowson wrote her play, public reaction to the ongoing piracy had reached a high pitch. Citizen groups were petitioning the government for action and holding fundraisers to pay ransoms, and dozens of narratives and plays were published on the subject.

While Rowson's depiction of Algiers suggests little knowledge of or interest in the real place or its people, *Slaves in Algiers* does reflect Rowson's extensive knowledge of British theater, and her portrayal of Islamic and Jewish characters especially draws upon stereotypes that were commonplace on the English stage in her era. In the character of Ben Hassan, for example, Rowson deploys the anti-Semitic trope of the deceitful, selfish Jewish moneylender, a character both villainized in other Barbary narratives and ridiculed in other stage comedies. Another stock type in the play is Muley Moloc, who embodies the trope of the cruelly repressive, sexually licentious Muslim tyrant. Even Muley Moloc's name is borrowed from theater history; variations on the name are attached to Islamic rulers in a variety of British plays, including John Dryden's *Don Sebastian* (1689), where the villain is the brutal "Muley-Moluch, Emperor of Barbary." Parallel plot elements and character relationships in *Don Sebastian* and *Slaves in Algiers* suggest that Dryden's play may have directly influenced Rowson's—as, it appears, did Aaron Hill's *Zara* (1735), a tragedy surrounding a Christian held captive by a tyrannical Muslim.

Rowson also follows several London playwrights—Isaac Bickerstaffe, Elizabeth Inchbald, and Hannah Cowley among them—by setting the action of her play in a harem, and by using this setting to depict women as slaves to men, establishing an implicit link between gender equality and "civilized" (i.e., white) society. Yet, while a few years later Rowson would denounce the slave trade as "a disgrace to humanity," *Slaves in Algiers* does not explicitly draw the analogy—made by many other Barbary narratives—between white slavery in Africa and black slavery in America. *Slaves in Algiers* was written four years after the Naturalization Act designated only "free white persons" as "citizens" of America, and Rowson's characterization, plot, and nationalistic rhetoric does not challenge this narrow definition of who was to be accorded the rights of citizenship in the new republic.

The theater scene in Philadelphia in the late eighteenth century included a season of "benefits," individual performances in which ticket sales were given to lead actors. The premiere of *Slaves in Algiers* on 30 June 1794 was one such benefit performance, in which Susanna Rowson and her husband were assigned the profits. They both acted in the play, with Susanna taking the role of Olivia and delivering the epilogue as herself, while William performed a song between acts. The playbill in the *Philadelphia Gazette* also advertised "Mrs. Rowson" as the writer of the play, capitalizing on her fame as the author of the popular sentimental novel *Charlotte Temple* as a means to draw in a full house. A review in the *Gazette* praised Rowson's acting and moral rectitude, her "delicatesse and sound sense." The play enjoyed modest success in America, with performances in New York City and Baltimore, and was sufficiently popular to be released in print in the same year it was staged. It was also revived in Boston in 1816 after renewed

American hostilities with the Barbary states spurred fresh interest in the subject matter. In recent decades, critics have given increased attention to *Slaves in Algiers*, explicating its interwoven feminist, nationalist, and imperialist themes, as well as its treatment of Muslim and Jewish characters.

SLAVES IN ALGIERS;

OR, A

STRUGGLE FOR FREEDOM:

A PLAY,

INTERSPERSED WITH SONGS,

IN THREE ACTS.

BY MRS. ROWSON.

AS PERFORMED

AT THE

NEW THEATRES,

IN

PHILADELPHIA AND BALTIMORE.

PHILADELPHIA:

PRINTED FOR THE AUTHOR, BY WRIGLEY AND BERRIMAN, N°. 149, CHESNUT-STREET.

M,DCC,XCIV.

Slaves in Algiers; or, A Struggle for Freedom
A Play, Interspersed with Songs, In Three Acts

To the Citizens of the United States
of North America.
This First Dramatic Effort Is Inscribed,
By Their Obliged Friend, and Humble Servant,
S. Rowson

Preface

In offering the following pages to the public, I feel myself necessitated to apologize for the errors which I am fearful will be evident to the severe eye of criticism.

The thought of writing a dramatic piece was hastily conceived, and as hastily executed; it being not more than two months, from the first starting of the idea, to the time of its being performed.

I feel myself extremely happy in having an opportunity thus publicly to acknowledge my obligation to Mr. Reinagle,[1] for the attention he manifested, and the taste and genius he displayed in the composition of the music. I must also return my thanks to the performers, who so readily accepted, and so ably supported their several characters: since it was chiefly owing to their exertions, that the play was received with such unbounded marks of approbation.

Since the first performance, I have made some alterations; and flatter myself those alterations have improved it: But of that, as well as of its merits in general, I am content to abide the decision of a candid and indulgent public.

Some part of the plot is taken from the story of the captive, related by Cervantes, in his inimitable romance of *Don Quixote*;[2] the rest is entirely the off-spring of fancy.

I am fully sensible of the many disadvantages under which I consequently labour from a confined education; nor do I expect my style will be thought equal in elegance or energy to the productions of those who, fortunately, from their sex, or situation in life, have been instructed in the classics, and have reaped both pleasure and improvement by studying the ancients in their original purity.

My chief aim has been to offer to the public a dramatic entertainment, which, while it might excite a smile, or call forth the tear of sensibility, might contain no one sentiment in the least prejudicial to the moral or political principles of the government under which I live.[3] On the contrary, it has been my endeavour, to place the social virtues in the fairest point of view, and hold up, to merited contempt and ridicule, their opposite vices. If, in this attempt, I have been the least successful, I shall reap the reward to which I aspire, in the smiles and approbation of a liberal public.

Prologue

Written and Spoken by Mr. Fennel.[4]

When aged Priam, to Achilles' tent
To beg the captive corse° of Hector[5] went, *corpse*
The silent suppliant spoke the father's fears,
His sighs his eloquence—his prayers his tears.
5 The noble conqueror by the sight was won,
And to the weeping sire restored the son.

No great Achilles holds *your* sons in chains,
No heart alive to friends' or father's pains,
No generous conqueror who is proud to show,
10 That valour vanquished is no more his foe;
But one, whose idol is his pilfered gold,
Got, or° by piracy, or subjects sold. *either*
Him no fond father's prayers nor tears can melt,
Untaught to feel for what he never felt.

1 *Mr. Reinagle* Alexander Reinagle (1756–1809), American composer and musician. He was an important influence in the Philadelphia music and theater scene through the 1790s.

2 *story of the captive ... Don Quixote* In chapters 40–41 of Miguel de Cervantes's *Don Quixote* (1605, 1615), a soldier tells Don Quixote about his captivity in Algiers and his subsequent escape. A young woman, Zoraida, gives him ransom money so he can free himself; Zoraida and the soldier escape to Spain, Zoraida converts to Christianity, and the two are married.

3 *government under which I live* I.e., the American government.

4 *Mr. Fennel* James Fennell (1766–1816), an English actor who was a star in the Philadelphia theater scene.

5 *Priam ... Hector* In Book 24 of the *Iliad*, Priam, king of Troy, pleads with the Greek warrior Achilles, who has killed Priam's son Hector in battle and refused to return the body, instead mistreating it out of rage toward Hector.

15 What then behoves it, they who helped to gain,
A nation's freedom, feel the galling chain?
They, who a more than ten year's war[1] withstood,
And stamped their country's honour with their blood?
Or, shall the noble Eagle see her brood,
20 Beneath the pirate kite's° fell claw subdued? *bird of prey*
View her dear sons of liberty enslaved,
Nor let them share the blessings which they saved?
It must not be—each heart, each soul must rise,
Each ear must listen to their distant cries;
25 Each hand must give, and the quick sail unfurled
Must bear their ransom to the distant world.

Nor *here* alone Columbia's° sons be free, *America's*
Where'er they breathe there must be liberty.
There *must*! There *is*, for he who formed the whole,
30 Entwined blest freedom with th' immortal soul.
Eternal twins, whose mutual efforts fan,
That heavenly flame that gilds the life of man,
Whose light, 'midst manacles and dungeons drear,
The sons of honour, must forever cheer.

35 What tyrant then the virtuous heart can bind?
'Tis vices only can enslave the mind.
Who barters country, honour, faith, to save
His life, though free in person, is a slave.
While he, enchained, imprisoned though he be,
40 Who lifts his arm for liberty, is free.

Tonight, our author boldly dares to choose,
This glorious subject for her humble muse;
Though tyrants check the genius which they fear,
She dreads no check, nor persecution *here*;
45 Where safe asylums every virtue guard,
And every talent meets its just reward.

Some say—the Comic muse, with watchful eye,
Should catch the reigning *vices* as they fly,
Our author boldly has reversed that plan,
50 The reigning virtues she has dared to scan,
And though a woman, plead the Rights of Man.

Thus she, with anxious hope her fate abides,
And to your care, the tender plant confides,
Convinced you'll cherish, what to freedom's true;
55 She trusts its life, to candour and to you.

Dramatis Personae

Men

Muley Moloc, Dey[2] of Algiers
Mustapha
Ben Hassan, a Renegado[3]
Sebastian, a Spanish Slave
Augustus, American Captive
Frederic, American Captive
Henry, American Captive
Constant, American Captive
Sadi
Selim

Women

Zoriana, Moriscan[4] Woman
Fetnah, Moriscan Woman
Selima, Moriscan Woman
Rebecca, American Woman
Olivia, American Woman

Slaves.—Guards, etc.

Act I, Scene I

(*Apartment at the Dey's.* [*Enter*] *Fetnah and Selima.*)

FETNAH. Well, it's all vastly pretty, the gardens, the
house and these fine clothes, I like them very well,
but I don't like to be confined.
SELIMA. Yet, surely, you have no reason to complain;
5 chosen favourite of the Dey, what can you wish for
more.
FETNAH. O, a great many things—in the first place,
I wish for liberty. Why do you talk of my being a

1 *ten year's war* I.e., the American Revolutionary War (1775–1783).

2 *Dey* Title of the absolute ruler of Algiers.

3 *Renegado* Traitor or turncoat.

4 *Moriscan* Moorish (term used to describe a person from North Africa).

favourite; is the poor bird that is confined in a cage (because a favourite with its enslaver) consoled for the loss of freedom? No! Though its prison is of golden wire, its food delicious, and it is overwhelmed with caresses, its little heart still pants for liberty: gladly would it seek the fields of air, and even, perched upon a naked bough, exulting, carol forth its song, nor once regret the splendid house of bondage.

SELIMA. Ah! But then our master loves you.

FETNAH. What of that, I don't love him.

SELIMA. Not love him?

FETNAH. No—he is old and ugly, then he wears such tremendous whiskers; and when he makes love, he looks so grave and stately, that I declare, if it was not for fear of his huge scimitar,[1] I should burst out a-laughing in his face.

SELIMA. Take care you don't provoke him too far.

FETNAH. I don't care how I provoke him, if I can but make him keep his distance. You know I was brought here only a few days since—well, yesterday, as I was amusing myself, looking at the fine things I saw everywhere about me, who should bolt into the room, but that great, ugly thing, Mustapha. What do you want, said I? Most beautiful Fetnah, said he, bowing till the tip of his long, hooked nose almost touched the toe of his slipper—most beautiful Fetnah, our powerful and gracious master, Muley Moloc, sends me, the humblest of his slaves, to tell you, he will condescend to sup in your apartment tonight, and commands you to receive the high honour with proper humility.

SELIMA. Well—and what answer did you return?

FETNAH. Lord, I was so frightened, and so provoked, I hardly know what I said, but finding the horrid looking creature didn't move, at last I told him, that if the Dey was determined to come, I supposed he must, for I could not hinder him.

SELIMA. And did he come?

FETNAH. No—but he made me go to him, and when I went trembling into the room, he twisted his whiskers and knit his great beetle brows.[2] Fetnah, said he, you abuse my goodness, I have condescended to request you to love me. And then he gave me such a fierce look, as if he would say, and if you don't love me, I'll cut your head off.

SELIMA. I dare say you were finely frightened.

FETNAH. Frightened! I was provoked beyond all patience, and thinking he would certainly kill me one day or other, I thought I might as well speak my mind, and be dispatched out of the way at once.

SELIMA. You make me tremble.

FETNAH. So, mustering up as much courage as I could; great and powerful Muley, said I—I am sensible I am your slave; you took me from an humble state, placed me in this fine palace, and gave me these rich clothes; you bought my person of my parents, who loved gold better than they did their child; but my affections you could not buy. I can't love you. How! cried he, starting from his seat: how, can't love me? And he laid his hand upon his scimitar.

SELIMA. Oh dear! Fetnah.

FETNAH. When I saw the scimitar half drawn, I caught hold of his arm. Oh! good my lord, said I, pray do not kill a poor little girl like me; send me home again, and bestow your favour on some other, who may think splendor a compensation for the loss of liberty. Take her away, said he, she is beneath my anger.

SELIMA. But, how is it Fetnah, that you have conceived such an aversion to the manners of a country where you were born.

FETNAH. You are mistaken. I was not born in Algiers. I drew my first breath in England; my father, Ben Hassan, as he is now called, was a Jew. I can scarcely remember our arrival here, and have been educated in the Moorish religion,[3] though I always had a natural antipathy to their manners.

SELIMA. Perhaps imbibed from your mother.

FETNAH. No; she has no objection to any of their customs, except that of their having a great many wives at a time. But some few months since, my father, (who sends out many corsairs,[4]) brought home a female captive, to whom I became greatly attached; it was she who nourished in my mind the love of liberty, and taught me woman was never formed to be the abject slave of man. Nature made

[1] *scimitar* Short, curved sword used primarily in the Middle East.

[2] *beetle brows* Heavy, dark eyebrows, associated with surliness.

[3] *Moorish religion* I.e., Islam.

[4] *corsairs* Cruisers sent to pillage foreign ships and capture those on board.

95 us equal with them, and gave us the power to render
ourselves superior.

SELIMA. Of what nation was she?

FETNAH. She came from that land, where virtue in
either sex is the only mark of superiority. She was
100 an American.

SELIMA. Where is she now?

FETNAH. She is still at my father's, waiting the arrival
of her ransom, for she is a woman of fortune. And
though I can no longer listen to her instructions, her
105 precepts are engraven on my heart. I feel that I was
born free, and while I have life, I will struggle to
remain so.

SONG.

I.

The rose just bursting into bloom,
Admired where'er 'tis seen;
110 Diffuses round a rich perfume,
The garden's pride and queen.
When gathered from its native bed,
No longer charms the eye;
Its vivid tints are quickly fled,
115 'Twill wither, droop, and die.

II.

So woman when by nature dressed,
In charms devoid of art;
Can warm the stoic's icy breast,
Can triumph o'er each heart.
120 Can bid the soul to virtue rise,
To glory prompt the brave,
But sinks oppressed, and drooping dies,
When once she's made a slave.

(*Exit.*)

ACT I, SCENE 2

(*Ben Hassan's house.* [*Enter*] *Rebecca.*)

REBECCA. (*Discovered reading.*) The soul, secure in its
existence, smiles
At the drawn dagger, and defies its point.
The stars shall fade away, the sun itself

Grow dim with age, and nature sink in years,
5 But thou shall flourish in immortal youth,
Unhurt, amidst the war of elements,
The wreck of matter, or the crush of worlds.[1]

[*Puts down the book.*]

Oh! Blessed hope, I feel within myself that spark of
intellectual heavenly fire, that bids me soar above
10 this mortal world, and all its pains or pleasures—its
pleasures! Oh! Long—long since I have been dead to
all that bear the name. In early youth, torn from the
husband of my heart's election, the first only object
of my love—bereft of friends, cast on an unfeeling
15 world, with only one poor stay[2] on which to rest the
hope of future joy. I have a son—my child!—my dear
Augustus—where are you now? In slavery. Grant me
patience, Heaven! Must a boy born in Columbia,[3]
claiming liberty as his birth-right, pass all his days in
20 slavery? How often have I gazed upon his face, and
fancied I could trace his father's features; how often
have I listened to his voice, and thought his father's
spirit spoke within him? Oh! My adored boy! Must
I no more behold his eyes beaming with youthful
25 ardour, when I have told him, how his brave coun-
trymen purchased their freedom with their blood?
Alas! I see him now but seldom; and when we meet,
to think that we are slaves, poor, wretched slaves
each serving different masters, my eyes overflow
30 with tears. I have but time to press him to my heart,
entreat just Heaven to protect his life, and at some
future day restore his liberty.

(*Enter Ben Hassan.*)

BEN HASSAN. How do you do, Mrs. Rebecca?

REBECCA. Well, in health, Hassan, but depressed in
35 spirit.

1 *The soul … crush of worlds* Rebecca is reading from *Cato* (1712),
a play by Joseph Addison. See *Cato* 5.1.24–30. Cato the Younger
(95–46 BCE) was a Roman political figure who died by suicide
rather than accept the dictatorship of Julius Caesar. At this point in
Addison's play, Cato is contemplating the immortality of his soul as
he determines to kill himself rather than lose his freedom.

2 *stay* Support.

3 *Columbia* The United States, personified as Lady Liberty.

BEN HASSAN. Ah! Dat be very bad—come, come, cheer up, I vants to talk vid you, you must not be so melancholy, I be your very good friend.

REBECCA. Thank you, Hassan, but if you are in real-
40 ity the friend you profess to be, leave me to indulge my grief in solitude. Your intention is kind, but I would rather be alone.

BEN HASSAN. You likes mightily to be by yourself, but I must talk to you a little; I vantsh to know ven
45 you think your ransom vil come, 'tis a long time, Mrs. Rebecca, and you knows.

REBECCA. Oh yes, I know, I am under many obliga-tions to you, but I shall soon be able to repay them.

BEN HASSAN. That may be, but 'tis a very long time,
50 since you wrote to your friends, 'tis above eight months; I am afraid you have deceived me.

REBECCA. Alas! Perhaps I have deceived myself.

BEN HASSAN. Vat, den you have no friends—you are not a voman's of fortune?

55 REBECCA. Yes, yes, I have both friends and ability—but I am afraid my letters have miscarried.

BEN HASSAN. Oh! dat ish very likely, you may be here dish two or three years longer; perhaps all your lifetimes.

60 REBECCA. Alas! I am very wretched. (Weeps.)

BEN HASSAN. Come, now don't cry so; you must consider I never suffered you to be exposed in the slave market.

REBECCA. But, my son. Oh! Hassan; why did you
65 suffer them to sell my child?

BEN HASSAN. I could not help it, I did all I could—but you knows I would not let you be sent to the Dey, I have kept you in my own house, at mine own expense. (Aside.) For which I have been more than
70 doubly paid.

REBECCA. That is indeed true, but I cannot at present return your kindness.

BEN HASSAN. Ah! You be very sly rogue—you pre-tend not to know how I loves you.

75 REBECCA. (Aside.) What means the wretch?

BEN HASSAN. You should forget your Christian friends, for I dare say they have forgot you. I vill make you my vife, I vill give you von, two, tree slaves to vait on you.

80 REBECCA. Make me your wife! Why, are you not already married?

BEN HASSAN. Ish, but our law gives us great many vives. Our law gives liberty in love; you are an American, and you must love liberty.

85 REBECCA. Hold, Hassan; prostitute not the sacred word by applying it to licentiousness; the sons and daughters of liberty take justice, truth, and mercy for their leaders when they list[1] under her glorious banners.

90 BEN HASSAN. Your friends will never ransom you.

REBECCA. How readily does the sordid mind judge of others by its own contracted feelings. You, who much I fear worship no deity but gold, who could sacrifice friendship, nay, even the ties of nature at
95 the shrine of your idolatry, think other hearts as self-ish as your own; but there are souls to whom the afflicted never cry in vain, who, to dry the widow's tear, or free the captive, would share their last posses-sion. Blest spirits of philanthropy, who inhabit my
100 native land, never will I doubt your friendship, for sure I am, you never will neglect the wretched.

BEN HASSAN. If you are not ransomed soon, I must send you to the Dey.

REBECCA. Even as you please. I cannot be more
105 wretched than I am; but of this be assured; however depressed in fortune, however sunk in adversity, the soul secure in its own integrity will rise superior to its enemies, and scorn the venal wretch who barters truth for gold.

(Exit [Rebecca].)

110 BEN HASSAN. (Solus.[2]) 'Tis a very strange voman, very strange indeed; she does not know I got her pocket-book, with bills of exchange in it; she thinks I keep her in my house out of charity, and yet she talks about freedom and superiority, as if she was in
115 her own country. 'Tis devilish hard indeed, when masters may not do what they please with their slaves. Her ransom arrived yesterday, but den she don't know it. Yesh, here is the letter; ransom for Rebecca Constant, and six other Christian slaves;
120 vell I vill make her write for more, she is my slave, I must get all I can by her. Oh, here comes that wild

1 list Enlist or enroll.
2 Solus Latin: Alone.

young Christian, Frederic, who ransomed himself a few days since.

(*Enter Frederic.*)

FREDERIC. Well, my little Israelite, what are you
125 muttering about; have you thought on my propos-
als, will you purchase the vessel and assist us?
BEN HASSAN. Vat did you say you would give me?
FREDERIC. We can amongst us muster up two thou-
sand sequins,[1] 'tis all we have in the world.
130 BEN HASSAN. You are sure you can get no more?
FREDERIC. Not a farthing more.
BEN HASSAN. Den I vill be satisfied with dat, it will
in some measure reward me—(*Aside.*) for betraying
you.
135 FREDERIC. And you will purchase the vessel.
BEN HASSAN. I will do everything that is necessary—
(*Aside.*) for my own interest.
FREDERIC. You have conveyed provision to the cavern
by the sea side, where I am to conceal the captives to
140 wait the arrival of the vessel.
BEN HASSAN. Most shartingly,[2] I have provided for
them as—(*Aside.*) as secure a prison as any in Algiers.
FREDERIC. But, are you not a most extortionate old
rogue to require so much, before you will assist a
145 parcel of poor devils to obtain their liberty?
BEN HASSAN. Oh! Mr. Frederic, if I vash not your
very good friend, I could not do it for so little; the
Moors are such uncharitable dogs, they never think
they can get enough for their slaves, but I have a
150 vasht deal of compassion; I feels very mush for the
poor Christians; I should be very glad—(*Aside.*) to
have a hundred or two of them my prisoners.
FREDERIC. You would be glad to serve us?
BEN HASSAN. Shartingly. (*Aside.*) Ven I can serve
155 myself at the same time.
FREDERIC. Prithee, honest Hassan, how came you to
put on the turban?[3]
BEN HASSAN. I'll tell you.

[1] *sequins* Gold coins.

[2] *shartingly* Ben Hassan is likely combining "certainly" and "surely" here.

[3] *put on the turban* I.e., become a Muslim.

SONG.[4]

Ven I vas a mighty little boy,
160 Heart-cakes[5] I sold and pepper-mint drops;
Wafers and sweet chalk[6] I used for to cry,
Alacumpaine[7] and nice lolly-pops.

The next thing I sold vas the rollers for the
macs[8]
To curl dere hair, 'twas very good;
165 Rosin I painted for[9] sealing wax
And I forged upon it vel brand en vast hood.[10]

Next to try my luck in the alley I vent,
But of dat I soon grew tired and wiser;
Monies I lent out at fifty per cent,
170 And my name was I.H. in the Public
Advertiser.[11]

The next thing I did was a spirited prank,
Which at one stroke my fortune was made;
I wrote so very like the cashiers of the bank,
The clerks did not know the difference, and the
monies was paid.

175 So, having cheated the Gentiles, as Moses
commanded,[12]

[4] *SONG* Rowson did not write this song; its authorship is unknown.

[5] *Heart-cakes* Heart-shaped cakes.

[6] *sweet chalk* Type of candy.

[7] *Alacumpaine* Elecampane, otherwise known as horse-heal, a plant used as a tonic.

[8] *rollers* Curling papers (for styling hair); *macs* Macaronies, i.e., dandies.

[9] *for* To look like.

[10] *vel brand en vast hood* Dutch: burn well and hold fast. This phrase, used to indicate the superior quality of Dutch sealing wax, was often dishonestly placed on poor-quality imitations.

[11] *Public Advertiser* London newspaper consisting primarily of advertisements.

[12] *Gentiles* Non-Jewish people; *Moses commanded* See Deuteronomy 23.19–20, where the Israelites are permitted to charge interest only when lending money to gentiles. This portion of Ben Hassan's song reflects a stereotypical association between Jews and moneylending. Moneylending was a common profession for Jewish people, as for hundreds of years social and legal discrimination [continued …]

Oh! I began to tremble at every gibbet° *gallows*
 that I saw;
But I got on board a ship, and here was safely
 landed,
In spite of the judges, counsellors, attorneys,
 and law.

FREDERIC. And so to complete the whole, you turned
180 Mahometan.

BEN HASSAN. Oh 'twas the safest way.

FREDERIC. But Hassan, as you are so fond of cheating the Gentiles, perhaps you may cheat us.

BEN HASSAN. Oh no! I swear by Mahomet.

185 FREDERIC. No swearing, old Trimmer.[1] If you are true to us you will be amply rewarded, should you betray us, (*Sternly.*) by heaven you shall not live an hour after. Go, look for a vessel, make every necessary preparation; and remember, instant death shall
190 await the least appearance of treachery.

BEN HASSAN. But I have not got monies.

FREDERIC. Go, you are a hypocrite; you are rich enough to purchase an hundred vessels, and if the Dey knew of your wealth—

195 BEN HASSAN. Oh! Dear Mr. Frederic, indeed I am very poor, but I vill do all you desire, and you vill pay me afterwards. (*Aside.*) Oh, I wish I could get you well paid with the bastinado.[2]

(*Exit.*)

FREDERIC. (*Solus.*) I will trust this fellow no farther.
200 I am afraid he will play us false—but should he, we have yet one resource, we can but die; and to die in a struggle for freedom, is better far than to live in ignominious bondage.

(*Exit.*)

in Europe prevented them from working in most professions, while religious doctrine forbade Christians from making loans for profit (a prohibition not always obeyed in practice).

[1] *Trimmer* One who changes sides out of self-interest.

[2] *bastinado* Stick used to torture people by striking them on the soles of the feet.

ACT 1, SCENE 3

(*Another Apartment at the Dey's. [Enter] Zoriana and Olivia.*)

ZORIANA. Alas! It was pitiful, pray proceed.

OLIVIA. My father's ill health obliging him to visit Lisbon, we embarked for that place, leaving my betrothed lover to follow us—but ere we reached
5 our destined port, we were captured by an Algerine corsair, and I was immediately sent to the Dey, your father.

ZORIANA. I was then in the country, but I was told he became enamoured of you.

10 OLIVIA. Unfortunately he did; but my being a Christian has hitherto preserved me from improper solicitations, though I am frequently pressed to abjure my religion.

ZORIANA. Were you not once near making your
15 escape?

OLIVIA. We were; my father, by means of some jewels which he had concealed in his clothes, bribed one of the guards to procure false keys to the apartments, but on the very night when we meant to put our
20 plan in execution, the Dey, coming suddenly into the room, surprized my father in my arms.

ZORIANA. Was not his anger dreadful?

OLIVIA. Past description. My dear father was torn from me and loaded with chains, thrown into a
25 dungeon where he still remains, secluded from the cheering light of heaven; no resting place but on the cold, damp ground; the daily portion of his food so poor and scanty, it hardly serves to eke out an existence lingering as it is forlorn.

30 ZORIANA. And where are the false keys?

OLIVIA. I have them still, for I was not known to possess them.

ZORIANA. Then banish all your sorrow; if you have still the keys, tomorrow night shall set us all at
35 liberty.

OLIVIA. Madam!

ZORIANA. Be not alarmed sweet Olivia, I am a Christian in my heart, and I love a Christian slave, to whom I have conveyed money and jewels, sufficient
40 to ransom himself and several others. I will appoint

him to be in the garden this evening; you shall go with me and speak to him.

OLIVIA. But how can we release my father?

ZORIANA. Every method shall be tried to gain admit-
45 tance to his prison; the Christian has many friends, and if all other means fail, they can force the door.

OLIVIA. Oh! heavens, could I but see him once more at liberty, how gladly would I sacrifice my own life to secure his.

50 ZORIANA. The keys you have will let us out of the house when all are locked in the embraces of sleep; our Christian friends will be ready to receive us, and before morning we shall be in a place of safety. In the meantime, let hope support your sinking spirits.

SONG.

55 Sweet cherub clad in robes of white,
 Descend celestial Hope;
 And on thy pinions,° soft, and light, wings
 Oh bear thy votary° up. devotee
 'Tis thou can soothe the troubled breast,
60 The tear of sorrow dry;
 Can'st lull each doubt and fear to rest,
 And check the rising sigh.
 Sweet cherub etc.

(*Exit.*)

ACT I, SCENE 4

(*A garden—outside of a house, with small high lattices.
[Enter] Henry and Frederic.*)

FREDERIC. Fearing the old fellow would pocket our cash and betray us afterwards, I changed my plan, and have entrusted the money with a Spaniard, who will make the best bargain he can for us: have you
5 tried our friends, will they be staunch?

HENRY. To a man. The hope of liberty, like an electric spark, ran instantly through every heart, kindling a flame of patriotic ardour. Nay, even those whom interest or fear have hitherto kept silent, now openly
10 avowed their hatred of the Dey and swore to assist our purpose.

FREDERIC. Those whose freedom we have already purchased, have concerted proper measures for lib-
erating many others, and by twelve o'clock tomor-
15 row night, we shall have a party large enough to surround the palace of the Dey, and convey from thence in safety the fair Zoriana.

(*Window opens and a white handkerchief is waved.*)

HENRY. Soft! Behold the signal of love and peace.

FREDERIC. I'll catch it as it falls.

(*He approaches, it is drawn back.*)

20 HENRY. 'Tis not designed for you, stand aside.

(*Henry approaching; the handkerchief is let fall, a hand waved, and then the lattice shut.*)

'Tis a wealthy fall, and worth receiving.

FREDERIC. What says the fair Mahometan?

HENRY. Can I believe my eyes; here are English char-
acters; and, but I think 'tis impossible, I should say,
25 this was my Olivia's writing.

FREDERIC. This is always the way with you happy fel-
lows, who are favourites with the women; you slight the willing fair one and dote on those who are only to be obtained with difficulty.

30 HENRY. I wish the lovely Moor had fixed her affec-
tions on you instead of me.

FREDERIC. I wish she had with all my soul—Moor or Christian, slave or free woman, 'tis no matter; if she was but young, and in love with me, I'd kneel down
35 and worship her. But I'm a poor miserable dog; the women never say civil things to me.

HENRY. But, do you think it can be possible that my adorable Olivia is a captive here?

FREDERIC. Prithee man, don't stand musing and
40 wondering, but remember this is the time for action. If chance has made your Olivia a captive, why, we must make a bold attempt to set her at liberty, and then I suppose you will turn over the fair Moriscan to me. But what says the letter.

45 HENRY. (*Reads.*) "As you have now the means of free-
dom in your power, be at the north garden gate at ten o'clock, and when you hear me sing, you will

be sure all is safe, and that you may enter without danger; do not fail to come, I have some pleasant
50 intelligence to communicate." Yes, I will go and acquaint her with the real state of my heart.

FREDERIC. And so make her our enemy.

HENRY. It would be barbarous to impose on her generous nature. What? Avail myself of her liberal-
55 ity to obtain my own freedom; take her from her country and friends, and then sacrifice her a victim to ingratitude and disappointed love?

FREDERIC. Tush, man, women's hearts are not so easily broken; we may, perhaps, give them a slight
60 wound now and then, but they are seldom or never incurable.

HENRY. I see our master coming this way. Begone to our friends; encourage them to go through with our enterprise: the moment I am released I will join you.
65 FREDERIC. 'Till when, adieu.

(Exit severally.)

ACT 2, SCENE 1

(Moonlight—A garden. [Enter] Zoriana and Olivia.)

ZORIANA. Sweet Olivia, chide me not; for though I'm fixed to leave this place and embrace Christianity, I cannot but weep when I think what my poor father will suffer. Methinks I should stay to console him for
5 the loss of you.

OLIVIA. He will soon forget me; has he not already a number of beautiful slaves, who have been purchased to banish me from his remembrance?

ZORIANA. True, but he slights them all; you only are
10 the mistress of his heart.

OLIVIA. Hark, did you not hear a footstep?

ZORIANA. Perhaps it is the young Christian; he waits the appointed signal. I think all is safe; he may approach.

SONG

15 Wrapped in the evening's soft and pensive shade,
 When passing zephyrs° scarce the *breezes*
 herbage moves;

Here waits a trembling, fond, and anxious maid,
 Expecting to behold the youth she loves.
 Though Philomela[1] on a neighbouring tree,
20 Melodious warbles forth her nightly strain
 Thy accents would be sweeter far to me,
 Would from my bosom banish doubt and pain.
 Then come dear youth, come haste away,
 Haste to this silent grove,
25 The signal's given, you must obey,
 'Tis liberty and love.

(Enter Henry.)

HENRY. Lovely and benevolent lady, permit me thus humbly to thank you for my freedom.

OLIVIA. Oh Heavens, that voice!

30 ZORIANA. Gentle Christian, perhaps I have overstepped the bounds prescribed my sex. I was early taught a love of Christianity, but I must now confess, my actions are impelled by a tenderer passion.

HENRY. That passion which you have so generously
35 avowed has excited my utmost gratitude, and I only wish for power to convince you, how much you have bound me to your service.

OLIVIA. Oh! *(Faints.)*

ZORIANA. What ails my friend? Help me to support
40 her; she is an amiable creature and will accompany us in our flight. She revives; how are you? Speak; my Olivia.

HENRY. Olivia, did you say?

OLIVIA. Yes, Henry, your forsaken Olivia.

45 HENRY. Oh my beloved! Is it possible that I see you here in bondage? Where is your father?

OLIVIA. In bondage too—but, Henry, you had forgot me; you could renounce your vows and wed another.

HENRY. Oh no; never for one moment has my
50 thoughts strayed from my Olivia—I never regretted slavery, but as it deprived me of your sweet converse, nor wished for freedom, but to ratify my vows to you.

[1] *Philomela* A nightingale. In Greek mythology, Philomela is transformed into a nightingale after she is raped by her brother-in-law Tereus, who ripped her tongue out so she could not denounce him.

ZORIANA. (*Aside*.) How? Mutual lovers! My disap-
pointed heart beats high with resentment, but in
vain; I wish to be a Christian, and I will, though my
heart breaks, perform a Christian's duty.

HENRY. Pardon, beauteous lady, an involuntary
error. I have long loved this Christian maid; we are
betrothed to each other. This evening I obeyed your
summons, to inform you that grateful thanks and
fervent prayers were all the return I could make for
the unmerited kindness you have shown me.

OLIVIA. Generous Zoriana, blame not my Henry.

ZORIANA. Think not so meanly of me, as to suppose
I live but for myself—that I loved your Henry, I can
without a blush avow, but, 'twas a love so pure, that
to see him happy will gratify my utmost wish; I still
rejoice that I've procured his liberty; you shall with
him embrace the opportunity, and be henceforth as
blest—(*Aside*.) as I am wretched.

HENRY. You will go with us.

ZORIANA. Perhaps I may—but let us now separate;
tomorrow, from the lattice, you shall receive instruc-
tions how to proceed: in the meantime here is more
gold and jewels. I never knew their value, till I found
they could ransom you from slavery.

HENRY. Words are poor.

ZORIANA. Leave us. My heart's oppressed, I wish to
be alone; doubt not the safety of your Olivia; she
must be safe with me, for she is dear to you.

(*Henry kisses her hand, bows and exits. They stand
sometime without speaking.*)

ZORIANA. Olivia!

OLIVIA. Madam!

ZORIANA. Why are you silent, do you doubt my
sincerity?

OLIVIA. Oh no—but I was thinking, if we should fail
in our attempt; if we should be taken—

ZORIANA. Gracious heaven forbid!

OLIVIA. Who then could deprecate[1] your father's
wrath? Yourself, my Henry, and my dearest father,
all, all, would fall a sacrifice.

ZORIANA. These are groundless fears.

OLIVIA. Perhaps they are; but yet, I am resolved to
stay behind.

[1] *deprecate* Alleviate.

ZORIANA. Do not think of it.

OLIVIA. Forgive me; I am determined, and that
so firmly, it will be in vain to oppose me. If you
escape—the Power who protects you, will also give
to me the means of following; should you be taken, I
may perhaps move the Dey to forgive you, and even
should my prayers and tears have no effect, my life
shall pay the forfeiture of yours.

ZORIANA. I will not go.

OLIVIA. Yes, gentle lady, yes; you must go with
them; perhaps you think it will be a painful task
to meet your father's anger; but indeed it will not.
The thought of standing forth the preserver of the
dear author of my being, of the man who loves me
next to heaven, of the friend who could sacrifice her
own happiness to mine, would fill my soul with such
delight, that even death, in its most horrid shape,
could not disturb its tranquility.

ZORIANA. But, can you suppose your father, and
your lover—

OLIVIA. You must assist my design, you must tell
them I am already at liberty, and in a place of safety;
when they discover the deception, be it your task,
my gentle Zoriana, to wipe the tear of sorrow from
their eyes. Be a daughter to my poor father, com-
fort his age, be kind and tender to him, let him not
feel the loss of his Olivia. Be to my Henry (Oh! my
bursting heart) a friend, to soothe him in his deep
affliction; pour consolation on his wounded mind,
and love him if you can, as I have done.

(*Exit.*)

ACT 2, SCENE 2

(*Dawn of the day. Another part of the garden—with an
alcove. Enter Frederic.*)

FREDERIC. What a poor unfortunate dog I am; last
night I slipped into the garden behind Henry, in
hopes I should find some distressed damsel, who
wanted a knight-errant to deliver her from captivity;
and here have I wandered through windings, turn-
ings, alleys, and labyrinths, till the Devil himself could
not find the way out again: someone approaches—by
all that's lovely 'tis a woman—young, and handsome

too, health glows upon her cheek, and good humour
10 sparkles in her eye; I'll conceal myself, that I may not
alarm her.

(*Exit into the alcove.*)

(*Enter Fetnah.*)

FETNAH.

SONG.

Aurora,[1] lovely blooming fair,
Unbarred the eastern skies;
While many a soft pellucid tear,
15 Ran trickling from her eyes.
Onward she came, with heart-felt glee,
Leading the dancing hours;
For though she wept, she smiled to see,
Her tears refresh the flowers.
20 Phoebus,[2] who long her charms admired,
With bright refulgent ray;
Came forth, and as the maid retired,
He kissed her tears away.

What a sweet morning, I could not sleep, so the
25 moment the doors were open, I came out to try and
amuse myself. 'Tis a delightful garden, but I believe
I should hate the finest place in the world, if I was
obliged to stay in it, whether I would or no. If I am
forced to remain here much longer, I shall fret myself
30 as old and as ugly as Mustapha. That's no matter;
there's nobody here to look at one, but great, black,
goggle-eyed creatures, that are posted here and there
to watch us. And when one speaks to them, they
shake their frightful heads, and make such a horrid
35 noise—lord, I wish I could run away, but that's
impossible; there is no getting over these nasty high
walls. I do wish some dear, sweet, Christian man,
would fall in love with me, break open the garden
gates, and carry me off.
40 FREDERIC. (*Stealing out.*) Say you so my charmer,
then I'm your man.

FETNAH. And take me to that charming place, where
there are no bolts and bars; no mutes[3] and guards;
no bow-strings and scimitars. Oh! It must be a dear
45 delightful country, where women do just what they
please.

FREDERIC. I'm sure you are a dear, delightful creature.

([*Fetnah,*] *turning, sees him, and shrieks.*)

FREDERIC. Hush, my sweet little infidel, or we shall
be discovered.

50 FETNAH. Why, who are you, and how came you here?

FREDERIC. I am a poor forlorn fellow, beautiful crea-
ture, over head and ears in love with you, and I came
here to tell you how much I adore you.

FETNAH. (*Aside.*) Oh dear! what a charming man. I
55 do wish he would run away with me.

FREDERIC. Perhaps this is the lady who wrote to
Henry; she looks like a woman of quality, if I may
judge from her dress. I'll ask her. You wish to leave
this country, lovely Moor?

60 FETNAH. Lord, I'm not a Moriscan; I hate 'em all,
there is nothing I wish so much as to get away from
them.

FREDERIC. Your letters said so.

FETNAH. Letters!

65 FREDERIC. Yes, the letters you dropped from the
window upon the terrace.

FETNAH. (*Aside.*) He takes me for some other, I'll not
undeceive him, and maybe, he'll carry [me] off. Yes,
sir; yes, I did write to you.

70 FREDERIC. To me!

FETNAH. To be sure; did you think it was to anybody
else?

FREDERIC. Why, there has been a small mistake.

FETNAH. (*Aside.*) And there's like to be a greater if
75 you knew all.

FREDERIC. And do you indeed love me?

FETNAH. Yes, I do, better than anybody I ever saw
in my life.

FREDERIC. And if I can get you out of the palace, you
80 will go away with me?

FETNAH. To be sure I will, that's the very thing I wish.

FREDERIC. Oh! thou sweet, bewitching, little—

[1] *Aurora* In Roman mythology, the goddess of the dawn.

[2] *Phoebus* Name applied to the Greek god Apollo in his role as
sun god.

[3] *mutes* Term formerly used to refer to deaf people employed in
Turkish and Algerian courts on account of their discretion.

(*Catching her in his arms.*)

MULEY MOLOC. (*Without.*) Tell him Fetnah shall be sent home to him immediately.

85 FETNAH. Oh lord! what will become of us? That's my lord the Dey—you'll certainly be taken.

FREDERIC. Yes, I feel the bow-string round my neck already; what shall I do—where shall I hide?

FETNAH. Stay, don't be frightened—I'll bring you 90 off; catch me in your arms again.

(*She throws herself in his arms as though fainting.*)

(*Enter Muley Moloc and Mustapha.*)

MULEY MOLOC. I tell thee, Mustapha, I cannot banish the beautiful Christian one moment from my thoughts. The women seem all determined to perplex me; I was pleased with the beauty of Fetnah, 95 but her childish caprice—

MUSTAPHA. Behold, my lord, the fair slave you mention, in the arms of a stranger.

FREDERIC. (*Aside.*) Now, good-bye to poor Pil-garlic.[1]

FETNAH. (*Pretending to recover.*) Are they gone, and 100 am I safe? Oh! Courteous stranger, when the Dey my master knows—

MULEY MOLOC. What's the matter Fetnah; who is this slave?

FETNAH. (*Kneeling.*) Oh mighty prince, this stranger 105 has preserved me from the greatest outrage.

MULEY MOLOC. What outrage?

FETNAH. Now, do not look angry at your poor little slave, who, knowing she had offended you, could not rest, and came early into the garden to lament 110 her folly.

FREDERIC. (*Aside.*) Well said, woman.

MULEY MOLOC. Rise, Fetnah; we have forgot your rashness—proceed.

FETNAH. So, as I was sitting, melancholy and sad, 115 in the alcove, I heard a great noise, and presently four or five Turks leaped over the wall, and began to plunder the garden. I screamed; did not you hear me, Mustapha?

FREDERIC. (*Aside.*) Well said, again.

120 FETNAH. But, the moment they saw me, they seized me, and would have forced me away, had not this gallant stranger run to my assistance. They, thinking they were pursued by many, relinquished their hold and left me fainting in the stranger's arms.

125 MULEY MOLOC. 'Tis well.

MUSTAPHA. But, gracious sir, how came the stranger here?

FREDERIC. (*Aside.*) Oh! Confound your inquisitive tongue.

130 MULEY MOLOC. Aye, Christian; how came you in this garden?

FETNAH. He came from my father. Did not you say my father sent you here?

FREDERIC. (*Bows. Aside.*) Now, who the devil is her 135 father?

FETNAH. He came to beg leave to gather some herbs for a salad, while they were still fresh with morning dew.

FREDERIC. (*Aside.*) Heaven bless her invention!

140 MULEY MOLOC. Go to your apartment.

FETNAH. Oh dear! If he should ask him any questions when I am gone, what will become of him?

(*Exit Fetnah.*)

MULEY MOLOC. Christian, gather the herbs you came for, and depart in peace. Mustapha, go to my 145 daughter Zoriana; tell her I'll visit her some two hours hence, 'till when, I'll walk in the refreshing morning air.

(*Exit Muley and Mustapha.*)

FREDERIC. (*Solus.*) Thanks to dear little infidel's ready wit; I breathe again. Good Mr. Whiskers,[2] I 150 am obliged by your dismission of me—I will depart as fast as I can; and yet I cannot but regret leaving my lovely little Moor behind. Who comes here? The apostate[3] Hassan. Now could I swear some mischief was afoot. I'll keep out of sight and try to learn his 155 business.

(*Frederic retires.*)

[1] *Pil-garlic* Bald, slovenly, or foolish person; the term was often used self-pityingly (as here), meaning "poor foolish me."

[2] *Mr. Whiskers* I.e., Muley Moloc.

[3] *apostate* One who has abandoned one's religion.

(*Enter Ben Hassan and Mustapha.*)

BEN HASSAN. Indeed, I am vashtly sorry that my daughter has offended my good lord the Dey; but if he will admit me to his sublime presence, I can give him intelligence of so important a nature, as I makes no doubt will incline him to pardon her, for my sake.

MUSTAPHA. I will tell him you wait his leisure.

(*Exit Mustapha.*)

FREDERIC. The traitor is on the point of betraying us. I must if possible prevent his seeing the Dey. (*Runs to Ben Hassan with all the appearance of violent terror.*) Oh! my dear friend Hassan, for heaven's sake what brought you here? Don't you know the Dey is so highly offended with you that he vows to have you impaled alive?

BEN HASSAN. Oh dear! Mr. Frederic, how did you know?

FREDERIC. It was by the luckiest chance in the world; I happened to be in this garden when I overheard a slave of yours informing the Dey that you had not only amassed immense riches, which you intended to carry out of his territories; but, that you had many valuable slaves, which you kept concealed from him, that you might reap the benefit of their ransom.

BEN HASSAN. Oh, what will become of me! But, come, come; Mr. Frederic, you only say this to frighten me.

FREDERIC. Well, you'll see that; for I heard him command his guards to be ready to seize you when he gave the signal, as he expected you here every moment.

BEN HASSAN. Oh! What shall I do?

FREDERIC. If you stay here, you will certainly be bastinadoed—impaled—burnt.

BEN HASSAN. Oh dear! Oh dear!

FREDERIC. Make haste my dear friend; run home as fast as possible; hide your treasure and keep out of the way.

BEN HASSAN. Oh dear! I wish I was safe in Duke's Place.[1]

(*Exit.*)

[1] *Duke's Place* Area of London known for its Jewish community.

FREDERIC. Let me but get you once safe into your own house, and I'll prevent your betraying us I'll warrant.

(*Exit.*)

ACT 2, SCENE 3

(*Fetnah's Apartment. [Enter] Fetnah and Selima.*)

FETNAH. Now will you pretend to say you are happy here, and that you love the Dey.

SELIMA. I have been here many years; the Dey has been very good to me, and my chief employment has been to wait on his daughter, Zoriana, till I was appointed to attend you. To you perhaps, he may be an object of disgust; but, looking up to him as a kind and generous master, to me he appears amiable.

FETNAH. Oh! To be sure, he is a most amiable creature; I think I see him now, seated on his cushion, a bowl of sherbet by his side, and a long pipe in his mouth. Oh! How charmingly the tobacco must perfume his whiskers—here, Mustapha, says he, "Go, bid the slave Selima come to me." Well it does not signify, that word "slave" does so stick in my throat—I wonder how any woman of spirit can gulp it down.

SELIMA. We are accustomed to it.

FETNAH. The more's the pity: for how sadly depressed must the soul be, to whom custom has rendered bondage supportable.

SELIMA. Then, if opportunity offered, you would leave Algiers?

FETNAH. That I would, most cheerfully.

SELIMA. And perhaps, bestow your affections on some young Christian.

FETNAH. That you may be sure of; for say what you will, I am sure the woman must be blind and stupid, who would not prefer a young, handsome, good-humoured Christian, to an old, ugly, ill-natured Turk.

(*Enter Sadi—with robe, turban, etc.*)

FETNAH. Well, what's your business?

SADI. I—I—I—I'm afraid I'm wrong.

SELIMA. Who sent you here?

SADI. I was told to take these to our master's son,
35 young Soliman. But somehow, in the turnings and
windings in this great house, I believe I have lost
myself.
SELIMA. You have mistaken—
FETNAH. Mistaken—no, he is very right; here, give
40 me the clothes, I'll take care of them, (*Takes them.*)
there, there, go about your business, it's all very well.

(*Exit Sadi.*)

Now, Selima, I'll tell you what I'll do; I'll put these
on—go to the Dey, and see if he will know me.
SELIMA. He'll be angry.
45 FETNAH. Pshaw! You're so fearful of his anger. If you
let the men see you are afraid of them, they'll hector
and domineer finely. No, no, let them think you
don't care whether they are pleased or no, and then
they'll be as condescending and humble. Go, go—
50 take the clothes into the next apartment.

(*Exit Selima.*)

Now, if by means of these clothes, I can get out of
the palace, I'll seek the charming young Christian
I saw this morning. We'll get my dear instructress
from my father's and fly together from this land of
55 captivity to the regions of Peace and Liberty.

(*Exit.*)

ACT 3, SCENE 1

(*A kind of grotto.* [*Enter*] *Frederic, Henry, Sebastian,
and Slaves.*)

SEBASTIAN. Now, if you had trusted me at first, I'll
answer for it, I had got you all safe out; aye, and
that dear, sweet creature, madam Zoriana too!
What a pity it is she's Mahometan, your true bred
Mahometans never drink any wine. Now, for my
5 part, I like a drop of good liquor, it makes a body feel
so comfortable, so … so, I don't know howish, as if
they were friends with all the world—I always keep
a friend or two hid here. (*Takes out some bottles.*)

10 Mum, don't be afraid, they are no tell-tales—only
when they are trusted too far.
FREDERIC. Well, Sebastian, don't be too unguarded
in trusting these very good friends tonight.
SEBASTIAN. Never fear me; did not I tell you I'd show
15 you a place of safety; well, haven't I performed my
promise? When I first discovered this cave, or cavern,
or grotto, or cell, or whatever your fine-spoken folks
may call it; this, said I, would be a good place to hide
people in. So I never told my master.
20 HENRY. This fellow will do some mischief, with his
non-sensical prate.[1]
FREDERIC. I don't fear him, he has an honest heart,
hid under an appearance of ignorance. It grows
duskish, Sebastian, have we good sentinels placed at
25 the entrance of the cell?
SEBASTIAN. Good sentinels! Why do you suppose
I would trust any with that post but those I could
depend on?
HENRY. Two hours past midnight we must invest[2]
30 the garden of the Dey; I have here a letter from
Zoriana, which says she will at that time be ready
to join us—and lead us to the prison of my Olivia's
father. Olivia is by some means already at liberty.
SENTINEL. (*Without.*) You must not not pass.
35 FETNAH. No—but I must. I have business.
SEBASTIAN. What, what, what's all this?

(*Exit.*)

FETNAH. Nay, for pity's sake, don't kill me.

(*Re-enter Sebastian, forcing in Fetnah habited[3] like a
boy.*)

SEBASTIAN. No, no, we won't kill you; we'll only
make you a slave, and you know that's nothing.
40 FETNAH. (*Aside.*) There is my dear Christian, but I
won't discover myself, till I try if he will know me.
HENRY. Who are you, young man and for what pur-
pose were you loitering about this place?
FETNAH. I am Soliman, son to the Dey, and I heard
45 by chance that a band of slaves had laid a plot to

1 *prate* Talk.

2 *invest* Surround.

3 *habited* Dressed.

invest the palace, and so I traced some of them to this cell and was just going—

FIRST SLAVE. To betray us.

SECOND SLAVE. Let us dispatch him, and instantly
50 disperse till the appointed hour.

SEVERAL SLAVES. Aye, let us kill him.

HENRY. Hold; why should we harm this innocent youth?

FIRST SLAVE. He would be the means of our suffering
55 most cruel tortures.

HENRY. True, but he is now in our power: young, innocent, and unprotected. Oh my friends! Let us not, on this auspicious night, when we hope to emancipate ourselves from slavery, tinge the bright
60 standard[1] of liberty with blood.

SLAVES. 'Tis necessary; our safety demands it.

(*They rush on Fetnah; in her struggle her turban falls off—she breaks from them and runs to Frederic.*)

FETNAH. Save me, dear Christian! It's only poor little Fetnah.

FREDERIC. Save you my sweet little infidel—why, I'll
65 impale the wretch, who should move but a finger against you.

SEBASTIAN. Oh! Oh! a mighty pretty boy to be sure.

FREDERIC. But tell me—how got you out of the palace, and how did you discover us?

70 FETNAH. I have not time now, but this I will assure you, I came with a full intention to go with you, if you will take me, the whole world over.

FREDERIC. Can you doubt—

FETNAH. Doubt, no to be sure I don't, but you must
75 comply with one request, before we depart.

FREDERIC. Name it.

FETNAH. I have a dear friend, who is a captive at my father's; she must be released, or Fetnah cannot be happy, even with the man she loves.

([*Fetnah*] *draws aside and confers with Henry.*)

80 SEBASTIAN. Well, here am I, Sebastian; who have been a slave, two years, six months, a fortnight and three days, and have, all that time worked in the

garden of the Alcaide,[2] who has twelve wives, thirty concubines, and two pretty daughters; and yet not
85 one of the insensible hussies ever took a fancy to me. 'Tis devilish hard, that when I go home, I can't say to my honoured father, the barber, and to my reverend mother, the laundress: this is the beautiful princess who fell in love with me; jumped over the garden-
90 wall of his serene holiness her father, and ran away with your dutiful son, Sebastian—then, falling on my knees—thus.

HENRY. What's the matter, Sebastian? There is no danger, don't be afraid, man.

95 FREDERIC. Sebastian, you must take a party of our friends, go to the house of Ben Hassan, and bring from thence an American lady. I have good reason to think you will meet with no opposition; she may be at first unwilling to come, but tell her—friends and
100 countrymen await her here.

FETNAH. Tell her, her own Fetnah expects her.

FREDERIC. Treat her with all imaginable respect: Go, my good Sebastian; be diligent, silent, and expedi-tious. You, my dear Fetnah, I will place in an inner
105 part of the grotto, where you will be safe, while we effect the escape of Olivia's father.

FETNAH. What, shut me up! Do you take me for a coward?

HENRY. We respect you as a woman and would
110 shield you from danger.

FETNAH. A woman! Why, so I am; but in the cause of love or friendship, a woman can face danger with as much spirit, and as little fear, as the bravest man amongst you. Do you lead the way, I'll follow to the
115 end.

(*Exit Fetnah, Frederic, Henry, etc.*)

SEBASTIAN. (*Solus.*) Bravo! Excellent! Bravissimo! Why, 'tis a little body; but ecod,[3] she's a devil of a spirit. It's a fine thing to meet with a woman that has a little fire in her composition. I never much
120 liked your milk-and-water ladies; to be sure, they are easily managed—but your spirited lasses require taming; they make a man look about him—dear, sweet, angry creatures, here's their health. This is the

[1] *standard* Flag.

[2] *Alcaide* Commander of a fortress or prison warden.

[3] *ecod* Variant of the oath "by God!"

summum-bonum[1] of all good: If they are kind, this,
125 this, makes them appear angels and goddesses: If they
are saucy, why then, here, here, in this we'll drown
the remembrance of the bewitching, froward,[2] little
devils. In all kind of difficulties and vexations, noth-
ing helps the invention, or cheers the courage, like a
130 drop from the jorum.[3]

SONG.

When I was a poor, little innocent boy,
About sixteen or eighteen years old;
At Susan and Marian I cast a sheep's eye,
But Susan was saucy and Marian was shy;
135 So I flirted with Flora, with Cecily and Di.
But they too, were frumpish and cold.
Says Diego, one day, what ails you I pray?
I fetched a deep sigh—Diego, says I,
Women hate me. Oh! how I adore 'em.
140 Pho;° nonsense, said he, *pshaw (dismissive sound)*
never mind it my lad.
Hate you? Then hate them boy, come, never
be sad,
Here, take a good sup of the jorum.
If they're foolish and mulish, refuse you, abuse
you,
No longer pursue,
145 They'll soon buckle too
When they find they're neglected,
Old maids, unprotected,
Ah! then 'tis their turn to woo;
But bid them defiance, and form an alliance,
150 With the mirth-giving, care-killing jorum.
I took his advice, but was sent to the war,
And soon I was called out to battle;
I heard the drums beat, Oh! how great was my
fear,
I wished myself sticking, aye, up to each ear
155 In a horse-pond—and skulked away into the
rear.
When the cannon and bombs 'gan to rattle,
Said I to myself, you're a damned foolish elf,
Sebastian keep up, then I took a good sup.

[1] *summum-bonum* Latin: highest good.

[2] *froward* Difficult to manage.

[3] *jorum* Drinking cup.

Turkish villains, shall we fly before 'em;
160 What, give it up tamely and yield ourselves
slaves,
To a pack of rapscallions, vile infidel knaves,
Then I kissed the sweet lips of my jorum.
No, hang 'em, we'll bang 'em, and rout 'em,
and scout 'em.
If we but pursue,
165 They must buckle too:
Ah! then without wonder,
I heard the loud thunder,
Of cannon and musketry too,
But bid them defiance, being firm in alliance,
170 With the courage-inspiring jorum.

(*Exit.*)

ACT 3, SCENE 2

(*Ben Hassan's house.* [*Enter*] *Rebecca and Augustus.*)

AUGUSTUS. Dear mother, don't look so sorrowful; my
master is not very hard with me. Do, pray, be happy.

REBECCA. Alas! My dear Augustus, can I be happy
while you are a slave? My own bondage is nothing.
5 But you, my child—

AUGUSTUS. Nay, mother, don't mind it; I am but a
boy you know. If I was a man—

REBECCA. What would you do my love?

AUGUSTUS. I'd stamp beneath my feet the wretch
10 that would enslave my mother.

REBECCA. There burst forth the sacred flame which
heaven itself fixed in the human mind; Oh! my brave
boy! (*Embracing him.*) Ever may you preserve that
independent spirit, that dares assert the rights of the
15 oppressed, by power unawed, unchecked by servile
fear.

AUGUSTUS. Fear, mother? What should I be afraid of?
Ain't I an American, and I am sure you have often
told me, in a right cause the Americans did not fear
20 anything.

(*Enter Ben Hassan.*)

BEN HASSAN. So, here's a piece of vork; I'se be like to
have fine deal of troubles on your account. Oh! that

ever I should run the risk of my life by keeping you concealed from the Dey.

25 REBECCA. If I am a trouble to you, if my being here endangers your life, why do you not send me away?

BEN HASSAN. There be no ships here for you to go in; besides, who will pay me?

REBECCA. Indeed, if you will send me to my native
30 land, I will faithfully remit to you my ransom; aye, double what you have required.

BEN HASSAN. If I thought I could depend—

(*Enter Servant.*)

SERVANT. Sir, your house is surrounded by armed men.

35 BEN HASSAN. What, Turks?

SERVANT. Slaves, sir; many of whom I have seen in the train of the Dey.

BEN HASSAN. Vhat do they vant?

SERVANT. One of my companions asked them, and
40 received for answer, they would shew us presently.

SEBASTIAN. (*Without.*) Stand away, fellow; I will search the house.

REBECCA. Oh heavens! What will become of me?

BEN HASSAN. What will become of me? Oh! I shall
45 be impaled, burnt, bastinadoed, murdered, where shall I hide, how shall I escape them?

(*Runs through a door, as though into another apartment.*)

SEBASTIAN. (*Without.*) This way, friends; this way.

REBECCA. Oh, my child, we are lost!

AUGUSTUS. Don't be frightened, mother, through
50 this door is a way into the garden. If I had but a sword, boy as I am, I'd fight for you till I died.

(*Exit with Rebecca.*)

(*Enter Sebastian etc.*)

SEBASTIAN. I thought I heard voices this way; now my friends, the lady we seek, is a most lovely, amiable creature, whom we must accost with respect
55 and convey hence in safety. She is a woman of family and fortune and is highly pleased with my person

and abilities; let us therefore, search every cranny of the house till we find her; she may not recollect me directly, but never mind, we will carry her away first
60 and assure her of her safety afterwards. Go search the rooms in that wing, I will myself investigate the apartments on this side.

(*Exit Slaves.*)

Well I have made these comrades of mine believe I am a favoured lover in pursuit of a kind mistress,
65 that's something for them to talk of; and I believe many a fine gentleman is talked of for love affairs that has as little foundation; and so one is but talked of as a brave or gallant man, what signifies whether there is any foundation for it or no. And yet, hang
70 it, who knows but I may prove it a reality. If I release this lady from captivity, she may cast an eye of affection—may—why I dare say she will. I am but poor Sebastian, the barber of Cordova's son, 'tis true; but I am well made, very well made. My leg is not amiss—
75 then I can make a graceful bow. And as to polite compliments, let me but find her, and I'll show them what it is to have a pretty person, a graceful air, and a smooth tongue. But I must search this apartment.

(*Exit.*)

ACT 3, SCENE 3

(*Another apartment. Enter Ben Hassan with a petticoat and robe on, a bonnet, and deep veil in his hand.*)

BEN HASSAN. I think now, they vill hardly know me, in my vife's clothes; I could not find a turban, but this head dress of Rebecca's vill do better, because it vill hide my face—but, how shall I hide my monies?
5 I've got a vast deal, in bills of exchange and all kinds of paper; if I can but get safe off with this book in my pocket, I shall have enough to keep me easy as long as I live.

(*Puts it in his pocket and drops it.*)

Oh! This is a judgment fallen upon me for betraying
10 the Christians.

(*Noise without.*)

Oh lord! Here they come.

(*Ties on the bonnet and retires into one corner of the apartment.*)

(*Enter Sebastian etc.*)

SEBASTIAN. There she is, I thought I traced the sweep
of her train this way. Don't mind her struggles or
entreaties but bring her away. Don't be alarmed,
15 madam, you will meet with every attention, you will
be treated with the greatest respect, and let me whis-
per to you there is more happiness in store for you,
than you can possibly imagine. Friends, convey her
gently to the appointed place.

(*They take up Ben Hassan and carry him off.*)

20 BEN HASSAN. Oh!—o—o—o!

(*Exit.*)

(*Enter Augustus and Rebecca.*)

AUGUSTUS. See, my dear mother, there is no one
here, they are all gone; it was not you they came to
take away.
REBECCA. It is for you, I fear, more than for myself. I
25 do not think you are safe with me—go, my beloved,
return to your master.
AUGUSTUS. What, go and leave my mother without
a protector?
REBECCA. Alas, my love, you are not able to protect
30 yourself. And your staying here only adds to my dis-
tress. Leave me for the present. I hope the period is
not far off, when we shall never be separated.
AUGUSTUS. Mother! Dear mother! My heart is so big
it almost chokes me. Oh! how I wish I was a man.

(*Exit Augustus.*)

35 REBECCA. (*Solus.*) Heaven guard my precious child!
I cannot think him quite safe anywhere, but with
me, his danger would be imminent. The emotions of
his heart hang on his tongue, and the least outrage

40 offered to his mother he would resent at peril of his
life. My spirits are oppressed—I have a thousand
fears for him, and for myself. The house appears
deserted—all is silent—what's this?

(*Takes up the pocket-book.*)

Oh heaven! Is it possible! Bills, to the amount of
45 my own ransom and many others—transporting
thought! My son—my darling boy, this would
soon emancipate you! Here's a letter addressed to
me—the money is my own. Oh joy beyond expres-
sion! My child will soon be free. I have also the
50 means of cheering many children of affliction with
the blest sound of liberty. Hassan, you have dealt
unjustly by me, but I forgive you—for, while my
own heart overflows with gratitude for this unex-
pected blessing, I will wish every human being as
happy as I am this moment.

(*Exit.*)

ACT 3, SCENE 4

(*Dey's garden. [Enter] Zoriana.*)

ZORIANA. (*Solus.*) How vain are the resolves, how
treacherous the heart of a woman in love; but a few
hours since, I thought I could have cheerfully relin-
quished the hope of having my tenderness returned;
5 and found a relief from my own sorrow in reflect-
ing on the happiness of Henry and Olivia. Then
why does this selfish heart beat with transport at
the thought of their separation? Poor Olivia—how
deep must be her affliction. Ye silent shades, scenes
10 of content and peace, how sad would you appear to
the poor wretch who wandered here, the victim of
despair. But the fond heart, glowing with all the joys
of mutual love, delighted views the beauties scat-
tered round, thinks every flower is sweet, and every
15 prospect gay.

SONG.

In lowly cot° or mossy cell, *cottage*
With harmless nymphs and rural swains,[1]
'Tis there contentment loves to dwell,
'Tis there soft peace and pleasure reigns;
20 But even there, the heart may prove,
The pangs of disappointed love.
But softly, hope persuading,
Forbids me long to mourn;
My tender heart pervading,
25 Portends my love's return.
Ah! then how bright and gay,
Appears the rural scene,
More radiant breaks the day,
The night is more serene.

(*Enter Henry.*)

30 HENRY. Be not alarmed, madam. I have ventured
here earlier than I intended, to enquire how my
Olivia effected her escape.
ZORIANA. This letter will inform you—but, early as
it is, the palace is wrapped in silence. My father is
35 retired to rest. Follow me, and I will conduct you to
the old man's prison.
HENRY. Have you the keys?
ZORIANA. I have; follow in silence, the least alarm
would be fatal to our purpose.

(*Exit.*)

ACT 3, SCENE 5

(*The grotto again. [Enter] Sebastian, leading in Ben
Hassan.*)

SEBASTIAN. Beautiful creature, don't be uneasy, I
have risked my life to procure your liberty, and will
at the utmost hazard convey you to your desired
home: but, Oh! most amiable—most divine—most
5 delicate lady, suffer me thus humbly on my knees
to confess my adoration of you; to solicit your pity,
and—

BEN HASSAN. (*In a feigned tone.*) I pray tell me why
you brought me from the house of the good Ben
10 Hassan, and where you design to take me.
SEBASTIAN. Oh! thou adorable, be not offended
at my presumption, but having an opportunity of
leaving this place of captivity, I was determined to
take you with me, and prevent your falling into the
15 power of the Dey, who would no doubt be in rap-
tures, should he behold your exquisite beauty. Sweet
innocent charmer, permit your slave to remove the
envious curtain that shades your enchanting visage.
BEN HASSAN. Oh no! Not for the world; I have in
20 consideration of many past offences, resolved to take
the veil and hide myself from mankind for ever.
SEBASTIAN. That my dear, sweet creature, would be
the highest offence you could commit. Women were
never made, with all their prettiness and softness,
25 and bewitching ways, to be hid from us men, who
came into the world for no other purpose, than to
see, admire, love and protect them. Come, I must
have a peep under that curtain; I long to see your
dear little sparkling eyes, your lovely blooming
30 cheeks—and I am resolved to taste your cherry lips.

(*In struggling to kiss him, the bonnet falls off.*)

Why, what in the devil's name, have we here?
BEN HASSAN. Only a poor old woman—who has
been in captivity—
SEBASTIAN. These fifty years at least, by the length of
35 your beard.
FREDERIC. (*Without.*) Sebastian—bring the lady to
the waterside, and wait till we join you.
BEN HASSAN. I wish I was in any safe place.
SEBASTIAN. Oh ma'am, you are in no danger any-
40 where—come make haste.
BEN HASSAN. But give me my veil again, if anyone
saw my face it would shock me.
SEBASTIAN. And damme,[2] but I think it would shock
them—here, take your curtain, though I think to be
45 perfectly safe, you had best go barefaced.
BEN HASSAN. If you hurry me I shall faint; consider
the delicacy of my nerves.
SEBASTIAN. Come along, there's no time for fainting
now.

[1] *nymphs … swains* A nymph is a sexually desirable young
woman; a swain is a young male suitor. The terms are commonly
used to refer to lovers in pastoral poetry.

[2] *damme* I.e., damn me.

50 BEN HASSAN. The respect due—

SEBASTIAN. To old age—I consider it all—you are very respectable. Oh! Sebastian what a cursed ninny you were to make so much fuss about a woman old enough to be your grandmother.

(*Exit.*)

ACT 3, SCENE 6

(*Inside the Palace.* [*Enter*] *Muley Moloc and Mustapha.*)

MULEY MOLOC. Fetnah gone, Zoriana gone … and the fair slave Olivia?

MUSTAPHA. All, dread[1] sir.

MULEY MOLOC. Send instantly to the prison of the
5 slave Constant. 'Tis he who has again plotted to rob me of Olivia.

(*Exit Mustapha.*)

My daughter, too, he has seduced from her duty. But he shall not escape my vengeance.

(*Re-enter Mustapha.*)

MUSTAPHA. Some of the fugitives are overtaken and
10 wait in chains without.

MULEY MOLOC. Is Zoriana taken?

MUSTAPHA. Your daughter is safe. The old man, too, is taken, but Fetnah and Olivia have escaped.

MULEY MOLOC. Bring in the wretches.

(*Henry, Constant, and several Slaves brought in, chained.*)

15 Rash old man, how have you dared to tempt your fate again? Do you not know the torments that await the Christian who attempts to rob the harem of a Mussulman?[2]

CONSTANT. I know you have the power to end my
20 being, but that's a period[3] I more wish than fear.

MULEY MOLOC. Where is Olivia?

[1] *dread* Revered.

[2] *Mussulman* Muslim.

[3] *period* End.

CONSTANT. Safe, I hope, beyond your power. Oh, gracious heaven, protect my darling from this tyrant, and let my life pay the dear purchase of her freedom.

25 MULEY MOLOC. Bear them to the torture. Who and what am I, that a vile slave dares brave me to my face?

HENRY. Hold off! We know that we must die, and we are prepared to meet our fate like men. Impotent,
30 vain boaster, call us not slaves. You are a slave indeed, to rude, ungoverned passion, to pride, to avarice and lawless love. Exhaust your cruelty in finding tortures for us, and we will smiling tell you the blow that ends our lives strikes off our chains and sets our souls
35 at liberty.

MULEY MOLOC. Hence! Take them from my sight.

(*Captives taken off.*)

Devise each means of torture. Let them linger months, years, ages, in their misery.

(*Enter Olivia.*)

OLIVIA. Stay,[4] Muley, stay. Recall your cruel sentence.

40 MULEY MOLOC. Olivia here; is it possible?

OLIVIA. I have never left the palace. Those men are innocent. So is your daughter. It is I alone deserve your anger; then on me only let it fall. It was I procured false keys to the apartments; it was I seduced
45 your daughter to our interest. I bribed the guards and with entreaty won the young Christian to attempt to free my father. Then, since I was the cause of their offenses, it is fit my life should pay the forfeiture of theirs.

50 MULEY MOLOC. Why did you not accompany them?

OLIVIA. Fearing what has happened, I remained, in hopes, by tears and supplications, to move you to forgive my father. Oh, Muley, save his life! Save all his friends, and if you must have blood to appease
55 your vengeance, let me alone be the sacrifice.

MULEY MOLOC. (*Aside.*) How her softness melts me.

(*To Olivia.*)

Rise, Olivia. You may on easier terms give them both life and freedom.

[4] *Stay* Stop.

OLIVIA. No. Here I kneel till you recall your orders.
60 Haste, or it may be too late.
MULEY MOLOC. Mustapha, go bid them delay the
execution.

(*Exit Mustapha.*)

OLIVIA. Now teach me to secure their lives and free-
dom, and my last breath shall bless you.
65 MULEY MOLOC. Renounce your faith. Consent to be
my wife. Nay, if you hesitate—
OLIVIA. I do not. Give me but an hour to think.
MULEY MOLOC. Not a moment. Determine instantly.
Your answer gives them liberty or death.
70 OLIVIA. Then I am resolved. Swear to me, by
Mohammed—an oath I know you Musselmen never
violate—that the moment I become your wife my
father and his friends are free.
MULEY MOLOC. By Mohammed I swear, not only to
75 give them life and freedom, but safe conveyance to
their desired home.
OLIVIA. I am satisfied. Now leave me to myself a few
short moments, that I may calm my agitated spirits
and prepare to meet you in the mosque.
80 MULEY MOLOC. Henceforth I live but to obey you.

(*Exits.*)

OLIVIA. On what a fearful precipice I stand. To go
forward is ruin, shame and infamy; to recede is to
pronounce sentence of death upon my father and
my adored Henry. Oh, insupportable! There is one
85 way, and only one, by which I can fulfill my promise
to the Dey, preserve my friends, and not abjure my
faith. Source of my being, Thou canst read the heart
which Thou hast been pleased to try in the school of
adversity. Pardon the weakness of an erring mortal,
90 if, rather than behold a father perish—if, rather than
devote his friends to death, I cut the thread of my
existence and rush unbidden to Thy presence. Yes,
I will to the mosque, perform my promise, preserve
the valued lives of those I love, then sink at once into
95 the silent grave and bury all my sorrow in oblivion.

(*Exits.*)

ACT 3, SCENE 7

(*Another apartment. Enter Olivia with Muley Moloc.*)

MULEY MOLOC. Yes, on my life, they are free. In a
few moments they will be here.
OLIVIA. Spare me the trial; for the whole world I
would not see them now, nor would I have them
5 know at what a price I have secured their freedom.

(*Enter Henry and Constant.*)

CONSTANT. My child—
HENRY. My love—
OLIVIA. My Henry! O my dear father! Pray excuse
these tears.

(*Enter Mustapha.*)

10 MUSTAPHA. Great sir, the mosque is prepared, and
the priest waits your pleasure.
MULEY MOLOC. Come, my Olivia.
HENRY. The mosque—the priest—what dreadful
sacrifice is then intended?
15 OLIVIA. Be not alarmed. I must needs attend a
solemn rite which gratitude requires—go my dear
father—dearest Henry leave me; and be assured,
when next you see Olivia, she will be wholly free.

(*Enter Rebecca.*)

REBECCA. Hold for a moment.
20 MULEY MOLOC. What means this bold intrusion?
REBECCA. Muley, you see before you a woman
unused to forms of state, despising titles: I come to
offer ransom for six Christian slaves. Waiting your
leisure, I was informed a Christian maid, to save
25 her father's life, meant to devote herself a sacrifice
to your embraces. I have the means: make your
demand of ransom, and set the maid, with those she
loves, at liberty.
MULEY MOLOC. Her friends are free already; but for
30 herself, she voluntarily remains with me.
REBECCA. Can you unmoved behold her anguish?
Release her Muley. Name but the sum that will pay
her ransom, 'tis yours.

MULEY MOLOC. Woman, the wealth of Golconda[1] could not pay her ransom. Can you imagine that I, whose slave she is; I, who could force her obedience to my will and yet gave life and freedom to those Christians to purchase her compliance, would now relinquish her for paltry gold? Contemptible idea. Olivia, I spare you some few moments to your father. Take leave of him, and as you part, remember his life and liberty depends on you.

(*Exits.*)

REBECCA. Poor girl—what can I do to mitigate your sufferings?

OLIVIA. Nothing. My fate, alas, is fixed. But, generous lady, by what name shall we remember you— what nation are you of?

REBECCA. I am an American—but while I only claim kindred with the afflicted, it is of little consequence where I first drew my breath.

CONSTANT. An American—from what state?

REBECCA. New York is my native place; there did I spend the dear delightful days of childhood, and there, alas, I drained the cup of deep affliction, to the very dregs.

CONSTANT. My heart is strangely interested. Dearest lady, will you impart to us your tale of sorrow, that we may mourn with one who feels so much for us?

REBECCA. Early in life, while my brave countrymen were struggling for their freedom,[2] it was my fate to love and be beloved by a young British officer, to whom, though strictly forbid by my father, I was privately married.

CONSTANT. Married! Say you?

REBECCA. My father soon discovered our union; enraged, he spurned me from him, discarded, cursed me, and for four years I followed my husband's fortune. At length my father relented; on a sick bed he sent for me to attend him. I went, taking with me an infant son, leaving my husband and a lovely girl, then scarcely three years old. Oh heavens! What sorrows have I known from that unhappy hour. During my absence the armies met—my husband fell—my daughter was torn from me; what then availed the wealth my dying father had bequeathed me? Long— long did I lose all sense of my misery, and returning reason showed me the world only one universal blank. The voice of my darling boy first called me to myself. For him I strove to mitigate my sorrow; for his dear sake I have endured life.

CONSTANT. Pray proceed.

REBECCA. About a year since[3] I heard a rumour that my husband was still alive. Full of the fond hope of again beholding him, I, with my son, embarked for England; but before we reached the coast we were captured by an Algerine.[4]

CONSTANT. Do you think you should recollect your husband?

REBECCA. I think I should, but fourteen years of deep affliction has impaired my memory and may have changed his features.

CONSTANT. What was his name? Oh! speak it quickly!

REBECCA. His name was Constant—but wherefore—

CONSTANT. It was—it was—Rebecca, don't you know me?

REBECCA. Alas—how you are altered. Oh! Constant, why have you forsaken me so long?

CONSTANT. In the battle you mention, I was indeed severely wounded, nay, left for dead in the field; there, my faithful servant found me, when some remaining signs of life encouraged him to attempt my recovery, and by his unremitting care I was at length restored. My first returning thought was fixed on my Rebecca, but after repeated enquiries all I could hear was that your father was dead and yourself and child removed farther from the seat of war. Soon after, I was told you had fallen a martyr to grief for my supposed loss. But see my love, our daughter, our dear Olivia; heaven preserved her to be my comforter.

OLIVIA. (*Kneeling and kissing Rebecca.*) My mother, blessed word. Oh! Do I live to say I have a mother?

REBECCA. Bless you my child, my charming duteous girl; but tell me, by what sad chance you became captives?

[1] *Golconda* Fort in India. The area surrounding it is famous for its diamond mines, and the name "Golconda" became synonymous with great riches.

[2] *struggling for their freedom* In the American Revolutionary War (1775–83).

[3] *since* Ago.

[4] *Algerine* Algerian pirate ship.

CONSTANT. After peace was proclaimed with America, my duty called me to India, from whence I returned with a ruined constitution. Being advised to try the air of Lisbon, we sailed for that place, but Heaven ordained that here, in the land of captivity, I should recover a blessing which will amply repay me for all my past sufferings.

(*Enter Muley Moloc.*)

MULEY MOLOC. Christians you trifle with me. Accept your freedom, go in peace, and leave Olivia to perform her promise. For should she waver or draw back, on you I will wreak my vengeance.

REBECCA. Then let your vengeance fall. We will die together; for never shall Olivia, a daughter of Columbia, and a Christian, tarnish her name by apostacy, or live the slave of a despotic tyrant.

MULEY MOLOC. Then take your wish. Who's there?

(*Enter Mustapha hastily.*)

MUSTAPHA. Arm, mighty sir! The slaves throughout Algiers have mutinied—they bear down all before them—this way they come—they say, if all the Christian slaves are not immediately released, they'll raze the city.

REBECCA. Now! Bounteous heaven, protect my darling boy, and aid the cause of freedom.

MULEY MOLOC. Bear them to instant death.

MUSTAPHA. Dread sir—consider.

MULEY MOLOC. Vile abject slave, obey me and be silent! What, have I power over these Christian dogs, and shall I not exert it? Dispatch, I say!

(*Huzza[1] and clash of swords without.*)

Why am I not obeyed?

(*Clash again—confused noise—several huzzas.*)

AUGUSTUS. (*Without.*) Where is my mother? Save, oh! save my mother.

FREDERIC. (*Speaking.*) Shut up the palace gates, secure the guards, and at your peril suffer none to pass.

AUGUSTUS. (*Entering.*) Oh! Mother are you safe?

CONSTANT. Bounteous heaven! And am I then restored to more—much more than life—my Rebecca! my children! Oh! This joy is more than I can bear.

(*Enter Frederic, Fetnah, Sebastian, Ben Hassan, Slaves, etc.*)

SEBASTIAN. Great and mighty Ottoman, suffer my friends to show you what pretty bracelets these are. Oh, you old dog, we'll give you the bastinado presently.

FREDERIC. Forbear Sebastian. Muley Moloc, though your power over us is at end, we neither mean to enslave your person, or put a period to your existence. We are freemen, and while we assert the rights of men, we dare not infringe the privileges of a fellow creature.

SEBASTIAN. By the law of retaliation, he should be a slave.

REBECCA. By the Christian law, no man should be a slave; it is a word so abject, that, but to speak it dyes the cheek with crimson. Let us assert our own prerogative, be free ourselves, but let us not throw on another's neck the chains we scorn to wear.

SEBASTIAN. But what must we do with this old gentlewoman?

BEN HASSAN. Oh, pray send me home to Duke's Place.

FREDERIC. Ben Hassan, your avarice, treachery and cruelty should be severely punished; for, if any one deserves slavery, it is he who could raise his own fortune on the miseries of others.

BEN HASSAN. Oh! that I was but crying "old clothes"[2] in the dirtiest alley in London.

FETNAH. So, you'll leave that poor old man behind?

FREDERIC. Yes, we leave him to learn humanity.

FETNAH. (*Going to Ben Hassan.*) Very well, good bye Frederic—good bye dear Rebecca: while my father was rich and had friends, I did not much think about my duty; but now he is poor and forsaken, I know it too well to leave him alone in his affliction.

MULEY MOLOC. Stay, Fetnah—Hassan stay. I fear from following the steps of my ancestors, I have greatly erred: teach me then, you who so well know how to practice what is right, how to amend my faults.

[1] *Huzza* Exuberant shout made in unison.

[2] *old clothes* Street call used by London used-clothing dealers, many of whom were Jewish.

CONSTANT. Open your prison doors; give freedom to your people. Sink the name of subject in the endearing epithet of fellow-citizen. Then you will be loved
195 and reverenced—then will you find, in promoting the happiness of others, you have secured your own.

MULEY MOLOC. Henceforward, then, I will reject all power but such as my united friends shall think me incapable of abusing. Hassan, you are free—to you,
200 my generous conquerors, what can I say?

HENRY. Nothing, but let your future conduct prove how much you value the welfare of your fellow-creatures. Tomorrow we shall leave your capital and return to our native land, where liberty has estab-
205 lished her court—where the warlike Eagle extends his glittering pinions in the sunshine of prosperity.

OLIVIA. Long, long, may that prosperity continue. May freedom spread her benign influence through every nation, till the bright Eagle, united with the
210 dove and olive-branch, waves high the acknowledged standard of the world.

EPILOGUE.
WRITTEN AND SPOKEN BY MRS. ROWSON

PROMPTER. (*Behind.*) Come—Mrs. Rowson! Come! Why don't you hurry?

MRS. ROWSON. (*Behind.*) Sir I am here—but I'm in such a flurry,
Do let me stop a moment! just for breath,

(*Enter.*)

5 Bless me! I'm almost terrified to death.
Yet sure, I had no real cause for fear,
Since none but liberal, generous friends are here.
Say, will you kindly overlook my errors?
You smile. Then to the winds I give my terrors.
10 Well, ladies, tell me—how d'ye like my play?
"The creature has some sense," methinks you say;
"She says that we should have supreme dominion,
And in good truth, we're all of her opinion.
Women were born for universal sway,
15 Men to adore, be silent, and obey."

True, Ladies—bounteous nature made us fair,
To strew sweet roses round the bed of care.

A parent's heart, of sorrow to beguile,
Cheer an afflicted husband by a smile.
20 To bind the truant that's inclined to roam,
Good humour makes a paradise at home.
To raise the fallen, to pity and forgive,
This is our noblest, best prerogative.
By these, pursuing nature's gentle plan,
25 We hold in silken chains—the lordly tyrant man.

But pray, forgive this flippancy—indeed,
Of all your clemency I stand in need.
To own the truth, the scenes this night displayed,
Are only fictions—drawn by fancy's aid.
30 'Tis what I wish. But we have cause to fear,
No ray of comfort the sad bosoms cheer,
Of many a Christian, shut from light and day,
In bondage, languishing their lives away.

Say! You who feel humanity's soft glow,
35 What rapt'rous joy must the poor captive know;
Who, freed from slavery's ignominious chain,
Views his dear native land and friends again?

If there's a sense, more exquisitely fine,
A joy more elevated, more divine;
40 'Tis felt by those, whose liberal minds conceived,
The generous plan, by which he was relieved.

When first this glorious universe began,
And heaven to punish disobedient man
Sent to attend him, through life's dreary shade,
45 Affliction—poor dejected, weeping maid.
Then came Benevolence, by all revered,
He dried the mourner's tears, her heart he cheered;
He wooed her to his breast—made her his own,
And Gratitude appeared, their first-born son.
50 Since when, the father and the son has joined,
To shed their influence o'er the human mind:
And in the heart, where either deign to rest,
Rise transports, difficult to be expressed.
Such, as within your generous bosoms glow,
55 Who feel returned the blessings you bestow.
Oh! ever may you taste those joys divine,
While Gratitude—sweet Gratitude—is mine.

—1794

HANNAH WEBSTER FOSTER

1758 – 1840

When Hannah Webster Foster's first novel, *The Coquette*, was published in 1797, it quickly became one of the eighteenth century's most widely read works of American fiction. Often referred to today as a "seduction novel," the book's title page declared it to be "Founded on Fact"—in other words, based on the true story of Elizabeth Whitman, who had earned notoriety throughout New England in the previous decade after the still birth of her illegitimate child and her subsequent death. Both the content of *The Coquette* and the public response to it over subsequent decades shed considerable light on the ways gender roles, sexual mores, and class hierarchies were expressed in the late-eighteenth century—and the ways in which sexual, gender, and class conventions were sometimes resisted. They help as well to illuminate a moment at which the novel—and questions about truth and fiction—were taking on a new importance in American life.

Hannah Webster was born to Grant Webster, a prosperous merchant, and Hannah Wainwright Webster on 10 September 1758, in Salisbury, Massachusetts. Very little is known about her early life, though the content of her novels strongly suggests that she received a formal education. In her youth she moved to Boston, probably to attend a boarding school, and eventually began to write anonymous political articles for Boston periodicals. None of these articles are known to scholars today. Her writing attracted the attention of minister John Foster; the two married in 1785, and went on to have six children.

In July 1788, New England society was shaken by scandal when a young woman died at the Bell Tavern in Danvers, Massachusetts, after having had a miscarriage; she had been staying at the inn under a false name for several weeks, claiming to be awaiting the arrival of her husband. When the woman's identity was revealed to be that of Elizabeth Whitman, the unmarried daughter of a respected Connecticut minister, she quickly became the subject of widespread gossip. Prior to her disappearance, Whitman had been known regionally as an accomplished poet, and a friend of notable men of letters such as Joel Barlow, Noah Webster, and the poet John Trumbull; the circumstances of her death were rendered the more scandalous by her respectable background. Newspapers such as Boston's *Independent Chronicle* concluded that Whitman had brought on her fate by having previously "refused two as good offers of marriage as she deserved, because she aspired higher than to be a clergyman's wife; and having coquetted till past her prime, fell into criminal indulgences." From journalism to religious sermons, Whitman's death came to be interpreted as "a good moral lecture to young ladies"—a warning against flirtation, against refusing respectable offers of marriage, and against aspiring beyond the station of one's birth.

Nine years after Whitman's death, Hannah Foster—whose husband was a cousin of Whitman—released her first novel, *The Coquette; or, The History of Eliza Wharton*. The story of Eliza Wharton, clearly a thinly veiled portrait of Whitman, was an immediate success. At the peak of its popularity, editions could be found "in every cottage within [New England's] borders, beside the family Bible," as reflected in the "Historical Preface" to the 1855 edition. By 1802, *The Coquette* was being adapted for the stage by J. Horatio Nichols in Salem; it remained in high demand for several decades, with eight printings released in the 1820s alone.

Told entirely in an epistolary format, *The Coquette* was among the first novels published in the United States, but followed a narrative format that had been rendered popular in England in previous decades by the epistolary novels of writers such as Samuel Richardson, whose "seduction novels" *Pamela; or, Virtue Rewarded* (1740) and *Clarissa: Or the History of a Young Lady* (1748) told of virtuous young women striving to resist the seductions of immoral men. While Foster's name was not given on the book's title page—which attributed it simply to "A Lady of Massachusetts"—her authorship was something of an open secret among those of her social class, who were also aware of her familial relationship to Whitman. This relationship led some to believe that Foster had based her novel on real letters to

which she had had access. To some degree, the novel's epistolary format and supposed resemblance to reality may have worked to assuage the anxieties held by many at the time that novels were an indulgent and potentially immoral genre—especially for women readers. Indeed, among the many criticisms of Elizabeth Whitman's conduct that circulated after her death was the accusation, voiced notably by the *Massachusetts Sentinel*, that she was "a great reader of romances, and [had] formed her notions of happiness from that corrupt source."

The Coquette, with its tragic conclusion, appeared to provide a clear moral lesson to many eighteenth-century readers. Yet many modern readers find it difficult to discern any clear moral. Is Eliza Wharton's death a tragedy, or an unfortunate but just punishment for her immoral behavior? Are readers to blame Eliza for her own unhappiness and death, or are they rather to condemn the selfish and immoral behavior of her seducer, Major Sanford? Does Foster's narrative affirm the social and sexual mores that were dominant in the late eighteenth century, or does it in fact indict them? Critics continue to disagree on the answers.

The novel's merits and faults remained vigorously debated throughout the nineteenth century, with much discussion centered on how well Foster represented the factual story of Elizabeth Whitman. In the late nineteenth century critics increasingly came to the defense of Whitman's character. Caroline Dall, in 1875, claimed that Whitman had been secretly married before her death; Mary C. Crawford, in 1903, agreed, adding that Foster had "maliciously misrepresented" Whitman's character, and dismissed *The Coquette* as "crudely sensational." Interest in *The Coquette* has rarely waned since its publication, though in the early twentieth century some critics considered it largely as a representative text of what Herbert Ross Brown, in 1939, referred to as the "sentimental, 'handkerchiefly' novels written somewhat apologetically by American women in the eighteenth century." In more recent decades, scholarship has placed a more serious emphasis on *The Coquette*'s relationship to some of the central social concerns of its era—but Elizabeth Whitman remains at the core of many analyses.

After *The Coquette*, Foster published only one further novel, *The Boarding School; or, Lessons of a Preceptress to Her Pupils* (1798). Presented largely as a series of letters between a teacher and her students at a girls' academy, the novel was less successful than *The Coquette*, and has received less attention from scholars, many of whom have found it to be overly didactic and disjointed in its narrative—and on both counts have compared it unfavorably with *The Coquette*. Nevertheless, scholarship focused on *The Boarding School* has seen an increase in the twenty-first century, as readers have become more interested in the development of female education in the early United States.

After the death of her husband in 1829, Foster moved to Montreal, where two of her daughters, both of whom had also become successful authors, then resided. Foster died in 1840. Her authorship of *The Coquette* was first openly acknowledged in 1855, in the introduction to an edition which appeared that year; the first edition to carry her name on the title page was published in 1866.

NOTE ON THE TEXT: The text presented below is based on the 1797 first edition of *The Coquette; or, The History of Eliza Wharton; a Novel; Founded on Fact. By a Lady of Massachusetts*. Spelling and punctuation have been modernized in accordance with the practices of this anthology; Foster's occasional inconsistency in her use of American and British spellings, however, has been retained.

⌘ ⌘ ⌘

The Coquette;[1] or, The History of Eliza Wharton; a Novel; Founded on Fact

LETTER 1
TO MISS LUCY FREEMAN

New-Haven

An unusual sensation possesses my breast; a sensation which I once thought could never pervade it on any occasion whatever. It is *pleasure*; pleasure, my dear Lucy, on leaving my paternal roof! Could you have believed that the darling child of an indulgent and dearly beloved mother would feel a gleam of joy at leaving her? but so it is. The melancholy, the gloom, the condolence which surrounded me for a month after the death of Mr. Haly, had depressed my spirits, and palled every enjoyment of life. Mr. Haly was a man of worth; a man of real and substantial merit. He is therefore deeply and justly regretted by *his* friends; he was chosen to be a future guardian and companion for me, and was, therefore, beloved by *mine*. As their choice; as a good man, and a faithful friend, I esteemed him. But no one acquainted with the disparity of our tempers and dispositions, our views and designs, can suppose my heart much engaged in the alliance. Both nature and education had instilled into my mind an implicit obedience to the will and desires of my parents. To them, of course, I sacrificed my fancy in this affair; determined that my reason should concur with theirs; and on that to risk my future happiness. I was the more encouraged, as I saw from our first acquaintance his declining health, and expected that the event[2] would prove as it has. Think not, however, that I rejoice in his death. No; far be it from me; for though I believe that I never felt the passion of love for Mr. Haly, yet a habit of conversing with him, of hearing daily the most virtuous, tender, and affectionate sentiments from his lips, inspired emotions of the sincerest friendship and esteem.

He is gone. His fate is unalterably and, I trust, happily fixed. He lived the life, and died the death of the righteous. O that my last end may be like his! This event will, I hope, make a suitable and abiding impression upon my mind, teach me the fading nature of all sublunary[3] enjoyments, and the little dependence which is to be placed on earthly felicity. Whose situation was more agreeable, whose prospects more flattering, than Mr. Haly's? Social, domestic, and connubial joys were fondly anticipated, and friends and fortune seemed ready to crown every wish! Yet animated by still brighter hopes, he cheerfully bid them all adieu. In conversation with me, but a few days before his exit, "There is," said he, "but one link in the chain of life, undissevered; that, my dear Eliza, is my attachment to you. But God is wise and good in all his ways; and in this, as in all other respects, I would cheerfully say, His will be done."

You, my friend, were witness to the concluding scene; and therefore, I need not describe it.

I shall only add on the subject that if I have wisdom and prudence to follow his advice and example; if his prayers for my temporal and eternal welfare be heard and answered, I shall be happy indeed.

The disposition of mind which I now feel, I wish to cultivate. Calm, placid, and serene; thoughtful of my duty, and benevolent to all around me, I wish for no other connection than that of friendship.

This letter is all egotism, I have even neglected to mention the respectable and happy friends with whom I reside; but will do it in my next. Write soon, and often; and believe me sincerely yours,

Eliza Wharton

LETTER 2
TO THE SAME

New-Haven

Time, which effaces every occasional impression, I find gradually dispelling the pleasing pensiveness which the melancholy event, the subject of my last,[4] had dif-

[1] *Coquette* Derisive term for a woman who behaves provocatively, invites the attentions of men, and toys with the feelings of her admirers.

[2] *event* Outcome.

[3] *sublunary* Earthly.

[4] *my last* I.e., my last letter.

fused over my mind. Naturally cheerful, volatile, and unreflecting, the opposite disposition[1] I have found to contain sources of enjoyment which I was before unconscious of possessing.

My friends here are the picture of conjugal felicity. The situation is delightful. The visiting parties perfectly agreeable. Everything tends to facilitate the return of my accustomed vivacity. I have written to my mother, and received an answer. She praises my fortitude, and admires the philosophy[2] which I have exerted under what she calls my heavy bereavement. Poor woman! She little thinks that my heart was untouched; and when that is unaffected, other sentiments and passions make but a transient impression. I have been, for a month or two, excluded from the gay world; and, indeed, fancied myself soaring above it. It is now that I begin to descend and find my natural propensity for mixing in the busy scenes and active pleasures of life returning. I have received your letter; your moral lecture rather; and be assured, my dear, your monitorial[3] lessons and advice shall be attended to. I believe I shall never again resume those airs, which you term *coquettish*, but which I think deserve a softer appellation, as they proceed from an innocent heart, and are the effusions of a youthful and cheerful mind. We are all invited to spend the day tomorrow at Col. Farington's, who has an elegant seat in the neighbourhood. Both he and his Lady are strangers to me; but the friends by whom I am introduced will procure me a welcome reception. Adieu.

Eliza Wharton

LETTER 3
TO THE SAME

New-Haven

Is it time for me to talk again of conquests? or must I only enjoy them in silence? I must write to you the impulses of my mind; or I must not write at all. You are not so morose, as to wish me to become a nun, would our country and religion allow it. I ventured yesterday to throw aside the habiliments[4] of mourning, and to array myself in those more adapted to my taste. We arrived at Col. Farington's about one o'clock. The Col. handed me out of the carriage, and introduced me to a large company assembled in the Hall. My name was pronounced with an *emphasis*; and I was received with the most flattering tokens of respect. When we were summoned to dinner, a young gentleman in a clerical dress offered me his hand, and led me to a table furnished with an elegant and sumptuous repast, with more gallantry and address than commonly fall to the share of students. He sat opposite me at the table; and whenever I raised my eye, it caught his. The ease and politeness of his manners, with his particular attention to me, raised my curiosity, and induced me to ask Mrs. Laiton who he was? She told me that his name was Boyer; that he was descended from a worthy family; had passed with honor and applause through the university where he was educated; had since studied divinity with success; and now had a call to settle as a minister in one of the first parishes in a neighbouring state.

The gates of a spacious garden were thrown open, at this instant; and I accepted with avidity an invitation to walk in it. Mirth and hilarity prevailed, and the moments fled on downy wings, while we traced the beauties of art and nature so liberally displayed and so happily blended in this delightful retreat. An enthusiastic admirer of scenes like these, I had rambled some way from the company, when I was followed by Mrs. Laiton to offer her condolence on the supposed loss which I had sustained in the death of Mr. Haly. My heart rose against the woman, so ignorant of human nature as to think such conversation acceptable at such a time. I made her little reply and waved the subject, though I could not immediately dispel the gloom which it excited.

The absurdity of a custom authorizing people at a first interview to revive the idea of griefs which time has lulled, perhaps obliterated, is intolerable. To have our enjoyments arrested by the empty compliments of unthinking persons, for no other reason than a

[1] *the opposite disposition* I.e., the disposition of "pleasing pensiveness."

[2] *philosophy* Calm acceptance or composure.

[3] *monitorial* Admonishing.

[4] *habiliments* Clothes.

compliance with fashion, is to be treated in a manner which the laws of humanity forbid.

We were soon joined by the gentlemen, who each selected his partner, and the walk was prolonged.

Mr. Boyer offered me his arm, which I gladly accepted; happy to be relieved from the impertinence of my female companion. We returned to tea, after which the ladies sung, and played by turns on the pianoforte,[1] while some of the gentlemen accompanied with the flute, the clarinet, and the violin, forming in the whole a very decent concert. An elegant supper, and half an hour's conversation after it, closed the evening, when we returned home, delighted with our entertainment and pleased with ourselves and each other. My imagination is so impressed with the scenes of the day, that Morpheus waves his ebon-wand in vain.[2] The evening is fine beyond the power of description! All nature is serene and harmonious, in perfect unison with my present disposition of mind. I have been taking retrospect of my past life; and a few juvenile follies excepted, which I trust the recording angel had blotted out with the tear of charity, find an approving conscience and a heart at ease. Fortune, indeed, has not been very liberal of her gifts to me; but I presume on a large stock in the bank of friendship, which, united with health and innocence, give me some pleasing anticipations of future felicity.

Whatever my fate may be, I shall always continue your

Eliza Wharton

LETTER 4
TO MR. SELBY

New-Haven

You ask me, my friend, whether I am in pursuit of truth, or a lady? I answer, both. I hope and trust they are united, and really expect to find truth and the virtues and graces besides in a fair form. If you mean by the first part of your question, whether I am searching into the sublimer doctrines of religion? To these I would by no means be inattentive; but to be honest, my studies of that kind have been very much interrupted of late. The respectable circle of acquaintances with which I am honored here, has rendered my visits very frequent and numerous. In one of these I was introduced to Miss Eliza Wharton; a young lady whose elegant person, accomplished mind, and polished manners have been much celebrated. Her fame has often reached me; but, as the queen of Sheba said to Solomon, the half was not told me.[3] You will think that I talk in the style of a lover. I confess it, nor am I ashamed to rank myself among the professed admirers of this lovely fair one. I am in no danger, however, of becoming an enthusiastic devotee. No, I mean to act upon just and rational principals. Expecting soon to settle in an eligible situation, if such a companion as I am persuaded she will make me may fall to my lot, I shall deem myself as happy as this state of imperfection[4] will admit. She is now resident at Gen. Richman's. The general and his lady are her particular friends. They are warm in her praises. They tell me, however, that she is naturally of a gay disposition. No matter for that; it is an agreeable quality, where there is discretion sufficient for its regulation. A cheerful friend, much more a cheerful wife, is peculiarly necessary to a person of a studious and sedentary life. They dispel the gloom of retirement and exhilarate the spirits depressed by intense application. She was formerly addressed by the late Mr. Haly of Boston. He was not, it seems, the man of her choice; but her parents were extremely partial to him and wished the connection to take place. She, like a dutiful child, sacrificed her own inclination to their pleasure, so far as to acquiesce in his visits. This she more easily accomplished, as his health, which declined from their first acquaintance, led her to suppose, as the event has proved, that he would not live to enter into any lasting engagements. Her father, who died some months before him, invited him to reside at his house, for the

1 *pianoforte* Early form of piano.

2 *Morpheus ... vain* In Greek mythology, Morpheus is the god of sleep and dreams; he is sometimes depicted using a wand to induce sleep; *ebon* Ebony.

3 *queen of Sheba ... not told me* In 1 Kings 10.4–7, the Queen of Sheba visits the Israelite King Solomon to see his rumored wealth for herself; when she sees the true extent of his riches, she remarks that "the half was not told me: thy wisdom and prosperity exceedeth the fame which I heard."

4 *state of imperfection* I.e., the condition of humanity.

benefit of a change of air, agreeably to the advice of his physicians. She attended him during his last illness, with all the care and assiduity of a nurse; and with all the sympathising tenderness of a sister.

I have had several opportunities of conversing with her. She discovers[1] an elevated mind, a ready apprehension, and an accurate knowledge of the various subjects which have been brought into view. I have not yet introduced the favorite subject of my heart. Indeed she seems studiously to avoid noticing any expression which leads towards it. But she must hear it soon. I am sure of the favor and interest of the friends with whom she resides. They have promised to speak previously in my behalf. I am to call as if accidentally this afternoon, just as they are to ride abroad. They are to refer me to Miss Wharton for entertainment, till their return. What a delightful opportunity for my purpose! I am counting the hours, nay, the very moments. Adieu. You shall soon hear again from your most obedient,

J. Boyer

LETTER 5
TO MISS LUCY FREEMAN

New-Haven

These bewitching charms of mine have a tendency to keep my mind in a state of perturbation. I am so pestered with these admirers; not that I am so very handsome neither; but I don't know how it is, I am certainly very much the taste of the other sex. Followed, flattered, and caressed; I have cards and compliments in profusion. But I must try to be serious; for I have, alas! one serious lover. As I promised you to be particular in my writing, I suppose I must proceed methodically. Yesterday we had a party to dine. Mr. Boyer was of the number. His attention was immediately engrossed; and I soon perceived that every word, every action, and every look was studied to gain my approbation. As he sat next to me at dinner, his assiduity and politeness were pleasing; and as we walked together afterwards, his conversation was improving. Mine was sentimental

and sedate; perfectly adapted to the taste of my gallant. Nothing, however, was said particularly expressive of his apparent wishes. I studiously avoided every kind of discourse which might lead to this topic. I wish not for a declaration from anyone, especially from one whom I could not repulse and do not intend to encourage at present. His conversation, so similar to what I had often heard from a similar character, brought a deceased friend to mind, and rendered me somewhat pensive. I retired directly after supper. Mr. Boyer had just taken leave.

Mrs. Richman came into my chamber as she was passing to her own. Excuse my intrusion, Eliza, said she; I thought I would just step in and ask you if you have passed a pleasant day?

Perfectly so, madam; and I have now retired to protract the enjoyment by recollection. What, my dear, is your opinion of our favorite Mr. Boyer? Declaring him your favorite, madam, is sufficient to render me partial to him. But to be frank, independent of that, I think him an agreeable man. Your heart, I presume, is now free? Yes, and I hope it will long remain so. Your friends, my dear, solicitous for your welfare, wish to see you suitably and agreeably connected. I hope my friends will never again interpose in my concerns of that nature. You, madam, who have ever known my heart, are sensible that had the Almighty spared life, in a certain instance, I must have sacrificed my own happiness, or incurred their censure. I am young, gay, volatile. A melancholy event has lately extricated me from those shackles, which parental authority had imposed on my mind. Let me then enjoy that freedom which I so highly prize. Let me have opportunity, unbiassed by opinion, to gratify my natural disposition in a participation of those pleasures which youth and innocence afford. Of such pleasures, no one, my dear, would wish to deprive you. But beware, Eliza! Though strewed with flowers when contemplated by your lively imagination, it is, after all, a slippery, thorny path. The round of fashionable dissipation is dangerous. A phantom is often pursued, which leaves its deluded votary[2] the real form of wretchedness. She spoke with an emphasis, and taking up her candle, wished me a good night. I had not power to return the compliment. Something seemingly prophetic in her looks and expressions, cast

[1] *discovers* Exhibits, reveals.

[2] *votary* Enthusiast, devotee.

a momentary gloom upon my mind! But I despise those contracted ideas which confine virtue to a cell. I have no notion of becoming a recluse. Mrs. Richman has ever been a beloved friend of mine; yet I always thought her rather prudish. Adieu,

Eliza Wharton

LETTER 6
TO THE SAME

New-Haven

I had scarcely seated myself at the breakfast table this morning, when a servant entered with a card of invitation from Major Sanford, requesting the happiness of my hand this evening at a ball given by Mr. Atkins, about three miles from this. I showed the billet[1] to Mrs. Richman, saying, I have not much acquaintance with this gentleman, madam; but I suppose his character sufficiently respectable to warrant an affirmative answer. He is a gay man, my dear, to say no more, and such are the companions we wish, when we join a party avowedly formed for pleasure. I then stepped into my apartment, wrote an answer, and dispatched the servant. When I returned to the parlour, something disapprobating appeared in the countenances of both my friends. I endeavoured, without seeming to observe, to dissipate it by chit chat; but they were better pleased with each other than with me, and soon rising, walked into the garden, and left me to amuse myself alone. My eyes followed them through the window. Happy pair, said I. Should it ever be my fate to wear the hymenial chain,[2] may I be thus united! The purest and most ardent affection, the greatest consonance of taste and disposition, and the most congenial virtue and wishes distinguish this lovely couple. Health and wealth, with every attendant blessing preside over their favored dwelling and shed their benign influence without alloy. The consciousness of exciting their displeasure gave me pain; but I consoled myself with the idea that it was ill founded.

They should consider, said I, that they have no satisfaction to look for beyond each other.

There every enjoyment is centered; but I am a poor solitary being, who need some amusement beyond what I can supply myself. The mind, after being confined at home for a while, sends the imagination abroad in quest of new treasures, and the body may as well accompany it, for ought I can see.

General Richman and lady have ever appeared solicitous to promote my happiness since I have resided with them. They have urged my acceptance of invitations to join parties, though they have not been much themselves, of late; as Mrs. Richman's present circumstances render her fond of retirement. What reason can be assigned for their apparent reluctance to this evening's entertainment is to me incomprehensible; but I shall apply the chymical[3] powers of friendship and extract the secret from Mrs. Richman tomorrow, if not before. Adieu. I am now summoned to dinner, and after that shall be engaged in preparation till the wished for hour of hilarity and mirth engrosses every faculty of your

Eliza Wharton

LETTER 7
TO MR. SELBY

New-Haven

Divines[4] need not declaim, nor philosophers expatiate on the disappointments of human life! Are they not legibly written on every page of our existence? Are they not predominantly prevalent over every period of our lives?

When I closed my last letter to you, my heart exulted in the pleasing anticipation of promised bliss; my wishes danced on the light breezes of hope, and my imagination dared to arrest the attention, and even claim a return of affection from the lovely Eliza Wharton! But imagination only, it has proved; and that dashed with the bitter ranklings of jealousy and suspicion.

[1] *billet* Informal note.

[2] *hymenial chain* Bonds of marriage. Hymen is the Greek god of marriage.

[3] *chymical* Alchemical; i.e., magical, transformative.

[4] *Divines* Members of the clergy.

But to resume my narrative. I reached the mansion of my friend about four. I was disagreeably stuck with the appearance of a carriage at the door, as it raised an idea of company which might frustrate my plan; but still more disagreeable were my sensations when, on entering the parlour, I found Major Sanford evidently in a waiting posture. I was very politely received; and when Eliza entered the room with a brilliance of appearance and gaiety of manner, which I had never connected with her character, I rose, as did Major Sanford who offered his hand, and led her to a chair. I forgot to sit down again, but stood transfixed by the pangs of disappointment. Miss Wharton appeared somewhat confused; but soon resuming her vivacity, desired me to be seated; inquired after my health, and made some commonplace remarks on the weather. Then apologizing for leaving me, gave her hand again to Major Sanford, who had previously risen, and reminded her that the time and their engagements made it necessary to leave the good company; which, indeed, they both appeared very willing to do. General Richman and the lady[1] took every method in their power to remove my chagrin and atone for the absence of my fair one, but ill did they succeed. They told me that Miss Wharton had not the most distant idea of my visiting there this afternoon, much less of the design[2] of my visit; that for some months together, she had been lately confined by the sickness of Mr. Haly, whom she attended during the whole of his last illness; which confinement had eventually increased her desire of indulging her natural disposition for gaiety. She had, however, they said, an excellent heart and reflecting mind, a great share of sensibility,[3] and a temper peculiarly formed for the enjoyments of social life. But this gentleman, madam, who is her gallant this evening—is his character unexceptionable? Will a lady of delicacy associate with an immoral, not to say profligate man? The rank and fortune of Major Sanford, said Mrs. Richman, procure him respect.

His specious[4] manners render him acceptable in public company; but I must own that he is not the person with whom I wish my cousin to be connected, even for a moment. She never consulted me so little on any subject as on that of his card this morning. Before I had time to object, she dismissed the servant; and I forbore to destroy her happiness, by acquainting her with my disapprobation of her partner. Her omission was not design; it was juvenile indiscretion. We must, my dear sir, continued she, look with a candid eye on such eccentricities. Faults, not foibles, require the severity of censure. Far, madam, be it from me to censure any conduct, which as yet I have observed in Miss Wharton; she has too great an interest in my heart to admit of that.

We now went into more general conversation. Tea was served; and I soon after took leave. General Richman, however, insisted on my dining with him on Thursday, which I promised. And here I am again over head and ears in the hypo.[5] A disease, you will say, peculiar to students. I believe it peculiar to lovers; and with that class I must now rank myself, though I did not know, until this evening, that I was so much engaged as I find I really am. I knew, indeed, that I was extremely pleased with this amiable girl; that I was interested in her favor; that I was happier in her company than anywhere else, with innumerable other circumstances which would have told me the truth, had I examined them. But be that as it may; I hope and trust that I am, and ever shall be, a reasonable creature; and not suffer my judgment to be misled by the operations of a blind passion.

I shall now lay aside this subject, endeavor to divest even my imagination of the charmer, and return, until Thursday, to the contemplation of those truths and duties, which have a happy tendency to calm the jarring elements which compose our mortal frame. Adieu.

J. Boyer

1 *the lady* I.e., Mrs. Richman.

2 *design* Plan or purpose.

3 *sensibility* Heightened emotional or aesthetic awareness.

4 *specious* Deceptively pleasant.

5 *hypo* I.e., low spirits, melancholy, or anxiety.

LETTER 8
TO MR. CHARLES DEIGHTON

New-Haven

We had an elegant ball last night, Charles; and what is still more to the taste of your old friend, I had an elegant partner; one exactly calculated to please my fancy: gay, volatile, apparently thoughtless of everything but present enjoyment. It was Miss Eliza Wharton, a young lady whose agreeable person, polished manners, and refined talents have rendered her the toast of the country around for these two years; though for half that time she has had a clerical lover imposed on her by her friends; for I am told it was not agreeable to her inclination. By this same clerical lover of hers, she was for several months confined as a nurse. But his death has happily relieved her, and she now returns to the world with redoubled lustre. At present she is a visitor to Mrs. Richman, who is a relation. I first saw her on a party of pleasure at Mr. Frazier's, where we walked, talked, sung, and danced together. I thought her cousin watched her with a jealous eye; for she is, you must know, a prude; and immaculate, more so than you or I must be the man who claims admission to her society. But I fancy this young lady is a coquette; and if so, I shall avenge my sex, by retaliating the mischiefs she meditates against us. Not that I have any ill designs; but only to play off her own artillery, by using a little unmeaning gallantry. And let her beware of the consequences. A young clergyman came in at Gen. Richman's yesterday, while I was waiting for Eliza, who was much more cordially received by the general and his lady, than was your humble servant: but I lay that up.

When she entered the room, an air of mutual embarrassment was evident. The lady recovered her assurance much more easily than the gentleman. I am just going to ride, and shall make it in my way to call and inquire after the health of my dulcinea.[1] Therefore, adieu for the present.

Peter Sanford

[1] *dulcinea* Name of the idealized beloved of the title character in Miguel de Cervantes's novel *Don Quixote* (1605, 1615). *Dulce* means "sweet" in Spanish.

LETTER 9
TO MISS LUCY FREEMAN

New-Haven

I am not so happy today in the recollection of last evening's entertainment, as I was in the enjoyment.

The explanation which I promised you from Mrs. Richman yesterday, I could not obtain. When I went down to dinner, some friends of General Richman's had accidentally dropped in, which precluded all particular conversation. I retired soon to dress, and saw Mrs. Richman no more, till I was informed that Major Sanford waited for me. But I was surprised on going into the parlour to find Mr. Boyer there. I blushed and stammered; but I know not why; for certain I am, that I neither love nor fear the good man yet, whatever I may do some future day. I would not be understood that I do not respect and esteem him; for I do both. But these are calm passions, which soothe rather than agitate the mind. It was not the consciousness of any impropriety of conduct; for I was far from feeling any. The entertainment for which I was prepared was such as virtue would not disapprove, and my gallant was a man of fortune, fashion, and for ought I knew, of unblemished character.

But Mr. Boyer was much more disconcerted than myself. Indeed he did not recover his philosophy while I stayed. I believe, by some hints I have received since, that he had some particular views, in which he was disappointed.

Our ball had every charm which could render a ball delightful. My partner was all ease, politeness, and attention; and your friend was as much flattered and caressed as variety itself could wish. We returned to General Richman's about two. Major Sanford asked leave to call and inquire after my health, this morning, and I am now expecting him. I rose to breakfast. The late hour of retiring to rest had not depressed, but rather exhilarated my spirits. My friends were waiting for me in the parlor. They received me sociably, inquired after my health, my last evening's entertainment, the company, etc. When, after a little pause, Mrs. Richman said, and how do you like Major Sanford, Eliza? Very well indeed, madam: I think him a finished[2] gentleman. Will you, who are a

[2] *finished* Accomplished; complete.

connoisseur, allow him that title? No, my dear; in my opinion, he falls far below it; since he is deficient in one of the great essentials of the character, and that is, *virtue*. I am surprised, said I: but how has he incurred so severe a censure? By being a professed libertine; by having but too successfully practised the arts of seduction; by triumphing in the destruction of innocence and the peace of families!

O, why was I not informed of this before? But, perhaps, these are old affairs; the effects of juvenile folly; crimes of which he may have repented, and which charity ought to obliterate. No, my dear, they are recent facts; facts which he dares not deny; facts for which he ought to be banished from all virtuous society. I should have intimated this to you before, but your precipitate acceptance of his invitation deprived me of an opportunity, until it was too late to prevent your going with him; and we thought it best to protract your enjoyment as long as possible, not doubting but your virtue and delicacy would, in future, guard you against the like deception.

Must I then become an avowed prude at once; and refuse him admission, if he call, in compliance with the customary forms? By no means. I am sensible that even the false maxims of the world must be complied with in a degree. But a man of Major Sanford's art can easily distinguish between a forbidding, and an encouraging reception. The former may, in this case, be given without any breach of the rules of politeness. Astonished, and mortified, I knew not what further to say. I had been so pleased with the man, that I wished to plead in his favor; but virtue and prudence forbade. I therefore rose and retired. He is this moment, I am told, below stairs. So that I must bid you adieu, until the next post.

Eliza Wharton

LETTER 10
TO THE SAME

New-Haven

Upon closing my last, I walked down, and found Major Sanford alone. He met me at the door of the parlor; and taking my hand with an air of affectionate tenderness, led me to a seat, and took one beside me. I believe the gloom of suspicion had not entirely forsaken my brow. He appeared, however, not to notice it; but after the compliments of the day had passed, entered into an easy and agreeable conversation on the pleasures of society: a conversation perfectly adapted to my taste, and calculated to dissipate my chagrin, and pass the time imperceptibly. He inquired the place of my native abode; and having informed him, he said he had thoughts of purchasing the seat of Capt. Pribble, in that neighborhood, for his residence; and could he be assured of my society and friendship, his resolution would be fixed. I answered his compliment only by a slight bow. He took leave, and I retired to dress for the day, being engaged to accompany my cousin to dine at Mr. Laurence's, a gentleman of fortune and fashion, in this vicinity. Mr. Laurence has but one daughter, heiress to a large estate, with an agreeable form, but a countenance, which to me, indicates not much soul. I was surprised in the afternoon to see Major Sanford alight at the gate. He entered with the familiarity of an old acquaintance; and, after accosting each of the company, told me, with a low bow, that he did not expect the happiness of seeing me again so soon. I received his compliment with a conscious awkwardness. Mrs. Richman's morning lecture still rung in my head; and her watchful eye now traced every turn of mine, and every action of the major's. Indeed, his assiduity was painful to me; yet I found it impossible to disengage myself a moment from him, till the close of the day brought our carriage to the door; when he handed me in, and, pressing my hand to his lips, retired.

What shall I say about this extraordinary man? Shall I own to you, my friend, that he is pleasing to me? His person, his manners, his situation, all combine to charm my fancy; and to my lively imagination, strew the path of life with flowers. What a pity, my dear Lucy, that the graces and virtues are not oftener united! They must, however, meet in the man of my choice; and till I find such a one, I shall continue to subscribe my name

Eliza Wharton

LETTER 11
TO MR. CHARLES DEIGHTON

New-Haven

Well, Charles, I have been maneuvering today, a little revengefully. That, you will say, is out of character. So baleful a passion does not easily find admission among those softer ones, which you well know I cherish. However, I am a mere Proteus[1] and can assume any shape that will best answer my purpose.

I called this forenoon, as I told you I intended, at Gen. Richman's. I waited some time in the parlor alone, before Eliza appeared; and when she did appear, the distant reserve of her manners and the pensiveness of her countenance convinced me that she had been vexed, and I doubted not but Peter Sanford was the occasion. Her wise cousin, I could have sworn, had been giving her a detail of the vices of her gallant and warning her against the danger of associating with him in future. Notwithstanding, I took no notice of any alteration in her behavior; but entered with the utmost facetiousness into a conversation which I thought most to her taste. By degrees, she assumed her usual vivacity; cheerfulness and good humor again animated her countenance. I tarried as long as decency would admit. She having intimated that they were to dine at my friend Laurence's, I caught at this information; and determined to follow them and tease the jealous[2] Mrs. Richman, by playing off all the gallantry I was master of in her presence.

I went, and succeeded to the utmost of my wishes, as I read in the vexation, visible in the one; and the ease and attention displayed by the other. I believe too, that I have charmed the eye, at least, of the amiable Eliza. Indeed, Charles, she is a fine girl. I think it would hurt my conscience to wound her mind or reputation. Were I disposed to marry, I am persuaded she would make an excellent wife; but that you know is no part of my plan, so long as I can keep out of the noose. Whenever I do submit to be shackled, it must be from a necessity of mending my fortune. This girl would be far from doing that. However, I am pleased with her acquaintance, and mean not to abuse her credulity and good nature, if I can help it.

Peter Sanford

LETTER 12
TO MISS LUCY FREEMAN

New-Haven

The heart of your friend is again besieged. Whether it will surrender to the assailants or not, I am unable at present to determine. Sometimes I think of becoming a predestinarian,[3] and submitting implicitly to fate, without any exercise of free will; but, as mine seems to be a wayward one, I would counteract the operations of it, if possible.

Mrs. Richman told me this morning that she hoped I should be as agreeably entertained this afternoon, as I had been the preceding; that she expected Mr. Boyer to dine and take tea; and doubted not but he would be as attentive and sincere to me, if not as gay and polite, as the gentleman who obtruded his civilities yesterday. I replied that I had no reason to doubt the sincerity of the one, or the other, having never put them to the test, nor did I imagine I ever should. Your friends, Eliza, said she, would be very happy to see you united to a man of Mr. Boyer's worth; and so agreeably settled, as he has a prospect of being. I hope, said I, that my friends are not so weary of my company, as to wish to dispose of me. I am too happy in my present connections to quit them for new ones. Marriage is the tomb of friendship. It appears to me a very selfish state. Why do people, in general, as soon as they are married, centre all their cares, their concerns, and pleasures in their own families? Former acquaintances are neglected or forgotten. The tenderest ties between friends are weakened, or dissolved; and benevolence itself moves in a very limited sphere. It is the glory of the marriage state, she rejoined, to refine, by circumscribing our enjoyments. Here we can repose in safety.

[1] *Proteus* Greek sea-god capable of changing into any form he wishes.

[2] *jealous* Vigilantly protective, suspicious.

[3] *predestinarian* One who believes in the Calvinist tenet of predestination, which posits that all souls are marked by God as bound either for Heaven or Hell, and that no human action has any effect on these pre-ordained fates.

The friendships of the world are oft
Confed'racies in vice, or leagues in pleasure:
Our's has the purest virtue for its basis;
And such friendship ends not but with life.[1]

True, we cannot always pay that attention to former associates which we may wish; but the little community which we superintend is quite as important an object; and certainly renders us more beneficial to the public. True benevolence, though it may change its objects, is not limited by time or place. Its effects are the same, and, aided by a second self, are rendered more diffusive and salutary.

Some pleasantry passed, and we retired to dress. When summoned to dinner, I found Mr. Boyer below. If what is sometimes said be true, that love is diffident, reserved, and unassuming, this man must be tinctured with it. These symptoms were visible in his deportment when I entered the room. However, he soon recovered himself, and the conversation took a general turn. The festive board was crowned with sociability, and we found in reality, "The feast of reason, and the flow of soul."[2] After we rose from table, a walk in the garden was proposed, an amusement we are all peculiarly fond of. Mr. Boyer offered me his arm. When at a sufficient distance from our company, he begged leave to congratulate himself on having an opportunity which he had ardently desired for some time, of declaring to me his attachment; and of soliciting an interest in my favor; or, if he might be allowed the term, affection. I replied, that, Sir, is indeed laying claim to an important interest. I believe you must substitute some more indifferent epithet for the present. Well then, said he, if it must be so, let it be esteem, or friendship. Indeed, Sir, said I, you are entitled to them both. Merit has always a share in that bank; and I know of none who has a larger claim on that score, than Mr. Boyer. I suppose my manner was hardly serious enough for what he considered a weighty cause. He was a little disconcerted; but soon regaining his presence of mind, entreated me, with an air of earnestness, to encourage his suit, to admit his addresses, and, if possible,

to reward his love. I told him, that this was rather a sudden affair to me; and that I could not answer him without consideration. Well then, said he, take what time you think proper, only relieve my suspense as soon as may be. Shall I visit you again tomorrow? O, not so soon, said I. Next Monday, I believe will be early enough. I will endeavor to be at home. He thanked me even for that favor, recommended himself once more to my kindness; and we walked towards the company, returned with them to the house, and he soon took leave. I immediately retired to write this letter, which I shall close, without a single observation on the subject, until I know your opinion.

Eliza Wharton

LETTER 13
TO MISS ELIZA WHARTON

Hartford

And so you wish to have my opinion before you know the result of your own. This is playing a little too much with my patience. But, however, I will gratify you this once, in hopes that my epistle may have a good effect. You will ask, perhaps, whether I would influence your judgment? I answer, no; provided you will exercise it yourself; but I am a little apprehensive that your fancy will mislead you. Methinks I can gather from your letters a predilection for this Major Sanford. But he is a rake,[3] my dear friend; and can a lady of your delicacy and refinement, think of forming a connection with a man of that character? I hope not. Nay, I am confident you do not. You mean only to exhibit a few more girlish airs, before you turn matron. But I am persuaded, if you wish to lead down the dance of life with regularity, you will not find a more excellent partner than Mr. Boyer. Whatever you can reasonably expect in a lover, husband, or friend, you may perceive to be united in this worthy man. His taste is undebauched, his manners not vitiated, his morals uncorrupted. His situation in life is, perhaps, as elevated as you have a right to claim. Forgive my plainness, Eliza. It is the task

[1] *The friendships ... with life* See Joseph Addison's 1712 play *Cato: A Tragedy* 3.1.7–10.

[2] *The feast ... flow of soul* See *The First Satire of the Second Book of Horace* (1733) by Alexander Pope, line 128.

[3] *rake* Fashionable man, usually of high social status, who is driven by pleasure and has a habit of seducing women.

of friendship sometimes to tell disagreeable truths. I know your ambition is to make a distinguished figure in the first class of polished society; to shine in the gay circle of fashionable amusements, and to bear off the palm[1] amidst the votaries of pleasure. But these are fading honors, unsatisfactory enjoyments; incapable of gratifying those immortal principles of reason and religion which have been implanted in your mind by nature; assiduously cultivated by the best of parents, and exerted, I trust, by yourself. Let me advise you then, in conducting this affair, an affair big,[2] perhaps, with your future fate, to lay aside those coquettish airs which you sometimes put on; and remember that you are not dealing with a fop,[3] who will take advantage of every concession; but with a man of sense and honor, who will properly estimate your condescension and frankness. Act then with that modest freedom, that dignified unreserve which bespeaks conscious rectitude and sincerity of heart.

I shall be extremely anxious to hear the process and progress of this business. Relieve my impatience, as soon as possible, and believe me yours, with undissembled affection.

Lucy Freeman

LETTER 14
TO MISS LUCY FREEMAN

New-Haven

I have received, and read again and again, your friendly epistle. My reason and judgment entirely coincide with your opinion; but my fancy claims some share in the decision, and I cannot yet tell which will preponderate. This was the day fixed for deciding Mr. Boyer's cause. My friends here gave me a long dissertation on his merits. Your letter, likewise, had its weight, and I was candidly summing up the *pros* and *cons* in the garden, whither I had walked (Gen. Richman and lady having rode out) when I was informed that he was waiting in the parlor. I went immediately in (a good symptom,

you will say) and received him graciously. After the first compliments were over, he seemed eager to improve the opportunity to enter directly on the subject of his present visit. It is needless for me to recite to you, who have long been acquainted with the whole process of courtship, the declarations, propositions, protestations, entreaties, looks, words and actions of a lover. They are, I believe, much the same in the whole sex, allowing for their different dispositions, educations, and characters. But you are impatient I know for the conclusion. You have hastily perused the preceding lines, and are straining your eye forward to my part of the farce; for such it may prove after all. Well then, not to play too long with the curiosity, which I know to be excited, and actuated by real friendship, I will relieve it. I think you would have been pleased to have seen my gravity, on this important occasion. With all the candor and frankness which I was capable of assuming, I thus answered his long harangue, to which I had listened, without interrupting him. Self-knowledge, sir, that most important of all sciences, I have yet to learn. Such have been my situations in life, and the natural volatility of my temper, that I have looked but little into my own heart, in regard to its future wishes and views. From a scene of constraint and confinement, ill suited to my years and inclination, I have just launched into society. My heart beats high in expectation of its fancied joys. My sanguine imagination paints, in alluring colors, the charms of youth and freedom, regulated by virtue and innocence. Of these, I wish to partake. While I own myself under obligations for the esteem which you are pleased to profess for me, and in return, acknowledge, that neither your person nor manners are disagreeable to me, I recoil at the thought of immediately forming a connection, which must confine me to the duties of domestic life, and make me dependent for happiness, perhaps too, for subsistence, upon a class of people, who will claim the right of scrutinising every part of my conduct; and by censuring those foibles, which I am conscious of not having prudence to avoid, may render me completely miserable. While, therefore, I receive your visits, and cultivate towards you sentiments of friendship and esteem, I would not have you consider me as confined to your society, or obligated to a future connection. Our short acquaintance renders it impossible for me to decide what the operations

[1] *bear off the palm* Claim victory, of which the palm is a symbol.

[2] *big* Literally, pregnant; here, full of potential or significance.

[3] *fop* Vain or conceited man; dandy.

of my mind may hereafter be. You must either quit the subject, or leave me to the exercise of my free will, which perhaps may coincide with your present wishes. Madam, said he, far is the wish from me to restrain your person or mind. In your breast I will repose my cause. It shall be my study to merit a return of affection; and I doubt not but generosity and honor will influence your conduct towards me. I expect soon to settle among a generous and enlightened people, where I flatter myself I shall be exempt from those difficulties, and embarrassments, to which too many of my brethren are subject. The local situation is agreeable, the society refined and polished; and if, in addition, I may obtain that felicity which you are formed to bestow, in a family connection, I shall be happy indeed.

He spoke with emphasis. The tear of sensibility sparkled in his eye. I involuntarily gave him my hand, which he pressed with ardor to his lips. Then rising, he walked to the window to conceal his emotion. I rang the bell and ordered tea; during, and after which, we shared that social converse which is the true zest of life, and in which, I am persuaded, none but virtuous minds can participate. General Richman and lady returned with the shades of the evening. The penetrating eye of my cousin traced in *our* countenances the progress of the cause, and the smile of approbation animated *hers*. Mr. Boyer asked the favor of my company to ride tomorrow morning, which was granted. He tarried to supper, and took his leave. I retired immediately to my chamber, to which I was followed by Mrs. Richman. I related to her the conversation, and the encouragement which I had given to Mr. Boyer. She was pleased; but insisted that I should own myself somewhat engaged to him. This, I told her I should never do to any man, before the indissoluble knot is tied. That, said I, will be time enough to resign my freedom. She replied that I had wrong ideas of freedom, and matrimony; but she hoped that Mr. Boyer would happily rectify them.

I have now, my dear friend, given you an account of my present situation, and leave you to judge for yourself concerning it. Write me your opinion, and believe me ever yours.

Eliza Wharton

LETTER 15
TO MISS ELIZA WHARTON

Hartford

I congratulate you, my dear Eliza, on the stability of your conduct towards Mr. Boyer. Pursue the system which you have adopted, and I dare say that happiness will crown your future days. You are indeed very tenacious of your freedom, as you call it; but that is a play about words. A man of Mr. Boyer's honor and good sense will never abridge any privileges which virtue can claim.

When do you return to embellish our society, here? I am impatient to see you, and likewise this amiable man. I am much interested in his favor. By the way, I am told that Major Sanford has been to look at the seat of Captain Pribble, which is upon sale. It is reported that he will probably purchase it. Many of our gentry are pleased with the prospect of such a neighbor. As an accomplished gentleman, say they, he will be an agreeable addition to our social parties; and as a man of property, and public spirit, he will be an advantage to the town; but, from what I have heard of him, I am far from supposing him a desirable acquisition in either of these respects. A man of a vicious character cannot be a good member of society. In order to that,[1] his principles and practice must be uncorrupted: in his morals, at least, he must be a man of probity and honor. Of these qualifications, if I mistake not, this gallant of yours cannot boast. But I shall not set up for a censor. I hope neither you nor I shall have much connection with him. My swain[2] interests himself very much in your affairs. You will possibly think him impertinent; but I give his curiosity a softer name. Should I own to you that I place great confidence in his integrity and honor, you would, perhaps, laugh at my weakness; but, my dear, I have pride enough to keep me above coquetry, or prudery; and discretion enough, I hope, to secure me from the errors of both. With him I have determined to walk the future round of life. What folly then would it be to affect reserve and distance, relative to an affair in which I have so much interest? Not

[1] *In order to that* In order to be that.

[2] *swain* Suitor.

that I am going to betray your secrets. These I have no right to divulge; but I must be the judge what may, and what may not be communicated. I am very much pressed for an early day of consummation; but I shall not listen to a request of that kind, till your return. Such is my regard for you, that a union of love would be imperfect, if friendship attended not the rites. Adieu.

Lucy Freeman

LETTER 16
TO MISS LUCY FREEMAN

New-Haven

We go on charmingly here; almost as soft and smooth as your ladyship. It seems to me that love must stagnate, if it have not a light breeze of discord once in a while to keep it in motion. We have not tried any yet, however. We had a lovely tour this forenoon; were out three long hours, and returned to dinner in perfect harmony.

Mr. Boyer informed me that he should set out tomorrow morning for his future residence, and soon put on the sacred bands.[1] He solicited an epistolary correspondence, at the same time, as an alleviation of the care which that weighty charge would bring on his mind. I consented; telling him, that he must not expect anything more than general subjects from me.

We were somewhat interrupted in our confidential intercourse, in the afternoon, by the arrival of Major Sanford. I cannot say that I was not agreeably relieved. So sweet a repast, for several hours together, was rather sickening to my taste. My enamorato[2] looked a little mortified at the cheerful reception which I gave the intruder, and joined not so placidly in the social conversation as I could have wished.

When Mr. Boyer, after the Major took leave, pressed me to give him some assurance of my constancy, I only reminded him of the terms of our engagement. Seeing me decided, he was silent on the subject and soon bid

me an affectionate adieu; not expecting, as he told me, the pleasure of a personal interview again, for two or three months.

Thus far we have proceeded in this sober business. A good beginning, you will say. Perhaps it is. I do not, however, feel myself greatly interested in the progress of the negotiation. Time may consolidate my affections and enable me to fix them on some particular object. At present the most lively emotions of my heart are those of friendship; that friendship which I hope you will soon participate with your faithful

Eliza Wharton

LETTER 17
TO MR. SELBY

New-Haven

I have succeeded in my addresses to the lovely Eliza Wharton; as far at least as I had any reason to expect from our short acquaintance. I find the graces of her person and mind rise in my esteem; and have already enjoyed, in her society, some of the happiest hours of my life. She is kind, affable, and condescending;[3] yet I must own that I have not been able to infuse into her bosom the ardor which I feel in my own. I know that the native modesty of the sex would restrain the discovery; but there is an animation of countenance, which betrays the sensations of the heart, that I find wanting[4] in hers on this occasion.

I have just taken leave of my fair, and propose returning tomorrow morning; to take upon me the solemn charge, which lies with such weight upon my mind that I need every support, both human and divine. Eliza has promised to correspond with me. From this I anticipate a source of pleasure, which alone can atone for her absence. I am, etc.

J. Boyer

[1] *put on the sacred bands* Enter into the ministry.

[2] *enamorato* Italian: lover.

[3] *condescending* Agreeable, yielding.

[4] *wanting* Lacking.

Letter 18
to Mr. Charles Deighton

New-Haven

Do you know, Charles, that I have commenced[1] lover? I was always a general one; but now I am somewhat particular. I shall be the more interested, as I am likely to meet with difficulties; and it is the glory of a rake, as well as a Christian, to combat obstacles. This same Eliza, of whom I have told you, has really made more impression on my heart, than I was aware of; or than the sex, take them as they rise, are wont to do. But she is besieged by a priest (a likely lad though). I know not how it is, but they are commonly successful with the girls, even the gayest of them. This one, too, has the interest of all her friends, as I am told. I called yesterday at General Richman's, and found this pair together, apparently too happy in each other's society for my wishes. I must own, that I felt a glow of jealousy, which I never experienced before; and vowed revenge for the pain it gave me, though but momentary. Yet Eliza's reception of me was visibly cordial; nay, I fancied my company as pleasing to her as that which she had before. I tarried not long, but left him to the enjoyment of the pleasure which I flatter myself will be short-lived. O, I have another plan in my head; a plan of necessity, which, you know, is the mother of invention. It is this: I am very much courted and caressed by the family of Mr. Laurence, a man of large property in this neighborhood. He has only one child; a daughter, with whom I imagine the old folks intend to shackle me in the bonds of matrimony. The girl looks very well. She has no soul though, that I can discover. She is heiress, nevertheless, to a great fortune; and that is all the soul I wish for in a wife. In truth, Charles, I know of no other way to mend my circumstances. But lisp not a word of my embarrassments for your life. Show and equipage[2] are my hobby-horse; and if any female wish to share them with me, and will furnish me with the means of supporting them, I have no objection. Could I conform to the sober rules of wedded life, and renounce those dear enjoyments of dissipation in which I have so long indulged, I know not the lady in the world with whom I would sooner form a connection of this sort than with Eliza Wharton. But it will never do. If my fortune or hers were better, I would risk a union; but as they are, no idea of the kind can be admitted. I shall endeavor, notwithstanding, to enjoy her company as long as possible. Though I cannot possess her wholly myself, I will not tamely see her the property of another.

I am now going to call at General Richman's, in hopes of an opportunity to profess my devotion to her. I know I am not a welcome visitor to the family; but I am independent of their censure or esteem, and mean to act accordingly.

Peter Sanford

Letter 19
to Miss Lucy Freeman

New-Haven

I find the ideas of sobriety and domestic solitude I have been cultivating for three days past, somewhat deranged by the interruption of a visitor, with whom, I know, you will not be pleased. It is no other than Major Sanford. I was walking alone in the garden yesterday, when he suddenly appeared to my view. How happy am I, said he, seizing my hand, in this opportunity of finding you alone; an opportunity, Miss Wharton, which I must improve in expatiating on a theme that fills my heart, and solely animates my frame.

I was startled at his impetuosity and displeased with his freedom. Withdrawing my hand, I told him, that my retirement was sacred. He bowed submissively; begged pardon for his intrusion, alleged, that he found nobody but the servants in the house; that they informed him, I was alone in the garden, which intelligence was too pleasing for him to consult any forms of ceremony for the regulation of his conduct. He then went on rhapsodically to declare his passion, his suspicions that I was forming a connection with Mr. Boyer, which would effectually destroy all his hopes of future happiness. He painted the restraint, the confinement, the embarrassments to which a woman, connected with a man of Mr. Boyer's profession, must

[1] *commenced* Taken up the role of.

[2] *equipage* I.e., articles of fashionable life.

be subjected, however agreeable his person might be. He asked if my generous mind could submit to cares and perplexities like these; whether I could not find greater sources of enjoyment in a more elevated sphere of life, or share pleasures better suited to my genius and disposition, even in a single state? I listened to him involuntarily. My heart did not approve of his sentiments, but my ear was charmed with his rhetoric, and my fancy captivated by his address.

He invited my confidence by the most ardent professions of friendship, and labored to remove my suspicions by vows of sincerity. I was induced by his importunity gradually to disclose the state of affairs between Mr. Boyer and myself. He listened eagerly; wished not, he said, to influence me unduly; but if I were not otherwise engaged, might he presume to solicit a place in my friendship and esteem; be admitted to enjoy my society, to visit me as a acquaintance, and to attend my excursions and amusements, as a brother, if no more? I replied, that I was a pensioner of friendship, at present; that my friends were extremely refined in their notions of propriety, and that I had no right to receive visitants independent of them. I understand you, madam, said he. You intimate that my company is not agreeable to them, but I know not why. Surely my rank in life is as elevated; and my knowledge of, and acceptance in the world, are as extensive as General Richman's. I hope, said I, since we are engaged in the conversation, that you will excuse my frankness, if I tell you that the understanding and virtue of this worthy couple, induce them, without any regard to rank, to bestow their esteem wherever it is merited. I cannot say that you are not a sharer. Your own heart can best determine, whether upon their principles, you are, or not! He appeared mortified and chagrined; and we had walked some distance without exchanging a word, or a look. At last, he rejoined, I plead guilty to the charge, madam, which they have undoubtedly brought against me, of imprudence and folly in many particulars; yet of malignancy and vice I am innocent. Brought up in affluence; inured from my infancy to the gratification of every passion; the indulgence of every wish; it is not strange, that a life of dissipation and gaiety should prove alluring to a youthful mind, which had no care but to procure what it deemed enjoyment. In this

pursuit I have perhaps deviated from the rigid rules of discretion, and the harsher laws of morality.

But let the veil of charity be drawn over my faults; let the eye of candor impartially examine my present behavior; let the kind and lenient hand of friendship assist in directing my future steps; and, perhaps, I may not prove unworthy of associating with the respectable inhabitants of this happy mansion; for such I am sure it must be, while honored with Miss Wharton's presence. But, circumstanced as you and I are at present, I will not sue for your attention as a lover; but rest contented, if possible, with that share of kindness and regard, which your benevolence may afford me as a friend. I bowed in approbation of his resolution. He pressed my hand with ardor to his lips; and at that instant General Richman entered the garden. He approached us cheerfully, offered Major Sanford his hand with apparent cordiality, and told us pleasantly, that he hoped he should not be considered as an intruder. By no means, sir, said Major Sanford. It is I who have incurred that imputation. I called this afternoon to pay you my respects; when being informed that you and your lady were abroad, and that Miss Wharton was in the garden, I took the liberty to invade her retirement. She has graciously forgiven my crime, and I was just affixing the seal to my pardon as you entered.

We then returned into the house. Mrs. Richman received us politely. During tea, the conversation turned on literary subjects, in which I cannot say that the Major bore a very distinguished part. After he was gone, Mrs. Richman said, I hope you have been agreeably entertained, Miss Wharton? I did not choose my company, madam, said I. Nor, said she, did you refuse it, I presume. Would you not have me respect the rights of hospitality towards your guests when you are absent, madam? If you had acted from that motive, I own my obligations to you, my dear; but even that consideration can hardly reconcile me to the sacrifice of time, which you have made to the amusement of a seducer. I hope, madam, you do not think me an object of seduction! I do not think you seducible; nor was Richardson's Clarissa, till she made herself the victim by her own indiscretion. Pardon me, Eliza, this

is a second Lovelace.[1] I am alarmed by his artful intrusions. His insinuating attentions to you are characteristic of the man. Come, I presume you are not interested to keep his secrets, if you know them. Will you give me a little sketch of his conversation? Most willingly, said I; and, accordingly, related the whole. When I had concluded, she shook her head, and replied, beware, my friend, of his arts. Your own heart is too sincere to suspect treachery and dissimulation in another; but suffer not your ear to be charmed by the siren voice of flattery; nor your eye to be caught by the phantom of gaiety and pleasure. Remember your engagements to Mr. Boyer. Let sincerity and virtue be your guides, and they will lead you to happiness and peace. She waited not for an answer, but immediately rising, begged leave to retire, alleging that she was fatigued. Gen. Richman accompanied her, and I hastened to my apartment, where I have written thus far, and shall send it on for your comments. I begin to think of returning soon to your circle. One inducement is that I may be free from the intrusions of this man. Adieu.

Eliza Wharton

LETTER 20
TO MRS. M. WHARTON

New-Haven

From the conversation of the polite, the sedate, the engaging and the gay; from corresponding with the learned, the sentimental and the refined, my heart and my pen turn with ardor and alacrity to a tender and affectionate parent, the faithful guardian and guide of my youth; the unchanging friend of my riper years. The different dispositions of various associates, sometimes perplex the mind, which seeks direction; but in the disinterested affection of the maternal breast, we fear no dissonance of passion, no jarring interests,

no disunion of love. In this seat of felicity is every enjoyment which fancy can form, or friendship, with affluence, bestow; but still my mind frequently returns to the happy shades of my nativity. I wish there to impart my pleasures and share the counsels of my best, my long tried and experienced friend. At this time, my dear mamma, I am peculiarly solicitous for your advice. I am again importuned to listen to the voice of love; again called upon to accept the addresses of a gentleman of merit and respectability. You will know the character of the man, when I tell you, it is Mr. Boyer. But his situation in life! I dare not enter it. My disposition is not calculated for that sphere. There are duties arising from the station, which I fear I should not be able to fulfil; cares and restraints to which I could not submit. *This* man is not disagreeable to me; but if I must enter the connubial state, are there not *others*, who may be equally pleasing in their persons, and whose profession may be more conformable to my taste? You, madam, have passed through this scene of trial, with honor and applause. But alas! can your volatile daughter ever acquire your wisdom; ever possess your resolution, dignity and prudence?

I hope soon to converse with you personally upon the subject, and to profit by your precepts and example. I anticipate the hour of my return to your bosom, with impatience. My daily thoughts and nightly dreams restore me to the society of my beloved mamma; and, till I enjoy it in reality, I subscribe myself your dutiful daughter,

Eliza Wharton

LETTER 21
TO MISS ELIZA WHARTON

Hartford

How welcome to me, my dear Eliza, are the tidings of your return! My widowed heart has mourned your absence, and languished for the company of its now dearest connection. When stripped of one dependence, the mind naturally collects, and rests itself in another. Your father's death deprived me, for a while, of every enjoyment. But a reviving sense of the duties

[1] *Richardson's Clarissa … a second Lovelace* Reference to Samuel Richardson's popular epistolary novel *Clarissa* (1748). It recounts the protagonist Clarissa Harlowe's efforts to keep her virtue while being pursued by the rake Robert Lovelace, who imprisons her in a brothel and then drugs and rapes her. Clarissa dies as a result. The "indiscretion" mentioned here is likely Clarissa's mistake in trusting Lovelace to help her escape her family's unkind machinations.

which I owed to a rising family roused me from the lethargy of grief. In my cares I found an alleviation of my sorrows. The expanding virtues of my children soothed and exhilarated my drooping spirits; and my attention to their education, and interest, was amply rewarded by their proficiency and duty. In them, every hope, every pleasure now centres. They are the axis on which revolves the temporal felicity of their mother. Judge then, my dear, how anxiously I must watch, how solicitously I must regard every circumstance which relates to their welfare and prosperity! Exquisitely alive to these sensations, your letter awakens my hopes and my fears. As you are young and charming, a thousand dangers lurk unseen around you. I wish you to find a friend and protector, worthy of being rewarded by your love and your society. Such a one, I think, Mr. Boyer will prove. I am, therefore, sorry, since there can be no other, that his profession should be an objection in your mind. You say, that I have experienced the scenes of trial, connected with that station. I have, indeed; and I will tell you the result of this experience. It is, that I have found it replete with happiness. No class of society has domestic enjoyment more at command, than clergymen. Their circumstances are generally a decent competency.[1] They are removed alike from the perplexing cares of want,[2] and from the distracting parade of wealth. They are respected by all ranks, and partakers of the best company. With regard to its being a dependent situation, what one is not so? Are we not all links in the great chain of society, some more, some less important; but each upheld by others, throughout the confederated whole? In whatever situation we are placed, our greater or less degree of happiness must be derived from ourselves. Happiness is in a great measure the result of our own dispositions and actions. Let us conduct uprightly and justly; with propriety and steadiness; not servilely cringing for favor, nor arrogantly claiming more attention and respect than our due; let us bear with fortitude the providential, and unavoidable evils of life, and we shall spend our days with respectability and contentment, at least.

I will not expatiate on the topic of your letter, till we have a personal interview, for which I am, indeed, impatient. Return, my daughter, as soon as politeness

will allow, to your expecting friends; more especially, to the fond embraces of your affectionate mother,

M. Wharton

LETTER 22
TO MISS ELIZA WHARTON

Hampshire

Can time, can distance, can absence allay or extinguish the sentiments of refined affection, the ardor of true love? No, my dear Eliza. If I may judge by my own heart, I shall say they cannot. Amidst the parade which has attended me, the interesting scenes in which I have been engaged, and the weighty cares, which have occupied my attention, your idea has been the solace of my retired moments; the soother of every anxious thought. I recall, with pleasure, the conversation which we have shared. I dwell with rapture on the marks of favor which I have received from you. My first wish is the continuance and increase of these favors; my highest ambition, to deserve them. I look forward and anticipate with impatience, the future enjoyment of your society; and hope we shall one day experience the reality of those beautiful lines of Thompson:

——An elegant sufficiency,
Content, retirement, rural quiet, friendship;
Books, ease and alternate labor, useful life;
Progressive virtue, and approving heaven;
These are the matchless joys of virtuous love.[3]

Mr. Selby, my particular friend, will have the honor of delivering this letter. He will be able to give you any information, relative to our public transactions, which you may wish. May I solicit the favor of a line, through him, in return? It will relieve, in some measure, the tediousness of this separation. I intend to pay my respects to you personally, in about a fortnight; till when, I subscribe myself your sincere and affectionate friend,

J. Boyer

1 *competency* Comfortable but not excessive wealth.

2 *want* Lack; poverty.

3 *An elegant ... virtuous love* Lines 1158–62 of the poem "Spring" from James Thomson's highly popular poem cycle *The Seasons* (1726–30).

LETTER 23
TO THE REV. J. BOYER

New-Haven

I have executed your commission, and been amply rewarded for my trouble, by the pleasure I enjoyed in the society of the agreeable family to which I was introduced; especially of the amiable and accomplished lady, who is the object of your particular regard. I think she fully justifies your partiality to her. She appears to possess both the virtues and the graces. Her form is fine, and her countenance interests us at once in her favor. There is a mixture of dignity and ease, which commands respect, and conciliates affection. After these encomiums,[1] will you permit me to say, there is an air of gaiety in her appearance and deportment, which favors a little of coquetry. I am persuaded, however, that she has too much good sense to practice its arts. She received your letter very graciously, asked leave to retire a few moments; and returned with a smile of complacency on her brow, which I construe favorably to you.

There was a Mr. Laurence, with his lady and daughter, and a certain Major Sanford, at the house. The latter, I believe, in the modern sense of the phrase, *is much of a gentleman*, that is, a man of show and fashion.

Miss Wharton asked me when I should leave town, and when I should return, or have an opportunity of conveyance to Hampshire? I told her I should write by the next post, and if she had any commands, would be happy to execute them. She would send a line to her friend, she said, if I would take the trouble to enclose it in my letter. I readily consented, and told her that I would call and receive her favor tomorrow morning. This chit-chat was a little aside, but I could not but observe, that the foresaid Major Sanford had dropped his part in the conversation of the rest of the company, and was attending to us, though he endeavored to conceal his attention, by looking carelessly over a play, which lay on the window by him. Yet he evidently watched every word and action of Miss Wharton, as if he were really interested in her movements.

It is said she has many admirers, and I conceive it very possible that this may be one of them; though, truly, I do not think that she would esteem such a conquest any great honor. I now joined in the general topic of conversation, which was politics. Mrs. Richman and Miss Wharton judiciously, yet modestly bore a part; while the other ladies amused themselves with Major Sanford, who was making his sage remarks on the play, which he still kept in his hand. General Richman at length observed, that we had formed into parties. Major Sanford, upon this, laid aside his book. Miss Laurence simpered and looked as if she was well pleased with being in a party with so fine a man; while her mother replied that she never meddled with politics; she thought they did not belong to ladies. Miss Wharton and I, said Mrs. Richman, must beg leave to differ from you, madam. We think ourselves interested in the welfare and prosperity of our country; and, consequently, claim the right of inquiring into those affairs, which may conduce to, or interfere with the common weal.[2] We shall not be called to the senate or the field to assert its privileges, and defend its rights, but we shall feel for the honor and safety of our friends and connections, who are thus employed. If the community flourish and enjoy health and freedom, shall we not share in the happy effects? If it be oppressed and disturbed, shall we not endure our proportion of the evil? Why then should the love of our country be a masculine passion only? Why should government, which involves the peace and order of the society, of which we are a part, be wholly excluded from our observation? Mrs. Laurence made some slight reply and waived the subject. The gentlemen applauded Mrs. Richman's sentiments as truly Roman; and what was more, they said, truly republican.

I rose to take leave, observing to Miss Wharton, that I should call tomorrow as agreed. Upon this, Gen. Richman politely requested the favor of my company at dinner. I accepted his invitation, and bid them good night. I shall do the same to you for the present; as I intend, tomorrow to scribble the cover, which is to enclose your Eliza's letter.

T. Selby

[1] *encomiums* Praises.

[2] *common weal* Common welfare; commonwealth.

LETTER 24
TO THE REV. J. BOYER

New-Haven

I resume my pen, having just returned from Gen. Richman's; not with an expectation, however, of your reading this, till you have perused, and reperused the enclosed. I can bear such neglect, in this case, as I have been alike interested myself.

I went to Gen. Richman's at twelve o'clock. About a mile from thence, upon turning a corner, I observed a gentleman and lady on horseback, some way before me, riding a very moderate pace, and seemingly in close conversation. I kept at the same distance from them, till I saw them stop at the General's gate. I then put on, and coming up with them, just as they alighted, and was surprised to find them no other than Major Sanford and Miss Wharton. They were both a little disconcerted at my salutation; I know not why. Miss Wharton invited him in; but he declined, being engaged to dine. Gen. Richman received us at the door. As I handed Miss Wharton in, he observed jocosely that she had changed company. Yes sir, she replied, more than once, since I went out, as you doubtless observed. I was not aware, said Mrs. Richman, that Major Sanford was to be of your party today. It was quite accidental, madam, said Miss Wharton. Miss Laurence and I had agreed last evening, to take a little airing, this forenoon. A young gentleman, a relation of hers, who is making them a visit, was to attend us. We had not rode more than two miles, when we were overtaken by Major Sanford, who very politely asked leave to join our party. Miss Laurence very readily consented; and we had a very sociable ride. The fineness of the day induced me to protract the enjoyment of it abroad; but Miss Laurence declined riding so far as I proposed, as she had engaged company to dine. We therefore parted till evening, when we are to meet again. What, another engagement! said Mrs. Richman. Only to the assembly,[1] madam. May I inquire after your gallant, my dear? But I have no right, perhaps, to be inquisitive, said Mrs. Richman.

Miss Wharton made no reply; and the conversation took a general turn. Miss Wharton sustained her part with great propriety. Indeed, she discovers a fund of useful knowledge, and extensive reading, which render her peculiarly entertaining; while the brilliancy of her wit, the fluency of her language, the vivacity and ease of her manners, are inexpressibly engaging. I am going myself to the assembly this evening, though I did not mention it to General Richman; I therefore took my leave soon after dinner.

I have heard so much in praise of Miss Wharton's penmanship, in addition to her other endowments, that I am almost tempted to break the seal of her letter to you; but I forbear. Wishing you much happiness in the perusal of it, and more in the possession of its writer, I subscribe myself, yours, etc.

T. Selby

LETTER 25
TO THE REV. J. BOYER

New-Haven

Sir,

Your favor of the 4th inst.[2] came to hand yesterday. I received it with pleasure, and embrace this early opportunity of contributing my part to a correspondence, tending to promote a friendly and social intercourse. An epistolary communication between the sexes has been with some a subject of satire and censure; but unjustly, in my opinion. With persons of refinement and information, it may be a source of entertainment and utility. The knowledge and masculine virtues of your sex may be softened, and rendered more diffusive by the inquisitiveness, vivacity, and docility of ours; drawn forth and exercised by each other.

In regard to the *particular* subject of yours I shall be silent. Ideas of that kind are better conveyed, on my part, by words, than by the pen.

I congratulate you on your agreeable settlement, and hope it will be productive of real and lasting happiness. I am convinced that felicity is not confined to any

[1] *assembly* Elegant gathering for the purposes of dancing and other entertainment (a regular feature of upper-middle-class life during this period).

[2] *inst.* Instant; of the present month.

particular station, or condition in life; yet methinks some are better calculated to afford it to me, than others.

Your extract from a favorite poet is charmingly descriptive; but is it not difficult to ascertain what we can pronounce "an elegant sufficiency"? Perhaps you will answer as some others have done, We can attain it by circumscribing our wishes within the compass of our abilities. I am not very avaricious; yet I must own that I should like to enjoy it without so much trouble as that would cost me.

Excuse my seeming levity. You have flattered my cheerfulness by commending it; and must, therefore, indulge me in the exercise of it. I cannot conveniently be at the pains of restraining its sallies, when I write in confidence.

Is a sprightly disposition, in your view, indicative of a giddy mind, or an innocent heart? Of the latter, I presume; for I know you are not a misanthrope.

We expect the pleasure of Mr. Selby's company to dinner. You are, certainly, under obligations to his friendship for the liberal encomiums he bestowed on you, and your prospects yesterday. Mrs. Richman rallied me after he was gone, on my listening ear. The General and she unite in requesting me to present their respects. Wishing you health and happiness, I subscribe myself your friend,

Eliza Wharton

LETTER 26
TO MISS LUCY FREEMAN

New-Haven

I am perplexed and embarrassed, my friend, by the assiduous attentions of this Major Sanford. I shall write circumstantially and frankly to you, that I may have the benefit of your advice. He came here, last Monday, in company with Mr. Laurence, his wife, and daughter, to make us a visit. While they were present, a Mr. Selby, a particular friend of Mr. Boyer, came in, and delivered me a letter from him. I was really happy in the reception of this proof of his affection. His friend gave a very flattering account of his situation and prospects.

The watchful eye of Major Sanford traced every word and action, respecting Mr. Boyer, with an attention which seemed to border on anxiety. That, however, did not restrain, but rather accelerate my vivacity and inquisitiveness on the subject; for I wished to know whether it would produce any real effect upon him, or not.

After Mr. Selby's departure, he appeared pensive and thoughtful the remainder of the evening; and evidently sought an opportunity of speaking to me aside; which I studiously avoided. Miss Laurence and I formed an engagement to take an airing in the morning on horseback; attended by a relation of hers, who is now with them. They called for me about ten, when we immediately set out upon our preconcerted excursion. We had not proceeded far, before we were met by Major Sanford. He was extremely polite, and finding our destination was not particular, begged leave to join our party. This was granted, and we had an agreeable tour for several miles; the time being passed in easy and unstudied remarks upon obvious occurrences. Maj. Sanford could not, however, conceal his particular attention to me, which rather nettled Miss Laurence. She grew somewhat serious, and declined riding so far as we had intended; alleging that she expected company to dine.

Major Sanford understanding that she was going to the assembly in the evening with Mr. Gordon, solicited me to accept a ticket and form a party with them. The entertainment was alluring, and I consented. When we had parted with Miss Laurence, Major Sanford insisted on my riding a little farther; saying, he must converse with me on a particular subject; and if I refused him this opportunity, that he must visit me, at my residence, let it offend whom it would. I yielded to his importunity; and we rode on. He then told me that his mind was in a state of suspense and agitation, which was very painful to bear; and which I only could relieve; that my cheerful reception of Mr. Boyer's letter, yesterday, and deportment respecting him, had awakened in his breast all the pangs of jealousy, which the most ardent love could feel; that my treatment of Mr. Boyer's friend convinced him that I was more interested in his affairs than I was willing to own; that he foresaw himself to be condemned to an eternal separation; and the total loss

of my favor and society, as soon as time and circumstances would allow.

His zeal, his pathos, alarmed me. I begged him to be calm. To you, said I, as a friend, I have intrusted my situation in relation to Mr. Boyer. You know that I am under no special obligation to him; and I do not intend to form any immediate connection. Mr. Boyer must have different ideas, madam; and he has reason for them, if I may judge by appearances. When do you expect another visit from him? In about a fortnight. And is my fate to be then decided; and so decided, as I fear it will be, through the influence of your friends, if not by your own inclination? My friends, sir, will not control; they will only advise to what they think most for my interest; and I hope, that my conduct will not be unworthy of their approbation. Pardon me, my dear Eliza, said he, if I am impertinent; it is my regard for you which impels me to the presumption. Do you intend to give your hand to Mr. Boyer? I do not intend to give my hand to any man at present. I have but lately entered society;[1] and wish, for a while, to enjoy my freedom, in the participation of pleasures, suited to my age and sex. These, said he, you are aware, I suppose, when you form a connection with that man, you must renounce; and content yourself with a confinement to the tedious round of domestic duties, the pedantic conversation of scholars, and the invidious criticisms of a whole town. I have been accustomed, said I, and am therefore attached to men of letters; and as to the praise or censure of the populace, I hope always to enjoy that approbation of conscience, which will render me superior to both. But you forget your promise, not to talk in this style; and have deviated far from the character of a friend and brother, with which you consented to rest satisfied. Yes, but I find myself unequal to the task. I am not stoic enough, tamely to make so great a sacrifice. I must plead for an interest in your favor, till you banish me from your presence, and tell me plainly that you hate me. We had by this time reached the gate; and as we dismounted, were unexpectedly accosted by Mr. Selby, who had come agreeably to his promise, to dine with us, and receive my letter to Mr. Boyer.

Major Sanford took his leave as General Richman appeared at the door. The General and his lady rallied[2] me on my change of company; but very prudently concealed their sentiments of Major Sanford, while Mr. Selby was present. Nothing material occurred before, and during dinner; soon after which, Mr. Selby went away. I retired to dress for the assembly; and had nearly completed the labor of the toilet,[3] when Mrs. Richman entered. My friendship for you, my dear Eliza, said she, interests me so much in your affairs, that I cannot repress my curiosity to know who has the honor of your hand this evening. If it be any honor, said I, it will be conferred on Major Sanford. I think it far too great to be thus bestowed, returned she. It is perfectly astonishing to me, that the virtuous part of my sex will countenance, caress, and encourage those men, whose profession it is to blast their reputation, destroy their peace, and triumph in their infamy! Is this, madam, the avowed design of Major Sanford? I know not what he avows; but his practice too plainly bespeaks his principles and views. Does he now practice the arts you mention; or do you refer to past follies? I cannot answer for his present conduct; his past has established his character. You, madam, are an advocate for charity; that, perhaps, if exercised in this instance might lead you to think it possible for him to reform; to become a valuable member of society; and, when connected with a lady of virtue and refinement, to be capable of making a good husband. I cannot conceive that such a lady would be willing to risk her all upon the slender prospect of his reformation. I hope the one with whom I am conversing, has no inclination to so hazardous, an experiment. Why, not much. Not much! If you have any, why do you continue to encourage Mr. Boyer's addresses? I am not sufficiently acquainted with either yet, to determine which to take. At present, I shall not confine myself in any way. In regard to these men, my fancy and my judgment are in scales. Sometimes one preponderates, sometimes the other. Which will finally outweigh, time alone can reveal. O my cousin, beware of the delusions of fancy! Reason must be our guide, if we would expect durable happiness. At this instant a servant opened the door, and told me that

[1] *entered society* I.e., begun engaging in social activities after the period of mourning for her fiancé.

[2] *rallied* Teased.

[3] *the labor of the toilet* I.e., getting dressed, styling one's hair, and other aspects of personal grooming.

Major Sanford waited in the parlor. Being ready, I wished Mrs. Richman a good evening, and went down. Neither General Richman nor his lady appeared. He therefore handed me immediately into his phaeton,[1] and we were soon in the assembly room.

I was surprised, on my entrance, to find Mr. Selby there, as he did not mention, at dinner, his intention of going. He attached himself to our party; and, in the intervals of dancing, took every opportunity of conversing with me. These, however, were not many; for Major Sanford assiduously precluded the possibility of my being much engaged by anyone else. We passed the evening very agreeably; but the Major's importunity was rather troublesome, as we returned home. He insisted upon my declaring whether Mr. Boyer really possessed my affections; and whether I intended to confer myself on him or not. If, said he, you answer me in the affirmative, I must despair; but if you have not absolutely decided against me, I will still hope, that my persevering assiduity, my faithful love, may at last be rewarded. I told him that I was under no obligation to give him any account of my disposition towards another; and that he must remember the terms of our present association, to which he had subscribed. I therefore begged him to wave the subject now, if not forever. He asked my pardon, if he had been impertinent; but desired leave to renew his request, that I would receive his visits, his friendly visits. I replied that I could not grant this; and that he must blame himself, not me, if he was an unwelcome guest at General Richman's. He lamented the prejudices which my friends had imbibed against him; but flattered himself that I was more liberal than to be influenced by them, without any positive proof of demerit; as it was impossible that his conduct towards me should ever deviate from the strictest rules of honor and love.

What shall I say now, my friend? This man, to an agreeable person[2] has superadded graceful manners, an amiable temper, and a fortune sufficient to ensure the enjoyments of all the pleasing varieties of social life. Perhaps a gay disposition, and a lax education may have betrayed him into some scenes of dissipation. But is it not an adage generally received, that "*a reformed rake makes the best husband*"? My fancy leads me for

happiness to the festive haunts of fashionable life. I am at present, and know not but I ever shall be, too volatile for a confinement to domestic avocations, and sedentary pleasures. I dare not, therefore, place myself in a situation where these must be indispensable. Mr. Boyer's person and character are agreeable. I really esteem the man. My reason and judgment, as I have observed before, declare for a connection with him, as a state of tranquillity and rational happiness. But the idea of relinquishing those delightful amusements and flattering attentions, which wealth and equipage bestow, is painful. Why were not the virtues of the one, and the graces and affluence of the other combined? I should then have been happy indeed! But, as the case now stands, I am loath to give up either; being doubtful which will conduce most to my felicity.

Pray write me impartially; let me know your real sentiments, for I rely greatly upon your opinion. I am, etc.

Eliza Wharton

LETTER 27
TO THE REV. MR. BOYER

New-Haven

I am quite a convert to Pope's assertion that "Every woman is, at heart, a rake."[3] How else can we account for the pleasure which they evidently receive from the society, the flattery, the caresses of men of that character? Even the most virtuous of them seem naturally prone to gaiety, to pleasure, and, I had almost said, to dissipation! How else shall we account for the existence of this disposition, in your favorite fair? It cannot be the result of her education. Such a one as she has received, is calculated to give her a very different turn of mind. You must forgive me, my friend, for I am a little vexed and alarmed on your account. I went last evening to the assembly, as I told you in my last that I intended. I was purposely without a partner, that I might have the liberty to exercise my gallantry, as circumstances should invite. Indeed, I must own that my particular

1 *phaeton* Light four-wheeled carriage.

2 *agreeable person* Pleasant physical appearance.

3 *Every woman ... a rake* See Alexander Pope's "Epistle Two: To a Lady" (1735).

design was to observe Miss Wharton's movements, being rather inclined to jealousy in your behalf. She was handed into the assembly room by Major Sanford. The brilliance of their appearance, the levity of their manners, and the contrast of their characters I found to be a general subject of speculation. I endeavored to associate with Miss Wharton, but found it impossible to detach her a moment from the coxcomb[1] who attended her. If she has any idea of a connection with you, why does she continue to associate with another, especially with one of so opposite a description? I am seriously afraid that there is more intimacy between them than there ought to be, considering the encouragement she has given you.

I hope you will not be offended by my freedom in this matter. It originates in a concern for your honor and future happiness. I am anxious, lest you should be made the dupe of a coquette, and your peace of mind fall a sacrifice to an artful debauchee.[2] Yet I must believe, that Miss Wharton has, in reality, all that virtue and good sense of which she enjoys the reputation; but her present conduct is mysterious.

I have said enough (more than I ought, perhaps) to awaken your attention to circumstances, which *may* lead to important events. If they appear of little or no consequence to you, you will at least ascribe the mention of them to motives of sincere regard, in your friend and humble servant,

T. Selby

LETTER 28
TO MR. CHARLES DEIGHTON

New-Haven

I go on finely with my amour. I have every encouragement that I could wish. Indeed my fair one does not verbally declare in my favor; but then, according to the vulgar proverb *that actions speak louder than words*, I have no reason to complain; since she evidently approves my gallantry, is pleased with my company,

and listens to my flattery. Her sagacious friends have undoubtedly given her a detail of my vices. If, therefore, my past conduct has been repugnant to her notions of propriety, why does she not act consistently, and refuse at once to associate with a man whose character she cannot esteem? But no; that, Charles, is no part of the female plan: our entrapping a few of their sex, only discovers the gaiety of our dispositions, the insinuating graces of our manners, and the irresistible charms of our persons and address.[3] These qualifications are very alluring to the sprightly fancy of the fair. They think to enjoy the pleasures which result from this source; while their vanity and ignorance prompt each one to imagine herself superior to delusion; and to anticipate the honor of reclaiming the libertine, and reforming the rake! I don't know, however, but this girl will really have that merit with me; for I am so much attached to her, that I begin to suspect I should sooner become a convert to sobriety than lose her. I cannot find that I have made much impression on her heart as yet. Want of success in this point mortifies me extremely, as it is the first time I ever failed. Besides, I am apprehensive that she is prepossessed in favor of the other swain, the clerical lover, whom I have mentioned to you before. The chord, therefore, upon which I play the most, is the dissimilarity of their dispositions and pleasures. I endeavor to detach her from him, and disaffect her towards him; knowing, that if I can separate them entirely, I shall be more likely to succeed in my plan. Not that I have any thoughts of marrying her myself; that will not do at present. But I love her too well to see her connected with another for life. I must own myself a little revengeful too in this affair. I wish to punish her friends, as she calls them, for their malice towards me; for their cold and negligent treatment of me whenever I go to the house. I know that to frustrate their designs of a connection between Mr. Boyer and Eliza would be a grievous disappointment. I have not yet determined to seduce her, though, with all her pretensions to virtue, I do not think it impossible. And if I should, she can blame none but herself, since she knows my character, and has no reason to wonder if I act consistently with it. If she will play with a lion, let her beware of his paw, I say. At present, I wish innocently to enjoy her society; it is a luxury which

1 *coxcomb* Foolish, ostentatious man.

2 *debauchee* Immoral pleasure seeker (especially with regard to sexual relationships).

3 *address* Manners.

I never tasted before. She is the very soul of pleasure. The gayest circle is irradiated by her presence, and the highest entertainment receives its greatest charm from her smiles. Besides, I have purchased the seat of Capt. Pribble, about a mile from her mother's; and can I think of suffering her to leave the neighborhood, just as I enter it? I shall exert every nerve to prevent that, and hope to meet with the usual success of

Peter Sanford

Letter 29
to Miss Eliza Wharton

Hartford

You desire me to write to you, my friend; but if you had not, I should by no means have refrained. I tremble at the precipice on which you stand; and must echo, and re-echo the seasonable admonition of the excellent Mrs. Richman, "Beware of the delusions of fancy!" You are strangely infatuated by them! Let not the magic arts of that worthless Sanford lead you, like an *ignis fatuus*[1] from the path of rectitude and virtue!

I do not find, in all your conversations with him, that one word about marriage drops from his lips. This is mysterious? No, it is characteristic of the man. Suppose, however, that his views are honorable; yet what can you expect, what can you promise yourself from such a connection? "A reformed rake," you say, "makes the best husband"; a trite, but a very erroneous maxim, as the fatal experience of thousands of our sex can testify. In the first place, I believe that rakes very seldom *do* reform, while their fortunes and constitutions enable them to pursue their licentious pleasures. But even allowing this to happen, can a woman of refinement and delicacy enjoy the society of a man, whose mind has been corrupted, whose taste has been vitiated, and who has contracted a depravity both of sentiment and manners, which no degree of repentance can wholly efface? Besides, of true love they are absolutely incapable. Their passions have been too

much hackneyed to admit so pure a flame. You cannot anticipate sincere and lasting respect from them. They have been so long accustomed to the company of those of our sex, who observe no esteem, that the greatest dignity and purity of character can never excite it in their breasts. They are naturally prone to jealousy. Habituated to an intercourse with the baser part of the sex, they level the whole, and seldom believe any to be incorruptible. They are always hard hearted and cruel. How else could they triumph in the miseries which they frequently occasion? Their specious manners may render them agreeable companions abroad; but at home the evil propensities of their minds will invariably predominate. They are steeled against the tender affections, which render domestic life delightful; strangers to the kind, the endearing sympathies of husband, father, and friend! The thousand nameless attentions which soften the rugged path of life are neglected and deemed unworthy of notice by persons who have been inured to scenes of dissipation and debauchery! and is a man of this description to be the partner, the companion, the bosom friend of my Eliza? Forbid it heaven! Let not the noble qualities, so lavishly bestowed upon her, be thus unworthily sacrificed!

You seem to be particularly charmed with the fortune of Major Sanford; with the gaiety of his appearance; with the splendor of his equipage; with the politeness of his manners; with what you call the graces of his person! These, alas! are superficial, ensnaring endowments. As to fortune, prudence, economy, and regularity are necessary to preserve it, when possessed. Of these Major Sanford is certainly destitute; unless common fame (which more frequently tells truth than some are willing to allow) does him great injustice. As to external parade, it will not satisfy the rational mind, when it aspires to those substantial pleasures for which yours is formed. And as to the graces of person and manners, they are but a wretched substitute for those virtues which adorn and dignify human life. Can you, who have always been used to serenity and order in a family, to rational, refined and improving conversation, relinquish them, and launch into the whirlpool of frivolity, where the correct taste and the delicate sensibility which you possess must constantly be wounded by the frothy and illiberal sallies of licentious wit?

[1] *ignis fatuus* Phosphorescent light sometimes seen hovering above marshy land; in many stories, travelers become lost after following the lights, which they mistake for lanterns.

This, my dear, is but a faint picture of the situation to which you seem inclined! Reverse the scene, and you will perceive the alternative, which is submitted to your option, in a virtuous connection with Mr. Boyer. Remember that you are acting for life; and that your happiness in this world, perhaps in the next, depends on your present choice!

I called, last evening, to see your mamma. She is fondly anticipating your return, and rejoicing in the prospect of your agreeable and speedy settlement. I could not find it in my heart to distress her by intimating that you had other views. I wish her benevolent bosom never more to feel the pangs of disappointed hope.

I am busily engaged in preparing for my nuptials. The solemn words "as long as ye both shall live" render me thoughtful and serious. I hope for your enlivening presence soon; which will prove a seasonable cordial to the spirits of your

Lucy Freeman

LETTER 30
TO MISS LUCY FREEMAN

New-Haven

I believe your spirits need a cordial indeed, my dear Lucy, after drawing so dreadful a portrait of my swain. But I call him mine no longer. I renounce him entirely. My friends shall be gratified. And if their predictions are verified, I shall be happy in a union with the man of their choice. General Richman and lady have labored abundantly to prove that my ruin was inevitable if I did not immediately break all intercourse with Major Sanford. I promised a compliance with their wishes; and have accomplished the task, though a hard one I found it. Last Thursday he was here, and desired leave to spend an hour with me. I readily consented, assuring my friends it should be the last hour, which I would ever spend in his company.

He told me that he was obliged to leave town for a few days; and, as I should probably see Mr. Boyer, before his return, he could not depart in peace without once more endeavoring to interest me in his favor; to obtain some token of esteem, some glimpse of hope, that I would not utterly reject him, to support him in his absence. I thanked him for the polite attention he had paid me, since our acquaintance; told him that I should ever retain a grateful sense of his partiality to me; that he would ever share my best wishes; but that all connection of the kind, to which he alluded, must from that time, forever cease.

He exerted all his eloquence to obtain a retraction of that sentence, and ran, with the greatest volubility, through all the protestations, prayers, entreaties, professions and assurances which love could feel or art contrive. I had resolution, however, to resist them, and to command my own emotions on the occasion, better than my natural sensibility gave me reason to expect.

Finding every effort vain, he rose precipitately, and bade me adieu. I urged his tarrying to tea; but he declined, saying that he must retire to his chamber, being, in his present state of mind, unfit for any society, as he was banished from mine. I offered him my hand, which he pressed with ardor to his lips, and bowing in silence, left the room.

Thus terminated this affair; an affair, which, perhaps, was only the effect of mere gallantry on his part, and of unmeaning pleasantry on mine; and which, I am sorry to say, has given my friends so much anxiety and concern. I am under obligations to them for their kind solicitude, however causeless it may have been.

As an agreeable companion, as a polite and finished gallant, Major Sanford is all that the most lively fancy could wish. And as you have always affirmed that I was a little inclined to coquetry, can you wonder at my exercising it upon so happy a subject? Besides, when I thought more seriously, his liberal fortune was extremely alluring to me, who, you know, have been hitherto confined to the rigid rules of prudence and economy, not to say, necessity in my finances.

Miss Laurence called on me yesterday, as she was taking the air, and asked me whether Major Sanford took leave of me when he left town? He was here last week, said I, but I did not know that he was gone away. O yes, she replied, he is gone to take possession of his seat, which he has lately purchased of Captain Pribble. I am told it is superb; and it ought to be, if it have the honor of his residence. Then you have a great opinion of Major Sanford, said I. Certainly; and has not

everybody else? said she. I am sure he is a very fine gentleman. Mrs. Richman smiled rather contemptuously, and I changed the subject.

I believe that the innocent heart of this simple girl is a little taken in.

I have just received a letter from Mr. Boyer, in the usual style. He expects the superlative happiness of kissing my hand next week. O dear! I believe I must begin to fix my phiz.[1] Let me run to the glass[2] and try if I can make up one that will look *madamish*. Yes, I succeed very well.

I congratulate you on your new neighbor; but I advise friend George to have the guardian knot tied immediately, lest you should be ensnared by his bewitching squire.

I have been trying to seduce General Richman to accompany me to the assembly, this evening, but cannot prevail. Were Mrs. Richman able to go with us, he would be very happy to wait on us together; but to tell the truth, he had rather enjoy her company at home, than any which is to be found abroad. I rallied him on his old fashioned taste; but my heart approved and applauded his attachment. I despise the married man or woman who harbors an inclination to partake of separate pleasures.

I am told, that a servant man inquires for me below; the messenger of some enamoured swain, I suppose. I will step down and learn what message he brings——

Nothing extraordinary; it is only a card of compliments from a Mr. Emmons, a respectable merchant of this city, requesting the honor to wait on me to the assembly this evening. A welcome request, which I made no hesitation to grant. If I must resign these favorite amusements, let me enjoy as large a share as possible, till the time arrive. Adieu. I must repair to the toilet and adorn for a new conquest, the person of

Eliza Wharton

Letter 31
to Miss Eliza Wharton

Hartford

I am very happy to find you are in so good spirits, Eliza, after parting with your favorite swain. For I perceive that he is really the favorite of your fancy, though your heart cannot esteem him; and, independent of that, no sensations can be durable.

I can tell you some news of this strange man. He has arrived, and taken possession of his seat. Having given general invitations, he has been called upon and welcomed by most of the neighboring gentry. Yesterday he made an elegant entertainment. Friend George (as you call him) and I were of the number, who had cards. Twenty-one couples went, I am told. We did not go. I consider my time too valuable to be spent in cultivating acquaintance with a person from whom neither pleasure nor improvement are to be expected. His profuseness may bribe the unthinking multitude to show him respect; but he must know, that though

Places and honors have been bought for gold,
Esteem and love were never to be sold.[3]

I look upon the vicious habits, and abandoned[4] character of Major Sanford, to have more pernicious effects on society, than the perpetrations of the robber and the assassin. These, when detected, are rigidly punished by the laws of the land. If their lives be spared, they are shunned by society, and treated with every mark of disapprobation and contempt. But to the disgrace of humanity and virtue, the assassin of honor; the wretch, who breaks the peace of families, who robs virgin innocence of its charms, who triumphs over the ill placed confidence of the inexperienced, unsuspecting, and too credulous fair, is received, and caressed, not only by his own sex, to which he is a reproach, but even by ours, who have every conceivable reason to despise and avoid him. Influenced by these principles, I am neither ashamed nor afraid openly to avow my

1 *phiz* Facial expression.

2 *glass* Mirror.

3 *Places and honors ... sold* See Alexander Pope's 1733–34 *Essay on Man* 4.187–88: "Judges and senates have been bought for gold, / Esteem and love were never to be sold."

4 *abandoned* Unrestrained; immoral.

sentiments of this man, and my reasons for treating him with the most pointed neglect.

I write warmly on the subject; for it is a subject in which I think the honor and happiness of my sex concerned. I wish they would more generally espouse their own cause. It would conduce to the public weal, and to their personal respectability. I rejoice, heartily, that you have had resolution to resist his allurements, to detect and repel his artifices. Resolution, in such a case, is absolutely necessary; for,

> In spite of all the virtue we can boast,
> The woman that deliberates is lost.[1]

As I was riding out, yesterday, I met your mamma. She wondered that I was not one of the party at our new neighbor's. The reason, madam, said I, is that I do not like the character of the man. I know nothing of him, said she; he is quite a stranger to me, only as he called at my house, last week, to pay me his respects, as he said, for the sake of my late husband, whose memory he revered; and because I was the mother of Miss Eliza Wharton, with whom he had the honor of some little acquaintance. His manners are engaging, and I am sorry to hear that his morals are corrupt.

This, my dear, is a very extraordinary visit. I fear that he has not yet laid aside his arts. Be still on your guard, is the advice of your sincere and faithful friend,

Lucy Freeman

LETTER 32
TO MR. CHARLES DEIGHTON

Hartford

I am really banished and rejected; desired never more to think of the girl I love, with a view of indulging that love, or of rendering it acceptable to its object! You will perhaps, dispute the propriety of the term, and tell me it is not love, it is only gallantry, and a desire to exercise it with her, as favorite nymph.[2] I neither know, nor

care by what appellation you distinguish it, but it truly gives me pain. I have not felt one sensation of genuine pleasure since I heard my sentence; yet I acquiesced in it, and submissively took my leave; though I doubt not but I shall retaliate the indignity one time or other.

I have taken possession of my new purchase, an elegant and delightful residence. It is rendered more so by being in the vicinity of my charmer's native abode. This circumstance will conduce much to my enjoyment, if I can succeed in my plan of separating her from Mr. Boyer. I know that my situation and mode of life are far more pleasing to her than his, and shall therefore trust to my appearance and address for a reestablishment in her favor. I intend, if possible, to ingratiate myself with her particular friends. For this purpose, I called last week at her mother's, to pay my respects to her (so I told the good woman) as an object of my particular regard; and as the parent of a young lady, whom I had the honor to know and admire. She received me very civilly, thanked me for my attention, and invited me to call whenever I had opportunity; which was the very thing I wanted. I intend likewise to court popularity. I don't know but I must accept, by and by, some lucrative office in the civil department. Yet I cannot bear the idea of confinement to business. It appears to me quite inconsistent with the character of a gentleman; I am sure it is, with that of a man of pleasure. But something I must do; for I tell you, in confidence, that I was obliged to mortgage this place, because I had not wherewithal to pay for it. But I shall manage matters very well, I have no doubt, and keep up the appearance of affluence, till I find some lady in a strait for a husband, whose fortune will enable me to extricate myself from these embarrassments. Do come and see me, Charles; for, notwithstanding all my gaiety and parade, I have some turns of the hypo, some qualms of conscience, you will call them; but I meddle not with such obsolete words. And so good bye to you, says

Peter Sanford

1 *In spite ... is lost* See Addison's *Cato* 4.1.30–31.

2 *nymph* Sexually desirable young woman, especially one pursued by a swain.

LETTER 33
TO MISS LUCY FREEMAN

New-Haven

My Dear Friend,

I believe I must begin to assume airs of gravity; and they will not be quite so foreign to my feelings now, as at some other times. You shall know the reason. I have been associated for three days, with sentiment and sobriety, in the person of Mr. Boyer. I don't know but this man will seduce me into matrimony. He is very eloquent upon the subject; and his manners are so solemn, that I am strongly tempted, yet I dare not to laugh. Really, Lucy, there is something extremely engaging and soothing too, in virtuous and refined conversation. It is a source of enjoyment which cannot be realised by the dissolute and unreflecting. But then, this particular theme of his, is not a favorite one to me; I mean, as connected with its consequences, care and confinement. However, I have compounded the matter with him, and conditioned that he shall expatiate on the subject, and call it by what name he pleases, *platonic* or *conjugal*, provided he will let me take my own time for the consummation. I have consented that he shall escort me, next week, to see my mamma and my Lucy. O, how the idea of returning to that revered mansion, to those beloved friends, exhilarates my spirits!

General Richman's politeness to me has induced him to invite a large party of those gentlemen and ladies who have been particularly attentive to me, during my residence here, to dine and take tea, tomorrow. After that, I expect to be engaged in making farewell visits, till I leave the place. I shall, therefore, forego the pleasure of telling you any occurrences, subsequent to this date, until you see and converse with your sincere friend,

Eliza Wharton

LETTER 34
TO MRS. RICHMAN

Hartford

Dear Madam,

The day after I left your hospitable dwelling, brought me safe to that of my honored mamma; to the seat of maternal and filial affection; of social ease and domestic peace; of every species of happiness which can result from religion and virtue; from refinement in morals, and manners.

I found my brother and his wife, with Lucy Freeman and Mr. Sumner, waiting to receive and bid me welcome. I flew with ecstasy to the bosom of my mamma, who received me with her accustomed affection, testified by the expressive tears of tenderness which stole silently down her widowed cheek. She was unable to speak. I was equally so. We therefore indulged, a moment, the pleasing emotions of sympathising sensibility. When disengaged from her fond embrace, I was saluted by the others in turn; and having recovered myself, I presented Mr. Boyer to each of the company, and each of the company to him. He was cordially received by all, but more especially by my mamma.

The next day I was called upon and welcomed by several of my neighboring acquaintance; among whom I was not a little surprised to see Major Sanford. He came in company with Mr. Stoddard and Lady, whom he overtook, as he told me, near by; and, as they informed him that the design of their visit was to welcome me home, he readily accepted their invitation to partake of the pleasure which everyone must receive on my return. I bowed slightly at his compliment, taking no visible notice of any peculiarity of expression either in his words or looks.

His politeness to Mr. Boyer appeared to be the result of habit. Mr. Boyer's to him, to be forced by respect to the company to which he had gained admission. I dare say, that each felt a conscious superiority; the one on the score of merit; the other on that of fortune. Which ought to outweigh, the judicious mind will easily decide. The scale, as I once observed to you, will turn as fancy or reason preponderates. I believe the esteem which I now have for Mr. Boyer will keep me

steady; except, perhaps, some little eccentricities, now and then, just by way of variety. I am going tomorrow morning to spend a few days with Lucy Freeman; to assist in the preparation for, and the solemnization of her nuptials. Mr. Boyer, in the meantime, will tarry among his friends in town. My mamma is excessively partial to him; though I am not yet jealous that she means to rival me. I am not certain, however, but it might be happy for him if she should. For I suspect, notwithstanding the disparity of her age, that she is better calculated to make him a good wife than I am or ever shall be.

But to be sober. Please, madam, to make my compliments acceptable to those of your neighbors, whose politeness and attention to me, while at your house, have laid me under particular obligations of gratitude and respect. My best regards attend General Richman. Pray tell him, that though I never expect to be so good a wife as he is blessed with; yet I intend, after a while (when I have sowed all my wild oats) to make a tolerable one.

I am anxious to hear of a wished for event and of your safety. All who know you, feel interested in your health and happiness; but none more warmly than your obliged and affectionate

Eliza Wharton

LETTER 35
TO MISS ELIZA WHARTON

New-Haven

I write a line, at Mrs. Richman's request, just to inform you, Eliza, that yesterday, that lovely and beloved woman presented me with a daughter. This event awakens new sensations in my mind; and calls into exercise a kind of affection which had before lain dormant. I feel already the tenderness of a parent; while imagination fondly traces the mother's likeness in the infant form. Mrs. Richman expects to receive your congratulations, in a letter by the next post. She bids me tell you, moreover, that she hopes soon to receive an invitation, and be able to attend to the consummation you talk of. Give Mrs. Richman's and my particular regards

to your excellent mother; and to the worthy Mr. Boyer. With sentiments of esteem and friendship, I am, etc.

S. Richman

LETTER 36
TO MRS. RICHMAN

Hartford

From the scenes of festive mirth, from the conviviality of rejoicing friends, and from the dissipating amusements of the gay world, I retire with alacrity, to hail my beloved friend on the important charge which she has received; on the accession to her family, and, may I not say, on the addition to her care; since that care will be more than counterbalanced by the pleasure it confers. Hail happy babe! Ushered into the world by the best of mothers; entitled by birth-right to virtue and honor; defended by parental love, from the weakness of infancy and childhood, by guardian wisdom from the perils of youth, and by affluent independence from the griping hand of poverty, in more advanced life! May these animating prospects be realised by your little daughter; and may you long enjoy the rich reward of seeing her all that you wish!

Yesterday, my dear friend, Lucy Freeman gave her hand to the amiable and accomplished Mr. George Sumner. A large circle of congratulating friends were present. Her dress was such as wealth and elegance required. Her deportment was everything that modesty and propriety could suggest. They are, indeed, a charming couple. The consonance of their dispositions, the similarity of their tastes, and the equality of their ages are a sure pledge of happiness. Every eye beamed with pleasure on the occasion, and every tongue echoed the wishes of benevolence. Mine only was silent. Though not less interested in the felicity of my friend than the rest, yet the idea of a separation; perhaps, of an alienation of affection, by means of her entire devotion to another, cast an involuntary gloom over my mind. Mr. Boyer took my hand, after the ceremony was past. Permit me, Miss Wharton, said he, to lead you to your lovely friend; her happiness must be heightened by your participation of it. Oh no; said I, I

am too selfish for that. She has conferred upon another that affection which I wished to engross. My love was too fervent to admit a rival. Retaliate then, said he, this fancied wrong, by doing likewise. I observed that this was not a proper time to discuss that subject; and, resuming my seat, endeavored to put on the appearance of my accustomed vivacity. I need not relate the remaining particulars of the evening's entertainment. Mr. Boyer returned with my mamma, and I remained at Mrs. Freeman's.

We are to have a ball here, this evening. Mr. Boyer has been with us, and tried to monopolize my company; but in vain. I am too much engaged by the exhilarating scenes around, for attending to a subject which affords no variety. I shall not close this till tomorrow.

——I am rather fatigued with the amusements of last night, which were protracted to a late hour. Mr. Boyer was present; and I was pleased to see him not averse to the entertainment, though his profession prevented his taking an active part. As all the neighboring gentry were invited, Mr. Freeman would, by no means, omit Major Sanford, which his daughter earnestly solicited. It happened (unfortunately, shall I say?) that I drew him for a partner. Yet I must own, that I felt very little reluctance to my lot. He is an excellent dancer, and well calculated for a companion in the hours of mirth and gaiety. I regretted Mr. Boyer's being present, however; because my enjoyment seemed to give him pain. I hope he is not inclined to the passion of jealousy. If he is, I fear it will be somewhat exercised.

Lucy Freeman, now Mrs. Sumner, removes, next week, to Boston. I have agreed to accompany her, and spend a month or two in her family. This will give variety to the journey of life. Be so kind as to direct your next letter to me there.

Kiss the dear little babe for me. Give love, compliments, etc. as respectively due; and believe me, with every sentiment of respect, your affectionate

Eliza Wharton

Letter 37
To Mr. Charles Deighton

Hartford

Dear Charles,

My hopes begin to revive. I am again permitted to associate with my Eliza; invited to the same entertainment! She does not refuse to join with me in the mazy[1] dance, and partake the scenes of festive mirth. Nay, more; she allows me to press her hand to my lips; and listens to the sighing accents of love. Love her, I certainly do. Would to heaven I could marry her! Would to heaven I had preserved my fortune; or she had one to supply its place! I am distracted at the idea of losing her forever. I am sometimes tempted to solicit her hand in serious earnest; but if I should, poverty and want must be the consequence. Her disappointment in the expectation of affluence and splendor, which I believe her ruling passion, would afford a perpetual source of discontent and mutual wretchedness.

She is going to Boston with her friend, Mrs. Sumner. I must follow her. I must break the connection, which is rapidly forming, between her and Mr. Boyer; and enjoy her society a while longer, if no more.

I have had a little intimation from New-Haven, that Miss Laurence is partial to me, and might easily be obtained, with a handsome property into the bargain. I am neither pleased with, nor averse to the girl. But she has money, and that may supply the place of love, by enabling me to pursue independent pleasures. This she must expect, if she marries a man of my cast. She doubtless knows my character; and if she is so vain of her charms or influence, as to think of reforming or confining me, she must bear the consequences.

However, I can keep my head up, at present, without recourse to the noose of matrimony; and shall, therefore, defer any particular attention to her, till necessity requires it.

I am, etc.

Peter Sanford

1 *mazy* Intricate; also the name of a specific dance popular at the end of the eighteenth century.

LETTER 38
TO MRS. M. WHARTON

Boston

You commanded me, my dear mamma, to write you. That command I cheerfully obey, in testimony of my ready submission and respect. No other avocation could arrest my time, which is now completely occupied in scenes of amusement.

Mrs. Sumner is agreeably settled and situated. She appears to be possessed of every blessing which can render life desirable. Almost every day, since our arrival, has been engrossed by visitants. Our evenings, we have devoted to company abroad; and that more generally than we should otherwise have done, as my stay is limited to so short a period. The museum, the theatres, the circus and the assemblies have been frequented.

Mrs. Sumner has made me several presents, notwithstanding which, the articles requisite to a fashionable appearance, have involved me in considerable expense. I fear that you will think me extravagant when you are told how much.

Mr. Boyer tarried in town about a week, having business. He appeared a little concerned at my taste for dissipation, as he once termed it. He even took the liberty to converse seriously on the subject.

I was displeased with his freedom; and reminded him that I had the disposal of my own time, as yet; and that while I escaped the censure of my own heart, I hoped that no one else would presume to arraign it. He apologized, and gave up his argument.

I was much surprised, the first time I went to the play, to see Major Sanford in the very next box. He immediately joined our party; and wherever I have been since, I have been almost sure to meet him.

Mr. Boyer has taken his departure; and I do not expect to see him again, till I return home.

O mamma! I am embarrassed about this man. His worth I acknowledge; nay, I esteem him very highly. But can there be happiness with such a disparity of dispositions?

I shall soon return to the bosom of domestic tranquillity, to the arms of maternal tenderness, where I can deliberate and advise at leisure, about this important matter. Till when,

I am, etc.

Eliza Wharton

LETTER 39
TO MR. T. SELBY

Hampshire

Dear Sir,

I believe that I owe you an apology for my long silence. But my time has been much engrossed of late; and my mind much more so. When it will be otherwise, I cannot foresee. I fear, my friend, that there is some foundation for your suspicions respecting my beloved Eliza. What pity it is, that so fair a form, so accomplished a mind, should be tarnished, in the smallest degree, by the follies of coquetry! If this be the fact, which I am loth to believe, all my regard for her shall never make me the dupe of it.

When I arrived at her residence, at New-Haven, where, I told you in my last, I was soon to go, she gave me a most cordial reception. Her whole behavior to me was correspondent with those sentiments of esteem and affection which she modestly avowed. She permitted me to accompany her to Hartford, to restore her to her mother, and to declare my wish to receive her again from her hand. Thus far, all was harmony and happiness. As all my wishes were consistent with virtue and honor, she readily indulged them. She took apparent pleasure in my company, encouraged my hopes of a future union, and listened to the tender accents of love.

But the scenes of gaiety, which invited her attention, reversed her conduct. The delightful hours of mutual confidence, of sentimental converse, and of the interchange of refined affection, were no more! Instead of these, parties were formed, unpleasing to my taste; and every opportunity was embraced to join in diversions, in which she knew I could not consistently take a share. I, however, acquiesced in her pleasure, though I sometimes thought myself neglected,

and even hinted it to her mother. The old lady apologized for her daughter, by alleging that she had been absent for a long time; that her acquaintances were rejoiced at her return, and welcomed her by striving to promote her amusement.

One of her most intimate friends was married during my stay; and she appeared deeply interested in the event. She spent several days in assisting her, previous to the celebration. I resided, in the meantime, at her mamma's, visiting her at her friend's, where Major Sanford, among others, was received as a guest. Mrs. Sumner acquainted me that she had prevailed on Miss Wharton to go and spend a few weeks with her at Boston, whither she was removing; and urged my accompanying them. I endeavored to excuse myself, as I had been absent from my people a considerable time, and my return was now expected. But their importunity was so great, and Eliza's declaration that it would be very agreeable to her, so tempting, that I consented. Here I took lodgings and spent about a week, taking every opportunity to converse with Eliza, striving to discover her real disposition towards me. I mentioned the inconvenience of visiting her so often as I wished, and suggested my desire to enter, as soon as might be, into a family relation. I painted in the most alluring colours the pleasures resulting from domestic tranquillity, mutual confidence, and conjugal affection; and insisted on her declaring frankly whether she designed to share this happiness with me, and when it should commence. She owned that she intended to give me her hand; but when she should be ready, she could not yet determine. She pretended a promise from me[1] to wait her time; to consent that she should share the pleasures of the fashionable world, as long as she chose, etc.

I then attempted to convince her of her mistaken ideas of pleasure; that the scenes of dissipation, of which she was so passionately fond, afforded no true enjoyment; that the adulation of the coxcomb could not give durability to her charms, or secure the approbation of the wise and good; nor could the fashionable amusements of brilliant assemblies, and crowded theatres furnish the mind with

That which nothing earthly gives, or can destroy,
The soul's calm sunshine, and the heart felt joy.[2]

These friendly suggestions, I found were considered as the theme of a priest; and my desire to detach her from such empty pursuits, as the selfishness of a lover. She was even offended at my freedom, and warmly[3] affirmed that no one had a right to arraign her conduct. I mentioned Major Sanford who was then in town, and who (though she went to places of public resort with Mr. and Mrs. Sumner) always met and gallanted her home. She rallied me upon my jealousy, as she termed it; wished that I would attend her myself, and then she should need no other gallant. I answered that I had rather resign that honor to another; but wished, for her sake, that he might be a gentleman whose character would not disgrace the company with which he associated. She appeared mortified and chagrined in the extreme. However, she studiously suppressed her emotions; and even soothed me with the blandishments of female softness. We parted amicably. She promised to return soon, and prepare for a compliance with my wishes. I cannot refuse to believe her! I cannot cease to love her! My heart is in her possession. She has a perfect command of my passions. Persuasion dwells on her tongue. With all the boasted fortitude and resolution of our sex, we are but mere machines. Let love once pervade our breasts; and its object may mould us into any form that pleases her fancy, or even caprice.

I have just received a letter from Eliza, informing me of her return to Hartford. Tomorrow I shall set out on a visit to the dear girl; for, my friend, notwithstanding all her foibles, she is very dear to me. Before you hear from me again, I expect that the happy day will be fixed; the day which shall unite, in the most sacred bands, this lovely maid, and your faithful friend,

J. Boyer

1 *pretended ... from me* I.e., claimed (not necessarily falsely) that I had made a promise.

2 *That which ... felt joy* See Pope's *Essay on Man* 4.167–68.

3 *warmly* Passionately.

LETTER 40
TO MR. T. SELBY

Hampshire

I have returned; and the day, indeed, is fixed; but Oh! How different from my fond expectations! It is not the day of union, but the day of final separation; the day which divides me from my charmer; the day which breaks asunder the bands of love; the day on which my reason assumes its empire, and triumphs over the arts of a finished coquette! Congratulate me, my friend, that I have thus overcome my feelings, and repelled the infatuating wiles of a deceitful girl. I would not be understood to impeach Miss Wharton's virtue; I mean her chastity. Virtue in the common acceptation of the term, as applied to the sex, is confined to that particular, you know. But in my view, this is of little importance, where all other virtues are wanting!

When I arrived at Mrs. Wharton's, and inquired for Eliza, I was told that she had rode out; but was soon expected home. An hour after, a phaeton stopped at the door, from which my fair one alighted, and was handed into the house by Major Sanford, who immediately took leave. I met her and offered my hand, which she received with apparent tenderness.

When the family had retired after supper, and left us to talk on our particular affairs, I found the same indecision, the same loathness[1] to bring our courtship to a period,[2] as formerly. Her previous excuses were renewed, and her wishes to have a union still longer delayed, were zealously urged. She could not bear the idea of confinement to the cares of a married life at present; and begged me to defer all solicitation on that subject to some future day. I found my temper rise, and told her plainly, that I was not thus to be trifled with; that if her regard for me was sincere; if she really intended to form a connection with me, she could not thus protract the time, try my patience, and prefer every other pleasure to the rational interchange of affection, to the calm delights of domestic life. But in vain did I argue against her false notions of happiness; in vain did I represent the dangerous system of conduct, which she now pursued, and urge her to accept, before it was too late, the hand and heart which were devoted to her service. That, she said, she purposed ere long to do; and hoped amply to reward my faithful love; but she could not fix the time this evening. She must consider a little further; and likewise consult her mother. Is it not Major Sanford whom you wish to consult, madam? said I. She blushed, and gave me no answer. Tell me, Eliza, I continued, tell me frankly, if he has not supplanted me in your affections; if he be not the cause of my being thus evasively, thus cruelly treated? Major Sanford, sir, replied she, has done you no harm. He is a particular friend of mine; a polite gentleman, and an agreeable neighbor; and therefore I treat him with civility; but he is not so much interested in my concerns, as to alter my disposition towards any other person. Why, said I, do you talk of friendship with a man of his character? Between his society and mine, there is a great contrast. Such opposite pursuits and inclinations cannot be equally pleasing to the same taste. It is therefore necessary that you renounce the one, to enjoy the other. I will give you time to decide which. I am going to a friend's house to spend the night, and will call on you tomorrow, if agreeable, and converse with you further upon the matter. She bowed assent, and I retired.

The next afternoon I went as agreed; and found her mamma and her alone in the parlor. She was very pensive and appeared to have been in tears. The sight affected me. The idea of having treated her harshly, the evening before, disarmed me of my resolution to insist on her decision that day. I invited her to ride with me and visit a friend, to which she readily consented. We spent our time agreeably. I forebore to press[3] her on the subject of our future union; but strove rather to soothe her mind, and inspire her with sentiments of tenderness towards me. I conducted her home, and returned early in the evening to my friend's, who met me at the door; and jocosely told me, that he expected I should now rob them of their agreeable neighbor. But, added he, we have been apprehensive that you would be rivaled, if you delayed your visit much longer. I did not suspect a rival, said I. Who can the happy man be? I can say nothing from personal observation, said he; but fame, of late, has talked loudly of Major Sanford and Miss Wharton. Be not alarmed, continued he,

1 *loathness* Reluctance.

2 *period* Conclusion.

3 *forebore to press* Abstained from pressing.

seeing me look grave. I presume no harm is intended. The Major is a man of gallantry, and Miss Wharton is a gay lady; but I dare say that your connection will be happy, *if it be formed*. I noticed a particular emphasis on the word *if*; and as we were alone, I followed him with questions, till the whole affair was developed. I informed him of my embarrassment; and he gave me to understand that Eliza's conduct had, for some time past, been a subject of speculation in the town; that formerly, her character was highly esteemed; but that her intimacy with a man of Sanford's known libertinism, more especially as she was supposed to be engaged to another, had rendered her very censurable; that they were often together; that wherever she went, he was sure to follow, as if by appointment; that they walked, talked, sung and danced together in all companies; that some supposed he would marry her; others, that he only meditated adding her name to the black catalogue of deluded wretches whom he had already ruined!

I rose, and walked the room in great agitation. He apologized for his freedom; was sorry if he had wounded my feelings; but friendship alone had induced him frankly to declare the truth, that I might guard against duplicity and deceit.

I thanked him for his kind intensions, and assured him that I should not quit the town till I had terminated this affair, in one way or another.

I retired to bed, but sleep was a stranger to my eyes. With the dawn I rose; and after breakfast walked to Mrs. Wharton's, who informed me that Eliza was in her chamber, writing to a friend, but would be down in a few minutes. I entered into conversation with the old lady on the subject of her daughter's conduct; hinted my suspicions of the cause, and declared my resolution of knowing my destiny immediately. She endeavored to extenuate, and excuse her as much as possible; but frankly owned that her behavior was mysterious; that no pains had been wanting, on her part, to alter and rectify it; that she had remonstrated, expostulated, advised and entreated, as often as occasion required. She hoped that my resolution would have a good effect, as she knew that her daughter esteemed me very highly.

In this manner we conversed till the clock struck twelve; and Eliza, not appearing, I desired her mamma to send up word that I waited to see her. The maid returned with an answer that she was indisposed,

and had lain down. Mrs. Wharton observed that she had not slept for several nights, and complained of the headache in the morning. The girl added, that she would wait on Mr. Boyer in the evening. Upon this information I rose and abruptly took my leave. I went to dine with a friend, to whom I had engaged myself the day before; but my mind was too much agitated to enjoy either the company or the dinner. I excused myself from tarrying to tea, and returned to Mrs. Wharton's. On inquiry, I was told that Eliza had gone to walk in the garden; but desired that no person might intrude on her retirement. The singularity of the request awakened my curiosity, and determined me to follow her. I sought her in vain, in different parts of the garden, till, going towards an arbor, almost concealed from sight, by surrounding shrubbery, I discovered her, sitting in close conversation with Major Sanford! My blood chilled in my veins, and I stood petrified with astonishment at the disclosure of such baseness and deceit. They both rose in visible confusion. I dared not trust myself to accost them. My passions were raised, and I feared that I might say or do something unbecoming my character. I therefore gave them a look of indignation and contempt, and retreated to the house. I traversed the parlor hastily, overwhelmed with chagrin and resentment! Mrs. Wharton inquired the cause. I attempted to tell her, but my tongue refused utterance! While in this situation, Eliza entered the room. She was not less discomposed than myself. She sat down at the window and wept. Her mamma wept likewise. At length she recovered herself, in a degree, and desired me to sit down. I answered no; and continued walking. Will you, said she, permit me to vindicate my conduct and explain my motives? Your conduct, said I, cannot be vindicated; your motives need no explanation; they are too apparent! How, Miss Wharton, have I merited this treatment from you? But I can bear it no longer. Your indifference to me proceeds from an attachment to another; and forgive me if I add, to one who is the disgrace of his own sex, and the destroyer of yours. I have been too long the dupe of your dissimulation and coquetry. Too long has my peace of mind been sacrificed to the arts of a woman whose conduct has proved her unworthy of my regard; insensible to love, gratitude and honor!

To you, madam, said I, turning to her mother, I acknowledge my obligations for your friendship, politeness and attention. I once hoped for the privilege of rocking for you the cradle of declining age. I am deprived of that privilege; but I pray that you may never want a child, whose love and duty shall prove a source of consolation and comfort!

Farewell! If we never meet again in this life, I hope and trust we shall in a better; where the parent's eye shall cease to weep for the disobedience of a child; and the lover's heart to bleed for the infidelity of his mistress!

I turned to Eliza, and attempted to speak; but her extreme emotion softened me, and I could not command my voice. I took her hand, and bowing, in token of an adieu, went precipitately out of the house. The residence of my friend, with whom I lodged, was at no great distance, and thither I repaired. As I met him in the entry, I rushed by him, and betook myself to my chamber.

The fever of resentment and the tumult of passion began now to give place to the softer emotions of the soul. I found myself perfectly unmanned. I gave free scope to the sensibility of my heart; and the effeminate relief of tears materially lightened the load which oppressed me.

After this arduous struggle I went to bed; and slept more calmly than for several nights before. The next morning I wrote a farewell letter to Eliza (a copy of which I shall enclose to you) and ordering my horse to be brought, left town immediately.

My resentment of her behavior has much assisted me in erasing her image from my breast. In this exertion I have succeeded beyond my most sanguine expectations. The more I reflect on her temper and disposition, the more my gratitude is enlivened towards the wise Disposer of all events for enabling me to break asunder the snares of the deluder. I am convinced that the gaiety and extravagance of her taste, the frivolous levity of her manners, disqualify her for the station in which I wished to have placed her. These considerations, together with that resignation to an overruling Providence which the religion I profess, and teach, requires me to cultivate, induce me cheerfully to adopt the following lines of an ingenious poet:

Since all the downward tracts of time,
 God's watchful eye surveys,
Oh, who so wise to choose our lot,
 Or regulate our ways?

Since none can doubt his equal love,
 Unmeasurably kind,
To his unerring gracious will,
 Be every wish resigned.

Good, when he gives, supremely good,
 Not less when he denies,
E'en crosses from his sovereign hand,
 Are blessings in disguise.[1]

I am, etc.

J. Boyer

TO MISS ELIZA WHARTON

Hartford

Madam,

Fearing, that my resolution may not be proof against the eloquence of those charms, which have so long commanded me, I take this method of bidding you a final adieu. I write not as a lover. That connection between us is forever dissolved; but I address you as a friend; a friend to your happiness, to your reputation, to your temporal and eternal welfare. I will not rehearse the innumerable instances of your imprudence and misconduct, which have fallen under my observation. Your own heart must be your monitor! Suffice it for me to warn you against the dangerous tendency of so dissipated a life; and to tell you that I have traced (I believe aright) the cause of your dissimulation and indifference to me. They are an aversion to the sober, rational, frugal mode of living, to which my profession leads; a fondness for the parade, the gaiety, not to say the licentiousness, of a station calculated to gratify such a disposition; and a prepossession for Major Sanford, infused into your giddy mind by the frippery,

[1] *Since all ... in disguise* See "Reflections on a Flower-Garden" (1748) by English poet and priest James Hervey.

flattery and artifice of that worthless and abandoned man. Hence you preferred a connection with him, if it could be accomplished; but a doubt whether it could, together with the advice of your friends, who have kindly espoused my cause, have restrained you from the avowal of your real sentiments, and led you to continue your civilities to me. What the result of your coquetry would have been, had I waited for it, I cannot say, nor have I now any desire or interest to know. I tear from my breast the idea which I have long cherished of future union and happiness with you in the conjugal state. I bid a last farewell to these fond[1] hopes, and leave you forever!

For your own sake, however, let me conjure you to review your conduct, and before you have advanced beyond the possibility of returning to rectitude and honor, to restrain your steps from the dangerous path in which you now tread!

Fly Major Sanford. That man is a deceiver. Trust not his professions. They are certainly insincere, or he would not affect concealment; he would not induce you to a clandestine intercourse! Many have been the victims of his treachery! O Eliza! add not to the number! Banish him from your society, if you wish to preserve your virtue unsullied, your character unsuspicious! It already begins to depreciate. Snatch it from the envenomed tongue of slander, before it receive an incurable wound!

Many faults have been visible to me, over which my affection once drew a veil. That veil is now removed. And, acting the part of a disinterested friend, I shall mention some few of them with freedom. There is a levity in your manners, which is inconsistent with the solidity and decorum becoming a lady who has arrived to years of discretion. There is also an unwarrantable extravagance betrayed in your dress. Prudence and economy are such necessary, at least, such decent virtues, that they claim the attention of every female, whatever be her station or her property. To these virtues you are apparently inattentive. Too large a portion of your time is devoted to the adorning of your person.

Think not that I write thus plainly from resentment. No; it is from benevolence. I mention your foibles, not to reproach you with them, but that you may consider their nature and effects, and renounce them.

I wish you to regard this letter as the legacy of a friend; and to improve it accordingly. I shall leave town before you receive it. O, how different are my sensations at going, from what they were when I came! But I forbear description.

Think not, Eliza, that I leave you with indifference! The conflict is great; the trial is more than I can calmly support! Yet the consciousness of duty affords consolation. A duty I conceive it to be, which I owe to myself, and to the people of my charge,[2] who are interested in my future connection.

I wish not for an answer; my resolution is unalterably fixed. But should you hereafter be convinced of the justice of my conduct, and become a convert to my advice, I shall be happy to hear it.

That you may have wisdom to keep you from falling, and conduct you safely through this state of trial to the regions of immortal bliss, is the fervent prayer of your sincere friend, and humble servant,

J. Boyer

LETTER 41
TO MRS. LUCY SUMNER

Hartford

The retirement of my native home is not so gloomy, since my return from Boston, as I expected, from the contrast between them.

Indeed, the customs and amusements of this place are materially altered, since the residence of Major Sanford among us. The dull, old fashioned sobriety which formerly prevailed, is nearly banished; and cheerfulness, vivacity, and enjoyment are substituted in its stead. Pleasure is now diffused through all ranks of the people, especially the rich; and surely it ought to be cultivated, since the wisest of men informs us that "a merry heart doth good like a medicine."[3] As human life has many diseases which require medicines, are we not right in selecting the most agreeable and palatable? Major Sanford's example has had great influence upon

[1] *fond* Foolish, doting.

[2] *the people of my charge* I.e., Boyer's parishioners.

[3] *a merry … medicine* See Proverbs 17.22: "A merry heart doeth good like a medicine: but a broken spirit drieth the bones."

our society in general; and though some of our old dons[1] think him rather licentious, yet, for aught I can see, he is as strict an observer of decorum as the best of them. True, he seldom goes to church; but what of that? The Deity is not confined to temples made with hands. He may worship him as devoutly elsewhere, if he chooses; and who has a right to say he does not?

His return from Boston was but a day or two after mine. He paid me an early visit; and, indeed, has been very attentive ever since. My mamma is somewhat precise in her notions of propriety; and of course, blames me for associating so freely with him. She says that my engagements to Mr. Boyer ought to render me more sedate, and more indifferent to the gallantry of mere *pleasure-hunters*, to use her phrase. But I think otherwise. If I am to become a recluse, let me, at least, enjoy those amusements, which are suited to my taste, a short time first. Why should I refuse the polite attentions of this gentleman? They smooth the rugged path of life, and wonderfully accelerate the lagging wheels of time.

Indeed, Lucy, he has an admirable talent for contributing to vary and increase amusement. We have few hours unimproved. Some new plan of pleasure and sociability is constantly courting our adoption. He lives in all the magnificence of a prince; and why should I, who can doubtless share that magnificence if I please, forego the advantages and indulgences it offers, merely to gratify those friends who pretend to be better judges of my happiness than I am myself?

I have not yet told my mamma that he entertains me with the lover's theme; or, at least, that I listen to it. Yet I must own to you, from whom I have never concealed an action or idea, that his situation in life charms my imagination; that the apparent fervor and sincerity of his passion affect my heart. Yet there is something extremely problematical in his conduct. He is very urgent with me to dissolve my connection with Mr. Boyer, and engage not to marry him without his consent; or knowledge, to say no more. He warmly applauds my wish, still longer to enjoy the freedom and independence of a single state; and professedly adopts it for his own. While he would disconnect me from another, he mysteriously conceals his own intentions and views. In conversation with him yesterday, I plainly told him that his conduct

was unaccountable; that if his professions and designs were honorable he could not neglect to mention them to my mamma; that I should no longer consent to carry on a clandestine intercourse with him; that I hourly expected Mr. Boyer, whom I esteemed, and who was the favorite of my friends; and that unless he acted openly in this affair before his arrival, I should give my hand to him.

He appeared thunderstruck at this declaration. All his words and actions were indicative of the most violent emotions of mind. He entreated me to recall the sentence; for I knew not, he said, his motives for secrecy; yet he solemnly swore that they were honorable. I replied in the words of the poet,

> Trust not a man, they are by nature cruel,
> False, deceitful, treacherous, and inconstant.
> When a man talks of love, with caution hear him;
> But if he swear, he'll certainly deceive you.[2]

He begged that he might know by what means he had provoked my suspicions; by what means he had forfeited my confidence? His importunity vanquished my fortitude; and before we parted, I again promised to make him acquainted, from time to time, with the progress of my connection with Mr. Boyer.

Now, my dear friend, I want your advice more than ever. I am inadvertently embarrassed by this man; and how to extricate myself, I know not. I am sensible that the power is in my hands; but the disposition (shall I confess it) is wanting!

> I know the right, and I approve it too;
> I know the wrong, and yet the wrong pursue![3]

I have just received a card from Major Sanford, inviting me to ride this afternoon. At first I thought of returning a negative answer; but recollecting that Mr. Boyer must soon be here, I concluded it best to embrace this opportunity of talking further with him. I must now prepare to go, but shall not close this letter,

[1] *dons* Men of local importance.

[2] *Trust not ... deceive you* See Thomas Otway's 1680 play *The Orphan* 2.1.311–14.

[3] *I know ... wrong pursue!* Slight misquotation from Nahum Tate's 1717 translation of Ovid's *Metamorphoses* 7.34–35.

for I intend writing in continuation, as events occur, till this important business is decided.

Tuesday evening. The little tour which I mentioned to you this afternoon was not productive of a final determination. The same plea was repeated over and over again, without closing the cause. On my return I found Mr. Boyer waiting to receive me. My heart beat an involuntary welcome. I received him very cordially, though with a kind of pleasure mixed with apprehension. I must own that his conversation and manners are much better calculated to bear the scrutinising eye of a refined understanding and taste, than Major Sanford's. But whether the fancy ought not to be consulted about our settlement for life, is with me a question.

When we parted last, I had promised Mr. Boyer to inform him positively, at this visit, when my hand should be given. He therefore came, as he told me in the course of our conversation, with the resolution of claiming the fulfilment of this promise.

I begged absolution; told him that I could not possibly satisfy his claim; and sought still to evade, and put off the important decision. He grew warm; and affirmed that I treated him ungenerously, and made needless delays. He even accused me of indifference towards him; and of partiality to another. Major Sanford, he believed, was the man who robbed him of the affection which he had supposed his due. He warned me against any intercourse with him, and insisted that I must renounce the society of the one or the other immediately. He would leave me, he said, this evening and call tomorrow to know the result of my determination. It was late before he bade me good night; since which I have written these particulars. It is now time to lay aside my pen, and deliberate what course to take.

Wednesday Evening. Last night I closed not my eyes. I rose this morning with the sun, and went into the garden till breakfast. My mamma doubtless saw the disorder of my mind, but kindly avoided any inquiry about it. She was affectionately attentive to me, but said nothing of my particular concerns. I mentioned not my embarrassment to her. She had declared herself in favor of Mr. Boyer; therefore I had no expectation that she would advise impartially. I retired to my chamber, and remained in a kind of reverie, for more than an hour; when I was roused by the rattling of a carriage at the door. I hastened to the window, and saw Major Sanford just driving away. The idea of his having been to converse with my mamma gave me new sensations. A thousand perplexities occurred to my mind relative to the part most proper for me to act in this critical situation. All these might have been avoided, had I gone down and inquired into the matter; but this I delayed till dinner. My mamma then informed me that Major Sanford had been with her, and inquired for me; but that she thought it unnecessary to call me, as she presumed I had no particular business with him. I knew the motives by which she was actuated, and was vexed at her evasions. I told her plainly that she would never carry her point in this way; that I thought myself capable of conducting my own affairs, and wished her not to interfere, except by her advice, which I should always listen to, and comply with when I could possibly make it consistent with my inclination and interest. She wept at my undutiful anger (of which I have severely repented since) and affectionately replied, that my happiness was the object of her wishes and prayers; conformably to which she felt constrained freely to speak her mind, though it incurred my displeasure. She then went through again with all the comparative circumstances and merits of the two candidates for my favor, which have perpetually rung in my ears for months. I shed tears at the idea of my embarrassment; and in this condition Mr. Boyer found us. He appeared to be affected by my visible disorder; and without inquiring the cause, endeavored to dissipate it. This was kindly done. He conversed upon indifferent subjects, and invited me to ride, and take tea with your mamma, to which I readily consented. We found her at home; and passed the time agreeably, excepting the alloy of your absence. Mr. Boyer touched lightly on the subject of our last evening's debate; but expatiated largely on the pleasing power of love, and hoped that we should one day both realize and exemplify it in perfection. When we returned, he observed that it was late, and took his leave, telling me that he should call tomorrow; and begged that I would then relieve his suspense. As I was retiring to bed, the maid gave me a hint that Major Sanford's servant had been here and left a letter. I turned instantly back to my mamma, and telling her my information, demanded the letter. She hesitated, but I insisted on having it; and seeing

me resolute, she reluctantly gave it into my hand. It contained the following words:

Am I forsaken? Am I abandoned? Oh my adorable Eliza, have you sacrificed me to my rival? Have you condemned me to perpetual banishment, without a hearing?

I came this day, to plead my cause at your feet; but was cruelly denied the privilege of seeing you! My mind is all anarchy and confusion! My soul is harrowed up with jealousy! I will be revenged on those who separate us, if that distracting[1] event take place! But it is from your lips only that I can hear my sentence! You must witness its effects! To what lengths my despair may carry me, I know not! You are the arbitress of my fate!

Let me conjure you to meet me in your garden tomorrow at any hour you shall appoint. My servant will call for an answer in the morning. Deny me not an interview; but have pity on your faithful

Sanford.

I wrote for answer that I would meet him tomorrow, at five o'clock in the afternoon.

I have now before me another night for consideration; and shall pass it in that employment. I purpose not to see Mr. Boyer, till I have conversed with Major Sanford.

Thursday Morning. The morning dawns, and ushers in the day; a day, perhaps big with the fate of your friend! What that fate may be is wrapped in the womb of futurity; that futurity which a kind Providence has wisely concealed from the penetration of mortals!

After mature consideration; after revolving and re-revolving every circumstance on both sides of the question, I have nearly determined, in compliance with the advice of my friends, and the dictates of my own judgment, to give Mr. Boyer the preference, and with him to tread the future round of life.

As to the despair of Major Sanford, it does not much alarm me. Such violent passions are seldom so deeply rooted as to produce lasting effects. I must, however, keep my word, and meet him according to promise.

Mr. Boyer is below. My mamma has just sent me word that he wished to see me. My reply was that I had lain down, which was a fact.

One o'clock. My mamma, alarmed by my indisposition, has visited my apartment. I soon convinced her that it was but trifling, owing principally to the want of sleep; and that an airing in the garden, which I intended towards night, would restore me.

Ten o'clock, at night. The day is past! and such a day it has been, as I hope never more to see!

At the hour appointed, I went tolerably composed and resolute into the garden. I had taken several turns, and retired into the little arbor, where you and I have spent so many happy hours, before Major Sanford entered. When he appeared, a consciousness of the impropriety of this clandestine intercourse suffused my cheek, and gave a coldness to my manners. He immediately penetrated the cause, and observed that my very countenance told him he was no longer a welcome guest to me. I asked him if he ought so to be; since his motives for seeking admission were unworthy of being communicated to my friends. That he said was not the case, but that prudence in the present instance required a temporary concealment.

He then undertook to exculpate himself from blame, assuring me that as soon as I should discountenance the expectations of Mr. Boyer, and discontinue the reception of his address, his intentions should be made known. He was enlarging upon this topic, when we heard a footstep approaching us; and looking up saw Mr. Boyer within a few paces of the arbor. Confusion seized us both! We rose involuntarily from our seats, but were mute as statues! He spoke not a word, but casting a look of indignant accusation at me, a glance which penetrated my very soul, turned on his heel, and walked hastily back to the house.

I stood a few moments, considering what course to take, though shame and regret had almost taken from me the power of thought.

Major Sanford took my hand. I withdrew it from him. I *must* leave you, said I. Where will you go? said he. I will go and try to retrieve my character. It has suffered greatly by this fatal interview.

He threw himself at my feet and exclaimed, leave me not, Eliza, I conjure you not to leave me. Let me go now, I rejoined, or I bid you farewell forever. I flew

[1] *distracting* Distressing; maddening.

precipitately by him, and went into the parlor, where I found Mr. Boyer and my mamma, the one traversing the room in the greatest agitation; the other in a flood of tears! Their appearance affected me; and I wept like an infant! when I had a little recovered myself, I begged him to sit down; He answered no. I then told him, that however unjustifiable my conduct might appear, perhaps I might explain it to his satisfaction, if he would hear me; that my motives were innocent, though they doubtless wore the aspect of criminality, in his view. He sternly replied, that no palliation could avail; that my motives were sufficiently notorious! He accused me of treating him ill, of rendering him the dupe of coquetting artifice, of having an intrigue with Major Sanford, and declared his determination to leave me forever, as unworthy of his regard, and incapable of love, gratitude, or honor! There was too much reason in support of his accusations for me to gainsay them, had his impetuosity suffered me to attempt it.

But in truth I had no inclination to self defence. My natural vivacity had forsaken me; and I listened without interrupting him to the fluency of reproachful language, which his resentment inspired. He took a very solemn and affectionate leave of my mamma; thanking her for her politeness, and wishing her much future felicity. He attempted to address me, I suppose somewhat in the same way, but his sensibility overcame him; and he only took my hand, and bowing in silence, departed.

The want of rest for two long nights together, the exercise of mind, and conflict of passions, which now tortured my breast, were too much for me to support!

When I saw that he was gone; that he had actually forsaken me, I fainted. My mamma, with the assistance of the maid, soon restored me.

When I opened my eyes, and beheld this amiable and tender parent, watching and attending me with the most anxious concern; without one reproachful word, without one accusing look, my reflections upon the part I had acted, in defeating her benevolent wishes, were exquisitely afflictive! But we mutually forbore to mention the occasion of my illness; and I complied with her advice to take some refreshment, and retire to my chamber. I am so much fatigued by the exertions of the day, that rest is absolutely necessary; and I lay aside my pen to seek it.

Friday Morning. When I shall again receive the balmy influence of sleep, I know not. It has absolutely forsaken me at present. I have had a most restless night. Every awakening idea presented itself to my imagination; whether I had sustained a real loss in Mr. Boyer's departure; reflections on my own misconduct, with the censure of my friends, and the ill-natured remarks of my enemies, excited the most painful anxiety in my mind!

I am going down, but how shall I see my mamma? To her will I confess my faults, in her maternal breast repose my cares, and by her friendly advice regulate my conduct. Had I done this before, I might have escaped this trouble, and saved both her and myself many distressing emotions!

Friday Evening. I have had a long conversation with my mamma, which has greatly relieved my mind. She has soothed me with the most endearing tenderness.

Mr. Atkins, with whom Mr. Boyer lodged, while in town, called here this afternoon. I did not see him, but he told my mamma that Mr. Boyer had returned home, and left a letter for me, which he had promised to convey with his own hand. By this letter I am convinced that the die is absolutely cast, with respect to him, and that no attempts on my part to bring about a reconciliation would be either prudent or successful. He has penetrated the cause of my proceedings; and such is his resentment, that I am inclined not much to regret his avoiding another interview.

My excuses would be deemed utterly insufficient, and truth would not befriend and justify me.

As I know you are impatient to hear from me, I will now dispatch this long letter without any other addition, than that I am your sincere friend,

Eliza Wharton

LETTER 42
TO MR. CHARLES DEIGHTON

Hartford

Well, Charles, the show is over, as we yankees say; and the girl is my own. That is, if I will have her. I shall take my own time for that, however. I have carried my

point, and am amply revenged on the whole posse of those dear friends of hers. She was entangled by a promise (not to marry this priest without my knowledge) which her conscience would not let her break. Thank God, I have no conscience. If I had, I believe it would make wretched work with me! I suppose she intended to have one or the other of us; but preferred me. I have escaped the noose, this time, and I'll be fairly hanged, if I ever get so near it again. For indeed Charles, I was seriously alarmed. I watched all their motions; and the appearances of harmony between them awakened all my activity and zeal. So great was my infatuation, that I verily believe I should have asked her in marriage, and risked the consequences, rather than to have lost her!

I went to the house, while Mr. Boyer was in town, but her mamma refused to call her, or to acquaint her that I was there. I then wrote a despairing letter, and obtained a conference with her in the garden. This was a fortunate event for me. True, Eliza was very haughty, and resolutely insisted on immediate declaration or rejection. And I cannot say what would have been the result, if Mr. Boyer had not surprized us together. He gave us a pretty harsh look and retired without speaking a word.

I endeavored to detain Eliza, but in vain. She left me on my knees, which are always ready to bend on such occasions.

This finished the matter, it seems. I rose, and went into a near neighbor's to observe what happened; and in about half an hour saw Mr. Boyer come out, and go to his lodgings.

This, said I to myself, is a good omen. I went home, and was informed next day that he had mounted his horse and departed.

I heard nothing more of her till yesterday, when I determined to know how she stood affected towards me. I therefore paid her a visit, her mamma being luckily abroad.

She received me very placidly, and told me, on inquiry, that Mr. Boyer's resentment at her meeting me in the garden was so great, that he had bid her a final adieu. I congratulated myself on having no rival; hoped that her favor would now be unbiased, and that in due time I should reap the reward of my fidelity. She begged me not to mention the subject; said she had been perplexed by our competition, and wished

not to hear anything further about it at present. I bowed in obedience to her commands and changed the discourse.

I informed her, that I was about taking a tour to the southward; that I should be absent several months, and trusted that on my return her embarrassments would be over.

I left her with regret. After all, Charles, she is the *summum bonum*[1] of my life. I must have her in some way or other. Nobody else shall, I am resolved.

I am making preparations for my journey; which, between you and me, is occasioned by the prospect of making a speculation, by which I hope to mend my affairs. The voyage will at least lessen my expenses, and screen me from the importunity of creditors till I can look about me.

Peter Sanford

LETTER 43
TO MISS ELIZA WHARTON

New-Haven

My Dear Eliza,

Through the medium of my friends at Hartford I have been informed of the progress of your affairs, as they have transpired. The detail which my sister gave me of your separation from Mr. Boyer was painful; as I had long contemplated a happy union between you. But still more disagreeable sensations possessed my breast, when told that you had suffered your lively spirits to be depressed, and resigned yourself to solitude and dejection!

Why, my dear friend, should you allow this event thus to affect you? Heaven, I doubt not, has happiness still in store for you—perhaps greater than you could have enjoyed in that connection. If the conviction of any misconduct on your part give you pain, dissipate it by the reflection, that unerring rectitude is not the lot of mortals, that few are to be found who have not deviated in a greater or less degree from the maxims

[1] *summum bonum* Latin: greatest good.

of prudence. Our greatest mistakes may teach lessons which will be useful through life.

But I will not moralize. Come and see us; and we will talk over the matter once, and then dismiss it forever. Do prevail on your mamma to part with you a month or two at least. I wish you to witness how well I manage my nursery business. You will be charmed with little Harriot. I am already enough of the mother to think her a miniature of beauty and perfection.

How natural, and how easy the transition from one stage of life to another! Not long since[1] I was a gay, volatile girl, seeking satisfaction in fashionable circles and amusements; but now I am thoroughly domesticated. All my happiness is centered within the limits of my own walls; and I grudge every moment that calls me from the pleasing scenes of domestic life. Not that I am so selfish as to exclude my friends from my affection or society. I feel interested in their concerns, and enjoy their company. I must own, however, that conjugal and parental love are the main springs of my life. The conduct of some mothers in depriving their helpless offspring of the care and kindness which none but a mother can feel, is to me unaccountable. There are many nameless attentions which nothing short of maternal tenderness and solicitude can pay; and for which the endearing smiles and progressive improvements of the lovely babe are an ample reward.

How delightful to trace from day to day the expansion of reason and the dawnings of intelligence! Oh, how I anticipate the time, when these faculties shall be displayed by the organs of speech; when the lisping accent shall heighten our present pleasure, and the young idea be capable of direction "how to shoot"![2] General Richman is not less interested by these enjoyments than myself. All the father beams in his eye! All the husband reigns in his heart, and pervades his every action!

Miss Laurence is soon to be married to Mr. Laiton. I believe he is a mere fortune-hunter. Indeed she has little to recommend her to any other. Nature has not been very bountiful, either to her body, or mind. Her parents have been shamefully deficient in her education; but have secured to her what they think the chief good; not considering that happiness is by no means the invariable attendant of wealth.

I hope this incoherent scroll will amuse, while it induces you speedily to favor us with another visit.

My best wishes attend your honored mamma, while I subscribe myself, etc.

A. Richman

LETTER 44
TO MRS. LUCY SUMNER

Hartford

I am extremely depressed, my dear Lucy! The agitating scenes, through which I have lately passed, have broken my spirits, and rendered me unfit for society.

Major Sanford has visited me, and taken his leave. He is gone to the southward on a tour of two or three months. I declined any further conversation with him, on the subject of love. At present, I wish not to hear it mentioned by anyone.

I have received a very friendly and consolatory letter from Mrs. Richman. She invites me to spend a few months with her; which with my mamma's consent I shall do. I hope the change of situation and company will dissipate the gloom which hangs over my mind.

It is a common observation, that we know not the value of a blessing but by deprivation.

This is strictly verified in my case. I was insensible of my regard for Mr. Boyer, till this fatal separation took place. His merit and worth now appear in the brightest colors. I am convinced of that excellence which I once slighted; and the shade of departed happiness haunts me perpetually! I am sometimes tempted to write him, and confess my faults; to tell him the situation of my mind, and to offer him my hand. But he has precluded all hopes of success, by the severity of his letter to me. At any rate, I shall do nothing of the kind, till my return from New-Haven.

I am the more willing to leave home, as my affairs are made a town talk. My mamma persuades me to disregard it. But how can I rise superior to "The world's

[1] *since* Ago.

[2] *how to shoot* See Thomson's *The Seasons*, "Spring" 1069–70: "Delightful task! to rear the tender thought, / To teach the young idea how to shoot."

dread laugh, which scarce the firm philosopher can scorn"?[1]

Pray remember me to Mr. Sumner. You are happy, my friend, in the love and esteem of a worthy man; but more happy still, in deserving them. Adieu.

Eliza Wharton

LETTER 45
TO THE SAME

Hartford

I have returned to the once smiling seat of maternal affection; but I find not repose and happiness, even there!

In the society of my amiable friends at New-Haven, I enjoyed everything that friendship could bestow; but rest to a disturbed mind was not in their power.

I was on various parties of pleasure, and passed through different scenes of amusement; but with me they have lost their charms. I relished them not as formerly.

Mrs. Richman advises me to write to Mr. Boyer, and I have concluded to act accordingly. If it answer no other purpose, it will be a relief to my mind. If he ever felt for me the tenderness and regard which he professed, methinks they cannot be entirely obliterated. If they still remain, perhaps I may rekindle the gentle flame, and we may both be happy. I may at least recall his esteem, and that will be a satisfaction to my conscious mind.

I wonder what has become of Major Sanford! Has he too forsaken me? Is it possible for him willfully to neglect me? I will not entertain so injurious a suspicion.

Yet, if it were the case, it would not affect me like Mr. Boyer's disaffection; for I frankly own that my fancy, and a taste for gaiety of life, induced me to cherish the idea of a connection with Major Sanford; while Mr. Boyer's real merit has imprinted those sentiments of esteem and love in my heart, which time can never efface.

Instead of two or three, more than twelve months have elapsed, and I have not received a line from Major Sanford in all that time, which I fully expected, though he made no mention of writing; nor have I heard a syllable about him, except a report circulated by his servants, that he is on the point of marrying, which I do not believe. No, it is impossible! I am persuaded that his passion for me was sincere, however deceitful he may have been with others. But I will not bestow an anxious thought upon him. My design relative to Mr. Boyer demands my whole attention.

My hopes and fears alternately prevail, and my resolution is extremely fluctuating. How it finally terminates you shall hear in my next. Pray write to me soon. I stand in need of the consoling power of friendship. Nothing can beguile my pensive hours, and exhilarate my drooping spirits, like your letters.

Let me know how you are to be entertained this winter at the theatre. That, you know, is a favorite amusement of mine. You see I can step out of myself a little. Afford an assisting hand, and perhaps I may again be fit for society.

Eliza Wharton

LETTER 46
TO THE REV. J. BOYER

Hartford

Sir,

It is partly in compliance with your desire, in your last letter to me, in which you tell me, "that when I am convinced of the justice of your conduct, and become a convert to your advice, you shall be happy to hear it"; and partly from a wish to inform you that such is in truth my present state of mind, that I now write to you.

I cannot but hope that this letter, coming from the hand which you once sought, will not be unacceptable.

Pope very justly observes, "that every year is a critic on the last."[2] The truth of this observation is fully

1 *The world's ... can scorn* See "Autumn" from Thomson's *The Seasons*, 230–31.

2 *that every ... the last* See Alexander Pope's *Essay on Criticism* (1711), lines 570–71: "But you, with pleasure own your errors past, / And make each day a critic on the last."

exemplified in my years! How severely this condemns the follies of the preceding, my own heart alone can testify!

I shall not offer any palliation or apology for my misconduct. You told me it admitted none. I frankly confess it; and if the most humble acknowledgement of my offences, with an assurance that they have cost me the deepest repentance, can in any degree atone for them, I now make the atonement. Casting off the veil of dissimulation, I shall write with frankness; believing you possessed of more honor than to make any ungenerous use of the confidence reposed in you.

To say that I ever esteemed you, may, perhaps, appear paradoxical, when compared with certain circumstances which occurred during our acquaintance; but to assert that I loved you, may be deemed still more so. Yet these are real facts, facts of which I was then sensible, and by which I am now more than ever affected.

I think you formerly remarked that absence served but to heighten real love. This I find by experience. Need I blush to declare these sentiments, when occasion like this calls for the avowal? I will go even further, and offer you that heart which once you prized; that hand which you once solicited. The sentiments of affection, which you then cultivated, though suppressed, I flatter myself are not wholly obliterated. Suffer me then to rekindle the latent flame; to revive that friendship and tenderness, which I have so foolishly neglected. The endeavor of my future life shall be to reward your benevolence, and perhaps we may yet be happy together.

But let not this offer of myself constrain you. Let not pity influence your conduct. I would have your return, if that pleasing event take place, a voluntary act. Receive or consent not to confer happiness.

I thought it a duty which I owed to you, and to myself, to make this expiation; this sacrifice of female reserve, for the wrongs I have done you. As such I wish you to accept it; and if your affections are entirely alienated, or otherwise engaged; if you cannot again command the respect and love which I would recall, do not despise me for the concessions I have made. Think as favorably of my past faults, and of my present disposition, as charity will allow. Continue, if possible, to be my friend, though you cease to be my lover.

Should this letter find you in the full possession of happiness, let not the idea of your once loved Eliza, thus intruding itself again upon your thoughts, interrupt your enjoyments. May some distinguished female, as deserving, as fair, partake with you of that bliss which I have forfeited.

Whatever may be my destiny, my best wishes shall ever attend you, and a pleasing remembrance of your honorable attentions preside, till death, in the breast of,

Eliza Wharton

LETTER 47
TO MISS ELIZA WHARTON

Hampshire

Madam,

As I was sitting last evening in my study, a letter was handed me by a servant; upon which I no sooner cast my eye, than I recognized, with surprise, the hand and seal of my once loved, but to me long lost Eliza! I opened it hastily, and with still greater surprise, read the contents!

You write with frankness. I shall answer in the same manner.

On reviewing our former intercourse, be assured that I have not an accusing thought in my heart. The regard which I felt for you was tender and animated, but it was not of that passionate kind which ends in death or despair. It was governed by reason, and had a nobler object in view than mere sensual gratification. It was excited by the appearance of excellent qualities. Your conduct, at length, convinced me it was misplaced; that you possessed not, in reality, those charms which I had fondly ascribed to you. They were inconsistent, I conceived, with that artifice and dissimulation of which you strove to render me the dupe. But thank heaven, the snare was broken. My eyes were opened to discover your folly; and my heart, engaged as it was, exerted resolution and strength to burst asunder the chain by which you held me enslaved, and to assert the rights of an injured man.

The parting scene, you remember. I reluctantly bade you adieu. I tore myself from you, determined to eradicate your idea from my breast! Long and severe was the struggle. I at last vanquished, as I thought, every tender passion of my soul (for they all centered in you), and resigned myself to my God, and my duty; devoting those affections to friendship, which had been disappointed in love. But they are again called into exercise. The virtuous, the amiable, the accomplished Maria Selby possesses my entire confidence and esteem; and I trust I am not deceived, when I think her highly deserving of both. With her I expect soon to be united in the most sacred and endearing of human relations; with her to pass my future days in serenity and peace.

Your letter, therefore, came too late, were there no other obstacle to the renewal of our connection. I hope at the close of life, when we take a retrospect of the past, that neither of us shall have reason to regret our separation.

Permit me to add that, for your own sake, and for the sake of your ever valued friends, I sincerely rejoice that your mind has regained its native strength and beauty; that you have emerged from the shade of fanciful vanity. For although to adopt your own phrase, I cease to style myself your lover, among the number of your friends, I am happy to be reckoned. As such, let me conjure you, by all that is dear and desirable, both in this life, and another, to adhere, with undeviating exactness, to the path of rectitude and innocence; and to improve the noble talents, which heaven has liberally bestowed upon you, in rendering yourself amiable, and useful to your friends. Thus will you secure your own, while you promote the happiness of all around you.

I shall ever cherish sentiments of kindness towards you, and with gratitude remember your condescension, in the testimony of regard, which you have given me in your last letter.

I hope soon to hear that your heart and hand are bestowed on some worthy man, who deserves the happiness you are formed to communicate. Whatever we may have called errors will, on my part, be forever buried in oblivion; and for your own peace of mind, I entreat you to forget that any idea of a connection between us ever existed.

I shall always rejoice at the news of your welfare, and my ardent prayers will daily arise for your temporal and eternal felicity.

I am, etc.

J. Boyer

LETTER 48
TO MRS. LUCY SUMNER

Hartford

Health, placid serenity, and every domestic pleasure, are the lot of my friend; while I, who once possessed the means of each, and the capacity of tasting them, have been tossed upon the waves of folly, till I am shipwrecked on the shoals of despair!

Oh my friend, I am undone! I am slighted, rejected by the man who once sought my hand, by the man who still retains my heart! and what adds an insupportable poignancy to the reflection, is self-condemnation! From this inward torture, where shall I flee? Where shall I seek that happiness which I have madly trifled away?

The enclosed letters[1] will show you whence this tumult of soul arises. But I blame not Mr. Boyer. He has acted nobly. I approve his conduct, though it operates my ruin!

He is worthy of his intended bride, and she is what I am not, worthy of him. Peace and joy be their portion, both here and hereafter! But what are now my prospects? what are to be the future enjoyments of my life?

Oh that I had not written to Mr. Boyer! By confessing my faults, and by avowing my partiality to him, I have given him the power of triumphing in my distress; of returning to my tortured heart all the pangs of slighted love! and what have I now to console me? My bloom is decreasing; my health is sensibly impaired. Those talents, with the possession of which I have been flattered, will be of little avail when unsupported by respectability of character!

My mamma, who knows too well the distraction of my mind, endeavors to sooth and compose me, on Christian principles; but they have not their desired

1 [Foster's note] See the two preceding letters.

effect. I dare not converse freely with her on the subject of my present uneasiness, lest I should distress her. I am therefore obliged to conceal my disquietude, and appear as cheerful as possible in her company, though my heart is ready to burst with grief!

Oh that you were near me, as formerly, to share and alleviate my cares! to have some friend in whom I could repose confidence, and with whom I could freely converse, and advise, on this occasion, would be an unspeakable comfort!

Such a one, next to yourself, I think Julia Granby to be. With your leave and consent I should esteem it a special favor if she would come and spend a few months with me. My mamma joins in this request. I would write to her on the subject, but cannot compose myself at present. Will you prefer my petition for me?

If I have not forfeited your friendship, my dear Mrs. Sumner, write to me, and pour its healing balm into the wounded mind of your

Eliza Wharton

LETTER 49
TO MISS ELIZA WHARTON

Boston

Your truly romantic letter came safe to hand. Indeed, my dear, it would make a very pretty figure in a novel. A bleeding heart, slighted love, and all the *et ceteras* of romance, enter into the composition!

Excuse this raillery; and I will now write more seriously. You refer yourself to my friendship for consolation. It shall be exerted for the purpose. But I must act the part of a skilful surgeon, and probe the wound which I undertake to heal.

Where, O Eliza Wharton! Where is that fund of sense and sentiment which once animated your engaging form? Where that strength of mind, that independence of soul, that alacrity and sprightliness of deportment, which formerly raised you superior to every adverse occurrence? Why have you resigned these valuable endowments, and suffered yourself to become the sport of contending passions?

You have now emerged from that mist of fanciful folly, which, in a measure obscured the brilliance of your youthful days.

True, you figured among the first rate coquettes; while your friends, who knew your accomplishments, lamented the misapplication of them; but now they rejoice at the returning empire of reason.

True, you have erred; misled by the gaiety of your disposition, and that volatility, and inconsideration, which were incident to your years; but you have seen and nobly confessed your errors. Why do you talk of slighted love? True, Mr. Boyer, supposing you disregarded him, transferred his affections to another object; but have you not your admirers still among men of real merit? Are you not esteemed and caressed by numbers, who know you capable of shining in a distinguished sphere of life? Turn then, my friend, from the gloomy prospect, which your disturbed imagination has brought into view. Let reason and religion erect their throne in your breast; obey their dictates and be happy. Past experience will point out the quicksands which you are to avoid in your future course.

Date then, from this, a new era of life; and may every moment be attended with felicity. Follow Mr. Boyer's advice, and forget all former connections.

Julia accepts your invitation. Nothing short of your request could induce me to part with her. She is a good girl; and her society will amuse and instruct you.

I am, etc.

Lucy Sumner

LETTER 50
TO MRS. LUCY SUMNER

Hartford

My Julia Granby has arrived. She is all that I once was; easy, sprightly, debonair. Already has she done much towards relieving my mind. She endeavors to divert and lead my thoughts into a different channel from that to which they are now prone. Yesterday, we had each an invitation to a ball. She labored hard to prevail on me to go; but I obstinately refused. I cannot yet mix

with gay and cheerful circles. I therefore alleged that I was indisposed, and persuaded her to go without me.

The events of my life have always been unaccountably wayward. In many instances I have been ready to suppose that some evil genius[1] presided over my actions, which has directed them contrary to the sober dictates of my own judgment.

I am sometimes tempted to adopt the sentiment expressed in the following lines of the poet,

> To you, great gods, I make my last appeal;
> O, clear my conscience, or my crimes reveal!
> If wand'ring through the paths of life I've run;
> And backward trod the steps, I sought to shun,
> Impute my errors to your own decree;
> My feet were guilty, but my heart was free.[2]

I suppose you will tell me that the fate I accuse, through the poet, is only the result of my own imprudence. Well, be it what it may; either the impulse of my own passions, or some higher efficiency; sure I am, that I pay dear for its operation.

I have heard it remarked that experience is the preceptor of fools; but that the wise need not its instruction. I believe I must be content to rank accordingly, and endeavor to reap advantage from its tuition.

Julia urges me to revisit the scenes of amusements and pleasure; in which she tells me she is actuated by selfish motives. She wishes it for her own sake. She likes neither to be secluded from them, nor to go alone. I am sometimes half inclined to seek, in festive mirth, a refuge from thought and reflection. I would escape, if possible, from the idea of Mr. Boyer. This I have never been able to accomplish, since he dropped a tear upon my hand, and left me. I marked the spot with my eye; and twenty times in a day do I view it, and fondly imagine it still there! How could I give him pain! I hope his happy Maria never will! I hope she will reward that merit, which I have slighted! but I forbear. This theme carries away my pen, if I but touch upon it. And no wonder; for it is the sole exercise of my thoughts! Yet I will endeavor to divert them. Send me some new books; not such, however, as will require

much attention. Let them be plays or novels, or anything else, that will amuse and extort a smile.

Julia and I have been rambling in the garden. She insisted upon my going with her into the arbor, where I was surprised with Major Sanford. What a crowd of painful ideas rushed upon my imagination! I believe she repented her rashness. But no more of this. I must lay aside my pen; for I can write nothing else!

<div align="right">Eliza Wharton</div>

<div align="center">

LETTER 51
TO MRS. LUCY SUMNER

</div>

<div align="right">Hartford</div>

Dear Madam,

You commanded me to write you respecting Miss Wharton; and I obey. But I cannot describe to you the surprising change which she has undergone. Her vivacity has entirely forsaken her; and she has actually become, what she once dreaded above all things, a recluse! She flies from company as eagerly as she formerly sought it! Her mamma is exceedingly distressed by the settled melancholy which appears in the darling child; but neither of us think it best to mention the subject to her. We endeavor to find means to amuse her; and we flatter ourselves that the prospect of success rather increases. It would add greatly to my happiness, to contribute, in any degree, to restore her to herself, to her friends, and to society.

We are all invited to dine abroad tomorrow; and to oblige me, she has consented to go.

Pray madam, write to her often. Your letters may do much for her. She is still feelingly alive to the power of friendship; and none can exercise it upon her to greater acceptance, or with more advantage than yourself.

Major Sanford's house is undergoing a complete repair. The report is, that he is soon to be married. Miss Wharton has heard, but does not believe it. I hope, for her sake, it will prove true. For, at any rate, he is about returning; and from her mamma's account of his past conduct towards Eliza, were he to return unconnected, he would probably renew his attentions; and though

[1] *genius* Protective spirit who governs an individual's fortune.

[2] *To you ... was free* Slight misquotation from John Dryden's 1679 play *Oedipus: A Tragedy* 3.1.588–93.

they might end in marriage, her happiness would not be secured. She has too nice a sense of love and honor to compound with his licentious principles. A man who has been dissolute before marriage will very seldom be faithful afterwards.

I went into Eliza's chamber the other day, and found her with a miniature picture in her hand. You pretend to be a physiognomist,[1] Julia, said she. What can you trace in that countenance? I guessed whose it was; and looking wistfully at it, replied, I believe the original is an artful, designing man. He looks to me like a Chesterfieldian.[2] Pray who is he? Major Sanford, said she; and I am afraid you have hit his character exactly. Sure I am, that the appearance of those traits in it has made my heart ache! She wept, as she spoke it.

Poor girl! I wish he may never give you greater cause to weep! She is strongly blind to the vices and imperfections of this man. Though naturally penetrating, he has somehow or other cast a deceptious mist over her imagination, with respect to himself. She professes neither to love nor esteem him; and owns that his ungenerous artifice misled her in her treatment of Mr. Boyer. Yet she has forgiven him, and thinks him a pleasing companion!

How prone to error is the human mind! How much lighter than the breath of zephyrs[3] the operations of fancy! Strange then, it should ever preponderate over the weightier powers of the understanding!

But I will not moralize. My business here is to dissipate, not to collect ideas; and I must regulate myself accordingly.

I am endeavoring to prepare Eliza, by degrees, to accompany me to Boston, the ensuing winter; but think it doubtful whether I shall succeed. I shall, however, return myself; till when, I am, etc.

Julia Granby

LETTER 52
TO MISS ELIZA WHARTON

Boston

My Dear Eliza,

I received yours of the 24th ult.[4] and thank you for it; though it did not afford me those lively sensations of pleasure which I usually feel at the perusal of your letters. It inspired me both with concern and chagrin. With concern, lest your dejection of mind should affect your health; and with chagrin at your apparent indulgence of melancholy. Indeed, my friend, your own happiness and honor, require you to dissipate the cloud which hangs over your imagination.

Rise then above it; and prove yourself superior to the adverse occurrences which have befallen you. It is by surmounting difficulties, not by sinking under them, that we discover our fortitude. True courage consists not in flying from the storms of life, but in braving and steering through them with prudence. Avoid solitude. It is the bane of a disordered mind; though of great utility to a healthy one. Your once favorite amusements court your attention. Refuse not their solicitations. I have contributed my mite[5] by sending you a few books, such as you requested. They are of the lighter kind of reading; yet perfectly chaste; and if I mistake not, well adapted to your taste.

You wish to hear from our theatre. I believe it will be well supplied with performers this winter. Come and see whether they can afford you any entertainment. Last evening I attended a tragedy; but never will I attend another. I have not yet been able to erase the gloom which it impressed upon my mind. It was Romeo and Juliet. Distressing enough to sensibility this! Are there not real woes (if not in our own families, at least among our own friends, and neighbors) sufficient to exercise our sympathy and pity, without introducing fictitious ones into our very diversions? How can that be a diversion, which racks the soul with grief, even though that grief be imaginary. The introduction of a funeral solemnity, upon the stage, is shocking indeed!

[1] *physiognomist* One who can read a person's facial features and thereby determine their character.

[2] *Chesterfieldian* Allusion to Philip Stanhope, Earl of Chesterfield (1694–1773), whose posthumously published *Letters to His Son* (1774) contained extensive advice for gentlemen on topics including what he called "the art of pleasing" and ways to seduce women.

[3] *zephyrs* Light breezes.

[4] *ult* Latin: ultimo; of the preceding month.

[5] *mite* Small donation.

Death is too serious a matter to be sported with! An opening grave cannot be a source of amusement to any considerate mind! The closing scene of life can be no pastime, when realized! it must therefore awaken painful sensations, in the representation!

The circus is a place of fashionable resort of late, but not agreeable to me. I think it inconsistent with the delicacy of a lady even to witness the indecorums which are practised there; especially, when the performers of equestrian feats are of our own sex. To see a woman depart so far from the female character as to assume the masculine habit and attitudes, and appear entirely indifferent even to the externals of modesty, is truly disgusting, and ought not to be countenanced by our attendance, much less by our approbation. But setting aside this circumstance, I cannot conceive it to be a pleasure to sit a whole evening, trembling with apprehension, lest the poor wight of a horseman, or juggler, or whatever he is to be called, should break his neck in contributing to our entertainment.

With Mr. Bowen's museum,[1] I think you were much pleased. He has made a number of judicious additions to it since you were here. It is a source of rational and refined amusement. Here the eye is gratified, the imagination charmed, and the understanding improved. It will bear frequent reviews without palling on the taste. It always affords something new; and for one, I am never a weary spectator.

Our other public and private places of resort, are much as you left them.

I am happy in my present situation; but when the summer returns, I intend to visit my native home. Again, my Eliza, will we ramble together in those retired shades which friendship has rendered so delightful to us. Adieu, my friend, till then. Be cheerful, and you will yet be happy.

Lucy Sumner

LETTER 53
TO MRS. LUCY SUMNER

Hartford

Gracious Heaven! What have I heard? Major Sanford is married! Yes, the ungrateful, the deceitful wretch, is married! He has forsworn, he has perjured, and given himself to another! That, you will say, is nothing strange. It is characteristic of the man. It may be so; but I could not be convinced of his perfidy,[2] till now!

Perhaps it is all for the best. Perhaps, had he remained unconnected, he might still have deceived me; but now I defy his arts!

They tell me, he has married a woman of fortune. I suppose he thinks, as I once did, that wealth can ensure happiness. I wish he may enjoy it.

This event would not affect me at all, were it not for the depression of spirits which I feel, in consequence of a previous disappointment; since which, everything of the kind agitates and overcomes me. I will not see him. If I do, I shall betray my weakness, and flatter his vanity; as he will doubtless think he has the power of mortifying me by his connection with another.

Before this news discomposed me, I had attained to a good degree of cheerfulness. Your kind letter, seconded by Julia's exertions, has assisted me in regulating my sensibility. I have been frequently into company, and find my relish for it gradually returning.

I intend to accept the pleasure to which you invite me, of spending a little time with you this winter. Julia and I will come together. Varying the scene may contribute effectually to dissipate the gloom of my imagination. I would fly to almost any resort, rather than my own mind. What a dreadful thing it is to be afraid of one's own reflections, which ought to be a constant source of enjoyment! But I will not moralize. I am sufficiently melancholy, without any additional cause to increase it!

Eliza Wharton

1 *Mr. Bowen's museum* Boston museum run by Daniel Bowen (c. 1760–1856), exhibiting wax figures, animal specimens, and other curiosities.

2 *perfidy* Deceitfulness.

LETTER 54
TO MR. CHARLES DEIGHTON

Hartford

Dear Deighton,

Who do you think is writing to you? Why, it is your old friend, metamorphosed into *a married man*! You stare, and can hardly credit the assertion. I cannot realize it myself; yet, I assure you, Charles, it is absolutely true! Necessity, dire necessity, forced me into this *dernier*[1] resort. I told you, some time ago, it would come to this.

I stood aloof, as long as possible; but in vain did I attempt to shun the noose. I must either fly to this resource; or give up all my show, equipage, and pleasure, and degenerate into a downright plodding money-catcher, for a subsistence. I chose the first; and who would not? yet I feel some remorse at taking the girl to wife, from no better motives. She is really too good for such an imposition. But she must blame herself, if she suffer hereafter; for she was visibly captivated by my external appearance; and wanted but very little solicitation to confer herself, and fortune, on so charming a fellow. Her parents opposed her inclination for a while, because I was a stranger, and rather too gay for their taste. But she had not been used to contradiction, and could not bear it; and therefore they ventured not to cross her. So I bore off the prize; and a prize she really is. Five thousand pounds in possession, and more in reversion,[2] if I do not forfeit it. This will compensate for some of my past mistakes, and set matters right for the present. I think it doing much better than to have taken the little Laurence girl I told you of, with half the sum. Besides, my Nancy is a handsomer and more agreeable person. But that is of little consequence to me, you know. "Beauty soon grows familiar to the lover."[3] Were I a lover, it would be of no great avail. A lover I am; yet not of my wife. The dart which I received from Miss Wharton sticks fast in my heart; and I assure you, I could hardly persuade myself even

to appear unfaithful to her. O, Eliza, accuse me not of infidelity; for your image is my constant companion! A thousand times have I cursed the unpropitious stars, which withheld from her a fortune. That would have enabled me to marry her; and with her, even wedlock would have been supportable.

I am told that she is still single. Her sober lover never returned. Had he loved as I did, and do, he could not have been so precipitate. But these stoic souls are good for nothing, that I know of, but

> Fixed like a plant, to one peculiar spot,
> To draw nutrition, propagate, and rot.[4]

I want to see Eliza, and I must see her; yet I dread an interview. I shall frankly confess my motives for marrying; and the reasons of my conduct, before I went away. I shall own that my circumstances would not allow me to possess her; and yet that I could not resign her to another.

When I make up the matter with her, I shall solicit her friendship for my wife. By this mean I may enjoy her society, at least, which will alleviate the confinement of a married state. To my spouse I must be as civil as possible. I really wish she has less merit, that I might have a plausible excuse for neglecting her.

Tomorrow I shall go to Mrs. Wharton's. I am very much taken up with complimental visits, at present. What a difference is always paid to equipage! They may talk of this virtue, their learning, and what not; but without either of them, I shall bear off the palm of respect from those, who have them, unadorned with gold, and its shining appendages.

Everything hereabouts recalls Eliza to my mind. I impatiently anticipate the hour, which will convey me to her presence.

Peter Sanford

[1] *dernier* French: last.

[2] *in reversion* I.e., to be inherited in the future.

[3] *Beauty soon ... the lover* See Joseph Addison's *Cato: A Tragedy* 1.4.145.

[4] *Fixed like ... and rot* See Alexander Pope's *An Essay on Man* 3.63–64.

LETTER 55
TO MRS. LUCY SUMNER

Hartford

A new scene has opened upon us today, my dear Mrs. Sumner; a visit from Major Sanford. My mamma, Miss Granby, and myself, were sitting together in the chamber. Miss Granby was entertaining us by reading aloud in Millot's[1] elements of history, when a servant rapped at the door, and handed in the following billet.

Will Miss Wharton condescend to converse a few moments with her once favored Sanford? He is but too sensible that he has forfeited all claim to the privilege. He therefore presumes not to request it on the score of merit, or of former acquaintance; but solicits it from her benevolence, and pity.

I read and showed it to my mamma, and Julia. What, said I, shall I do? I wish not to see him. His artifice has destroyed my peace of mind; and his presence may open the wounds which time is closing. Act, said my mamma, agreeably to the dictates of your own judgment. I see no harm in conversing with him, said Julia. Perhaps it may remove some disagreeable thoughts, which now oppress and give you pain. And as he is no longer a candidate for your affections, added she, with a smile, it will be less hazardous than formerly. He will not have the insolence to speak; nor you the folly to hear, the language of love.

He was accordingly invited in. When I rose to go down, I hesitated, and even trembled. I fear, said I, to myself, it will be too much for me; yet why should it? Conscious innocence will support me. This he has not. When I entered the room he stepped forward to meet me. Confusion and shame were visibly depicted in his countenance. He approached me hastily; and without uttering a word, took my hand. I withdrew it. O! Miss Wharton, said he, despise me not. I am convinced that I deserve your displeasure, and disdain; but my own heart has avenged your cause. To your own heart, then, said I, I will leave you! But why do you again seek an interview with one whom you have endeavored to mislead; with one whom you have treated with unmerited neglect? Justice to myself required my appearing before you; that by confessing my faults, and obtaining your forgiveness, I might soften the reproaches of my own mind. Will you be seated, sir? said I. Will you, rejoined he, condescend to sit with me, Eliza? I will, sir, answered I. The rights of hospitality I shall not infringe. In my own house, therefore, I shall treat you with civility. Indeed, said he, you are very severe; but I have provoked all the coldness and reserve which you can inflict!

I am a married man, Eliza. So I understand, said I; and I hope you will never treat your wife with the dissimulation and falsehood which you have exercised towards me. Would to heaven, exclaimed he, that you were my wife! I should not then fail in my love or duty as a husband! Yet she is an amiable girl; and, had I a heart to give her, I might still be happy! but that, alas! I can never recall. Why, then, said I, did you marry her? You were doubtless master of your own actions. No, said he, I was not. The embarrassed state of my affairs precluded the possibility of acting as I wished. Loving you most ardently, I was anxious to prevent your union with another, till I could so far improve my circumstances, as to secure you from poverty and want in a connection with me. My regard was too sincere to permit me to deceive you, by a marriage which might have proved unhappy for us both. My pride forbad my telling you the motives of my delay; and I left you to see if I could place myself in a situation worthy of your acceptance. This I could not effect; and therefore have run the risk of my future happiness, by marrying a lady of affluence. This secures to me the externals of enjoyment; but my heart, I fear, will never participate it. Yet it affords me some degree of satisfaction that I have not involved you in distress. The only alleviation of which my banishment from you is capable, is your forgiveness. In compassion, then, refuse it not! It cannot injure you! To me it will be worth millions! He wept! Yes, Lucy, this libertine, this man of pleasure and gallantry, wept! I really pitied him from my heart. I forgive you, said I, and wish you happy; yet, on this condition only, that you never again pollute my ears with the recital of your infamous passion. Yes, infamous, I call it, for what softer appellation can be given

[1] *Millot* Claude-François-Xavier Millot, French historian and author of *Elements of General History* (1772–83).

to such professions from a married man? Harbor not an idea of me, in future, inconsistent with the love and fidelity which you owe your wife; much less, presume to mention it, if you wish not to be detested by me; and forever banished from my presence. He expressed gratitude for his absolution even upon these terms; and hoped his future conduct would entitle him to my friendship and esteem. That, I replied, time only can determine.

One favor more he begged leave to solicit; which was, that I would be a neighbor to his wife. She was a stranger, he said, and would deem my society a particular privilege. This, I told him, I could not grant, at present, whatever I might do hereafter. He did not urge it any further, but inquired after my mamma, and expressed a wish to see her. I rung the bell, and ordered her and Miss Granby to be called. When they came, he was very polite to them both; and, after usual compliments, told my mamma that he was to be happy in having obtained my forgiveness, to which he was anxious to have her seal affixed. My daughter, said she, is the injured party; and if she be satisfied, I shall not complain. He thanked her for her condescension; informed her that he was married, and requested her to visit his wife. We then conversed upon different subjects for a short time, and he took his leave. A sigh escaped him as he departed; and a gloom was visible in his countenance, which I never observed before.

I must acknowledge that this interview has given me satisfaction. I have often told you that if I married Major Sanford, it would be from a predilection for his situation in life. How wretched must have been my lot, had I discovered, too late, that he was by no means possessed of the independence which I fondly anticipated. I knew not my own heart, when I contemplated a connection with him. Little did I think that my regard for Mr. Boyer was so deeply rooted, as I now find it. I foolishly imagined that I could turn my affections into what channel I pleased. What then must have been my feelings, when I found myself deprived both of inward peace, and outward enjoyment! I begin now to emerge from darkness, in which I have been long benighted! I hope the tragic comedy, in which I have acted so conspicuous a part, will come to a happy end.

Julia and I talk, now and then, of a journey to Boston. As yet I have not resolution to act with much decision upon the subject. But, wherever I am, and whatever may be my fate, I shall always be yours in truth,

Eliza Wharton

LETTER 56
TO MRS. LUCY SUMNER

Hartford

I begin to hope we shall come to rights here, by and by. Major Sanford has returned; has made us a visit; and a treaty of peace, and amity (but not of commerce) is ratified.

Eliza appears to be rapidly returning to her former cheerfulness, if not gaiety. I hope she will not diverge too far from her present sedateness and solidity; yet I am not without apprehensions of danger, on that score. One extreme commonly succeeds another. She tells me that she assiduously cultivates her natural vivacity; that she finds her taste for company and amusements increasing; that she dreads being alone, because past scenes arise to view which vex and discompose her.

These are indications of a mind not perfectly right. I flatter myself, however, that the time is not far distant, when her passions will vibrate with regularity.

I need not repeat to you anything relative to Major Sanford's conciliatory visit. Eliza has given you a particular, and I believe, a faithful detail. I was called down to see this wonderful man; and disliked him exceedingly. I am astonished that Eliza's penetrating eye has not long since read his vices in his very countenance. I am told by a friend, who has visited them, that he has an agreeable wife; and I wish she may find him a husband of the same description; but I very much doubt the accomplishment of my wish. For I have no charity for these reformed rakes.

We were walking abroad the other afternoon, and met Major Sanford and lady. Eliza did not see them till they were very near us. She started, turned pale, and then colored like crimson. I cannot but think, a little envy rankled in her heart. Major Sanford very politely accosted us; and congratulated Mrs. Sanford on this opportunity of introducing her to a particular friend; presenting Eliza. She received her with an easy dignity,

and bid her welcome to this part of the country. Mrs. Sanford answered her modestly; hoped for the pleasure of a further acquaintance; and urged us, as we were not far from their house, to return with them to tea. We declined; and, wishing each other a good evening, parted. Major Sanford's eyes were rivetted on Eliza, the whole time we were together; and he seemed loath to remove them, when we separated. I suspect there is some truth in his tale of love. I shall therefore discourage Eliza from associating with him under any pretext whatever. She appeared more pensive and thoughtful than common, as we returned home; and said little the rest of the evening; but next morning was as chatty as ever.

She is warm in the praises of Mrs. Sanford, thinks her an accomplished woman, and wonders that the major could suggest an idea of marrying her for her money. She intends, she says, to visit her soon; and wishes me to accompany her. This, for her own sake, I shall defer, as long as possible.

I am, etc.

Julia Granby

LETTER 57
TO MRS. LUCY SUMNER

Hartford

By Julia's advice, we have neglected the repeated invitations of Major Sanford to visit and commence neighborhood with them, till yesterday; when we received a polite billet, requesting the honor of our company to dine. My mamma declined going; but said she had no objection to our compliance with the message, if we thought proper. Julia and I accordingly went. We found a large company assembled in a spacious hall, splendidly furnished and decorated. They were all very polite and attentive to me; but none more so than Major Sanford and his lady, who jointly strove to dissipate the pensiveness of my mind, which I found it impossible to conceal. When we were summoned to dinner, the major, being near me, offered his hand, and leading me into the dining room, seated me at a table furnished with all the variety which could please the eye, or regale the taste of the most luxurious epicure.

The conversation turned on various subjects, literary, political, and miscellaneous. In the evening we had a ball. Major Sanford gave the hand of his wife to a Mr. Grey, alleging that he was a stranger, and therefore entitled to particular attention; and then solicited mine for himself. I was on the point of refusing him, but recollecting that it might have the appearance of continued resentment, contrary to my declaration of forgiving what was past, I complied. He was all kindness, and assiduity; the more so, I imagine, with a view to make amends for his former ingratitude and neglect. Tenderness is now peculiarly soothing to my wounded heart. He took an opportunity of conversing with his wife and me together; hoped she would be honored with my friendship and acquaintance; and begged, for her sake, that I would not be a stranger at his house. His Nancy, he said, was far removed from her maternal friends; but I could supply their place, if I would generously undertake the task. She joined in expressing the same sentiments and wishes. Alas! Sir, said I, Eliza Wharton is not now what she once was! I labor under a depression of spirits, which must render my company rather painful than pleasing to my friends. The idea of what I had been, contrasted with what I then was, touched my sensibility; and I could not restrain the too officious tear from stealing down my cheek. He took me by the hand, and said, you distress me, Miss Wharton, indeed, you distress me! Happiness must, and shall attend you! Cursed be the wretch, who could wound a heart like yours!

Julia Granby now joined us. An inquisitive concern was visible in her countenance.

I related this conversation to her, after we returned home; but she approved it not.

She thought Major Sanford too particularly attentive to me, considering what had previously happened. She said it would be noticed by others, and the world would make unfavorable remarks upon any appearance of intimacy between us. I care not for that, said I. It is an ill-natured, misjudging world; and I am not obliged to sacrifice my friends to its opinion. Were Major Sanford a single man I should avoid his society; but since he is married; since his wife is young, beautiful and lovely, he can have no temptation to injure me. I therefore see no evil which can arise from the cultivation of friendship with *her*, at least. I relish company

so little, that I may surely be indulged in selecting that which is most agreeable to my taste, to prevent my becoming quite a misanthrope.

I thank you, my dear Mrs. Sumner, for your kind letter. It was a seasonable cordial to my mind; and I will endeavor to profit by your advice.

Your remarks on the public entertainments are amusing, and as far as I am a judge, perfectly just.

I think it a pity they have not female managers for the theatre. I believe it would be under much better regulations, than at present.

With cordial respects to Mr. Sumner, I subscribe myself, yours in sincerity,

Eliza Wharton

LETTER 58
TO MR. CHARLES DEIGHTON

Hartford

Rejoice with me, my friend, that I have made peace with the mistress of my heart. No devotee could have been more sincere in his penitence, than I was in mine. Indeed, Charles, I never knew I had so much sensibility before! Why, I was as much a woman as the very weakest of the sex!

But I dealt very plainly and sincerely with her, to be sure; and this atones for all the past offences, and procures absolution for many others yet to be committed.

The dear girl was not inexorable; she was as placable and condescending as I could expect, considering the nature of the crime, which was apparently slighting her person and charms, by marrying another. This you know is one of the nicest points with the ladies. Attack their honor, that is their chastity, and they construe it to be the effect of excessive love, which hurries you a little beyond the bounds of prudence. But touch their vanity by preferring another, and they will seldom pardon you. You will say I am very severe upon the sex. And have I not reason to be so, since I have found so many frail ones among them. This, however, is departing from my subject.

Eliza is extremely altered! Her pale dejected countenance, with the sedateness of her manners, so different from the lively glow of health, cheerfulness and activity which formerly animated her appearance and deportment, struck me very disagreeably.

With all my gallantry and fluency in love matters, I was unable to acquit myself tolerably; or to address her with any degree of ease and confidence. She was very calm; and spoke with great indifference about my marriage, etc., which mortified me exceedingly. Yet I cannot consent to believe that her present depression of spirits arises solely from Mr. Boyer's infidelity. I flatter myself that I am of sufficient consequence to her, to have contributed in a degree.

When I inquired after her health, she told me she had been indisposed; but was now much better. This indisposition, I am informed, was purely mental; and I am happy to observe her recovering from it. I frequently visit her, sometimes with, and sometimes without my wife; of whom, through my mediation, she has become a favorite. I have married, and according to the general opinion, reformed. Yet I suspect my reformation, like most others of the kind, will prove instable as "the baseless fabric of vision";[1] unless I banish myself entirely from her society. But that I can never do; for she is still lovely in my eyes, and I cannot control my passions. When absent from her, I am lost to everything but her idea. My wife begins to rally me on my fondness for Miss Wharton. She asked me the other day if she had a fortune? No, said I, if she had I should have married her. This wounded her sensibility. I repented of my sincerity, and made my peace for that time. Yet, I find myself growing extremely irritable, and she must take heed how she provokes me; for I do not love her; and I think the name of wife becomes more and more distasteful to me every day.

In my mind Eliza has no competitor. But I must keep up appearances, though I endeavor to regain her love. I imagine that the enjoyment of her society, as a neighbor and friend, may content me for the present, and render my condition supportable.

Farewell, Charles. I hope you will never be embarrassed with a wife, nor lack some favorite nymph to supply the place of one.

Peter Sanford

[1] *the baseless fabric of vision* See Shakespeare's *The Tempest* 4.1.168.

LETTER 59
TO MRS. LUCY SUMNER

Hartford.

Dear Lucy,

I intended, this week, to have journeyed to Boston with Julia Granby; but my resolution fails me. I find it painful even to think of mixing again with the gay multitude. I believe the melancholy reflections by which I am oppressed will be more effectually, if not more easily, surmounted by tarrying where they are rendered familiar, than by going from them awhile, and then returning.

Julia will therefore go without me. I envy her no enjoyment there, except your company.

The substitution of friendship in the place of love for Major Sanford, I find productive of agreeable sensations. With him, he assures me, it is a far more calm and rational pleasure. He treats me with affection and tenderness of a brother; and his *wife*, who exceeds him in professions of regard, with all the consoling softness and attention of a sister. Indeed, their politeness has greatly contributed to revive the cheerfulness of my natural disposition.

I believe the major's former partiality to me, as a lover, is entirely obliterated; and for my part, I feel as little restraint in his company, and his lady's, as in that of any other in the neighborhood.

I very much regret the departure of Julia, and hope you will permit her to return to me again, as soon as possible. She is a valuable friend. Her mind is well cultivated; and she has treasured up a fund of knowledge and information, which renders her company both agreeable and useful in every situation of life. We lately spent the afternoon and evening at Mr. Smith's. They had a considerable number of visitants; and among the rest, Major Sanford. His wife was expected, but did not come, being indisposed.

I believe, my friend, you must excuse me if my letters are shorter than formerly. Writing is not so agreeable to me as it used to be. I love my friends as well as ever; but I think they must be weary of the gloom and dullness which pervades my present correspondence. When my

pen shall have regained its original fluency and alertness, I will resume and prolong the pleasing task.

I am, my dear Lucy, yours most affectionately,

Eliza Wharton

LETTER 60
TO THE SAME

Hartford

Dear Madam,

Agreeably to your desire, every art has been tried, every allurement held out, every argument used, and every plan adopted which Mrs. Wharton and I could devise to induce Eliza to accompany me to Boston; but all in vain. Sometimes she has been almost persuaded to a compliance with our united request; but soon has resolutely determined against it. I have observed her sentiments to be suddenly changed after being in company with Major Sanford. This alarms us exceedingly. Indeed the major seems to have insinuated himself into her good opinion more than ever. She is flattered into the belief that his attention to her is purely the result of friendship and benevolence.

I have not so favorable an opinion of the man as to suppose him capable of either. He has become very familiar here. He calls in almost every day. Sometimes he but just inquires after our health; and sometimes makes long visits. The latter is his invariable practice, when he finds Eliza alone. Mrs. Wharton always avoids seeing him if she can. She dreads, she says, his approaching the house.

I entered the parlor the other day, somewhat suddenly, and found him sitting very near Eliza, in a low conversation. They both rose in apparent confusion, and he soon retired.

When he was gone; I suspect, said I, that the major was whispering a tale of love, Eliza? Do you imagine, said she, that I would listen to such a theme from a married man? I hope not, said I; but his conduct towards you indicates a revival of his former sentiments, at least. I was not aware of that, said she. As yet

I have observed nothing in his behavior to me inconsistent with the purest friendship.

We drank tea not long since at Mr. Smith's. Late in the afternoon, Major Sanford made his appearance to apologize, as he said, for Mrs. Sanford, who was indisposed, and could not enjoy the pleasure of the visit she had contemplated. He was very gay the whole evening; and when the company separated, he was the first to present his arm to Eliza, who accepted it without hesitation. A Mr. Newhall attended me, and we endeavored to keep them company; but they evidently chose to walk by themselves. Mr. Newhall observed that if Major Sanford were not married, he should suspect he still intended a union with Miss Wharton. I replied that their former intercourse, having terminated in friendship, rendered them more familiar with each other, than with the generality of their acquaintance.

When we reached the house, Mr. Newhall chose not to go in, and took his leave. I waited at the door for Eliza and Major Sanford. At some little distance I saw him press her hand to his lips. It vexed me exceedingly; and no sooner had they come up, than I sullenly bade him good night, and walked directly in. Eliza soon followed me. I sat down by the fire in a thoughtful posture. She did the same. In this situation we both remained for some time, without speaking a word. At length she said, you seem not to have enjoyed your walk, Miss Granby; did you not like your gallant? Yes, said I, very well; but I am mortified that you were not better provided for. I make no complaint, rejoined she; I was very well entertained. That is what displeases me, said I; I mean your visible fondness for the society of such a man. Were you averse to it, as you ought to be, there would be no danger. But he has an alluring tongue, and a treacherous heart. How can you be pleased and entertained by his conversation? To me it appears totally repugnant to that refinement and delicacy for which you have always been esteemed.

His assiduity, and obtrusion ought to alarm you. You well know what his character has been. Marriage has not changed his disposition. It is only a cloak which conceals it. Trust him not then, my dear Eliza! If you do, depend upon it, you will find his professions of friendship to be mere hypocrisy and deceit! I fear that he is acting over again the same unworthy arts which formerly misled you. Beware of his wiles! Your friends are anxious for you. They tremble at your professed regard, and apparent intimacy with that unprincipled man. My friends, said she, are very jealous of me, lately. I know not how I have forfeited their confidence, or incurred their suspicion. By encouraging that attention, I warmly replied, and receiving those caresses from a married man, which are due from him to none but his wife! He is a villain, if he deceived her into marriage by insincere professions of love. If he had then an affection for her, and has already discarded it, he is equally guilty! Can you expect sincerity from the man, who withholds it from an amiable and deserving wife? No, Eliza; it is not love which induces him to entertain you with the subject! It is a baser passion; and if you disdain not his artifice, if you listen to his flattery, you will, I fear, fall victim to his evil machinations! If he conducted like a man of honor, he would merit your esteem; but his behavior is quite the reverse! Yet vile as he is, he would not dare to lisp his insolent hopes of your regard, if you punished his presumption with the indignation it deserves; if you spurned from your presence the ungrateful wretch, who would requite your condescension by triumphing in your ruin!

She now burst into tears, and begged me to drop the subject. Her mind, she said, was racked by her own reflections. She could bear but little. Kindness deceived, and censure distressed her!

I assured her of my good intentions; that as I saw her danger, I thought it a duty of the friendship and affection I bore her, solemnly to warn her against it before we parted. We talked over the matter more calmly, till she professed herself resolved in future to avoid his company, and reject his insinuations.

The next day, as I walked out, I met Major Sanford. He accosted me very civilly. I barely bid him good morning, and passed on.

I made it in my way to call at his house, and bid Mrs. Sanford adieu; not expecting another opportunity equally favorable. When I entered the parlor, she was playing a melancholy air[1] on the harpsichord. She rose, and gave me a polite and graceful reception. I told her, as I was soon to leave town, I called to take my leave of her; a compliment, which her attention to me required. Are you going to leave us then, Miss

[1] *air* Musical composition with a simple melody.

Granby? said she. I shall regret your departure exceedingly. I have so few friends in this part of the country, that it will give me sensible pain to part with one I so highly value.

I told her in the course of conversation, that I expected the pleasure of seeing her yesterday at Mr. Smith's; and was very sorry for the indisposition, which prevented her favoring us with her company. Indeed said she, I did not know I was expected there! Were you there pray? Yes, said I; and Major Sanford excused your not coming, on the account I have mentioned. Well, said she, this is the first word I ever heard about it; he told me that business led him abroad! Did he gallant any lady? O, said I, he was with us all together. We had no particular gallants.

Seeing her curiosity excited, I heartily repented saying anything of the matter, and waved the subject. Little did I suspect him to have been guilty of so base an artifice! It was evidently contrived to facilitate an interview with Eliza.

When I returned I related this affair to Mrs. Wharton and her daughter. The old lady and I expatiated largely on the vileness of this conduct, and endeavored to expose it to Eliza's view in its true colors. She pretended not to justify it. Yet she looked as if she wished it in her power.

I am now preparing for my journey to Boston, which I must however defer another week, for the sake of a more agreeable passage in the stage.[1] I regret leaving Eliza! I tremble at her danger! She has not the resolution to resist temptation which she once possessed. Her mind is surprisingly weakened! She appears sensible of this; yet adds to it by yielding to her own imbecility. You will receive a letter from her with this; though I had much difficulty to persuade her to write. She has unfortunately become very averse to this, her once favorite amusement.

As I shall soon have the pleasure of conversing with you personally, I conclude without any other addition to this scroll, than the name of your obliged

Julia Granby

LETTER 61
TO MISS ELIZA WHARTON

Boston

My Dear Friend,

I have received your letters, and must own to you that the perusal of them gave me pain. Pardon my suspicions, Eliza: they are excited by real friendship. Julia, you say, approves not Major Sanford's particular attention to you. Neither do I. If you recollect, and examine his conversation in his conciliatory visit, you will find it replete with sentiments, for the avowal of which he ought to be banished from all virtuous society.

Does he not insidiously declare that you are the only object of his affections; that his union with another was formed from interested[2] views; and though that other is acknowledged to be amiable and excellent, still he has not a heart to bestow, and expects not happiness with her? Does this discover even the appearance of amendment? Has he not, by false pretensions, misled a virtuous woman, and induced her to form a connection with him? She was a stranger to his manner of life; and doubtless allured, as you have been, by flattery, deceit, and external appearance, to trust his honor; little thinking him wholly devoid of that sacred tie! What is the reward of her confidence? Insensibility to her charms, neglect of her person, and professed attachment to another!

Is he the man, my dear Eliza, whose friendship you wish to cultivate? Can that heavenly passion reside in a breast, which is the seat of treachery, duplicity, and ingratitude? You are too sensible of its purity and worth to suppose it possible. The confessions of his own mouth condemn him. They convince me that he is still the abandoned libertine, and that marriage is but the cloak of his intrigues. His officious attentions to you are alarming to your friends. You own your mind weakened, and peculiarly susceptible of tender impressions. Beware how you receive them from him. Listen not a moment to his flattering professions. It is an insult upon your understanding for him to offer them. It is derogatory to virtue for you to hear them.

[1] *stage* Stagecoach.

[2] *interested* I.e., self-interested.

Slight not the opinion of the world. We are dependent beings; and while the smallest traces of virtuous sensibility remain, we must feel the force of that dependence, in a greater or less degree. No female whose mind is uncorrupted can be indifferent to reputation. It is an inestimable jewel, the loss of which can never be repaired. While retained, it affords conscious peace to our own minds, and ensures the esteem and respect of all around us.

Blessed with the company of so disinterested and faithful a friend as Julia Granby, some deference is certainly due to her opinion and advice. To an enlarged understanding, a cultivated taste, and an extensive knowledge of the world, she unites the most liberal sentiments, with a benevolence and candor of disposition which render her equally deserving of your confidence and affection.

I cannot relinquish my claim to a visit from you this winter. Marriage has not alienated, or weakened my regard for my friends. Come, then, to your faithful Lucy. Have you sorrows? I will sooth, and alleviate them. Have you cares? I will dispel them. Have you pleasures? I will heighten them. Come then, let me fold you to my expecting heart. My happiness will be partly suspended till your society render it complete. Adieu.

Lucy Sumner

LETTER 62
TO MISS JULIA GRANBY

Hartford

Dear Julia,

I hope Mrs. Sumner and you will excuse my writing but one letter, in answer to the number I have received from you both. Writing is an employment which suits me not at present. It was pleasing to me formerly, and therefore, by recalling the idea of circumstances and events which frequently occupied my pen in happier days, it now gives me pain. Yet I have just written a long consolatory letter to Mrs. Richman. She has buried her babe; her little Harriot, of whom she was dotingly fond.

It was a custom with some of the ancients, we are told, to weep at the birth of their children.

Often should we be impelled to a compliance with this custom, could we foresee the future incidents of their lives. I think, at least, that the uncertainty of their conduct and condition in more advanced age, may reconcile us to their removal to a happier state, before they are capable of tasting the bitterness of woe.

Happy the babe who, privileged by fate,
To shorter labors, and a lighter weight,
Received but yesterday the gift of breath;
Ordered tomorrow to return to death.[1]

Our domestic affairs are much as when you left us. Nothing remarkable has occurred in the neighborhood, worth communicating. The company and amusements of the town are as usual, I suppose. I frequent neither of them. Having incurred so much censure by the indulgence of a gay disposition, I am now trying what a recluse and solitary mode of life will produce. You will call me splenetic.[2] I own it. I am pleased with nobody; still less with myself. I look around for happiness, and find it not. The world is to me a desert! If I indulge myself in temporary enjoyment, the consciousness or apprehension of doing amiss destroys my peace of mind. And when I have recourse to books, if I read those of serious description, they remind me of an awful futurity for which I am unprepared; if history, it discloses facts in which I have no interest; if novels, they exhibit scenes of pleasures which I have no prospect of realizing!

My mamma is solicitously attentive to my happiness; and though she fails of promoting it, yet I endeavor to save her the pangs of disappointment, by appearing what she wishes.

I anticipate, and yet I dread your return; a paradox, this, which time alone can solve.

Continue writing to me, and entreat Mrs. Sumner, in my name, to do likewise. Your benevolence must be your reward.

Eliza Wharton

[1] *Happy the babe ... death* Paraphrased from Matthew Prior's 1718 poem *Solomon on the Vanity of the World* 2.231–34.

[2] *splenetic* Ill-humored; prone to sadness.

LETTER 63
TO MISS ELIZA WHARTON

Boston

A paradox, indeed, is the greater part of your letter to us, my dear Eliza. We had fondly flattered ourselves that the melancholy of your mind was exterminated. I hope no new cause has revived it. Little did I intend, when I left you, to have been absent so long; but Mrs. Sumner's disappointment, in her plan of spending the summer at Hartford, induced me, in compliance with her request, to prolong my residence here.

But for your sake, she now consents to my leaving her, in hopes I may be so happy as to contribute to your amusement.

I am both pleased and instructed by the conduct of this amiable woman. As I always endeavored to imitate her discreet and modest behavior in a single state; so likewise shall I take her for a pattern, should I ever enter a married life. She is most happily united. Mr. Sumner, to all the graces and accomplishments of the gentleman, adds the still more important and essential properties of virtue, integrity, and honor. I was once present when a person was recommended to her for a husband. She objected that he was a rake. True, said the other, he has been, but he has reformed. That will never do for me, rejoined she; I wish my future companion to need no reformation: a sentiment worthy the attention of our whole sex; the general adoption of which, I am persuaded, would have a happy influence upon the manners of the other.

I hope neither you, nor I, Eliza, shall ever be tried by a man of debauched principles. Such characters I conceive to be totally unfit for the society of women who have any claim to virtue and delicacy.

I intend to be with you in about a month. If agreeable to you, we will visit and spend a few weeks with the afflicted Mrs. Richman. I sincerely sympathize with her under her bereavement. I know her fondness for you will render your company very consoling to her; and I flatter myself that I should not be an unwelcome guest.

Make my respects to your mamma; and believe me ever yours,

Julia Granby

LETTER 64
TO MRS. LUCY SUMNER

Hartford

Dear Madam,

I have arrived in safety to the mansion of our once happy and social friends. But I cannot describe to you how changed, how greatly changed this amiable family appears since I left it. Mrs. Wharton met me at the door; and tenderly embracing, bade me a cordial welcome. You are come, Julia, said she, I hope, to revive and comfort us. We have been very solitary during your absence. I am happy madam, said I, to return; and my endeavors to restore cheerfulness and content shall not be wanting. But where is Eliza? By this time we had reached the back parlor, whither Mrs. Wharton led me; and the door being open, I saw Eliza reclined on a settee,[1] in a very thoughtful posture. When I advanced to meet her, she never moved, but sat "like patience on a monument, smiling at grief!"[2]

I stopped involuntarily and, involuntarily raising my eyes to heaven, exclaimed, is that Eliza Wharton! She burst into tears, and attempted to rise, but sunk again into her seat. Seeing her thus affected, I sat down by her; and throwing my arms about her neck, why these tears? said I. Why this distress, my dear friend? Let not the return of your Julia give you pain! She comes to sooth you with the consolations of friendship! It is not pain, said she, clasping me to her breast; it is pleasure, too exquisite for my weak nerves to bear! See you not, Julia, how I am altered? Should you have known me for the sprightly girl, who was always welcome at the haunts of hilarity and mirth? Indeed, said I, you appear indisposed, but I will be your physician. Company and change of air will, I doubt not, restore you. Will these cure disorders of the mind, Julia? They will have a powerful tendency to remove them, if rightly applied; and I profess considerable skill in that art. Come, continued I, we will try these medicines in the morning. Let us

1 *settee* Couch.

2 *like patience … at grief* See Shakespeare's *Twelfth Night* 2.4.126–27. The image refers to statues of personified virtues that sometimes decorated early modern burial sites.

rise early, and step into the chaise;[1] and after riding a few miles, call and breakfast with Mrs. Freeman. I have some commissions from her daughter. We shall be agreeably entertained there, you know.

Being summoned to supper, I took her by the hand, and we walked into another room, where we found her brother, and his wife, with her mamma waiting for us. We were all very chatty; even Eliza resumed, in a degree, her former sociability. A settled gloom, notwithstanding, brooded on her countenance; and a deep sigh often escaped her, in spite of her evident endeavors to suppress it. She went to bed before us; when her mamma informed me that her health had been declining for some months, that she never complained, but studiously concealed every symptom of her indisposition. Whether it were any real disorder of the body, or whether it arose from her depression of spirits, she could not tell; but supposed they operated together, and mutually heightened each other.

I inquired after Major Sanford; whether he and Eliza had associated together during my absence? Sometimes, she said, they seemed on good terms; and he frequently called to see her; at others, they had very little, if any, correspondence at all. She told me that Eliza never went abroad, and was very loath to see company at home; that her chief amusement consisted in solitary walks; that the dreadful idea of her meeting Major Sanford in these walks, had now and then intruded upon her imagination; that she had not the least evidence of the fact, however; and indeed, was afraid to make any inquiries into the matter, lest her own suspicions be discovered; that the major's character was worse than ever; that he was much abroad, and frequently entertained large parties of worthless bacchanalians[2] at his house; that common report said he treated his wife with indifference, neglect, and ill nature; with many other circumstances, which it is not material to relate.

Adieu, my dear friend, for the present. When occasion requires, you shall hear again from your affectionate

Julia Granby

1 *chaise* Light open carriage.

2 *bacchanalians* Drunken revelers; with reference to Bacchus, the Roman god of wine.

LETTER 65
TO MR. CHARLES DEIGHTON

Hartford

Good news, Charles, good news! I have arrived to the utmost bounds of my wishes; the full possession of my adorable Eliza! I have heard a quotation from a certain book; but what book it was I have forgotten, if I ever knew. No matter for that; the quotation is that "stolen waters are sweet, and bread eaten in secret is pleasant."[3] If it has references to the pleasures which I have enjoyed with Eliza, I like it hugely, as Tristram Shandy's father said of Yorick's sermon;[4] and I think it fully verified.

I had a long and tedious siege. Every method which love could suggest, or art invent, was adopted. I was sometimes ready to despair, under an idea that her resolution was unconquerable, her virtue impregnable. Indeed, I should have given over the pursuit long ago, but for the hopes of success I entertained from her parleying with me, and in reliance upon her own strength, endeavoring to combat and counteract my designs. Whenever this has been the case, Charles, I have never yet been defeated in my plan. If a lady will consent to enter the lists[5] against the antagonist of her honor, she may be assured of losing the prize. Besides, were her delicacy genuine, she would banish the man at once, who presumed to doubt, which he certainly does, who attempts to vanquish it!

But, far be it from me to criticize the pretensions of the sex. If I gain the rich reward of my dissimulation and gallantry, that you know is all I want.

3 *stolen waters … is pleasant* See Proverbs 9.13–18: "A foolish woman is clamorous: she is simple, and knoweth nothing. For she sitteth at the door of her house, on a seat in the high places of the city, to call passengers who go right on their ways: Whoso is simple, let him turn in hither: and as for him that wanteth understanding, she saith to him, Stolen waters are sweet, and bread eaten in secret is pleasant. But he knoweth not that the dead are there; and that her guests are in the depths of hell."

4 *I like … Yorick's sermon* Reference to Laurence Sterne's influential novel *The Life and Opinions of Tristram Shandy, Gentleman* (nine volumes, 1759–67), in which the protagonist Tristram's uncle (not, as Sanford writes, his father) praises the parson Yorick's sermon.

5 *lists* Term historically used for competitions such as jousts.

To return then to the point. An unlucky, but not a miraculous accident, has taken place, which must soon expose our amour.[1] What can be done? At the first discovery, absolute distraction seized the soul of Eliza, which has since terminated in a fixed melancholy. Her health is too much impaired. She thinks herself rapidly declining; and I tremble when I see her emaciated form!

My wife has been reduced very low, of late. She brought me a boy a few weeks past, a dead one though.

These circumstances give me neither pain nor pleasure. I am too much engrossed by my divinity to take an interest in anything else. True, I have lately suffered myself to be somewhat engaged here and there by a few jovial lads, who assist me in dispelling the anxious thoughts which my perplexed situation excites. I must, however, seek some means to relieve Eliza's distress. My finances are low; but the last fraction shall be expended in her service, if she need it.

Julia Granby is expected at Mrs. Wharton's every hour. I fear her inquisitorial eye will soon detect our intrigue, and obstruct its continuation. Now there's a girl, Charles, I should never attempt to seduce; yet she is a most alluring object, I assure you. But the dignity of her manners forbid all assaults upon her virtue. Why, the very expression of her eye blasts in the bud every thought derogatory to her honor, and tells you plainly that the first insinuation of the kind would be punished with eternal banishment and displeasure! Of her there is no danger! But I can write no more, except that I am, etc.

Peter Sanford

LETTER 66
TO MRS. LUCY SUMNER

Hartford

Oh, my friend! I have a tale to unfold; a tale which will rend every nerve of sympathizing pity, which will rack the breast of sensibility, and unspeakably distress your benevolent heart! Eliza—Oh the ruined, lost Eliza!

I want words to express the emotions of indignation and grief which oppress me! But I will endeavor to compose myself, and relate the circumstances as they came to my knowledge.

After my last letter, Eliza remained much in the same gloomy situation as I found her. She refused to go, agreeably to her promise, to visit your mamma; and under one pretext or another, has constantly declined accompanying me anywhere else, since my arrival.

Till last Thursday night she slept in the same bed with me; when she excused herself by saying she was restless, and should disturb my repose. I yielded to her humor of taking a different apartment, little suspecting the real cause! She frequently walked out; and though I sometimes followed, I very seldom found her. Two or three times, when I happened to be awake, I heard her go downstairs; and on inquiry in the morning, she told me that she was very thirsty, and went down for water. I observed a degree of hesitancy in her answers, for which I could not account. But last night, the dreadful mystery was developed! A little before day, I heard the front door opened with great caution. I sprang from my bed and, running to the window, saw by the light of the moon a man going from the house. Soon after I perceived a footstep upon the stairs, which carefully approached and entered Eliza's chamber.

Judge of my astonishment, my surprise, my feelings, upon this occasion! I doubted not but Major Sanford was the person I had seen; and the discovery of Eliza's guilt, in this infamous intrigue, almost deprived me of thought and recollection! My blood thrilled with horror at this sacrifice of virtue! After a while I recovered myself, and put on my clothes. But what to do, I knew not; whether to go directly to her chamber, and let her know that she was detected; or to wait another opportunity.

I resolved on the first. The day had now dawned. I tapped at her door; and she bid me come in. She was sitting in an easy chair by the side of her bed. As I entered she withdrew her handkerchief from her face; and looking earnestly at me, said, what procures me the favor of a visit at this early hour, Miss Granby? I was disturbed, said I, and wished not to return to my bed. But what breaks your rest and calls you up so unseasonably, Eliza? Remorse and despair, answered she, weeping. After what I have witnessed this morning,

1 *An unlucky ... our amour* I.e., Eliza has become pregnant.

rejoined I, I cannot wonder at it! Was it not Major Sanford whom I saw go from the house some time ago? She was silent, but tears flowed abundantly. It is too late, continued I, to deny, or evade. Answer my question sincerely; for believe me, Eliza, it is not malice, but concern for you, which prompts it. I will answer you, Julia, said she. You have discovered a secret which harrows up my very soul! A secret which I wished you to know, but could not exert resolution to reveal! Yes! It was Major Sanford; the man who has robbed me of my peace; who has triumphed in my destruction; and who will cause my sun to sit at noon![1]

I shudder, said I, at your confession! Wretched, deluded girl! Is this a return for your parent's love, and assiduous care; for your friends' solicitude and premonitory advice? You are ruined, you say! You have sacrificed your virtue to an abandoned, despicable profligate! And you live to acknowledge and bear your infamy! I do, said she; but not long shall I support this burden! See you not, Julia, my decaying frame, my faded cheek, and tottering limbs? Soon shall I be insensible to censure and reproach! Soon shall I be sequestered in that mansion, "where the wicked cease from troubling, and where the weary are at rest!"[2] Rest! said I, can you expect to find rest, either in this world or another, with such a weight of guilt on your head? She exclaimed, with great emotion, add not to the upbraidings of a wounded spirit! Have pity upon me, Oh! my friend, have pity upon me!

Could you know what I suffer, you would think me sufficiently punished! I wish you no other punishment, said I, than what may effect your repentance and reformation. But your mother, Eliza! She cannot long be ignorant of your fall; and I tremble to think of her distress! It will break her widowed heart! How has she loved; how has she doted upon you! Dreadful is the requital which you have made! My mother, rejoined she—Oh, name her not! The very sound is distraction to me! Oh! my Julia, if your heart be not shut against mercy and compassion towards me, aid me through this trying scene! Let my situation call forth your pity, and induce you, undeserving as I am, to exert it on my behalf!

During this time, I had walked the chamber. My spirits had been raised above their natural key, and were exhausted. I sat down, but thought I should have fainted, till a copious flood of tears gave me relief. Eliza was extremely affected. The appearance of calamity which she exhibited would have softened the most obdurate anger. Indeed, I feared some immediate and fatal effect. I therefore seated myself beside her; and assuming an air of kindness, compose yourself, Eliza, said I; I repeat what I told you before, it is the purest friendship, which thus interests me in your concerns. This, under the direction of charity, induces me to again offer you my hand. Yet you have erred against knowledge and reason; against warning and counsel. You have forfeited the favor of your friends; and reluctant will be their forgiveness. I plead guilty, said she, to all your charges. From the general voice I expect no clemency. If I can make my peace with my mother, it is all I seek or wish on this side the grave.

In your benevolence I confide for this. In you, I hope to find an intercessor. By the remembrance of our former affection and happiness, I conjure you, refuse me not. At present, I entreat you to conceal from her this distressing tale. A short reprieve is all I ask. Why, said I, should you defer it? When the painful task is over, you may find relief in her lenient kindness. After she knows my condition, I cannot see her, resumed she, till I am assured of her forgiveness. I have not strength to support the appearance of her anger and grief. I will write to her what I cannot speak. You must bear the melancholy message, and plead for me, that her displeasure may not follow me to the grave; whither I am rapidly hastening. Be assured, replied I, that I will keep your secret as long as prudence requires. But I must leave you now; your mamma will wonder at our being thus closeted together. When opportunity presents, we will converse further on the subject. In the meantime, keep yourself as composed as possible, if you would avoid suspicion. She raised her clasped hands, and with a piteous look, threw her handkerchief over her face, and reclined in her chair, without speaking a word. I returned to my chamber, and endeavored to dissipate every idea which might tend to disorder

[1] *my sun ... at noon* See Amos 8.9: "And it shall come to pass in that day, saith the Lord God, that I will cause the sun to go down at noon, and I will darken the earth in the clear day."

[2] *where the wicked ... at rest* See Job 3.17.

my countenance, and break the silence I wished to observe, relative to what had happened.

When I went down, Mrs. Wharton desired me to step up, and inform Eliza that breakfast was ready. She told me she could not yet compose herself sufficiently to see her mamma; and begged me to excuse her absence as I thought proper. I accordingly returned for answer to Mrs. Wharton, that Eliza had rested but indifferently, and being somewhat indisposed, would not come down, but wished me to bring her a bowl of chocolate, when we had breakfasted. I was obliged studiously to suppress even my thoughts concerning her, lest the emotions they excited might be observed. Mrs. Wharton conversed much of her daughter, and expressed great concern about her health and state of mind. Her return to this state of dejection, after having recovered her spirits and cheerfulness, in a great degree, was owing, she feared, to some cause unknown to her; and she entreated me to extract the secret, if possible. I assured her of my best endeavors, and doubted not, I told her, but I should be able in a few days to effect what she wished.

Eliza came down and walked in the garden before dinner; at which she commanded herself much better than I expected. She said that a little ride might, she imagined, be of service to her; and asked me if I would accompany her a few miles in the afternoon. Her mamma was much pleased with the proposition; and the chaise was accordingly ordered.

I observed to Eliza, as we rode, that with her natural and acquired abilities, with her advantages of education, with her opportunities of knowing the world, and of tracing the virtues and vices of mankind to their origin, I was surprised at her becoming the prey of an insidious libertine, with whose character she was well acquainted, and whose principles she was fully apprised would prompt him to deceive and betray her. Your surprise is very natural, said she. The same will doubtless be felt and expressed by everyone to whom my sad story is related. But the cause may be found in that unrestrained levity of disposition, that fondness for dissipation and coquetry which alienated the affections of Mr. Boyer from me. This event fatally depressed and enfeebled my mind. I embraced with avidity the consoling power of friendship, ensnaringly offered by my seducer; vainly inferring, from his

marriage with a virtuous woman, that he had seen the error of his ways, and forsaken his licentious practices, as he affirmed, and I, fool that I was, believed it.

It is needless for me to rehearse the perfidious arts by which he insinuated himself into my affections and gained my confidence. Suffice it to say, he effected his purpose! But not long did I continue in the delusive dream of sensual gratification. I soon awoke to a most poignant sense of his baseness, and of my own crime and misery. I would have fled from him; I would have renounced him forever; and by a life of sincere humility and repentance, endeavored to make my peace with heaven, and to obliterate, by the rectitude of my future conduct, the guilt I had incurred; but I found it too late! My circumstances called for attention; and I had no one to participate my cares, to witness my distress, and to alleviate my sorrows, but him. I could not therefore prevail on myself wholly to renounce his society. At times I have admitted his visits; always meeting him in the garden, or grove adjoining; till of late, the weather and my ill health induced me to comply with his solicitations, and receive him into the parlor.

Not long, however, shall I be subject to these embarrassments. Grief has undermined my constitution. My health has fallen a sacrifice to a disordered mind. But I regret not its departure! I have not a single wish to live. Nothing which the world affords can restore my former serenity and happiness!

The little innocent I bear will quickly disclose its mother's shame! God Almighty grant it may not live as a monument of my guilt, and a partaker of infamy and sorrow, which is all I have to bequeath it! Should it be continued in life, it will never know the tenderness of a parent; and, perhaps, want and disgrace may be its wretched portion! The greatest consolation I can have will be to carry it with me to a state of eternal rest; which, vile as I am, I hope to obtain, through the infinite mercy of heaven, as revealed in the gospel of Christ.

I must see Major Sanford again. It is necessary to converse further with him, in order to carry my plan of operation into execution. What is this plan of operation, Eliza? said I. I am on the rack of anxiety for your safety. Be patient, continued she, and you shall soon be informed. Tomorrow I shall write my dreadful story to my mother. She will be acquainted with my future

intentions; and you shall know, at the same time, the destination of your lost friend. I hope, said I, that you have formed no resolution against your own life. God forbid, rejoined she. My breath is in his hands, let him do what seemeth good in his sight! Keep my secret one day longer, and I will never more impose so painful a silence upon you.

By this time we had reached home. She drank tea with composure, and soon retired to rest. Mrs. Wharton eagerly inquired whether I had found out the cause of Eliza's melancholy. I have urged her, said I, on the subject; but she alleges that she has particular reasons for present concealment. She has, notwithstanding, promised to let me know, the day after tomorrow. Oh, said she, I shall not rest till the period arrives. Dear, good woman, said I to myself, I fear you will never rest afterwards!

This is our present situation. Think what a scene rises to the view of your Julia! She must share the distresses of others, though her own feelings, on this unhappy occasion, are too keen to admit a moment's serenity! My greatest relief is in writing to you; which I shall do again by the next post. In the meantime, I must beg leave to subscribe myself, sincerely yours,

Julia Granby

LETTER 67
TO THE SAME

Hartford

All is now lost; lost, indeed! She is gone! Yes, my dear friend, our beloved Eliza is gone! Never more shall we behold this once amiable companion, this once innocent and happy girl. She has forsaken, and, as she says, bid an everlasting adieu to her home, her afflicted parent, and her friends! But I will take up my melancholy story where I left it in my last.

She went, as she told me she expected, into the garden, and met her detestable paramour. In about an hour she returned, and went directly to her chamber. At one o'clock I went up, and found her writing, and weeping. I begged her to compose herself, and go down to dinner. No; she said, she could not eat; and

was not fit to appear before anybody. I remonstrated against her immoderate grief, represented the injury she must sustain by the indulgence of it, and conjured her to suppress the violence of its emotions.

She entreated me to excuse her to her mamma; said she was writing to her, and found it a task too painful to be performed with any degree of composure; that she was almost ready to sink under the weight of her affliction; but hoped and prayed for support, both in this and another trying scene which awaited her. In compliance with her desire, I now left her; and told her mamma that she was very busy in writing; wished not to be interrupted at present; but would take some refreshment, an hour or two hence. I visited her again, about four o'clock; when she appeared more calm and tranquil.

It is finished, said she, as I entered her apartment, it is finished. What said I, is finished? No matter, replied she; you will know all tomorrow, Julia. She complained of excessive fatigue, and expressed an inclination to lie down; in which I assisted her, and then retired. Some time after her mamma went up, and found her still on the bed. She rose, however, and accompanied her downstairs. I met her at the door of the parlor, and taking her by the hand, inquired how she did? Oh, Julia, miserably indeed, said she. How severely does my mother's kindness reproach me! How insupportably it increases my self-condemnation! She wept; she wrung her hands, and walked the room in the greatest agony! Mrs. Wharton was exceedingly distressed by her appearance. Tell me, Eliza, said she, tell me the cause of your trouble! Oh, kill me not by your mysterious concealment! My dear child, let me, by sharing, alleviate your affliction! Ask me not, madam, said she; O my mother, I conjure you not to insist on my divulging tonight the fatal secret which engrosses and distracts my mind! Tomorrow I will hide nothing from you. I will press you no further, rejoined her mamma. Choose your own time, my dear; but remember, I must participate your grief, though I know not the cause.

Supper was brought in, and we endeavored to prevail on Eliza to eat, but in vain. She sat down, in compliance with our united importunities; but neither of us tasted food. It was removed untouched. For a while, Mrs. Wharton and I gazed in silent anguish upon the spectacle of woe before us! At length, Eliza rose to

retire. Julia, said she, will you call at my chamber, as you pass to your own? I assented. She then approached her mamma, fell upon her knees before her, and clasping her hand, said, in broken accents, Oh madam! can you forgive a wretch, who has forfeited your love, your kindness, and your compassion? Surely, Eliza, said she, you are not that being! No, it is impossible! But however great your transgression, be assured of my forgiveness, my compassion, and my continued love! Saying this, she threw her arms about her daughter's neck, and affectionately kissed her. Eliza struggled from her embrace, and looking at her with wild despair, exclaimed, this is too much! Oh, this unmerited goodness is more than I can bear! She then rushed precipitately out of the room, and left us overwhelmed in sympathy and astonishment!

When Mrs. Wharton had recovered herself a little, she observed that Eliza's brain was evidently disordered. Nothing else, continued she, could impel her to act in this extraordinary manner. At first she was resolved to follow her; but I dissuaded her from it, alleging that, as she had desired me to come into her chamber, I thought it better for me to go alone. She acquiesced; but said she should not think of going to bed; but would, however, retire to her chamber, and seek consolation there. I bade her good night; and went up to Eliza, who took me by the hand and led me to the toilet,[1] upon which she laid the two enclosed letters, the one to her mamma, and the other to me. These, said she, contain what I had not resolution to express. Promise me, Julia, that they shall not be opened until tomorrow morning. I will, said I. I have thought and wept, continued she, till I have almost exhausted my strength, and my reason. I would now obtain a little respite, that I may prepare my mind for the account I am one day to give at a higher tribunal than that of earthly friends. For this purpose, what I have written, and what I shall yet say to you, must close the account between you and me. I have certainly no balance against you, said I. In my breast you are fully acquitted. Your penitential tears have obliterated your guilt, and blotted out your errors with your Julia. Henceforth, be they all forgotten. Live, and be happy. Talk not, said she, of life. It would be a vain hope, though I cherished it myself.

That I must die, it is my only comfort;
Death is the privilege of human nature;
And life without it were not worth our taking.
Thither the poor, the prisoner and the mourner
Fly for relief, and lay their burdens down![2]

You have forgiven me, Julia; my mother has assured me of her forgiveness, and what have I more to wish? My heart is much lightened by these kind assurances, they will be a great support to me in the dreadful hour which awaits me! What mean you, Eliza? said I. I fear some desperate purpose labors in your mind. Oh, no, she replied; you may be assured that your fear is groundless. I know not what I say; my brain is on fire; I am all confusion! Leave me, Julia; when I have had a little rest, I shall be composed. These letters have almost distracted me; but they are written, and I am comparatively easy. I will not leave you, Eliza, said I, unless you will go directly to bed, and endeavor to rest. I will, said she, and the sooner the better. I tenderly embraced her, and retired, though not to bed. About an hour after, I returned to her chamber, and opening the door very softly, found her apparently asleep. I acquainted Mrs. Wharton with her situation, which was a great consolation to us both; and encouraged us to go to bed. Having suffered much in my mind, and being much fatigued, I soon fell asleep; but the rattling of a carriage, which appeared to stop at a little distance from the house, awoke me. I listened a moment, and heard the door turn slowly on its hinges. I sprang from my bed, and reached the window just in time to see a female handed into a chaise by a man who hastily followed her, and drove furiously away! I at once concluded they could be no other than Eliza and Major Sanford. Under this impression I made no delay, but ran immediately to her chamber. A candle was burning on the table; but Eliza was not there! I thought it best to acquaint her mamma with the melancholy discovery; and stepping to her apartment for the purpose, found her rising. She had heard me walk, and was anxious to know the cause. What is the matter, Julia, said she; what is the matter? Dear madam, said I, arm yourself with fortitude! What new occurrence

1 *toilet* Dressing table.

2 *That I ... burdens down!* See Nicholas Rowe's 1703 play *The Fair Penitent* 5.1.137–41. The play centers partially on the sexual exploits of an unfaithful wife.

demands it? rejoined she. Eliza has left us! Left us! what mean you? She is just gone! I saw her handed into a chaise, which instantly disappeared!

At this intelligence she gave a shriek, and fell back on her bed! I alarmed the family, and by their assistance soon recovered her. She desired me to inform her of every particular relative to her elopement, which I did; and then delivered her the letter which Eliza had left for her. I suspect, said she, as she took it; I have long suspected, what I dared not believe! The anguish of my mind has been known only to myself, and my God! I could not answer her, and therefore withdrew. When I had read Eliza's letter to me, and wept over the sad fall—and, as I fear, the total loss of this once amiable and accomplished girl—I returned to Mrs. Wharton. She was sitting in her easy chair, and still held the fatal letter in her hand. When I entered, she fixed her streaming eyes upon me, and exclaimed, O Julia, this is more than the bitterness of death! True, madam, said I, your affliction must be great; yet that all-gracious Being, who controls every event, is able, and I trust, disposed to support you! To Him, replied she, I desire humbly to resign myself; but I think I could have borne almost any other calamity with greater resignation and composure than this. With how much comparative ease could I have followed her to the grave, at any period since her birth! Oh, my child, my child! dear, very dear hast thou been to my fond heart! Little did I think it possible for you to prepare so dreadful a cup of sorrow for your widowed mother! But where, continued she, where can the poor fugitive have fled? Where can she find that protection and tenderness which, notwithstanding her great apostacy, I should never have withheld? From whom can she receive those kind attentions, which her situation demands?

The agitation of her mind had exhausted her strength; and I prevailed on her to refresh, and endeavor to compose herself to rest; assuring her of my utmost exertions to find out Eliza's retreat, and restore her to a mother's arms.

I am obliged to suppress my own emotions; and to bend all my thoughts towards the alleviation of Mrs. Wharton's anxiety and grief.

Major Sanford is from home, as I expected; and I am determined, if he return, to see him myself, and extort from him the place of Eliza's concealment. Her

flight, in her present state of health, is inexpressibly distressing to her mother; and, unless we find her soon, I dread the effects!

I shall not close this, till I have seen or heard from the vile miscreant who has involved a worthy family in wretchedness!

Friday Morning—Two days have elapsed without affording us much relief. Last evening, I was told that Major Sanford was at home. I immediately wrote him a billet, entreating and conjuring him to let me know where the hapless Eliza had fled. He returned me the following.

Miss Granby need be under no apprehensions, respecting the situation of our beloved Eliza. She is well provided for, conveniently accommodated, and has everything to make her happy, which love or affluence can give.

Major Sanford has solemnly sworn not to discover her retreat. She wishes to avoid the accusations of her friends, till she is better able to bear them.

Her mother may rest assured of immediate information, should any danger threaten her amiable daughter; and also of having seasonable notice of her safety.

Although little dependence can be placed upon this man, yet these assurances have, in a great degree, calmed our minds. We are, however, contriving means to explore the refuge of the wanderer; and hope, by tracing his steps, to accomplish our purpose. This we have engaged a friend to do.

I know, my dear Mrs. Sumner, the kind interest you will take in this disastrous affair. I tremble to think what the event may be! To relieve your suspense, however, I shall write you every circumstance, as it occurs. But at present, I shall only enclose Eliza's letters to her mamma, and me, and subscribe myself your sincere and obliged friend,

Julia Granby

LETTER 68
TO MRS. M. WHARTON

Tuesday

My Honored And Dear Mamma,

In what words, in what language shall I address you? What shall I say on a subject which deprives me of the power of expression? Would to God I had been totally deprived of that power before so fatal a subject required its exertion! Repentance comes too late, when it cannot prevent the evil lamented. For your kindness, your more than maternal affection towards me, from my infancy to the present moment, a long life of filial duty and unerring rectitude could hardly compensate. How greatly deficient in gratitude must I appear then, while I confess that precept and example, counsel and advice, instruction and admonition, have been all lost upon me!

Your kind endeavors to promote my happiness have been repaid by the inexcusable folly of sacrificing it. The various emotions of shame and remorse, penitence and regret, which torture and distract my guilty breast, exceed description. Yes, madam, your Eliza has fallen; fallen, indeed! She has become the victim of her own indiscretion, and of the intrigue and artifice of a designing libertine, who is the husband of another! She is polluted, and no more worthy of her parentage! She flies from you, not to conceal her guilt, that she humbly and penitently owns; but to avoid what she has never experienced, and feels herself unable to support: a mother's frown; to escape the heart-rending sight of a parent's grief, occasioned by the crimes of her guilty child!

I have become a reproach and disgrace to my friends. The consciousness of having forfeited their favor, and incurred their disapprobation and resentment, induces me to conceal from them the place of my retirement; but, lest your benevolence should render you anxious for my comfort in my present situation, I take the liberty to assure you that I am amply provided for.

I have no claim even upon your pity; but from my long experience of your tenderness, I presume to hope it will be extended to me. Oh, my mother, if you knew what the state of my mind is, and has been, for months

past, you would surely compassionate my case! Could tears efface the stain which I have brought upon my family, it would long since have been washed away! But, alas, tears are vain; and vain is my bitter repentance! It cannot obliterate my crime, nor restore me to innocence and peace! In this life I have no ideas of happiness. These I have wholly resigned! The only hope which affords me any solace, is that of your forgiveness. If the deepest contrition can make an atonement; if the severest pains, both of body and mind, can restore me to your charity, you will not be inexorable! Oh, let my sufferings be deemed a sufficient punishment; and add not the insupportable weight of a parent's wrath! At present, I cannot see you. The effect of my crime is too obvious to be longer concealed, to elude the invidious eye of curiosity. This night, therefore, I leave your hospitable mansion! This night I become a wretched wanderer from thy paternal roof! Oh, that the grave were this night to be my lodging! Then should I lie down and be at rest! Trusting in the mercy of God, through the mediation of his son; I think I could meet my heavenly father with more composure and confidence, than my earthly parent!

Let not the faults and misfortunes of your daughter oppress your mind. Rather let the conviction of having faithfully discharged your duty to your lost child support and console you in this trying scene.

Since I wrote the above, you have kindly granted me your forgiveness, though you knew not how great, how aggravated was my offence! You forgive me, you say: Oh, the harmonious, the transporting[1] sound! It has revived my drooping spirits; and will enable me to encounter, with resolution, the trials before me!

Farewell, my dear mamma! pity and pray for your ruined child; and be assured that affection and gratitude will be the last sentiments which expire in the breast of your repenting daughter,

Eliza Wharton

[1] *transporting* Causing overwhelming joy or ecstasy.

LETTER 69
TO MISS JULIA GRANBY

Tuesday

My Dear Friend,

By that endearing title you permit me still to address you, and such you have always proved yourself, by a participation of my distresses, as well as by the consoling voice of pity and forgiveness. What destiny Providence designs for me, I know not; but I have my forebodings that this is the last time I shall ever accost you! Nor does this apprehension arise merely from a disturbed imagination. I have reason to think myself in a confirmed consumption,[1] which commonly proves fatal to persons in my situation. I have carefully concealed every complaint of the kind from my mamma, for fear of distressing her; yet I have never been insensible of their probable issue,[2] and have bidden a sincere welcome to them, as the harbingers of my speedy release from a life of guilt and woe!

I am going from you, Julia. This night separates us, perhaps, forever! I have not resolution to encounter the tears of my friends, and therefore seek shelter among strangers where none knows or is interested in my melancholy story. The place of my seclusion I studiously conceal; yet I shall take measures that you may be apprized of my fate.

Should it please God to spare and restore me to health, I shall return, and endeavour, by a life of penitence and rectitude, to expiate my past offences. But should I be called from this scene of action, and leave behind me a helpless babe, the innocent sufferer of its mother's shame, Oh, Julia, let your friendship for me extend to the little stranger! Intercede with my mother to take it under her protection, and transfer to it all her affection for me; to train it up in the ways of piety and virtue, that it may compensate her for the afflictions which I have occasioned!

One thing more I have to request. Plead for me with my two best friends, Mrs. Richman and Mrs. Sumner. I ask you not to palliate my faults—that cannot be done—but to obtain, if possible, their forgiveness. I cannot write all my full mind suggests on this subject. You know the purport; and can better express it for me.

And now, my dear Julia, recommending myself again to your benevolence, to your charity and (may I add?) to your affection; and entreating that the fatal consequences of my folly, now fallen upon my devoted head, may suffice for my punishment; let me conjure you to bury my crimes in the grave with me, and to preserve the remembrance of my former virtues, which engaged your love and confidence; more especially of that ardent esteem for you, which will glow till the last expiring breath of your despairing

Eliza Wharton

LETTER 70
TO MR. CHARLES DEIGHTON

Hartford

I have, at last, accomplished the removal of my darling girl, from a place where she thought every eye accused, and every heart condemned her.

She has become quite romantic in her notions. She would not permit me to accompany her, lest it should be reported that we had eloped together. I provided amply for her future exigencies, and conveyed her by night to the distance of ten or twelve miles, where we met the stage, in which I had previously secured her a seat. The agony of her grief at being thus obliged to leave her mother's house baffles all description.

It very sensibly affected me, I know. I was almost a penitent. I am sure I acted like one, whether I were sincere or not. She chose to go where she was totally unknown. She would leave the stage, she said, before it reached Boston, and take passage in a more private carriage to Salem, or its vicinity, where she would fix her abode; chalking the initials of my name over the door, as a signal to me of her residence.

She is exceedingly depressed; and says she neither expects nor wishes to survive her lying in.[3] Insanity, for aught I know, must be my lot, if she should die. But I will not harbor the idea. I hope, one time or

[1] *consumption* Tuberculosis.

[2] *issue* Outcome.

[3] *lying in* Period of confinement and bedrest surrounding childbirth, often lasting many weeks.

other, to have the power to make her amends, even by marriage. My wife may be provoked, I imagine, to sue for a divorce. If she should, she would find no difficulty in obtaining it; and then I would take Eliza in her stead. Though I confess that the idea of being thus connected with a woman whom I have been able to dishonor would be rather hard to surmount. It would hurt even my delicacy, little as you may think me to possess, to have a wife whom I know to be seducible. And, on this account, I cannot be positive that even Eliza would retain my love.

My Nancy and I have lived a pretty uncomfortable life, of late. She has been very suspicious of my amour with Eliza, and now and then expressed her jealous sentiments a little more warmly than my patience would bear. But the news of Eliza's circumstances and retirement, being publicly talked of, have reached her ears, and rendered her quite outrageous. She tells me she will no longer brook my indifference and infidelity; intends soon to return to her father's house, and extricate herself from me entirely. My general reply to all this is that she knew my character before we married, and could reasonably expect nothing less than what has happened. I shall not oppose her leaving me, as it may conduce to the execution of the plan I have hinted above.

Tomorrow I shall set out to visit my disconsolate fair one. From my very soul I pity her; and wish I could have preserved her virtue consistently with the indulgence of my passion. To her I lay not the principal blame, as in like cases, I do to the sex in general. My finesse was too well planned for detection, and my snares too deeply laid for anyone to escape who had the least warmth in her constitution, or affection in her heart. I shall, therefore, be the less whimsical about a future connection, and the more solicitous to make her reparation, should it ever be in my power.

Her friends are all in arms about her. I dare say I have the imprecations[1] of the whole fraternity. They may thank themselves in part; for I always swore revenge for their dislike and coldness towards me. Had they been politic, they would have conducted more like the aborigines of the country, who are said to worship the devil out of fear.

I am afraid I shall be obliged to remove my quarters; for Eliza was so great a favorite in town, that I am looked upon with an evil eye. I plead with her before we parted last, to forgive my seducing her; alleged my ardent love, and my inability to possess her in any other way. How, said she, can that be love which destroys its object? But granting what you say, you have frustrated your own purpose. You have deprived yourself of my society, which might have been innocently enjoyed. You have cut me off from life in the midst of my days. You have rendered me the reproach of my friends, the disgrace of my family, and a dishonor to virtue and my sex! but I forgive you, added she. Yes, Sanford, I forgive you; and sincerely pray for your repentance and reformation. I hope to be the last wretched female sacrificed by you to the arts of falsehood and seduction!

May my unhappy story serve as a beacon to warn the American fair of the dangerous tendency and destructive consequences of associating with men of your character, of destroying their time, and risking their reputation by the practice of coquetry and its attendant follies! But for these, I might have been honorably connected; and capable, at this moment, of diffusing and receiving happiness! But for your arts, I might have remained a blessing to society, as well as the delight and comfort of my friends!

Your being a married man unspeakably aggravates both your guilt and mine. This circumstance annexes indelible shame to our crime! You have rent asunder the tenderest ties of nature! You have broken the bonds of conjugal love, which ought ever to be kept sacred and inviolate! You have filled with grief and discontent the heart of your amiable wife, whom gratitude, if no other principle, should have induced you to cherish with tenderness; and I, wretch that I am, have been your accomplice!

But I cease to reproach you. You have acted but too consistently with the character which I was sufficiently apprised you sustained. The blame then may be retorted on myself, for disregarding the counsels, warnings and admonitions of my best friends. You have prided yourself in the character of a libertine. Glory no longer in your shame! You have accomplished your designs; your dreadful designs against me! Let this suffice. Add not to the number of those deluded creatures,

[1] *imprecations* Curses.

who will one day rise up in judgment against you, and condemn you.

By this time we had nearly reached the inn, and were soon to part. I seized her hand and exclaimed, you must not leave me, Eliza, with that awful anathema on your lips! Oh, say that you will forget my past faults. That, said she, I shall soon do; for in the grave there is no remembrance! This, to my mind, was a harsher sentence than the other; and almost threw me into despair. Never was I so wrought upon before! I knew not what to say or do! She saw my distress, and kindly softened her manner. If I am severe, said she, it is because I wish to impress your mind with such a sense of your offences against your Maker, your friends and society in general, as may effect your repentance and amendment. I wish not to be your accuser, but your reformer. On several accounts, I view my own crime in a more aggravated light than yours; but my conscience is awakened to a conviction of my guilt. Yours, I fear is not. Let me conjure you to return home, and endeavor by your future kindness and fidelity to your wife to make her all the amends in your power. By a life of virtue and religion, you may yet become a valuable member of society, and secure happiness both here and hereafter.

I begged leave to visit her retirement next week, not in continuation of our amour, but as a friend, solicitous to know her situation and welfare. Unable to speak, she only bowed assent. The stage being now ready, I whispered some tender things in her ear, and kissing her cheek, which was all she would permit, suffered her to depart.

My body remains behind; but my soul, if I have any, went with her!

This was a horrid lecture, Charles! She brought every charge against me, which a fruitful and gloomy imagination could suggest! But I hope, when she recovers, she will resume her former cheerfulness, and become as kind and agreeable as ever. My anxiety for her safety is very great. I trust, however, it will soon be removed; and peace and pleasure be restored to your humble servant,

Peter Sanford

LETTER 71
TO MRS. LUCY SUMNER

Hartford

The drama is now closed! A tragical one indeed it has proved!

How sincerely, my dear Mrs. Sumner, must the friends of our departed Eliza sympathize with each other; and with her afflicted, bereaved parent!

You have doubtless seen the account, in the public papers, which gave us the melancholy intelligence. But I will give you a detail of circumstances.

A few days after my last was written, we heard that Major Sanford's property was attached,[1] and he a prisoner in his own house. He was the last man to whom we wished to apply for information respecting the forlorn wanderer; yet we had no other resource. And after waiting a fortnight in the most cruel suspense, we wrote a billet, entreating him, if possible, to give some intelligence concerning her. He replied that he was unhappily deprived of all means of knowing himself; but hoped soon to relieve his own, and our anxiety about her.

In this situation we continued, till a neighbor (purposely, we since concluded) sent us a Boston paper. Mrs. Wharton took it, and unconscious of its contents, observed that the perusal might divert her a few moments. She read for some time; when it suddenly dropped upon the floor. She clasped her hands together, and raising her streaming eyes to heaven, exclaimed, It is the Lord; let him do what he will! Be still, O my soul, and know that he is God![2]

What, madam, said I, can be the matter? She answered not; but with inexpressible anguish depicted in her countenance, pointed to the paper. I took it up, and soon found the fatal paragraph. I shall not attempt to paint our heart felt grief and lamentation upon this occasion; for we had no doubt of Eliza's being the person described, as a stranger, who died at Danvers, last July. Her delivery of a child; her dejected state of mind; the marks upon her linen; indeed, every circumstance in the advertisement convinced us beyond dispute that it could be no other. Mrs. Wharton retired immediately

[1] *attached* Legally transferred to his creditors.

[2] *Be still ... is God* See Psalm 46.10.

to her chamber, where she continued overwhelmed with sorrow that night and the following day. Such, in fact, has been her habitual frame ever since; though the endeavors of her friends, who have sought to console her, have rendered her somewhat more conversable. My testimony of Eliza's penitence before her departure is a source of comfort to this disconsolate parent. She fondly cherished the idea that, having expiated her offence by sincere repentance and amendment, her deluded child finally made a happy exchange of worlds. But the desperate resolution which she formed, and executed, of becoming a fugitive—of deserting her mother's house and protection, and of wandering and dying among strangers—is a most distressing reflection to her friends; especially to her mother, in whose breast so many painful ideas arise, that she finds it extremely difficult to compose herself to that resignation which she evidently strives to exemplify.

Eliza's brother has been to visit her last retreat, and to learn the particulars of her melancholy exit. He relates that she was well accommodated, and had every attention and assistance which her situation required. The people where she resided appear to have a lively sense of her merit and misfortunes. They testify her modest deportment, her fortitude under the sufferings to which she was called, and the serenity and composure with which she bid a last adieu to the world. Mr. Wharton has brought back several scraps of her writing, containing miscellaneous reflections on her situation, the death of her babe, and the absence of her friends. Some of these were written before, some after her confinement.[1] These valuable testimonies of the affecting sense and calm expectation she entertained of her approaching dissolution, are calculated to sooth and comfort the minds of mourning connections. They greatly alleviate the regret occasioned by her absence at this awful period.

Her elopement can be equalled only by the infatuation which caused her ruin.

But let no one reproach her memory.
Her life has paid the forfeit of her folly.
Let that suffice.[2]

I am told that Major Sanford is quite frantic. Sure I am that he has reason to be. If the mischiefs he has brought upon others return upon his own head, dreadful indeed must be his portion! His wife has left him, and returned to her parents. His estate, which has been long mortgaged, is taken from him; and poverty and disgrace await him! Heaven seldom leaves injured innocence unavenged! Wretch that he is, he ought forever to be banished from human society! I shall continue with Mrs. Wharton, till the lenient hand of time has assuaged her sorrows; and then make my promised visit to you. I will bring Eliza's posthumous papers with me, when I come to Boston, as I have not time to copy them now.

I foresee, my dear Mrs. Sumner, that this disastrous affair will suspend your enjoyments, as it has mine. But what are our feelings, compared with the pangs which rend a parent's heart? This parent, I here behold, inhumanly stripped of the best solace of her declining years by the ensnaring machinations of a profligate debauchee! Not only the life, but what was still dearer, the reputation and virtue of the unfortunate Eliza, have fallen victims at the shrine of *libertinism*! Detested be the epithet! Let it henceforth bear its true signature, and candor itself shall call it *lust* and *brutality*!

Execrable is the man, however arrayed in magnificence, crowned with wealth, or decorated with the external graces and accomplishments of fashionable life, who shall presume to display them, at the expense of virtue and innocence! Sacred names! attended with real blessings; blessings too useful and important to be trifled away! My resentment at the base arts which must have been employed to complete the seduction of Eliza, I cannot suppress. I wish them to be exposed, and stamped with universal ignominy! Nor do I doubt but you will join with me in execrating the measures by which *we* have been robbed of so valuable a friend; and *society*, of so ornamental a member. I am, etc.

Julia Granby

[1] *confinement* I.e., her lying-in.

[2] *But let … that suffice* The source of this quotation is uncertain.

LETTER 72
TO MR. CHARLES DEIGHTON

Hartford

Confusion, horror and despair are the portion of your wretched, unhappy friend! Oh, Deighton, I am undone! Misery irremediable is my future lot! She is gone; yes, she is gone forever! The darling of my soul, the centre of all my wishes and enjoyments, is no more! Cruel fate has snatched her from me; and she is irretrievably lost! I rave, and then reflect; I reflect, and then rave! I have not patience to bear this calamity, nor power to remedy it! Where shall I fly from the upbraidings of my mind, which accuses me as the murderer of my Eliza? I would fly to death, and seek a refuge in the grave; but the forebodings of a retribution to come, I cannot away with! Oh, that I had seen her; that I had once more asked her forgiveness! But even that privilege, that consolation, was denied me! The day on which I meant to visit her, most of my property was attached, and to secure the rest, I was obliged to shut my doors, and become a prisoner in my own house! High living, and old debts incurred by extravagance, had reduced the fortune of my wife to very little, and I could not satisfy the clamorous demands of my creditors.

I would have given millions, had I possessed them, to have been at liberty to see, and to have had power to preserve Eliza from death! But in vain was my anxiety; it could not relieve; it could not liberate me! When I first heard the dreadful tidings of her exit, I believe I acted like a madman! Indeed, I am little else now!

I have compounded with my creditors, and resigned the whole of my property.

Thus, the splendor and equipage, to secure which I have sacrificed a virtuous woman, is taken from me; that poverty, the dread of which prevented my forming an honorable connection with an amiable and accomplished girl, the only one I ever loved, has fallen, with redoubled vengeance, upon my guilty head; and I must become a vagabond in the earth![1]

I shall fly my country as soon as possible; I shall go from every object which reminds me of my departed Eliza! But never, never shall I eradicate from my bosom the idea of her excellence; or the painful remembrance of the injuries I have done her! Her shade[2] will perpetually haunt me! The image of her, as she appeared when mounting the carriage which conveyed her forever from my sight, she waved her hand in token of a last adieu, will always be present to my imagination! The solemn counsel she gave me before we parted, never more to meet, will not cease to resound in my ears!

While my being is prolonged, I must feel the disgraceful and torturing effects of my guilt in seducing her! How madly have I deprived her of happiness, of reputation, of life! Her friends, could they know the pangs of contrition, and the horror of conscience which attend me, would be amply revenged!

It is said she quitted the world with composure and peace. Well she might! She had not that insupportable weight of iniquity, which sinks me to despair! She found consolation in that religion, which I have ridiculed as priestcraft and hypocrisy! But whether it be true, or false, would to heaven I could now enjoy the comforts which its votaries evidently feel!

My wife has left me. As we lived together without love, we parted without regret.

Now, Charles, I am to bid you a long, perhaps a last, farewell. Where I shall roam in future, I neither know nor care; I shall go where the name of Sanford is unknown; and his person and sorrows unnoticed.

In this happy clime I have nothing to induce my stay. I have not money to support me with my profligate companions; nor have I any relish, at present, for their society. By the virtuous part of the community, I am shunned as the pest and bane of social enjoyment. In short I am debarred from every kind of happiness. If I look back, I recoil with horror from the black catalogue of vices which have stained my past life, and reduced me to indigence and contempt. If I look forward, I shudder at the prospects which my foreboding mind presents to view, both in this and a coming world! This is a deplorable, yet just picture of myself! How totally the reverse of what I once appeared!

Let it warn you, my friend, to shun the dangerous paths which I have trodden, that you may never be involved in the hopeless ignominy and wretchedness of

Peter Sanford

[1] *vagabond in the earth* See Genesis 4.14, where Cain, having murdered his brother and been punished by God, declares that he "shall be a fugitive and a vagabond in the earth."

[2] *shade* Ghost.

LETTER 73
TO MISS JULIA GRANBY

Boston

A melancholy tale have you unfolded, my dear Julia; and tragic indeed is the concluding scene!

Is she then gone! gone in this most distressing manner! Have I lost my once loved friend; lost her in a way which I could never have conceived to be possible.

Our days of childhood were spent together in the same pursuits, in the same amusements. Our riper years increased our mutual affection, and maturer judgment most firmly cemented our friendship. Can I then calmly resign her to so severe a fate! Can I bear the idea of her being lost to honor, to fame, and to life! No; she shall still live in the heart of her faithful Lucy; whose experience of her numerous virtues and engaging qualities, has imprinted her image too deeply on the memory to be obliterated. However she may have erred, her sincere repentance is sufficient to restore her to charity.

Your letter gave me the first information of this awful event. I had taken a short excursion into the country, where I had not seen the papers; or if I had, paid little or no attention to them. By your directions I found the distressing narrative of her exit. The poignancy of my grief, and the unavailing lamentations which the intelligence excited, need no delineation. To scenes of this nature you have been habituated in the mansion of sorrow where you reside.

How sincerely I sympathize with the bereaved parent of the dear, deceased Eliza, I can feel, but have not power to express. Let it be her consolation, that her child is at rest. The resolution which carried this deluded wanderer thus far from her friends, and supported her through her various trials, is astonishing! Happy would it have been, had she exerted an equal degree of fortitude in repelling the first attacks upon her virtue! But she is no more; and heaven forbid that I should accuse or reproach her!

Yet in what language shall I express my abhorrence of the monster whose detestable arts have blasted one of the fairest flowers in creation? I leave him to God, and his own conscience! Already is he exposed in his true colors! Vengeance already begins to overtake him!

His sordid mind must now suffer the deprivation of those sensual gratifications, beyond which he is incapable of enjoyment!

Upon your reflecting and steady mind, my dear Julia, I need not inculcate the lessons which may be drawn from this woe-fraught tale; but for the sake of my sex in general, I wish it engraved upon every heart, that virtue alone, independent of the trappings of wealth, the parade of equipage, and the adulation of gallantry, can secure lasting felicity. From the melancholy story of Eliza Wharton, let the American fair[1] learn to reject with disdain every insinuation derogatory to their true dignity and honor. Let them despise and forever banish the man who can glory in the seduction of innocence and the ruin of reputation. To associate, is to approve; to approve, is to be betrayed!

I am, etc.

Lucy Sumner

LETTER 74
TO MRS. M. WHARTON

Boston

Dear Madam,

We have paid the last tribute of respect to your beloved daughter. The day after my arrival, Mrs. Sumner proposed that we should visit the sad spot which contains the remains of our once amiable friend. The grave of Eliza Wharton, said she, shall not be unbedewed by the tears of friendship.

Yesterday we went accordingly, and were much pleased with the apparent sincerity of the people, in their assurances that everything in their power had been done to render her situation comfortable. The minutest circumstances were faithfully related; and from the state of her mind in her last hours, I think much comfort may be derived to her afflicted friends.

We spent a mournful hour in the place where she is interred, and then returned to the inn, while Mrs. Sumner gave orders for a decent stone to be erected over her grave, with the following inscription:

[1] *fair* Women.

THIS HUMBLE STONE,
IN MEMORY OF
ELIZA WHARTON,
IS INSCRIBED BY HER WEEPING FRIENDS,
TO WHOM SHE ENDEARED HERSELF BY UNCOMMON
TENDERNESS AND AFFECTION.
ENDOWED WITH SUPERIOR ACQUIREMENTS,
SHE WAS STILL MORE DISTINGUISHED BY
HUMILITY AND BENEVOLENCE.
LET CANDOR THROW A VEIL OVER HER FRAILTIES,
FOR GREAT WAS HER CHARITY TO OTHERS.
SHE SUSTAINED THE LAST
PAINFUL SCENE, FAR FROM EVERY FRIEND;
AND EXHIBITED AN EXAMPLE
OF CALM RESIGNATION.
HER DEPARTURE WAS ON THE 25TH DAY OF
JULY, A.D. ——,
IN THE 37TH YEAR OF HER AGE,
AND THE TEARS OF STRANGERS WATERED HER
GRAVE.[1]

I hope, madam, that you will derive satisfaction from these exertions of friendship, and that, united to the many other sources of consolation with which you are furnished, they may alleviate your grief; and while they leave the pleasing remembrance of her virtues, add the supporting persuasion, that your Eliza is happy.

I am, etc.

Julia Granby

Finis
——1797

<div style="text-align: center">1</div>

1 *THIS HUMBLE STONE ... GRAVE* The text here is almost identical to that inscribed on the real Elizabeth Whitman's headstone.

POPULAR LITERATURE AND PRINT CULTURE

In the twenty-first century "popular literature" and "popular culture" tend to be thought of almost entirely in secular terms. In seventeenth-century America, though, popular literary forms among the white settler population were primarily religious; more than that, they were primarily Protestant Christian. Given the motivations of the settler colonists for crossing the Atlantic, it should be no surprise that the first book printed in America should be a book of psalms. And as Samuel Sewall's 1701 broadside shows, religious themes retained a prominent place in eighteenth-century American popular literature as well. The weekly newspapers that began to proliferate in the early eighteenth century, though, were inevitably more secular in their focus. Newspapers covered developments in colonial politics (and were often fiercely partisan) and provided such information as was available regarding developments overseas; they presented the news as best as they were able in an age when news would typically take over a month to cross the Atlantic, and travel overland in the interior of America was even slower. But they presented a good deal more than the news; they also aimed to provide, as Benjamin Franklin said with regard to the *Pennsylvania Gazette*, "as agreeable and useful an entertainment as the nature of the thing will allow." They published a wide range of poetry, for example, and they paid a good deal of attention to cultural matters (as the selections here from the *Philadelphia Repository and Weekly Register* and the *New York Weekly Inspector* demonstrate).

Whereas poetry tends nowadays to be conceived of primarily as a lyric genre, in the seventeenth and eighteenth centuries one very significant function of poetry was storytelling. In broadsides, in newspapers—even (as with "Forty Shillings Reward") in advertisements—ballads and other narrative poetic forms played a prominent role. "The Poor, Unhappy, Transported Felon" and "New England Bravery" are examples of narrative poetry serving purposes that modern readers have come to think of as being more naturally served by prose.

This section provides some sense of the range of popular literature and print culture beyond that which may be found under the author entries in this volume. But it should not be supposed that the works gathered in those entries were *unpopular* in their own time; the list of authors represented elsewhere in this anthology (among them Rowlandson, Wheatley, Crèvecoeur, Franklin, Paine, Freneau, Rowson, Foster, and Irving) who reached a broad popular audience is long and distinguished.

⌘ ⌘ ⌘

Bay Psalm Book

In 1638 the young colony on Massachusetts Bay acquired a printing press, and in 1640 the first book printed in the English colonies was issued—*The Whole Book of Psalms, Faithfully Translated into English Meter*, a book that has come to be known familiarly as the *Bay Psalm Book*. The project involved 30 ministers and was supervised by Richard Mather, Thomas Welde, and John Eliot; exactly who translated what is not known. But the background to the book's printing is plain. Like many other Protestant congregations, those in the Bay area were keen to engage all worshippers in singing the word of God. Many were concerned, however, that *only* the word of God be sung (rather than hymns or other religious songs composed by Christians but not deriving directly from the words of the Bible). For that reason, they focused on the biblical Book of Psalms as offering the most appropriate texts to set to music and to sing.

The resulting book was very widely used in American churches in the seventeenth and eighteenth centuries; by the end of the seventeenth century no fewer than nine editions had been published, and revised editions continued to appear into the second half of the eighteenth century.

Much of the preface to the *Bay Psalm Book* is devoted to justifying the decision to translate the psalms into "such meter as English poetry is wont to run in" rather than into prose (as was employed in the King James Bible, the version authorized by the Church of England). The compilers of the *Bay Psalm Book* evidently take the term *meter* to refer not only to rhythm (for the most part, the patterns of stressed and unstressed syllables are iambic), but also to rhyme; the *Bay Psalm Book* version of the 23rd psalm, for example, follows an ABAB rhyme scheme.

The compilers caution in their preface that their renderings may not be "so smooth and elegant as some may desire or expect," and not a few later readers have concurred in that assessment. Samuel Kettell, in his *Specimens of English Poetry* (1828), declared that "the versification is harsh and unmusical to the last degree"; and Barrett Wendell, in his *Literary History of America* (1900) termed the *Bay Psalm Book*'s imitations of meters used by earlier English poets "barbarous." But the *Bay Psalm Book*'s style has in the twentieth and early twenty-first centuries had numerous defenders as well, with many admiring its rough-hewn rhythms.

from THE PREFACE

The singing of Psalms, though it breathe forth nothing but holy harmony and melody, yet such is the subtlety of the enemy,[1] and enmity of our nature against the Lord and his ways, that our hearts can find matter of discord in this harmony[.] ...

There have been three questions especially stirring concerning singing. First, what psalms are to be sung in churches? whether David's and other scripture psalms,[2] or the psalms invented by the gifts of godly men in every age of the church. Secondly, if scripture psalms, whether in their own words, or in such metre as English poetry is wont to run in? Thirdly, by whom are they to be sung? whether by the whole churches together with their voices? Or by one man singing alone and the rest joining in silence, and in the close saying amen.

Touching the first, certainly the singing of David's psalms was an acceptable worship of God, not only in his, but in succeeding times. ...

As for the scruple that some take at the translation of the Book of Psalms into metre, because David's psalms were sung in his own words without metre, we answer—First, there are many verses together in several psalms of David which run in rhythms (as those that know Hebrew [are aware]. ...), which shows at least the lawfulness of singing psalms in English rhythms.

Secondly, the psalms are penned in such verses as are suitable to the poetry of the Hebrew language, and not in the common style of such other books of the Old Testament as are not poetical; now no Protestant doubts but that all the books of scripture should by God's ordinance be extant in the mother tongue of each nation, that they may be understood of all. Hence the psalms are to be translated into our English tongue; and if in our English tongue we are to sing them, then as all our English songs (according to the course of our English poetry) do run in metre, so ought David's psalms to be translated into metre, that so we may sing the Lord's songs as in our English tongue, so in such verses as are familiar to an English ear, which are commonly metrical. And as it can be no just offense to any good conscience to sing David's Hebrew songs in English words, so neither to sing his poetical verses in English poetical metre. ...

Neither let any think that, for the metre['s] sake, we have taken liberty or poetical license to depart from the true and proper sense of David's words in the Hebrew verses; no, but it has been one part of our religious care and faithful endeavour to keep close to the original text. ...

If ... the verses are not always so smooth and elegant as some may desire or expect; let them consider that

1 *subtlety of the enemy* Cunning of the devil.

2 *David's and other scripture psalms* Many of the psalms in the Bible are attributed to David, who had earned fame as a musician prior to becoming King of Israel. The writer here contrasts the "scripture psalms," i.e., those included in the Book of Psalms, with the "psalms" or hymns written by later Christians.

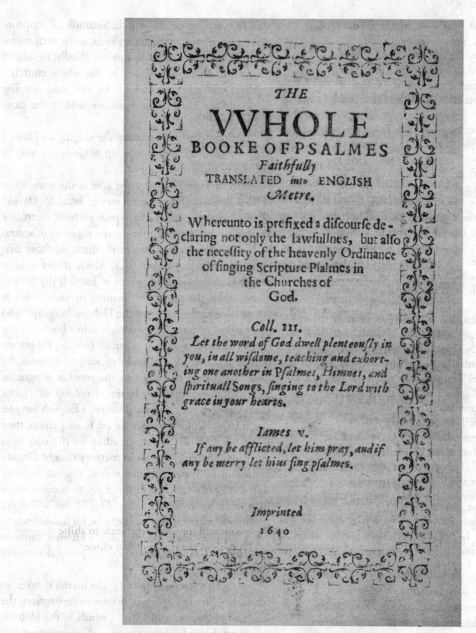

Title page from the *Bay Psalm Book* (1640).

God's altar needs not our polishings; ... for we have respected rather a plain translation, than to smooth our verses with the sweetness of any paraphrases, and so have attended conscience rather than elegance, fidelity rather than poetry, in translating the Hebrew words into English language, and David's poetry into English metre; that so we may sing in Sion[1] the Lord's songs of praise according to his own will until he take us from hence, and wipe away all out tears, and bid us enter into our Master's joy to sing eternal hallelujahs.

—1640

[1] *Sion* Zion; elevated spiritual state.

Psalm 23 [*King James Version*]

The Lord is my shepherd; I shall not want.
 He maketh me to lie down in green pastures; he
 leadeth me beside the still waters.
He restoreth my soul. He leadeth me in the paths of
5 righteousness for his name's sake.
Yea, though I walk through the valley of the shadow of
 death, I will fear no evil, for thou art with me; thy
 rod and thy staff they comfort me.
Thou preparest a table before me in the presence of
10 mine enemies. Thou anointest my head with oil;
 my cup runneth over.
Surely goodness and mercy shall follow me all the days
 of my life; and I will dwell in the house of the Lord
 for ever.
—1611

Psalm 23 [*Bay Psalm Book*]

The Lord to me a shepherd is,
 Want therefore shall not I,
He in the folds of tender grass
 Doth cause me down to lie.
5 To waters calm me gently leads,
 Restore my soul doth He;
He doth in paths of righteousness
 For his name's sake lead me.
Yea, though in valley of death's shade
10 I walk, none ill I'll fear;
Because thou art with me, thy rod
 And staff my comfort are.
For me a table thou hast spread
 In presence of my foes;
15 Thou dost anoint my head with oil,
 My cup it overflows.
Goodness and mercy surely shall
 All my days follow me;
And in the Lord's house I shall dwell
20 So long as days shall be.
—1640

Samuel Sewall, ["Verses upon a New Century"]

Samuel Sewall (1652–1730) is today best remembered for the part he took as a judge in the infamous Salem Witch Trials (a part he later came to regret), but he was also a prominent printer and writer and occasional poet. The following poem was first printed by Sewall as a broadside—a large-format sheet meant to be pasted on public walls or sold cheaply—on the first of January, 1701; he arranged for the poem to be read aloud at the Boston Common, accompanied by trumpets. Though Sewall did not provide a conventional title for the poem, he referred to it in his diary as his "Verses Upon a New Century."

Excerpts from Sewall's diary, and his antislavery tract *The Selling of Joseph*, are included in the website component of this anthology.

WEDNESDAY
January 1. 1701

A little before Break-a-day at Boston of Massachusetts

Once more! Our God, vouchsafe to shine
 Tame thou the rigour of our clime.
Make haste with thy impartial light,
And terminate this long dark night.

5 Let the transplanted *English* vine
Spread further still: still call it thine.
Prune it with skill: for yield it can
More fruit to thee the husbandman.° *farmer*

Give the poor *Indians* eyes to see
10 The light of life: and set them free;
That they religion may profess,
Denying all ungodliness.

From hardened *Jews* the veil remove,
Let them their martyred Jesus love;
15 And homage unto Him afford,
Because He is their rightful Lord.

So false religions shall decay,
And darkness fly before bright day:

So men shall God in Christ adore;
20 And worship idols vain, no more.

So *Asia*, and *Africa*,
Europa, with *America*;
All four, in consort joined, shall sing
Now songs of praise to Christ our King.
—1701

WEDNESDAY, *January* 1. 1701.
A little before Break-a-Day, at *Boston* of the *Massachusetts*.

ONCE more! Our GOD, vouchsafe to Shine:
Tame Thou the Rigour of our Clime.
Make haste with thy Impartial Light,
And terminate this long dark Night.

Let the transplanted English Vine
Spread further still : still Call it Thine.
Prune it with Skill : for yield it can
More Fruit to Thee the Husbandman.

Give the poor Indians Eyes to see
The Light of Life : and set them free ;
That they Religion may profess,
Denying all Ungodliness.

From hard'ned Jews the Vail remove,
Let them their Martyr'd JESUS love ;
And Homage unto Him afford,
Because He is their Rightfull LORD.

So false Religions shall decay,
And Darkness fly before bright Day :
So Men shall GOD in CHRIST adore ;
And worship Idols vain, no more.

So Asia, and Africa,
Europa, with America ;
All Four, in Consort join'd, shall Sing
The Songs of Praise to CHRIST our KING.

Sewall's 1701 broadside.

from Benjamin Harris, *The New England Primer; or, An Easy and Pleasant Guide to the Art of Reading/The New English Tutor, Enlarged for the More Easy Attaining the True Reading of English*

Harris, a British journalist who moved to Boston when his religious and political writings had excited an uncomfortable amount of controversy in England, had in 1679 published a little textbook called *The Protestant Tutor*. He adapted and expanded the earlier work and re-titled it *The New England Primer*, the first edition of which he published in Boston in 1690. Frequently revised and re-issued under various titles, the book remained in common use in American schools for more than 150 years.

Harris returned to Britain in 1695; sometime between 1702 and 1714 he published a new version of his textbook for English audiences, this time calling it *The New English Tutor, Enlarged*. No copies of the first edition of c. 1690 have survived; the earliest extant version of Harris's textbook is that of c. 1702–14.

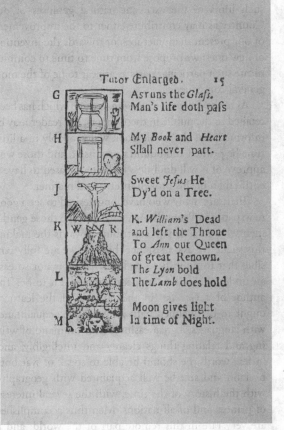

Page from *The New English Tutor, Enlarged for the More Easy Attaining the True Reading of English*. The reference to "Ann[e], our queen of great renown" places the book's publication date as during the reign of Queen Anne (1702–14).

Page from an 1830 edition of *The New England Primer*, published in Pittsburgh by Luke Loomis and Co. The entries under "K" vary widely in the book's many editions. Many eighteenth-century editions have "Our king, the good / No man of blood"; different wording was adopted in editions published after the American Revolution.

from Benjamin Franklin, *The Printer to the Reader*

A true polymath, Benjamin Franklin earned great respect as, among other things, a writer, publisher, inventor, scientist, and diplomat. Formally schooled only until the age of ten, he soon became an apprentice to his brother James, a printer, and began publishing letters to James's paper under a pseudonym when he was denied the opportunity to publish under his own name. Years later, when he was twenty-three, Franklin became the publisher of *The Pennsylvania Gazette*, which with him at the helm—and contributing pieces under various aliases—quickly became the most successful newspaper in the colonies, and remained one of the United States' most prominent newspapers for the better part of a century.

Franklin began his first issue with a statement of intention, outlining the ways in which the *Pennsylvania Gazette* would differ from its predecessor, the *Universal Instructor in All Arts and Sciences, and Pennsylvania Gazette*, thirty-nine issues of which had been published to little sustained readership by Samuel Keimer. Keimer's failure to attract and keep readers was no doubt exacerbated by Franklin's harsh criticism of the paper under the pen name "Busy Body."

The *Pennsylvania Gazette* being now to be carried on by other hands, the reader may expect some account of the method we design to proceed in.

Upon a view of Chambers' great dictionaries, from whence were taken the materials of the *Universal Instructor in all Arts and Sciences*, which usually made the first part of this paper,[1] we find that besides their containing many things abstruse or insignificant to us, it will probably be fifty years before the whole can be gone through in this manner of publication. There are likewise in those books continual references from things under one letter of the alphabet to those under another, which relate to the same subject, and are necessary to explain and complete it; these taken in

their turn may perhaps be ten years distant, and since it is likely that they who desire to acquaint themselves with any particular art or science would gladly have the whole before them in much less time, we believe our readers will not think such a method of communicating knowledge to be a proper one.

Moreover, though we do not intend to continue the publication of those dictionaries in a regular alphabetical method, as has hitherto been done; yet as several things exhibited from them in the course of these papers have been entertaining to such of the curious, who never had and cannot have the advantage of good libraries; and as there are many things still behind, which being in this manner made generally known may perhaps become of considerable use, by giving such hints to the excellent natural geniuses of our Country as may contribute either to the improvement of our present manufactures, or towards the invention of new ones; we propose from time to time to communicate such particular parts as appear to be of the most general consequence.

As to the *Religious Courtship*,[2] part of which has been retailed to the public in these papers, the reader may be informed that the whole book will probably in a little time be printed and bound up by itself, and those who approve of it will doubtless be better pleased to have it entire than in this broken interrupted manner.

There are many who have long desired to see a good newspaper in Pennsylvania, and we hope those gentlemen who are able will contribute towards the making this such. We ask assistance, because we are fully sensible that to publish a good newspaper is not so easy an undertaking as many people imagine it to be. The author of a *Gazette* (in the opinion of the learned) ought to be qualified with an extensive acquaintance with languages, a great easiness and command of writing and relating things cleanly and intelligibly, and, in few words, he should be able to speak of war both by land and sea; be well acquainted with geography, with the history of the time, with the several interests of princes and of all nations. Men thus accomplished are very rare in this remote part of the world; and it

[1] *Chambers' great dictionaries … first part of this paper* Under Keimer's leadership, each issue of the paper had begun with an extract from Ephraim Chambers's encyclopedia: *Cyclopaedia, or a Universal Dictionary of Arts and Sciences* (1728–53).

[2] *Religious Courtship* Extracts from this 1797 conduct manual by Daniel Defoe were printed by Keimer in his later issues of the *Universal Instructor*.

would be well if the writer of these papers could make up among his friends what is wanting[1] in himself.

Upon the whole, we may assure the public that as far as the encouragement we meet with will enable us, no care and pains shall be omitted that may make the *Pennsylvania Gazette* as agreeable and useful an entertainment as the nature of the thing will allow.

—1729

anonymous ("A Lady"), "Woman's Hard Fate"

This poem appears to have first been published in the *South Carolina Gazette* in 1743; it was reprinted in numerous other papers over the following decades.

How wretched is poor woman's fate!
No happy change her fortune knows:
Subject to man in every state,
 How can she then be free from woes?
5 In youth, a father's stern command,
 And jealous eyes, control her will;
A lordly brother watchful stands,
 To keep her closer captive still.

The tyrant husband next appears,
10 With awful[2] and contracted brow;
No more a lover's form he wears:
 Her slave's become her sov'reign now,
If from this fatal bondage free,
 And not by marriage chains confined,
15 If, blessed with single life, she see
 A parent fond, a brother kind—

Yet love usurps her tender breast,
 And paints a phoenix to her eyes;
Some darling youth disturbs her rest;
20 And painful sighs in secret rise.
Oh cruel pow'rs, since you've designed,
 That man, vain man, should bear the sway,
To slavish chains add slavish mind,
 That I may thus your will obey.

—1743?

[1] *wanting* Lacking.

[2] *awful* Inspiring a mix of awe and fear; intimidating.

anonymous, *New England Bravery, Being a Full and True Account of the Taking of the City of Louisbourg by the New England Forces under the Command of the Gallant General Pepperell, on the 17th of June, 1745*

Broadsides were a common form of popular literature in America from the late seventeenth century until well into the nineteenth. Printed on one side of a sheet of paper, broadsides provided an everyday means of disseminating information of all sorts. Some broadsides were posted for passers-by to read, while others—including many "broadside ballads"—were printed for sale. This mid-eighteenth-century broadside (which was, as the notice at the bottom informs us, "sold at the Heart and Crown in Cornhill, Boston") offers a poetic version of the capture of the French fortress of Louisburg by colonial forces during King George's War. The expedition was an initiative of the colonial government of Massachusetts, but support was also enlisted from the other New England colonies (as well as, somewhat belatedly, from the Royal Navy). When King George's War ended in 1748, the terms of the treaty provided for the return of the fortress of Louisburg to the French; it was not until 1758 (during the Seven Years' War) that the fortress fell permanently to the British.

New-England Bravery:

Being a full and true Account of the taking of the City of *Louisbourg*, by the *New-England* Forces under the Command of the gallant General *Pepperell*, on the 17th of *June*, 1745.

Tune of, *Chivey-Chace*.

Come all *New-England*'s gallant Lads,
 and lend to me an Ear,
And of your Brethren's mighty Acts
 I will in short declare.
Brave PEP'RELL with three Thousand Men,
 (perhaps some hundreds more)
Did land the very first of *May*,
 upon *Cape-Breton* Shore:
And tho' opposed by *Morepang*
 with full two hundred Men,
A handful of our gallant Lads
 did drive them back again.
Some few were taken Prisoners,
 and many kill'd out-right,
Which taught the *French* at *Louisbourg*
 New-England Men can fight.
The *Monsieurs* all astonished
 to see our Armament,
Were griev'd to see that they must be
 within Stone Walls all pent.
In haste they call in to their Aid
 the Men upon the Isle,
Forgetting their own Poverty,
 (such Things would make one smile)
But what is vastly more absurd
 Than any thing like this,
They quitted the *Grand Battery*,
 the Glory of the Place.
Of which our *English* Lads did take

And with the Guns did ever since
 the Enemy annoy.
They also did with mighty Toil
 their Batteries erect,
Against the Town and Citidel,
 which play'd with good Effect.
They sent such Showers of Bombs and Balls
 as made the *Frenchmen* quake,
And sputter out such Words as these,
 Those Dogs the Place will take.
Our Men did also batter down
 the West Gate and the Wall,
And made therein so large a Breach
 that to the *French* they'd call ;
Come out, Jack Frenchman, *come to us,*
 and drink a Bowl of Punch,

The *Frenchmen* cry, *you English Dogs,*
 come, here's a pretty Wench.
But by and by they change their Tones,
 and offer Terms of Peace,
Which if consented to they would
 surrender up the Place.
(For they were so severely maul'd
 by Cannon Shot and Shells,
That they no Place of Safety found
 on Platforms or in Cells.)
Their Island Battery likewise,
 on which they much depended,
Was so annoyed by our Men
 it could not be defended.
For they did wisely plant some Guns
 upon the Light-House Point,
And also one good Mortar Piece,
 which put them out of Joint.
Our Lads they fir'd so furiously
 into that Island Fort,
The Soldiers jump'd into the Sea,
 which made our Men good Sport.
Our Gen'ral upon this Success
 did send *Monsieurs* Word,
If they would not give up the Place,
 He'd put them to the Sword.
And now not daring to withstand
 the Force of all our Bands,
They gave up all their Fortresses
 to our *English* Hands.
With Beat of Drums and Colours spread,
 the Seventeenth of *June*,
Our gallant Army marched in,
 'bout Twelve o'Clock at Noon.
The Gentlemen and Ladies too
 they did caress our Men,
For having them delivered
 from worse than Lion's Den.
They all are to be sent to *France*,
 with all the Islanders,
Which needs must ease our Countrymen
 of many Cares and Fears.
And all the Men are strictly bound
 (that is as we do hear)
Not to bear Arms against King GEORGE,
 at least for one whole Year.

Sold at the *Heart and Crown* in *Cornhill*, *Boston*.

Jonathan Livermore His Verses

Mary Nelson, "Forty Shillings Reward"

Advertisements offering rewards were common in early American newspapers; Mary Nelson's advertisement in the *Pennsylvania Chronicle* was highly unusual, however, for being written in rhyming couplets rather than in prose. Aside from her authorship of this poem, nothing is known of Nelson. As the advertisements from *The Pennsylvania Gazette* that are reproduced below attest, forty shillings was a sum frequently offered as a reward at the time.

Valuing money in the Thirteen Colonies was (and is) extraordinarily complicated. Most colonies followed Britain in using pounds, shillings, and pence, but the value of these denominations in each colony was not the same as the value of the same denominations in Britain—or as the same denominations in other colonies. Further complicating matters was the prevalence of the Spanish dollar as a standard currency unit throughout the colonies. In Pennsylvania the dollar was valued in the 1760s at 7.5 shillings. A half-crown was a denomination equivalent to 2.5 shillings; thus—in Pennsylvania at least—40 shillings was equivalent to five dollars plus a half crown.

Last Wednesday morn, at break of day,
From Philadelphia run away,
An Irish man, named John M'Keoghn,
To fraud and imposition prone;
5 About five feet five inches high,
Can curse and swear as well as lie;
How old he is I can't engage,
But forty-five is near his age;
He came (as all reports agree)
10 From Belfast town in sixty-three,
On board the *Culloden*,[1] a ship
Commanded by M'Lean that trip;
Speaks like a Scotchman, very broad,
Is round shouldered, and meagre jawed;
15 Has thick short hair, of sandy hue,
Breeches and hose of maz'reen[2] blue;
Of lightish cloth an outside vest,

In which he commonly is dressed;
Inside of which two more I've seen,
20 One flannel, th' other coarse nankeen.[3]
He stole, and from my house conveyed,
A man's blue coat, of broadcloth[4] made;
A grey great coat, of bearskin stuff,
(Nor had the villain yet enough);
25 Some chintz (the ground was pompadour)[5]
I lately purchased in a store,
Besides a pair of blue ribbed hose,
Which he has on as I suppose.
He oft in conversation chatters,
30 Of scripture and religious matters,
And fain would to the world impart,
That virtue lodges in his heart;
But take the rogue from stem to stern,
The hypocrite you'll soon discern
35 And find (though his deportment's civil)
A saint without, within a devil.
Whoe'er secures said John M'Keoghn,
(Provided I should get my own)
Shall have from me, in cash paid down,
40 Five Dollar-Bills, and Half-a-Crown.

Water-street, Jan. 10, 1769

1 *Culloden* Launched in 1747, the *Culloden* was a ship in the British Navy until April 1770.

2 *maz'reen* Mazarine; deep shade of blue.

3 *nankeen* Pale yellow cloth made of cotton.

4 *broadcloth* Plain woven cloth with double width, historically made of wool.

5 *chintz* Cotton cloth decorated with flowered designs, imported from India, that gained widespread popularity in Europe and America during the mid-eighteenth century; *the ground was pompadour* The fabric's background color was pompadour pink, a rosy shade.

IN CONTEXT

Forty Shillings Reward

Advertisements, *The Pennsylvania Gazette* (4 May 1769)

RUN away from his bail, in Uwchland township, Chester county, on the 7th of this inst. March, one John Benson, this country born, a blacksmith by trade, with short black hair, about 5 feet 8 or 9 inches high, 24 years of age, has a scar above his right eye; had on, when he went away, a blanket coat, old felt hat, new buckskin breeches, new leather apron, much given to drink; it is likely he may change his clothes for money. Whoever takes up and secures the said John Benson, in any of his Majesty's goals, shall have Forty Shillings reward, if taken within this province; and if taken out of the province, FIVE POUNDS, with reasonable charges, paid by
 WILLIAM MELCHIOR.
¶

RUN away, the 13th of this inst. March, from the subscriber, in Tredyffrin, Chester county, a servant man, named PEARCE CHESSEY, about 35 years old, or more; he is a very lusty healthy man, stoops much, is a weaver by trade, and very handy at the carpenter's trade, as he says; has a down look, and black complexion. He took with him one handkerchief, with diamond squares on one side, and blue and white on the other, and two pitching axes; also another handkerchief, with diamonds on both sides; one walnut coloured stocking, and one pale blue ditto, footed; a short blue mended coat, a jacket made of a blanket, and faced with linsey, leather breeches, and shoes, with thongs in them. He was bought out of Chester goal, where he was confined for stealing a watch; and some time ago, he took away two pair of silver buckles, one pair 30 penny weight, the other 26. Whoever takes up and secures said servant, if in the province, shall have Forty Shillings; and if out of the province, Three Pounds reward, and reasonable charges, from
 DAVID EVANS. ¶

from James Revel, "The Poor, Unhappy, Transported Felon"

"The Poor, Unhappy, Transported Felon" recounts the story of a young man transported from Britain to Virginia during the third quarter of the seventeenth century as punishment for theft. It is unclear when the poem was written, or indeed whether Revel was an actual person, especially since fictional tales of transported criminals were common fodder for ballads and other forms of popular literature during the eighteenth century. However, certain details in the poem itself disclose a familiarity with the geography of seventeenth-century Virginia and suggest firsthand knowledge on the part of the author. The earliest extant published versions of the poem date to the mid-eighteenth century; the following text is based on an undated chapbook printed c. 1767–80.

from PART 1

My loving countrymen pray lend an ear,
To this relation that I bring you here,
My present sufferings at large I will unfold,
Although it's strange, 'tis true as e'er was told.

5 Of honest parents I did come though poor,
Who besides me had children never more,
Near Temple Bar[1] was born their darling son,
In virtue's paths he for some time did run.

My parents in me took a vast delight,
10 And sent me unto school to read and write,
And cast accompts[2] likewise as it appears,
Until that I was aged thirteen years.

Then to a tin man[3] I was apprentice bound,
My master and my mistress good I found,

15 They liked me well, my business I did mind,[4]
From me my parents comfort hoped to find.

My master near unto Moorfields[5] did dwell,
Here into wicked company I fell;
To wickedness I quickly was inclined,
20 So soon is tainted any youthful mind.

I from my master then did run away,
And roved about the streets both night and day,
Did with a gang of thieves a robbing go,
Which filled my parents' hearts with grief and
 woe. …

25 A wicked life I lived I must confess,
In fear and dread, and great uneasiness,
Which does attend those actions most unjust,
For thieves can never one another trust.

Strong liquor banished the thoughts of fear,
30 But justice stopped us in our full career;
One night was taken up one of our gang,
Who five impeached, and three of them were hanged.

I was one of the five was tried and cast,° *convicted*
Yet transportation I did get at last,[6]
35 A just reward for my vile actions base;
So justice overtook me at the last.

My father vexed, my mother she took on,[7]
And said, alas! alas! my only son;
My father said, it cuts me to the heart,
40 To think on such a cause as this we part.

1 *Temple Bar* Gate forming the entrance to the western edge of the City of London.

2 *cast accompts* Perform basic arithmetic.

3 *tin man* Tinsmith; someone who works with tin.

4 *mind* Attend to diligently.

5 *Moorfields* Plot of open, marshy land just outside London's northern wall. In the early eighteenth century, the dwellings around Moorfields housed mostly the poor, and the district had a reputation for hiding thieves and other criminals.

6 *Yet transportation … at last* If found guilty of grand larceny (defined as the theft of property valued over twelve pence), an individual could be sentenced to death; as was often the case with similar capital crimes during this period, Revel was spared this conviction and was instead sentenced to transportation, or banishment to a penal colony.

7 *took on* Became greatly agitated and distressed.

To see him grieve pierced my very soul,
My wretched case I sadly did condole,
With grief and shame my eyes did overflow,
I did much rather choose to die than go.

45 In vain I grieved and in vain my parents wept,
For I was quickly sent on board the ship,
With melting kisses, and a heavy heart,
I from my parents then did part.

from PART 3

Down to the harbour I was took again
On board a ship loaded with chains;
Which I was forced to wear both night and day,
For fear I from the sloop should run away.

5 My master was a man but of ill fame,[1]
Who first of all a transport thither came,
In Rappahannock county[2] he did dwell,
In Rappahannock river known full well.

When the ship was laden and home sent,
10 An hundred miles we up the river went,
The weather cold, and very hard my fare,
My lodgings on the deck both hard and bare.

At last to my new master's house I came,
To the town of Wicowoco[3] called by name,
15 Here my European clothes were took from me,
Which never after I could ever see.

A canvas shirt and trousers me they gave,
A hopsack frock[4] in which I was a slave,
No shoes or stockings had I for to wear,
20 Nor hat nor cap, my head and feet were bare.

Thus dressed, into the field I next did go,
Among tobacco plants all day to hoe,
At daybreak in the morn our work begun,
And lasted till the setting of the sun.

25 My fellow slaves were five transports more,
With eighteen negroes, which is twenty-four,
Besides four transport women in the house,
To wait upon his daughter and his spouse.

We and the negroes both alike did fare,
30 Of work and food we had an equal share;
And in a piece of ground called our own,
The food we eat first by ourselves is sown.

No other time to us they will allow,
But on a Sunday we the same must do,
35 Six days we slave for our master's good,
The seventh is to produce our homely food.

And when we a hard day's work have done,
Away unto the mill we must be gone.
'Till twelve or one o'clock a-grinding corn,
40 And must be up by daylight in the morn. ...

from PART 6

My countrymen take warning e'er too late,
Lest you should share my unhappy fate,
Although but little crimes you here have done,
Think of seven or fourteen years to come.

5 Forced from your friends and country to go,
Among the negroes to work at the hoe,
Indifferent countries void of all relief,
Sold for a slave because you proved a thief.

Now young me all with speed your lives amend
10 Take my advice, as one that is your friend,
For though so slight you do make of it here,
Hard is your lot if you once get there.
—C. 1767–80 (WRITTEN LATE 1600S?)

1 *ill fame* Reputation for being immoral or vicious.

2 *Rappahannock county* Today often known as Old Rappahannock County to distinguish it from the current county by that name, this Virginia county was in existence between 1656 and 1692.

3 *Wicowoco* Wicomico; town near the York River in Virginia.

4 *hopsack frock* Sack in which hops have been packed, repurposed as clothing.

from Philip Freneau, "The Country Printer"

In his four-part poem "The Country Printer," Freneau laments what he sees as the decline of the press in 1790s America, praising those who in revolutionary times "with press and pen attacked the royal side" and mocking (as in the excerpt below) much of what has come to pass for news in the popular press. In the end, he praises the press for the contribution it has made ("to the pen and press so much we owe") and calls on readers—"ye Guardians of your country and her laws"—to exhort writers and printers to have the courage to "favour freedom's sacred cause."

from PART 2

All is not truth ('tis said) that travellers tell—
So much the better for this man of news;
For hence the country round, that know him well,
Will, if he prints some lies, his lies excuse.
5 Earthquakes, and battles, shipwrecks, myriads slain—
If false or true—alike to him are gain. ...

Some miracles he makes, and some he steals;
Half nature's works are giants in his eyes:
Much, very much, in wonderment he deals—
10 New Hampshire apples grown to pumpkin size,
Pumpkins almost as large as country inns,
And ladies bearing, each, three lovely twins.

He, births and deaths with cold indifference views;
A paragraph from him is all they claim:
15 And here the rural squire, amongst the news
Sees the fair record of some lordling's fame;
All that was good, minutely brought to light,
All that was ill—concealed from vulgar sight!

—1794

anonymous, "Every Man His Own Politician"

In the years following the Revolution, many Americans found themselves disillusioned with the form their new government was seeming to take, believing that the administrations of George Washington and, especially, of John Adams displayed a worryingly aristocratic interpretation of the Constitution. These critics formed what came to be known as the Democratic-Republican Party, whose leader, Thomas Jefferson, defeated the incumbent Federalist Adams in the presidential election of 1800. Jefferson officially began his first term as president in March 1801. The following poem was published as a broadside around this period and clearly voices support for the values and policies of the Jeffersonians.

Let every man of Adam's line
In social contact freely join
To extirpate monarchic power,
That kings may plague the earth no more.

5 As pow'r results from you alone,
Ne'er trust it on a single throne,
Kings oft betray their sacred trust,
And crush their subjects in the dust.

Nor yet confide in men of show,
10 Aristocrats reduce you low;
Nobles, at best, are fickle things,
And oft, far worse than cruel kings.

Nobles combine in secret fraud,
(Though in pretence for public good)
15 To frame a law the most unjust,
And sink the people down to dust.

When laws are framed, the poor must lie,
Distressed beneath the noble's eye;
Unpitied there, to waste their breath,
20 In fruitless prayers 'till freed by death.

A year is long enough to prove
A servant's wisdom, faith and love,

Release him from temptation then
And change the post to other men.

25 Now is the prime important hour
The people may improve their pow'r
To stop aristocratic force,
And walk in reason's peaceful course.
 —c. 1801

from *The Philadelphia Repository and Weekly Register*

The Philadelphia Repository and Weekly Register, which was published between 1800 and 1804, included in each issue a literary page, under the heading "Temple of the Muses."[1] That page brought together short lyrics on a wide variety of topics, poems in dialogue, puzzle poems, and the occasional letter of literary commentary. The poems reproduced here both appeared in the 17 March 1804 issue; the author of L'Embonpoint was identified simply as "Alithean," while "The Mother" was printed anonymously.

L'EMBONPOINT[2]

Though *Cloe* boasts her slender limb,
 Her little foot and arm so slim,
 I slight her meagre charms;
Give me, O Cupid! her whose waist,
5 When fondly she's by me embraced
 Will fill my 'raptured° arms. *enraptured*

The lath-like *Cloe* strives in vain;
 A slender waist will never gain
 My little flutt'ring heart;
10 Long since, to a plump, rosy maid,
The little truant wand'rer strayed—
 From her 'twill ne'er depart

For though 'tis held a captive there,
 Its prisons so divinely fair,
15 With bondage 'tis content;

Nay, so delighted 'tis to dwell,
In her sweet bosom—charming cell!
 To change 'twill ne'er consent.

Cloe, I ne'er loved lath-like belles;
20 But her I love whose plumpness tells,
 Good-nature dwells within:
Me, skin and bones could never charm;
A full, red cheek and plump white arm
 Alone could ever win.

25 Cupid and Hymen,[3] gods benign
 I pray that *Rosa* may be mine
 O, grant my fervent pray'r!
O, grant me her whose plump white arm,
A hoary anchorite[4] would warm,
30 *Rosa*, Health's fav'rite fair!

O, Hymen! make plump *Rosa* mine:
 The slender waist I will resign,
 For her superior charms.
Give me, O Cupid! her whose waist,
35 When fondly she's by me embraced
 Will fill my 'raptured arms.
 —1804

THE MOTHER[5]

So when the *Mother*, bending o'er his charms,
 Claps the fair *nursling* in delightful arms;
Throws her thin 'kerchief from her neck of snow,
And half unveils the pearly orbs below;
5 With sparkling eye the blameless plunderer owns
Her soft embraces and endearing tones;
Seeks the salubrious fount with opening lips,
Spreads his inquiring hands, and smiles and sips.
Connubial fair![6] whom no fond transport[7] warms,
10 To lull your infant in maternal arms,
Who, blest in vain with tumid° bosoms, hear *swollen*

1 *Temple of the Muses* The editors wish to thank Edward White of Tulane University for drawing this material to their attention.

2 *L'EMBONPOINT* French: The curvy one.

3 *Hymen* Classical god of marriage.

4 *hoary* White-haired; *anchorite* Religious hermit; monk.

5 Though printed anonymously in the *Philadelphia Repository*, this poem was originally part of a much longer 1791 poem by English naturalist Erasmus Darwin, *The Botanic Garden*.

6 *Connubial fair* Married woman.

7 *transport* Rapturous emotion.

His tender wailings with unfeeling ear;
The soothing kiss, and milky rill,° deny stream
To the sweet pouting lip and glist'ning eye!
15 Ah! what avails the cradle's damask roof,
The silken bolster, and embroidered woof![1]
Oft hears the gilded couch unpitied plains,° complaints
And many a tear the tasseled cushion stains!
No voice so sweet attunes his cares to rest,
20 So soft no pillow as his mother's breast.
Thus charmed to sweet repose when twilight hours
Shed their sweet influence in celestial bow'rs,
The cherub *Innocence*, with smile divine,
Shuts his white wings, and sleeps on *Beauty's* shrine.
—1804

from anonymous ("Volina"), "You Say We're Fond of Fops—Why Not?"

The 6 September 1806 issue of the *New York Weekly Inspector* included a poem by "Dr. Caustick" satirizing fops (overly fashionable and flirtatious men) and the women who admired them. "Dr. Caustick" was the pen name of Thomas Fessenden, a popular author and the editor of the *Weekly Inspector*. Shortly thereafter, the Vermont *Brattleborough Reporter* printed a response piece by an author identified only as "Volina," and the response was then reprinted in the *Weekly Inspector* on 1 November 1806. A short paragraph prefacing Volina's poem in the latter paper suggested that the satirical response might "induce [Fessenden] to correct some of his own faults and foibles, before he falls pell-mell upon the fair sex."

You say we're fond of fops—why not,
When men of sense cannot be got?
A woman, *something* must admire,
Or else with *ennui* expire.

5 O Doctor! listen to my prayer—
A lesson for proud man prepare;
There is a fault you must confess,
Most men of wit and worth possess.

They seem to think in woman's mind,
10 But very little sense to find;
And therefore when they condescend,
Perchance an hour with us to spend—

Think it impossible to please,
With their profound sublime ideas;
15 But sit in silence, most heroic,
Plodding, like philosophic stoic.

…

Most women will the fop despise,
When men of sense shall be so wise

As to discard, Turk-like[2] opinions,
20 That women are but Nature's minions;
Made for a while to please the eye,
To nourish man, and then to die!

When you do this we'll bid adieu,
To lap-dogs, fops, and monkeys[3] too;
25 Reserving all our admiration,
FOR MAN, THE GLORY OF CREATION.
—1806

Samuel Woodworth, "The Patriotic Diggers"

During the War of 1812, thousands of ordinary citizens came together to help build fortifications around key locations that were vulnerable to British attacks, most notably New York Harbor. This voluntary communal effort was the inspiration for "The Patriotic Diggers," a song by poet and journalist Samuel Woodworth that proved enduringly popular and was reprinted in newspapers and anthologies long after the end of the war. The following text is based on that published in John Lossing's *Pictorial Field-Book of the War of 1812* (1868).

1 *woof* Fabric (the terms *warp* and *woof* refer to the interlocking lengthwise and transverse threads that make up a woven material).

2 *Turk-like* The term "Turk" was often used to denote Arabic peoples as a whole; the author's usage reflects the false but commonly held belief that Muslim cultures were inherently more sexist than Christian cultures.

3 *monkeys* The last line of Fessenden's poem suggests that women would be better off having romantic attachments with "gallants / From Afric's coast, or that of France, / … or monkeys."

Johnny Bull,[1] beware,
 Keep at proper distance,
Else we'll make you stare
 At our firm resistance;
5 Let alone the lads
 Who are freedom tasting,
Recollect our dads
 Gave you once a basting.° *beating*
 Pickaxe, shovel, spade,
10 Crowbar, hoe, and barrow,
 Better not invade,
 Yankees have the marrow.

To protect our rights
 'Gainst your flints and triggers,
15 See on Brooklyn Heights
 Our patriotic diggers;
Men of every age,
 Color,[2] rank, profession,
Ardently engage,
20 Labor in succession.
 Pickaxe, etc.

Here the mason builds
 Freedom's shrine of glory,
While the painter gilds,
25 The immortal story
Blacksmiths catch the flame,
 Grocers feel the spirit,
Printers share the fame,
 And record their merit.
30 Pickaxe, etc.

Scholars leave their schools
 With their patriot teachers;
Farmers seize their tools,
 Headed by the preachers.
35 How they break the soil!
 Brewers, butchers, bakers;
Here the doctors toil,
 There the undertakers.
 Pickaxe, etc.

40 Bright Apollo's sons[3]
 Leave their pipe and tabor,[4]
'Mid the roar of guns
 Join the martial labor;
Round the embattled plain
45 In sweet concord rally,
And in freedom's strain
 Sing the foe's finale!
 Pickaxe, etc.

Plumbers, founders,[5] dyers,
50 Tinmen, turners,[6] shavers,
Sweepers, clerks, and criers,
 Jewelers, engravers,
Clothiers, drapers,° players,° *fabric sellers / actors*
 Cartmen, hatters, tailors,
55 Gaugers, sealers, weighers,[7]
 Carpenters and sailors.
 Pickaxe, etc.

Better not invade;
 Recollect the spirit
60 Which our dads displayed,
 And their sons inherit.
If you still advance,
 Friendly caution slighting,
You may get, by chance,
65 A bellyful of fighting.
 Pickaxe, shovel, spade,
 Crowbar, hoe, and barrow,
 Better not invade,
 Yankees have the marrow.

—1812

1 *Johnny Bull* Common personification of England.

2 *Men of every … Color* Many free African Americans participated in the digging.

3 *Bright Apollo's sons* I.e., musicians. Apollo is the Greek god of music, among other things.

4 *tabor* Small drum, especially one meant to accompany pipes as a marching instrument.

5 *founders* Workers who deal with cast metal.

6 *turners* Workers who manufacture objects on a lathe.

7 *Gaugers, sealers, weighers* Workers engaged in different parts of the importing and exporting process.

TECUMSEH
c. 1768 – 1813

One of the most energetic and eloquent exponents of Native American unity and resistance to U.S. expansion, the Shawnee leader Tecumseh was also, ironically, one of the first Native Americans to become a full-blown U.S. folk hero. His foremost adversary, the military officer and politician William Henry Harrison, summarized Tecumseh's insurgent stature while also anticipating his appropriation by the very white American society he fought so hard against: "The implicit obedience and respect which the followers of Tecumseh pay him bespeaks him one of those uncommon geniuses, which spring up occasionally to produce revolutions and overturn the established order of things." Together with his brother Tenskwatawa, also known as "The Prophet," Tecumseh envisioned and worked indefatigably to create a confederation of the Indigenous nations of the Great Lakes region (and beyond) that would be able to halt the relentless march of white colonization and form an independent Indigenous state. Much of his reputation and many of his achievements stemmed from the universally acknowledged power of his oratory, which drew on and reshaped longstanding Indigenous rhetorical traditions, and his legacy looms large in both white American and Native American history and culture.

Tecumseh's nation, the Shawnee, had been scattered by Haudenosaunee expansion into the Ohio River valley during the century before his birth; at the time Tecumseh was born, they were attempting to return to their traditional territories in what is now Ohio. Tecumseh was born around 1768 in those traditional territories (most likely in the vicinity of present-day Chillicothe, Ohio), although his parents had met and married in what is now Alabama and his mother may have been Muscogee (Creek). No sooner had the Shawnee begun reestablishing themselves in their Ohio Valley homelands than they found themselves facing a new foreign influx, this time that of Euro-American colonists. Tecumseh spent much of the 1780s and 1790s alternately taking part in the fight against American expansion into the Ohio Country—in the course of which both his father and his older brother died in battle—and traveling further afield in an (unsuccessful) attempt to outpace that expansion. In 1794, an American victory at the Battle of Fallen Timbers (at which Tecumseh was present) ended the so-called Northwest Indian War and caused the collapse of the Indigenous confederation that had formed to resist the Americans. Many Indigenous leaders signed the subsequent Treaty of Greenville (1795), ceding most of present-day Ohio to the U.S., but Tecumseh did not.

In 1805, Tecumseh's younger brother Lalawéthika reportedly experienced a series of visions that earned him the new name "Tenskwatawa," meaning "Open Door." Tenskwatawa began preaching a new religion, which held that white Americans were "the children of the Evil Spirit" who "poisoned the land," and enjoined Native Americans to forswear alcohol and other Euro-American products and customs, to revive their traditional ways of life, and to surrender no more land to the whites. Tecumseh joined Tenskwatawa in proclaiming that Indigenous land was the common possession of all Indigenous nations, which could not be ceded without the consent of all, and in calling for the fractured Indigenous confederacy to reunite around this imperative. White writers have long tended to apportion Tenskwatawa and Tecumseh to separate "religious" and "political" spheres and to build up Tecumseh at Tenskwatawa's expense. It is clear from the historical record, however, that the two brothers shared the same beliefs and ideas—and that, at least in the early days of their movement, Tenskwatawa overshadowed Tecumseh. The originality of the brothers' message has also been exaggerated, when in fact they were building on prior movements for political unity, and related spiritual revivalist movements, among the Indigenous peoples

of the Great Lakes region, including the earlier confederacies organized by the Odawa leader Pontiac (in conjunction with the religious revival led by the Lenape prophet Neolin) and the Mohawk Joseph Brant (who anticipated the later course of Tecumseh's career by allying with the British against the Americans during the Revolutionary War).

Tenskwatawa and Tecumseh's new movement spread quickly, and in 1808 they founded (in what is now Indiana) a base for it, known in English as "Prophetstown," which soon grew into a large multinational Indigenous community. The brewing conflict between the brothers' movement and U.S. authorities came to a head after the signing of the Treaty of Fort Wayne in 1809, whereby accommodationist Indigenous leaders ceded millions more acres of present-day Indiana and Illinois in negotiations at which other Indigenous groups with a stake in the land in question were not represented. Tecumseh, outraged, met in August 1810 with William Henry Harrison, the governor of the Indiana Territory, in an attempt to get the treaty rescinded. The encounter was tense and left both sides convinced that war was impending.

Tecumseh's speech at his meeting with Harrison, in which he laid out his objections to the Fort Wayne treaty in the context of a broader history of Indigenous relations with white colonizers, is one of the first extant examples of his oratory. Like the other speeches attributed to him, the speech has roots in Shawnee political and rhetorical culture, with its emphasis on using public speaking to foster consensus; it also shows how Tecumseh, like other Indigenous leaders at the time, adapted his rhetoric for white audiences and in response to the exigencies of Indigenous–white contact. Tecumseh's recorded speeches also attest—however imperfectly, given their translation and likely embellishment by white writers—to his oratory's incisive power. In the words of one white American recollection of Tecumseh from shortly after his death, "His eloquence was nervous [i.e., forceful], concise, impressive, figurative and sarcastic."

During the two years following his meeting with Harrison, Tecumseh devoted himself to building a common front among Indigenous peoples both near and far, visiting nations as distant as the Choctaw, Chickasaw, and Muscogee (Creek) of what is now Mississippi and Alabama and the Osage of what is now Missouri and Arkansas. Tecumseh's travels, and the speeches and anecdotes that stem from them, bear ample witness to his political and diplomatic abilities; however, few of the more distant Indigenous nations he visited ended up joining his confederacy. In November 1811, William Henry Harrison took advantage of Tecumseh's absence to launch a preventive strike on Prophetstown, defeating Tenskwatawa at the Battle of Tippecanoe and burning the town—although this battle was not the crippling blow to the Indigenous confederacy that American propaganda later made it out to be.

When war broke out between the U.S. and Britain in 1812, Tecumseh's war with the U.S. bled into this broader conflict. Tecumseh quickly made common cause with the British and fought successfully with them in the first year of the war, helping to fend off an American invasion of Canada and later to capture Detroit. The esteem in which Tecumseh was held by his British allies gave rise to the mistaken belief that he was made a general in the British army. By the fall of 1813, however, the British had been forced to retreat into Canada, reluctantly accompanied by Tecumseh. When the British and Indigenous force confronted their American pursuers at the Battle of the Thames, in what is now the Canadian province of Ontario, the British contingent fled the field, and Tecumseh, left to fight alone, was killed. After his death, his confederacy crumbled, leaving the way clear for U.S. domination of the entire region between the Ohio River, the Great Lakes, and the Mississippi.

Tecumseh's death in battle sealed his swift transformation, in white American culture, into the paradigmatic "noble Indian": a worthy foe whose courageous but doomed struggle (as American commentators characterized it) underscored the supposed inevitability of U.S. conquest. As a contributor to the *Indiana Sentinel* put it in 1820, "Every schoolboy in the Union now knows that Tecumseh was a great man. He was truly great—and his greatness was his own, unassisted by science or the aid of education." His legend inspired and was embroidered by works such as the 1841 biography *Life of Tecumseh*, the 1844 play *Tecumseh; or, The Prophet of the West*, and a slew of similar novels, poems, plays, and films that continued into the twentieth century. At the same time, Tecumseh's words and actions—together with those of his brother—helped inspire an ongoing lineage of Indigenous resistance and assertion of autonomy. The Sauk leader Black Hawk, who led his own war against U.S. expansion twenty years after Tecumseh's death, was reported to have "often boasted of his being at the right hand of Tecumseh," and

his 1833 autobiography—a landmark in Native American literature—refers specifically and prophetically to Tenskwatawa (who also inspired Black Hawk's spiritual counterpart, Wabokieshiek). In the late nineteenth century, the kind of apocalyptic Indigenous spiritual ideas, transcending tribal boundaries and blending aspects of various religions, that were developed by Tenskwatawa and articulated in Tecumseh's speeches reemerged in the Ghost Dance movement, while in the twentieth century, Tecumseh's example was frequently cited by the organizers of the American Indian Movement. Scholars today continue to work to counteract Tecumseh's mythologization by the people who defeated him, demonstrating the extent of his collaboration with Tenskwatawa and the way in which his speeches and ideas built on existing Indigenous political, religious, and rhetorical traditions.

NOTE ON THE TEXTS: The text of Tecumseh's 1810 speech to William Henry Harrison is based on the manuscript text of the English translation of the speech included in the collection of Harrison's papers held by the Indiana Historical Society, a facsimile of which appears on the society's website. The text of the speech to the Osages is based on that printed in John Dunn Hunter's *Memoirs of a Captivity among the Indians of North America* (1824). (Hunter [c. 1796–1827] was a white captive who was raised from early childhood among the Osage and other Indigenous nations; the authenticity of his account, including its report of speeches such as Tecumseh's, has been disputed since its publication, but while some modern scholars continue to doubt its veracity, others take it more seriously.) Spelling and punctuation have been modernized according to the practices of this anthology.

⌘ ⌘ ⌘

Speech to William Henry Harrison

Brother, I wish you to listen to me well. I wish to reply to you more explicitly, as I think you do not clearly understand what I before said to you. I shall explain it again.

When we were first discovered it was by the French,[1] who told us that they would adopt us as their children and gave us presents, without asking anything in return but our considering them as our fathers. Since we have changed our fathers, we find it different.

Brother, this is the manner that the treaty was made by us with the French. They gave us many presents and treated us well. They asked us for a small piece of country to live on, which they were not to leave, and continued to treat us as their children. After some time, the British and French came to quarrel.[2] The British

were victorious, yet the French promised to think of us as their child and if they ever could serve us, to do it: "Now, my red children, I know I was obliged to abandon you in disagreeable circumstances, but we have never ceased to look upon you, and if we now could be of service to you, we would still be your friends."

The next father we found was the British, who told us that they would now be our fathers and treat us in the same manner as our former fathers the French. They would occupy the same land they did and not trouble us on ours, but would look on us as their children.

Brother, we were very glad to hear the British promise to treat us [as] our fathers the French had done. They began to treat us in the same way, but at last they changed their good treatment by raising the tomahawk against the Americans and put it into our hands, by which we have suffered the loss of a great many of our young men.

[1] *When we ... the French* Explorers from the French colonies in Canada and the Illinois Country first encountered Shawnee along the Ohio River in the seventeenth century.

[2] *the British ... quarrel* Conflicts between the French and British colonies in North America over control of the Great Lakes region and the Ohio River valley, in which both sides were supported by their respective mother countries and by Native American allies, took

place regularly throughout the late seventeenth and early eighteenth centuries. These conflicts culminated in the French and Indian War (1754–63), in which Britain forced France to give up nearly all of its North American possessions. The Shawnee supported the French in the early stages of the war but made peace with the British colonies in 1758.

Brother, now we began to discover the treachery of the British. They never troubled us for our lands, but they have done worse by inducing us to go to war. The Hurons have particularly suffered during the war and have at length become certain of it—they have told us we must bury the British tomahawk entirely—that if we do not, they (the British) would ere long ask us to take it up.

You ought to know that after we agreed to bury the tomahawk at Greenville[1] we then found new fathers in the Americans, who told us they would treat us well, not like the British who gave us but a small piece of pork every day.

I want now to remind you of the promises of the white people. You recollect that the time the Delawares lived near the white people (Americans) and [were] satisfied with the promises of friendship and remained in security, yet one of their towns was surprised and the men, women and children murdered.[2]

The same promises were given to the Shawnees. Flags were given to them and [they] were told by the Americans that they were now children of the Americans: "These flags will be as security for you; if the white people intend to do you harm hold up your flags and no harm will be done you." This was at length practised, and the consequence was that the person bearing the flag was murdered with others in their village.[3] How, my Brother, after this conduct can you

blame me for placing little confidence in the promises of our fathers the Americans?

Brother, since the peace was made you have killed some of the Shawnees, Winebagoes, Delawares and Miamies, and you have taken our lands from us, and I do not see how we can remain at peace with you if you continue to do so. You have given goods to the Kickapoos for the sale of their land, which has been the cause of many deaths among them. You have promised us assistance, but I do not see that you have given us any.

You try to force the red people to do some injury. It is you that is pushing them on to do mischief. You endeavour to make distinctions. You wish to prevent the Indians to do as we wish them: to unite and let them consider their land common property of the whole. You take tribes aside and advise them not to come into this measure, and until our design is accomplished, we do not wish to accept of your invitation to go and visit the President.

The reason I tell you this is—you want by your distinctions of Indian tribes, in allotting to each a particular track of land, to make them to war with each other. You never see an Indian come and endeavour to make the white people do so. You are continually driving the red people; when at last you will drive them into the great Lake where they can't either stand or walk.

Brother, you ought to know what you are doing with the Indians. Perhaps it is by direction of the President to make those distinctions. It is a very bad thing and we do not like it. Since my residence at Tippecanoe,[4] we have endeavoured to level all the distinctions, to destroy village chiefs, by whom all mischief is done. It is they who sell our land to the Americans. Our object is to let all our affairs be transacted by warriors.

Brother, this land that was sold and the goods that [were] given for it was only done by a few. The treaty was afterwards brought here and the Weas[5] were induced to give their consent because of their small

1 *we agreed ... Greenville* Reference to the 1795 Treaty of Greenville, which ended the Northwest Indian War (1785–95). Under the terms of the treaty, the defeated Northwestern Confederacy of Native American nations, including the Shawnee, ceded most of the present-day state of Ohio in exchange for yearly grants of money and supplies.

2 *one ... murdered* In the Gnadenhutten Massacre of 1782, ninety-six men, women, and children from the Lenape (Delaware) and other Indigenous nations, who had converted to the pacifist Moravian Christian denomination and were living in a Moravian missionary settlement in Gnadenhutten, Ohio, were killed by American militia who suspected them of spying for the British.

3 *the consequence ... their village* Reference to the murder of the Shawnee chief Moluntha during Logan's raid, an American military expedition led by General Benjamin Logan against largely undefended Shawnee villages in October 1786, during the Northwest Indian War. Moluntha had signed the Treaty of Fort Finney between the United States and the Shawnee the year before, in token of which he was flying an American flag over his lodge, and he met Logan's troops holding a copy of the treaty, but he was killed (against Logan's orders) by one of Logan's officers.

4 *Tippecanoe* Known in English as Prophetstown, the community of Indigenous people from various nations founded by Tecumseh and his brother Tenskwatawa ("The Prophet") at the confluence of the Tippecanoe and Wabash Rivers in what is now Indiana.

5 *Weas* Indigenous nation whose traditional territory is located in what is now western Indiana.

numbers. The treaty at Fort Wayne[1] was made through the threats of Winamac,[2] but in the future we are prepared to punish those chiefs who may come forward to propose to sell their land. If you continue to purchase of them, it will produce war among the different tribes, and at last I do not know what will be the consequence to the white people.

Brother, I was glad to hear your speech. You said if we could show that the land was sold by persons that had no right to sell, you would restore it. Those that did sell did not own it. It was *me*—these tribes set up a claim but the tribes with me will not agree to their claim. If the land is not restored to us, you will soon see, when we return to our homes, how it will be settled. We shall have a great council at which all the tribes shall be present, when we will show to those who sold that they had no right to sell the claim they set up, and we shall see what will be done with those chiefs that did sell the land to you. I am not alone in this determination. It is the determination of all the warriors and red people that listen to me.

I now wish you to listen to me. If you do not, it will appear as if you wished me to kill all the chiefs that sold you the land. I tell you so because I am authorized by all the tribes to do so. I am at the head of them all. I am a warrior, and all the warriors will meet together in two or three moons from this. Then I will call for those chiefs that sold you the land and shall know what to do with them. If you do not restore the land, you will have a hand in killing them.

Brother, do not believe that I came here to get presents from you. If you offer us anything we will not take it. By taking goods from you, you will hereafter say that with them you purchased another piece of land from us. If we want anything we are able to buy it from your traders. Since the land was sold to you, no traders come among us. I now wish you would clear all the roads and let the traders come among us. Then perhaps some of our young men will occasionally call on you to get their guns repaired. This is all the assistance we ask of you.

Brother, I should now be very glad to know immediately: what is your determination about the land, also of the traders I have mentioned?

Brother, it has been the object of both myself and my brother[3] from the beginning to prevent the lands being sold. Should you not return the land, it will occasion us to call a great council that will meet at the Huron Village,[4] where the council fire has already been lighted, at which those who sold the land shall be called and shall suffer for their conduct.

Brother, I wish you would take pity on all the red people and do what I have requested. If you will not give up the land and do cross the boundary of your present settlement, it will be very hard and produce great troubles among us. How can we have confidence in the white people? When Jesus Christ came upon the earth, you killed and nailed him on a cross. You thought he was dead, but you were mistaken. You have Shakers[5] among you, and you laugh and make light of their worship.

1 *The treaty at Fort Wayne* In 1809, William Henry Harrison, governor of the Indiana Territory, began negotiations at Fort Wayne with representatives of the Potawatomi, Lenape (Delaware), Eel Rivers, and Miami nations—although not with the Shawnee—to open a large swath of Indigenous land in the territory to white American settlement. The Treaty of Fort Wayne, signed in the fall of 1809 and finalized in 1810, sold over three million acres of Indigenous land to the United States. Opposition to the treaty by other Native Americans led to attacks on white settlements in 1810; Tecumseh was particularly incensed by the treaty, and his hostility to it motivated the negotiations with Harrison during which he gave this speech.

2 *Winamac* Potawatomi chief, whose name is also spelled Winnemac; he led the Potawatomi delegation in the negotiations that led to the Treaty of Fort Wayne and played a key part in persuading other, more reluctant Indigenous representatives to sign the treaty.

3 *my brother* I.e., Tenskwatawa, also known as "The Prophet" (1775–1836), Tecumseh's younger brother. An influential religious figure, Tenskwatawa led a separatist Indigenous spiritual movement that provided much of the basis for unified Indigenous opposition to further U.S. expansion in the Great Lakes region in the first decades of the nineteenth century.

4 *the Huron Village* Today the site of Brownstown, Michigan, near Detroit; the Wendat (Huron) community located there in the early nineteenth century was the symbolic headquarters of the alliance of Indigenous nations around the Great Lakes that formed to resist U.S. expansion in 1783 and of which Tecumseh's confederacy was the continuation.

5 *Shakers* Christian sect, founded in England in the mid-eighteenth century, that settled in America in the 1770s and 1780s; their ecstatic worship services (which earned them the name "Shakers"), celibate and communal lifestyle, pacifism, and egalitarian beliefs, which particularly emphasized equality of the sexes, prompted bemusement or hostility among many other Americans. A group of Shaker missionaries visited Tecumseh and Tenskwatawa's community in 1807, under the belief that it represented a religious revival similar to that which had given rise to the Shakers themselves, and were cordially received there.

Everything I have said to you is the truth. The Great Spirit has inspired me, and I speak nothing but the truth to you. In two moons we shall assemble at the Huron Village (addressing himself to the Weas and Pottawatomies), where the great belts of all the tribes[1] are kept, and there settle our differences.

Now, Brother, I hope you will confess that you ought not to have listened to those bad birds who bring you bad news. I have declared myself freely to you, and if you want any explanation from our town, send a man who can speak to us.

If you think [it] proper to give us any presents, and we can be convinced that they are given through friendship alone, we will accept them. As we intend to hold our council at the Huron Village that is near the British, we may probably make them a visit. Should they offer us any presents of goods, we will not take them, but should they offer us powder[2] and the tomahawk, we will take the powder and refuse the tomahawk.

I wish you, Brother, to consider [that] everything I have said is true and that it is the sentiments of all the red people who listen to me.

By your giving goods to the Kickapoos, you killed many. They were seized with the smallpox, by which many died.

—1810

Illustration by John Reuben Chapin, engraved by William Ridgway, of the 1810 confrontation between Tecumseh and William Henry Harrison (c. 1818). This illustration has been characterized as "extremely inaccurate," especially for its depiction of the clothing of Tecumseh and his party, but it exemplifies white American culture's rapid appropriation of Tecumseh.

[1] *the great ... tribes* Belts and strings of wampum, a type of bead made from shells, are used among the Indigenous nations of eastern North America for numerous purposes, including the recording of treaties, stories, and historical events as well as ceremonial exchange, trade, and decorative art.

[2] *powder* I.e., gunpowder.

Speech to the Osages

Brothers—We all belong to one family; we are all children of the Great Spirit; we walk in the same path; slake our thirst at the same spring; and now affairs of the greatest concern lead us to smoke the pipe around the same council fire!

Brothers—We are friends; we must assist each other to bear our burdens. The blood of many of our fathers and brothers has run like water on the ground, to satisfy the avarice of the white men. We, ourselves, are threatened with a great evil; nothing will pacify them but the destruction of all the red men.

Brothers—When the white men first set foot on our grounds, they were hungry; they had no place on which to spread their blankets, or to kindle their fires. They were feeble; they could do nothing for themselves. Our fathers commiserated their distress, and shared freely with them whatever the Great Spirit had given his red children. They gave them food when hungry, medicine when sick, spread skins for them to sleep on, and gave them grounds, that they might hunt and raise corn. Brothers, the white people are like poisonous serpents: when chilled, they are feeble and harmless; but invigorate them with warmth, and they sting their benefactors to death.

The white people came among us feeble; and now we have made them strong, they wish to kill us, or drive us back, as they would wolves and panthers.

Brothers—The white men are not friends to the Indians: at first, they only asked for land sufficient for a wigwam; now, nothing will satisfy them but the whole of our hunting grounds, from the rising to the setting sun.

Brothers—The white men want more than our hunting grounds; they wish to kill our warriors; they would even kill our old men, women and little ones.

Brothers—Many winters ago, there was no land; the sun did not rise and set: all was darkness. The Great Spirit made all things. He gave the white people a home beyond the great waters. He supplied these grounds with game, and gave them to his red children; and he gave them strength and courage to defend them.

Brothers—My people wish for peace; the red men all wish for peace; but where the white people are, there is no peace for them, except it be on the bosom of our mother.[1]

Brothers—The white men despise and cheat the Indians; they abuse and insult them; they do not think the red men sufficiently good to live.

The red men have borne many and great injuries; they ought to suffer them no longer. My people will not; they are determined on vengeance; they have taken up the tomahawk; they will make it fat with blood; they will drink the blood of the white people.

Brothers—My people are brave and numerous; but the white people are too strong for them alone. I wish you to take up the tomahawk with them. If we all unite, we will cause the rivers to stain the great waters with their blood.

Brothers—If you do not unite with us, they will first destroy us, and then you will fall an easy prey to them. They have destroyed many nations of red men because they were not united, because they were not friends to each other.

Brothers—The white people send runners[2] amongst us; they wish to make us enemies that they may sweep over and desolate our hunting grounds, like devastating winds, or rushing waters.

Brothers—Our Great Father, over the great waters,[3] is angry with the white people, our enemies. He will send his brave warriors against them; he will send us rifles, and whatever else we want—he is our friend, and we are his children.

Brothers—Who are the white people that we should fear them? They cannot run fast, and are good marks to shoot at: they are only men; our fathers have killed many of them; we are not squaws,[4] and we will stain the earth red with blood.

1 *on the ... mother* I.e., in the earth—in other words, dead and buried.

2 *runners* I.e., messengers.

3 *Our Great ... waters* The British king. During the decades after the Revolutionary War, Britain backed Indigenous resistance to U.S. expansion into the Great Lakes region out of a desire to prevent the U.S. from becoming dominant there. A year after Tecumseh gave this speech, these and other tensions between the U.S. and Britain helped spark the War of 1812.

4 *squaws* Now considered indisputably offensive, this word likely has roots in languages (such as Massachusett) belonging to the Algonquian language family, to which Shawnee also belongs; however, Shawnee belongs to a different branch of the [continued ...]

Brothers—The Great Spirit is angry with our ene-
mies; he speaks in thunder, and the earth swallows
up villages,[1] and drinks up the Mississippi. The great
waters will cover their lowlands; their corn cannot
grow, and the Great Spirit will sweep those who escape
to the hills from the earth with his terrible breath.

Brothers—We must be united; we must smoke the
same pipe; we must fight each other's battles; and more
than all, we must love the Great Spirit: he is for us; he
will destroy our enemies, and make all his red children
happy.

—1811

family from that to which the word's roots have been traced. By the
early nineteenth century, the word had become common in white
American usage as a generic term for Indigenous women; while it
was still often intended as a neutral term during this period, its con-
notations were becoming increasingly derogatory.

[1] *the earth ... villages* On 16 December 1811, a powerful earth-
quake, today known as the New Madrid earthquake, occurred in
the Mississippi Valley near the present-day site of New Madrid,
Missouri; two similarly strong earthquakes in the same area followed
in January and February 1812. The quakes, which were felt over a huge
stretch of the central and eastern United States, were interpreted by
many Indigenous people of the region as an omen of imminent war
with the U.S. and helped build support for Tecumseh's confederacy.

Washington Irving
1783 – 1859

Washington Irving was the United States' first literary celebrity, and among the first American writers to be widely read and respected—including in Britain, where critics had long scoffed at literature in America. Over the course of his highly varied career, Irving earned fame for his urbane satire and ambitious, pseudohistorical parody; for his small-scale literary portraits of rural New York; and for works of nonfiction that capitalized on the emerging cultural importance of the American "frontier." As an important advocate for writers' financial rights, and one of the first Americans to attain financial success through his writings alone, Irving played a vital role in giving shape to an American literary market—and stature to a national literature that was struggling for recognition.

Born to English and Scottish parents in Manhattan in 1783, Irving was raised primarily in the growing metropolis, but also experienced the landscapes and cultural heritage of rural Dutch New York, whose influence would be seen in some of his earliest writings. Though he was initially pushed toward a career in the law, Irving had by his early twenties established a local reputation as a satirist and occasional theater critic; he wrote a popular series of letters under the pen name of Jonathan Oldstyle for New York's *Morning Chronicle* in 1802, and from 1807 to 1808 collaborated with his brother William and friend James Kirke Paulding on the periodical *Salmagundi*, which was among the first publications to refer to New York City by the nickname "Gotham."

By 1809, Irving was piecing together his first major book, a unified work that quickly evolved from an extension of the satirical *Salmagundi* project into a work of much broader literary and cultural scope. Published late that year, *A History of New York, from the Beginning of the World to the End of the Dutch Dynasty* was a lively parody of American historical publications. Written in the persona of the elderly and rather unreliable Dutch historian Diedrich Knickerbocker, the book's account of New York's colonial history was composed of both farce and fact; though parodic in tone, the text was nevertheless based on serious archival research on Irving's part, and worked to feed the growing post-revolutionary hunger of Euro-Americans for an account of their national heritage. In this sense, Irving's *History* responded to the appeals of writers like Charles Brockden Brown, who had in the *American Review* of 1802 called for an American historian who could "vie with those who have so recently shone in Great-Britain." The *History* became the most lucrative single literary work yet published in the United States. Abroad, its humor won the admiration (and won Irving the friendship) of Scottish Romantic poet Sir Walter Scott, who claimed the volume had given him an "uncommon degree of entertainment," and who favorably compared Irving's writing to that of the famous satirists Jonathan Swift and Laurence Sterne. The immensely popular Scott would prove an important influence on Irving's later fiction.

Irving's next publication, written while he was living abroad in England, constituted a considerable change in his literary vision. The stories and sketches that made up *The Sketch Book of Geoffrey Crayon, Gent.* (1819–20) were written under yet another pseudonym. Lightly comic in tone, they also exhibited Irving's increasingly romantic sensibility and interest in European myth. Much of the text was inspired by Irving's recent readings of German folktales, to which he had been introduced by Scott; "Rip Van Winkle," for example, is an Americanized adaptation of the German tale "Peter Klaus."

The *Sketch Book* was published in the United States between 1819 and 1820 to extraordinary and lasting acclaim; years later, American poet Henry Wadsworth Longfellow would call the collection his

"first book," "the one book among all others" that first captivated him as a chid. The *Sketch Book* was soon re-published in Britain by the prestigious publisher John Murray. In an age of rampant and unchecked book piracy—especially when it came to international publication—Irving established a copyright in England and subsequently became one of the first American authors to make a profit from books printed abroad. The English volumes of the *Sketch Book* contained a number of both major and minor revisions, some likely designed to capitalize on the new literary market; particularly noteworthy were two added sketches depicting and commenting on Native American culture and life. In England, the *Sketch Book* was admired by writers such as Lord Byron and Charles Dickens; Irving's numerous tales of English Christmas traditions contributed to a tradition that would later influence Dickens's famous Christmas tales. Overall, indeed, the *Sketch Book*'s focus was almost overwhelmingly English—yet its most popularly enduring stories, "Rip Van Winkle" and "The Legend of Sleepy Hollow," have acquired near-mythic status as quintessentially American fables.

Irving's next two books, *Bracebridge Hall* (1822) and *Tales of a Traveller* (1824), were also written under the Geoffrey Crayon pseudonym and inspired by Irving's European travels. He then wrote *The Life and Voyages of Christopher Columbus* (1828) while on a political assignment in Madrid. Though a rather fanciful account of the explorer's life, the work long remained a standard educational text in American schools; as such, it contributed to an enduring historical misconception: the notion that Europeans had believed the earth to be flat until Columbus's voyage had proved them wrong.

After seventeen years abroad Irving finally returned to the United States and was recognized there as a celebrity. He embarked on a tour of the western regions of the country, which provided the raw material for three lucrative volumes of travel writing. These books—*A Tour on the Prairies* (1833), *Astoria: Or, Enterprise Beyond the Rocky Mountains* (1836), and *The Adventures of Captain Bonneville* (1837)—represent another significant shift in Irving's literary vision and cultural focus. Irving encourages his readers to take excursions into the west such as he had done. He wrote, in *A Tour*: "We send our youth abroad to grow luxurious and effeminate in Europe; it appears to me that a previous tour on the prairies would be more likely to produce that manliness, simplicity, and self-dependence most in unison with our political institutions." These books both contributed to and were shaped by the growing culture of western expansion—exemplified in fiction by the works of James Fenimore Cooper—with *A Tour* influentially describing the frontier as a place "between civilized and savage life." Though Irving shows some sympathy for the struggles of Indigenous Americans, he nevertheless portrays western expansion—reliant on the genocidal Indian Removal Act—in broadly romantic terms.

The travel volumes proved lucrative, and allowed Irving to purchase property in the region that has since 1996 been named Sleepy Hollow in his honor. He spent the last two decades of his life writing several biographical works, including a life of Irish writer Oliver Goldsmith (whose *Citizen of the World* [1760–61] Irving had admired as a child), and the substantial *Life of George Washington* (1855–59). Irving died a few months after the release of the latter work's final volume, and was buried in the cemetery at Sleepy Hollow. Upon Irving's death, the English novelist William Makepeace Thackeray described him as "the first ambassador whom the New World of Letters sent to the Old." In that so-called New World, Irving's work had bolstered and brought life to American literature as a whole, and the American short story in particular. Though American authors would continue throughout much of the nineteenth century to struggle against a literary market that privileged British writing, Irving helped open the door to the idea that American writers could be worth reading. His depictions of the American landscape, from the Hudson River and the Catskill Mountains to Oregon, helped define a whole set of romantic associations with those regions in America's popular imagination.

NOTE ON THE TEXTS: Unless otherwise noted, the texts of the writings presented here have been prepared based on their first American editions, the 1809 edition of *A History of New York*, and the 1819–20 edition of *The Sketch Book of Geoffrey Crayon, Gent.* Spelling and punctuation have been modernized in accordance with the practices of this anthology.

⌘ ⌘ ⌘

from *A History of New York, from the Beginning of the World to the End of the Dutch Dynasty, by Diedrich Knickerbocker*

FROM CHAPTER 5[1]

. . . Thus were the European worthies who first discovered America, clearly entitled to the soil; and not only entitled to the soil, but likewise to the eternal thanks of these infidel savages, for having come so far, endured so many perils by sea and land, and taken such unwearied pains, for no other purpose under heaven but to improve their forlorn, uncivilized and heathenish condition—for having made them acquainted with the comforts of life, such as gin, rum, brandy, and the small-pox; for having introduced among them the light of religion, and finally—for having hurried them out of the world, to enjoy its reward!

But as argument is never so well understood by us selfish mortals, as when it comes home to ourselves, and as I am particularly anxious that this question should be put to rest forever, I will suppose a parallel case, by way of arousing the candid attention of my readers.

Let us suppose then, that the inhabitants of the moon, by astonishing advancement in science, and by profound insight into that ineffable lunar philosophy, the mere flickerings of which, have of late years, dazzled the feeble optics, and addled the shallow brains of the good people of our globe—let us suppose, I say, that the inhabitants of the moon, by these means, had arrived at such a command of their *energies*, such an enviable state of *perfectibility*, as to control the elements, and navigate the boundless regions of space. Let us suppose a roving crew of these soaring philosophers, in the course of an aerial voyage of discovery among the stars, should chance to alight upon this outlandish planet.

And here I beg my readers will not have the impertinence to smile, as is too frequently the fault of volatile readers, when perusing the grave speculations of philosophers. I am far from indulging in any sportive vein

at present, nor is the supposition I have been making so wild as many may deem it. It has long been a very serious and anxious question with me, and many a time, and oft, in the course of my overwhelming cares and contrivances for the welfare and protection of this my native planet, have I lain awake whole nights, debating in my mind whether it was most probable we should first discover and civilize the moon, or the moon discover and civilize our globe. Neither would the prodigy of sailing in the air or cruising among the stars be a whit more astonishing and incomprehensible to us, than was the European mystery of navigating floating castles through the world of waters, to the simple savages. We have already discovered the art of coasting along the aerial shores of our planet, by means of balloons, as the savages had, of venturing along their sea coasts in canoes; and the disparity between the former, and the aerial vehicles of the philosophers from the moon, might not be greater, than that, between the bark canoes of the savages, and the mighty ships of their discoverers. I might here pursue an endless chain of very curious, profound and unprofitable speculations; but as they would be unimportant to my subject, I abandon them to my reader, particularly if he be a philosopher, as matters well worthy his attentive consideration.

To return then to my supposition—let us suppose that the aerial visitants I have mentioned, possessed of vastly superior knowledge to ourselves; that is to say, possessed of superior knowledge in the art of extermination—riding on Hippogriffs, defended with impenetrable armour—armed with concentrated sun beams, and provided with vast engines, to hurl enormous moon stones: in short, let us suppose them, if our vanity will permit the supposition, as superior to us in knowledge, and consequently in power, as the Europeans were to the Indians, when they first discovered them. All this is very possible, it is only our self-sufficiency, that makes us think otherwise; and I warrant the poor savages, before they had any knowledge of the white men, armed in all the terrors of glittering steel and tremendous gun-powder, were as perfectly convinced that they themselves, were the wisest, the most virtuous, powerful and perfect of created beings, as are, at this present moment, the lordly inhabitants of old England, the volatile populace of

[1] The full text of this chapter appears in the website component of this anthology.

France, or even the self-satisfied citizens of this most enlightened republic.

Let us suppose, moreover, that the aerial voyagers, finding this planet to be nothing but a howling wilderness, inhabited by us, poor savages and wild beasts, shall take formal possession of it, in the name of his most gracious and philosophic excellency, the man in the moon. Finding however, that their numbers are incompetent to hold it in complete subjection, on account of the ferocious barbarity of its inhabitants; they shall take our worthy President, the King of England, the Emperor of Haiti, the mighty little Bonaparte, and the great King of Bantam,[1] and returning to their native planet, shall carry them to court, as were the Indian chiefs led about as spectacles in the courts of Europe.

Then making such obeisance as the etiquette of the court requires, they shall address the puissant man in the moon, in, as near as I can conjecture, the following terms:

"Most serene and mighty Potentate, whose dominions extend as far as eye can reach, who rideth on the Great Bear,[2] useth the sun as a looking glass and maintaineth unrivalled control over tides, madmen, and sea-crabs. We thy liege subjects have just returned from a voyage of discovery, in the course of which we have landed and taken possession of that obscure little scurvy planet, which thou beholdest rolling at a distance. The five uncouth monsters, which we have brought into this august presence, were once very important chiefs among their fellow savages; for the inhabitants of the newly discovered globe are totally destitute of the common attributes of humanity, inasmuch as they carry their heads upon their shoulders, instead of under their arms—have two eyes instead of one—are utterly destitute of tails, and of a variety of unseemly complexions, particularly of horrible whiteness—whereas all the inhabitants of the moon are pea green!

"We have moreover found these miserable savages sunk into a state of the utmost ignorance and depravity, every man shamelessly living with his own wife, and rearing his own children, instead of indulging in that community of wives, enjoined by the law of nature, as expounded by the philosophers of the moon. In a word they have scarcely a gleam of true philosophy among them, but are, in fact, utter heretics, ignoramuses and barbarians. Taking compassion therefore on the sad condition of these sublunary wretches, we have endeavoured, while we remained on their planet, to introduce among them the light of reason—and the comforts of the moon. We have treated them to mouthfuls of moonshine and draughts of nitrous oxide, which they swallowed with incredible voracity, particularly the females; and we have likewise endeavoured to instil into them the precepts of lunar Philosophy. We have insisted upon their renouncing the contemptable shackles of religion and common sense, and adoring the profound, omnipotent, and all perfect energy, and the ecstatic, immutable, immovable perfection. But such was the unparalleled obstinacy of these wretched savages, that they persisted in cleaving to their wives and adhering to their religion, and absolutely set at naught the sublime doctrines of the moon—nay, among other abominable heresies they even went so far as blasphemously to declare, that this ineffable planet was made of nothing more nor less than green cheese!"

At these words, the great man in the moon (being a very profound philosopher) shall fall into a terrible passion, and possessing equal authority over things that do not belong to him, as did whilome[3] his holiness the Pope, shall forthwith issue a formidable bull, specifying "That—whereas a certain crew of Lunatics[4] have lately discovered and taken possession of that little dirty planet, called *the earth*—and that whereas it is inhabited by none but a race of two legged animals, that carry their heads on their shoulders instead of under their arms; cannot talk the Lunatic language; have two eyes instead of one; are destitute of tails, and of a horrible whiteness, instead of pea green—therefore

1 *Emperor of Haiti* Following the Haitian Revolution (1791–1804), the First Empire of Haiti was ruled by Emperor Jean-Jacques Dessalines until his assassination in 1806. By the time Irving was writing the *History*, however, Haiti was a republic; *Bantam* Sultanate in present-day Indonesia.

2 *Great Bear* Constellation also colloquially known as the Big Dipper.

3 *whilome* Once; formerly.

4 *Lunatics* Punning on the Latin word for moon, "Luna." (In its original use, the word "lunatic" referenced those whose insanity was affected by the lunar cycles.)

and for a variety of other excellent reasons—they are considered incapable of possessing any property in the planet they infest, and the right and title to it are confirmed to its original discoverers. And furthermore, the colonists who are now about to depart to the aforesaid planet, are authorized and commanded to use every means to convert these infidel savages from the darkness of Christianity, and make them thorough and absolute Lunatics."

In consequence of this benevolent bull, our philosophic benefactors go to work with hearty zeal. They seize upon our fertile territories, scourge us from our rightful possessions, relieve us from our wives, and when we are unreasonable enough to complain, they will turn upon us and say—miserable barbarians! ungrateful wretches! Have we not come thousands of miles to improve your worthless planet—have we not fed you with moon shine—have we not intoxicated you with nitrous oxide—does not our moon give you light every night—and have you the baseness to murmur, when we claim a pitiful return for all these benefits? But finding that we not only persist in absolute contempt to their reasoning and disbelief in their philosophy, but even go so far as daringly to defend our property, their patience shall be exhausted, and they shall resort to their superior powers of argument—hunt us with hippogriffs, transfix us with concentrated sun-beams, demolish our cities with moonstones; until having by main force, converted us to the true faith, they shall graciously permit us to exist in the torrid deserts of Arabia, or the frozen regions of Lapland,[1] there to enjoy the blessings of civilization and the charms of lunar philosophy—in much the same manner as the reformed and enlightened savages of this country, are kindly suffered to inhabit the inhospitable forests of the north, or the impenetrable wilderness of South America.

Thus have I clearly proved, and I hope strikingly illustrated, the right of the early colonists to the possession of this country—and thus is this gigantic question, completely knocked in the head—so having manfully surmounted all obstacles, and subdued all opposition, what remains but that I should forthwith conduct my impatient and wayworn readers, into the renowned city, which we have so long been in a manner besieging. But hold, before I proceed another step, I must pause to take breath and recover from the excessive fatigue I have undergone, in preparing to begin this most accurate of histories. And in this I do but imitate the example of the celebrated Hans Von Dunderbottom, who took a start of three miles for the purpose of jumping over a hill, but having been himself out of breath by the time he reached the foot, sat himself quietly down for a few moments to blow, and then walked over it at his leisure.

—1809

The Wife[2]

The treasures of the deep are not so precious
As are the concealed comforts of a man
Lock'd up in woman's love. I scent the air
Of blessings, when I come but near the house.
What a delicious breath marriage sends forth—
The violet bed's not sweeter![3]
 MIDDLETON

I have often had occasion to remark the fortitude with which women sustain the most overwhelming reverses of fortune. Those disasters which break down the spirit of a man, and prostrate him in the dust, seem to call forth all the energies of the softer sex, and give such intrepidity and elevation to their character, that at times it approaches to sublimity. Nothing can be more touching than to behold a soft and tender female, who had been all weakness and dependence, and alive to every trivial roughness while treading the prosperous paths of life, suddenly rising in mental force, to be the comforter and supporter of her husband, under misfortune, and abiding, with unshrinking firmness, the bitterest blasts of adversity.

As the vine which has long twined its graceful foliage around the oak, and been lifted by it into sunshine, will, when the hardy plant is rifted by the thunderbolt, cling round it with its caressing tendrils, and bind

[1] *Lapland* Northernmost region of Finland.

[2] Irving placed this tale immediately before "Rip Van Winkle" in the first American edition of *The Sketch Book* (1819).

[3] *The treasures ... not sweeter!* See Thomas Middleton's Jacobean play *Women Beware Women* 3.1 (1657).

up its shattered boughs; so is it beautifully ordered by Providence, that woman, who is the mere dependant and ornament of man in his happier hours, should be his stay and solace when smitten with sudden calamity, winding herself into the rugged recesses of his nature, tenderly supporting the drooping head, and binding up the broken heart.

I was once congratulating a friend, who had around him a blooming family, knit together in the strongest affection. "I can wish you no better lot," said he, with enthusiasm, "than to have a wife and children—if you are prosperous, there they are to share your prosperity; if otherwise, there they are to comfort you." And, indeed, I have observed that married men falling into misfortune, are more apt to retrieve their situation in the world than single men; partly because they are more stimulated to exertion by the necessities of the helpless and beloved beings who depend upon them for subsistence; but chiefly because their spirits are soothed and relieved by domestic endearments, and their self-respect kept alive by finding, that though all abroad is darkness and humiliation, yet there is still a little world of love, of which they are monarchs. Whereas a single man is apt to run to waste and self neglect; to fancy himself lonely and abandoned, and his heart to fall to ruin like some deserted mansion, for want of an inhabitant.

These observations call to mind a little domestic story, of which I was once a witness. My intimate friend, Leslie, had married a beautiful and accomplished girl, who had been brought up in the midst of fashionable life. She had, it is true, no fortune, but that of my friend was ample; and he delighted in the anticipation of indulging her in every elegant pursuit, and administering to those delicate tastes and fancies, that spread a kind of witchery about the sex. "Her life," said he, "shall be like a fairy tale."

The very difference in their characters produced an harmonious combination: he was of a romantic, and somewhat serious, cast; she was all life and gladness. I have often noticed the mute rapture with which he would gaze upon her in company, of which her sprightly powers made her the delight; and how, in the midst of applause, her eye would still turn to him, as if there alone she sought favour and acceptance. When leaning on his arm, her slender form contrasted finely with his tall, manly person. The fond confiding air with which she looked up to him, seemed to call forth a flush of triumphant pride and cherishing tenderness, as if he doted on his lovely burden for its very helplessness. Never did a couple set forward on the flowery path of early and well-suited marriage with a fairer prospect of felicity.

It was the mishap of my friend, however, to have embarked his fortune in large speculations; and he had not been married many months, when, by a succession of sudden disasters, it was swept from him, and he found himself reduced almost to penury. For a time he kept his situation to himself, and went about with a haggard countenance, and a breaking heart. His life was but a protracted agony; and what rendered it more insupportable, was the necessity of keeping up a smile in the presence of his wife; for he could not bring himself to overwhelm her with the news. She saw, however, with the quick eyes of affection, that all was not well with him. She marked his altered looks and stifled sighs, and was not to be deceived by his sickly and vapid attempts at cheerfulness. She tasked all her sprightly powers and tender blandishments to win him back to happiness; but she only drove the arrow deeper into his soul. The more he saw cause to love her, the more torturing was the thought that he was soon to make her wretched. A little while, thought he, and the smile will vanish from that cheek—the song will die away from those lips—the lustre of those eyes will be quenched with sorrow; and the happy heart which now beats lightly in that bosom, will be weighed down, like mine, by the cares and miseries of the world.

At length he came to me one day, and related his whole situation in a tone of the deepest despair. When I had heard him through, I inquired, "does your wife know all this?" At the question he burst into an agony of tears. "For God's sake!" cried he, "if you have any pity on me, don't mention my wife; it is the thought of her that drives me almost to madness!"

"And why not?" said I. "She must know it sooner or later: you cannot keep it long from her, and the intelligence may break upon her in a more startling manner, than if imparted by yourself; for the accents of those we love soften the harshest tidings. Besides, you are depriving yourself of the comforts of her sympathy; and not merely that, but also endangering the only

bond that can keep hearts together—an unreserved community of thought and feeling. She will soon perceive that something is secretly preying upon your mind; and true love will not brook reserve, but feels undervalued and outraged, when even the sorrows of those it loves are concealed from it."

"Oh, but, my friend! to think what a blow I am to give to all her future prospects—how I am to strike her very soul to the earth, by telling her that her husband is a beggar! that she is to forego all the elegancies of life—all the pleasures of society—to shrink with me into indigence and obscurity! To tell her that I have dragged her down from the sphere in which she might have continued to move in constant brightness—the light of every eye—the admiration of every heart! How can she bear poverty? she has been brought up in all the refinements of opulence. How can she bear neglect? she has been the idol of society. Oh, it will break her heart, it will break her heart!"

I saw his grief was eloquent, and I let it have its flow; for sorrow relieves itself by words. When his paroxysm had subsided, and he had relapsed into moody silence, I resumed the subject gently, and urged him to break his situation at once to his wife. He shook his head mournfully, but positively.

"But how are you to keep it from her? It is necessary she should know it, that you may take the steps proper to the alteration of your circumstances. You must change your style of living—nay," observing a pang to pass across his countenance, "don't let that afflict you. I am sure you have never placed your happiness in outward show—you have yet friends, warm friends, who will not think the worse of you for being less splendidly lodged: and surely it does not require a palace to be happy with Mary—"

"I could be happy with her," cried he convulsively, "in a hovel! I could go down with her into poverty and the dust! I could—I could—God bless her! God bless her!" cried he, bursting into a transport of grief and tenderness.

"And believe me, my friend," said I, stepping up, and grasping him warmly by the hand, "believe me, she can be the same with you. Aye, more: it will be a source of pride and triumph to her—it will call forth all the latent energies and fervent sympathies of her nature; for she will rejoice to prove that she loves you for yourself. There is in every true woman's heart a spark of heavenly fire, which lies dormant in the broad daylight of prosperity; but which kindles up, and beams and blazes in the dark hour of adversity. No man knows what the wife of his bosom is—no man knows what a ministering angel she is—until he has gone with her through the fiery trials of this world."

There was something in the earnestness of my manner, and the figurative style of my language, that caught the excited imagination of Leslie. I knew the auditor I had to deal with; and following up the impression I had made, I finished by persuading him to go home and unburden his sad heart to his wife.

I must confess, notwithstanding all I had said, I felt some little solicitude for the result. Who can calculate on the fortitude of one whose whole life has been a round of pleasures? Her gay spirits might revolt at the dark, downward path of low humility, suddenly pointed out before her, and might cling to the sunny regions in which they had hitherto revelled. Besides, ruin in fashionable life is accompanied by so many galling mortifications, to which, in other ranks, it is a stranger. In short, I could not meet Leslie, the next morning, without trepidation. He had made the disclosure.

"And how did she bear it?"

"Like an angel! It seemed rather to be a relief to her mind, for she threw her arms around my neck, and asked if this was all that had lately made me unhappy—but, poor girl," added he, "she cannot realize the change we must undergo. She has no idea of poverty but in the abstract: she has only read of it in poetry, where it is allied to love. She feels as yet no privation: she experiences no want of accustomed conveniences or elegancies. When we come practically to experience its sordid cares, its paltry wants, its petty humiliations—then will be the real trial."

"But," said I, "now that you have got over the severest task, that of breaking it to her, the sooner you let the world into the secret the better. The disclosure may be mortifying; but then it is a single misery, and soon over; whereas you otherwise suffer it, in anticipation, every hour in the day. It is not poverty, so much as pretence, that harasses a ruined man—the struggle between a proud mind and an empty purse—the keeping up a hollow show that must soon come to an end.

Have the courage to appear poor, and you disarm poverty of its sharpest sting." On this point I found Leslie perfectly prepared. He had no false pride himself, and as to his wife, she was only anxious to conform to their altered fortunes.

Some days afterwards he called upon me in the evening. He had disposed of his dwelling house, and taken a small cottage in the country, a few miles from town. He had been busied all day in sending out furniture. The new establishment required few articles, and those of the simplest kind. All the splendid furniture of his late residence had been sold, excepting his wife's harp. That, he said, was too closely associated with the idea of herself; it belonged to the little story of their loves; for some of the sweetest moments of their courtship were those when he had leaned over that instrument, and listened to the melting tones of her voice. I could not but smile at this instance of romantic gallantry in a doting husband.

He was now going out to the cottage, where his wife had been all day, superintending its arrangement. My feelings had become strongly interested in the progress of this family story, and as it was a fine evening, I offered to accompany him.

He was wearied with the fatigues of the day, and as we walked out, fell into a fit of gloomy musing.

"Poor Mary!" at length broke, with a heavy sigh, from his lips.

"And what of her," asked I, "has any thing happened to her?"

"What," said he, darting an impatient glance, "is it nothing to be reduced to this paltry situation—to be caged in a miserable cottage—to be obliged to toil almost in the menial concerns of her wretched habitation?"

"Has she then repined at the change?"

"Repined! she has been nothing but sweetness and good humour. Indeed, she seems in better spirits than I have ever known her; she has been to me all love, and tenderness, and comfort!"

"Admirable girl!" exclaimed I. "You call yourself poor, my friend; you never were so rich—you never knew the boundless treasures of excellence you possessed in that woman."

"Oh, but my friend, if this first meeting at the cottage were over, I think I could then be comfortable.

But this is her first day of real experience. She has been introduced into a humble dwelling—she has been employed all day in arranging its miserable equipments—she has for the first time known the fatigues of domestic employment—she has for the first time looked around her on a home destitute of everything elegant, and almost convenient;[1] and may now be sitting down, exhausted and spiritless, brooding over a prospect of future poverty."

There was a degree of probability in this picture that I could not gainsay, so we walked on in silence.

After turning from the main road, up a narrow lane, so thickly shaded by forest trees, as to give it a complete air of seclusion, we came in sight of the cottage. It was humble enough in its appearance for the most pastoral poet; and yet it had a pleasing rural look. A wild vine had overrun one end with a profusion of foliage; a few trees threw their branches gracefully over it; and I observed several pots of flowers tastefully disposed about the door, and on the grass plot in front. A small wicket gate opened upon a footpath that wound through some shrubbery to the door. Just as we approached, we heard the sound of music—Leslie grasped my arm; we paused and listened. It was Mary's voice, in a style of the most touching simplicity, singing a little air[2] of which her husband was peculiarly fond.

I felt Leslie's hand tremble on my arm. He stepped forward, to hear more distinctly. His step made a noise on the gravel walk. A bright beautiful face glanced out at the window, and vanished—a light footstep was heard—and Mary came tripping forth to meet us. She was in a pretty rural dress of white; a few wild flowers were twisted in her fine hair; a fresh bloom was on her cheek; her whole countenance beamed with smiles—I had never seen her look so lovely.

"My dear George," cried she, "I am so glad you are come; I've been watching and watching for you; and running down the lane, and looking out for you. I've set out a table under a beautiful tree behind the cottage; and I've been gathering some of the most delicious strawberries, for I know you are fond of them—and we have such excellent cream—and every thing is so

[1] *destitute of ... convenient* Lacking not only in things of elegance, but also in everyday conveniences.

[2] *air* Style of song, often played on the piano at polite gatherings.

sweet and still here—Oh!" said she, putting her arm within his, and looking up brightly in his face, "Oh, we shall be so snug!"

Poor Leslie was overcome.—He caught her to his bosom—he folded his arms around her—he kissed her again and again—he could not speak, but the tears gushed into his eyes. And he has often assured me, that though the world has since gone prosperously with him, and his life has been a happy one, yet never has he experienced a moment of such unutterable felicity. —1819

Rip Van Winkle

[The following Tale was found among the papers of the late Diedrich Knickerbocker, an old gentleman of New York, who was very curious in the Dutch history of the province,[1] and the manners of the descendants from its primitive settlers. His historical researches, however, did not lay so much among books, as among men; for the former are lamentably scanty on his favourite topics; whereas he found the old burghers,[2] and still more, their wives, rich in that legendary lore, so invaluable to true history. Whenever, therefore, he happened upon a genuine Dutch family, snugly shut up in its low-roofed farm house, under a spreading sycamore, he looked upon it as a little clasped volume of black-letter,[3] and studied it with the zeal of a bookworm.

The result of all these researches was a history of the province, during the reign of the Dutch governors, which he published some years since. There have been various opinions as to the literary character of his work, and, to tell the truth, it is not a whit better than it should be. Its chief merit is its scrupulous accuracy, which, indeed, was a little questioned, on its first appearance, but has since been completely established; and it is now admitted into all historical collections, as a book of unquestionable authority.

The old gentleman died shortly after the publication of his work, and now, that he is dead and gone, it cannot do much harm to his memory, to say, that his time might have been much better employed in weightier labours. He, however, was apt to ride his hobby his own way; and though it did now and then kick up the dust a little in the eyes of his neighbours, and grieve the spirit of some friends, for whom he felt the truest deference and affection; yet his errors and follies are remembered "more in sorrow than in anger,"[4] and it begins to be suspected, that he never intended to injure or offend. But however his memory may be appreciated by critics, it is still held dear among many folk, whose good opinion is well worth having; particularly certain biscuit bakers, who have gone so far as to imprint his likeness on their new year cakes, and have thus given him a chance for immortality, almost equal to being stamped on a Waterloo medal, or a Queen Anne's farthing.[5]]

Rip Van Winkle
A Posthumous Writing of Diedrich Knickerbocker

By Woden, God of Saxons,
From whence comes Wensday, that is Wodensday,
Truth is a thing that ever I will keep
Unto thylke day in which I creep into
My sepulchre—

CARTWRIGHT[6]

[1] *Diedrich Knickerbocker* Allusion to the fictional author of Irving's parody *History of New York* (1809); *curious* interested; *Dutch history ... province* In the early to mid-seventeenth century, the Dutch Republic colonized land on the east coast of North America, calling this territory New Netherland. The territory was ceded to Britain in 1664 and renamed the Province of New York, with the town of New Amsterdam also being named New York.

[2] *burghers* Citizens.

[3] *black-letter* Gothic-style typeface used in early printed material; black-letter books were regarded as valuable and important, and therefore often fitted with clasps and locks.

[4] [Irving's note] Vide the excellent discourse of G.C. Verplanck, Esq. before the New-York Historical Society. [Gulian C. Verplanck was a politician, writer, and founder of the New York Historical Society, who had disparaged Irving's parodic *History of New York*; also see Horatio's description of the King's ghost in Shakespeare's *Hamlet* 1.2.232: "A countenance more in sorrow than in anger."]

[5] *Waterloo medal ... Anne's farthing* Waterloo medals were widely distributed to those who fought in the battles leading up to the defeat of Napoleon in 1815; Queen Anne's farthings, small coins worth a quarter of a penny, were only accidentally circulated after the Queen's death in 1714, and then incorrectly believed to be highly valuable.

[6] *By Woden ... CARTWRIGHT* Excerpt from William Cartwright's 1635 play *The Ordinary* (3.1.1050–54), lines spoken by a pedantic antiquarian named Moth; *Woden* Foremost god in Norse mythology.

Whoever has made a voyage up the Hudson[1] must remember the Kaatskill mountains. They are a dismembered branch of the great Appalachian family, and are seen away to the west of the river, swelling up to a noble height, and lording it over the surrounding country. Every change of season, every change of weather, indeed, every hour of the day, produces some change in the magical hues and shapes of these mountains, and they are regarded by all the good wives, far and near, as perfect barometers. When the weather is fair and settled, they are clothed in blue and purple, and print their bold outlines on the clear evening sky; but sometimes, when the rest of the landscape is cloudless, they will gather a hood of gray vapours about their summits, which, in the last rays of the setting sun, will glow and light up like a crown of glory.

At the foot of these fairy mountains, the voyager may have descried[2] the light smoke curling up from a village, whose shingle roofs gleam among the trees, just where the blue tints of the upland melt away into the fresh green of the nearer landscape. It is a little village of great antiquity, having been founded by some of the Dutch colonists, in the early times of the province, just about the beginning of the government of the good Peter Stuyvesant[3] (may he rest in peace!), and there were some of the houses of the original settlers standing within a few years, with lattice windows, gable fronts surmounted with weathercocks, and built of small yellow bricks brought from Holland.

In that same village, and in one of these very houses (which, to tell the precise truth, was sadly time-worn and weather-beaten), there lived many years since, while the country was yet a province of Great Britain, a simple, good-natured fellow, of the name of Rip Van Winkle. He was a descendant of the Van Winkles who figured so gallantly in the chivalrous days of Peter Stuyvesant, and accompanied him to the siege of Fort Christina.[4] He inherited, however, but little of the martial character of his ancestors. I have observed that he was a simple, good-natured man; he was moreover a kind neighbour, and an obedient, henpecked husband. Indeed, to the latter circumstance might be owing that meekness of spirit which gained him such universal popularity; for those men are most apt to be obsequious and conciliating abroad, who are under the discipline of shrews[5] at home. Their tempers, doubtless, are rendered pliant and malleable in the fiery furnace of domestic tribulation, and a curtain lecture[6] is worth all the sermons in the world for teaching the virtues of patience and long suffering. A termagant[7] wife may, therefore, in some respects, be considered a tolerable blessing; and if so, Rip Van Winkle was thrice blessed.

Certain it is, that he was a great favourite among all the good wives of the village, who, as usual with the amiable sex, took his part in all family squabbles, and never failed, whenever they talked those matters over in their evening gossippings, to lay all the blame on Dame Van Winkle. The children of the village, too, would shout with joy whenever he approached. He assisted at their sports, made their playthings, taught them to fly kites and shoot marbles, and told them long stories of ghosts, witches, and Indians. Whenever he went dodging about the village, he was surrounded by a troop of them, hanging on his skirts, clambering on his back, and playing a thousand tricks on him with impunity; and not a dog would bark at him throughout the neighbourhood.

The great error in Rip's composition was an insuperable aversion to all kinds of profitable labour.[8] It could not be for the want of assiduity or perseverance; for he would sit on a wet rock, with a rod as long and heavy as a Tartar's lance, and fish all day without a murmur, even though he should not be encouraged by a single

[1] *Hudson* Hudson River, which runs through what is now New York State; the river was named after English explorer Henry Hudson, who sailed for the Dutch East India Company in the early seventeenth century.

[2] *descried* Discerned; caught sight of.

[3] *Peter Stuyvesant* Last director-general of the colony of New Netherland, from 1647 until 1664, when he ceded the territory to the English.

[4] *Fort Christina* Swedish colony in what is now the state of Delaware, where Swedish troops were defeated by Stuyvesant in 1655, effectively ending Swedish colonialism in North America.

[5] *shrews* Derogatory term for controlling or nagging women.

[6] *curtain lecture* Archaic term describing the scolding by a wife of her husband, with the further implication that she denies his sexual advances, while behind the curtains of their bed.

[7] *termagant* Bad-tempered; shrewish.

[8] *The great error ... profitable labour* I.e., Rip's greatest character flaw was his constant distaste for doing useful work.

nibble. He would carry a fowling piece[1] on his shoulder for hours together, trudging through woods and swamps, and up hill and down dale, to shoot a few squirrels or wild pigeons. He would never even refuse to assist a neighbour in the roughest toil, and was a foremost man at all country frolics for husking Indian corn, or building stone fences; the women of the village, too, used to employ him to run their errands, and to do such little odd jobs as their less obliging husbands would not do for them—in a word, Rip was ready to attend to anybody's business but his own; but as to doing family duty, and keeping his farm in order, it was impossible.

In fact, he declared it was no use to work on his farm; it was the most pestilent little piece of ground in the whole country; everything about it went wrong, and would go wrong, in spite of him. His fences were continually falling to pieces; his cow would either go astray, or get among the cabbages; weeds were sure to grow quicker in his fields than anywhere else; the rain always made a point of setting in just as he had some outdoor work to do. So that though his patrimonial estate had dwindled away under his management, acre by acre, until there was little more left than a mere patch of Indian corn and potatoes, yet it was the worst conditioned farm in the neighbourhood.

His children, too, were as ragged and wild as if they belonged to nobody. His son Rip, an urchin begotten in his own likeness, promised to inherit the habits, with the old clothes of his father. He was generally seen trooping like a colt at his mother's heels, equipped in a pair of his father's cast-off galligaskins,[2] which he had much ado to hold up with one hand, as a fine lady does her train in bad weather.

Rip Van Winkle, however, was one of those happy mortals, of foolish, well-oiled dispositions, who take the world easy, eat white bread or brown, whichever can be got with least thought or trouble, and would rather starve on a penny than work for a pound. If left to himself, he would have whistled life away in perfect contentment; but his wife kept continually dinning in his ears about his idleness, his carelessness, and the ruin he was bringing on his family. Morning, noon, and night, her tongue was incessantly going, and

everything he said or did was sure to produce a torrent of household eloquence. Rip had but one way of replying to all lectures of the kind, and that, by frequent use, had grown into a habit. He shrugged his shoulders, shook his head, cast up his eyes, but said nothing. This, however, always provoked a fresh volley from his wife, so that he was fain to draw off his forces,[3] and take to the outside of the house—the only side which, in truth, belongs to a henpecked husband.

Rip's sole domestic adherent was his dog Wolf, who was as much henpecked as his master; for Dame Van Winkle regarded them as companions in idleness, and even looked upon Wolf with an evil eye, as the cause of his master's so often going astray. True it is, in all points of spirit befitting an honourable dog, he was as courageous an animal as ever scoured the woods—but what courage can withstand the ever-during and all-besetting terrors of a woman's tongue? The moment Wolf entered the house, his crest fell, his tail drooped to the ground, or curled between his legs, he sneaked about with a gallows air,[4] casting many a sidelong glance at Dame Van Winkle, and at the least flourish of a broomstick or ladle, would fly to the door with yelping precipitation.

Times grew worse and worse with Rip Van Winkle as years of matrimony rolled on; a tart temper never mellows with age, and a sharp tongue is the only edge tool that grows keener[5] by constant use. For a long while he used to console himself, when driven from home, by frequenting a kind of perpetual club of the sages, philosophers, and other idle personages of the village, that held its sessions on a bench before a small inn, designated by a rubicund portrait of his majesty George the Third.[6] Here they used to sit in the shade, of a long lazy summer's day, talk listlessly over village gossip, or tell endless sleepy stories about nothing. But it would have been worth any statesman's money to have heard the profound discussions that sometimes took place,

1 *fowling piece* Small gun for hunting wild birds.

2 *galligaskins* Loose-fitting style of breeches or trousers.

3 *fain to … his forces* I.e., inclined to withdraw from the interaction.

4 *gallows air* Appearance of one ready for the gallows, to be hanged.

5 *keener* Sharper.

6 *George the Third* King of Great Britain from 1760 to 1820, and the last British monarch to rule over the Thirteen Colonies preceding the American Revolutionary War.

when by chance an old newspaper fell into their hands, from some passing traveller. How solemnly they would listen to the contents, as drawled out by Derrick Van Bummel, the schoolmaster, a dapper, learned little man, who was not to be daunted by the most gigantic word in the dictionary; and how sagely they would deliberate upon public events some months after they had taken place.

The opinions of this junto[1] were completely controlled by Nicholas Vedder, a patriarch of the village, and landlord of the inn, at the door of which he took his seat from morning till night, just moving sufficiently to avoid the sun, and keep in the shade of a large tree; so that the neighbours could tell the hour by his movements as accurately as by a sun dial. It is true, he was rarely heard to speak, but smoked his pipe incessantly. His adherents, however (for every great man has his adherents), perfectly understood him, and knew how to gather his opinions. When anything that was read or related displeased him, he was observed to smoke his pipe vehemently, and send forth short, frequent, and angry puffs; but when pleased, he would inhale the smoke slowly and tranquilly, and emit it in light and placid clouds, and sometimes taking the pipe from his mouth, and letting the fragrant vapour curl about his nose, would gravely nod his head in token of perfect approbation.

From even this stronghold the unlucky Rip was at length routed by his termagant wife, who would suddenly break in upon the tranquility of the assemblage, [and][2] call the members all to nought; nor was that august personage, Nicholas Vedder himself, sacred from the daring tongue of this terrible virago,[3] who charged him outright with encouraging her husband in habits of idleness.

Poor Rip was at last reduced almost to despair; and his only alternative to escape from the labour of the farm and the clamour of his wife, was to take gun in hand, and stroll away into the woods. Here he would sometimes seat himself at the foot of a tree, and share the contents of his wallet[4] with Wolf, with whom he sympathised as a fellow sufferer in persecution. "Poor

Wolf," he would say, "thy mistress leads thee a dog's life of it; but never mind, my lad, while I live thou shalt never want a friend to stand by thee!" Wolf would wag his tail, look wistfully in his master's face, and if dogs can feel pity, I verily believe he reciprocated the sentiment with all his heart.

In a long ramble of the kind on a fine autumnal day, Rip had unconsciously scrambled to one of the highest parts of the Kaatskill mountains. He was after his favourite sport of squirrel shooting, and the still solitudes had echoed and re-echoed with the reports of his gun. Panting and fatigued, he threw himself, late in the afternoon, on a green knoll, covered with mountain herbage, that crowned the brow of a precipice. From an opening between the trees, he could overlook all the lower country for many a mile of rich woodland. He saw at a distance the lordly Hudson, far, far below him, moving on its silent but majestic course, the reflection of a purple cloud, or the sail of a lagging bark,[5] here and there sleeping on its glassy bosom, and at last losing itself in the blue highlands.

On the other side he looked down into a deep mountain glen, wild, lonely, and shagged, the bottom filled with fragments from the impending cliffs, and scarcely lighted by the reflected rays of the setting sun. For some time Rip lay musing on this scene, evening was gradually advancing, the mountains began to throw their long blue shadows over the valleys, he saw that it would be dark long before he could reach the village, and he heaved a heavy sigh when he thought of encountering the terrors of Dame Van Winkle.

As he was about to descend, he heard a voice from a distance, hallooing, "Rip Van Winkle! Rip Van Winkle!" He looked around, but could see nothing but a crow winging its solitary flight across the mountain. He thought his fancy must have deceived him, and turned again to descend, when he heard the same cry ring through the still evening air; "Rip Van Winkle! Rip Van Winkle!"—at the same time Wolf bristled up his back, and giving a low growl, skulked to his master's side, looking fearfully down into the glen. Rip now felt a vague apprehension stealing over him; he looked anxiously in the same direction, and perceived a strange figure slowly toiling up the rocks, and bending under the weight of something he carried on his back.

[1] *junto* Self-organized political committee or club.

[2] *[and]* Irving added this word in later editions.

[3] *virago* Fierce woman.

[4] *wallet* Knapsack.

[5] *bark* Small type of sailing boat.

He was surprised to see any human being in this lonely and unfrequented place, but supposing it to be someone of the neighbourhood in need of his assistance, he hastened down to yield it.

On nearer approach, he was still more surprised at the singularity of the stranger's appearance. He was a short, square-built old fellow, with thick bushy hair, and a grizzled beard. His dress was of the antique Dutch fashion—a cloth jerkin[1] strapped round the waist—several pairs of breeches, the outer one of ample volume, decorated with rows of buttons down the sides, and bunches at the knees. He bore on his shoulder a stout keg, that seemed full of liquor, and made signs for Rip to approach and assist him with the load. Though rather shy and distrustful of this new acquaintance, Rip complied with his usual alacrity, and mutually relieving each other, they clambered up a narrow gully, apparently the dry bed of a mountain torrent. As they ascended, Rip every now and then heard long rolling peals, like distant thunder, that seemed to issue out of a deep ravine, or rather cleft between lofty rocks, toward which their rugged path conducted. He paused for an instant, but supposing it to be the muttering of one of those transient thunder showers which often take place in mountain heights, he proceeded. Passing through the ravine, they came to a hollow, like a small amphitheatre, surrounded by perpendicular precipices, over the brinks of which impending trees shot their branches, so that you only caught glimpses of the azure sky, and the bright evening cloud. During the whole time, Rip and his companion had laboured on in silence; for though the former marvelled greatly what could be the object[2] of carrying a keg of liquor up this wild mountain, yet there was something strange and incomprehensible about the unknown, that inspired awe, and checked familiarity.[3]

On entering the amphitheatre, new objects of wonder presented themselves. On a level spot in the centre was a company of odd-looking personages playing at nine-pins.[4] They were dressed in a quaint, outlandish fashion: some wore short doublets,[5] others jerkins, with long knives in their belts, and most had enormous breeches, of similar style with that of the guide's. Their visages, too, were peculiar: one had a large head, broad face, and small piggish eyes; the face of another seemed to consist entirely of nose, and was surmounted by a white sugarloaf hat,[6] set off with a little red cockstail. They all had beards, of various shapes and colours. There was one who seemed to be the commander. He was a stout old gentleman, with a weather-beaten countenance; he wore a laced doublet, broad belt and hanger,[7] high crowned hat and feather, red stockings, and high-heeled shoes, with roses in them. The whole group reminded Rip of the figures in an old Flemish painting, in the parlour of Dominie[8] Van Schaick, the village parson, and which had been brought over from Holland at the time of the settlement.

What seemed particularly odd to Rip was that, though these folks were evidently amusing themselves, yet they maintained the gravest faces, the most mysterious silence, and were, withal, the most melancholy party of pleasure he had ever witnessed. Nothing interrupted the stillness of the scene, but the noise of the balls, which, whenever they were rolled, echoed along the mountains like rumbling peals of thunder.

As Rip and his companion approached them, they suddenly desisted from their play, and stared at him with such fixed statue-like gaze, and such strange, uncouth, lacklustre countenances, that his heart turned within him, and his knees smote together. His companion now emptied the contents of the keg into large flagons, and made signs to him to wait upon the company. He obeyed with fear and trembling;[9]

[1] *jerkin* Style of jacket fashionable during the seventeenth century, but no longer worn by the time of this story.

[2] *object* Purpose.

[3] *checked familiarity* I.e., discouraged overt friendliness.

[4] *nine-pins* Lawn game similar to modern-day bowling.

[5] *doublets* Another form of male upper-body garment.

[6] *sugarloaf hat* Tall, conical sort of hat, often associated with English Puritans and Pilgrims who settled the eastern Americas in the early 1600s.

[7] *hanger* Short sword worn at the belt.

[8] *old Flemish painting* Flemish art, hailing from Belgium and the Netherlands, developed its distinctive style during the late Renaissance; *Dominie* Title for a minister or parson, commonly used in the former Dutch colonies.

[9] *fear and trembling* Cf. Philippians 2.12: "Wherefore, my beloved, as ye have always obeyed, not as in my presence only, but now much more in my absence, work out your own salvation with fear and trembling."

they quaffed the liquor in profound silence, and then returned to their game.

By degrees, Rip's awe and apprehension subsided. He even ventured, when no eye was fixed upon him, to taste the beverage, which he found had much of the flavour of excellent Hollands.[1] He was naturally a thirsty soul, and was soon tempted to repeat the draught. One taste provoked another, and he reiterated his visits to the flagon so often, that at length his senses were overpowered, his eyes swam in his head, his head gradually declined, and he fell into a deep sleep.

On awakening, he found himself on the green knoll from whence he had first seen the old man of the glen. He rubbed his eyes—it was a bright sunny morning. The birds were hopping and twittering among the bushes, and the eagle was wheeling aloft, and breasting the pure mountain breeze. "Surely," thought Rip, "I have not slept here all night." He recalled the occurrences before he fell asleep. The strange man with the keg of liquor—the mountain ravine—the wild retreat among the rocks—the woebegone party at nine-pins—the flagon—"Oh! that flagon! that wicked flagon!" thought Rip—"what excuse shall I make to Dame Van Winkle?"

He looked round for his gun, but in place of the clean, well-oiled fowling piece, he found an old firelock lying by him, the barrel encrusted with rust, the lock falling off, and the stock worm-eaten. He now suspected that the grave roysters[2] of the mountain had put a trick upon him, and having dosed him with liquor, had robbed him of his gun. Wolf, too, had disappeared, but he might have strayed away after a squirrel or partridge. He whistled after him, shouted his name, but all in vain; the echoes repeated his whistle and shout, but no dog was to be seen.

He determined to revisit the scene of the last evening's gambol,[3] and if he met with any of the party, to demand his dog and gun. As he arose to walk he found himself stiff in the joints, and wanting in his usual activity.[4] "These mountain beds do not agree with me," thought Rip, "and if this frolic should lay me up with a fit of the rheumatism, I shall have a blessed time with

Dame Van Winkle." With some difficulty he got down into the glen: he found the gully up which he and his companion had ascended the preceding evening, but to his astonishment a mountain stream was now foaming down it, leaping from rock to rock, and filling the glen with babbling murmurs. He, however, made shift to scramble up its sides, working his toilsome way through thickets of birch, sassafras, and witch hazel, and sometimes tripped up or entangled by the wild grape vines that twisted their coils and tendrils from tree to tree, and spread a kind of network in his path.

At length he reached to where the ravine had opened through the cliffs, to the amphitheatre; but no traces of such opening remained. The rocks presented a high impenetrable wall, over which the torrent came tumbling in a sheet of feathery foam, and fell into a broad deep basin, black from the shadows of the surrounding forest. Here, then, poor Rip was brought to a stand. He again called and whistled after his dog; he was only answered by the cawing of a flock of idle crows, sporting high in air about a dry tree that overhung a sunny precipice; and who, secure in their elevation, seemed to look down and scoff at the poor man's perplexities. What was to be done? the morning was passing away, and Rip felt famished for his breakfast. He grieved to give up his dog and gun; he dreaded to meet his wife; but it would not do to starve among the mountains. He shook his head, shouldered the rusty firelock, and, with a heart full of trouble and anxiety, turned his steps homeward.

As he approached the village, he met a number of people, but none that he knew, which somewhat surprised him, for he had thought himself acquainted with everyone in the country round. Their dress, too, was of a different fashion from that to which he was accustomed. They all stared at him with equal marks of surprise, and whenever they cast eyes upon him, invariably stroked their chins. The constant recurrence of this gesture induced Rip, involuntarily, to do the same, when, to his astonishment, he found his beard had grown a foot long!

He had now entered the skirts of the village. A troop of strange children ran at his heels, hooting after him, and pointing at his gray beard. The dogs, too, not one of which he recognized for his old acquaintances, barked at him as he passed. The very village seemed

[1] *Hollands* Dutch gin.

[2] *roysters* Revelers.

[3] *gambol* Festivity; frolic.

[4] *wanting in his usual activity* I.e., lacking his usual energy.

altered: it was larger and more populous. There were rows of houses which he had never seen before, and those which had been his familiar haunts had disappeared. Strange names were over the doors—strange faces at the windows—everything was strange. His mind now began to misgive him, that both he and the world around him were bewitched. Surely this was his native village, which he had left but the day before. There stood the Kaatskill mountains—there ran the silver Hudson at a distance—there was every hill and dale precisely as it had always been—Rip was sorely perplexed. "That flagon last night," thought he, "has addled my poor head sadly!"

It was with some difficulty he found the way to his own house, which he approached with silent awe, expecting every moment to hear the shrill voice of Dame Van Winkle. He found the house gone to decay—the roof fallen in, the windows shattered, and the doors off the hinges. A half-starved dog, that looked like Wolf, was skulking about it. Rip called him by name, but the cur snarled, showed his teeth, and passed on. This was an unkind cut indeed. "My very dog," sighed poor Rip, "has forgotten me!"

He entered the house, which, to tell the truth, Dame Van Winkle had always kept in neat order. It was empty, forlorn, and apparently abandoned. This desolateness overcame all his connubial fears—he called loudly for his wife and children—the lonely chambers rung for a moment with his voice, and then all again was silence.

He now hurried forth, and hastened to his old resort, the little village inn—but it too was gone. A large rickety wooden building stood in its place, with great gaping windows, some of them broken, and mended with old hats and petticoats, and over the door was painted, "The Union Hotel, by Jonathan Doolitle." Instead of the great tree that used to shelter the quiet little Dutch inn of yore, there now was reared a tall naked pole, with something on top that looked like a red night cap,[1] and from it was fluttering a flag, on which was a singular assemblage of stars and stripes—all this was strange and incomprehensible.

He recognized on the sign, however, the ruby face of King George, under which he had smoked so many a peaceful pipe, but even this was singularly metamorphosed. The red coat was changed for one of blue and buff,[2] a sword was stuck in the hand instead of a sceptre, the head was decorated with a cocked hat,[3] and underneath was painted in large characters, GENERAL WASHINGTON.

There was, as usual, a crowd of folk about the door, but none that Rip recollected. The very character of the people seemed changed. There was a busy, bustling, disputatious tone about it, instead of the accustomed phlegm and drowsy tranquillity. He looked in vain for the sage Nicholas Vedder, with his broad face, double chin, and fair long pipe, uttering clouds of tobacco smoke instead of idle speeches; or Van Bummel, the schoolmaster, doling forth the contents of an ancient newspaper. In place of these, a lean, bilious-looking fellow, with his pockets full of handbills, was haranguing vehemently about rights of citizens—election—members of congress—liberty—Bunker's hill—heroes of seventy-six[4]—and other words, that were a perfect Babylonish jargon[5] to the bewildered Van Winkle.

The appearance of Rip, with his long, grizzled beard, his rusty fowling piece, his uncouth dress, and the army of women and children that had gathered at his heels, soon attracted the attention of the tavern politicians. They crowded around him, eyeing him from head to foot, with great curiosity. The orator bustled up to him, and drawing him partly aside, inquired "which side he voted?" Rip stared in vacant stupidity. Another short but busy little fellow pulled him by the arm, and raising on tiptoe, inquired in his ear, "whether he

[1] *tall naked pole ... red night cap* The pole and the red cap were both widespread symbols of liberty, especially after their use in the French Revolution; similar loose-fitting caps had been worn in ancient Rome by people emancipated from slavery.

[2] *blue and buff* Colors worn by American Revolutionary soldiers.

[3] *cocked hat* Style of hat worn in the late eighteenth century (especially as part of military uniforms), worn with one side of the brim folded up or "cocked."

[4] *Bunker's hill* First major battle of the Revolutionary war; *heroes of seventy-six* The Declaration of Independence was drafted in 1776.

[5] *Babylonish jargon* Incomprehensible gibberish, referring to the biblical story of the Tower of Babel (Genesis 11.1–9), which relates how it came to be that humans speak different languages and cannot understand one another; technically, the more correct term would be "Babelish."

was Federal or Democrat."[1] Rip was equally at a loss to comprehend the question, when a knowing, self-important old gentleman, in a sharp cocked hat, made his way through the crowd, putting them to the right and left with his elbows as he passed, and planting himself before Van Winkle, with one arm akimbo, the other resting on his cane, his keen eyes and sharp hat penetrating, as it were, into his very soul, demanded, in an austere tone, "what brought him to the election with a gun on his shoulder, and a mob at his heels, and whether he meant to breed a riot in the village?" "Alas! gentlemen," cried Rip, somewhat dismayed, "I am a poor quiet man, a native of the place, and a loyal subject of the King, God bless him!"

Here a general shout burst from the bystanders—"A tory![2] a tory! a spy! a refugee! hustle him! away with him!" It was with great difficulty that the self-important man in the cocked hat restored order; and having assumed a tenfold austerity of brow, demanded again of the unknown culprit, what he came there for, and whom he was seeking. The poor man humbly assured them that he meant no harm, but merely came there in search of some of his neighbours, who used to keep about the tavern.

"Well—who are they?—name them."

Rip bethought himself a moment, and inquired, "where's Nicholas Vedder?"

There was a silence for a little while, when an old man replied, in a thin piping voice, "Nicholas Vedder? why he is dead and gone these eighteen years! There was a wooden tombstone in the churchyard that used to tell all about him, but that's rotted and gone too."

"Where's Brom Dutcher?"

"Oh he went off to the army in the beginning of the war; some say he was killed at the battle of Stoney Point—others say he was drowned in a squall, at the foot of Antony's Nose.[3] I don't know—he never came back again."

"Where's Van Bummel, the schoolmaster?"

"He went off to the wars too, was a great militia general, and is now in Congress."

Rip's heart died away, at hearing of these sad changes in his home and friends, and finding himself thus alone in the world. Every answer puzzled him, too, by treating of such enormous lapses of time, and of matters which he could not understand: war—congress—Stoney Point—he had no courage to ask after any more friends, but cried out in despair, "does nobody here know Rip Van Winkle?"

"Oh, Rip Van Winkle!" exclaimed two or three, "Oh, to be sure! that's Rip Van Winkle yonder, leaning against the tree."

Rip looked, and beheld a precise counterpart of himself as he went up the mountain: apparently as lazy, and certainly as ragged. The poor fellow was now completely confounded. He doubted his own identity, and whether he was himself or another man. In the midst of his bewilderment, the man in the cocked hat demanded who he was, and what was his name?

"God knows," exclaimed he, at his wit's end; "I'm not myself—I'm somebody else—that's me yonder—no—that's somebody else, got into my shoes—I was myself last night, but I fell asleep on the mountain, and they've changed my gun, and everything's changed, and I'm changed, and I can't tell what's my name, or who I am!"

The bystanders began now to look at each other, nod, wink significantly, and tap their fingers against their foreheads. There was a whisper, also, about securing the gun, and keeping the old fellow from doing mischief; at the very suggestion of which, the self-important man in the cocked hat retired with some precipitation. At this critical moment a fresh likely[4] woman pressed through the throng to get a peep at the graybearded man. She had a chubby child in her arms, which, frightened at his looks, began to cry. "Hush, Rip," cried she, "hush, you little fool, the old man

[1] *Federal or Democrat* Opposing political parties that arose in the 1790s, led respectively by Alexander Hamilton (1755–1804) and Thomas Jefferson (1743–1826); the policies of the Federalists emphasized a strong central government and favored stronger ties to Britain in foreign affairs, while Jefferson's Democratic-Republicans placed more emphasis on states' rights, defended the values of an agrarian society in opposition to the perceived elitism of the Federalists, and believed in the capability of common people to participate fully in democracy.

[2] *tory* Royalist.

[3] *Stoney Point* British fortress which was captured by the Continental Army in 1779; *Antony's Nose* Small mountain along the Hudson River, which is also mentioned in Irving's *History of New York*.

[4] *likely* Pretty (later revised editions have "comely" here).

won't hurt you." The name of the child, the air of the mother, the tone of her voice, all awakened a train of recollections in his mind.

"What is your name, my good woman?" asked he.

"Judith Gardenier."

"And your father's name?"

"Ah, poor man, his name was Rip Van Winkle; it's twenty years since he went away from home with his gun, and never has been heard of since—his dog came home without him; but whether he shot himself, or was carried away by the Indians, nobody can tell. I was then but a little girl."

Rip had but one question more to ask; but he put it with a faltering voice:

"Where's your mother?"

Oh, she too had died but a short time since; she broke a blood vessel in a fit of passion at a New England pedlar.

There was a drop of comfort, at least, in this intelligence. The honest man could contain himself no longer. He caught his daughter and her child in his arms. "I am your father!" cried he—"Young Rip Van Winkle once—old Rip Van Winkle now! Does nobody know poor Rip Van Winkle?"

All stood amazed, until an old woman, tottering out from among the crowd, put her hand to her brow, and peering under it in his face for a moment, exclaimed, "Sure enough! it is Rip Van Winkle—it is himself. Welcome home again, old neighbour—why, where have you been these twenty long years?"

Rip's story was soon told, for the whole twenty years had been to him but as one night. The neighbours stared when they heard it; some were seen to wink at each other, and put their tongues in their cheeks; and the self-important man in the cocked hat, who, when the alarm was over, had returned to the field, screwed down the corners of his mouth, and shook his head—upon which there was a general shaking of the head throughout the assemblage.

It was determined, however, to take the opinion of old Peter Vanderdonk, who was seen slowly advancing up the road. He was a descendant of the historian of that name,[1] who wrote one of the earliest accounts of the province. Peter was the most ancient inhabitant of the village, and well versed in all the wonderful events and traditions of the neighbourhood. He recollected Rip at once, and corroborated his story in the most satisfactory manner. He assured the company that it was a fact, handed down from his ancestor the historian, that the Kaatskill mountains had always been haunted by strange beings. That it was affirmed that the great Hendrick Hudson, the first discoverer of the river and country, kept a kind of vigil there every twenty years, with his crew of the Half-moon,[2] being permitted in this way to revisit the scenes of his enterprise, and keep a guardian eye upon the river, and the great city called by his name. That his father had once seen them in their old Dutch dresses playing at nine pins in a hollow of the mountain; and that he himself had heard, one summer afternoon, the sound of their balls, like long peals of thunder.

To make a long story short, the company broke up, and returned to the more important concerns of the election. Rip's daughter took him home to live with her; she had a snug, well-furnished house, and a stout cheery farmer for a husband, whom Rip recollected for one of the urchins that used to climb upon his back. As to Rip's son and heir, who was the ditto of himself, seen leaning against the tree, he was employed to work on the farm; but evinced an hereditary disposition to attend to anything else but his business.

Rip now resumed his old walks and habits; he soon found many of his former cronies, though all rather the worse for the wear and tear of time; and preferred making friends among the rising generation, with whom he soon grew into great favour.

Having nothing to do at home, and being arrived at that happy age when a man can do nothing with impunity, he took his place once more on the bench, at the inn door, and was reverenced as one of the patriarchs of the village, and a chronicle of the old times "before the war." It was some time before he could get into the regular track of gossip, or could be made to comprehend the strange events that had taken place during his torpor. How that there had been a revolutionary war—that the country had thrown off the yoke of old

1 *historian of that name* Adriaen van der Donk, who wrote *Description of New Netherland* (1655).

2 *crew of the Half-moon* Referring to Hudson's ship, the *Halve Maen*; following a mutiny in 1611, Hudson and seven other crew members disappeared into the Hudson Bay, their fates remaining unknown.

England—and that, instead of being a subject of his Majesty George the Third, he was now a free citizen of the United States. Rip, in fact, was no politician; the change of states and empires made but little impression on him. But there was one species of despotism under which he had long groaned, and that was—petticoat government. Happily, that was at an end; he had got his neck out of the yoke of matrimony, and could go in and out whenever he pleased, without dreading the tyranny of Dame Van Winkle. Whenever her name was mentioned, however, he shook his head, shrugged his shoulders, and cast up his eyes; which might pass either for an expression of resignation to his fate, or joy at his deliverance.

He used to tell his story to every stranger that arrived at Mr. Doolittle's hotel. He was observed, at first, to vary on some points every time he told it, which was doubtless owing to his having so recently awakened. It at last settled down precisely to the tale I have related, and not a man, woman, or child in the neighbourhood, but knew it by heart. Some always pretended to doubt the reality of it, and insisted that Rip had been out of his head, and that this was one point on which he always remained flighty. The old Dutch inhabitants, however, almost universally gave it full credit. Even to this day they never hear a thunderstorm of a summer afternoon about the Kaatskill, but they say Hendrick Hudson and his crew are at their game of nine pins; and it is a common wish of all henpecked husbands in the neighbourhood, when life hangs heavy on their hands, that they might have a quieting draught out of Rip Van Winkle's flagon.

NOTE

The foregoing tale, one would suspect, had been suggested to Mr. Knickerbocker by a little German superstition about Charles V.[1] and the Kypphauser

mountain; the subjoined note, however, which he had appended to the tale, shows that it is an absolute fact, narrated with his usual fidelity:

"The story of Rip Van Winkle may seem incredible to many, but nevertheless I give it my full belief, for I know the vicinity of our old Dutch settlements to have been very subject to marvellous events and appearances. Indeed, I have heard many stranger stories than this, in the villages along the Hudson; all of which were too well authenticated to admit of a doubt. I have even talked with Rip Van Winkle myself, who, when last I saw him, was a very venerable old man, and so perfectly rational and consistent on every other point, that I think no conscientious person could refuse to take this into the bargain; nay, I have seen a certificate on the subject taken before a country justice, and signed with a cross, in the justice's own hand writing. The story, therefore, is beyond the possibility of doubt.
 D.K."
—1819

[1] *Charles V.* Holy Roman Emperor from 1519 to 1556. In later editions, Irving changed this to "the Emperor Frederick der Rothbart," another Holy Roman Emperor who reigned from 1152 to 1190. According to legend, der Rothbart, also known as Frederick Barbarossa ("redbeard"), did not die but rather fell asleep in the Kyffhäuser mountains in Germany, and will one day reawaken and return Germany to its past greatness. In reality, Irving's source for "Rip Van Winkle" is likely the German folktale "Peter Klaus," which was written down by Johann Karl Christoph Nachtigal in 1800.

IN CONTEXT

Images of Rip Van Winkle

John Quidor, *Rip Van Winkle and His Companions at the Inn Door of Nicholas Vedder*, 1839.

John Quidor, *The Return of Rip Van Winkle*, 1849 (see also the color insert).

The first illustrated edition of Irving's *Sketch Book* appeared in 1848, with 17 illustrations by Felix O.C. Darley. (Irving contributed a new preface for the edition, but made no comment in it on the addition of illustrations to the texts.) Darley's one illustration for "Rip Van Winkle," which appeared without a caption, is reproduced here.

F.O.C. Darley, *Rip Van Winkle Awaking*, 1848.

Joseph Jefferson (1829–1905) became famous in the latter half of the nineteenth century very largely for his portrayals of Rip Van Winkle in the dramatic adaptation by Irish playwright Dion Boucicault (*Rip Van Winkle, or The Sleep of Twenty Years* [1865]); the play was a hit for many years in London as well as throughout America. The 30 September 1865 issue of *The Illustrated London News* featured the following short piece on the new play. The same issue included an illustration of Jefferson starring in the production. Both that image and a photograph of Jefferson starring in the same role almost thirty years later are reproduced on the following pages.

The new play of "Rip Van Winkle," a dramatised version, by Mr. Dion Boucicault, of Washington Irving's most genial and humorous story—in which the hero, one of the early Dutch settlers in New York, falls in with the goblins who haunt the Katskill mountains, and drinks their magic liquor, causing him a sleep of twenty years—is likely to have a long run at the Adelphi Theatre. The new American actor, Mr. Jefferson, who appears as Rip Van Winkle, seems as though he had created the character himself, so perfectly does he enter into the author's conception of the loose-lived, lazy, lounging fellow, who lets his wife turn him out of doors and then becomes the victim of the mischievous imps, with the ghost of the old pirate, Hendrik Hudson, at their head. Our Illustration shows the scene in which poor Rip Van Winkle is compelled to quaff the fatal potion.

Scene from "Rip Van Winkle," at the Adelphi Theatre, 1865.

Benjamin Joseph Falk, *Joseph Jefferson as Rip Van Winkle*, c. 1894.

Glossary of Terms

Abolitionism: a social and political movement in the pre-Civil War era that sought to bring an end to the institution of slavery.

Accent: the natural emphasis (or stress) that speakers place on a syllable.

Accentual-Syllabic Verse: the most common metrical system in traditional English verse, in which a line is measured by the number of syllables and by the pattern of accented (stressed) and unaccented (unstressed) syllables.

Allegory: a narrative with both a literal meaning and secondary, often symbolic meaning or meanings, in which nearly every element, including such things as setting, characters, objects, and plot lines, may contribute to that symbolic meaning. See, for example, Nathaniel Hawthorne's "Young Goodman Brown."

Alliteration: the grouping of words with the same initial consonant (e.g., Longfellow's "In the world's broad field of battle / In the bivouac of Life"). The repetition of sound acts as a connector and adds auditory (and sometimes also thematic) emphasis.

Allusion: a reference, often indirect or unidentified, to a person, thing, or event. A reference in one literary work to another literary work, whether to its content or its form, also constitutes an allusion.

Almanac: an annual publication compiling information on many subjects, such as weather predictions for the year, cures for ailments, lists of roads, lists of government officials, poetry, and essays on current topics of interest.

Ambiguity: an "opening" of language created by the writer to allow for multiple meanings or differing interpretations. In literature, ambiguity may be deliberately employed by the writer to enrich meaning; this differs from any unintentional, unwanted ambiguity in non-literary prose.

Analogy: a broad term that refers to our processes of noting similarities among things or events. Specific forms of analogy in poetry include *simile* and *metaphor* (see below).

Antebellum: before, or existing before, a war; in American usage, particularly the period before the American Civil War but after the War of 1812. See also *postbellum*.

Antinomian Controversy / Free Grace Controversy: a conflict that took place from 1636 to 1638 involving religious and political leaders in the Massachusetts Bay Colony. The dispute originated with a difference in interpretation of the relationship between "works" (an individual's good acts) and "grace" (bestowed by God) as markers of spiritual salvation. Puritans generally agreed that salvation came through God's grace alone—people could not bring about their own salvation through good works—but most thought that a person who had been saved would necessarily think and act in accordance with the rules set out in the Bible. Proponents of "free grace" (called *antinomians* by their opponents) took the more extreme position that individuals who had been saved would simply know it, and that one's actions should not be treated as evidence of salvation—including one's adherence to civil or biblical law. Political and religious leaders responded to this challenge to their authority by banishing some of the movement's leaders—including, most famously, Anne Hutchinson—from the colony.

Aphorism: a pithy observation or saying that contains a general truth. For example: "Three may keep a secret, if two of them are dead" (Benjamin Franklin).

Apostrophe: a figure of speech (a trope; see *figures of speech* below) in which a writer directly addresses an object—or a dead or absent person—as if the imagined audience were actually listening. For example, James Monroe Whitfield's "America, it is to thee / Thou boasted land of liberty, / It is to thee I raise my song."

Archetype: in literature and mythology, a recurring idea, symbol, motif, character, or place. To some scholars and psychologists, an archetype represents universal human thought-patterns or experiences.

Arminianism: the theological doctrine that grew in opposition to the idea of predestination in Calvinism, holding instead that salvation was available to those who had faith in God and practiced good works; the movement influenced Methodism and, later, Unitarianism.

Autobiography: an account of a person's life, or portions of it, as written by that person and presumed to be factual.

Ballad: a folk song, or a poem originally recited to an audience, which tells a dramatic story based on legend or history. See, for example, Longfellow's "Paul Revere's Ride."

Ballad Stanza: a quatrain with alternating four-stress and three-stress lines, rhyming abcb. A variant is "common measure," in which the alternating lines are strictly iambic, and rhyme abab. Emily Dickinson used the technique to great effect; see, for example, "There is no Frigate like a Book."

Baptist: a member of a Protestant denomination that tends to adhere to Calvinist doctrine and advocates baptism for adult believers only—by total immersion, and after a confession of faith—in contrast to the practice of infant baptism among other denominations. See *Calvinism, Separatists.*

Bathos: an anticlimactic effect brought about by a writer's descent from an elevated subject or tone to the ordinary or trivial.

Bildungsroman: from the German words *Bildung* (education) and *Roman* (novel), a narrative (often a novel) of personal development as a young or innocent person grows through a series of social, sexual, and political experiences, among others.

Blank Verse: unrhymed lines written in iambic pentameter. See George Moses Horton's "Division of an Estate."

Bombast: inappropriately inflated or grandiose language.

Broadside: individual sheet of paper printed on only one side. Broadsides of a variety of different sorts (e.g., ballads, political tracts, short satires) were sold on the streets; they were also used to distribute information or as advertisements.

Brownists: a group of Separatists from the Church of England who adhered to the principles of church government espoused by Robert Browne (1550–1633), the founder of Congregationalism. See *Congregationalism.*

Burlesque: satire of a particularly exaggerated sort, particularly that which mocks its subject by emphasizing its vulgar or ridiculous aspects.

Calvinism: a branch of Protestantism based on the teachings of John Calvin (1509–64), stressing the absolute power of God and humanity's total depravity; central to Calvinist doctrine is the idea that human beings are innately and irreversibly sinful, and that only those who are predestined at birth to be saved—the elect—will be granted salvation. Many of the Separatists and Puritans who first settled in America followed Calvinist doctrine. See also *Protestantism.*

Canon: in literature, those works that are commonly accepted as possessing authority or importance. In practice, "canonical" texts or authors are those that are discussed most frequently by scholars and taught most frequently in university courses.

Canto: a sub-section of a long (usually epic) poem. See Melville's *Clarel* and Ezra Pound's *The Cantos.*

Captivity Narrative: a genre of literature that relates the experiences of a person who has been kidnapped; in American literature, the "Indian captivity narrative" was especially popular from the seventeenth through the nineteenth centuries. Conventions of this genre include a focus on the perspective of white captives, usually women; an emphasis on the subject's piety during the captivity; a tendency toward dehumanizing representations of Indigenous people; and detailed but prejudiced descriptions of Indigenous ways of life. *A Narrative of the Captivity and Restoration of Mrs. Mary Rowlandson* (1682) serves as an excellent example.

Catharsis: the arousal through the performance of a dramatic tragedy of "emotions of pity and fear" to a point where "purgation" or "purification" occurs and the feelings are released or transformed. The concept was developed by Aristotle in his *Poetics* from an ancient Greek medical concept, and adapted by him into an aesthetic principle.

Chiasmus: a figure of speech (a scheme) that reverses word order in successive parallel clauses; if the word order is A-B-C in the first clause, it becomes C-B-A in the second. See, for example, Frederick Douglass's phrase: "You have seen how a man was made a slave; you shall see how a slave was made a man."

Church of England/Anglican Church: Christian church established in the 1530s when the English King Henry VIII broke from the Roman Catholic Church and papal authority. In the sixteenth and seventeenth centuries, there was substantial conflict over whether or not the Anglican Church was sufficiently Protestant in its ideology and aesthetics; Puritans, Separatists, and related groups argued that the Church retained too much of what they saw as Catholic corruption. Some of the reforms advocated by the Puritans were taken up by the Anglican Church, but different factions within the Church continue to express a wide range of opinions on rituals and organization, from elaborate ceremony and a strict hierarchy to relatively informal religious services and more egalitarian governance. After the American Revolution, Anglican churches in America separated from the Church of England and, eventually, formed the Episcopal Church.

Civil Disobedience: title commonly applied to an 1849 essay by Henry David Thoreau ("Resistance to Civil Government"); more generally, a political view that recommends passive resistance to authority whenever laws or social obligations contradict individual beliefs.

Classical: originating in or relating to ancient Greek or Roman culture. As commonly conceived, classical implies a strong sense of formal order. The term neoclassical is often used with reference to literature (particularly of the eighteenth century) that was strongly influenced by ancient Greek and Roman models.

Closet Drama: a play (typically in verse) written for private performance. The term came into use in the first half of the nineteenth century.

Colonialism/Colonization: the system or policy by which a nation acquires control of another nation or nations by means of settlement, economic exploitation, and the subjugation of the region's original inhabitants. The term "colonization" may also refer to the idea, popular among white Americans in the early and mid-nineteenth century, of transporting freed enslaved people to Africa.

Colony: a settled area that is connected with a parent, often distant, country; the community of people in that area, and their descendants.

Color Line: a reference to the division between blacks and whites after the abolition of slavery, so named after an 1881 article by Frederick Douglass.

Colored Narrative: alternative term for *free indirect discourse*.

Comedy: as a literary term, used originally to denote that class of ancient Greek drama in which the action ends happily. More broadly the term has been used to describe a wide variety of literary forms of a more or less light-hearted or humorous character.

Conceit: an unusually elaborate metaphor or simile that presents a striking parallel between two apparently dissimilar things (see, for example, Edward Taylor's poem "Huswifery," in which God is cast as a cloth-maker and the speaker His spinning wheel). Ingenious or fanciful images and comparisons were especially popular with the metaphysical poets of seventeenth-century England, giving rise to the term "metaphysical conceit."

Confederacy: a group of people or nations joined together in political or social union for a particular purpose or mutual support; as, for example, the Iroquois Confederacy. The term is also used to denote the Confederate States of America, the self-proclaimed national government formed by the southern states that supported slavery and seceded from the United States.

Congregationalism: a Protestant religious movement in the Calvinist tradition in which each congregation runs its own affairs, independently from others. See also *Protestantism, Calvinism*.

Connotation: the implied, often unspoken meaning(s) of a given word, as distinct from its denotation, or literal meaning. Connotations may have highly emotional undertones and are usually culturally specific.

Contact: a reference to the physical and cultural meeting between European explorers and Indigenous peoples of North America, the repercussions of which included extensive loss of land and epidemic disease and death for the Indigenous population.

Convention: aesthetic approach, technique, or practice accepted as characteristic and appropriate for a particular form. It is a convention of certain sorts of plays, for example, that the characters speak in blank verse, of other sorts of plays that characters speak in rhymed couplets, and of still other sorts of dramatic performances that characters frequently break into song to express their feelings.

Coverture: a common-law doctrine stipulating that a married woman had no legal identity separate from that of her husband, and so was "covered" or controlled by him in the eyes of the law, with no property or economic rights of her own.

Creation Story: a story that narrates the origins of the world and its first inhabitants; creation stories may present a culture's fundamental worldview, including its moral and spiritual values; some may also chronicle significant geographical or historical events. The telling of creation stories is an act of great importance in many Indigenous cultures.

Creole: originally, a person of European descent who was born in the West Indies or Latin America; also, an enslaved person of African descent born in the colonies. These diverse groups of people settled in a variety of regions and established distinct social and political identities, and the term today can be defined variously; in Louisiana, the term refers to people who are descended from (mainly French) colonial settlers of the Louisiana region before the Louisiana Purchase in 1803. "Creole" may also refer to the hybrid language that develops as a result of the mixing of two or more such groups who speak a different parent language.

Declaration of Independence: the pronouncement adopted on 4 July 1776 that sets out to explain why the Thirteen Colonies felt it necessary to leave the British Empire and declare themselves independent states.

Deism: a school of religious and philosophical thought that grew to prominence during the Enlightenment, proposing

that God exists only as the creator of the universe, and has had little or no influence on the world since creation; more generally, deists deny the literal truth of the Bible and other teachings of formal religion.

Democratic Party: a political party established in 1828; led by Andrew Jackson, the party supported a somewhat limited federal government, states' rights, and the removal of the central banking system. The party's nineteenth-century platform differed substantially from that of the Democratic Party in the twenty-first century. See also *Democratic-Republican Party*, *Whig Party*.

Democratic-Republican Party: one of the first two political parties of the United States; established in 1792 and led by Thomas Jefferson and James Madison, the party advocated a limited, decentralized federal government, agrarian and anti-aristocratic policies, and stronger ties to France in foreign affairs. Originally known as just the Republican Party, or the Jeffersonian Republicans, the party embraced the "Democratic-Republican Party" label in 1798, a name that had been intended by Federalist opponents to link them to the radicalism of the French Revolution. The party grew enormously during and after Jefferson's presidency—so much so that in 1824 it ran four candidates for the presidency; however, political division ensued, and the party eventually split in two, giving rise over the next decade to the Democratic Party and the Whig Party.

Denotation: See *connotation* above.

Dialogue: words spoken by characters to one another. (When a character is addressing themselves or the audience directly, the words spoken are referred to as a *monologue*.)

Diaspora: a group of people with a similar heritage or homeland who disperse across the globe to different locations, especially involuntarily; or, the dispersion itself.

Diction: word choice; the diction of a literary work (or of a literary character), whether colloquial, conversational, formal, or of some other type, contributes significantly to the tone of the text as well as to characterization.

Didacticism: aesthetic approach emphasizing moral instruction. See, for example, Harriet Beecher Stowe's novel, *Uncle Tom's Cabin*, or Frances Harper's temperance poems.

Disenfranchisement: the state of being deprived of civil privileges, especially the right to vote.

Doppelgänger: a look-alike (from the German *doppel-* double + *-gänger* walker); in folklore and literature, often an apparition of a living person, the sight of which spells doom or bad luck.

Dramatic Irony: This form of irony occurs when the audience's reception of a speech by a character on the stage is affected by the possession by the audience of information not available to the character.

Dred Scott v. Sandford: an 1857 Supreme Court decision in which the Court held that people of African descent were not United States citizens and so were not entitled to the rights and privileges laid out in the U.S. Constitution. The decision also held that the Missouri Compromise was unconstitutional, nullifying Congress's power to prevent the spread of slavery into new states. The decision came after the formerly enslaved Dred Scott attempted to secure the court's further confirmation of his freedom so that the children of his deceased former enslaver could not claim inherited ownership of Scott's daughters.

Elegy: a poem or other similar form of expression which formally mourns the death of a particular person (e.g., Whitman's "When Lilacs Last in the Dooryard Bloom'd") or in which the poet or speaker meditates on other serious subjects (e.g., Chief Seattle's 1854 speech concerning Indigenous worldviews and the environment).

Ellipsis: the omission of a word or words necessary for the complete grammatical construction of a sentence, but not necessary for our understanding of the sentence.

End-Stopped: a line of poetry is said to be end-stopped when the end of the line coincides with a natural pause in the syntax, such as the conclusion of a sentence; an end-stopped line is usually but not always marked by punctuation. For example, the first two lines of Longfellow's "The Arrow and the Song": "I shot an arrow into the air, / It fell to earth, I knew not where." Compare *enjambement*.

Enjambement: the "running-on" of the sense from one line of poetry to the next, with no pause created by punctuation or syntax. Longfellow's poem "The Arrow and the Song" provides an example, which follows on the heels of an end-stopped line: "For, so swiftly it flew, the sight / Could not follow it in its flight." Compare *end-stopped*.

Enlightenment: an intellectual movement of the seventeenth and eighteenth centuries broadly characterized by radically new scientific, political, and philosophical ideas that ushered in a wholesale reappraisal of society. Also referred to as the "Age of Reason," the period placed great stock in empirical observation and in the belief that human rationality, rather than faith and religious doctrine, would improve society. Enlightenment thinkers frequently called for the reform of existing political, religious, and social institutions, extending to—in the case of more radical

figures—the separation of church and state, constitutional government, freedom of expression, and other kindred individual liberties. Enlightenment ideals directly inspired the American and other national revolutions.

Epic: a lengthy narrative poem, often divided into sections, that generally celebrates heroic deeds or events, and the style of which tends to be lofty and grand. Examples include Anne Bradstreet's *The Four Monarchies* and Michael Wigglesworth's *The Day of Doom.*

Epigraph: a quotation placed at the beginning of a discourse to indicate or foreshadow the theme.

Epiphany: a moment at which matters of significance are suddenly illuminated for a literary character (or for the reader), typically triggered by something small and seemingly of little import.

Episodic Plot: plot comprising a variety of episodes that are only loosely connected by threads of story material (as opposed to plots that present one or more continually unfolding narratives where successive episodes build one on another).

Eulogy: text expressing praise, especially for a distinguished person recently deceased. While not necessarily typical of the form, William Apess's *Eulogy on King Philip* provides an example.

Euphemism: mode of expression through which aspects of reality considered to be vulgar, crudely physical, or unpleasant are referred to indirectly rather than named explicitly. A variety of euphemisms exist for the processes of urination and defecation; *passed away* is often used as a euphemism for *died.*

Exposition: the setting out of material in an ordered form, either in speech or in writing. In a play those parts of the action that do not occur on stage but are rather recounted by the characters are frequently described as being presented in exposition. Similarly, when the background narrative is filled in near the beginning of a novel, such material is often described as having been presented in exposition.

Federalist Party: one of the first two political parties of the United States; led by Alexander Hamilton, George Washington, and John Adams, and favored by conservatives and business owners, the party dominated the national government from 1791 to 1801. Federalists advocated a strong centralized federal government, a national bank, and stronger ties to Britain in foreign affairs. The party faded after 1801 and dissolved soon thereafter. See also *Democratic-Republican Party.*

Fifteenth Amendment: an 1870 amendment to the U.S. Constitution guaranteeing that the right to vote could not be denied to anyone based on "race, color, or previous condition of servitude." Even after the amendment passed, threats, violence, and poll taxes continued to prevent some populations from voting in many places, and women were excluded from the amendment.

Figures of Speech: deliberate, highly concentrated uses of language intended to achieve particular purposes or effects on an audience. There are two kinds of figures: schemes and tropes. Schemes involve changes in word-sound and word-order, such as *alliteration* and *chiasmus*. Tropes play on our understandings of words to extend, alter, or transform meaning, as in *metaphor* and *personification*.

Fireside Poets: a group of nineteenth-century American poets who became widely popular especially in the latter half of the century, including Henry Wadsworth Longfellow, John Greenleaf Whittier, James Russell Lowell, William Cullen Bryant, and Oliver Wendell Holmes Sr. Their fame stemmed from their tendency to write in conventional meter on domestic themes and familiar moral and political issues.

First Great Awakening: the period of increased religious fervor that swept through the American colonies beginning in the 1730s. Having originated in Europe, the movement was introduced to New England through the preaching of figures like George Whitefield and Jonathan Edwards; it influenced many denominations, and led to, among other things, the emergence of evangelical Christianity. Proponents reinvigorated concepts of Calvinism as a reaction against the confidence placed in science and reason during the Age of Enlightenment and as an antidote to the prevailing materialism in the colonies. See also *Second Great Awakening.*

First-Person Narrative: narrative recounted using *I* and *me*. See also *narrative perspective.*

Folklore: the traditions and cultural artifacts shared by a given group of people; these include such things as tales and proverbs, handmade items and building styles, rituals and celebratory practices, and so on.

Folktale: a story that is passed down through generations orally and that, while often featuring fictional elements or characters, can communicate key aspects of a culture's knowledge, history, or beliefs; a genre of folklore.

Foot: a unit of a line of verse which contains a particular combination of stressed and unstressed syllables. Dividing a line into metrical feet (*iambs, trochees,* etc.), then counting the number of feet per line, is part of *scansion*. See also *meter.*

Founders/Founding Fathers: the leading figures in the founding of the United States who worked to unite the Thirteen Colonies, draft the Declaration of Independence and Constitution, lead the war for independence in various capacities, and build the ideological and functional framework of the country's democratic government.

Fourteenth Amendment: an 1868 amendment to the U.S. Constitution that granted citizenship to formerly enslaved people and guaranteed them "equal protection of the laws," thereby nullifying the Supreme Court's 1857 *Dred Scott* decision that had prevented people of African descent from becoming citizens. The amendment also gave the federal government authority to punish states for restricting citizens' right to vote; introduced hurdles that made it difficult for former Confederate leaders to hold office; invalidated federal and state debts owed to the now defunct Confederate states; and prohibited compensation to be paid to former enslavers.

Free Indirect Discourse: in prose fiction, third-person narration in which a seemingly objective and omniscient narrative voice assumes the point of view of one or more characters, and in which the thoughts and expressions are not typically set apart with indicators such as "he said" or "she thought"; the term may also be applied to situations in which it may not be entirely clear if the thoughts expressed emanate from the character, the narrator, or some combination of the two. When we hear through the third-person narrative voice of Melville's *Benito Cereno*, for example, the unsettling description of enslaved black sailors, we are likely to take it as being the view of the character Captain Delano. The narrator ascribes to the sailors the traits of "docility," "good-humour," and "cheerfulness"—"as though God had set the whole negro to some pleasant tune"—but it is difficult to imagine that the extreme incongruity between their enslavement and the narrator's description of their disposition is an objective statement of perceived truth on the part of the novel's third-person narrative voice.

Free Verse: poetry that does not follow any regular meter, line length, or rhyming scheme. In many respects, though, free verse follows the complex natural "rules" and rhythmic patterns (or cadences) of speech. Walt Whitman's long poetic lines provide a fine example.

Frontier: an extreme limit of settled land; as a concept in American history and culture, the frontier was an imagined border in the west beyond which lay wilderness. To many colonists, the idea of the frontier represented the opportunity for leading a new and better life; however, this idea frequently distorted the reality of the conditions in the frontier territory and either minimized or dismissed outright the Indigenous people who already inhabited it.

Fugitive Slave Acts: two federal laws, enacted in 1793 and 1850, that provided for the capture and return of escapees from slavery and imposed penalties on anyone who harbored or helped them; both acts were meant to quell the unrest emerging in southern states as a result of increasing antislavery sentiment in the north.

Genre: a particular literary form. The concept of genre may be used with different levels of generality. At the most general, poetry, drama, and prose fiction are distinguished as separate genres. At a lower level of generality various sub-genres are frequently distinguished, such as (within drama) comedy and tragedy, or, at a still lower level of generality, minstrelsy, puppetry, burlesque, and so on.

Gilded Age: a period between the end of the Civil War and the start of the twentieth century in which tremendous industrial and technological growth led to extreme economic disparity between wealthy industrialists and financiers, on one hand, and the working class and immigrants, on the other; the term was coined by Mark Twain in reference to the façade of respectability that masked the era's greed and corruption.

Gold Coast: a region in West Africa named by imperial nations after its chief export, gold; modern-day Ghana. It was one of many coastal regions from Senegambia (modern-day Senegal) to Angola that were exploited during the era of the transatlantic slave trade.

Goodman/Goodwife: polite terms of address used in colonial America, generally in reference to those of lower or middling social status—laborers or farmers (and their wives)—as opposed to merchants and others of the wealthier classes.

Gospel: historically, the first four books of the New Testament, which narrate the life and relate the teachings of Jesus Christ, or the biblical message of Christ in general; also, a genre of music in which songs echo and elevate Christian worship, often featuring evangelical lyrics. See also *spiritual*.

Gothic: in literature, a term used to describe work with a sinister or grotesque tone that seeks to evoke a sense of terror on the part of the reader or audience. The term was used originally to describe styles prevalent in architecture and the visual arts in late Medieval Europe; Gothic literature originated in eighteenth-century England as a distinct genre in which works often featured medieval settings or themes, supernatural elements, and fantastic, macabre plots. Examples in American literature include much of Edgar

Allan Poe's work, Charles Brockden Brown's *Edgar Huntly*, and "The Legend of Sleepy Hollow" by Washington Irving.

Gullah/Geechee: a distinct group of African Americans who live in parts of Georgia, North Carolina, South Carolina, and Florida; the culture developed as various ethnic groups of enslaved people from Africa were forced to work on large and relatively isolated plantations in the region; also, the creole language that they speak.

Haitian Revolution: a large-scale revolution in Haiti that began in 1791 and was led by black and mixed-race Haitians, many of whom were enslaved; it ultimately resulted in the expulsion of French colonial forces and the establishment of Haiti as an independent nation in 1804. The revolution's success, along with Haiti's proximity to the fledgling United States, had a profound impact on American racial, social, and political history.

Homestead Act: a law enacted by Congress during the Civil War in 1862 that granted public lands to any private citizen or citizens-to-be who had not taken up arms against the Federal government; the law dealt a severe blow to Indigenous peoples.

Hoodoo: a set of spiritual practices and folk magic based in part on traditions and beliefs of enslaved Africans, including African spiritualism and Christianity. Hoodoo practice is also known as conjure or rootwork. See also *Obeah, Voodoo*.

Hudson River School: a group of New York-based landscape artists in the nineteenth century who were influenced by the ideas of Romanticism.

Humors: The four humors were believed until the sixteenth and seventeenth centuries to be elements in the makeup of all humans; a person's temperament was thought to be determined by the way in which the humors were combined. When the *choleric* humor was dominant, the person would tend toward anger; when the *sanguine* humor was dominant, toward pleasant affability; when the *phlegmatic* humor was dominant, toward a cool and calm attitude and/or a lack of feeling or enthusiasm; and when the *melancholic* humor was dominant, toward withdrawal and melancholy.

Hymn: a song whose theme is usually religious, in praise of divinity. Literary hymns may praise more secular subjects. African American spirituals provide abundant examples; see, for instance, "Swing Low, Sweet Chariot."

Hyperbole: a *figure of speech* (a trope) that deliberately exaggerates or inflates meaning to achieve particular effects, such as the theatrical tale of Pocahontas by John Smith, who describes her as laying her own head upon his to prevent him

from being clubbed to death (see Smith's *General History of Virginia*), or, to more humorous effect, when Joel Chandler Harris's Uncle Remus describes sleep as an old man "ridin' on my eyeleds."

Iamb: the most common metrical foot in English verse, containing one unstressed syllable followed by a stressed syllable (e.g., between, achieve).

Idyll: traditionally, a short pastoral poem that idealizes country life, conveying impressions of innocence and happiness. See, for example, Longfellow's "The Village Blacksmith."

Image: the recreation in words of objects perceived by the senses, sometimes thought of as "pictures," although other senses besides sight are involved. Besides this literal application, the term also refers more generally to the descriptive effects of figurative language, especially in *metaphor* and *simile*.

Incantation: a chant or recitation of words that are believed to have magical power. A poem can achieve an "incantatory" effect through a compelling rhyme scheme and other repetitive patterns. For example, see Edgar Allan Poe's "The Raven."

Indentured Servant/Apprentice: a person who was bound to work without pay for a fixed period of time; indentures were usually at least somewhat voluntary, but the contracts were often liable to be sold to different employers with little to no consultation with the servant or apprentice in question.

Indian Expulsion: the forced removal of Indigenous people from their homes to facilitate settlement by predominantly white settlers, codified in the 1830 Indian Removal Act; also called Indian Removal.

Indian Territory: areas in modern-day Oklahoma, Missouri, and Kansas designated by the Federal government for Indigenous nations who had been forcibly removed from their homes; the territory shifted continuously throughout the eighteenth and nineteenth centuries, decreasing over time.

Indigenous people: the inhabitants of a region who are the descendants of the people who lived there prior to another ethnic group settling or colonizing that region.

Individualism: an ideology that emphasizes self-reliance, independence, and the value of one's own instincts and intelligence, especially with respect to aesthetic, social, or ethical judgments; in religion, an ideology that affirms the individual as the sole source of an authentic relationship with God, and the sole arbiter of one's social and intellectual responsibilities.

Irony: a subtle form of humor in which a statement is understood to convey a quite different (and often entirely opposite) meaning. A writer achieves this by carefully making sure that the statement occurs in a context which undermines or twists the statement's "literal" meaning. *Hyperbole* and *litotes* are often used for ironic effect. *Sarcasm* is a particularly strong or crude form of irony (usually spoken), in which the meaning is conveyed largely by the tone of voice adopted; something said sarcastically is meant clearly to imply its opposite.

See, for example, Washington Irving's *History of New York*, in which the narrator employs irony to relate one of the more disastrous effects that European colonization had on Indigenous people:

> ... no sooner did the benevolent inhabitants of Europe behold their sad condition than they immediately went to work to ameliorate and improve it. They ... made known to them a thousand remedies, by which the most inveterate diseases are alleviated and healed, and that they might comprehend the benefits and enjoy the comforts of these medicines, they previously introduced among them the diseases, which they were calculated to cure. By these and a variety of other methods was the condition of these poor savages, wonderfully improved. ...

Künstlerroman: from the German for *Künstler* (artist) and *Roman* (novel), a narrative (often in novel form) about the personal and aesthetic growth of an artist, as he or she apprentices in an art form (music, literature, painting, or sculpture). See, for example, Louisa May Alcott's *Little Women*.

Jacksonian Democracy: a nineteenth-century political movement associated with the presidency of Andrew Jackson; the movement saw expanded suffrage (for white men), a hands-off approach to the economy, and aggressive expansionism. While the movement had an egalitarian drive, many changes came at the expense of black and Indigenous people.

Jeffersonian Democracy: a late eighteenth-century and early nineteenth-century political movement named after Thomas Jefferson whose advocates staunchly supported the common people and ideas of republicanism, the tenets of which underpinned the values of the Democratic-Republican Party. See also *Democratic-Republican Party, Republicanism*.

Jeremiad: a literary work, often a sermon or speech, that expresses mourning, sorrow, or moral and spiritual disapproval; the form laments or decries perceived social or moral evils and prophesies doom unless the supposedly more wholesome spirit of an earlier time can be reawakened.

Jesuit: a member of the Society of Jesus, an order of the Roman Catholic Church; founded in the mid-sixteenth century during the rise of Protestantism, the order professed total obedience to the pope and sought to advance the Catholic faith, often by education or missionary activity.

Jim Crow: comic character commonly depicted by blackface performers in minstrel shows in the mid-nineteenth century; due to the popularity of such shows, "Jim Crow" was often used as a racist epithet for African Americans, and in the late nineteenth century the term came to refer to the legal and social systems that enforced racial segregation in southern states.

Know-Nothing Movement: an anti-immigrant and anti-Catholic movement that formed in the mid-nineteenth century in opposition to widespread German and Irish immigration.

Ku Klux Klan: a white supremacist group that emerged in the South in the wake of the Civil War and whose early members used organized violence, terror, and murder as a way to intimidate and abuse formerly enslaved people; the initial Klan's activities declined by the early 1880s, but there have been various resurgences throughout the twentieth and twenty-first centuries.

Ledger Art/Ledger Drawing: narrative drawings developed by the Indigenous nations of the Great Plains as a means of historical representation; made with pencil, ink, crayon, and/or watercolor, and drawn on the pages of old ledgers (i.e., account books) that had earlier been used by white settlers. The practice flourished from the 1860s to the 1920s, continuing a long history of recording oral histories pictorially.

Litotes: a *figure of speech* (a trope) in which a writer deliberately uses understatement to paradoxically highlight significance, or, conversely, to convey an ironic attitude; this is often accomplished by affirming something through the negation of the opposite thing. For example, when the narrator of Melville's "Bartleby, the Scrivener" states that he was "not unemployed" by John Jacob Astor and "not insensible" to Astor's good opinion, the oddly constructed understatements cause the reader to pause, even stumble, and to call the narrator's reliability or purpose into question.

Local Color: a style of writing from the latter half of the nineteenth century that captures the character of a specific locale and the people who live there; practitioners sought to reproduce regional dialects and to give color to distinctive features of landscape, custom, and folklore. See also *Regionalism*.

Loyalist: a colonist who remained loyal to Britain in the American War of Independence. See also *Tory*.

Lyric: a poem, usually short, expressing an individual speaker's feelings or private thoughts. Originally a song performed with accompaniment on a lyre, the lyric poem is often noted for musicality of rhyme and rhythm. The lyric genre includes a variety of forms, including the *sonnet*, the *elegy*, the *ode*, and the *hymn*.

Manifest Destiny: a term, originating in the 1840s, used to communicate the belief that the United States was destined to expand westward across the North American continent; the doctrine of expansionism was couched in the terms of moral duty and God-given destiny, and its implementation had dire consequences for Indigenous and Hispanic people.

Mason-Dixon Line: Eighteenth-century survey line separating Pennsylvania and Delaware from Maryland and Virginia. In the *antebellum* United States, it and the Ohio River formed much of the dividing line between free and slave states and hence between North and South.

Mass: within Christianity, a church service that includes the sacrament of the Eucharist (Holy Communion), in which bread and wine are consumed; these are believed by those of many Christian denominations, especially Roman Catholics, to have been transubstantiated into the body and blood of Christ. Protestants do not generally use the term "Mass" and are more likely to believe that the bread and wine merely symbolize the body and blood.

Mayflower Compact: a document signed in 1620 aboard the *Mayflower* before it landed at Plymouth that committed the settlers to majority-rule government.

Melodrama: originally a term used to describe nineteenth-century plays featuring sensational story lines and a crude separation of characters into moral categories, with the pure and virtuous pitted against evil villains. Early melodramas employed background music throughout the action of the play as a means of heightening the emotional response of the audience. By extension, certain sorts of prose fictions or poems are often described as having melodramatic elements.

Mesoamerica: cultural region of Mexico and most of Central America where the Maya, Aztec, and other Indigenous peoples flourished before the Spanish Conquest. While the peoples of the region shared some cultural traits, geographical and linguistic differences were many.

Mestizo: a term used in Spanish America for a person of mixed Indigenous and European ancestry; from the Spanish word, meaning "mixed."

Metaphor: a *figure of speech* (in this case, a trope) in which a comparison is made or identity is asserted between two unrelated things or actions without the use of "like" or "as." The primary subject is known as the *tenor*; to illuminate its nature, the writer links it to wholly different images, ideas, or actions referred to as the *vehicle*. Unlike a *simile*, which is a direct comparison of two things, a metaphor "fuses" the separate qualities of two things, creating a new idea. For example, Dickinson's "'Hope' is the thing with feathers" is a metaphorical statement. The tenor, or primary subject, is "hope"; the vehicle of the metaphor is the image of an initially unnamed "thing with feathers," a bird. The line fuses the idea of hope with the qualities of a delicate bird perched in the soul and forever singing.

Meter: the pattern of stresses, syllables, and pauses that constitutes the regular rhythm of a line of verse. The meter of a poem is determined by identifying the stressed and unstressed syllables in a line of verse, and grouping them into recurring units known as feet. See also *accent, accentual-syllabic verse, foot,* and *scansion*.

Methodist: a member of a Protestant denomination formed in the eighteenth century as part of the religious movement led by John and Charles Wesley. Originally a sect within the Church of England, Methodism entailed enthusiastic evangelism, a strong emphasis on free will, and a strict, methodical regimen of Christian worship and living.

Metonymy: a *figure of speech* (a trope), meaning "change of name," in which a writer refers to an object or idea by substituting the name of another object or idea closely associated with it: for example, the substitution of "crown" for monarchy, "the press" for journalism, or "the pen" for writing. *Synecdoche* (see below) is a kind of metonymy.

Middle Passage: in the slave trade, the transatlantic journey from the coasts of Africa to the Americas and the West Indies; for the enslaved people in the slave ships, the one- to two-month voyage was horrific, brutal, and often deadly.

Minstrel Show/Minstrelsy: a form of Vaudeville theater popularized in the mid-nineteenth century that featured entertainers performing in blackface.

Miscegenation: the mixing of different racial or ethnic groups, or sexual relationships or reproduction between individuals of those groups, especially between white and non-white people; the term was coined in 1863.

Missouri Compromise: a deal made by Congress in 1820 to resolve the political imbalance that would have resulted if Missouri was admitted as a slave state; Maine was admitted

as a free state, and slavery was prohibited thereafter anywhere north of Missouri's southern border.

Monologue: words spoken by a character to him or herself or to an audience directly.

Mood: This can describe the writer's attitude, implied or expressed, toward the subject (see *tone* below); or it may refer to the atmosphere that a writer creates in a passage of description or narration.

Mormonism: the teachings and doctrines of the Latter-Day Saint movement; started by Joseph Smith in the 1820s, Mormon theology embraces as sacred scripture both the Bible and the Book of Mormon; Smith claimed to have translated the latter from an ancient record shown to him by an angel.

Motif: an idea, image, action, or plot element that recurs throughout a literary work, creating new levels of meaning and strengthening structural coherence. The term is taken from music, where it describes recurring melodies or themes. See also *theme*.

Mulatto: term for a person with one white and one black parent; more loosely, a person with the appearance of being mixed-race. The designation is today considered offensive.

Myth: a traditional story that provides an explanation for a society or culture's early history or spiritual beliefs, or features of the natural world, usually involving a supernatural element of some kind.

Narrative Perspective: in fiction, the point of view from which the story is narrated. A first-person narrative is recounted using *I* and *me*, whereas a third-person narrative is recounted using *he*, *she*, *they*, and so on. When a narrative is written in the third person and the narrative voice evidently "knows" all that is being done and thought, the story is typically described as being recounted by an "omniscient narrator."

Neoclassical: adapted from or substantially influenced by the cultures of ancient Greece and Rome. The term *neoclassical* is often used to describe the ideals of eighteenth-century writers, thinkers, and artists who looked to ancient Greek and Roman civilization for models.

Non-Alphabetic Literature: a transmission or recording of knowledge, or a literary expression, that is inscribed without employing an alphabet; Indigenous literacies of this sort include objects such as baskets, wampum, pottery, tattoos, textiles, pictographs, and rock art.

Nonconformist: general term used to describe one who does not subscribe to the Church of England.

Obeah: a practice of spiritual healing and witchcraft, or folk medicine, originating among enslaved West Africans and developed in the Caribbean; the practice is more individual than it is collective. See also *Hoodoo*, *Voodoo*.

Ode: in English poetry, a long lyric poem of some gravity that is typically elevated in tone and complex in structure. Originally a classical poetic form, the ode was used by the Greeks and Romans to convey serious themes; later imitations of the form stemmed from the examples set by the Greek poet Pindar and the Roman poet Horace.

Onomatopoeia: a *figure of speech* (a scheme) in which a word "imitates" a sound, or in which the sound of a word seems to reflect its meaning.

Oral Literature: a form of literature communicated by spoken word and passed down from generation to generation; often taking the form of stories, oral literature may serve as a repository of history, mythology, spiritual belief, etc.

Oratory: the formal art of public speaking, especially with eloquence and with an eye toward persuasion.

Over-Soul: all-encompassing spiritual "unity" that animates the universe and resides in each human soul, and through which all of humanity is connected. The term was coined in 1841 by Ralph Waldo Emerson, but the concept is also a central principle in a number of Eastern religions.

Oxymoron: a *figure of speech* (a trope) in which two words whose meanings seem contradictory are placed together: for example, Fitzgerald's description in *The Great Gatsby* of Wolfsheim eating with "ferocious delicacy."

Parliament: in Britain, the combined legislative body, comprising both the House of Commons (the "lower house," made up of elected officials) and the House of Lords (the "upper house," comprised of members of the aristocracy). Unlike the American system, the British parliamentary system does not separate the executive and legislative functions of government.

Parody: a close, usually mocking imitation of a particular literary work, or of the well-known style of a particular author, in order to expose or magnify weaknesses. Parody is a form of satire—that is, humor that may ridicule and scorn its object. The poem "Counter-Jumps" parodies Whitman's sprawling "Song of Myself": "I am the shop, and the counter, and the till, / But particularly the last. / And I explore and rummage the till, and am at home in it."

Pastiche: a discourse which borrows or imitates other writers' characters, forms, style, or ideas. Unlike a parody, a

pastiche is usually intended as a compliment to the original writer.

Pastoral: in general, pertaining to country life; in prose, drama, and poetry, a stylized type of writing that idealizes the lives and innocence of country people, particularly shepherds and shepherdesses. See *idyll*.

Pathetic Fallacy: a form of personification in which inanimate objects are given human emotions: for example, rain clouds "weeping." The word "fallacy" in this connection is intended to suggest the distortion of reality or the false emotion that may result from an exaggerated use of personification.

Pathos: the emotional quality of a discourse; or the ability of a discourse to appeal to our emotions. It is usually applied to the mood conveyed by images of pain, suffering, or loss that arouse feelings of pity or sorrow in the reader.

Persona: the assumed identity or "speaking voice" that a writer projects in a discourse. The term "persona" literally means "mask." Even when a writer speaks in the first person, we should be aware that the attitudes or opinions we hear may not necessarily be those of the writer in real life. Much of Herman Melville's shorter fiction and essays, especially "Bartleby, the Scrivener" and *Benito Cereno*, makes extensive use of personas.

Personification: a *figure of speech* (a trope) in which a writer refers to inanimate objects, ideas, or animals as if they were human, or creates a human figure to represent an abstract entity such as Philosophy or Peace. For example, see Allen Ginsberg's "America": "America, when will you be angelic? / When will you take off your clothes?"

Picaresque: a genre of fiction that deals with the adventures of an unscrupulous but charismatic individual.

Pilgrims: Puritans who broke with the Church of England and settled the Plymouth Colony in 1620; their break from the church led to them being labeled Separatists. See also *Separatists*.

Pioneer: a person who is (or is deemed to be) among the first to explore or settle a new or unknown region or territory; the term is often used without considering prior Indigenous habitation.

Plantation: a large-scale agricultural enterprise that produces cash crops; in the American south, plantations varied greatly in size, but all relied on the forced labor of enslaved people. The term was also used in the seventeenth and eighteenth centuries to refer to the American colonies themselves.

Plot: the organization of story materials within a literary work. The order in which story material is presented (especially causes and consequences); the inclusion of elements that allow or encourage the reader or audience to form expectations as to what is likely to happen; the decision to present some story material through exposition rather than in more extended form as part of the main action of the narrative—all these are matters of plotting.

Postbellum: after, or existing after, a war; in American usage, especially the American Civil War. See also *antebellum*.

Predestination: the Calvinist belief that God has predetermined who is saved and who is damned. The belief thereby advances a doctrine of grace (rather than a doctrine of works): the actions, or works, of a person while alive have no influence on their fate. Rather, their salvation comes as a predetermined gift from God. See also *Calvinism*.

Presbyterian: term applied to a group of Protestants who advocated replacing the traditional hierarchy of the church (in which bishops and archbishops governed lower-level members of the clergy) with a system in which all presbyters, or ministers, would be equal; the Presbyterians were strongly influenced by Calvinism.

Prosody: the study and analysis of meter, rhythm, rhyme, stanzaic pattern, and other devices of versification.

Protagonist: the central character in a literary work.

Protestant Reformation/Reformation: a religious movement of the sixteenth century that set out to reform the Roman Catholic Church, and which resulted in the establishment of various Protestant churches throughout Europe and Britain and, eventually, its colonies; the movement effected a profound religious, political, intellectual, and cultural upheaval. See also *Protestantism*.

Protestantism: a branch of Christianity that formed as a result of the Protestant Reformation in the early sixteenth century. Protestant denominations reject the authority of the pope and of the Catholic Church, and they tend to place a greater emphasis than the Catholic Church on the Bible as the primary or sole source of religious doctrine.

Pun: a play on words, in which a word with two or more distinct meanings, or two words with similar sounds, may create humorous ambiguities.

Puritan: term applied to sixteenth- and seventeenth-century Protestants who felt that the Anglican Church was too similar to the Catholic Church and required further reform. Puritans played a leading role in the settlement of

many New England colonies, including the Massachusetts Bay Colony in 1630. See also *Separatists*.

Quakerism/Religious Society of Friends: a Protestant sect committed to pacifism and the spiritual equality of all worshippers, and whose members stressed a direct relationship with God through Jesus Christ; many Quakers were also abolitionists and advocates of various social reforms.

Radical Republican: a mid-nineteenth century group within the Republican Party that, prior to the Civil War, was vehemently opposed to slavery and any form of compromise with the south; the group later advocated equal civil and political rights for former enslaved people during Reconstruction. See also *Republican Party*.

Realism: a literary movement that gained in prominence with the rise of social reform movements of the late nineteenth century. Proponents rejected the grandeur, sentimentalism, and idealism of Romanticism in favor of logic, fact, and objectivity; works feature a candid and detailed treatment of ordinary people living everyday lives. Rebecca Harding Davis's "Life in the Iron-Mills" (1861) provides a prime early example.

Reconstruction: the period from 1865 to 1877 during which the states that had seceded from the United States during the Civil War were readmitted to the federal system of government and reorganized; also, the process by which this reorganization was effected. The reorganization of the former secessionist states prominently featured efforts to secure the rights and promote the welfare of formerly enslaved people, including the ratification of the Fourteenth and Fifteenth Amendments. These efforts, however, were largely negated by the violent reimposition of white supremacy throughout the South and by the federal government's abandonment of Reconstruction in 1877.

Regionalism: a category of literature that emerged after the Civil War and that centers on the distinctiveness of regional, or local, culture and geography, rather than on broader national themes and issues. Bret Harte's coverage of the California Gold Rush in "The Luck of Roaring Camp" (1868) is an example. See also *local color*.

Renaissance, American: a term coined by literary critic F.O. Matthiessen to refer to the period in American literature between 1830 and 1865 during which, in Matthiessen's opinion, five main writers—Ralph Waldo Emerson, Nathaniel Hawthorne, Herman Melville, Henry David Thoreau, and Walt Whitman—helped to forge a literary style that was unique to the national spirit of the United States. Subsequent critics have taken Matthiessen to task for his exclusion of women and of African American and Indigenous writers, and have much broadened the list of those responsible for defining a national literature of the period. Some have also questioned whether such a uniform literature even exists. See also *Transcendentalism*, *Romanticism*.

Republican Party: a political party established in 1854 by a group of Whigs, Democrats, and other politicians who left their respective parties to form a party opposed to slavery's expansion. The Republicans nominated Abraham Lincoln as their presidential candidate in 1860; after the Civil War, the party sought for a time to protect and promote the rights of newly emancipated African Americans during Reconstruction, but the party gradually became more oriented toward economic and industrial growth. Not to be confused with the earlier political party of the same name that formed in opposition to the Federalist Party in the early 1790s. See also *Democratic-Republican Party*.

Republicanism: a political philosophy of the eighteenth century that rejected aristocracies and monarchies, and instead stressed liberty, the virtue of common citizens, and the uninfringeable rights of individuals. See also *Jeffersonian democracy*.

Reservation: an area of land set aside for a special purpose; in the context of America's Indigenous peoples, reservations were created by treaty, legislation, or executive order, and very often involved the forcible removal of Indigenous populations from their homelands.

Rhetoric: in classical Greece and Rome, the art of persuasion and public speaking. From the Middle Ages onwards, the study of rhetoric gave greater attention to style, particularly figures of speech. Today in poetics, the term rhetoric may encompass not only figures of speech, but also the persuasive effects of forms, sounds, and word choices.

Rhyme: the repetition of identical or similar sounds, usually in pairs and generally at the ends of metrical lines.

> **End-Rhyme:** a rhyming word or syllable at the end of a line.
>
> **Eye-Rhyme:** rhyming that pairs words whose spellings are alike but whose pronunciations are different: for example, move/love.
>
> **Feminine Rhyme:** a two-syllable (also known as "double") rhyme. The first syllable is stressed and the second unstressed: for example, hasty/tasty. See also *triple rhyme*.
>
> **Interlocking Rhyme:** the repetition of rhymes from one stanza to the next, creating links that add to the poem's continuity and coherence.

Internal Rhyme: the placement of rhyming words within lines so that at least two words in a line rhyme with each other.

Masculine Rhyme: a correspondence of sound between the final stressed syllables at the end of two or more lines, as in grieve/leave, arr-ive/sur-vive.

Slant Rhyme: an imperfect or partial rhyme (also known as "near" or "half" rhyme) in which the final consonants of stressed syllables match but the vowel sounds do not. E.g., spoiled/spilled, taint/stint.

Triple Rhyme: a three-syllable rhyme in which the first syllable of each rhyme-word is stressed and the other two unstressed (e.g., greenery/scenery).

True Rhyme: a rhyme in which everything but the initial consonant matches perfectly in sound and spelling.

Rhythm: in speech, the arrangement of stressed and unstressed syllables creates units of sound. In song or verse, these units usually form a regular rhythmic pattern, a kind of beat, described in prosody as *meter*.

Romanticism: a major social and cultural movement that originated in Europe as a reaction against the rationalism of the Enlightenment and that shaped much of Western artistic thought in the late eighteenth and nineteenth centuries; the movement emphasized the essential roles played by subjectivity and emotion in knowing and experiencing the world. Romantic works in literature tend to elevate the individual, to disparage the conventional, and to stress the value of contact with the natural world. Examples include William Cullen Bryant's poem "Thanatopsis" (1817). See also *Transcendentalism*.

Sarcasm: See *irony*.

Satire: literary work designed to make fun of or seriously criticize its subject. According to many literary theories of the Renaissance and neoclassical periods, the ridicule through satire of a certain sort of behavior may function for the reader or audience as a corrective of such behavior.

Scansion: the formal analysis of patterns of rhythm and rhyme in poetry. Each line of verse will have a certain number of fairly regular "beats" consisting of alternating stressed and unstressed syllables. To "scan" a poem is to count the beats in each line, to mark stressed and unstressed syllables and indicate their combination into "feet," to note pauses, and to identify rhyme schemes with letters of the alphabet.

Scheme: See *figures of speech*.

Secession: the action of withdrawing from membership of a political state, religious organization, or other similar alliance; in the United States, the insurrectionist withdrawal of eleven Southern states from the federal government that brought about the Civil War.

Second Great Awakening: a widespread Protestant religious revival during the early nineteenth century; the heart of the new evangelical movement stressed God's benevolence and humans' ability to endeavor to save themselves (where earlier Calvinist tradition emphasized the deep depravity of humanity, the inability to alter our fate, and salvation through God). See *Great Awakening*.

Sermon: a discourse based upon scripture for the purpose of giving religious instruction or encouragement.

Seneca Falls Convention: 1848 New York convention often viewed as having launched the women's suffrage movement in America.

Separatists: a Protestant group in the Calvinist tradition whose members believed that the Church of England was too corrupt to be reformed and that it was necessary to separate from it; the Pilgrims aboard the *Mayflower* were Separatists. See also *Calvinism*, *Pilgrims*.

Simile: a *figure of speech* (a trope) which makes an explicit comparison between a particular object and another object or idea that is similar in some (often unexpected) way. A simile always uses "like" or "as" to signal the connection. Compare with *metaphor*.

Slave Narrative: an autobiographical account of the experiences of an enslaved person; numerous slave narratives were published in the United States from the late-eighteenth to the mid-nineteenth century, and they contributed greatly to the rise of the abolitionist movement and the spread of opposition to slavery.

Sonnet: a highly structured lyric poem, which normally has fourteen lines of iambic pentameter. See the glossary of poetic terms in this anthology's online component.

Sons of Liberty: a loosely connected group of underground, grassroots organizations in Colonial America that formed in response to the Stamp Act with the goal of undermining British rule through acts of radical civil disobedience.

Spiritual: a genre of religious song that grew out of the collective experience of enslaved people and was adopted by black Christians of the southern United States especially; blending African, American, and African American musical elements, spirituals often express ideals of hope, justice, and

salvation in the face of the oppressive experience of enslavement. See also *gospel, work song.*

Spiritualism: a nineteenth-century religious movement, especially popular among the upper and middle classes, whose adherents believed it was possible for the living to communicate with the spirits of the dead. It was closely linked to widely discussed scientific and pseudoscientific ideas.

Stanza: any lines of verse that are grouped together in a poem and separated from other similarly structured groups by a space.

Stress: See *accent.*

Sublime: a concept of the qualities of grandeur, power, and awe that may be inherent in or produced by undomesticated nature or great art. The sublime is generally thought of as higher and loftier than something that is merely beautiful; the concept plays a central role in many Romantic works.

Subplot: a line of story that is subordinate to the main storyline of a narrative. (Note that properly speaking a subplot is a category of story material, not of plot.)

Subtext: implied or suggested meaning of a passage of text, or of an entire work.

Suffrage: the right to vote.

Sun Dance: a large annual ceremony practiced primarily by Plains Indigenous cultures to honor the earth and sun, prove bravery, and pray for prowess in, for example, hunting or fighting; over several days, individuals endure exhaustion and self-torture as a path to spiritual renewal and enhanced prestige, or to establish stronger personal or tribal relationships.

Syllable: vocal sound or group of sounds forming a unit of speech; a syllable may be formed with a single effort of articulation. Some syllables consist of a single phoneme (e.g., the word *I*, or the first syllable in the word *u*-ni-ty) but others may be made up of several phonemes (as with one-syllable words such as *lengths, splurged,* and *through*). By contrast, the much shorter words *ago, any,* and *open* each have two syllables.

Symbol: a word, image, or idea that represents something more, or other, than for what it at first appears to stand. Like metaphor, the symbol extends meaning; but while the components of a metaphor are bound in a specific relationship, a symbol may have a range of connotations. For example, the image of a rose may call forth associations of love, passion, transience, fragility, youth, and beauty, among others. Often,

such meaning is implied rather than explicitly stated; indeed, much of the power of symbolic language lies in the reader's ability to make meaningful sense of it.

Synecdoche: a kind of *metonymy* in which a writer substitutes the name of a part of something to signify the whole: for example, "sail" for ship or "hand" for a member of the ship's crew.

Tall Tale: a form of folktale in which unbelievably exaggerated details are related as though they are historically factual. Tall tales may describe one's own supposed adventures or the adventures of a larger-than-life folk hero; examples of the latter include narratives about figures such as Davy Crockett and Johnny Appleseed, as well as African American oral stories such as "Big Sixteen."

Theme: the governing idea of a discourse, conveyed through the development of the subject, and through the recurrence of certain words, sounds, or metrical patterns. See also *motif.*

Third-Person Narrative: See *narrative perspective.*

Thirteenth Amendment: an 1865 amendment to the U.S. Constitution that abolished slavery throughout the nation; it was the first of three Reconstruction amendments following the Civil War that attempted to secure equal status and rights for African Americans.

Three-Fifths Clause: a provision in the U.S. Constitution that allowed for three-fifths of the enslaved population to be counted when determining each state's representation in the House of Representatives, thereby bolstering southern states' political power.

Tone: the writer's attitude toward a given subject or audience, as expressed through an authorial persona or "voice." Tone can be projected through particular choices of wording, imagery, figures of speech, and rhythmic devices. Compare *mood.*

Tory: a person who supported the British Crown; more generally, a political conservative who supports traditional political and social institutions. See also *Loyalist.*

Tragedy: in the traditional definition originating in discussions of ancient Greek drama, a serious narrative recounting the downfall of the protagonist. More loosely, the term has been applied to a wide variety of literary forms in which the tone is predominantly a dark one and the narrative does not end happily.

Trail of Tears: the expression used generally to invoke the suffering that Indigenous nations experienced when forcibly

removed from their ancestral lands and driven, despite the threats of disease, exposure, starvation, and death, to "Indian Territory" west of the Mississippi; more specifically, the route traversed by the Cherokee nation during its expulsion in 1838 and 1839. See also *Indian Expulsion, Indian Territory.*

Transcendentalism: a philosophical and literary movement, centered mainly in New England, that flourished in the 1830s and 1840s; linked with the Romantic movement, its adherents held to a mystical, idealistic belief in the unity of all creation and the innate goodness of nature and of people, as well as a trust in one's own insight and intellect as a pathway to the deepest truths. Its members included Margaret Fuller, Ralph Waldo Emerson, and Henry David Thoreau. See also *Romanticism.*

Trickster: a figure in the mythology or oral literature of many cultures, including Indigenous peoples and African Americans, that turns its intelligence toward playing tricks or breaking rules and challenging conventions; in different cultures the figure takes different forms—often an animal such as Coyote or Raven (in various Indigenous cultures) or Brer Rabbit (in African American folklore).

Trope: any figure of speech that plays on our understandings of words to extend, alter, or transform "literal" meaning. Common tropes include *metaphor, simile, personification, hyperbole, metonymy, oxymoron, synecdoche,* and *irony.* See also *figures of speech.*

Uncle Sam: a personification of the United States and its people, typically represented as a white man with a severe gaze, white hair and chin whiskers, dressed in red, white, and blue; a symbol of American patriotism.

Uncle Tom: the enslaved title character of Harriet Beecher Stowe's 1852 novel; theatrical adaptations of the novel frequently transformed Uncle Tom into a subservient apologist for slavery, and the term "Uncle Tom" subsequently became a derogatory epithet for someone who accepts or willingly participates in their own subordination.

Underground Railroad: the secret network of support and safehouses by means of which many enslaved people escaped to the North, to Canada, or (in some cases) to Mexico.

Union: the United States; specifically, the group of northern states that were opposed to slavery and that remained loyal to the Federal government during the Civil War.

Unitarianism: a Christian movement beginning in the late eighteenth century that emphasized free will and universal salvation: the idea that all human beings can and will be saved, regardless of whether or not they belong to or accept the beliefs of a particular church. The movement was particularly influential upon Transcendentalists in the early nineteenth century (though it was also criticized by several of them, including by Emerson, himself a former Unitarian minister).

Verse: a general term for works of poetry, usually referring to poems that incorporate some kind of metrical structure. The term may also describe a line of poetry, though more frequently it is applied to a stanza.

Visual Literature: a form of literature in which images make up the primary means of communication, for example, sign language, rock art, winter counts, ledger art, etc.

Voodoo, or Vodou: a religion developed in the sixteenth century in Hispaniola (now Haiti) by enslaved Africans that blends elements from African religions with aspects of Roman Catholicism. See also *Hoodoo, Obeah.*

Wampum: beads made from shells, often threaded together in strings or belts, used by Indigenous peoples for ornamental, ceremonial, and record-keeping purposes.

Whig: during the American Revolution, a supporter of American independence; more generally, a supporter of the British or American Whig Party or its principles.

Whig Party: a political party that emerged in 1834 in opposition to the political platform of Andrew Jackson and his strong executive power; the party splintered in the 1850s over the issue of slavery, the northern faction joining with antislavery Democrats to form the Republican Party. See also *Democratic Party, Democratic-Republican Party.*

Winter Count: a pictographic record or calendar that records the major events in the history of an Indigenous community, especially Indigenous nations of the Plains.

Work Song: a song sung by physical laborers, especially enslaved people, as they worked, and usually linked rhythmically to the work being done. See also *spiritual.*

Yankee: a New Englander or, more generally, a person from a Northern state; outside of the United States, the term is often used to refer to any American.

Zeugma: a *figure of speech* (trope) in which one word links or "yokes" two others in the same sentence, often to comic or ironic effect. For example, a verb may govern two objects, as when Twain describes the fight between Tom Sawyer and the "new boy": "They ... covered themselves with dust and glory."

MAPS

INDIGENOUS TRADE NETWORKS, NORTH AMERICA (c. 1450)

Uug Han, or Yuukan (Gwich'in)

Kuukpak (Inuvialuktun)

Hudson Bay

Pacific Ocean

Missinipe (Cree)

Nch'i-Wana (Sahaptin)

Mnisose (Siouan)

Great Lakes

Kisiteku (Abenaki)

Ojibwean

Muhheakantuck (Lenni-Lenape)

Atlantic Ocean

Aha Kwahwat (Mohave)

Mo'sooneo'he'e (Cheyenne)

Mississippi

Kiskepila Sepe (Shawnee)

Bah'hatteno (Caddoan)

To Bá áádi (Navajo)

Gulf of Mexico

This map suggests major Indigenous trade routes prior to European contact. Before contact, trade networks between and within Indigenous nations covered all manner of distances; many, of course, were smaller, localized networks, but major routes crisscrossed the continent. Traded items included products such as canoes, pottery, woven fabrics, and fishing nets; furs, shells, and feathers; turquoise, obsidian, and copper; and dried fish, maize, and tobacco—among many other goods. Trade centers also served as points for the exchange of oral literature and other forms of cultural expression.

Note that rivers, of significant importance to the trade networks depicted, are identified by Indigenous names; it should be recognized that these names are likely one of many applied to each river (or portion thereof) by different peoples over the centuries.

North American Indigenous Nations at Contact

The map on the following pages does not depict a specific historical moment, but rather shows the approximate locations of individual Indigenous nations at the time that each made contact with Europeans—a process that began in 1492 but extended over centuries. It is important to recognize that the names, locations, and cultures of many Indigenous groups changed significantly in the centuries before and after contact, and that individual peoples' relationships to their territories varied: some formed cities or other permanent settlements, others regularly migrated over vast distances, and some did both. We have attempted to include as many as possible of the nations that are named in works included in this anthology; regrettably, space constraints have necessitated the omission of hundreds of others. Despite its many limitations, we have included this map as a gesture toward representing the immense diversity of North America's Indigenous peoples, and as a rough geographical reference for readers encountering Indigenous peoples unfamiliar to them.

Indigenous nations appearing on the map are listed below, organized alphabetically within very general geographical regions. Where possible, the nations are identified by the names they use for themselves (autonyms), but variations in name, spelling, and orthography are many and may lead to irregularities. We have also included commonly used names imposed by Europeans or other Indigenous nations (exonyms); in a few cases, these exonyms are all we have available. Some modern nations formed after contact and are thus not represented on the map.

Many Indigenous scholars and knowledge-keepers have created maps intended to better represent Indigenous understandings of place and counter misrepresentations in traditional Euro-American maps. We encourage you to visit such resources as the Decolonial Atlas, Lisa Brooks's digital awikhigan, and Claudio Saunt's *Invasion of America*, all available online.

North

Aleut (Unangan)	1
Algonquin (Odishkwaagamiig)	24
Assiniboine (Nakoda)	18
Beothuk	28
Blackfoot (Siksika)	15
Chipewyan (Dene Suline)	16
Chippewa (Ojibwe)	22
Dogrib (Thlingchadine)	9
East Cree (Iyiniwak)	23
Eastern Swampy Cree (Omaskekowak)	21
Gwich'in	6
Haida	11
Hare (Kawchottine)	8
Huron (Wendat)	25
Inuit	19
Inupiat	5
Koyukon	4
Kwakiutl (Kwakwaka'wakw)	12
Mi'kmaq (Lnu'k)	29
Montagnais, Naskapi (Innu)	27
Nootka (Nuu-chah-nulth)	13
Ottawa (Odawa)	26
Plains Cree (Nehiyawak)	17
Slavey (Dene Tha)	14
Tanaina (Dena'ina)	3
Tlingit	10
Tutchone	7
Western Swampy Cree (Maskekowak)	20
Yup'ik	2

West

Arapaho (Hinono'eino)	41
Cheyenne (Tsistsistas)	40
Coast Salish Peoples	30
Crow (Apsáalooke)	39
Eastern Shoshone	38
Flathead (Selis)	32
Klamath	34
Luiseño (Payomkawichum)	48
Maidu	44
Miwok	45
Mono (Numa/Nim)	46
Nez Perce (Nimiipuu)	33
Northern Paiute (Numu)	35
Northern Shoshone (Nimi)	36
Pomo	43
Chinook (Tsinuk)	31
Salinan (Te'po'ta'ahl)	47
Serrano (Taaqtam)	49
Ute (Nunt'zi)	42
Western Shoshone (Newe)	37

Southwest

Atakapa (Akokisa)	70
Coahuiltecan	68
Comanche (Nʉmʉnʉʉ)	63
Hopi (Hopi'sinom)	54
Jicarilla Apache (Ndee)	62
Karankawa (Auia)	69
Kiowa (Ka'igwu)	64
Lipan Apache (Ndee)	67
Mescalero Apache (Ndee)	61
Mojave (Pipa Aha Macav)	51
Navajo (Diné)	57
Pima (Akimel O'odham)	53
Quechan (Kwatsaan)	52
Southern Paiute (Nuwuvi)	50
Taos Pueblo	59
Tewa	60
Tiwa (Tíwan)	58
Tonkawa (Tickanwatic)	66
Western Apache (Ndee)	56
Wichita (Kitikiti'sh)	65
Zuni (Ashiwi)	55

Midwest

Fox (Meskwaki)	88
Hidatsa (Hiraaca)	71
Illinois (Illiniwek)	82
Iowa (Baxoje)	80
Kansa (Kaw)	84
Kaskaskia (Kaskaskahamwa)	81
Kickapoo (Kiikaapoi)	89
Lakota (Teton)	74
Mandan (Numakaki)	72
Menominee (Mamaceqtaw)	78
Miami (Myaamia)	90
Missouria (Nutachi)	83
Omaha (Umonhon)	75
Osage (Wazhazhe)	85
Pawnee (Chahiksichahik)	76
Potawatomi (Neshnabek)	86
Santee Dakota (Isanti)	77
Sauk (Asakiwaki)	87
Shawnee (Shaawanwaki)	92
Wea (Waayaahtanwa)	91
Winnebago (Ho-Chunk)	79
Yankton-Yanktonai Dakota (Wiciyela)	73

Southeast

Apalachee	101
Caddo (Kadohadacho)	94
Calusa	103
Catawba (Iswa)	105
Cherokee (Aniyunwiya)	99
Chickasaw (Chikashsha)	97
Choctaw (Chahta)	96
Creek (Muscogee)	98
Cusabo	104
Mannahoac	109
Monacan	108
Natchez	95
Powhatan	107
Quapaw (Ugakpa)	93
Timucua	102
Tuscarora (Skaru·rę?)	106
Yamasee	100

Northeast

Abenaki (Alnobak)	125
Cayuga (Gayogohono)	114
Delaware (Lenni Lenape)	111
Erie	112
Massachusett	122
Mohawk (Kanien'keha:ka)	117
Mohegan	120
Mohican (Muhhekunneuw)	118
Narragansett	123
Nipmuc	121
Oneida (Onyota'a:ka)	116
Onondaga (Ononda'gaga')	115
Passamaquoddy (Peskotomuhkati)	126
Pequot	119
Seneca (Onondowahgah)	113
Susquehannock	110
Wampanoag	124

South

Aztec (Mexica)	136
Cochimí	127
Huichol (Wixáritari)	131
K'iche' Maya	141
Lenca	143
Maya Nations	140
Mayo (Yoreme)	129
Mixe (Ayuujkja'ay)	139
Mixtec (Tu'un savi)	137
Otomi (Hñähñu)	134
Pame (Xi'iuy)	132
Paya (Pech)	144
Pipil (Cuzcatlec)	142
Taino	145
Tarascan (Purépecha)	133
Tepehuan	130
Totonac (Tachiwin)	135
Yaqui (Yoeme)	128
Zapotec (Binizaa)	138

Pacific Ocean

Hudson Bay

Atlantic Ocean

Gulf of Mexico

Columbia R.

Missouri R.

St. Lawrence R.

Ohio R.

Mississippi R.

Colorado R.

Rio Grande

NORTH AMERICAN INDIGENOUS NATIONS AT CONTACT

Please refer to the table on the previous page in order to identify the Indigenous nations that correspond to numbers.

MASSACHUSETTS AND SURROUNDINGS (c. 1645)

SELECTED INDIGENOUS TERRITORY

SELECTED COLONIAL CLAIM

● Selected Indigenous Village ○ Selected Settler Village

Ktsi Mskodak

Schaghticoke

SOKWAKIK (SOKOKI)

PENACOOK

Merrimack R.

Wamesit

Salem

Wachusett

MUHHEKUNNEUW (MOHICAN)

POCUMTUC

Norwottuck

MASSACHUSETTS BAY COLONY

Boston

Cohasset

MASSACHUSETT

Meeshawm

Connecticut R.

NIPMUC

Plymouth

Hudson R.

NARRAGANSETT

WAMPANOAG

Providence

PLYMOUTH COLONY

NAUSET

Mannamoyik

Hartford

MATTABESIC

RHODE ISLAND COLONY

Sakonnet

Mashpee

DUTCH CLAIMS

CONNECTICUT COLONY

MOHEGAN

Newport

Aquinnah

PEQUOT

NIANTIC

New Haven

Nantucket

LENNI LENAPE

Atlantic Ocean

MONTAUKETT

SHINNECOCK

COLONIAL SETTLEMENT (1607–1733)

SELECTED INDIGENOUS REGIONS

EUROPEAN SETTLEMENTS

(dates of settlement)

MI'KMAQ

MALISEET

ABENAKI

NARRAGANSETT

Boston NEW HAMPSHIRE (1623)

MOHEGAN MASSACHUSETTS BAY (1630)

PEQUOT

HAUDENO-SAUNEE

RHODE ISLAND (1636)

New York CONNECTICUT (1636)

SHAWNEE

Philadelphia NEW YORK (1624)

LENNI LENAPE NEW JERSEY (1664)

PENNSYLVANIA (1681)

MANNAHOAC DELAWARE (1638)

Jamestown MARYLAND (1633)

POWHATAN

TUSCARORA VIRGINIA (1607)

CATAWBA

CHEROKEE CAROLINAS (1670)

MUSCOGEE (CREEK) Charlestown GEORGIA (1733)

YAMASEE

ATLANTIC
TRADE ROUTES
(18TH CENTURY)

Main sources of
enslaved people for the
Americas

Main areas of
importation of enslaved
people in the Americas

EUROPEAN CLAIMS IN
NORTH AMERICA (1763)

British Claims French Claims

Spanish Claims Russian Claims

EUROPEAN CLAIMS IN
NORTH AMERICA (1754)

British Claims French Claims

Spanish Claims Russian Claims

Claimed by more than one European power

RUSSIA

*Pacific
Ocean*

*Hudson
Bay*

Great Lakes

NEW
SPAIN

Maine (Mass.)
New Hampshire
Massachusetts
Rhode Island
Connecticut
New Jersey
New York
Pennsylvania
Delaware
Maryland
Virginia
North Carolina
South Carolina
Georgia

Western Territory

*Atlantic
Ocean*

Gulf of Mexico

Santo
Domingo
Cuba
Saint-Domingue
Jamaica

*Caribbean
Sea*

NORTH AMERICA AFTER THE AMERICAN WAR OF INDEPENDENCE (1783)

United States of America

British Claims

Spanish Claims

French Claims

Russian Claims

Disputed Claims (U.S. and Spain)

Disputed Claims (U.S. and Britain)

Disputed Claims (Britain, Spain, and Russia)

The Treaty of Paris in 1783 concluded the American War of Independence and established a boundary for the newly independent colonies that stretched west to the Mississippi River. States' claims to this new Western Territory were varied, overlapping, and dynamic, and are not depicted here.

Pacific Ocean

DISPUTED TERRITORY

Columbia R.

NEW SPAIN

Colorado R.

Rio Grande

LOUISIANA PURCHASE

Missouri R.

BRITISH NORTH AMERICA

St. Lawrence R.

Maine (Mass.)
Vermont
New Hampshire
Massachusetts
Rhode Island
Connecticut
New York
New Jersey
Delaware
Maryland
Pennsylvania
Virginia
North Carolina
South Carolina
Georgia
Ohio
Ohio R.
Kentucky
Tennessee
Indiana Territory
Mississippi Territory
Mississippi R.

SPANISH FLORIDA

Atlantic Ocean

Gulf of Mexico

Cuba

Saint-Domingue
Jamaica

NORTH AMERICA AFTER THE LOUISIANA PURCHASE (1803)

Spanish Claims

British Claims

Louisiana Purchase

United States of America

Disputed Claims (Spain and Britain)

NORTH AMERICA DURING
NORTHWEST EXPANSION (c. 1820)

Free States and territories

Slave States and territories

Disputed Territory
(United States and Britain)

Open to slavery
by Missouri Compromise

Closed to slavery
by Missouri Compromise

Permissions Acknowledgments

Adams, Abigail and John Adams. Excerpted from *Adams Family Correspondence, Volumes 1 and 2: December 1761–March 1778*, ed. L.H. Butterfield. Cambridge, Mass.: The Belknap Press of Harvard University Press. Copyright © 1963 by the Massachusetts Historical Society. Reprinted by permission of Harvard University Press.

Amador, José María and Lorenzo Asisara. Excerpt from Chapter 3, *Californio Voices: The Oral Memoirs of José María Amador and Lorenzo Asisara*, ed./trans. Gregorio Mora-Torres. Denton, TX: University of North Texas Press, 2005. Copyright © 2005 Gregorio Mora-Torres. Reprinted by permission.

Anonymous. Excerpts from "Manuscript of Tlatelolco (1528)," *The Broken Spears,* ed. Miguel León-Portilla. Copyright © 1962, 1990 by Miguel León-Portilla. Expanded and Updated Edition © 1992 by Miguel León-Portilla. Reprinted by permission of Beacon Press, Boston.

Anonymous. *Prospect of the City of New-York*, 1771. Courtesy of the John Carter Brown Library. CC BY 4.0 https://creativecommons.org/licenses/by/4.0/legalcode

Ashbridge, Elizabeth. "Some Account of the Fore Part of the Life of Elizabeth Ashbridge," from *Journeys in New Worlds*, ed. William L. Andrews. Copyright © 1990 by the Board of Regents of the University of Wisconsin System. All rights reserved. Reprinted by permission of the University of Wisconsin Press.

"Battle at Sea: A Northern Lushootseed Historical Narrative," and "Maiden of Deception Pass: A Traditional Samish Story," from *Salish Myths and Legends: One People's Stories*, edited by M. Terry Thompson and Steven M. Egesdal. Copyright © 2008 by the Board of Regents of the University of Nebraska. (pp. 219–22, 395–400) Reproduced by permission of the University of Nebraska Press.

Cabeza de Vaca, Alvar Núñez. Excerpted from *Alvar Núñez Cabeza de Vaca: his account, his life, and the expedition of Pánfilo de Narváez, Vol. 1,* eds./trans. Rolena Adorno and Patrick Charles Pautz. Copyright © 1999 University of Nebraska Press. (pp. 15–265) Reproduced by permission of the University of Nebraska Press.

Casas, Bartolomé de las. Excerpted from *A Short Account of the Destruction of the Indies*, trans. Nigel Griffin, Penguin Classics, 1992. Translation and notes copyright © Nigel Griffin, 1992. Reproduced by permission of Penguin Books Limited.

Columbus, Christopher. "Letter on the First Voyage (1493)," from *The Four Voyages*, trans. J.M. Cohen, Penguin Classics, 1969. Copyright © 1969 J.M Cohen. Reproduced by permission of Penguin Books Limited.

Cortés, Hernán. Excerpts from "The Second Letter [to the Spanish Crown, 1522]," *Letters from Mexico*, trans. Anthony Pagden, revised edition published by Yale University Press, 1986. Copyright © 1971 by Anthony Pagden. Revised edition copyright © 1986 Yale University. Reproduced by permission of Yale University Press.

Covered Basket, made by Mohegan People, c. 1815, plain-woven ash and oak. Object no.1950.488.0a,b. Image courtesy of the Connecticut Historical Society, Hartford, CT.

Cruz, Sor Juana Inés de la. Excerpted from *A Sor Juana Anthology*, trans. Alan S. Trueblood, foreword by Octavio Paz. Cambridge, Mass.: Harvard University Press. Copyright © 1988 by the President and Fellows of Harvard College. (pp. 41, 43, 81, 111, 113, 205, 208–15, 224–47) Used by permission. All rights reserved.

Cuneo, Michele de. "Letter on the Second Voyage, 28 October 1495," from *Journals and Other Documents on the Life and Voyages of Christopher Columbus*, ed./trans. Samuel Eliot Morison. New York: Heritage Press, 1963. (pp. 212, 224–47)

Davidson, Basil. "Letter from Alfonso I to King Joao [English translation]," *The African Past: Chronicles from Antiquity to Modern Times*. An Atlantic Monthly Press Book. Boston and Toronto: Little, Brown and Company, 1964. Copyright © 1964 by Basil Davidson. (p. 191ff)

Document no. 22. Dukes County Registry of Deed (DD 1:349) from *Native Writings in Massachusett*, ed. Ives Goddard and Kathleen J. Bradon. Vol. 1. Philadelphia: American Philosophical Society, 1988. (p. 94) Reproduced by permission of the American Philosophical Society.

Excerpt from *Popol Vuh: The Definitive Edition of the Mayan Book of the Dawn of Life and the Glories of Gods and Kings*, revised/expanded by Dennis Tedlock, Translator. Copyright © 1985, 1996 Dennis Tedlock. Reprinted with the permission of Touchstone, a division of Simon & Schuster, Inc. All rights reserved.

Excerpt from "The Birth of Nenabozho," *Voices from Four Directions: Contemporary Translations of the Native Literatures of North America*, ed. Brian Swann. Copyright © 2004 by the Board of Regents of the University of Nebraska. Reproduced by permission of the University of Nebraska Press.

Excerpts from *Algonquian Spirit: Contemporary Translations of the Algonquian Literatures of North America*, ed. Brian Swann. Copyright © 2005 University of Nebraska Press. (pp. 59–61) Reproduced courtesy of the University of Nebraska Press.

Excerpts from Chapter 22, Section 22:6, "1518 Memorial of Fray Bernardino de Manzanedo on the government of Hispaniola," and Chapter 21: Expansion from Hispaniola, 1509–1515, Section 21:1, "Las Casas on the depopulation of the Bahamas by Spanish slave raiders," *New Iberian World, Volume II: The Caribbean*, eds. John H. Parry & Robert G. Keith. New York, NY: Times Books (The New York Times Book Co., Inc.) 1984. Copyright © 1984 Joyce Parry, Executrix, Estate of John H. Parry. (pp. 282–83, 334–40) Reproduced by permission of Taylor

and Francis Group, LLC, a division of Informa plc, conveyed through Copyright Clearance Center, Inc.

Franklin, Benjamin. "The Autobiography," from *Franklin: Writings*, ed. J.A. Leo Lemay, Library of America # 37, 1987. Reprinted with the permission of Dr. Kate Clarke Lemay.

Hasteen Klah. Excerpted from *Navajo Creation Myth: The Story of the Emergence*, recorded by Mary C. Wheelwright. Navajo Religion Series, Vol. 1. Copyright © 1942 Museum of Navajo Ceremonial Art, Santa Fe, NM. (pp. 78–79, 81–85) Reproduced by permission of the Wheelwright Museum of the American Indian.

Hochbruck, Wolfgang and Beatrix Dudensing-Reichel. Excerpt from "'Honoratissimi Benefactores': Native American Students and Two Seventeenth-Century Texts in the University Tradition," *Early Native American Writing: New Critical Essays*, ed. Helen Jaskoski. Copyright © Cambridge University Press, 1996. (pp. 5–6) Reproduced with the permission of Cambridge University Press through PLSclear.

House post belonging to Chief Chowitsoot, Lummi, mid-nineteenth century, photograph by Harlan Smith, image [X. 2782.1] held by The Whatcom Museum of History and Art, Bellingham, WA. Image courtesy of The Whatcom Museum. https://www.whatcommuseum.org/

The Maiden of Deception Pass, story pole carved by Tracy W. Powell, a joint project of the Samish Tribe and the Skagit County Centennial Commission, dedicated in 1983 at Rosario Beach, Deception Pass State Park, Fidalgo Island, WA. Item ID: 2013.050.001, 2013.050.003. Photographs by Pam Bagnall (July 2013), courtesy of the Anacortes Museum, with the kind permission of the Samish Indian Nation.

Manuscript of a Mi'kmaq prayer book, c. 1790, Image M18836. Copyright © McCord Museum. Reproduced by permission of the McCord Museum, Montreal, QC.

Mi'kmaq petroglyph of human figure and sun, c. pre-1500 CE, Bedford, Nova Scotia. Ownership/collection: Mylar tracing: R.H. Whitehead, 1983. Image ref # P179/N-17,124. Image courtesy of Nova Scotia Museum.

"Mittark, Agreement of Gay Head Indians Not to Sell Land to the English, 1681," from *Native Writings in Massachusett, 2 Volumes*, eds. Ives Goddard and Kathleen J. Bradon. Copyright © 1988 by The American Philosophical Society. (pp. 196–97) Reproduced by permission of the American Philosophical Society.

"Nanabozho," from *Ojibwa Narratives: Of Charles and Charlotte Kawbawgam and Jacques LePique, 1893–1895*, ed. Arthur P. Bourgeois, recorded with Notes by Homer H. Kidder. Copyright © 1994 Wayne State University Press. Reprinted with the permission of Wayne State University Press.

"Nanabush Eats the Artichokes," from *Coming to Light: Contemporary Translations of the Native Literatures of North America*, edited by Brian Swann, as told by Waasaagoneshkang, recorded

and translated by William Jones, and revised by Ridie Wilson Ghezzi. Copyright © Brian Swann, 1994; Vintage Books, 1996. Reprinted with the permission of Brian Swann.

Occom, Samson. Excerpt from "The Most Remarkable and Strange State Situation and Appearence [sic] of Indian Tribes in This Great Continent," from *The Collected Writings of Samson Occom, Mohegan*, ed. Joanna Brooks. Copyright © 2006 by Oxford University Press, Inc. (pp. 58–59) Reproduced with the permission of Oxford University Press through PLSclear.

Petroglyph traced by George Creed, 1888. Retrieval #: George Creed Nova Scotia Archives MG 15 Vol. 15 M20. Image courtesy of Nova Scotia Archives.

Samson Occom Box, c. 1785, on display at the Tantaquidgeon Museum. Image courtesy of The Mohegan Tribe.

Sequoyah. *Cherokee Number System and Syllabary*, 1839, ink on paper. Manuscript Collection: Sequoyah (George Guess). GM 4926.488. Copyright © Gilcrease Museum. Image courtesy of Gilcrease Museum, Tulsa, OK.

Tac, Pablo. "Conversion of the San Luiseños of Alta California (manuscript 1840)," from *Pablo Tac, Indigenous Scholar*, ed./trans. Lisbeth Haas, University of California Press, 2011. Copyright © 2011 by The Regents of the University of California. (pp. 169, 171, 173) Republished with the permission of the University of California conveyed through Copyright Clearance Center, Inc.

"Thanksgiving Address: Greetings to the Natural World," as told by Rokwaho (Dan Thompson) and translated by John Stokes and Kanawahienton (David Benedict). Copyright © 1993 Six Nations Indian Museum and The Tracking Project. Reprinted by permission of The Tracking Project, Corrales, New Mexico.

Two-Row Wampum Belt, 1613. Six Nations Legacy Consortium Collection. Local identifier: SNPL000066v00i. Image courtesy of the Six Nations Public Library.

White, John. *A wife of an Indian 'werowance'*; *An Indian man and woman eating on rush mat*; *La Virginea Pars, map*; and *The Town of Secoton*, c. 1585–93, The British Museum. Asset numbers: 25876001, 25883001, 26038001, 25868001. Copyright © The Trustees of the British Museum. Used with permission.

Wigglesworth, Michael. Entry for 15 September 1655, containing sketch of pillar, *Michael Wigglesworth diary, 1653–1657*, Ms. SBd-20. Collection of the Massachusetts Historical Society. Reproduced with permission.

Wigglesworth, Michael. Excerpts from *The Diary of Michael Wigglesworth*, ed./trans. Edmund S. Morgan, Volume 35: Transactions, 1942–46, Colonial Society of Massachusetts, 1951. Reprinted with the permission of the Colonial Society of Massachusetts.

Color Insert

Anonymous. *John Freake* and *Mrs Elizabeth Freake and Baby Mary*, c. 1671–74, oil on canvas. Copyright © Worcester Art Museum / Bridgeman Images. Image no: WAM183405; WAM183406. Reproduced with permission.

Anonymous. *Plan of Civilization*, c. 1800, oil on canvas. Purchased by the Greenville County Museum of Art with funds from the Museum Association's 1990 and 1991 Collectors Groups and the 1989, 1990, and 1991 Museum Antiques Shows, sponsored by Elliott, Davis & Company, CPAs. Corporate Benefactors: Ernst and Young; Fluor Daniel; Mr. and Mrs. Alester G. Furman III; Mr. and Mrs. M. Dexter Hagy; Thomas P. Hartness; Mr. and Mrs. E. Erwin Maddrey II; Mary M. Pearce; Mr. and Mrs. John D. Pellett, Jr.; Mr. W. Thomas Smith; Mr. and Mrs. Edward H. Stall; Eleanor and Irvine Welling. Image courtesy of the Greenville County Museum of Art.

Barralet, John James. *The Apotheosis of Washington*, c. 1802. Image ID: BAWDNC. Contributor: John James Barralet / Alamy Stock Photo. Used with permission.

Dighton, Robert. *Keep Within Compass*, 16 August 1785, object no. 1958-629,1; *Keep Within Compass*, 9 November 1784, object no. 1958-629,2. The Colonial Williamsburg Foundation. Museum Purchase. Used with permission.

Fernández, Alejo. *The Virgin of the Navigators*, c. 1531–36. Image ID: BTGWT0. Contributor: Peter Horree / Alamy Stock Photo. Used with permission.

Krimmel, John Lewis. *Fourth of July Celebration in Center Square*, 1819. Image ID: 2E2MDAR. Contributor: ClassicStock / Alamy Stock Photo. Used with permission.

Punderson, Prudence. *The First, Second, and Last Scene of Mortality*, c. 1776–83. Item no. 1962.28.4. Image courtesy of the Connecticut Historical Society, Hartford, CT.

White, John. *The Manner of Their Fishing*, c. 1585–93, The British Museum. Asset number: 22109001. Copyright © The Trustees of the British Museum. Used with permission.

Cover image: detail from *Pocket*, c. 1784, American, cotton and wool. Brooklyn Museum Costume Collection at The Metropolitan Museum of Art, Gift of the Brooklyn Museum, 2009; Bequest of Marie Bernice Bitzer, by exchange, 1996. The Metropolitan Museum of Art, New York, NY, U.S.A. Accession number 2009.300.2241. Copyright © The Metropolitan Museum of Art. Image courtesy of Art Resource, NY. Reproduced with permission.

Index of Authors and Titles

165: [Détente, Sombra de mi bien Esquivo] / [Semblance of my elusive love, hold still—] online

165: [Semblance of my elusive love, hold still—] 330

82: [Divina Lysi mía] / [My divine Lysis] 328

92: [Hombres necios] / [Silly, you men] online

92: [Silly, you men] 329

Abigail Adams to John Adams 8 February 1777 online

Abigail Adams to John Adams, 19 August 1774 496

Abigail Adams to John Adams, 27 November 1775 496

Abigail Adams to John Adams, 31 March 1776 497

[Account of Mission Life] 130

Account of the Life of David George, An online

Account of the Massacre in St. Domingo in May 1806 online

[Acrostic Love Poem to Elizabeth Fitch] online

Act for the Encouragement of the Importation of White Servants, An online

Adams, Abigail 494, online

Adams, John 494, online

Address to the Government of the US on the Cession of Louisiana to the French, An online

Address to the Negroes in the State of New York, An 587

Address to the New York African Society for Mutual Relief, An online

[Address] to the Right Honourable Both Houses of the High Court of Parliament 244

Address to the Sons of Liberty, An online

advertisement, The Pennsylvania Gazette (10 August 1738) online

advertisement, The Pennsylvania Gazette (29 October 1766) online

Age of Reason, The online

Agreement of Mittark and His People Not to Sell Land to the English 114

Ahaton, William online

Alarm to the Legislature of the Province of New York, Occasioned by the Present Political Disturbances in North America, Addressed to the Honourable Representatives in General Assembly Convened, An online

Algerine Captive, The online

Allen, Richard online

American Crisis, The 517

American Liberty online

American Maid's Choice, The 665

Announcement of the Formation of the Association of the Sons of Liberty in New York (15 December 1773) online

anonymous manuscript of Tlatelolco, the 72

Another [Letter to Her Husband, Absent upon Public Employment I] online

Another [Letter to Her Husband, Absent upon Public Employment II] online

Apology of the Paxton Volunteers, Adapted to the Candid and Impartial World, The online

Appamatahqeen, John online

As Weary Pilgrim online

Ascención, Antonio de la 124

Ashbridge, Elizabeth 366

Asisara, Lorenzo 130

Author to Her Book, The 259

[Autobiographical Narrative] 458

Autobiography of Thomas Jefferson, The 522

Autobiography, The 403, online

Banneker, Benjamin 588

Bars Fight 390

Bartram, William online

Battle at Sea 49

Battle of Lexington, The 663

Bay Psalm Book 848

Before the Birth of One of Her Children 259

Belinda (Sutton) 584

Belt that Would Not Burn, The 34

Birth of Nenabozho, The 20

Bishop, Abraham 683

Blind African Slave, or Memoirs of Boyrereau Brinch, Nick-named Jeffrey Brace, The 594

Bloody Tenet of Persecution, The 244

Boarding-School; Lessons of a Preceptress to Her Pupils, The online

Bradford, William 120, 169, 193, online

Bradstreet, Anne 249, online

Brief and Candid Answer to a Late Printed Sheet, Entitled, The Selling of Joseph, A online

Brief and True Report of the New Found Land of Virginia, A 105

Brief Report of the Discovery in the South Sea, A 124

Brinch, Boyrereau 594

British Prison Ship, The online

Brown, Charles Brockden online

Brown, William Wells 688

"Brutus" online

Bryant, Ruth 665

Cabeza de Vaca, Álvar Núñez 132

Camp Ballad, A 667

Canassatego 343, online

Casas, Bartolomé de las 53, 62, 575

Cassacinamon 206

Champlain, Samuel de online

Channing, William Ellery online

Charge Delivered to the African Lodge, 24 June 1797, A online

Charlotte Temple online

Cheeshateaumauk, Caleb 114

Cherokee Syllabary 33

Columbus, Christopher 53, 57

Coming of the Whites, The 102

Common Sense 505

Confession of John Joyce, Alias Davis, Who Was Executed on Monday, the 14th of March, 1808 online

Constitution of the United States, The online

Contemplations 253

Contrast, A Comedy; In Five Acts, The online

Conversion of the San Lusieños of Alta California 128

Coquette; or, The History of Eliza Wharton, The 774

Cortés, Hernán 68

Country Printer, The 861

Coyote and Rock (audio selection) online

Creation Story (Haudenosaunee / Iroquois) 10

Creation Story, The (Navajo / Diné) 41

Creation, The (Haudenosaunee / Iroquois) online

Crèvecoeur, J. Hector St. John de 469, online

Cruz, Sor Juana Inés de la 326, online

Cuneo, Michele de 60

Cushman, Robert 199

Davies, Samuel online

Day of Doom, Or A Poetical Description of the Great and Last Judgment, The 279

Deceiver Unmasked, The 515

Declaration by the Representatives of the People of the Colony and Dominion of Virginia, Assembled in General Convention 671

Declaration by the Representatives of the United States of America, A 522

Declaration of the Independence of the Blacks of St. Domingo online

Declaration of the Rights of Man and of the Citizen 676

Declaration of the Rights of Woman, The online

Declaration of the State of the Colony and Affairs in Virginia, A 578

Dessalines, Jean-Jacques 684

Détente, Sombra de mi bien Esquivo online

Diary of Michael Wigglesworth, The 271

Diary of Samuel Sewall, The online

Dickinson, John online

Discourse on Some of the Distinguishing Opinions of Unitarians, A ["The Baltimore Sermon"] online

dispatch to King Charles I of Spain 576

Divina Lysi mía 328

Dresden Codex, The 36

Drinking Song online

Dunmore's Proclamation (7 November 1775) 669

Duty of Christians to Propagate Their Religion Among Heathens, Earnestly Recommended to the Masters of Negro Slaves in Virginia, The online

Easton, John 315

Ebb and Flow, The online

Edwards, Jonathan 352, online

Elegy upon That Honourable and Renowned Knight, Sir Philip Sidney, An online

Elm Bark Box 468

English Writers on America online

Equiano, Olaudah or Gustavus Vassa 598, online
Erik the Red's Saga online
Escobedo, Alonso Gregorio de 78
Every Man His Own Politician 861
Examination and Relation of James Quannapaquait,
 alias James Rumny-March, The 316
Examination into the Leading Principles of the
 Federal Constitution, An online
Examination of Mrs. Anne Hutchinson at the Court
 at Newtown, The 231
Farewell Address online
Farewell to America. To Mrs. S.W., A 723
Faugères, Margaretta 669
Federalist, The 549, online
Female Review, The online
Figure of the Indians' Fort or Palizado in New
 England and the Manner of Destroying It by
 Captain Underhill and Captain Mason 204
Flesh and the Spirit, The 257
For Deliverance from a Fever 261
Forty Shillings Reward 857
Foster, Hannah Webster 772, online
Four Monarchies, The online
Franklin, Benjamin 396, 658, 854, online
Freneau, Philip 710, 861, online
General History of Virginia, New England, and the
 Summer Isles 153, online
George III 650, 652
George, David online
Gleaner Contemplates the Future Prospects of
 Women in This "Enlightened Age," The 702
God's Determinations Touching His Elect online
Gookin, Daniel 320
Gottlieb Mittelberger's Journey to Pennsylvania in
 the Year 1750 and Return to Germany in the Year
 1754 online
Gouges, Olympe de online
Grainger, James 582
Griffitts, Hannah 666
Gronniosaw, James Albert Ukawsaw online
Ha:yëwënta' (Hiawatha) Belt 18
Haitian Declaration of Independence online
Hall, Prince online
Hamilton, Alexander 550, online
Hamilton, William online
Hammon, Briton 704

Hammon, Jupiter 587
Handsome Lake 115
Hariot, Thomas 105
Harris, Benjamin 853
Haynes, Lemuel 663, 737, online
Henry, Patrick online
Hireling Ministry None of Christ's online
Historical Account of the Doings and Sufferings
 of the Christian Indians in New England in the
 Years 1675, 1676, 1677, An 320
History of New Mexico online
History of New York, A 875, online
History of the Indies 575
History of the Rise, Progress, and Termination of
 the American Revolution 672, online
History of the Work of Redemption, A online
Hombres necios online
Hopkinson, Francis 667
How the Spaniards Came to Shung-Opovi, How
 They Built a Mission, and How the Hopi
 Destroyed the Mission 97
How the White Race Came to America and Why
 the Gai'wiio' Became a Necessity 115
Hubbard, William 207
Hul'q'umi'num House Post 48
Hurricane, The 712
Huswifery 324
Hutchinson, Anne 229
Hymn to the Morning, An 735
In Honour of That High and Mighty Princess, Queen
 Elizabeth of Most Happy Memory online
In Memory of My Dear Grand-Child Elizabeth
 Bradstreet 261
In Memory of My Dear Grand-Child Simon
 Bradstreet 261
In Reference to Her Children, 23 June 1659 online
Indian Account of the First Arrival of the Dutch at
 New York Island 103
Indian Burying Ground, The 712
Inglis, Charles 515
Interesting Narrative of the Life of Olaudah Equiano,
 The 601, online
Irving, Washington 873, online
Jefferson, Thomas 519, 680, online
Jemison, Mary online

John Adams to Abigail Adams, 16 September 1774 online

John Adams to Abigail Adams, 29 October 1775 online

John Adams to Abigail Adams, 7 February 1777 online

John Adams to Abigail Adams, first letter of 3 July 1776 499

John Adams to Abigail Adams, second letter of 3 July 1776 499

John Adams to Thomas Jefferson, 2 September 1813 online

John Adams to Thomas Jefferson, 15 November 1813 online

Johnson, Samuel online

Join or Die 659

Jones, Absalom 642, online

Journal of John Winthrop, The online

Journal of Madame Knight, The online

Journal of Major George Washington, The 347

Journal of the First Voyage to America 53

Journal of the Pontiac Conspiracy 647

Key into the Language of America, A 238

King Alfonso I 575

Knight, Sarah Kemble online

L'Embonpoint 862

La Florida 78

La Florida del Inca 85

Lawrence, George online

LeClerq, Chrestien online

Legend of Sleepy Hollow online

Letter [Concerning Columbus's Second Voyage] 60

Letter of Columbus to Various Persons Describing the Results of His First Voyage and Written on the Return Journey 57

letter on the Pueblo Revolt of 1680, 8 September 1680 91

Letter Sent from New England to a Friend in These Parts, A 119

letter to Colonel David Wooster, 18 October 1773 730

letter to Dr. William Robertson, 6 August 1776 671

letter to Edmond Hector, 10 October 1756 online

letter to her daughter [Julia Stockton Rush], 22 March 1793 678

Letter to Her Husband, Absent upon Public Employment, A 260

letter to John Sprigs, 22 September 1756 online

letter to Josiah Winslow, 26 May 1675 315

letter to King João III of Portugal, 18 October 1526 575

letter to Obour Tanner, 19 May 1722 729

letter to Obour Tanner, 30 October 1773 731

letter to Ralph Izard, 8 December 1775 670

letter to Samson Occom, 11 February 1774 732

letter to Selina Hastings, 27 June 1773 729

letter to Sir Edwin Sandys, January 1620 578

letter to the Society for the Propagation of the Gospel in New England, 1663 114

letter to the South Carolina Gazette, 14 October 1732 579

Letter to the Town of Providence 247

letter to Thomas Henchman, November 1675 318

letter to Thomas Jefferson, 19 August 1791 588

Letters from a farmer in Pennsylvania to the Inhabitants of the British Colonies online

Letters from an American Farmer 472, online

Liberty Further Extended: Or Free Thoughts on the Illegality of Slave-keeping 738, online

Liberty or Death. Proclamation. Jean Jacques Dessalines, Governor General, to the People of Hayti 684

Ligon, Richard online

Lincoln, Abraham 120

Lindsay, Reverend John 671

Line, John 318

Lloyd, Thomas online

Logan 533

Louverture, Toussaint 680

Madison, James 552, online

Mague, John 321

Maiden of Deception Pass (oral story) 44

Maiden of Deception Pass, The (story pole) 47

Mann, Herman online

Manzanedo, Bernardino de 576

Map of New-England, A 207

Marrant, John online

Martin, Joseph Plumb online

Massachusetts Council, order regarding Indigenous allies 318
Mather, Cotton 336, online
Meat Out of the Eater online
Meditations Divine and Moral 265
Memoir of Old Elizabeth, a Coloured Woman 585
Mittark 114
Mittelberger, Gottlieb online
Model of Christian Charity, A 219
Moral Argument against Calvinism, The online
Morton, Thomas 208, online
[Moshup Story] 4
Most Remarkable and Strange State, Situation, and Appearance of Indian Tribes in This Great Continent, The 467
Mother, The 862
Murray, Judith Sargent 694
My divine Lysis 328
Nanabozho 26
Nanabush Eats the Artichokes 25
Nanabush Story (audio selection) online
Narrative of Some of the Adventured, Dangers and Sufferings of a Revolutionary Soldier, A online
Narrative of the Late Massacres, in Lancaster County, of a Number of Indians, Friends of This Province, By Persons Unknown. With Some Observations on the Same, A online
Narrative of the Life and Adventures of Venture, A Native of Africa, A 559
Narrative of the Life of Mrs. Mary Jemison, A online
Narrative of the Lord's Wonderful Dealings with John Marrant, a Black, A online
Narrative of the Most Remarkable Particulars in the Life of James Albert Ukawsaw Gronniosaw, an African Prince, as Related by Himself, A online
Narrative of the Proceedings of the Black People, During the Late Awful Calamity in Philadelphia, A online
Narrative of the Uncommon Sufferings and Surprising Deliverance of Briton Hammon, A Negro Man, A 705
Negroes Character, The 579
Nelson, Mary 857
New England Bravery 855

New England Courant, The [The "Silence Dogood" Papers] online
New England Primer, The 853
New English Canaan, The 210, online
New Relation of Gaspesia, with the Customs and Religion of the Gaspesian Indians online
New Song, Addressed to the Sons of Liberty, on the Continent of America; Particularly to the Illustrious, Glorious and Never to Be Forgotten Ninety-two of Boston, A 661
News from America 204
Ninigret 206
Notes on the State of Virginia 531, online
notice, New York Independent Journal (24 January 1784) online
Numphow 318
Nzinga Mbemba 575
Occom, Samson 455
Odell, Jonathan 668
Of Plymouth Plantation 120, 171, online
Ojibwe Pictographs 29
"Old Elizabeth" 585
Old Year and the New: A Prophecy, The 668
On a Survey of the Heavens online
On Being Brought from Africa to America 721
On Imagination 721
On Mr. Paine's Rights of Man 713
On Recollection 735
On the Consequences of Abolishing the Slave Trade to the West Indian Colonies online
On the Death of a Young Gentleman 735
On the Death of a Young Lady of Five Years of Age 734
On the Death of General Wooster online
On the Death of the Rev. Mr. George Whitefield 726
On the Equality of the Sexes 695
On the Fourteenth Query of Thomas Jefferson's Notes on Virginia 545
On the Religion of Nature 717
On the Slave Trade 401
On the Universality of Other Attributes of the God of Nature online
Oration on the Abolition of the Slave Trade, An (Lawrence) online

Oration on the Abolition of the Slave Trade, An (Williams) 590
Origin of Folk Stories 12
Otermín, Antonio de 91
Page of a Mi'kmaq Prayer Book 7
Paine, Thomas 501, online
Painted Wood-Splint Storage Basket 8
Patriotic Diggers, The 863
[Personal Narrative] (Edwards) online
Peters, Phillis Wheatley 718, online
Petition of Belinda, an African, The 584
Petition of the People of Color, The 643
petition to the Boston Court of Assistants, 5 September 1676 online
petition to the Governor and Council of the Massachusetts Colony, June 1676 321
petition to the Governor and Council of the Massachusetts Colony, July 1676 online
Petroglyph of Human Figure and Sun 6
Petroglyph Tracing 6
Philadelphia Minerva, The 679
Pittimee, Andrew 321
Plan of the Pequot Country and Testimony of Uncas, Cassacinamon, and Wesawegun 206
Poem on the Rising Glory of America, A online
Poor, Unhappy, Transported Felon, The 859
Popol Vuh, The 39
Powell, Tracy 47
Powhatan (Chief) 164
Prediction of the Arrival of the White People 102
Preface to Phillis Wheatley's Poems on Various Subjects, Religious and Moral 733
Preparatory Meditations before My Approach to the Lord's Supper online
Printer to the Reader, The 854
Printer, James 319, 320
Proceedings of Farmington, Connecticut, on the Boston Port Act online
Proclamation by Leger-Felicite Sonthonax, Civil Commissioner of the Republic, delegate to the French Islands of Leeward America, in order to restore order and public tranquility online
Proclamation, 29 August 1793 680
Proclamation, A (Lincoln) 120
Prologue (Bradstreet) 251
Quanahphokit 321

Quannapaquait, James 316
Raguet, Condy online
Reasons and Considerations Touching the Lawfulness of Removing out of England into the Parts of America 199
Reflections on the Gradual Progress of Nations from Democratical States to Despotic Empires online
Relación of Álvar Núñez Cabeza de Vaca, The 134
Relation of the Discoveries and Voyages of Cavalier de La Salle from 1679 to 1681 online
Relation or Journal of the Proceedings of the Plantation Settled at Plymouth in New England, A [Mourt's Relation] 193
Remarks Concerning the Savages of North America 398
[Reply to President Washington, 31 March 1792] online
Reply to Sor Philothea, the 330
[Reply to the Missionary Jacob Cram] 393
Response of the House of Commons, 8 December 1774 653
Revel, James 859
review of "Observations sur la Virginie, par M.J., traduites de l'Anglais" 544
Rights of Black Men, The 683
Rights of Man, Part Two online
Rip Van Winkle 881
Risings Glory of America, The online
Rolfe, John 578
Rowlandson, Mary 283
Rowson, Susanna Haswell 744, online
Royal Proclamation of 1763, The 650
Rule of Equity, The online
Rules by Which a Great Empire May Be Reduced to a Small One online
Rutledge, Edward 670
Saffin, John 579, online
Saga of the Greenlanders, The online
Sagoyewatha 391
Salute to the Fourteenth Anniversary of American Independence, A 669
Sampson, Deborah online
Sansay, Leonora 686
Seabury, Samuel online
Second Letter to the Spanish Crown 68

Secret History, Or, the Horrors of St.
 Domingo 686
Selling of Joseph: A Memorial, The online
Semblance of my elusive love, hold still— 330,
 online
Sequoyah 33
Sermon, Preached at the Execution of Moses Paul, an
 Indian, A 462
Sewall, Samuel 851, online
Short Account of the Destruction of the Indies,
 A 62
["Silence Dogood" Papers] online
Silly, you men 329, online
Sinners in the Hands of an Angry God 354
Sketches of the Life and Character of Patrick
 Henry 654
Slaves in Algiers; or, A Struggle for Freedom 746
Smith, James McCune 545
Smith, John 150, online
Smith, Venture 557
Some Account of the Capture of the Ship
 Aurora online
Some Account of the Fore Part of the Life of
 Elizabeth Ashbridge 367
Some Considerations on the Keeping of
 Negroes 580
Some Verses upon the Burning of Our House,
 July 10th, 1666 262
Somnambulism: A Fragment online
Sor Philothea's Letter to Sor Juana online
South Carolina Negro Act, The online
Sovereignty and Goodness of God, The 285
Speech at Lancaster, 4 July 1744 online
Speech at Lancaster, 26 July 1744 345
Speech of Miss Polly Baker, The online
Speech to Parliament, 30 November 1774 652
Speech to the Osages 871
Speech to William Henry Harrison 867
Speen, James 321
Sprigs, Elizabeth online
St. Domingo: Its Revolutions and Its Patriots 688
Stansbury, Joseph 666
Stockton, Annis Boudinot 678
Sufferings of Christ, The 466
Sugar-Cane, The 582
Sutcliff, Robert 693

Sutton, Belinda 584
Tac, Pablo 128
Taxation No Tyranny: An Answer to the Resolutions
 and Address of the American Congress online
Taylor, Edward 322, online
Tecumseh 865
Terry, Lucy 389
Thanksgiving Address 13
Thanksgiving Sermon, A online
Thomas Jefferson to John Adams, 28 October
 1813 online
Thought on the Inestimable Blessing of Reason,
 A online
Timberlake, Henry online
Tinker, John 206
To Her Father with Some Verses online
To His Excellency General Washington 725
To Maecenas 719
To My Dear and Loving Husband 260
To My Dear Children 263
To S.M., a Young African Painter, on Seeing His
 Works 723
To Sir Toby 714
To the Free and Loyal Inhabitants of the City and
 Colony of New York online
To the King's Most Excellent Majesty 721
To the Memory of My Dear and Ever Honored
 Father Thomas Dudley Esq. online
To the Right Honourable William, Earl of
 Dartmouth 722
To the University of Cambridge, in
 New-England 720
Traits of Indian Character online
Translation of the War-Song [of the Cherokee],
 A online
Travels in Some Parts of North America in the Years
 1804, 1805, and 1806 693
Travels through North and South Carolina, Georgia,
 East and West Florida, the Cherokee Country,
 the Extensive Territories of the Muscogulges
 or Creek Confederacy, and the Country of the
 Chactaws online
True and Exact History of the Island of Barbados,
 A online
Tse'Hone / Newspaper Rock 43
Two Row Wampum 18

Tyler, Royall online
Uncas 206
Underhill, John 204
United States, The 667
Universal Salvation: A Very Ancient
 Doctrine online
Upon a Spider Catching a Fly online
Upon a Wasp Chilled with Cold online
Upon Reading a Book Entitled Common
 Sense 666
Upon Wedlock, and Death of Children 324
Vega, Inca Garcilaso de la 85
Verses to the Tories 666
Verses upon a New Century 851
Villagrá, Gaspar Pérez de online
Virginia Banishing Tea 662
Virginia Stamp Act Resolutions (29 May
 1765) online
Voyage to Saint Domingo, in the Years 1788, 1789,
 and 1790, A online
Voyages of Samuel Champlain online
Wahunsonacock 164
Wannukhow, Joseph online
Wannukhow, William online
Warren, Mercy Otis 672, online

Washington, George 347, online
Waterhouse, Edward 578
Way to Wealth: Preface to Poor Richard Improved,
 The online
Webster, Noah online
Wesawegun 206
What Would Satisfy the Americans? 659
Wheatley, Phillis 718, online
White, John 109
Why the Possum's Tail Is Bare 33
Wife, The 877
Wigglesworth, Michael 269, online
Wild Honey Suckle, The 712
Williams, Peter Jr. 590
Williams, Roger 236, online
Wimpffen, Baron de online
Winslow, Edward 119, 193
Winthrop, John 217, online
Wirt, William 654
Woman's Hard Fate 855
Wonders of the Invisible World, The 338
Woodworth, Samuel 863
Woolman, John 580
Wright, Harry 206
You Say We're Fond of Fops—Why Not? 863

From the Publisher

A name never says it all, but the word "Broadview" expresses a good deal of the philosophy behind our company. We are open to a broad range of academic approaches and political viewpoints. We pay attention to the broad impact book publishing and book printing has in the wider world; for some years now we have used 100% recycled paper for most titles. Our publishing program is internationally oriented and broad-ranging. Our individual titles often appeal to a broad readership too; many are of interest as much to general readers as to academics and students.

Founded in 1985, Broadview remains a fully independent company owned by its shareholders—not an imprint or subsidiary of a larger multinational.

To order our books or obtain up-to-date information, please visit www.broadviewpress.com.

broadview press

www.broadviewpress.com

From the Publisher

A name never says it all, but the word "Broadview" expresses a good deal of the philosophy behind our company. We are open to a broad range of academic approaches and political viewpoints. We pay attention to the broad impact book publishing and book printing has in the wider world; for some years now we have used 100% recycled paper for most titles. Our publishing program is internationally oriented and broad-ranging. Our individual titles often appeal to a broad readership too; many are of interest as much to general readers as to academics and students.

Founded in 1985, Broadview remains a fully independent company owned by its shareholders—not an imprint or subsidiary of a larger multinational.

To order our books or obtain up-to-date information, please visit www.broadviewpress.com.

broadview press

www.broadviewpress.com